P9-DDX-454

PRINCIPLES OF PUBLIC INTERNATIONAL LAW

PRINCIPLES OF PUBLIC INTERNATIONAL LAW

BY

IAN BROWNLIE, Q.C., D.C.L., F.B.A.
Associé de l'Institut de Droit International
Professor of International Law in the University of London

THIRD EDITION

CLARENDON PRESS · OXFORD
1979

Oxford University Press, Walton Street, Oxford OX2 6DP
OXFORD LONDON GLASGOW
NEW YORK TORONTO MELBOURNE WELLINGTON
NAIROBI DAR ES SALAAM CAPE TOWN
KUALA LUMPUR SINGAPORE JAKARTA HONG KONG TOKYO
DELHI BOMBAY CALCUTTA MADRAS KARACHI

Published in the United States by
Oxford University Press, New York

FIRST EDITION 1966
SECOND EDITION 1973
REPRINTED 1977
THIRD EDITION 1979

Russian edition of the second edition,
by Professor G. I. Tunkin,
Moscow, 1977.

British Library Cataloguing in Publication Data

Brownlie, Ian
Principles of public international law. – 3rd ed.
1. International law
I. Title
341 JX3091 79–41139

ISBN 0–19–876066–3
ISBN 0–19–876067–1

PRINTED IN GREAT BRITAIN
BY WILLIAM CLOWES & SONS LIMITED,
BECCLES AND LONDON

FROM THE PREFACE OF THE SECOND EDITION

THE prime object remains that of the first edition: to present the subject matter in terms of law and legal technique, whilst making appropriate reference to the influence of policy and political conflicts. With the inclusion of new chapters the book provides a reasonably comprehensive account of the law of peace based upon the modern practice of states, the practice of organizations of states, and the decisions of international and municipal courts. In preparing the text reference has been made to available evidence of the practice of states generally. The writer has attempted to observe the professional standard which requires the recording of what is happening in the world at large and not merely what is pleasing to the eye. A true estimate of consensus or possibly emergent rules will not relate neatly to the view of any single state or group of states. Of course, in some areas of the law it is not possible to do more than to indicate the divergent tendencies.

A high proportion of the references are to sources and literature in English and French. In preparing a book of this kind I have been indebted to various useful contemporary sources and, in particular, the International Law Reports, edited by Mr. E. Lauterpacht, Q.C. The document reproduced at pp. 310–13 is taken from the same learned editor's *British Practice in International Law*, 1967, p. 58.

I am beholden to a number of friends and reviewers for criticisms and suggestions. Particular assistance came from Richard Baxter, Judge of the International Court of Justice (formerly of Harvard Law School), Professor K. Skubiszewski, of the Polish Academy of Sciences (formerly of the Adam Mickiewicz University, Poznań), Professor R. Y. Jennings, Q.C., of Cambridge University, and Dr. D. R. Harris, of Nottingham University. Of course, the text now presented remains my responsibility alone. Finally, I am grateful for the help and courtesy of the staff of the Clarendon Press. Neither the work for nor the publication price of the present book has been subsidised by any official source or private foundation.

I. B.

Oxford
4 September 1972

PREFACE TO THE THIRD EDITION

THE work has been revised to reflect recent developments in various areas of the law, including the law of the sea, state immunity, and the status of foreign investments. In certain areas, which have attracted more attention in recent years, the scale of treatment did not stand in need of revision for the reason that such areas as human rights and the law of the sea have been given wide coverage since the first edition of the book.

I am grateful to Professor F. G. Jacobs, University of London, for helpful suggestions relating to Chapter XXIV.

43 Fairfax Road,
Chiswick, W4 1EN.
12 June 1979

I. B.

CONTENTS

PART II
PERSONALITY AND RECOGNITION

PART III
TERRITORIAL SOVEREIGNTY

PART IV
LAW OF THE SEA

PART VI
STATE JURISDICTION

PART VIII
THE LAW OF RESPONSIBILITY

PART X
INTERNATIONAL TRANSACTIONS

PART XI
TRANSMISSION OF RIGHTS AND DUTIES

PART XII

INTERNATIONAL ORGANIZATIONS AND TRIBUNALS

ABBREVIATIONS

(of titles of books, etc., quoted in the text)

Acta Scandinavica. *Acta Scandinavica Juris Gentium (Nordisk Tidsskrift for International Ret.)*.
A.J. *American Journal of International Law*.
Ann. Digest. *Annual Digest of Public International Law Cases*.
Annuaire de l'Inst. *Annuaire de l'Institut de droit international*.
Annuaire français. *Annuaire français de droit international*.
A.S.I.L. Proceedings. *Proceedings of the American Society of International Law*.
Austral. Y.B.I.L. *Australian Year Book of International Law*.
B.F.S.P. *British and Foreign State Papers*.
Bishop. Bishop, *International Law: Cases and Materials*, 3rd ed., 1971.
Brierly. Brierly, *The Law of Nations*, 6th ed., 1963, by Sir Humphrey Waldock.
Briggs. Briggs, *The Law of Nations: Cases, Documents and Notes*, 2nd ed., 1952.
British Digest. C. Parry (ed.), *A British Digest of International Law* (1965–).
British Practice in I.L. E. Lauterpacht (ed.), *British Practice in International Law*.
Brownlie, *Documents*. Brownlie (ed.), *Basic Documents in International Law*, 2nd ed., 1972.
B.Y. *British Year Book of International Law*.
Camb. L.J. *Cambridge Law Journal*.
Canad. Yrbk. *Canadian Yearbook of International Law*.
Cmd., Cmnd. United Kingdom, Command Papers.
Colombos. Colombos, *International Law of the Sea*, 6th ed., 1967.
Curr. Leg. Problems. *Current Legal Problems*.
Gidel. Gidel, *Le droit international public de la mer*, 3 vols.
Green. Green, *International Law Through the Cases*, 4th ed., 1979
Grot. Soc. *Transactions of the Grotius Society*.
Guggenheim. Guggenheim, *Traité de droit international public*, 2 vols., 1953; Vol. I, 2nd ed., 1967.
Hackworth. Hackworth, *Digest of International Law*, 8 vols.
Hague Court Reports. Scott (ed.), Hague Court Reports.
Hague *Recueil*. *Recueil des cours de l'Académie de droit international*.
Harv. L. R. *Harvard Law Review*.
Harv. Research. Research in International Law under the Auspices of the Harvard Law School.
Hudson, *Cases*. *Cases and Other Materials on International Law*, 3rd ed., 1951.
Hudson, *Int. Legis*. Hudson (ed.), *International Legislation*, 9 vols.
Hyde. Hyde, *International Law Chiefly as Interpreted and Applied by the United States*, 3 vols., 2nd ed., 1945.
I.C.J. Pleadings. International Court of Justice: Pleadings, Oral Arguments, Documents.

I.C.J. Reports. Reports of Judgments, Advisory Opinions and Orders of the International Court of Justice.

I.C.L.Q. *International and Comparative Law Quarterly.*

I.L.C. International Law Commission.

I.L.Q. *International Law Quarterly.*

Indian Journ. *Indian Journal of International Law.*

Int. Conciliation. *International Conciliation.*

Int. Leg. Materials. *International Legal Materials.*

Int. L.R. International Law Reports (continuation of the *Annual Digest*).

Int. Organization. *International Organization.*

J.D.I. *Journal du droit international.*

La Fontaine. La Fontaine, *Pasicrisie internationale.*

La Pradelle and Politis. *Recueil des arbitrages internationaux*, 3 vols., 2nd ed., 1957.

L.N.T.S. League of Nations Treaty Series.

L.Q.R. *Law Quarterly Review.*

McDougal and Burke. McDougal and Burke, *Public Order of the Oceans.*

McNair, *Opinions.* McNair, *International Law Opinions*, 3 vols.

Mod. L.R. *Modern Law Review.*

Moore, *Arbitrations.* Moore, *History and Digest of the International Arbitrations to which the United States has been a Party*, 6 vols.

Moore, *Digest.* Moore, *Digest of International Law*, 8 vols.

Neths. Int. L.R. *Netherlands International Law Review* (*Nederlands tijdschrift voor international recht*).

O'Connell. O'Connell, *International Law*, 2 vols., 2nd ed., 1970.

Oppenheim. Oppenheim, *International Law*, Vol. I, 8th ed., 1955; Vol. II, 7th ed., 1952.

P.C.I.J. Publications of the Permanent Court of International Justice.

R.D.I. (La Pradelle). *Revue de droit international* (Paris, ed. by La Pradelle).

R.D.I.L.C. *Revue de droit international et de législation comparée* (Brussels).

R.G.D.I.P. *Revue générale de droit international public* (Paris).

R.I.A.A. United Nations, *Reports of International Awards.*

Rousseau. Rousseau, *Droit international public*, 1953

Rousseau i, ii, iii. *Droit international public*, 3 vols., 1970– .

Sørensen. Sørensen (ed.), *Manual of Public International Law* (1968).

Treaty Series. *United Kingdom Treaty Series.*

U.K. Contemp. Practice. E. Lauterpacht, *The Contemporary Practice of the United Kingdom in the Field of International Law.*

U.N.T.S. United Nations Treaty Series.

U.S. United States; or United States Supreme Court Reports.

Whiteman. Whiteman, *Digest of International Law* (1963–).

World Court Reports. Hudson, *World Court Reports*, 4 vols. (1934–43).

Yrbk., I.L.C. United Nations, *Yearbook of the International Law Commission.*

Z.a.ö. R.u.V. *Zeitschrift für ausländisches öffentliches Recht und Völkerrecht.*

TABLE OF CASES

Principal references are printed in heavy type

GLOSSARY

amicus curiae. A person permitted to present arguments bearing upon issues before a tribunal yet not representing the interests of any party to the proceedings.

animus. An intention, a state of mind.

compromis. A special agreement between states to submit a particular issue either to an arbitral tribunal or to the International Court.

conflict of laws. Or, private international law. A part of the municipal law of each state which provides rules for deciding cases involving foreign factual elements, for example, a contract made abroad.

culpa. The civil law or Roman law term employed by lawyers from non-common law countries to refer to negligence, lack of reasonable care.

de lege ferenda. Relating to the law as it should be if the rules were changed to accord with good policy.

détournement de pouvoir. A term of French administrative law originally, meaning abuse of administrative powers by public officials.

dicta. The lesser propositions of law stated by tribunals or by individual members of tribunals; propositions not directed to the principal matters in issue.

diligentia quam in suis. The standard of care normally exercised by a particular person in the conduct of his affairs.

dolus. The intention to inflict some harm, together with the foreseeable consequences of the intended harm.

erga omnes. Opposable to, valid against, 'all the world', i.e. all other legal persons, irrespective of consent on the part of those thus affected.

inter se. Between the parties to a specific agreement or other transaction.

lex ferenda. See *de lege ferenda.*

litispendence. The principle that a tribunal should refuse to admit an issue before it when the same issue is pending before another tribunal.

locus delicti. The place, or more usually, the particular state or jurisdiction, in which a wrong was committed.

locus standi. The power to apply to a tribunal for a particular remedy; more specifically, the existence of a sufficient legal interest in the matter in issue.

ne bis in idem. No man should be proceeded against twice over the same matter.

obiter dicta. See *dicta.*

pacta sunt servanda. Simply, the principle that agreements are binding and are to be implemented in good faith.

prima facie. In principle; presumptively.

ratio; ratio decidendi. The principal proposition or propositions of law determining the outcome of a case; or, the only legal consideration necessary for the decision of a particular case.

ratione materiae. By reason of the subject matter.

ratione temporis. Conditioned by reference to time.

res inter alios acta. A matter affecting third parties and not opposable to the legal persons between whom there is an issue.

res judicata. The principle that an issue decided by a court should not be reopened.

res nullius. An asset susceptible of acquisition but presently under the ownership or sovereignty of no legal person.

stare decisis. The principle that a tribunal should follow its own previous decisions and those of other tribunals of equal or greater authority.

travaux préparatoires. Preparatory work; preliminary drafts, minutes of conferences and the like, relating to the conclusion of a treaty.

PART I
PRELIMINARY TOPICS

CHAPTER I
SOURCES OF THE LAW[1]

1. *Introductory*

As objects of study, the sources of international law and the law of treaties (treated in Chapter XXV) must be regarded as fundamental: between them they provide the basic particles of the legal regime.

It is common for writers to distinguish the formal sources and the material sources of law. The former are those legal procedures and methods for the creation of rules of general application which are legally binding on the addressees. The material sources provide evidence of the existence of rules which, when proved, have the status of legally binding rules of general application. In systems of municipal law the concept of formal source refers to the constitutional machinery of law-making and the status of the rule is established by constitutional law: for example, a statute is binding in the United Kingdom by reason of the principle of the supremacy of Parliament. In the context of international relations the use of the term 'formal source' is awkward and misleading since the reader is put in mind of the constitutional machinery of law-making which exists within states. No such machinery exists for the creation of rules of international law. Decisions of the International Court, unanimously

[1] See generally Sørensen, *Les Sources de droit international* (1946); id., 101 Hague *Recueil* (1960, III), 16–108; Fitzmaurice, 92 Hague *Recueil* (1957, II), 97–108; id., *Symbolae Verzijl* (1958), pp. 153–76; Briggs, *Law of Nations* (2nd ed.), pp. 43–52; Guggenheim, 94 Hague *Recueil* (1958, II), 5–81; Kopelmanas, 18 *B.Y.* (1937), 127–51; id., 21 *R.D.I.* (La Pradelle) (1938), 101–50; de Visscher, 58 *R.G.D.I.P.* (1955), 353–69; Scelle, in *Recueil d'études sur les sources du droit en l'honneur de François Gény* iii (1936), 400–30; Parry, *The Sources and Evidences of International Law* (1965); Tunkin, *Theory of International Law* (1970; English trans. by Butler, 1974), pp. 89–203; Marek, Furrer and Martin, *Les sources du droit international* (1967) (a collection of materials of the P.C.I.J. and I.C.J.); Verzijl, *International Law in Historical Perspective* i (1968), 1–89; Quadri, 113 Hague *Recueil* (1964, III), 319–72; Bishop, ibid., 115 (1965, II), 214–50; Jennings, ibid., 121 (1967, II), 329–45; Rousseau, *Droit international public* i (1970), 55–443; Lauterpacht, *International Law: Collected Papers* i. 58–135; Elias, in Friedmann, Henkin and Lissitzyn (eds.), *Transnational Law in a Changing Society* (1972), pp. 34–69; *Z.a.ö.R.u.V.*, Vol. 36 (1976), Nos. 1–3; *Völkerrecht als Rechtordnung, Grundlagen und Quellen.*

supported resolutions of the General Assembly of the United Nations concerning matters of law, and important multilateral treaties concerned to codify or develop rules of international law, are all lacking the quality to bind states generally in the same way that Acts of Parliament bind the people of the United Kingdom. In a sense 'formal sources' do not exist in international law. As a substitute, and perhaps an equivalent, there is the principle that the general consent of states creates rules of general application. The definition of custom in international law[1] is essentially a statement of this principle (and not a reference to ancient custom as in municipal law).

The consequence is that in international law the distinction between formal and material sources is difficult to maintain. The former in effect consist simply of a quasi-constitutional principle of inevitable but unhelpful generality. What matters then is the variety of material sources, the all-important *evidences* of the existence of consensus among states concerning particular rules or practices. Thus decisions of the International Court, resolutions of the General Assembly of the United Nations, and 'law-making' multilateral treaties are very material evidence of the attitude of states toward particular rules, and the presence or absence of consensus. Moreover, there is a process of interaction which gives these evidences a status somewhat higher than mere 'material sources'. Thus neither an unratified treaty nor a report of the International Law Commission to the General Assembly have any binding force either in the law of treaties or otherwise. However, such instruments stand as candidates for public reaction, approving or not, as the case may be: they may stand for a threshold of consensus and confront states in a significant way.

The law of treaties concerns the question of the content of obligations between individual states: the incidence of obligations resulting from express agreement.[2] In principle, the incidence of particular obligations is a matter distinct from the sources. Terminology presents some confusion in this respect. Thus treaties binding a few states only are dubbed 'particular international law' as opposed to 'general international law' comprising multilateral 'law-making' treaties[3] to which a majority of states are parties. Yet in strictness there is no fundamental distinction here: both types of treaty only create particular obligations and treaties are *as such* a source of obligation and not a

[1] *Infra*, pp. 4–5.

[2] And obligations may arise apart from treaties properly so-called; see *infra*, Chapter XXVI. [3] See *infra*, p. 12.

source of rules of general application. Treaties may form an important material source, however: see section 4 below.

It is perhaps useful to remark on two other usages of the term 'sources' which raise questions not of immediate concern in this chapter. Thus the term may refer to the source of the binding quality of international law as such and also to the literary sources of the law as sources of information.[1]

2. *The Statute of the International Court of Justice*

The pertinent provisions are as follows:

Article 38. 1. The Court, whose function is to decide in accordance with international law such disputes as are submitted to it, shall apply:

(a) international conventions, whether general or particular, establishing rules expressly recognized by the contesting States;
(b) international custom, as evidence of a general practice accepted as law;
(c) the general principles of law recognized by civilized nations;
(d) subject to the provisions of Article 59, judicial decisions and the teachings of the most highly qualified publicists of the various nations, as subsidiary means for the determination of rules of law.

2. This provision shall not prejudice the power of the Court to decide a case *ex aequo et bono*, if the parties agree thereto.

Article 59. The decision of the Court has no binding force except between the parties and in respect of that particular case.

These provisions are expressed in terms of the function of the Court, but they represent the previous practice of arbitral tribunals, and Article 38 is generally regarded as a complete statement of the sources of international law.[2] Yet the article itself does not refer to 'sources' and, if looked at closely, cannot be regarded as a straightforward enumeration of the sources. The first question which arises is whether paragraph 1 creates a hierarchy of sources. They are not stated to represent a hierarchy, but the draftsmen intended to give an order and in one draft the word 'successively' appeared.[3] In practice the Court may be expected to observe the order in which they appear: (a) and (b)

[1] This role may assume the character of law creation: see *infra*, pp. 25–26.

[2] See Hudson, *The Permanent Court of International Justice*, pp. 601 seq. See also the Revised General Act for the Pacific Settlement of International Disputes, Art. 28; Model Rules on Arbitral Procedure adopted by the I.L.C., Art. 10, *Yrbk., I.L.C.* (1958), ii. 83; Report of Scelle, ibid., p. 8. Article 38 has often been incorporated textually or by reference in the *compromis* of other tribunals: Simpson and Fox, *International Arbitration*, p. 130 n. See also *infra*, p. 16, note 1.

[3] Cf. *Castillo* v. *Zalles*, Int. L.R. 22 (1955), 540. See also Quadri, 113 Hague *Recueil*, 342–5; Judge Tanaka, diss. op., *South West Africa Cases* (Second Phase), I.C.J. Reports (1966), p. 300; Akehurst, 47 *B.Y.* (1974–5), 273–85.

are obviously the important sources, and the priority of (a) is explicable by the fact that this refers to a source of mutual obligations of the parties. Source (a) is thus not primarily a source of rules of general application, although treaties may provide evidence of the formation of custom. Sources (b) and, perhaps, (c) are formal sources, at least for those who care for such classification. Source (d), with its reference 'as subsidiary means for the determination of rules of law', relates to material sources. Yet some jurists regard (d) as a reference to formal sources, and Fitzmaurice has criticized the classification of judicial decisions as 'subsidiary means'.[1]

In general Article 38 does not rest upon a distinction between formal and material sources, and a system of priority of application depends simply on the order (a) to (d), and the reference to subsidiary means. Moreover, it is probably unwise to think in terms of hierarchy dictated by the order (a) to (d) in all cases.[2] Source (a) relates to *obligations* in any case; and presumably a treaty contrary to a custom or to a general principle part of the *jus cogens*[3] would be void or voidable. Again, the interpretation of a treaty may involve resort to general principles of law or of international law.[4] A treaty may be displaced or amended by a subsequent custom, where such effects are recognized by the subsequent conduct of the parties.[5]

The function of the International Court raises the question whether parties going before the Court can lay down the law to be applied to the particular dispute. Precedents for such a course of action can be found in the practice of arbitral tribunals, and the *Alabama Arbitration* of 1872[6] was on the basis of a convention in which the rules of neutrality to be applied by the tribunal were formulated. It is not yet clear whether the Court would act on a *compromis* containing an agreement on the law applicable.[7]

3. *International Custom*[8]

Definition. Article 38 refers to 'international custom, as evi-

[1] *Symbolae Verzijl*, at p. 174.

[2] See Judge Moreno Quintana, *Right of Passage Case*, I.C.J. Reports (1960), p. 90.

[3] *Infra*, Chapter XXII, on *jus cogens* and its effects.

[4] See *infra*, pp. 15–20.

[5] *Air Transport Services Agreement Arbitration*, 1963, Int. L.R. 38, p. 182; *R.I.A.A.* xvi. 5; Award, Part IV, sect. 5.

[6] Hudson, p. 665; Green, p. 27; Briggs, p. 1026. Cf. the Nuremberg Charter: *Treaty Series*, no. 27 (1946), Cmd. 6903; Hudson, *Int. Legis.* ix., nos. 659, 659a.

[7] Article 38 might suggest that acceptance of such a *compromis* would be incompatible with the judicial function. *Quaere* if the objection applies to waiver of procedural rules.

[8] See *supra*, p. 1, n. 1, and see further: MacGibbon, 31 *B.Y.* (1954), 150–1; id., 33

dence of a general practice accepted as law', and Brierly[1] remarks that 'what is sought for is a general recognition among States of a certain practice as obligatory'. Although occasionally the terms are used interchangeably, 'custom' and 'usage' are terms of art and have different meanings. A usage is a general practice which does not reflect a legal obligation,[2] and examples are ceremonial salutes at sea and, apart from a recent convention, the giving of customs exemption to the personal baggage of diplomatic agents.[3]

Evidence. The material sources of custom are very numerous and include the following:[4] diplomatic correspondence, policy statements, press releases, the opinions of official legal advisers, official manuals on legal questions, e.g. manuals of military law, executive decisions and practices, orders to naval forces etc., comments by governments on drafts produced by the International Law Commission, state legislation,[5] international and national judicial decisions,[6] recitals in treaties and other international instruments, a pattern of treaties in the same form, the practice of international organs,[7] and resolutions relating to legal questions in the United Nations General Assembly. Obviously the value of these sources varies and much depends on the cir-

B.Y. (1957), 115–45; Lauterpacht, *The Development of International Law by the International Court* (1958), pp. 368–93; Guggenheim, in *Études en l'honneur de Georges Scelle* (1950), i. 275–84; id., *Traité* (2nd ed.), i. 93–113; Tunkin, 95 Hague *Recueil* (1958, III), 9–21; id., 49 *California L.R.* (1961), 419–30; Sériadès, 43 *R.G.D.I.P.* (1936), 129–96; Suy, *Les Actes juridiques unilatéraux en droit international public* (1962), pp. 215–67; Silving, 31 *Iowa L.R.* (1945–46), 614–33; Fitzmaurice, 27 *B.Y.* (1950), 17–18; 30 *B.Y.* (1953), 67–69; 35 *B.Y.* (1959), 229–30; Kunz, 47 *A.J.* (1953), 662–9; Jenks, *The Prospects of International Adjudication*, pp. 225–65; Verdross, 7 *Jap. Annual* (1963), 1–7; id., 29 *Z.a.ö.R.u.V.* (1969), 635–53; Skubiszewski, ibid., 31 (1971), 810–54; D'Amato, *The Concept of Custom in International Law* (1971); Verzijl, op. cit., pp. 31–47; Wolfke, *Custom in Present International Law* (1964); Thirlway, *International Customary Law and Codification* (1972); Naganathan, 2 *Colombo L.R.* (1971), 68–82; Barberis, *Neths. Int. L.R.* (1967), 367–81; Manin, 80 *R.G.D.I.P.* (1976), 7–54; P. de Visscher, 136 Hague *Recueil* (1972, II), 61–77; Akehurst, 47 *B.Y.* (1974–75), 1–53. The last provides a cogent critique of the position of D'Amato and Thirlway. On the function of custom see Dupuy, *Mélanges Offerts à Charles Rousseau* (1974), pp. 75–87

1 *The Law of Nations* (6th ed), p. 61. See also Judge Read in the *Fisheries* case, I.C.J. Reports (1951), p. 191: 'Customary international law is the generalization of the practice of States'; and Hudson, A/CN.4/16, p. 5, in Briggs, p. 25.

2 See further *infra*, pp. 8–10, on the *opinio juris*.

3 Cf. Art. 36 of the Vienna Convention on Diplomatic Relations, 1961.

4 See in particular Parry, 44 *Grot. Soc.* (1958, 1959), 145–86; McNair, *Opinions* i, Preface. Custom apart from the practice of *states* may be influential, e.g. in the general law of the sea; cf. the *Tolten* [1946] P. 135; *Ann. Digest* (1946), no. 42.

5 Cf. the *Scotia* (1871) 14 Wallace 170; Briggs, p. 25.

6 The latter provided a basis for the concept of the historic bay.

7 In its advisory opinion in the *Genocide* case the I.C.J. refers to the practice of the Council of the League of Nations in the matter of reservations to multilateral conventions: I.C.J. Reports (1951), p. 25. See also the joint dissenting opinion, ibid., pp. 34 seq.

cumstances. Moreover, internal law sources require careful handling. A statute may create powers which are not exercised to their greatest extent in actual practice. Thus in the United Kingdom the Customs Consolidation Act is not applied in practice so as to maintain a contiguous zone,[1] and it is the *actions* of states which build up practice.[2] Nevertheless, even as evidence of a presumptive nature, legislation has immense value, witness the volumes of the *United Nations Legislative Series* produced for the use of the International Law Commission in its work.

The elements of custom

(a) *Duration*. Provided the consistency and generality of a practice are proved, no particular duration is required: the passage of time will of course be a part of the evidence of generality and consistency. A long (and much less, an immemorial) practice[3] is not necessary, and rules relating to airspace and the continental shelf[4] have emerged from fairly quick maturing of practice. The International Court does not emphasize the time element as such in its practice.

(b) *Uniformity, consistency of the practice*. This is very much a matter of appreciation and a tribunal will have considerable freedom of determination in many cases. Complete uniformity is not required, but substantial uniformity is, and thus in the *Fisheries* case[5] the Court refused to accept the existence of a ten-mile rule for bays.[6] Moreover, the Court may take the view that uniformity in one respect does not preclude the application of a different rule when there are serious reasons for allowing exceptions to the normal rule.[7]

The leading pronouncements by the Court appear in the judgment in the *Asylum*[8] case:

[1] McNair, *Opinions* i. 344, 345–6. On contiguous zones see *infra*, pp. 210 seq. Similarly the executive has not followed the interpretation of the Herring Fishery (Scotland) Act, 1889, adopted by the High Court of Justiciary in *Mortensen* v. *Peters* (1906) 8 S.C. 93; Briggs, p. 52: see *U.K. Contemp. Practice* (1962), i. 48.

[2] See Judge Altamira, P.C.I.J., Ser. A, no. 10, pp. 96–97; Judge Read, I.C.J. Reports (1951), p. 191, and Fitzmaurice, 30 *B.Y.* (1953), 67–68.

[3] See the unhappy reference by Deputy-Judge Negulesco, *European Commission of the Danube*, P.C.I.J., Ser. B, no. 14, p. 114. Hudson, in a working paper on Art. 24 of the I.L.C. Statute, required 'continuation or repetition of the practice over a considerable period of time' (see Briggs, p. 25).

[4] See now the Convention on the Continental Shelf, *infra*, pp. 220–8. See also Lauterpacht, 27 *B.Y.* (1950), 376–433.

[5] I.C.J. Reports (1951), p. 116 at p. 131. See also the *Genocide* case, ibid., p. 25: 'In fact, the examples of objections made to reservations appear to be too rare in international practice to have given rise to such a rule.'

[6] See *infra*, pp. 199–200. [7] On the *Fisheries* case generally see *infra*, pp. 186 seq.

[8] I.C.J. Reports (1950), at pp. 276–7. See also *U.S. Nationals in Morocco* case, I.C.J.

The party which relies on a custom . . . must prove that this custom is established in such a manner that it has become binding on the other party . . . that the rule invoked . . . is in accordance with a constant and uniform usage practised by the States in question, and that this usage is the expression of a right appertaining to the State granting asylum and a duty incumbent on the territorial State. This follows from Article 38 of the Statute of the Court, which refers to international custom 'as evidence of a general practice accepted as law'.

The facts brought to the knowledge of the Court disclose so much uncertainty and contradiction, so much fluctuation and discrepancy in the exercise of diplomatic asylum[1] and in the official views expressed on different occasions; there has been so much inconsistency in the rapid succession of conventions on asylum, ratified by some States and rejected by others, and the practice has been so much influenced by considerations of political expediency in the various cases, that it is not possible to discern in all this any constant and uniform usage, accepted as law. . . .

(c) *Generality of the practice*. This is an aspect which complements that of consistency. Certainly universality is not required, but the real problem is to determine the value of abstention from protest by a substantial number of states in face of a practice followed by some others. Silence may denote either tacit agreement or a simple lack of interest in the issue. It may be that the Court in the *Lotus* case[2] misjudged the consequences of absence of protest and also the significance of fairly general abstention from prosecutions by states other than the flag state.[3] In the *Fisheries Jurisdiction Case* (United Kingdom v. Iceland) the International Court referred to the extension of a fishery zone up to a 12 mile limit 'which appears now to be generally accepted' and to 'an increasing and widespread acceptance of the concept of preferential rights for coastal states' in a situation of special dependence on coastal fisheries.[4]

Reports (1952), p. 200; *Nottebohm* case (Second Phase), I.C.J. Reports (1955), p. 30 per Judge Klaestad; *Right of Passage* case (*Merits*), I.C.J. Reports (1960), pp. 40, 43; ibid., p. 62 per Judge Wellington Koo; p. 99 per Judge Spender, and ibid., p. 136 per Fernandes, Judge *ad hoc*; *North Sea Continental Shelf Cases*, I.C.J. Reports (1969), p. 43; ibid., p. 86 per Judge Padilla Nervo; ibid., p. 229 per Judge Lachs; ibid., p. 246 per Judge Sørensen. Cf. *Fisheries* case, I.C.J. Reports (1951), pp. 191–2, per Judge Read. See also *Borga* v. *Russian Trade Delegation*, Int. L.R. 22 (1955), 235.

[1] The Court was concerned with the right to decide whether the offence was political and whether the case was one of urgency.

[2] See *infra*, pp. 8, 254–5, 301.

[3] Lauterpacht, *The Development of International Law by the International Court*, pp. 384–6. See also the *Paquete Habana* (1900) 175 U.S. 677; Briggs, p. 30; Bishop, p. 26.

[4] I.C.J. Reports (1974), p. 3 at pp. 23–6. See also the *North Sea Continental Shelf Cases*, I.C.J. Reports (1969), p. 4 at p. 42. For reliance on the practice of a limited number of states see the *Wimbledon* (1923) P.C.I.J., Ser. A, no. 1; Green, p. 311; and see *infra*, p. 278.

(d) *Opinio juris et necessitatis.*[1] The Statute of the International Court refers to 'a general practice *accepted as law*'.[2] Brierly[3] speaks of recognition by states of a certain practice 'as obligatory', and Hudson[4] requires a 'conception that the practice is required by, or consistent with, prevailing international law'. Some writers do not consider this psychological element to be a requirement for the formation of custom,[5] but it is in fact a necessary ingredient. The sense of legal obligation, as opposed to motives of courtesy, fairness, or morality, is real enough, and the practice of states recognizes a distinction between obligation and usage. The essential problem is surely one of proof, and especially the incidence of the burden of proof. The position is probably as follows. The proponent of a custom has to establish a general practice and, having done this in a field which is governed by legal categories, the tribunal can be expected to presume the existence of an *opinio juris*.[6] In other words, the opponent on the issue has a burden of proving its absence.[7] In only two cases has the International Court, or its predecessor, referred to the *opinio juris* in regard to general customs. The first case in which it was found necessary to advert to this element was the *Lotus*, in which the Permanent Court said:[8]

Even if the rarity of the judicial decisions to be found among the reported cases were sufficient to prove in point of fact the circumstances alleged by the Agent for the French Government, it would merely show that States had often, in practice, abstained from instituting criminal proceedings, and not that they recognized themselves as being obliged to do so; for only if such abstention were based on their being conscious of a duty to abstain would it be possible to speak of an international custom. The alleged fact does not allow one to infer that States have been conscious of having such

[1] See generally Chaumont, 129 Hague *Recueil* (1970, I), 434–45; Verzijl, *International Law in Historical Perspective* i. 37–41; Barberis, 50 *Rivista di d.i.* (1967), 563–83; P. de Visscher, 136 Hague *Recueil* (1972, II), 70–5.

[2] Italics supplied.

[3] *The Law of Nations* (6th ed), p. 61.

[4] Quoted in Briggs, p. 25.

[5] See Guggenheim, op. cit., pp. 275–80; Fischer Williams, *Aspects of Modern International Law*, pp. 44–6. See now Guggenheim, *Traité* (2nd ed.), i. 103–5. For Kelsen the *opinio juris* is a fiction to disguise the creative powers of the judge: see *Revue internationale de la théorie du droit* (1939), pp. 253–74; and cf. *Principles of International Law*, p. 307; (2nd ed.), pp. 450–1.

[6] See Lauterpacht, *The Development of International Law by the International Court*, 1958, p. 380; id., *Coll. Papers* i. 63; Baxter, 129 Hague *Recueil* (1970, I), 69; Guggenheim, *Traité* (2nd ed.), i. 103–5. Cf. Sørensen, p. 134.

[7] Cf. Verzijl, op. cit., pp. 41–3.

[8] Ser. A, no. 10, p. 28. See also the individual opinions of Nyholm and Altamira, ibid., pp. 60, 97; the *European Commission of the Danube*, Ser. B, no. 14, p. 114 per Deputy-Judge Negulesco. Cf. the passage from the judgment in the *Asylum* case quoted *supra*.

a duty; on the other hand . . . there are other circumstances calculated to show that the contrary is true.

Presumably the same principles should apply to both positive conduct and abstention, yet in the *Lotus* the Court was not ready to accept continuous conduct as *prima facie* evidence of a legal duty and required a high standard of proof on the issue of *opinio juris*.[1]

In the *North Sea Continental Shelf Cases*[2] the International Court was also strict in requiring proof of the *opinio juris*. The Court did not presume the existence of *opinio juris* either in the context of the argument that the equidistance-special circumstances basis of delimiting the continental shelf had become a part of general or customary law at the date of the Geneva Convention of 1958, or in relation to the proposition that the *subsequent* practice of states based upon the Convention had produced a customary rule. However, it is incorrect to regard the precise findings as in all respects incompatible with the view that the existence of a general practice raises a presumption of *opinio juris*. In regard to the position *before* the Convention concerning the equidistance principle, there was little 'practice' apart from the records of the International Law Commission, which revealed the experimental aspect of the principle prior to 1958.[3] In considering the argument that practice *based upon* the Convention had produced a customary rule the Court made it clear that its unfavourable reception to the argument rested primarily upon two factors: (a) the peculiar form of the equidistance principle in Article 6 of the Convention was such that the rules were not of a norm creating character;[4] (b) the Convention had only been in force for less than three years when the proceedings were brought and consequently:[5]

Although the passage of only a short period of time is not necessarily, or of itself, a bar to the formation of a new rule of customary international law on the basis of what was originally a purely conventional rule, an indispensable requirement would be that within the period in question, short though it might be, State practice, including that of States whose interests are specially affected, should have been both extensive and virtually uniform in the sense of the provision invoked;—and should moreover have occurred in such a way as to show a general recognition that a rule of law or legal obligation is involved.

[1] See the criticisms of Lauterpacht, op. cit., p. 386. See, however, MacGibbon, 33 *B.Y.* (1957), 131. [2] I.C.J. Reports (1969), p. 3.
[3] Ibid., pp. 28, 32–41. [4] Ibid., pp. 41–2. [5] Ibid., p. 43.

Nevertheless, the general tenor of the Judgment[1] is hostile to the presumption as to *opinio juris* and the Court quoted the passage from the *Lotus* case set out above.[2]

Bilateral relations and local customs. In the case concerning *U.S. Nationals in Morocco*[3] the Court quoted the first of the passages from the *Asylum* case quoted earlier[4] and continued: 'In the present case there has not been sufficient evidence to enable the Court to reach a conclusion that a right to exercise consular jurisdiction founded upon custom or usage has been established *in such a manner that it has become binding on Morocco.*'[5]

In this case the Court may seem to have confused the question of law-making and the question of opposability, i.e. the specific relations of the United States and Morocco.[6] The fact is that general formulae concerning custom do not necessarily help in penetrating the complexities of the particular case. The case concerning a *Right of Passage over Indian Territory*[7] raised an issue of bilateral relations, the existence of a local custom in favour of Portugal in respect of territorial enclaves inland from the port of Daman (Damão). In this type of case the general law is to be varied and the proponent of the special right has to give affirmative proof of a sense of obligation on the part of the territorial sovereign: *opinio juris* is here not to be presumed on the basis of continuous practice and the notion of *opinio juris* merges into the principle of acquiescence.[8]

The persistent objector. The way in which, as a matter of practice, custom resolves itself into a question of special relations is illustrated further by the rule that a state may contract out of a custom in the process of formation.[9] Evidence of objection must be clear and there is probably a presumption of acceptance which

[1] Ibid., pp. 43–5.

[2] For comment see Baxter, 129 Hague *Recueil* (1970, I), pp. 67–9; D'Amato, 64 *A.J.* (1970), 892–902; Marek, *Revue Belge*, 1970, 44–78. For the views of dissenting Judges see I.C.J. Reports (1969), pp. 156–8 (Koretsky), 175–9 (Tanaka), 197 (Morelli), 221–32 (Lachs), 241–2 (Sørensen). See also the Separate Opinion of Judge Petrén in the *Nuclear Tests Case*, I.C.J. Reports (1974), p. 253 at pp. 305–6.

[3] I.C.J. Reports (1952), pp. 199–200. See Lauterpacht, op. cit., pp. 388–92.

[4] *Supra*, pp. 6–7. [5] Italics supplied.

[6] See Fitzmaurice, 92 Hague *Recueil* (1957, II), 106. On opposability in general see *infra*, pp. 89–90. The *Asylum* case itself concerned a regional custom.

[7] I.C.J. Reports (1960), p. 6 at pp. 39–43. Cf. Judges Wellington Koo at pp. 62–3; Armand-Ugon at pp. 82–4; and Spender at p. 110. See also Deputy-Judge Negulesco, *European Commission of the Danube*, P.C.I.J., Ser. B, no. 14, p. 114; and Judge Klaestad, *Nottebohm* (Second Phase), I.C.J. Reports (1955), p. 30.

[8] See generally MacGibbon, 33 *B.Y.* (1957), 125–31; D'Amato, 63 *A.J.* (1969), 211–23.

[9] See the views of Judge Gros in his Separate Opinion in the *Nuclear Tests Case* (Australia v. France), I.C.J. Reports (1974), p. 253 at pp. 286–9.

is to be rebutted. The toleration of the persistent objector is explained by the fact that ultimately custom depends on the consent of states.

The subsequent objector. In the *Fisheries* case[1] part of the Norwegian argument was that certain rules were not rules of general international law, and, even if they were, they did not bind Norway, which had 'consistently and unequivocally manifested a refusal to accept them'. The United Kingdom admitted the general principle of the Norwegian argument here whilst denying that, as a matter of fact, Norway had consistently and unequivocally manifested a refusal to accept the rules. Thus the United Kingdom regarded the question as one of persistent objection. The Court did not deal with the issue in this way, however, and the *ratio* in this respect was that Norway had departed from the alleged rules, if they existed, *and other states had acquiesced* in this practice. But the Court is not too explicit about the role of acquiescence in validating a subsequent contracting out of rules.[2] Here one has to face the problem of change in a customary regime.[3] Presumably, if a substantial number of states assert a new rule, the momentum of increased defection, complemented by acquiescence, may result in a new rule,[4] as in the case of the law on the continental shelf. If the process is slow and neither the new rule nor the old have a majority of adherents then the consequence is a network of special relations based on opposability, acquiescence, and historic title.[5]

Proof of custom. In principle a court is presumed to know the law and may apply a custom even if it has not been expressly pleaded. In practice the proponent of a custom has a burden of proof the nature of which will vary according to the subject-matter and the form of the pleadings. Thus in the *Lotus* case[6] the Court spoke of the plaintiff's burden in respect of a general custom. Where a local or regional custom is alleged, the pro-

[1] I.C.J. Reports (1951), p. 116. On which generally see *infra*, pp. 186 seq.

[2] See Fitzmaurice, 30 *B.Y.* (1953), 24–6; id., 92 Hague *Recueil* (1957, II), 99–101; Sørensen, 101 Hague *Recueil* (1960, III), 43–7. The dictum which requires explanation, at p. 131 of the Reports, is: 'In any event the ten-mile rule would appear to be inapplicable as against Norway inasmuch as she had always opposed any attempt to apply it to the Norwegian coast.'

[3] See *Lauritzen et al.* v. *Government of Chile*, Int. L.R. 23 (1956), p. 708 at pp. 710–12.

[4] Since delict cannot be justified by an allegation of a desire to change the law, the question of *opinio juris* arises in a special form and in the early stages of change can amount to little more than a plea of good faith.

[5] Both forms of objection are restricted in any case by the norms of *jus cogens*: on which see *infra*, Chapter XXII, section 5.

[6] P.C.I.J., Ser. A, no. 10, p. 18.

ponent 'must prove that this custom is established in such a manner that it has become binding on the other Party'.[1]

4. '*Lawmaking*' *Treaties and Other Material Sources*

It may seem untidy to depart from discussion of the 'formal' sources, of which custom is the most important, and yet a realistic presentation of the sources involves giving prominence to certain forms of evidence of the attitude of states to customary rules and general principles of the law.[2] 'Lawmaking' treaties, the conclusions of international conferences, resolutions of the United Nations General Assembly, and drafts adopted by the International Law Commission have a direct influence on the content of the law, an influence the significance of which is not conveyed adequately by their designation as material sources.

'*Lawmaking*' *treaties*.[3] Such treaties create legal obligations the observance of which does not dissolve the treaty obligation. Thus a treaty for the joint carrying out of a single enterprise is not lawmaking, since fulfilment of its objects will terminate the obligation. Lawmaking treaties create *general* norms for the future conduct of the parties in terms of legal propositions, and the obligations are basically the same for all parties. The Declaration of Paris, 1856 (on neutrality in maritime warfare), the Hague Conventions of 1899 and 1907 (on the law of war and neutrality), the Geneva Protocol of 1925 (on prohibited weapons), the General Treaty for the Renunciation of War of 1928, and the Genocide Convention of 1948, are examples of this type. Moreover, those parts of the United Nations Charter which are not concerned with constitutional questions concerning competence of organs, and the like, have the same character.[4] Such treaties are in principle binding only on parties,[5] but the number of parties, the explicit acceptance of rules of law, and, in some cases, the declaratory nature of the provisions produce a strong law-creating effect at least as great as the general practice considered

[1] *Asylum* case, I.C.J. Reports (1950), p. 276. [2] See *infra*, pp. 15–20.

[3] See McNair, *Law of Treaties* (1961), pp. 5, 124, 749–52; id., 11 *B.Y.* (1930), 100–18 (reprinted in *Law of Treaties*, p. 739); id., 19 *Iowa L.R.* (1934) (reprinted in *Law of Treaties*, p. 729); Hyde, *International Law*, para. 34 c; Sørensen, 101 Hague *Recueil* (1960, III), 72–90; Gihl, *International Legislation*, pp. 46–73; Starke, 23 *B.Y.* (1946), 341–6; de Visscher, 59 *R.G.D.I.P.* (1955), 362–9; Tunkin, 95 Hague *Recueil* (1958, III), 21–3; Baxter, 41 *B.Y.* (1965–66), 275–300; id., 129 Hague *Recueil* (1970, I), 31–75; Shihata, 22 *Rev. Egyptienne* (1966), 51–90; Manin, 80 *R.G.D.I.P.* (1976), 7–54. See further Chapter XXV, section 11.

[4] In particular the principles in Article 2. [5] But see Chapter XXV, section 8.

sufficient to support a customary rule.[1] By their conduct non-parties may accept the provisions of a multilateral convention as representing general international law:[2] this has been the case with Hague Convention IV[3] of 1907 and the rules annexed relating to land warfare. Even an unratified treaty may be regarded as evidence of generally accepted rules, at least in the short run.[4]

In the *North Sea Continental Shelf Cases*[5] the principal issue was to what extent, if at all, the German Federal Republic was bound by the provisions of the Continental Shelf Convention which it had signed but not ratified. The International Court concluded, by eleven votes to six, that only the first three articles of the Convention were emergent or pre-existing customary law.[6] The principles on which the Court discriminated between articles included reference to the faculty of making unilateral reservations which applied to some articles but not to those which, by inference, had a more fundamental status. With respect it may be doubted if the existence of reservations of itself destroys the probative value of treaty provisions.[7] The Court concluded, further, that the provision on delimitation of shelf areas in Article 6 of the Convention had not become a rule of customary law by virtue of the subsequent practice of states and, in particular, of non-parties.[8] The six dissenting Judges regarded the Convention as having greater potency, more particularly in generating rules after its appearance.[9]

Other treaties. Bilateral treaties may provide evidence of custo-

[1] See McNair, *Law of Treaties* (1961), pp. 216–18, for expression of a firm opinion on the effect of Article 2, paragraphs 3 and 4, of the Charter, which he describes as the 'nearest approach to legislation by the whole community of States that has yet been realised'.

[2] There must be evidence of consent to the extension of the rule, particularly if the rule is found in a regional convention: in the *Asylum* case the Court was unwilling to hold Peru bound by the rule contained in the Montevideo Convention. Cf. the *European Human Rights Convention Case*, Int. L.R. 22 (1955), p. 608 at p. 610.

[3] Scott, *The Hague Conventions and Declarations of 1899 and 1907* (3rd ed.), p. 100; Briggs, p. 1004. See the Nuremberg judgment, *Ann. Digest*, 13 (1946), no. 92; Green, p. 707; and the declarations of both sides in the Korean war.

[4] See Baxter, 129 Hague *Recueil* (1970, I), p. 61; *Nottebohm* case (Second Phase), I.C.J. Reports (1955), p. 23; *Namibia Opinion*, ibid. (1971), p. 47. Cf. *North Sea Continental Shelf Cases*, ibid. (1969), p. 41.

[5] I.C.J. Reports (1969), p. 3.

[6] Ibid., pp. 32–41. See also Padilla Nervo, sep. op., pp. 86–9; Ammoun, sep. op., pp. 102–6, 123–4.

[7] See Baxter, 129 Hague *Recueil* (1970, I), 47–51. See also Judges Tanaka, diss. op., I.C.J. Reports (1969), p. 182; Morelli, diss. op., p. 198; Lachs, diss. op., pp. 223–5; Sørensen, diss. op., p. 248.

[8] I.C.J. Reports (1969), pp. 41–5.

[9] Ibid., pp. 56 (Bengzon); 156–8, 163, 169 (Koretsky); 172–80 (Tanaka); 197–200 (Morelli); 221–32 (Lachs); 241–7 (Sørensen).

mary rules,[1] and indeed there is no clear and dogmatic distinction between 'lawmaking' treaties and others. If bilateral treaties, for example on extradition, are habitually framed in the same way, a court may regard the usual form as the law even in the absence of a treaty obligation.[2] However, considerable caution is necessary in evaluating treaties for this purpose.

The conclusions of international conferences.[3] The 'Final Act' or other statement of conclusions of a conference of states may be a form of multilateral treaty, but, even if it be an instrument recording decisions not adopted unanimously, the result may constitute cogent evidence of the state of the customary law on the subject concerned. Even before the necessary ratifications are received, a convention embodied in a Final Act and expressed as a codification of existing principles has obvious importance.[4]

Resolutions of the United Nations General Assembly.[5] The lawmaking role of organizations is considered further in Chapter XXX, Section 10. In general these resolutions are not binding on member states, but, when they are concerned with general norms of international law, then acceptance by a majority vote constitutes *evidence* of the opinions of governments in the widest forum for the expression of such opinions. Even when they are framed as general principles, resolutions of this kind provide a basis for the progressive development of the law and the speedy consolidation of customary rules. Examples of important 'law-

[1] See Baxter, 129 Hague *Recueil* (1970, I), 75–91; Kopelmanas, 18 *B.Y.* (1937), 136–7; Sørensen, *Les Sources de droit international*, pp. 96–8. See also *The Wimbledon*, P.C.I.J., Ser. A, no. 1, p. 25; *Panevezys–Saldutiskis Railway*, Ser. A/B, no. 76, pp. 51–2, per Judge Ehrlich; *Nottebohm*, I.C.J. Reports (1955), pp. 22–3; see also *In re Lechin et al.*, Ann. Digest, 16 (1949), no. 1; *In re Dilasser et al.*, Int. L.R., 18 (1951), no. 99; *The State (Duggan)* v. *Tapley*, ibid., no. 109; *Lagos* v. *Baggianini*, ibid., 22 (1955), 533; *Lauritzen* v. *Government of Chile*, ibid., 23 (1956), p. 708 at pp. 715–16.

[2] Cf. *In re Muzza Aceituno*, Int. L.R., 18 (1951), no. 98; *Re Tribble*, ibid., 20 (1953), 366.

[3] See Johnson, 35 *B.Y.* (1959), 1–33. See also *infra*, Chapter XXVI, on international transactions.

[4] See *Re Cámpora et al.*, Int. L.R., 24 (1957), 518; *Namibia Opinion*, I.C.J. Reports (1971), p. 47.

[5] Generally see Cheng, 5 *Indian Journ.* (1965), 23–48; Castañeda, *Legal Effects of United Nations Resolutions* (1969); id., 129 Hague *Recueil* (1970, I), 211–331; Bastid, *Recueil d'études en hommage à Guggenheim*, 132–45; Verdross, 26 *Z.a.ö.R.u.V.* (1966), 690–6; Wolfke, 1 *Polish Yrbk.* (1966–7), 183–94; Asamoah, *The Legal Significance of the Declarations of the General Assembly of the United Nations* (1966); Skubiszewski, 41 *B.Y.* (1965–6), 198 at pp. 242–8; Bishop, 115 Hague *Recueil* (1965, II), 241–5; Yepes, 46 *R.G.D.I.P.* (1939), 550 at p. 558; Sørensen, 160–2; O'Connell i. 26–8; Arangio-Ruiz, 137 Hague *Recueil* (1972, III), 431–628; Hambro, *Scand. Studies in Law*, 17 (1973), 75–93; P. de Visscher, 136 Hague *Recueil* (1972, II), 123–33. See further *South West Africa Cases* (Second Phase), I.C.J. Reports (1966), pp. 171–2 (sep. op., van Wyk), pp. 291–3 (diss. op., Tanaka), pp. 432–41 (diss. op., Jessup), pp. 455–7, 464–70 (diss. op., Padilla Nervo).

making' resolutions are the resolution[1] which affirmed 'the principles of international law recognized by the Charter of the Nuremberg Tribunal and the Judgment of the Tribunal'; the resolution on Prohibition of the Use of Nuclear Weapons for War Purposes;[2] the Declaration on the Granting of Independence to Colonial Countries and Peoples;[3] the Declaration on Permanent Sovereignty over Natural Resources;[4] and the Declaration of Legal Principles Governing Activities of States in the Exploration and Use of Outer Space.[5] Literature in English all too often fails to indicate the significance of such instruments. In some cases a resolution may have direct legal effect as an authoritative interpretation and application of the principles of the Charter.[6]

Drafts adopted by the International Law Commission. See *infra*, p. 31.

5. *General Principles of Law*[7]

Article 38 (1) (c) of the Statute of the International Court refers to 'the general principles of law recognized by civilized

[1] Resol. no. 95; 11 December 1946. Adopted unanimously.

[2] Resol. no. 1653 (XVI); 24 November 1961. Adopted by 55 votes to 20; 26 abstentions.

[3] Resol. no. 1514 (XV), 14 December 1960. Adopted by 89 votes to none; 9 abstentions.

[4] Resol. no. 1803 (XVII), 14 December 1962; *U.K. Contemp. Practice* (1962), ii. 283. Adopted by 87 votes to 2; 12 abstentions.

[5] Resol. no. 1962 (XVIII), 13 December 1963; 3 *Int. Leg. Materials* (1964), 160; 58 *A.J.* (1964), 477. Adopted unanimously.

[6] See, for example, the Declaration on the Elimination of All Forms of Racial Discrimination; adopted 20 November 1963; Art. 1 (in Resol. 1904 (XVIII)); 3 *Int. Leg. Materials* (1964), 164; Declaration on Principles of International Law Concerning Friendly Relations; adopted without vote, 24 October 1970; Resol. 2625; Brownlie, *Documents*, p. 32.

[7] Sørensen, 101 Hague *Recueil* (1960, III), 16–34; id., *Les Sources de droit international*, pp. 123–52; Kopelmanas, 43 *R.G.D.I.P.* (1936), 285–308; Guggenheim, 94 Hague *Recueil* (1958, II), 72–79; id., *Traité* (2nd ed.), i. 291–312; Verzijl, *International Law in Historical Perspective* i. 47–74; Tunkin, 95 Hague *Recueil* (1958, III), 23–6; Verdross, in *Recueil d'études sur les sources du droit en l'honneur de François Gény* iii (1936), 383–8; Lauterpacht, *Private Law Sources and Analogies of International Law* (1927); id., *International Law: Collected Papers* ii. 173–212; id., *The Function of Law in the International Community*, pp. 115–18; id., *The Development of International Law by the International Court*, pp. 158–72; Cheng, *General Principles of Law as Applied by International Courts and Tribunals* (1953), pp. 163–80; McNair, 33 *B.Y.* (1957), 1–19; Rousseau, *Principes généraux du droit international public*, i (1944), 889–929; id., *Droit international public* i (1970), 370–97; Schlesinger, 51 *A.J.* (1957), 734–53; Gutteridge, 38 *Grot. Soc.* (1952), 125–34; Jenks, *The Prospects of International Adjudication*, pp. 266–315; Parry, op. cit., pp. 83–91; Verdross, *Recueil d'études en hommage à Guggenheim*, 521–30; Paul, 10 *Indian Journ.* (1970), 324–50; Bartoš, *Mélanges Andrassy*, pp. 1–12; Akehurst, 25 *I.C.L.Q.* (1976), 813–25. For the view that general principles of law provide a third system for disputes between corporations and governments see McNair, op. cit., and the *Abu Dhabi* award (1951), 1 *I.C.L.Q.* (1952), 247.

nations', a source which comes after those depending more immediately on the consent of states and yet escapes classification as a 'subsidiary means' in paragraph (d). The formulation appeared in the *compromis* of arbitral tribunals in the nineteenth century, and similar formulae appear in draft instruments concerned with the functioning of tribunals.[1] In the committee of jurists which prepared the Statute there was no very definite consensus on the precise significance of the phrase. The Belgian jurist, Baron Descamps, had natural law concepts in mind, and his draft referred to 'the rules of international law recognized by the legal conscience of civilized peoples'. Root considered that governments would mistrust a court which relied on the subjective concept of principles of justice. However, the committee realized that the Court must be given a certain power to develop and refine the principles of international jurisprudence. In the result a joint proposal by Root and Phillimore was accepted and this is the text we now have.[2]

Root and Phillimore regarded the principles in terms of rules accepted in the domestic law of all civilized states, and Guggenheim[3] holds the firm view that paragraph (c) must be applied in this light. However, the view expressed in Oppenheim[4] is to be preferred: 'The intention is to authorize the Court to apply the general principles of municipal jurisprudence, in particular of private law, in so far as they are applicable to relations of States.' The latter part of this statement is worthy of emphasis. It would be incorrect to assume that tribunals have in practice adopted a mechanical system of borrowing from domestic law after a census of domestic systems. What has happened is that international tribunals have employed elements of legal reasoning and private law analogies in order to make the law of nations a viable system for application in a judicial process. Thus, it is impossible, or at least difficult, for state practice to evolve the rules of procedure and evidence which a court must employ. An international tribunal chooses, edits, and adapts elements from better developed systems: the result is a new element of inter-

[1] See the draft treaty for the establishment of an international prize court, 1907, Art. 7 (general principles of justice and equity), and see *supra*, p. 4. See also the European Conv. for the Protection of Human Rights and Fundamental Freedoms, Art. 7, para. 2: Robertson, *Human Rights in Europe*, pp. 26, 179, 182.

[2] *Procès-Verbaux*, pp. 316, 335, 344. Sørensen remarks that the compromise formula has an inherent ambiguity which is inimical to any rational interpretation of the provision: *Les Sources*, p. 125.

[3] Op. cit., p. 78.

[4] *International Law* i (8th ed.), 29.

national law the content of which is influenced historically and logically by domestic law.[1]

In practice tribunals show considerable discretion in the matter. The decisions on the acquisition of territory[2] tend not to reflect the domestic derivatives on the subject to be found in the textbooks, and there is room for the view that domestic law analogies have caused more harm than good in this sphere. The evolution of the rules on the effect of duress on treaties[3] has not depended on changes in domestic law. In the *North Atlantic Fisheries*[4] case the tribunal considered the concept of servitude and then refused to apply it. Moreover, in some cases, for example the law relating to expropriation of private rights, reference to domestic law might give uncertain results and the choice of models might reveal ideological predilections.[5]

General principles of law in the practice of tribunals

(a) *Arbitral tribunals.*[6] Arbitral tribunals have frequently resorted to municipal analogies. In the *Fabiani*[7] case between France and Venezuela the arbitrator had recourse to municipal public law on the question of the responsibility of the state for the acts of its agents, including judicial officers, committed in the exercise of their functions. Reliance was also placed on general principles of law in the assessment of damages. The Permanent Court of Arbitration applied the principle of moratory interest on debts in the *Russian Indemnity* case.[8] Since the original Statute of the International Court came into force in 1920, tribunals not otherwise bound by it have treated Article 38 (1) (c) as declaratory of the law applicable.[9]

[1] See Tunkin, loc. cit.; and de Visscher, *Theory and Reality in Public International Law*, pp. 356–8. Cf. McNair, I.C.J. Reports (1950), pp. 148–50. A problem worth examination is whether public law is a better source of analogies in the present state of international law and institutions. [2] See *infra*, Chapter VII.

[3] See *infra*, Chapter XXV, section 7. Nineteenth century writers took the view that duress had no vitiating effect. Since 1920 the contrary view has been gaining ground.

[4] (1910) Hague Court Reports, i. 141; Green, p. 301; Briggs, p. 313; Hudson, pp. 241, 273.

[5] See Sørensen, 101 Hague *Recueil* (1960, III), 19–22.

[6] See Simpson and Fox, *International Arbitration*, pp. 132–7; Jenks, op. cit., pp. 306–9; Lauterpacht, *Analogies*, pp. 60–7; id., *Function of Law*, pp. 115–18; Seidl-Hohenveldern, 53 *A.J.* (1959), 853–72; U.S. argument in the *Behring Sea* arbitration, Moore, *Arbitrations* i. 755, that the property in the seals rested on the principle of *animus revertendi*.

[7] (1896), Lafontaine, *Pasicrisie internationale*, p. 344; *R.I.A.A.* x. 83. The claim was based on denial of justice by the Venezuelan courts.

[8] (1912), Hague Court Reports, p. 297; Briggs, p. 37. See also *Sarropoulos* v. *Bulgarian State* (1927), *Ann. Digest* 4 (1927–8), no. 173 (extinctive prescription).

[9] Admin. Decision no. II (1923), Mixed Claims Commission, U.S.–Germany; *Ann. Digest* 2 (1923–4), no. 205; *Goldenberg & Sons* v. *Germany* (1928), ibid., 4 (1927–8), no. 369; *Lena Goldfields* arbitration (1930), ibid., 5 (1929–30), no. 1; 36 *Cornell L.Qtly.* 42.

(b) *The International Court of Justice and its predecessor.*[1] The Court has used this source sparingly, and it normally appears, without any formal reference or label, as a part of judicial reasoning. However, the Court has on occasion referred to general notions of responsibility. In the *Chorzów Factory* case[2] the Court observed: '. . . one Party cannot avail himself of the fact that the other has not fulfilled some obligation, or has not had recourse to some means of redress, if the former Party has, by some illegal act, prevented the latter from fulfilling the obligation in question, or from having recourse to the tribunal which would have been open to him'. In a later stage of the same case[3] the following statement was made: '. . . the Court observes that it is a principle of international law, and even a general conception of law, that any breach of an engagement involves an obligation to make reparation'. In a number of cases the principle of estoppel or acquiescence (*préclusion*) has been relied on by the Court,[4] and on occasion rather general references to abuse of rights and good faith may occur.[5] Perhaps the most frequent and successful use of domestic law analogies has been in the field of evidence, procedure, and jurisdictional questions. Thus there have been references to the rule that no one can be judge in his own suit,[6] litispendence,[7] *res judicata*,[8] various 'principles governing the judicial process',[9] and 'the principle universally accepted by international tribunals . . . to the effect that the parties to a case must abstain from any measure capable of exercising a prejudicial

[1] See Jenks, op. cit., pp. 268–305; Lauterpacht, *The Development of International Law by the International Court*, pp. 158–72; Fitzmaurice, 35 *B.Y.* (1959), 216–29; Waldock, 106 Hague *Recueil* (1962, II), 57–69; Beckett, *Corfu Channel* case, I.C.J. Pleadings iii. 267 seq.; Blondel, *Recueil d'études en hommage à Guggenheim*, 201–36.

[2] *Chorzów Factory* (Indemnity; Jurisdiction), P.C.I.J., Ser. A, no. 9, p. 31.

[3] *Chorzów Factory* (Merits), P.C.I.J., Ser. A, no. 17, p. 29.

[4] See the *Eastern Greenland* case (1933), P.C.I.J., Ser. A/B, no. 53, pp. 52 seq., 62, 69; *Arbitral Award of the King of Spain*, I.C.J. Reports (1960), p. 192 at pp. 209, 213; the *Temple case*, I.C.J. Reports (1962), at pp. 23, 31, 32 (see Chapter XXVI, section 4); ibid., individual opinion of Judge Alfaro, pp. 39–51. See also ibid., p. 26, where the Court said: 'it is an established rule of law that a plea of error cannot be allowed as an element vitiating consent if the party advancing it contributed by its own conduct to the error'.

[5] e.g. the *Free Zones* case (1930), P.C.I.J., Ser. A, no. 24, p. 12; and (1932), Ser. A/B, no. 46, p. 167. For references to individual judges' use of analogies see Lauterpacht, op. cit., p. 167, n. 20, and see also I.C.J. Reports (1960), pp. 66–7, 90, 107, 136.

[6] *Mosul Boundary* case (1925), P.C.I.J., Ser. B, no. 12, p. 32.

[7] *German Interests in Polish Upper Silesia* (1925), P.C.I.J., Ser. A, no. 6, p. 20.

[8] *Effect of Awards of the U.N. Administrative Tribunal*, I.C.J. Reports (1954), p. 53.

[9] Advisory Opinion, *Application for Review of Judgement No. 158*, I.C.J. Reports (1973), p. 166 at pp. 177, 181, 210.

effect in regard to the execution of the decision to be given . . .'.[1] In the *Corfu Channel* case[2] the Court had recourse to circumstantial evidence and remarked that 'this indirect evidence is admitted in all systems of law, and its use is recognized by international decisions'. In his Dissenting Opinion in the *South West Africa* cases (Second Phase),[3] Judge Tanaka referred to Article 38 (1) (c) of the Court's Statute as a basis for human rights concepts and pointed out that the provision contains natural law elements. The reasoning of the Court in the *Barcelona Traction* case (Second Phase)[4] related very closely to the general conception of the limited liability company to be found in systems of municipal law.

6. *General Principles of International Law*[5]

The rubric may refer to rules of customary law, to general principles of law as in Article 38 (1) (c), or to logical propositions resulting from judicial reasoning on the basis of existing pieces of international law and municipal analogies. What is clear is the inappropriateness of rigid categorization of the sources. Examples of this type of general principle are the principles of consent, reciprocity, equality of states, finality of awards and settlements, the legal validity of agreements, good faith, domestic jurisdiction, and the freedom of the seas. In many cases these principles are to be traced to state practice. However, they are primarily abstractions from a mass of rules and have been so long and so generally accepted as to be no longer *directly* connected with state practice. In a few cases the principle concerned, though useful, is unlikely to appear in ordinary state practice. In general the subject-matter of 'general principles of law' over-

[1] *Electricity Company of Sofia and Bulgaria* (1939), P.C.I.J., Ser. A/B, no. 79, p. 199.

[2] I.C.J. Reports (1949), p. 18; Green, p. 228; Briggs, p. 291. See also *Right of Passage over Indian Territory* (Preliminary Objection), I.C.J. Reports (1957), pp. 141–2; *German Interests in Polish Upper Silesia*, P.C.I.J., Ser. A, no. 6 (1925), p. 19; and, on *forum prorogatum*, *infra*, Chapter XXXI, section 9.

[3] I.C.J. Reports (1966), p. 6 at pp. 294–9.

[4] Ibid. (1970), at pp. 33–5. See generally *infra*, Chapter XXI, section 5.

[5] See Rousseau i. 389–95; id., *Principes généraux* i. 913–24; Fitzmaurice, 92 Hague *Recueil* (1957, II), 57–8; Sørensen, *Les Sources*, pp. 112–22; Friedmann, 57 *A.J.* (1963), 281; Waldock, 106 Hague *Recueil* (1962, II), 62–4; Briggs, p. 48; Simpson and Fox, op. cit., p. 132. See also I.C.J. Reports (1958), pp. 106–7 (Moreno Quintana); ibid. (1960), pp. 136–7 (Fernandes); and ibid. (1962), p. 143 (Spender); Verdross, *Recueil d'études en hommage à Guggenheim*, pp. 521–30; Virally, ibid., pp. 531–54. Cf. Fitzmaurice, 30 *B.Y.* (1953), 2; 35 *B.Y.* (1959), 185, rubric 'General Principles'; and id., *Symbolae Verzijl*, pp. 161–8.

laps that of the present section. However, certain fundamental principles have recently been set apart as overriding principles of *jus cogens* which may qualify the effect of more ordinary rules.[1]

7. *Judicial Decisions*[2]

(a) *Decisions of international tribunals.* Judicial decisions are not strictly speaking a formal source, but in some instances at least they are regarded as authoritative evidence of the state of the law, and the practical significance of the label 'subsidiary means' in Article 38 (1) (d) is not to be exaggerated.[3] A coherent body of jurisprudence will naturally have important consequences for the law.

Arbitral tribunals. The literature of the law contains frequent reference to decisions of arbitral tribunals. The quality of arbitral tribunals has varied considerably, but there have been a number of awards which contain notable contributions to the development of the law by eminent jurists sitting as arbitrators, umpires, or commissioners.[4]

Reference to arbitral awards by the International Court of Justice and its predecessor. The Court has referred to particular decisions on only four occasions,[5] but on other occasions[6] has referred compendiously to the jurisprudence of international arbitration.

Decisions of the International Court of Justice and its predecessor.

[1] See Chapter XXII, section 5.

[2] Lauterpacht, *The Development of International Law by the International Court*, pp. 8–22; Waldock, 106 Hague *Recueil* (1962, II), 88–95; Fitzmaurice, *Symbolae Verzijl*, pp. 168–73; Tunkin, 95 Hague *Recueil* (1958, III), 28–30; Sørensen, *Les Sources*, pp. 153–76.

[3] Fitzmaurice, *Symbolae Verzijl*, p. 174, criticizes the classification.

[4] See, for example, the *Alabama Claims* arbitration (1872), Moore, *Arbitrations* i. 653; Green, p. 27; Briggs, p. 1026; and the *Behring Sea Fisheries* arbitration (1893), Moore, *Arbitrations* i. 755. See also *infra*, pp. 144–5 on the *Palmas Island* case, and pp. 399 seq. on the *Canevaro* case, and, generally, the series of *Reports of International Arbitral Awards* published by the U.N. since 1948, and the foreword to volume i.

[5] *Polish Postal Service in Danzig* (1925), P.C.I.J., Ser. B, no. 11, p. 30 (to the P.C.A. in the case of the *Pious Funds of the Californias*, *R.I.A.A.* ix. 11); the *Lotus* (1927), P.C.I.J., Ser. A, no. 10, p. 26 (to the *Costa Rica Packet* case, Moore, *Arbitrations* v. 4948); *Eastern Greenland* case (1933), P.C.I.J., Ser. A/B, no. 53, pp. 45–6; Hague Court Reports iii, at p. 170 (to the *Island of Palmas* case, *infra*, pp. 144–5); *Nottebohm*, I.C.J. Reports (1953), p. 119 (to the *Alabama* arbitration, *supra*, p. 4).

[6] *Chorzów Factory* (Jurisdiction) (1927), P.C.I.J., Ser. A, no. 9, p. 31; *Chorzów Factory* (Merits) (1928), P.C.I.J., Ser. A, no. 17, pp. 31, 47; *Fisheries* case, I.C.J. Reports (1951), p. 131. See also *Peter Pázmány University* (1933), P.C.I.J., Ser. A/B, no. 61, p. 243 (consistent practice of mixed arbitral tribunals); *Barcelona Traction* case (Second Phase), I.C.J. Reports (1970), at p. 40. The Court has also referred generally to decisions of other tribunals without specific reference to arbitral tribunals: *Eastern Greenland* case, *supra*, at p. 46; *Reparation for Injuries*, I.C.J. Reports (1949), p. 186.

The Court applies the law and does not make it, and Article 59 of the Statute[1] in part reflects a feeling on the part of the founders that the Court was intended to settle disputes as they came to it rather than to shape the law. Yet it is obvious that a unanimous, or almost unanimous, decision has a role in the progressive development of the law. Since 1947 the decisions and advisory opinions in the *Reparation*,[2] *Genocide*,[3] *Fisheries*,[4] and *Nottebohm*[5] cases have had decisive influence on general international law. The last three cases have provided a basis for the work of the International Law Commission in the fields involved. However, some discretion is needed in handling decisions. The *Lotus* decision, arising from the casting vote of the President, and much criticized, was rejected by the Commission in its draft articles[6] on the law of the sea, and at its third session the Commission refused to accept the principles emerging from the *Genocide* case (a stand which was reversed at its fourteenth session).[7] On occasion the General Assembly has not adopted the advice tendered by the Court on legal matters.[8] Moreover, the view may be taken that it is incautious to extract general propositions from opinions and judgments devoted to a specific problem or settlement of disputes entangled with the special relations of two states.[9]

Judicial precedent and the Statute of the Court. It will be remembered that Article 38 (1) (d) of the Statute starts with a proviso: 'Subject to the provisions of Article 59, judicial decisions . . . as subsidiary means for the determination of rules of law.' Article 59 provides: 'The decision of the Court has no binding force except as between the parties and in respect of that particular case.' Lauterpacht has argued[1] that Article 59 does not refer to the major question of judicial precedent but to the particular question of intervention. In Article 63 it is provided that, if a third state avails itself of the right of intervention, the construction given in the judgment shall be equally binding upon it. Lauterpacht concludes that 'Article 59 would thus seem

[1] *Supra*, p. 3. [2] *Infra*, Chapter XXX. [3] *Infra*, Chapter XXV, section 3.
[4] *Infra*, pp. 186–90. [5] *Infra*, Chapter XVIII. [6] See *infra*, pp. 254–5.
[7] See *infra*, Chapter XXV, section 3.
[8] Cf. the *Admissions* case, I.C.J. Reports (1947–8), p. 65, and the later U.N. practice; and see Rosenne, 39 *B.Y.* (1963), p. 1 at pp. 40–3.
[9] On the *Genocide* case see McNair, *Law of Treaties* (1961), pp. 167–8. On the *Nottebohm* case see the *Flegenheimer* case, Int. L.R. 25 (1958, I), p. 91 at pp. 148–50. On the implications for the law relating to the use of force of the *Corfu Channel* case, see Brownlie, *International Law and the Use of Force by States*, pp. 283–9; and, for a different view, Brierly, *Law of Nations* (6th ed.), pp. 421–30.
[1] *Development*, p. 8. He relies on the final report of the committee of jurists in 1920.

to state directly what Article 63 expresses indirectly'. Beckett[1] took the view that Article 59 refers to the actual decision as opposed to the legal principles on which it is based. However, the debate in the committee of jurists responsible for the Statute indicates clearly that Article 59 was not intended merely to express the principle of *res judicata* but to rule out a system of binding precedent.[2] Thus in one judgment the Court said:[3] 'The object of [Article 59] is simply to prevent legal principles accepted by the Court in a particular case from being binding on other States or in other disputes.' In its practice, however, it has not treated earlier decisions in such a narrow spirit.

Judicial precedent in the practice of the Court.[4] Strictly speaking, the Court does not observe a doctrine of precedent,[5] but strives nevertheless to maintain judicial consistency. Thus, in the case on *Exchange of Greek and Turkish Populations*,[6] the Court referred to 'the precedent afforded by its Advisory Opinion No. 3', i.e. the *Wimbledon* case, in respect of the view that the incurring of treaty obligations was not an abandonment of sovereignty. In the *Reparation*[7] case the Court relied on a pronouncement in a previous advisory opinion[8] for a statement of the principle of effectiveness in interpreting treaties. Such references are often a

[1] 39 Hague *Recueil* (1932, I), 141.

[2] See Descamps, *Procès-Verbaux*, pp. 332, 336, 584. See also Sørensen, *Les Sources*, p. 161; Hudson, *The Permanent Court of International Justice 1920–1942*, p. 207, and Waldock, op. cit., p. 91. The latter observes: 'It would indeed have been somewhat surprising if States had been prepared in 1920 to give a wholly new and untried tribunal explicit authority to lay down law binding upon all States.'

[3] *German Interests in Polish Upper Silesia* (1926), P.C.I.J., Ser. A, no. 7, p. 19; World Court Reports i. 510; Green, p. 533.

[4] See Lauterpacht, 12 *B.Y.* (1931), 60; id., *Development*, pp. 9–15; Beckett, 39 Hague *Recueil* (1932, I), 138; Sørensen, *Les Sources*, pp. 166–76.

[5] But precedent is firmly adhered to in matters of procedure.

[6] (1925), P.C.I.J., Ser. B, no. 10, p. 21. See also *German Interests in Polish Upper Silesia* (Merits) (1926), P.C.I.J., Ser. A, no. 7, p. 31; *Corfu Channel* case, I.C.J. Reports (1947–8), p. 28; *Admissions* case, I.C.J. Reports (1947–8), p. 63; *Corfu Channel* case (Merits), I.C.J. Reports (1949), p. 24; *U.S. Nationals in Morocco*, I.C.J. Reports (1952), pp. 200, 206; *Ambatielos* case, I.C.J. Reports (1953), p. 19; *Nottebohm* case (Preliminary Objection), ibid., p. 121; *Peace Treaties* case, I.C.J. Reports (1950), pp. 89, 103, 106 (Winiarski, Zoričić, and Krylov, dissenting); *South West Africa* cases, I.C.J. Reports (1962), pp. 328, 345; *Cameroons* case, ibid. (1963), pp. 27–8, 29–30, 37; *Aerial Incident* case, ibid. (1959), p. 192 (joint dissent); *South West Africa* cases (Second Phase), I.C.J. Reports (1966), pp. 240–1 (Koretsky, diss. op.); *North Sea Continental Shelf Cases*, ibid. (1969), p. 3 at pp. 44, 47–9; ibid., pp. 101–2, 121, 131, 138 (Ammoun, sep. op.); ibid., p. 210 (Morelli, diss. op.); ibid., pp. 223, 225, 229, 231, 232–3, 236, 238 (Lachs, diss. op.); ibid., pp. 243–4, 247 (Sørensen, diss. op.); *Namibia Opinion* (ibid.), 1971, pp. 26 seq., 53–4 (and there are numerous references in the sep. and diss. opinions).

[7] I.C.J. Reports (1949), pp. 182–3.

[8] *Competence of the I.L.O. to regulate, incidentally, the Personal Work of the Employer* (1926), P.C.I.J., Ser. B, no. 13, p. 18.

matter of 'evidence' of the law, but a fairly substantial consistency is aimed at and so the technique of distinguishing previous decisions may be employed. In the case on *Interpretation of Peace Treaties*[1] certain questions were submitted by the General Assembly to the Court for an advisory opinion. The questions concerned the interpretation of clauses in the peace treaties with Bulgaria, Hungary, and Rumania, clauses relating to the settlement of disputes concerning the interpretation or execution of these treaties. In fact the request arose from allegations against these three states by other parties of breaches of the provisions of the treaties on the maintenance of human rights, a matter of substance. The Court rejected arguments to the effect that it lacked the power to answer the request for an opinion. The Court said:[2]

Article 65 of the Statute is permissive. It gives the Court the power to examine whether the circumstances of the case are of such a character as should lead it to decline to answer the Request. In the opinion of the Court, the circumstances of the present case are profoundly different from those which were before the Permanent Court of International Justice in the Eastern Carelia case[3] (Advisory Opinion No. 5), when that Court declined to give an Opinion because it found the question put to it was directly related to the main point of dispute actually pending between two States, so that answering the question would be substantially equivalent to deciding the dispute between the parties, and that at the same time it raised a question of fact which could not be elucidated without hearing both parties.

. . . the present Request for an Opinion is solely concerned with the applicability to certain disputes of the procedure for settlement instituted by the Peace Treaties, and it is justifiable to conclude that it in no way touches the merits of those disputes.

(b) *Decisions of the Court of Justice of the European Communities.*[4] Several decisions of this Court have involved issues of general importance.

(c) *Decisions of national courts.*[5] Article 38 (1) (d) of the Statute

[1] I.C.J. Reports (1950), p. 65; Green, p. 567.

[2] I.C.J. Reports (1950), p. 72 (this is not the only significant passage). See Lauterpacht, *Development*, pp. 352–7, for criticism of the distinction between procedure and substance. See further Fitzmaurice, 29 *B.Y.* (1952), 50–2; Rosenne, *The International Court of Justice*, pp. 463–7; and the dissenting opinions. Cf. joint dissenting opinion of Spender and Fitzmaurice, *South West Africa* cases, I.C.J. Reports (1962), pp. 471–3; the *Cameroons* case, ibid. (1963), pp. 35, 37–8, 62–4 (Wellington Koo, sep. op.), pp. 68–73 (Sir Percy Spender, sep. op.); pp. 108, 125–7 (Sir Gerald Fitzmaurice, sep. op.); 140–1 (Morelli, sep. op.); 150–1 (Badawi, diss. op.); 156–9, 170, 182 (Bustamante, diss. op.); 187–91, 194–6 (Beb a Don, diss. op.). The *Eastern Carelia* case was also distinguished in the *Namibia Opinion*, I.C.J. Reports (1971), p. 16 at p. 23.

[3] (1923), P.C.I.J., Ser. B, no. 5, at p. 27.

[4] See Reuter, *Recueil d'études en hommage à Guggenheim*, p. 665 at pp. 673–85.

[5] See Lauterpacht, 10 *B.Y.* (1929), 65–95 (also in *International Law: Collected Papers* ii. 238–68); Schwarzenberger, *International Law*, i (3rd ed.), 32–4; Briggs, p. 49.

of the International Court is not confined to international decisions and the decisions of national tribunals have evidential value. Some decisions provide indirect evidence of the practice of the state of the *forum* on the question involved;[1] others involve a free investigation of the point of law and consideration of available sources, and may result in a careful exposition of the law. Hall, Oppenheim, Moore, Hyde, McNair, and other writers from common law jurisdictions, make frequent reference to municipal decisions, and such use is universal in monographs from this source. French, German, and Italian jurists tend to use fewer case references,[2] whilst Soviet jurists are even more sparing. In the recent past there has been a great increase in the availability of decisions as evidence of the law.[3] Municipal decisions have been an important source for material on recognition of belligerency, of governments and of states, state succession, sovereign immunity, diplomatic immunity, extradition, war crimes, belligerent occupation, the concept of a 'state of war', and the law of prize.[4] However, the value of these decisions varies considerably, and many present a narrow national outlook[5] or rest on a very inadequate use of the sources.

(d) *International military tribunals.* Tribunals set up by agreement between a number of states, for some *ad hoc* purpose, may produce valuable pronouncements on delicate issues, much depending on the status of the tribunal and its members and the conditions under which it does its work. The judgment of the International Military Tribunal for the trial of German major war criminals contains a number of significant findings on issues of law.[6]

(e) *Municipal courts and disputes between parts of composite states.*[7] The Supreme Court of the United States, the Swiss

[1] Note the relation between English decisions and the Foreign Office Certificates: see Lyons, 23 *B.Y.* (1946), 240–81. See also the *Lotus*, P.C.I.J., Ser. A, no. 10, pp. 23, 28–30; and the dissenting opinions of Judges Finlay and Moore, pp. 54, 68–9 respectively; and the *Eichmann* case (1961), 56 *A.J.* (1962), 805; Int. L.R., 36, 5.

[2] It depends very much on the individual. Rousseau and Guggenheim, authors of excellent general works, use cases extensively. The former is French; the latter Swiss.

[3] See the *Journal du droit international* (Clunet) and the *Annual Digest of Public International Law Cases*, now the International Law Reports.

[4] See also the *Scotia* (1871), 14 Wallace 170, Briggs, p. 25; the *Paquete Habana* (1900), 175 U.S. 677, Briggs, p. 30; the *Zamora* [1916] 2 A.C. 77; *Gibbs* v. *Rodriguez* (1950), Int. L.R. 18 (1951), no. 204; *Lauritzen* v. *Government of Chile*, Int. L.R. 23 (1956), 708.

[5] A decision may even present a view of national practice which does not correspond with the actual state of affairs: *supra*, p. 6, n. 1.

[6] Cmd. 6964; *Ann. Digest* 13 (1946), no. 92; Green, p. 707.

[7] See 10 *B.Y.* (1929), 74–5. See e.g. *New Jersey* v. *Delaware* (1934), 291 U.S. 361; 29 *A.J.* (1935), 309; Briggs, p. 253; *Labrador Boundary* case (1927), 43 T.L.R. 289.

Federal Court, and the *Staatsgerichtshof* of the Weimar Republic have had occasion to decide disputes between members of the federal communities involved on the basis of doctrines of international law. The practice of the first of these is of importance in view of the fact that the United States has its origin in a union of independent states and this gives an international element to its internal relations.[1]

(f) *Pleadings in cases before international tribunals.* Pleadings before the International Court contain valuable collations of material and, at the least, have value as comprehensive statements of the opinions of particular states on legal questions.[2]

8. *The Writings of Publicists*[3]

The Statute of the International Court includes, among the 'subsidiary means for the determination of rules of law', 'the teachings of the most highly qualified[4] publicists of the various nations' or, in the French text, 'la doctrine'. Once again the source only constitutes evidence of the law, but in some subjects individual writers have had a formative influence. Thus Gidel has had some formative influence on the law of the sea.[5] Writers of general works, such as Hall, Oppenheim, Hyde, Guggenheim, Verdross, and Rousseau, have earned international reputations. It is, however, obvious that subjective factors enter into any assessment of juristic opinion, that individual writers reflect national and other prejudices, and, further, that some publicists see themselves to be propagating new and better views rather than providing a passive appraisal of the law. Some quite eminent jurists have rested their opinions on a rather restricted selection of state practice and national decisions.

Whatever the need for caution, the opinions of publicists are used widely. The law officers' opinions tendered confidentially

[1] See also *infra*, pp. 62–3.

[2] Thus the British view on expropriation of foreign property occurs in the U.K. memorial in the *Anglo-Iranian Oil Co.* case; I.C.J. Pleadings (1951), p. 106.

[3] See Sørensen, *Les Sources*, pp. 177–90; Rousseau, *Principes généraux* i. 816–23; Lauterpacht, *Development*, pp. 23–5; Waldock, 106 Hague *Recueil* (1962, II), 95–6; Schwarzenberger, *International Law* i. 36–7. See also *infra*, p. 31, on the International Law Commission.

[4] This phrase is not given a restrictive effect by tribunals; but authority naturally affects the weight of the evidence.

[5] *Droit international public de la mer*, 3 vols. (1932–4). His work is associated with the concept of the contiguous zone. See also Colombos, *The International Law of the Sea* (6th ed., 1967), translated into French, Italian, Russian, Spanish, German, Portuguese, and Greek. Cf. the writings of Makarov on nationality; of Kelsen on the United Nations Charter.

to the executive in Great Britain contain references to the views of Vattel, Calvo, Hall, and others, and the opinions themselves represent the views of experts, including Harcourt, Phillimore, and Finlay.[1] Arbitral tribunals[2] and national courts[3] make extensive use of the writings of jurists. National courts are unfamiliar with state practice and are ready to lean on secondary sources. Superficially the International Court might seem to make little use of doctrine,[4] and majority judgments contain few references: but this is because of the process of collective drafting of judgments, and the need to avoid a somewhat invidious selection of citations. The fact that writers are used by the Court is evidenced by the dissenting and separate opinions[5] in which the 'workings' are set out in more detail and reflect the actual methods of approach of the Court as a whole. Many references to writers are to be found in the pleadings before the Court.

Sources analogous to the writings of publicists, and at least as authoritative, are the draft articles produced by the International Law Commission,[6] reports and secretariat memoranda prepared for the Commission,[7] Harvard Research drafts,[8] the bases of discussion of the Hague Codification Conference of 1930,[9] and the resolutions of the Institute of International Law and other scientific bodies.

[1] See McNair, *International Law Opinions* i, Preface; iii. 402–6. Robert Joseph Phillimore (1810–85) was author of the *Commentaries on International Law* (4 vols.).

[2] Particularly in the period 1793 to 1914, using Grotius, Vattel, and Bynkershoek.

[3] See the judgments in the *Eichmann* case (1961), 56 *A.J.* (1962), 805; Int. L.R., 36, 5; *R.* v. *Keyn* (1876), 2 Ex. D. 63; Green, p. 220; *Public Prosecutor* v. *Oie Hee Koi* [1968] A.C. 829.

[4] But see the *Wimbledon* (1923), P.C.I.J., Ser. A, no. 1, p. 28 ('general opinion'); *German Settlers in Poland* (1923), P.C.I.J., Ser. B, no. 6, p. 36 ('almost universal opinion'); *Jaworzina* case (1923), P.C.I.J., Ser. B, no. 8, p. 37 (French text, 'une doctrine constante'); *German Interests in Polish Upper Silesia* (1925), P.C.I.J., Ser. A, no. 6, p. 20 ('the "teachings of legal authorities"'; 'the jurisprudence of the principal countries'); the *Lotus* (1927), P.C.I.J., Ser. A, no. 10, p. 26 ('teachings of publicists', 'all or nearly all writers'); *Nottebohm* (Second Phase), I.C.J. Reports (1955), p. 22 ('the writings of publicists').

[5] *Diversion of Water from the Meuse* (1937), P.C.I.J., Ser. A/B, no. 70, pp. 76–7 (Hudson); *South West Africa* case, I.C.J. Reports (1950), pp. 146 seq. (McNair); *Peace Treaties* case, ibid., p. 235 (Read); *Asylum* case, ibid., pp. 335 seq. (Azevedo); *Genocide* case, I.C.J. Reports (1951), pp. 32 seq. (joint dissent, Guerrero, McNair, Read, Hsu Mo); *Temple* case, I.C.J. Reports (1962), pp. 39 seq. (Alfaro); *Aerial Incident* case, I.C.J. Reports (1959), p. 174 (joint diss., Lauterpacht, Wellington Koo, Spender).

[6] But see the *Abu Dhabi* award (1951), Int. L.R. 18 (1951), no. 37, pp. 156–7; 1 *I.C.L.Q.* (1952), 247. And see *infra*, p. 31.

[7] See generally the *Yearbook of the International Law Commission*.

[8] See *A.J.* 26 (1932), Suppl., 29 (1935), Suppl., 33 (1939), Suppl., and the *Genocide* case, I.C.J. Reports (1951), pp. 32 seq.

[9] See *A.J.* 24 (1930), Suppl., and *In re Eschauzier, Ann. Digest* 6 (1931–2), no. 110. See also the work of the committee of experts, *A.J.* 20 (1926), Suppl.; 22 (1928), Suppl.

9. *Equity in Judgments and Advisory Opinions of the International Court*[1]

'Equity' is used here in the sense of considerations of fairness, reasonableness, and policy often necessary for the sensible application of the more settled rules of law. Strictly, it cannot be a source of law, and yet it may be an important factor in the process of decision. Equity may play a dramatic role in supplementing the law or appear unobtrusively as a part of judicial reasoning. The principle of the 'exception' whereby existing rules are qualified to meet special cases, is a form of equity which takes on the form of judicial legislation.[2] In the case on *Diversion of Water from the River Meuse*[3] Judge Hudson applied the principle that equality is equity[4] and stated as a corollary that a state seeking the interpretation of a treaty must itself have completely fulfilled the obligations of that treaty. He observed that under 'Article 38 of the Statute, if not independently of that Article, the Court has some freedom to consider principles of equity as part of the international law which it must apply'.

In the *North Sea Continental Shelf Cases*[5] the Court had to resort to the formulation of equitable principles concerning the lateral delimitation of adjacent areas of continental shelf, as a consequence of its opinion that no rule of customary or treaty law bound the states parties to the dispute over the seabed of the North Sea. Considerations of equity advanced by Belgium in the *Barcelona Traction* case (Second Phase)[6] did not cause the Court to modify its views on the legal principles and considerations of policy. In the *Fisheries Jurisdiction Case* (United Kingdom v.

[1] Sørensen, *Les Sources*, pp. 191–209; Jenks, *The Prospects of International Adjudication*, pp. 316–427; Rousseau, *Principes généraux* i. 932–50; Lauterpacht, *Analogies*, pp. 63–7; id., *Function*, pp. 313–15; id., *Development*, pp. 213–17; Hudson, *The Permanent Court of International Justice*, pp. 615–21; Moore, *Collected Papers* vii. 322–8; Schwarzenberger, *International Law* i. 49–54; *American and British Claims Arbitration, Report of Fred K. Nielsen* (1926), pp. 51–72; Akehurst, 25 *I.C.L.Q.* (1976), 801–25; Pirotte, 77 *R.G.D.I.P.* (1973), 92–135. See also Green, index, *sub voc.* 'Equity'. Cf. *supra*, pp. 15–19 on 'general principles of law', including good faith and abuse of rights.

[2] See the *Fisheries* case, *infra*, pp. 186 seq. and Fitzmaurice, 30 *B.Y.* (1953), 18–24. And see also *infra*, on 'legitimate interests'.

[3] (1937), P.C.I.J., Ser. A/B, no. 70, p. 77. See also the *Wimbledon* (1923), P.C.I.J., Ser. A, no. 1, p. 32; World Court Reports i. 163 (on the currency in which the damages were to be paid). Instances of equity in arbitral jurisprudence: *Orinoco Steamship Co.* case (1910); Hague Court Reports i. 228; *R.I.A.A.* xi. 237; *Norwegian Shipowners'* claims (1922), Hague Court Reports ii. 40; *R.I.A.A.* i. 309; *Eastern Extension, Australasia and China Telegraph Co., Ltd.* (1923), *R.I.A.A.* vi. 112; *Trail Smelter* arbitration (1938, 1941), *R.I.A.A.* iii. 1905.

[4] See also *supra*, p. 19, on 'general principles of international law'.

[5] I.C.J. Reports (1969), p. 3 at pp. 46–52. See also ibid., pp. 131 seq. (sep. op., Ammoun), pp. 165–8 (diss. op., Koretsky), pp. 192–6 (diss. op., Tanaka), pp. 207–9 (diss. op., Morelli), p. 257 (diss. op., Sørensen).

[6] Ibid. (1970), p. 3 at pp. 48–50.

Iceland) the International Court outlined the elements of an 'equitable solution' of the differences over fishing rights and directed the Parties to negotiate accordingly.[1]

Equity, in the present context, is encompassed by Article 38 (1) (c) of the Statute, and not by Article 38 (2),[2] which provides: 'This provision [paragraph 1, *supra*, p. 3] shall not prejudice the power of the Court to decide a case *ex aequo et bono*, if the parties agree thereto.'

This power of decision *ex aequo et bono* involves compromise, conciliation, and legislation in a friendly settlement, whereas equity in the English sense is applied as a part of the normal judicial function. In the *Free Zones* case[3] the International Court, under a special agreement between France and Switzerland, was asked to settle the questions involved in the execution of the relevant provision in the Treaty of Versailles. Whilst the Court was to declare on the future customs regime of the zones, the agreement contained no reference to decision *ex aequo et bono*. Switzerland argued that the Court should work on the basis of existing rights, and, by a technical majority including the vote of the President, the Court agreed with the argument. The Court said:[4]

> ... even assuming that it were not incompatible with the Court's Statute for the Parties to give the Court power to prescribe a settlement disregarding rights recognized by it and taking into account considerations of pure expediency only, such power, which would be of an absolutely exceptional character, could only be derived from a clear and explicit provision to that effect, which is not to be found in the Special Agreement....

The majority of the Court expressed doubts as to the power of the Court to give decisions *ex aequo et bono*, but it would be unwise to draw general conclusions from such doubts since much depended on the nature of the special agreement. In any case the majority of the Court regarded the power to decide *ex aequo et bono* as distinct from the English notion of equity. However, the terminology of the subject is not well settled. The draftsmen of the General Act of Geneva, 1928,[5] seem to regard the power to decide *ex aequo et bono* and equity as synonymous. The converse, 'equity' to mean settlement *ex aequo et bono*, occurs in some

[1] I.C.J. Reports (1974), p. 3 at pp. 30–35.

[2] Judge Kellogg in the *Free Zones* case (1930), P.C.I.J., Ser. A, no. 24, pp. 39–40, thought otherwise, but was in error. See the *North Sea Cases*, I.C.J. Reports (1969), p. 48.

[3] (1930), P.C.I.J., Ser. A, no. 24. See the earlier phase: (1929), Ser. A, no. 22; and Lauterpacht, *Development*, pp. 213–17; and *Function*, p. 318.

[4] Ser. A, no. 24, p. 10.

[5] Article 28. See Brierly, 11 *B.Y.* (1930), 124–33. The provision was copied in other treaties.

arbitration agreements.[1] On occasion equity is regarded as an equivalent of the general principles of law.[2]

10. *Considerations of Humanity*

Considerations of humanity may depend on the subjective appreciation of the judge, but, more objectively, they may be related to human values already protected by positive legal principles which, taken together, reveal certain criteria of public policy[3] and invite the use of analogy. Such criteria have obvious connexions with general principles of law[4] and with equity, but they need no particular justification. References to principles or laws of humanity appear in preambles to conventions,[5] in resolutions of the United Nations General Assembly,[6] and also in diplomatic practice. The classical reference is the passage from the judgment of the International Court in the *Corfu Channel* case,[7] in which the Court relied on certain 'general and well-recognized principles', including 'elementary considerations of humanity, even more exacting in peace than in war'. In recent years the provisions of the United Nations Charter concerning the protection of human rights and fundamental freedoms,[8] and references to the 'principles' of the Charter, have been used as a more concrete basis for considerations of humanity, for example in matters of racial discrimination and self-determination.[9]

[1] See Simpson and Fox, *International Arbitration*, pp. 128–9, 137; Lauterpacht, *Function*, p. 314; Green, pp. 65–7 (*Cayuga Indians* claim (1926), *R.I.A.A.* vi. 173), pp. 723–5, 726 (*Georges Pinson* claim (1928), *R.I.A.A.* v. 327).

[2] *Norwegian Shipowners'* claim (1922), Hague Court Reports ii. 40; *R.I.A.A.* i. 309.

[3] In connexion with the use of weapons of mass destruction, the chairman of the U.S.S.R. Council of Ministers referred to 'principles of humanity, the standards of international law and the conscience of mankind': statement to the Pugwash Conference, 24 August 1959.

[4] See Lauterpacht, *Development*, p. 168; cf. *Annual Digest* 16 (1949), 3.

[5] Cf. Hague Conv. Concerning the Laws and Customs of War on Land, 1907, preamble, 'until a more complete code of the laws of war can be drawn up, the High Contracting Parties deem it expedient to declare that, in cases not covered by the rules adopted by them, the inhabitants and the belligerents remain under the protection and governance of the principles of the law of nations, derived from the usages established among civilized peoples, from the laws of humanity, and from the dictates of the public conscience'. This is known as the 'de Martens clause'. See also the draft provisions on war criminals debated at the Paris Peace Conference, 1919–20.

[6] See the resolution on the Prohibition of the Use of Nuclear Weapons for War Purposes, 24 November 1961.

[7] I.C.J. Reports (1949), p. 22; Green, p. 228; Briggs, p. 291. The statement was in respect of Albania's duty to warn of the presence of mines in her waters.

[8] See generally Chapter XXIV, section 7.

[9] In approaching the issues of interpretation in the *South West Africa* cases (Second Phase), I.C.J. Reports (1966), p. 6 at p. 34, the International Court held that humanitarian considerations were not decisive. See also, in the same cases, Judge Tanaka, diss. op., 252–3, 270, 294–9.

11. *Legitimate Interests*

In particular contexts rules of law may depend on criteria of good faith, reasonableness, and the like, and legitimate interests, including economic interests, may then be taken into account. However, legitimate interests may play a role in creating exceptions to existing rules and bringing about the progressive development of international law. Recognition of legitimate interest explains the extent of acquiescence in face of claims to the continental shelf[1] and fishing zones.[2] In this type of situation it is, of course, acquiescence and recognition which provide the formal bases for development of the new rules. In the *Fisheries* case[3] the International Court did not purport to do anything other than apply existing rules, but it had to justify the special application of the normal rules to the Norwegian coastline. In doing so the Court stated:[4] 'Finally, there is one consideration not to be overlooked . . . that of certain economic interests peculiar to a region, the reality and importance of which are clearly evidenced by a long usage.' Moreover, the Court referred to traditional fishing rights buttressed by 'the vital needs of the population' in determining particular baselines.[5]

Judge McNair, dissenting in the *Fisheries* case,[6] expressed disquiet:

> In my opinion the manipulation of the limits of territorial waters for the purpose of protecting economic and other social interests has no justification in law; moreover, the approbation of such a practice would have a dangerous tendency in that it would encourage States to adopt a subjective appreciation of their rights instead of conforming to a common international standard.

This caution is no doubt justified, but the law is inevitably bound up with the accommodation of the different interests of states, and the rules often require an element of appreciation. Examples of such rules are those concerning the invalidity of treaties,[7] excuses for delictual conduct,[8] and the various compromises in conventions between the standard of civilization and the necessities of war.[9]

[1] See *infra*, pp. 222 seq. [2] See *infra*, pp. 214–15. [3] See *infra*, pp. 186 seq.

[4] I.C.J. Reports (1951), p. 133. See also at p. 128: 'In these barren regions the inhabitants of the coastal zone derive their livelihood essentially from fishing.' See also Fitzmaurice, 30 *B.Y.* (1953), 69–70; id., 92 Hague *Recueil* (1957, II), 112–16.

[5] I.C.J. Reports (1951), p. 142.

[6] p. 169.

[7] See Chapter XXV, section 5. [8] See Chapter XX, section 3.

[9] On the provisions in the Hague Regulations on Land Warfare and the Geneva Conventions of 1949 see Schwarzenberger, in *Mélanges Séfériadès* (1961), pp. 13–21.

Note on comity. International comity, *comitas gentium*, is a species of accommodation not unrelated to morality but to be distinguished from it nevertheless. Neighbourliness, mutual respect, and the friendly waiver of technicalities are involved, and the practice is exemplified by the exemption of diplomatic envoys from customs duties.[1] Oppenheim[2] writes of 'the rules of politeness, convenience and goodwill observed by States in their mutual intercourse without being legally bound by them'. Particular rules of comity, maintained over a long period, may develop into rules of customary law.

Apart from the meaning just explained, the term 'comity' is used in four other ways: (1) as a synonym for international law;[3] (2) as equivalent to private international law (conflict of laws);[4] (3) as a policy basis for, and source of, particular rules of conflict of laws;[5] and (4) as the reason for and source of a rule of international law.[6]

Note on codification. Narrowly defined, codification involves the setting down, in a comprehensive and ordered form, of rules of existing law and the approval of the resulting text by a law-determining agency. The process in international relations has been carried out by international conferences, such as the First and Second Hague Peace Conferences of 1899 and 1907, and by groups of experts whose drafts were the subjects of conferences sponsored by the League of Nations or the American states. However, the International Law Commission, created as a subsidiary organ of the General Assembly of the United Nations, has had more success than the League bodies. Its membership combines technical qualities and experience of government work, so that its drafts are more likely to adopt solutions which are acceptable to governments. Moreover, its membership reflects a variety of political standpoints and thus its agreed drafts provide a realistic basis for legal obligations. In practice the Commission has not maintained a strict separation of its tasks of codification

[1] Cf. now Art. 36 of the Vienna Convention on Diplomatic Relations, 1961.

[2] *International Law* i (8th ed.), 34, n. 1. French usage is 'convenance et courtoisie internationale'. See the *Alabama* arbitration, Moore, *Arbitrations* i. 653; Green, p. 27; the *Paquete Habana* (1900), 175 U.S. 677; Briggs, p. 30.

[3] British and American courts often use the term thus, e.g. the *Parlement Belge* (1880), 5 P.D. 197, 214, 217, per Brett, L.J.

[4] See Phillimore, *Commentaries* iv, para. 1.

[5] i.e., as an aspect of public policy. See *Hilton* v. *Guyot* (1895), 159 U.S. 113; Briggs, p. 398; *Oetjen* v. *Central Leather Co.* (1918), 246 U.S. 297, 303; Green, p. 127; *Foster* v. *Driscoll* [1929] 1 K.B. 470; and Briggs, pp. 407–8.

[6] *The Cristina* [1938] A.C. 485, 502, per Lord Wright; *Re A.B.* [1941] 1 K.B. 454, 457; *Krajina* v. *Tass Agency* [1949] 2 A.E.R. 274, 280, per Cohen, L.J.

and 'progressive development' of the law. Its work on various topics, including the law of the sea, has provided the basis for fairly successful conferences of plenipotentiaries and the resulting multilateral conventions. On codification and especially the International Law Commission see Hurst, 32 *Grot. Soc.* (1946), 135–53; Oppenheim i. 57–70; Jennings, 24 *B.Y.* (1947), 301–29; id., 13 *I.C.L.Q.* (1964), 385–97; Johnson, 35 *B.Y.* (1959), 1–33; U.N. Secretariat Memo. A/AC.10/5 (1947), in 41 *A.J.* (1947), 29 (and see ibid., pp. 111 seq.); Liang, 73 Hague *Recueil* (1948, II), 411–527; id., 42 *A.J.* (1948), 66–97; Cheng, 5 *Curr. Leg. Problems* (1952), 251–73; Lauterpacht, 49 *A.J.* (1955), 16–43 (also in *International Law: Collected Papers* ii. 269–303); Rosenne, 36 *B.Y.* (1960), 104–73; Stone, 57 *Columbia L.R.* (1957), 16–51; Lee, 59 *A.J.* (1965), 545–69; Briggs, *The International Law Commission* (1965); id., 126 Hague *Recueil* (1969, I), 242–316; Gross, 19 *Int. Organization* (1965), 537–61; Ago, *Recueil d'études en hommage à Guggenheim*, pp. 93–131; Baxter, ibid., pp. 146–66; Dhokalia, *The Codification of Public International Law* (1970); Marek, 31 *Z.a.ö.R.u.V.* (1971), 489–520; Ramcharan, *The International Law Commission* (1977).

On a project for a Declaration on the Rights and Duties of States, see *Preparatory Study Concerning a Draft Declaration on the Rights and Duties of States*, I.L.C. (1948), A/CN.4/2; and Rosenne, op. cit., pp. 142–4. On the Covenants of Human Rights and the Universal Declaration of Human Rights see Chapter XXIV. On the United Nations Special Committee on the Principles of International Law Concerning Friendly Relations and Co-operation between States in accordance with the Charter, see Hazard, 58 *A.J.* (1964), 952; Lee, 14 *I.C.L.Q.* (1965), 1296–313; Houben, 61 *A.J.* (1967), 703–36; Briggs, 126 Hague *Recueil*, pp. 284–93; U.N. Documents A/5746, A/6230, A/6799, A/7326; Declaration on Principles of International Law Concerning Friendly Relations, U.N. Gen. Ass., Resol. 2625, 24 October 1970; Brownlie, *Documents*, p. 32.

CHAPTER II

THE RELATION OF MUNICIPAL AND INTERNATIONAL LAW

1. *Theoretical Problems*[1]

THE present section has the modest object of presenting the various theories on the nature of the relation between municipal and international law in broad outline and in doing so to explore the nature of the problems. An extended theoretical exposition would be out of place in this book, and yet theoretical questions have had a certain, though not decisive, influence on writers dealing with substantive issues and also on courts. A simple example will indicate the type of situation to which the theoretical controversy relates. An alien vessel may be arrested and the alien crew tried before a municipal court of the arresting authority for ignoring customs laws. The municipal law prescribes a customs enforcement zone of x miles. The defendants argue that international law permits a customs zone of x — 4 miles and that the vessel, when arrested, had not yet entered the zone in which enforcement was justified under international law.

The theoretical issue is normally presented as a clash between dualism (or pluralism) and monism. Both these schools of thought assume that there is a common field in which the international and municipal legal orders can operate simultaneously in regard to the same subject-matter, and the problem then is, which is to be master? It is at once obvious that when the issue is taken up in this form a limit has already been set to the controversy and certain solutions ruled out. Dualist doctrine[2] points to

[1] See Fitzmaurice, 92 Hague *Recueil* (1957, II), 68–94; Starke, 17 *B.Y.* (1936), 66–81; id., *Studies*, pp. 1–19; Kunz, 10 *Grot. Soc.* (1924), 115–41; and in 6 *R.D.I.L.C.* (1925), 556–98; Triepel, Hague *Recueil* (1923), 77–121; Kelsen, 14 Hague *Recueil* (1926, IV), 231–329; id., *Principles of International Law*, pp. 190–6, 401–50; ibid. (2nd ed.), 290–4, 551–88; id., 84 Hague *Recueil* (1953, III), 182–200; Rousseau, 93 Hague *Recueil* (1958, I), 464–74; id., *Droit international public* i (1970), 37–48; Morgenstern, 27 *B.Y.* (1950), 42–92; Ziccardi, 95 Hague *Recueil* (1958, III), 263–405; Verzijl, *International Law in Historical Perspective* i (1968), pp. 90–183; van Panhuys, 112 Hague *Recueil* (1964, II), pp. 7–87; Quadri, 113 Hague *Recueil* (1964, III), pp. 280–318; Lauterpacht, *International Law: Collected Papers* i (1970), pp. 151–77; *Wengler*, 72 *R.G.D.I.P.* (1968), 921–90

[2] Exponents: Triepel, *Völkerrecht und Landesrecht* (1899); id., 1 Hague *Recueil* (1923), 77–121; Oppenheim i. 37 (not the view of the editor); Strupp, *Élements*; id., 47 Hague *Recueil* (1934, I), 389–418.

the essential difference of international law and municipal law, consisting primarily in the fact that the two systems regulate different subject-matter. International law is a law between sovereign states: municipal law applies within a state and regulates the relations of its citizens with each other and with the executive. On this view neither legal order has the power to create or alter rules of the other. When municipal law provides that international law applies in whole or in part within the jurisdiction, this is merely an exercise of the authority of municipal law, an adoption or transformation of the rules of international law. In case of a conflict between international law and municipal law the dualist would assume that a municipal court would apply municipal law. Dualism is closely connected with positivist doctrine, which tends to deny the validity of sources of international law apart from the practice of states.

Monism is represented by a number of jurists whose theories diverge in significant respects. In the United Kingdom Hersch Lauterpacht[1] has been a forceful exponent of the doctrine. In his hands the theory has been no mere intellectual construction, and in his work monism takes the form of an assertion of the supremacy of international law even within the municipal sphere, coupled with well-developed views on the individual as a subject of international law.[2] Such a doctrine is antipathetic to the legal corollaries of the existence of sovereign states, and reduces municipal law to the status of pensioner of international law. The state is disliked as an abstraction and distrusted as a vehicle for maintaining human rights: international law, like municipal law, is ultimately concerned with the conduct and welfare of individuals. International law is seen as the best available moderator of human affairs, and also as a logical condition of the *legal* existence of states and therefore of the municipal systems of law within the sphere of the legal competence of states.[3]

Kelsen[4] has developed monist principles on the basis of formal

[1] See Oppenheim i. 38; 25 *Grot. Soc.* (1939), 62–67; 62 Hague *Recueil* (1937, IV), 129–48. See also the views of Scelle, *Précis de droit des gens* ii. 5; and Bourquin, 35 Hague *Recueil* (1931, I), 75–80. See also Lauterpacht, *International Law and Human Rights* (1950).

[2] See generally *infra*, Chapter XXIV.

[3] See Oppenheim i. 38: '... it is only by reference to a higher legal rule in relation to which they are all equal, that the equality and independence of a number of sovereign States can be conceived. Failing that superior legal order, the science of law would be confronted with the spectacle of some sixty sovereign States, each claiming to be the absolutely highest and underived authority.'

[4] *General Theory of Law and the State* (1945), pp. 363–80; 43 *R.G.D.I.P.* (1936), 5–49; *Principles of International Law* (1952), pp. 401–47; ibid. (2nd ed.), pp. 553–88. For views related to but not identical with those of Kelsen see the work of Verdross, 16 Hague

methods of analysis dependent on a theory of knowledge. According to the bases of Kelsen's thought, monism is scientifically established if international and municipal law are part of the same system of norms receiving their validity and contents by an intellectual operation from a basic norm. This basic norm he formulates as follows:[1] 'The states ought to behave as they have customarily behaved.' When the basic norm came to support a system of international law, the principle of effectiveness contained therein,[2] which allows revolution to be a law-creating fact, and accepts the first legislators of a state, provided the basic norm of national legal orders, i.e. the effectiveness of the new internal legal orders established on the basis of acts which may be contrary to the previous constitution. Then, it follows: 'Since the basic norms of the national legal orders are determined by a norm of international law, they are basic norms only in a relative sense. It is the basic norm of the international legal order which is the ultimate reason of validity of the national legal orders, too.'[3] Whilst Kelsen establishes monism on the formal bases of his own theory, he does not support the 'primacy' of international law over municipal law: in his view the question of 'primacy' can only be decided on the basis of considerations which are not strictly legal. One may speculate whether Kelsen has avoided an element of assumption when he establishes that the basic norm of international law in some sense determines the validity of the national basic norm: the validity of each could rest on a relation of interdependence rather than a 'hierarchical' relation.

There is also a monist-naturalist theory, which, superficially at least, resembles Kelsen's provision of a universal basic norm. According to this theory the international and municipal legal orders are subordinate to a third legal order, usually postulated in terms of natural law or 'general principles of law', superior to both and capable of determining their respective spheres.[4]

Recueil (1927, I), 287–96; 30 Hague *Recueil* (1929, V), 290–3; Kunz, 10 *Grot. Soc.* (1924), 115–41; id., 6 *R.D.I.L.C.* (1925), 556–98; Guggenheim i. 24–7; id. (2nd ed.), i. 58–61; Starke, 17 *B.Y.* (1936), 66–81; id., *Studies*, pp. 1–19.

[1] *General Theory*, p. 369; *Principles of International Law*, pp. 417–18, ibid. (2nd ed.), p. 564.

[2] *General Theory*, p. 367.

[3] *General Theory*, pp. 367–8; *Principles of International Law*, p. 415; ibid. (2nd ed.), p. 562; 84 Hague *Recueil* (1953, III), 196.

[4] See Lauterpacht, *Private Law Sources and Analogies of International Law*, p. 58, 7, for citations. Cf. the views of Scelle, *Précis* ii. 5. See also Starke, in *Law, State and International Legal Order: Essays in Honor of Hans Kelsen*, pp. 308–16, referring to certain 'functional or constitutional norms' of international law.

2. *Theories of Co-ordination*

An increasing number of jurists wish to escape from the dichotomy of monism and dualism, holding that the logical consequences of both theories conflict with the way in which international and national organs and courts behave. Thus Sir Gerald Fitzmaurice[1] challenges the premiss adopted by monists and dualists that international and municipal law have a common field of operation. The two systems do not come into conflict as *systems* since they work in different spheres. Each is supreme in its own field. However, there may be a conflict of *obligations*, an inability of the state on the domestic plane to act in the manner required by international law: the consequence of this will not be the invalidity of the internal law but the responsibility of the state on the international plane.[2] Rousseau[3] has propounded similar views, characterizing international law as a law of co-ordination which does not provide for automatic abrogation of internal rules in conflict with obligations on the international plane. These and other writers express a preference for practice over theory, and it is to the practice that attention will now be turned.

3. *The Relation between Obligations of States and Municipal Law*[4]

The law in this respect is well settled. A state cannot plead provisions of its own law or deficiencies in that law in answer to a claim against it for an alleged breach of its obligations under international law.[5] The acts of the legislature and other sources of

[1] 92 Hague *Recueil* (1957, II), 68–94. In particular this writer criticizes monist doctrine on the role of the state. In his view the state cannot be regarded merely as an aggregation of individuals. At p. 77 he says that 'the concept of the State or nation as an indivisible entity possessing its own separate personality, is a necessary initial hypothesis, which has to be made before it is possible to speak significantly of international law at all . . .'

[2] Ibid., pp. 79–80. Anzilotti, *Cours de droit international* i. 57, puts forward this view, but is often classified as a dualist (cf. Oppenheim i. 37, n. 1). See also Sørensen, 101 Hague *Recueil* (1960, III), 125–6; Kozhevnikov (ed.), *International Law* (English ed.), p. 15; and Ginsburgs, 59 *A.J.* (1965), 523–44 (references to Soviet doctrine).

[3] *Droit international public*, pp. 10–12; 93 Hague *Recueil* (1958, I), 473–4. Rousseau asserts the primacy of international law—but by this means primacy in its own field.

[4] See Marek, *Droit international et droit interne* (1961), pp. 23 seq.; Lauterpacht, *The Development of International Law by the International Court*, pp. 262, 314–15, 332; Morgenstern, 27 *B.Y.* (1950), 43–47; Fitzmaurice, 30 *B.Y.* (1953), 26–7, 53–4, 35 *B.Y.* (1959), 185–94, and 92 Hague *Recueil* (1957, II), 85–8; and Briggs, pp. 60–3. See also the *Wollemborg* claim, Int. L.R. 24 (1957), 654; *Ottoz* claim, ibid., 18 (1951), no. 136.

[5] See the Vienna Conv. on the Law of Treaties, 1969, Art. 27, referring to justification for failure to perform a treaty. See also *infra*, Chapter XXV, section 8.

internal rules and decision-making are not to be regarded as acts of some third party for which the state is not responsible, and any other principle would facilitate evasion of obligations. In the *Alabama Claims* arbitration[1] the United States successfully claimed damages from Great Britain for breach of its obligations as a neutral during the American Civil War. The absence of legislation to prevent the fitting out of commerce raiders in British ports and their journey to join the Confederate forces was no defence. The Permanent Court of Arbitration,[2] the Permanent Court of International Justice,[3] and the International Court of Justice[4] have produced a consistent jurisprudence. In the *Free Zones* case[5] the Permanent Court observed '. . . it is certain that France cannot rely on her own legislation to limit the scope of her international obligations . . .' And the advisory opinion in the *Greco-Bulgarian Communities* case[6] contains the statement: 'it is a generally accepted principle of international law that in the relations between Powers who are contracting Parties to a treaty, the provisions of municipal law cannot prevail over those of the treaty'. The same principle applies where the provisions of a constitution are relied upon; in the words of the Permanent Court:[7]

> It should . . . be observed that . . . a State cannot adduce as against another State its own Constitution with a view to evading obligations incumbent upon it under international law or treaties in force. Applying these principles to the present case, it results that the question of the treatment of Polish nationals or other Persons of Polish origin or speech must be settled exclusively on the basis of the rules of international law and the treaty provisions in force between Poland and Danzig.

[1] (1872), Moore, *Arbitrations*, p. 653; Green, p. 27; Briggs, p. 1026; Hudson, p. 665.

[2] References: Schwarzenberger, *International Law* i (3rd ed.), pp. 68–9.

[3] See the *Wimbledon* (1923), P.C.I.J., Ser. A, no. 1, p. 29; *Mavrommatis*, Ser. A, no. 5; *German Interests in Polish Upper Silesia* (1926), Ser. A, no. 7, p. 19; *Chorzów Factory* (Merits) (1928), Ser. A, no. 17, pp. 33, 34; *Jurisdiction of the Courts of Danzig* (1928), Ser. B, no. 15, pp. 26, 27; *Free Zones Case* (1929), Ser. A, no. 24, p. 12. See also notes 4, 5 and 6, *infra*. Further references: Schwarzenberger, op. cit., pp. 69–70.

[4] The leading cases are the *Fisheries* case, I.C.J. Reports (1951), p. 116 at p. 132; and the *Nottebohm* case, ibid. (1955), p. 4 at pp. 20–1. See also *infra*, p. 291 on domestic jurisdiction. See further the *Guardianship* case, I.C.J. Reports (1958), p. 55 at p. 67. For the views of individual judges: I.C.J. Reports (1951), p. 152 (Alvarez); ibid., p. 181 (McNair); ibid. (1953), p. 125 (Klaestad); ibid. (1957), pp. 37–8 (Lauterpacht); ibid. (1958), p. 74 (Badawi); ibid., p. 83 (Lauterpacht); ibid., pp. 125–6, 128–9 (Spender); ibid., pp. 137–8 (Winiarski); ibid., p. 140 (Córdova).

[5] (1932), P.C.I.J., Ser. A/B, no. 46, p. 167; Green, p. 741.

[6] (1930), P.C.I.J., Ser. B, no. 17, p. 32.

[7] *Polish Nationals in Danzig* (1931), P.C.I.J., Ser. A/B, no. 44, p. 24. See also the *Pinson* claim (1928), *R.I.A.A.* v. 327; *Ann. Digest* 4 (1927–8), no. 4; Green, p. 722.

Arising from the nature of treaty obligations and from customary law, there is a general duty to bring internal law into conformity with obligations under international law.[1] However, in general a failure to bring about such conformity is not in itself a direct breach of international law, and a breach arises only when the state concerned fails to observe its obligations on a specific occasion.[2] In some circumstances legislation could of itself constitute a breach of a treaty provision and a tribunal might be requested to make a declaration to that effect. Another principle connected with these rules is to the effect that a change of government is not as such[3] a ground for non-compliance with obligations.[4]

4. *The Position of the Individual*[5]

International law imposes duties of certain kinds on individuals as such, and thus national and international tribunals may try persons charged with crimes against international law, including war crimes and genocide.[6] The International Military Tribunal at Nuremberg and many national tribunals did not admit pleas by accused persons charged with war crimes that they had acted in accordance with their national law.[7] Conversely, in a great number of situations an individual or corporation may plead that a treaty has legal consequences affecting interests of the claimant which must be recognized by a municipal court.[8] And again, on a charge of crime, such as homicide, under municipal law, a plea of justification may be based on rules of international law, for example, that an act of killing was a lawful act of war.

[1] Briggs, p. 61; Fitzmaurice, 92 Hague *Recueil* (1957, II), 89; Oppenheim i. 44–5; Guggenheim i. 31–3; *Exchange of Greek and Turkish Populations* (1925), P.C.I.J., Ser. B, no. 10, p. 20. The principle applies to both unitary and federal states, but cf. Oppenheim i. 340.

[2] McNair, *Law of Treaties* (1961), p. 100. Cf. Fitzmaurice, op. cit., p. 89.

[3] Apart from the doctrine of *rebus sic stantibus*, on which see Chapter XXV, section 7.

[4] On continuity of states: *infra*, pp. 84–8.

[5] On the status of the individual in international law see generally Chapter XXIV.

[6] See Chapter XXIV, section 6.

[7] See Morgenstern, 27 *B.Y.* (1950), 47–8. For duties arising under a commercial treaty: *Institut National* v. *Mettes*, Int. L.R. 24 (1957), 584.

[8] See: *Restraint at Lobith* case, Int. L.R. 19 (1952), no. 34; *Pokorny* v. *Republic of Austria*, ibid., no. 98; *Soviet Requisition* case, ibid., no. 143; *People of the Philippines* v. *Acierto*, ibid. 20 (1953), 148; *Falcon Dam Constructors* v. *United States*, ibid. 23 (1956), 360; *Public Trustee* v. *Chartered Bank of India, Australia and China*, ibid., p. 687; *Revici* v. *Conference of Jewish Material Claims, Inc.*, ibid. 26 (1958, II), 362; *Indochina Railway* case, ibid. 28, p. 269; *Richuk* v. *State of Israel*, ibid., p. 442. See also *infra*, pp. 44 seq., on incorporation.

5. *Issues of Municipal Law before International Tribunals*

(a) Cases in which a tribunal dealing with issues of international law has to examine the municipal law of one or more states are by no means exceptional.[1] As a matter of evidence, the spheres of competence *claimed* by states, represented by state territory and the territorial sea, jurisdiction, and nationality of individuals and legal persons, are delimited by means of legislation and judicial and administrative decisions.[2] The substantive law of nations brings the same matters in issue by setting limits of competence, represented especially by the concept of domestic jurisdiction[3] against which the municipal law on a given topic has to be measured. Thus a tribunal may have to examine municipal law relating to expropriation,[4] fishing limits,[5] nationality,[6] or the guardianship and welfare of infants[7] in order to decide whether particular acts are in breach of obligations under treaties or customary law. Issues relating to obligations to protect human rights,[8] the treatment of civilians during belligerent occupation, and the exhaustion of local remedies (as a question of the admissibility of claims)[9] concern internal law in nearly every case.

(b) A considerable number of treaties contain provisions referring directly to internal law or employing concepts which by implication are to be understood in the context of a particular national law. Many treaties refer to 'nationals' of the contracting parties, and the presumption is that the term connotes persons having that status under the internal law of one of the parties. Similarly, claims settlements involve references to legal interests of individuals and corporations existing within the cadre of a given national law.[1]

[1] See generally Jenks, 19 *B.Y.* (1938), 67–103; id., *The Prospects of International Adjudication*, pp. 547–603; Marek, *Droit international et droit interne* (1961), pp. 267 seq.; id., 66 *R.G.D.I.P.* (1962), 260–98; Stoll, *L'Application et l'interprétation du droit interne par les juridictions internationales* (1962); Strebel 31 *Z.a.ö.R.u.V.* (1971), 855–84.

[2] See the *United Nations Legislative Series*. On municipal law as evidence of the intention of a government see the *Anglo-Iranian Oil Co.* case, I.C.J. Reports (1952), p. 93.

[3] *Infra*, pp. 291 seq.

[4] *German Interests in Polish Upper Silesia* (1926), P.C.I.J., Ser. A, no. 7; Green, p. 533. See further Chapter XXIII, section 9.

[5] *Fisheries* case, I.C.J. Reports (1951), p. 116. See further *infra*, pp. 186 seq.

[6] *Nottebohm* case, I.C.J. Reports (1955), p. 4; Green, p. 503. See further *infra*, Chapter XVIII.

[7] *Guardianship of Infants* case, I.C.J. Reports (1958), p. 55.

[8] Chapter XXIV and especially section 8 on the European Commission of Human Rights and the European Court of Human Rights.

[9] Chapter XXI, section 6.

[1] See also Fitzmaurice, 35 *B.Y.* (1959), 191. On extradition treaties see *infra*, p. 315.

(c) In the *Guardianship of Infants* case several of the individual judges rested their conclusions on the issues in the case on a principle of treaty law according to which the interpretation of treaties concerned with matters of private international law should take into account the nature of the subject-matter, in particular by the recognition of the principle of *ordre public* as applied locally.[1] In his separate opinion Judge Spender criticized this view of treaty interpretation, pointing to the variable content of *ordre public* and the importance of the principle *pacta sunt servanda*.[2]

(d) Treaties having as their object the creation and maintenance of certain standards of treatment of minority groups or resident aliens may refer to a national law as a method of describing the status to be created and protected. The protection of rights may be stipulated for 'without discrimination' or as 'national treatment' for the categories concerned.[3]

(e) On occasion an international tribunal may be faced with the task of deciding issues solely on the basis of the municipal law of a particular state. Such a case was the *Serbian Loans* case[4] before the Permanent Court. This arose from a dispute between the French bondholders of certain Serbian loans and the Serb-Croat-Slovene Government, the former demanding loan-service on a gold basis from 1924 or 1925 onwards, the latter holding that payment in French paper currency was in conformity with the terms of the contracts. This was not a dispute involving international law. The French Government, by virtue of the right of diplomatic protection,[5] took up the case of the French bondholders, and by a special agreement the dispute was sub-

[1] I.C.J. Reports (1958), pp. 72–3 (Spiropoulos); 74–8 (Badawi); 91 seq. (Lauterpacht); 102–9 (Moreno Quintana). See Fitzmaurice, 35 *B.Y.* (1959), 190–1. The Court, at p. 70, left the point open.

[2] pp. 120–31. See also Judge Córdova, separate opinion, pp. 140–1, for a similar view.

[3] See *Memel Statute* case (1932), P.C.I.J., Ser. A/B, no. 49; *Jurisdiction of the Danzig Courts*, Series B, no. 15; *German Settlers in Poland* (1923), Ser. B, no. 6; *Minority Schools in Albania* (1935), Ser. A/B, no. 64. The Permanent Court did not regard a formal equality in law as the only criterion of equality. See further Fitzmaurice, 35 *B.Y.* (1959), 191–2. Cf. the United Nations Charter, Arts. 55 and 56, and the European Convention of Human Rights, 1950, Art. 14.

[4] (1929), P.C.I.J., Ser. A, no. 20; Green, p. 29; Briggs, p. 655. See also the *Brazilian Loans* case (1929), P.C.I.J., Ser. A, no. 21; Green, p. 29; Jenks, 19 *B.Y.* (1938), 95–7; and Schwarzenberger, *International Law* i (3rd ed.), 72–8. Cf. the *Norwegian Shipowners* claims (1922), *R.I.A.A.* i. 309; Green, p. 3; the *Diverted Cargoes* arbitration (1955), Int. L.R. 22 (1955), 820; and *Case No.* 1, Arbitration Tribunal for the Agreement on German External Debts, 34 *B.Y.* (1958), 363.

[5] States may present, and negotiate concerning, claims which do not relate to international law. Sympathetic consideration may be given to such claims as a matter of general relations between the states concerned.

mitted to the Permanent Court. The Court considered whether it had jurisdiction under its Statute in a case where the point at issue was a question which must be decided by application of a particular municipal law. The conclusion was that jurisdiction existed, the basis for this important finding being the wide terms of Article 36 (1) of the Statute, which refers especially to cases brought by special agreement, and the duty of the Court to exercise jurisdiction when two states have agreed to have recourse to the Court, in the absence of a clause on the subject in the Statute. Applying itself to the issues arising from the loans the Court had to decide an issue of conflict of laws: did Serbian or French law govern the obligations at the time they were entered into? Public international law (as the law of the forum) provided no ready-made rules of conflict of laws, and the Court prescribed certain principles:[1]

> The Court, which has before it a dispute involving the question as to the law which governs the contractual obligations at issue, can determine what this law is only by reference to the actual nature of these obligations and to the circumstances attendant upon their creation, though it may also take into account the expressed or presumed intentions of the Parties. Moreover, this would seem to be in accord with the principles of municipal courts in the absence of rules of municipal law concerning the settlement of conflicts of law.

In the event the Court held that the substance of the debt and the validity of the clause defining the obligation of the debtor state was governed by Serbian law, but, with respect to the method of payment, the money of payment was the local currency of the place in which the debtor state was bound to discharge the debt. The money of payment was thus paper francs and the amount due in this currency was to be calculated, in accordance with the intention of the parties, by reference to gold francs, the money of account. The rate of conversion from the money of account to the money of payment was that prevailing at the time of the payment of the debt.

6. *Municipal Laws as 'Facts' before International Tribunals*

In the case of *Certain German Interests in Polish Upper Silesia*, the Permanent Court of International Justice observed:[2]

> It might be asked whether a difficulty does not arise from the fact that the Court would have to deal with the Polish law of July 14th, 1920. This,

[1] P.C.I.J., Ser. A, no. 20, p. 41. References to similar functions by arbitral tribunals are in Schwarzenberger, op. cit., p. 78.

[2] P.C.I.J., Ser. A, no. 7, p. 19.

however, does not appear to be the case. From the standpoint of International Law and of the Court which is its organ, municipal laws are merely facts which express the will and constitute the activities of States, in the same manner as do legal decisions or administrative measures. The Court is certainly not called upon to interpret the Polish law as such; but there is nothing to prevent the Court's giving judgment on the question whether or not, in applying that law, Poland is acting in conformity with its obligations towards Germany under the Geneva Convention.

This statement is to the effect that municipal law may be simply evidence of conduct attributable to the state concerned which creates international responsibility. Thus a decision of a court or a legislative measure may constitute evidence of a breach of a treaty or a rule of customary international law.[1] In its context the principle stated is clear. However, the general proposition that international tribunals take account of municipal laws only as facts 'is, at most, a debatable proposition the validity and wisdom of which are subject to, and call for, further discussion and review'.[2] In the practice of the International Court and other international tribunals the concept of 'municipal law as mere facts' has six distinct aspects, as follows.

(a) Municipal law may be evidence of conduct in violation of a rule of treaty or customary law, as stated already.

(b) Judicial notice does not apply to matters of municipal law. The tribunal will require proof of municipal law and will hear evidence of it, and, if necessary, may undertake its own researches.[3]

(c) Interpretation of their own laws by national courts is binding on an international tribunal.[4] This principle rests in part on the concept of the reserved domain of domestic jurisdiction[5]

[1] See *Anglo-Iranian Oil Co.* case (Jurisdiction), I.C.J. Reports (1952), 106–7; Judge Badawi, sep. op., *Norwegian Loans* case, ibid. (1957), 31–2; Judge Lauterpacht, sep. op., ibid., 36–8, 40; Judge Morelli, *Barcelona Traction* case (Second Phase), ibid. (1970), 234; Judge Gros, sep. op., ibid., 272.

[2] Jenks, *Prospects of International Adjudication*, p. 552; and see, in that work, pp. 548–53, 569–70; and Jenks, 19 *B.Y.* (1938), 89–92. See further Marek, *Répertoire des décisions et des documents de la cour permanente de justice internationale et la cour internationale de justice* i (1961).

[3] The *Mavrommatis Jerusalem Concessions* case, P.C.I.J., Ser. A. no. 5, pp. 29, 30; *Brazilian Loans*, ibid., nos. 20/21, p. 124; Judge Klaestad, diss, op., *Nottebohm* case (Second Phase), I.C.J. Reports (1955), 28–9; Judge Read, diss. op., ibid., 35–6; Judge Guggenheim, diss. op., ibid., 51–2; *Flegenheimer* claim, Int. L.R. 25 (1958, I), at p. 98. But see Judge Fitzmaurice, diss. op., Advisory Opinion, *Presence of South Africa in Namibia*, I.C.J. Reports (1971), p. 222.

[4] *Serbian Loans*, P.C.I.J., Ser. A. nos. 20/21, p. 46; *Brazilian Loans*, ibid., p. 124; Judge McNair, sep. op., *Fisheries* case, I.C.J. Reports (1951), p. 181; Judge Klaestad, diss. op., *Nottebohm* case (Second Phase), ibid. (1955), 28–9. See also the *Lighthouses* case, P.C.I.J., Ser. A/B, no. 62, p. 22; and the *Panevezys-Saldutiskis Railway* case, ibid., no. 76, p. 19.

[5] *Infra*, p. 291.

and in part on the practical need of avoiding contradictory versions of the law of a state from different sources.

(d) The *dicta* of international tribunals (already cited) rest to some extent on the assumption that, for any domestic issue of which a tribunal is seised, there must always be some applicable rule of municipal law, which will be ascertainable in the same way as other 'facts' in the case. This assumption is not uncommonly unsafe since municipal law may be far from clear.[1]

(e) International tribunals cannot declare the internal invalidity of rules of national law since the international legal order must respect the reserved domain of domestic jurisdiction.[2]

(f) Certain judges of the International Court have stated as a corollary of the proposition that 'municipal laws are merely facts' that an international tribunal 'does not interpret national law as such'.[3] This view is open to question. When it is appropriate to apply rules of municipal law, an international tribunal will apply domestic rules as such.[4] The special agreement may require the application of rules of municipal law to the subject matter of the dispute.[5] International law may designate a system of domestic law as the applicable law.[6] Moreover, in cases in which vital issues (whether classified as 'facts' or otherwise) turn on investigation of municipal law, the International Court has duly examined such matters, including the application of nationality laws,[7] the availability of local remedies[8] and the law concerning guardianship of infants.[9] It is also necessary to make the point that in the particular state national courts may have a power to overrule local legislation on the ground that it is contrary to international law, for example, as laid down by the International Court.[1]

[1] See *R.* v. *Keyn*, *infra*, p. 46; *Burmah Oil* case [1965] A.C. 75.

[2] *Interpretation of the Statute of the Memel Territory*, P.C.I.J. Ser. A/B, no. 49, p. 336; Judge Morelli, sep. op., *Barcelona Traction* case (Second Phase), I.C.J. Reports (1970), p. 234.

[3] See Judge Lauterpacht, *Guardianship* case, I.C.J. Reports (1958), sep. op., p. 91.

[4] The dictum of the P.C.I.J. in the *Upper Silesia* case (quoted earlier) is not unequivocal in its remark that the Court was 'not called upon to interpret the Polish law as such'. See Judge Read, diss. op., *Nottebohm* case (Second Phase), I.C.J. Reports (1955), p. 36; Judge Guggenheim, ibid., p. 52. See also Judge Córdova, diss. op., *Administrative Tribunal of the I.L.O.*, ibid. (1956), p. 165; Judge Moreno Quintana, sep. op., *Guardianship* case, ibid. (1958), p. 108.

[5] *Lighthouses* case, P.C.I.J., Ser. A/B, no. 62, pp. 19–23. See also the *Lighthouses Arbitration*, 1956, P.C.A., Int. L.R., 23 (1956), p. 659.

[6] *Serbian and Brazilian Loans*, above.

[7] *Nottebohm* case (Second Phase), I.C.J. Reports (1955), p. 4. See also the *Flegenheimer* claim, Int. L.R., 25 (1958, I), at pp. 108–10.

[8] *Panevezys-Saldutiskis Railway* case, P.C.I.J., Ser. A/B, no. 76, pp. 18–22.

[9] *Guardianship* case, above.

[1] See Judge Lauterpacht, sep. op., *Norwegian Loans* case, I.C.J. Reports (1957), pp. 40–1.

7. *Issues of International Law before Municipal Courts*

In general. English courts take judicial notice of international law: once a court has ascertained that there are no bars within the internal system of law to applying the rules of international law or provisions of a treaty,[1] the rules are accepted as rules of law and are not required to be established by formal proof, as in the case of matters of fact and foreign law. However, in the case of international law and treaties, the taking of judicial notice has a special character. In the first place, there is in fact a serious problem involved in finding reliable evidence on points of international law in the absence of formal proof and resort to the expert witness.[2] Secondly, issues of public policy and difficulties of obtaining evidence on the larger issues of state relations combine to produce the procedure whereby the executive is consulted on questions of mixed law and fact, for example, the existence of a state of war or the status of an entity claiming sovereign immunities.[3] The special considerations involved in this procedure do not affect the general character of rules of international law before the courts. Where, in a conflict of laws case, an expert gives evidence as to matters of foreign law, the method of ascertaining that law does not affect its character as law. However, in the absence of evidence offered by the parties, a court may presume that the foreign law is the same as the law of the forum in a conflict of laws case, but such a presumption cannot apply to matters of international law.

When a municipal court, in England or elsewhere, has decided, as a preliminary issue, that a rule of customary or treaty law is applicable to a case before it, the rule is applied as though it is a rule of the law of the forum.[4] For reasons set forth subsequently,[5] the practice of municipal courts in this respect does not provide conclusive evidence for or against the dualist doctrine.[6] It is now necessary to examine the conditions in which rules of customary law and treaty provisions are given effect in the municipal sphere, a process variously described as 'incorporation', 'adoption', and 'transformation'. Whether the variant terminology reflects issues of substance is a question which must be reserved until later.[7]

[1] See *infra*, p. 45, on incorporation.

[2] See *infra*, pp. 45–8, on the decisions in *R.* v. *Keyn* and *West Rand Central Gold Mining Co.* v. *R.* See also *infra* on the sources employed by English courts.

[3] On the Foreign Office Certificate see *infra*, p. 54.

[4] See Seidl-Hohenveldern, 12 *I.C.L.Q.* (1963), 90–4; Fawcett, *The British Commonwealth in International Law*, pp. 16–74.

[5] *Infra*, pp. 58–9.

[6] Cf. Morgenstern, 27 *B.Y.* (1950), 48–66.

[7] See *infra*, pp. 58–9.

8. *The Doctrine of Incorporation in British and Commonwealth Courts*[1]

(a) *Customary international law.* The dominant principle, normally characterized as the doctrine of incorporation, is that customary rules are to be considered part of the law of the land and enforced as such, with the qualification that they are incorporated only so far as is not inconsistent with Acts of Parliament or prior judicial decisions of final authority.[2] This principle is supported by a long line of authority[3] and represents a practical rather than theoretical policy in the courts. It would seem that the courts must first make a choice of law depending on the nature of the subject-matter. Where it is appropriate to apply international law, rather than the law of the forum or a foreign law, then the courts will take judicial notice of the applicable rules, whereas formal evidence is required of foreign (municipal) law. However, the courts still have to ascertain the existence of the rules of international law and their effect *within the municipal sphere*: the latter task is a matter of some difficulty on which the rules of international law may provide no real guidance. Lastly, the courts have to make sure that what they are doing is consonant with the conditions of (internal) competence under which they must work. Thus the rule of international law will not be applied if it is contrary to a statute,[4] and the courts will observe

[1] See generally Lauterpacht, 25 *Grot. Soc.* (1939), 51–88 (also in *International Law: Collected Papers* ii (1975), 537–69); Oppenheim i. 39–41; Lauterpacht, *International Law: Collected Papers* i (1970), pp. 154–69, 218–22; Holdsworth, *Essays in Law and History*, pp. 260–72; Westlake, 22 *L.Q.R.* (1906), 14–26; and in Westlake, *Collected Papers*, pp. 498–518; Fawcett, *The British Commonwealth in International Law*, pp. 16–74; Dickinson, 26 *A.J.* (1932), 239–60; Alexandrowicz, 13 *I.C.L.Q.* (1964), 78–95; Castel, *International Law* (3rd ed.), pp. 28–40; O'Connell (ed.), *International Law in Australia* (1965), pp. 48–51; Macdonald, Morris and Johnston, *Canadian Perspectives on International Law and Organization* (1974), pp. 88–136.

[2] Blackstone, *Commentaries* iv., Chapter 5; Oppenheim i. 39–40; Brierly, *Law of Nations* (6th ed.), pp. 86–8. Cf. Lord Finlay in the *Lotus* (1927), P.C.I.J., Ser. A, no. 10, p. 54; and the *Eichmann* case (1961), 56 *A.J.* (1962), p. 805 at pp. 806–7 (District Court); Int. L.R. 36, p. 18 at pp. 24–5. (District Court); ibid., p. 277 at pp. 280–1 (Israel, S.C.).

[3] *Barbuit's* case (1737), Cas. *temp.* Talbot. 281; *Triquet* v. *Bath* (1764), 3 Burr. 1478; *Heathfield* v. *Chilton* (1767), 4 Burr. 2015; *Dolder* v. *Lord Huntingfield* (1805), 11 Ves. 283; *Viveash* v. *Becker* (1814), 3 M. & S. 284, 292, 298; *Wolff* v. *Oxholm* (1817) 6 M. & S. 92, 100–6; *Novello* v. *Toogood* (1823) 1 B. & C. 554; *De Wütz* v. *Hendricks* (1824) 2 Bing. 314, 315; *Emperor of Austria* v. *Day* (1861) 30 L.J. Ch. 690, 702 (reversed on appeal on another point); *Trendtex Trading Corporation* v. *Central Bank of Nigeria* [1977] 1 Q.B. 529, C.A. Cf. *R.* v. *Secretary of State, ex p. Thakrar* [1974] 1 Q.B. 694, C.A.

[4] See *Mortensen* v. *Peters* (1906) 8 F. (J.C.) 93; Bishop, p. 84; Briggs, p. 52 (Scotland: High Court of Justieiary); *Polites* v. *The Commonwealth* (1945), 70 C.L.R. 60 (High Court of Australia), *Ann. Digest* 12 (1943–5), no. 61; *Roussety* v. *A.-G.*, Int. L.R., 44, p. 108. See further Morgenstern, 27 *B.Y.* (1950) at p. 70.

the principle of *stare decisis*.[1] These aspects of the work of the courts to some extent explain judicial pronouncements which are at first sight inimical to the principle of incorporation set out above.

However, the cases decided since 1876 are interpreted by some authorities[2] in such a way as to displace the doctrine of incorporation by that of transformation, *viz.*: customary law is a part of the law of England *only in so far as* the rules have been clearly adopted and made part of the law of England by legislation, judicial decision, or established usage.[3] The principal source of authority for this view is assumed by most writers to be the decision of the Court for Crown Cases Reserved in *Regina* v. *Keyn*.[4] In that case the *Franconia*, a German ship, collided, as a result of the negligence of the captain, with a British ship in British territorial waters. The British ship sank and a passenger was drowned. The German captain was indicted for manslaughter at the Central Criminal Court, and the question for the opinion of the Court for Crown Cases Reserved was whether the Central Criminal Court, successor to the jurisdiction of the Admiral, had jurisdiction. In a Court of thirteen it was decided by a majority of one that there was no jurisdiction, the main ground for this opinion being that no English statute conferred jurisdiction to try offences by foreigners on board foreign ships, whether within or without the limit of territorial waters. The majority of the judges were concerned primarily with heads of criminal jurisdiction in English law.[5] Cockburn, C.J., whose long judgment is often a source for quotation, after considering the English law, goes on to seek the relevant rule of international law.[6] He concludes that the littoral sea beyond low-water is not a part of British territory according to English law,[7] and then, assuming that the law of nations says otherwise, he seeks evidence of British assent to the rule of the law of nations, in the form of

[1] See *Chung Chi Cheung* v. *The King* [1939] A.C. 160, 169. For criticism of this application of *stare decisis* see Fawcett, op. cit., p. 39; Morgenstern, op. cit., pp. 80–2; and *County of Saint John* v. *Fraser-Brace* (1958), 13 D.L.R. (2d) 177; Int. L.R. 26 (1958, II), 165. In *Trendtex Trading Corporation* v. *Central Bank of Nigeria* [1977] 1 Q.B. 529, Lord Denning, M.R., and Shaw L.J. stated that international law knows no rule of *stare decisis* (see pp. 554, 579).

[2] Halsbury, *Laws of England* (3rd ed.), vii. 4, 264.

[3] Analytically the distinction between incorporation and transformation is probably only one of presumption for or against incorporation.

[4] (1876) 2 Ex D. 63, 202, 203. See Fawcett, op. cit., pp. 48–50. Cf. *Reg.* v. *Kent Justices, ex p. Lye* [1967] 2 Q.B. 153, D.C.; 42 *B.Y.* (1967), p. 293.

[5] Cf. Cockburn, C.J., pp. 161–73. [6] pp. 173–93.

[7] pp. 193–202. See now the Territorial Waters Jurisdiction Act, 1878, and *infra*, p. 192.

treaty or other express concurrence of a government, or by implication from established usage.[1] Further on[2] he introduces two special factors: the need for *evidence* of assent by the British Government and the constitutional consideration that the courts could not apply what would practically amount to a new law without usurping the province of the legislature. He is in general exercised by the vagueness and differing views of jurists on the precise point involved:[3] the exercise of criminal jurisdiction as a corollary of the territorial status of the littoral sea.

Holdsworth[4] considered that the court in *Keyn* displaced the doctrine of incorporation. On the other hand it is very doubtful if the majority of the judges directed themselves to the issue between incorporation and transformation.[5] The elements of 'transformation' in the judgment of Cockburn, C.J., are entirely compatible with the doctrine of incorporation if it is seen that he was concerned with proof of the rules of international law: if the evidence is inconclusive and the issue affects the liberty of persons, then assent by the legislature of the forum is needed to supplement the evidence. Yet as a *general* condition he does not require express assent or a functional transformation by Act of Parliament.[6] In cases of first impression the courts are ready to apply international law without looking for evidence of 'assent'.[7]

In any case *Keyn* remains a somewhat ambiguous precedent for the present purpose, and the later cases must be considered. In *West Rand Central Gold Mining Co.* v. *R.*[8] a petition of right was denied on the basis that the conquering state (Great Britain) was not successor to the financial liabilities of the conquered state (the South African Republic) before the outbreak of war. The issue of incorporation was properly argued, and Lord Alverstone, C.J., dealt with the question at length. As the rules of international law did not favour the suppliants in any case his remarks are *obiter*. However, his words seem to rest on an assump-

[1] p. 202. [2] p. 203.

[3] pp. 193, 203. The point was less obvious then than it would be now. See also the minority views of Brett, J.A., and Grove, J.

[4] Op. cit., pp. 263–6; and see Halsbury, loc. cit. Oppenheim i. 40 regards the statements on the need for assent as *dicta*. See also Morgenstern, op. cit., pp. 52, 67.

[5] Sir Robert Phillimore, at p. 68, expressly reserves the question. See also Lauterpacht, *International Law: Collected Papers* i (1970), pp. 218–22.

[6] Indeed Halsbury vii. 5 remarks that 'there seems little, if any, practical distinction between the two views expressed'.

[7] See *In re Piracy Jure Gentium* [1934] A.C. 586; Green, p. 493; *Molvan* v. *A.G. for Palestine* [1948] A.C. 351; Green, p. 556.

[8] [1905] 2 K.B. 391; Green p. 39; Briggs, p. 218.

tion that the doctrine of incorporation holds good. At the same time he shares the concern of Cockburn, C.J., with questions of evidence of the rules of international law. He requires 'assent' in relation to rules based on the 'opinions of text-writers' as opposed to a subject-matter on which there is a 'particular and recognized rule of international law'.[1] Thus his judgment *appears* to contain elements of the principle of transformation in the form of some 'assent' by Great Britain.[2]

In *Mortensen* v. *Peters*[3] Lord Dunedin, the Lord Justice-General, regarded the question as to the extent of jurisdiction in the Moray Firth as one of construing the relevant legislation. The *ratio* of the case was that the clear words of a statute bind the court even if the provisions are contrary to international law. The judgment contains the following dictum which must be seen in the context of the *ratio*: 'It is a trite observation that there is no such thing as a standard of international law extraneous to the domestic law of a kingdom, to which appeal may be made. International law, so far as this Court is concerned, is the body of doctrine . . . which has been adopted and made a part of the law of Scotland.' This is equivocal but is commonly understood to be in favour of the transformation doctrine.

In *Commercial and Estates Co. of Egypt* v. *Board of Trade*, Atkin, L.J.,[4] as he then was, uttered the following dictum which, not unambiguously, supports transformation: 'International Law as such can confer no rights cognisable in the municipal courts. It is only in so far as the rules of International Law are recognized as included in the rules of municipal law that they are allowed in municipal courts to give rise to rights and obligations.' Giving the opinion of the Privy Council in *Chung Chi Cheung* v. *The King*,[5] Lord Atkin stated that:

so far, at any rate, as the Courts of this country[6] are concerned, international

[1] pp. 407–8.

[2] And so Holdsworth, *Essays*, p. 269, and Halsbury vii. 4, note (d), consider the case to uphold the view of the majority in *Keyn*, *supra*. Oppenheim i. 40 regards the case as 'a reaffirmation of the classical doctrine', i.e., of incorporation. See also Brierly, *Law of Nations* (6th ed.), p. 87 and Stephenson, L.J., in *Trendtex* (*supra*, p. 45, n. 3) at pp. 568–9.

[3] *Supra*, p. 45, n. 4.

[4] [1925] 1 K.B. 271, 295. A case of first impression on the right of a belligerent to seize neutral ships by way of necessity (the right of angary). See Morgenstern, op. cit., pp. 51–2.

[5] [1939] A.C. 160, 167–8. Quoted: *Reference on Powers of City of Ottawa to Levy Rates on Foreign Legations* [1943] S.C.R. 208; *Ann. Digest* 10 (1941–2), no. 106; the *Rose Mary* [1953] 1 W.L.R. 246; *Fraser-Brace* v. *Saint John County*, Int. L.R. 23 (1956), 217.

[6] An anomalous way of expressing the matter in the Judicial Committee, but correct as a matter of form.

law has no validity save in so far as its principles are accepted and adopted by our own domestic law. There is no external power that imposes its own rules upon our own code of substantive law or procedure. The Courts acknowledge the existence of a body of rules which nations accept amongst themselves. On any judicial issue they seek to ascertain what the relevant rule is, and, having found it, they will treat it as incorporated into the domestic law, so far as it is not inconsistent with rules enacted by statutes or finally declared by their tribunals.

This statement harks back to the problem of evidence of the relevant rules and is by no means incompatible with the principle of incorporation.[1]

These authorities, taken as a whole, support the doctrine of incorporation, and the less favourable dicta are equivocal to say the least. Commonwealth decisions reflect the English accent on incorporation.[2]

(b) *Treaties.*[3] In England, and also it seems in most Commonwealth countries, the conclusion and ratification of treaties are within the prerogative of the Crown (or its equivalent), and if a transformation doctrine were not applied, the Crown could legislate for the subject without parliamentary consent. As a consequence treaties are only part of English law if an enabling Act of Parliament has been passed. This rule applies to treaties which affect private rights or liabilities, result in a charge on public funds, or require modification of the common law or statute for their enforcement in the courts.[4] The rule does not apply to treaties relating to the conduct of war or treaties of cession. In any case, the words of a subsequent Act of Parliament

[1] Significantly, as with the *West Rand* case, writers draw conflicting conclusions from the dictum. See Oppenheim i. 39, n. 5; Brierly, op. cit., p. 88; Starke, op. cit., pp. 86–7. See further the dicta of Lords Macmillan and Wright in the *Cristina* [1938] A.C. 485 at pp. 497 (quoting Lord Dunedin in *Mortensen* v. *Peters*) and 502 respectively, which also have these ambiguous aspects. But cf. *In re Ferdinand, Ex-Tsar of Bulgaria* [1921] 1 Ch. 107, especially the dictum of Warrington, L.J., at p. 137.

[2] See *The Ship 'North'* v. *The King* [1906] 37 S.C.R. 385 (Canada); *Wright* v. *Cantrell* [1943] 44 S.R. (N.S.W.), 45; *Ann. Digest* 12 (1943–5), no. 37; *Chow Hung Ching* v. *The King* (1948), 77 C.L.R. 449 (Australia); *Virendra Singh* v. *State of Uttar Pradesh*, Int. L.R. 22 (1955), 131 (India). See also, on S. African cases, Bridge, 20 *I.C.L.Q.* (1971), 746.

[3] See McNair, *The Law of Treaties* (1961), pp. 81–97; Mann, 44 *Grot. Soc.* (1958–9), 29–62; Fawcett, *The British Commonwealth in International Law*, pp. 56–72; Doeker, *The Treaty-Making Power in the Commonwealth of Australia* (1966); Gotlieb, *Canadian Treaty-Making* (1968).

[4] See *The Parlement Belge* [1880] 5 P.D. 197; *In re Californian Fig Syrup Co.* (1888), L.R. 40 Ch. D. 620 (Stirling, J., *obiter*); *Walker* v. *Baird* [1892] A.C. 491; *A.-G. for Canada* v. *A.-G. for Ontario* [1937] A.C. 326, 347, per Lord Atkin; *Theophile* v. *Solicitor-General* [1950] A.C. 186, 195–6; *Republic of Italy* v. *Hambro's Bank* [1950] 1 A.E.R. 430; *Cheney* v. *Conn* [1968] 1 W.L.R. 242; Int. L.R., 41, p. 421. Commonwealth cases: Fawcett, p. 57, n. 34.

will prevail over the provisions of a prior treaty in case of inconsistency between the two.[1]

9. *Treaties and the Interpretation of Statutes in the United Kingdom*[2]

The rule, stated in the previous section, is that in case of conflict statute prevails over treaty: this is a principle of constitutional law and not a rule of construction. There is, however, a well-established rule of construction which is normally stated thus: where domestic legislation is passed to give effect to an international convention, there is a presumption that Parliament intended to fulfil its international obligations.[3] The question then arises: what means should the courts use to discover the intention of Parliament in this connection?

Legislation to give effect in domestic law to the provisions may take various forms.[4] A statute may directly enact the provisions of the international instrument, which will be set out as a schedule to the Act. Alternatively, the statute may employ its own substantive provisions to give effect to a treaty, the text of which is not directly enacted. In the latter situation, the international convention may be referred to in the long and short titles of the Act and also in the preamble and schedule. In *Ellerman Lines* v. *Murray*[5] their lordships adopted the view that if the relevant section of the Act had a 'natural meaning' it was improper to resort to the text of the Convention as an aid to interpretation. In recent cases, however, the Court of Appeal has held that the text of the relevant convention may be used as an aid to interpretation even if the statute does not in terms incorporate the convention nor even refer to it.[6] In the *Salomon* case Diplock, L.J.,[7]

[1] *I.R.C.* v. *Collco Dealings Ltd.* [1962] A.C. 1; Int. L.R. 33, p. 1 (see Bowett, 37 *B.Y.* (1961), p. 548); *Woodend Rubber Company* v. *Commissioner of Inland Revenue* [1971] A.C. 321.

[2] See Mann, 62 *L.Q.R.* (1946), 278–91; Sinclair, 12 *I.C.L.Q.* (1963), 508–51; *The Interpretation of Statutes*, The Law Commission and the Scottish Law Commission, 1969, paras. 12–14, 74–76; Lasok, 70 *R.G.D.I.P.* (1966), 961–94; *Halsbury's Laws of England* (3rd ed.), vol. 36, 394, 411, 414.

[3] *Salomon* v. *Commissioners of Customs and Excise* [1967], 2 Q.B. 116, C.A., at pp. 141 (per Lord Denning, M.R.), 143 (per Diplock, L.J.); Int. L.R. 41, p. 1; *Post Office* v. *Estuary Radio* [1967] 1 W.L.R. 1396, C.A., at p. 1404; [1968] 2 Q.B. 740 at p. 757 (Diplock, L.J., delivering the judgment of the Court); Green, p. 499. *Corocraft Ltd.* v. *Pan American Airways Inc.* [1969] 1 Q.B. 616; [1968] 3 W.L.R. 1273, C.A. at p. 1281 per Lord Denning; Int. L.R. 41, p. 426.

[4] See Sinclair, op. cit., pp. 528–34; *British Practice* (1964), ii. 232–3.

[5] [1931] A.C. 126, at p. 147 per Lord Tomlin. See also *Barras* v. *Aberdeen Steam Trawling Co. Ltd.* [1933] A.C. 402; *Burns Philp & Co. Ltd.* v. *Nelson and Robertson Proprietaries Ltd.* (1957–8), 98 C.L.R. 495, H.C. of A.

[6] *Salomon* v. *Commissioners of Customs and Excise*, *supra*; *Post Office* v. *Estuary Radio*, *supra*.

[7] [1967] 2 Q.B. at pp. 143, 144.

stated two conditions for resort to the convention: (a) that the terms of the legislation are not clear but are reasonably capable of more than one meaning; (b) that there be cogent extrinsic evidence to the effect that the enactment was intended to fulfil obligations under a particular convention. These principles seem to represent the present law on the subject yet it is surely the case that Lord Diplock's second condition is the only necessary principle. The difficulty with the first condition is that it maintains the basic fault of the *dicta* in the *Ellerman Lines* decision, which is the question-begging involved. If the convention may be used on the correct principle that the statute is intended to implement the convention then, it follows, the latter becomes a proper aid to interpretation, and, more especially, may reveal a latent ambiguity in the text of the statute even if this was 'clear in itself'. Moreover, the principle or presumption that the Crown does not intend to break an international treaty must have the corollary that the text of the international instrument is a primary source of meaning or 'interpretation'. The courts have lately accepted the need to refer to the relevant treaty even in the absence of ambiguity in the legislative text when taken in isolation.[1] This approach is more readily adopted, as in the *Corocraft* case, when the statute expressly gives effect to the text of the Convention as such and the text appears in a schedule as a translation into English of the only official text.[2] It is not clear, however, that the method chosen to give legislative effect to the treaty should determine whether reference should be made to the text of the convention, providing Lord Diplock's second condition (above) is satisfied. In recent years the English courts have recognized the relevance of treaty provisions concerning human rights to the construction of statutes.[3]

British, American and Commonwealth courts normally[4] employ methods of interpretation similar in a general way to those of international tribunals and international law.[5]

[1] See *Post Office* v. *Estuary Radio* [1968] 2 Q.B. 740 at p. 755 per Diplock L.J., *The Abadesa (No. 2)* [1968] P. 656; *Benin* v. *Whimster* [1975] 3 W.L.R. 542, C.A.; *The Huntingdon* [1974] 1 W.L.R. 505, H.L.; *Wilson, Smithett and Cope Ltd.* v. *Terrazzi* [1976] 2 W.L.R. 418, C.A.; *The Jade, The Eischersheim* [1976] 1 W.L.R. 430, H.L.; *Pan-American World Airways Inc.* v. *Department of Trade* [1976] 1 Ll. L.R. 257, C.A.

[2] [1969] 1 Q.B. 616; [1968] 3 W.L.R. 1273.

[3] References and comment: 47 *B.Y.I.L.* (1974–5), 356–61; ibid., 48 (1976–7), 348–53; Dale, 25 *I.C.L.Q.* (1976), 292–309. Also: *Ahmad* v. *I.L.E.A.* [1978] 1 Q.B. 36, C.A.

[4] But not invariably: *The Katikiro of Buganda* v. *A.-G. of Uganda*, Int. L.R. 27, p. 260, Ct. of Appeal, Eastern Africa.

[5] See *James Buchanan & Co. Ltd.* v. *Babco* [1978] A.C. 141, H.L.; Sinclair, *supra*; American Law Inst., Restatement, Second, *For. Relations Law*, para. 151.

10. *The Reception of International Law in Other States*[1]

A very considerable number of states follow the principle of the incorporation, or adoption, of customary international law.[2] The principle may be applied in judicial practice or on the basis of constitutional provisions as interpreted by the courts. An increasing number of states make appropriate provision in their constitutions, and thus Article 10 of the Italian Constitution of 1947 provides that 'Italian law shall be in conformity with the generally recognized rules of international law'. In general it may be said that governments and lawyers are lately more conscious of the need to establish a constructive relationship between the municipal law and the system of international law. However, the subject-matter is complicated by issues of constitutional law peculiar to the given state and especially the distribution of power in a federal structure. Legal systems rarely adhere to any very pure form of incorporation. In Italy, to take an example already quoted, the courts have held that Article 10 of the Constitution does not affect the validity of legislation passed before the Constitution was brought into force. In the majority of states the rule obtains that international law must give way to national legislation. An important consideration is the fact that many rules of customary international law do not provide precise guidance for their application on the national plane. The principal task remains that of creating a sensible working relationship between the two systems within the jurisdiction of the particular state, an accommodation between them rather than the attainment of a formal 'harmony', or the 'primacy' of international law. The problems are obscured if they are placed in the context of the conflict between monists and dualists.[3]

These considerations apply with even greater force to the role of treaties in national courts. A number of countries adhere to the principle that treaties made in accordance with the constitution

[1] See generally Morgenstern, 27 *B.Y.* (1950), 42–92; Seidl-Hohenveldern, 12 *I.C.L.Q.* (1963), 88–124; Fawcett, op. cit., chapter 2; Masters, *International Law in National Courts* (1932); Mosler, 91 Hague *Recueil* (1957, I), 625–705; Lapidoth, *Les Rapports entre le droit international public et le droit interne en Israël* (1959); Carsten Smith, 12 *Scandinavian Studies in Law* (1968), 153–201; *Norwegian Dentists Association* case, 96 *J.D.I.* (1969), 419, Supr. Ct., Norway; Holloway, *Modern Trends in Treaty Law* (1967), pp. 253–88, 294–316.

[2] Current evidence may be found in the International Law Reports. For use of English sources on the question: *Stampfer* v. *A.-G.*, Int. L.R. 23 (1956), 284 (Israel); *Re Lawless* Int. L.R. 24 (1957) 420 (Eire). American authorities: *Hilton* v. *Guyot* (1895), 159 U.S. 113; Briggs, p. 399; the *Paquete Habana* (1900), 175 U.S. 677; Briggs, p. 30; *U.S.* v. *Melekh* (1960), 190 F. Supp. 67.

[3] *Supra*, pp. 33–35.

bind the courts without any specific act of incorporation.[1] In fact in such states the principle is often applied with significant qualifications. Thus, in the United States, a later act of federal legislation overrides a treaty. Furthermore, a self-executing treaty may not be enforced internally until it has been published, and control over due publication introduces elements of formal constitutionality.[2] What is probably the more generally accepted principle requires specific legislative incorporation as a condition of internal force.[3]

There also arises the category of 'self-executing' treaties. The term 'self-executing' may be used to state a principle of the particular system of national law that certain rules of international law do not need incorporation in order to have internal effect. However, the term is also used to describe the character of the rules themselves. Thus a national court may hold that, as a matter of interpretation, a treaty obligation could not be applicable internally without specific local legislation.[4] Both uses of the term appear in the decisions of American courts. The second of the uses described appears in *Fujii* v. *State of California*.[5] There the Supreme Court of California held that Articles 55 and 56 of the Charter of the United Nations, relating to human rights, were not self-executing and could not be applied in regard to individuals without the requisite legislation. The whole subject resists generalization, and the practice of states reflects the characteristics of the individual constitution.

[1] Argentina, Austria, France, Luxembourg, Belgium, Greece, German Federal Republic (probably), Spain, the Netherlands, Switzerland, United States, U.S.S.R., Mexico. See generally Mosler, op. cit., pp. 651–88; Ginsburgs, 59 *A.J.* (1965), 523–44; P. de Visscher, *Recueil d'études en hommage à Paul Guggenheim*, pp. 605–12; Blishchenko, 69 *A.J.* (1975), 819–27.

[2] See Seidl-Hohenveldern, op. cit., pp. 105–7.

[3] See Morgenstern, op. cit., pp. 53–5. British and Commonwealth practice: *supra*, p. 49. See also *Custodian of Absentee Property* v. *Samra*, Int. L.R. 22 (1955), 5; *Re Lawless*, Int. L.R. 24 (1957), 420.

[4] See Alona Evans, 30 *B.Y.* (1953), pp. 178–205; Bishop, 115 Hague *Recueil* (1965, II) pp. 202–9.

[5] (1952), 38 Cal. 2d. 718, 242 P. 2d. 617; Int. L.R. 19 (1952), no. 53; applied by the Supreme Court of Iowa in *Rice* v. *Sioux City Memorial Park Cemetery Inc.*, Int. L.R. 20 (1953), 244 and a District Court in *Comacho* v. *Rogers*, Int. L.R. 32, p. 368. See also Evans, 30 *B.Y.* (1953), 178–205; Preuss, 51 *Michigan L.R.* (1953) 117; *A.J.K.* v. *Public Prosecutor*, Int. L.R. 28, p. 268; *Re Masini*, Int. L.R. 24 (1957), 11; *Rossier* v. *Court of Justice of Canton of Geneva*, Int. L.R. 32, p. 348. On the effect of the European Convention of Human Rights: Golsong, 33 *B.Y.* (1957), 317–21; and 38 *B.Y.* (1962), 445–56; Drzemczewski, *Legal Issues of European Integration* (1979), 1–50. *European Convention on Human Rights* case, Int. L.R. 40 p. 238, Austrian Constitutional Court, 27 June 1960; *Ex parte Püschel*, Int. L.R. 38, p. 174, Austrian Constitutional Court, 14 October 1961; *Deprivation of Liberty* case, Int. L.R. 40, p. 244, Austria, Administrative Court, 15 December 1961; *Kannas* v. *The Police*, Int. L.R. 41, p. 360, Cyprus, S.C.

11. *Relation of Executive and Judiciary*

To a great extent the problems of applying international law in the municipal sphere are related to the distribution of power within the state, and many of the principles noticed in the previous sections depend on a concern to maintain a proper relation between the courts and the legislature. Yet another field of problems arises when the relation of the executive and the courts is considered.[1] This relation has a number of facets. One of these is illustrated by the case of *Mortensen* v. *Peters*[2] in which the High Court of Justiciary of Scotland interpreted the Herring Fishery (Scotland) Act, 1889, in such a way that it could apply in a manner contrary to international law—to prohibit fishing by aliens in areas outside the territorial sea. In fact the enforcement agencies have not applied the Act in this way.[3] In the realm of international relations the English courts seek the guidance of the appropriate department of government on the determination of a variety of issues, including the status of entities claiming to be independent states, the recognition of governments, the existence of a state of war, and the incidence of diplomatic immunity. This is formally a matter of evidence, a procedure for taking judicial notice of material facts, but the certificate of the Secretary of State is conclusive of the matter,[4] unless the certificate deliberately leaves the court free to construe a particular word or phrase, for example, 'war' in a time charter-party.[5] The effect of this procedure is where necessary to subject the courts to the determination of important legal issues by the executive and so avoid the embarrassment of a conflict of opinion.[6]

[1] Of course, where the executive has the treaty-making power, a pure doctrine of incorporation applied by the courts would have the effect of bypassing the legislature: hence the English practice, *supra*, p. 49.

[2] (1906), 8 F. (J.C.), 93; Briggs, p. 52.

[3] *U.K. Contemporary Practice* (1962), i. 48. Similarly where an Act, without the interpretative intervention of the courts, could be applied in a particular way, the executive may enforce the law in such a way as to accord with international law as it is assumed to be by the executive: on the application of the Customs Consolidation Act, 1876, so as to avoid a contiguous zone, see McNair, *Opinions* i. 344, 345–6.

[4] See Lyons, 23 *B.Y.* (1946), 240–81; 29 *B.Y.* (1952), 227–64. But cf. *The Zamora* [1916] 2 A.C. 77 on the evidential effect of an Order in Council in respect of the effectiveness of a blockade. On American practice: id., 24 *B.Y.* (1947), 116–47. On Continental and Latin-American practice: id., 25 *B.Y.* (1948), 180–210. See also *A.-G. of Israel* v. *Kamiar*, Int. L.R. 44, p. 197 at pp. 250–2.

[5] See *Kawasaki Kisen Kabushiki Kaisha of Kobe* v. *Bantham Steamship Co. Ltd.* [1939] 2 K.B. 544; Green, p. 685; *Luigi Monta of Genoa* v. *Cechofracht Co. Ltd.* [1956] 2 Q.B. 552; *In re Al-Fin Corporation's Patent* [1970] 1 Ch. 160; 44 *B.Y.* (1970), 213. See also Merrills, 20 *I.C.L.Q.* (1971), 476–99.

[6] In the United States on the issue of the immunity from suit of state-owned vessels

Policy considerations of a similar kind have led courts to apply a form of the Act of State doctrine[1] and, by holding a claim to be barred, because it concerned the acts of a foreign state, to leave the executive free in its conduct of foreign relations. Thus in the *Sabbatino* case[2] the United States Supreme Court refused to foreclose to any extent issues outstanding between the governments of the United States and Cuba. Furthermore, in a number of states, the courts follow the executive in matters of treaty interpretation.[3]

12. Res Judicata *and the Two Systems*

There is no effect of *res judicata* from the decision of a municipal court so far as an international jurisdiction is concerned, since, although the subject-matter may be substantially the same, the parties will not be, and the issues will have a very different aspect. In the municipal court the legal person claiming is an individual or corporation: before an international tribunal the claimant will be a state exercising diplomatic protection with respect to its national.[4] Considerations of admissibility may have the effect of creating an exception to the general rule. Thus a respondent in an international claim may plead successfully that adequate remedies have been obtained before another tribunal, either national or international.[5] In the *Cysne*[6] an arbitral tribunal held that in matters of prize the judgments of national prize courts of final instance constituted international titles, which were generally recognized, and so had the force of *res judicata* as to the passing of property. The policy behind this ruling was based on considerations of security for third persons acquiring title in prize: however, the prize court's decision might create international responsibility for the state

engaged in commerce the Supreme Court and State Department at one time held conflicting views: 28 *B.Y.* (1951), 268–70.

[1] See generally Morgenstern, 27 *B.Y.* (1950), 73–80.

[2] *Banco Nacional de Cuba* v. *Sabbatino,* 84 Sup. Ct. 923 (1964); see Henkin, 64 *Col. L.R.* (1964), 805–32; and Falk, *The Role of Domestic Courts in the International Legal Order* (1964). The effect of the decision has been substantially reduced by legislation.

[3] Morgenstern, pp. 79–80.

[4] See *Certain German Interests in Polish Upper Silesia* (1925), P.C.I.J., Ser. A, no. 6, p. 20; Schwarzenberger, *International Law* i (3rd ed.), p. 142.

[5] See the *Ottoz* claim, Int. L.R. 18 (1951), no. 136 and the *Nartnick* and *Mayer* claims, Int. L.R. 21 (1954), 149, 150 respectively. It could be argued, however, that the commission deciding these claims (U.S. International Claims Commission) was not strictly speaking an international tribunal.

[6] (1930), *R.I.A.A.* ii. 1035. See also Oppenheim ii. 475, n. 2.

of the *forum* if it constituted a violation of international law. And of course an international tribunal may be bound by its constituent instrument, usually an agreement between two or more states, to accept certain categories of national decisions as conclusive of particular issues.[1]

In principle decisions by organs of international organizations are not binding on national courts without the co-operation of the internal legal system,[2] which may adopt a broad constitutional provision for 'automatic' incorporation of treaty norms or require specific acts of incorporation at least for certain categories of treaties.[3] It follows that a decision of the International Court, though it concerns substantially the same issues as those before a municipal court, does not of itself create a *res judicata* for the latter.[4] However, the decisions of international courts could be justifiably regarded as evidence of title to property and of personal status, particularly of nationality in terms of international law.

In a considerable number of countries municipal courts, in dealing with cases of war crimes and issues arising from belligerent occupation, for example the validity of acts of administration, of requisition, and of transactions conducted in occupation currency, have relied upon the findings of the International Military Tribunals at Nuremberg and Tokyo as evidence, even conclusive evidence, of the illegality of the war which resulted in the occupations.[5] In general the decisions of international tribunals provide evidence of the legally permitted extent of the jurisdiction and territorial sovereignty of the particular states involved.[6]

[1] Cf. the *Pinson* claim (1928), *R.I.A.A.* v. 327; Green, p. 722.

[2] See Sørensen, 101 Hague *Receuil* (1960, III), 120–5; Skubiszewski, 41 *B.Y.* (1965–6), 198 at pp. 267–71; id., 2 *Polish Yrbk.* (1968–9), 80–108; id., 46 *B.Y.* (1972–3), 353–64; Schreuer, 27 *I.C.L.Q.* (1978), 1–17; *Diggs* v. *Richardson*, *Digest of U.S. Practice*, 1976, p. 50 (Security Council resol. held not to be self-executing); *Bradley* v. *Commonwealth of Australia* (1973), 1 A.L.R. 241; 101 *J.D.I.* (1974), 865.

[3] *Supra*, pp. 49–53.

[4] See '*Socobel*' v. *Greek State*, Int. L.R. 18 (1951), no. 2; 47 *A.J.* (1953), 580; Rosenne, *The Law and Practice of the International Court*, pp. 130–3; and Jenks, *The Prospects of International Adjudication*, pp. 706–15. In a treaty structure the Court of Justice of the European Communities has the power to hand down judgments enforceable within the municipal systems concerned. On the creation of issue estoppel by foreign decisions see *Carl Zeiss Stiftung* v. *Rayner and Keeler, Ltd.* (*No.* 2) [1967] 1 A.C. 853.

[5] See Brownlie, *International Law and the Use of Force by States*, pp. 185–6, 407. See also *Hong Kong and Shanghai Banking Corporation* v. *Luis Perez-Samanillo Inc.*, *Ann. Digest* 13 (1946), no. 157; *N.* v. *B.*, Int. L.R. 24 (1957), 941; *B.* v. *T.*, ibid., p. 962. On the special relationship between the Allied military tribunals in Germany under occupation and the I.M.T. at Nuremberg see *Law Reports of Trials of War Criminals*, U.N.W.C.C. xv. 17–20.

[6] See *Rex* v. *Cooper*, *Rex* v. *Martin*, Int. L.R. 20 (1953), 166, 167; *Administration des*

13. *Relation to the Sources of International Law*

Judicial decisions in the municipal sphere and acts of legislation provide *prima facie* evidence of the attitudes of states on points of international law and very often constitute the only available evidence of the practice of states. Thus collections of municipal cases, such as the *Annual Digest of Public International Law Cases* (continued as the *International Law Reports*), and of legislation, which appears in the *United Nations Legislative Series*, are important in any assessment of the customary law.[1] In the pleadings before an international tribunal points of law will be dealt with at length by experts and the tribunal will in any case be qualified to handle the legal sources. The issues may be of great significance and the process of argument and decision will take some time. When points of international law arise in a municipal court, and resort to the executive for guidance does not occur, the court will commonly face very real difficulty in obtaining reliable evidence, in convenient form, of the state of the law, and especially the customary law, on a particular point.[2] An *ad hoc*, yet extensive, research project is out of the question, and counsel cannot always fill the gap (unless a well prepared law officer of the Crown, or equivalent elsewhere, appears as an *amicus curiae*).[3] In these circumstances it is hardly surprising that courts have leaned heavily on the opinions of writers.[4] It can and does happen that a municipal court makes for itself a very full investigation of all the legal sources,[5] including treaties and state practice—yet here also works of authority may be relied upon as repositories and assessors of state practice. And of course refer-

Habous v. *Deal*, ibid. 19 (1952), no. 67; *Re Bendayan*, 49 *A.J.* (1955), 267; *Mackay Radio Company* v. *El Khadar*, Int. L.R. 21 (1954), 136; 49 *A.J.* (1955), 267, 413; *In re Krüger*, Int. L.R. 18 (1951), no. 68. See further *Anglo-Iranian Oil Co.* v. *Idemitsu Kosan Kabushiki Kaisha*, Int. L.R. 22 (1953), 305; *Anglo-Iranian Oil Co. Ltd.* v. *S.U.P.O.R.*, Int. L.R. 22 (1955), p. 23 at p. 41. Cf. *Steinberg* v. *Custodian of German Property*, Int. L.R. 24 (1957), 771; *Czechoslovak Agrarian Reform* (*Swiss Subjects*) case, *Ann. Digest* 4 (1927–8), no. 94. See also Schreuer, 24 *I.C.L.Q.* (1975), 153–83.

[1] See further *infra*, pp. 298 seq., 385 seq.

[2] See *supra*, pp. 44 seq.

[3] Cf. the information and protest filed by a law officer in cases involving the issue of sovereign immunity: see the *Parlement Belge* (1880) L. R. 5 P.D. 197.

[4] See *West Rand Central Gold Mining Co.* v. *R.* [1905] 2 K.B. 391 at pp. 407–8. In some jurisdictions resort will be made to an expert witness.

[5] See *R.* v. *Keyn* (1876), 2 Ex. D. 63; *In re Piracy Jure Gentium* [1934] A.C. 586; *The State* (*Duggan*) v. *Tapley* [1952] I.R. 62; Int. L.R. 18 (1951), no. 109; *State of the Netherlands* v. *Federal Reserve Bank*, ibid., no. 174; *Aboitiz & Co.* v. *Price* (1951), 99 F. Supp. 602; Int. L.R. 18 (1951), no. 182; *Haw Pia* v. *China Banking Corp.*, ibid., no. 203; *Lauritzen* v. *Government of Chile*, Int. L.R. 23 (1956), 708; *Indonesian Tobacco Estates Case*, Int. L.R. 28, p. 16.

ence may be made to decisions and dicta of international tribunals[1] and the work of the International Law Commission.[2] In this respect English courts have been reserved in their attitude, it seems, but it is to be remembered that opportunities for neat and conclusive citations are rare.[3] Since such reference arises from a desire to have evidence of the state of the law there is no distinction of principle to be made between judgments and advisory opinions of the International Court.[4] The picture is far from complete if it is not observed that municipal courts may, on the basis of precedents in the English sense or a *jurisprudence constante*, adopt a principle of international law with a modified content which after a time may diverge considerably from the view generally accepted by states.[5]

14. *Conclusion*

On the whole question of the relation between municipal and international law theoretical constructions have probably done much to obscure realities. If one has to choose between the theories considered earlier in this chapter,[6] then the views of Fitzmaurice and Rousseau might be preferred as coming closer to the facts.[7] Each system is supreme *in its own field*, and neither has a hegemony over the other. And yet any generalities offered can only provide a background to the complex relations between the two systems. Three factors operate on the subject-matter. The first is organizational: to what extent are the organs of states

[1] See e.g., *Eichmann* (1961), 56 *A.J.* (1962), 805; Int. L.R., 36, pp. 5, 18, 277; *Murarka* v. *Bachrack Bros., Inc.*, Int. L.R. 20 (1953), 52; *Lauritzen* v. *Larsen*, ibid., p. 197; *The Rose Mary* [1953] 1 W.L.R. 246; Int. L.R. 20 (1953), 316; *Heirs of Shababo* v. *Heilen* (no. 2), ibid., p. 400; *Stampfer* v. *A.-G.*, Int. L.R. 23 (1956), 284; *Lauritzen* v. *Government of Chile*, ibid., p. 708 at pp. 733, 738, 742, 750; *N.V. de Bataafsche Petroleum Maatschappij* v. *War Damage Commission*, ibid., p. 810 at p. 822, 832, 845; *Mobarik Ali Ahmed* v. *State of Bombay*, Int. L.R. 24 (1957), 156; *Re Application of Spanish-Swiss Conv. of Nov. 14, 1879*, Int. L.R. 28, p. 461.

[2] See *Cassirer and Geheeb* v. *Japan*, Int. L.R. 28, p. 396 at pp. 407 seq.

[3] See generally Jenks, 20 *B.Y.* (1939), 1–36; id., *The Prospects of International Adjudication*, pp. 727–56. And see the *Fagernes* [1927] P. 311, 325 (Lord Atkin); *Feist* v. *Société Intercommunale Belge* [1934] A.C. at p. 173 (Lord Russell of Killowen); *International Trustee* v. *Rex* [1936] 3 A.E.R. 406 at pp. 423, 426 (Lord Wright, M.R.); *Bank voor Handel* v. *Slatford* [1951] 2 A.E.R. 779 (Devlin, J.). See also *Civil Air Transport Inc.* v. *Central Air Transport Corp.* Int. L.R. 19 (1952), no. 20 at p. 103 (Hong Kong Court of Appeal).

[2] See *infra*, Chapter XXXI, section 8, 10.

[3] Cf. the lines of cases on recognition of governments and sovereign immunity in English law, *infra*, and prize law. See further Dicey, *Conflict of Laws* (8th ed.), pp. 995–6.

[4] *Supra*, pp. 33–6.

[5] Cf. also the views of Virally, *Mélanges offerts à Henri Rolin*, pp. 488–505.

willing to apply rules of international law internally and externally?[1] This raises the problem of state responsibility, sanctions, and non-recognition of illegal acts. Exceptionally, as a result of international action followed by occupation, a state may suffer external direction in the application of international law both internally and externally. The second factor is the difficulty of proving the existence of particular rules of international law. In case of difficulty municipal courts may rely on advice from the executive or existing internal precedents, and the result may not accord with an objective appreciation of the law. Thirdly, courts, both municipal and international, will often be concerned with the more technical question as to which is the *appropriate* system to apply to particular issues arising. The question of appropriateness emphasizes the distinction between organization, i.e. the nature of the jurisdiction as 'national' or 'international', and the character of the rules of both systems as flexible instruments for dealing with disputes and regulating non-contentious matters. An international court may find it necessary to apply rules of municipal law,[2] whilst bodies, such as the United States Foreign Claims Settlement Commission, which are national in terms of organization and competence, may find it appropriate, and be authorized, to apply rules of international law on a large scale.[3] When a municipal court applies a rule of international law because it is appropriate, it is pointless to ask if the rule applied has been 'transformed', except in so far as 'transformation' describes a special process required by a particular municipal system before certain organs are permitted, or are willing, to apply rules of international law.[4]

[1] Monists underestimate this aspect of the matter or gloss it over with conceptualism. The fact is that municipal law is more viable in terms of organization whereas international law is less of a system *in this sense*. From this point of view there is some substance in the view that international law derives from the activities of the constitutional organs of states. This view, characterized as monism in terms of internal law, was supported by Zorn, Kaufmann, Wenzel, and Decencière-Ferrandière (see the latter in 40 *R.G.D.I.P.* (1933), 45–70). Critics have tended to caricature this view in order to criticize it: in fact it accords with widely held views that international law is *international* and not dependent on a supranational coercive order.

[2] *Supra*, pp. 39–43.

[3] When it is lawful for it to do so, a municipal court applying international law to deal with the primary issues in a case may be designated an 'international court': cf. *infra*, Chapter XXIV, sections 6, 8.

[4] There are many areas of law in which the relation between the two systems has special features, for example the law of recognition, nationality of corporations, belligerent occupation, and the *res nullius*. Cf. Hackworth i. 476 on the latter; and see *infra*, pp. 62, 77–9, 136.

PART II

PERSONALITY AND RECOGNITION

CHAPTER III

SUBJECTS OF THE LAW[1]

1. *Introductory*

A SUBJECT of the law is an entity capable of possessing international rights and duties and having the capacity to maintain its rights by bringing international claims.[2] This definition, though conventional, is unfortunately circular since the *indicia* referred to depend on the existence of a legal person. All that can be said is that an entity of a type recognized by customary law as *capable* of possessing rights and duties and of bringing international claims, and having these capacities conferred upon it, is a legal person. If the first condition is not satisfied, the entity concerned may still have legal personality of a very restricted kind, dependent on the agreement or acquiescence of recognized legal persons and opposable on the international plane only to those agreeing or acquiescent. The principal formal contexts in which the question of personality has arisen have been: capacity to make claims in respect of breaches of international law, capacity to make treaties and agreements valid on the international plane, and the enjoyment of privileges and immunities from national jurisdictions. States have these capacities and immunities, and indeed the incidents of statehood as developed under the customary law have provided the *indicia* for, and instruments of personality in, other entities. Apart from states, organizations may have these capacities and immunities if certain conditions are satisfied.[3] The first of the capacities set

[1] See especially Verzijl, *International Law in Historical Perspective* ii (1969); Szászy, in *Mélanges offerts à Juraj Andrassy* (ed. Ibler), pp. 307–50; Lissitzyn, 125 Hague *Recueil* (1968, III), 5–87; Bishop, 115 Hague *Recueil* (1965, II), 251–74; Schwarzenberger, *International Law* i (3rd ed.), 89–179; O'Connell, 67 *R.G.D.I.P.* (1963), 5–43; Sørensen, 101 Hague *Recueil* (1960, III), 127–44; Mosler, in *Mélanges offerts à Henri Rolin*, pp. 228–51; Scelle, in *Law and Politics in the World Community* (1953), pp. 49–58; Eustathiades, 84 Hague *Recueil* (1953, III), 397–627; Berezowski, 65 Hague *Receuil* (1938, III), 5–82, Erich, 13 Hague *Receuil* (1926, III), 431–41; Lauterpacht, *International Law: Collected Papers*, ii. 487–533; Rousseau, *Droit International public* ii (1974); Lukashuk, 135 Hague *Recueil* (1972, I), 231–328.

[2] *Reparation for Injuries Case*, I.C.J. Reports (1949), p. 179.

[3] See *infra*, Chapter XXX, section 8.

out above, for organizations of a certain type, was established by the advisory opinion in the *Reparation for Injuries* case.[1] The first Waldock Report prepared for the International Law Commission on the law of treaties[2] recognized the capacity of international organizations to become parties to international agreements, and this recognition reflected the existing practice between organizations and also between states and organizations. Finally, whilst an organization probably cannot claim privileges and immunities like those of a sovereign state as of right, it can claim to be a suitable candidate for the conferment of like privileges and immunities.

It is states and organizations (if appropriate conditions exist) which represent the normal types of legal person on the international plane. However, as will become apparent in due course, the realities of international relations are not reducible to a simple formula and the picture is somewhat complex. The 'normal types' have congeners which create problems, and various entities, including non-self-governing peoples and the individual, have a certain personality.[3] Moreover, abstraction of types of acceptable persons at law falls short of the truth, since recognition and acquiescence may sustain an entity which is anomalous, and yet has a web of legal relations on the international plane. But in spite of the complexities, it is as well to remember the primacy of states as subjects of the law. As Professor Friedmann observes:[4]

> The basic reason for this position is, of course, that 'the world is to-day organized on the basis of the co-existence of States, and that fundamental changes will take place only through State action, whether affirmative or negative'.[5] The States are the repositories of legitimated authority over peoples and territories. It is only in terms of State powers, prerogatives, jurisdictional limits and law-making capabilities that territorial limits and jurisdiction, responsibility for official actions, and a host of other questions of co-existence between nations can be determined. . . . This basic primacy

[1] See generally Chapter XXX. See also Garcia Amador, *Yrbk., I.L.C.* (1956), ii. 195, 198.

[2] See *Yrbk., I.L.C.* (1962), ii. 31, 32, 35, 37. See also Brierly, ibid. (1950), ii. 230; Lauterpacht, ibid. (1953), ii. 96; Fitzmaurice, ibid. (1956), ii. 117–18; and 1958, ii. 24, 32: Waldock, ibid. (1962), ii. 31, 35–7. At a later stage the Commission decided to confine the specific provisions of the draft articles to the treaties of states: ibid. (1965), ii. 18; (1966), ii. 187, Article 1, commentary.

[3] It is true to say that personality is a quality which an entity either does or does not possess (see Broches, 98 Hague *Recueil* (1959, III), 320), but this proposition is not really very helpful.

[4] *The Changing Structure of International Law*, p. 213.

[5] Quoting Jessup, *A Modern Law of Nations* (1948), p. 17.

of the State as a subject of international relations and law would be substantially affected, and eventually superseded, only if national entities, as political and legal systems, were absorbed in a world State.

2. *Personality and Protected Status*

The questions of legal personality and protected status are connected but by no means identical. Minorities within states may receive guarantees of certain levels of treatment under an international agreement, but it does not follow that the minorities as such have legal personality, more especially when the individuals or groups themselves have no procedural rights before any international forum. In the case of the mandates system under the Covenant of the League of Nations, the United Nations Trusteeship System, and the Non-Self-Governing Territories to which Chapter XI of the Charter relates, the peoples concerned are given an international status,[1] but extraneous agencies—international organizations and their members—are given the task of supervising the carrying out of undertakings by the administering powers.[2] The particular instrument concerned, for example, the mandate agreement, may be interpreted in such a way as to give the populations concerned a direct legal interest in the carrying out of the undertakings contained in the instrument, although their limited legal capacity requires that they should have a representative.[3] The line between protected status, with no separate legal personality, and a special status with some limited legal capacity, is obviously not easily drawn.

3. *Established Legal Persons*

(a) *States*. This category, the most important, has its own problems. The existence of 'dependent' states[4] with certain qualified and delegated legal capacities complicates the picture, but, providing the conditions for statehood exist,[5] the 'dependent' state retains its personality. The position of members of federal unions is interesting. In the constitutions of Switzerland, the

[1] See Chapter XXIV, section 7.

[2] On the problems of *locus standi* and legal interest, see *infra*, pp. 466–73.

[3] This was the view of Judge Bustamante, separate opinion, in the *South West Africa* cases, I.C.J. Reports (1962) p. 354. But see the *South West Africa* cases (Second Phase), I.C.J. Reports, 1966, p. 6 and comment *infra*, pp. 468–70. On the personality of non-self-governing peoples see also Chapter XXIV, section 9. Cf. observations of Lord Finlay cited *infra*, p. 82, n. 3.

[4] See *infra*, p. 77. [5] See *infra*, pp. 74 seq.

German Federal Republic, and the U.S.S.R., component states are permitted to exercise certain of the capacities of independent states, including the power to make treaties. In the normal case, such capacities are probably exercised as agents for the union, even if the acts concerned are done in the name of the component state.[1] However, where the union originated as a union of independent states, the internal relations retain an international element, and the union may act as agent for the states.[2] The United States constitution enables the states of the Union to enter into agreements with other states of the Union or with foreign states with the consent of Congress.[3] In practice no such agreements have been made with foreign states. In Canada the federal government has the exclusive power to make treaties with foreign states.[4]

(b) *Political entities legally proximate to states.* Political settlements both in multilateral and bilateral treaties have from time to time produced political entities, such as the Free City of Danzig, which, possessing a certain autonomy, fixed territory and population, and some legal capacities on the international plane, are rather like states. Politically such entities are not sovereign states in the normal sense, yet legally the distinction is not very significant. The treaty origin of the entity and the existence of some form of protection by an international organization—the League of Nations in the case of Danzig—matter little if, in the result, the entity has autonomy and a nucleus of the more significant legal capacities, for example the power to make treaties, to maintain order and exercise jurisdiction within the territory, and to have an independent nationality law. The jurisprudence of the Permanent Court recognized that Danzig had international personality, except in so far as treaty obligations created special relations in regard to the League and to Poland.[5] The special relations of Danzig were based upon Articles 100–8 of the Versailles Treaty. The League of Nations had a supervisory function and Poland was placed in control of the foreign relations

[1] See 69 *R.G.D.I.P.* (1965), 775–80; Brierly, *Yrbk., I.L.C.* (1952), ii. 50; Lauterpacht, ibid. (1953), ii. 94–5, 137–9; Fitzmaurice, ibid. (1956), ii. 118; id., ibid. (1958), ii. 24, 32; Waldock, ibid. (1962), ii. 31, 36–7; Morin, 3 *Canad. Yrbk. Int. L.* (1965), 127–86; Lissitzyn, 125 Hague *Recueil* (1968, III), 24–50; Rousseau ii (1974), 138–213, 264–8; Uibopuu, 24 *I.C.L.Q.* (1975), 811–45; Wildhaber, 12 *Canad. Yrbk.* (1974), 211–21.

[2] This appears to be the position in Switzerland.

[3] See Whiteman, xiv. 15–17; Rodgers, 61 *A.J.* (1967), 1021–8.

[4] See Gotlieb, *Canadian Treaty-Making* (1968), pp. 27–32.

[5] See *Free City of Danzig and the I.L.O.* (1930), P.C.I.J., Ser. B, no. 18; and *Polish Nationals in Danzig* (1932), Ser. A/B, no. 44, pp. 23–24. Germany occupied the Free City in 1939 and since 1945 the area has been a part of Poland.

of Danzig. The result was very much a protectorate, the legal status and constitution of which were externally supervized. To describe legal entities like Danzig as 'internationalised territories'[1] is not very helpful since the phrase covers a number of juridically distinct entities and situations and begs the question of legal personality. The Italian Peace Treaty of 1947 provided for the creation of a Free Territory of Trieste with features broadly similar to those of the Free City of Danzig, but placed under the direct control of the United Nations Security Council.[2]

(c) *Condominia.* A *condominium*, as a joint exercise of state power within a particular territory[3] by means of an autonomous local administration, may bear a resemblance to entities of the type considered latterly. However, the local administration can only act as an agency of the states participating in the *condominium*, and normally even its capacity as agent is limited.[4]

(d) *Internationalized territories.*[5] The label 'internationalized territory' has been applied by writers to a variety of legal regimes. It may be applied very loosely to cases like Danzig and Trieste where a special status was created by multilateral treaty and protected by an international organization.[6] In these instances the special status was attached to entities with sufficient independence and legal capacity to admit of legal personality. However, a special status of this kind may attach without the creation of a legal person. An area within a sovereign state may be given certain rights of autonomy under treaty without this leading to any degree of separate personality on the international plane: this was the case with the Memel Territory, which enjoyed a special status in the period 1924 to 1939, yet remained a part of Lithuania.[7] Another type of regime, more truly international, involves ex-

[1] See Rousseau ii (1974), 413, 423; and cf. Ydit, *International Territories* (1961), *passim*. See generally Verzijl, op. cit. ii. 500–2, 510–45.

[2] The Permanent Statute of Trieste was not implemented: the administration of the territory was divided by agreement in 1954; the partition was made definitive by the Treaty of Osimo, in force 3 April 1977, *Rivista di d.i.* 60, 674. See Verzijl, op. cit. ii. 504–5; and, on the issue of sovereignty, *infra*, pp. 68–9. On the position of the Holy See and Formosa see *infra*, pp. 67, 68. If the given entity has very close relations with an international organization, coupled with some autonomy, it may approximate to an agency of the organization: see *infra*, p. 65.

[3] See *infra*, p. 65.

[4] See 9 *I.C.L.Q.* (1960), 258. On the New Hebrides see O'Connell, 43 *B.Y.* (1968–9), 71–145.

[5] See Ydit, *Internationalised Territories* (1961); Rousseau ii (1974), 413–48.

[6] *Supra*, p. 63.

[7] *Interpretation of the Statute of the Memel Territory* (1932) P.C.I.J., Ser. A/B, no. 49, p. 313. See also the complex legal status of the International Zone of Tangier wound up in 1956; for which Rousseau ii (1974), 430–40; Ydit, pp. 154–84; Whiteman i. 595–8; Gutteridge, 33 *B.Y.* (1957), 296–302.

clusive administration of a territory by an international organization or an organ thereof: this was the regime proposed for the city of Jerusalem by the Trusteeship Council in 1950 but never implemented.[1] In such a case no new legal person is established except in so far as an agency of an international organization may have a certain autonomy (*infra*).

(e) *International organizations.*[2] The conditions under which an organization acquires legal personality on the international plane and not merely as a legal person within a particular system of national law are examined in Chapter XXX. The most important person of this type is of course the United Nations.

(f) *Agencies of states.* Entities acting as the agents of states, with delegated powers, may have the appearance of enjoying a separate personality and considerable viability on the international plane. Thus components of federal states probably have treaty-making capacity, where this is provided for internally, as agents of the federal state.[3] By agreement states may create joint agencies with delegated powers of a supervisory, rule-making, and even judicial nature. Examples are the administration of a *condominium*,[4] an arbitral tribunal, the International Joint Commission set up under an agreement concerning boundary waters between Canada and the United States in 1909,[5] and the former European Commission of the Danube.[6] As the degree of independence and the legal powers of the particular agency increase it will approximate to an international organization.

(g) *Agencies of organizations.*[7] The constituent treaty or the exercise of powers conferred by the constituent treaty may create subsidiary organs of international organizations, and such organs may have a significant amount of independence and be invested with considerable administrative, rule-making, and judi-

[1] Ydit, pp. 273–314; Whiteman i. 593–5; Verzijl, op. cit. ii. 506–7. Cf. Fitzmaurice, *Yrbk., I.L.C.* (1958), ii. 24, 32 (para. 24). Cf. the Free City of Trieste, *supra*, p. 64.

[2] Friedmann, *The Changing Structure of International Law*, Chap. 13, describes, somewhat confusingly, organizations involving 'functional co-operation' as 'public international corporations'. For another use of this description see Kunz, 52 *A.J.* (1958), 570, referring to 'établissements publics internationaux', on which see *infra*, pp. 70–1.

[3] See Fitzmaurice, *Yrbk., I.L.C.* (1956), ii. 118 n.; and Morin, 3 *Canadian Yrbk.* of *I.L.* (1965), 127–86. See further the Draft Articles on the Law of Treaties, I.L.C., 1966, Art. 5 (2). On the role of the chartered companies such as the English East India Company and the Dutch East India Company, see Schwarzenberger, *International Law* i. (3rd ed.), 80–1; McNair, *Opinions* i. 41, 55; and the *Palmas* award, *R.I.A.A.* ii. at p. 858.

[4] *Supra*, p. 64; *infra*, pp. 118–19.

[5] See Baxter, *The Law of International Waterways*, p. 107.

[6] Ibid., pp. 103–6, 126–9.

[7] See Adam, *Les Organismes internationaux spécialisés* i. 12–18. See further Schachter, 109 Hague *Recueil* (1963, II), 240 and *Zoernsch* v. *Waldock* [1964] 1 W.L.R. 675.

cial powers without themselves acquiring a distinct legal personality. Thus the High Authority set up by the European Coal and Steel Community Treaty has the power to make administrative decisions and regulations which have legal effect within each member state, and to issue recommendations to governments of member states which are binding, although methods of implementation are within the discretion of members.[1] Again, the European Nuclear Energy Agency, an organ of O.E.C.D., has considerable powers in the sphere of security control.[2]

4. *Special Types of Personality*

(a) *Non-self-governing peoples.* Quite apart from the question of protected status,[3] and the legal effect of particular agreements under which territories have been placed under mandate or trusteeship, it is very probable that the populations of 'non-self-governing territories' within the meaning of Chapter XI of the United Nations Charter have legal personality, albeit of a special type. This proposition depends on the examination of the principle of self-determination to be found in Chapter XXIV, section 9.

(b) *States* in statu nascendi.[4] For certain legal purposes it is convenient to assume continuity in a political entity and thus to give effect, after statehood has been attained, to legal acts occurring before independence. Considerations relating to the principle of self-determination and the personality of non-self-governing peoples may of course reinforce a doctrine of continuity.

(c) *Legal constructions.* A state's legal order may be projected on the plane of time for certain purposes although politically it has ceased to exist.[5]

(d) *Belligerent and insurgent communities.* In practice, belligerent and insurgent bodies[6] within a state may enter into legal relations and conclude agreements valid on the international plane with states and other belligerents and insurgents. Sir Gerald Fitzmaurice[7] has attributed treaty-making capacity to

[1] See further Waldock, 106 Hague *Recueil* (1962, II), 96–101.

[2] See Arangio-Ruiz, 107 Hague *Recueil* (1962, III), 566 seq.

[3] *Supra*, p. 62. [4] *Infra*, p. 82. [5] See further *infra*, pp. 83–4.

[6] See further Chen, *Recognition*, pp. 303 seq.; and *infra*, pp. 90–6.

[7] *Yrbk., I.L.C.* (1958), ii. 24, 32; and see 92 Hague *Recueil* (1957, II), 10. The draft articles on the law of treaties adopted by the Commission referred to 'States or other subjects of international law': ibid. (1962), ii. 161. This phrase was intended to cover the case of insurgents. The 1966 draft articles related simply to treaties concluded between states. See also O'Connell, 67 *R.G.D.I.P.* (1963), 15–24; and Judge Moreno Quintana, diss. op. in the *Expenses* case, I.C.J. Reports (1962), p. 246.

'para-Statal entities recognized as possessing a definite if limited form of international personality, for example, insurgent communities recognized as having belligerent status—*de facto* authorities in control of specific territory'. This statement is correct as a matter of principle,[1] although its application to particular facts will require caution. The status of the particular belligerent community may be affected by the considerations offered elsewhere as to the principle of self-determination and the personality of non-self-governing peoples.[2] A belligerent community often represents a political movement aiming at independence and secession.

(e) *Entities* sui generis. Whilst due regard must be had to legal principle, the lawyer cannot afford to ignore entities which maintain some sort of existence on the international legal plane in spite of their anomalous character. Indeed, the role played by politically active entities such as belligerent communities indicates that, in the sphere of personality, effectiveness is an influential principle. Furthermore, as elsewhere in the law, provided that no rule of *jus cogens* is broken, acquiescence, recognition, and the incidence of voluntary bilateral relations can do much to obviate the more negative consequences of anomaly. Some of the special cases may be considered very briefly. In a Treaty and Concordat in 1929, Italy recognized 'the Sovereignty of the Holy See in the international domain' and its exclusive sovereignty and jurisdiction over the City of the Vatican.[3] A number of states recognize the Holy See, and have diplomatic relations with it and the Holy See has been a party to multilateral conventions, including those on the law of the sea concluded in 1958. Functionally, and in terms of its territorial and administrative organization, the Vatican City is proximate to a state. However, it has certain peculiarities. It has no population, apart from the resident functionaries, and its sole purpose is to support the Holy See as a religious entity. Some jurists regard the Vatican City as a state, although its special functions make this doubtful. However, it is widely recognized as a legal person with treaty-making capacity.[4] Its personality seems to rest partly on its approximation to a state in function, in spite of peculiarities, in-

[1] See Kelsen, *Principles* (2nd ed.), p. 252; McNair, *Law of Treaties* (1961), p. 676.

[2] *Supra*, pp. 62, 66; *infra*, Chapter XXXIV, section 9.

[3] See Whiteman i. 587–93; Kunz, 46 *A.J.* (1952), 308–14; Rousseau ii (1974), 353–77; Guggenheim i. 220–1; de la Brière, 63 Hague *Recueil* (1938, I), 371–464; Ehler, 104 Hague *Recueil* (1961, III), 5–63; Verzijl, op. cit. ii, 295–302, 308–38.

[4] See Fitzmaurice, ibid. (1956), ii. 107, 118.

cluding the patrimonial sovereignty of the Holy See, and partly on acquiescence and recognition by existing legal persons. More difficult to solve is the question of personality of the Holy See as a religious organ apart from its territorial base in the Vatican City.[1] It would seem that the personality of political and religious institutions of this type can only be relative to those states prepared to enter into relationships with such institutions on the international plane. Even in the sphere of recognition and bilateral relations, the legal capacities of institutions like the Sovereign Order of Jerusalem and Malta[2] must be limited simply because they lack the territorial and demographic characteristics of states. In the law of war the status of the Order mentioned is merely that of a 'relief society' within the meaning of the Prisoner of War Convention, 1949, Article 125.

Two other political animals require classification. 'Exile governments' may be accorded considerable powers within the territory of most states and be active in various political spheres. Apart from voluntary concessions by states and the use of 'exile governments' as agencies for illegal activities against lawfully established governments and states, the legal status of an 'exile government' is consequential on the legal condition of the community it claims to represent, which may be a state, belligerent community, or non-self-governing people. *Prima facie* its legal status will be established the more readily when its exclusion from the community of which it is an agency results from acts contrary to the *jus cogens*,[3] for example, an unlawful resort to force. Lastly, the case of territory the title to which is undetermined, and which is inhabited and has an independent administration, creates problems. On the analogy of belligerent communities and special regimes not dependent on the existence of the sovereignty of a particular state (for example, internationalized territories and trust territories), communities existing on territory with such a status may be treated as having a modified personality, approximating to that of a state. On one view of the

[1] For acceptance of such personality see Kelsen, *Principles* (2nd ed.), p. 251; Oppenheim i. 21; Ehler, op. cit.; Kunz, op. cit.; Guggenheim i. 214–16. The problem of personality divorced from territorial base is difficult to isolate because of the interaction of the Vatican City, the Holy See, and the Roman Catholic Church. See also Waldock, *Yrbk., I.L.C.* (1962), ii. 32, 36.

[2] See Farran, 3 *I.C.L.Q.* (1954), 217–34; id., 4 *I.C.L.Q.* (1955), 308–9; Whiteman i. 584–7; Guggenheim i. 216, n. 3, 489, n. 3; *Nanni* v. *Pace and the Sovereign Order of Malta, Ann. Digest* 8 (1935–7), no. 2; *Scarfò* v. *Sovereign Order of Malta*, Int. L.R. 24 (1957), 1; *Sovereign Order of Malta* v. *Soc. An. Commerciale*, ibid. 22 (1955), 1; O'Connell, 48 *B.Y.* (1976–7), 433–4.

[3] On this concept see *infra*, Chapter XXII, section 5.

facts, this is the situation of Taiwan (Formosa). Until March 1972 the United Kingdom, which regarded the island as territory the title to which was undetermined, had certain legal relations involving acceptance of passports with the authorities there and maintained a consulate.[1] Clearly it is undesirable that the population of such areas should be regarded as 'stateless' in law.

(f) *Individuals*. There is no general rule that the individual cannot be a 'subject of international law', and in particular contexts he appears as a legal person on the international plane. At the same time to classify the individual as a 'subject' of the law is unhelpful, since this may seem to imply the existence of capacities which do not exist and does not avoid the task of distinguishing between the individual and other types of subject. The position of the individual in international law is considered at large in Chapter XXIV.

5. *Controversial Candidatures*

Reference to states and similar political entities, to organizations, non-self-governing peoples, and to individuals, does not exhaust the tally of agencies active on the international scene. Thus corporations of municipal law, whether private or public corporations, engage in economic activity in one or more states other than the state under the law of which they were 'incorporated' or in which they have their economic seat. The resources available to the individual corporation may be greater than those of the smaller states, and they may have powerful diplomatic backing from governments. Such corporations can and do make agreements, including concession agreements, with foreign governments, and in this connexion in particular, jurists have argued that the relations of states and foreign corporations *as such* should be treated on the international plane[2] and not as an

[1] See the official statements reported in 5 *I.C.L.Q.* (1956), 413; 8 *I.C.L.Q.* (1959), 166; *British Practice in International Law* (1964), i. 25. See also *Rogers* v. *Cheng Fu Sheng* (1960), Int. L.R. 31, p. 349. Cf. the status of the Portuguese enclaves in Indian territory after 1954, when the Portuguese administration was expelled by the population; *Right of Passage case* (Merits), I.C.J. Reports (1960), p. 6 at p. 53 (Judge Spiropoulos), p. 87 (Judge Armand-Ugon). On the status of Trieste: *Società Teatro Puccini* v. *Commissioner-General*, Int. L.R. 40, p. 43, Italy, Council of State: the issue of sovereignty was finally settled by the Treaty of Osimo, in force 3 April 1977, *Rivista di d.i.* 60, 674. On the status of the islands of Abu Ail and Jabal at Tair in the Red Sea see the Treaty of Lausanne, 1923, 117 *B.F.S.P.* 543, Article 16; Agreement on Red Sea Lights, *U.K. Treaty Series* no. 8 (1967), Cmnd. 3191, Article 8.

[2] See, for example, Friedmann, *The Changing Structure of International Law*, pp. 221–31; 127 Hague *Recueil* (1969, II), 121–4, with reference to private corporations.

aspect of the normal rules governing the position of aliens and their assets on the territory of a state. In principle, corporations of municipal law do not have international legal personality. Thus a concession or contract between a state and a foreign corporation is not governed by the law of treaties.[1] The question will be pursued further in Chapter XXIII. However, in the present connexion it must be pointed out that it will not always be easy to distinguish corporations which are so closely controlled by governments as to be state agencies, with or without some degree of autonomy, and private corporations not sharing the international law capacity of a state. It will be clear that the conferment of separate personality by a particular national law is not necessarily conclusive of autonomy *vis-à-vis* the state for purposes of international law. Thus ownership of shares may give a state a controlling interest in a 'private law corporation'.[2]

Important functions are performed today by bodies which have been grouped under the labels 'intergovernmental corporations of private law' and 'établissements publics internationaux'.[3] The point is that states may by treaty create legal persons the status of which is regulated by the national law of one or more of the parties. However, the treaty may contain obligations to create a privileged status within the national law or laws to which the corporation is subjected. The parties by their agreement may accord certain immunities to the institution created and confer on it various powers. Where the independence from the national laws of the parties is marked, then the body concerned may simply be a joint agency of the states involved, with delegated powers effective on the international plane and with a privileged position *vis-à-vis* local law in respect of its activities.[4] Where there is, in addition to independence from national law, a considerable quantum of delegated powers and

[1] See Waldock, *Yrbk., I.L.C.* (1962), ii. 32; and cf. the *Anglo-Iranian Oil Company* case, I.C.J. Reports (1952), p. 93 at p. 112.

[2] See McNair, *Opinions* ii. 39. Cf. the experience in the context of the law of sovereign immunity, *infra*, pp. 341–3.

[3] See Adam, *Les Établissements publics internationaux* (1957); id., *Les Organismes internationaux spécialisés*, 4 vols. (1965–77); Sørensen, 101 Hague *Recueil* (1960, III), 139–41; Friedmann, *The Changing Structure*, pp. 181–4, 219–20; Sereni, 96 Hague *Recueil* (1959, I), 169 seq.; Goldman, 90 *J.D.I.* (1963), 321–89; Angelo, 125 Hague *Recueil* (1968, III), 482 seq. Kunz, 52 *A.J.* (1958), 570, suggests the labels 'public international corporations' or 'public international authorities'. Cp. Fawcett, *International Law and the Uses of Outer Space* (1968), pp. 47–52.

[4] For examples of such joint agencies see *supra*, p. 65. The treaty concerned may result in legal personality in terms of the national law of the parties: see *Vigoureux* v. *Comité des Obligataires Danube-Save-Adriatique*, Int. L.R. 18 (1951), 1.

the existence of organs with autonomy in decision and rule-making, then the body concerned has the characteristics of an international organization. It is when the institution created by treaty has a viability and special function which render the description 'joint agency' inappropriate, and yet has powers and privileges primarily within the *national* legal systems and jurisdictions of the various parties, that it calls for use of a special category. An example of intergovernmental enterprise of this kind is Eurofima, a company set up by a treaty involving fourteen states in 1955, with the object of improving the resources of railway rolling stock. The treaty[1] established Eurofima as a corporation under Swiss law with modifications in that law provided for in the treaty. The parties agreed that they would recognize this (Swiss) private law status, as modified by the treaty, within their own legal systems. The corporation is international in function and the fourteen participating railway administrations provide the capital. The corporation is also given privileges on the international plane, including exemption from taxation in Switzerland, the state of domicile. However, useful as the category 'établissements publics internationaux' may be, it is not an instrument of exact analysis, and does not represent a distinct species of legal person on the international plane. This type of arrangement is the product of a careful interlocking of the national and international legal orders on a treaty basis, and the nature of the product will vary considerably from case to case.

6. *Some Consequences*

The content of the previous sections must serve as a warning against facile generalizations on the subject of legal personality. In view of the complex nature of international relations and the absence of a centralized law of corporations, it would be strange if the legal situation had an extreme simplicity. The number of entities with personality *for particular purposes* is considerable. Moreover, the tally of autonomous bodies increases if agencies of states and organizations, with a quantum of delegated powers, are taken into account. The listing of candidates for personality, the characters the reader will encounter, has a certain value, and yet such a procedure has some pitfalls. In the first place, a great deal depends on the relation of the particular entity to the various aspects of the substantive law. Thus the individual is in certain contexts regarded as a legal person, and yet it is obvious that he

[1] Convention signed 20 October 1955; 378 U.N.T.S., 159.

cannot make treaties. The *context* of problems remains paramount. Further, subject to the operations of the *jus cogens*, comprising certain fundamental principles,[1] the institutions of acquiescence and recognition have been active in sustaining anomalous relations. And finally, the intrusion of agency and representation has created problems, both of application and of principle. Thus it is not always easy to distinguish a dependent state with its own personality from a subordinate entity with no independence, a joint agency of states from an organization, or a private or public corporation under some degree of state control from the state itself.

7. *Problems of Choice of Law*[2]

It has been pointed out already that much depends on the working of the rules of substantive law in the particular case, but one dimension of the law has particular impact on the question of personality and legal capacity. The rules of international law do not seem to prohibit the placing of legal relations affecting state interests within the sphere of a particular domestic law. As we have already seen, an institution like Eurofima, created by treaty, may be established as a corporation of a particular domestic law, in this case that of Switzerland. States may make contracts with each other which are intended to operate outside the rules of international law. In the case of international corporations, apart from special agreement on the choice of law to govern particular legal relations, the choice of law may not exist as such, but the question of nationality looms large, since this determines the way in which various rules both of public and private international law will apply.[3] In the absence of agreement to the contrary, it is public international law which provides the criteria for determination of nationality,[4] and also for determining whether a particular entity is sufficiently independent of other legal persons, whether states or organizations, to have a separate legal personality. A grant of separate personality by a particular domestic law would not be conclusive for all purposes on the international plane.[5]

[1] See *infra*, Chapter XXII, section 5.

[2] See Sereni, 96 Hague *Recueil* (1959, I), 133–232; Waldock, *Yrbk., I.L.C.* (1962), ii. 32.

[3] See *infra*, pp. 421–3. [4] *Infra*, Chapter XVIII.

[5] Cf. Judge Huber, award in the *Palmas* case, *R.I.A.A.* ii. p. 858; Cohen, L.J., in *Krajina* v. *Tass Agency* [1949] 2 A.E.R. 274 at p. 280 and *Baccus S.R.L.* v. *Servicio Nacional del Trigo* [1957] 1 Q.B. 438.

CHAPTER IV

INCIDENCE AND CONTINUITY OF STATEHOOD

1. *Introductory*

THE state is a type of legal person recognized by international law. Yet, since there are other types of legal person so recognized—as emerges from the previous chapter—the possession of legal personality is not in itself a sufficient mark of statehood. Moreover, the exercise of legal capacities is a normal consequence, rather than conclusive evidence, of legal personality: a puppet state may have all the paraphernalia of separate personality and yet be little more than an agency for another power. It is sometimes said that statehood is a question of fact, meaning that it is not a question of law. However, as lawyers are usually asking if an entity is a state with a specific legal claim or function in view, it is pointless to confuse issues of law with the difficulties, which undoubtedly exist, of applying the legal principles to the facts and of discovering the important facts in the first place. The criteria of statehood are laid down by the law. If it were not so, then statehood would produce the same type of structural defect that has been detected in certain types of doctrine concerning nationality.[1] In other words, a state would be able by its own unfettered discretion to contract out of duties owed to another state simply by refusing to characterize the obligee as a state. Thus a readiness to ignore the law may be disguised by a plea of freedom in relation to a key concept, determinant of many particular rights and duties, like statehood or nationality. In starting from this position it will be apparent that the writer has in part anticipated the results of the examination of recognition in the next chapter. Nevertheless, as a matter of presentation the question whether recognition by other states is an additional determinant will be ignored in the present chapter.[2] The subject of state succession is also excluded from the discussion, and the subject-matter conventionally described by that label is considered in Chapter

[1] See *infra*, Chapter XVIII.

[2] Certain special aspects of recognition and its congener, acquiescence, are noticed *infra*, at pp. 163–4.

XXVIII. However, when the continuity of states is considered some attempt will be made to distinguish this from state succession.[1]

In general the importance of the subject-matter is not reflected by the quantity of useful literature.[2] Three factors have contributed to the creation of this state of affairs. First, though the subject is important as a matter of principle, the issue of statehood does not often raise long-standing disputes. In practice disputes concern the facts rather than the applicable legal criteria. Moreover, many disputes do not concern statehood *simpliciter*, but specialized claims, for example, to membership of the United Nations.[3] Secondly, the literature is often devoted to the broad concepts of the sovereignty and equality of states[4] and so gives prominence to the incidents of statehood rather than its origins and continuity. Finally, the political and legal nature of many complete rifts in relations between particular states is represented by non-recognition of *governments* rather than of states.[5]

2. *Legal Criteria of Statehood*

Article I of the Montevideo Convention on Rights and Duties of States[6] provides: 'The State as a person of international law should possess the following qualifications: (a) a permanent population; (b) a defined territory; (c) government; and (d) capacity to enter into relations with the other States.' This brief enumeration of criteria is often adopted in substance by jurists,[7] but it is no more than a basis for further investigation. As will be

[1] See *infra*, pp. 84 seq.

[2] Generally see Crawford, 48 *B.Y.* (1976–7), 93–182; id., *The Creation of States in International Law* (1979); Higgins, *The Development of International Law Through the Political Organs of the United Nations*, pp. 11–57; Briggs, pp. 65–85; Rousseau, *Droit international public* ii (1974), 13–93, Chen, *The International Law of Recognition*, pp. 54–63, 74–7; Whiteman i. 221–33, 283–476; Guggenheim, 80 Hague *Recueil* (1952, I), 80–96; Marek, *Identity and Continuity of States in P.I.L.* (1954); Fawcett, *The British Commonwealth in I.L.*, pp. 88–143; Lauterpacht, *International Law: Collected Papers* iii. 5–25; Sørensen, 101 Hague *Recueil* (1960, III), 127–33; Alfaro, 97 Hague *Recueil* (1959, II), 95–103; Kelsen, *Principles of International Law* (2nd ed.), pp. 307–8, 343–4, 381–7; Rolin, 77 Hague *Recueil* (1950, II), 324–6; Mouskhély, 66 *R.G.D.I.P.* (1962), 469–85; *Yrbk., I.L.C.* (1949), pp. 37–8, 62 seq., 289; Verzijl, *International Law in Historical Perspective*, ii (1969), 62–294, 339–500; Lissitzyn, 125 Hague *Recueil* (1968, III), 5–87; Arangio-Ruiz, *L'état dans le sens du droit des gens et la notion du droit international* (1975).

[3] On the various specialized claims see *infra*, p. 84.

[4] See generally *infra*, Chapter XIII. [5] See *infra*, Chapter V, section 5.

[6] Signed 26 December 1933; Hudson, *Int. Legis.* vi. 620.

[7] See, for example, Fitzmaurice, 92 Hague *Recueil*, 13; Higgins, op. cit., p. 13; Fawcett, op. cit., p. 92. See further Jessup, as U.S. representative in the Security Council, 2 December 1948, quoted in Briggs, p. 69 and Whiteman i. 230.

seen, not all the conditions are peremptory, and in any case further criteria must be employed to produce a working legal definition of statehood. The four criteria enumerated above, and other conditions proposed from time to time, will now be considered.

(a) *Population.* The Montevideo Convention refers to 'a permanent population'. This criterion is intended to be used in association with that of territory, and connotes a stable community. Evidentially it is important, since in the absence of the physical basis for an organized community, it will be difficult to establish the existence of a state.

(b) *Defined territory.* There must be a reasonably stable political community and this must be in control of a certain area. It is clear from past practice that the existence of fully defined frontiers is not required and that what matters is the effective establishment of a political community.[1] In 1913 Albania was recognized by a number of states in spite of a lack of settled frontiers, and Israel was admitted to the United Nations in spite of disputes over her borders.

(c) *Government.* The shortest definition of a state for present purposes is perhaps a stable political community, supporting a legal order, in a certain area. The existence of effective government, with centralized administrative and legislative organs,[2] is the best evidence of a stable political community. However, the existence of effective government is in certain cases either unnecessary or insufficient to support statehood. Some states have arisen before government was very well organized, as, for example, Poland in 1919[3] and Burundi and Rwanda, admitted to membership of the United Nations at the seventeenth session of the General Assembly.[4] The principle of self-determination[5] will today be set against the concept of effective government, more particularly when the latter is used in arguments for continuation of colonial rule. The relevant question may now be: in whose interest and for what legal purpose is government 'effective'? Once a state has been established, extensive civil strife or the breakdown of order through foreign invasion or natural disasters are not considered to affect personality. Nor is effective government sufficient, since this leaves open the ques-

[1] See Jessup, op. cit.; *Deutsche Continental Gas-Gesellschaft* v. *Polish State*, *Ann. Digest* 5 (1929–30), no. 5, p. 15; *North Sea Continental Shelf Cases*, I.C.J. Reports, 1969, p. 3 at p. 32.

[2] See Guggenheim, op. cit., p. 83; Higgins, op. cit., pp. 20–5.

[3] Briggs, p. 104. See also ibid., pp. 108–13, 117–19, on the position in Albania 1913–24.

[4] Higgins, op. cit., p. 22.

[5] See further Chapter XXIV, section 9.

tions of independence and representation by other states to be discussed below.

(d) *Independence*. In the enumeration contained in the Montevideo Convention, the concept of independence is represented by the requirement of capacity to enter into relations with other states.[1] Independence has been stressed by many jurists as the decisive criterion of statehood.[2] Guggenheim[3] distinguishes the state from other legal orders by means of two tests which he regards as quantitative rather than qualitative. First, the state has a degree of centralization of its organs not found in the world community. Secondly, in a particular area the state is the sole executive and legislative authority. In other words the state must be independent of other state legal orders, and any interference by such legal orders, or by an international agency, must be based on a title of international law.[4] In the normal case independence as a criterion may create few problems. However, there are sources of confusion. In the first place, independence may be used in close association with a requirement of effective government,[5] leading to the issues considered earlier. Again, since a state is, in part, a legal order, there is a temptation to rely solely on formal criteria. Certainly, if an entity has its own executive and other organs, conducts its foreign relations through its own organs, has its own system of courts and legal system and, particularly important, a nationality law of its own, then there is *prima facie* evidence of statehood. However, there is no justification for ignoring evidence of foreign control which is exercised *in fact* through the ostensibly independent machinery of state. The question is that of foreign *control* overbearing the decision-making of the entity concerned on a wide range of matters of high policy and doing so systematically and on a permanent basis. The practice of states has been to ignore—so far as the issue of *statehood* is concerned—various forms of political and economic blackmail and interference directed against the weaker members

[1] See Jessup, op. cit.

[2] See, in particular, Rousseau, op. cit., pp. 68 seq; Marek, op. cit., pp. 161–90.

[3] Op. cit., pp. 83, 96. Cf. Rousseau, op. cit., pp. 68 seq.; and Marek, op. cit., p. 168.

[4] Cf. *infra*, pp. 77, 82, and Chapter XV.

[5] In the *Aaland Islands* case (1920) the committee of jurists referred to the disorder existing in Finland and observed: 'It is therefore difficult to say at what exact date the Finnish Republic in the legal sense of the term actually became a definitely constituted sovereign State. This certainly did not take place until a stable political organization had been created, and until the public authorities had become strong enough to assert themselves throughout the territories of the State without the assistance of foreign troops.' (*L.N.O.J* (1920), Spec. Suppl. no. 3, p. 3.) This standard would have embarrassing consequences if widely applied.

of the community. Whilst it is a matter of appreciation, there is a distinction between agency and control, on the one hand, and *ad hoc* interference and 'advice', on the other.

Dependent states. Foreign control of the affairs of a state may occur under a title of international law, for example as a consequence of a treaty of protection,[1] or some other form of consent to agency or representation in external relations, or of a lawful war of collective defence and sanction leading to an occupation of the aggressor and imposition of measures designed to remove the sources of aggression. Allied occupation of Germany under the Berlin Declaration of 5 June 1945 is an example of the latter: supreme authority was assumed in Germany by the Allies jointly.[2] Providing that the representation and agency exist in fact and in law, then there is no formal difficulty in saying that the criterion of independence is satisfied. Unfortunately writers have created confusion by rehearsing independence as an aspect of statehood and then referring to 'dependent states', which are presented as an anomalous category.[3] Here the incidents of personality are not sufficiently distinguished from its existence. The term 'dependent' is used to indicate the existence of one or more of the following distinct situations:

(1) the absence of statehood, where the entity concerned is subordinated to a state so completely as to be within its control and the origin of the subordination does not establish agency or representation;
(2) a state which has made concessions to another state in matters of jurisdiction and administration to such an extent that it has in some sense ceased to be sovereign;[4]
(3) a state which has legally conferred wide powers of agency and representation in foreign affairs on another state;[5]
(4) a state, which in fact suffers interference from another state and may be a 'client' state politically, but which quantitatively is not under the complete and permanent control of the 'patron';
(5) a legal person of a special type, appearing on the inter-

[1] On the possible effect of the *jus cogens* on such treaties see Chapter XXII, section 5.

[2] The occupation was not a belligerent occupation, nor was there a *debellatio* leading to extinction of Germany as a state: see Jennings, 23 *B.Y.* (1946), 112–41.

[3] See Hall, pp. 18, 20, 33; Oppenheim, pp. 118–19 ('sovereignty' used as a synonym for 'independence').

[4] See *infra*, pp. 80–1. On the former legal position of Kuwait: Whiteman i. 442–6.

[5] This may occur without subordination. Since 1919 by agreement the Swiss Federal Council has conducted the diplomatic relations of Liechtenstein.

national plane for certain purposes only, as in the case of mandated and trust territories [1] and some protectorates;[2]

(6) a state which fails to qualify as an 'independent' state for the purposes of a particular instrument.

The category of independence (or sovereignty used synonymously) can only be applied concretely in the light of the legal purpose with which the inquiry is made and the particular facts. In the *Austro-German Customs Union* case [3] the Permanent Court gave an advisory opinion on the question whether the proposed customs union was contrary to the obligations of Austria under a Protocol of 1922 'not to alienate its independence' and to 'abstain from any negotiations or from any economic and financial engagement calculated directly or indirectly to compromise this independence'. By a majority of eight to seven the Court held that the customs regime contemplated would be incompatible with these obligations. Here the term 'independence' referred to a specialized notion of economic relations in a treaty, and the obligations were not confined to abstention from actual and complete alienation of independence. In the case of the *Tunis and Morocco Nationality Decrees* [4] the Permanent Court emphasized that protectorates have 'individual legal characteristics resulting from the special conditions under which they were created, and the stage of their development'. A protected state may provide an example of international representation which leaves the personality and statehood of the entity represented intact, though from the point of view of the *incidents* of personality the entity may be 'dependent' in one or more of the senses noted above. In the case of *U.S. Nationals in Morocco* [5] the International Court, referring to the Treaty of Fez in 1912, and the creation of a French protectorate, stated: 'Under this Treaty, Morocco remained a sovereign State but it made an arrange-

[1] See *infra*, pp. 175–8, 181–2.

[2] e.g. areas autonomous to some degree according to municipal law whose autonomy is placed under international guarantee.

[3] (1931), P.C.I.J., Ser. A/B, no. 41; Green, p. 335; World Court Reports ii. 713.

[4] (1923), P.C.I.J., Ser. B, no. 4, p. 27; Briggs, p. 452; Green, p. 102; World Court Reports i. 145.

[5] I.C.J. Reports (1952), p. 176 at p. 188; Green, p. 339. See also Guggenheim, op. cit., p. 96. Cf. the separate but dependent personality of India 1919–47; on which see McNair, *Law of Treaties* (1938), p. 76; Poulouse, 44 *B.Y.* (1970), 201–12; Oppenheim i. 209; and the opinion of Judge Moreno Quintana, I.C.J. Reports (1960), p. 95. Cf. also the position of Monaco in relation to France. On the status of Hungary after German occupation in 1944 see *Effects of Jews Deported from Hungary* case, Int. L.R. 44, 301 at pp. 334–42 and on the status of the creation called Croatia in Yugoslavia during the German occupation see *Socony Vacuum Oil Company Claim*, Int. L.R. 21, 55 at pp. 58–62.

ment of a contractual character whereby France undertook to exercise certain sovereign powers in the name and on behalf of Morocco, and, in principle, all of the international relations of Morocco.' It should be pointed out that a common opinion is that the evidence supported the view that the relation was one of subordination and not agency.

It is sometimes said that international responsibility is a necessary correlative or criterion of independence.[1] Broadly this is true, but the principle must be qualified when a case of international representation arises and the 'protecting' state is the only available defendant.[2]

Federations. The federal state as such has indisputable legal personality, and it is the status of the constituent states which creates problems. A federal constitution may confer treaty-making capacity and a power to enter into separate diplomatic relations on the constituent members. In the normal case, the constituent state is simply acting as a delegate or agent of the parent state.[3] However, by agreement or recognition, a federated state may assume a separate personality, as an analogue of statehood, on the international plane. Thus the Ukrainian S.S.R. and Byelorussian S.S.R., members of the Union of Soviet Socialist Republics, conclude treaties on their own behalf and are members of the United Nations.[4]

Associations of states. Independent states may enter into forms of co-operation by consent and on an equal basis. The basis for the co-operation may be the constitution of an international organization, such as the United Nations or the World Health Organization. However, by treaty or custom other structures for maintaining co-operation may be created. One such structure, the confederation, has in practice either disintegrated or been transformed into a federation. In recent times the British Commonwealth of Nations[5] and the French Community[6] have provided examples of associations of states of a special type. Membership of these two associations would not necessarily affect the primary legal capacities and personality of member states any

[1] See Rousseau, 73 Hague *Recueil* (1948, II), p. 250; Marek, op. cit., p. 189.

[2] On agency and joint tortfeasors see *infra*, pp. 454–7.

[3] See Fitzmaurice, *Yrbk., I.L.C.* (1956), ii. 118; Reuter, *Mélanges offerts à Charles Rousseau* (1974), 199–218; Rousseau ii. 138–213, 264–8; and *supra*, p. 65. Cf. Lauterpacht, ibid. (1953), ii. 95, 137–9. The use of principles of international law by federal courts to settle intra-federal disputes is not decisive of the issue of legal personality.

[4] See Dolan, 4 *I.C.L.Q.* (1955), 629–36; Rousseau ii. 264–8.

[5] See Fawcett, *The British Commonwealth in International Law* (1963), especially at pp. 144–94 (on the *Inter Se* Doctrine); Whiteman i. 476–544; Rousseau ii. 214–64.

[6] See Whiteman i. 544–82.

more than membership of an organization and has less effect than membership of some organizations, for example, the European Economic Community, which has a slight federal element, albeit on a treaty basis. However, the French Community accommodated a variety of relations, some more intimate than others.

(e) *A degree of permanence.*[1] If one relies principally on the concept of a stable political community, it might seem superfluous to stipulate for a degree of permanence. Time is an element of statehood, as is space. However, *permanence* is not necessary to the existence of a state as a legal order, and a state which has only a very brief life may nevertheless leave an agenda of consequential legal questions on its extinction.[2]

(f) *Willingness to observe international law.* In modern literature, this is not often mentioned as a criterion,[3] and it has been subjected to trenchant criticism.[4] The delictual and other responsibilities of states are consequences of statehood, and logically it is inexcusable to express as a criterion of statehood a condition which the entity has a capacity to accept only if it is a state.

(g) *A certain degree of civilization.* Hyde[5] states four qualifications for statehood (the first four above), but adds a fifth: 'the inhabitants must have attained a degree of civilization, such as to enable them to observe . . . those principles of law which are deemed to govern the members of the international society in their relations with each other'. This has a similarity to the last point considered, but is more fundamental. However, it is usually omitted from enumerations of criteria and is redolent of the period when non-European states were not accorded equal treatment by the European Concert and the United States. In modern law it is impossible to regard a tribal society which refuses to conduct diplomatic relations with other societies as a *res nullius.*[6]

(h) *Sovereignty.*[7] The term 'sovereignty' may be used as a synonym for independence, an important element in statehood considered already. However, a common source of confusion lies

[1] See Kelsen, *Principles of International Law* (2nd ed.), pp. 381–3; Chen, *The International Law of Recognition*, pp. 59–60.

[2] Cf. the anti-Jewish legislation of the Italian Social Republic of Sálo: see the *Mosse* claim, Int. L.R. 20 (1953), 217; *Levi* claim, ibid. 24 (1957), 303; *Sonnino* claim, ibid., p. 647; *Wollemborg* claim, ibid., p. 654. British Somaliland became independent on 26 June 1960, but united with Somalia to form the Somali Republic on 1 July 1960.

[3] References: Chen, op. cit., p 61. See also Briggs, p. 100.

[4] See Chen, loc. cit.

[5] i. 23 (and see Chen, op. cit., pp. 127–9). See also Whiteman i. 223.

[6] On the independence of Western Samoa: Whiteman ii. 239.

[7] See generally *infra*, Chapter XIII.

in the fact that 'sovereignty' may be used to describe the condition where a state has not exercised its own legal capacities in such a way as to create rights, powers, privileges, and immunities in respect of other states.[1] In this sense a state which has consented to another state managing its foreign relations, or which has granted extensive extra-territorial rights to another state, is not 'sovereign'. If this or a similar content is given to 'sovereignty' and the same ideogram is used as a criterion of statehood,[2] then the *incidents* of statehood and legal personality are once again confused with their existence. Thus the condition of Germany after 1945 involved considerable diminution of German sovereignty in this sense, and yet Germany continued to exist as a state.[3] Considerations of this sort have led some jurists to reject sovereignty as a criterion.[4] An alternative approach is that of the International Court in the case of *U.S. Nationals in Morocco*, where the judgment described Morocco as a 'sovereign State', meaning that it had maintained its basic personality in spite of the French protectorate.[5] But it would be possible for a tribunal to hold that a state which had granted away piecemeal a high proportion of its legal powers had ceased to have a separate existence as a consequence. Obviously it may in law and fact be difficult to distinguish granting away of capacities and the existence of agency or representation.

(i) *Function as a state.* There remain some peripheral problems. Experience has shown that entities may exist which are difficult to regard as states in the political sense. The treaty of peace with Germany in 1919 created the Free City of Danzig, which had the legal marks of statehood in spite of the facts that it was placed under the guarantee of the League of Nations and Poland had the power to conduct its foreign relations.[6] The peace treaty with Italy in 1947 provided for the creation of the Free Territory of

[1] See *infra*, Chapter XVII.

[2] See Oppenheim i. 118–19; Korowicz, 102 Hague *Recueil* (1961, I), 10, 108; Alfaro, 97 Hague *Recueil* (1959, II), 95–6.

[3] *Supra*, p. 77.

[4] See Rousseau, 73 Hague *Recueil* (1948, II), 178 seq. Cf. the dissenting judges in the *Austro-German Customs Union* case, P.C.I.J., Ser. A/B, no. 41 at p. 77; and Viscount Finlay in *Duff Development Co.* v. *Government of Kelantan* [1924] A.C. 747 at p. 814. See further Fawcett, *The British Commonwealth in International Law*, pp. 88–93; and the case concerning the *Lighthouse in Crete and Samos*, for which see *infra*, p. 115.

[5] *Supra*, p. 78. See also Rolin, 77 Hague *Recueil* (1950, II), 326.

[6] *Supra*, pp. 63, 64. However, disputes between Danzig and Poland were referred to the Permanent Court of International Justice by means of its advisory jurisdiction in view of Article 34 of the Statute of the Court, which gives *locus standi* in contentious cases only to states.

Trieste, which was to be placed under the protection of the Security Council.[1] The type of legal personality involved in these two cases is a congener of statehood, and it is the specialized political function of such entities, and their relation to an organization, which inhibits use of the category of statehood.[2]

3. *States* in Statu Nascendi

A political community with considerable viability, controlling a certain area of territory and having statehood as its objective, may go through a period of travail before that objective has been achieved. In any case, since matters such as definition of frontiers and effective government are not looked at too strictly, the distinction between *status nascendi* and statehood cannot be very readily upheld.[3] States not infrequently first appear as independent belligerent entities under a political authority which may be called and function effectively as a provisional government. The influence of considerations of *jus cogens*, such as the principle of self-determination, on the status of belligerent entities is examined subsequently.[4] Apart from these considerations, once statehood is firmly established, it is justifiable, both legally and practically, to assume the retroactive validation of the legal order during a period prior to general recognition as a state, when some degree of effective government existed. Leaving questions of state succession on one side,[5] the principle of effectiveness dictates acceptance, for some legal purposes at least, of continuity before and after statehood is firmly established.[6] The legal consequences accorded by governments and foreign courts to the acts of governments recognized *de facto*[7] provide evidence for the views expressed above.

4. *Illegal Occupation and the Influence of* Jus Cogens

Earlier it was stated that a state remains 'independent', in the sense of retaining separate personality, if a foreign legal order

[1] *Supra*, pp. 63, 64.

[2] On the status of other entities *sui generis* see *supra*, pp. 67–9.

[3] Cf. the cases of Albania in 1913; Poland and Czechoslovakia in 1917–18; Estonia, Latvia, and Lithuania, 1918–20. See Briggs, pp. 103 seq.; Hackworth i. 199–222. See also the case of Indonesia, 1946–9: Whiteman ii. 165–7. Cf. the observations of Lord Finlay, *German Interests in Polish Upper Silesia* (Merits), P.C.I.J., Ser. A no. 7 (1926), p. 84.

[4] *Infra*, p. 83. [5] See Chapter XXVIII.

[6] See the *Annual Digest* 1 (1919–22), nos. 4–7, 24; ibid. 2 (1923–4), nos. 2, 122; ibid. 3 (1925–6), nos. 8, 9; ibid. 4 (1927–8), nos. 11, 94, 220: ibid. 5 (1929–30), no. 5.

[7] See *infra*, pp. 95–7. See, in particular, the *Gagara* [1919] P. 65.

impinges on it, provided that the impingement occurs under a title of international law. It follows that illegal occupation cannot of itself terminate statehood.[1] Elsewhere[2] the general question of balancing effectiveness and the principle *ex injuria non oritur jus* is considered. Here it must suffice to point out that, when elements of certain strong norms (the *jus cogens*[3]) are involved, it is less likely that recognition and acquiescence will offset the original illegality. These issues will receive discussion when the identity and continuity of states are considered subsequently. One aspect of *jus cogens*, the principle of self-determination,[4] may justify the granting of a higher status to certain types of belligerent entities and exile governments than would otherwise be the case.[5]

5. *Necessary Legal Constructions*

Political circumstances may lead to legal constructions which at first sight are excessively formalistic. A state's legal order may be projected on the plane of time for certain purposes although its physical and political existence has ceased. One view of the situation in Germany since 1945 is as follows. Subject to certain powers under the Berlin Declaration and the unconditional surrender, two German states currently exist. The German Federal Republic rests on a constitution of 1949 and certain agreements. The German Democratic Republic rests on a constitution of 1949 and an agreement with the U.S.S.R.[6] There is as yet no general peace treaty regulating certain territorial and other issues involving Germany left over from the Second World War. If such a treaty were concluded[7] three German states would be parties: the German Federal Republic, the German Democratic Republic, and the Germany which surrendered in 1945 and which technically would be the subject-matter of the general

[1] See Crawford, op. cit., pp. 144–8, 173–6; Marek, op. cit., pp. 553–87. Belligerent occupation clearly does not affect statehood: the occupant *ex hypothesi* does not displace the territorial sovereign though the *incidents* of statehood are affected. It is not correct to describe governments-in-exile as states without people or territory when the displacement is caused by a belligerent occupation (cf. Briggs, p. 66). Puppet states, such as Slovakia and Croatia, set up as a consequence of the illegal threat or use of force in 1939 and 1941 respectively, received recognition from very few states. On the status of Burma in the Second World War see *Chettiar* v. *Chettiar*, *Ann. Digest* 15 (1948), no. 178.

[2] *Infra*, Chapter XXII. [3] See *infra*, pp. 512–15. [4] See Chapter XXIV, section 9.

[5] See Crawford, op. cit., pp. 144–73; and see *infra*, pp. 173–4.

[6] The situation is complicated by the fact that the German Federal Republic claims to be the successor to all German territory within the frontiers of 1937.

[7] *Inter alia*, this hypothesis is affected by non-recognition of the German Democratic Republic by a number of states.

settlement.[1] In the *South-West Africa* cases[2] it was suggested by Judges Spender and Fitzmaurice in their joint dissenting opinion[3] that the principal Allied and associated powers of the First World War might retain a residual or reversionary interest in the ex-German territories placed under mandate. The five principal powers concerned were the United States,[4] the British Empire, France, Italy, and Japan, and, whilst they still exist as legal persons, their special capacity as principal Allied powers in 1919 may be projected on the plane of time.

6. *Membership of International Organizations and Agencies*

Membership in an international organization depends on the contractual terms arranged by the founding states. However, accession to membership may not be on the basis of right, by acceptance of a standing offer. Usually a leading organ of the institution will alone have competence to decide on qualifications for membership, and in practice political criteria may supplement the legal conditions laid down in a constituent instrument. These conditions will normally specify or assume the existence of statehood and may then refer to additional qualities.[5] Thus Article 4 of the United Nations Charter provides that membership of the organization 'is open to all peace-loving States which accept the obligations contained in the present Charter and, in the judgment of the Organization, are able and willing to carry out these obligations'. Admission to membership is to be by decision of the General Assembly upon the recommendation of the Security Council.[6]

7. *Identity and Continuity of States*[7]

The term 'continuity' of States is not employed with any

[1] See *infra*, p. 87, on the issue of continuity and survival in relation to the German Federal Republic.

[2] I.C.J. Reports (1962), p. 319.

[3] At pp. 482 (note), 486.

[4] The United States concluded a separate peace treaty in 1921: 16 *A.J.* (1922), Suppl., p. 10.

[5] See Rosalyn Higgins, *The Development of International Law Through the Political Organs of the United Nations*, pp. 11–57; and Fawcett, *The British Commonwealth in International Law*, pp. 223–39. On the concept of functional membership of organizations, see *infra*, Chapter XXX, section 6.

[6] See the *Admissions* case, I.C.J. Reports (1947–8), p. 63; Lauterpacht, *The Development of International Law by the International Court*, pp. 148–52; Rosenne, 39 *B.Y.* (1963), p. 1 at pp. 40–1.

[7] See, in particular, Whiteman ii. 754–99; Kelsen, *Principles of International Law* (2nd ed.), pp. 383–7; Marek, *Identity and Continuity of States in Public International Law*

precision, and may be used to preface a diversity of legal problems. Thus it may introduce the proposition that the legal rights and responsibility of states are not affected by changes in the head of state or the internal form of government.[1] This proposition can, of course, be maintained without reference to a concept of 'continuity' or 'succession', and it is in any case too general, since political changes may result in a change of circumstances sufficient to affect particular types of treaty relation.[2] More significantly, legal doctrine tends to distinguish between continuity (and identity) and state succession. The latter arises when one international personality takes the place of another, for example by union or lawful annexation. In general, it is assumed that cases of 'state succession'[3] are likely to involve important changes in the legal status and rights of the entities concerned, whereas if there is continuity, the legal personality and the particular rights and duties of the state remain unaltered.

Unfortunately the general categories of 'continuity' and 'state succession', and the assumption of a neat distinction between them, only make a difficult subject more confused by masking the variations of circumstance and the complexities of the legal problems which arise in practice. 'Succession' and 'continuity' are levels of abstraction unfitted to dealing with specific issues. Thus the view that Italy was formed not by union of other states with Sardinia, but by annexation to Sardinia, has the corollary that this was a case of continuity and not, with respect to Sardinia, a state succession.[4] Yet one may wonder if the difference in political procedure should make such a great legal difference. Further, political and legal experience provide several examples of situations in which there is 'continuity', but the precise circumstances, and the relevant principles of law and good policy, dictate solutions which are only partly conditioned by the element of 'continuity'. Legal techniques may well entail

(1954); Clute, *The International Legal Status of Austria* 1938–55 (1962); Briggs, pp. 209–13; O'Connell, *State Succession in Municipal Law and International Law*, 2 vols. (1967) (particular states in Index); Kunz, 49 *A.J.* (1955), 68–76; Crawford, op. cit., pp. 173–6. Cp. Green, in *Law, Justice and Equity* (ed. Keeton), pp. 152–67, on dissolution of states and membership of the League of Nations and the United Nations.

[1] Briggs, *ut supra*. See also Oppenheim i. 153–4; McNair, *Opinions* i. 3; Hackworth i. 387–92; *Tinoco Concessions* arbitration (1923), *R.I.A.A.* i. 369; Green, p. 113.

[2] See Chapter XXV, section 6. A treaty of military and political co-operation may be invalidated if one party undergoes a change of regime inimical to the basis of the treaty.

[3] See *infra*, Chapter XXVIII. There is no single legal criterion for distinguishing partial and total succession of states (the latter involving change of personality).

[4] Marek, pp. 191–8. See also Guggenheim i. 444–5; O'Connell, *State Succession in Municipal and International Law* i. 5; ii. 28–30, 365.

relying on continuity in one context, but denying its existence in another. Thus the political and legal transformation involved in destroying the Austro-Hungarian monarchy and establishing a new political settlement in central and south-east Europe produced Austria,[1] the Serb-Croat-Slovene state,[2] and Czechoslovakia,[3] which rested on new political and legal orders. Nevertheless for certain purposes principles of continuity with previous political entities were applied by state practice in these cases.

The functional approach has been prominent in a group of cases arising from the unlawful use of force. Ethiopia was conquered and annexed by Italy in 1936. Many states gave *de jure* or *de facto* recognition to Italian control, but Ethiopia remained formally a member of the League of Nations. After the outbreak of the Second World War the United Kingdom and other states treated Ethiopia, after liberation in 1941, as independent and co-belligerent.[4] Czechoslovakia was placed under German control in March 1939 as a result of the use and threat of force. *De jure* recognition was generally withheld in this case, and by 1941 an exile government was accepted by the Allies as a co-belligerent.[5] Albania was placed under Italian occupation in 1939 and was liberated in 1944.[6] Rather more difficult, since the community welcomed absorption, was the case of the Austrian Anschluss in 1938. Many states regarded this as illegal, and Austria was not regarded as responsible for her part in Axis aggression.[7] In all these cases foreign control can be

[1] The Treaty of St. Germain assumed continuity. State practice apart from this treaty favoured continuity in the matter of treaties. In respect of public debts and other matters, principles were applied indistinguishable from those related normally to 'state succession', i.e. continuity of obligation with modifications. See O'Connell, op. cit., index; Guggenheim, loc. cit.; Marek, op. cit., pp. 199–236 (who uses the category of continuity too dogmatically); Kelsen, *Principles* (2nd ed.), p. 384.

[2] See O'Connell, op. cit., i. 5, 6; Marek, pp. 237–62; *Katz and Klump* v. *Yugoslavia*, *Ann. Digest* 3 (1925–6), no. 24; *Ivanevic* v. *Artukovic*, Int. L.R. 21 (1954), p. 66.

[3] See O'Connell, op. cit., indices.

[4] See Marek, pp. 263–82; O'Connell, index; *Azazh Kebbeda Tesema* v. *Italian Government*, *Ann. Digest* 9 (1938–40), no. 36; U.K.–Ethiopia, Agreement of 31 January 1942; Cmd. 6334; Peace Treaty with Italy, 1947, sect. VII (cf. Fitzmaurice, 73 Hague *Recueil* (1948, II), 282).

[5] See Marek, pp. 283–330; *Hardtmuth* v. *Hardtmuth*, Int. L.R. 26 (1958, II), 40.

[6] See Marek, pp. 331–7; Briggs, pp. 119–21; Peace Treaty with Italy, 1947, sect. VI (cf. Fitzmaurice, 73 Hague *Recueil* (1948, II), 282).

[7] See Marek, pp. 338–68; Clute, *ut supra*; Guggenheim ii. 470; *Security for Costs (Austria)* case, Int. L.R. 22 (1955), 58; *Republic of Austria* v. *City of Vienna*, ibid. 26 (1958, II), 77; *Schleiffer* v. *Directorate of Finance*, ibid., p. 609. The Austrian State Treaty of 1955 (text: 49 *A.J.* (1955), Suppl., p. 162) is consonant with the view that Austria was re-established. See also p. 87, n. 1, *infra*. Cf. *In re Mangold's Patent*, Int. L.R. 18 (1951), no. 59; 28 *B.Y.* (1951), 406; 86 *J.D.I.* (1959), 1166.

ignored on the ground that its source was illegal: *ex injuria non oritur jus*. However, neither this principle nor that of continuity can provide an omnibus solution to the legal problems arising for solution after 1945. In all these cases, for slightly differing reasons, the occupation in fact and form went beyond belligerent occupation, since there was either absorption outright or the setting up of puppet regimes. Moreover, the control lasted for some time, and insistence on continuity is theoretical in these cases: what occurred on liberation was restoration, re-establishment of the former state. This is qualified continuity. Thus, in the case of Austria after 1945 state practice, including that of Austria, has supported the position that Austria is bound by pre-1938 treaties to which she was a party. Germany has been held responsible by the Allies for the payment of the bonded external debt of Austria for the period 1939–45: Austrian courts have not accepted succession in the public foreign debt from this period except where the principle of unjust enrichment required a different approach. Austria has accepted responsibility for the pre-Anschluss external debt. Nationality problems affecting Austria and Czechoslovakia show very clearly the need to approach issues free from the tyranny of concepts. After 1945 the governments of these two states did not revoke the nationality law of the usurping German administration retroactively. The law of the German Federal Republic allowed those who became German as a result of the Anschluss to maintain German nationality if since 1945 they had permanently resided on German territory (frontiers of 1937).[1]

Other types of qualified continuity exist. The relation of the German Federal Republic and German Democratic Republic to the former German Reich is a matter of some difficulty which cannot be pursued here.[2] In some instances, where the basis for continuity is tenuous, estoppel, special agreement, and principles of validation and effectiveness may provide elements of legal continuity. Moreover, the empirical elements in continuity must be distinguished from a concept of survival. Lastly, the operation of the principle of self-determination as a part of the *jus cogens* may support a doctrine of reversion: for example, rights of way granted by a colonial power may not be opposable

[1] See Brownlie, 39 *B.Y.* (1963), 326, 346; and the *Austrian Nationality* case, Int. L.R. 22 (1955), 430.

[2] See *German Civil Service* Case, Int. L.R. 22 (1955), 943; *Rex* v. *Bottrill, ex p. Kuechenmeister* [1947] 1 K.B. 41; Oppenheim i. 568–70; Bishop, 49 *A.J.* (1955), 125–47; Kunz, ibid. 210–16; Virally, *Annuaire français* (1955), pp. 31–52; Pinto, 86 *J.D.I.* (1959), 312; Plischke, 48 *A.J.* (1954), 245–64; Whiteman i. 332–8; Mann, 16 *I.C.L.Q.* (1967), 760–99.

to the state which, in replacing the colonial power, is recovering an independence which it formerly had.[1]

8. *Micro-States*[2]

Membership of the United Nations is not expressed to be conditioned by the size[3] of the state concerned. However, Article 4 of the United Nations Charter makes an ability to carry out the obligations contained in the Charter a requirement of admission to membership and the principalities of San Marino, Monaco, and Liechtenstein have not applied for membership. None the less, however small geographically or modest in resources, an entity is a 'state' for general purposes of international law provided the criteria of statehood are satisfied. Thus the very small principalities have become parties to the Statute of the International Court of Justice.

Since its early days quite small nations have been admitted to membership of the United Nations. Costa Rica, Luxembourg, and Iceland provide examples.[4] In recent years the increase in total membership and the modest size of some of the applicants for admission has caused United Nations organs to consider the possibility of establishing some form of associate membership of the United Nations. Such a regime might involve ineligibility for seats on the Security Council, the right to participate in General Assembly proceedings without a vote, favourable terms for contributions to expenses of the United Nations, and access to the resources of the specialized agencies, such as the World Health Organization. There are many problems to be faced, not least that of establishing criteria for ordinary membership.

[1] See the dissenting opinion of Judge Moreno Quintana in the *Right of Passage* case, I.C.J. Reports (1960), pp. 95–6. The majority of the Court did not deal with this issue; on the evidence the passage had been maintained for some years after the British left India.

[2] Other terms are 'diminutive' or 'mini-' states. See generally: UNITAR, *Status and Problems of Very Small States and Territories* (1969); Farran, *Festschrift für Walter Schätzel* (1960), pp. 131–47; Blair, *The Ministate Dilemma*, rev. ed. (1968); Saint-Girons, 76 *R.G.D.I.P.* (1972), 445–74; Rapoport, *A.S.I.L. Proceedings*, 1968, 155–63; Fisher, ibid., 164–70; Harris, *Columbia Journ. Trans. Law*, 1970, 23–53; de Smith, *Microstates and Micronesia* (1970); Rousseau ii. 329–47; Mendelson, 21 *I.C.L.Q.* (1972), 609–30; Schwebel, 67 *A.J.* (1973), 108–16; Gunter, 71 *A.J.* (1977), 110–24.

On comparable issues within the British Commonwealth see Fawcett, *Ann. Survey of Commonwealth Law* (1967), 709–11; ibid. (1968), 785–8; ibid. (1969), 558–9; Margaret Broderick, 17 *I.C.L.Q.* (1968), 368–403.

[3] The most common indicator used is population, as opposed to geographical area, gross national product, etc.

[4] Iceland: 146,000. More recent examples: the Maldive Islands, Bhutan; Comoros, Cape Verde, Samoa, Grenada, and São Tomé and Principe. Western Samoa and Nauru have not applied to join the U.N.

CHAPTER V

RECOGNITION OF STATES AND GOVERNMENTS[1]

1. *Recognition as a General Category*

WHENEVER a state acts in a way which may or does affect the legal rights or political interests of other states, the question arises of the legal significance of the reaction of other states to the event. In the *Eastern Greenland* case[2] it was held that Norway had, as a consequence of the declaration of her Foreign Minister, accepted Danish title to the disputed territory. There the acceptance by Norway of Denmark's claim was by informal agreement: in many instances formal treaty provisions will involve recognition of rights. However, apart from agreement, legally detrimental reaction may occur in the form of unilateral acts or conduct, involving estoppel, recognition, or acquiescence.[3] In the *Fisheries* case[4] between the United Kingdom and Norway, the former was held to have acquiesced in the Norwegian system of straight baselines for establishing exclusive fishery limits. Frequently acts of states which are not within their legal competence will meet with protest from other states. Illegal acts are not in principle opposable to other states in any case, and protest is not a condition of the illegality. Conversely, a valid

[1] State practice and other materials: Whiteman ii. 1–746; Hackworth i. 161–387; Moore, *Digest* i. 67–248; *British Practice in International Law*. Other literature: Chen, *The International Law of Recognition* (1951); Lauterpacht, *Recognition in International Law* (1947); id., 62 Hague *Recueil* (1937, IV), 244–80; id., *International Law: Collected Papers* i (1970), 308–48; Charpentier, *La Reconnaissance internationale* (1956); Fischer Williams, 44 Hague *Recueil* (1933, II), 203–314; id., 47 *Harv. L.R.* (1933–4), 776–94; Briggs, pp. 99–193; Raestad, 17 *R.D.I.L.C.* (1936), 257–313; Brown, *Annuaire de l'Inst.* (1934), pp. 302–57; ibid. (1936), i. 233–45; ii. 175–255, 300–5; id., 44 *A.J.* (1950), 617–40; Kelsen, 35 *A.J.* (1941), 605–17; id., *Principles of International Law* (2nd ed.), pp. 387–416; Wright, 44 *A.J.*, 548–59; Fitzmaurice, 92 Hague *Recueil* (1957, II), 16–35; Jessup, *A Modern Law of Nations* (1948), pp. 43–67; Erich, 13 Hague *Recueil* (1926, III), 457–502; Misra, 55 *A.J.* (1961), 398–424; American Law Institute, *Restatement of the Foreign Relations Law of the U.S.* (May, 1962), Part II, 'Recognition'; Jennings, 121 Hague *Recueil* (1967, II), 349–68; Mugerwa, in Sørensen, *Manual*, pp. 266–90; Verhoeven, *La Reconnaissance internationale dans la Pratique contemporaine* (1975); Blix, 130 Hague *Recueil* (1970, II), 587–704; Crawford, 48 *B.Y.I.L.* (1976–7), 93–107; Salmon, *La Reconnaissance d'état* (1971); Rousseau iii. 513–611.

[2] See *infra*, pp. 142 seq. The better view is that the facts disclosed an agreement rather than an estoppel.

[3] On unilateral acts in general see Chapter XXVI, section 3.

[4] See *infra*, pp. 186 seq.

claim to territory is not conditioned as to its validity by the acceptance of the claim by the defending state. However, acts of protest and recognition play a subsidiary but, in practice, not insubstantial role in the resolution of disputes. Protest and recognition by other states may provide good evidence of the state of the law on the issues involved. Furthermore, there is a spectrum of issues involving areas of uncertainty in the law, novel and potentially law-changing claims (cf. the development of claims to resources of the continental shelf), and actually illegal activity (apart from issues involving fundamental principles, *jus cogens*),[1] within which issues are most sensibly settled on an *ad hoc* and bilateral basis: indeed, cases concerned with relatively well-settled areas of law are often decided on the basis of facts, including elements of acquiescence, establishing a special content of obligation between the parties, and this quite apart from treaty. Finally, it may be observed that protest and recognition may be pure acts of policy not purporting to be legal characterizations of acts of other states, and, whether having this purport or not, the protest or recognition, if unfounded in law and backed by state activity, may be simply a declaration of intent to commit a delict or, otherwise, to act *ultra vires*.

2. *States and Governments in Relation to Recognition*

In international relations it is the recognition of states, governments, belligerency, and insurgency[2] which has been the most prominent aspect of the general category, and legal writing has adopted the emphasis and terminology of political relations. The dominance of the category 'recognition' has led to some perverse doctrine. When a state is in dispute over legal title to territory, for example, a legal forum will examine *all* the legally significant conduct and declarations of either party. A declaration by one party that it does not 'recognize' the title of the other will hardly determine the issue, and may be worth very little if it is simply a declaration of political interest and antagonism. Again, a statement registering the fact that at a certain date the opponent was in actual occupation will be a part of the evidence

[1] See *infra*, pp. 512–15.

[2] The complex and confused doctrines on belligerency and insurgency are omitted. The recognition of '*de facto* governments' is related to belligerency and insurgency (see *infra*, pp. 96–7). On these topics see the general works cited *supra*, p. 89, and see further McNair, *Opinions* ii. 325 seq.; Lauterpacht, 3 *Mod. L.R.* (1939–40), 1–20; McNair, 53 *L.Q.R.* (1937), 471–500; Walker, 23 *Grot. Soc.* (1937), 177–210; and Wehberg, 63 Hague *Recueil* (1938, I), 7–126.

in the case, but only within the context of the particular case will the statement have a specific legal significance. Unfortunately, when the existence of states and governments is in issue, a proper legal perspective seems to be elusive.

Absurdly, the complexity one may expect of legal issues in state relations is compacted into a doctrinal dispute between the declaratory and constitutivist views on recognition of states and (in so far as the two matters are interdependent)[1] governments. According to the declaratory view,[2] the legal effects of recognition are limited, since recognition is a mere declaration or acknowledgement of an existing state of law and fact, legal personality having been conferred previously by operation of law. As Hall says:[3] 'States being the persons governed by international law, communities are subjected to law . . . from the moment, and from the moment only, at which they acquire the marks of a State.' Thus, in a relatively objective forum, such as an international tribunal, it would be entirely proper to accept the existence of a state although the other party to the dispute, or third states, did not recognize it. The award in the *Tinoco Concessions* arbitration[4] adopted this approach. In that case Great Britain was allowed to bring a claim on the basis of concessions granted by the former revolutionary government of Costa Rica which had not been recognized by some other states, including Great Britain. The arbitrator, Taft, observed:

> The non-recognition by other nations of a government claiming to be a national personality, is usually appropriate evidence that it has not attained the independence and control entitling it by international law to be classed as such. But when recognition *vel non* of a government is by such nations

[1] See *infra*, p. 95.

[2] The number of adherents to this view has increased in the recent past. Modern adherents include Fischer Williams, *ubi supra*; Chen, op. cit.; Brierly, *Law of Nations* (6th ed.), p. 139; Briggs, p. 116; Rousseau iii. 534–8; Waldock, 106 Hague *Recueil* (1962, II), 147–51; Rolin, 77 Hague *Recueil* (1950, II), 326–37; Kunz, 44 *A.J.* (1950), 713; Kozhevnikov (ed.), *International Law*, pp. 117–18. Charpentier, op. cit., in substance is a declaratist. See also the resolution of the Institute of International Law: *Annuaire* 39, ii. 175–255, 300–5.

[3] p. 19.

[4] (1923), *R.I.A.A.* i. 369; Briggs, p. 197; Bishop, p. 368; Green, p. 113. See also *Socony Vacuum Oil Company Claim*, Int. L.R. 21 (1954), 55, U.S. Int. Claims Commission; *Standard Vacuum Oil Company Claim*, Int. L.R. 30, p. 168, U.S. Foreign Claims Settlement Commission, 1959; *Clerget* v. *Représentation Commerciale de la République démocratique du Viet-Nam*, 96 *J.D.I.* (1969), p. 894 at p. 898, Cour d'appel de Paris, 1969; *Wulfsohn* v. *R.S.F.S.R.* (1923), 234 N.Y. 372; Briggs, p. 148; *Sokoloff* v. *National City Bank* (1924), 239 N.Y. 158; Briggs, p. 162; *Salimoff* v. *Standard Oil Co.* (1933), 262 N.Y. 220; Briggs, p. 165; *Deutsche Continental Gas-Gesellschaft* v. *Polish State*, *Ann. Digest* 5 (1929–30), no. 5. Cf. the *Reparation for Injuries* case, *infra*, Chapter XXX, in which the United Nations was held to have personality *vis-à-vis* Israel, a non-member.

determined by inquiry, not into its *de facto* sovereignty and complete governmental control, but into its illegitimacy or irregularity of origin, their non-recognition loses something of evidential weight on the issue with which those applying the rules of international law are alone concerned. What is true of the non-recognition of the United States in its bearing upon the existence of a *de facto* government under Tinoco for thirty months is probably in a measure true of the non-recognition by her Allies in the European War. Such non-recognition for any reason, however, cannot outweigh the evidence disclosed by this record before me as to the *de facto* character of Tinoco's government, according to the standard set by international law.

The reasoning employed here applies also to recognition of states. In addition there is a substantial state practice behind the declaratory view. Unrecognized states are quite commonly the object of international claims, charges of aggression, and other breaches of the United Nations Charter, by the very states refusing recognition.[1]

The declaratory theory of recognition is opposed to the constitutive view. According to the latter, the political act of recognition is a precondition of the existence of legal rights: in its extreme form this is to say that the very personality of a state depends on the political decision of other states.[2] The result is as a matter of principle impossible to accept: it is clearly established that states cannot by their independent judgment establish any competence of other states which is established by international law and does not depend on agreement or concession.[3] Brierly comments:[4]

It is true that the present state of the law makes it possible that different states should act on different views of the application of the law to the same set of facts. This does not mean that their differing interpretations are all equally correct, but only that there exists at present no procedure for

[1] For example, Arab charges against Israel; United States charges against North Vietnam, 1964–5. On the latter: Falk (ed.), *The Vietnam War and International Law* i (1968), p. 583. See further *infra*, on implied recognition. See also the Montevideo Convention on Rights and Duties of States, 1933, Art. 3; Hudson, *Int. Legis.* vi. 620; Bogotá Charter, 1948, Art. 9; Briggs, p. 101.

[2] Constitutivist doctrine takes many forms, and in many cases the jurists concerned allow certain rights prior to recognition. Well-known adherents include Anzilotti, *Cours de droit international* i. 160; Oppenheim i. 126; Kelsen, *ut supra* (earlier he was a declaratist: 4 *R.D.I.* (1929), 617–18; and 42 Hague *Recueil* (1932, IV), 260–94); Lauterpacht, *ut supra*. See further Chen, op. cit., pp. 30 seq. The *Polish Upper Silesia* case (1926), P.C.I.J., Ser. A, no. 7 at p. 28, does not unequivocally support the constitutive view, since the issue was the existence of a contractual nexus between Germany and Poland. The fact that Poland could not invoke a treaty against Germany did not connote the non-existence of the former. For the view that U.N. Secretariat practice has supported the constitutivist position see Schachter, 25 *B.Y.* (1948), 109–15.

[3] See *infra*, pp. 291 seq., 380 seq. [4] p. 319.

determining which are correct and which are not. The constitutive theory of recognition gains most of its plausibility from the lack of centralized institutions in the system, and it treats this lack not as an accident due to the stage of development which the law has so far reached, but as an essential feature of the system.

Constitutivist doctrine creates a great many difficulties. Its adherents may feel a need to rationalize the position of the unrecognized state and in doing so may adopt near-declaratory views.[1] Reference to recognition leads to various difficulties. How many states must recognize? Can existence be relative only to those states which do recognize? Is existence dependent on recognition only when this rests on an adequate knowledge of the facts? Cogent arguments of principle and the preponderance of state practice thus dictate a preference for declaratory doctrine, yet to reduce, or to seem to reduce, the issues to a choice between the two opposing theories is to greatly oversimplify the legal situation.

3. *The Varied Legal Consequences of Acts of Recognition and Policies of Non-Recognition*

There is no such thing as a uniform type of recognition or non-recognition. The terminology of official communications and declarations is not very consistent: there may be '*de jure* recognition', '*de facto* recognition', 'full diplomatic recognition', 'formal recognition', and so on. The term 'recognition' may be absent, and thus recognition may take the form of an agreement, or declaration of intent, to establish diplomatic relations, or a congratulatory message on attainment of independence. The typical act of recognition has two legal functions. First, the determination of statehood, a question of law: such individual determination may have evidential[2] effect before a tribunal. Secondly, the act is a condition of the establishment of formal, optional, and bilateral relations, including diplomatic relations and the conclusion of treaties. It is this second function which has been described by some jurists as 'constitutivist', although here it is not a condition of statehood.[3] Since states cannot be required

[1] Cf. the views of Rivier, Fauchille, and Hyde: *infra*, note 3.

[2] Recognition is rarely 'cognitive' in a simple sense: the issue is one of law as well as fact, and cognition, which may involve no outward sign, occurs before, often long before, public recognition. Cf. Whiteman ii. 13 (Sec. of State, Dulles).

[3] Rivier, Fauchille, and Hyde draw the distinction between personality and the exercise of rights by a state.

Kelsen, Verdross, Kunz, and Guggenheim similarly regard recognition as declaratory of certain basic rights of existence but constitutive of more specific rights.

by the law (apart from treaty) actually to make a public declaration of recognition, and since they are obviously not required to undertake optional relations, the expression of state 'will' involved is political in the sense of being voluntary. But it may also be political in a more obvious sense. An absence of recognition may not rest on any legal basis at all, there being no attempt to pass on the legal question of statehood as such. Non-recognition may simply be part of a general policy of disapproval and boycott. Again, recognition may be part of a policy of aggression and the creation of puppet states: the legal consequences will here stem from the breaches of international law involved. The important point is that use of the term 'recognition' does not absolve the lawyer from inquiring into the intent of the government concerned and then placing this in the context of *all* the relevant facts and rules of law.

4. *Is there a Duty of Recognition?*

Lauterpacht[1] and Guggenheim[2] adopt the view that recognition is constitutive, but that there is a legal duty to recognize. This standpoint has been vigorously criticized[3] as bearing no relation to state practice and for its inconsistency, since in an oblique way it comes close to the declaratory view. In principle the legal duty can only be valid if it is in respect of an entity already bearing the marks of statehood and (although Lauterpacht does not express it thus) it is owed to the entity concerned. The argument postulates personality on an objective basis. However, discussion of Lauterpacht's views often reveals a certain confusion among the critics. Recognition, *as a public act of state*, is an optional and political act and there is no legal duty in this regard. However, in a deeper sense, if an entity bears the marks of statehood,[4] other states put themselves at risk legally if they ignore the basic obligations of state relations. Few would take the view that the Arab neighbours of Israel can afford to treat her as a non-entity: the responsible United Nations organs and individual states[5] have taken the view that Israel is pro-

[1] *Recognition in International Law* (1947); and in *International Law: Collected Papers* i (1970), 312–14. See also U.K. comment on the draft Declaration of the Rights and Duties of States: Whiteman ii. 15–17. [2] i. 190–1.

[3] See Kunz, 44 *A.J.* (1950), 713–19; Cohn, 64 *L.Q.R.* (1948), 404–8; Briggs, 43 *A.J.* 1949), 113–21. See also Jessup, 65 *A.J.* (1971), p. 214 at p. 217.

[4] Strictly speaking it is superfluous to call in aid rights of independence, sovereignty, and self-determination. Cf. Rolin, op. cit., p. 330; Higgins, p. 137.

[5] Arab representatives frequently discuss relations with Israel in terms of inter-state obligation.

tected, and bound, by the principles of the United Nations Charter governing the use of force. In this context of state *conduct* there is a duty to accept and apply certain fundamental rules of international law: there is a legal duty to 'recognize' for certain purposes at least, but no duty to make an express, public, and political determination of the question or to declare readiness to enter into diplomatic relations by means of recognition. This latter type of recognition remains political and discretionary. Even recognition is not determinant of diplomatic relations, and absence of diplomatic relations is not in itself non-recognition of the state.

5. *Recognition of Governments*

In principle most of the considerations set out previously apply equally to recognition of states and governments. It has been seen elsewhere[1] that the existence of an effective and independent government is the essence of statehood, and, significantly, recognition of states may take the form of recognition of a government. Thus in 1919 the British Foreign Office declared that the British Government recognized the Esthonian National Council as a *de facto* independent body with the capacity to set up a prize court.[2] Everything depends on the intention of the recognizing government and the relevant circumstances. Although recognition of government and state may be closely related, they are not necessarily identical. Non-recognition of a particular regime is not necessarily a determination that the state represented by that regime does not qualify for statehood. Non-recognition of a government may have two legal facets: that it is not a government in terms of independence and effectiveness (a facet which does *necessarily* affect statehood),[3] or, that the non-recognizing state is unwilling to have normal relations with the state concerned.[4] Non-recognition of governments seems more 'political' than that of states because unwillingness to enter into normal relations is more often expressed by non-recognition of the organs of government. Recognition in the context of voluntary relations may be made conditional on the democratic character of the regime, the acceptance of particular claims, or the giving of undertakings, for example on treatment of minorities.[5] The sphere of optional relations and voluntary obligations is one

[1] *Supra*, pp. 75 seq.
[2] See the *Gagara* [1919] P. 95; Briggs, p. 139. See also Briggs, p. 105.
[3] *Supra*, pp. 75–6. [4] See the *Tinoco Concessions* case, *supra*, p. 91.
[5] See Briggs, pp. 112–13, 130–2; Kelsen, *Principles* (2nd ed.), pp. 403–4.

of discretion and bargain. In terms of bilateral voluntary relations, an unrecognized government is no better off than an unrecognized state.[1]

6. De Jure *and* De Facto *Recognition*

General propositions about the distinction between *de jure* and *de facto* recognition are to be distrusted, since, as it was emphasized earlier, everything depends on the intention of the government concerned and the general context of fact and law. At least it is unlikely that the epithets refer to internal constitutionality. On the international plane a statement that a government is recognized as the '*de facto* government' of a state may involve a purely political judgment, involving either a reluctant or cautious acceptance of an effective government, lawfully established in terms of international law and not imposed from without, or an unwarranted acceptance of an unqualified agency. On the other hand, the statement may be intended to be or to include a legal determination of the existence of an effective government, but with reservations as to its permanence and viability. It may of course happen that the legal and political bases for caution coincide. The distinction between '*de jure/de facto* recognition' and 'recognition as the *de jure/de facto* government' is insubstantial, more especially as the question is one of intention and the legal consequences thereof in the particular case.[2] If there is a distinction it does not seem to matter legally. Certainly the legal and political elements of caution in the epithet *de facto* in either context are rarely regarded as significant, and courts both national[3] and international[4] accord the same strength to *de facto* recognition as evidence of an effective government as they do to *de jure* recognition. The distinction occurs exclusively in the political context of recognition of governments. It is sometimes said that *de jure* recognition is irrevocable whilst *de facto* recognition can be withdrawn.[5] In the political sense recognition

[1] There is a strong school of thought supporting the automatic recognition of *de facto* governments, exemplified by the 'Estrada doctrine' enunciated by the Mexican Secretary of Foreign Relations in 1930: Briggs, p. 123. As a means of reducing non-recognition as a source of interference in internal affairs this is laudable, but difficulties remain. Recognition cannot be automatic when competing governments appear or when there is an attempted secession and issues of government and statehood are linked.

[2] For a different approach: Chen, op. cit., pp. 273–300.

[3] See the *Gagara*, *supra*, p. 95, n. 2; and *Luther* v. *Sagor*, *infra*, p. 102.

[4] See the *Tinoco Concessions* case, *supra*, p. 91.

[5] Writers usually conduct their investigations on the assumption that no illegality was involved in giving recognition. If the situation recognized is the product of illegality, it is the case that the recognition is invalid and revocation legally superfluous.

of either kind can always be withdrawn: in the legal sense it cannot be unless a change of circumstances warrants it. Of course, if a statement involving a legal determination of effectiveness is made, withdrawal as a political gesture is embarrassing, but no more so than the withholding of recognition on political grounds.

Situations do occur where there is a serious legal distinction between *de jure* and *de facto* recognition as those terms are employed in the particular context. Thus some governments accepted certain legal consequences of German control of Austria, 1938–45, and Czechoslovakia, 1939–45, for example in the fields of nationality law and consular agents. Yet these same governments did not accept the legality of the *origin* of the factual control of Germany.[1] In documents relating to these matters '*de facto* recognition' may be used to describe acceptance of facts with a dubious legal origin: *de jure* recognition would be inappropriate and legally unjustifiable.[2] In this context it is legally hazardous to accept the full legal competence of an administration accorded only '*de facto* recognition'. Thus, in *Bank of Ethiopia* v. *National Bank of Egypt and Liguori*,[3] the Court gave effect to an Italian decree in Abyssinia on the basis that the United Kingdom had recognized Italy as the *de facto* government. In fact Italy at the time was no more than a belligerent occupant. Furthermore, in situations where rival governments were accorded *de jure* and *de facto* recognition in respect of the same territory, problems arise if the same legal consequences are given to both types of recognition.[4]

7. *Retroactivity*[5]

British and American courts have applied the principle of retroactivity in following or interpreting the views of the executive in matters of recognition,[6] but Oppenheim[7] describes the rule as 'one of convenience rather than of principle'. Once again

[1] On the policies of the United Kingdom and United States see Brownlie, *International Law and the Use of Force by States*, pp. 414–16.

[2] British *de jure* recognition in 1938 of the Italian conquest of Ethiopia in 1936 was avoided subsequently: cf. *supra*, p. 86.

[3] [1937] Ch. 513.

[4] On the policy of the United Kingdom and the response of the courts in the cases of the Spanish Civil War and Italo-Ethiopian war see *infra*, pp. 102–5. See further *Carl Zeiss Stiftung* v. *Rayner and Keeler, Ltd.* (*No.* 2) [1966] 3 W.L.R. 125 at pp. 135–7 (Lord Reid) and 180–2 (Lord Wilberforce).

[5] See generally Whiteman ii. 728–45; Fitzmaurice, op. cit., p. 23 n.; Hackworth i. 381–85; Chen, op. cit., pp. 172–86.

[6] See Briggs, p. 191; Oppenheim i. 150. [7] Loc. cit.

one ought not to generalize except to say that on the international plane there is no rule of retroactivity.[1] When a state makes a late acceptance of the existence of a state then, in the field of the basic rights and duties of existence, this recognition *ex hypothesi* cannot be 'retroactive' because in a special sense it is superfluous. In the sphere of optional relations and voluntary obligation it may or may not be, since the area is one of discretion.[2]

8. *Implied Recognition*[3]

Recognition is a matter of intention and may be express or implied. The implication of intention is a process aided by certain customary rules or, perhaps, presumptions. Thus Lauterpacht[4] concludes that, in the case of recognition of states, only the conclusion of a bilateral treaty which regulates comprehensively the relations between the two states, the formal initiation of diplomatic relations, and, probably, the issue of consular exequaturs, justify the implication. State practice shows that no recognition is implied from various forms of negotiation, the establishment of unofficial representation, the conclusion of a multilateral treaty to which the unrecognized entity is also a party, admission to an international organization (in respect to those opposing admission), or presence at an international conference in which the unrecognized entity participates. Confusion arises from two sources. First, the terminology of governmental statements may create confusion and lead tribunals to give high legal status to acts intended only to give a low level of recognition: for example, an authority with which only informal and limited contacts have been undertaken may be accorded sovereign immunity by national courts.[5] Secondly, different considerations ought to apply to different legal aspects of recognition, yet doctrine tends to generalize about the subject. Thus, in terms of evidence in an objective forum like an international tribunal, informal relations, without intent to recognize in the political sense, especially if these persist, have probative value on the

[1] See Mervyn Jones, 16 *B.Y.* (1935), 42–55; Kelsen, *Principles* (2nd ed.), p. 398; de Visscher, *Théories et réalités en droit international public* (4th ed.), p. 262. *Contra:* Chen, pp. 177–8.

[2] Cf. the *Polish Upper Silesia* case, P.C.I.J., Ser. A, no. 7 (1926), pp. 27–39 and 84 (Lord Finlay).

[3] See Lauterpacht, op. cit., pp. 369–408; id., 21 *B.Y.* (1944), 123–50; Chen, op. cit., pp. 201–16; Briggs, pp. 126–7; id., 34 *A.J.* (1940), 47–57; Hackworth i. 327–63; Whiteman ii. 48–59, 524–604; Lachs, 35 *B.Y.* (1959), 252–9.

[4] *Recognition*, p. 406. See also Oppenheim i. 146–8.

[5] See the *Arantzazu Mendi*, considered *infra*, pp. 103–5.

issue of statehood.[1] However, as a matter of optional bilateral relations and readiness to undertake normal relations, recognition depends precisely on intention.

9. *Collective Recognition: Membership of Organizations*[2]

Collective recognition may take the form of a joint declaration by a group of states, for example the Allied Supreme Council after the First World War, or of permitting a new state to become a party to a multilateral treaty of a political character, such as a peace treaty. The functioning of international organizations of the type of the League of Nations and United Nations provides a variety of occasions for recognition, of one sort or another, of states. Recognition by individual members of other members, or of non-members, may occur in the course of voting on admission to membership[3] and consideration of complaints involving threats to or breaches of the peace. Indeed, it has been argued that admission to the League and the United Nations entailed recognition by operation of law by all other members, whether or not they voted against admission. The position, supported by principle and state practice, would seem to be as follows. Admission to membership is *prima facie* evidence of statehood,[4] and non-recognizing members are at risk if they ignore the basic rights of existence of another state the object of their non-recognition. United Nations organs have consistently acted on the assumption that Israel is protected by the principles of the Charter on the use of force *vis-à-vis* her Arab neighbours. However, there is probably nothing in the Charter, or customary law apart from the Charter, which requires a non-recognizing state to give 'political' recognition and to enter into optional bilateral relations with a fellow member.[5]

[1] But not *incidental* relations like attendance at an international conference not primarily concerned with relations between the unrecognized state and non-recognizing state.

[2] See Briggs, pp. 106, 109–10, 117; id., *A.S.I.L. Proceedings* (1950), 169–81; Rosenne, 26 *B.Y.* (1949), 437–47; Kelsen, *Principles* (2nd ed.), pp. 398–9; Aufricht, 43 *A.J.* (1949), 679–704; Schachter, 25 *B.Y.* (1948), 109–15; Oppenheim i. 147; Rousseau iii. 548–51; Wright, 44 *A.J.* (1950), 548–59; Higgins, *The Development of International Law Through the Political Organs of the United Nations*, pp. 131–2, 140–4, 146–50; Jessup, *A Modern Law of Nations*, pp. 43–51; Lauterpacht, *Recognition*, pp. 400–3; Chen, op. cit., pp. 211–16, 221–3; Jennings, 121 Hague *Recueil* (1967, II), 352–4.

[3] Cf. *Cameroons* case (Prelim. Objections), I.C.J. Reports (1963), pp. 119–20, sep. op. of Judge Fitzmaurice.

[4] Apart from the possibility of error and bad faith affecting determinations by individual members, it is well known that membership both in the League and United Nations might be accorded to entities which, though states in one sense, were not possessed of all the legal capacities of statehood. On dependent states and components of federal states, see *supra*, pp. 77, 79.

[5] See Secretariat Memo., Doc. S/1466; Kelsen, *Law of the United Nations*, p. 946 n.

There are other elements in the situation in the case of organizations, adequate treatment of which cannot be given here. Can the Organization and its organs (including the Secretariat), *as such*, accord recognition? For the purposes of the Charter numerous determinations of statehood are called for: thus, for example, the U.N. Secretary-General acts as depositary for important treaties. Certainly such determinations are binding within the particular constitutional and functional context of the Charter. Whether, and to what extent, such determinations provide evidence of statehood for general purposes must depend on the relevance to general international law of the criteria employed in a given case.[1] Attitudes of non-recognition may depend on the political prejudices of individual members and the view that in any case the special qualifications for membership contained in Article 4 are not fulfilled: statehood may be necessary but is not sufficient. The approval of the credentials of state representatives by organs of the United Nations raises problems similar to, but not identical with, those concerning admission, since in practice the formal requirements for approving credentials have been linked with a challenge to the representation of a state by a particular government.[2]

10. *Non-Recognition and Sanctions*

One form of collective non-recognition commonly seen in practice is the resolution or decision of an organ of the League of Nations, and now the United Nations, based on a determination that an illegal act has occurred.[3] It is possible, though by no means necessary, to refer to such practice as collective non-recognition. There is no doubt a duty of states parties to a system of collective security or other multilateral conventions not to support or condone acts or situations contrary to the treaty concerned.[4] In some contexts such a duty will be carefully spelled out

[1] United Nations organs have been involved in varying degrees in the process of political creation of some states, viz., Indonesia, Israel, Libya, Republic of Korea (South Korea), and the Somali Republic. On the U.N. role in such cases see Chapter VIII.

[2] See Higgins, loc. cit.; Kelsen, loc. cit.

[3] See Lauterpacht, *International Law: Collected Papers* i (1970), p. 321; Charles de Visscher, *Théories et réalités en droit international public* (4th ed.), p. 266; Kelsen, *Principles* (2nd ed.), pp. 415–16; Mugerwa, in Sørensen, *Manual*, pp. 278–9; Whiteman v. 874–965; Radojković, *Mélanges Andrassy*, 225–36.

[4] Cf. the Stimson Doctrine of 1932 on non-recognition of illegal changes brought about by the use of force contrary to the Kellogg–Briand Pact. See Lauterpacht, op. cit., pp. 337–48.

and a duty of non-recognition may be associated with measures recommended or commanded by an organ of the United Nations as a form of sanction or enforcement against a wrongdoer. The Security Council resolutions of 1965 and 1966 characterized the Smith regime in Rhodesia as unlawful in terms of the Charter of the United Nations[1] and called upon all states not to recognize the illegal regime.[2] In this case, assuming that Rhodesia satisfies the normal criteria of statehood, particular matters of fact and law provide a basis for a duty of non-recognition. Similar issues arise in relation to the situation in South-West Africa (Namibia) following the termination of the Mandate.[3]

11. *Issues of Recognition before National Courts*[4]

Within the sphere of domestic law, recognition may have important practical consequences. Where the local courts are willing or are, as a matter of public law, obliged to follow the advice of the executive, the unrecognized state or government cannot claim immunity from the jurisdiction, obtain recognition for purposes of conflict of laws of its legislative and judicial acts or sue in the local courts as plaintiff. These are the normal consequences of non-recognition in British and American courts.[5] The attitude to questions of recognition adopted by municipal courts may thus reflect the policies of a particular state, and quite apart from this, the issue of recognition appears in relation to the special problems of private international law (conflict of laws). The manner in which municipal courts relate the generalities of pronouncements by the executive to specific cases is certainly a matter of interest, and it is proposed to examine some of the English cases on the subject. However, great caution is needed in using municipal cases to establish propositions about recognition in general international law. In particular, because of the constitutional position of the British and American courts in matters concerning foreign relations, it is unjustifiable to regard the cases as evidence supporting the constitutivist position.

[1] See 60 *A.J.* (1966), 921.

[2] On the U.N. resolutions concerning Rhodesia see Fawcett, 41 *B.Y.* (1965–6), 103–21; McDougal and Reisman, 62 *A.J.* (1968), 1–19; 71 *R.G.D.I.P.* (1967), 442–504.

[3] See the *Namibia Opinion,* I.C.J. Reports (1971), p. 16, where the legal consequences of non-recognition are examined.

[4] See generally Briggs, pp. 113–93; British International Law Cases i, vii and viii; Merrills, 20 *I.C.L.Q.* (1971), 476–99.

[5] Exceptionally an unrecognized state has been accorded procedural competence: *Wulfsohn* v. *R.S.F.S.R.*, 234 N.Y. 372 (1923); Briggs, p. 148; but the unrecognized government was not allowed to sue as plaintiff in *R.S.F.S.R.* v. *Cibrario*, 139 N.E. 259 (1923). Note the different approach to acts of the Executive in the *Zamora* [1916] 2 A.C. 77.

Luther v. *Sagor*.[1] The plaintiffs in this case were a company incorporated in the Russian Empire in 1898, and, it was held, retained Russian nationality at the time of the action. In pursuance of a decree of confiscation of June 1918 the Soviet authorities took possession of the plaintiff's factory and stock of manufactured wood. In August 1920 the defendants purchased a quantity of plywood boards from the Soviet authorities and imported them into England. The plaintiffs claimed a declaration that the goods were their property, an injunction restraining the defendants from dealing with them, and damages for conversion and detention of them. The defendants contended, *inter alia*, that the seizure and sale of the goods were acts of a sovereign state and had validly transferred the property in the goods to them. After judgment against the defendants in the court below, letters from the Foreign Office of April 1921 stated that the British Government recognized the Soviet Government as the '*de facto* Government of Russia', and that the former Provisional Government, recognized by the British Government, had been dispersed on 13 December 1917. The Court of Appeal found for the defendants. On the issues concerning recognition the Court held that for the present purpose no distinction was to be drawn between *de facto* and *de jure* recognition. Bankes, L.J., said:[2] 'The Government of this country having . . . recognized the Soviet Government as the Government really in possession of the powers of sovereignty in Russia, the acts of that Government must be treated by the courts of this country with all the respect due to the acts of a duly recognized foreign sovereign State.' Bankes, L.J., did not discuss retroactivity of the recognition as such, but looked at the evidence, including the information from the Foreign Office, and concluded that Soviet power dated from the end of 1917.[3] Warrington, L.J., observed:[4] 'Assuming that the acts in question are those of the government subsequently recognized I should have thought that in principle recognition would be retroactive at any rate to such date as our Government accept as that by which the government in question in fact established its authority.'

Haile Selassie v. *Cable and Wireless Ltd.* (*No.* 2).[5] On 9 May

[1] [1921] 3 K.B. 532. See also the *Gagara* [1919], P. 95, as to the status of a *de facto* government. [2] At p. 543. [3] At p. 544.

[4] At p. 549. See, to the same effect, Scrutton, L.J., at pp. 556–7. On retroactivity see also the *Jupiter* (no. 3) [1927] P. 122, 250; *Princess Paley Olga* v. *Weisz* [1929] 1 K.B. 718; *Lazard Bros.* v. *Midland Bank, Ltd.* [1933], A.C. 289.

[5] [1939] Ch. 182; Briggs, p. 213. See also *Haile Selassie* v. *Cable and Wireless, Ltd.* (No. 1) [1938] Ch. 545, 839.

1936 Italy proclaimed the annexation of Ethiopia following a war of conquest. Prior to this the plaintiff through an agent had made a contract with the defendants, and in 1937 he commenced proceedings to recover money due under the contract. Bennett, J., at first instance, held that the plaintiff, who was still recognized as *de jure* sovereign of Ethiopia by the United Kingdom, had not been divested of the right to sue for the debt in spite of the fact that British Government recognized the Italian Government 'as the Government *de facto* of virtually the whole of Ethiopia'. The defendants had relied, *inter alia*, on *Luther* v. *Sagor* to establish the exclusive power of the *de facto* government. Bennett, J., distinguished that decision,[1] confining it to acts of the *de facto* government in relation to persons or property in the territory which it is recognized as governing in fact. The present case was not concerned with acts in relation to persons or property in Ethiopia but with a debt, a chose in action, recoverable in England. While an appeal by the defendants was pending, the British Government recognized the King of Italy as *de jure* Emperor of Ethiopia, and it was not disputed that this related back to the date when recognition of the King of Italy as *de facto* sovereign occurred in December 1936. Thus, when the action commenced, the debt, which was a part of the public property of the state of Abyssinia, vested in the King of Italy and the appeal was allowed.[2]

The Arantzazu Mendi.[3] This case also concerned the comparative status of recognition *de facto* and *de jure*. The background was the civil war in Spain between rebel Nationalists under General Franco and the Republican Government which was finally overthrown in 1939. The *Arantzazu Mendi* was a Spanish vessel registered at Bilbao and at the material time was requisitioned by the Nationalist authorities exercising power in northern Spain. Her master and the managing director of the owners agreed to hold the vessel, which was in the London docks under arrest by the Admiralty Marshal, at the disposal of the Nationalist authorities. At that stage the Republican Govern-

[1] See also, at pp. 190–2, his comments on *Bank of Ethiopia* v. *National Bank of Egypt and Liguori* [1937] Ch. 513, and *Banco de Bilbao* v. *Sancha* [1938] 2 K.B. 176, which contain strong dicta favouring prevalence of the acts of the *de facto* government. Cf. Lauterpacht, *Recognition*, pp. 284–8. The substantial distinction from *Luther* v. *Sagor* was the provenance of the *de facto* government in the present case, an unlawful foreign invasion.

[2] The principle of retroactivity operated in a particular context, that of state succession in the matter of public debts.

[3] [1939] A.C. 256; [1939] 1 A.E.R. 719; Green, p. 125; Briggs, p. 142. In the Court of Appeal: [1939] P. 37; [1938] 4 A.E.R. 267.

ment issued the present writ, under which they claimed to have possession of the ship adjudged to them. The Nationalist authorities moved to set aside the writ on the ground that it impleaded a foreign sovereign state. The judge at first instance directed that inquiry be made of the Foreign Office as to the status of the Nationalist authorities. In reply[1] it was stated that the British Government recognized Spain as a foreign sovereign state and recognized the Goverment of the Spanish Republic as the only *de jure* Government of Spain or any part of it. It was also stated that:

5. His Majesty's Government recognises the Nationalist Government as a Government which at present exercises *de facto* administrative control over the larger portion of Spain.
6. His Majesty's Government recognizes that the Nationalist Government now exercises effective administrative control over all the Basque Provinces of Spain.
7. His Majesty's Government have not accorded any other recognition to the Nationalist Government.
8. The Nationalist Government is not subordinate to any other Government in Spain.
9. The question whether the Nationalist Government is to be regarded as that of a foreign Sovereign State appears to be a question of law to be answered in the light of the preceding statements and having regard to the particular issue with respect to which the question is raised.

The House of Lords held that the Foreign Office letter established that at the date of the writ the Nationalist Government of Spain was a foreign sovereign state and could not be impleaded. Lord Atkin said:[2]

> By 'exercising de facto administrative control' or 'exercising effective administrative control', I understand exercising all the functions of a sovereign government. . . . There is ample authority for the proposition that there is no difference for the present purposes between the recognition of a State de facto as opposed to de jure. All the reasons for immunity which are the basis of the doctrine in international law as incorporated in our law exist. . . .

This decision has some curious features.[3] Several sources of confusion existed. First, their Lordships[4] regarded the Foreign Office letter as conclusive as 'a statement of fact'. Yet they inter-

[1] See [1938] P. 233, 242. See also the letter before the Court of Appeal in *Banco de Bilbao* v. *Sancha* [1938] 2 K.B. 176.

[2] At pp. 264–5.

[3] For comment see Lauterpacht, 3 *Mod. L.R.* (1939), 1–20; id., *Recognition*, pp. 288–94, 365–8; Briggs, 33 *A.J.* (1939), 689–99.

[4] The other Lords substantially agreed with Lord Atkin.

preted and accepted it as conclusive on important issues of law. As a matter of interpretation, it was probably intended to be literally a statement of fact: its emphasis on 'administrative control' is significant. Moreover, at this time the Government had not 'recognized' the Franco authorities as *de facto* government of Spain.[1] Nor was the letter of the Foreign Office intended to be conclusive, as its terms (para. 9) indicate. In previous cases like the *Gagara*,[2] *Luther* v. *Sagor*,[3] and *Haile Selassie* v. *Cable and Wireless Ltd.* (*No.* 2)[4] the recognition *de facto* had occurred as a public political act and in respect of a government of the state as a whole. As a matter of interpretation, and in view of the still effective competition of the *de jure* government within the state, the Foreign Office letter did not necessarily accord equality to the governments. To equate a government in partial control of a state territory with the state itself in these circumstances was an odd procedure.[5] However, two other aspects of Lord Atkin's speech may be noticed as providing a more pragmatic basis for the decision. First, he seems to say that the rationale of sovereign immunity was in any case applicable on the facts: a proposition controversial in terms of international law, but not absurd, since a belligerent entity may soon become a *de jure* government. Secondly, and this point is connected with the foregoing, Lord Atkin states a principle of inadmissibility which is attractive:[6] 'The non-belligerent state which recognizes two Governments, one *de jure* and one *de facto*, will not allow them to transfer their quarrels to the area of the jurisdiction of its municipal courts.' Such a principle would obviate the dubious acceptance of belligerent entities engaged in civil war as soveriegn states for purposes of immunity from the jurisdiction.

Gdynia Ameryka Linie v. *Boguslawski*.[7] This case deals with the relations of *de facto* and *de jure* recognition in the context of retroactivity. On 28 June 1945 the Government of National Unity became *de facto* government of Poland, and at midnight, 5–6 July 1945, the British Government accorded *de jure* recognition to this government. Before this the exile Polish Government in London had been recognized *de jure* by the United

[1] See Briggs, 33 *A.J.* (1939), 689–99; 34 *A.J.* (1940), 47–57.

[2] *Supra*, p. 95, n. 2. [3] *Supra*, p. 102. [4] *Supra*, p. 102.

[5] One might add that this approach involved an assumption that the executive intended to act in breach of international law by giving such a measure of recognition to belligerents or insurgents.

[6] At p. 265.

[7] [1953] A.C. 11; [1952] 2 A.E.R. 470; Green, p. 127. See also Mann, 16 *Mod. L.R.* (1953), 266; Johnson, 29 *B.Y.* (1952), 462. In the Court of Appeal: [1951] 1 K.B. 162.

Kingdom. The issue was whether the *de jure* recognition of 5–6 July had retroactive effect on the validity of acts done by the London Government in respect of the Polish merchant marine and personnel under its control. The Foreign Office certificate stated that the question of the retroactive effect of recognition of a government was a question of law for decision by the courts. In spite of this, the House of Lords, with the exception of Lord Reid, regarded the case as one of construction of the certificate. This difficult exercise produced the conclusion that the recognition was not retroactive in spheres outside the effective control of the Polish Government in Warsaw, and the operative date was 5–6 July 1945. Lord Reid, and, it would seem, the other Law Lords, accepted retroactivity as a general principle, but, apart from the question of construction of the Foreign Office certificate, some of their Lordships considered that it should be confined to spheres of *de facto* control.[1] Such a principle runs contrary to the normal rules governing continuity of governments in respect of acts affecting nationals: full faith and credit should be accorded to jurisdiction on the plane of time. In any case the decision fails to provide a solution for the case where the metropolitan government purports to nullify acts of the exile government, no measures of this kind having been taken by the Warsaw Government.

Civil Air Transport Inc. v. *Central Air Transport Corp.*[2] In this case the Judicial Committee of the Privy Council dealt with very similar issues in much the same way as the Law Lords in the *Boguslawski* case. However, there was an interesting point of difference. In the *Civil Air Transport* case the aircraft concerned had fallen under the control of the Central People's Government of China as a result of the action within Hong Kong of pro-Communist employees of the Central Air Transport Corporation. Thus *de jure* recognition would preclude any other title. However, the Judicial Committee held that retroactivity does not validate acts which were unlawful under the local law, and the taking of possession by the employees was contrary to an ordinance issued by the Hong Kong authorities. The result is open to criticism, since it leaves questions on the international plane subject to a local law and introduces yet another qualification within the domestic law to the application of the principles of continuity and succession of states. As in the *Boguslawski* case,

[1] See Lord Porter at pp. 29–30 and 474–5 respectively; Lord Oaksey at pp. 39 and 477 respectively; Lord Reid at pp. 45–6 and 480 respectively.

[2] [1953] A.C. 70; [1952] 2 A.E.R. 733; Green, p. 131. See also Mann, op. cit.; Johnson, op. cit., p. 464; Anon., 4 *I.L.Q.* (1951), 159–77.

the *de jure* recognized government was not permitted to regulate the fate of national assets[1] by legislation not contrary to international law.

Carl Zeiss Stiftung v. *Rayner and Keeler, Ltd.* (*No* 2).[2] This case raised, as an interlocutory question, the issue of the validity of title to property based upon legislative and administrative acts of the German Democratic Republic (East Germany). The Foreign Office certificate available stipulated that since the withdrawal of Allied forces from the zone allocated to the U.S.S.R. in 1945 'Her Majesty's Government have recognized the State and government of the U.S.S.R. as *de jure* entitled to exercise governing authority in respect of that zone . . . and . . . have not recognized either *de jure* or *de facto* any other authority purporting to exercise governing authority in or in respect of the zone'. In the face of this the Court of Appeal[3] held that no effect could be given to the acts of the East German legal system. The House of Lords allowed the appeal by the East German foundation. In their view the case should be approached in terms of the conflict of laws and East Germany was a law district with an established legal system, even though the sovereignty on which this was based must be placed in the U.S.S.R.[4] In an *obiter dictum* of great interest Lord Wilberforce stated that in his view it was 'an open question', in English law, whether the courts must accept the doctrine of the absolute invalidity of all acts flowing from unrecognized governments.

The Rhodesian cases. Decisions of the Judicial Committee of the Privy Council concerning the validity of detentions in Rhodesia after the usurpation of power by the Smith regime in 1965,[5] and

[1] Cf. Denning, L.J., in the *Boguslawski* case [1951] 1 K.B. at p. 182; and Diplock, L.J., in *Buck* v. *A.-G.*, [1965] p. 145 1 A.E.R. at p. 887. See also *infra*, pp. 428–9, on the problem of property on the international plane.

[2] [1967] 1 A.C.853; [1966] 3 W.L.R. 125; Int. L.R., 43, 3; Green, p. 136. For comment see Jennings, 121 Hague *Recueil* (1967, II), 360–3; Greig, 83 *L.Q.R.* (1967), 96–145. Cf. *Salimoff* v. *Standard Oil Co.* (1933), 262 N.Y. 220; *Upright* v. *Mercury Business Machines Company*, 213 N.Y.S. (2d) 417 (1961); Int. L.R. 32, p. 65. See also *In re Al-Fin Corporation's Patent* [1970] 1 Ch. 160; *Hesperides Hotels Ltd.* v. *Aegean Turkish Holidays Ltd.* [1978] 1 Q.B. 205, C.A.; [1978] 3 W.L.R. 378 at p. 386, per Lord Wilberforce; and *supra*, p. 54.

[3] [1965] Ch. 596.

[4] This view has its difficulties since under the Allied arrangements of 1945 the four occupying Powers only had limited rights in their respective zones. United Kingdom declarations on the status of the East German Government were not intended to imply that the U.S.S.R. had sovereignty over East Germany. See Mann, 16 *I.C.L.Q.* (1967), p. 760 especially at pp. 773 (n. 73), 776, 788.

[5] *Madzimbamuto* v. *Lardner-Burke* [1967] A.C. 645; Int. L.R. 39, p. 61 at p. 374. The latter volume contains the decisions of the High Court, General and Appellate Divisions of Rhodesia. For comment see Eekelaar, 32 *Mod. L.R.* (1969), 19–34.

of the English courts as such concerning the recognition of Rhodesian divorce decrees,[1] raise substantially similar issues of policy to those presented by the *Carl Zeiss* proceedings. However, for English courts the major determinant has been the constitutional illegality of the Smith regime.[2] Thus even divorce decrees emanating from the Rhodesian courts were refused recognition by the English courts.[3]

[1] *Adams* v. *Adams* [1970] 3 A.E.R. 572, Sir Jocelyn Simon, P.

[2] See the Southern Rhodesia Act, 1965.

[3] See the Southern Rhodesia (Matrimonial Jurisdiction) Order 1970; S.I. 1970 No. 1540, which extends jurisdiction with respect to persons domiciled or resident in Southern Rhodesia.

PART III
TERRITORIAL SOVEREIGNTY

CHAPTER VI

TERRITORIAL SOVEREIGNTY

1. *The Concept of Territory*

IN spatial terms the law knows four types of regime: territorial sovereignty, territory not subject to the sovereignty of any state or states and which possesses a status of its own (mandated and trust territories, for example), the *res nullius*,[1] and the *res communis*.[2] Territorial sovereignty extends principally over land territory, the territorial sea appurtenant to the land, and the seabed and subsoil of the territorial sea.[3] The concept of territory includes islands, islets, rocks and reefs.[4] A *res nullius* consists of the same subject-matter legally susceptible to acquisition by states but not as yet placed under territorial sovereignty. The *res communis*, consisting of the high seas and also outer space, is not capable of being placed under state sovereignty.[5] In accordance with customary international law and the dictates of convenience, the airspace above and subsoil beneath state territory, the *res nullius*, and the *res communis* are included in each category.

2. *Sovereignty and Jurisdiction*

The state territory and its appurtenances (airspace and territorial sea), together with the government and population within its frontiers, comprise the physical and social manifestations of the primary type of international legal person, the state. The legal competence of states and the rules for their protection depend on and assume the existence of a stable, physically delimited, homeland.[6] The competence of states in respect of their

[1] See *infra*, p. 180. [2] See *infra*, p. 181.

[3] See further *infra*, pp. 120–3 on the parts of the territory of a state.

[4] See 67 *A.J.* (1973), 118–19; and the Award in the *Beagle Channel Arbitration*, 18 April 1977, Dispositif of the Decision.

[5] On the legal regime of the *res communis* see *infra*, p. 181, on the high seas, *infra*, pp. 237 seq.; on outer space, *infra*, pp. 266–70. See further *infra* pp. 233–6.

[6] On legal personality, see *supra*, Chapter III; on the criteria of statehood, *supra*, Chapter IV.

territory is usually described in terms of sovereignty and jurisdiction and the student is faced with a terminology which is not employed very consistently in legal sources such as works of authority or the opinions of law officers, or by statesmen, who naturally place political meanings in the foreground. The terminology as used by lawyers is also unsatisfactory in that the complexity and diversity of the rights, duties, powers, liberties, and immunities of states are obscured by the liberal use of omnibus terms like 'sovereignty' and 'jurisdiction'. At the same time, a degree of uniformity of usage does exist and may be noticed. The normal complement of state rights, the typical case of legal competence, is described commonly as 'sovereignty': particular rights, or accumulations of rights quantitatively less than the norm, are referred to as 'jurisdiction'.[1] In brief, 'sovereignty' is legal shorthand for legal personality of a certain kind, that of statehood; 'jurisdiction' refers to particular aspects of the substance, especially rights (or claims), liberties, and powers. Immunities are described as such.[2] Of particular significance is the criterion of consent. State A may have considerable forces stationed within the frontiers of state B. State A may also have exclusive use of a certain area of state B, and exclusive jurisdiction over its own forces. If, however, these rights exist with the consent of the host state then state A has no sovereignty over any part of state B.[3] In such a case there has been a derogation from the sovereignty of state B, but state A does not gain sovereignty as a consequence. It would be otherwise if state A had been able to claim that exclusive use of an area of state B was hers *as sovereign*, as of right by customary law and independently of the consent of any state.

3. *Sovereignty and Ownership*

The analogy between sovereignty and ownership is evident and, with certain reservations, useful. For the moment it is sufficient to establish certain distinctions. The legal competence of a state includes considerable liberties in respect of internal organization and the disposal of territory. This general power of government, administration, and disposition is *imperium*, a

[1] See Verzijl, *International Law in Historical Perspective*, i (1968), 256–92. On the various uses of 'jurisdiction', see *infra*, pp. 289–90, 298. On the concept of 'sovereign rights' in the Continental Shelf Convention of 1958 see *infra*, pp. 222–6.

[2] See *infra*, Chapter XV, on the jurisdictional immunities of states.

[3] See McNair, *Opinions* i. 69–74.

capacity recognized and delineated by international law. *Imperium* is thus distinct from *dominium* either in the form of public ownership of property within the state[1] or in the form ot private ownership recognized as such by the law.[2]

4. *Administration and Sovereignty*

It may happen that the process of government over an area, with the concomitant privileges and duties, falls into the hands of another state. Thus after the defeat of Nazi Germany in the Second World War the four major Allied powers assumed supreme power in Germany.[3] The legal competence of the German state did not, however, disappear. What occurred is akin to legal representation or agency of necessity. The German state continued to exist, and, indeed, the legal basis of the occupation depended on its continued existence. The very considerable derogation of sovereignty involved in the assumption of powers of government by foreign states, without the consent of Germany, did not constitute a transfer of sovereignty. A similar case, recognized by the customary law for a very long time, is that of the belligerent occupation of enemy territory in time of war.[4] The important features of 'sovereignty' in such cases are the continued existence of a legal personality and the attribution of territory to that legal person and not to holders for the time being.

5. *Sovereignty and Responsibility. The Ownership of Rights*

A possible source of confusion is the fact that sovereignty is not only used as a description of legal personality accompanied by independence[5] but also as a reference to various types of rights, indefeasible except by special grant, in the patrimony of a sovereign state, for example the 'sovereign rights' a coastal state has over the resources of the continental shelf,[6] or a prescriptive,

[1] Or elsewhere: cf. the John F. Kennedy Memorial Act, 1964, Sect. 1. But see *infra*, pp. 342, 428.

[2] Cf. Lauterpacht, *International Law: Collected Papers* i (1970), 367–70.

[3] For the purpose of argument it is assumed that the form which the occupation took was lawful. See Jennings, 23 *B.Y.* (1946), 112–41, and cf. *infra*, p. 376.

[4] See *L.* v. *N.*, *Ann. Digest* 14 (1947), no. 110. Another instance is provided by the situation in which the ceding state still administers the ceded territory, by agreement with the state taking cession: *Gudder Singh and Another* v. *The State*, Int. L.R. 20 (1953), 145. Further examples of delegated powers: Int. L.R. 19 (1952), nos. 32 and 33 (Italian Court of Cassation *in re* Italian administration of Trieste and Libya).

[5] See *supra*, pp. 80–1.

[6] At least according to the Convention on the Continental Shelf, see *infra*, p. 222.

or historic, right to fish in an area of territorial sea belonging to another state, or a prescriptive right of passage between the territorial homeland and an enclave.[1] Exercise of rights which are 'owned' and, therefore, in this special sense, 'sovereign' is not to be confused with *territorial* sovereignty. Thus a right of passage does not necessarily confer sovereignty over any particular area of territory.

6. *Administration Divorced from State Sovereignty*

Whilst the concept of territorial sovereignty normally applies in relation to states, there is the likelihood that international life will comprehend situations in which international organizations not only administer territory in the capacity of legal representatives[2] but also assume legal responsibility for territory in respect of which no state has territorial sovereignty.[3] Such a situation arose in 1966 when the General Assembly terminated the Mandate of South West Africa.[4] The nature of the legal relation of an organization to the territory would cause few difficulties of substance, but some difficulties of terminology can be foreseen solely because terms and concepts like 'sovereignty' and 'title' are historically associated with the patrimony of states with definable sovereigns.

7. *Territory the Sovereignty of which is Indeterminate*[5]

It may happen, and recent history has provided some interesting examples, that a piece of territory not a *res nullius* has no determinate sovereign. The situation envisaged is not that in which two states have conflicting legal claims to territory. In such a case a settlement of the dispute does not, apart from special agreement, have retroactive effect. If a disputed parcel of territory previously in the possession of state A is declared to belong to state B, it does not follow that, prior to the execution of the

[1] Cf. *infra*, pp. 374, 377. [2] See Chapter XXVI, section 5.

[3] The problem of substance is whether organizations have the capacity to acquire territory: see *infra*, pp. 175–9. In the case of the mandate and trust international organizations have assumed a large measure of legal responsibility in relation to territory: see *infra*, pp. 181–2.

[4] See *infra*, Chapter VIII, section 1.

[5] Pending final settlement territory the subject of dispute may be placed under a form of *condominium*: see the *Lighthouses* arbitration, Int. L.R. 23 (1956), p. 659 at pp. 664–6, 668–9; Oppenheim i. 454; Guggenheim i. 436; and *infra*, p. 118. It is not always obvious whether a particular disposition is final or not: see *Ditmar and Linde* v. *Ministry of Agriculture*, *Ann. Digest* 8 (1935–7), no. 52.

settlement, the sovereignty in respect of the land was indeterminate. The parcel was, until the settlement, the subject-matter of a claim, but its sovereignty was not, as a consequence, indeterminate'. Sovereignty may also be indeterminate in so far as the process of secession[1] may not be seen to be complete at any precise point in time.

Existing cases spring chiefly from the renunciation of sovereignty by the former holder and the coming into being of an interregnum with disposition postponed until a certain condition is fulfilled or the states having power of disposition for various reasons omit to exercise a power or fail to exercise it validly. For example, in a peace treaty Japan renounced all right to Formosa. However, Formosa has not been the subject of any act of disposition; it has not been transferred to any state. In the view of the British Government:[2] 'Formosa and the Pescadores are . . . territory the *de jure* sovereignty over which is uncertain or undetermined.' Of course, the Chinese claim may become consolidated by acquiescence on the part of other states.

8. *Terminable and Reversionary Rights*[3]

Territorial sovereignty may be defeasible in certain circumstances by operation of law, for example by fulfilment of a condition subsequent or the failure of the condition under which sovereignty was transferred where there is an express or implied condition that title should revert to the grantor. The first situation is exemplified by the status of Monaco,[4] the independence of which exists subject to there being no vacancy in the Crown of Monaco. Until such a condition operates the tenant has an interest equal in all respects to that of sovereignty.

The second type of case gives rise to many problems. On one view, the system of mandates created after the First World War

[1] i.e., rebellion having as its object the formation of a new state or union with another state. Cf. Jennings, *Acquisition of Territory*, pp. 7–8.

[2] Written answer by the Secretary of State, 4 February 1955, in 5 *I.C.L.Q.* (1956), 413–14. Cf. ibid. 8 (1959), 166. Whether there is a legal duty to transfer to China on the part of certain states is a separate question which cannot be pursued here. See also Jain, 57 *A.J.* (1963), 25–45. For further examples of a similar kind: 6 *I.C.L.Q.* (1957), 513–16; and *Contemporary Practice of the U.K.* (1962), i. 43. Cf. *De Wurts* v. *Wurts*, *Ann. Digest* 6 (1931–2), no. 52; *Re An Inquiry by the Italian Ministry for Foreign Affairs*, Int. L.R. 26 (1958, II), 68, and *Weiss* v. *Inspector-General of the Police*, ibid., p. 210 (and see note at p. 221). See also *infra*, pp. 175–9, on administration *ad interim* by the United Nations.

[3] Students are warned that no precise parallel with concepts of the English law of real property is intended.

[4] See Verzijl, *International Law in Historical Perspective* ii (1969), 459–61.

provides a useful example. The mandatories, or administering states for the various ex-German territories, were nominated by the five principal Allied and associated powers, in whose favour Germany had renounced sovereignty over these territories in the Treaty of Versailles. By reason of the facts that the principal Allied powers had taken the cession from Germany, and that it was they who took the decision to place the territories under mandate, it has been concluded[1] that in this capacity, 'the Principal Powers retained, and may still retain on a dormant basis, a residual or reversionary interest in the actual territories concerned except where these have attained self-government or independence'. The precise nature of such reversionary interests will depend on the facts of each case, but it seems clear that they do not necessarily amount to sovereignty but rather take the form of a power of disposition, or of intervention or veto in any process of disposition.

The concept of reversion is to be distinguished from that of 'residual sovereignty', considered subsequently, the principal point of difference consisting in the fact that reversion involves a change of sovereignty, whilst in the case of 'residual sovereignty', the territorial sovereign has not lost status as such.

9. *Residual Sovereignty*

Occupation of foreign territory in time of peace may occur on the basis of a treaty with the territorial sovereign. The grantee under the treaty may receive very considerable powers of administration amounting to a delegation of the exercise of many of the powers of the territorial sovereign to the possessor for a particular period. Thus, in Article 3 of the Treaty of Peace of 8 September 1951, Japan agreed that, pending any action to place the Ryukyu Islands under the trusteeship system of the United Nations, 'The United States will have the right to exercise all and any powers of administration, legislation and jurisdiction over the territory and inhabitants of these islands, including their territorial waters'. In 1951 the United States Secretary of State referred to the 'residual sovereignty' of Japan over the islands. United States courts, in holding that inhabitants of the Ryukyus were not nationals of the United States and that the islands were a

[1] See the joint dissenting opinion of Judges Spender and Fitzmaurice in the *South West Africa* cases (Preliminary Objections), I.C.J. Reports (1962), p. 482, footnote; and see ibid., p. 496. On the power of disposition in such a case, *infra*, p. 175.

'foreign country' in connexion with the application of various United States statutes, have referred to the '*de facto* sovereignty' of the United States and to the Japanese interest in terms of 'residual sovereignty' or '*de jure* sovereignty'.[1] Restoration of full Japanese sovereignty was the subject of bilateral agreements of 1968, 1969 and 1970.[2]

Referring to similar cases Oppenheim[3] describes the grantor's interest as 'nominal sovereignty', and points out that this type of interest may have practical consequences. For example, in the case concerning the *Lighthouses in Crete and Samos* (1937)[4] the Permanent Court of International Justice held that in 1913 the islands of Crete and Samos were under the sovereignty of Turkey, which therefore had the power to grant or renew concessions with regard to the islands. As regards Crete the Court said:

> Notwithstanding its autonomy, Crete had not ceased to be a part of the Ottoman Empire. Even though the Sultan had been obliged to accept important restrictions on the exercise of his rights of sovereignty in Crete, that sovereignty had not ceased to belong to him, however it might be qualified from a juridical point of view.

Another practical consequence of the grantor's interest in such a case is the continuance of his right of disposition—a far from insignificant proprietary right. Thus in the *Lighthouses* case the Court pointed out that evidence for the existence of Turkish sovereignty consisted, in part, in the fact that Turkey was able, subsequently, to carry out an act of disposition in regard to the islands by ceding them to Greece.

10. *International Leases*

The heading, it must be emphasized, is more a concession to usage than the product of legal analysis. The use of the term is excusable, but it cannot be regarded as more than a superficial guide to the nature of the interest concerned: each case depends on its particular facts and especially on the precise terms of the

[1] See *Brewer* v. *United States*, *Ann. Digest* 15 (1948), no. 169; *Cobb* v. *United States*, Int. L.R. 18 (1951), no. 173; *United States* v. *Ushi Shiroma*, Int. L.R. 21 (1954), 82; *Burna* v. *United States*, Int. L.R. 24 (1957), 89; 70 *R.G.D.I.P.* (1966), 160.

[2] *Int. Leg. Materials*, vii (1968), 554; 74 *R.G.D.I.P.* (1970) 717; 64 *A.J.* (1970), 647.

[3] i. 455.

[4] P.C.I.J., Ser. A/B, no. 71; World Court Reports iv. 241; *Ann. Digest* 8 (1935–7), no. 49. See also Lauterpacht, *International Law: Collected Papers* i (1970), 372–3; id., 62 Hague *Recueil* (1937, IV), 325–6; and the separate opinion of Judge Hudson in the case, P.C.I.J., Ser. A/B, no. 71, p. 117 at pp. 126–30.

grant. Certainly there is a presumption that the grantor retains residual sovereignty. By a Convention signed on 6 March 1898 China 'cedes to Germany on lease, provisionally for ninety-nine years, both sides of the entrance to the Bay of Kiao-Chau'. Article 3 of the Convention provides that China 'will abstain from exercising rights of sovereignty in the ceded territory during the term of the lease . . .'. In this case China clearly retained residual sovereignty, and the grantee has, for example, no right to dispose of the territory to a third state.[1]

The difficulties concerning the nature of the grantor's interest in this type of case, new examples of which are unlikely to arise, are not present in the amenity providing 'lease' of a railway station or a military, naval, or air base.[2] Here the rights conferred by a treaty, executive agreement, or other inter-governmental agreement are of a more limited nature: consequently the grantor has a right to revoke the 'contractual licence', and, after a reasonable time has elapsed, force may be employed to evict the trespasser.

11. *Use and Possession Granted in Perpetuity*

By a Convention of 18 November 1903 Panama granted to the United States 'in perpetuity the use, occupation and control of a zone of land and land under water for the construction . . . and protection' of the Panama Canal, ten miles in width.[3] In such a case the residual sovereignty remains with the grantor. How-

[1] In 1919 the rights under the lease were assigned to Japan. The lease was terminated in 1922. See generally Basdevant, *Dictionnaire, sub tit.* 'Bail'; Lauterpacht, *Private Law Sources and Analogies of International Law*, pp. 183–90; Verzijl, *International Law in Historical Perspective* iii (1970), 397–408; Brierly, pp. 189–90; Oppenheim i. 455–7; Lauterpacht, *International Law: Collected Papers* i (1970), 372; Guggenheim i. 402. See further *State of Madras* v. *Cochin Coal Co.*, Int. L.R. 26 (1958, II), 116. The British lease of territory on the Chinese mainland north of Kowloon expires in 1997. Certain types of 'lease' were, in fact and law, cessions of territory: see *Cook* v. *Sprigg* [1899] A.C. 572; and *Secretary of State for India* v. *Sardar Rustam Khan*, *Ann. Digest* 10 (1941–2), no. 21. See also *British and Foreign State Papers*, vol. 162, p. 92. On the dispute between the Philippines and Malaysia over Sabah (North Borneo) see 10 *Malaya L.R.* (1968), 306; 2 *Phil. Journ. of Int. L.* (1963), *passim*; Ortiz, *Legal Aspects of the North Borneo Question* (1964); Marston, *Australian Y.B.I.L.* (1967), 103; Rousseau, 66 *R.G.D.I.P.* (1962), 806.

[2] See, for example, the Agreement of 27 March, 1941 between the United States and the United Kingdom: 35 *A.J.* (1941), Suppl., pp. 134–59.

[3] See Hudson, *Cases*, pp. 222–3; Oppenheim i. 458; Lauterpacht, *Collected Papers*, i. 372; *In re Cia. de Transportes de Gelabert*, *Ann. Digest* 9 (1938–40), no. 45 (Panama, Supreme Court; held, that Panama retained 'its jurisdictional rights of sovereignty' in the airspace of the Canal Zone). Cf. *Stafford Allen & Sons, Ltd.* v. *Pacific Steam Navigation Co.* [1956] 1 W.L.R. 629; [1956] 2 A.E.R. 716; Int. L.R. 23 (1956), 116, C.A. The Panama Canal Treaty signed on 7 September 1977 will, if it is ratified, supersede the Convention of 1903: see 16 *Int. Leg. Materials* (1977), 1022.

ever, not only has the exercise of all rights of jurisdiction been delegated but the grantor might seem to have renounced even the right of disposition. A licence can be terminated; a grant in perpetuity by definition cannot. However, the grantee's right rests on an agreement and would be defeated by a disposition of the residual sovereignty to a third state in regard to which the grant was *res inter alios acta*. In other words, the restriction on disposition consists in an inability to grant similar rights to another state: the residual sovereignty remains transferable and the grantee has no power of disposition.

12. *Demilitarized and Neutralized Territory*

Restrictions on use of territory, accepted by treaty, do not affect territorial sovereignty as a title, even when the restriction concerns matters of national security and preparation for defence.[1]

13. *The Concept of Territory: the Principle of Effective Control Applied by National Courts*

National courts, though concerned indirectly with the large problems of residual sovereignty, territory the sovereignty of which is indeterminate, and the like, are usually presented with questions of narrow aspect which invite a pragmatic approach. Thus in a treaty or statute the term 'territory' may connote jurisdiction.[2] Moreover, courts are very ready to equate 'territory' with the actual and effective exercise of jurisdiction even when it is clear that the state exercising jurisdiction has not been the beneficiary of any lawful and definitive act of disposition. In the *Schtraks*[3] case the Israeli Government asked for the extradition of the appellant in pursuance of an agreement with the United Kingdom Government that the Extradition Act, 1870, should apply subject to the terms of the Israel (Extradition) Order, 1960. The appellant, having been committed to prison to await extradition, applied for a writ of habeas corpus on the grounds, *inter alia*, that Jerusalem, where the offences charged were alleged to have been committed, was not 'territory' within

[1] See *A.-G. of Israel* v. *El-Turani*, Int. L.R. 18 (1951), no. 39.

[2] *R.* v. *Governor of Brixton Prison, ex parte Minervini* [1959] 1 Q.B. 155; [1958] 3 W.L.R. 559, where the Div. Ct. held that 'territory' in a treaty of extradition meant jurisdiction and therefore included ships of the other party.

[3] [1964] A.C. 556; [1962] 3 W.L.R. 1013; [1962] 3 A.E.R. 529; Int. L.R. 33, p. 319. But cf. *In Re Ning Yi-Ching and Others* (1939), 56 T.L.R. 3; *Ann. Digest* 9 (1938–40), no. 44.

the meaning of the agreement. The basis of the argument was the fact that the United Kingdom Government did not recognize the *de jure* sovereignty of Israel in Jerusalem but only its *de facto* authority. On this point the House of Lords held that the instruments concerned were not concerned with sovereignty but with territory in which territorial jurisdiction is exercised.[1] Viscount Radcliffe[2] concluded that 'territory' in the present context included whatever is under the state's effective jurisdiction.

Such an approach avoids a legal vacuum in such territories and provides sensible solutions without the necessity for lengthy inquiry into roots of title,[3] or the legal quality of a protectorate or mandate. Further, the equation of territory and jurisdiction is theoretically sound. Abstract discussion as to whether ships, aircraft, territorial sea, and embassies are 'territory' lacks reality, since in a legal context the word denotes a particular sphere of legal competence and not a geographical concept. Ultimately territory cannot be distinguished from jurisdiction for certain purposes. Both terms refer to legal powers, and, when a concentration of such powers occurs, the analogy with territorial sovereignty justifies the use of the term 'territory' as a form of shorthand. Other applications of the principle of effective jurisdiction, outside the courts, may be found. For example, consular exequaturs[4] in respect of leased territory[5] are issued by the lessee state and not the grantor with residual sovereignty.[6]

14. *Condominia*

In spite of the influence of Austin and Salmond, it may be asserted that sovereignty is divisible both as a matter of principle and as a matter of experience. International law recognizes the *condominium*, of which Oppenheim[7] remarks: 'In this case a piece of territory consisting of land or water is under the *Joint Tenancy* of two or more States, these several States exercising

[1] Lord Reid at pp. 579, 1022, 532, respectively.

[2] Viscount Radcliffe at pp. 587, 1029, 537, respectively.

[3] See also, on the practical implication of the principles of non-recognition, *supra*, pp. 93–4.

[4] The evidence of official permission for admittance of a consul, granted by the Head of the admitting state.

[5] See *supra*, p. 115. [6] See Hackworth ii. 547–8.

[7] i. 453. See also Hudson, *Cases*, pp. 280–3; Verzijl, *International Law in Historical Perspective* iii (1970), 429–43; Lauterpacht, *International Law: Collected Papers* i (1970), 370–2; O'Connell, 43 *B.Y.* (1968–9), pp. 71–145; and Suzanne Bastid, 107 Hague *Recueil* (1962, III), 391–5; Rousseau iii. 22–30. Basdevant, *Dictionnaire*, p. 145, gives a wide definition.

sovereignty conjointly over it, and over the individuals living thereon.' Great Britain and Egypt had *condominium* over the Sudan between 1898 and 1956. Worthy of comment is the fact that the theoretical consequences of this type of regime may be qualified by agreement.[1] Moreover, national legislation and jurisdiction will not automatically extend to territory under the special regime of *condominium*. On occasion it has been suggested that in certain cases, for example with reference to land-locked lakes and bays[2] bounded by the territory of two or more states,[3] the riparian states have *condominium* over the area by the operation of law. This is doubtful, but it is possible for the regime to arise by prescription.[4]

In any case, as Professor Parry has pointed out,[5] the particular regime will depend on the facts of each case, and it is unsafe to rely on any general theory of the community of property. Thus the analogies of joint tenancy and tenancy in common do not give satisfactory results. This type of problem concerns a particular status *in rem*,[6] and the fact that one state cannot alienate the territory without the consent of the other or others[7] does not justify the application of the general category of joint tenancy, as opposed to tenancy in common.

15. *Vassalage, Suzerainty, and Protection*

Condominium is a case of sovereignty which is jointly exercised by two or more states on a basis of equality. Historically, other types of shared sovereignty have occurred in which the dominant partner, state A, has acquired a significant role in the government of state B, and particularly in the taking of executive decisions relating to the conduct of foreign affairs. The legal aspects of the relationship will vary with the circumstances of

[1] Thus, in the case of the New Hebrides, the two sovereigns, Great Britain and France, exercise a separate jurisdiction over their own (metropolitan) subjects. The legal regime may be used to deal with problems of neighbourhood relating to frontier rivers and the like: *Dutch-Prussian Condominium* (1816) case, *Ann. Digest* 6 (1931–2), no. 23. See also E. H. Brown, *The Saudi Arabia Kuwait Neutral Zone* (1963).

[2] See *Ann. Digest* 7 (1933–4), no. 53, for decisions on the position of Lake Constance.

[3] See *infra*, p. 123. [4] On which see *infra*, pp. 156 seq.

[5] *Nationality and Citizenship Laws of the Commonwealth and the Republic of Ireland* (1957), p. 18, n. 13.

[6] Cf. *International Status of South-West Africa*, I.C.J. Reports (1950), p. 128.

[7] See *Costa Rica* v. *Nicaragua* (1916), and *El Salvador* v. *Nicaragua* (1917), decisions of the Central American Court of Justice, cited by Parry, loc. cit., reported in 11 *A.J.* (1917), 181, 674, and discussed by Lauterpacht, *Private Law Sources and Analogies of International Law* (1927), pp. 288–9.

each case, and not too much can be deduced from the terminology of the relevant instruments.[1] It may be that the protected community or 'state' is a part of state A and, as a colonial protectorate, has no international legal personality, although for purposes of internal law it will have a special status.[2] However, the protected state may retain a measure of externally effective legal personality, although the exercise of its legal capacities be delegated to state A. In this latter case treaties by state A will not necessarily apply to state B. However, for certain purposes, including the law of neutrality and war, state B may be regarded as an agent of state A. Thus if state A declares war the protected state may be treated as belligerent also, although much will depend on the precise nature of the relations between states A and B.[3] These questions, though important for the determination of the legal status of territory, pertain closely to the question of the independence of states, considered previously.[4]

16. *Mandates and Trust Territories*

The nature of state authority over mandate and trust territories is not describable in terms of sovereignty, and the legal restraints on the exercise of power in such territories do not in general protect the ordinary legal interests of other states. This type of regime has close relations with the problem of representation in international law.[5]

17. *Parts of State Territory*

Apart from land permanently above low-water mark, territorial sovereignty may be exercised over various geographical features associated with or analogous to land territory. Permanence, accessibility, and natural appurtenance are the essential qualities. By reason of their practical importance certain forms of the sub-

[1] See Verzijl, *International Law in Historical Perspective* ii (1969), 339–454; Rousseau ii. 276–300; Oppenheim i. 188–96; and *supra*, pp. 77–9. On the unique co-seigneury of Andorra see *Cruzel* v. *Massip*, Int. L.R. 39, p. 412; *Re Boedecker and Ronski*, ibid., 44, p. 176; Verzijl, op. cit., iii (1970), 3, 325; Rousseau ii. 342–7; Crawford, 55 *R.D.I.* (Sottile), 258–72.

[2] See *Ex parte Mwenya* [1960] 1 Q.B. 241; [1959] 3 W.L.R. 509, C.A. (held, the sovereignty of the British Crown over the protectorate of Northern Rhodesia appeared to be indistinguishable in legal effect from that of a British colony or country acquired by conquest). See, however, Chapter XXIV, section 9, on self-determination.

[3] Cf. *Nationality Decrees in Tunis and Morocco* (1923), *supra*, p. 78. On other examples see Whiteman i. 431–53.

[4] *Supra*, pp. 76 seq.

[5] For discussion of various aspects of mandates and trust territories see *infra*, pp. 181–2, Chapter XX, section 14; Chapter XXIV, section 7.

ject-matter of sovereignty will be treated separately and in a more appropriate context. Thus discussion of the territorial sea occurs in Chapter IX. The consideration of specialized rights over the high seas in Chapters IX and X involves reference to legally protected interests, particularly in regard to the continental shelf,[1] proximate in varying degrees to the concept of territorial sovereignty. Other questions, for example international rivers, canals, and straits, commonly discussed in the present context, are reserved for Chapter XII on common amenities and co-operation in the use of resources. The topics which remain, though somewhat disparate, may be considered conveniently together.

Territorial subsoil. The rule universally accepted is that the subsoil belongs to the state which has sovereignty over the surface.[2]

Airspace.[3] The airspace superjacent to land territory, internal waters, and the territorial sea is in law a part of state territory, and as a consequence other states may only use such airspace for navigation or other purposes with the agreement of the territorial sovereign. With the development of aviation in the early years of the present century, and the impact of the First World War, the customary law emerged in a relatively short period.[4] Its content, the application of the maxim of private law *cujus est solum est usque ad caelum et ad inferos*, was dictated primarily by the concern of states for national security and the integrity of neutral states in time of armed conflict. To this factor may be added the desire to prevent aerial reconnaissance by potential enemies, a fear of surprise attack, and the economic value of granting the right to fly to foreign commercial agencies. Consequently, the law does not permit a right of innocent passage, even through airspace over the territorial sea.[5] Aerial trespass may be

[1] *Infra*, pp. 222–8; see also pp. 233–4 on ice territory, seabed and marine subsoil, and artificial constructions on the seabed, and pp. 171–2 on sedentary fisheries. For the distinction between territorial sovereignty and the ownership of rights see *supra*, p. 111; on 'international servitudes', *infra*, pp. 372–5.

[2] See Verzijl, *International Law in Historical Perspective* iii (1970), 47–51. For some interesting analogues in the law of trespass see Prosser, *Handbook of the Law of Torts* (3rd ed.), p. 73. See also *infra*, p. 124, on the concept of appurtenance.

[3] On jurisdiction over aircraft see *infra*, pp. 319–20. On the nationality of aircraft see *infra*, p. 426. Much of the 'law of the air' is devoted to the problems of private law, and chiefly conflict of laws, relating to international air traffic. On the public international law aspects see Oppenheim i. 516–30; Jennings, 22 *B.Y.* (1945), 191–209; id., 75 Hague *Recueil* (1949, II), 513–96; Goedhuis, 81 Hague *Recueil* (1952, II), 204–305; Johnson, *Rights in Air Space* (1965).

[4] For treaties embodying the rule, *infra*, p. 184, n. 3.

[5] Nor is there a right of innocent passage for aircraft through international straits apart from treaty. If the negotiating text before the Law of the Sea Conference in 1979 is adopted, the position of passage through straits will be considerably modified by the concept of 'transit passage': see *infra*, pp. 282–3.

met with appropriate measures of prevention, but does not normally justify instant attack with the object of destroying the trespasser.[1]

Two other issues must be noticed. First, the beginning of space exploration by satellites has led to discussion of the question of determining the outer limit of state sovereignty.[2] Secondly, airspace is generally assumed to be appurtenant to land territory and territorial waters.[3] It follows that a disposition of territory includes the superjacent airspace. However, the principle of appurtenance will not necessarily apply where the grantee is not to receive sovereignty but the possession and use of territory acknowledged to remain under the sovereignty of the grantor.[4]

Internal waters.[5] Lakes and rivers included in the land territory of a state, as well as waters on the landward side of baselines from which the breadth of the territorial sea is calculated, comprise internal waters subject to state sovereignty. Large bodies of water such as land-locked seas[6] and historic bays[7] come within this category. The legal regime is that of territorial sovereignty, but in the case of ports, rivers, and canals, special questions arise relating to the sharing of amenities: these will be considered in Chapter XII. In this connexion it is convenient to refer to the Convention on the Territorial Sea and Contiguous Zone of 1958,[8] which provides in Article 5:

1. Waters on the landward side of the baseline of the territorial sea form part of the internal waters of the State.
2. Where the establishment of a straight baseline in accordance with article 4[9] has the effect of enclosing as internal waters areas which previously had been considered as part of the territorial sea or of the high seas, a right of innocent passage, as provided in articles 11 to 23, shall exist in these waters.

It is to be emphasized that for purposes of international law the distinction between internal waters and territorial sea is important, in spite of the fact that the legal interest of the coastal

[1] See Lissitzyn, 47 *A.J.* (1953), 559–89; Anon., 61 *Columbia L.R.* (1961), 1074–102.

[2] See further *infra*, pp. 266–8.

[3] On the principle of appurtenance, *infra*, p. 124.

[4] Cf. *In re Cia. de Transportes de Gelabert, Ann. Digest* 9 (1938–40), no. 45.

[5] Otherwise described as national or interior waters. Generally see McDougal and Burke, *The Public Order of the Oceans*, pp. 89–173. A sea is not 'landlocked' in this sense if it is surrounded by the territory of two or more international persons: see *A.M.S.S.V.M. & Co.* v. *The State of Madras*, Int. L.R. 20 (1953), p. 167 and the note at p. 169. Distinguish also 'closed seas', on which *infra*, pp. 237–8.

[6] *Infra*, p. 123. [7] *Infra*, pp. 170–1.

[8] See *infra*, p. 183. [9] See *infra*, p. 190.

state amounts to sovereignty in either case. Thus no right of innocent passage for foreign vessels exists in the case of internal waters (apart from the treaty provision quoted above).[1] Again, the rules relating to jurisdiction over foreign vessels differ.[2]

In the case of lakes and inland seas bounded by the territory of two or more states the legal position in practice depends either on the creation of prescriptive rights or on a treaty regime.[3] Thus the water boundary through the Great Lakes of Ontario, Erie, Huron, and Superior rests on a Convention of 1909 between Canada and the United States.[4] No doubt in the absence of agreement there is a presumption in favour of the middle line where only two states are involved.[5]

18. *Restrictions on Disposition of Territory*

Treaty provisions. States may by treaty agree not to alienate certain parcels of territory in any circumstances, or they may contract not to transfer to a particular state or states.[6] Moreover, a state may agree not to unite with another state: in the State Treaty of 1955[7] Austria was placed under an obligation not to enter into political or economic union with Germany. Previously, in the Treaty of St. Germain of 1919, the obligation was expressed differently: the independence of Austria, it was provided,[8] 'is inalienable otherwise than with the consent of the Council of the League of Nations'. An obligation not to acquire

[1] On an alleged customary right of access to ports by foreign merchant vessels, see Guggenheim i. 419.

[2] On jurisdiction over vessels in the territorial sea, *infra*, pp. 207–9; on jurisdiction over vessels in internal waters, *infra*, pp. 316–19.

[3] See *Ann. Digest* 7 (1933–4), no. 53; Hackworth i. 615; Oppenheim i. 477; Verzijl, *International Law in Historical Perspective* iii (1970), 18–20, 95–103; Hyde i. 483; Riva, 24 *Ann. Suisse* (1967), 43–66; and 8 *I.C.L.Q.* (1959), 171 (refers to the Nyasaland–Mozambique Frontier Agreement of 18 November 1954). Cf. the case of bays, *infra*, p. 199. See also *infra*, pp. 237–8 on closed seas.

[4] Hudson, *Cases*, p. 245.

[5] Cf. Oppenheim i. 533; Rousseau iii. 263–5; Colombos (6th ed.), p. 165; Convention on the Territorial Sea and Contiguous Zone, 1958, Art. 12, *infra*, p. 200. Does the latter apply in any case? If it is confined to delimiting the territorial sea it may not, since in state practice the result of division is to produce internal waters. The difficult question of principle is to decide when an international lake includes, in the legal sense, 'high seas', or zones of a 'territorial sea' distinct from internal waters. The *travaux préparatoires* make it clear that the text was not intended to cover the present problem.

[6] Oppenheim i. 463 n., 547 n.; Rousseau iii. 197–8; Verzijl, *International Law in Historical Perspective* ii (1969), 477–8.

[7] Article 4. Text: 49 *A.J.* (1955), Suppl., p. 162.

[8] Article 88. Text: 14 *A.J.* (1920), Suppl., at p. 30; Hudson, *Cases*, p. 39. On the *Austro-German Customs Union* case see *supra*, p. 78.

territory may also be undertaken.[1] In case of a breach of a treaty obligation not to alienate, or acquire, territory, it is doubtful if the title of the grantee is affected. The grantee may regard the treaty as *res inter alios acta*, and it is doubtful if the existence of a claim by a third state for breach of a treaty can result in the nullity of the transfer.

The principle of appurtenance. The territory of a state by definition and legal implication includes a territorial sea and the airspace above land territory and the territorial sea. Thus if state A merges into state B the present extent of the latter includes by implication the territorial sea and the airspace of state A.[2] This simple proposition is sometimes described as the principle of appurtenance,[3] and high authority supports the view that as a corollary, the territorial sea cannot be alienated without the coast itself[4] (and no doubt similarly in the case of airspace). With respect, the logical, and therefore the legal, basis for the corollary is not compelling. Another form of the doctrine of appurtenance appears in the judgment of Judge McNair in the *Fisheries* case.[5] In his words: 'International law imposes upon a maritime State certain obligations and confers upon it certain rights arising out of the sovereignty which it exercises over its maritime territory. The possession of this territory is not optional, not dependent upon the will of the State, but compulsory.' Attractive though this view may seem at first sight, it raises many difficulties. How many of the various territorial extensions are possessed by compulsion of law?[6] The desire to invest the coastal state with responsibility for the maintenance of order and navigational facilities evinced by one authority[7] is not a sufficient basis for the rule supported by Judge McNair, and,

[1] Cf. Hackworth i. 397 (and see ibid. for a passage from Lindley, *Acquisition and Government of Backward Territory in International Law*, pp. 80–1).

[2] Claims to territory and treaties of transfer usually refer to territory as specified, or islands, without referring to territorial waters: see, for example, the Italian peace treaty, 1947, Arts. 11 and 14; treaty between U.S. and Cuba relating to the Isle of Pines, 19 *A.J.* (1925), 95; and correspondence between Canada and Norway, 27 *A.J.* (1933), 93.

[3] See the P.C.A. in the *Grisbadarna* case, Hague Court Reports, pp. 122, 487; Hudson, *Cases*, p. 258. Cf. *Procurator General* v. *D.*, *Ann. Digest* 15 (1948), no. 26, and, on the power of the mandatory to legislate for the territorial waters of the mandated territory, see *Molvan* v. *A.-G. for Palestine* [1948] A.C. 351; Green, p. 556.

[4] Oppenheim i. 463, 488 n. 2. What is the legal consequence of ignoring the supposed rule?

[5] I.C.J. Reports (1951), p. 160. See also Fitzmaurice, 31 *B.Y.* (1954), 372–3 and id., 92 Hague *Recueil* (1957, II), 137–8. This view is unhistorical: see *infra*, pp. 184–6. See also 8 *I.C.L.Q.* (1959), 171.

[6] The Continental Shelf Convention of 1958 adopts the principle of appurtenance: see *North Sea Continental Shelf Cases*, I.C.J. Reports (1969), p. 3 at p. 22, and *infra*, pp. 222–8.

[7] Fitzmaurice, loc. cit.

indeed, this kind of logic would equally support a doctrine of closed seas. States are permitted to abandon territory, leaving it a *res nullius*, whereas the presumable consequence of disclaiming the territorial sea is simply to extend a *res communis*, the high seas.

Whatever the difficulties surrounding the principle, it has two consequences. First, even if a state may disclaim its rights over the territorial sea or airspace, other states cannot treat these entities as *res nullius* open to occupation. Secondly, abandonment is not to be presumed, and an express disclaimer would be necessary to effect abandonment.

Transfer under conditions of illegality. Substantial problems of law and policy are created when the law postulates, or is thought to postulate, mandatory conditions (though the form taken may be that of prohibition) for the lawful transfer of territory. Two such conditions may arise as a consequence of the principles of self-determination and of prohibition of the use or threat of force as a means of settling disputes. These questions, and certain others, will be treated subsequently in Chapter XXII, section 5. This arrangement of the material may or may not be the most logical, but it is the more convenient.

19. *Capacity to Transfer or Acquire Territory*[1]

The last section relates to restrictions of a kind which may apply to transfer or acquisition by states with normal powers. However, the more basic questions of capacity may arise when a dependent state purports to acquire or transfer title.[2] When the principal or dominant state opposes the transaction entered into by the dependency, the effect of the transfer will depend on the operation of the law relating to prescription, acquiescence, and recognition.[3] In other cases the principal will tacitly or expressly ratify the transfer. Here the situation is cognate with the existence of agency, a delegation of power, and the question of capacity cannot arise as such.[4] Related issues, for example the powers of a mandatory in relation to the mandated territory, are better considered in relation to the principle *nemo dat quod non habet*.[5]

[1] On the capacity of the United Nations to administer and to make dispositions of territory, see *infra*, pp. 175–9.

[2] On the criteria of statehood, *supra*, pp. 74–81; on vassalage, suzerainty, and protection, *supra*, p. 119.

[3] *Infra*, pp. 156 seq.

[4] See *T.P. Sankara Rao* v. *Municipal Council of Masulipatam*, Int. L.R. 26 (1958, II), 104; Hyde i. 379.

[5] *Infra*, pp. 128–9.

20. *The Concept of Title*[1]

The content of sovereignty has been examined from various points of view elsewhere.[2] By and large the term denotes the legal competence which a state enjoys in respect of its territory. This competence is a consequence of title and by no means coterminous with it. Thus an important aspect of state competence, the power of disposition, may be limited by treaty,[3] but the restriction, provided it is not total, leaves the title unaffected.[4] However, the materials of international law employ the term sovereignty to describe both the concept of title and the legal competence which flows from it. In the former sense the term 'sovereignty' explains (1) why the competence exists and what its fullest possible extent may be; (2) whether claims may be enforced in respect of interference with the territorial aspects of that competence against a particular state.

The second aspect mentioned is the essence of title: the validity of claims to territorial sovereignty against other states. The equivalent concept in French, 'titre', has been defined as follows: 'Terme qui, pris dans le sens de titre juridique, désigne tout fait, acte ou situation qui est la cause et le fondement d'un droit.'[5] In principle the concept of ownership, opposable to all other states and unititular,[6] can and does exist in international law. Thus the first and undisputed occupation of land which is *res nullius*,[7] and immemorial and unchallenged attribution (as in the case of England and Wales), may give rise to title which is equivalent to the *dominium* of Roman law. However, in practice the concept of title employed to solve disputes approximates to the notion of the better right to possess familiar in the Common law.[8] The

[1] The student will find the following works helpful, since the problems in the sphere of international law are basically the same: Buckland and McNair, *Roman Law and Common Law* (2nd ed.), pp. 71–88 (Excursus by Lawson); Honoré, in *Oxford Essays in Jurisprudence* (ed. Guest), pp. 107–47 and especially at pp. 134–41. See also Chapter VII.

[2] *Supra*, pp. 109–12; *infra*, Chapter XIII.

[3] *Supra*, pp. 123–4.

[4] So also belligerent occupation and other forms of foreign control will not affect title: cf. *supra*, p. 111.

[5] *Dictionnaire de la terminologie du droit international* (1960), sub voc.

[6] See Honoré, op. cit., p. 137, for a definition of a unititular system: 'Under it, if the title to a thing is in A, no title to it can be acquired (independently) by B, except by a process which divests A. There is only one "root of title" for each thing, and the present title can ultimately be traced back to that root.'

[7] See *infra*, p. 180.

[8] Jennings, *The Acquisition of Territory in International Law*, pp. 5–6. The common law is 'multititular' (see Honoré, op. cit., p. 139). See also the *Eastern Greenland* case, P.C.I.J., Ser. A/B, no. 53 at p. 46; World Court Reports iii at p. 171; the *Palmas* award, *R.I.A.A.* ii at p. 480; and *infra*, pp. 166–8.

operation of the doctrines of prescription, acquiescence, and recognition[1] makes this type of approach inevitable, but in any case tribunals will surely favour an approach which reckons with the limitations inherent in a procedure dominated by the presentation of evidence by two claimants, the result of which is not automatically opposable to third states.[2]

21. *The Determination of Frontiers*

In a broad sense many questions of title arise in the context of 'frontier disputes', but as a matter of principle the determination of the location in detail of the frontier line is distinct from the issue of title. Considerable dispositions of territory may take place in which the grantee enjoys the benefit of a title derived from the grant although no determination of the precise frontier line is made.[3] On the other hand precise determination of the frontier may be made a suspensive condition in a treaty of cession. The process of determination is carried out in accordance with a special body of rules, the best known being the *thalweg* principle. According to the doctrine of the *thalweg* in the case of a navigable river, the middle of the principal channel of navigation is accepted as the boundary.[4] This and associated geographical doctrines are presumptions and principles of equity rather than mandatory rules.[5]

The practical aspects of frontiers must be emphasized. Agreement as to the precise details of a frontier, enshrined in a written instrument, is often followed by the separate procedure of demarcation, that is, the marking, literally, of the frontier on the ground by means of posts, stone pillars, and the like. A frontier may be legally definitive, for some purposes, and yet remain undemarcated. Frontiers which are '*de facto*', either because of the absence of demarcation or because of the presence of an

[1] *Infra*, pp. 156 seq.

[2] See, in particular, the Statute of the International Court of Justice, Art. 59.

[3] See on the effect of treaties of cession or renunciation relating to territories the frontiers of which are undetermined: the *Mosul* case, P.C.I.J., Ser. B, no. 12 (1925), at p. 21 (and see Jennings, op. cit., p. 14). Cf. Declaration of Potsdam, 2 August 1945; on which *infra*, p. 138. On occasion the distinction between cession and the fixing of a boundary involves considerations of convenience rather than logic: see the cases in *Ann. Digest* 6 (1931–2), no. 55.

[4] See Oppenheim i. 532; E. Lauterpacht, 9 *I.C.L.Q.* (1960), 208–36.

[5] Generally see Boggs, *International Boundaries* (1940); de Lapradelle, *La Frontière* (1928); Verzijl, *International Law in Historical Perspective* iii (1970), 513–621; Cukwurah, *The Settlement of Boundary Disputes in International Law* (1967); de Visscher, *Problèmes de Confins en droit international public* (1969). On submarine boundaries: Padwa, 9 *I.C.L.Q.* (1960), 628–53.

unsettled territorial dispute,[1] may nevertheless be accepted as the legal limit of sovereignty for some purposes, for example those of civil or criminal jurisdiction, nationality law, and the prohibition of unpermitted intrusion with or without the use of arms.[2]

22. *Nemo dat quod non habet*[3]

This maxim, together with some exceptions, is a familiar feature of English commercial law, and the principle which the maxim represents is undoubtedly a part of international law. In the *Palmas* case, Huber, arbitrator, stated:[4]

> The title alleged by the United States of America as constituting the immediate foundation of its claim is that of cession, brought about by the Treaty of Paris, which cession transferred all rights of sovereignty which Spain may have possessed in the region. . . . It is evident that Spain could not transfer more rights than she herself possessed.

The effect of the principle is in practice very much reduced by the operation of the doctrines of prescription, acquiescence, and recognition.[5]

Certain connected principles require consideration. Except when there are only two possible claimants, the adjudication by a tribunal of a piece of territory as between states A and B is not opposable to state C. The tribunal, in so far as adjudication of itself gives title,[6] only has jurisdiction to decide as between the parties before it.[7] The fact that state C claims a particular parcel of territory does not deprive the tribunal of power to adjudicate and does not prevent states A and B from defining their rights in relation to the parcel mutually.[8] In certain cases, the principle

[1] Example: the frontier between the Yemen and the former Aden Protectorate. There are many such frontiers in Latin America and Asia.

[2] On the concern of tribunals for effectiveness see *supra*, p. 117.

[3] Or, *nemo plus juris transferre potest quam ipse habet*: no man can give another any better title than he himself has.

[4] *R.I.A.A.* ii p. 829 at p. 842; Briggs, p. 239 at p. 241; Green, p. 421 at p. 423.
See also McNair, *The Law of Treaties* (1961), pp. 656, 665; Hyde i. 360; Fitzmaurice, 32 *B.Y.* (1955–6), 22; and O'Connell, *The Law of State Succession* (1st ed.), p. 50.

[5] See *infra*, pp. 156 seq. Indeed, if one accepts extreme forms of the doctrine of effective control as the basis of sovereignty, the principle can have no relevance except in relation to the actual construction of treaties of cession: cf. Guggenheim i. 443.

[6] See *infra*, pp. 140–1.

[7] *Brazil–British Guiana Boundary* arbitration (1904), Hudson, p. 214 at p. 215; *R.I.A.A.* xi, p. 21, at p. 22.

[8] See the Boundary Agreement between China and Pakistan, 2 March 1963, which is expressed as fixing 'the alignment of the boundary between China's Sinkiang and the contiguous areas the defence of which is under the actual control of Pakistan'. Thus India's rights in respect of Kashmir are not foreclosed (see Art. 6 of the Agreement).

operates through particular rules governing special problems. Thus an aggressor, having seized territory by force and committed a delict, may purport to transfer the territory to a third state. The validity of the cession will depend on the effect of specific rules relating to the use of force by states.[1] Again, a mandatory or independent state may transfer territory which it lacks the capacity to transfer. In this type of situation much turns on the extent to which such defects of title may be cured by prescription, acquiescence, and recognition.[2]

Under certain conditions it is possible that the law accepts the existence of encumbrances passing with territory ceded. Lord McNair[3] refers to 'treaties creating purely local obligations' and gives as examples territory over which the ceding state has granted to another state a right of transit or a right of navigation on a river, or a right of fishery in territorial or internal waters.[4] These matters are considered further in Chapter XXVIII.

[1] See *infra*, pp. 512–15, on *jus cogens*.

[2] See *infra*, pp. 156 seq.

[3] *The Law of Treaties* (1961), p. 656. Others speak of 'international servitudes'. See generally *infra*, pp. 372–5, where McNair's views are questioned. Cf. *supra*, pp. 115–16, on international leases and licences.

[4] On the Ethiopia–Somaliland frontier dispute and the question of the permanence of grazing rights of Somali tribes over Ethiopian territory: Brown, 10 *I.C.L.Q.* (1961), 167–78. See also the *Right of Passage over Indian Territory* case, I.C.J. Reports (1960), p. 6.

CHAPTER VII

THE CREATION AND TRANSFER OF TERRITORIAL SOVEREIGNTY[1]

1. *Introductory*

THE student of the materials on the acquisition of title to territory is apt to feel that he is studying the history of a class of disputes instances of which are unlikely to arise in the future. In fact a surprising proportion of frontiers are the subjects of legal disputes often involving large blocks of territory.[2] Many such disputes are dormant, and it is only when a dispute flares up, creating a threat to the peace or other political crisis, that it receives publicity. Even in the case of the acquisition of territory belonging to no state (*terra nullius*), while this may not occur currently, the relevance and existence of such occupation in the past are often issues in existing disputes. Legally relevant events may have occurred centuries ago.[3] The pressures of national sentiment, new forms of exploitation of barren and inaccessible areas, the strategic significance of areas previously neglected, and the pressure of population on resources, give good cause for a belief that territorial disputes will increase in significance. This is especially so in Africa and Asia, where the removal of foreign political domination has left the successor states with a long agenda of unsettled problems, legal and political. Moreover, the body of rules relating to title to land territory provides a basic apparatus applicable, within certain limits, in the sphere of maritime territory and the seabed.[4] Finally, the prin-

[1] Jennings, *The Acquisition of Territory in International Law* (1963); Whiteman ii. 1029–1172; Suzanne Bastid, 107 Hague *Recueil* (1962, III), 435–95; Fitzmaurice, 32 *B.Y.* (1955–6), 20–76; Schwarzenberger, 51 *A.J.* (1957), 308–24; Johnson, *Camb. L.J.* (1955), 215–25; id., 27 *B.Y.* (1950), 332–54; Lauterpacht, *International Law: Collected Papers* i (1970), 377–81; id., 27 *B.Y.* (1950), 415–19; id., *The Development of International Law by the International Court* (1958), pp. 240–2; McNair, *Opinions* i. 285–325; Hackworth i. 393–476; Waldock, 25 *B.Y.* (1948), 311–53; Verzijl, *International Law in Historical Perspective* iii (1970), 297–386; De Visscher, *Les Effectivités du droit international public* (1967), pp. 101–17; Blum, *Historic Titles in International Law* (1965); McEwen, *International Boundaries of East Africa* (1971); Munkman, 46 *B.Y.* (1972–3), 1–116; Sharma, *International Boundary Disputes and International Law* (1976). And see other works cited in the notes *infra*.

[2] The Sino-Indian frontier dispute is but a recent instance.

[3] In the *Minquiers and Ecréhos* case, I.C.J. Reports (1953), p. 47, the parties and, to a lesser extent, the Court considered it necessary to investigate legal transactions of the medieval period. See further *infra*, pp. 144 seq.

[4] *Infra*, p. 170.

ciples developed in relation to territorial areas provide useful resources for those engaged in building a legal regime for outer space.[1]

2. *Historical Changes in Concepts of Law*

In one sense at least law is history, and the lawyer's appreciation of the meaning of rules relating to acquisition of territory, and of the manner of their application in particular cases, will be rendered more keen by a knowledge of the historical development of the law. In the Middle Ages the ideas of state and kingship prevalent in Europe tended to place the ruler in the position of a private owner, since feudal law, as the applicable 'public law', conferred ultimate title on the ruler, and the legal doctrine of the day employed analogies of Roman private law in the sphere of property to describe the sovereign's power. The growth of absolutism in the sixteenth and seventeenth centuries confirmed the trend. A treaty ceding territory had the appearance of a sale of land by a private owner, and sales of territory did in fact occur. In the eighteenth and nineteenth centuries the significance of private law notions declined. In the field of theory sovereignty was recognized as an abstraction and thus the ruler was a bearer and agent of a legal capacity which belonged to the state. The nineteenth century witnessed some important and to some extent contradictory developments. In Europe and Latin America the principle of nationalities appeared, which, as 'the principle of self-determination', has become increasingly important.[2] At the same time the European powers made use of the concept of the *res nullius*, which was legal in form but often political in application, since it involved the occupation of areas in Asia and Africa which were often in fact the seat of organized communities.[3] More recently the rule has become established that the use or threat of force by states to settle disputes or otherwise to effect a territorial gain is illegal. This principle, like that of self-determination, requires harmonization with the pre-existing law on acquisition of territory.[4]

3. *The Doctrine of Inter-Temporal Law*[5]

The fact is that in many instances the rights of parties to a

[1] See *infra*, pp. 260–4, and McDougal, Lasswell, Vlasic, and Smith in 111 *U. Of Penn. L.R.* (1963), pp. 521–636 (also in McDougal, Lasswell, and Vlasic, *Law and Public Order in Space*, pp. 749 seq.). [2] See *infra*, Chapter XXIV, section 9.

[3] See *infra*, p. 166. [4] See *infra*, pp. 173–4.

[5] Jennings, op. cit., pp. 28–31; Waldock, 25 *B.Y.* (1948), 320–1; Fitzmaurice, 30 *B.Y.* (1953), 5–8; Lauterpacht, *The Function of Law in the International Community*, pp. 283–5; Schwarzenberger, *International Law* i (3rd ed.), 21–4; *Annuaire de l'Inst.*, 1973, p. 1; 1975, p. 537.

dispute derive from legally significant acts, or a treaty concluded, very long ago. Sir Gerald Fitzmaurice states the rule applicable in these cases:[1] 'It can now be regarded as an established principle of international law that in such cases the situation in question must be appraised, and the treaty interpreted, in the light of the rules of international law as they existed at the time, and not as they exist today.' In the *Island of Palmas* case Judge Huber stated the principle[2] and continued: 'The effect of discovery by Spain is therefore to be determined by the rules of international law in force in the first half of the 16th century—or (to take the earliest date) in the first quarter of it . . .'. The rule has also been applied in the interpretation of treaties.[3]

In the *Island of Palmas* case Judge Huber had to consider whether Spanish sovereignty over the island subsisted at the critical date[4] in 1898. In doing so he gave a new dimension to the rule under discussion. He said:

> As regards the question which of different legal systems prevailing at successive periods is to be applied in a particular case (the so-called intertemporal law), a distinction must be made between the creation of rights and the existence of rights. The same principle which subjects the act creative of a right to the law in force at the time the right arises, demands that the existence of the right, in other words its continued manifestation, shall follow the conditions required by the evolution of law.

This extension[5] of the doctrine has been criticized on the ground that logically the notion that title has to be maintained at every moment of time would threaten many titles and lead to instability.[6] It would seem that the principle represented by extension of the doctrine is logically inevitable, but that the criticism is in point in so far as it emphasizes the need for care in applying the rule.[7] In any case the principle cannot operate in a vacuum: its theoretical extent will in practice be reduced by

[1] Op. cit., p. 5. See also Westlake (2nd ed.), i. 114; Hyde i. 320 n. 5, 329 n. 27; Hackworth i. 393–5; Lindley, *Acquisition and Government of Backward Territory in International Law* (1926), pp. v–vi (quoted in Hackworth i. 395–6).

[2] Hague Court Reports ii. p. 83 at p. 100; Briggs, at p. 243; Green, at p. 425. See also the award in the *Grisbadarna* case (1909), 4 *A.J.* (1910), 226, 231, 232; Hackworth i. 395; *R.I.A.A.* xi, p. 155 at pp. 159, 160.

[3] The familiar label here is *contemporanea expositio*. See *U.S. Nationals in Morocco*, I.C.J. Reports (1952), p. 176 at p. 189; *Right of Passage over Indian Territory*, I.C.J. Reports (1960), p. 6 at p. 37.

[4] See *infra*, p. 133. [5] Lauterpacht, loc. cit.

[6] See Jessup, 22 *A.J.* (1928), p. 735 at pp. 739–40; Jennings, loc. cit. and 121 Hague *Recueil* (1967, II), 422.

[7] This form of the doctrine was applied sensibly in the *Minquiers and Ecrehos* case, I.C.J. Reports (1953), p. 47 at p. 56; and see also *Western Sahara* case, I.C.J. Reports, 1975, p. 12 at pp. 168–71 (Sep. Op. of Judge de Castro).

the effect of recognition, acquiescence, estoppel, prescription, the rule that abandonment is not to be presumed, and the general condition of the pleadings and evidence.[1]

4. *Critical Dates*[2]

In any dispute a certain date, or several dates, will assume prominence in the process of evaluating the facts. The choice of such a date, or dates, is within the province of the tribunal seised of the dispute and will depend in some circumstances on the inevitable logic of the law applicable to the particular facts and, in other cases, on the practical necessity of confining the process of decision to relevant and cogent facts and thus to acts prior to the existence of a dispute.[3] In the latter context the tribunal is simply employing judicial technique in the use of evidence and more especially the exclusion of evidence consisting of self-serving acts of parties at a stage when it was evident that a dispute existed. Of course, evidence of acts and statements occurring after the critical date may be admissible if not self-serving, as in the case of admissions against interest. There are several types of critical date, and it is difficult and probably misleading to formulate general definitions:[4] the facts of the case are dominant (including, for this purpose, the terms of the special agreement empowering the tribunal to hear the case) and there is no necessity for a tribunal to choose any date whatsoever. In many cases there will be several dates of varying significance.

The dispute between Norway and Denmark which led to the *Eastern Greenland* case arose from a Norwegian proclamation on 10 July 1931 announcing occupation of the area. The Court in that case said:[5] 'It must be borne in mind, however, that as the critical date is July 10th, 1931 . . . it is sufficient [for Denmark] to establish a valid title in the period immediately preceding the

[1] The doctrine had no very substantial effect in the *Minquiers and Ecrehos* case: see last note and Suzanne Bastid, 107 Hague *Recueil* (1962, III), 448–50.

[2] Fitzmaurice, 32 *B.Y.* (1955–6), 20–44; Goldie, 12 *I.C.L.Q.* (1963), 1251–84; Blum, *Historic Titles in International Law* (1965), pp. 208–22. For the problems arising in the context of treaties of cession and the rights of successor states see the *Lighthouses* arbitration (France/Greece), P.C.A., 1956; Int. L.R. 23 (1956), p. 659 at p. 668.

[3] Cf. the exceptions to the hearsay rule in the law of evidence based on statements *ante litem motam*, and the rules of English Equity evolved to regulate the evidence admissible to rebut a presumption of advancement: *Snell* (27th ed.), p. 176–9. See also Cross, *Evidence* (4th ed.), p. 22.

[4] See Jennings, *Acquisition*, pp. 31–5; id., 121 Hague *Recueil* (1967, II), 423–6.

[5] P.C.I.J., Ser. A/B no. 53, p. 45.

occupation.' In the *Palmas Island*[1] case the United States claimed as successor to Spain under a treaty of cession dated 10 December 1898, and everything turned on the nature of Spanish rights at that time. The Court did not specifically choose a critical date in the *Minquiers and Ecrehos* case.[2] In the *Argentine-Chile Frontier*[3] case the Tribunal reported that it 'had considered the notion of the critical date to be of little value in the present litigation and has examined all the evidence submitted to it, irrespective of the date of the acts to which such evidence relates.'

5. *The Modes of Acquisition*

Many of the standard textbooks,[4] and particularly those in English, classify the modes of acquisition in a stereotyped way which reflects the preoccupation of writers in the period before the First World War. According to this analysis (if the term is deserved) there are five modes of acquisition—occupation, accretion, cession, conquest,[5] and prescription. Apart from issues arising from the division and choice of the modes, the whole concept of modes of acquisition is unsound in principle and makes the task of understanding the true position much more difficult.[6] Labels are never a substitute for analysis. The inadequacies of the orthodox approach will perhaps be more apparent when the relevant questions have been examined in the sections which follow, but a few things may be usefully said here. A tribunal will concern itself with proof of the exercise of sovereignty at the critical date or dates, and in doing so will not apply

[1] See *infra*, p. 144.

[2] I.C.J. Reports (1953), p. 47. The French argument rested on the date of the Convention of 2 August 1839; that of the United Kingdom on the date of the *compromis* (29 December 1950). See Johnson, 3 *I.C.L.Q.* (1954), p. 189 at pp. 207–11. Critical dates *eo nomine* did not feature in the judgment in the case of the *Temple of Preah Vihear*, I.C.J. Reports (1962), p. 6. However, the Court treated two dates as material: 1904, the date of a frontier treaty between France and Thailand, and 1954, when Thailand sent military or police forces to occupy the area. See also the *Rann of Kutch* case; Award, 1968; *Int. Leg. Materials* vii, p. 633 at p. 666: Int. L.R. 50, 2 at p. 470.

[3] Award, 1966; Int. L.R., 38, p. 10 at pp. 79–80; *R.I.A.A.* xvi, p. 109 at pp. 166–7; 61 *A.J.* (1967), 1071.

[4] See Brierly, *Law of Nations* (6th ed.), pp. 163–73, and Akehurst, *Modern Introduction* (3rd ed.), pp. 140–6.

[5] This appears as 'subjugation' in Oppenheim i. 566.

[6] For critical comment see Johnson, *Camb. L.J.* (1955), pp. 215–17; Jennings, op. cit., pp. 6–7. See also Rousseau, 93 Hague *Recueil* (1958, I), 415–16; Schwarzenberger, *International Law* i (3rd ed.), 292–309. See also *infra*, pp. 168–9, on historical consolidation of title. For other types of treatment see Kozhevnikov (ed.), *International Law*, pp. 181–9; and Guggenheim i. 437–45.

the orthodox analysis to describe its process of decision.[1] The issue of territorial sovereignty, or title, is often complex, and involves the application of various principles of the law to the material facts. The result of this process cannot always be ascribed to any single dominant rule or 'mode of acquisition'. The orthodox analysis does not prepare the student for the interaction of principles of acquiescence and recognition with the other rules. Furthermore, a category like 'cession' or 'prescription' may bring quite distinct situations into unhappy fellowship.[2] Lastly, the importance of showing a better right to possess in contentious cases, i.e. of relative title,[3] is obscured if too much credit is given to the five 'models'. The headings employed in the sections of this chapter which follow represent categories of convenience and are not intended to prejudge any issues of principle.

6. *Original and Derivative Title*

It is common to classify the five orthodox modes of acquisition as 'original' or 'derivative'. Occupation and accretion are usually described as 'original' methods, cession as 'derivative'. Significantly, there are differences of opinion in regard to conquest and prescription, and the classification has no practical value.[4] In one sense all titles are original, since much depends on the acts of the grantee in the case of a cession.[5] In any case the dual classification oversimplifies the situation, and the modes described as 'derivative' are so in rather different ways. Moreover the usual analyses do not explain how title is acquired when a new state comes into existence.[6] Here title is created as a consequence of legal procedure relating to the establishment and recognition of new legal persons.[7] The events leading to independence of the new state are matters within the domestic jurisdiction of another legal person, and yet they are legally relevant to territorial disputes involving the new state.[8] In this

[1] Note the difficulty encountered in classifying the *Island of Palmas*, *Eastern Greenland*, and *Minquiers and Ecrehos* cases: *infra*, p. 142. And cf. *Case Concerning Sovereignty over Certain Frontier Land*, I.C.J. Reports (1959), p. 209.

[2] It may be noted that 'annexation' is not a term of art. The term commonly describes an official state act signifying an extension of sovereignty. It is not a root of title. See McNair, *Opinions* i. 285 n. 1, 289; Hyde i. 391; Hackworth i. 446–9; and *infra*, p. 151, on symbolic annexation.

[3] See *infra*, pp. 166–8.

[4] See Johnson, *Camb. L.J.* (1955), p. 217. Thus an 'original' mode does not necessarily give a title free of incumbrances: see I.C.J. Reports (1960), p. 6.

[5] Guggenheim i. 438, 443; and see *infra*.

[6] See Jennings, op. cit., pp. 7–11. See also Hyde i. 390; Hackworth i. 444–5.

[7] *Supra*, pp. 73 seq.

[8] For example, disputes between India and Pakistan involve examination of many constitutional issues and acts of state by the United Kingdom before independence.

type of case there is no 'root of title' *as such*: title is a by-product of the revolution, secession, or other events leading to the creation of a state as a new source of territorial sovereignty.

7. *Roots of Title*[1]

(a) *A treaty of cession*.[2] A right to possess certain territory as sovereign may be conferred by agreement between intending grantor and grantee, and, if the grantee takes possession in accordance with the treaty,[3] the treaty provides the legal basis of sovereignty.[4] An actual transfer is not of course possible or required if the grantee is already in occupation.[5] The date on which title changes may be determined by the treaty of cession. It will normally be the date on which the treaty comes into force.[6] Furthermore, the treaty itself gives the intending grantee an assignable interest, and the grantee can pass his interest to a third state. Presumably, for the third state to get title, transfer is still required, and, if the sovereign refuses to give possession, the assignee can be subrogated to the treaty right of the assignor.

(b) *Other dispositions by treaty*. Apart from cession and transfer in accordance with a treaty, title may exist on the basis of a treaty alone, the treaty marking a reciprocal recognition of sovereignty in solemn form and with attention to detail.[7] In the case of a disputed frontier line the boundary treaty which closes the dispute will *create* title, because previously the question of

[1] This is a general description of content and not strictly a term of art.

[2] The term 'cession' is used to cover a variety of types of transaction, and it is important to seek the legal realities behind the term in each case. Cf. *Différends Sociétés Dufay et Gigandet*, *R.I.A.A.*, xvi, p. 197 at pp. 208–12. On the effect of cessions accompanied by the use or threat of force see *infra*, p. 173. See also pp. 173–4, 512–15 on the relevance of the principle of self-determination and other rules.

[3] See Oppenheim i. 550; Redslob, *Traité*, p. 181; Rousseau iii. 173; Schwarzenberger, *International Law* i (3rd ed.), 302–4; *Franco-Ethiopian Railway Co.* claim, Int. L.R. 24 (1957), at pp. 616, 623. See also *San Lorenzo Title and Improvement Co.* v. *City Mortgage Co.*, *Ann. D gest* 6 (1931–2), no. 55 at p. 116. Cf. *German Interests in Polish Upper Silesia* (1926), P.C.I.J., Ser. A, no. 7, p. 30; Green, at pp. 537–8; *Lighthouses in Crete and Samos* (1937), Ser. A/B, no. 71, p. 103.

[4] See the United States argument in the *Island of Palmas* case.

[5] This situation is more properly classified as renunciation: *Sorkis* v. *Amed*, Int. L.R. 17 (1950), no. 24 at p. 103, and see *infra*, p. 139. However, the term cession is sometimes used thus: see the *German Reparations* case (1924), *R.I.A.A.* i, p. 429 at p. 443; *Banin* v. *Laviani and Ellena*, *Ann. Digest* 16 (1949), no. 27; *Différends Sociétés Dufay et Gigandet*, *R.I.A.A.* xvi, p. 197 at pp. 208–12.

[6] *Versailles Treaty* case, Int. L.R. 32, p. 339; *N. Masthan Sahib* v. *Chief Commissioner*, Int. L.R. 49, p. 484; and see Treaty of Cession relating to the Kuria Muria Islands, *U.K. Treaty Series* no. 8 (1968), Cmnd. 3505.

[7] Consequently disputes as to title may involve the interpretation of the given treaty exclusively: see the *Beagle Channel Arbitration*, Award of 18 April, 1977; H.M.S.O. 1977; Bilingual ed., Rep. of Chile, 1977; 17 *Int. Leg. Materials* (1978), 632.

title was unsettled; in contrast a treaty of cession transfers a definitive title.[1]

(c) *Consent in other forms*. The existence of consent to the transfer of territory may be evidenced without the conclusion of any formal agreement.[2] For example, a treaty of cession may be invalid, in the absence of appropriate legislation by one of the parties, in the courts of that state, yet if an actual transfer has taken place and a change of sovereignty is accepted by the interested parties, the validity or otherwise of the treaty is irrelevant.[3] Informal expression of consent is not far removed from consent implied from conduct and a unilateral rather than consensual recognition of sovereignty. This field of problems relates to acquiescence, estoppel, and recognition, and these topics will be considered later on.[4]

(d) *Uti possidetis (juris)*.[5] In the region of Latin America consent as a means of disposition of territory has assumed an indirect form. By their practice the successor states of Spain agreed to apply, as between themselves, and later in their disputes with Brazil, a principle for the settlement of frontier disputes in an area in which *terra nullius* (territory belonging to no state) by political definition, did not exist—the independent republics regarded their titles as co-extensive with that of the former Spanish empire. The principle has been expressed as follows:[6]

> When the common sovereign power was withdrawn, it became indispensably necessary to agree on a general principle of demarcation, since there was a universal desire to avoid resort to force, and the principle adopted was a colonial *uti possidetis*; that is, the principle involving the preservation of the demarcations under the colonial regimes corresponding to each of the colonial entities that was constituted as a State.

[1] See McNair, *Law of Treaties* (1961), pp. 656–7; id., *Opinions* i. 287; *Case Concerning Sovereignty over Certain Frontier Land*, I.C.J. Reports (1959), p. 209 at pp. 226, 231, 256; *Case of Temple of Preah Vihear*, I.C.J. Reports (1962), p. 6 at pp. 16, 52, 67, 73–74, 102–3; *Ditmar and Linde* v. *Ministry of Agriculture*, *Ann. Digest* 8 (1935–7), no. 52; *Willis* v. *First Real Estate and Investment Co.*, *Ann. Digest* 11 (1919–42), no. 52.

[2] Schwarzenberger, *International Law* i (3rd ed.), 302; *Frontier Land* case, I.C.J. Reports (1959), pp. 238–48, 251; *Temple* case, ibid. (1962), pp. 133–42.

[3] *Union of India* v. *Jain and Others*, Int. L.R. 21 (1954), p. 256 at p. 257.

[4] *Infra*, pp. 156 seq.

[5] For a full account: Hyde i. 498–510. See also Alvarez, *Le Droit International Américain* (1910), p. 65; the *Colombia-Venezuela Boundary* arbitration (1922), *R.I.A.A.*, i. 223; *Ann. Digest* 1 (1919–22), no. 54; *Beagle Channel Arbitration*, Award of 18 April 1977, *supra*, p. 136, n. 7, Decision, paras. 9–12; Whiteman ii. 1086–8; Hackworth i. 732–7. See also the use of *uti possidetis* as a general principle of law by two Latin-America judges in the *Case Concerning Sovereignty Over Certain Frontier Land*, I.C.J. Reports (1959), p. 209 at pp. 240, 255. Any use of a state of actual possession as a legal criterion may be so described: cf. *Dictionnaire de la terminologie du droit international*, *sub voc.*

[6] See Hyde i. 499, n. 3. See also Judge Urrutia Holguin, I.C.J. Reports (1960), p. 226.

The principle involves implied agreement to base territorial settlement on a rule of presumed possession by the previous Spanish administrative unit in 1821, in Central America, or in 1810, in South America.

The operation of such a principle does not give very satisfactory solutions, since much depends on the concept of possession to be employed, and, furthermore, the old Spanish administrative boundaries are frequently ill-defined or difficult of proof.[1] It must be emphasized that the principle is by no means mandatory and the states concerned are free to adopt other principles as the basis of a settlement.[2] However, the general principle, that pre-independence boundaries established by law remain in being, is in accordance with good policy and has been adopted by governments and tribunals concerned with boundaries in Asia[3] and Africa.[4]

(e) *Disposition by joint decision of the principal powers.* After the defeat of the Central Powers in the First World War, and the Axis Powers in the Second World War, the leading victor states assumed a power of disposition, to be exercised jointly, over the territory of the defeated states. In the years 1919 and 1920 decisions were taken by the Supreme Council of the Allied and Associated States; in 1943 and 1945 by meetings of leaders at Tehran, Yalta, and Potsdam,[5] and subsequently by meetings of Foreign Ministers. States losing territory as a consequence of dispositions in this wise might, and often did, renounce title[6] by the provisions of a peace treaty to the areas concerned, but the dispositions were assumed to be valid irrespective of such renunciation and the recipients were usually in possession prior to the coming into force of a peace treaty.[7] The existence of this power of disposition or assignment is recognized by jurists,[8]

[1] See the *Guatemala-Honduras Boundary* arbitration (1933), *R.I.A.A.* ii. 1322; *Ann. Digest* 7 (1933–4), no. 46. For comment see 27 *A.J.* (1933), 403–27. Cf. Waldock, 25 *B.Y.* (1948), at p. 325.

[2] See generally Hyde, loc. cit.; Hackworth i. 726–55.

[3] See the *Temple* case, I.C.J. Reports (1962), p. 6; Green, p. 457; *Rann of Kutch* case; Award, 1968; *Int. Leg. Materials*, vii. p. 633; Int. L.R. 50, p. 2.

[4] O.A.U. Resolution on Border Disputes, 21 July 1964; Touval, 21 *Int. Organization* (1967), 102–27.

[5] Text of declarations: 38 *A.J.* (1944), Suppl., p. 9; 39 *A.J.* (1945), Suppl., pp. 103, 245. See also Goodrich and Carroll (eds.), *Documents on American Foreign Relations* vii and viii.

[6] See *infra*, p. 139, on renunciation.

[7] See Hyde i. 360–3. Much depends on the particular facts of each case and especially the intentions of the parties involved. In this type of case the use of the term 'cession' does not aid legal analysis. The dismemberment of Austria-Hungary and its division among seven states was effected prior to the Treaties of St. Germain-en-Laye and Trianon. See also the *German Reparations* case (1924), *R.I.A.A.* i. 429 at p. 442.

[8] Verzijl, *International Law in Historical Perspective* i. (1968), 305–7; *Jaworzina*

but they find it difficult to suggest, or to agree upon, a satisfactory legal basis for it. Some translate political realities into legal forms by supposing that the community of states has delegated such a power to the 'principal' or 'great' powers.[1] Others, at least in relation to the Second World War, postulate a right to impose measures of security, which may include frontier changes, on an aggressor consequent on his defeat in a war of collective defence and sanction.[2]

Much turns on the extent to which recognition and acquiescence[3] may counteract any elements of illegality[4] which may infect such procedures in some cases. Dispositions of this kind normally are recognized by a multilateral peace treaty or otherwise.[5] In some cases, for example, the Geneva Conference of 1954,[6] in regard to Indo-China, the express delegation of power prior to agreed disposition of territory ensures that a certain number of states are bound to accept the results of the procedure.

(f) *Renunciation or relinquishment.*[7] It is not uncommon for states to renounce title over territory in circumstances in which the subject-matter does not thereby become *terra nullius* (territory belonging to no state). This distinguishes renunciation from abandonment.[8] Furthermore, there is no element of reciprocity, and no contract to transfer, as in the case of a treaty of cession. Renunciation may be a recognition that another state now has title[9] or a recognition of, or agreement to confer, a power of disposition to be exercised by another state or a group of states.[1]

Boundary, P.C.I.J., Ser. B, no. 8 (1923); *Monastery of Saint-Naoum*, ibid., no. 9; Joint dissenting opinion of Judges Spender and Fitzmaurice, I.C.J. Reports (1962), p. 482; P.C.A. in the *Lighthouses* arbitration (France/Greece), 1956; Int. L.R. 23 (1956), p. 659 at pp. 663–9. See also *L. and J.J.* v. *Polish State Railways*, Int. L.R. 24 (1957), 77.

[1] Cf. *infra*, p. 175.

[2] See Brownlie, *International Law and the Use of Force by States* (1963), pp. 408–9, and Kozhevnikov (ed.), *International Law*, pp. 188–9.

[3] On which *infra*, pp. 163–4.

[4] e.g. operation of the principle of self-determination (see *infra*, pp. 173–4) and the prohibition of the threat or use of force to acquire territory or settle disputes (see *infra*, p. 173, and also Brownlie, op. cit., pp. 74 seq., 251 seq.).

[5] In the case of the Polish western territories (those east of the Oder-Neisse line) the controversy relates in part to the actual meaning of the Potsdam Declaration, which states that the 'final delimitation of the western frontier of Poland should await the peace settlement.

[6] *Documents on International Affairs* (1954), p. 138; Cmd. 9186.

[7] See Hyde i. 385–6, 392, n. 2; Whiteman ii. 1229–32.

[8] *Infra*, p. 148.

[9] See *supra*, pp. 136–7, on consent. For examples see the Treaty of St. Germain-en-Laye of 10 September 1919; 14 *A.J.* (1920), Suppl., p. 1, Arts. 36, 43, 46, 47, 53, 54, 59. See also the *German Reparations* case (1924), *R.I.A.A.* i, p. 429 at p. 442.

[1] See the Treaty of St. Germain, Arts. 89–91; and the *Lighthouses* arbitration (1956), Int. L.R. 23 (1956), p. 659 at pp. 663–6 (as to the Treaty of London, 30 May, 1913). On

A series of unilateral acts may constitute evidence of an implicit voluntary relinquishment of rights.[1] Renunciation is to be distinguished from reversion, i.e. recognition by an aggressor that territory seized is rightfully under the sovereignty of the victim. Here, there is no title to renounce.[2] Since the procedure of renunciation involves title alone, it may happen that the state losing title retains powers of administration by delegation.[3]

(g) *Adjudication*. While the subject is generally neglected, some jurists accept adjudication by a judicial organ[4] as a mode of acquisition.[5] The award of a tribunal is certainly a valuable root of title, but the award is not of itself dispositive. There is some analogy here with the effect of a treaty of cession, and in general sovereignty changes only when there is an occupation in pursuance of the award. The award then gives the value of sovereignty to the possession.[6] However, in certain cases the award has a dispositive effect: (1) when the nature of the territory is such that no physical acts are necessary to its effective appropriation;[7] (2) where the two disputants are both exercizing acts of administration in respect of the territory concerned, and the award merely declares which of the two 'possessors' is a lawful holder;[8] (3) where the loser is to continue in possession with delegated powers of administration and jurisdiction; (4) when the success-

Italian renunciation of all right and title to Italian territories in Africa see the Treaty of Peace with Italy, 1947, Art. 23; *Banin* v. *Laviani and Ellena*, *Ann. Digest* 16 (1949), no. 27; *Sorkis* v. *Amed*, Int. L.R. 17 (1950), no. 24 at p. 103; *Farrugia* v. *Nuova Comp. Gen. Autolinee*, Int. L.R. 18 (1951), no. 32. See also *Différends Sociétés Dufay et Gigandet*, *R.I.A.A.* xvi, p. 197 at pp. 208–12; and Article 2 of the Japanese Peace Treaty of 8 September 1951; 46 *A.J.* (1952), Suppl., p. 71.

[1] See the *Rann of Kutch* case; Award, 1968; *Int. Leg. Materials* vii. 633 at pp. 667–73, 685–8; Int. L.R. 50, p. 2 at pp. 474–500, 516–18.

[2] See *infra*, p. 166, and a decision of the Franco-Italian Conciliation Commission in Int. L.R. 24 (1957), p. 602 at p. 605.

[3] See *supra*, p. 111, n. 4, and cf. the *constitutum possessorium*, so-called, in Roman Law.

[4] i.e., the International Court of Justice (and its predecessor), the Permanent Court of Arbitration, *ad hoc* arbitral tribunals, conciliation commissions, and other bodies acting judicially in respect of the issue of title, including, for example, the Council of the League of Nations. If a political organ like the Security Council does not decide the issue judicially and in accordance with the law, it is simply exercising a power of disposition which may be derived from the Charter (this is a difficult question) or from a treaty specially conferring such power.

[5] Rousseau iii. 186; Guggenheim i. 442, n. 2; Verzijl, *International Law in Historical Perspective* iii (1970), 378–81. See also Strupp, *Elements*, p. 155; *Minquiers and Ecrehos* case, I.C.J. Reports (1953), p. 56; *Brazil-British Guiana Boundary* arbitration (1905), Hudson, *Cases*, p. 214 at p. 215; *R.I.A.A.* xi, p. 21 at p. 22; Basdevant (ed.), *Dictionnaire de la terminologie de d.i., sub voc.*

[6] Thus, before execution of the award the successful claimant cannot seize the territory. See also the U.N. Charter, Art. 94, para. 2, and Brownlie, op. cit., p. 382.

[7] See *infra*, pp. 144 seq., on the *Island of Palmas*, *Clipperton Island*, and *Eastern Greenland* cases. [8] See *infra*, p. 142.

ful claimant is already in possession;[1] (5) where the award relates only to the detailed fixing of a frontier line.[2] In principle the International Court might be asked to declare the status of territory and subsequently find that at the critical date the territory belonged to no state.[3]

(h) *Agreements concluded with local rulers.* In the Advisory Opinion concerning *Western Sahara*[4] the International Court stated that in the period beginning in 1884:

'the State practice of the relevant period indicates that territories inhabited by tribes or peoples having a social and political organization were not regarded as *terrae nullius*. It shows that in the case of such territories the acquisition of sovereignty was not generally considered as effected unilaterally through "occupation" of *terrae nullius* by original title but through agreements concluded with local rulers . . . such agreements . . . were regarded as derivative roots of title, and not original titles obtained by occupation of *terrae nullius*.'

8. *Effective Occupation*[5]

The concept of effective occupation in international law represents the type of legal relation which in private law would be described as possession. In the absence of a formal basis for title in a treaty or judgment, and in a system without registration of title, possession plays a significant role. Naturally, as in private law, the concept is complex,[6] and many difficulties arise in applying principles to facts. It must be borne in mind that 'legal possession' involves a search for an interest worth protection by the law. Legal policy may lead a court to regard as sufficient a tenuous connexion between claimant and territory in certain conditions. Moreover, what is important is *state activity*, and especially acts of administration. 'Occupation' here derives from *occupatio* in Roman law and does not necessarily signify

[1] See the *Eastern Greenland* case, *infra*, p. 145.

[2] Rousseau, loc. cit. There are some objections to his view: (1) to distinguish disputes about frontier lines from other disputes is difficult (*supra*, p. 127; and (2) an award of this kind of its very nature demands careful execution, a process of demarcation, before the line is final (see I.C.J. Reports (1962), p. 69).

[3] Cf. P.C.I.J., Ser. A/B, no. 53, pp. 41–2; Hudson, World Court Reports iii. 167 (Norwegian suggestion).

[4] I.C.J. Reports, 1975, p. 12 at p. 39. See also ibid., pp. 123–4, Sep. Op. of Judge Dillard.

[5] See Waldock, 25 *B.Y.* (1948), 311–53; von der Heydte, 29 *A.J.* (1935), 448–71; Genet, 15 *R.D.I.L.C.* (1934), 285–324, 416–50; Fitzmaurice, 32 *B.Y.* (1955–6), at pp. 49–71; Lauterpacht, 27 *B.Y.* (1950), at pp. 415–31; Whiteman ii. 1030–62.

[6] See Pollock and Wright, *Possession in the Common Law*, pp. 28–36; de Zulueta, *Digest* 41, 1 & 2, pp. 83 seq.; Harris, in *Oxford Essays in Jurisprudence* (ed. Guest), pp. 69–106 (and note p. 73).

occupation in the sense of actual settlement and a physical holding.

Effective occupation is commonly related to extension of sovereignty to *terra nullius*, i.e. new land, for example a volcanic island, territory abandoned by the former sovereign, or territory not possessed by a community having a social and political organization.[1] The connexion with the *terra nullius* is pointed to as an important point of distinction between effective occupation and acquisitive prescription.[2] In the latter case land *previously* under the unchallenged sovereignty of one state is subjected to acts of sovereignty by a competitor. Where the conditions for acquisitive prescription are satisfied it is clear that a paradigm of effective occupation is an important element in the process of establishing sovereignty. In practice it is not easy to distinguish effective occupation and prescription, and in the *Island of Palmas* and *Eastern Greenland* cases the award and judgment, respectively do not employ the categories. Beckett[3] has classified the former as a case of prescription, the latter as resting on occupation.[4] However, it is submitted that in the *Palmas* case, as in the *Minquiers and Ecrehos* case in 1953, the issue was simply that of which of two competing sovereignties had the better right. Prescription classically involves usurpation, a sequence of peaceful possession and competition. Yet the two last-mentioned cases, as will appear subsequently, involve, for all practical purposes, contemporaneously competing acts of state sovereignty. In the *Minquiers and Ecrehos* case the Court stated the issue as one of possession,[5] which in the context was equated with sovereignty.[6] Its task, in part, was 'to appraise the relative strength of the opposing claims to sovereignty over the Ecrehos'.[7]

As a consequence much of the material to be considered under the heading 'effective occupation' has a relevance far beyond the acquisition of *terra nullius*. Its elements involve simply proof of possession by states, of manifestations of sovereignty legally more potent than those of the other claimant or claimants, or, in brief, proof of the better right. The intensity of state activity

[1] See the Advisory Opinion concerning *Western Sahara*, quoted in the text above. On the principle of self-determination see *infra*, pp. 173–4. On the regime of the *res nullius* see *infra*, p. 180.

[2] See *infra*, pp. 156 seq., on the nature of acquisitive prescription.

[3] 50 Hague *Recueil* (1934, IV), 218–55 at 220.

[4] The *Eastern Greenland* case, P.C.I.J., Ser. A/B, no. 53; Hudson, World Court Reports iii. 151; Green, p. 160; is commonly assumed to have been decided on the basis that the area concerned was *terra nullius* at the critical date: but see de Visscher, *Les Effectivités du droit international public* (1967), p. 105, citing the judgment at p. 45. See also on the *Clipperton Island* arbitration, *infra*, p. 145.

[5] I.C.J. Reports (1953), p. 57. See also ibid., pp. 55, 56.

[6] pp. 58–9.

[7] p. 67. Cf. the *Eastern Greenland* case, Series A/B, no. 53, at p. 46; Hudson iii at p. 171.

required will obviously be less in the case of *terra nullius* than in the case where a competing claimant takes an interest in territory.

Proof of animus occupandi. In the *Eastern Greenland* case the Permanent Court said:[1] '. . . a claim to sovereignty based not upon some particular act or title such as a treaty of cession but merely upon continued display of authority, involves two elements each of which must be shown to exist: the intention and will to act as sovereign, and some actual exercise or display of such authority'.

The requirement of an intention to act as sovereign, otherwise referred to as *animus occupandi*[2] or *animus possidendi*,[3] is generally insisted upon in the literature. However, it is notorious that the notion of *animus possidendi* may create more problems than it solves, and Ross has described the subjective requirement of the 'will to act as sovereign' as 'an empty phantom'.[4] In truth the subjective criterion involves the imputation of a state of mind, involving a *legal* assessment and 'judgment', to those ordering various state activities. This approach expects too much and is unrealistic in seeking a particular and coherent intention in a mass activity by numerous individuals. Furthermore, the criterion begs the question in many cases where there are competing acts of sovereignty. Significantly the award in the *Island of Palmas* case and the judgment in the *Minquiers and Ecrehos* case place emphasis on the objective facts of state activity, on manifestations of sovereignty.

In three contexts, however, the *animus occupandi*, or rules akin to the notion, have a necessary function. First, the activity must be *à titre de souverain* in the sense that the agency must be that of the state and not of unauthorized natural or legal persons.[5] Secondly, the concept has a negative role: if the activity is by the consent of another state or that other is otherwise recognized as the rightful sovereign[6] then no amount of state activity is capable

[1] Ser A/B, no. 53, at pp. 45–6; Hudson iii. 170–1. See also ibid., pp. 63 and 185 respectively; *Frontier Land* case, I.C.J. Reports (1959), p. 250 (diss. op. of Judge Armand-Ugon); Advisory Opinion concerning *Western Sahara*, I.C.J. Reports, 1975, p. 12 at pp. 42–3.

[2] Cf. Fitzmaurice, 32 *B.Y.* (1955–6), at pp. 55–8; award in the *Clipperton Island* arbitration, *R.I.A.A.* ii. 1105 at p. 1110.

[3] See Judge Anzilotti, dissenting opinion, *Eastern Greenland* case, ser. A/B, no. 53, p. 83; Hudson iii. 201. See also *Frontier Land* case, I.C.J. Reports (1959), p. 255 (diss. op. of Judge Moreno Quintana, referring to *animus domini*).

[4] *International Law*, p. 147; quoted with approval in Brierly, *Law of Nations* (5th ed.), p. 152 n.; 6th ed. by Waldock, p. 163, n. 2.

[5] See *infra*, p. 147. [6] See *supra*, pp. 111, 140.

of maturing into sovereignty.[1] Thirdly, the dominant nature of the activity taken as a whole must be explicable only on the basis that the existence of sovereignty is assumed.[2] Thus in the *Minquiers and Ecrehos* case the fact that both parties had conducted official hydrographic surveys of the area could not be regarded as necessarily referable to an assertion of sovereignty. But certain forms of activity, whilst not exclusively and necessarily connected with territorial sovereignty, have some probative value, for example the exercise of criminal jurisdiction in respect of territory. Generally, however, reference to a generalized intention, an *animus occupandi*, will cause confusion.

Effective and continuous display of state authority. Concrete acts of appropriation, or a display of state activity consonant with sovereignty, are the vital constituents of title. The older works on international law give the nineteenth-century view of occupation in terms of settlement and close physical possession.[3] In fact the law has been decisively changed as a consequence of three decisions.

In the *Island of Palmas* arbitration (1928)[4] the Netherlands and the United States agreed to submit to the Permanent Court of Arbitration a dispute concerning sovereignty over the Island of Palmas (or Miangas) lying about halfway between the Philippine Islands (then under United States sovereignty) and the Netherlands East Indies (as they then were). The United States founded its title upon the Treaty of Paris, under which all rights which Spain possessed in the region were transferred by cession to the United States. Everything turned on the nature of Spain's rights at the date when the treaty of cession came into force in 1898. Huber, arbitrator, stated that 'the continuous and peaceful display of territorial sovereignty (peaceful in relation to other states) is as good as a title', And further:

[1] This is subject to the possibilities of prescription, *infra*, pp. 156 seq.

[2] Fitzmaurice, op. cit., pp. 56–8.

[3] See Hall, *International Law* (8th ed.), p. 125. See also McNair, *Opinions* i. 291, 315–16; and Hyde i. 342.

[4] *R.I.A.A.* ii. 829; Green, p. 421; Hague Court Reports ii. 83; 22 *A.J.* (1928), 867; Briggs, p. 239; Hudson, *Cases*, p. 211. See also discussion by Jessup, 22 *A.J.*, 735–52; and F. de Visscher, 10 *R.D.I.L.C.* (1929), 735–62. See further the *Alp Cravairola* arbitration (1874), Moore, *Arbitrations* ii. 2027; *Jones* v. *United States* (1890), 136 U.S. 202; Hudson, *Cases*, p. 216; *Brazil-British Guiana Boundary* arbitration (1904), Hudson, *Cases*, p. 214; *R.I.A.A.* xi. 21; Hackworth i. 404; *Grisbadarna* arbitration (1909), 4 *A.J.* (1910), 226, 233; *R.I.A.A.* xi., p. 155 at pp. 161–2; Hague Court Reports i. 122, 130; Hackworth i. 405. See further the *Rann of Kutch* case; Award, 1968; *Int. Leg. Materials* vii, p. 633 at pp. 673–90; Int. L.R. 50, p. 2 at pp. 500–19; on which see Rousseau, 72 *R.G.D.I.P.* (1968), 1100–21; Salmon, 14 *Ann. français* (1968), 217–36; Untawale, 23 *I.C.L.Q.* (1974), 818–39; Anand, *Studies in International Adjudication* (1969), pp. 218–49.

Manifestations of territorial sovereignty assume, it is true, different forms, according to conditions of time and place. Although continuous in principle, sovereignty cannot be exercised in fact at every moment on every point of a territory. The intermittence and discontinuity compatible with the maintenance of the right necessarily differ according as inhabited or uninhabited regions are involved, or regions enclosed within territories in which sovereignty is incontestably displayed or again regions accessible from, for instance, the high seas.[1]

He then reiterated the view that 'the actual continuous and peaceful display of State functions is in case of dispute the sound and natural criterium of territorial sovereignty . . .'.[2] Having disposed of United States arguments based upon discovery,[3] recognition by treaty,[4] and contiguity,[5] and having decided that there was insufficient evidence of Spanish activities in relation to the Island of Palmas, the arbitrator then examined the Netherlands' arguments based upon peaceful and continuous display of state authority over the island. In his opinion the people of the island were connected with the East India Company, and thereby the Netherlands, by contracts of suzerainty[6] from 1677 onwards, and, allowing for the isolated position of the island and the relation of a colonial power and a vassal state[7] (which in turn controlled the island), there was evidence 'which tends to show that there were unchallenged acts of peaceful display of Netherlands sovereignty in the period from 1700 to 1906,[8] and which . . . may be regarded as sufficiently proving the existence of Netherlands sovereignty'.

In 1931 an award was made in the *Clipperton Island* arbitration[9] which resolved a dispute between France and Mexico, arising in 1898, on the subject of the sovereignty over an uninhabited[1] island in the Pacific Ocean. The reasoning of the award related very closely to the particular facts, and caution is needed in deducing principles from it.[2] However, the arbitrator stated une-

[1] See further on the degree of effectiveness required the *Clipperton Island* arbitration, *infra*; the *Eastern Greenland* case, *infra*, p. 153; Lauterpacht, *The Development of International Law by the International Court*, pp. 240–2; id., 27 *B.Y.* (1950), 415–19. Cf. *Frontier Land* case, I.C.J. Reports (1959), p. 228.

[2] See also *R.I.A.A.* ii. 867; Hague Court Reports ii. 126, and quotation thereof by the Permanent Court in the *Eastern Greenland* case, P.C.I.J., Ser. A/B, no. 53, p. 45; World Court Reports iii. at p. 170.

[3] *Infra*, p. 149. [4] *Infra*, p. 163. [5] *Infra*, pp. 153–4.

[6] See *supra*, p. 119. [7] See *supra*, p. 77.

[8] At which date the dispute arose. The critical date was in 1898.

[9] Award of the King of Italy; *R.I.A.A.* ii. 1105; 26 *A.J.* (1932), 390. Hudson, *Cases*, p. 209; Briggs, p. 247; Hackworth i. 404.

[1] A low coral lagoon reef, 670 miles south-west of Mexico.

[2] For further discussion see *infra*, pp. 151–2.

quivocally that 'the actual, and not the nominal, taking of possession is a necessary condition of occupation', and the taking of possession consisted of an exercise of state authority sufficient in the circumstances of the territory concerned.

The Permanent Court in the *Eastern Greenland* case[1] considered the status of the disputed area at the critical date, 10 July 1931, when Norway had proclaimed its occupation. Norway maintained that the area was then *terra nullius*. Denmark, in part,[2] argued that valid title in her favour had existed for a long time on the basis of the actual display of state authority over the whole of Greenland.[3] In deciding in favour of the Danish contention, the Permanent Court had regard to a pattern of activity between 1721 and 1931, including the enforcement of legislation of a state trade monopoly, the granting of trading, mining, and other concessions, the exercise of governmental functions and administration, and the making of numerous treaties in the terms of which Danish rights over Greenland were explicit. The Norwegian occupation was illegal and invalid, since Denmark, at the very least in the ten years previous to the Norwegian occupation, had 'displayed and exercized her sovereign rights to an extent sufficient to constitute a valid title to sovereignty'.

The emphasis on the display of state activity, and the interpretation of the facts in the light of a legal policy which favours stability and allows for the special characteristics of uninhabited and remote territories, are evidence of a change in the law. The modern law concentrates on title, evidence of sovereignty, and the notion of occupation has been refined accordingly.[4] In deciding in favour of the United Kingdom in the *Minquiers and Ecrehos* case,[5] the International Court applied, in a practical way, the modern law. Thus in relation to the Ecrehos group the Court was concerned with acts involving the exercise of jurisdiction, local administration, such as the holding of inquests in Jersey on corpses found on the Ecrehos,[6] and also an act of legislation, a British Treasury Warrant of 1875 constituting Jersey a Port of

[1] *Supra*, p. 142, n. 4. [2] See *infra*, pp. 153, 163.

[3] See *infra*, pp. 153–4, on the extent of sovereignty.

[4] See von der Heydte, 29 *A.J.* (1935), p. 448 at pp. 462 seq.; Rousseau iii. 169.

[5] I.C.J. Reports (1953), p. 47; Green, p. 8; 48 *A.J.* (1954), 316. See also Johnson, 3 *I.C.L.Q.* (1954), 189–216; Fitzmaurice, 32 *B.Y.* (1955–6), 20–76. See further *United States* v. *Fullard-Leo* (1943), 331 U.S. 256; *Case Concerning Sovereignty over Certain Frontier Land,* I.C.J. Reports (1959), p. 209 at pp. 228–9, 231–2, 248–50, 251, 255; *Case Concerning the Temple of Preah Vihear,* I.C.J. Reports (1962), p. 6 at pp. 12, 29–30, 59–60, 72, 91–6; Green, p. 457 at p. 462; and I.C.J. Pleadings, *Antarctica Cases* (*United Kingdom* v. *Argentina; United Kingdom* v. *Chile*), 1956.

[6] I.C.J. Reports (1953), pp. 65–66. On acts relating to the Minquiers see pp. 67–70.

the Channel Islands. In the *Frontier Land*[1] and *Temple*[2] cases the Court was reluctant to place reliance on acts of local administration.

Rann of Kutch *case, 1968*. The Award in this case remarked that in an agricultural and traditional economy, the distinction between state and private interests was not to be established with the firmness to be expected in a modern industrial economy.[3] In an agricultural economy grazing and other economic activities by private landholders may provide evidence of title.

Sovereignty and the duty of protection. In his award in the *Island of Palmas* case Huber states[4] that territorial sovereignty involves the right to exclude the activities of other states, and that, as a corollary of this, a duty exists 'to protect within the territory the rights of other States, in particular their right to integrity and inviolability in peace and in war, together with the rights which each State may claim for its nationals in foreign territory'. Maintenance of a reasonable standard of administration is thus strong evidence of sovereignty. However, it is doubtful if the fulfilment of the duty is an absolute condition for the existence of sovereignty, as some jurists assert.[5] It is generally admitted that slight activity will suffice in the case of uninhabited and remote regions, but, apart from the special circumstances of such territories, the view asserted will prejudice the rights of underdeveloped countries.[6] Failure to provide the minimum standard of protection to aliens will give rise to a claim for damages if injury ensues.[7]

Acts of appropriation by private persons. Acts by private persons purporting to appropriate territory for the state of which they are nationals may be ratified by the state and will then constitute evidence of effective occupation in the ordinary way.[8] The former

[1] I.C.J. Reports (1959), p. 209 at pp. 228–9, 231–2, 248–50, 251, 255.

[2] I.C.J. Reports (1962), p. 6 at pp. 29–30; Green, p. 457 at p. 462.

[3] *Int. Leg. Materials* vii., p. 633 at pp. 673–5; Int. L.R. 50, p. 2 at pp. 500–1.

[4] *R.I.A.A.* ii. 839; Hague Court Reports ii. 93. Cf. the *Clipperton Island* award, *infra*, pp. 151–2.

[5] See Waldock, 25 *B.Y.* (1948), 317; Fitzmaurice, 32 *B.Y.* (1955–6), 51.

[6] See also the criticism of Huber's extension to the doctrine of inter-temporal law, *supra*, pp. 131–3; and on the emphasis of the International Court on stability and effectiveness in acquisition of territory, Lauterpacht, *The Development of International Law by the International Court*, pp. 240–2. A logic similar to that in the passage in Huber's award has also given rise to a doctrine of the relativity of rights which would lead to considerable instability: see Bowett, *Self-Defence in International Law*, pp. 39, 51, 60, 66, 90–1, 152, 270. See also *infra*, pp. 149–50, 166–8, on inchoate title and relative title.

[7] *Infra*, Chapter XXIII.

[8] Oppenheim i. 544, 555; McNair, *Opinions* i. 295, 314, 316–19, 323–5. See also Orent and Reinsch, 35 *A.J.* (1941), 450–4.

doctrine, based upon agency in private law, was that ratification could only be of the acts of officials.

Acquisition by chartered companies.[1] The activity of chartered companies and corporations, such as the Dutch East India Company, to which a state may delegate considerable powers of acquisition and government, will be regarded as state activity in relation to the acquisition of sovereignty.

Notification of claims. Notice of a territorial claim or an intention to extend sovereignty to other governments constitutes evidence of occupation, but is not a condition for acquisition.[2] As between the contracting parties, conventions may provide for notification of claims.[3]

9. *Abandonment or* Derelictio[4]

In the face of competing activity and claims by another, a state may by conduct or by express admission acquiesce in the extension of its competitor's sovereignty. This process is more properly considered elsewhere.[5] In other cases, and more especially in the case where a claimant asserts that territory previously occupied by a rival claimant had been *res nullius* at a particular time and open to acquisition, 'abandonment' is simply the negative counterpart of effective occupation. Absence of a reasonable level of state activity may cause loss of title.[6] However, by reason of the need to maintain stability and to avoid temptations to 'squatting', abandonment is not to be presumed. Tribunals require little in the way of maintenance of sovereignty, particularly in regard to remote and uninhabited areas.[7] Thus in

[1] See Oppenheim i. 544–5; Rousseau iii. 154; McNair, 26 *B.Y.* (1949), pp. 41–4; id., *Opinions* i. 295; *Island of Palmas* arbitration, *R.I.A.A.* ii. 858–9; Hague Court Reports ii. 115–17.

[2] Oppenheim i. 559; McNair, *Opinions* i. 286, 292; Hackworth i. 408–9; Guggenheim i. 441. Notice was not regarded as necessary in the *Island of Palmas* or *Clipperton Island* cases. As a form of evidence see the award in the latter case, *infra*, pp. 151–2. On the effect of silence in the face of notice of claims see *infra*, pp. 163–5.

[3] See the General Act of the Berlin Congo Conference, abrogated by the Treaty of St. Germain, 1919. Some writers generalized from the General Act. Cf. Westlake i (2nd ed.), 112; Rousseau iii. 164; and see Hyde i. 343.

[4] Hyde i. 392–4; McNair, *Opinions* i. 299–305; Oppenheim i. 579–81; Moore, *Digest* i. 300; Beckett, 50 Hague *Recueil* (1934, IV), 252–5; Hackworth i. 442–3; Fitzmaurice, 32 *B.Y.* (1955–6), 67. See *supra*, p. 139, on renunciation or relinquishment.

[5] *Infra*, pp. 163–5.

[6] In principle the term 'abandonment' could be reserved for the rare situation in which a state *intends* to abandon and expressly and formally renounces title (without this involving a procedure by which the territory falls under another sovereignty: see *supra*, p. 139).

[7] Thus Huber in speaking of the duty of protection (*supra*, p. 147) in the *Island of Palmas* award was too dogmatic in the context of abandonment.

the *Clipperton Island* award[1] it is stated: 'There is no reason to suppose that France has subsequently lost her right by *derelictio*, since she never had the *animus* of abandoning the island, and the fact that she has not exercised her authority there in a positive manner does not imply the forfeiture of an acquisition already definitively protected.' In the *Eastern Greenland* case[2] Norway had argued that Greenland became *terra nullius* after the disappearance of the early settlements. The Court, rejecting the argument, observed: 'As regards voluntary abandonment, there is nothing to show any definite renunciation on the part of the Kings of Norway or Denmark'.

10. *Discovery*[3]

This category, though much employed, is less than satisfactory for the purpose of legal analysis. In principle it is to be distinguished from acts of state activity initiating an occupation, and also from symbolic annexation (the doubts existing in regard to this institution are considered subsequently). In practice discovery may be accompanied by symbolic acts, the planting of a flag and the like, and the distinction becomes blurred. At one time it was believed that in the fifteenth and sixteenth centuries discovery without more conferred a complete title.[4] Modern research has given cause to doubt that it gave more than an inchoate title in this period: an effective act of appropriation seems to have been necessary.[5] The view accepted by many jurists as to the modern law is that it gives an inchoate title, an option, as against other states, to consolidate the first steps by

[1] See *infra*, pp. 151–2. [2] *Supra* p. 142, n. 4.

[3] See Hyde i. 312–30; von der Heydte, 29 *A.J.* (1935), 448–71; Goebel, *The Struggle for the Falkland Islands* (1927), pp. 47–119; Keller, Lissitzyn, and Mann, *Creation of Rights of Sovereignty Through Symbolic Acts, 1400–1800* (1938); McDougal, Lasswell, Vlasic, and Smith, 111 *U. of Penn. L.R.* (1963), 543–4, 558–60, 598–611; McDougal, Lasswell, and Vlasic, *Law and Public Order in Space*, pp. 829–44; Waldock, 25 *B.Y.* (1948), 322–5.

[4] See Hall, p. 126.

[5] See Goebel, *The Struggle for the Falkland Islands* (1927), pp. 58, 69–73, 89–117; von der Heydte, op. cit., pp. 452 seq.; Hyde i. 324, 326. In the sixteenth century the Roman law relating to acquisition by finding was applied, and this emphasized actual taking. Bartolus, Gryphiander, and Grotius give a similar emphasis, and contemporary state practice usually demanded a first taking followed by a public and continuous possession evidenced by state activity. See the instructions of Charles V of Spain to his ambassador of 18 December, 1523 respecting the Spanish claim to the Moluccas: Goebel, pp. 96–7; Hyde i. 324. Keller, Lissitzyn, and Mann, op. cit., pp. 148–9 (and see Hackworth i. 398) consider that whereas mere discovery, 'visual apprehension', could not give a valid title, symbolic acts of taking of possession did have this result.

proceeding to effective occupation within a reasonable time.[1] In the *Island of Palmas* case[2] the United States argued that, as successor to Spain, title derived from Spanish discovery in the sixteenth century. While reserving his opinion on this point, Huber stated that, even if discovery without more gave title at that time, the continued existence of the right must be determined according to the law prevailing in 1898, at the critical date. In his opinion the modern law is that 'an inchoate title of discovery must be completed within a reasonable period by the effective occupation of the region claimed to be discovered'. Modern British[3] and Norwegian[4] practice supports this view. The official American view[5] is that mere discovery gives no title, inchoate or otherwise, and this view has much to commend it. The 'law of discovery' only makes sense if it is placed firmly in the context of effective occupation, and the modern law could avoid the category altogether.[6] Further, the notion of inchoate title is misleading. Title, which is in practice a question of the relative strength of state activity, is never 'inchoate', though it may be 'weak' in that it rests on a small amount of evidence of state activity.[7] The distinct though related question of symbolic annexation will be examined presently.

11. *Papal Grants*[8]

In the fifteenth century the Pope assumed a power to regulate the discovery and acquisition of lands which, in European terms, were 'unexplored' and 'unknown'. Best known are the Bulls of Pope Alexander VI of 1493 which assigned to Spain exclusive rights in land discovered or to be discovered west of the meridian one hundred leagues west of the Azores and Cape Verde, apart from lands already possessed by any Christian king or prince by

[1] Hall, p. 127; Oppenheim i. 559; Guggenheim i. 439; McNair, *Opinions* i. 285.

[2] *Supra*, p. 144. See also the *Clipperton Island* case, *infra*, pp. 151–2, in which Mexico relied unsuccessfully on alleged discovery by Spain.

[3] McNair, *Opinions* i. 285, 287, 320; Hackworth i. 455.

[4] Hackworth i. 400, 453, 469. See also ibid. 459 (French view on Adélie Land), and Orent and Reinsch, 35 *A.J.* (1941), 443–61, and cf. Hyde i. 325 (Portuguese view in 1782).

[5] Hackworth i. 398–400, 457, 460.

[6] The logical difficulty is the apparent assumption in some statements that mere discovery, without any state activity, bars any competitor 'for a reasonable time'. This seems to be clearly incompatible with the law on effective occupation. Cf. von der Heydte, op. cit., pp. 461–2.

[7] See further *infra*, p. 167.

[8] Hyde i. 323–4; von der Heydte, op. cit., pp. 451–2; Goebel, op. cit., pp. 49–54, 78–85, 95–6; Waldock, 25 *B.Y.* (1948), 321–2.

Christmas 1492. The legal nature of these 'grants' varied, but two general comments may be made. First, they were often in effect partitioning arrangements which could only bind the parties involved.[1] Secondly, they were not really 'grants' or titles as such, but either a recognition of the validity of existing claims by discovery and occupation, or licences to occupy territory, giving a provisional or inchoate title. Papal grants are sometimes cited in arbitration proceedings,[2] and the operation of the doctrine of inter-temporal law may give them significance. However, today their effect is minimized by the requirements for effective occupation.

12. *Symbolic Annexation*[3]

Symbolic annexation may be defined as a declaration or other act of sovereignty or an act of private persons, duly authorized, or subsequently ratified by a state, intended to provide unequivocal evidence of the acquisition of sovereignty over a parcel of territory or an island. The subject must be seen as a part of the general question of effective occupation. There is no magic in the formal declaration of sovereignty by a government, whether or not this is preceded, accompanied, or followed by a formal ceremony in the vicinity concerned. In the case of uninhabited, inhospitable, and remote regions little is required in the nature of state activity,[4] and a first and decisive act of sovereignty will suffice to create a valid title. In principle the state activity must satisfy the normal requirements of 'effective occupation'. 'Symbolic annexation' does not give title except in special circumstances (as in the *Clipperton Island* case below). However, in the case of a *res nullius*, or a situation of competing state activity,[5] it is a part of the evidence of state activity. It has been stated[6] that 'a prior State act of formal annexation cannot after a long interval prevail against an actual and continuous display of sovereignty by another State'. With respect it is thought that formal annexa-

[1] Henry VII of England and Francis I of France did not recognize the grants to Spain and Portugal in 1493.

[2] They played a very minor role in the *Island of Palmas* case; see Jessup, 22 *A.J.* (1928), 741. Papal grants were involved in the dispute between France and Brazil, Award of 1900, and concern the current issue between Venezuela and Guyana.

[3] von der Heydte, 29 *A.J.* (1935), 452 seq.; McDougal *et al.*, op. cit.; Hackworth i. 398–9; Waldock, 25 *B.Y.* (1948), 323–5; McNair, *Opinions* i. 314 seq.; Orent and Reinsch, 35 *A.J.* (1941), 443–61. Cf. the proclamation of rights over the continental shelf: see Waldock, 36 *Grot. Soc.* (1950), 140–2 and *infra*, p. 223.

[4] See the judgment in the *Eastern Greenland* case.

[5] *Supra*, p. 142.

[6] See Waldock, op. cit., p. 325. Cf. Fitzmaurice, 32 *B.Y.* (1955–6), 65.

tion creates something more than an 'inchoate title' and that the competitor can only succeed, if at all, on the basis of prescription[1] or acquiescence.[2] To require too much in respect of the maintenance of rights may well involve a return to the nineteenth-century concept of effectiveness and encourage threats to the peace.[3] In the case of remote islands, it is unhelpful to require a determinate minimum of 'effectiveness'.

In the *Clipperton Island* case[4] a lieutenant in the French navy, duly authorized, proclaimed French sovereignty in 1858 when cruising near the island, and the event was notified to the Government of Hawaii by the French consulate. In 1897, after inactivity in the intervening years, a French vessel called at the island and found three Americans collecting guano for an American company. The United States stated that it had no intention of claiming sovereignty. In the same year the island received its first visit from a Mexican gunboat and a diplomatic controversy began. The Mexican case rested on an allegation of Spanish discovery, and the arbitrator stated that even if an historic right existed it was not supported by any manifestation of Mexican sovereignty. Assuming the island to be *terra nullius* in 1858, the question was whether France had proceeded to an effective occupation. If she had not, Mexico had a right to treat the island as open to occupation in 1897. The arbitrator stated that a condition of occupation was an actual taking of possession which consisted in an act or series of acts by which the territory is reduced to possession. The award continues:

> Strictly speaking, and in ordinary cases, that only takes place when the State establishes in the territory itself an organization capable of making its laws respected. But this step is, properly speaking, but a means of proceeding to the taking of possession, and, therefore, is not identical with the latter. There may also be cases where it is unnecessary to have recourse to this method. Thus, if a territory, by virtue of the fact that it was completely uninhabited, is, from the first moment when the occupying State makes its appearance there, at the absolute and undisputed disposition of that State, from that moment the taking of possession must be considered as accomplished, and the occupation is thereby completed.

Thus France acquired the island when sovereignty was proclaimed on 17 November 1858 and the purported annexation, though symbolic in form, had legal effect.

[1] See *infra*, pp. 156 seq. [2] See *infra*, pp. 163–5.

[3] See *supra*, p. 148, on abandonment.

[4] References: *supra*, p. 145, n. 9. On the establishment of British sovereignty over Rockall in 1955: Verzijl, *International Law in Historical Perspective* iii (1970), 351.

13. *Extent of Sovereignty: Geographical Doctrines*[1]

We are here concerned with certain logical and equitable principles which are not roots of title[2] but are of importance in determining the actual extent of sovereignty derived from some orthodox source of title such as a treaty of cession or effective occupation. Principles of continuity, contiguity, and geographical unity come to the fore when the disputed territory is uninhabited, barren, or uncharted. In relation to islands contiguity is the relevant concept. The principles are simply a part of judicial reasoning, but have significance in other respects. In the context of effective occupation, continuity and contiguity are a facet of the modern view of sovereignty according to which it does not depend on close settlement but on state activity. State activity as evidence of sovereignty need not press uniformly on every part of territory.[3] Associated with this is the presumption of peripheral possession[4] based on state activity, for example, on the coast of a barren territory.[5] Lastly, in giving effect to principles of geographical unity in the *Eastern Greenland* case,[6] and thus concluding that somewhat localized Danish activity gave title over the whole of Greenland, the Permanent Court was not swayed by an intellectual significance of unity isolated from the context of effective occupation. In writing of the decision Lauterpacht[7] remarked on 'those principles of finality, stability and effectiveness[8] of international relations which have characterized the work of the Court'. Contiguity is in itself an earnest of effective-

[1] Hyde i. 331–6; Waldock, 25 *B.Y.* (1948), 339 seq.; von der Heydte, 29 *A.J.* (1935), 463–71; Fitzmaurice, 32 *B.Y.* (1955–6), 72–5; Kelsen, *Wehberg Festschrift* (1956), pp. 200–11; Lauterpacht, 27 *B.Y.* (1950), 423–31; McNair, *Opinions* i. 287–8, 292; Rousseau iii. 193–203.

[2] It would probably be truer to say that geographical doctrines are not independent roots of title: they are subsidiary to some other root of title, normally that of effective occupation.

[3] Thus the ordinary concept of effective occupation is the rationale of the *Eastern Greenland* case. It must be noted that some Danish legislation applied to Greenland as a whole.

[4] The legal force and procedural effect of which will depend on the facts of the case.

[5] *British Guiana Boundary* arbitration (1904), *R.I.A.A.* xi. 21; Hudson, p 214. Cf. the old hinterland doctrine. See also the *Island of Palmas* case, *R.I.A.A.* ii. 855; Green, p. 421; ind. op. of Judge Levi Carneiro, *Minquiers and Ecrehos* case, I.C.J. Reports (1953), p. 99; Jennings, *The Acquisition of Territory*, pp. 74–6.

[6] P.C.I.J., Ser. A/B, no. 53, pp. 45–52; World Court Reports iii. 170–7; and see the Advisory Opinion concerning *Western Sahara*, I.C.J. Reports, 1975, p. 12 at pp. 42–3.

[7] *The Development of International Law by the International Court*, p. 241.

[8] See also the diss. opinions of Judge Moreno Quintana, *Case Concerning Sovereignty over Certain Frontier Land*, I.C.J. Reports (1959), p. 257; and the *Temple* case, ibid. (1962), p. 71.

ness and has undoubtedly been an element in claims to the continental shelf.[1]

In conclusion it may be said that the 'principle of contiguity' is little more than a technique in the application of the normal principles of effective occupation.[2] In the case of islands in particular the notion of contiguity may be unhelpful. Huber in his award in the *Island of Palmas*[3] case said that 'the alleged principle itself is by its very nature so uncertain and contested that even governments of the same State have on different occasions maintained contradictory opinions as to its soundness. . . .'

14. *Arctic and Antarctic Sectors*[4]

Particularly in the case of the Arctic, the question of rights over frozen sea or 'ice territory' arises,[5] but otherwise the principles relating to discovery, symbolic annexation, effective occupation, and contiguity apply to territory situated in polar regions. In the making of claims to ice deserts and remote groups of islands, it is hardly surprising that governments should seek to establish the limits of territorial sovereignty by means of straight lines, and similar systems of delimitation may be found in different types of region, for example in North America.[6] In polar regions use has been made of lines of longitude converging at the Poles to produce a sector of sovereignty. Whilst the 'sector principle' does not give title which would not arise otherwise, if the necessary state activity occurs, it represents a

[1] Cf. *infra*, p. 202, on archipelagos.

[2] For a different opinion: Guggenheim i. 440–1. See also Whiteman ii. 1104–8.

[3] *R.I.A.A.* ii. 854; Hague Court Reports ii. 111. Other disputes involving arguments based on contiguity: *Bulama Island* case (1870), Moore, *Arbitrations* ii. 1909; Lobos Islands (1852), Moore, *Digest* i. 265–6, 575; Navassa Island (1872), Moore i. 266–7; *Aves Island* case (Netherlands/Venezuela) (1865), Moore, *Arbitrations* v. 5037 (Spanish Report); Lapradelle and Politis ii. 404, 412; *Aves Isalnd* (U.S./Venezuela; diplomatic controversy), Moore, *Digest* i. 266, 271. See further Hyde i. 343–6; McNair, *Opinions* i. 315.

[4] See for the Antarctic: Hackworth i. 399–400, 449–76; Waldock, 25 *B.Y.* (1948), 311–53; U.S. Naval War College, *Int. Law Docs.* (1948–9), pp. 217–45; Castles, in O'Connell (ed.), *International Law in Australia* (1965), pp. 341–67; Hayton, 50 *A.J.* (1956), 583–610; Toma, ibid., 611–26; Auburn, 19 *I.C.L.Q.* (1970), 229–56. On the Arctic: Lakhtine, 24 *A.J* (1930), 703–17; Hyde i. 349–50; Head, 9 *McGill L.J.* (1963), 200–26; Pharand, 19 *Univ. of Toronto L.J.* (1969), 210–33, Reid, 12 *Canad. Yrbk.* (1974), 111–36. See further Balch, 4 *A.J.* (1910); 265–75; Smedal, *Acquisition of Sovereignty over Polar Areas* (1931); Dollot, 75 Hague *Recueil* (1949, II), 121–9; Whiteman ii. 1051–61; Hyde, 19 *Iowa L.R.* (1933–4), 286–94; Rousseau iii. 203–30. On the status of Antarctica under the Antarctic Treaty see *infra*, pp. 265–6.

[5] Some writers take the view that permanently frozen ice shelves are susceptible to effective occupation. See Waldock, 25 *B.Y.* (1948), 317–18; Hackworth, i. 449–52; Fitzmaurice, 92 Hague *Recueil* (1957, II), 155; Whiteman ii. 1266–7; and, further, items in note 4 above.

[6] See also, on the determination of the territorial sea, pp. 186 seq.

reasonable application of the principles of effective occupation as they are now understood, and as they were applied in the *Eastern Greenland* case.[1] It remains a rough method of delimitation, and has not become a separate rule of law. Confusion of claims has arisen primarily from the indecisive nature of state activity in polar regions. However, three reservations may be made: the 'sector principle' has the defects of any doctrine based upon contiguity; its application is a little absurd in so far as there is claim to a narrow sliver of sovereignty stretching to the Pole; and, lastly, it cannot apply so as to include areas of the high seas.

The state practice is thought to support the propositions advanced. In the Arctic, Denmark, Finland, Norway, and the United States have refrained from sector claims linked to territories peripheral to the polar seas. On the other hand Canada[2] and the U.S.S.R.[3] support and have made use of the sector principle. It is very probable that it is recognition by treaty or otherwise which creates title[4] in the Arctic rather than the sector principle as such.[5] Sector claims in Antarctica have been made by the United Kingdom,[6] New Zealand, Australia, France, Norway, Germany, Argentina, and Chile.[7] The state practice calls for brief comment. First, some claims are made which do not depend in the first place on contiguity but on discovery. Secondly, claimants are not confined to peripheral neighbours as in the Arctic. And thirdly, recognition[8] is obviously important in establishing title in an otherwise fluid situation created by overlapping claims, many of which in law amount to little more than claims to first option or declarations of interest.

15. *Accretion, Erosion, and Avulsion*[9]

The three terms in the title describe similar processes resulting in the increase of territory through new formations.

[1] See Wall, 1 *I.L.Q.* (1947), 54–58.

[2] No precise declaration has been made, but see Hackworth i. 463.

[3] Decree of 15 April 1926; Hackworth i. 461; Kozhevnikov (ed.), *International Law*, p. 191.

[4] See *infra*, p. 163.

[5] See Hackworth i. 463–8.

[6] This claim, the first sector claim in the area, was by Letters Patent in 1917 defining the Falkland Islands Dependencies.

[7] For the various claims see: *Int. Law Docs.*, 1948–9, loc. cit.; Hackworth i. 456 seq.; Reeves, 33 *A.J.* (1939), 519–21; 34 *A.J.* (1940), Suppl., p. 83. There is doubt as to the existence of a clear claim by Germany.

[8] Thus the Norwegian proclamation of 1939 was accompanied by a minute of the Ministry of Foreign Affairs which recognized the British, New Zealand, Australian, and French claims. Norway does not accept the sector principle as such. Japan renounced her claims by the peace treaty of 8 September, 1951.

[9] See Oppenheim i. 563–6; Schwarzenberger, *International Law* (3rd ed.), pp. 294–6; Hackworth i. 409–21; Hyde i. 355; Huber, arbitrator, in the *Island of Palmas* award,

Thus, in the simple case, deposits on a sea coast may result in an extension of sovereignty. As Hyde puts it: 'No formal acts of appropriation are required.' The doctrine does not make an express choice between accretion, as a doctrine of appurtenance, and effective occupation: in the latter case there is a presumption of occupation (Hyde's formulation is in this sense correct), but the presumption could be met by evidence of renunciation. The usual assumption in the books is that accretion is a distinct 'mode of acquiring territory'. However, the general observations to be found under the heading are to be treated with reserve. Whenever, as, for example, in the case of boundary rivers and delta systems, the presumption of unchallenged occupation does not arise on the facts, accretion ceases to be a root of title. Thus, in relation to the southern boundary of New Mexico, the solution of disputes between the United States and Mexico depended on principles of acquiescence and the interpretation of agreements as to the outcome of natural changes.[1] In this type of case, even in the absence of applicable agreements, sudden, forcible, and significant changes in river courses (avulsion) will not be considered to have changed the frontier line,[2] which is normally the centre line of the former main channel or *thalweg*.[3] Accretion, the gradual and imperceptible addition of substance, is only valid in so far as the process gives rise to an extension to areas already under effective occupation[4] on the basis of principles of contiguity and certainty. The gradual nature of the process leads to a presumption of occupation by the riparian state and one of acquiescence by other states. Probably the use of the categories of accretion and avulsion cannot be avoided, but one may doubt if they are 'modes of acquisition'.

16. *Acquisitive Prescription*[5]

The reader will be well advised to regard the heading and the

R.I.A.A. ii, p. 829 at p. 839; the *Anna* (1805), 5 C. Rob. 373. Whatever the historical links, the Roman law cannot provide authoritative principles of law in this sphere except when the particular principle may be said to represent a general principle of law (or common sense). However, the texts on *alluvio, avulsio, insula nata,* and *alveus derelictus* give insight into the types of problem which may be encountered.

[1] See the *Chamizal* arbitration, 5 *A.J.* (1911), 785; *R.I.A.A.* xi. 316; Briggs, p. 258; Hudson, p. 267; Hackworth i. 409 seq.; and the *San Lorenzo* case, *Ann. Digest* 6 (1931–2), no. 55. See also the Chamizal Conv. of 1963, 58 *A.J.* (1964), 336.

[2] *Nebraska* v. *Iowa* (1892), 143 U.S. 359; Hudson, p. 265; *Kansas* v. *Missouri* (1943), 322 U.S. 213. Cf. the decision of the commission in the *Chamizal* case, *supra*, n. 1.

[3] See *infra*, p. 172, on the meaning of this term.

[4] See Huber, loc. cit.

[5] See generally Audinet, 3 *R.G.D.I.P.* (1896), 313–25; Whiteman ii. 1062–84; Johnson, 27 *B.Y.* (1950), 332–54; Verykios, *La Prescription en droit international public* (1934);

category it represents as no more than a conventional introduction to certain types of subject-matter, since the use of the general and convenient classification is very far from being a substitute for careful analysis. As a further preliminary it is necessary to distinguish extinctive prescription or 'prescription libératoire'. In English terms this concerns the limitation of actions. The failure to bring a claim before an international tribunal due to the negligence or laches of the claimant party may cause an international tribunal eventually seised of the dispute to declare the claim to be inadmissible. In a territorial dispute (or indeed a dispute over any property rights) lapse of time may create equities in favour of the possessor in the form of expenditure on, or investments in, the territory possessed.[1]

As a 'mode of acquisition' of territory prescription is accepted by many jurists, although some eminent opinions[2] of the nineteenth century denied that it was an institution of international law. The essence of prescription is the removal of defects in a putative title arising from usurpation of another's sovereignty by the consent and acquiescence of the former sovereign. The standard apology for the principle rests on considerations of good faith, the presumed voluntary abandonment of rights by the party losing title, and the need to preserve international order and stability.

Analysis of the concept. Since the concept, alleged to be a part of international law, depends on the views of writers, it is hardly surprising that in form it reflects the variety of view expressed as well as the internal inconsistencies of some expositions.[3] At least the doctrine[4] reveals clearly that the concept is regarded by jurists as having three forms:

(1) Immemorial possession. This is understood to give title when a state of affairs exists the origin of which is uncertain and may have been legal or illegal but is presumed to be legal.

(2) Prescription under conditions similar to those required for *usucapio* in Roman law: uninterrupted possession, *justus titulus* even if it were defective, good faith, and the

Jennings, *Acquisition of Territory*, pp. 20–3; Hackworth i. 432–42; MacGibbon, 31 *B.Y.* (1954), p. 143 at pp. 152–68; Fitzmaurice, 30 *B.Y.* (1953), p. 1 at pp. 27–43; id., 32 *B.Y.* (1955–6), p. 20 at pp. 31–7; Pinto, 87 Hague *Recueil* (1955, I), 433–8; Sørensen, 3 *Acta Scandinavica* (1932), 145–60; Blum, *Historic Titles in International Law* (1965), pp. 6–37.

[1] See King, 15 *B.Y.* (1934), 82–97.

[2] Heffter, F. de Martens, and Rivier.

[3] See Johnson, op. cit., pp. 334–40.

[4] Exclusive of writing since the Second World War.

continuance of possession for a period defined by the law.

(3) *Usucapio*, modified and applying under conditions of bad faith. Thus Hall, Oppenheim, and Fauchille do not require good faith in the context of international law.

This analysis is helpful in revealing some of the problems to be faced. The principle of immemorial possession is supported by many jurists as a source of title,[1] though some deny that it is a form of 'acquisitive prescription'.[2] Since the origin of the possession is unknown, it is illogical to classify the principle as a form of prescription. It is inelegant, moreover, to describe it as a mode of acquisition or source of title: the genuine source in this type of case is recognition of or acquiescence[3] in the consequences of unchallenged possession.[4] Apart from this there is the distinct issue of the procedural effect of the presumption of legality. The parts of the analysis which rest on *usucapio* reveal the malaise inherent in the general doctrine of prescription. The doctrine refers to concepts of municipal law, and it is sometimes said that the International Court would accept acquisitive prescription as a general principle of law.[5] However, there is a certain lack of congruity between the good faith of *usucapio* and the concept of acquiescence which English law,[6] for example, equates with prescription. A taking in bad faith may meet with acquiescence whilst an honest possession may meet with challenge. What is the content of the general principle, if indeed there is one? Furthermore, some writers do not require good faith and give acquiescence a very elastic interpretation.

Leaving aside the category of 'immemorial possession', the term 'prescription' is often used by contemporary jurists to describe two distinct situations.

Competing activities in the same parcel of territory. It has been remarked previously[7] that in particular cases the difference between prescription and effective occupation is not easy to establish. The points commonly made are, first, that prescription applies to land already appropriated and is a supplanting of title, whereas occupation is of a *res nullius*; and, secondly, the analytical

[1] Hall, p. 143; Johnson, loc. cit.; de Louter, *Le Droit international public positif* i. 341; Verykios, op. cit., p. 76.

[2] F. de Martens; Rivier. See also Fitzmaurice, 32 *B.Y.* (1955–6), 31, 34.

[3] See *infra*, pp. 163–4; and see further Johnson, *Camb. L.J.* (1955), pp. 218–19; and Schwarzenberger, *International Law* i (3rd ed.), 306, 332.

[4] The adjective 'immemorial' is superfluous and rather misleading.

[5] See Johnson, 27 *B.Y.* (1959), 343. See also *supra*, p. 15.

[6] Cheshire, *Modern Real Property* (12th ed.), pp. 542, 898–900.

[7] *Supra*, p. 142.

and not very relevant fact that prescription alone applies to rights over the sea.[1] However, in the *Island of Palmas* case and others like it,[2] the territory is not a *res nullius*, as it belongs to one of the two claimants, and yet there is no usurpation. There is simply contemporaneously competing state activity, and in deciding the question of title the tribunal concerned will apply the tests of effective control associated with 'effective occupation'. To speak of prescription here is unhelpful,[3] and significantly Huber in the *Palmas* arbitration avoided the terminology, apart from a passing reference to 'so-called prescription', by which he meant merely 'continuous and peaceful display of State sovereignty'.

Acquiescence by the displaced competitor. The writer's submission is that, in the second class of situation referred to above, acquiescence and estoppel may establish rights, and consequently an independent doctrine of 'prescription' has no function to fulfil. Some jurists have lately asserted the dependence of acquisitive prescription on acquiescence and consent.[4] For acquiescence and consent to operate they must have reference to a possession of territory.

The conditions for acquisitive prescription.[5] Assuming, without prejudice to later conclusions, that acquisitive prescription exists as a separate category, its content must be examined. The conditions usually specified are in fact interrelated and to some extent repetitive. They are also very similar to the criteria of effective occupation, with three differences. The first is that, in the case of competing state activities, the degree of possession must be greater, but this is hardly a vital difference and the case is not properly to be regarded as prescription. Secondly, unequivocal state acts will be required to provide a basis for conduct by the other party to a dispute which amounts to acquiescence in law. And, finally, there is the important difference—the criterion of acquiescence. The conditions as set forth by Fauchille and Johnson[6] may now be considered.

[1] *Infra*, p. 170. [2] *Supra*, pp. 144 seq.

[3] Examples of references to the *Palmas* case as an instance of prescription: Oppenheim i. 578; Beckett, 50 Hague *Recueil* (1934, IV), 220, 230; Johnson, 27 *B.Y.* (1950), 342, 348. Other cases misleadingly classified in this way: *British Guiana Boundary* arbitration, Great Britain and Brazil (1904), 99 B.F.S.P., p. 930; Hudson, p. 214; *R.I.A.A.* xi. 21; *Grisbadarna* arbitration, Sweden and Norway (1909), 4 *A.J.* (1910), 226; *R.I.A.A.* xi. 155; Hague Court Reports i. 121; *Guatemala-Honduras Boundary* arbitration (1933), *Ann. Digest* 7 (1933–4), no. 46; *R.I.A.A.* ii. 1322.

[4] MacGibbon, op. cit.; Schwarzenberger, *International Law* i (3rd ed.), 307. And see *infra*, pp. 163–4 on acquiescence and recognition. See also Anzilotti, diss. op. in the *Eastern Greenland case*, P.C.I.J., Ser. A/B, no. 53 at pp. 94–5.

[5] See Beckett, op. cit., p. 249.

[6] See Johnson, 27 *B.Y.* (1950), 343–8, adopting the classification of Fauchille, *Traité* i,

(1) Possession must be exercised *à titre de souverain*. This states an important and familiar element of effective occupation. There must be a display of state authority and the absence of recognition of sovereignty in another state, for example under conditions of a protectorate leaving the protected state with a separate personality.

(2) Possession must be peaceful and uninterrupted. Huber in the *Palmas* case refers to 'continuous and peaceful display of State authority'. Though quoted often, this formula must be construed with great care. In the context of the *Palmas* case itself, it can only represent a rule of thumb, a useful standard, since in a situation of competing acts of sovereignty, the condition cannot be mandatory. The question is, which claimant has done the most in the way of state activity?

Apart from the case of contemporaneously competitive acts of sovereignty, the principle would seem to be a statement to the effect that there must be acquiescence by the former sovereign. Two sources of difficulty exist. First, it would be better if the principle were expressed as one of acquiescence, since, if a piece of territory were occupied shortly before the pre-existing sovereign was forcibly occupied by an aggressor, the 'prescribing' state would have a peaceful and uninterrupted possession, but there would be no acquiescence.[1]

The second problem is to decide what suffices to prevent possession from being peaceful and uninterrupted. In principle the answer is clear: any conduct indicating a lack of acquiescence. Thus protests will be sufficient.[2] In the *Chamizal* arbitration[3] the United States claimed, as against Mexico, a tract of the Rio Grande on the basis of prescription, but the claim failed on the ground that the possession of the United States had not been without challenge. The United States was precluded from acquiring on a basis of prescription by the terms of a Convention of 1884. Furthermore, possession must be peaceable to provide a basis for prescription, and, in the opinion of the Commissioners,

Pt. ii, p. 759; Fauchille and Audinet, 3 *R.G.D.I.P.* (1896), 313–25, based their classifications on Art. 2229 of the French Civil Code.

[1] Except if there were an exile government with competence in this respect. See *infra*, p. 163 on recognition by third states, as opposed to acquiescence by the loser.

[2] This is the opinion of Hyde i. 387, 388; Oppenheim i. 576; Fauchille, *Traité* i, Pt. ii, p. 760. See generally MacGibbon, 30 *B.Y.* (1953), pp. 306–17. But see *infra*, p. 162 on those supporting adverse prescription.

[3] 5 *A.J.* (1911), 782; *R.I.A.A.* xi. 316; Hackworth i. 441; Hudson, p. 267. For the eventual resolution of the matter: 58 *A.J.* (1964), 336; and see Jessup, 67 *A.J.* (1973), 423–45. See also the *Walfisch Bay* arbitration (1911), Great Britain and Germany, Hertslet, *Treaties*, Vol. 26, pp. 187–250 at p. 249; 104 *B.F.S.P.* (1911), 50; *R.I.A.A.* xi. 267.

diplomatic protests by Mexico prevented title arising. A failure to take action which might lead to violence could not be held to jeopardize Mexican rights.[1]

Certain modern jurists regard the protest as effecting merely a postponement for a reasonable period of the process of prescription. Since 1920, it is argued, the protest must be followed by steps to use available machinery for the settlement of international disputes, at present primarily constituted by the United Nations and International Court.[2] This view lacks solid foundations. If acquiescence is the crux of the matter (and it is believed that it is) one cannot dictate what its content is to be, with the consequences that the rule that jurisdiction rests on consent may be ignored,[3] and failure to resort to certain organs is penalized by loss of territorial rights. In any case, as MacGibbon has pointed out,[4] in a number of situations it is quite inappropriate to require resort to an international tribunal or political organ.

(3) The possession must be public. Johnson has remarked:[5] 'Publicity is essential because acquiescence is essential.' In a complicated situation of competing state activity, as in the *Palmas* case, publicity will not play an important role because acquiescence may not be relevant except in minor respects.

(4) Possession must persist. Obviously the legal power of state activity depends in part on its persistence. In the case of a very recent possession it is difficult to adduce evidence of tacit acquiescence, and in cases like that of the *Island of Palmas* the principle is simply an element in the process of weighing the activity of the competing states. A few writers have prescribed fixed periods of years.[6] The appearance of such opinions is due to a yearning after municipal models and also to the influence of the view that 'acquiescence' may be 'implied' in certain conditions.[7] It is significant that modern writers usually hold the view that the length of time required is a matter of fact de-

[1] Today it is a principle of international law that force may not be used to settle international disputes: see Article 2, paragraphs 3 and 4, of the United Nations Charter.

[2] See MacGibbon, op. cit., pp. 312–17 (materials on the view of the Government of the United Kingdom). See also Johnson, 27 *B.Y.* (1950), 346, 353–4; Fitzmaurice, 30 *B.Y.* (1953), 28–9, 42–3; id., 32 *B.Y.* (1955–6), 33.

[3] See *infra*, p. 287, Chapter XXXI, section 8.

[4] Op. cit., pp. 314–17. See also Lauterpacht, 27 *B.Y.* (1950), 396–7.

[5] 27 *B.Y.* (1950), 347.

[6] Field, *Outlines of an International Code*, para. 52; fifty years. The fifty-year period specified in Article IV (a) of the arbitration treaty relative to the British Guiana–Venezuela boundary dispute, of 1897, represents an *ad hoc* rule of thumb. Incidentally, for Venezuela, the process was *res inter alios acta*: the parties were Great Britain and the United States. A good number of older authorities insist on immemorial possession.

[7] See *infra*, on adverse prescription.

pending on the particular case.[1] But this really eliminates time as a *special* requirement.

Adverse holding or negative prescription. Some writers[2] support, or seem to do so, the doctrine that prescriptive title arises even without acquiescence, simply by lapse of time and possession which is not disturbed by measures of forcible self-help. A similar result is reached by formulations which presume acquiescence under certain conditions. Such views are today exceptional and are not supported by state practice or jurisprudence. They commonly antedate the period when forcible self-help and conquest were prohibited.[3] It is probably the law that prescription cannot create rights out of situations brought about by illegal acts,[4] and it is unlikely that this form can be presented, with any plausibility, as a general principle of law, since it does not rest on good faith. Finally, it must be remembered that in the *Island of Palmas*[5] and *Minquiers and Ecrehos*[6] cases, and others like them, the possession ultimately upheld by the tribunal is adverse only in a special sense; in such cases there is no deliberate usurpation of sovereignty with a sequel of adverse holding, but a more or less contemporaneous competition.

Acquisitive prescription: an epitaph. In summary, the submission is that (if one excludes adverse holding or negative prescription) the situations described under the rubric of prescription by the writers, on analysis, fall into three categories: cases of immemorial possession; competing acts of sovereignty (*Island of Palmas* case); and cases of acquiescence. The first two categories are not really cases of prescription, but, as to the third, it may be said that acquiescence is a form of prescription and that the question ends as a matter of terminology. However, the doctrine is so tangled that it would be a help if the more candid and unambiguous label were used. And, of course, this would make clear the position of adverse holding in the law. However, it is important to notice that, whilst it is intended as an aid to understanding, the threefold analysis offered is not necessarily reflected neatly by life. In some cases it is not entirely clear whether there has been an occupation by one claimant of a *res nullius* followed

[1] Oppenheim i. 577–8; Fauchille, *Traité* i, Pt. ii, p. 762; Johnson, op. cit., pp. 347–8, 354; Hyde i. 388–9.

[2] See Hall, pp. 143–4 (but he refers to the acquiescence of other states); Moore, *Digest* i. 293–5 (ambiguous and diverse dicta of publicists collected); Hyde i. 386 (but at p. 387 he stresses the element of acquiescence); Guggenheim i. 442.

[3] See *infra*, pp. 173, 512.

[4] Lauterpacht, 27 *B.Y.* (1950), 397–8. See also *infra*, pp. 173–4, on the question of alienability.

[5] *Supra*, p. 144.

[6] *Supra*, p. 146.

later on by competing acts by another state, or whether there have been contemporaneously competing acts from the outset.[1] Again, in either case, a court will take acts of acquiescence into account:[2] in other words the second and third categories may overlap in practice.[3] In conclusion one may doubt whether there is any role in the law for a doctrine of prescription as such.[4]

17. *Acquiescence and Recognition*[5]

The effect of consent on the transfer of territory has been considered previously with respect to cession, which is a procedure which includes agreement to transfer. However, in many cases recognition and acceptance of territorial sovereignty may occur in contexts where there is no agreement to transfer, as the claimant is in possession already, the transaction may be unilateral, and the recognition is on the part of third states and not necessarily the 'losing' state. Recognition may take the form of a unilateral express declaration, or may occur in treaty provisions which make it clear that there has been no cession in the sense of transfer by agreement.[6] In the *Eastern Greenland* case[7]

[1] It is possible to take such a view of the *Palmas* case, since Spain had some sort of title by discovery before Holland took possession: Beckett, 50 Hague *Recueil* (1934, IV), 230.

[2] That is, in the process of weighing the significance of the various acts of state authority.

[3] See the *Minquiers and Ecrehos* case, I.C.J. Reports (1953), p. 47; Green, p. 8; MacGibbon, 31 *B.Y.* (1954), 156–66; Fitzmaurice, 32 *B.Y.* (1955–6), 58 seq. In that case Counsel for the U.K. referred to omissions amounting to 'virtual acquiescence' in the British claims, but no argument was rested on prescription expressly.

[4] Many modern writers admit the relation between acquiescence and prescription: see Schwarzenberger, *International Law* i (3rd ed.), 307; Rousseau, 93 Hague *Recueil* (1958, I), 422; Jennings, *Acquisition of Territory*, pp. 23, 39. See also *Case Concerning Sovereignty over Certain Frontier Land*, I.C.J. Reports (1959), p. 209 at pp. 227–30. Some jurists give only slight and rather sceptical treatment of prescription: see Redslob, *Traité*, p. 183.

[5] See generally MacGibbon, 31 *B.Y.* (1954), 143–86; Blum, *Historic Titles in International Law* (1965); Charpentier, *La Reconnaissance internationale et l'évolution du droit des gens*, pp. 69–79; Suy, *Les Actes juridiques unilatéraux en droit international public*, pp. 61–8; Fitzmaurice, 32 *B.Y.* (1955–6), 58–63; Lauterpacht, *Recognition*, pp. 409–12; Jennings, *Acquisition of Territory*, pp. 36–40; Schwarzenberger, 51 *A.J.* (1957), 316–23. Generally on unilateral acts in international relations see Chapter XXVI, section 3.

[6] See *supra*, pp. 138–9, on disposition by joint decision of the principal powers, and p. 139 on renunciation. See further *Ditmar and Linde* v. *Ministry of Agriculture*, *Ann. Digest* 8 (1935–7), no. 52 at p. 162; *Franco-Ethiopian Railway Co.* claim, Int. L.R. 24 (1957), p. 602 at p. 605; U.K. recognition of Norwegian sovereignty over Jan Mayen Island and Canadian recognition of Norwegian sovereignty over the Sverdrup Islands, 27 *A.J.* (1933), Suppl., pp. 92, 93; and McNair, *Opinions* i. 287.

[7] (1933), P.C.I.J., Ser. A/B, no. 53, pp. 51–2; World Court Reports iii. 175–6. See also the Advisory Opinion concerning *Western Sahara*, I.C.J. Reports, 1975, p. 12 at pp. 49–57: the Moroccan argument from recognition failed on the evidence. See also ibid., pp. 87–92 (Judge Ammoun).

the Court referred to treaties between Denmark and states other than Norway and observed: 'To the extent that these treaties constitute evidence of recognition of her sovereignty over Greenland in general, Denmark is entitled to rely upon them.'

Acquiescence has the same effect as recognition, but arises from conduct, the absence of protest when this might reasonably be expected. In appropriate circumstances a tribunal will infer recognition of sovereignty in a competitor. In the case of land territory the term acquiescence is applied to the attitude of the 'losing' state in a dispute, whereas recognition refers to the attitude of third states.[1] Acquiescence and recognition are not essential to title in the normal case, but they give significance to actual control of territory and acts of state authority in circumstances when these do not of themselves provide a complete foundation for title in the holder, for example where there are competing acts of possession.[2] Acquiescence and recognition may establish that at some material date a rival claimant regarded an area as *res nullius*.[3] Of contemporary significance is the effect in establishing title of a series of resolutions of the General Assembly of the United Nations: the strength of institutionalized and general recognition is obvious.[4]

18. *Estoppel*[5]

The principle of estoppel undoubtedly has a place in international law (see *infra*, Chapter XXVI), and it has played a significant role in territorial disputes which have come before international tribunals. Recognition, acquiescence, admissions constituting a part of the evidence of sovereignty,[6] and estoppel form an interrelated subject-matter, and it is far from easy to

[1] See further *infra*, pp. 166–8, on questions of relative title; and pp. 170–2 on maritime claims.

[2] See the *Grisbadarna* arbitration (1909), 4 *A.J.* (1910), p. 226 at pp. 233, 234–5; *R.I.A.A.* xi, p. 155 at pp. 161–2; *Island of Palmas* case, *supra*, *R.I.A.A.* ii, at pp. 868, 869; *Case Concerning Sovereignty Over Certain Frontier Land*, I.C.J. Reports (1959), p. 209 at pp. 227, 231, 248–50, 255. In the latter case the Court gave an appraisal of 'routine administrative acts' which contrasts with the significance given to British acts in the *Minquiers* case. In the *Frontier Land* case Belgium was held to be excusably ignorant of acts by the Netherlands and not to have made implied admissions. See further MacGibbon, 31 *B.Y.* (1954), 154 seq.

[3] *Minquiers and Ecrehos* case, I.C.J. Reports (1953), p. 47, at p. 67.

[4] Jennings, *Acquisition of Territory*, p. 85. See further the following chapter.

[5] See Bowett, 33 *B.Y.* (1957), 175–202; MacGibbon, 7 *I.C.L.Q.* (1958), p. 468 at pp. 506–9; Jennings, *Acquisition of Territory*, pp. 41–51. See also Chapter XXVI, section 3, on unilateral acts.

[6] See Fitzmaurice, 32 *B.Y.* (1955–6), 60–2; Bowett, 33 *B.Y.* (1957), 196–7.

establish the points of distinction. It is clear that in appropriate conditions acquiescence will have the effect of estoppel. In the *Temple* case[1] the Court held that by her conduct Thailand had recognized the frontier line contended for by Cambodia in the area of the temple, viz., that marked on the map drawn up by the Mixed Delimitation Commission set up by the treaty of 1904.

In many situations acquiescence and express admissions are but part of the evidence of sovereignty. Estoppel differs in that, if it exists, it suffices to settle the issue because of its unambiguous characterization of the situation. Resting on good faith and the principle of consistency in state relations, estoppel may involve holding a government to a declaration which in fact does not correspond to its real intentions.[2] Such a principle must be used with caution, more particularly in dealing with territorial issues.[3] However, in instances like the *Temple* case, where much of the evidence is equivocal, acquiescence over a long period may be treated as decisive: here it is not in itself a root of title but an aid in the interpretation of the facts and legal instruments.[4] Acquiescence of the kind which closes the principal issue (which therefore has an effect equivalent to estoppel) must rest on very cogent evidence. Express recognition in the treaty of the existence of title in the *other party* to a dispute (as opposed to recognition by third states) creates an effect equivalent to that of estoppel.[5]

19. *Novation*

Verzijl[6] refers to 'novation' as a distinct mode of acquisition and defines the principle thus: 'It consists in the gradual transformation of a right *in territorio alieno*, for example a lease, or a

[1] I.C.J. Reports (1962), p. 6 at p. 32. See also ibid., pp. 39–51 (sep. op. of Alfaro); 62–5 (sep. op. of Fitzmaurice); 96–7 (diss. op. of Wellington Koo); 129–31, 142–6 (diss. op. of Spender). For comment see Johnson, 11 *I.C.L.Q.* (1962), 1183–1204; Verzijl, 9 *Neths. Int. L.R.* (1962), 229–63. [2] See *infra*, p. 637.

[3] See Bowett, 33 *B.Y.* (1957), 197–201, 202; and the dissenting opinion of Judge Spender in the *Temple* case, I.C.J. Reports (1962), pp. 142–6 (in his view, on the facts, the elements of estoppel were not present in any case).

[4] Jennings, *Acquisition of Territory*, p. 51.

[5] See McNair, *Law of Treaties* (1961), p. 487, referring to the *Eastern Greenland* case, P.C.I.J., Ser. A/B, no. 53, at pp. 68–9; World Court Reports iii. 190: 'In accepting these bilateral and multilateral agreements [containing provisions which recognized that Greenland was part of Denmark] as binding upon herself, Norway reaffirmed that she recognized the whole of Greenland as Danish; and thereby she has debarred herself from contesting Danish sovereignty over the whole of Greenland, and, in consequence, from proceeding to occupy any part of it.' McNair takes a less strict view of estoppel than, for example, Bowett, loc. cit.: see *infra*, pp. 637–8.

[6] *International Law in Historical Perspective* iii (1970), 384–6.

pledge, or certain concessions of a territorial nature, into full sovereignty without any formal and unequivocal instrument to that effect intervening.' Several modern disputes relate to this type of problem. The dispute over British Honduras (Belice) is the example used by Verzijl. In his view 'it is beyond all doubt that the British claims in respect of Spanish, later Guatemalan, Belice were in origin nothing more than the right, guaranteed by Spain to Great Britain on behalf of her nationals by Article 17 of their Peace Treaty of Paris of 10 February 1763 . . ., not to be molested in their trade of cutting Campeachy wood in the Spanish territories bordering the Bay of Honduras.'[1] The article concerned makes no mention of territorial limits. Other modern disputes which have raised the same issue are as follows: the 'neutral ground' adjacent to the north face of the Rock of Gibraltar (United Kingdom and Spain);[2] the *Right of Passage* case (Merits) (Portugal and India);[3] and the issue of title to Sabah (North Borneo) (Philippines and Malaysia).[4]

Whilst it is useful to regard these disputes as a type, the issue of tacit novation is in no way unique and concerns the matters reviewed in earlier sections devoted to acquisitive prescription, acquiescence, recognition, and estoppel.

20. *Doctrine of Reversion*

When a transfer of sovereignty occurs, and the successor is generally recognized as recovering a previous state of independence, the question arises whether the successor is bound by territorial grants or recognition of territorial changes by the previous holder. The matter is considered in Chapter XXVIII, section 7.

21. *Relative Title*[5]

Title to territory may be relative in several quite different contexts.

(1) The principle *nemo dat quod non habet* (no donor can give a

[1] Ibid., p. 385. See further *British Digest* iib, 621–58; Bloomfield, *The British Honduras–Guatemala Dispute* (1953); Clegern, 52 *A.J.* (1958), 280–97.

[2] See Fawcett, 43 *International Affairs* (1967), p. 236 at pp. 238–43; White Papers, Misc. No. 12 (1965), Cmnd. 2632; Misc. No. 13 (1966), Cmnd. 3131; *Documents on Gibraltar*, Madrid, 1956; 69 *R.G.D.I.P.* (1965), 123–49; ibid., 70 (1966), 461–6; ibid., 71 (1967), 404–13; *British Digest*, iib, 748–9 (and see vol. iia).

[3] I.C.J. Reports (1960), p. 6.

[4] Materials cited *supra*, p. 116.

[5] See Fitzmaurice, 32 *B.Y.* (1955–6), p. 20 at pp. 64–6; Schwarzenberger, 51 *A.J.* (1957), p. 308 at pp. 320–2.

greater interest than that which he himself has) places a restrictive effect on titles dependent on bilateral agreement.[1]

(2) A judicial decision on issues of title cannot foreclose the rights of third parties.[2]

(3) In a situation where physical holding is not conclusive of the question of right, recognition becomes important, and this may be forthcoming from some states and not others. An example of this situation is provided by the Rumanian occupation of Bessarabia in 1918. A number of states accepted the change, but the R.S.F.S.R., and later the U.S.S.R., pursued a policy of non-recognition.

(4) The *compromis* or special agreement, on the basis of which a dispute is submitted to the International Court, or other tribunal, may assume that title is to go to one of the two claimants. Thus the Court interpreted the *compromis* in the *Minquiers and Ecrehos* case as excluding the examination of the status of the islets as *res nullius* or subject to a *condominium*.[3] In such a case, in the absence of any other claimant, the result, it seems, is a title valid against all: but the parties have not had to come up to any minimum requirements of effective control.

(5) Apart from the form of the *compromis*, in instances such as the *Island of Palmas* and *Minquiers and Ecrehos*,[4] the Court will assess the relative intensity of the competing acts of state authority. It is not a question here of, who possesses?[5] but, which has the better right?

(6) In appropriate circumstances the Court will lean in favour of title in one claimant even though there are grounds for a finding that the territory is *terra nullius*. Thus in the *Eastern Greenland* case[6] Danish activity in the disputed area had hardly been intensive, but the Court refused to declare the area *terra nullius*. In Lauterpacht's view:[7] 'Any such decision would have been contrary to those principles of finality, stability and effectiveness of international relations which have characterized the work of the Court.'

[1] See *supra*, p. 127. [2] Ibid.

[3] I.C.J. Reports (1953), p. 47 at p. 52. See also the special agreement in the *Island of Palmas* case, *R.I.A.A.* ii. 831, 869. For the doctrine of *uti possidetis*, see *supra*, p. 137.

[4] See also the *Temple* case, I.C.J. Reports (1962), p. 6 at p. 72 (Judge Moreno Quintana).

[5] In physical terms a test for possession may give no clear answer: both claimants are, as it were, squatting in the same field.

[6] *Supra*, p. 142, n. 4.

[7] *The Development of International Law by the International Court*, p. 241. See also the award in the *Clipperton Island* case, *supra*, p. 145; and *supra*, pp. 153–4, on the extent of sovereignty.

(7) In some cases the sheer ambiguity of the facts will lead the Court to rely on matters which are less than fundamental,[1] and in this class of case there is a tendency to seek evidence of acquiescence by one party.[2] Moreover, in this context it is academic to use the classification 'inchoate'. A title, though resting on very preliminary acts, is self-sufficient as against those without a better title.[3] In coming to a decision on the question of right, it may be necessary to measure 'titles', if this is the correct term, against each other. In the *Palmas* case Huber explained his approach clearly:[4]

> . . . the exercise of some act of State authority and the existence of external signs of sovereignty . . . has been proved by the Netherlands. . . .
>
> These facts at least constitute a beginning of establishment of sovereignty by continuous and peaceful display of State authority, of a commencement of occupation of an island not yet forming a part of the territory of a State; and such a state of things would create in favour of the Netherlands an inchoate title for completing the conditions of sovereignty. Such inchoate title, based on display of State authority, would . . . prevail over an inchoate title derived from discovery, especially if this latter title has been left for a very long time without completion by effective occupation; and it would equally prevail over any claim which, in equity, might be deduced from the notion of contiguity.

22. *Historical Consolidation of Title*

In the *Anglo-Norwegian Fisheries*[5] case the Court, having established that Norway had delimited her territorial sea by a system of straight baselines since 1869, had to decide whether, as against other states, she had title to waters so delimited. The Court said:[6]

> . . . it is indeed this system itself [of straight baselines] which would reap

[1] See the *Temple* case, *supra*, p. 164, and the *Case Concerning Sovereignty over Certain Frontier Land*, I.C.J. Reports (1959), p. 209 at pp. 231 (Judge Lauterpacht), 232 (Judge Spiropoulos), and 249–51 (Judge Armand-Ugon). In this latter case a title resting on an ambiguous treaty conflicted with various acts of administration.

[2] *Supra*, pp. 163–4.

[3] Cf. French rights as against Mexico in the *Clipperton* case; Danish rights as against Norway in the *Eastern Greenland* case. See Beckett, 50 Hague *Recueil* (1934, IV), 230, 254, 255. And see *supra*, pp. 148–9 (abandonment), pp. 149–50 (discovery), pp. 151–2 (symbolic annexation).

[4] *R.I.A.A.* ii, p. 831 at p. 870. See also ibid., p. 869: 'An inchoate title [i.e. discovery] however cannot prevail over a definite title founded on continuous and peaceful display of sovereignty.'

[5] See *infra*, pp. 186 seq.

[6] I.C.J. Reports (1951), p. 116 at pp. 138–9. The whole of this section of the judgment should be read with care. See also ibid., p. 130.

the benefit of general toleration, the basis of an historical consolidation which would make it enforceable as against all States.

The general toleration of foreign States with regard to the Norwegian practice is an unchallenged fact.

The notoriety of the facts, the general toleration of the international community, Great Britain's position in the North Sea, her own interest in the question, and her prolonged abstention would in any case warrant Norway's enforcement of her system against the United Kingdom.

The attitude of other states was taken as evidence of the legality of the system, but there were certain special features. The extension of sovereignty claimed here was over a *res communis*[1] and therefore the toleration of foreign states in general was of significance. Moreover, the Court appears to regard British silence as an independent basis of legality as against the United Kingdom.

Charles de Visscher[2] has explained the decision on these lines,[3] and has proceeded to take the decision as an example of the 'fundamental interest of the stability of territorial situations from the point of view of order and peace', which 'explains the place that consolidation by historic titles holds in international law'.[4] He continues:

This consolidation, which may have practical importance for territories not yet finally organized under a State regime as well as for certain stretches of sea-like bays, is not subject to the conditions specifically required in other modes of acquiring territory. Proven long use, which is its foundation, merely represents a complex of interests and relations which in themselves have the effect of attaching a territory or an expanse of sea to a given State.

'Consolidation' differs from prescription, occupation, and recognition, in de Visscher's doctrine. It is certain that the elements which he calls 'consolidation' are influential. In the preceding section such elements were examined in relation to the problems of relative title[5] and the principle of effectiveness. The essence of the matter is peaceful holding and acquiescence or toleration by other states[6] (but de Visscher has his own notion of acquiescence). Moreover, special factors, including economic

[1] See *infra*, p. 181.

[2] *Theory and Reality in Public International Law* (1957), p. 199; (4th ed.) (in French, 1970), p. 226. See also de Visscher, *Les Effectivités du droit international public* (1970), pp. 107–9.

[3] But he does not regard the case as one of 'acquiescence properly so called'.

[4] Works cited above, n. 2, see also Johnson, *Camb. L.J.* (1955), pp. 215–25.

[5] Cf. Johnson, op. cit., and see *supra*, p. 166.

[6] See Schwarzenberger, 51 *A.J.* (1957), p. 308 at pp. 316–24.

interests, may be entertained by a court faced with rather equivocal facts. However, it is probably confusing to overemphasize, and to lump together, this penumbra of equities by discovering the concept of consolidation.[1] Apart from the concept of consolidation, the rate of social, economic and other 'non-legal' considerations in the application by tribunals of the more orthodox legal principles is not to be denied[2].

23. *Acquisition of Maritime Territory*[3] *and Other Topics*

Rules of general international law, reinforced by the doctrine of necessary appurtenance, attribute internal waters and a territorial sea to littoral states. The issue here is inherent right. In other cases extension of rights over the high seas has occurred on the basis of historic title and prescription.[4] Since the high seas are *res communis*[5] in principle there must be *general* acquiescence or recognition from other states, and, partly for this reason and partly because the extension may be by means of relatively unpublicized municipal decrees, there must be affirmative evidence of acquiescence. Where a special claim has existed for a very long time the parallel is with the 'immemorial' possession of land territory:[6] in so far as adverse prescription exists (but this is doubtful) it is inappropriate to speak of it here, as the possession may well have existed before the now generally accepted criteria developed. Acquiescence is the key notion in this field, and yet one may assume certain limits set by public policy.[7]

[1] Jennings, *Acquisition of Territory*, pp. 23–8, is critical of the concept. He also reminds us that the concept 'is based upon the merest hint in the case reports'. The passage relied upon by de Visscher and Johnson is concerned with general acquiescence: see MacGibbon, 31 *B.Y.* (1954), 160.

[2] See the careful study by Munkman, 46 *B.Y.* (1972–3), 1–116.

[3] See Secretariat Memo., 1957, *U.N. Conf. on the Law of the Sea, Off. Recs.* i. 1–38; Gidel, *Le Droit international public de la mer* iii. 621–63; Fitzmaurice, 30 *B.Y.* (1953), 27–42; id., 31 *B.Y.* (1954), 375–6, 381–2, 400; MacGibbon, ibid., pp. 159 seq.; Waldock, 28 *B.Y.* (1951), 159–66; de Visscher, *Theory and Reality in Public International Law*, pp. 199–201; Bourquin, *Mélanges Georges Sauser-Hall* (1952), pp. 37–51; Bowett, 33 *B.Y.* (1957), 199–201; Johnson, 1 *I.C.L.Q.* (1952), 163–6; *Law of the Sea, Juridical Regime of historic waters, including historic bays*, U.N. Secretariat, A/CN. 4/143, 9 March 1962; *Yearbook, I.L.C.* (1952), i. 155, paras. 18, 24; ibid. (1955), i. 178, para. 8; ibid. (1962), ii. 1, 86, para. 12 (c), 190, para. 60; ibid. (1967) ii. 339, 340, 368; Whiteman iv. 233–58; Bouchez, *The Regime of Bays in International Law* (1964), pp. 199–302; Blum, *Historic Titles in International Law* (1965), pp. 241–334; McDougal and Burke, *The Public Order of the Oceans*, pp. 357–68; Hackworth i. 698–712; Hyde i. 469–70.

[4] See the *North Atlantic Fisheries* arbitration (1910), *R.I.A.A.* xi. 173; Scott, Hague Court Reports, p. 141; Green, p. 301; Hudson, p. 241; *El Salvador* v. *Nicaragua* (1917), 11 *A.J.* (1917), 693. [5] See *infra*, pp. 181, 237.

[6] *Supra*, p. 157. On the relation between acquiescence and historic title see MacGibbon, 31 *B.Y.* (1954), 165. [7] See *infra*, pp. 173–4, 499–502.

Historic bays (internal or national waters). By general acquiescence bays may become a part of internal waters although the closing line exceeds the limits permitted by the general law.[1] This proposition is supported, in a general way, by the judgment of the Court in the *Fisheries* case.[2] The principle of decision in the case was simply that the Norwegian system of baselines was in accordance with the general rules of international law. However, as a secondary basis for decision,[3] the Court relied upon general acquiescence or recognition: the terminology used by the Court itself is rather loose, but the purport is clear. Furthermore, the precise point was not acquiescence in the possession of specific waters but in the *general system* of baselines.[4] In seeking evidence of toleration of a system of this sort caution must be exercised.[5] Many states claim historic bays,[6] but it is to be noted that, in view of the fact that the closing line permitted by the Convention on the Territorial Sea (1958) is twenty-four miles, the significance of the doctrine is much reduced.[7] The Convention contains no provision on historic bays as such.

Historic waters (territorial sea). The rule regarding historic bays is framed, naturally in view of the result of having a closing line, in terms of accessions to internal waters.[8] However, it is assumed that *ex hypothesi* this affects the outer limit of the territorial sea. Moreover, there is in principle no obstacle to recognition of a special breadth for the territorial sea, for example in respect of one coast of a state which elsewhere maintains an orthodox regime. In the *Fisheries* case both parties and the Court[9]

[1] See the U.K. replies to the questionnaire of the Preparatory Committee of the League; McNair, *Opinions* i. 378; and see further the U.K. arguments in the *Fisheries* case and the view expressed at the Geneva Conference in 1958; 7 *I.C.L.Q.* (1958), 545.

[2] *Infra*, pp. 186 seq.

[3] See also the concurrence of Judge Hackworth based solely upon historic title, I.C.J. Reports (1951), p. 144.

[4] I.C.J. Reports (1951), pp. 138–9; and see Fitzmaurice, 30 *B.Y.* (1953), 27.

[5] Criticism of the decision rests in part on the weak evidence for British acceptance of a *general* system, which did not emerge as such until recent times: see Fitzmaurice, 30 *B.Y.* (1953), 33–42; and Wilberforce, 38 *Grot. Soc.* (1952), 165–7. See also the dissenting opinions of Judges McNair and Read: I.C.J. Reports (1951), pp. 171 seq., 199 seq., respectively. On the nature of acquiescence in this context see Fitzmaurice, op. cit., pp. 27–42.

[6] France: Bay of Cancale or Granville (17 miles wide); Sweden: Laholm Bay; the United States: Santa Monica (29), Chesapeake (12), and Delaware (10) Bays. Canada claims Hudson Bay (50); the U.S. opposes this, see 15 *B.Y.* (1934), 1. The U.S.S.R. claims Peter the Great Bay (102) in the Far East: see 7 *I.C.L.Q.* (1958), 112.

[7] See *infra*, p. 200.

[8] Gidel iii. 624.

[9] I.C.J. Reports (1951), pp. 130, 138–9. The Court does not express any precise opinion on the point, however. See further the dissenting opinion of Judge McNair, at p. 183, citing Lord Stowell in the *Twee Gebroeders* (1801), 3 C. Rob. 336, 339; and that of Judge

considered that historic title applied to both the territorial sea and internal waters.

Sedentary fisheries.[1] Continuous occupation and acquiescence on the part of other states may create rights in sedentary fisheries outside the normal ambit of the territorial sea. Sedentary fisheries, such as pearl and chank, are capable of possession: but it is probable that the rights obtained are less than sovereignty.[2]

Boundary between adjacent territorial seas and contiguous zones.[3] In the case of opposite and adjacent coasts there is, in the absence of a regime based upon acquiescence or express agreement, a rule that the line of division depends on the principle of equidistance, i.e. on a median line. The authority for the principle is primarily its basis in common sense: it is a general principle of law. Moreover, it has been adopted in Articles 12 and 24 of the Convention on the Territorial Sea and Contiguous Zone and Article 6 of the Convention on the Continental Shelf.[4] However, apart from cases where acquiescence or treaty provide a source of obligation, the precise legal effect of the principle of equidistance is not clear. It is probably not a rule of attribution as yet, but serves to support claims when they are made. Of course the logic of the principle of appurtenance[5] would make it a rule of automatic attribution irrespective of claim or state activity.

Boundary rivers.[6] The principle of delimitation apparently[7] established in the law is that of the *thalweg*, which may be presumed to mean the middle of the main navigable channel. However, the term may have another meaning in particular instruments and treaties, viz., the line of deepest soundings. The two definitions will no doubt often coincide.

Boundary lakes.[8] The principle of the median line applies, but

Read (at pp. 201 seq.). Note also the concurrence of Judge Hackworth (p. 144), referring to 'the disputed areas of water'. Gidel, op. cit., p. 626, has a contrary view. See further *Civil Aeronautics Board* v. *Island Airlines*, 235 F. Supp. 990 (1964); Int. L.R. 35, p. 68.

[1] See *infra*, pp. 233–4. See also *A.M.S.S.V.M.* v. *State of Madras*, Int. L.R. 20 (1953), 167.

[2] Cf. *infra*, pp. 225, 234, on the concept of 'sovereign rights' in the Continental Shelf Convention of 1958.

[3] Padwa, op. cit.; Gidel iii. 765–74. On bays shared by two or more states see *infra*, p. 200.

[4] See *infra*, pp. 200, 228. See also the dictum in the *Grisbadarna* arbitration. Hague Court Reports i. p. 129; *R.I.A.A.* xi. 160; and *infra* for the regime of boundary lakes.

[5] *Supra*, p. 124.

[6] McEwen, *International Boundaries of East Africa*, pp. 76–96; E.L., 9 *I.C.L.Q.* (1960), 208–36. See also *infra*, pp. 270–5.

[7] Cf. the treatment of Guggenheim i. 381–2, and see *supra*, on the principle of equidistance.

[8] Hackworth i. 615–16; Guggenheim i. 384–6; McEwen, op. cit., pp. 97–100, 201–5;

as usual express agreement or acquiescence may produce other modes of division. Moreover, a *condominium* might be adopted.

24. *Problems of Alienability*

Certain restrictions on the transfer of territory have been noticed earlier,[1] and the present section is devoted to consideration of more fundamental issues arising from principles of general international law. The even more general, and very complex, question of the effect of illegality on various situations is considered later in Chapter XXII.[2] The immediate concern is the effect of certain rules on the power of alienation. Two problems will be considered, viz., the effect of the prohibition of the use or threat of force as a means of acquiring territory and the consequences of the principle of self-determination.

Transfer by an aggressor. In the older customary international law, when conquest was regarded as a source of title, it was yet forbidden to annex territory during the currency of the war and in the absence of a peace treaty. The modern law prohibits conquest and regards a treaty of cession imposed by force as a nullity. Even if—and this is open to considerable doubt—the vice in title can be cured by recognition by third states, it is clear that the loser is not precluded thus from challenging any title based upon a transfer from the aggressor. It is the force of a powerful prohibition, the stamp of illegality, which operates here rather than the principle *nemo dat quod non habet.* Apparent exceptions, when the right of the loser is precluded, occur when there is a disposition of territory by the principal powers or some other international procedure valid as against states generally.[3] Such dispositions may result in an aggressor keeping territory he seized: but the title thenceforth is not based upon the illegal seizure.

Suppose that, objectively speaking, the result of the transfer were in accordance with the principle of self-determination: would this circumstance supersede the illegality of the seizure? It is probable that, at the very least, recognition of the title of the

Pondaven, *Les Lacs-Frontière* (n.d.). Examples: Swiss frontiers through Lac Leman (Lake of Geneva) and Bodensee (Lake Constance).

[1] *Supra*, pp. 123–5.

[2] For the effect of the principle of self-determination on the 'static' rights of the territorial sovereign see pp. 593–6; for the limits of prescription, acquiescence, and recognition in respect of the consequences of illegal acts or omissions see pp. 139, 512–15; on the concepts of *res nullius* and self-determination see *supra*, p. 131.

[3] See *supra*, pp. 138–9, and *infra*, p. 175.

transference by third states would then be justifiable and would consolidate the rights of the holder.[1]

The right of self-determination. Some other aspects of this question are dealt with elsewhere,[2] and the object here is to consider whether there is a rule of law inhibiting the transfer of territory if certain minimum conditions are not fulfilled. Of course, no problem exists if one denies the existence of the right of self-determination under customary international law. However, it is at least an optional principle which particular states may agree to observe in their relations between themselves. Dispositions by the principal powers, transfers under procedures prescribed by international organizations,[3] and bilateral cessions in the period since 1919 are not infrequently expressed to be in accordance with the principle of self-determination. The machinery of the plebiscite is sometimes applied to provide solutions.[4]

Some opinions[5] support the view that transfers must satisfy the principle. However, at present there is insufficient practice to warrant the view that a transfer is invalid simply because there is no sufficient provision for expression of opinion by the inhabitants. The position would change if more states refused to recognize cessions precisely because the principle had been ignored. At present most claims are made in terms which do not include a condition as to due consultation of the population concerned. Those jurists who insist on the principle refer to exceptions, the principal among them being the existence of a joint decision of states representing the international community to impose measures of security on an aggressor.[6]

[1] See further *infra*, pp. 593–6.

[2] *Infra*, pp. 593–6. The right of self-determination may be given a content which varies from one context to the next. For a treaty provision see the Treaty of Dorpat, 1920; reference, Green, p. 106.

[3] *Infra*, pp. 175–8.

[4] See Hyde i. 364–5, 372; Whiteman II. 1168–72.

[5] Kozhevnikov (ed.), *International Law*, pp. 175–7.

[6] Cf. the debate between West German and Polish jurists over the Oder-Neisse frontier established by the Potsdam Declaration in 1945. See Brownlie, *International Law and the Use of Force by States*, p. 409, n. 3, and, for the Potsdam Declaration, 39 *A.J.* (1945), Suppl., p. 245, Chapters VI and IX.

CHAPTER VIII

STATUS OF TERRITORY: FURTHER PROBLEMS

1. *International Procedures relating to Territorial Dispositions*[1]

(a) *Agreement between the states concerned.* A cession of territory may depend on the political decision of the states concerned in a dispute and may be the result of either a political claim, on grounds of justice or security, or a legal claim. The conditions under which transfer occurs may be influenced by the recommendations of political organs of international organizations and by the principle of self-determination.[2] On a number of occasions plebiscites have been organized under the auspices of the United Nations.[3]

(b) *Joint decision of the principal powers.* It was pointed out in the previous chapter[4] that on a number of occasions a group of leading powers, perhaps in association with a large number of other states, have assumed a power of disposition. It is possible that, as in the case of the creation of a new constitution by rebellion, the political and legal bases are indivisible:[5] certainly the legal consequences of this power of disposition are commonly accepted. The mandates system rested in part at least on such a power of disposition, and the International Court has accepted its consequences in its advisory opinions on the status of South-West Africa and its decisions in the *South West Africa* cases.[6]

(c) *Action by United Nations organs.* It is doubtful if the United Nations has a 'capacity to convey title', in part because the Organization cannot assume the role of territorial sovereign: in spite of the principle of implied powers[7] the Organization is not a state and the General Assembly only has a power of recommendation. Thus the resolution of 1947 containing a partition

[1] See especially Jennings, *The Acquisition of Territory in International Law*, pp. 69–87.

[2] This begs the question of the legal content of the principle, on which *supra*, pp. 173–4; *infra*, pp. 593–6.

[3] See Merle, *Annuaire français* (1961), pp. 425–45; Whiteman ii. 1168–72.

[4] pp. 138–9.

[5] Cf. the advisory opinion in the *Reparation* case, quoted *infra*, Chapter XXX, Section 2.

[6] I.C.J. Reports (1962), p. 319; see also the joint dissenting opinion of Judges Spender and Fitzmaurice, ibid., p. 482; ibid. (1966), p. 6.

[7] On which see *infra*, Chapter XXX, Section 4.

plan for Palestine was probably *ultra vires*, and, if it was not, was not binding on member states in any case.[1] However, this may be, the fact is that states may agree to delegate a power of disposition to a political organ of the United Nations, at least where the previous sovereign has relinquished title and there is no transfer of sovereignty and no disposition of a title inhering in the Organization. The latter acts primarily as a referee. The General Assembly played this type of role in relation to the creation of the new states of Libya and Somalia and in the case of territory relinquished by Italy under the peace treaty of 1947.[2] On similar principles, the General Assembly probably has a power to terminate a trusteeship status.[3] The application of such principles to the termination of a mandate is a matter of some difficulty, partly because the power of disposition technically inhered in the principal Allied powers participating in the Treaty of Versailles.[4] It may be that, in the cases of mandate and trusteeship, and also of territories to which Chapter XI of the Charter applies,[5] the United Nations does not 'confer sovereignty', but merely decides on the manner in which the principle of self-determination shall be implemented. Certainly resolutions of the General Assembly play an important element in the consolidation of title over territory already in possession, and this is especially the case with the resolutions based on Resolution 1514 containing a Declaration on the Granting of Independence to Colonial Countries and Peoples.[6]

The United Nations General Assembly assumed the power to terminate the Mandate for South West Africa in Resolution 2145 (XXI) adopted on 27 October 1966.[7] The operative paragraphs of the resolution are as follows:

1. *Reaffirms* that the provisions of General Assembly resolution 1514

[1] See Kelsen, *The Law of the United Nations* (1951), pp. 195–7 (n. 7).

[2] See Resolutions 289 (IV)A of 21 November 1949, 387 (V) of 17 November 1950, and 1418 (XIV) of 5 December 1959. See further Resolution 515 (VI) of 1 February 1952 on the transfer of Eritrea to Ethiopia. For these and other materials see Briggs, p. 84; and Whiteman iii. 4–32.

[3] This may be inferred from Articles 76 and 85 of the Charter: Jennings, op. cit., p. 81. No express provision appears. See Marston, 18 *I.C.L.Q.* (1969), 1–40.

[4] *Supra*, pp. 113–14. See also the sep. op. of Judge McNair, *Status of South-West Africa*, I.C.J. Reports (1950), p. 128 at p. 150; sep. op. of Judge Read, ibid., p. 168, diss. op. of Judge Alvarez, ibid., pp. 180–1; and E. Lauterpacht, 6 *I.C.L.Q.* (1957), 514–15.

[5] See *infra*, Chapter XXIV, section 7.

[6] See *infra*, pp. 593–6. See further Jennings, op. cit., pp. 82–7.

[7] Text: 5 *Int. Leg. Materials* (1966), 1190; Whiteman xiii. 760. For comment see Dugard, 62 *A.J.* (1968), 78–97; Marston, 18 *I.C.L.Q.* (1969), pp. 28 seq.; Rousseau, 71 *R.G.D.I.P.* (1967), 382–4.

(XV)[1] are fully applicable to the people of the Mandated Territory of South West Africa and that, therefore, the people of South West Africa have the inalienable right to self-determination, freedom and independence in accordance with the Charter of the United Nations;

2. *Reaffirms further* that South West Africa is a territory having international status and that it shall maintain this status until it achieves independence;

3. *Declares* that South Africa has failed to fulfil its obligations in respect of the administration of the Mandated Territory and to ensure the moral and material well-being and security of the indigenous inhabitants of South West Africa, and has, in fact, disavowed the Mandate;

4. *Decides* that the Mandate conferred upon His Britannic Majesty to be exercised on his behalf by the Government of the Union of South Africa is therefore terminated, that South Africa has no other right to administer the Territory and that henceforth South West Africa comes under the direct responsibility of the United Nations;

5. *Resolves* that in these circumstances the United Nations must discharge those responsibilities with respect to South West Africa;

6. *Establishes* an *Ad Hoc* Committee for South West Africa—composed of fourteen Member States to be designated by the President of the General Assembly—to recommend practical means by which South West Africa should be administered, so as to enable the people of the Territory to exercise the right to self-determination and to achieve independence, and to report to the General Assembly at a special session as soon as possible and in any event not later than April 1967;

7. *Calls upon* the Government of South Africa forthwith to refrain and desist from any action, constitutional, administrative, political or otherwise, which will in any manner whatsoever alter or tend to alter the present international status of South West Africa;

8. *Calls the attention* of the Security Council to the present resolution;

9. *Requests* all States to extend their whole-hearted co-operation and to render assistance in the implementation of the present resolution;

10. *Requests* the Secretary-General to provide all assistance necessary to implement the present resolution and to enable the *Ad Hoc* Committee for South West Africa to perform its duties.

Subsequently the General Assembly established the United Nations Council for South West Africa, appointed a United Nations Commissioner to administer the territory and renamed the territory 'Namibia'. South Africa failed to respond to these developments and the Security Council adopted resolutions in 1969 and 1970 'recognizing' the decision of the General Assembly to terminate the Mandate and calling upon all states to take measures to implement the finding that South Africa's continued presence in Namibia was illegal. In a further resolution the Inter-

[1] On which see *infra*, pp. 593–6.

national Court was requested to give an Advisory Opinion on the question, 'What are the legal consequences for States of the continued presence of South Africa in Namibia notwithstanding Security Council resolution 276 (1970)?' The principal views of the Court are considered elsewhere,[1] but as a preliminary to giving its views on the substance of the question posed the Court considered the validity of General Assembly resolution 2145 (XXI) in terms of the Charter.[2] The Court held that the power of the League of Nations, and therefore of the United Nations also, to revoke the Mandate for reasons recognized by general international law (termination on the ground of material breach of a treaty) was to be implied.[3] The role adopted by the General Assembly, assisted if need be by the Security Council, appears to involve taking such action as is necessary to ensure the application of the provisions of resolution 1514 (XV) to the people of Namibia.[4] In formal terms at least, this does not involve a power of disposition as such, divorced from the existing provisions of the Charter, as interpreted by the practice of the organs, relating to the principle of self-determination.[5]

The role of the General Assembly in the decolonization of Western Sahara involved a complex of issues concerning the principle of self-determination and the legal interests of Morocco and Mauretania.[6]

2. *Capacity of the United Nations to Administer Territory*[7]

The United Nations has supervisory functions specified in the Charter, and supported by practice, in relation to trusteeship and non-self-governing territories. Moreover, in the context of maintaining international peace and security United Nations organs have been prepared to assume administrative functions in relation to the City of Jerusalem,[8] the Free City of Trieste,[9] and

[1] See *infra*, p. 515–16. [2] I.C.J. Reports (1971), p. 16 at pp. 45–50.

[3] pp. 47–9; and see Dugard, 62 *A.J.* at pp. 84–8.

[4] See para. 1 of Resolution 2145 (XXI), *supra*.

[5] For criticism of the Opinion on the basis (i) that neither the General Assembly nor the Security Council has the power to abrogate or alter territorial rights and (ii) that the resolutions concerned had this purpose, see Judge Fitzmaurice, diss. op., I.C.J. Reports (1971), pp. 280–3, 294–5.

[6] See the Advisory Opinion concerning the *Western Sahara*, I.C.J. Reports, 1975, p. 12; and also the Decl. of Judge Gros at pp. 69–77; Sep. Op. of Judge Petrén at pp. 105–15; Sep. Op. of Judge Dillard at pp. 116–26; Sep. Op. of Judge de Castro at pp. 127–72.

[7] See Halderman, 70 *Duke L.J.* (1964), 95–108. [8] See *supra*, pp. 64–5.

[9] See *supra*, p. 64, and Whiteman iii. 68–109.

in West Irian.[1] The existence of such administrative powers rests legitimately on the principle of necessary implication and is not incompatible with the view that the United Nations cannot have territorial sovereignty.[2] In resolution 2145 (XXI) the General Assembly assumed a power of administration in respect of South West Africa (see the previous section).

3. *Legal Regimes apart from State Sovereignty*[3]

(a) *Territory* sub judice. The analogy here is perhaps with the right of possession which the *sequester* or stakeholder had in Roman law. The existing regime rests on acts in the law which in principle could not create sovereignty in the existing holder but which do not render the region *terra nullius*.[4] For practical purposes the present possessor may be regarded as exercising normal powers of jurisdiction and administration, subject only to external limitations arising from the legal instruments determining the status of the region. Thus the relevant agreement may contain provisions for demilitarization. Furthermore, there must be an implied obligation not to act in such a way as to render fulfilment of the ultimate objective of the arrangement impossible. Thus if the stated objective is to provide for an expression of opinion by certain minority groups it would be *ultra vires* to deport or to harass and blackmail the groups concerned.[5] The status of the inhabitants in terms of nationality and citizenship will depend on the circumstances of the particular case. If one accepts the obligations inherent in the doctrine of the ultimate objective then the conferment and deprivation of nationality would not be a matter of domestic jurisdiction for the administering state.

Another type of indeterminate status arises when two or more states carry out acts of administration in the same area of *res nullius*, or when two states severally support claims to inchoate

[1] On the United Nations Temporary Executive Authority see Bowett, *United Nations Forces*, pp. 255–61.

[2] See E. Lauterpacht, 5 *I.C.L.Q.* (1956), 409–13; and Seyersted, 37 *B.Y.* (1961), p. 351 at pp. 451–3. Cf. Kelsen, *Charter of the United Nations*, pp. 195–7 (n. 7), 684–7.

[3] Certain variants of territorial sovereignty were considered *supra*, pp. 112 seq. However, these all had a relation to the stock type: the present chapter is concerned with regimes which have a legal quality which is in each case more or less unique.

[4] Examples: the City of Jerusalem (*supra*, pp. 64–5), Trieste (*supra*, p. 64), the former Italian colonies after 1947 (*supra*, p. 139, n. 1), and perhaps Taiwan (Formosa) (*supra*, p. 68). For administration by the United Nations see *supra*, p. 175.

[5] Such activity might amount to a breach of the standards laid down by the Genocide Convention, which, on one view at least, represents general international law.

and competing titles in respect of the same region.[1] Here, apart from special agreement, a final disposition of the territory does not retroactively invalidate acts of jurisdiction and administration on the part of the unsuccessful claimant in respect of areas he 'loses' thereby.

(b) *Terra nullius.*[2] For practical purposes the cases of the *terra nullius* and territory *sub judice* may be to a certain extent assimilated.[3] In both cases activity is limited by principles similar to those protecting a reversioner's interest in municipal law. However, in the case of the *terra nullius* the state which is in the course of consolidating title[4] is in principle entitled to carry out acts of sovereignty. The important difference is that whereas the *terra nullius* is open to acquisition by any state, the territory *sub judice* is not susceptible to occupation, since the express conditions for its attribution may have been laid down already, and in any case there is an existing possessor whose interim possession may have received some form of general recognition.[5]

The *terra nullius* is subject to certain rules of law which depend on the two assumptions that such zones are free for the use and exploitation of all and that persons are not deprived of the protection of the law merely because of the absence of state sovereignty—the law of the sea provides the analogy for this. States may exercise jurisdiction in respect of individuals and companies carrying on activities in a *terra nullius.* Article 15 of the Convention on the High Seas[6] defines piracy to include acts directed 'against a ship, aircraft, persons or property in a place outside the jurisdiction of any State'. Acts in the nature of aggression or breaches of the peace, war crimes, or crimes against peace and humanity, will equally be so in *terra nullius.*[7] Unjustified interference from agencies of another state with lawful activity will create international responsibility in the ordinary way. It is doubtful whether private interests established prior to the reduction into sovereignty of a *terra nullius* must be respected by

[1] See *supra*, p. 142. On Antarctica see *infra*, p. 265.

[2] See *Island of Palmas* case, Hague Court Reports ii. 92; Fitzmaurice, 92 Hague *Recueil* (1957, II), 140–4; Guggenheim i. 456–7; Hackworth i. 427, 465–8, 471, 474–6. See further *supra*, pp. 141 seq. Cf. McNair, *Opinions* i. 314–25; *Jacobsen* v. *Norwegian Government*, *Ann. Digest* 7 (1933–4), no. 42.

[3] Cf. *U.K. Contemp. Practice* (1962), i. 43–5.

[4] Since states do not always advertise an *animus possidendi* this is probably to be presumed, except where representations from other states provoke a disclaimer.

[5] This is apart from the case of competing acts of state authority in the same region.

[6] See *infra*, p. 244. See further Articles 14 and 19 of the Convention and *Yrbk., I.L.C.* (1956), ii. 282–3 (Articles 38, 39, and 43 and commentary thereon).

[7] Fitzmaurice, op. cit., p. 142.

the new sovereign.[1] Several issues remain unsettled. Thus it is not clear that a *terra nullius* has a territorial sea, and if so, what is the breadth thereof: the logic, such as it is, of the doctrine of appurtenance[2] does not apply here, and it would be reasonable to regard the adjacent waters as high seas.[3]

(c) *Right of pre-emption* (droit de préférence).[4] Territory subject to a right of pre-emption is not subject to any special regime, since the right so created, usually by express agreement, is a matter of treaty, and neither the existence of the right nor the breach of the agreement can affect the title to the territory concerned. The same considerations apply to claims to a first option with respect to acquisition of *terra nullius*.[5]

(d) *Res communis*. The high seas are commonly described as *res communis omnium*,[6] and occasionally as *res extra commercium*.[7] The use of these terms is innocent enough providing not too much is read into them. They represent only a few basic rules and do not provide a viable regime of themselves. The *res communis* may not be subjected to the sovereignty of any state, general acquiescence apart,[8] and states are bound to refrain from any acts which might adversely affect the use of the high seas by other states or their nationals. It is now generally accepted that outer space and celestial bodies have the same general character.[9] Legal regimes similar in type may be applied by treaty to other resources, for example an oilfield underlying parts of two or more states.[1]

(e) *Mandated and trust territories*.[2] The role of the mandate and trusteeship systems in the protection of human rights is considered briefly elsewhere,[3] and the problems concerning the

[1] Guggenheim, loc. cit., says that they must. [2] *Supra*, p. 124.

[3] Article 1 of the Convention on the Territorial Sea and Contiguous Zone speaks of the extension of the sovereignty of a state. The provisions of the Convention on the Continental Shelf refer constantly to the 'coastal state'.

[4] Oppenheim i. 550; Hackworth i. 470–1; Rousseau iii. 197; Verzijl, *International Law in Historical Perspective*, iii. 478–83. [5] Cf. Hackworth i. 475.

[6] Guggenheim i. 445; Fitzmaurice, 92 Hague *Recueil* (1957, II), 143, 150–1, 156–7, 160–2. In Roman law the concept did not acquire a very definite content and was confused at times with *res publicae*.

[7] Schwarzenberger, *International Law* i (3rd ed.), 309. Lindley (quoted in Hackworth i. 397) uses the term *territorium nullius*.

[8] *Supra*, pp. 156 seq., 168 seq. [9] See *infra*, pp. 266–70.

[1] See Agreement relating to the Exploitation of Single Geological Structures extending across the Dividing Line on the Continental Shelf under the North Sea, U.K. and Netherlands, *U.K. Treaty Series* no. 24 (1967), Cmnd. 3254. Cf. the Antarctic Treaty, *infra*, p. 265.

[2] See Duncan Hall, *Mandates, Dependencies and Trusteeships* (1948); Whiteman i. 598–911; id., xiii. 679 seq.; Sayre, 42 *A.J.* (1948), 263–98; Toussaint, *The Trusteeship System of the United Nations* (1956); Roche, 58 *R.G.D.I.P.* (1954), 399–437; Verzijl, op. cit. ii. 545–73; Marston, 18 *I.C.L.Q.* (1969), 1–40. [3] *Infra*, Chapter XXIV, section 7.

power of disposition have been noticed earlier in the present chapter. Both the mandate and trusteeship systems create a special regime for territory described by Judge McNair as follows:[1]

> The Mandates System (and the 'corresponding principles' of the International Trusteeship System) is a new institution—a new relationship between territory and its inhabitants on the one hand and the government which represents them internationally on the other.... The doctrine of sovereignty has no application to this new system. Sovereignty over a Mandated Territory is in abeyance; if and when the inhabitants of the Territory obtain recognition as an independent State ... sovereignty will revive and rest in the new State. What matters ... is not where sovereignty lies, but what are the rights and duties of the Mandatory in regard to the area of territory being administered by it. The answer to that question depends on the international agreements creating the system and the rules of law which they attract. Its essence is that the Mandatory acquires only a limited title to the territory entrusted to it, and that the measure of its powers is what is necessary for the purpose of carrying out the Mandate.

(f) *Non-self-governing territories* (*Chapter XI of the Charter of the United Nations*). *See infra*, section 7, Chapter XXIV.

(g) *Territorial entities* (*other than states*) *enjoying legal personality*. In the Advisory Opinion concerning the *Western Sahara*[2] the International Court considered the legal status of the 'Mauritanian entity' at the time of colonization by Spain in the years 1884 onwards. It was accepted that the entity was not a State. The Court concluded that the emirates and tribes which existed in the region did not constitute a 'legal entity'. However, in coming to this conclusion the Court accepted as a principle that in certain conditions a legal entity, other than a state, 'enjoying some form of sovereignty', could exist distinct from the several emirates and tribes which composed it. These conditions were not described with any precision by the Court but were related to the existence of 'common institutions or organs' and of an entity which was in 'such a position that it possesses, in regard to its Members, rights which it is entitled to ask them to respect'.[3] Presumably, but the matter is far from clear, such legal entities will have rights and duties similar to those of states.

[1] Separate opinion, *International Status of South West Africa*, I.C.J. Reports (1950), p. 128 at p. 150. He refers to *Rex* v. *Christian* [1924] A.D. 101; *Ann. Digest*, 2 (1923–4), no. 12; *Ffrost* v. *Stevenson* (1937), 58 C.L.R. 528; *Ann. Digest* 8 (1935–7), no. 29; and *Jolley* v. *Mainka* (1933), 49 C.L.R. 242; *Ann. Digest* 7 (1933–4), no. 17. On nationality in mandate and trust territories see *infra*, p. 394; and, further, 39 *B.Y.* (1963), 315–17. See also *Fishwick* v. *Cleland*, Int. L.R. 32, p. 38.

[2] I.C.J. Reports, 1975, p. 12 at pp. 57–65, 67–8.

[3] Ibid. p. 63, referring to the *Reparation for Injuries* case, I.C.J. Reports, 1949, p. 178, and see *infra*, p. 678.

PART IV
LAW OF THE SEA

CHAPTER IX

TERRITORIAL SEA, CONTIGUOUS ZONES, AND ANALOGOUS CLAIMS[1]

A. TERRITORIAL SEA

1. *Introductory*

At the present time all states claim to exercise sovereignty, subject to treaty obligations and rules of general international law, over a belt of sea adjacent to their coastlines. On its outer edge this belt is bounded by the high seas, and it is founded on a baseline, related to the low-water mark and, in certain conditions, to other phenomena, which serves to divide the territorial sea from the interior or national waters comprised in rivers, bays, gulfs, harbours, and other water lying on the landward side of the baseline. The term of art now generally accepted is 'territorial sea', and it is employed in the most recent Conventions. Other terms employed to denote the same concept include 'the maritime belt', 'marginal sea', and 'territorial waters'.[2] The language of the Convention on the Territorial Sea and Contiguous Zone[3] seems to assume that every state

[1] Major sources on the modern law of the sea: Lay, Churchill and Nordquist, *New Directions in the Law of the Sea*, 6 vols. (1973–7); Zacklin (ed.), *The Changing Law of the Sea* (1974); Whiteman iv; McDougal and Burke, *The Public Order of the Oceans* (1962); Barabolya and others, *Manual of International Maritime Law* (Moscow, 1966; U.S. Navy transl., 1968); Colombos, *International Law of the Sea* (6th ed., 1967); Butler, *The Soviet Union and the Law of the Sea* (1971); Johnston, *The International Law of Fisheries* (1965); Bowett, *The Law of the Sea* (1967); id., *The Legal Regime of Islands in International Law* (1979); Alexander (ed.); Law of the Sea Institute, Proceedings of Annual Conferences; Oda, *The International Law of the Ocean Development: Basic Documents* (1972); *Third United Nations Conference on the Law of the Sea, Official Records*; Jennings, [1972B] *Camb L.J.* 32–49; *Thesaurus Acroasium of the Inst. of Public International Law and International Relations of Thessaloniki*, II, *The Law of the Sea* (1977).

[2] The term 'territorial waters' is perhaps confusing as it is used on occasion in national legislation to describe internal waters, or internal waters and territorial sea combined. Cf. also the *Fisheries* case, I.C.J. Reports (1951), p. 116, at p. 125. Constitutions, legislation, and treaties often refer to the 'maritime frontier'.

[3] *Infra*. This important multilateral convention entered into force on 10 September 1964. Together with three other Conventions, on the High Seas, on Fishing and Conservation of the Living Resources of the High Seas, and on the Continental Shelf, it was

necessarily has a territorial sea, and some jurists assert a doctrine of inseparable and natural appurtenance.[1]

The view generally accepted by writers,[2] and which has found expression in Article 1 of the Convention on the Territorial Sea of 1958, is that states have rights amounting to sovereignty over the territorial sea.[3] The provision in the Convention of 1958 states that the sovereignty is exercised 'subject to the provisions of these articles and to other rules of international law'. The first part of the proviso is obvious, and the second part was intended to make it clear that the limitations set out in the Convention are not exhaustive. The sovereignty of the coastal state extends also to the seabed and subsoil of the territorial sea and the airspace over it.[4]

An understanding of the modern law and of the problems which remain unsolved must depend to a considerable extent on obtaining an historical perspective. In the eighteenth century extravagant claims to sovereignty over the seas were obsolete in many cases and were nearly so in others.[5] Before the abandonment of such claims in the case of states which had not pursued extensive claims to the seas, and as a consequence of such abandonment in other cases, a test of appurtenance, a definition of the maritime marches of states, had to be sought. In a work published in 1702[6] the Dutch jurist Bynkershoek propounded the doctrine that the power of the territorial sovereign extended to vessels

adopted at the First United Nations Conference on the Law of the Sea in 1958. Only the Convention on the High Seas is 'generally declaratory of established principles of international law' but the Territorial Sea and Continental Shelf Conventions provide evidence of the generally accepted rules bearing on their subject-matter, the cogency of this depending in part on the number of ratifications. On the status of the provisions of the latter as rules of general law see Chapter X. On the status of the Territorial Sea Conv. as general law see *Reference Re Ownership of Offshore Mineral Rights* (1968), 65 D.L.R. (2d) 353, S.C. of Canada. The Conservation Convention creates new rules. Texts of the Conventions: Brownlie, *Documents*, p. 77; 52 *A.J.* (1958), 830. The other three conventions came into force as follows: Convention on the High Seas, 30 September 1962; Convention on the Continental Shelf, 10 June 1964; Convention on Fishing and Conservation, 20 March 1966. The U.K. is bound by all four instruments.

[1] See *supra*, p. 124. Presumably if a state may have a particular system of territorial waters on the basis of historic rights (*infra*, pp. 186 seq.), it may also happen that a state has no claim to a territorial sea. Compare the law relating to the continental shelf, *infra*, pp. 225–6.

[2] Oppenheim i. 487; Gidel iii. 181; O'Connell, 45 *B.Y.* (1971), 303–83.

[3] See the Air Navigation Convention, 1919, Art. 1; International Civil Aviation Convention, 1944, Art. 2; Hague Convention XIII on the Rights and Duties of Neutral Powers in Time of War, 1907, Art. 1; Treaty of Peace with Japan, 1951, Art. 1; the *David*, *Ann. Digest* 7 (1933–4), no. 52; *Yrbk., I.L.C.* (1956), ii. 265. For a different view: Colombos, pp. 89–91. See also *Bonser* v. *La Macchia*, Int. L.R. 51, p. 39; *N.S.W. and others* v. *Commonwealth of Australia*, ibid., p. 89.

[4] Convention on the Territorial Sea, Art. 2.

[5] See further *infra*, pp. 238 seq., on the freedom of the seas.

[6] *De Dominio Maris*, Chap. 2.

within the range of cannon mounted on the shore. At first this doctrine seems to have rested on the control of the actual guns of ports and fortresses over adjacent waters: it was not originally a concept of a maritime belt of uniform breadth.[1] However, in the latter half of the eighteenth century several states laid down limits for belts for purposes of customs or fishery control in legislation and treaties, and Danish practice—after 1745 based on a four-mile belt[2] as the extent of sovereignty—had some impact on European thinking on the matter.[3]

In the last quarter of the century two decisive developments occurred. Writers and statesmen began to conceive of a hypothetical cannon-shot rule, a *belt* over which cannon could range if they were placed along the whole seaboard. Further, as 'cannon-shot' was by no means a definite criterion, suggestions for setting up a convenient standard equivalent, or rather substitute, began to appear. In 1782 the Italian writer Galiani proposed three miles, or one marine league,[4] and the diplomatic birth of the three-mile limit appears to be the United States Note to Britain and France of 8 November 1793, in which the limit was employed for purposes of neutrality.[5] During and after the Napoleonic wars the British and American prize courts translated the cannon-shot rule into the three-mile rule.[6]

A significant aspect of the development of the law is the intimate relation between claims to jurisdiction for particular purposes over the high seas, and extension of sovereignty to a maritime belt. Some claims, such as those of Denmark and Sweden, though commencing as pronouncements for neutrality purposes, fairly soon developed into assertions of sovereignty,[7] especially when associated with exclusive fishery limits. In other cases it remained for long uncertain whether a claim was only to certain types of jurisdiction or was a general limit of sovereignty.[8] What is certain is that claims to jurisdiction have always

[1] This is the view of Walker, 22 *B.Y.* (1945), 210–31. The concept of actual control is probably referable to the diplomatic practice of Holland and France in the seventeenth and eighteenth centuries.

[2] So also Sweden, at least after 1779. Vattel in his influential *Le Droit des gens* (1758) adopted a theory of a maritime belt.

[3] See Kent, 48 *A.J.* (1954), 537–53; O'Connell, 45 *B.Y.* (1971), 320–3.

[4] Similar views were expressed by Azuni in 1795. See also Kent, op. cit., p. 548.

[5] Hyde i. 455. See also U.S. Proclamation of Neutrality, 22 April 1793, which refers to the range of cannon-ball 'usually stated at one sea league'.

[6] The *Twee Gebroeders* (1800), 3 C. Rob. 162; (1801), 3 C. Rob. 336; the *Anna* (1805), 5 C. Rob. 373; the *Brig Ann* (1815), 1 Gallison 62. See also McNair, *Opinions* i. 331.

[7] In the case of Denmark and Norway, probably in 1812. See also Fulton. *The Sovereignty of the Sea*, pp. 566 seq.; Verzijl, *International Law in Historical Perspective*, iii. 60–5.

[8] Cf. the Portuguese six-mile limit for customs and neutrality; on which see Jessup,

tended to harden into claims to sovereignty. This process was, however, arrested to some extent by general recognition of the basic legal distinction between territorial sea as an extension of sovereignty and special jurisdictional zones, 'contiguous zones' as they were later to be called, *over the high seas*.[1]

2. *Baseline for Measurement of the Territorial Sea*

The normal baseline from which the breadth of the territorial sea is measured is the low-water line along the coast. This follows from the concepts of maritime belt and appurtenance, and corresponds with state practice.[2] There is no uniform standard by which states in practice determine this line, and Article 3 of the Convention on the Territorial Sea defines the line 'as marked on large scale charts officially recognised by coastal States'.[3] In the case of tideless seas the baseline may be placed at the average waterline on the coast in question.[4] The regime of bays, islands in the vicinity of coasts, and archipelagos will be considered subsequently. For the present, attention must be turned to the *Anglo-Norwegian Fisheries* case, which has had a decisive effect on the baseline issue.

The Fisheries case.[5] British fishermen have fished off the Norwegian coast since about 1906, and at various times incidents led

The Law of Territorial Waters and Maritime Jurisdiction (1927), p. 41. The Spanish six-mile limit for a territorial sea appears to originate in customs legislation. The twelve-mile zone claimed by Imperial Russia related to customs and fisheries legislation.

[1] The 'general recognition' certainly existed by 1920 and perhaps as early as 1880. See generally Masterson, *Jurisdiction in Marginal Seas* (1929), pp. 375 seq. In 1914 Chile, which already had a territorial sea with a three-mile limit, declared the same limit for purposes of neutrality. British sources often refer to 'territorial jurisdiction'.

[2] Convention on the Territorial Sea and Contiguous Zone, Art. 4 (and see Art. 6); *I.L.C. Yrbk.* (1956), ii. 266; Colombos, p. 113; the *Fisheries* case, I.C.J. Reports (1951), p. 116 at p. 128; sep. op. of Judge Hsu Mo, p. 154; diss. op. of Judge McNair, p. 162. Note especially Waldock, 28 *B.Y.* (1951) at pp. 131–7; McDougal and Burke, *The Public Order of the Oceans*, pp. 305 seq.; Gihl, *Scand. Studies in Law* (1967), 119–74.

[3] The article states this as a definition and not as presumptive evidence: the relevant subcommittee of the Hague Codification Conference entered a proviso 'provided the latter line does not appreciably depart from the line of mean low-water spring tides': see Hackworth i. 643–4; and the critical comment in McDougal and Burke, op. cit., pp. 322–6.

[4] McDougal and Burke, op. cit., pp. 326–7.

[5] I.C.J. Reports (1951), p. 116; Int. L.R. 18 (1951), no. 36; 46 *A.J.* (1952), 348; Green, p. 369; MacChesney, U.S. Naval War College, *Int. Law Situation and Documents* (1956), p. 65. Literature: MacChesney, p. 62 (bibliographical note); Waldock (Counsel for U.K. in the case), 28 *B.Y.* (1951), 114–71; Fitzmaurice, 30 *B.Y.* (1953), 8–54 and 31 *B.Y.* (1954), 371–429; Lauterpacht, *The Development of International Law by the International Court*, pp. 190–9; Hudson, 46 *A.J.* (1952), 23–30; Johnson (U.K. Counsel), 1 *I.C.L.Q.* (1952), 145–80; Evensen, 46 *A.J.* (1952), 609–30; Wilberforce (U.K. Counsel), 38 *Grot. Soc.* (1952), 151–68; Auby, 80 *J.D.I.* (1953), 24–55.

to diplomatic correspondence about Norway's fishery limits. The Norwegian limit of four miles for territorial waters had been established by royal decree in 1812 and was not in issue in the case. However, later decrees of 1869, 1881, and 1889, and official explanations thereof, continued the measure of 1812 in terms of a system of straight lines drawn from certain outermost points of the 'skjaergaard' or rampart of rocks and islands which fringes much of the Norwegian coast.[1] By a decree of 12 July 1935 Norway applied the system in a more detailed way than before, and the validity of the new limits was challenged by the United Kingdom. After a series of incidents involving British vessels the United Kingdom took the case before the International Court by unilateral application, asking for the award of damages for interferences with British fishing vessels outside the permissible limits.[2] The Court took the view that the system of straight baselines following the general direction of the coast had been consistently applied by Norway and had encountered no opposition on the part of other states. The United Kingdom had not made a formal and definite protest on the issue of the position of baselines until 1933.[3] There is little doubt that, as the later parts of the judgment indicate, the validity of the decree of 1935 could have been upheld on the basis of acquiescence,[4] and, indeed, Judge Hackworth gave, as a separate reason for concurring in the judgment of the Court, the existence of historic title to the areas in question on the part of Norway.[5] However, while it is true that the Court refers to the absence of protest from other states, and also to the consolidation of the method 'by a constant and sufficiently long practice', the judgment as a whole makes abundantly clear the fact that the Court believed that the Norwegian system of baselines was, as a matter of principle, in accordance with international law.[6] The course of the Court's reasoning brings this out.

The Court commences with a description of the topography of the coast of the mainland:

[1] See the decision of the Norwegian Supreme Court in the *Saint Just* (1933), *Ann. Digest* 7 (1933–4), no. 51.

[2] The 1935 decree was not strictly enforced until 16 September 1948 and the U.K. claim was for interference between that date and the date of the application, 24 September 1949. 48 fixed points were employed: 18 of the lines exceeded 15 miles in length, one line was 44 miles in length. The decree refers to a fisheries zone, but both parties assumed in their arguments that it delimited the territorial sea: I.C.J. Reports (1951), p. 125.

[3] I.C.J. Reports (1951), p. 138. But see the diss. op. of Judge McNair, ibid., pp. 171–80.

[4] See *supra*, p. 163. [5] I.C.J. Reports (1951), p. 206.

[6] The later references to the attitude of other governments appear to have been intended, in part at least, as evidence of legality: see I.C.J. Reports (1951), p. 139.

Very broken along its whole length, it constantly opens out into indentations often penetrating for great distances inland.... To the West, the land configuration stretches out into the sea: the large and small islands, mountainous in character, the islets, rocks and reefs,[1] some always above water, others emerging only at low tide, are in truth but an extension of the Norwegian mainland.... The coast of the mainland does not constitute... a clear dividing line between land and sea. What matters, what really constitutes the Norwegian coast line, is the outer line of the 'skjaergaard'.[2]

The Court then states that the problem which arises concerns the baseline from which the breadth of the territorial sea is to be measured and that, while the parties agree that the criterion is the low-water mark, they differ as to its application. The Court decides that the relevant low-water mark is the outer line of the 'skjaergaard' and states that this solution 'is dictated by geographical realities'.[3] The question which now presented itself was how the baseline was to be drawn in the case of the Norwegian coast. The method of the *tracé parallèle*, that is, drawing a line which is an exact image of the coastline, assumed by the Court to be the normal method of applying the low-water mark rule,[4] did not apply to the type of coast in question, since in this case the baseline could only be determined by means of a geometric construction. In a crucial passage the judgment elaborates this concept:[5]

The principle that the belt of territorial waters must follow the general direction of the coast makes it possible to fix certain criteria valid for any delimitation of the territorial sea; these criteria will be elucidated later. The Court will confine itself at this stage to noting that, in order to apply this principle, several States have deemed it necessary to follow the straight baselines method[6] and that they have not encountered objections of principle by other States. This method consists of selecting appropriate points on the low-water mark and drawing straight lines between them. This has been done, not only in the case of well-defined bays, but also in cases of minor curvatures of the coastline where it was solely a question of giving a simpler form to the belt of territorial waters.

The Court proceeds to discount the British contention that straight lines could only be drawn across bays.[7] An argument

[1] The 'skjaergaard' or rock rampart, containing about 120,000 insular formations.

[2] I.C.J. Reports (1951), p. 127.

[3] Ibid., p. 128.

[4] See Waldock, 28 *B.Y.* (1951), 132–7.

[5] I.C.J Reports (1951), pp. 129–30.

[6] Annex 112 of the Norwegian Rejoinder. See Waldock, op. cit., pp. 142–3; and the diss. op. of Judge McNair, I.C.J. Reports (1951), p. 162.

[7] See *infra*, p. 199, on the ten-mile closing line for bays.

that, in any case, the length of straight lines must not exceed ten miles was criticized in these terms:[1]

In this connection, the practice of States does not justify the formulation of any general rule of law. . . . Furthermore, apart from any question of limiting the lines to ten miles, it may be that several lines can be envisaged. In such cases the coastal State would seem to be in the best position to appraise the local conditions dictating the selection.

Consequently, the Court is unable to share the view of the United Kingdom Government, that 'Norway, in the matter of base-lines, now claims recognition of an exceptional system'. . . all that the Court can see therein is the application of general international law to a specific case.

In the opinion of the Court certain basic considerations as to the nature of the territorial sea provided criteria by which the validity of systems of delimitation could be determined.[2] First, because of the close dependence of the territorial sea upon the land domain, 'the drawing of baselines must not depart to any appreciable extent from the general direction of the coast'. Secondly, a close geographical relationship between sea areas and land formations is a 'fundamental consideration' in deciding 'whether certain sea areas lying within [the baselines] are sufficiently closely linked to the land domain to be subject to the regime of internal waters'. The Court states that the other consideration is 'that of certain economic interests peculiar to a region, the reality and importance of which are evidenced by long usage'.[3]

The judgment is then devoted to an examination of the consistency of the application of the Norwegian system of baselines, and of the attitude of other states. The conclusion reached[4] is that the method of straight lines 'was imposed by the peculiar

[1] I.C.J. Reports (1951), p. 131. [2] Ibid., p. 133.

[3] See also the reference (p. 128) to the fact that 'in these barren regions the inhabitants of the coastal zone derive their livelihood essentially from fishing'.

[4] Ibid., p. 139. In an individual opinion Judge Alvarez expresses the view that each state may determine the extent of its territorial sea and the way in which it is reckoned if certain conditions are satisfied, *inter alia*, that the delimitation is carried out reasonably (p. 150). His criteria of reasonableness include geographic and economic considerations. Judge Hsu Mo agrees in his separate opinion with the findings of the Court on the legality of the method of straight lines, but does not consider that all the actual lines fixed by the decree of 1935 are in conformity with international law (p. 154). In a substantial dissenting opinion Judge McNair states that the system of straight lines is not in accordance with law, that it will create practical difficulties for mariners, and that the effect of the decree of 1935 will be to injure the principle of the freedom of the seas (pp. 158, 171, 185). Moreover, he considered reliance on 'economic and other social interests' as a basis for delimitation to be impermissible (pp. 161, 169, 171). See also pp. 171–80 on the issue of acquiescence on the part of the United Kingdom. The dissenting opinion of Judge Read presents similar conclusions (p. 186). See also Moore, *Digest* i. 785–8.

geography of the Norwegian coast', and had been consolidated by 'a constant and sufficiently long practice'.

3. *Straight Baselines: Recent Developments*

Even if one regards the judgment in the *Fisheries* case as an instance of judicial legislation, and not an application of pre-existing principles to the special facts, its significance for the development of the law cannot be underestimated.[1] The pronouncements on the straight lines method are intended to have general application to coasts of that type.[2] Hudson,[3] among others, has welcomed the decision as allowing a more sensible approach to the subject of the territorial sea. Adherents of a strict regime of delimitation are naturally critical of its substance and inevitable effects on state practice.[4] Another source of criticism is the reference to subjective factors in delimitation and the encouragement of unilateral claims which may result.

Article 4 of the Convention on the Territorial Sea[5] includes a provision (paragraph 4) the effect of which is that account may be taken of economic interests in determining baselines if the geographical criteria justifying straight lines are satisfied. Substantially the article confirms the place of the principles of the *Fisheries* case in the law. The system of straight lines applies both to territorial sea and to contiguous zones.[6] A good number of states employ straight baselines which apply the Norwegian

[1] See Oppenheim i. 489.

[2] Colombos, p. 117, considers that the case is not in any sense a precedent because the coast concerned was 'exceptional'. See the view of Fitzmaurice expressed during the Geneva Conference on the Law of the Sea, 7 *I.C.L.Q.* (1958), 542.

[3] 46 *A.J.* (1952), at p. 30.

[4] Judges McNair and Read, *ut supra*, p. 189, n. 4.

[5] 'Article 4. 1. In localities where the coastline is deeply indented and cut into, or if there is a fringe of islands along the coast in its immediate vicinity, the method of straight baselines joining appropriate points may be employed in drawing the baselines from which the breadth of the territorial sea is measured.

2. The drawing of such baselines must not depart to any appreciable extent from the general direction of the coast, and the sea areas lying within the lines must be sufficiently closely linked to the land domain to be subject to the regime of internal waters.

3. Baselines shall not be drawn to and from low-tide elevations, unless lighthouses or similar installations which are permanently above sea level have been built on them.

4. Where the method of straight baselines is applicable under the provisions of paragraph 1, account may be taken, in determining particular baselines, of economic interests peculiar to the region concerned, the reality and importance of which are clearly evidenced by long usage.

5. The system of straight baselines may not be applied by a State in such a manner as to cut off from the high seas the territorial sea of another State.

6. The coastal State must clearly indicate straight baselines on charts, to which due publicity must be given.'

[6] This is implicit in Article 24 of the Convention on the Territorial Sea.

system or are at least compatible with it,[1] leaving aside certain extensive closing lines for bays and lines enclosing archipelagoes. The provisions concerning baselines in the informal texts of the Third United Nations Conference on the Law of the Sea (UNCLOS III) affirm the existing principles governing straight baselines.

4. *Breadth of the Territorial Sea*[2]

This is a question on which there is no general consensus on the part of governments, and an understanding of present difficulties may be gained only by an examination of the historical evolution of the territorial sea. In the seventeenth century several forms of limit were known, including the range of vision on a fair day and the range of cannons on shore.[3] By the last quarter of the eighteenth century the cannon-shot rule obtained in western and southern Europe.[4] It was not dominant, however, and other claims rested simply on a belt with a stated breadth.[5] In 1793, as we have seen, the cannon-shot rule was first given a standard value of one marine league or three miles in diplomatic practice.[6] By 1862,[7] and probably earlier, the cannon-shot rule and the three-mile limit were generally regarded as synonymous in the practice of states supporting a three-mile rule. The cannon-shot rule in its original form had become obsolete.[8]

[1] Approximately 24 states employ such baselines: see U.S. Dept. of State, The Geographer, *Limits in the Seas*, No. 36. For the U.K. system of straight baselines: Territorial Waters Order in Council, 1964; *British Practice in I.L.* (1964, I), 49; *Limits in the Seas*, No. 23. The baselines off the west coast of Scotland constitute a fairly exuberant application of the Norwegian system. Certain states employ conspicuously eccentric lines. See further Law of the Sea Inst. (Rhode Island), Occasional Paper No. 13 (1972); Hydrographic Society (London), Special Publication No. 2; Voelckel, 19 *Ann. français* (1973), 820–36.

[2] See Gidel iii, 62 seq.; Fauchille, *Traité* ii, Pt. ii, pp. 126–422; McDougal and Burke, pp. 446–564; Fulton, *The Sovereignty of the Sea* (1911), pp. 537 seq.; Jessup, *The Law of Territorial Waters and Maritime Jurisdiction* (1927); Lay, Churchill and Nordquist, op. cit, VI, 843, 881; U.S. Dept. of State, The Geographer, *Limits in the Seas*, No. 36. Of particular importance are the materials to be found in the *Yearbook of the International Law Commission* (1952–6, inclusive), and I.C.J. Pleadings (1951), *U.K.–Norway*. On the techniques for determining the outer limit see Waldock, 28 *B.Y.* (1951), 132–7.

[3] *Supra*, pp. 185–6. [4] Fulton, pp. 566 seq.

[5] Denmark and Norway, 4 miles (1745); Sweden, 4 miles (1779); Spain, 6 miles (1760). On the relation to special zones of jurisdiction, *supra*, p. 185.

[6] *Supra*, p. 185. Units of measurements: the marine or nautical mile is equivalent to 1,853 metres and is the same as the geographic mile of 60 to a degree or one minute.

[7] Cf. Moore, *Digest* i. 706–7.

[8] An isolated case of reliance on the rule to justify a limit of 12 miles occurred in 1912, when Russia referred to the rule to justify extensions of jurisdiction for customs and fishery purposes: Hackworth i. 635. See also *Costa Rica Packet*, La Fontaine, p. 510;

The United States and the United Kingdom have supported the three-mile limit since the Napoleonic wars, and have protested in the face of claims to a wider territorial sea.[1] In the view of these governments other limits can only rest on historic title. British adherence to the three-mile limit was reinforced in the late nineteenth century by the abandonment of a special customs and excise jurisdiction over zones beyond three miles[2] and the embodiment of the limit in legislation, commencing with the Territorial Waters Jurisdiction Act, 1878.[3] The three-mile limit gained considerable currency in the course of the nineteenth century.[4] It appeared in a number of international agreements[5] and found an increasing number of partisans among writers.[6] However, the practice was far from

Moore, *Arbitrations* iv. 4948; the *Alleganean*, Moore, *Arbitrations* iv. 4332–5; La Pradelle and Politis ii. 257; and the view of Latvia in 1929, Gidel iii. 53 n.

[1] See *supra*, note 2. For the diplomatic practice on the three-mile limit: Hackworth i. 630–41; Hyde i. 455–9; McNair, *Opinions* i. 331–8. On recent American and British protests: MacChesney, op. cit., pp. 441, 448, 450, 452, 456, 457, 460, 463, 481, 488. For other British protests: 7 *I.C.L.Q.* (1958), 538; 9 *I.C.L.Q.* (1960), 278. Official British statements: 30 April 1923, Hackworth i. 631–2; 14 December 1953, MacChesney, p. 491; Exchange of Notes, U.K.–U.S.S.R., 25 May 1956, ibid., p. 395. This position was maintained at the United Nations Conferences on the Law of the Sea, 1958 and 1960, although there was a willingness to agree on other limits, and the United Kingdom does not consider that the failure to agree on a uniform breadth at these conferences has affected the status of the three-mile rule. See also I.C.J. Pleadings (1951), *U.K.–Norway*, vols. i–iv.

[2] See Masterson, op. cit. The Customs Consolidation Act of 1876 in fact still provided for acts of enforcement outside a three-mile zone, but the Act has not been so applied: McNair, *Opinions* i. 345–6. McDougal and Burke, pp. 586, 613; and Briggs, *Law of Nations* (2nd ed.), pp. 373–4; are wrong on this point. See also, on the interpretation and application of the Herring Fishery (Scotland) Act, 1889, the official statement in *U.K. Contemp. Practice* (1962), i. 48.

[3] Section 7. However, the legislation assumes and does not expressly state that the three-mile limit employed is fixed in accordance with the United Kingdom view of international law. See also the Sea-Fishing Industry Act, 1933; and the Customs and Excise Act, 1952. Some statutes refer to the 'limits of the territorial waters' with no limit stated: e.g. the Sea Fish Industry Acts, 1959 and 1962. See also the legislation of dominions and colonies.

[4] Adherents prior to 1914 included Argentina (1871), Austria (1846), Belgium (1832–91—fishing zone), Brazil (1859), Chile (1855), Ecuador (1889), France (1862—fishing zone), Greece (1869—fishing zone), Japan (1870), Liberia, Mexico (1902), Netherlands (1889), Panama, United Kingdom, and the United States. Germany is a possible claimant: see 20 *A.J.* (1926), Spec. Suppl., p. 71, and the German Supreme Court in the *Elida* (1915), 10 *A.J.*, 916; Briggs, p. 278. See Raestad, 21 *R.G.D.I.P.* (1914), 401–20; Baty, 22 *A.J.* (1928), 517–37; Riesenfeld, *Protection of Coastal Fisheries under International Law* (1942).

[5] Principal among them: North Sea Fishery Convention, 1882, Art. 2; Suez Canal Convention, 1888, Art. 4; Convention Relating to the Aaland Islands, 1921. Further details: Masterson, pp. 346–57; 23 *A.J.* (1929), Spec. Suppl., pp. 255–6. There is no significant arbitral practice, apart from a dictum in the *Behring Sea Fisheries* award (1893), *infra* (but see Hall, p. 192, n. 1).

[6] Wheaton, *Elements* (1866), para. 177; Jessup, op. cit., pp. 9–66; Lawrence, *Principles* (3rd ed., 1909), p. 175. Many writers of the nineteenth century continued to state the

uniform,[1] and some states, including France, Belgium, Portugal, Germany, and Imperial Russia, did not differentiate clearly in their practice between territorial sea and jurisdictional zones, and claimed zones for particular purposes. Many states supporting a three-mile limit claimed contiguous zones extending beyond three miles. Several states had not really faced the issue.

It is not surprising to find that several eminent jurists doubted whether the three-mile limit had been unequivocally settled.[2] Indeed, it was not until 1920 that claims to special jurisdictional zones were generally seen to be distinct from full claims to territorial sea. Thus the results of the Hague Codification Conference of 1930 provide a significant balance sheet in view of the stage of development reached and the obvious role of the Conference and its preliminaries in crystallizing governmental attitudes. The preparatory material and the proceedings showed that although a majority of states favoured a three-mile limit, some of these also claimed contiguous zones.[3] In its report to the Conference the second committee explained that, in view of differences of opinion, it had preferred not to express an opinion on what ought to be regarded as the existing law. At the time of writing it is obvious that, while a significant minority adheres to the three-mile limit, the majority of states favour six or twelve-mile limits or take intermediate positions.[4] Moreover, certain proponents of three miles also claim contiguous zones. Debates

cannon-shot rule without reducing it to a particular limit in miles. Cf. Judge Moore, the *Lotus*, P.C.I.J., Ser. A, no. 10 (1927), pp. 74–5. See also Baty, 22 *A.J.* (1928), 503.

[1] Spain had long had a 6-mile limit; Norway, Denmark, and Sweden claimed 4 miles. See also 20 *A.J.* (1926), Spec. Suppl., pp. 73–4, and Gidel iii. 69 seq., on treaty practice. Cf. Sørensen, 101 Hague *Recueil* (1960, III), 153.

[2] Hall, pp. 191–2; Westlake i. 184–6. See also Fulton, op. cit., p. 664. Oppenheim i. 490–2 is very cautious on the subject (and see the first edition (1905), pp. 241–2).

[3] For the views expressed in the second committee: 24 *A.J.* (1930), Suppl., p. 253; Hackworth i. 628. 17 (Colombos, p. 104, says 20) states favoured 3 miles; 4 favoured 4 miles; 12 states favoured 6 miles. Of the 17 states favouring 3 miles, 5 desired a contiguous zone. Gidel iii. 123, 134, rejects the three-mile limit except as a minimum, a rule of negative content. See also Guggenheim i. 388; id., 48 Hague *Recueil* (1934, II), 193; Rousseau, p. 437; and O'Connell i. 465–7. Generally: Report by François, *Yrbk., I.L.C.* (1952) ii. 28–32; and 3 *Int. Leg. Materials*, 551.

[4] Useful information on claims to territorial seas (and other zones) may be found in: U.S. Dept. of State, The Geographer, *Limits in the Seas* (set of fascicles on individual states), in particular No. 36: *National Claims to Maritime Jurisdictions*. The current situation is as follows. 19 states claim 3 miles: Australia, The Bahamas, Bahrain, Belgium, Chile, Denmark, German Democratic Rep., German Federal Rep., Ireland, Jordan, Netherlands, Nicaragua, Qatar, Singapore, Solomon Islands, Tuvalu, United Arab Emirates (except Sharjah), United Kingdom, United States. 4 states claim 4 miles: Finland, Iceland, Norway, Sweden. 4 states claim 6 miles: Dominican Republic, Greece, Israel, Turkey. Yugoslavia claims 10 miles. 73 states claim 12 miles: Algeria, Arab Republic of Egypt, Bangladesh, Barbados, Bulgaria, Burma, Cambodia, Canada, Cape

during the fourth, seventh, and eighth sessions of the International Law Commission indicated that a majority of members did not regard 'the three-mile rule' as a part of positive law. In 1970 the United States adopted an Oceans Policy one component of which was an effort to obtain international agreement on a maximum of twelve miles. In the work of the Third United Nations Conference on the Law of the Sea (1973–9) the provisional formulation of the breadth of the territorial sea is in terms of a limit not exceeding 12 nautical miles. The acceptance of this is bound up with provision for a generous exclusive economic zone extending not more than 200 miles from the baselines of the territorial sea, and also the strengthening of the regime governing passage through international straits.

5. *Is Delimitation a Liberty of Coastal States?*

The present position would seem to be that there is no general agreement on a uniform breadth for the territorial sea. However, while to accept the demise of 'the three-mile rule' (some would say it had never existed) is easy enough, considerable fortitude is required in determining the present regime, unless it is accepted that the coastal state has freedom to fix its limits. In plain words, the really grave issue is not what breadth is presently accepted, but whether the issue is governed by international law at all. To do away with a rule without agreement on a replacement presents this issue.

Apart from conflicts of view as to the permissible baseline or the breadth of the territorial sea, states have an occasion asserted

Verde, China, Colombia, Comoros, Costa Rica, Cuba, Cyprus, Djibouti, Equatorial Guinea, Ethiopia, Fiji, France, Grenada, Guatemala, Guinea-Bissau, Guyana, Haiti, Honduras, India, Indonesia, Iran, Iraq, Italy, Ivory Coast, Jamaica, Japan, Kenya, Kuwait, Libya, Malaysia, Malta, Mauritius, Mexico, Monaco, Morocco, Mozambique, Nauru, New Zealand, North Korea, Oman, Pakistan, Papua New Guinea, Poland, Portugal, Romania, São Tome and Principe, Saudi Arabia, Seychelles, South Africa, South Korea, Spain, Sri Lanka, Sudan, Surinam, Syria, Thailand, Trinidad and Tobago, Tunisia, U.S.S.R., Venezuela, Vietnam, Western Samoa, Yemen Arab Republic, Yemen P.D. Republic, Zaïre.

Claims in excess of 12 miles call for cautious evaluation. In particular, the incidence of protest and recognition by other states is significant. Moreover, certain of the claims are equivocal and may amount to fishery conservation zones rather than claims to territorial sea.

Albania claims 15 miles, Angola 20 miles. 2 states claim 30 miles: Togo, Nigeria. 4 states claim 50 miles: Cameroun, The Gambia, Malagasy, Tanzania. Mauritania claims 70 miles. Gabon claims 100 miles. Senegal claims 150 miles. 14 states claim 200 miles: Argentina (or, perhaps, 12), Benin, Brazil, Chile (or, perhaps, 3), Ecuador, El Salvador, Ghana, Guinea, Liberia, Panama, Peru, Sierra Leone, Somalia, Uruguay.

that the coastal state is at liberty to fix its own limits.[1] However, in spite of differences in practice, states have very generally taken up the position that their individual claim was in accordance with the law and was not a discretionary choice.[2] The International Law Commission was not of the opinion that states had freedom in the matter. In the *Fisheries* case, whilst the Court allowed that in relation to rugged coasts the coastal state would seem to be in the best position to appraise the local conditions dictating the selection of lines,[3] and referred to 'economic interests', the tenor of the judgment is that the straight lines system was an application of the general principles of the law to special facts. The Court stated:[4]

> The delimitation of sea areas has always an international aspect; it cannot be dependent merely upon the will of the coastal State as expressed in its municipal law. Although it is true that the act of delimitation is necessarily a unilateral act, because only the coastal State is competent to undertake it, the validity of the delimitation with regard to other States depends upon international law.

In other words states cannot unilaterally obliterate the major concept of a maritime belt associated with the line of the coast, appurtenant to the land, and partition the open sea. However, some jurists are prepared to deduce from the *Fisheries* case a power of unilateral delimitation qualified only by the requirement of reasonableness.[5] Such a power would in practice be

[1] See Italian Note to the United States, 6 November 1914; Hackworth i. 637. For a Norwegian view, Hyde i. 464. See also the Swedish reply of 1929 to the Preparatory Committee for the Hague Codification Conf. 1930 and the Yugoslav comment on I.L.C. draft, *Yrbk., I.L.C.* (1956), ii. 99–100. At the Hague Codification Conference in 1930 Spain took this position. For the view of the Philippines: 67 *R.G.D.I.P.* (1963), 395. Generally, McDougal and Burke, p. 489–98. Rousseau, p. 437, states such a view as an estimate of the existing position. See also Meyer, *The Extent of Jurisdiction in Coastal Waters* (1937), pp. 512–20; and Smith, *Great Britain and The Law of Nations* ii. 198–206. After the failure of the 1960 conference certain states have assumed a liberty of action.

[2] See the replies of governments to the questionnaire on territorial waters prepared by a Committee of Experts for the Progressive Codification of International Law (appointed by the League Council), published in 1927.

[3] I.C.J. Reports (1951), p. 131.

[4] Ibid., p. 132. See also Judge McNair, pp. 160–1; Judge Read, pp. 189–90.

[5] See Smith, *The Law and Custom of the Sea* (3rd ed.), pp. 20–2; and cf. Judge Alvarez, I.C.J. Reports (1951), p. 150. See also Resol. XIII, para. A, adopted at the third meeting of the Inter-American Council of Jurists, Mexico City, 1956: '2. Each State is competent to establish its territorial waters within reasonable limits, taking into account geographical, geological, and biological factors, as well as the economic needs of its population, and its security and defence.' Adopted by 15 votes to 4. However, 3 states, including Brazil, which had voted affirmatively, subsequently expressed reservations on this paragraph. See MacChesney, op. cit., p. 244. See further views expressed in the I.L.C. by Kozhevnikov, Amado, Žourek, Córdova, and Scelle, *Yrbk., I.L.C.* (1952), i. 153 seq.; by Krylov and Žourek, ibid. (1955), i. 156 seq.; and by Žourek, Padilla-Nervo, Amado, Salamanca, ibid. (1956), i. 161 seq. Cf. Comments of Peru, U.N. Conference on the Law of the Sea, Off. Recs. i. 97; Poland, ibid., p. 98; Sweden, ibid., p. 99.

little more than an uncontrolled discretion. States claiming freedom in fixing limits at least admit that the question of baselines is regulated by law, and their claims would seem to spring in part from a reaction against the restrictive three-mile limit supported by maritime nations. At the Geneva Conference in 1958 a Peruvian proposal based on a resolution adopted by the Inter-American Council of Jurists in 1956[1] did not receive any real support. No such proposals were put before the United Nations Conferences of 1960[2] or 1973–9.

6. *The Present Legal Regime*

To dismiss 'the three-mile rule' is not to produce anarchy, and the position is still governed by the law. This is implicit in the draft article on the breadth of the territorial sea produced by the International Law Commission:[3]

> Article 3. 1. The Commission recognizes that international practice is not uniform as regards the delimitation of the territorial sea.
>
> 2. The Commission considers that international law does not permit an extension of the territorial sea beyond twelve miles.
>
> 3. The Commission, without taking any decision as to the breadth of the territorial sea up to that limit, notes, on the one hand, that many States have fixed a breadth greater than three miles, and, on the other hand, that many States do not recognize such a breadth when that of their own territorial sea is less.

Subject to historic rights[4] and the question of acquiescence,[5] the formula provides two rules which are reliable in that they carry the persuasive authority of the Commission and correspond to present practice. First, the three-mile limit is a minimum[6] which must be recognized by all: to this extent the 'rule' has survived.[7] Secondly, any limit over twelve miles is invalid.[8] This corresponds to present practice, since some ninety-eight states claim twelve miles or less, and the provisional formulation adopted at the Third United Nations Conference on the Law of

[1] See last note. A Soviet proposal on similar lines but less radical was rejected. See McDougal and Burke, pp. 496–8.

[2] See, however, the '10-Power' proposal (see text, and comment by Bowett, in 9 *I.C.L.Q.* (1960), 431).

[3] *Yrbk., I.L.C.* (1956), ii. 265. Paragraph 4 reads: 'The Commission considers that the breadth of the territorial sea should be fixed by an international conference.'

[4] *Supra*, pp. 170–1. [5] *Supra*, pp. 163–4.

[6] See Gidel iii. 134; Alfaro, *Yrbk., I.L.C.* (1952), i. 159. Sørensen, 101 Hague *Recueil* (1960, III), 154–5, considers six miles to be the existing minimum.

[7] On one view states are under a duty to have a three-mile minimum.

[8] Sørensen, op. cit., p. 155.

the Sea presents twelve miles as the maximum permitted limit. It is possible to express the present position in terms of the proposition that a claim of more than twelve miles is not opposable to other states save as a result of express recognition. It might be thought that the draft article states or implies that three-mile states are not obliged to recognize the larger claims.[1] However, this construction is illogical, as it would involve an assumption that the article gives a higher value to the three-mile limit, which it does not. The text merely 'notes' that 'many States do not recognize [a breadth greater than three miles] when that of their own territorial seas is less'. The question which still remains is whether a twelve-mile claimant[2] is obliged to recognize, for example, a six-mile claimant: it would certainly be reasonable to suppose such an obligation.

7. *Attempts to Establish a Uniform Breadth by Multilateral Convention*

The Hague Codification Conference of 1930 failed to reach agreement on a uniform limit. When the International Law Commission of the United Nations General Assembly began its work of codification it was natural that the question of the territorial sea should make an early appearance on the agenda. The work of the Commission culminated in the convening of the Conference on the Law of the Sea, held at Geneva in 1958 under United Nations auspices.[3] Positions adopted at the Conference ranged from adherence to three miles with no special zones to opinions that each coastal state has the right to determine the limit. The proceedings centred on compromise proposals by states with three-mile limits, and there was a general acceptance of the connexion between the question of exclusive fishery zones and the limit of the territorial sea as such. Considerations of national policy were to the fore, although these also assumed a regional or bloc aspect to some extent. Communist states and newly independent states were concerned at the deployment of naval power as a means of policy and particularly the appearance of

[1] See the comments annexed to the draft and compare the 1955 draft article, *Yrbk., I.L.C.* (1955), ii. 35.

[2] That is, a state not relying on historic rights.

[3] Eighty-seven nations attended. General accounts of the work of the Conference: Fitzmaurice, 8 *I.C.L.Q.* (1959), 73–121; Dean, 52 *A.J.* (1958), 607–28; McDougal and Burke, pp. 496–8, 529–40, 549–54; Patey, 62 *R.G.D.I.P.* (1958), 446–68; Jessup, 59 *Columbia L.R.* (1959), 234–68; Verzijl, 6 *Neths. Int. L.R.* (1959), pp. 1–42, 115–39; Sørensen, *Int. Conciliation*, no. 520 (1958), p. 195; Franklin, *The Law of the Sea; Some Recent Developments*, U.S. Naval War College, vol. liii, pp. 84–126.

vessels within sight of a coast at times of internal crisis. The United States also placed emphasis on matters of military security, including the possible use of neutral waters by belligerent submarines in time of conflict. Economically weak states with interests in fisheries in 'home' waters favoured broad limits as a form of protection from well organized foreign fishing fleets appearing off their shores. Arguments from an international public policy tended to be sullied by selfish inspiration. Thus appeals to the principle of the freedom of the seas no longer have much effect. The total result is unfortunate: while claims made by underdeveloped states are just as vital to them as claims to freedom by states wishing to have freedom for their interests in naval strategy, the fact remains that a policy of he takes who can will in the end favour powerful states if it is taken up. There has to be *some* limit or there will be a return to the era of closed seas.

Compromise proposals at the conference failed: the essence of these proposals was acceptance of a six-mile territorial sea accompanied by a twelve-mile fishing zone. Similar proposals at the Second Conference on the Law of the Sea in 1960 also failed to obtain the necessary majority.[1] A proposal supported by the sixteen Afro-Asian powers, the U.S.S.R., Mexico, and Venezuela would have established twelve miles as a permissible limit. It was rejected in the Committee of the Whole.[2]

The United Kingdom has regulated its relations with states with whom it had differences on the law concerning the territorial sea and special fishery zones by means of bilateral treaties.[3] Indeed, special conventions, recognition, and acquiescence are important stabilizers in the present situation of the law. Regional solutions also play a role. The solution adopted in the European Fisheries Convention of 1964[4] shows adherence to a formula analogous to the 'six plus six' formula popular at the Geneva Conferences. The European Fisheries Convention provides for

[1] For the text of the proposals: Bowett, 9 *I.C.L.Q.* (1960), p. 415 at pp. 424–32. The key Canadian/United States proposal was amended to provide for preferential fishing rights of coastal states, as established by a special commission. It failed by only one vote (54 to 28, 5 abstentions). See, in addition to Bowett's very clear account of the conference Dean, 54 *A.J.* (1961), 104–9; Jessup, 55 *A.J.* (1962), 104–9; François, 7 *Neths. Int. L.R.* (1960), 249–54.

[2] See Bowett, op. cit., pp. 421–4. Voting: 39 to 36, 13 abstentions.

[3] e.g. the Fishery Agreement with Norway, in force 3 March 1961; 57 *A.J.* (1963), 490. See generally Johnson, 10 *I.C.L.Q.* (1961), 587–97; Whiteman iv. 1154 seq.

[4] Entry into force: 15 March 1966. Text: 581 U.N.T.S. 57; 58 *A.J.* (1964), 1070; 3 Int. Legal Materials (1964), 469. Thus, under the U.K. Fishery Limits Act of 1964, parties to this Convention are not excluded from the six to twelve belt. New agreements in 1964 gave Norway and Poland rights in the same belt, subject to time limits. See further Johnson, in *Recent Developments in the Law of the Sea 1958–1964*, pp. 48–91.

an exclusive fisheries zone of six miles, and, further, that 'within the belt between six and twelve miles measured from the baseline of the territorial sea, the right to fish shall be exercised only by the coastal state and by such other Contracting Parties, the fishing vessels of which have habitually fished in that belt between January 1, 1953 and December 31, 1962.' This provision is not to prejudice application of 'internationally agreed measures of conservation', and is without any time limit.

8. *Baselines: Further Problems*[1]

Bays.[2] It is necessary to determine the closing line which leaves internal waters on its landward side and provides a baseline for delimiting the territorial sea. The drawing of a closing line is possible only where the coast of the bay belongs to a single state. To justify assimilation to the land domain there must be a certain degree of penetration.[3] The straight closing line applicable to bays is quite distinct from the system of baselines applicable in special circumstances as established in the *Fisheries* case. The provision concerning bays in the Convention on the Territorial Sea is not intended to introduce the system of straight lines to coasts whose configuration does not justify this. A number of writers[4] have asserted the existence of a rule limiting the closing line to ten miles. Practice was, however, far from uniform,[5]

[1] On the baseline in frozen seas: Colombos, p. 129. Minor points are dealt with in Articles 8, 9 and 13 of the Convention on the Territorial Sea.

[2] Bibliography in Hyde i. 468. In particular see: Gidel iii. 532 seq.; Hurst, 3 *B.Y.* (1922–3), 42–54; Fitzmaurice, 8 *I.C.L.Q.* (1959), 79–85; McDougal and Burke, pp. 327–73; Waldock, 28 *B.Y.* (1951), 137–42; Whiteman iv. 207–33; *Fisheries* case, Pleadings, I; Gihl, *Scand. Studies in Law* (1967), 119–74; Bouchez, *The Regime of Bays in International Law* (1964); Blum, *Historic Titles in International Law* (1965), 261–81; Edeson, *Austral. Year Book*, 1968–9, 5–54; Law of the Sea Inst. (Rhode Island), Occasional Paper No. 13 (1972).

[3] See the Convention on the Territorial Sea, Art. 7, para. 2: 'For the purposes of these articles, a bay is a well-marked indentation whose penetration is in such proportion to the width of its mouth as to contain landlocked waters and constitute more than a mere curvature of the coast. An indentation shall not, however, be regarded as a bay unless its area is as large as, or larger than, that of the semi-circle, whose diameter is a line drawn across the mouth of that indentation.' On the application of this provision see *Post Office* v. *Estuary Radio* [1967] 1 W.L.R. 1396. And see para. 3. Gulfs, fjords, and the like are included in the legal concept of a bay. See also *U.S.* v. *California*, 381 U.S. 139; Int. L.R. 42, 86; *U.S.* v. *Louisiana et al.*, 394 U.S. 11 (1969); 63 *A.J.* (1969), 832.

[4] e.g. Bluntschli, Rivier, de Lapradelle; others have supported a six-mile or 'double cannon shot' rule. In 1917 the International Law Association supported a ten-mile rule.

[5] See statements in Hall, p. 197; Oppenheim i. 506–7; Hackworth i. 696 (quoting Meyer); and Briggs, p. 289. In the nineteenth century the content of the concept of a bay was assumed and not precisely defined: see McNair, *Opinions* i. 353–6, 360, and the views of the tribunal in the *North Atlantic Fisheries* case, Hague Court Reports, p. 141 at

and in the *Fisheries* case the International Court concluded that 'the ten-mile rule has not acquired the authority of a general rule of international law'.[1] In recent years various lengths have been employed, including six, ten, twelve, and twenty miles. In view of present uncertainties a generally accepted limit had to be sought: Article 7, paragraph 4 of the Convention on the Territorial Sea prescribes twenty-four miles.[2] Coastal states may derive title to bays as a consequence of the system of straight lines approved in the *Fisheries* case[3] where this is applicable. A considerable number of large claims related to 'bays' are based on historic title, a mode of acquisition which has been examined already as a question of general principle.[4]

Bays bounded by the territory of two or more states. Although the issue has not been uncontroversial, Article 12 of the Convention on the Territorial Sea probably represents the law as it has been generally understood.[5] Paragraph 1 provides:[6]

> Where the coasts of two States are opposite or adjacent to each other, neither of the two States is entitled, failing agreement between them to the contrary, to extend its territorial sea beyond the median line every point of which is equidistant from the nearest points of the baselines from which the breadth of the territorial seas of each of the two States is measured. The provisions of this paragraph shall not apply, however, where it is necessary by reason of historic title[7] or other special circumstances[8] to delimit the

pp. 187–8; Briggs, p. 284. The ten-mile limit finds support in the documents of the 1930 Codification Conference and the practice of Belgium, France, Germany, and Holland. The United States supports the rule in comments on the I.L.C. draft articles of 1955. The limit has figured from time to time in treaties relating to fisheries since 1839. See further Harv. Research, 23 *A.J.* (1929), Spec. Suppl., pp. 265–74.

[1] I.C.J. Reports (1951), p. 131. See also Judge McNair, at pp. 163–4. However, Judge Read, p. 188, regards the rule as a part of the customary law.

[2] The provisions of the 1958 Convention on the Territorial Sea and Contiguous Zone are maintained in the Informal Composite Negotiating Text of the Third United Nations Conference (1977), Art. 10.

[3] *Supra*, pp. 186 seq.

[4] *Supra*, pp. 170–1. For bays claimed as 'historic bays' (over thirty in all), see Colombos, pp. 180–8; Jessup, *The Law of Territorial Waters and Maritime Jurisdiction* (1927), pp. 383–439. See further McDougal and Burke, pp. 357–68 (discounting the basis in authority of some claims); Gidel iii. 621–63; and *infra*, note 7.

[5] See Oppenheim i. 508; Colombos, p. 188; Hyde i. 475.

[6] See Informal Composite Negotiating Text (1977), Art. 15.

[7] The Central American Court of Justice, in an opinion and decision of 9 March 1917, declared that the Gulf of Fonseca was 'an historic bay possessed of the characteristics of a closed sea' and further that, without prejudice to the rights of Honduras, El Salvador and Nicaragua had a right of co-ownership in the extra-territorial waters of the Gulf. See Hackworth i. 702–5. On claims to treat the Straits of Tiran and the Gulf of Aqaba as a closed sea see Gross, 53 *A.J.* (1959), p. 564 at pp. 566–72; Selak, 52 *A.J.* (1958), p. 660 at pp. 689–98.

[8] This is unfortunately vague. Geographical peculiarities and the elimination of practical

territorial seas of the two States in a way which is at variance with this provision.

Straits.[1] See the provision quoted above.

Occasional islands.[2] Whatever the size or population a formation is an island in the legal sense if two conditions are satisfied: (1) the formation must be natural and not an artificial installation; (2) it must always be above sea level. Formations visible only at low tide ('low-tide elevations'), and permanently submerged banks and reefs, do not in general produce a territorial sea, as islands do.

Low-tide elevations. In two cases these formations are permitted to produce an effect on the limit of the territorial sea. Article 4, paragraph 3, of the Convention on the Territorial Sea provides that straight baselines shall not be drawn to or from low-tide elevations unless lighthouses or similar installations which are permanently above sea level have been built on them.[3] Secondly, and apart from the effect of Article 4, the low-water line on an elevation situated at a distance not exceeding the breadth of the territorial sea from the mainland or an island may be used as the baseline.[4] Elevations not within the territorial sea have no territorial sea of their own.

Island and rock fingers of the Norwegian type. Such formations may be included in the system of straight lines considered previously.

Island fringes treated as natural appendages of the coast.[5] Quite apart from coasts to which a *system* of straight lines may properly apply, there is, in the opinion of Sir Humphrey Waldock, a 'considerable body of State practice' supporting the principle

problems are probably catered for. See the declaration on Article 12 by Venezuela: McDougal and Burke, p. 1184.

[1] See Gidel iii. 728 seq.; McDougal and Burke, pp. 432–7; Hyde i. 489; Harv. Research, 23 *A.J.* (1929), Spec. Suppl., pp. 280–7; Briggs, p. 290.

[2] See the Convention on the Territorial Sea, Art. 10; *Yrbk., I.L.C.* (1956), ii. 270; Fitzmaurice, 8 *I.C.L.Q.* (1959), 85–8; Gidel iii. 670 seq.; McNair, *Opinions* i. 363 seq.; McDougal and Burke, pp. 373, 391–8; Hyde i. 484–7. Note the role of the skjaergaard in the *Fisheries* case, *supra*, pp. 186 seq. For the contention that certain artificial islands have a territorial sea: Johnson, 4 *I.L.Q.* (1951), 203–15.

[3] See Marston, 46 *B.Y.* (1972–3), 405–23, for detailed consideration.

[4] Art. 11 of the Convention. See also the *Fisheries* case, I.C.J. Reports (1951), p. 128, and cf. U.N. Legis. Series, *Regime of the Territorial Sea*, pp. 14, 48, 54, 194, 245, 293, 563, 564; *Regina* v. *Kent Justices, ex p. Lye* [1967] 2 Q.B. 153; *U.S.* v. *Louisiana et al.*, 394 U.S. 11 (1969).

[5] See Gidel iii. 711, 719, 722; Colombos, pp. 122–3; Waldock, 28 *B.Y.* (1951), 142; Gihl, op. cit., 129–35. See also the *Anna* (1805), 5 C. Rob. 373; *U.S.* v. *Louisiana et al.*, n. 4 above and Third United Nations Conference, I.C.N. Text, Art. 6 (on reefs).

that under certain conditions coastal islands may be treated as part of the mainland.[1] The principle rests on considerations of geographical association and appurtenance, and some but by no means all claims are supported by historic title and acquiescence. A baseline—not necessarily a straight line—is drawn in such cases from the low-water line on the seaward shore of the island chain. Such an approach could be justified as an application of the principles expounded in the judgment in the *Fisheries* case[2] (in which the Court regarded the outer line of the 'skaergaard' as constituting 'a whole with the mainland') but receives no support in the Territorial Sea Convention.

Groups of islands; archipelagos.[3] Claims to a baseline drawn along the outer fringe of groups of islands in close association with the mainland may be justified on grounds considered in the last paragraph.[4] The International Law Commission failed to produce a draft article on the question, although in a comment (annexed to Article 10) it pointed out that the straight baselines system might be applicable. However, neither this system nor what has been said above provides a solution to the problem of baselines associated with large island systems unconnected with any mainland. Indonesia and the Philippines[5] employ straight baselines to enclose such island systems, and it may be that a polygonal system is the only feasible one in such special cases. It is arguable that this is only a further application, to special facts, of principles of unity and interdependence inherent in the *Fisheries* case. The difficulty is to allow for such special cases without giving a general prescription which, being unrelated to any clear concept of mainland, will permit of abuse.

At the Third United Nations Conference on the Law of the Sea the archipelagic states as a group[6] have had some success in

[1] 28 *B.Y.* (1951), 142. See also Hall, p. 149.

[2] I.C.J. Reports, 1951, p. 128.

[3] Gidel iii. 706–27; Evensen, U.N. Conf. on the Law of the Sea, Off. Recs. i. 289; Fitzmaurice, op. cit., pp. 88–90; Waldock, op. cit., pp. 142–7; McDougal and Burke, pp. 373–87; Sørensen, *Varia Juris Gentium*, pp. 315–31; *Yrbk., I.L.C.* (1953), ii. 69, 77; Whiteman iv. 274–303; Verzijl, *International Law in Historical Perspective* iii. 71–5; Pharand, 21 *Univ. of Toronto L.J.* (1971), 1–14; O'Connell, 45 *B.Y.* (1971), 1–77; Law of the Sea Inst. (Rhode Island), Occasional Paper No. 13 (1972); Amerasinghe, 23 *I.C.L.Q.* (1974), 539–75; Bowett, *The Legal Regime of Islands in International Law* (1979), pp. 73–113. See also *Civil Aeronautics Board* v. *Island Airlines*, 235 F. Supp. 990 (1964).

[4] See legislation of Cuba, Ecuador, Egypt, Ethiopia, Iran, Saudi Arabia, and Yugoslavia. See also *Fisheries* case, Pleadings, I. 79–83, 465–95.

[5] Philippines claim: *Yrbk., I.L.C.* (1956), ii. 69–70; MacChesney, op. cit., p. 487. For the Indonesian claim and the United Kingdom protest: 7 *I.C.L.Q.* (1958), 538.

[6] Comprising Fiji, Indonesia, Mauritius and Philippines.

advancing the cause of straight archipelagic baselines. Consequently the Informal Composite Negotiating Text of 1977 includes a set of articles concerning archipelagic states (Articles 46–54). These are defined as 'a state constituted wholly by one or more archipelagos and may include other islands'. For no very sound reason this definition excludes states, such as Ecuador and Canada, which consist in part of one or more archipelagos. According to the provisional draft archipelagic straight baselines may be employed subject to certain conditions: for example, that such baselines 'shall not depart to any appreciable extent from the general configuration of the archipelago'. The archipelagic state has sovereignty over the waters enclosed by the baselines subject to certain limitations created by the provisions of this Part of the draft. These limitations consist of the right of innocent passage (see below) for ships of all states, and, unless the archipelagic state designates sea lanes and air routes above, 'the right of archipelagic sea lanes passage . . . through the routes normally used for international navigation' (Article 53).

9. *Legal Regime of the Territorial Sea*

In practical terms, the coastal state has rights and duties inherent in sovereignty, although alien vessels have privileges, associated particularly with the right of innocent passage, which have no counterparts in respect of the land domain apart from special agreement or local customary rights. The coastal state may reserve fisheries for its own nationals, and indeed the first exercise of this power has often been the first evidence of a claim to a maritime belt. It may also exclude foreign vessels from navigation and trade along the coast (*cabotage*). Obviously, there is a general power of police in matters of security, customs, fiscal regulation, and sanitary and health controls. Particular limitations on this sovereignty to be found in general international law will now be considered.

Innocent passage.[1] Customary law recognizes the right of peaceful or innocent passage through the territorial sea.[2] Historically the right or, as some would call it, the privilege is re-

[1] Gidel iii. 193–291; Whiteman iv. 343–417; McDougal and Burke, pp. 174–269; Fitzmaurice, 8 *I.C.L.Q.* (1959), 90–108; Hackworth i. 645–51; Franklin, U.S. Naval War College, *The Law of the Sea: Some Recent Developments* (1961), pp. 127–56; Gross, 53 *A.J.* (1959), 564–94; François, Report, *Yrbk., I.L.C.* (1952), ii. 38; and for statements by U.K. delegates to the Geneva Conference, 7 *I.C.L.Q.* (1958), 543.

[2] Not through internal waters. For an exception resulting from the use of a straight baseline, see Article 5 of the Convention on the Territorial Sea.

lated to a state of affairs in which special zones of jurisdiction were not clearly distinguished from full-blooded claims and in principle the maritime belt was high seas but with restrictions in favour of the coastal state. As a question of policy innocent passage is a sensible form of accommodation between the necessities of sea communication and the interests of the coastal state. In the face of tendencies to claim a broader territorial sea in the practice of states any proposals to restrict the right will no doubt be met with considerable opposition. Definition of innocent passage is a matter of some difficulty, not only in respect of precision in stating the conditions of innocence, but also with regard to the question of a presumption in favour either of the visitor or of the coastal state in case of doubt. The starting point must be Article 14 of the Convention on the Territorial Sea:[1]

1. Subject to the provisions of these articles, ships of all States, whether coastal or not, shall enjoy the right of innocent passage through the territorial sea.
2. Passage means navigation through the territorial sea for the purpose either of traversing that sea without entering internal waters, or of proceeding to internal waters, or of making for the high seas from internal waters.
3. Passage includes stopping and anchoring, but only in so far as the same are incidental to ordinary navigation or are rendered necessary by *force majeure* or by distress.
4. Passage is innocent so long as it is not prejudicial to the peace, good order or security of the coastal State. Such passage shall take place in conformity with these articles and with other rules of international law.
5. Passage of foreign fishing vessels shall not be considered innocent if they do not observe such laws and regulations as the coastal State may make and publish in order to prevent these vessels from fishing in the territorial sea.[2]

In substance this article corresponds to the customary law,[3] but it is more specific in certain respects. Though to some degree the text speaks for itself some comment is necessary. Vessels engaged in coastal trade (*cabotage*) are excluded by the definition of passage. Fishing vessels are included, though by an ill-drafted provision which makes compliance with local laws and regu-

[1] Articles 14 to 17 inclusive appear under the rubric 'Rules applicable to All Ships'. Article 14 bears a close relation to Articles 3 and 4 of the draft produced by the Second Committee of the Hague Codification Conference in 1930.

[2] Paragraph 6 contains a simple condition of passage rather than a criterion of innocence: 'Submarines are required to navigate on the surface and to show their flag.'

[3] However, it relates innocent passage and the matter of access to ports, which are distinct issues historically.

lations relating to the prevention of fishing a criterion of innocence. This approach contradicts paragraph 4. Paragraph 4 states that passage is innocent if 'not prejudicial to the peace, good order or security of the coastal State', but does not make compliance with local laws and regulations a criterion of innocence.[1] Apparently the text was intended to place emphasis on the manner in which the passage was carried out[2] rather than on factors such as the object of the particular passage, the cargo carried, ultimate destination, and so on. However, several commentators understand the words to extend to the object of the journey.[3]

At the Third United Nations Conference on the Law of the Sea (1973–9) the right of innocent passage was a matter of particular interest. The maritime states, faced with expanding claims to territorial seas affecting many seaways, were concerned to provide firmer outlines for the right. Consequently, in the Informal Composite Negotiating Text of 1977 there is a more detailed definition of 'innocent passage'.[4]

[1] See Fitzmaurice, op. cit., p. 95.

[2] Cf. the *Corfu Channel* case (Merits), I.C.J. Reports (1949), pp. 30–2; and Fitzmaurice, 27 *B.Y.* (1950), 28–31.

[3] Fitzmaurice, 8 *I.C.L.Q.*, pp. 95–6; Sørensen, 101 Hague *Recueil* (1960, III), 188; id. *Int. Conciliation*, no. 520 (1958), p. 334. *Contra*, Gross, op. cit., p. 582. Example of non-innocent passage on this interpretation: carriage of weapons to a state helping guerrillas operating against the coastal state.

[4] Article 19 of the draft:

'*Meaning of innocent passage*

1. Passage is innocent so long as it is not prejudicial to the peace, good order or security of the coastal State. Such passage shall take place in conformity with the present Convention and with other rules of international law.

2. Passage of a foreign ship shall be considered to be prejudicial to the peace, good order or security of the coastal State, if in the territorial sea it engages in any of the following activities:

(a) Any threat or use of force against the sovereignty, territorial integrity or political independence of the coastal State, or in any other manner in violation of the principles of international law embodied in the Charter of the United Nations;

(b) Any exercise or practice with weapons of any kind;

(c) Any act aimed at collecting information to the prejudice of the defence or security of the coastal State;

(d) Any act of propaganda aimed at affecting the defence or security of the coastal State;

(e) The launching, landing or taking on board of any aircraft;

(f) The launching, landing or taking on board of any military device;

(g) The embarking or disembarking of any commodity, currency or person contrary to the customs, fiscal, immigration or sanitary regulations of the coastal State;

(h) Any act of wilful and serious pollution, contrary to the present Convention;

(i) Any fishing activities;

(j) The carrying out of research or survey activities;

(k) Any act aimed at interfering with any systems of communication or any other facilities or installations of the coastal State;

(l) Any other activity not having a direct bearing on passage.'

Passage of warships.[1] Several opinions of considerable authority deny the right of passage of warships in peacetime;[2] others allow such a right 'when the territorial waters are so placed that passage through them is necessary for international traffic'.[3] It is clear that a significant number, and perhaps a majority, of states require prior authorization for the passage of warships, and, as a consequence, dogmatic assertions of a right of passage have an aspect of advocacy. A draft article formulated by the International Law Commission at its eighth session gave the coastal state the right to make passage subject to prior authorization or notification.[4] At the Geneva Conference of 1958 this formula did not get the necessary support. However, Professor Sorensen[5] is of the opinion that a majority of delegations did not intend warships to have a right of passage, but no article in the Convention on the Territorial Sea deals with this question directly. The draft article of the Commission bearing directly on the subject was omitted.[6]

Certain jurists have deduced from the text of the Convention the sense that it recognizes a right of passage. In support of this position Sir Gerald Fitzmaurice, as he then was, states that Articles 14–17 are titled 'Rules applicable to All Ships', and the provision relating to submarines (Art. 14, para. 6) makes it clear by implication that 'All Ships' includes warships.[7] The *travaux préparatoires* contradict this implication.[8] It has also been argued [9] that the right of passage arises by implication from

[1] See McDougal and Burke, pp. 192–4, 216–21; Colombos, p. 133; Gidel iii. 277–89; Jessup, 59 *Columbia L.R.* (1959), 247–9; Harv. Research, 23 *A.J.* (1929), Spec. Suppl., pp. 295–6; François, *Yrbk., I.L.C.* (1952), ii. 42–3; U.N. Legis. Series, *The Territorial Sea*, pp. 361–420; Verzijl, *International Law* iii. 59–60; McNair, *Opinions* ii. 191–2; de Vries Reilingh, 2 *Neths. Yrbk.* (1971), 29–67. On passage through territorial waters forming part of an international strait, *infra*, Chapter XII.

[2] Hall, p. 198; Sørensen, 101 Hague *Recueil* (1960, III), 192. Is 'peacetime' a bilateral relation, or is it applicable to a war situation proximate geographically?

[3] Oppenheim i. 494 (temporizes somewhat); Colombos, loc. cit. Cf. Guggenheim i. 421–2; Hyde i. 516–18. Gidel iii. 280 quotes Oppenheim with approval. Cf. *Corfu Channel* case (Merits), I.C.J. Reports (1949), p. 28.

[4] *Yrbk., I.L.C.* (1956), ii. 276–7. States requiring prior authorization or notification: (*inter alia*) Belgium, Bulgaria, Colombia, Egypt, France, Honduras, Italy, Norway, Poland, Rumania, U.S.S.R., Yugoslavia. See also reservations to Art. 23 of the Conv. on the Territorial Sea by Bulgaria, Byelorussia, Czechoslovakia, Hungary, Rumania, and the Ukraine. Those permitting a right of passage: (*inter alia*) Denmark, Netherlands, United Kingdom (see 7 *I.C.L.Q.* (1958), 544), United States, German Federal Republic, Iran, Peru, Sweden. The materials of the Hague Codification Conference are inconclusive.

[5] *Int. Conciliation*, no. 520 (1958), p. 235.

[6] See U.N. Conference on the Law of the Sea, Off. Recs. ii. 66–8.

[7] Op. cit., pp. 98–9, 102–3.

[8] Cf. *Yrbk., I.L.C.* (1956), ii. 272 (comment on Art. 15).

[9] Jessup, op. cit., p. 248; and cf. Franklin, U.S. Naval War College, *The Law of the Sea: Some Recent Developments* (1961), pp. 133–7; and O'Connell ii. 637–8.

Article 23, which is the sole article under the title 'Rule applicable to Warships'. This provides: 'If any warship does not comply with the regulations of the coastal State concerning passage through the territorial sea and disregards any request for compliance which is made to it, the coastal State may require the warship to leave the territorial sea.'

The object of this provision was to deal with the case where a warship, having commenced passage in accordance with international law, being subject to local laws and regulations, has refused to comply therewith.[1] The immunity from jurisdiction[2] which warships enjoy necessitated a special provision: the hypothesis on which the article rests does not preclude the issue as to a *right* of passage. Moreover, the textual arguments advanced involve the unwarranted assumption that a question with a background of controversy was ultimately settled by leaving the issue dependent on inference. The provisional draft produced at the Third United Nations Conference contains the same unresolved obscurities as the provisions of 1958 (Informal Composite Negotiating Text of 1977, Articles 17–32).

Rights of the coastal state.[3] The coastal state may take the necessary steps in its territorial sea to prevent passage which is not innocent (Convention on the Territorial Sea, Art. 16, para. 1). Vessels exercising the right of passage are subject to local laws and regulations, providing these conform with international law and treaty obligations (Art. 16, para. 2; Art. 17).[4] The substance of such laws and regulations and the mode of enforcing compliance should not be such as to render passage impossible or impracticable. Article 16, paragraph 3, confers on the coastal state a right to suspend innocent passage *temporarily* in specified areas of the territorial sea if such suspension 'is essential for the protection of its security'. Article 18 provides that no charge may be levied on foreign vessels by reason only of their passage, but only for specific services rendered to the ship.

Criminal jurisdiction over ships in passage.[5] This question does

[1] See *Yrbk., I.L.C.* (1956), ii. 276–7: in this draft Subsection D 'Warships', has two sub-heads, 'Passage' and 'Non-observance of the regulations'. Article 23 repeats the article under the latter sub-head. [2] See *infra*, pp. 325, 366.

[3] See McDougal and Burke, pp. 233–4, 247–58, 289–91.

[4] The right of the coastal state to enforce its laws and regulations on ships passing through the territorial sea is implicit in Article 17: McDougal and Burke, pp. 272–3.

[5] See McDougal and Burke, pp. 294–301; Lee, 55 *A.J.* (1961), p. 77 at pp. 86–93; Fitzmaurice, 8 *I.C.L.Q.* (1959), 103–6; U.N. Legis. Series, *The Territorial Sea*, pp. 319 seq.; Guggenheim i. 423; Rousseau, p. 443; Hyde i. 749; Report of François, *Yrbk., I.L.C.* (1952), ii. 40–1; *Yrbk., I.L.C.* (1956), ii 274–5 (draft article and comment). Cf. the Territorial Waters Jurisdiction Act, 1878.

not arise in the case of warships or non-commercial government vessels, which enjoy complete immunity from local jurisdiction. Article 19 of the Convention on the Territorial Sea substantially reproduces rules assumed to represent international law:[1]

1. The criminal jurisdiction of the coastal State should not be exercised on board a foreign ship passing through the territorial sea to arrest any person or to conduct any investigation in connexion with any crime committed on board the ship during its passage, save only in the following cases:
(a) If the consequences of the crime extend to the coastal State; or
(b) If the crime is of a kind to disturb the peace of the country or the good order of the territorial sea; or
(c) If the assistance of the local authorities has been requested by the captain of the ship or by the consul of the country whose flag the ship flies; or
(d) If it is necessary for the suppression of illicit traffic in narcotic drugs.

Subsection (d) is an innovation, however. A matter of controversy concerned the legality of arrest or investigation in connexion with any crime committed before a ship entered the territorial sea if the vessel was merely passing through the territorial sea without entering internal waters. Gidel was of the opinion that arrest was permitted.[2] Paragraph 5 of Article 19 expressly prohibits the exercise of jurisdiction in this way, although logically the prohibition is inherent in the first paragraph. Paragraph 2 of Article 19 reserves a right of arrest and investigation on board foreign vessels passing through the territorial sea after leaving internal waters. The provisional draft produced by the Third United Nations Conference (1973–9) affirms the provisions of 1958 (Informal Composite Negotiating Text of 1977, Article 27).

Civil jurisdiction over ships in passage[3]

(a) *Persons on board.* It is impermissible to stop or divert a foreign ship passing through the territorial sea for the purpose of exercising civil jurisdiction in relation to a person on board. The good sense of the rule is obvious, and it appears in the Territorial Sea Convention.[4]

[1] Fitzmaurice, p. 104, is not prepared to regard the rules as strict law but rather as international practice. Cf. the view of Fitzmaurice as delegate to the Geneva Conference, 7 *I.C.L.Q.* (1958), 545.

[2] iii. 261. Contradicted by other writers. See also Hyde i. 749–50.

[3] See McDougal and Burke, pp. 273–82; Lee, 55 *A.J.* (1961), p. 77 at pp. 93–5; Fitzmaurice, 8 *I.C.L.Q.* (1959), 106–8; U.N. Legis. Series, *The Territorial Sea*, pp. 319 seq.; Report of François, *Yrbk., I.L.C.* (1952), ii. 41–2; ibid. (1956), ii. 275–6 (draft article and comment); Jessup, 27 *A.J.* (1933), 747–50.

[4] Art. 20, para. 1; Colombos, p. 318; Art. 9, draft of Hague Codification Conference,

(b) *Process against the vessel.* Paragraph 2 of Article 20 of the Convention on the Territorial Sea provides that the coastal state may not levy execution against or arrest a foreign ship for the purpose of any civil proceedings 'save only in respect of obligations or liabilities assumed or incurred by the ship itself in the course or for the purpose of its voyage through the waters of the coastal State'.[1] Under this provision the rights of the coastal states are more restricted than they would be under the Brussels Convention for the Unification of Certain Rules Relating to the Arrest of Sea-going Ships, 1952.[2] If the latter does not apply to arrest during passage through the territorial sea, as opposed to internal waters, there is, of course, no conflict. In any case many states have not ratified the Brussels Convention.[3]

Ships at anchor in the territorial sea. The rules considered previously apply, since stopping and anchoring, if these acts are incidental to ordinary navigation, or are rendered necessary by *force majeure* or by distress, are a part of passage.[4] In other cases ships at anchor may be treated in the same way as ships in internal waters: in such cases vessels are not exercising the right of innocent passage.[5]

Foreign vessels in internal waters. See *infra*, pp. 316–19.

B. SPECIALIZED RIGHTS OVER THE HIGH SEAS

1. *Introductory*

The territorial sea is by no means the only form in which the power of the coastal state is manifested over sea areas. It is, however, the form which involves a concentration of legal rights justifying the term 'sovereignty',[6] and the limit of the territorial sea marks the seaward frontier of states. Beyond this line stretch the high seas. A general interest in maintaining the substance of

1930, 24 *A.J.* (1930), Suppl., p. 244. See also the Informal Composite Negotiating Text of 1977, Article 28, para. 1.

[1] See Art. 9, Hague draft, last note; *The Ship 'D. C. Whitney'* v. *St. Clair Navigation Co.* (1907), 38 S.C.R. 303, 311. For a contrary opinion: *The David* (1933), *R.I.A.A.* vi. 382, relied on by Hyde i. 749. See further the proviso in Art. 20, para 3, of the Territorial Sea Conv.; and see the Informal Composite Negotiating Text of 1977, Article 28, paras 2, 3.

[2] 439 U.N.T.S., no. 6330.

[3] For the position of parties to both, see the Convention on the Territorial Sea, Art. 25: 'The provisions of this Convention shall not affect conventions or other international agreements already in force, as between States Parties to them.'

[4] *Supra*, p. 203. [5] Hyde ii. 750; Gidel iii. 276. [6] *Supra*, pp. 109–10.

the principle of freedom of the seas outside the territorial sea has been reconciled with the tendencies of coastal states to extend their power seawards, by the development of generally recognized specialized extensions of jurisdiction, and of rights analogous to legally protected possession of land areas.

2. *The Concept of the Contiguous Zone*[1]

The historical development of the territorial sea, and the appearance of a clear distinction between the plenitude of legal rights over the territorial sea called sovereignty and specialized rights arising from particular types of jurisdiction and control in contiguous zones, are matters which have been considered previously.[2] The opinions of jurists and of governments give very wide recognition to the fact that contiguous zones give jurisdiction *over the high seas* for special purposes. In the Convention on the Territorial Sea the sole article on the contiguous zone, Article 24, refers to control by the coastal state 'in a zone of the high seas contiguous to its territorial sea', and article 1 of the Convention on the High Seas defines 'high seas' as 'all parts of the sea that are not included in the territorial sea or in the internal waters of a State'. It follows that the rights of the coastal state in such a zone do not amount to sovereignty,[3] and thus other states have rights exercisable over the high seas except as they are qualified by the existence of jurisdictional zones. Moreover, these zones are not appurtenant as in the case of the territorial sea—they must be claimed.[4] However, like the territorial sea, they are contiguous, and they share the latter's baseline.[5] They are distinct in origin and legal quality from the legal concepts based on the continental shelf[6] and special zones of various spatial characteristics which may not even be adjacent to the territorial sea.[7]

[1] McDougal and Burke, pp. 565–630; Gidel iii. 361–492; id., 48 Hague *Recueil* (1934, II), 241–73; François, Second Report, *Yrbk., I.L.C.* (1951), ii. 91–4; Fitzmaurice, 8 *I.C.L.Q.* (1959), 108–21; Briggs, pp. 372–7; Jessup, *The Law of Territorial Waters and Maritime Jurisdiction* (1927), pp. 75–112; 241–352; Oda, 11 *I.C.L.Q.* (1962), 131–53; Fell, 62 *Michigan L.R.* (1964), 848–64.

[2] *Supra*, pp. 183–6.

[3] See Fitzmaurice, op. cit., pp. 111–13; id., 92 Hague *Recueil* (1957, II), 157; Sørensen, 101 Hague *Recueil* (1960, III), 155–8.

[4] *Supra*, p. 124. Note the permissive language of Article 24 of the Convention on the Territorial Sea and compare the terms of Art. 1 of the Convention.

[5] *Supra*, pp. 186–91, 199–202.

[6] *Infra*, pp. 222–6. The rubric 'contiguous zone' is applied too widely in the work of McDougal and Burke.

[7] *Infra*, p. 217.

The most important question concerns the purposes for which special rights of jurisdiction and policy may be asserted. Difficulty arises from two sources. From the doctrinal point of view it is only in relatively recent times that a consistent general doctrine of contiguous zones has made an appearance,[1] and systematic development had not proceeded very far when the International Law Commission took up these problems. With regard to state practice consistency has been less than it might have been in part because some states, favouring a narrow breadth for the territorial sea, have remained reluctant to recognize contiguous zones, which they look upon as ultimately just as subversive of their policies as extensions to the territorial sea.[2]

The Informal Composite Negotiating Text produced in 1977 by the Third United Nations Conference on the Law of the Sea provides for the creation of contiguous zones for the same purposes and on the same basis as before (Article 33), except that (1) the contiguous zone is no longer expressed to be 'a zone of the high seas'; and (2) the maximum limit is expressed to be twenty-four miles.

In the recent period more contiguous zones have been eliminated as a result of extended territorial seas. However, the contiguous zones of a number of states with narrow territorial seas survive and two states have recently claimed twenty-four mile contiguous zones,[3] apparently in reaction to the Third United Nations Conference. Another recent development, anomalous to a degree, is the promulgation of customs, pollution or sanitary zones, commonly of six miles in breadth, measured from the outer limits of the territorial sea.[4]

3. *Permissible Types of Zone*

In considering the purposes for which zones may be maintained, Article 24 of the Convention on the Territorial Sea may

[1] Gidel (vol. iii, published in 1934) may be given the credit for giving the concept authority, system, and coherence. Cf. the materials of the Hague Codification Conference; and Renault, 11 *Annuaire de l'Inst.* (1889–92), 150. Generally see Gidel iii. 372 seq. Colombos gives a rather idiosyncratic treatment.

[2] The United Kingdom had no contiguous zone between 1876 and 1964 (*infra*, pp. 212, 214). The United Kingdom has not given explicit recognition of the validity of claims to contiguous zones by other states, but as a party to the Convention on the Territorial Sea it has recognized the principle of the contiguous zone. The United Kingdom has now established a twelve-mile zone for exclusive fisheries: Fishery Limits Act, 1964; *British Practice in International Law* (1964), i. 44.

[3] Legislation of India (1976), and Sri Lanka (1976).

[4] Legislation of Bangladesh (1974), Brazil (1966, 1967), Dominican Republic (1967),

be taken as a point of departure. The article refers to exercise of control necessary to prevent infringement of 'customs, fiscal, immigration or sanitary regulations within the territory or territorial sea of the coastal State'. Subsequently other claims, including fishery and security zones, will be considered.

Customs zones. The exercise of this type of jurisdiction is very frequent and no doubt rests on customary international law.[1] Article 24 of the Convention on the Territorial Sea refers compendiously to 'customs and fiscal' regulations, other sources refer to 'revenue laws'. Modern vessels would find smuggling only too easy if a narrow enforcement area were employed, and customs zones of six and twelve miles are common. The United States has exercised customs jurisdiction over foreign vessels bound for the United States within a four-league zone since 1790.[2] The United Kingdom had similar 'hovering acts' operating against foreign vessels from 1736 until 1876.[3] The content of the claim to enforcement of national legislation in areas of the high seas is presumably limited by a requirement of reasonableness, and regulations designed for revenue enforcement cannot be employed in such a way as to accomplish another purpose, for example the exclusion of foreign vessels.[4] Treaty regimes may be created for the mutual recognition of zones and enforcement procedures, thus reducing the likelihood of incidents.[5]

Immigration zones. In general, standard works do not contain any reference to such zones, and there is little state practice relating to this type as such. In practice customs and fiscal regulations might be applied to deal with the question, and this type of jurisdiction shares the same basis in policy as the customs zone. Immigration zones are given a significant measure of recognition

Arab Rep. of Egypt (1958), Haiti (1972), Saudi Arabia (1958), Sudan (1970), Syrian Arab Rep. (1963), Yemen P.D. Rep. (1970), Yemen Arab Rep. (1967).

[1] See Briggs, pp. 373–6; Whiteman iv. 483–94; Gidel iii. 379–454, 476–9; Jessup, *The Law of Territorial Waters and Maritime Jurisdiction*, p. 95; Oppenheim i. 496–7; Hackworth i. 663 seq. Some customs zones, for example those of Spain, Sweden, and the United Kingdom, coincide with territorial sea limits and are not significant for the present purpose. However, it is useful to notice that in some cases a former customs zone has been eliminated by an extension of the territorial sea.

[2] See also the Anti-Smuggling Act of 1935, Briggs, p. 371.

[3] On the British and American legislation and the diplomatic repercussions see Masterson, *Jurisdiction in Marginal Seas* (1929).

[4] See the opinion excerpted in Hackworth i. 657–9.

[5] See the Helsingfors Convention of 19 August 1925; U.N. Legis. Series, *The Territorial Sea*, p. 709, signed and ratified by eleven European states; ibid., Second Part, Chap. II, for bilateral treaties. On the 'liquor treaties' concluded by the United States see Masterson, op. cit., pp. 326 seq.

by inclusion in the Convention on the Territorial Sea.[1] The limitation to immigration is perhaps significant, although in the relevant draft of the International Law Commission the term was intended to include emigration.

Zones for sanitary purposes. Such zones are included in Article 24 of the Convention on the Territorial Sea. The comment of the International Law Commission on the relevant draft article states:[2] 'Although the number of States which claim rights over the contiguous zone for the purpose of applying sanitary regulations is fairly small,[3] the Commission considers that, in view of the connexion between customs and sanitary regulations, such rights should also be recognized for sanitary regulations.' Doctrine supports the validity of this type of claim.[4]

Prevention of pollution of the sea. The zones considered in the previous paragraph might well be held to accommodate measures to prevent pollution, particularly by oil, but the position is by no means clear.[5] In recent years jurisdiction to police pollution has been advanced principally by extension of the territorial sea and the appearance of the exclusive economic zone (see below), in which the coastal state has the right of *conserving* the natural resources.

Security zones. The Convention on the Territorial Sea does not recognize such zones, and it is submitted that they have not received general acceptance in the practice of states.[6] In a commentary on the relevant draft article the International Law Commission states:[7]

> The Commission did not recognize special security rights in the contiguous zone. It considered that the extreme vagueness of the term 'security' would open the way for abuses and that the granting of such rights was not necessary. The enforcement of customs and sanitary regulations will be

[1] The type had appeared in the I.L.C. draft articles in 1955, but was deleted from the draft of the eighth session in 1956. *Yrbk., I.L.C.* (1956), ii. 295, comment (7). See Fitzmaurice, 8 *I.C.L.Q.* (1959), 117–18 (critical of inclusion); and Oda, 11 *I.C.L.Q.* (1962), 146.

[2] *Yrbk., I.L.C.* (1956), ii. 294–5.

[3] Examples: Dominican Republic (12 miles), Saudi Arabia (18 miles), Venezuela (15 miles). The Netherlands, New Zealand, Norway, and South Africa have zones coinciding with the limits of the territorial sea.

[4] See Gidel iii. 455–7, 476, 486; Oppenheim i. 496–7; Rousseau, p. 440; Fitzmaurice, 8 *I.C.L.Q.*, 117.

[5] See Briggs, pp. 376–7, and references therein.

[6] See Gidel iii. 455, 458–62, 476, 486–7; Whiteman iv. 495–8. Many standard works contain no reference to such zones. See also Secretariat Memo., 1950, paras. 81–107, and François, Second Report, *Yrbk., I.L.C.* (1951), ii. 93, paras. 117–18. Twenty states have claimed security zones in the recent past, apart from security zones not greater in breadth than the territorial sea.

[7] *Yrbk., I.L.C.* (1956), ii. 295. See also Oda, 11 *I.C.L.Q.* (1962), 147–8.

sufficient in most cases to safeguard the security of the State. In so far as measures of self-defence against an imminent and direct threat to the security of the State are concerned, the Commission refers to the general principles of international law and the Charter of the United Nations.

To this it may be added that recognition of such rights would go far toward equating rights over the contiguous zone and rights in the territorial sea.

Neutrality zones.[1] These are claimed infrequently, and the same objections of principle advanced in relation to security zones apply, though with less force. It will be recalled that claims to the territorial sea sometimes originated in claims to restrict belligerent activity near the coast of a neutral state.

Fisheries zones.[2] The source of existing territorial sea limits is found in several cases to lie in a claim by the coastal state to exclude foreign fishing vessels from an adjacent belt, and the monopoly of the living resources of the sea very nearly amounts to proprietorship. Indeed, frequently the principal reason for recent unilateral extension of the limits of the territorial sea has been the desire to reserve offshore fisheries for nationals of the coastal state. At the two United Nations Conferences on the Law of the Sea it was clear that agreement on territorial sea limits was related to agreement on a contiguous zone for fisheries. Formerly the majority of jurists denied the legality of fisheries zones.[3] However, a considerable number of states claim such zones including former opponents of such zones such as Canada, the United Kingdom, the United States, France, and New Zealand.[4] The International Law Commission was not willing to recognize an exclusive right to engage in fishing in a contiguous zone, and the outcome of the Geneva Conferences evidences a lack of agreement on the subject, but some twenty-two states have a fishery limit more extensive than that of the territorial sea.

[1] U.N. Legis. Series, *The Territorial Sea*, pp. 615–74; Harvard draft, 33 *A.J.* (1939), Suppl., pp. 343–53; Jessup, *The Law of Territorial Waters and Maritime Jurisdiction*, pp. 96–105 (sympathetic to such claims in principle); Hackworth i. 660–3. Such zones as exist usually coincide with the limit of the territorial sea.

[2] See Gidel iii. 463–73; U.N. Legis. Series, *The Territorial Sea*, pp. 421–614; Briggs, pp. 382–3; Weissberg, 16 *I.C.L.Q.* (1967), 704–24; U.S. Dept. of State, The Geographer, *Limits in the Seas*, No. 36; and revisions thereof.

[3] See François, Second Report, *Yrbk., I.L.C.* (1951), ii. 93, para. 119; Gidel iii. 468 seq.; Briggs, p. 376; Sørensen, 101 Hague *Recueil* (1960, III), 157; Fitzmaurice, 8 *I.C.L.Q.* (1959), 118–21; Hyde i. 459; Oppenheim i. 499–501.

[4] France has recently claimed a twelve mile territorial sea. See the U.K. Fishery Limits Act, 1964; 3 *Int. Leg. Materials* (1964), 1067; *British Practice in Int. Law* (1964), i. 44–7; and the Canadian Territorial Sea and Fishing Zones Act, 1964; 3 *Int. Legal Materials* (1964), 922.

A good number of twelve mile fishing zones have been overlaid by new extensions of territorial sea. The number is substantial enough to justify the view that Article 24 of the Territorial Sea Convention has been modified by the subsequent practice of the parties so as to include fishery zones of twelve miles in breadth. The practice also involves modification of Article 2 of the High Seas Convention, which stipulates freedom of the high seas in respect of fishing. In the *Fisheries Jurisdiction Case* (United Kingdom v. Iceland) the International Court expressed the view that the extension of a fishery limit to twelve miles 'appears now to be generally accepted'.[1]

4. *Delimitation of the Contiguous Zone*

Baselines. It has always been assumed that the baselines for the delimitation of both contiguous zones and the territorial sea are identical.[2] State practice and the terms of Article 24 of the Convention on the Territorial Sea confirm the assumption.

Breadth. The question of breadth is not often discussed, but there is a definite tendency in State practice for claims not to exceed twelve miles, or twenty kilometres, whether the zone concerned relates to customs, fisheries, or security.[3] The question is now dealt with by Article 24 of the Convention on the Territorial Sea, which established a twelve-mile limit for all purposes.[4] At the Third United Nations Conference the Informal Composite Negotiating Text of 1977 prescribes twenty-four miles (Article 33).

5. *Problems of Enforcement*

As a matter of general international law the coastal state may take any steps necessary to enforce compliance with its laws and regulations in the prescribed zone or zones. The power is one of police and control, and transgressors cannot be visited with consequences amounting to reprisal or summary punishment. Forcible measures of self-help may not be resorted to as readily as in the case of trespass over a state frontier.

[1] I.C.J. Reports, 1974, p. 3 at p. 23.

[2] See, however, Gidel iii. 779–80.

[3] See the views expressed in Oppenheim i. 497, n. 1; Gidel iii. 479–80; and Rousseau, p. 438. Cf. I.L.C. draft article, *Yrbk., I.L.C.* (1953), ii. 219.

[4] Paragraph 3 of the Article provides for the case where the coasts of two states are opposite or adjacent to each other. Cf. Article 12 of the Convention. The provision in Article 24 does not provide for exceptions 'by reason of historic title or other special circumstances', contrasting thus with the provision on the territorial sea.

In this respect the text adopted both by the International Law Commission and by the Conference on the Law of the Sea in 1958 may be more restrictive from the point of view of a coastal state than general international law.[1] Article 24, paragraph 1, of the Convention on the Territorial Sea provides:

In a zone of the high seas contiguous to its territorial sea, the coastal State may exercise the control necessary to:

(a) Prevent infringement of its customs, fiscal, immigration or sanitary regulations within its territory or territorial sea.

(b) Punish infringement of the above regulations committed within its territory or territorial sea . . .

Sir Gerald Fitzmaurice was prominent in promoting this text, and the interpretation which he has placed upon it deserves attention. In his view:[2]

It . . . is control, not jurisdiction, that is exercised. . . . Although the two ensuing subheads (a) and (b) of the paragraph envisage punishment as well as prevention, yet taken as a whole, the power is essentially supervisory and preventative. The basic object is anticipatory. No offence against the laws of the coastal State is actually being committed at the time. The intention is to avoid such an offence being committed *subsequently*, when, by entering the territorial sea, the vessel comes within the jurisdiction of the coastal State; or else to punish such an offence already committed when the vessel was within such jurisdiction . . . it would seem that the following distinction can be drawn between the powers the coastal States can exercise under heads (a) and (b) of this paragraph, respectively . . . it is . . . clear that just as head (b)—punishment—can only apply to outgoing ships, head (a)—prevention—can only apply to incoming ones. But what are the ('necessary') powers of control which the coastal State can exercise in the case of an incoming ship, or rather, do they, in particular, include arrest and conduct into port? So far as arrest, as such, is concerned, the answer must be in the negative. Whatever the eventual designs of the vessel, she cannot *ex hypothesi* at this stage have committed an offence 'within [the coastal State's] territory or territorial sea.' There is consequently nothing in respect of which an arrest, as such, can be effected. . . . As regards ordering, or conducting, the vessel into port under escort, the case is less clear. Though formally distinct from arrest, enforced direction into port is, in the circumstances, almost tantamount to it, and should therefore in principle be excluded: any necessary inquiries, investigation, examination, search, etc., should take place at sea while the ship is still in the contiguous zone. . . . In case this may seem to be unduly restrictive, it must be observed that only

[1] See the article by Oda, 11 *I.C.L.Q.* (1962), 131–53; and McDougal and Burke, pp. 621–30.

[2] 8 *I.C.L.Q.* (1959), p. 73 at p. 113. See also id., 31 *B.Y.* (1954), p. 371 at pp. 378–9.

by insistence on such limitations is it possible to prevent coastal States from treating the contiguous zone as virtually equivalent to territorial sea.

Whilst this interpretation is perfectly possible as a matter of textual exegesis, nevertheless in case of controversy reference may be made to the *travaux préparatoires*. From these it is apparent that the majority of states at the Law of the Sea Conference did not intend to restrict rights in contiguous zones, as hitherto understood,[1] by establishing the distinction between 'control' and 'jurisdiction'.

6. *Other Zones for Special Purposes*

The twentieth century has produced a number of national claims to non-contiguous, but adjacent, zones for special purposes, which represent attempts to apply the logic of claims to contiguous zones in a manner calculated to protect national interests to the utmost. Thus defence zones[2] in polygonal or similar forms extending beyond the territorial sea, and zones for purposes of air identification[3] have made their appearance in the practice of states. In so far as those zones represent claims to extraterritorial jurisdiction over nationals they are not necessarily in conflict with general international law, and, furthermore, groups of states may co-operate and be mutually obligated to respect such zones by convention. Again, such zones may take the form of a lawful aspect of belligerent rights in time of war. Beyond these limits such zones would be incompatible with the status of waters beyond the limit of the territorial sea, at least if they involved the application of powers of prevention or punishment in regard to foreign vessels or aircraft.

Fishery Conservation Zones. We are not concerned here either with zones established by virtue of the Convention on Fishing

[1] See Oda, op. cit.; O'Connell ii. 643–4; and other literature cited *supra*, p. 210, n. 1. Note Article 23 of the Convention on the High Seas, which permits hot pursuit to commence within the contiguous zone (*infra*, pp. 250–2), thus strengthening the powers of the coastal state.

[2] See U.S. Naval War College, *Int. Law Documents* (1941), pp. 83–90; ibid. (1943), pp. 51–67; ibid. (1948–9), pp. 157 seq., 169 seq.; MacChesney, op. cit., Part iii; legislation of Ethiopia and South Korea, U.N. Legis. Series, *Regime of the Territorial Sea*, pp. 128, 175. Cf. for the U.K., the Land Powers (Defence) Act, 1958, sect. 7. See also *supra*, pp. 213–14, on security and neutrality zones. On defence zones in the territorial sea: Article 16, paragraph 3, of the Convention on the Territorial Sea.

[3] Such zones have appeared in recent American and Canadian practice: MacChesney, op. cit., pp. 577 seq.; Murchison, *The Contiguous Air Space Zone in International Law* (1956); Whiteman iv. 495–8.

and Conservation of the Living Resources of the High Seas[1] or with exclusive fishery zones in the form of contiguous zones of twelve miles in breadth starting from the same baseline as the territorial sea.[2]

For some time coastal states with particular interest in offshore fisheries have sought means of limiting major operations by extra-regional fishing fleets. Paradoxically it was the United States, historically an opponent of fishing zones, which sowed the seeds of change. In the first place the United States took an important initiative in claiming the mineral resources of the continental shelf in 1945,[3] on the basis of the generous concept of 'adjacency'. It would not be surprising if other states were ready to claim the biological resources of the adjacent waters or 'epicontinental sea' by a general parity of reasoning. Secondly, the United States produced a Fisheries Proclamation of 28 September 1945,[4] which empowered the Government to establish 'explicitly bounded' conservation zones in areas of the high seas 'contiguous to the United States'.

Beginning in 1946 a number of Latin American states made claims to the natural resources of the epicontinental sea, in effect a fishery conservation zone of two hundred miles breadth.[5] Icelandic legislation on these lines began in 1948. Similar steps were taken by India (100 miles zone, 1956), Pakistan (100 miles zone, 1966), and Sri Lanka (100 miles zone, 1957), in each case measured from the outer limit of the territorial sea. For a long while the tendency was lacking in coherence. Adherents were scattered and the legal quality of some of the claims was uncertain and varied. Some, for example, the Peruvian claim, were, on one view, an extended territorial sea with a concession of the rights of overflight and free navigation. In 1970 only nine out of twenty Latin American states subscribed to the Montevideo Declaration on the Law of the Sea.[6] In this instrument a two hundred mile zone is asserted by the states concerned, involving 'sovereignty and jurisdiction to the extent necessary to conserve, develop and exploit the natural resources of the maritime area

[1] *Infra*, p. 264.

[2] See *supra*, p. 214. [3] See Chapter X.

[4] Briggs, p. 377; 40 *A.J.* (1946), Supp., p. 45; Whiteman iv, 954. The Proclamation has never been implemented by Executive Order.

[5] Argentina (1946), Panama (1946), Peru (1947), Chile (1947), Ecuador (1947), Honduras (1950), El Salvador (1950). See Enrique Garcia Sayán, *The Position of Peru* (Geneva, 1958) at p. 17; and Zacklin (ed.), *The Changing Law of the Sea* (1974).

[6] Text: 64 *A.J.* (1970), 1021. See further the Lima Declaration, 8 August 1970; 10 *Int. Leg. Materials* (1971), 207.

adjacent to their coasts, its soil and its subsoil', but without prejudice to freedom of navigation and overflight.

By 1978 some seventy-four states had fishing zones of 200 miles, whilst ten states had claims greater than twelve but less than two hundred miles.[1] The adherents to two hundred mile zones included the United States,[2] Japan[3] and the members of the E.E.C. (including the United Kingdom). Clearly the fishery conservation zone, not greater than 200 miles from the usual baselines, is in the process of crystallizing as a principle of customary international law. However, in the early phase of the formation of the new rule such limits are opposable to non-adherents only on the basis of express recognition. Thus in the *Fisheries Jurisdiction Case* (United Kingdom v. Iceland)[4] an Icelandic fishing zone fifty miles in breadth was held to be not valid as against the United Kingdom as a consequence of the terms of a bilateral agreement of 1961. The Court avoided taking a position on the validity of the Icelandic claim in general international law. In a Joint Separate Opinion[5] five judges expressed the firm view that no rule of customary law concerning maximum fishery limits had yet emerged. Whilst the views expressed by different members of the Court reflect the difficulty of assessing the shifts in state practice, nonetheless in 1979 there is considerable evidence of the general acceptance of a maximum limit of two hundred miles.[6]

Preferential rights for the coastal state. In the *Fisheries Jurisdiction Case* (United Kingdom v. Iceland)[7] the International Court held that the concept of preferential rights had crystallized as customary law: that is to say, 'preferential rights of fishing in adjacent waters in favour of the coastal state in a situation of special dependence on its coastal fisheries, this preference operating in regard to other states concerned in the exploitation of the same fisheries'.

[1] U.S. Dept. of State, The Geographer, *Limits in the Seas*, No. 36 and revisions; Lay, Churchill and Nordquist, *New Directions in the Law of the Sea*, VI, 843, 881. For the U.K., see the Fishery Limits Act, 1976.

[2] Fishery Conservation and Management Act of 1976; 15 *Int. Leg. Materials* (1976), 635. This legislation has some controversial features: see the statement by the President, ibid., 634.

[3] In 1977 on the basis of reciprocity.

[4] I.C.J. Reports, 1974, p. 3 at p. 24. See also *Fisheries Jurisdiction Case* (Fed. Rep. of Germany v. Iceland), ibid., p. 175. For comment: Fitzmaurice, *The Times*, 13 September, 1974.

[5] I.C.J. Reports, 1974, p. 45 at p. 46.

[6] See Jiménez de Aréchaga, Hague *Recueil* (1978, I), 21.

[7] I.C.J. Reports, 1974, p. 3 at pp. 23, 24–31.

Exclusive Economic Zones.[1] The increase in claims to exclusive rights in respect of the fisheries in an adjacent maritime zone, described above, led eventually to claims encompassing all natural resources in and of the seabed and superjacent waters in a zone two hundred miles in breadth. By 1972 this development was presented, in more or less programmatic form, as a 'patrimonial sea',[2] or 'economic zone'.[3] In 1973 documents presented at the meetings of the United Nations Committee on the Peaceful Uses of the Seabed and Ocean Floor proclaimed the right to establish 'an exclusive economic zone' with limits not exceeding two hundred miles.[4]

At the Third United Nations Conference on the Law of the Sea (1973–9) there has been widespread support for the exclusive economic zone. The Informal Composite Negotiating Text of 1977 provides a detailed structure (Articles 55–75). The zone is to extend no further than two hundred miles from the baselines of the territorial sea. In the text the zone is not defined as a part of the high seas (Article 86) and is *sui generis*. Apart from the freedom of fishing, the freedoms of the high seas apply (see Article 87 and see generally below, pp. 238–42). The rights of the coastal state are described as follows (Article 56, para. 1):

'In the exclusive economic zone, the coastal State has:

(a) sovereign rights for the purpose of exploring and exploiting, conserving and managing the natural resources, whether living or non-living, of the seabed and subsoil and the superjacent waters, and with regard to other activities for the economic exploitation and exploration of the zone, such as the production of energy from the water, currents and winds;

(b) jurisdiction as provided for in the relevant provisions of the present Convention with regard to:

(i) the establishment and use of artificial islands, installations and structures;

(ii) marine scientific research;

(iii) the preservation of the marine environment;

(c) other rights and duties provided for in the present Convention.'

[1] Brown, *Maritime Policy and Management*, 1977, 325–50, 377–408; Phillips, 26 *I.C.L.Q.* (1977), 585–618; Queneudec, 79 *R.G.D.I.P.* (1975), 321–53; Gastines, ibid., 447–57; Nawaz, 16 *Indian J.I.L.* (1976), 471–88.

[2] See the Declaration of Santo Domingo, 9 June 1972; 11 *Int. Leg. Materials* (1972), 892; Castañeda, 12 *Indian J.I.L.* (1972), 535–42; Nelson, 22 *I.C.L.Q.* (1973), 668–86; Gastines, 79 *R.G.D.I.P.* (1975), 447–57; cf. the Declaration of Lima, 8 August 1970, 10 *Int. Leg. Materials* (1971), 207.

[3] Yaoundé Seminar of African States, Recommendations, 30 June 1972; Lay, Churchill and Nordquist, *New Directions in the Law of the Sea*, I, 250.

[4] 12 *Int. Leg. Materials* (1973), 1200, 1235, 1246, 1249. Other proposals of similar content did not use the same label. For an early reference to the 'exclusive economic zone concept': ibid., 33 (proposal of Kenya, 1972).

Essentially the zone involves exclusive rights to economic resources[1] with ancillary powers relating to control of pollution and other matters, without prejudice to freedom of navigation and overflight. At the Third United Nations Conference the maritime powers have been prepared to accept this model, although the inclusion of control over pollution and scientific research has been a matter of controversy. It is not apparently the case that the rights are inherent, like those relating to continental shelf, but some uncertainty persists in this respect.

A matter of crucial importance concerns the legal status of the E.E.Z. There can be little doubt that exclusive *fishery* zones of two hundred miles have become a part of customary law (see above). Some commentators are prepared to equate these with the E.E.Z. (as featured in the Informal Composite Text). This equation is not justified on the evidence so far. The United States and many other states would not accept all aspects of the E.E.Z. in the Text except on the basis of acceptance of a general political 'package' of proposals at the United Nations Conference. The position may change if state practice evolves explicitly along the lines of E.E.Z. in the Informal Composite Negotiating Text.[2]

Anti-pollution measures. Such measures may be taken within a territorial sea or in a contiguous zone as provided in Article 24 of the Territorial Sea Convention.[3] Other measures can only be based upon special arrangements by treaty or, perhaps, a plea of necessity in relation to particular remedial action.[4] Canada, pleading the inadequacy of the existing law, has provided for a special belt of jurisdiction, one hundred miles in breadth, on her Arctic seaboard.[5] The United States does not accept the legality of this extension of jurisdiction.[6]

[1] But certain qualifications are foreseen: see Article 62, para. 2 (access of other states to surplus allowable catch); Article 69 (right of participation of land-locked states); and Article 70.

[2] A number of states have created an E.E.Z. *eo nomine* in recent legislation (including Bangladesh, France, Guatemala, India, Mexico, Norway and Sri Lanka): see Lay, Churchill and Nordquist, V, 286–327.

[3] *Supra*, p. 211. [4] *Infra*, p. 464.

[5] Arctic Waters Pollution Prevention Act, Statutes of Canada 1969–70, Chap. 47; assent, 26 June 1970. Also in 9 *Int. Leg. Materials* (1970), 543.

[6] See generally Morin, op. cit., at pp. 206–15; 9 *Int. Leg. Materials* (1970), 598–615; Fawcett, *Ann. Survey of Commonwealth Law*, 1970, 418–21; Bilder, 69 *Michigan L.R.* (1970–1), 1–37; Green, 50 *Oregon L.R.* (1971), 462–90.

CHAPTER X

SUBMARINE AREAS: CONTINENTAL SHELF, SEABED, AND OCEAN FLOOR

1. *Classification of Submarine Areas*

SUBMARINE areas may be classified as follows: (a) the seabed of the internal waters and territorial seas of coastal states; (b) the continental shelf area; (c) the seabed of the exclusive economic zone;[1] (d) the seabed and ocean floor beyond the outer limits of the continental shelf and exclusive economic zone. The first case is under the legal regime of territorial sovereignty. The continental shelf has a specialized regime which is considered subsequently. The fourth category partakes of the legal regime of the high seas but this relation is not necessarily exclusive, since the continental shelf area is in principle governed by the regime of the high seas. The presumption is that each of the categories includes the marine subsoil to the extent that the rules of the particular legal regime are intended so to apply.

2. *Continental Shelf*[2]

(a) *Background*

Much of the seabed consists of the deep ocean floor (the abyssal plain), several thousand metres deep. In many parts of the world the deep ocean floor is separated from the coast of the land masses by a terrace or shelf, which in geological terms is a part of

[1] The status of the E.E.Z. in general international law is not yet certain. On the E.E.Z. in general see Chapter IX.

[2] See generally: Whiteman iv. 740–931; Lauterpacht, 27 *B.Y.* (1950), 376–433; Waldock, 36 *Grot. Soc.* (1950), 115–48; Mouton, *The Continental Shelf* (1952); id., 85 Hague *Recueil* (1954, I), 357–465; Scelle, 59 *R.G.D.I.P.* (1955), 5–62; Gutteridge, 35 *B.Y.* (1959), 102–23; McDougal and Burke, pp. 630–729; MacChesney, op. cit., pp. 297 seq.; Franklin, U.S. Naval War College, *The Law of the Sea: Some Recent Developments* (1961), pp. 8–83; Secretariat Memo., *Yrbk., I.L.C.* (1950), ii. 87–113; François, Fourth Report, ibid. (1953) ii. 1–50; Jennings, 121 Hague *Recueil* (1967, II), 387–408; Brown, *The Legal Regime of Hydrospace* (1971), pp. 3–78; O'Connell i. 503–15; Andrassy, *International Law and the Resources of the Sea* (1970); Burke and others, *Towards a Better Use of the Ocean* (SIPRI, 1969); Henkin, *Law for the Sea's Mineral Resources* (ISHA Monograph, 1968); Alexander (ed.), *Proceedings*, Annual Conferences of the Law of the Sea Institute, 1967– ; International Law Association, *Report of the Fifty-Third Conference* (1968), 191–247; Butler, 63 *A.J.* (1969), 103–7; Goldie, 3 *I.C.L.Q.* (1954), 535–75; Slouka, *International Custom and the Continental Shelf* (1968); Oda, 127 Hague *Recueil* (1969, II), 433–57.

the continent itself, overlain by the relatively shallow waters of the continental margin. The width of the shelf varies from a mile or so to some hundreds of miles and the depth ranges from 50 to 550 metres. The configuration of the seabed has certain regularities. The increase in depth is gradual until the shelf edge or break is reached, when there is a steep descent to the ocean floor. The average depth of the edge is between 130 and 200 metres. The relatively steep incline of the continental slope gives way to the often large apron of sediments, which masks the boundary between the deep ocean floor and the pedestal of the continental mass, and is called the continental rise.

The shelf carries substantial oil and gas deposits in many areas and the seabed itself provides fishery resources. In 1944 an Argentine Decree created zones of mineral reserves in the epicontinental sea. However, the decisive event in state practice was a United States proclamation on 28 September 1945 relating to the natural resources of the subsoil and seabed of the continental shelf.[1] The shelf was regarded as a geological feature and a press release stated that the shelf was regarded as extending up to the 100 fathoms line.[2] The resources concerned were described as 'appertaining to the United States, subject to its jurisdiction and control'. Of particular importance are the limitations of the claim to the resources themselves and the declaration that 'the character as high seas of the waters of the continental shelf and the right to their free and unimpeded navigation are in no way thus affected'.

The lines of the Truman proclamation were in substance followed by Orders in Council of 1948 relating to the Bahamas and Jamaica, and by proclamations issued by Saudi Arabia, in 1948, and nine sheikhdoms in the Persian Gulf under United Kingdom protection, in 1949.[3] The practice showed certain variations, however. The Truman proclamation and an Australian proclamation of 10 September 1953 relate the claim to the purpose of *exploitation of the resources* of the seabed and subsoil of the continental shelf, and stipulate that the legal status of the super-

[1] Text: 40 *A.J.* (1946), Suppl., p. 45: Briggs, p. 378; Whiteman iv. 756. For the background: Hollick, 17 *Virginia J.I.L.* (1976), 23–55.

[2] Approximately 200 metres or 600 feet.

[3] Surveys of state practice: Whiteman iv. 752–814; U.N. Legis. Series, *The Regime of the High Seas* i (1951); ibid., Suppl. (1959); MacChesney, op. cit., pp. 407–501; U.N. Secretariat, Survey of National Legislation Concerning the Seabed and the Ocean Floor, and the Subsoil thereof, underlying the High Seas beyond the Limits of Present National Jurisdiction, A/AC. 135/11, 4 June 1968; U.N. Legis. Series, *National Legislation and Treaties Relating to the Territorial Sea* . . ., ST/LEG/SER.B/15, 1970, pp. 319–476; U.S. Dept. of State, The Geographer, *Limits in the Seas* No. 36.

jacent waters as high seas shall not be affected. A number of states claimed sovereignty over the seabed and subsoil of the shelf as such but without prejudice to the status of the waters above as high seas.[1] Certain Latin American states claimed sovereignty over the shelf, the waters above and the airspace also, whilst reserving 'freedom of navigation'.[2]

In this development principles of geological continuity, self-protection, and effective control played a part and the development parallels, in a new sphere, the concepts of the territorial sea and contiguous zone.

(b) *The Continental Shelf Convention, 1958*[3]

The thesis contained in the Truman Proclamation proved attractive to a diversity of states. The new principle provided a stable basis for exploitation of petroleum and at the same time made a reasonable accommodation for freedom of fishing and navigation in the superjacent waters. However, the practice was far from uniform[4] and the discussions in the International Law Commission in the years 1951–6 indicated the immaturity of the legal regime. As a consequence the text of the Convention adopted at the Law of the Sea Conference of 1958 represented in part at least an essay in the progressive development of the law. Nevertheless, the first three articles reflect pre-existing or at least emergent rules of customary international law:[5]

Article 1

For the purpose of these Articles, the term 'continental shelf' is used as referring (a) to the seabed and subsoil of the submarine areas adjacent to the coast but outside the area of the territorial sea, to a depth of 200 metres or, beyond that limit, to where the depth of the superjacent waters admits of the exploitation of the natural resources of the said areas; (b) to the seabed and subsoil of similar submarine areas adjacent to the coasts of islands.

Article 2[6]

1. The coastal State exercises over the continental shelf sovereign rights for

[1] e.g. Bahamas (1948), Saudi Arabia (1949), Pakistan (1950), India (1955).

[2] e.g. Argentina (1946), El Salvador (1950).

[3] Text: 52 *A.J.* (1958), 858; Brownlie, *Documents*, p. 107. Entered into force 10 June 1964. For discussion see Whiteman, 52 *A.J.* (1958), 629–53; Young, 55 *A.J.* (1961), 359–73; McDougal and Burke, pp. 656 seq.; Samuels, in *Recent Developments in the Law of the Sea 1958–1964*, pp. 155–73; Gutteridge, 35 *B.Y.* (1959), 102–23.

[4] See the award of Lord Asquith as umpire in the *Abu Dhabi* arbitration, Int. L.R. 18 (1951), no. 37; Whiteman iv. 747.

[5] *North Sea Continental Shelf* cases, I.C.J. Reports (1969), p. 3 at p. 39; Int. L.R. 41, 29; 73 *R.G.D.I.P.* (1969), 508.

[6] See also the Third United Conference, Informal Composite Negotiating Text of 1977, Article 77; and Article 81 (on drilling).

the purpose of exploring it and exploiting its natural resources.
2. The rights referred to in paragraph 1 of this Article are exclusive in the sense that if the coastal State does not explore the continental shelf or exploit its natural resources, no one may undertake these activities, or make a claim to the continental shelf, without the express consent of the coastal State.
3. The rights of the coastal State over the continental shelf do not depend on occupation, effective or notional, or on any express proclamation.
4. The natural resources referred to in these Articles consist of the mineral and other non-living resources of the seabed and subsoil together with living organisms belonging to sedentary species, that is to say, organisms which, at the harvestable stage, either are immobile on or under the seabed or are unable to move except in constant physical contact with the seabed or the subsoil.

Article 3[1]

The rights of the coastal State over the continental shelf do not affect the legal status of the superjacent waters as high seas, or that of the air space above those waters.

The remainder of the Convention is not so clearly declaratory of the existing law[2] though the provisions, together with the subsequent practice of both parties and non-parties, constitute cogent evidence of the existence of rules of general international law.[3] By 1978 fifty-four states had ratified the Convention and on several occasions non-parties had treated its provisions as declaratory of the law on the subject.

(c) *Rights of the Coastal State*

The coastal state exercises 'sovereign rights for the purpose of exploring [the continental shelf] and exploiting its natural resources'. The term 'sovereignty' was deliberately avoided as it was feared that this term, redolent of territorial sovereignty and three dimensional control, would prejudice the status as high seas of the waters over the shelf. According to the High Seas Convention[4] the area of the shelf is high seas and therefore, apart from the express provisions of the Continental Shelf Convention, the freedom of the high seas is preserved in respect of navigation, fishing, the laying of submarine cables and pipelines, and flying

[1] See also the Third United Nations Conference, Informal Composite Negotiating Text of 1977, Article 78.
[2] But see the diss. op. of Judges Koretsky (pp. 156–8), Tanaka (pp. 173–9), Morelli (pp. 197–8), Lachs (pp. 221–32), and Sørensen (pp. 241–7), in the *North Sea Continental Shelf* cases, previous note.
[3] For a rather different view: Jennings, 18 *I.C.L.Q.* (1969), 819–21.
[4] *Infra*, p. 237.

over the high seas. The Shelf Convention recognizes that in practice the activities of the coastal state may impede the exercise of these freedoms. Thus article 4[1] provides that, 'subject to its right to take reasonable measures for the exploitation of the continental shelf and the exploitation of its natural resources' the coastal state may not impede the laying or maintenance of cables and pipelines. Article 5, paragraph 1, provides:

> The exploration of the continental shelf and the exploitation of its natural resources must not result in any unjustifiable interference with navigation, fishing or the conservation of the living resources of the sea, nor result in any interference with fundamental oceanographic or other scientific research carried out with the intention of open publication.[2]

A major objective has been to provide a stable basis for operations on the seabed and to avoid squatting by offshore interests. Thus the 'sovereign rights' inhere in the coastal state by operation of law and are not conditioned by occupation or express claim. They are not defeasible except by express grant. It is incorrect to fit this regime into a dichotomy of either territorial sovereignty or the mere exercise of jurisdictional rights.[3] Whilst it is true that coastal states apply various parts of criminal and civil law to activities in the shelf area, it is by no means clear that states do this either on the basis that the shelf is territorial or even as an aspect of their international law rights in the shelf area as such. Legislation of the United Kingdom[4] and other states indicates that the shelf regime is not assimilated to state territory.[5]

(d) *Delimitation*

(i) *Inner limit.* The inner limit is the outer edge of the territorial sea and seabed.

(ii) *Outer limit.* There has been much debate over the interpretation of Article 1 of the Convention and it is generally agreed that the provisions stand in need of clarification. The issue has practical importance since the United States has granted exploitation leases and exploration permits at depths of 4000 and 5000 feet respectively. One view of Article 1 is to the effect that the outer limit is a shifting line dependent on the technological

[1] See also the Third United Nations Conference, Informal Composite Negotiating Text, Article 79.

[2] The Informal Composite Negotiating Text of 1977 has no similar provision.

[3] Cf. O'Connell i. 507.

[4] Continental Shelf Act 1964 c29; *British Practice* (1964), pp. 53–7.

[5] See *In re Ownership and Jurisdiction over Offshore Mineral Rights*, 65 D.L.R. 2d (1967) 353; Int. L.R. 43, 93; S.C. of Canada; *Bonser* v. *La Macchia*, 43 *A.L.J.R.* 275 (1969); 64 *A.J.* (1970), 435; Int. L.R. 51, p. 39; High Ct. of Australia.

possibilities of exploration and exploitation. According to this view[1] the United States practice constitutes an assertion of rights based upon such an interpretation of the Convention and thus opposable to other states. Other commentators consider that the United States has not yet adopted a definitive position. It is, of course, necessary to distinguish assertions of right from the exercise of jurisdiction over the extraterritorial activities of citizens. Legislation of the various states either reproduces the formula in the Convention or makes no provision for determining the outer limit.[2] The Truman Proclamation and the United Kingdom Act are silent in this respect. Some twenty states employ the exploitability criterion but it is not clear that this is intended to outstrip the limit of the geological feature of the shelf.[3] Some legislation expressly refers to the 'continental platform', 'continental margin', or 'natural prolongation'.[4]

The correct interpretation of Article 1 of the Convention would seem to be as follows.[5] The 200 metre depth criterion is subject to the exploitability criterion, but the latter is controlled by the overall general conception of the shelf as a geological feature, and by the principle of adjacency in Article 1. It is clear from the preparatory materials (the records of the International Law Commission) that the legal conception was based substantially upon the geological conception. It was not thought that the whole ocean floor could be divided up as continental shelf and be subject ultimately to a median line division in accordance with Article 6. It makes no material difference that the legal conception was not based *exclusively* upon the geological conception.[6] Thus the legal definition *includes* (a) the shelves of islands; (b) shallow basins such as the North Sea and the Persian

[1] Brown, *Legal Regime of Hydrospace*, pp. 17–20. The author relies upon an opinion, unpublished, of the Associate Solicitor of the Dept. of the Interior, submitted to the Depts. of State and Justice in 1961. This opinion does not appear in Whiteman iv, a volume released in April 1965. See also Stone, 17 *I.C.L.Q.* (1968), 103–17.

[2] Continental Shelf Acts of U.K. (1964) and Rep. of Ireland (1968). See also the Petroleum (Submerged Lands) Act, 1967, of Australia.

[3] Including: Norway (1963); Philippines (1968); Iceland (1969); Italy (1967).

[4] Bangladesh (1974); Cameroon (1967); Cyprus (1972); Guatemala (1949). See also the Australian measure: Petroleum and Minerals Authority Act, 1973, section 3, defining 'Australian continental land mass.'

[5] See further Jennings, 121 Hague *Recueil*, 392–400; id., 18 *I.C.L.Q.* (1969), 819–32; O'Connell i. 509–11; Goldie, 8 *Natural Resources Journal* (1968), 434–77; id. 1 *Journ. of Maritime Law and Commerce* (1970), 461–72; Weissberg, 18 *I.C.L.Q.* (1969), 62–83; Henkin, *Law for the Sea's Mineral Resources*, 14–24; id., 63 *A.J.* (1969), 504–10; Finlay, 64 *A.J.* (1970), 42–61; Henkin, op. cit., pp. 62–72; Andrassy, op. cit., pp. 70–90; Brown, op. cit., pp. 3–36; Burke, *Towards a Better Use of the Ocean*, pp. 22, 24–5, 27–8, 30.

[6] *Yrbk., I.L.C.* (1956), ii. 296–7 (Commentary on draft art. 67).

Gulf; (c) steep buttresses like that adjacent to the coast of Chile which can be exploited by tunnels from the mainland; and *excludes* the seabed of the territorial sea. The assumption that, with exploitability at greater depths, the 200 metres criterion becomes otiose is unjustified. If exploitability be applied as a dominant test the result would be that state A would concede part of a broad shelf 'opposite' to state B's narrow shelf [but separated from it by abyssal plain] since the median line would fall across the 200 metre zone adjacent to state A. The median line solution in Article 6 only applies when states share the same shelf in the geological context. In other terms the submarine area extending to the 200 metre contour is always 'adjacent'.[1] The outcome is that when exploitability extends to great depths the coastal state will have rights over the entire shelf as a geological feature, including the continental slope and the continental rise.

(iii) *Opposite or adjacent states.*[2] Article 6 of the Continental Shelf Convention[3] is concerned with the cases where the 'same continental shelf' extends between two opposite or two adjacent states.[4] In separate provisions for the two cases the Convention stipulates that the boundary shall be determined by agreement but 'in the absence of agreement, and unless another boundary line is justified by special circumstances', the boundary shall be determined by a median line, that is, the principle of equidistance from the nearest points of the baselines from which the breadth of the territorial sea of each state is measured. This principle has been applied in the conclusion of various bilateral agreements.[5]

In the *North Sea Continental Shelf* cases[6] the International Court decided that Article 6 of the Convention was not declaratory of existing or emergent rules of law and consequently the

[1] See Jennings, 121 Hague *Recueil*, p. 398; and also in 18 *I.C.L.Q.* (1969), 819–32.

[2] See *North Sea Continental Shelf* cases, Pleadings; Oda, 12 *Japanese Annual* (1968), 264–84; Brown, *The Legal Regime of Hydrospace*, pp. 41–73; Verzijl, *International Law in Historical Perspective*, iii. 84–94; Young, 59 *A.J.* (1965), 505–22; Andrassy, op. cit., pp. 91–107; Padwa, 9 *I.C.L.Q.* (1960), 628–53; Feulner, 17 *Virginia J.I.L.* (1976), 77–105; U.S. Dept. of State, The Geographer, *Limits in the Seas*, (various items in this series).

[3] See the Fr. decl., *British Practice* (1965), p. 141; U.K. reaction, ibid. (1966), p. 101.

[4] On the meaning of 'opposite' or 'adjacent' see the *North Sea Continental Shelf* cases, I.C.J. Reports (1969), at pp. 27–8; and also Judge Sørensen, diss. op., pp. 250–2.

[5] Italy–Yugoslavia, 1968; 7 *Int. Leg. Materials* (1968), 547; U.S.S.R.–Finland, 1965; ibid., 6 (1967), 727; U.S.S.R.–Finland, 1967; ibid., 7 (1968), 560; Iran–Saudi Arabia, 1969; ibid., 8 (1969), 493; U.K.–Denmark, 1967, Cmnd. 3278; U.K.–Netherlands, 1967, Cmnd. 3253; U.S.S.R.–Poland, 1969.

[6] I.C.J. Reports (1969), p. 3; Int. L.R. 41, p. 29; 73 *R.G.D.I.P.* (1969), 508. For comment see Jennings, 18 *I.C.L.Q.* (1969), 819–32; Brown, *Curr. Leg. Problems* (1970), pp. 187–215; Münch, 29 *Z.a.ö.R.u.V.* (1969), 455–75; Monconduit, *Ann. Français* (1969), 213–44; Friedmann, 64 *A.J.* (1970), 229–40; Grisel, ibid., 562–93; Eustache, 74 *R.G.D.I.P.* (1970), 590–639; Goldie, 16 *N.Y. Law Forum* (1970), 325–77.

equidistance method of delimitation was not binding on the German Federal Republic, which had not ratified the Convention. Thus, in order to regulate the difference between the German Federal Republic, on the one hand, and the Netherlands and Denmark, on the other hand, over the apportionment of the bed of the North Sea, delimitation must occur by agreement between the parties in accordance with certain equitable principles 'in such a way as to leave as much as possible to each Party all those parts of the continental shelf that constitute a natural prolongation of its land territory into and under the sea, without encroachment on the natural prolongation of the land territory of the other'.

The application of the principles elaborated by the Court in the *North Sea Cases* is a matter of particular difficulty in the case of the presence of islands belonging to one state off a coast of another sovereignty.[1] Examples of such situations include the disputes involving delimitation of shelf in the Aegean Sea (Greece and Turkey[2]), adjoining St. Pierre and Miquelon (Canada and France),[3] and in the Persian (Arabian) Gulf.[4] In the *Western Approaches Arbitration* (United Kingdom and France),[5] the problems presented to the Court of Arbitration included the delimitation of the shelf in the English Channel with appropriate adjustments for the presence of the Scilly Islands, Ushant and the Channel Islands. The Court in a general way affirmed and applied the principles formulated by the International Court in the *North Sea Continental Shelf Cases* (above). In particular, the Court of Arbitration stressed that the 'fundamental norm' was that 'delimitation must be in accordance with equitable principles' (para. 97).[6] Moreover, there is no presumption in favour of equidistance: 'this Court considers that the appropriateness of

[1] See Northcutt Ely, 6 *The Int. Lawyer* (1972), 219–36; Hodgson, in *Law of the Sea: The Emerging Regime of the Oceans* (Law of the Sea Inst., 1973), pp. 137–99; Goldie, 4 *Neths. Int. L. R.* (1973), 237–61; Symmons, 26 *Northern Ireland L. Qtly.* (1975), 65–93; Karl, 71 *A.J.* (1977), 642–73.

[2] See *Aegean Sea Continental Shelf Case* (Greece v. Turkey); Request for Interim Measures of Protection; I.C.J. Reports, 1976, p. 3; Gross, 71 *A.J.* (1977), 31–59; Rousseau, 80 *R.G.D.I.P.* (1976), 1252–6. See also I.C.J. Reports, 1978, p. 3.

[3] See 72 *R.G.D.I.P.* (1968), 167; 7 *Canad. Yrbk.* (1969), 308.

[4] See U.S. Dept. of State, The Geographer, *Limits of the Seas*, No. 12 (Bahrain–Saudi Arabia); No. 18 (Abu Dhabi–Qatar); No. 24 (Iran–Saudi Arabia); No. 25 (Iran–Qatar); No. 58 (Bahrain–Iran); No. 63 (Iran–U.A.E.); No. 67 (Iran–Oman).

[5] Decision of 30 June 1977. Comment: Colson, 72 *A.J.* (1978), 95–112; McRae, 15 *Canad. Yrbk.* (1977), 173–97; Bowett, 49 *B.Y.* (1978), 1–29; Brown, 16 *San Diego L.R.* (1979), 461–530. See also Bowett, 48 *B.Y.* (1976–7), 67–92. For the text: H.M.S.O. Misc. No. 15 (1978), Cmnd. 7438.

[6] See also paras. 194, 195, 239–42.

the equidistance or of any other method for the purpose of effecting an equitable delimitation is a function or reflection of the geographical and other relevant circumstances of each particular case'. The use of equitable principles in this broad form results in discretionary rather than substantially articulated decisions. Thus the Court gave the Scillies 'half effect' in drawing a modified equidistance line, gave full effect to Ushant in doing so, and gave the Channel Islands a restricted and enclaved area of shelf. In all these cases general references such as 'an inequitable distortion of the equidistance line' were used to explain the process of decision.[1]

Article 83 of the Informal Composite Negotiating Text of 1977 contains a formula derived from the jurisprudence; paragraph 1 provides:

> The delimitation of the continental shelf between adjacent or opposite States shall be effected by agreement in accordance with equitable principles, employing, where appropriate, the median or equidistance line, and taking account of all the relevant circumstances.

A further development at the Third United Nations Conference has been an attempt to redefine the concept of an island. This is done, obliquely, in paragraph 3 of Article 121 of the provisional Text of 1977, which provides that 'rocks which cannot sustain human habitation or economic life of their own shall have no exclusive economic zone or continental shelf'. This formula would be extremely difficult to apply and is incompatible with the general practice of employing rocks as turning points for baselines.

(iv) *Trenches and depressions*.[2] The Convention does not provide for the situations in which either deep depressions are enclosed within a shelf area or an otherwise continuous shelf area is trenched by deep depressions, such as the Norwegian trench of 500 metres depth. The United Kingdom has accepted a division of the North Sea which ignores this trench.[3] The test would seem to be whether the area has a substantial geological unity: but in any case the opposite or adjacent states may choose to ignore such trenches.[4]

(v) *The Third United Nations Conference*. At the Third United

[1] Decision, para. 243 and see also paras. 196, 199, 244, 248–51.

[2] See Feulner, 17 *Virginia J.I.L.* (1976), 77–105.

[3] *British Practice* (1964), p. 58; Anglo-Norwegian Agreement, 1965, Cmnd. 2757. See also the Soviet Decree, 1968; 7 *Int. Leg. Materials* (1968), 392.

[4] See the *North Sea Continental Shelf* cases, I.C.J. Reports (1969), p. 32; *Western Approaches Arbitration*, Decision of 30 June 1977, paras. 107, 108.

Nations Conference on the Law of the Sea, the provisional draft articles of 1977 contain a novel definition of the continental shelf as follows:[1]

> The continental shelf of a coastal State comprises the seabed and subsoil of the submarine areas that extend beyond its territorial sea throughout the natural prolongation of its land territory to the outer edge of the continental margin, or to a distance of 200 nautical miles from the baselines from which the breadth of the territorial sea is measured where the outer edge of the continental margin does not extend up to that distance.

So far as this definition refers to the 'natural prolongation' of land territory it consolidates the geological elements present in the definition contained in the 1958 Convention and emphasized by the International Court in the *North Sea Continental Shelf Cases*.[2] At the same time the precise content of the phrase 'outer edge of the continental margin'[3] is undefined. The remainder of the definition—the numerical supplement to the geological conception—is a reflection of a desire at the conference to introduce equity by creating norms. The 'double definition' is provisional and its future is contingent upon the outcome of the conference as a whole.

The work of the conference, as reflected in the Informal Composite Negotiating Text, leads to certain difficult questions concerning the relationship between legal concepts. In particular, the exclusive economic zone as presented in the Text must be related to the continental shelf. For example, the possible effect of the draft articles relating to delimitation between opposite or adjacent states would be to have part of an exclusive economic zone of one state overriding the natural prolongation forming part of the continental shelf of another state (where the latter is much broader than the shelf of the former).[4] A further issue concerns the overlap of continental shelves more than two hundred miles in breadth and the 'area' of seabed which may be placed under an International Sea-bed Authority[5] (on which see below). A more general feature of the provisional draft is the apparent assimilation of E.E.Z. and continental shelf. The principal differences appear to be that (a) the E.E.Z. is optional whilst shelf rights are inherent by operation of law (but this is

[1] Informal Composite Negotiating Text of 1977, Article 76.

[2] See above, pp. 228–9.

[3] See Hedberg, 17 *Virginia J.I.L.* (1976), 57–75.

[4] Cf. Informal Composite Negotiating Text of 1977, Articles 74, 76 and 83. Article 83 does not apply to *separated* 'opposite' continental shelf areas, but applies to states abutting upon the same shelf.

[5] See the Text of 1977, Article 82.

uncertain); and (b) the existence of shelf rights (in some form) beyond the two hundred miles limit between E.E.Z. and the 'international seabed area'.

(e) *Definition of Natural Resources*[1]

The Truman Proclamation of 1945 was concerned with the mineral resources of the shelf. Subsequently Latin American states pressed for recognition of the interest of coastal states in the fisheries of the shelf. The International Law Commission had decided to include sedentary fisheries;[2] and Article 2, paragraph 4, of the Convention defines 'natural resources' so as to include 'living organisms belonging to the sedentary species, that is to say, organisms which, at the harvestable stage, either are immobile on or under the seabed or are unable to move except in constant physical contact with the seabed or the subsoil'. The application of this distinction has met difficulties in relation to king crabs[3] and particular species of lobster.[4] The definition excludes in principle demersal species, such as halibut and plaice, which swim close to the seabed.

(f) *Regime of the Subsoil: Tunnels*[5]

Article 7 of the Continental Shelf Convention provides that the Convention 'shall not prejudice the right of the coastal State to exploit the subsoil by means of tunnelling irrespective of the depth of water above the subsoil'.[6] In other words such activity falls outside the scope of the Convention and is governed by customary international law.[7] There is a notable distinction inherent in this arrangement. If exploitation of the subsoil occurs from above the shelf, the continental shelf regime applies; whereas if exploitation is by tunnels from the mainland then a different regime applies.

[1] See Whiteman iv. 856–71; Lumb, 7 *Univ. of Queensland L.J.* (1970–1), 111–14; Goldie, 63 *A.J.* (1969), 86–97; Goldie, ibid., 536–43; Gutteridge, 35 *B.Y.* (1959), 116–19; *British Practice* (1964), pp. 58–9; Report on Law of the Sea Conf., 1958, Cmnd. 584, para. 31.

[2] *Yrbk., I.L.C.* (1956), ii. 297–8.

[3] Oda, 127 Hague *Recueil* (1969, II), 427–30.

[4] Azzam, 13 *I.C.L.Q.* (1964), 1453–9; 67 *R.G.D.I.P.* (1965), 364. See also decl. with French ratif.: *British Practice* (1965), p. 141.

[5] See Whiteman iv. 918–20; Gutteridge, op. cit., 122. On the Channel tunnel project: van den Mensbrugghe, 71 *R.G.D.I.P.* (1967), 325–41; Marston, 47 *B.Y.* (1974–5), 290–300.

[6] See also the Informal Composite Negotiating Text of 1977, Article 85.

[7] Generally, on the seabed and subsoil, *infra*, section 4.

(g) *Installations and other devices on the Shelf*[1]

Article 5 of the Continental Shelf Convention provides in part:

> 2. Subject to the provisions of paragraphs 1 and 5 of this article,[2] the coastal State is entitled to construct and maintain on the continental shelf installations necessary for the exploration and exploitation of its natural resources, and to establish safety zones at a reasonable distance around such installations and take in those zones measures necessary for their protection.

Such installations do not have a territorial sea of their own.

The Convention provides no basis for the construction of defence installations on the shelf: nor does it prohibit such installations, so that they may be lawful if some other legal justification exists.[3] To suggest that the coastal state may create defence installations and prohibit comparable activities by other states[4] is to run the risk of justifying a security zone over the whole shelf area. The well-known North Sea Installations Act (1964) of the Netherlands asserted certain rights of jurisdiction over fixed installations on the shelf as a means of control over 'pirate' broadcasting. However, this measure was not based upon the doctrine of the continental shelf.[5]

3. *Seabed and Ocean Floor*

(a) *The existing regime*[6]

The legal status of the high seas beyond the outer limit of the territorial sea is considered in Chapter XI. In principle the seabed of the high seas is *res communis* and not susceptible of appropriation by states or private persons. However, some authorities consider the area to be *res nullius* and open to effective occupation. In any case historic title and prescription have played a role.[7] Title to certain seabed fisheries (for example, pearl, oyster, and sponge

[1] Whiteman iv. 888–903. [2] *Supra*, p. 226.

[3] See Gutteridge, 35 *B.Y.* (1959), 119–22; Franklin, op. cit., pp. 65–7; Jennings, op. cit., p. 389.

[4] See O'Connell i. 507.

[5] See van Panhuys and van Emde Boas, 60 *A.J.* (1966), p. 303 at pp. 326–36. See further François, Bos, and Woodliffe, 12 *Neths. Int. L.R.* (1965), 113, 337, 365, respectively; Verzijl, *International Law in Historical Perspective* iv. 145–51.

[6] See Gidel i. 493–501; Hackworth ii. 672–9; Oppenheim i. 589 note, 629–35; Lauterpacht, 27 *B.Y.* (1950), 392 seq.; Hyde i, para. 145A; Jonkheer P.R. Feith and others, Int. Law Assoc., *Report of the Forty-third Conference* (1948), pp. 168–206; Hurst, 4 *B.Y.* (1923–4), 34–43; Waldock, 36 *Grot. Soc.* (1950), 116–20; Verzijl, *International Law in Historical Perspective* iv. 277–84; O'Connell, 49 *A.J.* (1955), 185–209; Goldie, 1 *Sydney L.R.* (1953), 84–95; François, *Yrbk., I.L.C.* (1951), ii. 94–9.

[7] See the *Fisheries* case, *supra*, p. 186; and Chapter VII, section 22.

fisheries) has been obtained on the basis of prescription[1] and the rights, it seems, have related to the exclusive right to take the harvest rather than to the seabed as such.[2] The existing regime includes rights deriving from the doctrine of the continental shelf in the appropriate areas (section 2, above).

The appearance of the doctrine relating to the continental shelf (and also the concept of a two hundred mile fishing zone/or exclusive economic zone)[3] has displaced the subject of the sedentary fisheries of the shelf area. However, sedentary fisheries remain as a separate issue in two situations: (a) where certain historic rights are maintained on a shelf appurtenant to another state; (b) where historic rights to sedentary fisheries of a coastal state on its own shelf are more extensive than the rights to sedentary species as defined in the Convention of 1958.[4]

(b) *Improvement of the legal structure for management of the resources of the seabed and ocean floor*[5]

In recent years exploration and even exploitation of mineral resources have occurred at considerable depths. Such developments have prompted controversy in the United Nations and elsewhere concerning an improved legal structure for the use and exploitation of the seabed beyond the limits of national jurisdiction. The need for improvement may be appreciated in the light of the following considerations. First, the regime of the high seas as a *res communis* does not provide a sufficiently stable legal basis for extensive development and competing claims. Secondly, the provisions of the Continental Shelf Convention relating to the definition of the outer limit of the shelf area stand in need of clarification.

[1] *Supra*, p. 172. Prior to the appearance of continental shelf claims the United Kingdom and Venezuela had partitioned and annexed the bed of the Gulf of Paria: Treaty of 26 Feb. 1942; Whiteman iv. 789. See also Saudi Arabia Decree of 7 Sept. 1968; 8 *I.L.M.* (1969), 606.

[2] See McNair, *Opinions*, i. 258–64. See also the Conv. on Fishing and Conservation, 1958; Brownlie, *Documents*, p. 99, Art. 13.

[3] Above, pp. 217–21.

[4] See Young, 55 *A.J.* (1961), 359–73; Goldie, 63 *A.J.* (1969), 86–97; Papandreou, 11 *Revue hellénique de d.i.* (1958), 1–148.

[5] Friedmann, *The Future of the Oceans* (1971); Henkin, *The Law of the Sea's Mineral Resources* (1968); id., 63 *A.J.* (1969), 504–10; Lévy, 75 *R.G.D.I.P.* (1971), 356–91; Auburn, 20 *I.C.L.Q.* (1971), 173–94; Goldie, 64 *A.J.* (1970), 905–19; id., 1 *Journal of Maritime Law and Commerce* (1970), 461–72; ibid., 2 (1970), 173–7; Jennings, 20 *I.C.L.Q.* (1971), 433–52; Weissberg, 18 *I.C.L.Q.* (1969), 41–102; Oda, 127 Hague *Recueil* (1969, II), 458–72; *United States Foreign Policy 1971*, Dept. of St. Public. 8634 (March 1972); Alexander in Churchill, Simmonds and Welch, *New Directions in the Law of the Sea*, III, 119–33; Bowett, *Camb. L.J.* (1972B), 50; Adede, 69 *A.J.* (1975), 31–49.

Pressure for the development of a new regime developed in the General Assembly Committee on Peaceful Uses of the Seabed. In 1970 the General Assembly adopted a resolution containing a Declaration of Principles Governing the Seabed and Ocean Floor, and the Subsoil Thereof, Beyond the Limits of National Jurisdiction.[1] The resolution represented a substantial consensus on certain principles: (a) the area shall not be subject to appropriation by states or by natural or legal persons; (b) an international regime should be created to govern the management of the natural resources; (c) the area shall be open to use for exclusively peaceful purposes. The legal purport of the resolution is a matter of uncertainty.[2] Primarily the instrument is programmatic and directory. Some states consider that a moratorium on exploitation of the seabed exists as a consequence of the Declaration.[3] This is doubtful except in so far as particular states have unilaterally accepted such an obligation. The United States Government has adopted a policy of voluntarily avoiding action which would preempt the outcome of the Third United Nations Conference;[4] in the view of the United States 'high seas freedoms do not include exclusive rights to the exploration or exploitation of the mineral resources of an area'.[5]

A major aspect of the Third United Nations Conference on the Law of the Sea (1973–9) has been the effort to design an appropriate regime for 'the Area', that is, 'the sea-bed and ocean floor and subsoil thereof beyond the limits of national jurisdiction'. The regime provisionally envisaged appears as Part XI of the Informal Composite Negotiating Text of 1977. Article 136 provides that 'the Area and its resources[6] are the common

[1] Resol. 2749 (XXV) of 17 December 1970; Brownlie, *Documents*, p. 112. 108 votes; 14 abstentions.

[2] See Skubiszewski, *Annals of International Studies* (Geneva), 1973, pp. 237–48; Friedmann, 65 *A.J.* (1971), 757–70; Jennings, 20 *I.C.L.Q.* (1971), 433 at pp. 438–40; Jiménez de Aréchaga, Hague *Recueil* (1978, I), 32–33, 228–30.

[3] And see also the 'Moratorium' resolution, G.A. resol. 2574 (XXIV), 15 December 1969; 62 in favour, 28 against, 28 abstentions; Lay, Churchill and Nordquist, *New Directions*, II, 737.

[4] *Digest of U.S. Practice*, 1973, pp. 263–7.

[5] Ibid., 1974, pp. 339–43 at pp. 342–3.

[6] Article 133 provides in part: (b) '"Resources" means mineral resources *in situ*. When recovered from the Area, such resources shall, for the purposes of this Part of the present Convention, be regarded as minerals.' (c) 'Minerals shall include the following categories: (i) Liquid or gaseous substances such as petroleum, gas, condensate, helium, nitrogen, carbon dioxide, water, steam, hot water, and also sulphur and salts extracted in liquid form in solution; (ii) Useful minerals occurring on the surface of the seabed or at depths of less than three metres beneath the surface and also concretions of phosphorites and other minerals; (iii) Solid minerals in the ocean floor at depths of more than three metres from the surface; (iv) Ore-bearing silt and brine.'

heritage of mankind'. Negotiations are proceeding in order to reach agreement on the precise features of the Area and the role of the International Sea-bed Authority. Problems to be solved include the composition and voting procedure within the organs of the Authority, and the regime of exploitation involving both the Enterprise (as an organ of the Authority) directly and contractors (who may be states or state entities or natural or legal persons). Further issues concern the system of dispute settlement, and the policies and preferences to be applied in management of the Area and its resources. Excess revenues are to be paid into a Special Fund by the Authority and such surplus may be apportioned or made available according to criteria not yet determined. It is to be noted that within the framework of the Informal Composite Negotiating Text the area beyond the limits of national jurisdiction would start at 200 miles from the baselines of the territorial sea.[1] The emplacement of weapons of mass destruction on the seabed beyond a twelve mile coastal zone is prohibited by the provisions of a multilateral treaty.[2]

4. *Special Cases*

It is necessary to record that the regime of the Antarctic Treaty of 1959 applies to the area south of 60° South Latitude, whether sea or land.[3] Oil and natural gas structures (single geological structures) may extend across the line dividing a continental shelf between states and exploitation may then occur in accordance with treaty arrangements.[4]

[1] See Article 82 of the text, which relates to the rights of coastal states with continental shelf extending beyond 200 miles.

[2] Treaty on the Prohibition of the Emplacement of Nuclear Weapons and Other Weapons of Mass Destruction on the Sea-bed . . . In force 18 May 1972. Text: 10 *Int. Leg. Materials* (1971), 145.

[3] Antarctic Treaty, art. VI; and see *infra*, pp 265–6.

[4] e.g. U.K.–Neths. Agreement, 6 October 1965, Cmnd. 3254. See further Onorato, 17 *I.C.L.Q.* (1968), 85–102; id., 26 *I.C.L.Q.* (1977), 324–37; Woodliffe, ibid., 338–53; *North Sea Continental Shelf* cases, I.C.J. Reports (1969), at pp. 51–2; ibid., pp. 81–2 (Judge Jessup).

CHAPTER XI

THE REGIME OF THE HIGH SEAS[1]

1. *Introductory*

THE acquisition of title to sea areas, and problems relating to contiguous zones, continental shelf, other special zones, and sedentary fisheries, are commonly treated under the rubric 'regime of the high seas', but it has been thought convenient to deal with these questions separately.[2] At the outset, it must be emphasized that 'the term "high seas" means all parts of the sea that are not included in the territorial sea or in the internal waters of a State',[3] and therefore comprehends contiguous zones and the waters over the continental shelf and outside the limit of the territorial sea. The term, and the rules which it draws in its train, do not apply to international lakes and land-locked seas, and these are not open to free navigation except by special agreement.[4] However, by acquiescence and custom, perhaps reinforced by conventions on particular questions, seas which are virtually land-locked may acquire the status of high seas or open sea: this is the case of the Baltic and Black Seas. In such cases much turns on the maintenance of freedom of transit through the straits communicating with other large bodies of sea.[5] It is doubtful whether, apart from acquiescence and special agree-

[1] Of considerable value and authority is the Secretariat Memo. of 14 July 1950, A/CN. 4/32, *Yrbk., I.L.C.* (1950), ii. 67–79 (believed to be the work of Gidel). See also: Hackworth ii. 651 seq.; H. A. Smith, *The Law and Custom of the Sea* (3rd ed., 1959); Colombos, *The International Law of the Sea* (6th ed.), Chaps. II and IX; Gidel i. 125 seq.; McDougal and Burke, pp. 730 seq.; Oppenheim i. 588–627; Hyde i. 751 seq.; François, Reports on the Regime of the High Seas, *Yrbk., I.L.C.* (1950), ii. 36; ibid. (1951), ii. 75; ibid. (1952), ii. 44; ibid. (1954), ii. 7; Green, 12 *Curr. Leg. Problems* (1959), 224–46; Bierzanek, 65 *R.G.D.I.P.* (1961), 233–59; Whiteman iv. 499–739; Verzijl, *International Law in Historical Perspective* iv (1971).

On the legal status of the *res communis, supra*, p. 181; on the regulation of the high seas as a shared resource, *infra*, pp. 263–5.

[2] *Supra*, pp. 170–2, 209 seq., 222.

[3] Convention on the High Seas, Article 1. This multilateral convention entered into force on 30 September 1962. See *Treaty Series* No. 5 (1963). Cmnd. 1929; Brownlie, *Documents*, p. 89. In the preamble its provisions are expressed to be 'generally declaratory of established principles of international law'.

[4] Oppenheim i. 477–9, 587–8. Lakes and land-locked seas entirely enclosed by the land of a single state are part of the territory of that state.

[5] On access to the Black Sea and its status see the Montreux Convention, 1936, 31 *A.J.* (1937), Suppl., p. 1. Does the Convention recognize the status of the Black Sea as an open or a closed sea?

ments on access and other issues, the Baltic and Black Seas would have the status of open seas.[1]

2. *The Freedom of the High Seas*

The modern law governing the high seas has its foundation in the rule that the high seas are not open to acquisition by occupation on the part of states individually or collectively: it is *res extra commercium*.[2] Historically the emergence of the rule is associated with the rise to dominance of maritime powers and the decline of the influence of states which had favoured closed seas.[3] In the fifteenth century states were in favour of appropriation of or at least an exercise of exclusive rights over large expanses of sea, and Papal Bulls of 1493 and 1506 partitioned the oceans of the world between Spain and Portugal. The Spanish monopoly of commerce in the West Indies was challenged by Tudor policies, and Elizabeth I affirmed the freedom of the seas in answer to a Spanish protest arising from the expedition of Drake.[4] After 1609 Stuart policies extended the principle of closed seas from Scotland to England and Ireland, and the political concept of the 'British Seas' appeared. The areas claimed extended to the opposite shores of the Continent.[5] The seventeenth century marked the heyday of the *mare clausum* (closed sea) with claims by England, Denmark, Spain, Portugal, Genoa, Tuscany, the Papacy, Turkey, and Venice.

In the eighteenth century the position changed completely. Dutch policies had favoured freedom of navigation and fishing in the previous century, and the great publicist Grotius had written against the Portuguese monopoly of navigation and commerce in the East Indies.[6] After the accession of William of Orange to the English throne in 1689 English disputes with

[1] See Kozhevnikov (ed.), *International Law*, pp. 226–7.

[2] But encroachment may occur as a result of acquisition by general acquiescence, see *supra*, p. 186 on the *Fisheries* case and historic waters.

[3] For the history see Fulton, *The Sovereignty of the Sea* (1911).

[4] However, in instructions to her ambassadors in 1602, whilst contesting a Danish claim to dominion over the seas between Norway, on the one hand, and Iceland and Greenland, on the other, the Queen recognized a right of 'oversight and jurisdiction'. Russia asserted the principle of the freedom of the seas in 1587.

[5] See Selden, *Mare Clausum* (1635). The King's Chambers were a different concept. In 1604 James I caused the limits of bays, from which hostile acts of belligerents were excluded, to be marked on charts (see the map in Fulton, p. 123). No claim to sovereignty was intended. It seems that no special rights exist today in respect of the King's Chambers: see the *Fagernes* [1927] P. 311, C.A.; Hudson, p. 284.

[6] *Mare Liberum sive de jure quod Batavis competit ad Indicana commercia dissertatio* (1609), being a chapter of the work *De iure praedae*.

Holland over fisheries ceased. However, sovereignty of the sea was still asserted against France, and in general the formal requirement of the salute to the flag was maintained. By the late eighteenth century the claim to sovereignty was obsolete and the requirement of the flag ceremony was ended in 1805. After 1691 extensive Danish claims were reduced by stages to narrow fixed limits. By the late eighteenth century the cannon-shot rule predominated, and claims to large areas of sea faded away.[1] In the nineteenth century naval power and commercial interests dictated British, French, and American support for the principle of freedom of the seas. However, whatever special interests the principle may have served historically, it has obviously commended itself to states generally, as representing a sensible and wholesome concept of shared use.

The principle of the freedom of the high seas has been described by Gidel[2] as 'multiforme et fugace', and in truth it is a 'general principle of international law', or a policy concept, from which particular rules must be deduced. Its application to specific problems often fails to give precise results. Weapon testing which involves the closure of large areas of ocean is regarded by some as a legitimate form of enjoying the freedom of the seas and by others as a serious denial of that freedom.[3] The problems of reasonableness and mutuality involved are reminiscent of the law of nuisance and the doctrine of abuse of rights.[4] Like guarantees of freedoms in written constitutions the only successful form of prescription is that of specifying exceptions. Gidel regards the concept as essentially negative. However, the substance of the principle and its character as a principle provide certain presumptions which may aid in the resolution of particular problems, and some consideration of its positive content is, therefore, useful. Grotius stated two principles: first, that the sea could not be the object of private or state appropriation; secondly, that the use of the high seas by one state would leave the medium available for use by another.[5]

Gidel has stated his views as follows:[6]

[1] *Supra*, pp. 184–5. The extravagant Portuguese and Spanish pretensions had ended before this. Spain supported a six-mile limit in 1760.

[2] *Yrbk., I.L.C.* (1950), ii. 68.

[3] See Whiteman iv. 544 seq.; Gidel, in *Festschrift für Jean Spiropoulos*, pp. 173–205; *Yrbk., I.L.C.* (1956), ii. 278 (Article 27, Commentary, para. 3); and the Applications of Australia and New Zealand in the *Nuclear Tests Case*, I.C.J. Reports, 1974, p. 253 (Australia v. France); p. 457 (New Zealand v. France). The claims were found to be without object: see below, p. 472. Useful material may be found in the *Pleadings*. Nuclear tests are restricted by the Test Ban Treaty signed in 1963.

[4] See *infra*, pp. 285–6, 443–5.

[5] *Mare Liberum*, cap. v.

[6] *Ubi supra*, p. 69. See also the *Lotus* (1927), P.C.I.J., Ser. A, no. 10, p. 25; Briggs, p. 10; Green, p. 211; Hudson, p. 372.

La liberté de la haute mer, essentiellement négative, ne peut pas cependant ne pas comporter des conséquences positives. Dirigée contre l'exclusivité d'usage elle se résout nécessairement en une idée d'égalité d'usage. . . . Tous les pavillons maritimes ont un droit égal à tirer de la haute mer les diverses utilités qu'elle peut comporter. Mais l'idée d'égalité d'usage ne vient qu'en second lieu. L'idée essentielle contenue dans le principe de liberté de la haute mer est l'idée d'interdiction d'interférence de tout pavillon dans la navigation en temps de paix de tout autre pavillon.

To these propositions it is necessary to add that the general principle applies in time of war or armed conflict as well as time of peace.[1] An attempt to describe, in part, the content of the freedom of the seas is to be found in Article 2 of the Convention on the High Seas, which provides:

The high seas being open to all nations, no State may validly purport to subject any part of them to its sovereignty. Freedom of the high seas is exercised under the conditions laid down by these articles and by the other rules of international law. It comprises, *inter alia*, both for coastal and non-coastal States:[2]

(1) Freedom of navigation;
(2) Freedom of fishing;[3]
(3) Freedom to lay submarine cables and pipelines;
(4) Freedom to fly over the high seas.

These freedoms, and others which are recognized by the general principles of international law,[4] shall be exercised by all States with reasonable regard to the interests of other States in their exercise of the freedom of the high seas.

The four freedoms itemized, and particularly the first two, are supported by arbitral jurisprudence and are inherent in many particular rules of law. Freedom of fishing is an assumption at the base of the decision in the *Fisheries* case[5] and the awards in the

[1] This aspect of the matter is obscured by the treatment in some works: naturally the exceptions to the principle are different if the status of belligerent is acquired, but the principle is not thereby obliterated.

[2] The view has been expressed that these rights inhere in *states* and not in ships not registered in any state, e.g. vessels used in pirate broadcasting. See *British Practice in International Law* (1964), i. 42–3 and *infra*, p. 298, n. 3.

[3] See also Article 1 of the Convention on Fishing and Conservation of the Living Resources of the High Seas.

[4] The United Kingdom in its comment on the I.L.C. draft articles advocated the addition of two others: '5. Freedom of research, experiment and exploration. 6. The right to regulate the operation of foreign vessels in the coastal trade in those cases where such ships are permitted to engage in that trade.'

[5] *Supra*, pp. 186 seq. Cf. Judge Read, diss. op., I.C.J. Reports (1951), pp. 187–9.

Behring Sea Fisheries arbitrations in 1893[1] and 1902.[2] Both arbitrations arose from attempts to enforce conservation measures on the high seas.[3] In the former case the United States had arrested Canadian sealers, and in the latter Russian vessels had arrested American sealers, with the object of preventing the depletion of seal stocks. The awards in both arbitrations rejected claims to enforce conservation measures against foreign vessels on the high seas. In the absence of a treaty, a coastal state could only apply such measures to vessels flying its own flag.[4] Of the questions submitted for decision to the tribunal of 1892 the fifth concerned an issue of general law: '5. Has the United States any right, and if so, what right of protection or property in the fur-seals frequenting the islands of the United States in Behring Sea when such seals are found outside the ordinary three-mile limit?' The arbitrators found, by a majority that 'the United States has not any right of protection or property in the fur-seals frequenting the islands of the United States in Behring Sea, when such seals are found outside the ordinary three-mile limit'.

In conclusion it is necessary to give some account of the changes scheduled in the Informal Composite Negotiating Text of the Third United Nations Conference on the Law of the Sea. The major change envisaged is the legitimation of the exclusive economic zone (see above, pp. 219–21) two hundred miles in breadth. According to the provisional Text the zone does not form part of the High Seas (see Articles 55 and 86), although some significant aspects of the regime of the high seas apply to the zone. A further change would be the creation of a special regime for the resources of the seabed and subsoil beyond the limits of national jurisdiction under the control and management of the International Sea-bed Authority. These changes are reflected in the chronicle of freedoms of the high seas included in the provisional Text. The four freedoms set forth in the Convention of 1958 are formulated but freedom of fishing is subject (principally) to the reduction of area consequent upon

1 See Moore, *Digest* i, para. 172; McNair, *Opinions* i. 241.

2 See Moore, *Digest* i, para. 173; *R.I.A.A.* ix. 51. The seal fishery was later regulated by the Convention of Washington, 1911, between Great Britain, the United States, Russia, and Japan. See further Johnston, *The International Law of Fisheries*, pp. 205–11, 264–9.

3 The arbitration between Great Britain and the United States involved the question of compensation for abstention from fishing by Great Britain during the pendency of the arbitration; the arbitration between the United States and Russia concerned claims for indemnity arising from seizures by Russian cruisers.

4 On fishery conservation zones see *supra*, p. 217.

exclusive economic zones, as well as the activities involved in exploitation of the Sea-bed Area under control of the International Sea-bed Authority. The Text formulates additional freedoms (Article 87, para. 1):

> '(d) Freedom to construct artificial islands and other installations permitted under international law, subject to Part VI[1] of the present Convention; . . .
>
> (f) Freedom of scientific research, subject to Parts VI[1] and XIII[2] of the present Convention.'

It is to be noted that the exclusive economic zone as described in the provisional Text would confer jurisdiction on coastal States in respect of marine scientific research (Article 56, para. 1).

3. *The Maintenance of Order on the High Seas*

States may agree among themselves to accept special procedures for the repression of the slave trade and other wrongdoing on the high seas. In some cases the Convention on the High Seas confers the power to stop and seize foreign vessels by way of enforcement. In others the parties are obliged only to incorporate the prohibition in their national legislation, and enforcement is by national courts in respect of vessels flying the flag of the forum and persons subject to the jurisdiction of the forum state. The system of enforcement, whether specified by treaty or custom, rests on the co-operation of international law and the national laws of states possessing a maritime flag. Every state is under a duty to fix the conditions for the grant of nationality to its ships, for the registration of ships in its territory, and for the right to fly its flag. Ships have the nationality of the state whose flag they are entitled to fly, and each state has an obligation to issue to ships to which it has granted the right to fly its flag documents to that effect.[3]

The essential elements are the nationality of the ship;[4] the exclusive jurisdiction of the flag state over the ship (apart from treaty provisions to the contrary); the right of approach to verify the right of a ship to fly its flag; and the imposition on the flag state of obligations in respect of the maintenance of good order and general security on the high seas by customary rules and by

[1] Concerning the continental shelf.

[2] Concerning marine scientific research in general.

[3] See Oppenheim i. 590; Convention on the High Seas, Article 5.

[4] On the nationality of ships: *infra*, p. 424.

treaties. The right to enjoy the protection of the law balances the responsibility of the flag state for the behaviour of its ships. The ship without nationality[1] loses the protection of the law with respect to boarding and seizure on the high seas.[2] However, such ships are not outside the law altogether, and their occupants are protected by elementary considerations of humanity.[3] The seizure of ships by insurgents has created some difficult problems, and the issues have been obscured by a tendency for courts to describe ships under the control of insurgents as pirates.[4] Such ships, it seems, should not be interfered with provided they do not attempt to exercise belligerent rights against foreign vessels and the lives of any 'neutral' aliens on board are not threatened.

4. *Exceptions to the Principle of the Freedom of the High Seas*

(a) *Rules of customary law*

(i) *Piracy*.[5] The dissenting opinion of Judge Moore in the *Lotus* case provides a useful starting point.[6] He said that:

> in the case of what is known as piracy by law of nations, there has been conceded a universal jurisdiction, under which the person charged with the offence may be tried and punished by any nation into whose jurisdiction he may come. I say 'piracy by law of nations', because the municipal laws of many States[7] denominate and punish as 'piracy' numerous acts which do not constitute piracy by law of nations, and which therefore are not of universal cognizance, so as to be punishable by all nations. Piracy by law of nations, in its jurisdictional aspects, is *sui generis*. Though statutes may provide for its punishment, it is an offence against the law of nations; and as the scene of the pirate's operations is the high seas, which it is not the right

[1] To which will be assimilated a vessel flying a flag without authority of the flag state and a ship sailing under the flags of two or more states, using them according to convenience: see Oppenheim i. 595–6; Convention on the High Seas, Article 6, paragraph 2.

[2] See *Naim Molvan* v. *A.-G. for Palestine* [1948] A.C. 351 at p. 369, P.C.; Green, p. 556; and Report of François, *Yrbk., I.L.C.* (1950), ii. 36 at p. 38. On the status of derelict vessels see the *Costa Rica Packet* case, La Fontaine, 510; Pitt Cobbett i. 278.

[3] *Supra*, p. 29. On pirate ships, *infra*, p. 245.

[4] See Colombos, pp. 450 seq.; and *infra*, p. 246. On the *Santa Maria* incident in 1961: Green, 37 *B.Y.* (1961), 496–505; Goyard, 66 *R.G.D.I.P.* (1962), 123–42.

[5] Gidel i. 303–55; Whiteman iv. 648–67; McDougal and Burke, pp. 809–23, 875–9; Secretariat Memo., *Yrbk., I.L.C.* (1950), ii. at p. 70; Oppenheim i. 608–17; Johnson, 43 *Grot. Soc.* (1957), 63–85; Pella, 15 Hague *Recueil* (1926, V), 149–257; Harv. Research, 26 *A.J.* (1932), Suppl., pp. 739 seq.; McNair, *Opinions* i. 265–81; Shubber, 43 *B.Y.* (1968–9), 193–204. Bibliographies: Oppenheim i. 608; Gidel i. 303.

[6] P.C.I.J., Ser. A, no. 10 (1927), p. 70.

[7] See, for example, the British legislation: Piracy Acts of 1698, 1837; Slave Trade Act, 1834.

or duty of any nation to police, he is denied the protection of the flag which he may carry, and is treated as an outlaw, as the enemy of all mankind—*hostis humani generis*—whom any nation may in the interest of all capture and punish.

The definition of piracy has long been a source of controversy,[1] but it is thought that Article 15 of the Convention on the High Seas represents the existing customary law.[2] This provides:

Piracy consists of any of the following acts:

(1) Any illegal acts of violence, detention or any act of depredation, committed for private ends by the crew or the passengers of a private ship or a private aircraft, and directed:

(a) On the high seas, against another ship or aircraft, or against persons or property on board such ship or aircraft;

(b) Against a ship, aircraft, persons or property in a place outside the jurisdiction of any State;

(2) Any act of voluntary participation in the operation of a ship or of an aircraft with knowledge of facts making it a pirate ship or aircraft;

(3) Any act of inciting or of intentionally facilitating an act described in sub-paragraph (1) or sub-paragraph (2) of this article.

The only clear innovation in the provision just quoted is the reference to aircraft, a sensible application of analogy.[3] The essential feature of the definition is that the acts must be committed for private ends. It follows that piracy cannot be committed by warships or other government ships, or government aircraft, except where the crew 'has mutinied and taken control of the ship or aircraft' (Article 16). Acts committed on board a ship by the crew and directed against the ship itself, or against persons or property on the ship, are not within the definition.[4]

The Convention confines piracy to acts on the high seas or

[1] By way of caution, it may be pointed out that definitions by municipal courts are often out of date, and may involve an amalgam of municipal rules and international law, or the narrow issue of the meaning of 'piracy' in an insurance policy. The treatment in Oppenheim i. 610–14 presents an unusually wide conception of piracy. For judicial essays in definition see *The Serhassan Pirates* (1845), 2 Wm. Rob. 354; *The Magellan Pirates* (1853), 1 Sp. Ecc. & Ad. 81; *Republic of Bolivia* v. *Indemnity Mutual Marine Assurance Co.* [1909] K.B. 785; *In re Piracy Jure Gentium* [1934] A.C. 586, P.C.; Green, p. 493; Hudson, p. 364.

[2] See also the I.L.C. draft and comment: *Yrbk., I.L.C.* (1956), ii. 282. See further the Third United Nations Conference, Informal Composite Negotiating Text of 1977, Article 101.

[3] The I.L.C. draft did not refer to attacks by aircraft on aircraft. Cf. Johnson, op. cit., p. 67 n. See further the U.K. Tokyo Convention Act 1967, s. 4 and Sched.

[4] *Contra*, Oppenheim i. 614, n. 2; Hall, p. 314.

'in a place outside the territorial jurisdiction of any State'. The latter phrase refers primarily to an island constituting *terra nullius* or the shore of an unoccupied territory.[1] In excluding acts within the territorial sea the International Law Commission and the Geneva Conference were prepared to ignore a not inconsiderable weight of contrary authorities.[2]

Article 19 of the Convention on the High Seas provides:

On the high seas, or in any other place outside the jurisdiction of any State, every State may seize a pirate ship or aircraft,[3] or a ship taken by piracy and under the control of pirates, and arrest the persons and seize the property on board. The courts of the State which carried out the seizure may decide upon the penalties to be imposed, and may also determine the action to be taken with regard to the ships, aircraft or property, subject to the rights of third parties acting in good faith.[4]

The second part of this provision preserves the effect of the maxim '*pirata non mutat dominium*': the rightful owner is not deprived of his title by virtue of acts of piracy relating to his goods.[5] Seizures on account of piracy may only be carried out by warships or military aircraft, or other government ships or aircraft authorized to that effect (Article 21). Capture may occur in other circumstances as a consequence of acts of self-defence by an intended victim of piratical action.

(ii) *Other illegal acts committed by ships on the high seas.* The use of force by ships against foreign vessels on the high seas may be unlawful and yet may not fall within the definition of piracy. However, from time to time tribunals, governments, and writers have assimilated certain categories of acts to piracy. The tendency to enlarge the concept of piracy thus evident is explicable partly by the existence of doubts relating to the definition of piracy and partly by a desire to affirm the illegality of certain types of activity in the most unequivocal manner. The subject as a whole is dominated by the problem of keeping order outside the territorial jurisdiction of states[6] and, in particular, of maintaining

[1] On the legal regime of the *res nullius*, see *supra*, p. 180.

[2] Cf. Oppenheim i. 615, n. 5; *People* v. *Lol-Lo and Saraw*, *Ann. Digest* 1 (1919–22), no. 112.

[3] Defined in Article 17: 'A ship or aircraft is considered a pirate ship or aircraft if it is intended by the persons in dominant control to be used for the purpose of committing one of the acts referred to in article 15. The same applies if the ship or aircraft has been used to commit any such act, so long as it remains under the control of the persons guilty of that act.' (And see also the Informal Composite Negotiating Text of 1977, Article 103.)

[4] And see also the Informal Composite Negotiating Text of 1977, Article 105.

[5] See Wortley, 24 *B.Y.* (1947), 258–72; id., 33 *Grot. Soc.* (1948), 25–35. According to English law the crew of a British warship capturing the pirate is entitled to a salvage of 12½ per cent: Piracy Act, 1850, sect. 5.

[6] See generally *supra*, pp. 242–3.

legal controls in respect of those not identifiable with a state on which responsibility may be placed. Thus Hall[1] considered piracy to include acts done 'by persons not acting under the authority of any politically organized community, notwithstanding that the objects of the persons so acting may be professedly political'. The categories of act causing difficulties of classification will now be briefly reviewed.

Insurgency. Ships controlled by insurgents may not, without a recognition of belligerency by third states,[2] exercise belligerent rights against the shipping of other states. Forcible interference of this kind is unauthorized by law and may be resisted by all available means. However, it is very doubtful if it is correct to characterize such acts as piracy,[3] and this proposition is reinforced by the terms of the Convention on the High Seas. However, it may be that it is lawful to punish acts constituting *mala prohibita*—murder, robbery, and so on—carried out *ultra vires* by insurgents.[4] Opinions which favour the treatment of insurgents as such as 'pirates' are surely incorrect.[5]

Unlawful acts committed with the authority of a lawful government. Illegal attacks on or seizures of innocent merchant ships by warships or government ships result in the delictual responsibility of the aggressor's flag state, but the offending ships do not become pirate ships.[6] Again, a privateer, authorized by a belligerent to act in her service, is not a pirate,[7] even if acts of violence are committed against neutral ships.[8] In the latter case the belligerent is responsible as principal.

Politically motivated operations by organized groups. Harassing operations by organized groups deploying forces on the high seas may have political objectives, and yet may be neither connected with insurgency against a particular government nor performed by agents of a lawful government. Ships threatened by

[1] 8th ed., p. 314 (and see p. 311). See also Johnson, op. cit., p. 77 n.

[2] *Supra*, p. 90, n. 2.

[3] For the view doubted see: Hall, pp. 314, 318–19; Oppenheim i. 610–12; Law Officers of the Crown *in re* the *Huascar* incident in 1877 (McNair, *Opinions* i. 274–80); Lauterpacht, 46 *R.G.D.I.P.* (1939), 513–49; Secretariat Memo., *Yrbk., I.L.C.* (1950), ii. 70. See further van Zwanenberg, 10 *I.C.L.Q.* (1961), 798–817; Green, 37 *B.Y.* (1961), 496–505.

[4] See the Convention on the Rights and Duties of States in the Event of Civil Strife, 1928; Hudson, *Int. Legis.* iv. no. 195.

[5] See an American court in the case of the *Ambrose Light* [1885] 25 Fed. Rep. 408; Hudson, p. 132.

[6] *Supra*, pp. 243–5; Oppenheim i. 609–10; McNair i. 267, 268.

[7] McNair iii. 82–9; Hall, p. 316.

[8] *Contra*, Oppenheim i. 610. If a neutral vessel took letters of marque from both belligerents its actions might well be regarded as 'for private ends' and therefore piratical.

such activities may be protected, and yet the aggressors may not be regarded as pirates.

Unrestricted submarine warfare. The term 'piracy' is employed on occasion to describe acts by ships acting on the orders of a recognized government 'which are in gross breach of International Law and which show a criminal disregard of human life'.[1] Thus by the Nyon Agreement of 14 September 1937[2] eight states agreed on collective measures 'against piratical acts by submarines' with regard to attacks on merchant ships in the Mediterranean during the Spanish Civil War. The acts were stated to be 'acts contrary to the most elementary dictates of humanity which should be justly treated as acts of piracy'. In this case the condemnation rests on the convention, and the use of the term 'piracy' adds nothing to the legal result.

(iii) *The right of approach in time of peace.*[3] In order to make a success of the system for maintaining order on the high seas, reviewed earlier, it is necessary to provide for an approach by warships in order to verify the identity and nationality of ships. Such a right of approach (*droit d'approche; enquête ou vérification du pavillon; reconnaissance*) is recognized by customary law. The right of approach exists in all circumstances, but does not involve the actual examination of papers or seizure of the vessel.[4]

(iv) *Visit, search, and capture in time of peace.*[5] There is no general power of police exercisable over foreign merchant ships, and the occasion on which ships can be visited and seized by warships in time of peace are limited. In a report of a Law Officer of the Crown of 25 October 1854 there appears the statement:[6] 'I have further to observe that all interference with British Vessels on the High Seas by the Mexican Authorities

[1] See Oppenheim i. 612.

[2] Treaty Series, no. 38 (1937); 31 *A.J.* (1937), Suppl., p. 179. See also the unratified Treaty of Washington, 1922, Art. 3; 16 *A.J.* (1922), Suppl., p. 57 (attacks on merchant ships contrary to the laws of war); and Johnson, op. cit., pp. 81–5.

[3] Oppenheim i. 604; Gidel i. 299; Colombos, p. 311; Report by François, *Yrbk., I.L.C.* (1950), ii. 41; Second Report by François, ibid. (1951), ii. 81; the *Marianna Flora* (1826), 11 Wheaton 1. See also, note 5 *infra*.

[4] The treatments in Oppenheim, Colombos, and other Anglo-American sources do not show clarity on this point. In the context of piracy the right of approach tends to merge with the right of visit and capture. See Gidel i. 290–3; and the reports by François *supra*, n. 3.

[5] McNair, *Opinions* i. 229–45; Colombos, pp. 310–14; Gidel i. 288–300; McDougal and Burke, pp. 885–93; van Zwanenberg, 10 *I.C.L.Q.* (1961), 785–93; O'Connell ii. 645–7.

[6] McNair, op. cit., p. 233. Note 1 on p. 231 reads: 'It is believed that, apart from cases of suspected piracy . . . and cases permitted by treaty (e.g. slave traffic treaties), Great Britain has always resisted the visit and search of her merchant ships on the high seas in time of peace. . . .' See also the U.S. Dept. of State memo. and diplomatic correspondence set out in Hackworth ii. 659–65; and Moore, *Digest* ii. 987–1001.

on any pretence beyond the limit of three miles from the shore is *prima facie* illegal. No general right of search of foreign ships can be claimed on the High Seas by any Nation not a belligerent.'

The jurists have generally agreed that a right to resort to a threat or use of force to effect visit, search, and, if justified, seizure of a ship[1] only existed in the case of a known pirate ship or a ship the behaviour of which gave reasonable grounds for suspecting her of piracy.[2] This proposition is a corollary of the principle of the freedom of the seas and also of the rule that in general a merchant ship can only be boarded by a warship flying the same flag and therefore having a right of jurisdiction.[3] British and American jurisprudence refused to admit a right of visit in the case of ships suspected of taking part in the slave trade,[4] and, apart from piracy, the right could only exist on the basis of treaty or if a ship refused to show its flag.

The legal regime outlined here has met with three threats to its stability. The first, attempts to extend the concept of piracy, has been noticed already.[5] Claims to a right of self-defence on the high seas constitute another source of instability, and some writers, having presented a strict regime in the matter of visit, somewhat inconsistently refer later to a right of self-defence without defining its limits. The third source of confusion lies in the definition of the right of approach or verification of flag. Some English writers link this closely with the right of visit and lay down the conditions for visit in seemingly expansive terms requiring only 'suspicion' of piracy.[6] However, it was realized by governments in the last century that the right of visit could be

[1] As a matter of customary law visit, search, and capture are a legal unity. For an attempt to distinguish visit and search see Wilson, 44 *A.J.* (1950), p. 505 at p. 516. The right to interfere may be delimited by treaty: see the International Convention for the Protection of Submarine Telegraph Cables, 1884, Art. 10.

[2] Gidel i. 301, 303, 355; Colombos, p. 310–11; Briggs, p. 389; Brierly (6th ed.), pp. 306–7; Wheaton, *Elements* (1866), sect. 106; Moore, *Digest* ii. 886; Guggenheim i. 449–50; Rousseau, pp. 418 seq.; Hyde i. 764.

[3] In the judgment in the *Lotus* case, P.C.I.J., Ser. A/10, p. 25, the Permanent Court expressed the rule: 'Vessels on the high seas are subject to no authority except that of the State whose flag they fly. In virtue of the principle of the freedom of the seas, that is to say, the absence of any territorial sovereignty upon the high seas, no State may exercise any kind of jurisdiction over foreign vessels upon them.' Cf. the *Jessie*, etc. (1921), *R.I.A.A.* vi. 57; the *Wanderer* (1921), ibid., 68.

[4] See the decisions of Lord Stowell in *Le Louis* (1817), 2 Dods. 210; Green, p. 487; Pitt Cobbett i. 302; and of the U.S. Supreme Court in the *Antelope* (1825), 10 Wheaton 66. See further Moore, *Digest* ii. 914–18.

[5] *Supra*, pp. 245–6. Activities described there as illegal may give rise to rights of self-defence but not *ipso facto* to a right of visit, search, and capture (except perhaps when insurgent vessels have foreign nationals on board).

[6] See Oppenheim i. 604, 605; Colombos, p. 311.

abused and that there must be reasonable ground for suspicion, for example a refusal by a ship to hoist her flag.[1]

The provisions of the Convention on the High Seas in general confirm the validity of the strict regime in these matters and include slaving as a justification for visit:

Article 22. 1. Except where acts of interference derive from powers conferred by treaty, a warship which encounters a foreign merchant ship on the high seas is not justified in boarding her unless there is reasonable ground for suspecting:[2]

(a) That the ship is engaged in piracy; or
(b) That the ship is engaged in the slave trade; or
(c) That, though flying a foreign flag or refusing to show its flag, the ship is, in reality, of the same nationality as the warship.

2. In the cases provided for in sub-paragraphs (a), (b) and (c) above, the warship may proceed to verify the ship's right to fly its flag. To this end, it may send a boat under the command of an officer to the suspected ship. If suspicion remains after the documents have been checked, it may proceed to a further examination on board the ship, which must be carried out with all possible consideration.

3. If the suspicions prove to be unfounded, and provided that the ship boarded has not committed any act justifying them, it shall be compensated for any loss or damage that may have been sustained.

A few comments may be made. The right to board a foreign merchant ship is conditional on the existence of 'reasonable ground' for suspecting piracy etc. This would be difficult to establish in areas of the high seas in which piracy and the slave trade are unknown. Moreover, the act of boarding, even when 'reasonable ground' for boarding existed, is a privilege, and, if no act justifying the suspicions has been committed by the ship boarded, there is strict liability, and the flag state of the warship must compensate for 'any loss or damage'.[3] In its comment[4] the International Law Commission stated that the severe penalty 'seems justified in order to prevent the right of visit being abused'.

[1] See Gidel i. 299; Colombos, pp. 312–13; McNair, *Opinions* i. 233, 240 ('vehement suspicion of Piracy'); Hall, pp. 317–18 ('when weighty reasons exist for suspecting'); François, Second Report, *Yrbk., I.L.C.* (1951), ii. 81–3.

[2] In the Informal Composite Negotiating Text of 1977 (Third United Nations Conference) Article 110 adds the cases of unauthorized broadcasting (see Article 109) and that the ship is without nationality.

[3] In the comment on the I.L.C. draft the Yugoslav Government thought that the search of merchant ships by warships should not be discouraged by too strict sanctions: 'It is necessary therefore to consider whether a provision should be inserted freeing the warship from *damnum emergens*, if *dolus* or *culpa lata* cannot be charged to the warship.' (*Yrbk., I.L.C.* (1956), ii. 97.) Cf. the *Marianna Flora* (1826), 11 Wheaton 1; Moore, *Digest* ii. 886.

[4] *Yrbk., I.L.C.* (1956), ii. 284.

(v) *The right of self-defence.* The particular claim to visit and seize vessels on the high seas may take the form of a 'security zone', a 'defence zone', or a 'neutrality zone', and the legality of these zones has been considered briefly in Chapter IX. However, quite apart from claims to contiguous and other zones some states, and particularly the United Kingdom, have on occasion asserted a right to use force to detain vessels on the ground of security or self-defence, and many of the English authorities support such a right.[1] Nevertheless it may be said here that the legal basis of such a right, in the absence of an attack on other shipping by the vessel sought to be detained, is lacking. In the present context it is significant that the International Law Commission, and the majority of states, do not accept the legality of security zones and therefore are unlikely to regard an ambulatory exercise of a right of (anticipatory) self-defence with any favour. In its comment on the draft article which later appeared as Article 22 of the Convention on the High Seas the Commission stated:[2]

> The question arose whether the right to board a vessel should be recognized also in the event of a ship being suspected of committing acts hostile to the State to which the warship belongs, at a time of imminent danger to the security of that State. The Commission did not deem it advisable to include such a provision, mainly because of the vagueness of terms like 'imminent danger' and 'hostile acts', which leaves them open to abuse.

(vi) *Blockade and contraband.* In time of war the exercise of belligerent rights will be justified and may take the form of a blockade of the enemy's ports and coast. Enforcement of the blockade may take place on the high seas adjoining the coast, and neutral merchant ships may be confiscated if they attempt to break the blockade. The right of visit, search, and capture may be exercised against neutral ships carrying contraband or engaged in acts of unneutral service.[3]

(vii) *The right of hot pursuit;* droit de poursuite.[4] The law as

[1] See e.g. Colombos, pp. 314–15; Hall, p. 328. See also U.S. memo. in *Yrbk., I.L.C.* (1950), ii. 61–2. Generally on the use of force under this title see Brownlie, *International Law and the Use of Force by States*, pp. 305–8.

[2] *Yrbk., I.L.C.* (1956), ii. 284. See also the Secretariat Memo., *Yrbk., I.L.C.* (1950), ii. 71; and the view of the Commission on security zones, *supra*, p. 213.

[3] For useful accounts see Colombos, Chaps. XVII–XX.

[4] Gidel iii. 339–60; Colombos, pp. 168–75; McDougal and Burke, pp. 893–923; Glanville Williams, 20 *B.Y.* (1939), 83–97; Beck, 9 *Can. B.R.* (1931), 176–202, 249–70, 341–65; Hackworth ii. 700–9; Report by François, *Yrbk., I.L.C.* (1950), ii. 43–5; Second Report by François, ibid. (1951), ii. 89–91; Bowett, *Self-Defence in International Law*, pp. 82–6; Briggs, pp. 385–8; McNair, *Opinions* i. 253–5; Whiteman iv. 677–87. Whilst not the *ratio decidendi*, the question of hot pursuit was among the issues raised by the *I'm Alone*

understood in the nineteenth century, and its rationale, is expressed by Hall as follows:[1]

> . . . when a vessel, or some one on board her, while within foreign territory commits an infraction of its laws she may be pursued into the open seas, and there arrested. It must be added that this can only be done when the pursuit is commenced while the vessel is still within the territorial waters or has only just escaped from them. The reason for the permission seems to be that pursuit under these circumstances is a continuation of an act of jurisdiction which has been begun, or which but for the accident of immediate escape would have been begun, within the territory itself, and that it is necessary to permit it in order to enable the territorial jurisdiction to be efficiently exercised.

The right of pursuit[2] is thus an act of necessity, institutionalized and delimited by state practice. In its present form it had appeared in Anglo-American practice in the first half of the nineteenth century, and it was not until the Hague Codification of 1930 that there was sufficient evidence of general recognition by states. Article 11 of the regulations adopted by the second committee of the Conference provided the basis for the draft article adopted by the International Law Commission,[3] which, with some amendment, became Article 23 of the Convention on the High Seas.

Paragraph 1 of Article 23 provides:

> The hot pursuit of a foreign ship may be undertaken when the competent authorities of the coastal State have good reason to believe that the ship has violated the laws and regulations of that State. Such pursuit must be commenced when the foreign ship or one of its boats[4] is within the internal waters or the territorial sea or the contiguous zone of the pursuing State, and may only be continued outside the territorial sea or the contiguous zone if the pursuit has not been interrupted. It is not necessary that, at the time when the foreign ship within the territorial sea or the contiguous zone receives the order to stop, the ship giving the order should likewise be within

arbitration between the United States and Canada (1933–5); *R.I.A.A.* iii. 1609; Green, p. 472; Briggs, p. 385. For discussion of the case see Fitzmaurice, 17 *B.Y.* (1936), 82–111; McDougal and Burke, pp. 900–1.

[1] p. 309 (written in the first ed., 1880). The Canadian courts relied on Hall to a great extent in the *North* (1905), 11 Exch. Rep. 141; (1906), 37 S.C.R. 385; 2 *A.J.* (1908), 688; Hudson, p. 361.

[2] For other legal contexts in which the right might appear see Glanville Williams, op. cit.

[3] See *Yrbk., I.L.C.* (1956), ii. 284–5.

[4] Note the restrictive effect of the words 'one of its boats' (see *Yrbk., I.L.C.* (1956), ii. 285) and the different effect of paragraph 3. On the doctrine of 'constructive presence' see the *Araunah* (1888); Moore, *Arbitrations*, p. 824; McNair, *Opinions* i. 245; the *Grace and Ruby* (1922), 283 Fed. 475; Briggs, p. 360; the *Henry L. Marshall* (1923), 292 Fed. 486; François, Second Report, *Yrbk., I.L.C.* (1951), ii. 89; Masterson, *Jurisdiction in Marginal Seas*, pp. 308–21; McNair, *Opinions* i. 245.

the territorial sea or the contiguous zone.[1] If the foreign ship is within a contiguous zone, as defined in article 24 of the Convention on the Territorial Sea and the Contiguous Zone, the pursuit may only be undertaken if there has been a violation of the rights for the protection of which the zone was established.[2]

The British position has been to oppose any right of pursuit commencing within a contiguous zone,[3] but some continental[4] and American[5] opinions have been otherwise. The draft articles produced by the International Law Commission[6] provided that, whilst pursuit may *commence* in the contiguous zone, acts committed in the contiguous zone cannot confer a right of pursuit. However, during the Conference on the Law of the Sea a proposal was accepted to insert the words 'or the contiguous zone' in four places in the draft article. Sir Gerald Fitzmaurice[7] has argued that the paragraph provides for pursuit from a contiguous zone only if there 'has been a violation', a phrase appearing in the final sentence; and thus the right of pursuit only applies in respect of outgoing ships as regards violations already committed by them in the coastal state's internal waters or territorial sea. With respect, this construction is at variance both with the text of the article as a whole and with the *travaux préparatoires*.[8] Pursuit and arrest may relate to acts committed within the contiguous zone.

Paragraph 2 of the article is uncontroversial: 'The right of hot pursuit ceases as soon as the ship pursued enters the territorial sea of its own country or of a third state.'[9] Paragraph 3 states the conditions on which pursuit may commence:[1]

> Hot pursuit is not deemed to have begun unless the pursuing ship has satisfied itself by such practicable means as may be available that the ship pursued or one of its boats or other craft working as a team and using the ship pursued as a mother ship are within the limits of the territorial sea, or as the case may be within the contiguous zone. The pursuit may only be com-

[1] Thus patrol vessels will often cruise just outside the territorial sea.

[2] See also the Informal Composite Negotiating Text of 1977 (Third United Nations Conference), Article 111, para. 1.

[3] See Fitzmaurice, 8 *I.C.L.Q.* (1959), 115–17; *Yrbk., I.L.C.* (1956), ii. 82.

[4] Gidel iii. 348–9; François, Second Report, p. 90.

[5] Judicial interpretation of the Anglo-American Liquor Treaty, 1924, e.g. in the *Vinces* (1927), 20 Fed. (2d) 164, 174–5; U.S. arguments in the *I'm Alone* case.

[6] *Yrbk., I.L.C.* (1956), ii. 284–5.

[7] 31 *B.Y.* (1954), p. 380; and in 8 *I.C.L.Q.* (1959), 116.

[8] See McDougal and Burke, pp. 906–8, 910–13.

[9] See Colombos, p. 171; and the American-Chilean Claims Commission in the *Itata*, Moore, *Arbitrations*, iii. 3067.

[1] Cf. Glanville Williams, op. cit., p. 96 n. 5; François, Second Report, *ubi supra*.

menced after a visual or auditory signal to stop has been given at a distance which enables it to be seen or heard by the foreign ship.

Paragraph 4 stipulates that pursuit must be undertaken by warships, military aircraft,[1] 'or other ships or aircraft on government service specially authorized to that effect'.[2]

Paragraph 7 provides for compensation for 'any loss or damage' consequent on unjustified exercise of the right of pursuit. The criterion here is presumably the existence of reasonable ground for suspicion, since paragraph 1 refers to 'good reason' for belief that a violation of the laws of the coastal state has occurred, and the text of paragraph 7 differs significantly from the form of Article 22, paragraph 3.[3]

The Informal Composite Negotiating Text of 1977 (Third United Nations Conference) provides that the right of hot pursuit shall apply to violations of laws of the coastal state relating to and occurring in the exclusive economic zone and on the continental shelf (Article 111, para. 2).

(viii) *Ships flying without a flag*. Ships flying no flag, and refusing to show a flag when called upon to do so in a proper manner, may be boarded by the ships of any state.

(b) *Restrictions by treaty*.[4] Treaties conferring powers of visit and capture above and beyond those permitted to states by the customary law relate to a variety of subject-matter. Great Britain was a party to numerous bilateral treaties after 1815 concerning repression of the slave trade, and on 20 December 1841 the Treaty of London, to which five states became parties,[5] was concluded. This provided that warships with special warrants could search, detain, or send in for trial suspected merchant ships flying the flags of contracting states. The General Act for the Repression of the Slave Trade, signed at Brussels on 2 July 1890, provided for a limited right of search of suspected vessels in a defined zone.[6] The General Act was in major part abrogated

[1] In this respect the Convention developed the law. See also para. 5 of Article 23.

[2] The latter category comprehends customs and police vessels. The ship finally arresting need not necessarily be the same as the one which began the pursuit, but must not be a mere interceptor. Cf. the facts of the *I'm Alone* case. The validity of an arrest is not affected by the fact that the ship arrested was escorted across a portion of the high seas (paragraph 6).

[3] Cf. the provision on visit on the high seas, *supra*, p. 249; and see Glanville Williams, op. cit., p. 96, n. 2, and Colombos, p. 168. Paragraph 7 is, however, not unequivocal.

[4] It will be noticed that questions to which the Convention on the High Seas relates have been considered already since for the most part the provisions are closely related to general international law.

[5] Austria, Great Britain, Prussia, and Russia. Belgium acceded. France signed but did not ratify.

[6] U.N. Legis. Series, *The High Seas* i. 269.

as between parties to the Treaty of St. Germain, and the Slavery Conventions of 1926 and 1956 do not provide for visit, search, and seizure: such a power is provided for, however, in Article 23 of the Convention on the High Seas. Mutual powers of visit and search are provided for in the Convention for the Regulation of the Police of the Fisheries in the North Sea of 1882[1] and the Convention concerning the Abolition of the Liquor Traffic among the Fishermen of the North Sea of 1887.[2] Similar powers are conferred by bilateral treaties the parties to which are concerned to conserve fish stocks, to control smuggling, or to repress certain aspects of the trade in arms. The important multilateral Convention for the Protection of Submarine Cables of 1884, in Article 10, confers the right to stop and verify the nationality of merchant ships suspected of breaking the treaty on warships of the signatories.[3] The relevant provisions of the Convention on the High Seas (Articles 26 to 29) do not refer to such a right, but the Convention[4] is not intended to supersede the Convention of 1884 automatically. States have also been willing to provide for the mutual exercise of the right of hot pursuit in treaties.

5. *Jurisdiction over Ships on the High Seas*

The Convention on the High Seas of 1958 affirms the general principle enunciated by the Permanent Court in the *Lotus* case:[5] 'Vessels on the high seas are subject to no authority except that of the State whose flag they fly. In virtue of the principle of the freedom of the seas, that is to say, the absence of any territorial sovereignty upon the high seas, no State may exercise any kind of jurisdiction over foreign vessels upon them.' Thus Article 6, paragraph 1, of the Convention provides that 'Ships shall sail under the flag of one State only and, save in exceptional cases expressly provided for in international treaties or in these articles, shall be subject to its exclusive jurisdiction on the high seas'. The exceptions in the Convention, dealt with earlier, are piracy, the

[1] 73 *B.F.S.P.* 39. Parties formerly: Belgium, Denmark, France, Germany, Great Britain, and Holland. The Treaty has been denounced by several parties, including the U.K. [2] 79 *B.F.S.P.* 894.

[3] The parties numbered 26, including Great Britain. Text: U.N. Legis. Series, *The High Seas* i. 251. See also McDougal and Burke, p. 843; Franklin, U.S. Naval War College liii; *The Law of the Sea: Some Recent Developments*, pp. 157–78; Whiteman iv. 727–39.

[4] Article 30 provides: 'The provisions of this Convention shall not affect Conventions or other international agreements already in force, as between States Parties to them.'

[5] (1927), P.C.I.J., Ser. A, no. 10, p. 25.

slave trade, hot pursuit, and the right of approach by warships where reasonable grounds exist for suspecting that a ship is of the same nationality as the warship.[1]

Article 11, paragraph 1, of the Convention provides:[2] 'In the event of a collision or of any other incident of navigation[3] concerning a ship on the high seas, involving the penal or disciplinary responsibility of the master or of any other person in the service of the ship, no penal or disciplinary proceedings may be instituted against such persons except before the judicial or administrative authorities either of the flag State or[4] of the State of which such person is a national.' This provision negatives the decision of the Permanent Court in the *Lotus*[5] case and reflects the view of the International Law Commission.[6] In its commentary on the relevant draft article, the Commission commented on the *Lotus* case as follows:

> This judgement, which was carried by the President's casting vote after an equal vote of six to six, was very strongly criticized and caused serious disquiet in international maritime circles. A diplomatic conference held at Brussels in 1952 disagreed with the conclusions of the judgment. The Commission concurred with the decisions of the conference, which were embodied in the International Convention for the Unification of Certain Rules relating to Penal Jurisdiction in matters of Collisions and Other Incidents of Navigation. . . .[7] It did so with the object of protecting ships and their crews from the risk of penal proceedings before foreign courts in the event of collision on the high seas, since such proceedings may constitute an intolerable interference with international navigation.

6. *Oil Pollution Casualties and 'Pirate' Radio*

States may claim special zones of jurisdiction over areas of high sea adjacent to their coasts in order to regulate activities of various kinds: the contiguous zone and certain other claims have

[1] *Supra*, p. 249.

[2] See also paragraph 3: 'No arrest or detention of the ship, even as a measure of investigation, shall be ordered by any authorities other than those of the flag State.' See also the Informal Composite Negotiating Text of 1977 (Third United Nations Conference), Article 97.

[3] e.g. damage to a submarine telegraph, telephone, or high voltage cable or pipeline.

[4] Thus states issuing certificates of competence and the like may wish to consider the conduct of the holders serving on board foreign vessels: hence the reference also to 'disciplinary proceedings'.

[5] Considered also *infra*, p. 301.

[6] *Yrbk., I.L.C.* (1956), ii. 281. See also François, ibid. (1950), ii. 38, 39–40; Secretariat Memo., ibid., pp. 74–5; François, ibid. (1951), ii. 77–80; ibid. (1952), ii. 45–6; ibid. (1953), ii. 51–3; ibid. (1954), ii. 13; Gidel i. 281; Oppenheim i. 334; O'Connell, pp. 654–5; Whiteman ix. 58–62; Brierly, 44 *L.Q.R.* (1928), 154–63; McNair, *Opinions* ii. 180–85; Fischer Williams, *Chapters*, pp. 209–31 (and in 35 *R.G.D.I.P.* (1928), 361–76); Verzijl, 55 *R.D.I.L.C.* (1928), 1–32.

[7] Signed at Brussels 10 May 1952; Cmd. 8954.

been examined elsewhere.[1] Recently, a number of incidents have raised new problems relating to control of sources of harm to the coastal states, and perhaps states generally, which are sited beyond the territorial sea or any existing contiguous zone. Major accidents involving large tankers may release huge quantities of oil. The *Torrey Canyon*, registered in Liberia, ran aground on a reef off the Cornish coast in 1967 and lost some 60,000 tons of oil. The British Government ordered that the wreck be bombed, after salvage attempts had failed, in order to reduce the pollution. Even so, British and French coasts received serious pollution. This type of incident raises a variety of interesting legal issues.[2] Remedial action may be justified on the ground of necessity (but not of self-defence). The status of the Canadian anti-pollution zone in the Arctic is considered elsewhere.[3] Agreement on the use of remedial measures against ships of other nations on the high seas is obviously desirable and events led to the signing in Brussels in 1969 of an International Convention Relating to Intervention on the High Seas in Cases of Oil Pollution Casualties.[4] The discharge of oil into the sea by ships is regulated by conventions.[5]

The use of ships, aircraft, or installations fixed on a continental shelf, outside the territorial sea of any state, for broadcasting unregulated by any national legal system, has increased of late. This is regarded as a threat to national interests by states at whose population the broadcasts are aimed and may cause interference with licensed broadcasts and frequencies used for distress calls. Moreover, international regulation of telecommunications and allocation of radio frequencies depends upon the capacity of states to regulate these matters through their legal systems.[6] The Netherlands has based certain claims to control pirate radio upon the protective principle of jurisdiction.[7] The United Kingdom has preferred to take measures carefully restricted to the exercise

[1] *Supra*, pp. 209 seq.

[2] See Brown, 21 *Curr. Leg. Problems* (1968), 113–36; Queneudec, *Ann. français* (1968), 701–18.

[3] *Supra*, p. 221.

[4] Text: 64 *A.J.* (1970), 471; 9 *Int. Leg. Materials* (1970), 25.

[5] Int. Conv. for the Prevention of Pollution of the Sea by Oil, 1954; 327 U.N.T.S., p. 3; amended, 1962, *Treaty Series* No. 59 (1967), Cmnd. 3354; Agreement for Co-operation in Dealing with Pollution of the North Sea by Oil, 1969; *Treaty Series* No. 78 (1969), Cmnd. 4205. See further Green, 50 *Oregon L.R.* (1971), 462–90; Caflisch, 8 *Revue belge* (1972), 7–33.

[6] Generally on 'pirate' radio see: Evensen, 115 Hague *Recueil* (1965, II), 563–78; Bowett, *The Law of the Sea*, pp. 52–5; van Panhuys and van Emde Boas, 60 *A.J.* (1966), 303–41; Hunnings, 14 *I.C.L.Q.* (1965), 410–36; François, 12 *Neths. Int. L.R.* (1965), 113–23; Bos, ibid., 337–64; Woodliffe, ibid., 365–84; Sørensen, in *Festschrift Castberg* (1963), pp. 319–31; Whiteman ix. 789–809.

[7] See further *supra*, p. 233; *infra*, p. 303.

of territorial jurisdiction.[1] The Council of Europe sponsored the conclusion in 1965 of an Agreement for the Prevention of Broadcasts Transmitted from Stations outside National Territories.[2] This provides for the use, in effective co-ordination, of criminal sanctions in national legal systems, aimed both at nationals and aliens. The provisions of the Convention are concerned to punish acts supporting 'pirate' broadcasting which are committed *within* the national jurisdiction of the states which are parties and do not warrant external interference with foreign ships, aircraft, or nationals. The Informal Composite Negotiating Text of 1977 (Third United Nations Conference on the Law of the Sea) provides for broad bases of jurisdiction and powers of arrest in respect of 'the transmission of sound radio or television broadcasts from a ship or installation on the high seas intended for reception by the general public contrary to international regulations, but excluding the transmission of distress calls' (Article 109).

[1] See the Marine Broadcasting (Offences) Act 1967.
[2] U.K. *Treaty Series* No. 1, 1968, Cmnd. 3497; 4 *Int. Leg. Materials* (1965), 115.

PART V

COMMON AMENITIES AND CO-OPERATION IN THE USE OF RESOURCES

CHAPTER XII

COMMON AMENITIES AND CO-OPERATION IN THE USE OF RESOURCES

1. *Introduction*

INTERNATIONAL law has tended so far to ape the individualistic manners of municipal law. Apart from the concept of *res communis*,[1] as applied to the high seas and outer space, international law depends to a great extent on 'voluntarist' devices, in the form of concessions by private law methods, treaties, and various types of international agencies and organizations, in order to provide access to resources outside national territory. Indeed, the use of 'voluntarist' devices in the political conditions of the past has led to a situation where the law, as applied by some states, had prevented a weak or ex-colonial state from having a reasonable level of command over its own resources and general economy: however, issues concerning vested rights[2] and expropriation[3] are considered elsewhere. Apart from these questions of economic self-determination, the subject as a whole is concerned with machinery and organization and also the influence of technical considerations to a degree uncommon in other areas of the law. Co-operation may take the form of internationalization of a territory,[4] a qualitative change in its status, but this type of regime is more often employed to provide a solution to territorial problems creating political disputes and to maintain local conditions conducive to the maintenance of peace and security. In the subjects now to be considered customary international law plays a role, and at times a dynamic role,

[1] *Supra*, p. 181. [2] *Infra*, pp. 653–8. [3] *Infra*, pp. 531 seq.

[4] See Ydit, *Internationalized Territories* (1961); Mouton, 107 Hague *Recueil* (1962, III), 269–76. On Antarctica see *infra*, pp. 265–6.

but caution may be needed to avoid giving normative effect to rules which merely reflect local or temporary factors. It must also be observed that the agenda must tend to grow with changes in technology, and lawyers are already concerned with activities which radically affect the environment of the earth, such as weapon testing and experiments in weather control.[1]

2. *Economic Aid*

Though some distance from a genuine sharing of world resources, both of material wealth and of skill and knowledge, the provision of economic aid and technical assistance to underdeveloped areas is an object of the first importance in creating conditions of justice and stable foundations for peace. The United Nations Charter, in Chapters IX and X, recognizes the urgent need to deal with economic and social problems, and certain of its provisions create obligations for governments to maintain human rights. There is probably also a collective duty of member states to take responsible action to create reasonable living standards both for their own peoples and for those of other states.[2] The means by which economic aid may be provided are varied and include loans by governments, construction or technical assistance projects with no provision for payment or collateral advantages, loans by specialized agencies of the United Nations, and loans from, and aid projects supported by, private corporations with or without government sponsorship and support, for example by the requirement of guarantees from the recipient state on the international plane. These various forms of aid give rise to issues of private and public international law, although governments and corporations adopt devices to prevent issues arising from loans and concessions going before the national jurisdiction of the recipient or 'host' state.[3] Delicate problems in the law of diplomatic protection appear, some of which will be considered in Chapter XXI.[4]

The objectives of aid must be lawful, and aid agreements may

[1] See the *Draft Rules Concerning Changes in the Environment of the Earth*, David Davies Memorial Institute of International Studies (London, 1964); Stockholm Conference, Decl. on the Human Environment, 16 June 1972; 11 *Int. Leg. Materials* (1972), 1416.

[2] See Resol. 1316 (XIII) of the U.N. General Assembly, 12 December 1958, which refers to Art. 56 of the Charter; and Resol. 2158 (XXI) on Permanent Sovereignty over Natural Resources, 25 November 1966; 6 *Int. Leg. Materials* (1967), 147. See further Wilkins, 55 *California L.R.* (1967), 977–1019. For a criticism of the view expressed in the text: Johnson, 83 *L.Q.R.* (1967), 463.

[3] See Sereni, 96 Hague *Recueil* (1959, I), 133–237.

[4] *Infra*, pp. 480 seq.

be affected by the *jus cogens*[1] and thus, for example, should not be intended to further preparation for unlawful resort to force. Nor should aid be given under conditions which lead to infringement of the principles of the sovereign equality of states and of permanent sovereignty over natural resources.[2] In 1964 the United Nations Conference on Trade and Development recommended certain principles to be observed in the giving of aid.[3]

A high proportion of aid is given on the basis of bilateral agreements, and so it is subject to conditions imposed by the giving states, whilst its incidence is governed by political factors. Some technical assistance programmes are sponsored by the United Nations directly by means of the United Nations technical assistance programme. The Special United Nations Fund for Economic Development, and the Expanded Programme of Technical Assistance were merged in 1965 as the United Nations Development Programme.[4] Matters of study, planning, and expert advice on co-ordination of policies of states are within the sphere of the four United Nations Economic Commissions for Europe, Asia and the Far East, Latin America, and Africa. Apart from these sources the International Bank for Reconstruction and Development and its affiliates[5] provide very large sums for development projects. The Bank has the primary purpose of assisting in the reconstruction and development of its member countries by facilitating the investment of capital for productive purposes. The Bank is a specialized agency of the United Nations, but has more autonomy than other such agencies. Unfortunately, in its long-term loan operations, it is confined to promotion of private enterprise, and there is discrimination in favour of governments willing to pursue *laissez-faire* policies. Moreover, all members of the Bank must be members of the International Monetary Fund and comply with its policy.

In 1964 the United Nations Conference on Trade and Development (UNCTAD) was established as a subsidiary organ of the General Assembly of the United Nations. In 1966 the United

[1] See *infra*, pp. 512–15.

[2] *Infra*, pp. 287 seq., 540. These principles may also be considered to be a part of the *jus cogens*.

[3] *U.N. Monthly Chronicle* (July 1964), p. 49.

[4] *Yrbk. of the U.N.* (1965), 283–300.

[5] The International Development Association and the International Finance Corporation. Institutions serving Communist states are the Council for Mutual Economic Assistance and the International Bank for Economic Co-operation: see Grzybowski, *The Socialist Commonwealth of Nations, Organizations and Institutions* (1964); Agoston, *Le Marché Commun Communiste* (2nd ed., 1965); and 3 *Int. Leg. Materials*, 324. Regional institutions include the Inter-American, Asian, and African Development Banks.

Nations Capital Development Fund was brought into operation also as a subsidiary organ of the General Assembly.[1] A further, associated, step was the establishment in 1966 of the United Nations Industrial Development Organization (UNIDO).[2]

3. *Access to Resources: the Peaceful Uses of Atomic Energy*

By analogy with the legal duty which may exist to provide economic aid to underdeveloped countries, it is possible to suggest that there is a general duty to provide access to resources under reasonable conditions binding all states. However, it is not easy to describe the precise incidents of such a duty in respect of resources governed by a regime of territorial sovereignty, and the real issues relate to forms of organization between states rather than general legal principles. Because of its importance, the relation to questions of security and disarmament, and the immense cost of development, the utilization of atomic energy for peaceful purposes has been a fruitful field for co-operation between states and between organizations and states. The most important organization, the International Atomic Energy Agency, was established in 1957[3] and has a relationship agreement with the United Nations. The Agency provides assistance of various kinds for the development of atomic energy in particular states under a system of inspection and control to ensure, *inter alia*, that the aid is not used for military purposes. Other organizations and agencies existing include the European Atomic Energy Community (Euratom),[4] the European Nuclear Agency of O.E.E.C.,[5] the Moscow Joint Institute for Nuclear Research,[6] the European Organization for Nuclear Research,[7] and the Inter-American Nuclear Energy Commission.[8]

[1] *Yrbk. of the U.N.* (1966), 285–91.

[2] *Yrbk. of the U.N.* (1965), 338–47; (1966), 297–301. See Gutteridge, *The United Nations in a Changing World*, pp. 78–80.

[3] Text of Statute: 51 *A.J.* (1957), 466.

[4] In existence 1 January 1958; text of treaty: U.N.T.S., vols. 294–8; 51 *A.J.* (1957), 955.

[5] Statute in force 1 February 1958; text: 53 *A.J.* (1959), 1012. Subsequently O.E.E.C. was replaced by the O.E.C.D. (the Organization for Economic Co-operation and Development).

[6] Set up by a Convention signed in Moscow, 26 March 1956. Twelve Communist states are members.

[7] Or, C.E.R.N., set up by a Convention of 1 July 1953, under the auspices of U.N.E.S.C.O.

[8] Set up by the Organization of American States in 1959.

4. *Restrictive Practices*

The maintenance of standards of economic policy which accord with an international public policy is not a problem which can be approached very readily through customary law, and 'international economic law', whilst it has a certain coherence, is a body of principles dependent on treaties and the powers of organizations of states.[1] The General Agreement on Trade and Tariffs[2] and the International Monetary Fund[3] regulate respectively trade and currency exchange. However, a well-developed anti-trust law on the international plane exists only, on a regional basis, within the European Communities. Within the European Economic Community certain restrictive practices between enterprises are prohibited, and the Commission, an institution of the Community, can make regulations with a view to bringing national standards into conformity with the law of the Community.[4] Two general aspects of international economic law require notice. First, it is still a treaty law, and the problems are those of interpreting instruments, with reference to a community or treaty policy if one is extant. The task of deciding whether obligations to provide 'equality' of treatment have been fulfilled is delicate, since formal equality may not suffice.[5] Moreover it may be arguable that a treaty is subject to implied qualifications, for example with respect to the consequences of measures of exchange control to deal with conditions of economic crisis.[6] Secondly, there has been a move away from generalized *laissez faire* principles, which favoured the economically strong, toward regimes of sophisticated balance between control and flexibility. The relativity of freedom in economic matters is indicated by the European Economic Community,

[1] Cf. Schwarzenberger, *The Frontiers of International Law*, pp. 210–33; id., 117 Hague *Recueil* (1966, I), 5–98; id., *Economic World Order* (1970); Fawcett, 123 Hague *Recueil* (1968, I), 219–310.

[2] See Jackson, *The Law of GATT* (Problems, Cases and Materials) (rev. ed. 1966); Flory, *Le GATT* (1968); Fawcett, op. cit., pp. 260–81.

[3] See Fawcett, 40 *B.Y.* (1964), 32–76; id., 123 Hague *Recueil*, 282–99.

[4] See Articles 85–7 of the E.E.C. Treaty; the *Bosch* case in the Community Court; Brinkhorst and Schermers, *Judicial Remedies in the European Communities*, p. 182 (on which, Thompson, 11 *I.C.L.Q.* (1962), 721–41); and Campbell, 14 *I.C.L.Q.* (1965), 1375–82. See also Articles 66 and 67 of the European Coal and Steel Community Treaty. Further references, *infra*, pp. 694–5.

[5] See the *Oscar Chinn* case (1934), P.C.I.J., Ser. A/B, no. 63; *U.S. Nationals in Morocco*, I.C.J. Reports (1952), p. 186; Schwarzenberger, *International Law* i (3rd ed.), 23 seq.; id., 117 Hague *Recueil* (1966, I), 50–1; Kopelmanas, 81 *J.D.I.* (1954), 64–107; Lauterpacht, *The Development of International Law by the International Court*, pp. 262–6.

[6] See *U.S. Nationals in Morocco* case and literature cited in the previous note.

which promotes free interchange internally whilst appearing externally as a multilateral protectionist arrangement.

5. *Conservation of the Living Resources of the High Seas*

The high seas, having the character of *res communis*, are open to the use and enjoyment of all states on an equal basis.[1] This principle of freedom, applied to fishing, has threatened to cause depletion of certain fish stocks and so to destroy the content of the right to fish by unregulated exploitation. States, by means of extension of their territorial sea, the creation of contiguous zones for fisheries purposes, and the exercise of rights over the resources of the continental shelf, have been successful in extending their legal powers not only to fish but to regulate fishing in given areas. *Ad hoc*, somewhat anomalous, claims to fishery conservation zones as such on the high seas have been made, notably in a proclamation by the United States President in 1945.[2] Whatever the justification for extended claims to take fish exclusively, unilateral claims to take conservation measures involving abstention by other states have been resisted;[3] in other words, the reference to conservation as a reason for unilateral assertion of rights to control fish stocks makes no legal difference.

Clearly treaty arrangements may provide a reasonably stable conservation regime involving also a negotiated distribution of marine resources. The object of a treaty will often be the maintenance of the maximum sustainable yield of the fish stock combined with principles of equal access and equal limitations on fishing. Conservation thus appears in conjunction with allocation of resources. Another relevant factor is a dislike of the principle of 'free competition' by states unable to compete on the same basis and which, as underdeveloped countries, claim a priority of needs. Moreover, commercial fishing by non-regional interests generates regional maritime zones.[4]

In the last decade attempts have been made to provide a broad multilateral basis for conservation. The United States has urged acceptance of the principle of abstention,[5] which

[1] *Supra*, pp. 237 seq.

[2] 28 September 1945; Briggs, p. 377; contemporaneous with a Continental Shelf proclamation.

[3] Cf. the *Behring Sea Fisheries* arbitrations of 1893 and 1902, *supra*, pp. 240–1.

[4] The famous 200-mile claims by Peru, Ecuador, and Chile in 1952 were based on conservation rather than a concept of territorial sea. See García Amador, *The Exploitation and Conservation of the Resources of the Sea* (2nd ed.), pp. 73–9; *Yrbk., I.L.C.* (1956), i. 169.

[5] See, for example, *Yrbk., I.L.C.* (1956), ii. 91, 93. The principle first appeared in the North Pacific Fisheries Convention of 1952. See Allen, 46 *A.J.* (1952), 319–23; Bishop,

relates to situations where States have, through the expenditure of time, effort and money on research and management, and through restraints on their fishermen, increased and maintained the productivity of stocks of fish, which without such action would not exist or would exist at far below their most productive level. Under such conditions and when the stocks are being fully utilized, that is, under such exploitation that an increase in the amount of fishing would not be expected to result in any substantial increase in the sustainable yield, then States not participating, or which have not in recent years participated in exploitation of such stocks of fish, excepting the coastal state adjacent to the waters in which the stocks occur, should be required to abstain from participation.

This principle has been criticized as resting on a one-sided principle of allocation, akin to acquisitive prescription and contrary to the principle of the freedom of the high seas,[1] and it did not find a place in the Convention on Fishing and Conservation of the Living Resources of the High Seas opened for signature in 1958.[2] The Convention is concerned with creating powers to institute conservation measures, establishing priorities of interest, and providing machinery for the settlement of disputes arising from the implementation of its provisions on matters of substance. Article 6, paragraph 1, recognizes that 'a coastal State has a special interest in the maintenance of the productivity of the living resources in any area of the high seas adjacent to its territorial sea'. Article 7 gives content to the special interest as follows:

1. . . . any coastal State may, with a view to the maintenance of the productivity of the living resources of the sea, adopt unilateral measures of conservation . . . in any area of the high seas adjacent to its territorial sea, provided that negotiations to that effect with the other States concerned have not led to an agreement within six months.

2. The measures . . . shall be valid as to other States only if the following requirements are fulfilled:

(a) That there is a need for urgent application of conservation measures in the light of the existing knowledge of the fishery;
(b) That the measures adopted are based on appropriate scientific findings;
(c) That such measures do not discriminate in form or in fact against foreign fishermen.

62 *Columbia L.R.* (1962), 1206–29; id., 115 Hague *Recueil* (1965, II), 315–17; Yamamoto, 43 *Washington L.R.* (1967–8), 45–61.

[1] See Oda, *International Control of Sea Resources* (1963), pp. 89–90, 139–42; and Van der Molen, *Liber Amicorum presented to J.P.A. François* (1959), pp. 203–12.

[2] Text: 52 *A.J.* (1958), 851; Brownlie, *Documents*, p. 99; *Treaty Series* No. 39 (1966), Cmnd. 3028. In force 20 March 1966. The Convention was signed by only 37 states, although 86 states were represented at the Geneva Conference. The United Kingdom and United States have ratified it.

Articles 6 and 7 may well be subjected to a restrictive interpretation in the interest of those favouring fisheries off foreign shores.[1] In the Informal Composite Negotiating Text of 1977 (Third United Nations Conference on the Law of the Sea) the provisions concerning the exclusive economic zone[2] (Articles 61–67) constitute a regime of management based upon the specified powers and duties of the coastal state. In the same Text (Articles 116–120) certain duties are prescribed for all states in respect of the management and conservation of the living resources of the high seas, such duties being of a very general nature.

6. *Antarctica*

The issues arising from territorial claims in polar regions have been noticed earlier,[3] and it is now proposed to give a short account of the regime of co-operation established by the Antarctic Treaty.[4] The object of the treaty is to ensure that Antarctica is used for peaceful purposes only, and that freedom of scientific investigation, and co-operation towards that end, as applied during the International Geophysical Year, shall continue. However, military personnel and equipment may be used in pursuing peaceful purposes. Nuclear explosions, for whatever purpose, are prohibited. Article VI provides for the application of the treaty to the area south of 60° south latitude, includes all the shelves, but reserves the rights of states (and not only contracting parties) with regard to the high seas in the area. Article IV reserves the rights and claims of contracting parties to territorial sovereignty in the area and provides as follows:

> No acts or activities taking place while the present Treaty is in force shall constitute a basis for asserting, supporting or denying a claim to territorial sovereignty in Antarctica or create any rights of sovereignty in Antarctica. No new claim, or enlargement of an existing claim, to territorial sovereignty in Antarctica shall be asserted while the present Treaty is in force.

[1] Cf. Oda, op. cit., pp. 116–18; McDougal and Burke, pp. 981 seq.; Gros, 97 Hague *Recueil* (1959, II), 42–54.

[2] On which: *supra*, pp. 219–21.

[3] *Supra*, pp. 154–5.

[4] Text: Cmnd. 913, Misc. no. 21 (1959); 54 *A.J.* (1960), 476; 9 *I.C.L.Q.* (1960), 475; and Whiteman ii. 1232. Signed 1 December 1959 by Argentina, Australia, Belgium, Chile, France, Japan, New Zealand, Norway, South Africa, U.S.S.R., the United Kingdom, and the United States. See also 10 *I.C.L.Q.* (1961) 562. At least sixteen states are parties. For the U.K. see now the Antarctica Treaty Act 1967, c. 65. See further U.S. Dept. of State Memo.; 70 *A.J.* (1976), 115; *Digest of U.S. Practice*, 1975, p. 107.

This last-quoted provision is not expressed to apply only to contracting parties, and this, and indeed the treaty as a whole, leads to the question of the obligation of non-parties.[1] In principle the treaty as such can only bind parties to it,[2] although Article IV (2) quoted above may constitute a joint establishment by the parties of a policy of closed options, i.e., non-parties are not physically excluded, but they cannot by their activities create a basis for new territorial claims. Thus the states with outstanding claims are protected from new sources of competition. In addition, however, the parties may also intend to reserve previously unclaimed areas for disposal by agreement among themselves. The validity of such a policy of options *vis-à-vis* non-parties and joint reservation will depend on general international law and not on the fact that the policy is expressed in a treaty.

Two other matters may be mentioned. First, there is a liberal inspection system involving a right to designate observers unilaterally and provision for complete freedom of access for such observers at any time to any or all areas of Antarctica. Secondly, the jurisdiction cannot in the context rest on the principle of territoriality. From the jurisdictional point of view the area is treated as *res nullius* and the nationality principle presumably governs. However, general principles will have to be resorted to when a national of one party commits an offence or civil wrong against a national of another party or of a non-party.[3]

7. *Outer Space*

There is no reason for believing that international law is spatially restricted, although, obviously, new areas of human activity will create problems, as in the case of exploitation of the continental shelf. The General Assembly of the United Nations has in any case adopted the view that 'International law, including the Charter of the United Nations, applies to outer space and celestial bodies'.[4] The analogy most applicable is that of the

[1] See generally *infra*, pp. 619–22.

[2] Nevertheless, the treaty bears some resemblance to treaties classified as 'constitutive or semi-legislative' by Lord McNair, *Law of Treaties* (1961), Chap. XIV. Cf. also Art. X of the Antarctic Treaty: 'Each of the Contracting Parties undertakes to exert appropriate efforts, consistent with the Charter of the United Nations, to the end that no one engages in any activity in Antarctica contrary to the principles or purposes of the present Treaty.' This provision could be read as a clear admission that non-parties are not bound by the treaty itself.

[3] See *infra*, pp. 298 seq. The nationality principle (see *infra*, p. 303) is applied to observers and scientific personnel exchanged under the treaty: Art. VIII (1).

[4] Resol. 1721 (XVI), adopted 20 December 1961; 56 *A.J.* (1962), 946. See also Art. 3 of the Outer Space Treaty of 1967, *infra*.

high seas, a *res communis*, but such a category is not a source of many precise rules. However, although much remains to be done, particularly in relation to controlling military uses of space, a solid area of agreement on some basic rules has been achieved since space exploration began in 1957. The basis for agreement has been an early acceptance of the principle that outer space and celestial bodies are not susceptible to appropriation by states.[1] Evidence of generally accepted principles is provided by the General Assembly resolution of 13 December 1963,[2] adopted unanimously, which contains 'a declaration of legal principles' governing activities of states in the exploration and use of outer space.

In 1967 as a sequel to the resolution of 1963 there was signed the Treaty on Principles governing the Activities of States in the Exploration and Use of Outer Space, Including the Moon and Other Celestial Bodies.[3] This will be binding on the parties and, apart from that obvious feature, will replace the resolution as the best evidence of the applicable principles for non-parties. The regime created is similar to that of the Antarctica Treaty of 1959. Article I provides that exploration and use of outer space 'shall be carried out for the benefit and in the interests of all countries . . . and shall be the province of all mankind'; and further, outer space (including the moon and other celestial bodies) 'shall be free for exploration and use by all states without discrimination of any kind, on a basis of equality and in accordance with international law, and there shall be free access to all areas of celestial bodies'. Freedom of scientific investigation is established.[4] Article 2 provides that outer space 'is not subject to national appropriation by claim of sovereignty, by means of use or occupation, or any other means'. There is no provision on the precise boundary between outer space and airspace, or, more precisely, between the regime of *res communis*[5] and the sovereignty of states over national territory. Until there is agreement on the legality of

[1] Although existing principles on acquisition of territory would have been applicable, as they are to uninhabited polar regions. On the same problem relating to the continental shelf cf. Waldock, 36 *Grot. Soc.* (1950), 115–48.

[2] Resol. 1962 (XVIII); 58 *A.J.* (1964), 477; 3 *Int. Leg. Materials*, 157; Gen. Ass., Off. Recs., 18th Sess., Suppl. no. 15 (A/5515), p. 15. On the relations of the Outer Space Treaty of 1967 and the resolution see Fawcett, *International Law and the Uses of Outer Space*, pp. 4–14.

[3] U.K. *Treaty Series* No. 10 (1968), Cmnd. 3519; 61 *A.J.* (1967), 644; 41 *B.Y.* (1965–6), 426; Brownlie, *Basic Documents*, p. 116. In force 10 October 1967; approx. 60 parties. For comment see Jennings, 121 Hague *Recueil* (1967, II), 410–15; Darwin, 42 *B.Y.* (1967), 278–89; Cheng, 95 *J.D.I.* (1968), 532–45; McMahon, 41 *B.Y.* (1965–6), 417–25.

[4] See Articles 1, 10, 11, and 12.

[5] *Supra*, p. 181.

certain types of activity on the fringes of national airspace, states will tend to reserve their positions on a boundary line beyond which the application of sanctions against unlawful activities may be problematical. The lowest limit above the earth sufficient to permit free orbit of spacecraft would make a sensible criterion: this limit would be of the order of 100 miles since this is the lowest technically desirable altitude of orbit. Fawcett[1] has, on this basis, suggested that it would be necessary to convert the criterion into the arbitrary but precise limit of 100 miles. There may be a customary rule that satellites in orbit cannot be interfered with unless interference is justified in terms of the law concerning individual or collective self-defence.

The general regime is, like that of the high seas, based upon free use and a prohibition of claims to sovereignty by individual states. However, when the moon and other bodies are the objects of regular human activity, bases will be set up which may create some sort of possessory title. At any rate the existing rules need development to cope with the practical problems of peaceful but competing uses and matters of jurisdiction.[2] In Article 8 it is provided that 'a State Party to the Treaty on whose registry an object launched into outer space is carried shall retain jurisdiction and control over such object, and over any personnel thereof, while in outer space or on a celestial body'. The same article provides that the ownership of space objects is not affected by their presence in outer space or on a celestial body or by their return to earth. In 1974 the General Assembly adopted the Convention on Registration of Objects Launched into Outer Space.[3]

Article 6 provides that states parties to the Treaty shall bear responsibility for national activities in space, whether such activities are carried on by governmental agencies or by non-governmental entities. Article 7 is as follows:

> Each State Party to the Treaty that launches or procures the launching of an object into outer space, including the Moon and other celestial bodies, and each State Party from whose territory or facility an object is launched, is internationally liable for damage to another State Party to the Treaty or to its natural or juridical persons by such object or its component parts on the Earth, in airspace or in outer space, including the Moon and other celestial bodies.

[1] Op. cit., pp. 23–4. See also McMahon, 38 *B.Y.* (1962), 340–57.

[2] See the Soviet proposal for a Moon Treaty, May 1971; 10 *Int. Leg. Materials* (1971), 839.

[3] Resol. 3235 (XXIX). The Convention came into force on September 15, 1976. For the text see 14 *Int. Leg. Materials* (1975), 43; and see also *Digest of U.S. Practice*, 1974, 398–404.

The Legal Sub-Committee of the Space Committee of the United Nations General Assembly has prepared a more comprehensive treaty on these matters.[1] In the context of responsibility Article 9 contains some important provisions creating standards of conduct for states engaged in exploration and use of outer space. Thus activities shall be conducted 'with due regard to the corresponding interests of all other States Parties to the Treaty' and study and exploration shall be carried out so as to avoid harmful contamination of outer space and celestial bodies and also 'adverse changes in the environment of the Earth resulting from the introduction of extraterrestrial matter'. In recent years debate has proceeded on the compatibility or otherwise of various activities with the Outer Space Treaty, and, in particular, of remote sensing of the earth's surface by satellites.[2] There has also been discussion of the principles which apply to direct television broadcasting by satellites.

Article 4 creates a regime of demilitarization:[3]

> States Parties to the Treaty undertake not to place in orbit around the Earth any objects carrying nuclear weapons or any other kinds of weapons of mass destruction, install such weapons on celestial bodies, or station such weapons in outer space in any other manner.
>
> The Moon and other celestial bodies shall be used by all States Parties to the Treaty exclusively for peaceful purposes. The establishment of military bases, installations and fortifications, the testing of any type of weapons and the conduct of military manoeuvres on celestial bodies shall be forbidden. The use of military personnel for scientific research or for any other peaceful purposes shall not be prohibited. The use of any equipment or facility necessary for peaceful exploration of the Moon and other celestial bodies shall also not be prohibited.

Assistance to astronauts in case of emergency is the subject of Article 5 of the Outer Space Treaty and also of the Agreement on the Rescue of Astronauts, the Return of Astronauts and the Return of Objects Launched into Outer Space, signed on 22 April 1968.[4]

[1] See now the Conv. on International Liability for Damage Caused by Space Objects, signed 29 March 1972; 66 *A.J.* (1972), 702. See further Hailbronner, 30 *Z.a.ö.R.u.V.* (1970), 125–41; Malik, 6 *Indian Journ.* (1966), 335–62; Fawcett, op. cit., pp. 57–60; Cheng, *Curr. Leg. Problems* (1970), 216–39; Foster, 10 *Canad. Yrbk.* (1972), 137–85.

[2] See *Digest of U.S. Practice*, 1975, pp. 473–9.

[3] See also Article 3. Earlier developments: the Nuclear Test Ban Treaty signed on 5 August 1963; 57 *A.J.* (1963), 1026; and General Assembly Resol. 1884 (XVIII), adopted on 17 November 1963, prohibiting the placing in orbit around the earth of objects carrying weapons of mass destruction, the installing of such weapons on celestial bodies, or stationing such weapons in outer space in any other manner. See also Brownlie, 40 *B.Y.* (1964), 1–31; Fawcett, op. cit., pp. 29–42.

[4] Text: 63 *A.J.* (1969), 382; *Treaty Series* No. 56 (1969), Cmnd. 3997. For comment see Hall, 63 *A.J.* (1969), 197–210; Cheng, 23 *Yr. Bk. of World Affairs* (1969), 185–208.

An important feature of the use of outer space, as opposed to its exploration, has been the employment of satellites in orbit to develop world-wide telecommunications. The major developments so far have been based upon a private American corporation, COMSAT, and a consortium of interests of various nationalities known as INTELSAT, limited to ITU members. The consortium is not an international legal person but is nevertheless regulated by an Agreement establishing Interim Arrangements for a Global Commercial Communications Satellite System of 1964,[1] and its associated agreements.[2] The governing body of INTELSAT is the Interim Committee. COMSAT is the operating agency of INTELSAT and has a dominant position on the Interim Committee. In 1971 a number of socialist countries concluded an agreement for the creation of a satellite communications system called INTERSPUTNIK.[3] Problems created by these developments include the conservation of the radio frequency spectrum and the powers of the ITU and UNESCO to take action in the matter,[4] and also the legal responsibility of international organizations for space activities. Article 6 of the Outer Space Treaty of 1967 provides that 'responsibility for compliance with this Treaty shall be borne both by the international organization [which carries on activities in outer space] and by the States Parties to the Treaty participating in such organization'.[5]

8. *International Rivers*

The term 'international' with reference to rivers is merely a general indication of rivers which geographically and economically affect the territory and interests of two or more states. Associated with rivers will be lakes and canals and other artificial works forming part of the same drainage system. Conceivably a river could be 'internationalized', i.e. given a status entirely distinct from the territorial sovereignty and jurisdiction of any

[1] *Treaty Series* No. 12 (1966), Cmnd. 2940; 3 *Int. Leg. Materials* (1964), 805, 810.

[2] Supplementary Agreement on Arbitration, 1965; *Treaty Series* No. 71 (1967), Cmnd. 3375; 4 *Int. Leg. Materials* (1965), 735.

[3] Generally on these developments see Fawcett, op. cit., pp. 43–54; Cheng, 24 *Curr. Leg. Problems* (1971), 211–45; Doyle, 55 *California L.R.* (1967), 431–48; id., 15 *Villanova L.R.* (1969), 83–105; Gotlieb and Dalfen, 7 *Canad. Yrbk.* (1969), 33–60; Batailler, *Ann. français* (1965), 145–73.

[4] See Leive, *International Telecommunications and International Law: The Regulation of the Radio Spectrum* (1970).

[5] See also Article 13. For comment see Fawcett, op. cit., pp. 44–6; Darwin, op. cit., pp. 286–8.

state, on the basis of treaty or custom, either general or regional. However, in practice rivers separating or traversing the territories of two or more states are subject to the territorial jurisdiction of riparian states up to the *medium filum aquae*, usually taken to be the deepest channel of navigable waters.[1] For the most part the legal regime of rivers, creating rights for other riparians and non-riparian states and limiting the exercise of territorial jurisdiction for individual riparians, depends on treaty. Particularization of the regimes for various river systems would seem to be inevitable, since each system has its own character and technical problems. Moreover, no longer may general principles be founded on the assumption that the primary use will be navigation. Irrigation, hydro-electricity generation, and industrial uses are more prominent in many regions than navigation, fishing, and floating of timber.

In this field the lawyer has to avoid the temptation to choose rough principles of equity governing relations between riparians, reflected in some treaty provisions and the work of jurists and learned bodies, as rules of customary law.[2] On some sets of facts, however, unilateral action, creating conditions which may cause specific harm, and not just loss of amenity, to other riparian states, may create international responsibility on the principles laid down in the *Trail Smelter* arbitration[3] and the decision in the *Corfu Channel* case (Merits).[4] The arbitral award concerning the waters of *Lake Lanoux*[5] in 1957 was concerned with the interpretation of a treaty between France and Spain. However, the tribunal made observations on certain Spanish arguments based on customary law. On the one hand, the tribunal seemed to accept the principle that an upstream state is acting unlawfully if it

[1] On the problems of river boundaries see E. Lauterpacht, 9 *I.C.L.Q.* (1960), p. 208 at pp. 216–26. As in the case of maritime indentations a river may be subjected to a *condominium*.

[2] Cf. Brierly, pp. 231–2; Verzijl, *International Law in Historical Perspective* iii. 106–7. See, however, certain official American statements in 1944, in Berber, *Rivers in International Law* (1959), pp. 116–18. On the validity of established rights of user, see E. Lauterpacht, 6 *I.C.L.Q.* (1957), 135–7; Batstone, 8 *I.C.L.Q.* (1959), p. 523 at pp. 540–5, 558; van Alstyne, *Duke L.J.* (1964), p. 307 at pp. 330–4.

[3] *Infra*, p. 285.

[4] *Infra*, p. 441.

[5] Green, p. 318; 62 *R.G.D.I.P.* (1958), 79; *R.I.A.A.* xii. 281; 53 *A.J.* (1959), 156; Int. L.R., 24 (1957), p. 101. See also Duléry, 62 *R.G.D.I.P.* (1958), 469–516; and Griffin, 53 *A.J.* (1959), 50–80. The arbitration concerned the diversion of water by the upstream state, France, opposed by the lower state, Spain. For the Convention made subsequently by the parties, see 4 *Annuaire français* (1958), 708. See Berber, op. cit., p. 150, for a suggestion of local European customary rules; and Brownlie, 10 *I.C.L.Q.* (1960), 656. See further the Treaty Relating to Co-operative Development of the Water Resources of the Columbia River Basin, 1961; U.S. and Canada, 59 *A.J.* (1965), 989.

changes the waters of a river in their natural conditions to the serious injury of a downstream state. On the other, the tribunal stated that 'the rule according to which States may utilize the hydraulic force of international watercourses only on condition of a prior agreement between the interested States cannot be established as a custom, or even less as a general principle of law'.

In the case of navigable rivers[1] it is generally accepted that customary law does not recognize a right of free navigation.[2] Significantly, only a minority of states have accepted the Barcelona Convention on the Regime of Navigable Waterways of International Concern of 1921,[3] which provided for free navigation as between the parties on navigable waterways of international concern. Several treaty regimes for specific river systems provide for free navigation and equality of treatment for riparian states only.[4] However, this is not always the case, and the treaty regime for the Danube for long conferred rights of navigation and control on non-riparians. The Belgrade Convention of 1948 maintained free navigation for all states whilst retaining powers of control for riparian states.[5] Navigation by warships of non-riparian states is prohibited. In construing a treaty which creates machinery for supervision of an international regime of navigation, a tribunal may prefer not to employ a restrictive interpretation of the powers of the agency of control as against the territorial sovereigns.[6] In its judgment in the case on the *Jurisdiction of the International Commission of the River Oder*, the Permanent Court stated its view as to the conception on which international river law, as developed in conventions since the Act of the Congress of Vienna in 1815, is based. This conception was 'a community of

[1] See generally International Law Association, Report of the Fiftieth Conference (Brussels, 1962), pp. 453 seq.; Baxter, *The Law of International Waterways* (1964), pp. 149–59.

[2] Baxter, op. cit., p. 155; Oppenheim i. 474; Guggenheim i. 405. For a different view: Westlake, *International Law* i. 157; Kaeckenbeeck, *International Rivers* (1918), p. 23. See also the *Faber* case, Briggs, p. 263; *R.I.A.A.* x. 441; *British Digest* iib. 55–190.

[3] *Treaty Series* No. 28 (1923), Cmd. 1993; 7 L.N.T.S., 51; Briggs, p. 268. Some 23 states have become parties.

[4] See, for example, the Boundary Waters Treaty of 1909 between the United States and Canada; in Baxter (ed.), *Documents on the St. Lawrence Seaway* (1960), p. 7.

[5] Text: 33 U.N.T.S. 181. The United Kingdom, the United States, and France, *inter alia*, contend that the previous Danube Convention of 1921 is still in force. See Kunz, 43 *A.J.* (1949), 104–13; Sinclair, 25 *B.Y.* (1948), 398–404; Bokor-Szegö, 8 *Annuaire français* (1962), 192–205. Only the Rhine Commission contains representatives of non-riparian states, viz., the United Kingdom and the United States.

[6] See the *International Commission of the River Oder*, P.C.I.J., Ser. A, no. 23, p. 29 (1929); Briggs, p. 270; *Jurisdiction of the European Commission of the Danube*, P.C.I.J., Ser. B, no. 14, pp. 61, 63–4.

interest of riparian States', which in a navigable river 'becomes the basis of a common legal right, the essential features of which are the perfect equality of all riparian States in the use of the whole course of the river and the exclusion of any preferential privilege of any one riparian State in relation to the others'.[1]

In modern economic conditions these principles of equality of treatment for aliens and nationals are under pressure.[2] Freedom of navigation and equality of treatment need not necessarily exist in association. Moreover, within the European Economic Community there exist forms of regulation which have eroded the principle of navigational freedom.[3] The classical principles of 'international fluvial law' in the decisions referred to tend to reflect policies of economic liberalism and the 'open door', in other words, penetration by powerful outside interests, often as a result of peace treaties.[4]

In 1966 the International Law Association adopted the Helsinki Rules on the Uses of Waters of International Rivers as a statement of existing rules of international law.[5] The first two chapters are set out below. Other chapters deal with pollution, navigation, timber floating, and the prevention and settlement of disputes. In 1970 the United Nations General Assembly recommended that the International Law Commission should take up the study of the law of the non-navigational uses of international watercourses with a view to its progressive development and codification.[6]

The Helsinki Rules

CHAPTER I

General

Article I

The general rules of international law as set forth in these chapters are applicable to the use of the waters of an international drainage basin except

[1] *Ut supra*, p. 27. Ibid., p. 28, the Court referred also to the interest of non-riparian states in navigation on the waterways in question.

[2] *Supra*, pp. 262–3, on restrictive practices and, in particular, the *Oscar Chinn* case. There is a consideration of the notion of free navigation in the judgment in the latter, at p. 83.

[3] See especially Johnson, 62 *Mich. L.R.* (1963–4), 465–84.

[4] See Oppenheim i. 466–71 for details.

[5] *Report of the Fifty-Second Conference*, pp. 477–533. On the status of the Rules: 17 *Ann. Suisse* (1971), p. 179. Further work by the I.L.A.: *Report of the Fifty-Sixth Conference*, pp. xiii, 102–54; *Report of the Fifty-Seventh Conference*, pp. xxxiv, 213–66.

[6] See further Survey of International Law, U.N. Doc. A/CN. 4/245, pp. 141–5; *Yrbk., I.L.C.* (1971), ii. 207–8; ibid. (1973), ii. 95–6; ibid. (1974), ii (Pt. 1) 300–4; ibid. (1974), ii (Pt. 2). 33–366; ibid. (1976), ii (Pt. 2). 153–62; Report of Schwebel to I.L.C. (1979), A/CN. 4/320.

as may be provided otherwise by convention, agreement or binding custom among the basin States.

Article II

An international drainage basin is a geographical area extending over two or more States determined by the watershed limits of the system of waters, including surface and underground waters, flowing into a common terminus.

Article III

A 'basin State' is a state the territory of which includes a portion of an international drainage basin.

CHAPTER 2

Equitable Utilization of the Waters of an International Drainage Basin

Article IV

Each basin State is entitled, within its territory, to a reasonable and equitable share in the beneficial uses of the waters of an international drainage basin.

Article V

1. What is a reasonable and equitable share within the meaning of Article IV is to be determined in the light of all the relevant factors in each particular case.

2. Relevant factors which are to be considered include, but are not limited to:

(a) the geography of the basin, including in particular the extent of the drainage area in the territory of each basin State;

(b) the hydrology of the basin, including in particular the contribution of water by each basin State;

(c) the climate affecting the basin;

(d) the past utilization of the waters of the basin, including in particular existing utilization;

(e) the economic and social needs of each basin State;

(f) the population dependent on the waters of the basin in each basin State;

(g) the comparative costs of alternative means of satisfying the economic and social needs of each basin State;

(h) the availability of other resources;

(i) the avoidance of unnecessary waste in the utilization of waters of the basin;

(j) the practicability of compensation to one or more of the co-basin States as a means of adjusting conflicts among uses; and

(k) the degree to which the needs of a basin State may be satisfied, without causing substantial injury to a co-basin State;

3. The weight to be given to each factor is to be determined by its importance in comparison with that of other relevant factors. In determining

what is a reasonable and equitable share, all relevant factors are to be considered together and a conclusion reached on the basis of the whole.

Article VI

A use or category of uses is not entitled to any inherent preference over any other use or category of uses.

Article VII

A basin State may not be denied the present reasonable use of the waters of an international drainage basin to reserve for a co-basin State a future use of such waters.

Article VIII

1. An existing reasonable use may continue in operation unless the factors justifying its continuance are outweighed by other factors leading to the conclusion that it be modified or terminated so as to accommodate a competing incompatible use.

2. (a) A use that is in fact operational is deemed to have been an existing use from the time of the initiation of construction directly related to the use or, where such construction is not required, the undertaking of comparable acts of actual implementation.

(b) Such a use continues to be an existing use until such time as it is discontinued with the intention that it be abandoned.

3. A use will not be deemed an existing use if at the time of becoming operational it is incompatible with an already existing reasonable use.

9. *Canals*

Canals, like rivers, are in principle subject to the territorial sovereignty and jurisdiction of the state or states which they separate or traverse. Where the canal serves more than one state or otherwise affects the interests of more than one state a treaty regime may be created to regulate user and administration. The history of three canals of international concern, by reason of use by foreign vessels, has provided the basic materials for jurists seeking to establish general rules applicable to all such canals, and these must be examined.

The Suez Canal was built and opened in 1869 under a private law[1] concession for ninety-nine years by the Egyptian Government to the Universal Suez Maritime Canal Company. For most of its history the latter was a joint Franco-Egyptian com-

[1] There are arguments that the firmans granted should be regarded as on the international plane.

pany with the various aspects of its existence and function subjected either to French or to Egyptian municipal law. However, the British Government was the largest shareholder.[1] Eventually the affairs of the Canal were regulated by the Convention of Constantinople in 1888,[2] signed by nine states and to receive six accessions. In Article 1 it was provided that the Canal 'shall always be free and open, in time of war as in time of peace, to every vessel of commerce or of war, without distinction of flag'. The parties agreed not to interfere with the free use of the Canal and not to subject it to the right of blockade. It was further provided that, even if the territorial sovereign was a belligerent, no act of war should be committed in the Canal or its ports, as well as within a radius of three miles from these ports (Article IV). However, in Article X there is a stipulation that the restrictions in Article IV, and similar restrictions in other articles, should not interfere with the measures which the territorial sovereign 'might find it necessary to take for securing by [his] own forces the defence of Egypt and the maintenance of public order'. Legal issues of some complexity arise when the territorial sovereign is engaged in hostilities, or is otherwise in a 'state of war', and Egyptian measures against Israeli shipping in the Canal since the Rhodes Armistice of 1949 between Egypt and Israel have been the subject of acute controversy.[3]

In 1954 Britain and Egypt concluded an agreement[4] under which British forces withdrew from the Suez Canal base (with rights of use reserved under certain conditions), and the parties recognized 'that the Suez Maritime Canal, which is an integral part of Egypt, is a waterway economically, commercially and strategically of international importance', and expressed a determination to uphold the Convention of Constantinople. In 1956 the Egyptian Government nationalized the Canal Company, under a law making provision for compensation,[5] but made no claim to alter the status of the Canal itself. Britain, France, and other states argued for the illegality of this measure, linking the status of the Company and the concession from the Egyptian Government with the status of the Canal, and alleging that the nationalization was unlawful both in itself and as being

[1] On the problems of nationality and diplomatic protection see *infra*, pp. 485 seq.

[2] See *The Suez Canal, A Selection of Documents* . . . (London, Soc. of Comp. Legis. and Int. Law, 1956), p. 48; *British Digest* iib. 193–281, 341–67.

[3] See Mensbrugghe, *Les Garanties de la Liberté de navigation dans le Canal de Suez* (1964), pp. 147 seq.

[4] *Treaty Series* No. 67 (1955), Cmd. 9586; *Documents, ut supra*, p. 69.

[5] For the law: *Documents, ut supra*, p. 41. On nationalization see *infra*, pp. 531 seq.

incompatible with the 'international status' of the Canal. As a result of the Franco-British invasion later in the same year Egypt abrogated her agreement with Britain of 1954. On 24 April 1957 Egypt made a declaration[1] to the effect that she would respect the rights and obligations arising from the Convention of Constantinople and would 'afford and maintain free and uninterrupted navigation for all nations within the limits and in accordance with the provisions' of that Convention. Egypt registered the instrument with the U.N. Secretariat as an 'international agreement', but it would seem that it has legal force as a unilateral act.[2] The Canal is operated by the Suez Canal Authority, which is a legal person under Egyptian law, attached to the Ministry of Commerce.

Until 1978 the Panama Canal Zone was occupied and administered by the United States under a treaty with Panama under which the latter had a residual sovereignty.[3] The United States administered the Canal directly and independently of Panama under the bilateral Hay-Banau-Varilla Treaty of 1903,[4] which, *inter alia*, provided that the Canal should be neutral in perpetuity and open to the vessels of all nations. Before the construction of the Canal had been provided for in this latter treaty, the United States had already concluded the Hay-Pauncefote Treaty[5] with Great Britain, under which free navigation, even in time of war, was guaranteed in terms borrowed from the Convention of Constantinople. Under the terms of a treaty signed in 1977[6] Panama is recognized as 'territorial sovereign' with rights of management of the Canal granted to the United States for the duration of the Treaty. Associated agreements[7] deal with 'permanent neutrality' of the Canal and aspects of implementation of the Panama Canal Treaty. The Treaty was ratified in 1978 by both Panama and the United States on the basis of certain 'amendments, conditions, reservations and understandings'.[8]

The Kiel Canal, though important for international commerce, was controlled by Germany untrammelled by special obligations

[1] Text: 51 *A.J.* (1957), 673; E. Lauterpacht, *The Suez Canal Settlement* (1960), p. 35; Mensbrugghe, op. cit., p. 397.

[2] On such transactions see *infra*, p. 634.

[3] On the type of territorial status involved see *supra*, p. 116.

[4] See Hyde i. 63. See also *supra*, p. 116.

[5] Text: Moore, *Digest* iii. 219. See further *British Digest* iib. 281–338.

[6] Text: 16 *Int. Leg. Materials* (1977), 1022.

[7] Texts: ibid., 1040–98.

[8] Text: 17 *Int. Leg. Materials* (1977), 817.

until, in the Treaty of Versailles, it was provided that, except when Germany was a belligerent, the Canal was to be open to vessels of commerce and of war of all nations on terms of equality (Article 380). In 1936 the relevant provisions of the Treaty of Versailles were denounced by Germany. Apart from the specific question of the voidable character of the treaty by reason of duress applied to Germany, other states seem to have acquiesced in German avoidance of the Versailles provisions.[1]

It is very doubtful if the existing materials justify a general theory of international canals. However, there is some authority to the contrary in the majority judgment of the Permanent Court in the case of the *Wimbledon*.[2] In 1921 a British vessel chartered by a French company, *en route* to Danzig with munitions for the Polish Government, was refused access to the Kiel Canal by the German Government. The issue before the Court was whether, on the assumption that Poland and Russia were at war, Germany was justified in taking the view that Article 380 of the Versailles Treaty did not preclude the observance of neutral duties on her part. The question was primarily one of treaty interpretation, but the majority judgment, against Germany, referred[3] to the Suez and Panama Canals as 'precedents' which were

> merely illustrations of the general opinion according to which when an artificial waterway connecting two open seas has been permanently dedicated to the use of the whole world, such waterway is assimilated to natural straits in the sense that even the passage of a belligerent man-of-war does not compromise the neutrality of the sovereign State under whose jurisdiction the waters in question lie.

It will be noted that this proposition was ancillary to an exercise in treaty interpretation and that even the general proposition as such depends on the incidence of 'permanent dedication', a notion to be examined later on. Moreover, interested states are reluctant to generalize: in 1956 the United States regarded the Suez Canal as having an 'international status', whilst denying this in the case of the Panama Canal.

If the legal regime of a particular canal is not to rest on territorial sovereignty as qualified by treaty obligations, when these

[1] Some authors take another view: see Brierly, p. 236. See also the *Kiel Canal Collision* case, Int. L.R. 17 (1950), no. 34 and Barabolya (and Others), *Manual of International Maritime Law* (1966); U.S. Edition (1968), i. 162, 180–1.

[2] P.C.I.J., Ser. A, no. 1; World Court Reports i. 163; Green, p. 311. Judges Anzilotti, Huber, and Schücking dissented.

[3] P. 28. For criticism see Schwarzenberger, *International Law* i (3rd ed.), 223–6.

exist, one has to look for some special circumstance which renders interference with shipping unlawful in relation to states which are not parties to a treaty with the riparian sovereign. One approach, which does not constitute a principle specific to canals, is to see the particular treaty regime as 'constitutive or semi-legislative' and therefore creative of third-party rights.[1] The basis of this principle is examined more appropriately in Chapter XXV. Another basis is the solemn unilateral act which may create rights independent of a treaty regime.[2] Baxter prefers a principle of permanent dedication, reminiscent of the *Wimbledon* decision, but coupled with the requirement of reliance, of actual user.[3] Apparently reliance by the international shipping community suffices to support a complaint by any state, user or not. This principle Baxter regards as applicable to both the Panama and Suez Canals.[4] It has attractions, but also the weakness of novelty, since user as such can be legally ambiguous. Moreover, the notion of dedication only leads back to the problem of deciding when, if at all, treaties bind third states and create permanent regimes. Its legal core is the concept of historic rights, but it is not easy to apply this to the present subject-matter, partly because, where there has been for long a treaty obligation to allow free navigation, it is difficult to read a radical significance into the fulfilment of the treaty obligation by the territorial sovereign.[5] In conclusion, it can be pointed out that, assuming a canal has an international status on one basis or another, this is not necessarily incompatible with control by an administrative body which is merely a legal person under the law of the territorial sovereign.

10. *Straits*[6]

Narrow seas joining two large zones of the high seas do not create any real problems providing the territorial seas of the littoral states do not meet, as is the case in the Straits of Dover.

[1] See McNair, *Law of Treaties* (1961), pp. 265–8.

[2] See *infra*, p. 634.

[3] Op. cit., pp. 182, 308, 343.

[4] For the view that the Panama Canal is within the exclusive jurisdiction of the U.S. see Colombos, p. 213.

[5] In the case of the Panama Canal Zone has the United States the legal capacity to allow historic rights to accrue which affect territory in which Panama has at least a residual sovereignty?

[6] See generally Whiteman iv. 417–80; Brüel, *International Straits* (1947), 2 vols.; Kennedy, U.N. Conf. on the Law of the Sea, 1958, Off. Recs. i. 114 (U.N. Doc. A/CONF. 13/38); Giuliano, *Italian Yrbk.*, 1975, 16–26.

When the territorial seas do meet then problems arise as to the drawing of the boundary between them, although the applicable principle is generally that of a median line.[1] In general there is a right of innocent passage for foreign ships (with the possible exception of warships) through straits which are used for international navigation between one part of the high seas and another. This right is recognized by the customary law and is incorporated in the Convention on the Territorial Sea and Contiguous Zone of 1958 (Article 16 (4)).[2] Before the particular incidents of this right are considered, certain special cases may be mentioned. Functions in some respects similar to those of straits are fulfilled by boundary rivers linking international lakes with the high seas. Where this occurs, as in the case of the St. Lawrence Seaway and the Great Lakes in North America, the rights of the riparians are regulated by agreement between them and the analogy with straits is not accepted in general legal principle.[3] A process of unilateral dedication may create an estoppel in favour of one or a number of states or, perhaps, states generally. Assuming that it could be argued that the Baltic and Black Seas are not open seas,[4] then a process of acquiescence, together with agreement on particular issues, may create rights of access which would not otherwise exist. Thus Denmark has ceased to demand tolls for passage through the Great and Little Belts and the Sound, although treaties on the subject exist with only a restricted number of states.[5] In the case of the Black Sea, passage through the Dardanelles, the Sea of Marmara, and the Bosphorus is regulated by the Montreux Convention of 1936.[6] Powers which are non-littoral states of the Black Sea have only a limited access in respect of total tonnage of warships in time of peace, but otherwise there is freedom of transit and navigation for all vessels in peacetime. In time of war, but only when Turkey is not a belli-

[1] *Supra*, p. 201.

[2] Generally on the territorial sea see *supra*, pp. 203 seq. If twelve miles becomes a widely accepted breadth for the territorial sea, it is obvious that the law of straits will become much more prominent.

[3] On the rights, if any, of non-riparian states see Eek, *Scand. Studies in Law* (1965), 75–6. See also *British Digest* iib. 132–52; and Baxter, *The Law of International Waterways*, pp. 46–7.

[4] See *supra*, pp. 237–8; and *British Digest* iib. 12–28. If the Baltic Sea is an open sea by general acquiescence (which it almost certainly is), does this leave Denmark subject to the ordinary regime of international straits as a consequence, without acquiescence by Denmark in relation to this status for the straits?

[5] See Brüel, *International Straits* i. 198–200; ii. 11–115.

[6] Cmd. 5249; 31 *A.J.* (1937), Suppl., p. 1; Hudson, *Int. Legis.* vii. 386. See Brüel ii. 252–426; de Visscher, 17 *R.D.I.L.C.* (1936), 669–718.

gerent, warships have freedom of transit and navigation; with the proviso that belligerent vessels shall not pass except in pursuance of obligations arising out of the sanctions provisions of the Covenant of the League of Nations (see the Montreux Convention, Article 25) and in cases of assistance rendered to a state victim of aggression in virtue of a treaty of mutual assistance binding Turkey, concluded within the framework of the League Covenant (Article 19). Obviously the Convention is in need of revision, but it is doubtful if it is, as a whole, invalidated by change of circumstances, and the parties have not used the power of denunciation after twenty years provided for in Article 28. The analogue of the formation of a general right of access by estoppel, acquiescence, and general user is the acquisition of historic rights converting a strait broader than the sum of the normal territorial seas into a territorial strait.[1] Article 16 (4) of the Convention on the Territorial Sea takes care of another special case, since it refers to straits 'which are used for international navigation between one part of the high seas and another part of the high seas *or the territorial sea of a foreign State*'.[2]

Before the decision in the *Corfu Channel* case (Merits)[3] a number of authorities[4] considered that a strait was 'international' for legal purposes if it was *essential* to passage between two sections of the high seas and was used by considerable numbers of foreign ships. However, in the *Corfu Channel* case, the International Court of Justice stated that the test was not relative importance for navigation. Of the North Corfu Channel between Greek and Albanian territory it observed:[5]

> the decisive criterion is rather its geographical situation as connecting two parts of the high seas and the fact of its being used for international navigation. Nor can it be decisive that this strait is not a necessary route between

[1] Cf. the Juan de Fuca Strait, ten miles across at its narrowest, divided between Canada and the United States. Presumably historic rights may form the basis for denial of a right of passage also.

[2] Italics supplied. On the Arab-Israeli dispute over the Straits of Tiran, see Gross, 53 *A.J.* (1959), 564–94; Hammad, 15 *Revue égyptienne* (1959), 118–51; Lapidoth, 40 *R.G.D.I.P.* (1969), 30–51.

[3] I.C.J. Reports (1949), p. 4.

[4] See Hyde i. 488; Fauchille, *Traité* (8th ed.), I. ii. 246–7; Brüel, *International Straits* i. 43–5 (and see next note). Essentiality is a relative conception, as Brüel's examples show. See also Gidel iii. 729–64.

[5] I.C.J. Reports (1949), pp. 28–9. For criticism of the views of the Court on this point and its acceptance of the information provided by the British Agent see Brüel, *Festschrift für Rudolf Laun* (1953), p. 259 at pp. 273, 276. The passage in the *Corfu Channel* judgment is not easy to reconcile with the judgment in the *Anglo-Norwegian Fisheries* case, I.C.J. Reports (1951), p. 116 at p. 132, referring to the Indreleia (the name of a navigational route): see Fitzmaurice, 31 *B.Y.* (1954), p. 419.

two parts of the high seas, but only an alternative passage between the Aegean and the Adriatic Seas. It has nevertheless been a useful route for international maritime traffic.

In its final articles on the law of the sea the International Law Commission referred to straits 'normally used' for international navigation.[1] The intention was to follow the *Corfu Channel* judgment, but some thought the formulation was more restrictive. Article 16 (4) of the Territorial Sea Convention refers broadly to 'straits which are used for international navigation'.

The coastal state has less control over passage than in the case of innocent passage through the territorial sea.[2] The coastal state may not suspend passage, but it can take precautions to safeguard its security and make rules concerning safe navigation, lighting, and buoys. Where passage through a territorial sea not forming part of a strait is concerned, the right of passage may be suspended temporarily by the coastal state 'if such suspension is essential for its security' (Territorial Sea Convention, Article 16 (3)). Suspension of passage through a strait is not permitted (ibid., Article 16 (3) and (4)), but particular vessels may be objected to in respect of particular passages not considered innocent.[3] The provisions in Article 16 leave the question of the passage of warships shrouded in obscurity: this problem of interpretation has already been considered in connexion with passage through the territorial sea in general.[4] However, it must be said that the *Corfu Channel* case[5] and the International Law Commission support a right of innocent passage for warships without prior authorization, although the Commission did require previous authorization or notification when passage was not through a strait.[6] Nevertheless the controversy at the first Law of the Sea Conference as to the passage of warships was overall and extended to territorial seas both in straits and in ordinary circumstances.[7] Thus the interpretation of Article 16 (4)

[1] *Yrbk., I.L.C.* (1956), ii. 273 (Article 17).

[2] *Supra*, p. 203.

[3] Article 16 (1) provides: 'The coastal State may take the necessary steps in its territorial sea to prevent passage which is not innocent.'

[4] *Supra*, pp. 203–5. [5] I.C.J. Reports (1949), p. 28.

[6] *Yrbk., I.L.C.* (1956), ii. 276–7 (Article 24).

[7] On the connexions between the two parts of the subject-matter, and the authorities denying a right of passage for warships, see Judge Azevedo, diss. op., I.C.J. Reports (1949), at pp. 97–106; and cf. Gidel iii. 278–89 and especially pp. 283–4; and *British Digest* iib. 3–11. At the Hague Codification Conference in 1930 the United States denied the existence of a right of passage for warships. Affirming passage for warships through straits are Fauchille, I. ii. 257; Oppenheim i. 511–12; Sibert, *Traité* i. 725; Colombos, pp. 133, 198; McDougal and Burke, pp. 199–208; Sub-Committee no. 11 of the Hague

of the Territorial Sea Convention turns on the main issue, viz., what types of vessel qualify for innocent passage *ab initio*?

At the Third United Nations Conference on the Law of the Sea (1973–9) the question of passage through straits was regarded as a matter of the first importance by the United States, together with other maritime powers. The Informal Composite Negotiating Text of 1977 contains provisional articles concerning straits which have radical features involving a severe limitation on the powers of some coastal states. It is uncertain whether the regime envisaged will find its way into a final treaty text unchanged. The concept of strait is characterized loosely, as before, in terms of 'straits used for international navigation' (Article 34). The radical element is 'transit passage', which is 'the exercise ... of the freedom of navigation and overflight solely for the purpose of continuous and expeditious transit of the strait between one area of the high seas or an exclusive economic zone and another area of the high seas or an exclusive economic zone'. (Article 38, para. 2). Whilst ship and aircraft exercising this right have specified duties the coastal state has no power either to impede, hamper or suspend 'transit passage' (Article 44). There is no condition of innocence as such attached to 'transit passage'. However, 'if the strait is formed by an island of a state bordering the strait and its mainland, transit passage shall not apply if a high seas route or a route in an exclusive economic zone of similar convenience with respect to navigational and hydrographic characteristics exists seaward of the island' (Article 38, para. 1). In the latter case and in straits 'between one area of the high seas or an exclusive economic zone and the territorial sea of a foreign state' non-suspendable innocent passage would exist (Article 45).

11. *Landlocked States and Enclaves*

There are twenty-four landlocked states and principalities in existence and numerous enclaves detached from a parent entity (and lacking access to the sea).[1] Rights of transit, particularly for trade purposes, are normally arranged by treaty,

Conference, 1930 (see Briggs, p. 290); Baxter, *The Law of International Waterways*, pp. 167–8; Fitzmaurice, 8 *I.C.L.Q.* (1959), 100–1; Brüel, *International Straits* i. 54–69, 202. See also *British Practice* (1964), ii. 178.

[1] See generally *British Digest* iib. 727–38, 745–7; Whiteman ix. 1143–63; Palazzoli, 70 *R.G.D.I.P.* (1966), 667–735; Ibler, *Annales d'études Internationales* (Geneva), 1973, pp. 55–65.

but they may exist by revocable licence or local custom.[1] A right of transit may be posited as a general principle of law in itself[2] or on the basis of a principle of servitudes or other general principles of law.[3] However, a general right of transit is difficult to sustain, and the principle of servitudes, and the other possibly available instruments, are controversial and depend, in any case, on the existence of special circumstances.

Against this unpromising background must be considered the recent attempts to improve the legal position of landlocked states. At the first United Nations Conference on the Law of the Sea the Fifth Committee considered the question of free access to the sea of landlocked states.[4] The result was Article 3 of the Convention on the High Seas, which provides as follows:

1. In order to enjoy the freedom of the seas on equal terms with coastal States, States having no sea-coast should have free access to the sea. To this end States situated between the sea and a State having no sea-coast shall by common agreement with the latter and in conformity with existing international conventions accord:

(a) To the State having no sea-coast, on a basis of reciprocity, free transit through their territory, and

(b) To ships flying the flag of that State treatment equal to that accorded to their own ships, or to the ships of any other States, as regards access to sea ports and the use of such ports.

2. States situated between the sea and a State having no sea-coast shall settle, by mutual agreement with the latter, and taking into account the rights of the coastal State or State of transit and the special conditions of the State having no sea-coast, all matters relating to freedom of transit and equal treatment in ports, in case such States are not already parties to existing international conventions.

Article 4 of the same Convention recognizes the right of every state, whether coastal or not, to sail ships under its flag on the high seas. The latest development is the adoption in 1965 of a United Nations Convention on the Transit Trade of Landlocked Countries,[5] which adopts the principle of free access and sets out the conditions under which freedom of transit will be granted.

[1] See the *Right of Passage* case (Merits), I.C.J. Reports (1960), p. 6; and, in particular at pp. 66 (Judge Wellington Koo), 79–80 (Judge Armand-Ugon).

[2] Farran, 4 *I.C.L.Q.* (1955), p. 294 at p. 304. See also *supra*, p. 15.

[3] See *infra*, p. 372. See also U.N. Conference on the Law of the Sea, Off. Recs. i, A/CONF. 13/29, paras. 41–4.

[4] There was a Preliminary Conference of Landlocked States in Geneva, 10–14 February 1958, at which a statement of principles was adopted. See Whiteman ix. 1150; Cmnd. 584, Misc. no. 15 (1958), pp. 12–13.

[5] In force 9 June 1967. Text: Whiteman ix. 1156.

The Convention provides a framework for the conclusion of bilateral treaties and is not directly dispositive with respect to rights of access. Mr. Fawcett has observed that 'the wide terms in which freedom of transit is granted in the GATT,[1] and in the High Seas Convention . . . suggests that a duty to accord freedom of transit on reasonable conditions to another is now a customary rule'.[2]

At the Third United Nations Conference on the Law of the Sea (1973–9) the provisional draft articles envisage an improvement in the position of land-locked states. Thus the Informal Composite Negotiating Text of 1977 contains stronger provisions on rights of transit than the Convention of 1958 (Articles 124–132). Moreover, land-locked states are accorded 'the right to participate in the exploitation of the exclusive economic zones[3] of adjoining coastal states on an equitable basis, taking into account the relevant economic and geographical circumstances' (Article 69, para. 1, of the provisional Text).

12. *Extra-Hazardous Activities and Problems of Neighbourhood*

The relations of adjacent territorial sovereigns are of course governed by the normal principles of international responsibility,[4] and these may sustain liability for the consequences of extra-hazardous operations.[5] In the *Trail Smelter* arbitration[6] the tribunal observed that 'under the principles of international law . . . no State has the right to use or permit the use of its territory in such a manner as to cause injury by fumes in or to the territory of another or the properties or persons therein, when the case is of serious consequence and the injury is established by clear and convincing evidence'. This duty was held to apply in relation to the activities of a private Canadian corporation. This liability for the consequences of operations likely to cause serious harm to other states, whether or not they are immediate neighbours, has considerable value in relation to uses of international rivers,[7]

[1] General Agreement on Tariffs and Trade, 1947; 55 U.N.T.S., 194; Art. V.

[2] 123 Hague *Recueil* (1968, I), 266–7.

[3] *Supra*, pp. 219–21.

[4] *Infra*, Chapter XX.

[5] *Infra*, p. 436.

[6] Award II, 1941; *R.I.A.A.* iii., p. 1905 at p. 1965; 35 *A.J.* (1941), 684. See also the *Corfu Channel* case (Merits), I.C.J. Reports (1949), p. 22 (and see *infra*, pp. 435 seq.); the *Lake Lanoux* case, *supra*, p. 271; and Sørensen, 101 Hague *Recueil* (1960, III), 194–8. On the activities of armed bands see Brownlie, 7 *I.C.L.Q.* (1958), 712–35.

[7] See *supra*, pp. 270–5.

atmospheric pollution and activities in outer space adversely affecting the earth's environment.[1] Use of this principle is preferable to reliance on the principle of abuse of rights[2] or on the concept of neighbourhood rights extrapolated from municipal systems.[3]

13. *The International Sea-bed Area*

On the proposed regime contained in the Informal Composite Negotiating Text of the Third United Nations Conference (1973–9), reference should be made to Chapter X, section 4 (b).

[1] See *Draft Rules Concerning Changes in the Environment of the Earth*, David Davies Memorial Institute, p. 11.

[2] Considered *infra*, p. 443.

[3] See Andrassy, 79 Hague *Recueil* (1951, II), 77–181; Sauser-Hall, 83 Hague *Recueil* (1953, II), 553–8; Berber, *Rivers in International Law*, pp. 211–23 (critical); and Goldie, 11 *I.C.L.Q.* (1962), 687–91.

PART VI
STATE JURISDICTION

CHAPTER XIII
SOVEREIGNTY AND EQUALITY OF STATES

1. *In General*[1]

THE sovereignty and equality of states represent the basic constitutional doctrine of the law of nations, which governs a community consisting primarily of states having a uniform legal personality. If international law exists, then the dynamics of state sovereignty can be expressed in terms of law, and, as states are equal and have legal personality, sovereignty is in a major aspect a relation to other states (and to organizations of states) defined by law. The principal corollaries of the sovereignty and equality of states are: (1) a jurisdiction, *prima facie* exclusive, over a territory and the permanent population living there; (2) a duty of non-intervention in the area of exclusive jurisdiction of other states; and (3) the dependence of obligations arising from customary law[2] and treaties on the consent of the obligor.[3] The last of these has certain special applications: thus jurisdiction of international tribunals depends on the consent of the parties;

[1] See Sukiennicki, *La Souveraineté des états en droit international moderne* (1927); Raestad, 17 *R.D.I.* (La Pradelle) (1936), 26–84; Rousseau, 73 Hague *Recueil* (1948, II), 171–253; Chaumont, *Hommage d'une génération de juristes au Président Basdevant*, pp. 114–51; Waldock, 106 Hague *Recueil* (1962, II), 156–91; van Kleffens, 82 Hague *Recueil* (1953, I), 5–130; Lauterpacht, *The Development of International Law by the International Court*, pp. 297–400; Fitzmaurice, 92 Hague *Recueil* (1957, II), 48–59; Kelsen, *Principles of International Law*, pp. 108–10, 155–7, 216–17, 315–17, 438–44; ibid. (2nd ed.), 190–4, 247–50, 446–8, 581–5; id., 53 *Yale L.J.* (1944), 207–20; McNair, *Law of Treaties* (1961), pp. 754–66; Korowicz, *Introduction to International Law* (1959), Chaps. I–VI; id., 102 Hague *Recueil* (1961, I), 1–119; de Visscher, 86 Hague *Recueil* (1954, II), 455–70, 483–96; Constantopoulos, *Spiropoulos Festschrift*, pp. 89–102; Suontausta, *La Souveraineté des états* (1955); *Preparatory Study Concerning a Draft Declaration on the Rights and Duties of States*, A/CN.4/2, 1948, pp. 49–74; Verzijl, *International Law in Historical Perspective* i. 256–92.

[2] See *supra*, pp. 4–9. But see pp. 512–15 on *jus cogens*. In any case the conditions for 'contracting out' of rules are not easy to fulfil.

[3] See, in particular, the Declaration on Principles of International Law Concerning Friendly Relations and Co-operation Among States, U.N. Gen. Ass., 1970, 65 *A.J.* (1971), 243; Brownlie, *Basic Documents*, p. 32. See further *British Practice* (1964), pp. 124–6, 128–30; ibid. (1966), pp. 41–9; ibid. (1967), pp. 35–41, 192–6.

membership of international organizations is not obligatory; and the powers of the organs of such organizations to determine their own competence, to take decisions by majority vote, and to enforce decisions, depend on the consent of member states.

The manner in which the law expresses the content of sovereignty varies, and indeed the whole of the law could be expressed in terms of the co-existence of sovereignties.[1] The problems can be approached through the concept of the reserved domain of domestic jurisdiction (section 6, *infra*, p. 284). Yet another perspective is provided by the notion of sovereignty as discretionary power within areas delimited by the law. Thus states alone can confer nationality for purposes of municipal law, delimit the territorial sea, and decide on the necessity for action in self-defence. Yet in all these cases the exercise of the power is conditioned by the law.[2]

2. *Sovereignty and the Application of Rules*[3]

(a) *The validity of obligations arising from treaties.* In the *Wimbledon* the Permanent Court firmly rejected the argument that a treaty provision could not deprive a state of the sovereign right to apply the law of neutrality to vessels passing through the Kiel Canal:[4] 'The Court declines to see, in the conclusion of any treaty by which a State undertakes to perform or refrain from performing a particular act, an abandonment of its sovereignty . . . the right of entering into international engagements is an attribute of State sovereignty.'

(b) *Interpretation of treaties.* The principles of treaty interpretation are considered in Chapter XXV. On occasion the International Court has referred to sovereign rights as a basis for a restrictive interpretation of treaty obligations,[5] but everything depends on the context, the intention of the parties, and the

[1] See Dupuis, 32 Hague *Recueil* (1930, II), 5–290; and cf. Lauterpacht, loc. cit.

[2] On nationality see *infra*, Chapter XVIII. On the territorial sea see the *Fisheries* case, *supra*, pp. 186 seq. On the right of self-defence see Brownlie, *International Law and the Use of Force by States*, pp. 235 seq. Cf. the problem of the automatic reservation of the optional clause (*infra*, pp. 725 seq.) and the regulation of rights (*infra*, p. 376).

[3] See Lauterpacht, op. cit., pp. 359–67; Waldock, op. cit., pp. 159–69; Fitzmaurice, loc. cit.; id., 30 *B.Y.* (1953), 8–18; McNair, loc. cit.

[4] (1923), P.C.I.J., Ser. A, no. 1, p. 25. Cf. the view of the International Court on reservations by states seeking to become parties to multilateral treaties: *Reservations to the Genocide Convention*, I.C.J. Reports (1951), at p. 24; and the views of certain members of the Court on the automatic reservation in acceptances of the optional clause, *infra*, pp. 725 seq.

[5] See the *Wimbledon*, *supra*, p. 24; and the *Free Zones* cases (1930), P.C.I.J., Ser. A, no. 24, p. 12; (1932), P.C.I.J., Ser. A/B, no. 46, p. 167.

relevance of other, countervailing, principles such as that of effectiveness.

(c) *Presumptions and burdens.* Many areas of international law are uncertain or contain principles which do not admit of easy application to concrete issues. Thus much could turn on the answer to the question whether there is a presumption in favour of sovereignty. In another form the issue is whether, in case of doubt as to the mode of application of rules or in case of an absence of rules, the presumption is that states have legal competence or is one of incompetence. In the *Lotus* case[1] the Court decided the issue of jurisdiction on the basis that 'restrictions upon the independence of States cannot be presumed'. However, there is no general rule, and in judicial practice issues are approached empirically. It is also the case that a general presumption of either kind would lead to inconvenience or abuse. The context of a problem will determine the incidence of particular burdens of proof, which may be described in terms of the duty to establish a restriction on sovereignty on the part of the proponent of the duty. The jurisdictional 'geography' of the problem may provide useful indications. Thus in the *Asylum* case[2] the Court stressed the fact that diplomatic asylum involves a derogation from sovereignty as represented by the normally exclusive jurisdiction of the territorial state. On the other hand, in the *Fisheries* case,[3] the dominant factor from this point of view was the international impact of the delimitation of frontiers, in that case the maritime frontier.

(d) *The regulation of rights.* See *infra*, p. 376.

3. *Sovereignty and Legal Personality*

Sovereignty, or sovereignty and independence, are often the terms used to describe both the legal personality of a state and the incidents of that personality. The problems involved in adopting this usage have been considered in Chapter IV.[4]

4. *Sovereignty and Competence*

Sovereignty is also used to describe the legal competence which states have in general, to refer to a particular function of this

[1] See *infra*, p. 301. Cf. *Lake Lanoux* Arbitration, *supra*, p. 271. See further *De Pascale Claim, R.I.A.A.* xvi. 227; Int. L.R. 40, p. 250 at p. 256; Sultan, *Mélanges Offerts à Andrassy*, pp. 294–306.

[2] See *infra*, p. 377.

[3] *Supra*, pp. 186 seq.

[4] At pp. 80–1.

competence, or to provide a rationale for a particular aspect of the competence.[1] Thus jurisdiction, including legislative competence over national territory, may be referred to in the terms 'sovereignty' or 'sovereign rights'. Sovereignty may refer to the power to acquire title to territory and the rights accruing from exercise of the power. The correlative duty of respect for territorial sovereignty,[2] and the privileges in respect of territorial jurisdiction, referred to as sovereign or state immunities, are described after the same fashion. In general 'sovereignty' characterizes powers and privileges resting on customary law and independent of the particular consent of another state.

5. *Membership of Organizations*[3]

The institutional aspects of organizations of states result in an actual, as opposed to a formal, qualification of the principle of sovereign equality.[4] Thus an organization may adopt majority voting and also have a system of weighted voting; and organs may be permitted to take decisions, and even to make binding rules, without the express consent of all or any of the member states.[5] Of course it can be said that on joining the organization each member consented in advance to the institutional aspects, and thus in a formal way the principle that obligations can only arise from the consent of states and the principle of sovereign equality are satisfied. In their practice the European Communities, whilst permitting integration which radically affects domestic jurisdiction for special purposes, have been careful not to jar the delicate treaty structures by a too ready assumption of implied powers.[6] In the case of the United Nations the organs, with the approval of the Court, have interpreted the Charter in accordance with the principles of effectiveness and implied powers at the

[1] See further Chapter VI.

[2] See the *Corfu Channel* case (Merits), I.C.J. Reports (1949), p. 4 at p. 35; and Article 2, paragraph 4, of the United Nations Charter.

[3] See Bourquin, *L'État souverain et l'organisation internationale* (1959); Broms, *The Doctrine of Equality of States as applied in International Organizations* (1959); Padirac, *L'Égalité des états et l'organisation internationale* (1953); Korowicz, *Organisations internationales et souveraineté des états membres* (1961); Bowett, *International Institutions* (3rd ed.), pp. 342–74; Waldock, 106 Hague *Recueil* (1962, II), 20–38, 171–2; van Kleffens, 82 Hague *Recueil* (1953, I), 107–26; Verzijl, *International Law in Historical Perspective* i. 304–8.

[4] Compare Article 2, paragraph 1, of the United Nations Charter with the provisions on the Security Council, Chapters V–VIII.

[5] See generally Chapter XXX.

[6] See Pescatore, 103 Hague *Recueil* (1961, II), 9–238; Hahn, 108 Hague *Recueil* (1963, I), 195–300.

expense, it may seem, of Article 2, paragraphs 1 and 7.[1] If an organization encroaches on the domestic jurisdiction of members to a substantial degree the structure may approximate to a federation, and not only the area of competence of members but their very personality will be in issue. The line is not easy to draw, but the following criteria of extinction of personality have been suggested: the obligatory nature of membership; majority decision-making; the determination of jurisdiction by the organization itself; and the binding quality of decisions of the organization apart from consent of member states.[2]

6. *The Reserved Domain of Domestic Jurisdiction*

The corollary of the independence and equality of states is the duty on the part of states to refrain from intervention in the internal or external affairs of other states.[3] The duty of non-intervention is a master principle which draws together many particular rules on the legal competence and responsibility of states. Matters within the competence of states under general international law are said to be within the reserved domain, the domestic jurisdiction, of states.[4] This is tautology, of course, and as a matter of general principle the problem of domestic jurisdiction is not very fruitful. However, as a source of confusion, it deserves some consideration. The general position is that the 'reserved domain' is the domain of state activities where the jurisdiction of the state is not bound by international law: the extent of this domain depends on international law and varies according

[1] See *infra*, pp. 678 seq., 702 seq., on the *Reparation* and *Expenses* cases.

[2] See van Kleffens, op. cit., pp. 117–26; Verzijl, *International Law in Historical Perspective* i. 283–92; Waldock, op. cit., pp. 171–2. See also *supra*, pp. 76–9, on independence as a criterion of statehood.

[3] See the draft Decl. on the Rights and Duties of States, *Yrbk., I.L.C.* (1949), p. 287, Art. 3. The duty binds international organizations also. One aspect of the duty concerns the illegality of the use or threat of force: see Brownlie, *International Law and the Use of Force by States*, pp. 74, 96–101, 117, 224–5. Cf. the *Lotus* case *infra*, p. 301. The duty includes large areas of law: see Whiteman v. 321–702.

[4] On domestic jurisdiction see generally *Annuaire de l'Inst.* 44, i (1952), 137–80; and 45, ii (1954), 108–99, 292, 299; Preuss, 74 Hague *Recueil* (1949, I), 553–652; Rajan, *United Nations and Domestic Jurisdiction* (2nd ed., 1961) (pp. 407–48, 509–25, for notes on literature and a very full biblio.); Berthoud, 4 *Annuaire suisse de dr. int.* (1947), 17–104; Jones, 46 *Illinois L.R.* (1951), 219–72; Brierly, 6 *B.Y.* (1925), 8–19; Waldock, 106 Hague *Recueil* (1962, II), 173–91; id., 31 *B.Y.* (1954), 96–142; Kelsen, *Principles of International Law*, pp. 62–4, 191–2, 196–201; ibid. (2nd ed.), 290–1, 294–300; Briggs, 93 Hague *Recueil* (1958, I), 309–63; id., *Mélanges Rolin*, pp. 13–29; Fitzmaurice, 92 Hague *Recueil* (1957, II), 59–67; Verzijl, op. cit., pp. 272–83 (also in *Scritti Perassi* ii. 389–403); Rousseau ii. 84–91. Cf. the local remedies rule, *infra*, pp. 495–505.

to its development.[1] It is widely accepted that no subject is irrevocably fixed within the reserved domain, but some jurists have assumed that a list of topics presently recognized as within the reserved domain can be drawn up, including categories such as nationality and immigration.[2] This approach is misleading, since everything depends on the precise facts and legal issues arising therefrom. When, by legislation or executive decree, a state delimits a fishing zone or the territorial sea, the manner and provenance of the exercise of state power is clearly a matter for the state.[3] But when it is a matter of enforcing the limit *vis-à-vis* other states, the issue is placed on the international plane. Similarly, the conferment and withdrawal of nationality may lead to a collision of interest between states if two states are in dispute over the right of one of them to exercise diplomatic protection.[4] One might conclude that the criterion depends on a distinction between internal competence—no outside authority can annul or prevent the internally valid act of state power—and international responsibility for the consequences of the *ultra vires* exercise of the competence declared by the legislation to exist. This distinction certainly has wide application, but is not absolute in character. Thus, in particular contexts, international law may place restrictions on the 'internal' territorial competence of states as a consequence of treaty obligations, for example, forbidding legislation which discriminates against certain groups among the population, or as a consequence of territorial privileges and immunities created by custom. In the case of various territorial privileges, created either by general or local custom or by treaty, other states are permitted to exercise governmental functions, sovereign acts, within the territorial domain.[5]

The relativity of the concept of the reserved domain is illustrated by the rule that a state cannot plead provisions of its own law or deficiencies in that law in answer to a claim against it for an alleged breach of its obligations under international law,[6] and also by the fact that a particular international obligation may refer to national law as a means of describing a status to be created or protected.[7]

[1] Resolution of the Institute of International Law, *Annuaire de l'Inst.* 45, ii (1954), 292, 299; and see also *Nationality Decrees in Tunis and Morocco* (1923), P.C.I.J., Ser. B, no. 4, p. 24; Briggs, p. 452; Green, p. 102.

[2] Cf. Rousseau, 73 Hague *Recueil* (1948, II), 239–46.

[3] But see *infra*, p. 448.

[4] See generally *infra*, pp. 398 seq.

[5] See *infra*, pp. 321 seq., 364 seq. Cf. belligerent occupation, described *infra*, p. 371.

[6] *Supra*, p. 36.

[7] *Supra*, pp. 39, 40. And see also the *Serbian Loans* case, *supra*, p. 40.

As a separate notion in general international law, the reserved domain is mysterious only because many have failed to see that it really stands for a tautology. However, if a matter is *prima facie* within the reserved domain because of its nature and the issue presented in the normal case, then certain presumptions against any restriction on that domain may be created.[1] Thus the imposition of customs tariffs is *prima facie* unrestricted by international law, whilst the introduction of forces into another state is not *prima facie* an internal matter for the sending state.[2]

7. *Article 2, Paragraph 7, of the United Nations Charter*[3]

The advent of international organizations with powers to settle disputes on a *political* basis caused some states to favour express references to the reserved domain. Thus in the League of Nations Covenant, Article 15, paragraph 8, provided, in relation to disputes submitted to the Council *and not to arbitration or judicial settlement*: 'If the dispute between the parties is claimed by one of them, and is found by the Council, to arise out of a matter which by international law is solely within the domestic jurisdiction of that party, the Council shall so report, and shall make no recommendation as to its settlement.'

In making a political settlement the Council might well touch on the reserved domain, since this contains matters frequently the cause of disputes, and the need to write in the legal limit of action was apparent.[4] During the drafting of the United Nations Charter similar issues arose, and the result was the provision in Article 2, paragraph 7:[5]

[1] Cf. the remarks on sovereignty, *supra*, pp. 288–9.

[2] See, however, Judge Lauterpacht, sep. op., *Norwegian Loans* case, I.C.J. Reports (1957), at pp. 51–2.

[3] See the items cited *supra*, p. 287, and also Bindschedler, 108 Hague *Recueil* (1963, I), 391–6; Kelsen, 55 *Yale L.J.* (1946), 997–1007; id., *The Law of the United Nations* (1951), pp. 769–91; Fincham, *Domestic Jurisdiction* (1948); Verdross, 36 *R.G.D.I.P.* (1965), 314–25; Gross, *Austral. Yr. Bk. of I.L.* (1965), 137–58; Gilmour, ibid. (1967), 153–210; id., 16 *I.C.L.Q.* (1967), 330–51; Verdross, *Mélanges offerts à Charles Rousseau*, pp. 267–76. For accounts of the practice of United Nations organs see *Repertory of Practice of United Nations Organs*, i. 55–156; Rajan, op. cit.; Higgins, *The Development of International Law through the political organs of the United Nations*, pp. 58–130; Fincham; Ross, *Mélanges Rolin*, pp. 284–99; Köck, 22 *Ost. Z. fur öff.R.* (1971–2), 327–61; Watson, 77 *A.J.* (1977), 60–83; Trindade, 25 *I.C.L.Q.* (1976), 715–65. See further the *Peace Treaties* case, I.C.J. Reports (1950), p. 65 at pp. 70–1, quoted *infra*, p. 297.

[4] But the limitation could not be relied upon too readily: see the *Nationality Decrees* case, P.C.I.J., Ser. B, no. 4 and Lauterpacht, *The Development of International Law by the International Court*, pp. 270–2. The limitation does not appear in Articles 12 to 14, which are concerned with arbitration and judicial settlement.

[5] See also Art. 10 of the Charter; Art. 1 (3) of the UNESCO Constitution, and Art. 3 D of the Statute of the International Atomic Energy Agency.

> Nothing contained in the present Charter shall authorize the United Nations to intervene in matters which are essentially within the domestic jurisdiction of any State or shall require the Members to submit such matters to settlement under the present Charter; but this principle shall not prejudice the application of enforcement measures under Chapter VII.

Certain contrasts with the provision of the Covenant quoted above will be apparent. There is no reference to international law, the reference is to matters 'essentially' within the domestic jurisdiction, and there is no designation of the authority which is to have the power to qualify particular matters. The provision in the Charter was intended to be flexible and non-technical. At the same time the restriction was meant to be thoroughgoing, hence the formula 'essentially within', because of the wide implications of the economic and social provisions of the Charter (Chapter IX). These intentions have in practice worked against each other. The flexibility of the provision, and the assumption in practice that it does not override other, potentially conflicting, provisions,[1] have resulted in the erosion of the reservation of domestic jurisdiction, although its draftsmen had intended its reinforcement. Moreover, the word 'intervene' has been approached empirically. Discussion, recommendations in general terms, and even resolutions addressed to particular states, have not been inhibited by the form of paragraph 7. At the same time the term 'intervene' is not to be conceived of only as dictatorial intervention in this context. Member states have proceeded empirically with an eye to general opinion and a clear knowledge that precedents created in one connexion may have a boomerang effect.

In practice United Nations organs, particularly on the basis of Chapters IX and XI of the Charter and the provisions on human rights in Articles 55 and 56, have taken action on a wide range of topics dealing with the relations of governments to their own people. Resolutions on breaches of human rights,[2] the right of self-determination[3] and colonialism, and non-self-governing territories (as qualified by the General Assembly), have been adopted regularly. If the organ concerned felt that the acts complained of were contrary to the purposes and principles of the Charter and also that the issue was 'endangering international

[1] In particular, the provisions of Chapters IX and X. See Kelsen, 55 *Yale L.J.* (1946), 1006–7; Guggenheim, 80 Hague *Recueil* (1952, I), 105; Verdross, 83 Hague *Recueil* (1953, II), 73.

[2] Generally on human rights: Chapter XXIV.

[3] *Infra*, pp. 593–6.

peace and security',[1] then a resolution was passed. Certain issues, principally those concerning the right of self-determination and the principle of non-discrimination in racial matters, are regarded as of international concern by the General Assembly, apart from express reference to any threat to international peace and security.[2] The Security Council has adopted a resolution concerning *apartheid only partly* on the basis that the situation 'constitutes a potential threat to international peace and security'.[3]

A question which lacks a clear answer is the relation of Article 2, paragraph 7, to general international law. On its face the provision is a matter of constitutional competence for organs of the United Nations, and, as we have seen, it lacks reference to international law. Moreover, in their practice the political organs have avoided express determination of technical points arising from the provision. Thus in principle it has no necessary and direct impact on general law.[4] However, in a general way in a political document like the Charter, the provision corresponds to the principles of non-intervention and the reserved domain. And, further, *in relation to other articles* and especially Articles 55, 56, and 73 (e), the interpretation of the provision by organs of the United Nations has had important effects on the reserved domain: but here we must again escape from tautology. What has happened is simply that a new content has been given to the obligations and legal competence of states through the medium of the Charter.

8. *International Tribunals and the Plea of Domestic Jurisdiction*[5]

The chief characteristic of the concept of domestic jurisdiction in relation to the practice of tribunals has been its lack of specific relevance. In the case of *Nationality Decrees in Tunis and Morocco*[6] the concept played a prominent role simply by reason of the special circumstances in which the League Council had requested

[1] Exceptionally, as in the Spanish question, and the issue of *apartheid* in South Africa, the form of government in a state was regarded as a potential threat to international peace.

[2] On the concept of international concern see Howell, 48 *A.S.I.L. Proceedings* (1954), 90; and Higgins, op. cit., pp. 77–81.

[3] See Resol. 282 (1970), 23 July 1970. It is relevant to notice that this and other resolutions of the S.C. on the same subject were adopted under Chapter VI of the U.N. Charter.

[4] Cf. Hambro, *Annuaire de l'Inst.* 44 i (1952), 167.

[5] See Briggs, op. cit., pp. 309–63; Waldock, 31 *B.Y.* (1954), 96–142; Fitzmaurice, 35 *B.Y.* (1959), 197–207; Trindade, 16 *Indian Journ.* (1976), 187–218. On the 'peremptory' or 'automatic' version of the reservation of domestic jurisdiction see *infra*, pp. 724–5.

[6] P.C.I.J., Ser. B, no. 4; Green, p. 102; Briggs, p. 452.

an advisory opinion. The dispute between Great Britain and France had been brought before the League Council by Britain, as France had rejected her request to accept a judicial settlement.[1] In the Council proceedings France pleaded Article 15, paragraph 8, of the League Covenant. Eventually the two governments agreed that the League Council should request the Permanent Court to give an advisory opinion on the nature of the dispute, in other words, on the issue whether the Council's jurisdiction was barred by Article 15, paragraph 8, of the Covenant. The Court stressed that it was not concerned with the actual legal rights of the parties as in contentious proceedings but with the general character of the legal issues for the purpose of establishing the competence of the Council. In this task the Court contented itself with reaching a 'provisional conclusion' on the international character of the issues in the case.[2] However, it is doubtful if this approach on the basis of a 'provisional conclusion' is justifiable in the case where there is a preliminary objection to jurisdiction in a contentious case,[3] where the question of domestic jurisdiction is raised in relation to the precise issues before the Court. In practice[4] the International Court has joined a plea of domestic jurisdiction to the merits,[5] since, although the plea is in form a preliminary objection,[6] it has an intimate connexion with the issues of substance.

A further question which arises is application of the reservation in Article 2, paragraph 7, of the Charter to the jurisdiction of the Court, the object of arguing for its application being to benefit from the extensive formula 'essentially within'.[7] Whether the reservation in the Charter applies to the contentious jurisdiction

[1] At this time neither state had accepted jurisdiction in advance under the optional clause in the Statute of the Permanent Court of International Justice (see *infra*, p. 723).

[2] pp. 24–6.

[3] This approach has its supporters: see Waldock, op. cit., pp. 111–14. For critical comment see Lauterpacht, *The Development of International Law by the International Court*, pp. 270–1; Verzijl, *The Jurisprudence of the World Court* i. 45–50; and Fitzmaurice, 35 *B.Y.* (1959), 200–7. See further the *South-West Africa* cases (Second Phase), 1966.

[4] Apart from observations on the request to order interim measures of protection in the *Anglo-Iranian Oil Co.* case, I.C.J. Reports (1951), pp. 92–3; and the *Interhandel* case (Preliminary Objections), ibid. (1959), p. 105.

[5] See the *Losinger* case, P.C.I.J., Ser. A/B, no. 67, pp. 23–5; *Right of Passage* case, I.C.J. Reports (1957), p. 125 at pp. 149–50.

[6] But see *Electricity Company of Sofia and Bulgaria*, P.C.I.J., Ser. A/B, no. 77, pp. 78, 82–3.

[7] In the *Anglo-Iranian Oil Co.* case the Court did not find it necessary to examine an Iranian argument on these lines. See the views of Judge Lauterpacht on the breadth of the formula employed in the French Declaration of acceptance of jurisdiction, I.C.J. Reports (1957), at pp. 51–2.

or not,[1] the plea of domestic jurisdiction is available by operation of law, its success depending on the particular legal relations of the parties concerned.[2] The case is rather different where the advisory jurisdiction is challenged on the basis that the political organ concerned was incompetent to request an opinion as a consequence of Article 2, paragraph 7. In this situation the relevance of the Charter reservation is indisputable. In the *Peace Treaties* case, the Court considered objections to its competence based (1) upon the incompetence of the requesting organ and (2) upon the application of Article 2, paragraph 7, to the Court itself. The objections involved the argument that a matter may be 'essentially' within the domestic jurisdiction of a state although it is governed by a treaty. As to the competence of the requesting organ of the United Nations, the Court observed:[3]

> The Court is not called upon to deal with the charges brought before the General Assembly since the Questions put to the Court relate neither to the alleged violations of the provisions of the Treaties concerning human rights and fundamental freedoms nor to the interpretation of the articles relating to these matters. The object of the request is much more limited. It is directed solely to obtaining from the Court certain clarifications of a legal nature regarding the applicability of the procedure for the settlement of disputes [in the peace treaties with Bulgaria, Hungary, and Rumania]. The interpretation of the terms of a treaty for this purpose could not be considered as a question essentially within the domestic jurisdiction of a State. It is a question of international law which, by its very nature, lies within the competence of the Court.

The Court then stated that these considerations sufficed to dispose of the objection based on Article 2, paragraph 7, directed specifically against the competence of the Court. Whilst this is not unequivocal evidence that Article 2, paragraph 7, applies to the advisory jurisdiction,[4] the incident indicates that the Court will not in any case give any specific, and from the point of view of its jurisdiction more restrictive, content to the 'essentially within' formula as compared with the normal version of the principle of domestic jurisdiction: a matter regulated by treaty does not remain 'essentially within' the domestic jurisdiction of a state.

[1] For references to the different views: Shihata, *The Power of the International Court to Determine its own Jurisdiction*, pp. 229–33.

[2] See the *Interhandel* case (Preliminary Objections), I.C.J. Reports (1959), pp. 24–5; *Right of Passage* case (Merits), ibid. (1960), pp. 32–3.

[3] See the *Peace Treaties* case, I.C.J. Reports (1950), p. 65 at pp. 70–1.

[4] See Waldock, op. cit., p. 138.

CHAPTER XIV

JURISDICTIONAL COMPETENCE

1. *In General*

'JURISDICTION' refers to particular aspects of the general legal competence of states often referred to as 'sovereignty'. Jurisdiction is an aspect of sovereignty and refers to judicial, legislative, and administrative competence.[1] Distinct from the power to make decisions or rules (the prescriptive or legislative jurisdiction) is the power to take executive action in pursuance of or consequent on the making of decisions or rules (the enforcement or prerogative jurisdiction). The starting point in this part of the law is the proposition that, at least as a presumption, jurisdiction is territorial. However, the territorial theory has been refined in the light of experience, and the law, which is still rather unsettled, is developing in the light of two principles. First, that the territorial theory, whilst remaining the best foundation for the law, fails to provide ready-made solutions for some modern jurisdictional conflicts. Secondly, that a principle of substantial and genuine connexion between the subject-matter of jurisdiction, and the territorial base and reasonable interests of the jurisdiction sought to be exercised, should be observed.[2] It should also be pointed out that the sufficiency of grounds for jurisdiction is an issue normally considered relative to the rights of other states and not as a question of basic competence.[3]

2. *Civil Jurisdiction*

In order to satisfy international law standards in regard to the

[1] The best treatment of the subject of jurisdiction is Mann, 111 Hague *Recueil* (1964, I), 9–162; also in Mann, *Studies in International Law* (1973), 1–139. See also Jennings, 33 *B.Y.* (1957), 146–75; id., 32 *Nord. Tids.* (1962), 209–29; id., 121 Hague *Recueil* (1967, II), 515–26; Whiteman v. 216–19; vi. 88–183; *Digest of U.S. Practice*, 1973 (Ann. vols., Chap. 6 in each); Akehurst, 46 *B.Y.* (1972–3), 145–257.

[2] Cf. the doctrine stated in the *Nottebohm* case, *infra*, in the matter of conferment of nationality; *Kingdom of Greece* v. *Julius Bär and Co.*, Int. L.R. 23 (1956), 195; and the statements in the *Guardianship* case, I.C.J. Reports (1958), pp. 109 (Judge Moreno Quintana), 135–6 (Judge Winiarski), 145 (Judge Córdova), and 155 (Judge *ad hoc* Offerhaus).

[3] The last question may arise in relation to stateless persons or jurisdiction over non-nationals by agreement with other states. Cf. the European Agreement for the Prevention of Broadcasts Transmitted from Stations outside National Territories, signed 22 January 1965, Cmnd. 2616; and see *British Practice in International Law* (1964), i. 39–44; 59 *A.J.*

treatment of aliens[1] a state must in normal circumstances maintain a system of courts empowered to decide civil cases and, in doing so, prepared to apply private international law where appropriate in cases containing a foreign element.[2] Municipal courts are often reluctant to assume jurisdiction in cases concerning a foreign element and adhere to the territorial principle conditioned by the *situs* of the facts in issue, and supplemented by criteria relating to the concepts of allegiance or domicile and doctrines of prior express submission to the jurisdiction and of tacit submission, for example on the basis of the ownership of property in the state of the forum.[3] Excessive and abusive assertion of civil jurisdiction could lead to international responsibility or protests at *ultra vires* acts. Indeed, as civil jurisdiction is ultimately reinforced by procedures of enforcement involving criminal sanctions, there is in principle no great difference between the problems created by assertion of civil and criminal jurisdiction over aliens.[4] However, as the latter has provoked more disputes on the diplomatic plane, it is to this that more attention need be given.

3. *Criminal Jurisdiction*[5]

The discussion which follows concerns the general principles on which municipal courts may exercise jurisdiction in respect of acts criminal under the law of the forum, but of course the issue

(1965), 715; van Panhuys and van Emde de Boas, 60 *A.J.* (1966), 303–41; Bos, 12 *Neths. Int. L.R.* (1965), 337–64; and Woodliffe, ibid., 365–84.

[1] On which see *infra*, Chap. XXIII.

[2] On the relations of public and private international law see Stevenson, 52 *Columbia L.R.* (1952), 563; Wortley, 85 Hague *Recueil* (1954, I), 245; Fitzmaurice, 92 Hague *Recueil* (1957, II), 218–22; Mann, op. cit., 10–22, 54–62; Akehurst, op. cit., 216–31.

[3] See Beale, 36 *Harv. L.R.* (1922–3), 241–62; *Rainford, Boston and Graham* v. *Newell-Roberts*, Int. L.R. 30, p. 106; *Royal Exchange Assurance* v. *Compania Naviera Santi, S.A.*, Int. L.R. 33, p. 173; *Colt Industries, Inc.* v. *Sarlie*, Int. L.R. 42, p. 108. For a different view see Akehurst, op. cit., 170–7; and see *Derby & Co. Ltd.* v. *Larsson* [1976] 1 W.L.R. 202, H.L.; 48 *B.Y.* (1976–7), p. 352 (note by Crawford). See also *Thai-Europe Tapioca Service* v. *Government of Pakistan* [1975] 1 W.L.R. 1485 at pp. 1491–2, per Lord Denning.

[4] There are many specialized areas, for example those relating to conscription and taxation. On the former see Parry, 31 *B.Y.* (1954), 437–52, and Whiteman viii. 540–72; on the latter see Mann, op. cit., pp. 109–19; Whiteman viii. 507–39; Albrecht, 29 *B.Y.* (1952), 145–85. See also *Rex* v. *Secretary of State, ex p. Greenberg* [1947] 2 A.E.R. 550 (extra-territorial jurisdiction to render a deportation order effective); and on the protection of alien infants see the *Guardianship* case, I.C.J. Reports (1958), p. 55 at p. 71; and *Re P. (G.E.) (an infant)* [1965] Ch. 568; Int. L.R., 40, p. 239.

[5] See Mann, op. cit., pp. 82 seq.; O'Connell ii. 823–31; Sarkar, 11 *I.C.L.Q.* (1962), 446–70; Jennings, 33 *B.Y.* (1957), 146–75; Fawcett, 38 *B.Y.* (1962), 181–215; Harv. Research, 29 *A.J.* (1935), Spec. Suppl., pp. 439–651. And see further: Beckett, 6 *B.Y.* (1925), 44–60; id., 8 *B.Y.* (1927), 108–28; Fitzmaurice, 92 Hague *Recueil* (1957, II), 212–17; Cybichowski, 12 Hague *Recueil* (1926, II), 264–382; Brierly and de Visscher,

on the international plane is only acute when aliens, or other persons under the diplomatic protection of another state,[1] are involved. The question only achieved prominence after about 1870, and the appearance of clear principles has been retarded by the prominence in the sources of the subject of municipal decisions, which exhibit empiricism and adherence to national policies, and also by the variety of the subject-matter. Several distinct principles have nevertheless received varying degrees of support from practice and opinion, and these will be examined individually before their relations with each other are established.

(a) *The territorial principle.* The principle that the courts of the place where the crime is committed may exercise jurisdiction has received universal recognition, and is but a single application of the essential territoriality of the sovereignty, the sum of legal competences, which a state has. In the case of crime, the principle has a number of practical advantages, including the convenience of the forum and the presumed involvement of the interests of the state where the crime is committed. In English and American decisions statements occur which suggest that the territorial principle is exclusive. However, the practice of states has not adopted this view,[2] and the United Kingdom legislature has conferred jurisdiction over nationals, *inter alia*, in respect of treason, murder, bigamy, and breaches of the Official Secrets Acts, wherever committed.[3] Both the United Kingdom and the United States have tended in judicial practice toward the principle of territorial security.[4] Moreover, in so far as they and other states have adopted the territorial principle, this principle has sometimes been given extensive application. In the first place, there is the subjective application, which creates jurisdiction over crimes commenced within the state, but completed or consummated abroad.[5] Generally accepted and often applied is the objective territorial principle, according to which jurisdiction is founded when any essential constituent element of a crime is consummated on state territory. The classical illustration is the

20 *A.J.* (1926), Spec. Suppl., pp. 252–9; Mercier, 12 *R.D.I.L.C.* (1931), 439–90; Travers, *Le Droit pénal international*, (1920–22); Donnedieu de Vabres, *Les Principes modernes du droit pénal international* (1928); Jescheck, *Internationales Recht und Diplomatie* (1956), pp. 75–95. On the question of nationality see *infra*, pp. 405–6.

[1] On the relation between nationality and diplomatic protection see *infra*, pp. 401–2.

[2] See Harv. Research, loc. cit.

[3] On American divergence from the strict principle: Preuss, 30 *Grot. Soc.* (1944), 184–208.

[4] *Infra*, p. 303.

[5] See Harv. Research, pp. 484–7; the *Tennyson*, 45 *J.D.I.* (1918), 739; *Public Prosecutor* v. *D.S.*, Int. L.R. 26 (1958, II), p. 209.

firing of a gun across a frontier causing a homicide on the territory of the forum, but the principle can be employed to found jurisdiction in cases of conspiracy,[1] violation of anti-trust[2] and immigration laws[3] by activity abroad, and in many other fields of policy.[4] The objective principle received general support, and a controversial application to collisions on the high seas, in the *Lotus* case[5] before the Permanent Court of International Justice.

The *Lotus* case[6] originated in a collision on the high seas between a French steamer and a Turkish collier in which the latter sank and Turkish crew members and passengers lost their lives. The French steamer having put into port in Turkey, the officers of the watch on board at the time of the collision were tried and convicted of involuntary manslaughter. The Permanent Court was asked to decide whether Turkey had acted in conflict with international law by instituting proceedings, i.e. by the fact of exercising criminal jurisdiction and, if so, what reparation was due. France contended that the flag state of the vessel alone had jurisdiction over acts performed on board on the high seas. Turkey argued in reply, in part, that vessels on the high seas form part of the territory of the nation whose flag they fly. By the casting vote of the President (the votes were equally divided, six on either side), the Court decided that Turkey had not acted in conflict with the principles of international law by exercising criminal jurisdiction. The majority of six Judges avoided dealing with the precise question of the compatibility of the relevant article of the Turkish penal code with international law. This

[1] *Board of Trade* v. *Owen* [1957], A.C. 602 at p. 634; *R.* v. *Cox* [1968] 1 A.E.R. 410 at p. 414, C.A.; *D.P.P.* v. *Doot* [1973] A.C. 807, H.L. (and see the speech of Lord Wilberforce, p. 817); *D.P.P.* v. *Stonehouse* [1977] 2 A.E.R. 909 at 916 *per* Lord Diplock; Glanville Williams, 81 *L.Q.R.* (1965), at p. 536; *U.S.* v. *Ford*, *Ann. Digest* 3 (1925–6), no. 110.

[2] See *U.S.* v. *Aluminium Company of America*, 148F. 2d. 416 (1944). In American anti-trust cases wide extension of the territorial principle might be explained by, though it is not expressed in terms of, a principle of protection: see Jennings, op. cit., pp. 155, 161 seq.; Baxter *et al.*, *U.B.C. L.R.* (1960), pp. 333–72; Verzijl, 8 *Neths. Int. K.R.* (1961), 3–30; George, 64 *Michigan L.R.* (1966), pp. 609–38.

[3] Cf. *Naim Molvan* v. *A.-G. for Palestine* [1948] A.C. 531; Green, p. 556.

[4] See *Mobarik Ali Ahmed* v. *State of Bombay*, Int. L.R. 24 (1957), 156; *Public Prosecutor* v. *Y.*, ibid., p. 264: and the *Cutting* case, Briggs, p. 571 (on which see also *infra*, p. 303).

[5] (1927), P.C.I.J., Ser. A, no. 10, p. 23; on which also see *supra*, pp. 254–5. The dissenting judges considered an objective application to be improper if the effects in the other jurisdiction were unintended: on this distinction see Beckett, 8 *B.Y.* (1927), 108–28, and *R.* v. *Keyn* (1876), 2 Ex. Div. 63.

[6] For comment see Verzijl, 8 *Neths. Int. L.R.* (1961), 7–8; id., *The Jurisprudence of the World Court* i (1965), 73–98; Fischer Williams, *Chapters on Current International Law and the League of Nations*, pp. 209–31; Jennings, 121 Hague *Recueil* (1967, II), 516–20; Mann, 111 Hague *Recueil* (1964, I), 33–6, 39, 92–3; Brierly, 44 *L.Q.R.* (1928), 154–63; *Annuaire de l'Inst.*, 43 (1) (1950), 295–365.

article provided for punishment of acts abroad by foreigners against Turkish nationals and involved the protective principle of jurisdiction.[1] Judge Moore, in a separate opinion, agreed with the majority as to the outcome but expressly rejected the protective principle.[2]

The basis of the majority view on the Court (with which Judge Moore concurred, aside from the question of the principle of protective jurisdiction) was the principle of objective territorial jurisdiction. This principle was familiar but to apply it the Court had to assimilate the Turkish vessel to Turkish national territory. On this view the collision had affected Turkish territory.[3] In most respects the judgment of the Court is unhelpful in its approach to the principles of jurisdiction, and its pronouncements are characterized by vagueness and generality. Thus, on the specific question of criminal jurisdiction, the Court observes that:

> Though it is true that in all systems of law the territorial character of criminal law is fundamental, it is equally true that all or nearly all these systems extend their jurisdiction to offences committed outside the territory of the State which adopts them and they do so in ways which vary from State to State. The territoriality of criminal law, therefore, is not an absolute principle of international law and by no means coincides with territorial sovereignty.[4]

On the question of jurisdiction in general the Court expressed its view in a passage which reads in part:

> Far from laying down a general prohibition to the effect that States may not extend the application of their laws and the jurisdiction of their courts to persons, property or acts outside their territory, it leaves them in this respect a wide measure of discretion which is only limited in certain cases by prohibitive rules; as regards other cases, every State remains free to adopt the principles which it regards as best and most suitable.[5]

The passage of which this forms a part has been criticized by a substantial number of authorities[6] and its emphasis on state discretion is contradicted by the views of the International Court in the *Fisheries*[7] and *Nottebohm*[8] cases, which concerned the comparable competences of states, respectively, to delimit the territorial sea and to confer nationality on individuals.

[1] Lauterpacht has stated that in the *Lotus* the Court 'declared the exercise of such protective jurisdiction to be consistent with international law'; 9 *Camb. L.J.* (1947), at p. 343. But see Verzijl, *The Jurisprudence of the World Court*, i. 78–80; and in 8 *Neths. Int. L.R.* (1961), 7–8. [2] pp. 65, 89–94. [3] p. 23. [4] p. 20. [5] pp. 18–19.

[6] See, for example, Brierly, 58 Hague *Recueil* (1936, IV), 146–8, 183–4; Basdevant, ibid., 594–7; Fitzmaurice, 92 Hague *Recueil* (1957, II), 56–7; Lauterpacht, *Collected Papers* i (1970), 488–9.

[7] *Supra*, p. 186. [8] *Infra*, p. 408.

(b) *The nationality principle.* Nationality,[1] as a mark of allegiance and an aspect of sovereignty, is also generally recognized as a basis for jurisdiction over extra-territorial acts.[2] The application of the principle may be extended by reliance on residence and other connexions as evidence of allegiance[3] owed by aliens and also by ignoring changes of nationality.[4] On the other hand, since the territorial and nationality principles and the incidence of dual nationality create parallel jurisdiction and possible double jeopardy, many states place limitations on the nationality principle,[5] and it is often confined to serious offences.

(c) *The passive personality principle.*[6] According to this principle aliens may be punished for acts abroad harmful to nationals of the forum. This is the least justifiable, as a general principle, of the various bases of jurisdiction, and in any case certain of its applications fall under the principles of protection and universality considered below. In the *Cutting* case[7] a Mexican court[8] exercised jurisdiction in respect of the publication of defamatory matter by an American in a Texas newspaper. The defamation was of a Mexican, and the court applied the passive nationality principle among others. This judgment led to diplomatic protests from the United States,[9] although the outcome of the dispute was inconclusive.

(d) *The protective or security principle.*[1] Nearly all states assume jurisdiction over aliens for acts done abroad which affect the security of the state, a concept which takes in a variety of political offences, but is not necessarily confined to political acts.[2] Cur-

[1] On which see generally *infra*, Chapter XVIII. On the difficult question of the nationality of juristic persons see Harv. Research, *ubi supra*, pp. 535–9, and *infra*, pp. 421–3.

[2] Judge Moore, separate opinion in the *Lotus*, *ubi supra*, p. 92; Harv. Research, pp. 519 seq.; Jennings, op. cit., p. 153; Sarkar, op. cit., pp. 456–61; Sørensen, pp. 356–62. See also *U.S.* v. *Baker*, Int. L.R. 22 (1955), 203; *Re Gutierrez*, ibid. 24 (1957), 265; *Weiss* v. *Inspector-General*, ibid. 26 (1958, III), 210.

[3] See *Public Prosecutor* v. *Drechsler*, *Ann. Digest* 13 (1946), no. 29; *Re Penati*, ibid., no. 30; *In re Buttner*, ibid. 16 (1949), no. 33; and cf. *D.P.P.* v. *Joyce* [1946] A.C. 347, and *Re P. (G.E.) (an infant)* [1964] 3 A.E.R. 977. See also Sørensen, p. 361.

[4] See *In re Mittermaier*, *Ann Digest* 13 (1946), no. 28; ibid. 14 (1947), 200–1 (Dutch decisions); *Ram Narain* v. *Central Bank of India*, Int. L.R. 18 (1951), No. 49. This type of case may rest on the protective principle: see *infra*.

[5] Harv. Research, loc. cit., and see *infra*, p. 305.

[6] See Jennings, op. cit., p. 154; Sarkar, op. cit., p. 461; Briggs, p. 579; Harv. Research, *ubi supra*, pp. 445, 579; Bishop, 115 Hague *Recueil* (1965, II), 324; Mann, op. cit., 40–1; Akehurst, op. cit., pp. 162–6.

[7] See Moore, *Digest* ii. 228–42; U.S. For. Rel. (1887), pp. 751–867.

[8] Decision set out in Briggs, p. 571.

[9] See also Whiteman vi. 103–5 and *Digest of U.S. Practice*, 1975, 339.

[1] See Harv. Research, *ubi supra*, pp. 543–63; *Annuaire de l'Inst.* (1931), 236; Sarkar, pp. 462–6; Garcia Mora, 19 *U. Pitt. L.R.* (1957–9), 567–90; van Hecke, 106 Hague *Recueil* (1962, II), 317–18; Bourquin, 16 Hague *Recueil* (1927, I), 121–89.

[2] See *Nusselein* v. *Belgian State*, Int. L.R. 17 (1950), no. 35; *Public Prosecutor* v. *L.*,

rency, immigration, and economic offences are frequently punished. The United Kingdom and the United States allow significant exceptions to the doctrine of territoriality though without express reliance upon the protective principle. Thus, courts of the former have punished aliens for abetment by acts on the high seas of illegal immigration,[1] and perhaps considerations of security helped the House of Lords in *Joyce* v. *D.P.P.*[2] to the view that an alien who left the country in possession of a British passport owed allegiance and was guilty of treason when he subsequently broadcast propaganda for an enemy in wartime. In so far as the protective principle rests on the protection of concrete interests, it is sensible enough: however, it is obvious that the interpretation of the concept of protection may vary widely.

(e) *The universality principle.*[3] A considerable number of states have adopted, usually with limitations, a principle allowing jurisdiction over acts of non-nationals where the circumstances, including the nature of the crime, justify the repression of some types of crime as a matter of international public policy. Instances are common crimes, such as murder, where the state in which the offence occurred has refused extradition and is unwilling to try the case itself, and also crimes by stateless persons in areas not subject to the jurisdiction of any state, i.e. a *res nullius* or *res communis*. Anglo-American opinion is hostile to the general principle involved, and the Harvard Research regards it as the basis only for an auxiliary competence, except for the offence of piracy.[4] Hijacking (unlawful seizure of aircraft) is subject to universal jurisdiction.[5]

ibid. 18 (1951), no. 48; *Re van den Plas*, ibid. 22 (1955), 205; *Rocha et al.* v. *U.S.*, 288 F. 2d 545 (1961), Int. L.R. 32, p. 112.

[1] *Naim Molvan* v. *A.-G. for Palestine* [1948] A.C. 531, *Ann. Digest*, 15, p. 115; Green, p. 556. See also *Giles* v. *Tumminello*, Int. L.R. 38, p. 120.

[2] [1946] A.C. 347; *Ann Digest*, 15 (1948), p. 91. On which see Lauterpacht, 9 *Camb. L.J.*, 330–48; also *Collected Papers* iii (1977), 221–41. See also *Board of Trade* v. *Owen* [1957] A.C. 602, at p. 634 per Lord Tucker; the Exchange Control Act, 1947, and the Strategic Goods (Control) Order 1959, 9 *I.C.L.Q.* (1960), 226. See further the U.S. Anti-Smuggling Act of 1935, Preuss, loc. cit., and Sarkar, op. cit., pp. 453–6.

[3] See Harv. Research, *ubi supra*, pp. 563–92; Jennings, op. cit., p. 156; Bishop, op. cit., pp. 323–4; *Universal Jurisdiction (Austria)* case, Int. L.R. 28, 341; *R.* v. *Martin* [1956] 2 Q.B. 272; Int. L.R. 20 (1953), p. 167; *Board of Trade* v. *Owen, supra*, and *Cox* v. *Army Council* [1963] A.C. 48; Int. L.R. 33, p. 194.

[4] The existence of multilateral treaties creating machinery to deal with international nuisances has given rise to the opinion that the slave trade, traffic in narcotics, counterfeiting, and the like are *delicta juris gentium* and by custom, can be assimilated to piracy; Harv. Research, pp. 569–71. Of course treaties may prescribe duties to punish certain crimes for the states which are parties.

[5] See Akehurst, op. cit., pp. 161–2; and cf. *Annuaire de l'Inst.* 54 (1971), ii. 455.

(f) *Crimes under international law.* It is now generally accepted that breaches of the laws of war, and especially of the Hague Convention of 1907 and the Geneva Conventions of 1949, may be punished by any state which obtains custody of persons suspected of responsibility. This is often expressed as an acceptance of the principle of universality,[1] but this is not strictly correct, since what is punished is the breach of international law; and the case is thus different from the punishment, under national law, of acts in respect of which international law gives a liberty to all states to punish, but does not itself declare criminal.[2] In so far as the invocation of the principle of universality in cases apart from war crimes and crimes against humanity creates misgivings, it may be important to maintain the distinction. Certainly universality in respect of war crimes finds expression in the Geneva Conventions of 1949.[3] Moreover, in the *Eichmann* case[4] the Israeli courts were concerned, *inter alia*, with charges of crimes against humanity arising from events before Israel appeared as a state.

4. *The Relations of the Separate Principles*

The status of crimes under international law involves special considerations and can be left on one side. The various principles held to justify jurisdiction over aliens are commonly listed as independent and cumulative, although writers may grade them with some subjectivity, by labelling one or more as 'subsidiary' to some other. However, it must be remembered that the 'principles' are in substance generalizations of a mass of national provisions which by and large do not directly reflect categories of jurisdiction in the same way that, for example, the more recent legislation on jurisdiction over the continental shelf involves reference to a definite quantity of interest recognized by international law. It may be that each individual principle is only

[1] See Cowles, 33 *Calif. L.R.* (1945), 177–218; Brand, 26 *B.Y.* (1949), 414–27; Baxter, 28 *B.Y.* (1951), 382–93; *In re Gerbsch, Ann. Digest* 16 (1949), no. 143; *In re Rohrig*, Int. L.R. 17 (1850), no. 125. Cf. Röling, 100 Hague *Recueil* (1960, II), 357–62.

[2] On piracy see *supra*, pp. 243–5.

[3] But Art. VI of the Genocide Convention gives jurisdiction to the *forum delicti commissi*. See generally Carnegie, 39 *B.Y.* (1963), 402–24. Cf. *In re Koch*, Int. L.R. 30, p. 496.

[4] Int. L.R. 36, pp. 5, 18, 277, 342 (biblio.). See Fawcett, 38 *B.Y.* (1962), p. 181 at pp. 202–8; Green, ibid., pp. 457–71; Lasok, 11 *I.C.L.Q.* (1962), 355–74; Silving, 55 *A.J.* (1961), 307–58; Baade, *Duke L.J.* (1961), 400–20. Another issue which arises is the application of municipal rules on limitation (*verjährung*) to charges of war crimes and other crimes under international law: see Levasseur, 93 *J.D.I.* (1966), 259–84; Conv. on the Non-Applicability of Statutory Limitations to War Crimes and Crimes Against Humanity, adopted by the U.N. Gen. Ass., 26 Nov. 1968; in force 11 Nov. 1970; 8 *Int. Leg. Materials* (1969), 68.

evidence of the reasonableness of the exercise of jurisdiction. The various principles often interweave in practice. Thus, the objective applications of the territorial principle and also the passive personality principle have strong similarities to the protective or security principle. Nationality and security may go together, or, in the case of the alien, factors such as residence may support a rather *ad hoc* notion of allegiance. These features of the practice have led some jurists, with considerable justification, to formulate a broad principle resting on some genuine or effective link between the crime and the state of the forum.[1] Such a formulation would not necessarily solve issues of concurrence of jurisdiction, for example of the state of the nationality of the accused and the *locus delicti*.[2] Moreover, the principle of universality may still require a separate regime, with qualifications on competence arising from general principles of law, including the rule *ne bis in idem*.[3] Where there are connexions with several law districts the forum which is not the *locus delicti* may allow the accused to plead the *lex loci delicti*.[4]

5. *Extra-territorial Enforcement Measures*[5]

The governing principle is that a state cannot take measures on

[1] Mann, 111 Hague *Recueil* (1964, I), 43–51, 82–126; Sarkar, op. cit., pp. 466–70; Fawcett, op. cit., pp. 188–90 (with particular reference to the *Eichmann* case, on which see literature cited *supra*, p. 305, n. 4). Cf. Fitzmaurice, 92 Hague *Recueil* (1957, II), 215–17. See also the proper law approach in *U.S.* v. *R.P. Oldham Co. et al.*, Int. L.R. 24 (1957), 673; and cf. Seyersted, 14 *I.C.L.Q.* (1965), p. 31 at pp. 33–43 (on jurisdiction over state organs on foreign territory). On the latter see also *Weiss* v. *Inspector-General*, Int. L.R. 26 (1958, II), 210. On the effective link doctrine in the law of nationality see *infra*, pp. 393 seq. Such a principle applied to criminal jurisdiction would place reins on the permissiveness of the security principle. On the problem of jurisdiction in respect to United Nations forces see Bowett, *United Nations Forces*, pp. 244–8.

[2] See Int. L.R. 28, pp. 143–4 (amnesty by state of nationality).

[3] Where the doctrine of substantial connexion (the equivalent of a proper law as in private international law) is not applied, as in the case of the universality principle, it is possible that a choice of law problem is left open and that there is a tendency to solve this instinctively by reference to general principles of international law. As Mann, op. cit., pp. 17–22, points out, the 'private international law approach' and the 'public international law approach' are or should in principle be integrated, both in civil and criminal jurisdiction. The tendency towards a proper law approach supports this opinion.

[4] For example, to obtain benefit of a prescription period or to place a limit on the severity of the punishment.

[5] See Mann, 111 Hague *Recueil* (1964, I), 126–58; id., 13 *I.C.L.Q.* (1964), 1460–5; Jennings, 33 *B.Y.* (1957), 146–75; Whiteman vi. 118–83; Katz and Brewster, *The Law of International Transactions and Relations* (1960), 549–778; Brewster, *Antitrust and American Business Abroad* (1958); I.L.A., *Report of the Fifty-First Conference* (1964), pp. 304–592; *Report of the Fifty-Second Conference* (1966), pp. 26–142; *Report of the Fifty-Third Conference* (1968), pp. 337–402; Verzijl, 8 *Neths. Int. L.R.* (1961), 3–30; van Hecke, 106 Hague *Recueil* (1962, II), 257–356; Haight, 63 *Yale L.J.* (1953–4), 639–54; Whitney, ibid., 655–62; Henry, 8 *Canad. Yrbk.* (1970), 249–83; Akehurst, op. cit., pp. 179–212.

the territory of another state by way of enforcement of national laws without the consent of the latter. Persons may not be arrested, a summons may not be served, police or tax investigations may not be mounted, orders for production of documents may not be executed, on the territory of another state, except under the terms of a treaty or other consent given.[1] In the field of economic regulation, and especially anti-trust legislation, controversy has arisen. It is probable that states will acquiesce in the exercise of enforcement jurisdiction in matters governed by the objective territorial principle of jurisdiction. Courts in the United States, for example, in the *Alcoa*[2] and *Watchmakers of Switzerland*[3] cases, have taken the view that whenever activity abroad has consequences or effects within the United States which are contrary to local legislation then the American courts may make orders requiring the disposition of patent rights and other property of foreign corporations, the reorganization of industry in another country, the production of documents and so on. The American doctrine appears to be restricted to agreements abroad intended to have effects within the United States and actually having such effects.[4] Such orders may be enforced by action within the United States against the individuals or property present within the territorial jurisdiction, and the policy adopted goes beyond the normal application of the objective territorial principle.[5]

American activities have provoked a strong reaction from a large number of foreign governments.[6] Protest was provoked in particular by the Bonner Amendment to the Shipping Act, under which the U.S. Federal Maritime Commission was given regulatory powers concerning the terms upon which non-American shipowners carry goods to and from the United States. The United Kingdom[7] and other states enacted legislation to provide

[1] The *Lotus* case, P.C.I.J., Ser. A, no. 10 (1927), p. 18; *Service of Summons Case,* Int. L.R. 38, p. 133, Austria, S.C.; *Répertoire suisse* ii. 986–1017.

[2] *U.S.* v. *Aluminium Co. of America,* 148 F. 2d 416 (1945); Whiteman vi. 136.

[3] *U.S.* v. *Watchmakers of Switzerland Information Center Inc.*, 133 F. Supp. 40 (1955); 134 F. Supp. 710 (1955).

[4] See O'Connell ii. 821–2. Intention was not a prominent requirement in *U.S.* v. *I.C.I.*, 100 F. Supp. 504 (1951); 105 F. Supp. 215 (1952); and in many circumstances it can be inferred. See *U.S.* v. *Holophane Co. Inc.*, 119 F. Supp. 114 (1954); *Zenith Radio Corp.* v. *Hazeltine Research,* 395 U.S. 100 (1969).

[5] See Mann, 111 Hague *Recueil,* at pp. 104–8. See further I.L.A., *Report of the Fifty-Fifth Conference* (1972), pp. 107–75, 744–5.

[6] See I.L.A., *Report of the Fifty-First Conference* (1964), pp. 565–92; *U.K. Contemporary Practice* (1962), i. 15–18. But see Judge Jessup, sep. op., *Barcelona Traction* case (Second Phase), I.C.J. Reports (1970), p. 166.

[7] Shipping Contracts and Commercial Documents Act 1964. See, e.g. *In re Mitsui S.S. Co.*, Int. L.R. 33, p. 158.

defensive measures against American policy. It must be noted that anti-cartel legislation in Austria, Denmark and the German Federal Republic imitates the American doctrine. Moreover, the Court of Justice of the European Communities has applied a principle similar to the American 'effects doctrine' in respect of company subsidiaries.[1]

The American courts, the United States Government,[2] and foreign governments in reacting to American measures, assume that there are *certain* limits to enforcement jurisdiction but there is no consensus on what those limits are.[3] The view of the United Kingdom appears to be that a state 'acts in excess of its own jurisdiction when its measures purport to regulate acts which are done outside its territorial jurisdiction by persons who are not its own nationals and which have no, or no substantial, effect within its territorial jurisdiction'.[4] Professor Jennings has stated[5] the principle 'that extraterritorial jurisdiction may not be exercised in such a way as to contradict the local law at the place where the alleged offence was committed'. In the case of corporations with complex structures and foreign-based subsidiaries, a principle of substantial or effective connection could be applied as a basis for jurisdiction.[6] This approach would accord with the highly relevant notions of the conflict of laws and, in particular, the notion of the 'proper law' of a transaction. The present position is probably this: a state has enforcement jurisdiction abroad only to the extent necessary to enforce its legislative jurisdiction.[7] This latter rests upon the existing principles of jurisdiction and these, it has been suggested already, are close to the principle of substantial connection.

[1] *I.C.I.* v. *E.E.C. Commission*, Int. L.R., 48, 106 at pp. 121–3.

[2] See Whiteman vi. 133, 159, 164; 8 *Canad. Yrbk.* (1970), 267–8.

[3] See Judge Fitzmaurice, sep. op., *Barcelona Traction* case (Second Phase), I.C.J. Reports (1970), pp. 103–6; the Belgian Memorial, I.C.J. Pleadings, *Barcelona Traction*, p. 114; I.C.J. Pleadings, *Barcelona Traction* (*New Application: 1962*), I. Belgian Memorial, p. 165 and, in particular, p. 167, para. 336. In tax cases the U.S. Courts appear to be inhibited much more than in the anti-trust cases: see *U.S.* v. *First National City Bank*, 321 F. 2d 14 (1963), at p. 24, 325 F. 2d 1020 (1964).

[4] The Attorney-General, Sir John Hobson, 15 July 1964; *British Practice* (1964), p. 146 at p. 153. Criticized by Mann, 13 *I.C.L.Q.* at p. 1464. See also the U.K. Monopolies Act, 1948, s. 10 (4); the U.K. Restrictive Trade Practices Act, 1956, s. 6 (1); and American Law Institute, *Restatement*, Second, *Foreign Relations Law*, 1965, paras. 18, 30, 40.

[5] 33 *B.Y.* (1957), 151. See also *British Nylon Spinners Ltd.* v. *I.C.I. Ltd.* [1952] 2 A.E.R. 780 and [1954] 3 A.E.R. 88; Kahn-Freund, 18 *M.L.R.* (1955), 65.

[6] See *supra*, p. 298, n. 2; and see also *Carron Iron Co.* v. *Maclaren* (1855), 5 H.L.C. 416, 442 per Lord Cranworth; *The Tropaioforos* (1962), 1 Lloyds List L.R. 410; Mann, 111 Hague *Recueil*, at pp. 149–50.

[7] Cf. Mann, op. cit., pp. 156–7.

6. *A General View of the Law*

There is some risk in presenting the law in a schematic form, yet the usual presentation of the different facets of jurisdiction in separate compartments can obscure certain essential and logical points.

(a) In the case of substantive or legislative jurisdiction (the power to make decisions or rules enforceable within state territory), there is no major distinction between the types of jurisdiction. The 'types' used by writers in presenting materials (principally the civil, criminal, fiscal, and monetary jurisdictions) are not the basis of significant distinctions in the principles limiting extra-territorial jurisdiction.[1] Thus the exercise of civil jurisdiction in respect of aliens presents essentially the same problems as the exercise of criminal jurisdiction over them.

(b) There is again no essential[2] distinction between the legal bases for and limits upon substantive (or legislative) jurisdiction, on the one hand, and, on the other, enforcement (or personal, or prerogative) jurisdiction. The one is a function of the other. If the substantive jurisdiction is beyond lawful limits, then any consequent enforcement jurisdiction is unlawful.

(c) The two generally recognized bases for jurisdiction of all types are the territorial and nationality principles, but the application of these principles is subject to the operation of other principles (para. (d));

(d) Extra-territorial acts can only lawfully be the object of jurisdiction if certain general principles are observed:

(i) that there should be a substantial and *bona fide* connection between the subject-matter and the source of the jurisdiction;[3]

(ii) that the principle of non-intervention in the domestic or territorial jurisdiction of other states should be observed;[4]

[1] But see Mann, op. cit., e.g. at p. 96; and Jennings, 121 Hague *Recueil* (1967, II), 517–18. The latter relies on the judgment in the *Lotus* case. It is doubtful if the Court was concerned to establish any significant distinction.

[2] But see Mann, op. cit., pp. 13–14, 128.

[3] The various principles of criminal jurisdiction overlap and could be synthesized in this way: *supra*. See further *supra*, p. 298, n. 2; Mann, op. cit., pp. 44–51, 126; *Survey of International Law* (Working Paper Prepared by the Sec.-Gen.), U.N. Document A/CN. 4/245, 23 April, 1971, paras 80–90; Judge Padilla Nervo, sep. op., *Barcelona Traction* case (Second Phase), I.C.J. Reports (1970), pp. 248–50, 262–3. Cf. Judge Fitzmaurice, sep. op., ibid., pp. 103–6.

[4] See *Buck* v. *Attorney-General* [1965] Ch. 745, C.A., per Diplock, L.J., at pp. 770–2; *Lauritzen* v. *Larsen*, 345 U.S. 571 (1953); Int. L.R., 20, p. 197; *Romero* v. *International Terminal Operating Co.*, 358 U.S. 554 (1959); Int. L.R. 28, p. 145.

(iii) that a principle based on elements of accommodation, mutuality and proportionality should be applied. Thus nationals resident abroad should not be constrained to violate the law of the place of residence.[1]

(3) The customary law and general principles of law relating to jurisdiction are emanations of the concept of domestic jurisdiction[2] and its concomitant, the principle of non-intervention in the internal affairs of other states. These basic principles do not apply or do not apply very helpfully to (a) certain cases of concurrent jurisdiction[3] and (b) crimes against international law.[4] In these areas special rules have evolved. Special regimes also apply to the high seas,[5] continental shelf,[6] outer space[7] and Antarctica.[8]

(f) The principle of territorial jurisdiction is to be placed in a proper relation to the other principles. Thus it is not completely exclusive in its application to aliens within national territory. This qualification has several ramifications. First, the jurisdiction of the alien's state of origin is not excluded.[9] Secondly, the territorial jurisdiction may be excluded if there is an absence of substantial links between the alien or foreign corporation and the state asserting jurisdiction.[1]

(g) Jurisdiction is not based upon a principle of exclusiveness: the same acts may be within the lawful ambit of one or more jurisdictions. However, an area of exclusiveness may be established by treaty,[2] as in the case of offences committed on board aircraft.[3]

Excursus: British Aide-Mémoire to the Commission of the European Communities[4]

Aide-Memoire

The United Kingdom Government have noted, in the *Journal Officiel* of the European Communities dated 7 August 1969, the publication of a

[1] Oppenheim I, 296. [2] *Supra*, p. 291, cf. Mann, op. cit., pp. 16, 30.

[3] *Infra*. On jurisdiction of the sending state in respect of diplomatic missions see the Vienna Conv. on Diplomatic Relations, Article 31 (4); Hardy, *Modern Diplomatic Law*, p. 55. [4] *Supra*, p 305. [5] Chapter XI. [6] Chapter X.

[7] *Supra*, p. 266. [8] *Supra*, p. 265.

[9] See Whiteman, v. 216–19, at p. 219; *Yrbk., I.L.C.* (1949), 99.

[1] See the Belgian case, I.C.J. Pleadings, *Barcelona Traction*, Belgian Memorial, p. 114, para. 225; I.C.J. Pleadings, *Barcelona Traction* (*New Application: 1962*), Belgian Memorial p. 165; Mann, 111 Hague *Recueil*, p. 50. Cf. Judge Fitzmaurice, sep. op., I.C.J. Reports (1970), pp. 103–6.

[2] There may exist a rule of exclusiveness based upon customary law in the case of international crimes.

[3] *Infra*, p. 319. [4] 20 October 1969. Text in *British Practice* (1967), p. 58.

decision of the Commission of 24 July 1969 (No. IV/26267) concerning proceedings pursuant to Article 85 of the Treaty establishing the European Economic Community in the matter of dyestuffs. Article 1 of this decision declares that 'the concerted practices of fixing the rate of price increases and the conditions of application of these increases in the dyestuffs sector . . . constitute violations of the provisions of Article 85 of the EEC Treaty'. Article 2 of the decision inflicts or purports to inflict certain fines upon the commercial undertakings who are alleged to have participated in these concerted practices. Among the undertakings specified in Articles 1 and 2 of the decision are Imperial Chemical Industries, Limited (hereinafter referred to as 'I.C.I.'), which is a company incorporated and carrying on business in the United Kingdom. Article 4 of the decision declares that 'the present decision is directed to the undertakings mentioned in Article 1'; it then goes on to state that as far as I.C.I. and certain Swiss undertakings are concerned, '[the decision] may likewise be notified to them at the seat of one of their subsidiaries established in the Common Market'.

The United Kingdom Government neither wish nor intend to take issue with the Commission about the merits of this particular case. They accept that it is for the undertakings to whom the decision is directed to pursue whatever remedies are available to them under the E.E.C. Treaty if they desire for their part to challenge the legality or correctness of this measure taken by the Commission. It is in any event their understanding that certain of the undertakings to whom the decision is directed have already indicated their intention to institute proceedings before the European Court of Justice challenging the decision on various grounds.

The concern of the United Kingdom Government in this matter is rather directed towards the more fundamental point concerning the reach and extent of the jurisdiction exercisable by the Commission *vis-à-vis* undertakings which are neither incorporated in the territory of a member-State of the European Economic Community, nor carrying on business nor resident therein.

The Commission will be aware that certain claims to exercise extra-territorial jurisdiction in anti-trust proceedings have given rise to serious and continuing disputes between Western European Governments (including the Governments of some E.E.C. member-States) and the United States Government, inasmuch as these claims have been based on grounds which the Western European Governments consider to be unsupported by public international law.

In particular, the United Kingdom Government have for their part consistently objected to the assumption of extra-territorial jurisdiction in anti-trust matters by the courts or authorities of a foreign state when that jurisdiction is based upon what is termed the 'effects doctrine'—that is to say, the doctrine that territorial jurisdiction over conduct which has occurred wholly outside the territory of the State claiming jurisdiction may be justified because of the resulting economic 'effects' of such conduct within the territory of that State. This doctrine becomes even more open to objection when, on the basis of the alleged 'effects' within the State claiming jurisdiction of the conduct of foreign corporations abroad (that is to say, conduct pursued outside the territory of that State), such corporations are actually made subject to penal sanctions.

The United Kingdom Government are of the view that certain of the 'considerations' advanced in the decision of the Commission of 24 July 1969 conflict with the principles of public international law concerning the basis upon which personal and substantive jurisdiction may be exercised over foreign corporations in anti-trust matters. A summary statement of these principles as seen by the United Kingdom Government, is annexed to this *aide-mémoire* for ease of reference.

In particular, it will be noted that the method by which the decision of the Commission was purportedly notified to I.C.I. (Article 4 of the decision) ignores the clear legal distinction between a parent company and its subsidiaries and the separate legal personalities of the latter. The United Kingdom Government consider that this attempted 'notification' of a parent company through its subsidiary is designed to support a doctrine of substantive jurisdiction which is itself open to objection as going beyond the limits imposed by the accepted principles of international law.

So far as substantive jurisdiction is concerned, the United Kingdom Government are of the view that the decision of the Commission incorporates an interpretation of the relevant provisions of the E.E.C. Treaty which is not justified by the accepted principles of international law governing the exercise of extra-territorial jurisdiction over foreigners in respect of acts committed abroad.

The United Kingdom Government deem it necessary to bring these considerations to the attention of the Commission lest there be any misunderstanding as to their position in the matter.

STATEMENT OF PRINCIPLES ACCORDING TO WHICH, IN THE VIEW OF THE UNITED KINGDOM GOVERNMENT, JURISDICTION MAY BE EXERCISED OVER FOREIGN CORPORATIONS IN ANTI-TRUST MATTERS

The basis on which personal jurisdiction may be exercised over foreign corporations

(1) Personal jurisdiction should be assumed only if the foreign company 'carries on business' or 'resides' within the territorial jurisdiction.

(2) A foreign company may be considered to 'carry on business' within the jurisdiction by an agent only if the agent has legal power to enter into contracts on behalf of the principal.

(3) A foreign parent company may not be considered to 'carry on business' within the jurisdiction by a subsidiary company, unless it can be shown that the subsidiary is the agent for the parent in the sense of carrying on the parent's business within the jurisdiction.

(4) The separate legal personalities of a parent company and its subsidiary should be respected. Such concepts as 'enterprise entity' and 'reciprocating partnership' when applied for the purpose of asserting personal jurisdiction

over a foreign parent company by reason of the presence within the jurisdiction of a subsidiary (and a foreign subsidiary by reason of the presence of its parent company) are contrary to sound legal principle in that they disregard the distinction of personality between parent and subsidiary.[1]

(5) The normal rules governing the exercise of personal jurisdiction should not be extended in such a manner as to extend beyond proper limits the exercise of substantive jurisdiction in respect of the activities of foreigners abroad. Nor can the assertion of extended personal jurisdiction be justified on the basis that it is necessary for the enforcement of legislation which in itself exceeds the proper limits of substantive jurisdiction.

(6) There is no justification for applying a looser test to methods of personal service in anti-trust matters than is permissible in relation to other matters.

The basis on which substantive jurisdiction may be exercised in anti-trust matters

(1) On general principles, substantive jurisdiction in anti-trust matters should only be taken on the basis of either

(a) the territorial principle, or
(b) the nationality principle.

There is nothing in the nature of anti-trust proceedings which justifies a wider application of these principles than is generally accepted in other matters; on the contrary there is much which calls for a narrower application.

(2) The territorial principle justifies proceedings against foreigners and foreign companies only in respect of conduct which consists in whole or in part of some activity by them in the territory of the State claiming jurisdiction. A State should not exercise jurisdiction against a foreigner who or a foreign company which has committed no act within its territory. In the case of conspiracies the assumption of jurisdiction is justified:

(a) if the entire conspiracy takes place within the territory of the State claiming jurisdiction; or
(b) if the formation of the conspiracy takes place within the territory of the State claiming jurisdiction even if things are done in pursuance of it outside its territory; or
(c) if the formation of the conspiracy takes place outside the territory of the State claiming jurisdiction, but the person against whom the proceedings are brought has done things within its territory in pursuance of the conspiracy.

(3) The nationality principle justifies proceedings against nationals of the State claiming jurisdiction in respect of their activities abroad only provided that this does not involve interference with the legitimate affairs of other States or cause such nationals to act in a manner which is contrary to the laws of the State in which the activities in question are conducted.

[1] See also the issues involving the Canadian Government: 5 *Canad. Yrbk.* (1967), 308–10, 313–17 (note inserted by author).

7. *Cognate Questions, Including Extradition*

Ancillary issues abound and are of some complexity: some at least of these must be mentioned. In the first place, what are the precise legal consequences of a wrongful exercise of jurisdiction? In principle excess of jurisdiction gives rise to state responsibility even in the absence of an intention to harm another state.[1] Moreover, the state of which the accused is a national has *locus standi* in respect of proceedings which by object or mode involve a breach of existing standards protecting human rights.[2] Secondly, a change of sovereignty does not have the effect of an amnesty for criminals: the rule is in part the result of a principle of substitution, but particular applications may depend on genuine connexion or the principle of universality.[3]

Apart from trial *in absentia*, an unsatisfactory procedure, states have to depend on the co-operation of the other states in order to obtain surrender of suspected criminals or convicted criminals who are, or have fled, abroad. Where this co-operation rests on a procedure of request and consent, regulated by certain general principles, the form of international judicial assistance is called extradition.[4] However, executive discretion to expel aliens may be employed *ad hoc* for similar ends.[5] With the exception of alleged crimes under international law,[6] in the absence of treaty, surrender of an alleged criminal cannot be demanded as of right.[7] On the other hand, no general rule forbids surrender, and this is lawful unless on the facts it constitutes complicity in conduct harmful to human rights or in crimes under international law, for example acts of genocide. Much of the material on extradition depends on questions of internal and particularly

[1] See the Belgian final submissions in the *Barcelona Traction* case (Second Phase), I.C.J. Reports, 1970, p. 4 at pp. 17–18. *Ultra vires* acts may justify diplomatic protests, of course: cf. U.S. reaction in the *Cutting* case, *supra*, p. 303. See also Beckett, 6 *B.Y.* (1925), 59–60.

[2] *Infra*, pp. 518 seq.

[3] See Rosenne, 27 *B.Y.* (1950), p. 267 at pp. 282–7; Fawcett, 38 *B.Y.* (1962), 181–215. Cf. the cases on the effect of a change of nationality: *supra*, p. 303, n. 4.

[4] Extradition is not easy to classify: McNair and Oppenheim place it under 'Individuals'; Briggs links it with jurisdiction over aliens.

[5] Cf. *R.* v. *Brixton Prison (Governor), ex. p. Soblen* [1963] 2 Q.B. 283; Int. L.R. 33, p. 255. And see Thornberry, 12 *I.C.L.Q.* (1963), 414–74; O'Higgins, 27 *Mod.L.R.* (1964), 521–39; Bowett, 28 *B.Y.* (1962), 479–83.

[6] i.e. war crimes, crimes against humanity, and crimes against peace. See Neumann, 45 *A.J.* (1951), 495–508; Green, 11 *I.C.L.Q.* (1962), 329–54.

[7] See generally Briggs, pp. 580–600; Harv. Research, 29 *A.J.* (1935), Suppl., pp. 15–434; McNair, *Opinions* ii. 40–66; Green, 6 *Curr. Leg. Problems* (1953), 274–96; *Annual Digest* and International Law Reports sub voc.; *British Digest* vi, ch. 17; Shearer, *Extradition in International Law* (1971); Whiteman vi, ch. 16; Verzijl, *International Law in Historical Perspective* V. 269–401.

of constitutional law and the effect of treaties on municipal rules. However, some courts, in giving extradition in the absence of a treaty, have abstracted from existing treaties and municipal provisions certain 'general principles of international law'.[1] The two leading principles are that of double criminality, that the act charged must be criminal under the laws of both the state of refuge and the requesting state, and that of specialty, according to which the person surrendered shall be tried and punished exclusively for offences for which extradition had been requested and granted. Extradition may also be refused if the requesting state is not expected to observe reasonable procedural standards and also if the offence alleged is political.[2] The granting of political asylum[3] is a power which is limited in law in respect of international crimes, including genocide,[4] in certain conventions for the suppression of terrorist acts,[5] and in practice by security measures between members of political and military alliances.[6] In general, states refuse to extradite nationals, but in some cases to do so without assuming responsibility for trying the suspect is an obvious abuse of power.

[1] See *Re D'Emilia*, Int. L.R. 24 (1957), 499; *Re Campora et al.*, ibid., p. 518; *Re Bachofner*, ibid., 28. 322.

[2] Courts in England approach the definition of 'political offence' empirically: see *In re Castioni* [1891] 1 Q.B. 149, Green, p. 369; *In re Meunier* [1894] 2 Q.B. 415; *R.* v. *Governor of Brixton Prison, ex. p. Kolczynski* [1955] 1 Q.B. 540; *Schtraks* v. *Government of Israel* [1964] A.C. 556; Int. L.R. 33, p. 319; (and note the Div. Ct., [1963] 1 Q.B. 55 at pp. 86–9 per Lord Parker, C.J.); *R.* v. *Governor of Brixton Prison, ex. p. Kotronis* [1969] 3 A.E.R. 304 at pp. 306–7, per Lord Parker, C.J. (point not taken in H. of Lds.); *Re Gross and Others* [1968] 3 A.E.R. 804 at pp. 807–10, per Chapman, J.; *Cheng* v. *Governor of Pentonville Prison* [1973] A.C. 931, H.L.; *R.* v. *Governor of Brixton Prison, ex. p. Keane* [1971] 2 W.L.R. 194, D.C.; [1971] 2 W.L.R. 1243, H.L.; *R.* v. *Governor of Winson Green Prison, ex. p. Littlejohn* [1975] 1 W.L.R. 893, D.C. The last two decisions relate to the hybrid procedure under the Republic of Ireland (Backing of Warrants) Act 1965, on which see O'Higgins, 15 *I.C.L.Q.* (1966), 369–94. See also Gutteridge, 31 *B.Y.* (1954), 430–6; Evans, 57 *A.J.* (1963), 1–24; Wortley, 45 *B.Y.* (1971), 219–53; *Hungarian Deserter* case, Int. L.R. 28, p. 343; *Algerian Irregular Army* case, Int. L.R. 32, p. 294; *Jimenez* v. *Aristeguieta*, 311 F. 2d 547 (1963); Int. L.R. 33, p. 353; *The State* v. *Schumann*, Int. L.R. 39, p. 433; *Public Prosecutor* v. *Zind*, Int. L.R. 40, p. 214; *Karadzole* v. *Artukovic*, 247 F. 2d 198; Int. L.R. 24 (1957), p. 510; 170 F. Supp. 383, Int. L.R. 28, p. 326; *In re Gonzalez*, 217 F. Supp. 717; Int. L.R. 34, p. 139; *Digest of U.S. Practice*, 1975, 168–75. See also the European Extradition Conv., 359 U.N.T.S. 273, art. 3.

[3] In some influential instruments there is provision for a *right* to seek asylum from persecution: Universal Decl. of Human Rights, Art. 14; and see also the materials in Whiteman viii. 660–84. On diplomatic and extraterritorial asylum generally see *infra*, pp. 367, 376–7.

[4] Genocide Conv., Art. VII. For the former attitude of the U.K.: *U.K. Contemp. Practice* (1962, II), p. 223.

[5] For example: European Convention on the Suppression of Terrorism, 1977; 15 *Int. Leg. Materials* (1976), 1272 (and see the U.K. Suppression of Terrorism Act, 1978).

[6] Cf. the process of rendition under the Fugitive Offenders Act, 1881; see *British Digest* vi. 767 seq. See now, for U.K., the Fugitive Offenders Act 1967, c. 68.

Whilst international responsibility may arise as a consequence of the illegal seizure of offenders, the violation of the law does not affect the validity of the subsequent exercise of jurisdiction over them.[1] The position is similar in respect of defective extradition procedures and mistaken surrender of fugitive criminals.[2]

8. *Special Cases of Concurrent Jurisdiction*

Elsewhere the exercise of jurisdiction over ships on the high seas[3] or enjoying the right of innocent passage through the territorial sea has been considered.[4] The matter which falls to be dealt with here is the relation between the territorial sovereign and the flag state in the matter of jurisdiction[5] over private[6] vessels in ports or other internal waters.[7] The view that a ship is a floating part of state territory has long fallen into disrepute, but the special character of the internal economy of ships is still recognized, the rule being that the law of the flag depends on the nationality of the ship[8] and the flag state has responsibility for and jurisdiction over the ship. But, when a foreign ship enters a port, except perhaps as a consequence of distress,[9] a temporary allegiance is owed to the territorial sovereign and a case of concurrent jurisdiction arises, since both the flag state and the local sovereign may exercise jurisdiction in respect of activities associated with the ship for breaches of their respective laws.[1] In the

[1] This is the view adopted by courts in many states and by some writers. Much depends on the existence of independently sustainable grounds for the actual exercise of jurisdiction or of a waiver of a claim to reconduction. See generally Harv. Research, op. cit., pp. 623–32; Dickinson, 28 *A.J.* (1934), 231–45; O'Higgins, 36 *B.Y.* (1960), 279–320; Fawcett, 38 *B.Y.* (1962), p. 181 at pp. 193–202 (on the *Eichmann* case).

[2] The award in the *Savarkar* case (1911), Hague Court Reports, p. 275, supports this statement in the case of mistaken surrender, although in fact the French Government had agreed that the fugitive should remain in British custody while on French territory (cf. McNair, *Opinions* ii. 64).

[3] *Supra*, pp. 242 seq.

[4] *Supra*, pp. 207–9.

[5] See Gidel ii. 39–252; Jessup, *The Law of Territorial Waters and Maritime Jurisdiction*, pp. 144–208; Charteris, 1 *B.Y.* (1920–1), 45–96; Harv. Research, 23 *A.J.* (1929), Spec. Suppl., pp. 307–28; and 29 *A.J.* (1935), Suppl., pp. 508–15; Brierly, pp. 223–6; McDougal and Burke, pp. 161–73; Colombos, pp. 318–30; Briggs, pp. 341–54; van Praag, *Juridiction et droit international public*, pp. 509 seq.; id., Supplement, pp. 272 seq.; Whiteman ix. 62–7.

[6] On the immunities from jurisdiction of public vessels and foreign armed forces, see *infra*, pp. 366 seq. Concurrence may arise in these cases also.

[7] On the nature of internal waters see *supra*, p. 122. For analogous cases of concurrence see Beale, 36 *Harv. L.R.* (1922–3), 247–51; Lauterpacht, 9 *I.C.L.Q.* (1960), p. 208 at pp. 231–2.

[8] On which see *infra*, p. 424. See also *Lauritzen* v. *Larsen*, Int. L.R. 20 (1953), p. 197 at pp. 205–7.

[9] See Oppenheim i. 503–4; Briggs, p. 354; Schwarzenberger i. 199.

[1] See *U.S.* v. *Flores* (1933), 289 U.S. 137; Briggs, p. 337; *Re Bianchi*, Int. L.R. 24 (1957), 173.

case of criminal jurisdiction there is some debate on the limits of the local jurisdiction. In principle, there are no limits provided action is taken with regard only to breaches of local law and not to breaches of rules set by the law of the flag state.[1] However, it has been customary to contrast the Anglo-American position with the French jurisprudence (which has been followed by some other states). During the preparatory work of the Hague Codification Conference of 1930, the United Kingdom stated its opinion on the issues as follows:[2]

> . . . the State is entitled to exercise jurisdiction over a foreign merchant vessel lying in its ports and over persons and goods on board.
>
> In criminal matters it is not usual for the authorities to intervene and enforce the local jurisdiction, unless their assistance is invoked by, or on behalf of the local representative of the flag State, or those in control of the ship, or a person directly concerned, or unless the peace or good order of the port is likely to be affected. In every case it is for the authorities of the State to judge whether or not to intervene.

Thus in the view of the United Kingdom derogation from the exercise of local criminal jurisdiction is a matter of comity and discretion. In *Wildenhus'* case[3] the United States Supreme Court took the view that a murder by one crew member of another, both Belgian nationals, committed on board a Belgian steamship in dock in Jersey City, *ipso facto* disturbed the public peace on shore. These Anglo-American attitudes are sometimes supposed to contrast with French practice based upon the opinion of the *Conseil d'État* in the cases of the *Sally* and the *Newton* in 1806.[4] The *Conseil d'État* maintained the principle of local jurisdiction in matters affecting the interest of the state, in matters of police, and for offences by members of the crew against strangers even on board. The local jurisdiction was stated not to apply to matters of internal discipline or offences by members of the crew not affecting strangers,[5] except when the peace and good order of the port are affected or the local authorities are asked for assistance. The French practice is said to be more liberal *vis-à-vis* the flag state and to involve a more explicit renunciation of jurisdiction in some cases than the Anglo-American doctrine. How-

[1] Oppenheim, loc. cit; Gidel ii. 204, 246.

[2] McNair, *Opinions* ii. 194. See also *Wildenhus'* case (1887), 120 U.S. 1; Bishop, p. 606; Briggs, p. 341.

[3] See last note.

[4] See Charteris, op. cit., p. 50 (translation of the opinion); 23 *A.J.* (1929), Spec. Suppl., p. 325. It received imperial approval and had the force of legislation. See also the *Albissola*, *Ann. Digest* 5 (1929–30), no. 67.

[5] The instant cases involved assaults by members of the crews of American vessels in French ports on other crew members.

ever, the points of contrast are seen to be minimal on closer examination, and the actual practice on both sides is fairly uniform.[1] The French practice accepts the overriding nature of the local jurisdiction, and French jurisprudence has adopted the view that homicide of a fellow crew-member compromises the peace of the port.[2] In general, the local jurisdiction does not apply to acts taking place on board a ship before the vessel entered internal waters.[3]

A problem of some consequence arises from the view of the New York Court of Appeals in *Incres Steamship Co. Ltd.* v. *International Maritime Workers Union et al.*[4] that a Federal statute, the National Labor Relations Act, applied to labour disputes between foreign nationals operating ships under foreign flags and therefore the National Labor Relations Board had jurisdiction in respect of disputes concerning Liberian-registered ships operating from New York. In seeking to make intervention as *amicus curiae* in the appeal to the Supreme Court, the United Kingdom Government stated in the brief that to hold that such jurisdiction existed if the foreign flag vessel called at a United States port with any degree of regularity opposed 'the traditional internal economy doctrine long applied by all nations to foreign flag vessels temporarily in their ports' and gave 'an unwarranted extraterritorial effect to domestic law'. In its argument the United Kingdom Government seems to regard the exception as to matters involving the tranquillity of the port as a matter of law and not a matter of comity.[5] The dispute is not directly an issue of criminal jurisdiction, but the national policy involved is an important one, and such legislation employs penal sanctions as a longstop. Certainly the law of the flag doctrine needs more integration with the regime of vessels in port, and it may be that a doctrine of effective connexion[6] is usable in questions of both criminal and civil jurisdiction. In the *Incres* case[7] and also in *McCulloch* v. *Sociedad Nacional*[8] the Supreme Court held that the

[1] Many states follow slight variants of the 'English' or 'French' rules: but the 'French' rule may be that of the *Tempest* (next note), not that laid down in 1806.

[2] *Cour de Cassation*: the *Tempest*, 1859, Dalloz i. 88; quoted in *Wildenhus*' case, *supra*, p. 317, n. 2. In the facts of the *Tempest* it will be found that disorder on shore had been caused.

[3] Colombos, pp. 301–3; Fitzmaurice, 92 Hague *Recueil* (1957, II), 211.

[4] 10 N.Y. 2d 218, 176 N.E. 2d 719 and other appeals (1963), 372 U.S. 10; 57 *A.J.* (1963), 659; Bishop, p. 586. The Supreme Court reaffirmed the jurisdiction of the flag state. See also May, 54 *Georgetown L.J.* (1966), 794–856.

[5] See *U.K. Contemp. Practice* (1962, I), p. 18.

[6] *Supra*, p. 306.

[7] 372 U.S. 24 (1963); Int. L.R. 34, p. 66.

[8] 372 U.S. 10 (1963); Int. L.R. 34, p. 51. See further May, 54 *Georgetown L.J.* (1966), 794–856; *Lopes* v. *S.S. Ocean Daphne*, 337 F. 2d 777; Int. L.R. 35, p. 97.

National Labor Relations Act had no application to the operations of foreign-flag ships employing alien crews. In *McCulloch* the Supreme Court relied principally on the construction of the Act but also referred to the 'well-established rule of international law that the law of the flag State ordinarily governs the internal affairs of a ship'.

Aircraft have not fitted very readily into the jurisdictional rules of either domestic or international law, and crimes on board civil aircraft over the high seas or in the airspace of foreign states or *terra nullius* have been the subject of considerable variations of opinion. In the United Kingdom the extra-territorial commission of common law offences such as murder and theft is punishable,[1] and many provisions, apart from aeronautical regulations made under the Civil Aviation Act, 1949, have no application to crimes on aircraft abroad or over the high seas.[2] The practice of states on the relation between the national law of the aircraft[3] and the law of any foreign territory overflown is not very coherent,[4] and no doubt the general practice on criminal jurisdiction, considered earlier, supplies some useful principles. However, work sponsored by the International Civil Aviation Organization has produced a Convention on Offences and Certain Other Acts Committed on Board Aircraft,[5] the jurisdictional provisions of which are as follows:

Art. 3

1. The State of registration of the aircraft is competent to exercise jurisdiction over offences and acts committed on board.

2. Each Contracting State shall take such measures as may be necessary to establish its jurisdiction as the state of registration over offences committed on board aircraft registered in such State.

[1] *R.* v. *Martin* [1956] 2 Q.B. 272 at pp. 285–6, Devlin, J., *obiter*; *R.* v. *Naylor* [1962] 2 Q.B. 527; Int. L.R. 33, p. 202.

[2] In *R.* v. *Martin* it was decided that sect. 62 (1) of the Civil Aviation Act has procedural effect and confers jurisdiction only if a substantive rule makes the act concerned criminal when committed on board a British aircraft. In that case the indictment was quashed, as the Dangerous Drugs Regulations, 1953, applied only to the United Kingdom. See generally Cheng, 12 *Curr. Leg. Problems* (1959), 177–207.

[3] On which see *infra*, p. 426.

[4] See the survey in Cheng, op. cit., pp. 180–1, based upon the U.N. Legis. Series, *Laws and Regulations on the Regime of the High Seas* ii (1952; Suppl., 1959). See generally Mankiewicz, *Annuaire français* (1958), pp. 112–43; Lemoine, *Traité de droit aérien* (1947), pp. 795 seq.; Honig, *The Legal Status of Aircraft* (1956); Oppenheim i. 520, n. 5; Treaty on International Penal Law, signed at Montevideo, 19 March 1940, Hudson, *Int. Legis.* viii, no. 582; Whiteman ix. 422–9.

[5] Signed at Tokyo, 14 September 1963; 58 *A.J.* (1964), 566; Cmnd. 2261; McNair, *The Law of the Air* (3rd ed.), p. 535. See Mendelsohn, 53 *Virginia L.R.* (1967), 509–63; and, for the U.K., the Tokyo Convention Act 1967, c. 52; comment by Samuels, 42 *B.Y.* (1967), 271.

3. This Convention does not exclude any criminal jurisdiction exercised in accordance with national law.

Art. 4

A Contracting State which is not the State of registration may not interfere with an aircraft in flight in order to exercise its criminal jurisdiction over an offence committed on board except in the following cases:

(a) the offence has effect on the territory of such state;
(b) the offence has been committed by or against a national or permanent resident of such state;[1]
(c) the offence is against the security of such state;
(d) the offence consists of a breach of any rules or regulations relating to the flight or manoeuvre of aircraft in force in such state;
(e) the exercise of jurisdiction is necessary to ensure the observance of any obligation of such state under a multilateral international agreement.

The practice of hijacking aircraft has prompted the promotion of multilateral conventions creating duties for states to punish the seizure of aircraft in flight and to exercise jurisdiction in specified conditions, for example, when the offence is committed on board an aircraft registered in the contracting state.[2]

[1] Cf. the principle of passive personality, *supra*, p. 303.

[2] Conv. for the Suppression of Unlawful Seizure of Aircraft, in force; 10 *Int. Leg. Materials* (1971), p. 133; 65 *A.J.* (1971), p. 440; U.K. Hijacking Act 1971; Conv. for the Suppression of Unlawful Acts Against Civil Aviation, in force 26 Jan. 1973; 10 *Int. Leg. Materials* (1971), p. 1151; 66 *A.J.* (1972), p. 455; U.K. Protection of Aircraft Act 1973. See further Institute of Int. Law, *Hijacking of Aircraft*, Provisional Report by McWhinney, 1970; McWhinney, (ed.), *Aerial Piracy and International Law* (1971); Green, 10 *Alberta L.R.* (1972), 72–88; Glaser, 76 *R.G.D.I.P.* (1972), 12–35; Int. Law Assoc., *Report of the Fifty-Fourth Conference*, 1970, 336–404. On the suppression of terrorism see also *infra*, pp. 362–3.

CHAPTER XV

PRIVILEGES AND IMMUNITIES OF FOREIGN STATES

1. *Introductory*

By licence[1] the agents of one state may enter the territory of another and there act in their official capacity. The acts may include the disposition and even the use in the field of military forces and the exercise of jurisdiction in the specific sense of setting up courts and using power to enforce the findings of such courts.[2] The privilege of the entrant in such cases stands against the exclusive power of the territorial sovereign to regulate, and to enforce decisions of its organs respecting, the territory and its population.[3] A concomitant of the privilege to enter and remain is normally the existence of an immunity from the jurisdiction of the local courts and the local agencies of law enforcement. However, as a general principle this immunity is delimited by a right on the part of the receiving state to use reasonable force to prevent or terminate activities which are in excess of the licence conferred or are otherwise in breach of international law.

The subject is related to two matters which must be given brief notice. First, it is a consequence of the equality and independence of states that municipal courts accept the validity of the acts of foreign states and their agents, including legislation.[4] This is a highly controversial subject, and in practice courts may refuse to recognize foreign acts considered to be contrary to international law[5] or the public policy of the forum.[6] A very common practice is for courts to refuse to exercise jurisdiction in cases involving foreign acts of state on the ground that to pass on the question would embarrass the executive in arriving at an appropriate diplomatic settlement.[7] This approach, whatever the

[1] Cf. the Vienna Conv. on Diplomatic Relations, 1961, Art. 2: 'The establishment of diplomatic relations between States, and of permanent diplomatic missions, takes place by mutual consent.'

[2] See *infra*, pp. 367 seq.

[3] See *supra*, pp. 289–90, on the relation between jurisdiction and sovereignty.

[4] See Briggs, pp. 404–8; Oppenheim i. 267.

[5] See *infra*, pp. 531 seq., on expropriation.

[6] There is also a rule, in effect an adjunct of the public policy proviso, that no effect will be given to foreign penal, fiscal, or political laws.

[7] See *Banco Nacional de Cuba* v. *Sabbatino*, 84 Sup. Ct. 923 (1964); and the comment

motivation, is akin to the notion that admissibility of a claim is related to the appropriateness of the forum.[1] The second related matter is the privilege, which as a matter of comity is usually allowed, of foreign states to appear as plaintiffs in national courts.[2] The generally recognized limits to the privilege are the non-enforcement of penal or revenue laws by this means and the refusal to admit disputes between the plaintiff state and the state of the forum (or a third state) to be presented as civil actions.[3] In the latter case there is no dogmatic objection to the exercise of jurisdiction and the issue becomes one of appropriate forum, either diplomatic negotiation, arbitration, or judicial settlement on the international plane. When a foreign state brings an action in the courts of another state there is a submission to the jurisdiction which extends to any counter-claim which is in the nature of a defence to the action rather than a cross-action.[4]

2. *The Distinction between Non-justiciability and Immunity as a Jurisdictional Bar*

The concept of state immunity is treated very often in the context of statements in which the immunity features as a bar to a jurisdiction of the state of the forum which would exist *but for* the doctrine of immunity, and which can be waived by the beneficiary state. The facts of well-known cases involve ships or other property actually within the territorial jurisdiction, the latter being 'excluded' by the existence of state immunity. Thus in *The Schooner Exchange*[5] the principles appear as implied conditions of a licence to enter foreign territory. It is, however, important to bear in mind that state immunity may appear as a doctrine of inadmissibility or non-justiciability rather than an immunity in a strict sense. In other words the national court has no competence to assert jurisdiction: it is a matter of the essential

by Henkin, 64 *Col. L.R.* (1964), 805–32. See further on *Sabbatino* Chapter XXI, Section II. Generally: Morgenstern, 27 *B.Y.* (1950), 73–80.

[1] See *infra*, pp. 495, 508.

[2] See Briggs, pp. 411–13; Harv. Research, 26 *A.J.* (1932), Suppl., pp. 493–526.

[3] Cf. *Secretary of State for India* v. *Kamachee Boye Sahaba* (1859), 13 Moo. P.C. 22; *Salaman* v. *Secretary of State for India* [1906] 1 K.B. 613. Cf. the *Arantzazu Mendi*, *supra*, pp. 103–5.

[4] See *High Commissioner for India* v. *Ghosh*, [1960] 1 Q.B. 134; *National City Bank* v. *Republic of China*, 348 U.S. 356 (1965); Int. L.R. (1955), 211; *Banco Nacional de Cuba* v. *First National City Bank*, 270 F. Supp. 1004 (1967); Int. L.R. 42, 45; and generally Simmonds, 9 *I.C.L.Q.* (1960), 334–43; Bishop, pp. 698–700.

[5] See *infra*.

competence of the local courts in relation to the subject-matter.[1] In *Buck* v. *A.-G.*[2] the Court of Appeal refused to make declarations on the validity or otherwise of the constitution of Sierra Leone as created by Order in Council at independence. The Court held that it had no jurisdiction to make a declaration of the kind claimed. Diplock, L.J.,[3] stated the principles as follows:

> 'The only subject-matter of this appeal is an issue as to the validity of a law of a foreign independent sovereign State, in fact, the basic law containing its constitution ...
>
> As a member of the family of nations, the Government of the United Kingdom (of which this court forms the judicial branch) observes the rules of comity, *videlicet* the accepted rules of mutual conduct as between State and State which each State adopts in relation to other States and expects other States to adopt in relation to itself. One of those rules is that it does not purport to exercise jurisdiction over the internal affairs of any other independent State, or to apply measures of coercion to it or to its property, except in accordance with the rules of public international law. One of the commonest applications of this rule ... is the well-known doctrine of sovereign immunity ... the application of the doctrine of sovereign immunity does not depend upon the persons between whom the issue is joined, but upon the subject-matter of the issue. For the English Court to pronounce upon the validity of a law of a foreign sovereign State within its own territory, so that the validity of that law became the *res* of the *res judicata* in the suit, would be to assert jurisdiction over the internal affairs of that State. That would be a breach of the rules of comity. In my view, this court has no jurisdiction so to do.

It is helpful to distinguish two principles on which sovereign immunity rests. The one, expressed in the maxim *par in parem non habet jurisdictionem*, is concerned with the status of equality attaching to the independent sovereign: legal persons of equal standing cannot have their disputes settled in the courts of one of them. This principle is satisfied if a sovereign state waives its immunity: the consent given upholds the status of equality. If there is a subject matter over which the national courts of the other state may properly exercise jurisdiction *in rem* or if there is a basis for acquiring jurisdiction *in personam*, then jurisdiction follows consent. The existence of a ship or a fund or other assets

[1] The same point arises in relation to diplomatic immunity: *infra*, p. 356.

[2] [1965] Ch. 745; Int. L.R., 42, 11; 41 *B.Y.* (1965–6), p. 435; Mann, 14 *I.C.L.Q.* (1965), pp. 985–7. See also *Zoernsch* v. *Waldock* [1964] 1 W.L.R. 675, at pp. 684, 688–9, 691–2.

[3] [1965] Ch. at p. 770–1. See further *Duke of Brunswick* v. *King of Hanover* (1848), 2 H.L.C. 1; *Johnstone* v. *Pedlar* [1921] 2 A.C. 262, 291; *Nissan* v. *A.-G.* [1970] A.C. 179, at pp. 216–18 per Lord Morris; Mann, 59 *L.Q.R.* (1943), pp. 42–57, 155–71.

may provide a basis in such cases for the exercise of civil jurisdiction in accordance with the principles of jurisdiction considered in Chapter XIV. The other principle on which immunity is based is that of non-intervention in the internal affairs of other states. This produces an area of issues which are in essence non-justiciable and are exemplified by *Buck* v. *A.-G.* (above). It is difficult to catalogue such issues but the nature of the subject matter will lead municipal courts to accept that the court is not an appropriate forum and can do nothing useful or effective.[1] A good example would be the immunity of arbitrations between states from the jurisdiction of the state in which the arbitration takes place.[2] This principle of non-justiciability overlaps with the cases in which courts refuse to exercise jurisdiction over transactions flowing from the execution of treaties the provisions of which do not provide for enforcement in the municipal courts of either party.[3] A related principle is the basis of the refusal of English and Canadian courts to be parties to the enforcement of foreign penal and revenue legislation.[4]

The first principle, stated above, as a rule setting the appropriate forum, is akin to the rule requiring prior exhaustion of local remedies as a pre-condition to the admissibility of certain types of claim on the international plane.[5] The principle of sovereign immunity keeps the domestic law out of the picture whereas the local remedies rule promotes domestic law as the most convenient recourse. It is a curiosity of the literature that writers who are critical of the local remedies rule are hostile to state immunity, at least partly, on the ground that it is 'contrary to the rule of law'. There are several practices which effectively exclude the operation of domestic law. Thus the United States has concluded treaties in which the government is subrogated automatically to the claims of American investors under the law of the other party as host state of the investor. There appears to be a need for an integrated view of the proper role of domestic law.

[1] *See National Institute of Agrarian Reform* v. *Kane*, 153 So. 2d 40 (1963); Int. L.R. 34, p. 12. Cp. the *Sabbatino* case in which, however, the U.S. Supreme Court applied the Act of State doctrine as a doctrine of municipal law, neither required nor prohibited by international law: Int. L.R. 35, p. 25.

[2] See Mann, 42 *B.Y.* (1967), 1–2.

[3] *Secretary of State* v. *Kamachee Boye Sahaba* (1859), 13 Moo. P.C. 22; *Cook* v. *Sprigg* [1899] A.C. 572; *Salaman* v. *Secretary of State* [1906] 1 K.B. 613; *Kingdom of Greece* v. *Gamet*, Int. L.R. 28, p. 153.

[4] See *Huntington* v. *Attrill* [1893] A.C. 150; *Government of India* v. *Taylor* [1955] A.C. 491; *United States* v. *Harden*, 41 D.L.R. 2d (1964), 721; Int. L.R. 42, p. 114; and Mann, 40 *Grot. Soc.* (1954), 25–47.

[5] *Infra*, p. 495.

The second principle, based upon the concept of non-intervention in internal affairs (or the reserved domain of domestic jurisdiction), extends to two situations. First, as in *Buck* v. *A.-G.*, cases in which the issue is not one which can be raised properly either in a domestic court or on the international plane. Secondly, cases in which the issues are not issues of municipal law but which can be the subject of international settlement, for example, questions concerning the execution of treaty provisions.

3. *The Rationale of Jurisdictional Immunity*

The most commonly quoted statement of the principle is the judgment of the United States Supreme Court in *The Schooner Exchange* v. *McFaddon*,[1] delivered by Marshall, C.J., who referred to the jurisdiction of a state within its own territory as being 'necessarily exclusive and absolute'. In his words:

> This full and absolute territorial jurisdiction being alike the attribute of every sovereign, and being incapable of conferring extra-territorial power, would not seem to contemplate foreign sovereigns nor their sovereign rights as its objects. One sovereign being in no respect amenable to another, and being bound by obligations of the highest character not to degrade the dignity of his nation, by placing himself or its sovereign rights within the jurisdiction of another, can be supposed to enter a foreign territory only under an express license, or in the confidence that the immunities belonging to his independent sovereign station, though not expressly stipulated, are reserved by implication, and will be extended to him.
>
> This perfect equality and absolute independence of sovereigns, and this common interest compelling them to mutual intercourse, and an interchange of good offices with each other, have given rise to a class of cases in which every sovereign is understood to waive the exercise of a part of that complete exclusive territorial jurisdiction, which has been stated to be the attribute of every nation.

The instances which were then enumerated were the exemption of the person of the sovereign from arrest or detention within a foreign territory, the immunity of foreign ministers, and the passage of foreign troops under licence. In an earlier period the immunity would be seen to attach to the person of the visiting sovereign, but in the view of the Supreme Court the immunity clearly extends to the various organs of the visiting nation, and the sovereign himself is considered somewhat in a

[1] (1812), 7 Cranch 116; Green, p. 237; Briggs, p. 413; Bishop, p. 659. See also *Municipality of St. John* v. *Fraser-Brace Overseas Corporation*, 13 D.L.R. (2d) 177 (1958); Int. L.R. 26 (1958, II), 165.

representative capacity. The immunity is primarily from the jurisdiction of the territorial courts, but it has other facets.[1] The rationale rests equally on the dignity of the foreign nation, its organs and representatives, and on the functional need to leave them unencumbered in the pursuit of their mission. Historically the immunity of diplomatic agents was established by a well developed practice before that of sovereigns and states.[2] However, the two doctrines are closely linked as to their underlying principles. They both contain an extra-territorial and a ceremonial element,[3] though the diplomatic immunity is more obviously functional.[4] It must be emphasized that the terms 'immunity', with or without the adjective 'absolute', and 'extraterritoriality' are no more than general guides to the legal regime involved in each case. The 'immunity' is not absolute, for it can be waived; and there are limits and exceptions varying with the nature of the occasion for the licence.[5] Moreover, it must be stressed that there is no immunity from international responsibility where this exists under general international law.

4. *State Immunity: Controversy over its Extent*[6]

In the course of the nineteenth century states appeared as commercial entrepreneurs on a considerable scale, creating

[1] See *infra*, pp. 343, 345.

[2] The immunity of sovereigns would not be in issue often and must have been presumed to exist. Sovereign immunity seems to have derived doctrinally from that of the ambassador.

[3] See Hall, *International Law* (8th ed.), pp. 217 seq., at p. 219; Fitzmaurice, 92 Hague *Recueil* (1957, II), 187–8; and Simmonds, 11 *I.C.L.Q.* (1962), 1204–10.

[4] Cf. Oppenheim i. 264–7, 271–5, 788, 792–3. Courts seeking to develop a restrictive doctrine of sovereign immunity are tempted to emphasize the distinction between state immunity and the very protected position of diplomatic agents: see *Lagos* v. *Baggianini*, Int. L.R. 22 (1955), 533; *Foreign Press Attaché* case, Int. L.R. 38, p. 160; Austrian S.C.; comment by Abel, 11 *I.C.L.Q.* (1962), 842–3; *Yugoslav Military Mission* case, Int. L.R. 38, p. 162; German Fed. Rep., Fed. Const. Ct. See also Lalive, 84 Hague *Recueil* (1953, III), 252–3; *S.* v. *British Treasury*, Int. L.R. 24 (1957), 223; *Reference on Powers of City of Ottawa to Levy Rates on Foreign Legations* [1943] S.C.R. 208; *Ann. Digest* 10 (1941–2), no. 106.

[5] It is now generally recognized that exterritoriality or 'extraterritoriality' of warships and diplomatic agents is a fiction, and an unhelpful fiction at that, since there is no necessary coincidence between territorial sovereignty and jurisdiction: see *Chung Chi Cheung* v. *The King* [1939] A.C. 160, P.C., at p. 175, quoting Brierly, *Law of Nations* (see the 6th ed., p. 223).

[6] See Whiteman vi. 553–726; Harv. Research, 26 *A.J.* (1932), Suppl., 451–738; Lémonon *et al.*, *Annuaire de l'Inst.* 44 (1952), i. 5 seq.; 44 (1952), ii. 424–6; 45 (1954), ii. 200–27; Lauterpacht, 28 *B.Y.* (1951), 220–72; Fitzmaurice, 14 *B.Y.* (1933), 101–24; Fawcett, 25 *B.Y.* (1948), 34–51; O'Connell ii. 841–79; Pugh and McLaughlin, 41 *N.Y.U.L.R.* (1966), 25–66; Vincke, 7 *Canad. Yrbk.* (1969), 224–54; Riad, 108 Hague *Recueil* (1963, I), 607–29; Sucharitkul, *State Immunities and Trading Activities* (1959); id., 149 Hague *Recueil* (1976, I), 87–216; Dunbar, 132 Hague *Recueil* (1971, I), 197–362;

monopolies in particular trades, and operating railway, shipping, and postal services. The First World War increased such activities, and the appearance of socialist and communist states has given greater prominence to the public sector in national economies. Moreover, countries such as India have found it necessary to have a public sector as a basis for a planned development of a modern economy. After earlier doctrinal developments Belgian and Italian courts responded to the extension of state activity by developing a distinction between acts of government, *jure imperii*, and acts of a commercial nature, *jure gestionis*, denying immunity from jurisdiction in the latter case. This approach, often called the doctrine of restrictive or relative immunity, has been adopted by the courts of at least thirteen countries.[1] The United States Supreme Court in *Berizzi Bros.* v. *S.S. Pesaro*[2] and the *Navemar*[3] upheld the principle of 'absolute immunity' in respect of state trading ships actually in possession of the foreign

Žourek, 86 *J.D.I.* (1959), 639–85; Seidl-Hohenveldern, ibid., pp. 1050–73; Lalive, 84 Hague *Recueil* (1953, III), 205–389; Report of Matsuda and Diena, 22 *A.J.* (1928), Spec. Suppl., pp. 118–32; Schmitthoff, 7 *I.C.L.Q.* (1958), 452–67; van Praag, 15 *R.D.I.L.C.* (1934), 652–82; id., 16 *R.D.I.L.C.* (1935), 100–37; Lissitzyn, in Friedmann, Henkin and Lissitzyn (eds.), *Essays in Honor of Philip C. Jessup* (1972), pp. 188–201.

[1] Belgium and Greece have long applied a restrictive doctrine. On Belgian law: Suy, 27 *Z.a.ö R.u.V.* (1967), 660–92. For Italy see *Borga* v. *Russian Trade Delegation*, Int. L.R. 22 (1955), 235; for Egypt see *F.P.R. of Yugoslavia* v. *Kafr El-Zayat Cotton Co. Ltd.*, Int. L.R. 18 (1951), no. 54 (following the jurisprudence of the Mixed Courts); for Switzerland see *Kingdom of Greece* v. *Julius Bär & Co.*, Int. L.R. 23 (1956), 195; for Austria see *Dralle* v. *Republic of Czechoslovakia*, Int. L.R. 17 (1950), no. 41 and *Collision* case, Int. L.R. 40, p. 73; for the German Federal Republic see decision of the Federal Constitutional Court, April 30 1963, Int. L.R., 45, 57 at pp. 61–82; noted in 27 *Mod.L.R.* (1964), 81; 59 *A.J.* (1965); 654; for the Netherlands see *Krol* v. *Bank of Indonesia*, Int. L.R. 26 (1958, II), 180; *N.V. Exploitatie-Maatschappij Bengkalis* v. *Bank Indonesia*, 13, *Neths. Int. L.R.* (1966), 318. French case law has fluctuated, but mainly supports the restrictive doctrine: see Hamson, 27 *B.Y.* (1950), 330; Lalive, op. cit., pp. 238–9, 248–9: *Guggenheim* v. *State of Vietnam*; 84 *J.D.I.* (1957), 408; Int. L.R. 22 (1955), 224; Int. L.R. 44, p. 74; *Societé Bauer-Marchal* v. *Ministre des Finances de Turquie*, Int. L.R. 10 (1957), 204; Int. L.R. 44, p. 75; and *Administration des Chemins de Fer iraniens* v. *Société Levant Express Transport*, 73 *R.G.D.I.P.* (1969), 883. The Irish High Court has denied immunity with respect to a trading vessel: the *Ramava*, *Ann. Digest* 10 (1941–2), no. 20. In Canada the Government favours the Tate letter, it seems; 7 *Canad. Yrbk.* (1969), 298–302, and the courts now favour restrictive immunity: *Allan Construction Ltd.* v. *Venezuela* [1968] R.P. 145; *Venne* v. *D.R. of the Congo* (1969), 5 D.L.R. (3d) 128; (1971), 22 D.L.R. (3d) 669, S.C. (non-commital: see Castel, 9 *Canad. Yrbk.* (1971), pp. 165–72); *Penthouse Studios Inc.* v. *Venezuela* (1969), 8 D.L.R. (3d) 686. The doctrine of absolute immunity was applied by the S.C. in *Dessaulles* v. *Rep. of Poland* [1944] S.C.R. 275, but viewed with reserve in *Flota Maritima de Browning Cuba S.A.* v. *The Steamship Canadian Conqueror* (1962), S.C.R. 598; 91 *J.D.I.* (1964), 830; Int. L.R. 42, p. 125. For Pakistan see *Secretary of State of the U.S.A.* v. *Gammon-Layton*, P.L.D. 1971, Kar. 314, favouring restrictive immunity. For general surveys of judicial practice see Lauterpacht, 28 *B.Y.* (1951), 250–72; and Sweeney, *The International Law of Sovereign Immunity* (U.S. Dept. of State, October 1963); Johnson, 6 *Austral. Y.B.I.L.*, 1–51.

[2] (1926), 271 U.S. 562; Briggs, p. 417; Bishop, p. 662.

[3] (1938), 303 U.S. 68.

state. However, in 1952 the Department of State announced its intention to follow the restrictive principle of immunity,[1] and it is apparent that the courts will adopt that principle.[2] In *Alfred Dunhill of London, Inc.* v. *Republic of Cuba*[3] four of the Justices of the Supreme Court expressed support for the restrictive approach to sovereign immunity. It should be noted that the decision concerned the issue of what constituted an act of state, a question of justiciability for the domestic law of the United States. The restrictive doctrine of immunity is now codified in the United States as a result of the Foreign Sovereign Immunities Act of 1976.[4] There is certainly a trend toward a restrictive principle, although the courts of a number of countries adhere to the wider principle.[5] The English courts adhered to the principle of absolute immunity but the House of Lords has

[1] In the 'Tate Letter': Bishop, p. 670; Dept. of St. Bull. 26 (1952), 984, on which see Bishop, 47 *A.J.* (1953), pp. 93–106; Note, 1 *Georgia Journ. of Int. and Comp. Law* (1970), pp. 133–78. In 1918 the Dept. of Justice had expressed a contrary opinion: see Leonard, *A.S.I.L. Proc.* (1958), pp. 95–104.

[2] See the views of Justices Frankfurter and Stone in *Republic of Mexico* v. *Hoffman* (1945), 324 U.S. 31; Bishop, p. 667; *Ann. Digest* 12 (1943–5), no. 39; the *Beaton Park*, 65 F. Supp. 213; *Plesch* v. *Banque Nationale de la République d'Haiti* (1948), 77 N.Y.S. (2nd) 41, 43; *Republic of China et al.* v. *National City Bank of New York* (1955), 348 U.S. 356, Int. L.R. 22 (1955), 210; Green, p. 308; Bishop, p. 695; *New York and Cuba Mail S.S. Co.* v. *Republic of Korea*, 132 F. Supp. 684 (1955); *Rich* v. *Naviera Vacuba*, 295 F. 2d 24 (1961); *Victory Transport* v. *Comisaria General*, 336 F. 2d 354 (1964); Int. L.R. 35, p. 110; 59 *A.J.* (1965), 388; Bishop, p. 673; *Petrol Shipping Corp.* v. *Kingdom of Greece*, 360 F. 2d 103 (1966); Int. L.R. 42, 173; 94 *J.D.I.* (1967), 668; *Chemical Natural Resources, Inc.* v. *Republic of Venezuela*, 125 A. 2d 864 (1966); Int. L.R. 42, 119; *Pan American Tankers Corp.* v. *Rep. of Vietnam*, 291 F. Supp. 49 (1968); 296 F. Supp. 261 (1969); *Amkor Corp.* v. *Bank of Korea*, 298 F. Supp. 143 (1969); *Republic of Iraq* v. *First National City Trust Company*, 207 F. Supp. 588 (1962); Int. L.R. 34, p. 81; *Isbrandtsen Tankers* v. *President of India*, 446 F. 2d. 1198 (1971). See also Cardozo, 67 *Harv. L.R.* (1954), 608–18; *Restatement of For. Rel. Law* (1965), sections 65, 69; Anon., 62 *Northwestern Univ. L.R.* (1967), 397–427; *Et Ve Balik Kurumu* v. *B.N.S.*, 204 N.Y.S. 2d 971 (1960); Int. L.R. 31, p. 247.

[3] 425 U.S. 682 (1976); 15 *Int. Leg. Materials* (1976), 735; 70 *A.J.* (1976), 828.

[4] In force 19 January, 1977. For the text: 15 *Int. Leg. Materials* (1976), 1388. For the Dept. of State circular to foreign embassies: 27 *I.C.L.Q.* (1978), 253; *Digest of U.S. Practice*, 1976, p. 327. For comment: Von Mehren, 17 *Columbia Journ. of Transnational Law* (1978), 33–66; Delaume, 71 *A.J.* (1977), 399–422; id., *Festschrift für F. A. Mann* (1977), pp. 338–65.

[5] For the United Kingdom see *Mighell* v. *Sultan of Johore* [1894] 1 Q.B. 149; the *Cristina* [1938] A.C. 485; Green, p. 243; *U.S.A. and France* v. *Dollfus Mieg et Cie S.A.* [1952] A.C. 582; *Rahimtoola* v. *Nizam of Hyderabad* [1958] A.C. 379; Int. L.R. 24 (1957), 175; *The Quillwark*, 1922 S.L.T. 68; Ann. Dig., Vol. 11, no. 80. Australia, India, and South Africa follow the English cases. See *Wright* v. *Cantrell*, (1943) 44 S.R. (N.S.W.) 45; *Van Heyningen* v. *Netherlands Indies Government* [1949] S.R. (Qd.) 54; *U.S.* v. *Republic of China* [1950] Queensland W.N. 5; *Grunfeld* v. *U.S.A.*, N.S.W.R. (1968), Vol. 3, p. 36; 97 *J.D.I.* (1970), 146; *Mirza Ali Akbar Kashani* v. *United Arab Rep.* (1966) 53 A.I.R.S.C. 230; Int. L.R. 23, pp. 212, 214; *G.D.R.* v. *Dynamic Industrial Undertaking Ltd.* (1972), A.I.R. Bomb. 27; *De Howarth* v. *S.S. India* [1921] S.A.L.R.C.P.D. 451; *Ex p. Sulman*

reserved the right to reconsider the principle and judicial opinion is increasingly in favour of denying immunity in respect of commercial transactions.[1]

Many states, including the United States and U.S.S.R., agree by treaty to waive immunity in respect of shipping and other commercial activities,[2] and it could be said either that such treaties assume a broad doctrine of immunity or that they are part of a contrary trend. Reference to treaty practice should include mention of the Brussels Convention of 1926,[3] which subjected vessels engaged in trade owned or operated by foreign states to the local jurisdiction as if they were private persons. This Convention received only thirteen ratifications and cannot be regarded as of general significance.[4] However, the provisions of two important treaties, the Convention on the Territorial Sea and Contiguous Zone and the Convention on the High Seas, signed at Geneva in 1958 and now in force,[5] tend to assimilate for the purposes of the Conventions the position of government ships operated for commercial purposes to that of non-government merchant ships. The former Convention, in dealing with the right of innocent passage through the territorial sea,[6] distinguishes the position of 'government ships operated for commercial purposes' from that of 'government ships operated for non-commercial purposes'.[7] Article 9 of the latter Convention provides:[8] 'Ships owned or operated by a State and used only on government non-commercial service shall, on the high seas, have complete immunity from the jurisdiction of any State other

[1943] S.A.L.R.N.P.D. 190; *Parkin* v. *Congo Government*, 1971 (1) S.A. 259 (W.); *Lendalease Finance* v. *Corporacion De Mercadeo Agricola*, 1975 (4) S.A. 397 (C.). Communist states support this view, see e.g. *In re Produst*, Int. L.R. 22 (1955), 242 (Czechoslovakia). However, the Polish courts emphasize the principle of reciprocity; *S.* v. *British Treasury*, Int. L.R. 24 (1957), 223; 90 *J.D.I.* (1963), 190; *French Consulate in Cracow*, Int. L.R. 26 (1958, II), 178; 87 *J.D.I.* (1960), 542. Japan, Brazil, Chile, Norway, Portugal, Luxembourg, and the Philippines support absolute immunity. The practice of some states remains uncertain: cf. *Kovtunenko* v. *U Law Yone*, Int. L.R. 31, p. 259, Burmese S.C.

1 See the *Cristina* [1938] A.C. 485 at pp. 495–6 (Lord Thankerton), 498 (Lord Macmillan), 511–12 (Lord Wright), 520–3 (Lord Maugham); and see further, *infra*, p. 336, on the English cases.

2 See Sucharitkul, op. cit., pp. 151–4, 196–7; Żourek, 86 *J.D.I.* (1959), 660.

3 Hudson, *Int. Legis.* iii, no. 154, Art. II.

4 But see *Yrbk., I.L.C.* (1956), ii. 276, commentary to Art. 22.

5 *Supra*, pp. 183, 237. On government ships employed in commerce see generally Sucharitkul, pp. 15–103; and Thommen, *Legal Status of Government Merchant Ships in International Law* (1962).

6 *Supra*, p. 203.

7 See Articles 20, 21, and 22; and *Yrbk., I.L.C.* (1956), ii. 276, Art. 22 and commentary.

8 Contrast the I.L.C. draft, *Yrbk., I.L.C.* (1956), ii. 280, Art. 33 and commentary.

than the flag State.' These provisions are by no means conclusive of the general issue as to the extent of sovereign immunity, but they establish the position[1] in the very important sector of state-operated merchant shipping.

5. *The Distinction between Acts* Jure Imperii *and* Jure Gestionis

In the face of the evidence some writers conclude that the law is uncertain,[2] and a number of these express this conclusion in the form of a denial that the wider principle of immunity, often called the doctrine of absolute immunity, represents the law.[3] Certain authorities continue to regard the wider principle as representing present law.[4] Finally, a considerable number of writers maintain that the preponderant practice supports a principle of restrictive immunity on the basis of the distinction between acts *jure imperii* and acts *jure gestionis*.[5] The merits of this distinction must now be examined. Difficulties in establishing and applying criteria for classifying state activities have led some critics of the wider principle to express objection to the distinction as an alternative regime.[6] The short point is that there is a logical contradiction in seeking to distinguish the 'sovereign' and 'non-sovereign' acts of a state.[7] The concept of acts *jure gestionis*, of commercial, non-sovereign, or less essential activity,

[1] However, Art. 20 (or Art. 21) of the Territorial Sea Convention drew reservations from seven Communist states; and Art. 9 of the High Seas Convention drew reservations from eight Communist states. See McDougal and Burke, pp. 1180–9. The U.K. Government has informed the Secretariat of its objection to these reservations. See *Treaty Series* No. 5 (1963), Cmnd. 1929. See also *British Digest* vii. 505; Lillich, 28 *George Washington L.R.* (1960), 408.

[2] e.g., Fitzmaurice, 14 *B.Y.* (1933), 117; and id., 92 Hague *Recueil* (1957, II), 187; Briggs, pp. 447–8; Brierly, *Law of Nations* (6th ed.), p. 250.

[3] e.g. Lalive, 84 Hague *Recueil* (1953, III), 251; Oppenheim i. 274; Lauterpacht, 28 *B.Y.* (1951), 225–6 (but he is not dogmatic); Cavaré, 58 *R.G.D.I.P.* (1954), 177–207; O'Connell ii. 844–6.

[4] See van Praag, 15 *R.D.I.L.C.* (1934), 652–82; id., 16 *R.D.I.L.C.* (1935), 100–37; Guggenheim i. 182–7; Žourek, 86 *J.D.I.* (1959), 639–85.

[5] e.g. Sørensen, 101 Hague *Recueil* (1960, III), 170; id. *Manual*, 430–7. However, many writers, whilst supporting this position as a matter of principle and policy, are cautious in stating their views in terms of *lex lata*: cf. Sucharitkul, *State Immunities and Trading Activities*, pp. 355–9. See further the Asian African Legal Consultative Committee, Third Session, 1960, *Report*, p. 66.

[6] See Lauterpacht, op. cit., pp. 222–7; Brierly, loc. cit.; Lalive, op. cit., pp. 255–7.

[7] Fitzmaurice, op. cit., p. 121, observes: 'The truth is that a sovereign State does not cease to be a sovereign State because it performs acts which a private citizen might perform.' See also Bishop, 115 Hague *Recueil* (1965, II), 327–8; O'Connell ii. 845–6; *Weber* v. *U.S.S.R.*, *Ann. Digest*, Suppl. 1919–42, No. 74; Belman, *A.S.I.L. Proceedings* (1969), pp. 183–4.

requires value judgments which rest on political assumptions as to the proper sphere of state activity and of priorities in state policies. Many economists consider that an extensive public sector, as a concomitant of a modicum of planning, is a necessary way forward for underdeveloped economies which face problems of poverty, health, nutrition, and education of a magnitude equal to that of a national emergency only created for some Western countries by war or threat of war.[1] Legal exponents of *laisser-faire* theories would disagree.

Jurists have offered various criteria for distinguishing between acts *jure imperii* and acts *jure gestionis*. Weiss suggested that the nature of the act was the determinant: if the transaction can be made by an individual then it is *jure gestionis*.[2] Thus an individual can make a contract, but cannot legislate or expel an alien. Yet this test breaks down or at least gives odd results, if one argues that the purchase of stores for the armed forces is *jure gestionis*: this is a contract, but is hardly one which could be made by an individual. Another approach is to inquire into the purpose of the act,[3] and certainly this seems a more appropriate criterion. In practice, however, the reference to purpose restates the problem and involves classifying acts according to variable criteria of social and economic policy.[4] The least objectionable technique is to abandon a search for *general* principles of distinction and to except from immunity, empirically and on the basis of general practice, a particular type of activity or subject-matter, for example government ships operated for commercial purposes.[5]

[1] Figures for average life expectation, infant mortality, and the relation of diseases and malnutrition support this comparison. In *Berizzi Bros.* v. *S.S. Pesaro* the U.S. Supreme Court observed: 'We know of no international usage which regards the maintenance and advancement of the economic welfare of a people in time of peace as any less a public purpose than the maintenance and training of a naval force.' See also Schwarzenberger, 117 Hague *Recueil* (1966, I), 335–6.

[2] Hague *Recueil* (1923), 525–49. See also Seidl-Hohenveldern, 86 *J.D.I.* (1959), 1058; *Annuaire de l'Inst.* 45, ii (1954), 212; Austrian Supreme Court, 10 February 1961; Int. L.R. 40, p. 73; 11 *I.C.L.Q.* (1962), 840; German Fed. Rep., Fed. Constitutional Court, 30 April 1963; 27 *Mod. L.R.* (1964), 81; 59 *A.J.* (1965), 654.

[3] See Niboyet, *Traité de droit international privé français* vi (1949), paras. 1758–92; and the case law of states adopting restrictive immunity.

[4] See generally Sucharitkul, op. cit., pp. 202 seq., 267 seq., for a survey of all the variants of the doctrines. See also *Rahimtoola* v. *Nizam of Hyderabad* [1958] A.C. 379, 422, per Lord Denning.

[5] See the Conventions referred to *supra*, p. 329. Cf. the Harv. Research, 26 *A.J.* (1932), Suppl., p. 597, Art. 11. This is the view of Friedmann, *The Changing Structure of International Law*, p. 345. Clearly even this does not remove all the difficulties: see Fawcett, 25 *B.Y.* (1948), 34–48; Sucharitkul, op. cit., pp. 272–6; Suy, 27 *Z.a.ö. R.u.V.* (1967), at pp. 677–82. Cf. the flexible principles relating to jurisdiction in general, on which, *supra*, pp. 298 seq.

As things stand courts proceed more empirically than they would care to admit, and there are differing decisions in the various states on the classification of the purchase of military equipment, the purchase of goods for sale to the population of the state, and the operation of railways.[1] In an action arising from a contract for repairs to an embassy heating system the Constitutional Court of the German Federal Republic contradicted the opinion of the Federal Minister of Justice that this was a matter of *imperium* and not a commercial act.[2] In the *Victory Transport*[3] case the U.S. Court of Appeals listed as exclusively sovereign acts, internal administrative acts, such as expulsion of an alien, legislative acts, such as nationalization, acts concerning the armed forces, acts concerning diplomatic activity, and public loans.[4]

6. *Some Questions of Policy and Principle*

Writers hostile to the wider principle of immunity have used a great variety of arguments. It has been said that the sovereign who engages in ordinary commerce should be held to have waived his immunity, and that the use of immunity for extensive state operations is incompatible with the sovereignty of the receiving state. Furthermore it is pointed out that the tendency of municipal law, exemplified by the Federal Tort Claims Act in the United States and the Crown Proceedings Act in the United Kingdom, is to place the state and state corporations on an equal footing with other legal persons. The rule of law, it is suggested, is not adequately observed when ordinary claims between legal persons with *locus standi* in municipal courts are placed on the diplomatic plane with its delays and compromises. The reasonableness of this outlook is, it is said, supported by the fact that in practice governments often waive their immunity. These arguments have some force, but on closer examination they are seen to be in varying degrees inconclusive. In the first place the approach of many jurists to the 'sovereign in the market place' is based on conceptions concerning the role of the state and the significance of state ownership which are inapplicable even to many modern capitalist economies. It is this political aspect which makes it difficult to find a rationale for a restrictive prin-

[1] See Harv. Research, *ut supra*, pp. 609–11; Lalive, op. cit., pp. 255–7.

[2] See Mann, 27 *Mod. L.R.* (1964), 81.

[3] *Supra*, p. 328, n. 2. See also *Isbrandtsen Tankers Inc.* v. *President of India*, 446 F. 2d 1198 (1971); 66 *A.J.* (1972), 396.

[4] For criticism: Lissitzyn, in Friedmann, Henkin and Lissitzyn (eds.), *Essays in Honor of Philip C. Jessup* (1972), p. 188 at pp. 198–9. See also the German Fed. Rep., Const. Ct., 30 April 1963; *supra*, p. 331, n. 2.

ciple: as it has been pointed out,[1] economic activity of the state remains state activity. Indeed, from this point of view it would be more logical to do away with the immunity.[2] The points about the sovereignty of the receiving state and the rule of law both involve a *petitio principii*. The former alone is not in issue: two sovereignties are in issue, and it is the manner of their relation which is the debated question of law. The rule of law in the present context is the rule of international law which operates normally on the international plane: the immunity is from the *local jurisdiction*, not from legal responsibility. If the matter be regarded as one of appropriate forum, then it is by no means clear that the plaintiff's place of residence should have precedence over the municipal courts of the defendant state,[3] or the procedures of diplomatic protection.[4] In the 'plaintiff's forum' the foreign state is involved in the idiosyncrasies of the local law and, in particular, the operation of its rules of public policy.

Whilst it is easy to register the trend toward a restrictive principle of immunity, it is difficult as yet to see a new principle which would satisfy the criteria of uniformity and consistency required for the formation of a rule of customary international law. Objectivity has been nudged aside by missionary zeal and proponents of the restrictive principle have, for example, failed to notice (a) that the practice based upon the Tate letter was discretionary, immunity being 'suggested' on a political basis from time to time; and (b) that it was only in 1973 that the United States ceased to rely upon absolute immunity in the context of action *by foreign courts*. A number of distinguished lawyers[5] have concluded that international law requires immunity for sovereign functions and leaves it to the law of the forum to decide whether to accord immunity to state commercial activities. In view of the lack of agreed principles for making the crucial distinction, this position involves the subjection of the major principle of immunity to the discretion of domestic courts. If this be a correct view of the present position, then the outcome is unsatisfactory and reform is needed.

[1] By Fitzmaurice, 14 *B.Y.* (1933), 121.

[2] Which is the object of Lauterpacht's theses in 28 *B.Y.* (1951), 220–50.

[3] Cf. the operation of the local remedies rule, *infra*, pp. 495–505. The general rule of private international law, in particular for actions *in personam*, is that the proper forum is that of the defendant's residence or domicile. Hence the concession that a state can sue a private defendant in foreign courts. See also *Kingdom of Greece* v. *Julius Bär & Co.*, Int. L.R. 23 (1956), 195, for a proper law or substantial link doctrine.

[4] On which see *infra*, pp. 480 seq.

[5] For example, Bishop, 47 *A.J.* (1953) at p. 105; 115 Hague *Recueil* (1965, II), at p. 328.

A fresh approach to the problem would be as follows. The concepts of sovereign immunity (see section 2 above), the exclusive jurisdiction of the state within its own territory, and the need for an express licence for a foreign state to operate within that national jurisdiction (see section 3 above), can be taken as starting points. Each state has an existing power, subject to treaty obligations, to exclude foreign public agencies, including even diplomatic representation. If a state chooses, it would enact a law governing immunities of foreign states which would enumerate those acts which would involve acceptance of the local jurisdiction. Such acts would probably include the making of contracts expressed to be subject to private law and the acceptance of arbitration clauses. The existence of such legislation would be notified to foreign states having trade relations with the host state; a commencement date would be set well in advance to allow convenient withdrawal if necessary; and vested rights could be reserved. States would thus be given a licence to operate within the jurisdiction with express conditions[1] and the basis of sovereign immunity, as explained in the *Schooner Exchange*,[2] would be observed. Such a legal regime would be subject to the inevitable immunity *ratione materiae* (considered in Section 2 above), and the principles of international law as to jurisdiction.[3] The approach suggested would avoid the difficulties of the distinction between acts *jure gestionis* and acts *jure imperii*. For example, if an agreement were made in private law form, without any reservation as to its legal character, for the purchase of supplies for armed forces of a foreign state, local law (including conflict of law rules) would be applicable. The legislation envisaged above could also specify which, if any, assets or types of asset, would be subject to attachment and execution.

7. *The European Convention on State Immunity*

The adoption in 1972 of the European Convention on State Immunity[4] is an important development and provides further evidence of the trend toward a restrictive approach to immunity.

[1] Cf. the Calvo clause. [2] *Supra*, p. 325.

[3] Cf. *Kingdom of Greece* v. *Julius Bär & Co.*, Int. L.R. 23 (1956), 195, Fed. Trib. of Switz. (requirement of some close connexion with state in which proceedings occur).

[4] Opened for signature on 16 May 1972. For the text: 11 *Int. Leg. Materials* (1972), 470. For comment: Sinclair, 22 *I.C.L.Q.* (1973), 254–83; Krafft, 31 *Ann. suisse* (1975), 11–30; Knierim, 12 *Columbia Journ. of Transnational Law* (1973), 130–54; Council of Europe, *Explanatory Reports on the European Convention on State Immunity and the Additional Protocol* (1972).

At the same time the provisions have a cadence and economy of their own, and the Convention represents a compromise between the doctrines of absolute and relative immunity. The principal provisions of interest are as follows:

Article 6

1. A Contracting State cannot claim immunity from the jurisdiction of a court of another Contracting State if it participates with one or more private persons in a company, association or other legal entity having its seat, registered office or principal place of business on the territory of the State of the forum, and the proceedings concern the relationship, in matters arising out of that participation, between the State on the one hand and the entity or any other participant on the other hand.

2. Paragraph 1 shall not apply if it is otherwise agreed in writing.

Article 7

1. A Contracting State cannot claim immunity from the jurisdiction of a court of another Contracting State if it has on the territory of the State of the forum an office, agency or other establishment through which it engages, in the same manner as a private person, in an industrial, commercial or financial activity, and the proceedings relate to that activity of the office, agency or establishment.

2. Paragraph 1 shall not apply if all the parties to the dispute are States, or if the parties have otherwise agreed in writing.

The Convention formulates these and other exceptions to the principle of immunity, which applies apart from the express provisions (Article 15). There is no immunity from execution but foreign States are obliged to give effect to judgments rendered against them (Article 20). It is to be noted that the provisions do not incorporate the restrictive principle of immunity in terms, but a major part of activities of a commercial character will fall within Articles 6 and 7. The specification of connecting links is a special feature deriving from the need to provide a basis for recognition and enforcement of any resulting judgment. In the United Kingdom the State Immunity Act of 1978[1] will make possible the ratification of the Convention of 1972, together with the Brussels Convention of 1926.[2] Incidentally, the Act will place limits upon the free-ranging suppositions concerning the precise content of the 'restrictive principle' of immunity to be found in recent English decisions.

[1] Chapter 36 of 1978; Royal assent 31 July 1978; see Bowett, 37 *Camb. L.J.* (1978), 193–6. [2] *Supra*, p. 329.

8. *The Evolution of the English Cases*

The Court of Appeal produced the first authoritative statement of principle in *The Parlement Belge*,[1] in the words of Brett L.J.:

> The principle to be deduced from the cases is that, as a consequence of the absolute independence of every sovereign authority, and of the international comity which induces every sovereign state to respect the independence and dignity of every other state, each and every one declines to exercise by means of its courts any of its territorial jurisdiction over the person of any sovereign or ambassador of any other state, or over the public property of any state which is destined to public use, or over the property of any ambassador, though such sovereign, ambassador or property be within its territory and, therefore, but for the common agreement, subject to its jurisdiction.

In that case immunity was accorded to a mail packet owned by the King of the Belgians and operated by Belgian navy personnel. The Court of Appeal accepted that the mail packet was destined to public use and the writ *in rem* against the ship was set aside. The principle was applied by the Court of Appeal in *The Porto Alexandre*[2] to a vessel which was the property of, or in the alternative, subject to the direction of the Portuguese Government. The vessel was German and had been lawfully condemned in prize. At the material time the vessel was being used for trading purposes.

In *The Cristina*[3] the issue of principle was canvassed by the House of Lords. This concerned a privately owned Spanish vessel which had been requisitioned by the Republican Government of Spain during the civil war. The majority of their Lordships adopted the view that the fact of requisition involved a public use and immunity was granted. However, there was a divergence of view concerning the alternative approach which involved saying that 'possession or control' by a foreign sovereign was decisive. Lords Thankerton, Macmillan and Maugham[4] expressed criticism of the immunity of 'public ships engaged in commerce', whilst, with no great consistency, they allowed that requisition by a government entailed immunity. In subsequent cases individual judges expressed opposition to immunity in the context of commercial activity.[5] However, the majority in the

[1] (1880) 5 P.D. 197 at pp. 214–15. [2] [1920] P. 30.

[3] [1938] A.C. 485; Briggs, p. 419.

[4] Respectively, at pp. 495–6, 498, 520–3.

[5] See *Baccus S.R.L.* v. *Servicio del Trigo* [1957] 1 Q.B. 438 at p. 464, *per* Singleton, L.J.; *Rahimtoola* v. *Nizam of Hyderabad* [1958] A.C. 379 at pp. 415–24, *per* Lord Denning.

Court of Appeal in *Thai-Europe Tapioca Service* v. *Government of Pakistan*[1] adopted the view that the Court of Appeal was bound to follow the rule of international law as incorporated into English law by previous decisions in accordance with the principle of *stare decisis*. In respect of proceedings *in personam* concerning a body representing a sovereign state the question of employment of the vessel in private trading did not arise.[2]

The Judicial Committee of the Privy Council came to deal with the issue of principle in *The Philippine Admiral*.[3] The vessel was a merchant ship owned by the Reparations Commission, which was an agent of the Republic of the Philippines, and which operated in accordance with the policies laid down in the Reparations Act. The vessel came into the possession of a private Philippine corporation, the Liberation Steamship Company, by virtue of a contract of conditional sale, and was operated for commercial purposes. When the ship was in Hong Kong various actions *in rem* were commenced by repairers and charterers in the local courts and the Reparations Commission sought to rely on the doctrine of sovereign immunity.

The Privy Council adopted the principle of restrictive immunity. More precisely, their Lordships did not favour the application of the doctrine of sovereign immunity to 'ordinary trading transactions'.[4] Since the vessel in question had been operated as an ordinary merchant ship, immunity was denied. The leading English decisions on the subject were disciplined by that form of judicial resourcefulness known as 'distinguishing'. *The Parlement Belge* (above) was authority for the proposition that a foreign sovereign cannot be sued *in personam*, but immunity from an action *in rem* only applied if the vessel is being used 'substantially for public purposes', as was the case of the Parlement Belge. *The Porto Alexandre* (above) was in effect stated to have been decided *per incuriam* in that the Court of Appeal had misconstrued *The Parlement Belge* which had left open the position of vessels engaged 'in ordinary commerce'. *The Cristina* (above) was distinguished on the basis that the ship

Cf. the reasoning in *Mellenger* v. *New Brunswick Development Corporation* [1971] 1 W.L.R. 603, C.A.

[1] [1975] 1 W.L.R. 1485, at p. 1495, *per* Scarman, L.J., with whom Lawton, L.J. agreed. Lord Denning, at pp. 1491–2, restated his views as set forth in the *Rahimtoola* case, but held that there was no basis for jurisdiction in any event.

[2] Reference was made to the Court of Appeal decision in *Compañia Mercantil Argentina*, 40 T.L.R. 601 (1924) at p. 602, *per* Bankes, L.J.

[3] [1976] 2 W.L.R. 214; 47 *B.Y.* (1974–5), 365. See also *I Congreso del Partido* [1978] Q.B. 500, Robert Goff, J.

[4] [1976] 2 W.L.R. at pp. 232–3.

concerned was clearly destined for public use, having been requisitioned by the government in order to assist it in putting down a rebellion. Consequently, in the view of the Judicial Committee, the question of immunity in an action *in rem* against a state owned vessel employed solely for trading purposes was not in issue in *The Cristina*.

The Judicial Committee's insistence on the distinction between proceedings *in personam* and proceedings *in rem* as a means of canalising the effects of *The Parlement Belge* is awkward in some respects. First, it involves a confirmation of the doctrine of immunity in the case of proceedings *in personam*. Secondly, it is unacceptable that the application of a principle of international law should depend upon concepts peculiar to the system of domestic law.[1] One final comment may be made. The ship was described by the Judicial Committee as 'an ordinary trading ship for the purposes of the doctrine of sovereign immunity', in spite of the facts that her operations were under the terms of a contract with the Reparations Commission and were subject to the provisions of the Reparations Act. In terms of Philippines law the vessel was operating for public purposes. The difference between this case and the cases of requisitioned ships is very fine indeed. The candid view of judicial policy in these cases would be that the English judges are in effect *classifying* public purposes as seen by other systems: some qualify for immunity, some do not.

In *Trendtex Trading Corporation* v. *Central Bank of Nigeria*[2] the Court of Appeal was faced with the very important and difficult question of the status of the transactions of a central bank. The Central Bank of Nigeria acted as the reserve bank for Nigeria and acted as banker to the Government of Nigeria. The bank was wholly owned by the central government, which exercised a considerable amount of control over its affairs. The plaintiff company was seeking to sue for payments due upon a letter of credit issued by the bank. The Court of Appeal denied immunity on the specific ground that the bank was not an *alter ego* or organ of the Government of Nigeria. However, the judges expressed views relating to the principle of restrictive immunity in response to the full argument on the general question of immunity. Stephenson, L.J., regarded the principle of absolute immunity as representing English law until the contrary was declared by the

[1] See the *U.S.A. and Republic of France* v. *Dollfus Mieg* [1952] A.C. 582, H.L., where their Lordships avoided use of the concepts peculiar to bailment in the context of sovereign immunity.

[2] [1977] 1 Q.B. 529; 48 *B.Y.* (1976–7), 353.

House of Lords or Parliament.[1] In any case his Lordship was not convinced that the restrictive principle had yet received sufficently general acceptance. Lord Denning, M.R., and Shaw L.J. were of the view that the principle of restrictive immunity was established in international law and was to be incorporated into English law accordingly.[2] Unfortunately their lordships took no great pains to define the principle of restrictive immunity: Shaw L.J., for example, referred to 'a narrower principle which excludes ordinary commercial transactions from the ambit of sovereign immunity'.[3] Moreover, their lordships were not in all respects well informed. Thus neither Lord Denning nor Shaw L.J. appreciated that the European Convention on State Immunity (see above), to which both referred, in fact represents a compromise between the absolute and restrictive doctrines of immunity. Furthermore, the Court makes no reference to the criteria for the existence of a rule of customary international law, although Stephenson L.J. was aware of the need for caution.

English law is now set by the State Immunity Act of 1978, which will place restraints upon judicial essays in public international law. However, the decisions examined above provide some lessons and some of the problems will continue to appear notwithstanding the statute. In particular it will still be necessary to identify ships and other property 'in use or intended for use for commercial purposes',[4] to distinguish departments of government and 'separate entities', distinct from the executive organs and capable of suing or being sued,[5] and to identify acts done by such separate entities 'in the exercise of sovereign authority'.[6] The property of central banks, whether separate entities or not, is immune from various forms of execution under the new Act.[7]

9. *Waiver of Immunity*[8]

Immunity here is not mandatory: subject to the distinction drawn in section 2 above, no fundamental principle prohibits the exercise of jurisdiction, and the immunity can be waived by the state concerned either expressly or by conduct. Waiver may occur, *inter alia*, in a treaty, in a diplomatic communication, by actual

[1] [1977] 1 Q.B. at pp. 569–72.
[2] At pp. 555–9 and 575–9, respectively.
[3] At p. 575; and see Lord Denning, M.R., at p. 555.
[4] Sect. 10; sect. 13 (4); sect. 14 (4). [5] Sect. 14 (1).
[6] Sect. 14 (2). [7] Sect. 14 (4).
[8] See Harv. Research, 26 *A.J.* (1932), Spec. Suppl., pp. 540–72; Sweeney, op. cit. *supra*, p. 55.

submission to the proceedings in the local court or by legislation which establishes a public foreign trade undertaking as an autonomous economic unit with legal personality.[1] Voluntary submission to jurisdiction does not extend to measures of execution.[2] Waiver is not to be implied, by law as it were, from the fact that a given activity is commercial.[3] The problems of waiver are of course related to the controversy over the extent of immunity, and some courts utilize a doctrine of 'implied waiver' to restrict immunity. English courts,[4] on the other hand, required a genuine and unequivocal submission in the face of the court: waiver was not constituted either by a prior contract to submit to the jurisdiction[5] or by an arbitration clause in a contract, even when an award had been made and the foreign state was applying to have it set aside.[6] Under the State Immunity Act 1978 immunity is denied when there is a prior written agreement to submit to the jurisdiction and when there is a written agreement to submit to arbitration: see sections 2 and 9 of the Act.

10. *The Principle of Reciprocity*

From time to time the courts and jurists give approval to the principle of reciprocity in the context of state immunity, but it is far from having a precise role in the general law.[7] This approach could encourage uncertainty and provide excuses for failure to accept established standards,[8] but it could find a place in a part of the law which depends in practice on mutual accommodation.

11. *Other Exceptions to the Principle of Immunity*

Apart from waiver and the operation of a principle of reciprocity, practice supports the denial of immunity in certain fairly well-defined situations.

(1) Whilst the matter is controverted, it seems that there is

[1] See *infra*, p. 342.

[2] For another view: *Government of Peru* v. *Sociedad Industrial*, Int. L.R. 26 (1958, II), 195.

[3] Such a doctrine of implied waiver has been employed by the Italian courts: *Storelli* v. *Governo della Repubblica francese*, *Ann. Digest* 2 (1923–4), no. 66; *Hungarian P.R.* v. *Onori*, Int. L.R. 23 (1956), 203.

[4] See Dicey, *Conflict of Laws* (9th ed.), pp. 154–7; Cohn, 34 *B.Y.* (1958), 260–73.

[5] See *Kahan* v. *Pakistan Federation* [1951] 2 K.B. 1003; Int. L.R. 18 (1951), no. 50; *Baccus S.R.L.* v. *Servicio Nacional del Trigo* [1957] 1 Q.B. 438; Int. L.R. 23 (1956), 160.

[6] *Duff Development Co.* v. *Government of Kelantan* [1924] A.C. 797. Cf. *Myrtoon Steamship Co.* v. *Agent Judiciaire du Trésor*, Int. L.R. 24 (1957), 205.

[7] See *Dollfus Mieg* v. *Bank of England* [1950] Ch. 333 (Court of Appeal); Carter, 3 *I.L.Q.* (1950), 413; *Immunity of U.K. from Jurisdiction (Germany)* case, Int. L.R. 24 (1957), 207.

[8] See Lauterpacht, 28 *B.Y.* (1951), 245–6.

no immunity where the proceedings relate to rights or interests in or use of immovable property which the defendant state owns or possesses or in which it has or claims an interest.[1] In this type of case the independence of the state of the *forum rei sitae* and principles of convenience establish a priority differing from the general rule of immunity. If the *forum rei sitae* has no jurisdiction then no other court has under the rules of the conflict of laws. However, premises devoted to use as diplomatic missions do have immunity: the functional rationale prevails here.[2]

(2) There is no immunity where the proceedings relate to the acquisition by a foreign state by succession or gift of movable or immovable property subject to the jurisdiction of the state of the forum.[3] Cases of this kind raise difficult issues of law, and it is equitable that the rights of the various claimants should be adjudicated on a basis of equality.

(3) In England at least the rule of immunity cannot apply if a trust fund is to be administered in which a foreign state or foreign sovereign is interested, unless the alleged trustee is a foreign sovereign.[4]

12. *Political Subdivisions and State Agencies*

The extent to which member states of federations and provinces of other types of state can claim immunity is unsettled.[5] Three approaches are possible: (1) on the basis that political subdivisions are organs of a state and entitled to the same immunity; (2) on the basis that sovereignty for this purpose inheres only in the central organs of a state; and (3) on a functional basis attempting to distinguish political acts (which are immune) from administrative acts. The existing case law is confused and reveals no

[1] Whiteman vi. 638–48; Harv. Research, Art. 9, *ubi supra*, pp. 572–90; Dicey, *Conflict of Laws* (9th ed.), p. 141. The rule has very wide acceptance in treaties and judicial decisions. See, for example, *Restitution of Property* (*Republic of Italy*) case, Int. L.R. 18 (1951), no. 52; *Limbin Hteik Tin Lat* v. *Union of Burma*, Int. L.R. 32, and cases in the next note. See also *Sultan of Johore* v. *Abubakar* [1952] A.C. 318. For another view: Hurst, *Collected Papers* (1950), pp. 233–7; Beckett, *Annuaire de l'Inst.* 44 (1952), I. 71–3; *Mahe* v. *Agent Judiciaire*, Int. L.R. 40, p. 80; U.K. State Immunity Act 1978, s. 6 (1).

[2] See *supra*, p. 332. See also the *Republic of Latvia* case, Int. L.R. 20 (1953), 180; and ibid. 22 (1955), 230; *Beckman* v. *Chinese P.R.*, ibid. 24 (1957), 221; *Tietz et al.* v. *P.R. of Bulgaria*, ibid. 28. 369; and see now Fed. Const. Ct. of West Germany, noted 59 *A.J.* (1965), 653, 654.

[3] Harv. Research, Art. 10, *ubi supra*, pp. 590–7; Fairman, 22 *A.J.* (1928), 568–9; Sweeney, op. cit., p. 25; U.K. State Immunity Act 1978, s. 6 (2).

[4] *Rahimtoola* v. *Nizam of Hyderabad* [1958] A.C. 379, 401; Int. L.R. 24 (1957), 175, 198; *British Digest* vii. 118–19; *Government of Aden* v. *East African Currency Board*, *British Practice* (1967), p. 66; Beckett, *Annuaire de l'Inst.* 44 (1952), i. 68–71; U.K. State Immunity Act 1978, s. 6 (3).

[5] See Sucharitkul, op. cit., pp. 106–12; Harv. Research, *ubi supra*, pp. 475, 484–7.

consistent principles.[1] Decisions allowing immunity on the ground that an entity is 'sovereign' under the law of the forum are not very much in point.[2]

Municipal courts have been prepared, apart from the effect of the restrictive doctrine, to extend immunity to various state agencies, including the United States Shipping Board,[3] the Spanish Servicio Nacional Del Trigo,[4] the Soviet Trade Delegation,[5] the Tass Agency[6] and the New Brunswick Development Corporation.[7] However, in this sphere also the principles on which courts act are still unsettled.[8] At least it is doubtful if separate incorporation as a legal person under municipal law should preclude immunity.[9] The general test seems to be that of effective control, and thus immunity may extend to a private corporation in which a foreign government has a controlling interest.[1] However, in decisions concerning central banks the

[1] See *Feldman* v. *State of Bahia* (1907), 26 *A.J.* (1932), 484; *Molina* v. *Comisión Reguladora del Mercado de Henequen* (1918), Hackworth ii. 402; *State of Céara* v. *Dorr* (1932), *Ann. Digest* 4 (1927–8), no. 21; *Van Heyningen* v. *Netherlands Indies* (1948), *Ann. Digest* 15 (1948), no. 43; *Montefiore* v. *Belgian Congo*, Int. L.R. 44, p. 72; *Mellenger* v. *New Brunswick Development Corporation* [1971] 1 W.L.R. 603, C.A.; 45 *B.Y.* (1971), 396. Some writers regard the jurisprudence as supporting a rule denying immunity: see de Visscher, 102 Hague *Recueil* (1961, I), 421; Harv. Research, loc. cit.

[2] See *Mighell* v. *Sultan of Johore* [1894] 1 K.B. 149; *Duff Development Co.* v. *Government of Kelantan* [1924] A.C. 797; *Kahan* v. *Federation of Pakistan* [1951] 2 K.B. 1003; *Sayce* v. *Bahawalpur* [1952] 2 A.E.R. 64.

[3] *Compania Mercantil Argentina* v. *United States Shipping Board* (1924), 131 L.T. 388; *Ann. Digest* 2 (1923–4), no. 73.

[4] *Baccus S.R.L.* v. *Servicio Nacional del Trigo* [1957] 1 Q.B. 438; Int. L.R. 23 (1956), 160.

[5] *Russian Trade Delegation in Sweden*, *Ann. Digest* (1946), no. 33; *Bank of Netherlands* v. *State Trust*, *Ann. Digest* (1943–5), No. 26. Cf. *Borga* v. *Russian Trade Delegation* (1953), Int. L.R. 22 (1955), 235, where the Italian Court of Cassation applied the restrictive doctrine of immunity to trading activity. See Fensterwald, 63 Harv. L.R. (1950), 614–42.

[6] *Krajina* v. *Tass Agency* [1949] 2 A.E.R. 274; *Ann. Digest* 16 (1949), no. 37.

[7] *Mellenger* v. *New Brunswick Development Corporation* [1971] 1 W.L.R. 603, C.A.

[8] See generally Fawcett, 123 Hague *Recueil* (1968, I), 227–9; Whiteman vi. 592–611; Riad, 108 Hague *Recueil* (1963, I), 598–629; Sweeney, pp. 54–5; Sucharitkul, pp. 104–61; Lalive, op. cit., pp. 243–7; Wedderburn, 6 *I.C.L.Q.* (1957), 290–300; Bishop, pp. 571–6; Cohn, 73 *L.Q.R.* (1957), 26–9. See also *Hungarian Academy in Rome* case, Int. L.R. 40, p. 59.

[9] See *Krajina* v. *Tass Agency*, *Baccus S.R.L.* v. *Servicio Nacional del Trigo*, *Mellenger*, *supra*; and *Czarnikow (C) Ltd.* v. *Rolimpex*, [1978] Q.B. 176, C.A. This is not the approach of French and other civil law courts: cf. *Passelaigues* v. *Mortgage Bank of Norway*, Int. L.R. 22 (1955), 227. See also de Visscher, op. cit., pp. 423–6.

[1] Cf. *Re Investigation of World Arrangements with Relation to Petroleum* (1952), 13 F. 280; Int. L.R. 19 (1952), no. 41; 47 *A.J.* (1953), 502, where the test applied was that of the 'object and purpose' of the Anglo-Iranian Oil Co., which was held to have a public purpose by reason of its connexion with the British Government. See also *U.S.* v. *Deutsches Kalisyndikat Gesellschaft*, 31 F. 2d 199 (1929), *Ann. Digest* (1929–31), no. 71; *Ulen* v. *Bank Gospodarstwa*, 24 N.Y.S. 2d 201 (1940); Sørensen, *Manual*, pp. 428–9; *In re Grand*

criteria have been applied with rather different results and reserve banks under substantial governmental control have been held not to be organs or agents of government.[1]

13. *Jurisdictional Immunities: Treaty Provisions*

It is necessary to emphasize the role of treaties in providing a stable basis for intercourse between states particularly in the field of commercial activities by state agencies. A considerable number of bilateral treaties provide for waiver of jurisdictional immunities in case of commercial activities. The commercial activities of state-owned ships are subjected to the jurisdiction of foreign courts by the Brussels Convention for the Unification of Certain Rules relating to the Immunity of State Owned Vessels of 1926[2] and the Montevideo Treaty on International Commercial Navigation Law of 1940.[3] In the sphere of air transport state enterprise is subjected to the rules of the Warsaw Convention for the Unification of Certain Rules relating to International Carriage by Air of 1929[4] with no reservation concerning immunity.[5]

The issue of state immunity is dealt with at the regional level in the Convention on Private International Law (the Bustamente Code) of 1928[6] and is the subject of the European Convention on State Immunity drawn up within the Council of Europe.[7]

14. *Attachment and Seizure in Execution*[8]

The majority of states concede immunity in respect of measures of execution directed against property of foreign states,[9] whilst a

Jury Investigation of the Shipping Industry, 186 F. Supp. 298 (1960); Int. L.R. 31, p. 209; *Et Ve Balik Kurumu* v. *B.N.S.*, 204 N.Y.S. 2d 971; Int. L.R. 31, p. 247.

[1] See *Swiss Israel Trade Bank* v. *Government of Salta* (1972), 1 Lloyd's Rep. 497; 46 *B.Y.* (1972–3), 427; *Trendtex Trading Corporation* v. *Central Bank of Nigeria* [1977] 1 Q.B. 529, C.A.; 48 *B.Y.* (1976–7), 353 at pp. 354–5 (further citations). See also the material in *Digest of U.S. Practice*, 1973, 227–30; and Delaume, 71 *A.J.* (1977), 399 at pp. 412–13.

[2] 176 L.N.T.S. 199; Hudson, *Int. Legis.*, iii. 1837.

[3] Hudson, *Int. Legis.*, viii. 460.

[4] 137 L.N.T.S. 11; Hudson, *Int. Legis.*, v. 100.

[5] See also the additional protocol of 1955, 478 U.N.T.S. 371, Article XXVI, concerning carriage for military purposes.

[6] 86 L.N.T.S. 254; Hudson iv. 2279; Articles 333–6.

[7] See above. [8] L'Exécution forcée.

[9] The rule is usually stated as one of immunity: cf. Sibert, *Traité* i. 272; Lauterpacht, 28 *B.Y.* (1951), at p. 243. Sørensen, 101 Hague *Recueil* (1960, III), 172, considers that the practice is not sufficiently uniform to support a customary rule. Hostile to immunity for acts *jure gestionis* at least are Oppenheim i. 274; Sucharitkul, pp. 247–51, 262–3, 347–50;

few apply the doctrine of restricted immunity for acts *jure gestionis* at this stage also.[1]

15. *Specialized Privileges and Immunities*

On the position of diplomats, consuls, and *ad hoc* missions see *infra*, Chapter XVI. On the immunities of foreign armed forces, *infra*, pp. 367–71. On the privileges and immunities of international organizations, *infra*, pp. 682–4. On the status of foreign warships and other public vessels, see further pp. 366–7.

García-Mora, 42 *Virginia L.R.* (1956), 354–9; Lémonon, *Annuaire d l'Inst.* (1952, I), 28–31; cf. Sørensen, *Manual*, pp. 440–1. See also Lalive, op. cit., pp. 272–81; resolution in *Annuaire d l'Inst.* (1954, II), 293, Art. 5; Whiteman vi. 709–26; *New York and Cuba Mail S.S. Co.* v. *Republic of Korea*, 132 F. Supp. 684 (1955); Bishop, p. 687; *Loomis* v. *Rogers*, 254 F. 2d 941 (1958); Int. L.R. 26 (1958, II), 161; *Weilamann and McCloskey* v. *The Chase Manhattan Bank*, 192 N.Y. Supp. 2nd 469 (1959); Int. L.R. 28, p. 165; *Stephen* v. *Zivnostenska Banka*, 15 App. Div. 2d 111, 222 N.Y.S. 2d 128 (1961), Int. L.R. 33, p. 184; *Rich* v. *Naviera Vacuba*, 295 F. 2d 24 (1961); Int. L.R. 32, p. 127; *Clerget* v. *Représentation commerciale de la Rép. du Viet-Nam*, 96 *J.D.I.* (1969), 894; *Hellenic Lines Ltd.* v. *Embassy of South Vietnam*, 275 F. Supp. 860 (1967); *R.S.F. de Yougoslavie* v. *Société européenne*, 98 *J.D.I.* (1971), 131.

[1] See *Socobel* v. *Greek State*, Int. L.R. 18 (1951), no. 2; 79 *J.D.I.* (1952), 244 (Belgium); *United Arab Republic* v. *Dame X*, 55 *A.J.* (1961), 167; 88 *J.D.I.* (1961), 458 (Switzerland). Cf. the French decision in *Procureur Général* v. *Vestwig. Ann. Digest* (1946), no. 32, on which see Castel, 46 *A.J.* (1952), 520–6. See further the important decision of the West German *Bundesverfassungsgerichts*, 13 December 1977; 38 *Z.a.ö.R.u.V.* (1978), 242; *N.J.W.* (1978), 485.

CHAPTER XVI

DIPLOMATIC AND CONSULAR RELATIONS

1. *Diplomatic Relations:*[1] *Introductory*

In its simplest sense diplomacy comprises any means by which states establish or maintain mutual relations, communicate with each other, or carry out political or legal transactions, in each case through their authorized agents. Diplomacy in this sense may exist between states in a state of war or armed conflict with each other, but the concept relates to communication, whether with friendly or hostile purpose, rather than the material forms of economic and military conflict.

Normally, diplomacy involves the exchange of permanent diplomatic missions, and similar permanent, or at least regular, representation is necessary for states to give substance to their membership of the United Nations and other major intergovernmental organizations.[2] Then there are the categories of special missions or *ad hoc* diplomacy, and the representation of states at *ad hoc* conferences.[3]

The rules of international law governing diplomatic relations were the product of long-established state practice evidenced not only by that practice but also by the legislative provisions and judicial decisions of national law. The law has now been codified to a considerable extent in the Vienna Convention on Diplomatic Relations.[4] Parts of the Convention are based on existing practice

[1] See Hardy, *Modern Diplomatic Law* (1968); Whiteman vii. 1–504; Denza, *Diplomatic Law* (1976); *Yrbk., I.L.C.* (1956) ii. 129; ibid. (1957), i. 2; ibid. (1958), i. 84; (1958), ii. 16, 89; Harv. Research Draft Conv., 26 *A.J.* (1932), Suppl., p. 15; U.N. Legis. Series, Vol. 7, Diplomatic and Consular Privileges and Immunities, 1958; Suppl. 1963; *British Digest,* vii, Chap. 19; Hackworth, iv. 393–654; vii. 1–504; Kiss, iii. 277–359; Havana Conv., 1928, Hudson, *Int. Legis.*, iv. 2385; Satow, *A Guide to Diplomatic Practice* (4th ed., 1957); Giuliano, 100 Hague *Recueil* (1960, II), 81–202; Lyons, 30 *B.Y.* (1953), 116–51; 31 *B.Y.* (1954), 299–370; 34 *B.Y.* (1958), 368–74. See also Cahier, *Le Droit diplomatique contemporain* (1962); Sen, *A Diplomat's Handbook of International Law and Practice* (1965), pp. 1–197; Eileen Young, 40 *B.Y.* (1964), 141–82; *Répertoire suisse* iii. 1431–1547; *Digest of U.S. Practice,* 1973 (Ann. vols., Chap. 4 in each); Dufour, 11 *Canad. Yrbk.* (1973), 123–65, ibid., 12 (1974), 3–37; do Nascimento e Silva, *Diplomacy in International Law* (1972).

[2] *Infra,* p. 677.

[3] *Infra,* p. 362.

[4] In force 24 April 1964. Text: 500 U.N.T.S., 95; Brownlie, *Basic Documents.*, p. 123; 10 *I.C.L.Q.* (1961), 600; 55 *A.J.* (1961), 1062. On the Convention see Kerley, 56 *A.J.* (1962), 88–129; Colliard, *Annuaire français* (1961), 3–42; Ahluwalia, 1 *Indian Journ.* (1961), 599. See further the Optional Protocol concerning Acquisition of Nationality and the Optional Protocol concerning the Compulsory Settlement of Disputes: 500 U.N.T.S., 223, 241; also in force 24 April 1964.

and other parts constitute a progressive development of the law. However, as ratifications mount up even the latter portions provide the best evidence of generally accepted rules.[1] The Convention presently has at least 123 parties. For English courts the Diplomatic Privileges Act of 1708 was declaratory of the common law. The Act of 1708 has been repealed and replaced by the Diplomatic Privileges Act of 1964.[2] which sets out in a schedule those provisions of the Convention which are incorporated into the law of the United Kingdom. The same Act replaces section 1(1) of the Diplomatic Immunities (Commonwealth Countries and Republic of Ireland) Act of 1952, which provided for immunity from suit. The Vienna Convention does not affect rules of customary law governing 'questions not expressly regulated' by its provisions, and, of course, states are free to vary the position by treaty and tacit agreements based upon subsequent conduct.

2. *General Legal Aspects of Diplomatic Relations*

(a) *Incidence.* Article 2 of the Vienna Convention provides that 'the establishment of diplomatic relations between States, and of permanent diplomatic missions, takes place by mutual consent'. There is no right of legation in general international law, though all independent states have the capacity to establish diplomatic relations. The mutual consent involved may be expressed quite informally.

(b) *Relation to recognition.* Whilst recognition[3] is a condition for the establishment and maintenance of diplomatic relations, the latter are not necessary consequences of recognition. The non-establishment or withdrawal of diplomatic representation may be the result of purely practical considerations or a form of non-military sanction.[4]

(c) *Rationale of privileges and immunities.*[5] The essence of diplomatic relations is the exercise by the sending government of state functions on the territory of the receiving state by licence

[1] Various sources refer to the Convention as representing generally accepted principles of international law: 7 *Canad. Yrbk.* (1969), 305–6; ibid., 8 (1970), 339–40; *Hellenic Lines Ltd.* v. *Moore*, 345 F. 2d 978; Int. L.R. 42, 239; *Digest of U.S. Practice*, 1974, 164; 1976, 189, 194, 198; 14 *Canad. Yrbk.* (1976), 326–7.

[2] 1964, c. 81. See *Empson* v. *Smith* [1966] 1 Q.B. 426; Int. L.R. 41, 407; C.A.; Buckley, 41 *B.Y.* (1965–6), 321–67.

[3] Chapter V.

[4] On several occasions the General Assembly has recommended severance of diplomatic relations. For the powers of the Security Council see the U.N. Charter, Art. 41.

[5] Hardy, op. cit., 8–12; *Yrbk., I.L.C.* (1956), ii. 157–61; Briggs, 761–3; Montell Ogden, *Juridical Bases of Diplomatic Immunity* (1936); *British Digest*, vii. 693–99; Preuss, 10 *N.Y.U.L.Q.R.* (1933), 170–87.

of the latter. Having agreed to the establishment of diplomatic relations, the receiving state must take steps to enable the sending state to benefit from the content of the licence. The process of giving 'full faith and credit' to the licence results in a body of 'privileges and immunities'. One explanation, now discredited, for this situation has been that the diplomatic agent and the mission premises were 'exterritorial', in other words for all purposes legally assimilated to the territorial jurisdiction of the sending state.[1] The consequences of this theory were never worked out and the existing rules of law simply do not rest on such a premiss. The existing legal position in truth rests on no particular theory or combination of theories, though in a very general way it is compatible with both the representative theory, which emphasizes the diplomat's role as agent of a sovereign state, and the functional theory, which rests on practical necessity.[2] The latter theory is fashionable but somewhat question-begging.

In the final analysis, the question must be related to the double aspect of diplomatic representation: the sovereign immunity (immunity *ratione materiae*) attaching to official acts of foreign states, and the wider and overlying, yet more conditional, elements of 'functional' privileges and immunities of the diplomatic staff and the premises.[3]

(d) *Fulfilment of duties by the host state.* The observance of legal duties by the host state requires the taking of a variety of steps, both legislative and administrative, in the municipal sphere. Appropriate care must be shown in providing police protection for personnel and premises[4] and the state may incur responsibility if the judiciary fails to maintain the requisite privileges and immunities.

(e) *Functions of missions.* Article 3 of the Vienna Convention provides:

1. The functions of a diplomatic mission consist *inter alia* in:
(a) representing the sending State in the receiving State;
(b) protecting in the receiving State the interests of the sending State and of its nationals, within the limits permitted by international law;[5]

[1] See 8 *Canad. Yrbk.* (1970), 337; and cases cited below, section 6.

[2] *Yrbk., I.L.C.* (1958), ii. 94–5; *Tietz* v. *People's Republic of Bulgaria*, Int. L.R. 28, p. 369; *Yugoslav Military Mission* case, Int. L.R. 38, p. 162. The preamble to the Vienna Convention refers to both considerations.

[3] See further section 7 below. Courts seeking to develop a restrictive doctrine of state immunity are tempted to emphasize the distinction between state immunity and the, in one sense, more extensive immunity of diplomatic agents: see *Foreign Press Attaché* case, Int. L.R. 38, p. 160 and *supra*, p. 326.

[4] See sections 4(a) and 5 below.

[5] See Art. 41 which provides, *inter alia*, that persons enjoying privileges and immunities have a duty not to interfere in the internal affairs of the receiving state.

(c) negotiating with the Government of the receiving State;
(d) ascertaining by all lawful means[1] conditions and developments in the receiving State, and reporting thereon to the Government of the sending State;
(e) promoting friendly relations between the sending State and the receiving State, and developing their economic, cultural and scientific relations.

2. Nothing in the present Convention shall be construed as preventing the performance of consular relations by a diplomatic mission.

3. *Staff, Premises, and Facilities of Missions*

(a) *Classification of personnel.* The Vienna Convention, in Article 1, divides the staff of the mission into the following categories:

1. The diplomatic staff, namely, members of the mission having diplomatic rank as counsellors, diplomatic secretaries or attachés.
2. The administrative and technical staff, such as clerical assistants and archivists.
3. The service staff, who are the other employees of the mission itself, such as drivers and kitchen staff, referred to in the Convention as 'in the domestic service of the mission'.

Two other terms are of importance in the Convention. A 'diplomatic agent' is the head of the mission or a member of the diplomatic staff of the mission; and the 'head of the mission' is 'the person charged by the sending State with the duty of acting in that capacity'.

(b) *Heads of Mission*

(i) *Accreditation and* agrément. Article 4 of the Vienna Convention provides as follows:

> 1. The sending State must make certain that the *agrément*[2] of the receiving State has been given for the person it proposes to accredit as head of the mission to that State.
>
> 2. The receiving State is not obliged to give reasons to the sending State for a refusal of *agrément*.

In this and other respects the receiving state is given a power of refusal and control in keeping with its role as licensor of the mission. In case of the appointment of a chargé d'affaires *ad interim* as provisional head of the mission, owing to the vacancy of the post of head or his inability, no *agrément* is required.[3]

[1] i.e. under local law. [2] A term of art meaning consent. [3] Article 19(1).

The actual taking up of functions is regulated by Article 13 of the Vienna Convention:

1. The head of the mission is considered as having taken up his functions in the receiving State either when he has presented his credentials or when he has notified his arrival and a true copy of his credentials has been presented to the Ministry for Foreign Affairs of the receiving State, or such other ministry as may be agreed, in accordance with the practice prevailing in the receiving State which shall be applied in a uniform manner.

2. The order of presentation of credentials or of a true copy thereof will be determined by the date and time of the arrival of the head of the mission.

(ii) *Classes and precedence.*[1] The principal provision is Article 14 of the Vienna Convention:

1. Heads of mission are divided into three classes, namely:

(a) that of ambassadors or nuncios[2] accredited to Heads of State, and other heads of mission of equivalent rank;

(b) that of envoys, ministers and internuncios, accredited to Heads of State;

(c) that of *chargé d'affaires* accredited to Ministers for Foreign Affairs.

2. Except as concerns precedence and etiquette, there shall be no differentiation between heads of mission by reason of their class.

Article 16, paragraph 1, provides:

Heads of mission shall take precedence in their respective classes in the order of the date and time of taking up their functions in accordance with Article 13.

(c) *Appointment of Members other than the Head of Mission.* Article 7 of the Vienna Convention provides as follows:

Subject to the provisions of Articles 5, 8, 9 and 11, the sending State may freely appoint the members of the staff of the mission. In the case of military, naval or air attachés, the receiving State may require their names to be submitted beforehand, for its approval.

In the International Law Commission there was considerable difference of opinion as to the extent to which the consent of the receiving state conditioned the appointment of members other than the head of mission. The text of Article 7 may seem sufficiently clear but at the Vienna Conference several delegations adopted the position that the Article was to be interpreted in

[1] For the background see Hardy, op. cit., pp. 21–4. The practice was regulated previously by the Congress of Vienna, 1815, and the Conference of Aix-la-Chapelle, 1818, which established four classes. See further *British Digest*, vii. 655–71.

[2] Representatives of the Holy See: on their precedence see Art. 16(3).

accordance with prevailing custom,[1] namely that the consent of the receiving state was required in all cases. It may be that, if Article 7 is not so interpreted by a majority of states, then the prevailing custom will have changed, and such a position can only be preserved by means of a reservation.[2] In any case the receiving state has special powers of control in case of appointments to more than one state (Article 5(1)), appointment of non-nationals (Article 8), and excessive appointments (see below).[3]

In recent years there has been some pressure for limitation on the size of missions. The consequence of this was the provision in Article 11 of the Vienna Convention:

> 1. In the absence of specific agreement as to the size of the mission, the receiving State may require that the size of a mission be kept within limits considered by it to be reasonable and normal, having regard to circumstances and conditions in the receiving State and to the needs of the particular mission.

The test is thus not an objective one but rests simply on the opinion of the receiving state.[4] However, a decision of the latter which was discriminatory or otherwise unrelated to the considerations of size as such would be in breach of the provision. Article 11, paragraph 2, provides that 'the receiving State may equally, within similar bounds and on a non-discriminatory basis, refuse to accept officials of a particular category'.

(d) *Termination of functions of individual diplomatic staff.*[5] The sending state may for its own reasons, practical or political, terminate the functions of individual staff members on notification of this to the receiving state.[6] The receiving state may act under Article 9[7] of the Vienna Convention:

> 1. The receiving State may at any time and without having to explain its decision, notify the sending State that the head of the mission or any member of the diplomatic staff of the mission is *persona non grata* or that any other member of the staff of the mission is not acceptable. In any such case, the sending State shall, as appropriate, either recall the person concerned or

[1] See Harvard Research Draft Conv., Art. 8. Comment: 26 *A.J.* (1932), Suppl., p. 67.

[2] Nepal has made a reservation.

[3] And see also on the *persona non grata* procedure, below.

[4] Article 11(1) has attracted reservations from certain states.

[5] Of course, diplomatic relations may be terminated by armed conflict, extinction of the sending or receiving state, and withdrawal of the mission at the will of either the sending or receiving state. See the Vienna Convention, Articles 44, 45(a). On the effect of death see Article 39(3) and (4). See further Whiteman vii. 83–108; Denza, op. cit., pp. 273–5.

[6] Article 43(a).

[7] See also Article 43(b).

terminate his functions with the mission. A person may be declared *non grata* or not acceptable before arriving in the territory of the receiving State.

2. If the sending State refuses or fails within a reasonable period to carry out its obligations under paragraph 1 of this Article, the receiving State may refuse to recognize the person concerned as a member of the mission.

The term *persona non grata* is simply the formal equivalent of 'not acceptable' in the case of staff not having diplomatic rank.

(e) *Premises and facilities*. Article 25 of the Vienna Convention provides that the receiving State 'shall accord full facilities for the performance of the functions of the mission'. Other provisions refer to freedom of movement for members of the mission, subject to legal restrictions established for reasons of national security,[1] and 'free communication on the part of the mission for all official purposes'.[2] A particular problem is the acquisition of premises since in some states the legal system may exclude a market in land or place restrictions on acquisition of land by aliens or foreign states. The International Law Commission draft[3] had required the receiving state either to permit acquisition by the sending state or to 'ensure adequate accommodation in some other way'. The Vienna Convention contains less decisive provisions in Article 21,[4] as follows:

1. The receiving State shall either facilitate the acquisition on its territory, in accordance with its laws, by the sending State of premises necessary for its mission or assist the latter in obtaining accommodation in some other way.

2. It shall also, where necessary, assist missions in obtaining suitable accommodation for their members.

4. *Inviolability*[5] *of Missions*

(a) *Premises*.[6] A necessary consequence of the establishment and functioning of a mission is the protection of the premises

[1] Article 26. See Denza, op. cit., pp. 115–18.

[2] Article 27(1). See Kerley, 56 *A.J.* (1962), 110–18; and Denza, op. cit., pp. 119–23.

[3] Article 19. See further Hardy, op. cit., pp. 33–4.

[4] Conditions governing the use of premises appear in Articles 12 and 41(3).

[5] Parry, in *British Digest*, vii. 700, observes that the term, which appears often in the Vienna Convention, is 'not particularly precise', and remarks: 'But it no doubt implies immunity from all interference, whether under colour of law or right or otherwise, and connotes a special duty of protection, whether from such interferences or from mere insult, on the part of the receiving State.' See also Giuliano, op. cit., 111 seq., 181–2; Whiteman vii. 353–5, 373–4; Harvard Research, 26 *A.J.* (1932), suppl., 52, 90–7; Guggenheim, i. 502–4; *Yrbk., I.L.C.* (1956), ii. 161, 170; 8 *Canad. Yrbk.* (1970), 355–6; *Répertoire suisse* iii. 1504–28.

[6] See *British Digest*, vii. 887–901; Giuliano, op. cit., pp. 181–93; Whiteman vii. 353–403; Dehaussy, 83 *J.D.I.* (1956), 596; *Digest of U.S. Practice*, 1976, 205.

from external interference. The mission premises, including the surrounding land, are the headquarters of the mission and benefit from the immunity of the sending state itself. The Vienna Convention recapitulates the position in the customary law in Article 22 as follows:

1. The premises of the mission shall be inviolable. The agents of the receiving State may not enter them, except with the consent of the head of mission.

2. The receiving State is under a special duty to take all appropriate steps to protect the premises of the mission against any intrusion or damage and to prevent any disturbance of the peace of the mission or impairment of its dignity.

3. The premises of the mission, their furnishings and other property thereon and the means of transport of the mission shall be immune from search, requisition, attachment or execution.

The provisions of paragraph 1 contain no proviso relating either to cases of emergency, for example, the situation in which the premises present a pressing danger to the surrounding district by reason of fire breaking out or use as a firing point, or to counter-measures in case of a use of the premises by the staff themselves for unlawful purposes. It is a nice question whether on general principles,[1] if remedial steps were taken by the host state, a defence of necessity or *force majeure* could be sustained.[2] It follows from article 22 that writs may not be served, even by post, within the premises of a mission but only through the local Ministry of Foreign Affairs.[3] Paragraph 2 of the Article creates a special standard of care apart from the normal obligation to show due diligence in protecting aliens present within the state.

On the question of the jurisdiction of local courts over actions against the sending state concerning the embassy premises see Chapter XV, pp. 323–5.[4]

(b) *Diplomatic asylum.*[5] The Vienna Convention contains no provision on diplomatic asylum, although in Article 41 the reference to 'special agreements' makes room for bilateral

[1] *Infra*, p. 464.

[2] See the case of Sun Yat Sen, detained in the Chinese Legation in London in 1896; McNair, *Opinions*, i. 85. See also Giuliano, op. cit., 192–3; Kerley, 56 *A.J.* (1962), 102–3; Guggenheim, i. 504; *Fatemi et al.* v. *United States*, 192 A. 2d 525 (1963); Int. L.R. 34, p. 148; *The Queen* v. *Turnbull, ex p. Petroff* (1971), 17 F.L.R. 438.

[3] See *Hellenic Lines, Ltd.* v. *Moore*, 345 F. 2d 978; Int. L.R. 41, p. 239.

[4] See also sect. 7 below.

[5] See Morgenstern, 25 *B.Y.* (1948), 236–61; Hackworth ii. 621–32; Whiteman vi. 428–95; *British Digest*, vii. 905–23; Ronning, *Diplomatic Asylum* (1965); Sørensen, *Manual*, pp. 409–12; 13 *Canad. Yrbk.* (1975), 338–9; ibid., 14 (1976), 335–6; *Digest of U.S. Practice*, 1974, 115–19; 1975, 158–9.

recognition of the right to give asylum to political refugees within the mission. The reason for the omission is substantially that it was deliberately excluded from the agenda during the preparatory work by the International Law Commission. It is very doubtful if a right of asylum for either political or other offenders is recognized by general international law.[1] There is a qualified right under the Havana Convention on Asylum of 1928[2] and it may be that a Latin-American regional custom exists.[3]

(c) *Archives, documents, and official correspondence.*[4] The Vienna Convention establishes the inviolability of the archives and documents of the mission 'at any time and wherever they may be'[5] and also of the official correspondence.[6] It is also provided simply that 'the diplomatic bag shall not be opened or detained'.[7]

(d) *Other property.* See the terms of the Vienna Convention, Article 22, paragraph 3, set out above.

5. *Inviolability*[8] *of Diplomatic Agents*

Article 29 of the Vienna Convention provides: 'The person of a diplomatic agent shall be inviolable. He shall not be liable to any form of arrest or detention. The receiving state shall treat him with due respect and shall take all appropriate steps to prevent any attack on his person, freedom or dignity.' This inviolability is distinct from the immunity from criminal jurisdiction (see below). As in the case of the inviolability of the mission premises, there is no express reservation for action in cases of emergency, for example, a drunken diplomat with a loaded gun in a public place.[9]

[1] Whiteman vi. 440, 458; McNair, *Opinions*, ii. 67, 76; Guggenheim i. 505; Harvard Research Draft, *ut supra*, Art. 6 and Comment, pp. 62–6; Sørensen, p. 409; *obiter dicta* of the International Court, *Asylum* case, I.C.J. Reports (1950), p. 266 at pp. 282–6. But see Morgenstern, loc. cit., and id., 67 *L.Q.R.* (1951), p. 362 at p. 381, for a different view.

[2] Hudson, *Int. Legis.*, iv. 2412; Article 2(1). See also the Montevideo Conv. on Political Asylum, 1933; Hudson vi. 607.

[3] See the *Asylum* case, I.C.J. Reports (1950), p. 266; ibid., 395, ibid. (1951), p. 71. See now the Inter-American Conv. on Diplomatic Asylum, 1954, Whiteman vi. 436, for a new Latin-American regime.

[4] See Hardy, p. 49; Cohen, 25 *B.Y.* (1948), 404; Whiteman vii. 389–92. Cf. *In re Estate of King Faisal II*, Int. L.R. 31, p. 395.

[5] Article 24.

[6] Article 27(2). See Denza, op. cit., pp. 124–5.

[7] Article 27(3); and see also Article 27(4). See Denza, op. cit., pp. 125–8.

[8] On this term see *supra*, p. 351, n. 5.

[9] See *British Digest*, vii. 785; Giuliano, op. cit., pp. 120–2; Denza, op. cit., pp. 135–6; *Fatemi et al.* v. *United States*, 192 A. 2d 525 (1963); Int. L.R. 34, p. 148.

Article 30 of the Vienna Convention provides as follows:

1. The private residence of a diplomatic agent shall enjoy the same inviolability and protection as the premises of the mission.

2. His papers, correspondence, and, except as provided in paragraph 3 of Article 31,[1] his property,[2] shall likewise enjoy inviolability.

The principle in paragraph 1 applies even to the temporary residence of an agent. However, there is no jurisdictional immunity in case of a real action concerning immovable property and, whilst no measures of execution may be taken against his property, courts may be unwilling to support measures of self-help undertaken by the diplomatic agent to recover premises from a person in possession under a claim of right made in good faith.[3]

6. *Personal Immunities from Local Jurisdiction*[4]

(a) *General.* Diplomatic agents enjoy an immunity from the jurisdiction of the local courts and not an exemption from the substantive law.[5] The immunity can be waived[6] and the local law will then apply. Moreover, the Vienna Convention, Article 41, paragraph 1, stipulates that 'it is the duty of all persons enjoying such privileges and immunities to respect the laws and regulations of the receiving State'.

In each jurisdiction a standard procedure will exist by which the qualification for immunity is established in such a way as to be conclusive for the local court.[7] In the United Kingdom, the Diplomatic Privileges Act 1964, provides as follows in section 4:

If in any proceedings any question arises whether or not any person is entitled to any privilege or immunity under this Act a certificate issued by or

[1] See below, p. 355.

[2] This includes goods in the agent's private residence, and also other property such as his motor car, his bank account and goods which are intended for his personal use or essential to his livelihood: *Yrbk., I.L.C.* (1958), ii. 98.

[3] *Agbor* v. *Metropolitan Police Commissioner* [1969] 2 A.E.R. 707, C.A.

[4] The jurisdiction of the sending state applies in principle: see Hardy, op. cit., p. 55; Vienna Convention, Article 31(4).

[5] *Dickinson* v. *Del Solar* [1930] 1 K.B. 376; *Empson* v. *Smith* [1966] 1 Q.B. 426, C.A.; *Fatemi* v. *U.S.*, 192 A. 2d 525 (1963); 34 Int. L.R. 148. Cf. *Regele* v. *Federal Ministry*, Int. L.R. 26 (1958, II), p. 544.

[6] See below, p. 356.

[7] For the position in the United States see *Trost* v. *Tompkins*, 44 A. 2d 226 (1945); *Carrera* v. *Carrera*, 174 F. 2d 496 (1949); Cardozo, 48 *Cornell L.Q.* (1963), 461; Whiteman vii. 108–26; Lyons, 24 *B.Y.* (1947), 116–47. On continental and Latin-American practice: Lyons, 25 *B.Y.* (1948), 180–210.

under the authority of the Secretary of State stating any fact relating to that question shall be conclusive evidence of that fact.

A court may act on information received from the executive by the parties.[1]

(b) *Immunity from criminal jurisdiction.*[2] Article 31, paragraph 1, of the Vienna Convention provides in simple terms and without qualification that 'a diplomatic agent shall enjoy immunity from the criminal jurisdiction of the receiving State'. This has long been the position in the customary law. A diplomatic agent guilty of serious or persistent breaches may be declared *persona non grata*.

(c) *Immunity from civil and administrative jurisdiction.*[3] Article 31, paragraph 1, also confers immunity from the local civil and administrative jurisdiction, except in the case of:

(a) a real action relating to private immovable property situated in the territory of the receiving State, unless he holds it on behalf of the sending State for the purposes of the mission;

(b) an action relating to succession in which the diplomatic agent is involved as executor, administrator, heir or legatee as a private person and not on behalf of the sending State;

(c) an action relating to any professional or commercial activity exercised by the diplomatic agent[4] in the receiving State outside his official functions.

The jurisdictions referred to 'comprise any special courts in the categories concerned, e.g. commercial courts, courts set up to apply social legislation, and all administrative authorities exercising judicial functions'.[5]

The exceptions to this form of immunity represent a modern development in the law and reflect the principle that the personal immunities of diplomatic agents should not be conferred without discrimination. The exceptions do not affect official acts and would rarely create a likelihood of criminal proceedings.

The exception relating to immovable property applies to the

[1] See generally, Lyons, 23 *B.Y.* (1946), 240–81; 26 *B.Y.* (1949), 433–7; 33 *B.Y.* (1957), 302–10; *British Digest*, vii. 186–216.

[2] See generally Hackworth iv. 515–33; *British Digest*, vii. 756–97; Giuliano, op. cit., pp. 91–2.

[3] See generally Hardy, op. cit., 58–63; Hackworth iv. 533–51; Giuliano, op. cit., pp. 92–104. On proceedings begun before immunity applied see *Ghosh* v. *D'Rozario* [1963] 1 Q.B. 106; Int. L.R. 33, p. 361.

[4] Article 42 provides that 'a diplomatic agent shall not in the receiving state practise for personal profit any professional or commercial activity'. The exception in Article 31 (1) applies (a) to cases in which the receiving state allows exceptions to the operation of Article 42; (b) to activities of members of the staff not of diplomatic rank.

[5] *Yrbk., I.L.C.* (1958), ii. 98. Cf. *British Digest*, vii. 798.

situation in which the property is the residence of the diplomatic agent. However, in that case such measures of execution as affect the inviolability of his person or of his residence are ruled out, as they are in respect of all three exceptions.[1]

(d) *Waiver*. This subject is dealt with in Article 32 of the Vienna Convention. It has always been accepted that the immunity from jurisdiction may be waived by the sending state.[2] Previous practice had been to some extent tolerant of implied waiver based on conduct but Article 32, paragraph 2, states that 'waiver must always be express'.[3] It further provides:

> 3. The initiation of proceedings . . . shall preclude [the person enjoying immunity] from invoking immunity from jurisdiction in respect of any counter-claim directly connected with the principal claim.[4]

The fourth paragraph provides that waiver of immunity from civil or administrative jurisdiction shall not be held to imply waiver in respect of the execution of the judgment, for which a separate waiver shall be necessary.

7. *Immunity from Jurisdiction for Official Acts* (Ratione Materiae)[5]

In the case of official acts the immunity is permanent, since it is that of the sending state.[6] In respect of private acts the immunity is contingent and supplementary and it ceases when the individual concerned leaves his post. Article 39, paragraph 2, of the Vienna Convention refers to the termination of diplomatic functions and the concomitant immunities, and provides: 'However, with respect to acts performed by such a person in the exercise of his functions as a member of the mission, immunity

[1] Article 31(3).

[2] The Vienna Conference adopted a Resolution II, on 'Consideration of Civil Claims', which recommended that the sending state should waive immunity 'in respect of civil claims of persons in the receiving State when this can be done without impeding the performance of the functions of the mission'. It recommended, further, 'that in the absence of waiver the sending state should use its best endeavours to bring about a just settlement of claims'.

[3] For the position in English law see *Engelke* v. *Musmann* [1928] A.C. 433; *Regina* v. *Madan* [1961] 2 Q.B. 1; 33 Int. L.R. 368, C.C.A.; Diplomatic Privileges Act 1964, s. 2(3); *British Digest*, vii. 867–75.

[4] See *High Commissioner for India* v. *Ghosh* [1960] 1 Q.B. 134; 28 Int. L.R. 150, C.A.

[5] See Hardy, op. cit., pp. 64–7; van Panhuys, 13 *I.C.L.Q.* (1964), 1193; Dinstein, 15 *I.C.L.Q.* (1966), 76; Harvard Research, 26 *A.J.* (1932), Supp., pp. 97–9, 104–6, 136–7; Niboyet, 39 *Revue critique de d.i. privé* (1950), 139; Giuliano, op. cit., pp. 166–80; *Yrbk., I.L.C.* (1956), ii. 145, para. 101; Parry, *Cambridge Essays*, p. 122 at pp. 127–32; *Foreign Press Attaché* case, Int. L.R. 38, p. 160, Austrian S.C.

[6] See *Zoernsch* v. *Waldock* [1964] 1 W.L.R. 675 at pp. 684, 688–9, 691–2, C.A., per Willmer, Danckwerts and Diplock, L.JJ.

shall continue to subsist.'[1] The definition of official acts is by no means self-evident. The conception presumably extends to matters which are essentially 'in the course of' official duties and this might include a road accident involving a car on official business.[2] It is possible that a distinction must be made between official acts which are amenable to the local law, *should the relevant immunity be waived*, and those which cannot be justiciable, sometimes described as acts of state. The former class is exemplified by dangerous driving of an official car; whilst a contractual promise made in negotiations for a concession with a legal person in private law would fall within the latter category as an act involving the sphere of policy and decision-making.

8. *Immunities from Application of Certain Local Laws*

Certain immunities from the application of the local law are obviously ancillary to the main body of privileges and immunities. Perhaps the most decisive of the ancillary immunities is that from measures of execution.[3] There is exemption from all dues and taxes with a number of exceptions, one of which is indirect taxes (normally incorporated in the price of goods or services).[4] Further immunities concern customs duties,[5] personal services, public service (for example, jury service), military obligations,[6] social security provisions,[7] and the giving of evidence as a witness.[8] The exemption from customs duties of articles for the personal use of the diplomatic agent or members of his family belonging to the household is a rendering of a long current practice into a rule of law. The exemption from dues and taxes probably existed in the previous customary law, though the practice was not very consistent.

9. *Some other Aspects of Immunity*

(a) *Beneficiaries of immunities.*[9] Diplomatic agents, who are not

[1] See also Article 37(2) and (3), set out *infra*, p. 358; and Article 38(1).

[2] See Kerley, 56 *A.J.* (1962), 120–1. Cf. *Re Cummings*, Int. L.R. 26 (1958, II), p. 549; *Caisse Industrielle d'Assurance Mutuelle* v. *Consul Général de la République Argentine*, Int. L.R. 45, 381.

[3] See *supra*, Articles 31(3) (see p.356, n. 1) and 32(4) (see p. 356).

[4] Vienna Convention, Articles 23 and 34. Cf. Article 37 concerning the family of the agent and administrative, technical, and service staff.

[5] Article 36. Cf. Article 37. [6] Article 35. Cf. Article 37.

[7] Article 33. This deals with a matter previously obscure. Cf. Article 37.

[8] Article 31(2). Cf. Giuliano, op. cit., pp. 118–19. Cf. also Article 37.

[9] See Hardy, op. cit., pp. 74–80; Giuliano, op. cit., pp. 141–65; Whiteman, op. cit., pp. 260–70; Wilson, 14 *I.C.L.Q.* (1965), 1265–95; Denza, op. cit., pp. 223–33.

nationals of or permanently resident in, the receiving state, are beneficiaries of the privileges and immunities set out in the Vienna Convention, Articles 29 to 36.[1] The extent to which administrative and technical staff (as non-diplomatic members of the staff) should have these privileges and immunities was a matter on which state practice had not been uniform[2] and on which there was considerable debate at the Vienna Conference. The position for this group and also for members of service staff[3] was regulated as follows in Article 37:[4]

> 2. Members of the administrative and technical staff of the mission, together with members of their families forming part of their respective households, shall, if they are not nationals of or permanently resident in the receiving State, enjoy the privileges and immunities specified in Articles 29 to 35, except that the immunity from civil and administrative jurisdiction of the receiving State specified in paragraph 1 of Article 31 shall not extend to acts performed outside the course of their duties. They shall also enjoy the privileges specified in Article 36, paragraph 1,[5] in respect of articles imported at the time of first installation.
>
> 3. Members of the service staff of the mission who are not nationals of or permanently resident in the receiving State shall enjoy immunity in respect of acts performed in the course of their duties, exemption from dues and taxes on the emoluments they receive by reason of their employment and the exemption[6] contained in Article 33.

In the case of diplomatic agents and the administrative and technical staff of the mission the respective immunities extend to 'members of the family' 'forming part of' their households. In view of variations in family law and social custom a precise definition was inappropriate.[7]

(b) *Duration of privileges and immunities.*[8] The termination of the functions of individual members of the diplomatic staff has been considered already.[9] Termination of the mission may occur, for example, through its recall, the outbreak of war between the

[1] Article 37(1). There had been some inconsistent practice in relation to diplomatic agents apart from heads of mission; see Gutteridge, 24 *B.Y.* (1947), 148–59; cf. Giuliano, op. cit., p. 142.

[2] See Gutteridge, loc. cit.; Giuliano, op. cit., pp. 153–8.

[3] On the previous position: Giuliano, pp. 159–62.

[4] This Article has provoked reservations from some states.

[5] Concerning customs duties.

[6] Concerning social security provisions.

[7] See *In re C. (an infant)* [1959] Ch. 363; Int. L.R. 26 (1958, II), 539; see generally O'Keefe, 25 *I.C.L.Q.* (1976), 329–50.

[8] See generally Whiteman vii. 436–45; Jones, 25 *B.Y.* (1948), 262–79; Hardy, op. cit., pp. 80–3; Lauterpacht, *International Law: Collected Papers* iii. 433–57; Denza, op. cit., pp. 87–9, 244–50.

[9] *Supra*, p. 350.

states concerned, or the extinction of one of the states concerned. The duration of privileges is governed by Article 39 of the Vienna Convention, the principal provisions being these:

> 1. Every person entitled to privileges and immunities shall enjoy them from the moment he enters the territory of the receiving State on proceeding to take up his post or, if already in its territory from the moment when his appointment is notified to the Ministry of Foreign Affairs or such other ministry as may be agreed.
>
> 2. When the functions of a person enjoying privileges and immunities have come to an end, such privileges and immunities shall normally cease at the moment when he leaves the country, or on expiry of a reasonable period in which to do so,[1] but shall subsist until that time even in case of armed conflict. However, with respect to acts performed by such a person in the exercise of his functions as a member of the mission,[2] immunity shall continue to subsist.

The Supreme Restitution Court of Berlin has held that premises or sites formerly occupied by diplomatic missions but no longer used for diplomatic purposes had lost their immunity from the local jurisdiction.[3]

10. *Consular Relations*[4]

Consuls are in principle distinct in function and legal status from diplomatic agents. Though agents of the sending state for particular purposes, they are not accorded the type of immunity from the laws and enforcement jurisdiction of the receiving state enjoyed by diplomatic agents. Consular functions are very varied indeed and include the protection of the interests of the sending state and its nationals, the development of economic and cultural relations, the issuing of passports and visas, the administration of the property of nationals of the sending state, the registration of births, deaths, and marriages, and supervision of vessels and aircraft attributed to the sending state.

Since the eighteenth century the status of consuls has been based upon general usage rather than law, together with special

[1] See *Magdalena Steam Navigation Co.* v. *Martin* (1859) 2 El. & El. 94; *Musurus Bey* v. *Gadban* [1894] 2 Q.B. 352; *Re Suarez* [1918] 1 Ch. 176, C.A.; *Shaffer* v. *Singh*, 343 F. 2d 324 (1965); Int. L.R. 35, p. 219.

[2] On immunity *ratione materiae*, see *supra*, sect. 7.

[3] See *Tietz* v. *People's Republic of Bulgaria*, Int. L.R. 28, p. 369. The Court emphasized that the non-user was permanent. See further Romberg, 35 *B.Y.* (1959), 235.

[4] *British Digest*, viii; Harvard Research, 26 *A.J.* (1932), Suppl., pp. 189–449; Hackworth iv. 655–949; Whiteman vii. 505–870; Guggenheim, i. 512–15; Briggs, pp. 812–35; *Yrbk., I.L.C.* (1961), ii. 55, 89, 129; Žourek, 106 Hague *Recueil* (1962, II), 365–497; id., 90 *J.D.I.* (1963), 4–67; Lee, *Consular Law and Practice* (1961); *Répertoire suisse* iii. 1552–93.

treaty provisions. The customary law as it has evolved is as follows.[1] The consul must have the authority of the sending state (his commission) and the authorization of the receiving state (termed an exequatur). The receiving state must give consular officials and premises special protection, i.e. a higher standard of diligence than that appropriate to protection of aliens generally.[2] The consular premises are not inviolable from entry by agents of the receiving state.[3] The consular archives and documents are inviolable[4] and members of the consulate are immune from the jurisdiction of the judicial and administrative authorities of the receiving state in respect of acts performed in the exercise of consular functions.[5] This immunity in respect of official acts is generally regarded as an aspect of state immunity.[6] Articles intended for the use of the consulate are exempt from customs duties, and members of the consulate, other than the service staff, are exempt from all public services, including military obligations. The authorities reveal differences of opinion concerning the personal inviolability of consular officials and in principle they are liable to arrest or detention.[7] In addition they are amenable to criminal and civil jurisdiction in respect of non-official acts, to local taxation and to customs duties. In a general way it could be said that the jurisdiction of the local sovereign is presumed in the customary law.

The existence of fairly uniform *practices* (whatever the customary law might be), evidenced by a large number of bilateral treaties, encouraged the International Law Commission to produce draft articles on consular relations, and subsequently the Vienna Convention on Consular Relations was signed in 1963.[8]

[1] See *Yrbk., I.L.C.* (1961), ii. 110 et seq. There are differing views on the ambit of the customary law: compare Žourek, 106 Hague *Recueil*, at p. 451; Beckett, 21 *B.Y.* (1944), 34–50; Guggenheim, op. cit.; Lee, op. cit.; *British Digest*, viii. 146, 151, 158, 164.

[2] *Infra*, p. 524.

[3] See *British Digest*, viii. 125; O'Connell ii. 920–1; Oppenheim i. 841–2; Briggs, p. 827; Beckett, op. cit.; *Yrbk., I.L.C.* (1961), ii. 109. Cp. Whiteman vii. 744.

[4] The authorities all agree on this.

[5] *Princess Zizianoff* v. *Kahn and Bigelow*, *Ann. Digest*, (1927–8), No. 266; Oppenheim, i. 841; *British Digest*, viii. 146; Beckett, op. cit.; Whiteman vii. 770; *Yrbk., I.L.C.* (1961), ii. 117, Article 43, Commentary; Parry, *Cambridge Essays*, p. 122 at pp. 127–32, 154.

[6] *Supra*, p. 315. See *Hallberg* v. *Pombo Argaez*, Int. L.R. 44, p. 190.

[7] Compare *British Digest*, viii. 103–22, 214; Whiteman, vii. 739; *Yrbk., I.L.C.* (1961), ii. 115, Article 41, Commentary.

[8] In force 19 March 1967. Text: 596 U.N.T.S. 261; 57 *A.J.* (1963), 993; 13 *I.C.L.Q.* (1964), 1230. For comment see Lee, *Vienna Convention on Consular Relations* (1966); Do Nascimento e Silva, 13 *I.C.L.Q.* (1964), 1214; Torres Bernardez, *Ann. français* (1963), 78. Substantial parts of the Convention are incorporated into the law of the United Kingdom: Consular Relations Act 1968, c. 18, sect. 1. The Act, except for sects. 7–11, was brought into operation on 1 Jan. 1971.

It is provided that the Convention 'shall not affect other international agreements in force as between parties to them'. The Convention has a strong element of development and reconstruction of the existing law and brings the status of career consuls, as opposed to honorary consuls, nearer to that of diplomatic agents. Career consuls are exempted from taxation and customs duties in the same way as diplomats. Consular premises are given a substantial degree of inviolability (Article 31) and are exempted from taxation (Article 32). Immunities and the duty of protection already recognized by customary law are maintained.[1] A significant extension of protection and immunity occurs as follows:

Article 41 (Personal inviolability of consular officers):

1. Consular officers shall not be liable to arrest or detention pending trial, except in the case of a grave crime and pursuant to a decision by the competent judicial authority.

2. Except in the case specified in paragraph 1 of this article, consular officers shall not be committed to prison or liable to any other form of restriction on their personal freedom save in execution of a judicial decision of final effect.

3. If criminal proceedings are instituted against a consular officer, he must appear before the competent authorities. Nevertheless, the proceedings shall be conducted with the respect due to him by reason of his official position and, except in the case specified in paragraph 1 of this article, in a manner which will hamper the exercise of consular functions as little as possible. When, in the circumstances mentioned in paragraph 1 of this article, it has become necessary to detain a consular officer, the proceedings against him shall be instituted with the minimum delay.

Although the Vienna Convention has attracted about forty ratifications it is unsafe to regard its provisions in general as conclusive evidence on the present state of general international law on the subject.[2] Nevertheless, states and municipal courts[3] may use its provisions as the best evidence of the present state of the law quite apart from its effect for actual parties. Two regional multilateral conventions should also be noted, namely the Pan-American Convention of 1928[4] and the European Convention on Consular Functions of 1967.[5]

[1] See especially Articles 40 (Protection of consular officers); 33 (Inviolability of consular archives and documents); 43 (Immunity from jurisdiction in respect of acts performed in the exercise of consular functions); and 52 (Exemption from personal services and contributions).

[2] On the *North Sea Continental Shelf Cases*, see *supra*, p. 13.

[3] Cf. *Republic of Argentina* v. *City of New York*, 25 N.Y. 2d 252 (1969), N.Y. Ct. of Appeals; Whiteman vii. 825–8; *Digest of U.S. Practice*, 1974, 183; 1975, 249–50, 259–60.

[4] Hudson, *Int. Legis.*, iv. 2394.

[5] European Treaty Series No. 61.

11. *Special Missions*[1]

Beyond the sphere of permanent relations by means of diplomatic missions or consular posts, states make frequent use of *ad hoc* diplomacy or special missions. These vary considerably in function: examples include a head of government attending a funeral abroad in his official capacity, a foreign minister visiting his opposite number in another state for negotiations and the visit of a government trade delegation to conduct official business. These occasional missions have no *special* status in customary law but it should be remembered that, since they are agents of states and are received by the consent of the host state, they benefit from the ordinary principles based upon sovereign immunity and the express or implied conditions of the invitation or licence received by the sending state. The United Nations General Assembly has adopted and opened for signature the Convention on Special Missions, 1969.[2] This provides a fairly flexible code of conduct based on the Vienna Convention on Diplomatic Relations with appropriate divergences.

12. *The Prevention and Punishment of Crimes against Internationally Protected Persons*

As a consequence of the fashion for political acts of violence directed against diplomats and other officials, the General Assembly of the United Nations adopted the Convention on the Prevention and Punishment of Crimes Against Internationally Protected Persons, including Diplomatic Agents, which was annexed to Resolution 3166 (XXVIII) of December 14, 1973.[3] The offences envisaged are primarily the 'murder, kidnapping or other attack upon the person or liberty of an internationally protected person', the latter category including Heads of State,

[1] Whiteman vii. 33–47; *Yrbk., I.L.C.* (1964), ii. 67; (1965), ii. 109; (1966), ii. 125; (1967), ii. 1; Hardy, op. cit., 89–94; Bartoš, 108 Hague *Recueil* (1963, I), 431–560; Waters, *The Ad Hoc Diplomat* (1963); Louis, 66 *R.G.D.I.P.* (1962), 601. On the arrest of the French Property Commission in the U.A.R. in 1961 see 12 *I.C.L.Q.* (1963), 1383; *Annuaire Français* (1962), 1064. See also *R.* v. *Governor of Pentonville Prison, ex p. Teja* [1971] 2 Q.B. 274, D.C.

[2] Resolution 2530 (XXIV), 8 December 1969, Annex: (a) Convention; (b) Optional Protocol concerning the Compulsory Settlement of Disputes. See also Resolution 2531 (XXIV) on settlement of civil claims. See Donnarumma, 8 *Revue belge* (1972), 34–79.

[3] The Convention came into force on 20 February 1977. For the text see: 68 *A.J.* (1974), 383; 13 *I.L.M.* (1974), 41. See also the U.K. Internationally Protected Persons Act, 1978. There is also an O.A.S. Convention, adopted on 2 February 1971; 10 *I.L.M.* (1971), 255. The European Convention on the Suppression of Terrorism, opened for signature on 27 January 1977, is concerned to render extradition more effective: for the text see 14 *I.L.M.* (1976), 1272. See also the U.K. Suppression of Terrorism Act, 1978.

foreign ministers and the like. Contracting Parties undertake to make these crimes punishable by 'appropriate penalties which shall take into account their grave nature', and either to extradite alleged offenders or to apply the domestic law.

CHAPTER XVII
RESERVATIONS FROM TERRITORIAL SOVEREIGNTY

1. *Territorial Privileges by Concession*

THE previous section relates the cases in which there exists immunity from territorial jurisdiction, primarily, but by no means exclusively, an immunity from the jurisdiction of the local courts. There is no very neat way of separating these instances from the cases of 'privilege' now to be considered. Thus, in the case of the diplomatic agent, the legal regime is by no means confined to negative rules of jurisdictional immunity: after all, these rules are only one facet of a situation involving privileges to carry out various governmental commissions and in certain cases even to grant diplomatic asylum on the basis of treaty or regional custom.[1] Conversely, the stay of foreign armed forces in time of peace involves both privileges and immunities. However, in this latter case and in some others placed under the present heading the aspect of privilege involving extraterritorial exercise of sovereign capacities is particularly prominent. Whilst the classification is to some extent empirical, it is believed that the special rights involved in the stationing of armed forces on foreign territory, and other instances of the exercise of governmental functions on the territory of another state, are relatively less normal and more prominently 'privileges' than the other cases of official intercourse including the sending and receiving of diplomatic agents. Technically these other cases are also privileges, but the cases now to be considered all display a number of idiosyncrasies and, in view of their character, may more readily lead to the application of a presumption in favour of the exclusive jurisdiction of the territorial sovereign[2] in case of doubt. However, the situations are rather disparate, and generalizations are unlikely to be very helpful. If it is not sufficiently obvious it should be pointed out that what follows is not exhaustive of all forms of privilege and licence granted by territorial sovereigns.[3]

[1] On extraterritorial asylum see *infra*, p. 364. On diplomatic agents see Chapter XVI.

[2] Cf. *supra*, p. 289.

[3] On the enforcement and recognition in England of foreign judgments and arbitration awards see Dicey, *Conflict of Laws* (8th ed.), Chaps. 29 and 30; U.N. Conv. on the Recognition and Enforcement of Foreign Arbitral Awards (in force, 7 June 1959), 7 *Int. Leg. Materials* (1968), 1046; and the U.K. Arbitration Act, 1975.

The group of cases depends on the existence of agreement or *ad hoc* consent on the part of the receiving state and not on the operation of law. However, once the *occasion* has arisen by concession, in the absence of variations by special agreement, the law regulates the nature and extent of the privilege.

(a) *Refugee and exile governments.*[1] Where there is no breach of legal duty[2] involved, a state may tolerate the establishment of a refugee or exile government of a foreign state on its territory. In this type of case a considerable quantum of sovereign powers may be exercised by the exile government over the nationals, armed forces, and both public and private vessels in the host state and on the high seas. During the Second World War the United Kingdom gave extensive privileges and immunities to exile governments and their representatives, and such governments were permitted to carry out legislative, administrative, and other functions in the United Kingdom. The basis for such competence can only be the invitation and consent of the territorial sovereign. Similar concessions may be made in favour of visiting sovereigns.

(b) *International Control Commissions.* The internal affairs of a state may give rise to issues of international concern, for example because the right of self-determination is denied, or there is foreign intervention in a civil war, or the state has recently been defeated by a group of lawful belligerents conducting a war of collective defence and sanction against a source of aggression.[3] In such a case, with or without the support of organs of the United Nations,[4] interested states may by agreement, or otherwise, bring about a political solution, the principles of which are to be applied under the supervision of an external agency. Thus, the Geneva Agreements of 1954[5] provided for an International Control Commission to supervise the application of a political settlement to the succession states of French Indo-China. The regime of supervision may involve a grant of privileges to agents

[1] See Oppenheim i. 326–7, 828; Oppenheimer, 36 *A.J.* (1942), 568–95; Stein, 46 *Michigan L.R.* (1948), 341–70; Whiteman vi. 354–78; McNair, *The Legal Effects of War* (4th ed.), pp. 424–46; id., *Opinions* i. 69–70, 72–4; *In re Amand* [1941] 2 K.B. 239; *Lorentzen* v. *Lydden* [1942] 2 K.B. 202. On deposed, abdicated, refugee, and captured monarchs see McNair, *Opinions* i. 104–10, 127. And see *supra*, p. 68.

[2] On recognition of governments see *supra*, p. 95.

[3] On the situation in Germany after 1945, see *supra*, pp. 83, 87.

[4] For cases of U.N. administration, *supra*, pp. 175–9.

[5] *Docs. on International Affairs* (1954), p. 138; Cmnd. 9239, Misc. no. 20 (1954); 23 *Rev. int. française du droit des gens* (1954), 172. See also the Protocol to the Declaration on the Neutrality of Laos, 23 July 1962, 456 U.N.T.S., no. 6564, p. 301. And see 9 *I.C.L.Q.* (1960), 259.

of other states, and may constitute a serious derogation from sovereignty.

(c) *Foreign public ships.*[1] The controversy as to the jurisdictional immunity of government ships used in commerce has been treated as an aspect of the general question of state control of economic activity,[2] and for the present purpose that issue will be left on one side. In any case the extraterritorial exercise of sovereign powers is normally the business of naval vessels and auxiliaries. The main principles are for the most part well settled[3] and have had influence on the law relating to the status of foreign armed forces in general. Apart from lawful belligerency, foreign warships using a police power in the territory of a state are violating the latter's territorial sovereignty and create a legal responsibility.[4] However, foreign public vessels lawfully entering territorial sea or internal waters have extensive privileges and immunities. The law was stated by Hyde[5] as follows:

> The ship cannot be lawfully subjected to a civil action arising, for example, from a claim for salvage, or to a criminal action arising from the violation of a local regulation. No occupant while remaining on board the vessel is subject to the local jurisdiction, notwithstanding his infraction of the local criminal code by an act committed on shore or taking effect there. . . . The vessel of war and its occupants owe, nevertheless, well-defined duties to the local sovereign. The former is obliged to respect, for example, local regulations pertaining to navigation and quarantine, and special obligations, when, in time of war, the vessel attached to a belligerent service enters a neutral port.

The foreign public vessel, in the classical case, a warship, attracts the character of sovereign immunity,[6] and the sources

[1] The position of warships and other government ships in innocent passage through the territorial sea is considered *supra*, pp. 203–7, 329, and their position on the high seas *supra*, pp. 236 seq. On concurrence of criminal jurisdiction in the case of non-governmental ships: *supra*, pp. 316–19.

[2] *Supra*, pp. 326 seq.

[3] See McNair, *Opinions* i. 90 seq.; Brierly, pp. 267–9; Briggs, pp. 446–7; Oppenheim i. 461, 851–9; Hall, pp. 237–49; Gidel ii. 253–315; Colombos, pp. 264–84; id., *Mélanges Gidel* (1961), pp. 159–65; Baldoni, 65 Hague *Recueil* (1938, III), 189–302; U.N. Legis. Series, *Laws and Regulations on the Régime of the Territorial Sea* (1957), Chap. III; *Annuaire de l'Inst.* 34 (1928), 475 seq.; Cheng, 11 *Curr. Leg. Problems* (1958), 225–57; Hackworth ii. 408–65; Whiteman ix. 74–83.

[4] See McNair, *Opinions* i. 74–83 and cf. the *Corfu Channel* case (Merits), I.C.J. Reports (1949), pp. 33–5 (on a British mine-sweeping operation in Albanian waters); and *Japan* v. *Kulikov*, Int. L.R. 21 (1954), 105.

[5] ii. 826–7.

[6] See Marshall, C.J., in the *Schooner Exchange* v. *McFaddon* (1812), 7 Cranch 116; Green, p. 237; Briggs, p. 413; *supra*, pp. 325–6; *infra*, p. 368. The decision influenced courts elsewhere: see the *Constitution* (1879), 4 P.D. 39; the *Parlement Belge* (1880), 5 P.D. 197, Green, p. 270; *Chung Chi Cheung* v. *The King* [1939] A.C. 160; *Wright* v. *Cantrell*

treat the subject as a facet of sovereign immunity. However, the armed public vessel, by its function and physical autonomy, has a special inviolability, and it was not absurd to regard such vessels as extraterritorial. However, this is not strictly the case. Thus in *Chung Chi Cheung* v. *The King*[1] the Privy Council held that a local court has jurisdiction if the immunity is waived and can punish a member of the crew for a breach of the local law, in this case a murder, on board a foreign public ship in territorial waters. Yet the warship remains for many purposes an independent area of foreign competence: the sending state can exercise governmental powers and undertake judicial action on the vessel. Members of the crew committing crimes when ashore on leave and recovering the ship are safe from apprehension by the local authorities. Moreover, it seems that members of the crew committing breaches of the local law when ashore on duty or on official mission are immune from the local jurisdiction.[2] The internal independence of the warship has led to opinions that political asylum may be granted on board, but no power exists in positive law.[3] If, however, asylum is granted, local fugitives from justice are taken on board, infractions of local regulations, particularly those relating to navigation, anchorage and public health, occur, or acts of violence issue from the vessel, no local police power may be exercised within the warship itself. The remedy lies in diplomatic representations and, ultimately, in termination of the licence to remain and measures of compulsion to enforce the withdrawal of consent or to prevent further acts of violence.

(d) *Foreign military and other public aircraft*.[4] The legal position is similar to that which obtains in the case of foreign military and other public ships.

(e) *Foreign armed forces* (*apart from public ships and aircraft*).[5]

(1943), 44 S.R.N.S.W. 45; *Ann. Digest* (1943–5), no. 37; *Municipality of Saint John* v. *Fraser-Brace Overseas Corp.* (1958), 13 D.L.R. (2d), 177; Int. L.R. 26 (1958, II), 165.

[1] *Ubi supra*, p. 366, n. 6.

[2] See Oppenheim i. 855; and *Ministère Public* v. *Triandafilou*, *Ann. Digest* (1919–42), no. 86; 39 *A.J.* (1945), 345. Some would deny this immunity; see Hyde ii. 830; Hall, p. 249. Cf. *Japan* v. *Smith and Stinner*, Int. L.R. 19 (1952), no. 47.

[3] Opinion of Lord Stowell, 18 November 1820; Hyde ii. 829; Gidel ii. 273–88. See also Baldoni, op. cit., pp. 285–92; Morgenstern, 25 *B.Y.* (1948), 253–5; McNair, *Opinions* ii. 67–73 (Stowell's opinion at p. 70). Other views: Hall, p. 247; Colombos, p. 278. See also the Havana Conv. on Asylum, 1928, 22 *A.J.* (1928), Suppl., p. 158.

[4] Oppenheim i. 521, 851; Cheng, 11 *Curr. Leg. Problems* (1958), 225–57; Brierly, p. 269; Whiteman ix. 75.

[5] See generally Whiteman vi. 379–427; Wijewardane, 41 *B.Y.* (1967), 122–54; Barton, 26 *B.Y.* (1949), 380–413; 27 *B.Y.* (1950), 186–234; and 31 *B.Y.* (1954), 341–70; King, 36 *A.J.* (1942), 539–67; 40 *A.J.* (1946), 257–79; van Praag, *Juridiction et droit inter-*

This subject has complexities to which justice cannot be done in the present treatment. Any statement of general principle must be provisional in view of the confused state of the sources, and states commonly rely on a treaty regime to govern the status of visiting forces. The problems are a little more tractable if some classification, based on the occasion for the presence of foreign forces, is attempted. Foreign public ships and aircraft have a special legal regime which justifies separate treatment (above).

(i) *A military force exercising a right of passage.* We are here concerned with a concession relating to a specific force on a specific occasion.[1] The decision in the *Schooner Exchange* has been used to support a variety of propositions about the immunities of armed forces, and it is important to recall that in this connexion Marshall, C.J., was concerned exclusively with the case of the grant of free passage and not the stationing or sojourn of troops.[2] There is, of course, an analogy with the visit of a warship by invitation, and there is an immunity from the supervisory and, though this is less certain, the criminal jurisdiction of the territorial sovereign.[3] Moreover, the sending state has wide powers of control and jurisdiction over the force.

(ii) *Forces stationed in defined camp or base areas.* If the rationale of the privilege given to forces in transit is based on their organized and hermetic nature and the warship analogy is drawn on, and if it is correct to say that forces in passage have extensive privileges, then it can obviously be argued that visiting forces in defined camp and base areas have similar characteristics and should have similar privileges. However, this is almost certainly not the modern law.[4]

(iii) *Visiting forces in general.* Some writers have applied the principles stated in the *Schooner Exchange*, which in regard to land forces were expressed in the context of a right of free passage, to visiting forces in general, and thus support a doctrine of 'absolute' immunity, which can nevertheless be waived.[5]

national public (1915), pp. 492 seq., Suppl. (1935), pp. 265 seq.; Whitton, 63 *R.G.D.I.P.* (1959), 5–20; Rousseau iii. 72–92.

[1] On the rights of passage as such see *infra*, pp. 377–8. The conditions in which the concession is made may create issues arising from the duties of neutrals in time of war.

[2] (1812), 7 Cranch 116 at pp. 139–40; Westlake, *International Law* i. 255; and see also Barton, 26 *B.Y.* (1949), 383–5; and 27 *B.Y.* (1950), 217–19; *In re Gilbert, Ann. Digest* 13 (1946), no. 37, per Nonato, J. (cf. Barton, 31 *B.Y.* (1954), 345).

[3] See Brierly, p. 269 ('passing through . . . another State's territory as organized units'); Hall, pp. 250–1.

[4] See Barton, 27 *B.Y.* (1950), 227–9; id., 31 *B.Y.* (1954), 342–50. For a statement supporting a wide immunity see Oppenheim i. 847–8. Cf. Brierly, p. 270. On lease of territory for bases see *Hans* v. *The Queen* [1955] A.C. 378; Int. L.R. 22 (1955), 154.

[5] King, *ubi supra*; van Panhuys, 2 *Neths. Int. L.R.* (1955), 255.

Others have interpreted the materials differently and, influenced by the content of the N.A.T.O. Status of Forces Agreement[1] and various recent bilateral agreements, have denied, as a general principle, the immunity of members of a visiting force from the criminal jurisdiction of the local courts.[2] A number of writers,[3] supported by some judicial practice,[4] support a qualified immunity, operating in certain situations: the rule is normally stated as an acceptance of immunity from criminal jurisdiction for offences committed within the quarters of the force and elsewhere when on duty. Yet another approach, which is the most satisfactory in principle and therefore, in a confused situation, has a good claim to be the law on the subject, involves a return to the rationale of the words of Marshall, C.J., in the *Schooner Exchange*.[5] Although he referred to the *passage* of a force, his rationale for the immunity was the implied waiver by the receiving state of the exercise of any powers which would seriously affect the integrity and efficiency of the force.[6] Thus, in principle the visiting force has exclusive jurisdiction over matters of discipline and internal organization and over offences by its members committed when on duty. In some situations it will not be immediately clear that the rationale precludes local jurisdiction—for example, where within the quarters one member of the visiting force not on duty murders another or a local civilian commits a breach of local law within the base area. In such cases it is thought that the principle of immunity should be comple-

[1] See *infra*, p. 370.

[2] See Barton, 31 *B.Y.* (1954), 341–70; Draper, 44 *Grot. Soc.* (1958, 1959), 12 seq.

[3] e.g. Oppenheim i. 847–8; Guggenheim i. 518–19; O'Connell ii. 879–86 (limited to matters of 'internal disciplinary organization').

[4] See Barton, 27 *B.Y.* (1950), 227–31; 31 *B.Y.* (1954), 342–63. Cf. Oppenheim i. 848–59; *Reference re Exemption of United States Forces from Canadian Criminal Law* (1943), 4 D.L.R. 11; *Ann. Digest* 12 (1943–5), no. 36, Duff, C.J.C., and Hudson, J.

[5] The key passage is as follows: 'In such case, without any express declaration waiving jurisdiction over the army to which this right of passage has been granted, the sovereign who should attempt to exercise it would certainly be considered as violating his faith. By exercising it, the purpose for which the free passage was granted would be defeated, and a portion of the military force of a foreign independent nation would be diverted from those national objects and duties to which it was applicable and would be withdrawn from the control of the sovereign whose power and safety might greatly depend on retaining the exclusive command and disposition of this force. The grant of a free passage therefore implies a waiver of all jurisdiction over the troops during their passage, and permits the foreign general to use that discipline and to inflict those punishments which the government of his army may require.' But see *Wilson* v. *Girard*, 354 U.S. 524 (1957).

[6] See *Wright* v. *Cantrell* (1943), 44 S.R.N.S.W. 45; *Ann. Digest* 12 (1943–5), no. 37, Supreme Court of New South Wales; and see the views of Starke, *Introduction to International Law* (8th ed.), pp. 291–4 and Brierly, pp. 269–70. See further *Chow Hung Ching* v. *The King* (1948), 77 C.L.R. 449; *Ann. Digest* 15 (1948), no. 47, High Court of Australia; and U.S. view in 58 *A.J.* (1964), 994.

mented by principles of interest[1] or substantial connexion.[2] In the case of forces stationed on territory, and not merely passing through it, it may be that the presumption should be in favour of the local jurisdiction.[3] In cases of doubt there is no reason why the modalities of an immunity should not be governed by the general principles governing jurisdiction over aliens.[4] The rationale referred to above provides a reasonable outcome to the difficult issue of civil jurisdiction: in most cases there will be no reason to allow a member of a visiting force immunity from civil action for harm caused to a local citizen even by acts committed in the course of duty.[5] On the other hand there will be immunity from local direct taxation.[6]

As a matter of political and administrative convenience, and no doubt partly because of the uncertainty of the customary law, states frequently rely on special agreement. In one case, that of the N.A.T.O. Status of Forces Agreement,[7] 1951, the matter is regulated by a multilateral convention. Its provisions have created some problems of application, but the general scheme is as follows. The military authorities of the sending state may exercise criminal jurisdiction within the receiving state over all persons subject to the military law of the sending state and committing offences against that law. The receiving state may punish any breach of its own law by members of the visiting force and their dependants: when the breach is not also a breach of the law of the sending state (as it applies to such forces) this jurisdiction is exclusive. However, there is a large area of concurrence, and for this the treaty provides rules to decide which state has the 'primary right' to exercise jurisdiction.[8] Thus the

[1] See Nonato, J. in *In re Gilbert*, *Ann. Digest* 13 (1946), no. 37; 31 *B.Y.* (1954), 345–6.

[2] Cf. *supra*, p. 305. See also bilateral treaties concluded by the Soviet Union with Hungary, Poland, and the German Democratic Republic: 52 *A.J.* (1958), 219–27. These provide for local jurisdiction, as a general principle, but crimes by Soviet forces or members of their families solely against the Soviet Union or other persons in the Soviet forces, and crimes committed by these forces while discharging their duties, are excluded. And cf. the Visiting Forces Act 1952, sects. 2 and 3.

[3] See *Wilson* v. *Girard*, 354 U.S. 524 (1957); Whiteman vi. 382, 384–6.

[4] *Supra*, Chapter XIV.

[5] See *Wright* v. *Cantrell*, *supra*, p. 369, n. 6.

[6] See Fairman and King, 38 *A.J.* (1944), 258–77, and cf. *Reference on Powers of City of Ottawa* (1943), S.C.R. 208, *Ann. Digest* 10 (1941–2), no. 106. See also N.A.T.O. Status of Forces Agreement, Art. 10.

[7] 48 *A.J.* (1954), Suppl., p. 83. See also the Visiting Forces Act, 1952; and the International Headquarters and Defence Organizations Act, 1964.

[8] See generally Snee and Pye, *Status of Forces Agreements and Criminal Jurisdiction* (1957); Rouse and Baldwin, 51 *A.J.* (1957), 29–62; Baxter, 7 *I.C.L.Q.* (1958), 72–81; Draper, 44 *Grot. Soc.* (1958, 1959), 9–28; id., *Civilians and the NATO Status of Forces Agreement* (1966); Lazareff, *Status of Military Forces under Current International Law*

sending state has primary jurisdiction if the offence arises out of any act or omission 'done in the performance of official duty'. Professor Baxter has expressed the view that the N.A.T.O. formula for allocation of jurisdiction may pass into customary law.[1]

(iv) *Co-belligerent forces conducting operations on national territory.*[2] It could be said that the rationale of the position of warships and, perhaps, of forces in passage applies equally to the lines of allied forces helping the territorial sovereign to expel hostile forces. However, the evidence suggests that, apart from defences to international claims and criminal charges offered by the contingencies of war operations, such forces have a status basically no different from that of visiting forces in other circumstances. It is, of course, difficult to distinguish between the case of co-belligerent forces stationed in a country not yet the field of land operations, co-belligerent forces in action on state territory, and allied forces given facilities for deployment in time of peace as part of preparation for effective action in case of attack. In all three cases the position will normally be regulated by treaty.[3] However, it is probable that a source of limitations on the belligerent powers of the allied forces in action on state territory lies in the ordinary rules on belligerent occupation,[4] although these are normally conceived to apply only to enemy occupants.

(f) *The inviolability of certain weapons deployed by foreign forces.* It is today not uncommon for states supplying weapons or components thereof in pursuance of a joint military programme to reserve full 'ownership, custody and control' of certain components, for example nuclear warheads for missiles.[5] The reservation is presumably necessary because otherwise the supply of

(1971); Whiteman vi. 392–427; van Panhuys, 2 *Neths. Int. L.R.* (1955), 253–78. See also *Re Labelle*, Int. L.R. 24 (1957), 251; *Whitley* v. *Aitchison*, ibid., 26 (1958, II), 196. Cf. *U.S.* v. *Copeland*, ibid., 23 (1956), 241; *Wilson* v. *Girard*, ibid., 24, 248; 354 U.S. 524 (1957); *Japan* v. *Girard*, ibid., 26 (1958, II), 203. For some other aspects: Meron, 6 *I.C.L.Q.* (1957), 689–94.

[1] Foreword to Lazareff, op. cit.

[2] See King, 36 *A.J.* (1942), 539–67; 40 *A.J.* (1946), 257–79; Barton, 26 *B.Y.* (1949), 387 seq.; 27 *B.Y.* (1950), 187 seq. See also *Société Anonyme* v. *Office d'Aide Mutuelle*, Int. L.R. 23 (1956), 205; *Office d'Aide Mutuelle* v. *Veuve Eugène Elias*, Int. L.R. 32, p. 588.

[3] e.g. Agreement between U.K. and Belgium on civil administration and jurisdiction in liberated territory, 1944, 90 U.N.T.S., p. 283; Agreement between U.S. and the Netherlands, 1944, 132 U.N.T.S., p. 355; U.S. and France, 1944, 138 U.N.T.S., p. 247.

[4] See *Jakub Ł.* v. *Teofil B.*, Int. L.R. 26 (1958, II), 730; and the U.K. *Manual of Military Law* iii (1958), 140, n. 3.

[5] United Kingdom and United States, Exchange of Notes, 22 February 1958, *Dept. of State Bull.* 38 (1958), 418–19.

such components might be regarded as a transfer of rights of ownership and control.

(g) *United Nations forces*. United Nations forces engaged in peace-keeping operations, not constituting enforcement action within the meaning of the Charter of the United Nations,[1] can only be deployed with the agreement of the state concerned. In the relevant formal agreements, considerable powers and immunities may be conferred, involving the establishing of bases and freedom of movement.[2]

(h) *Grants of interests in territory*. A state may grant a right of exclusive use over a part of its territory to another state, retaining sovereignty, but conceding the enjoyment of the liberties of the territorial sovereign. Such a grant may be described as a 'lease'.[3] However, the nature of the interest involved here is such that it is inappropriate to classify such grants with the privileges considered in this section. Nevertheless, in strictness, these grants do constitute privileges, and in principle their incidence depends on the consent of the territorial sovereign. In most cases where military and naval bases have been established by agreement the result is more akin to a contractual licence than it is to an interest in land in the English sense.[4]

(i) *Servitudes*.[5] The title 'servitudes' denotes only an area of problems, and its use as a legal category is a matter of controversy.[6] By treaty or otherwise, a state may have accommodation rights over the territory of a neighbour in the form of a right of way, user of a railway station or port facilities, maintenance of

[1] There is a large issue as to the constitutional status of such forces within the Charter: see the *Expenses* case, *infra*, pp. 699, 702.

[2] See generally Wijewardane, 41 *B.Y.* (1967), 154–97; Bowett, *United Nations Forces* (1964), pp. 428–67. See further *Jennings* v. *Markley*, 186 F. Supp. 611; 290 F. 2d 892; Int. L.R. 32, p. 367; *Nissan* v. *A.-G.* [1970] A.C. 179; 43 *B.Y.* (1968–9), 217. On the position of U.N. observer groups: Bowett, *op. cit.*, pp. 83–4.

[3] *Supra*, pp. 115–16.

[4] On areas 'retained under full British sovereignty' in Cyprus after independence see Cmnd. 679, Misc. no. 4 (1959). See also Whiteman ii. 1215–24.

[5] See generally McNair, 6 *B.Y.* (1925), 111–27; Crusen, 22 Hague *Recueil* (1928, II), 5–79; Schwarzenberger, *International Law* (3rd ed.), pp. 209–15; Lauterpacht, *Private Law Sources and Analogies*, pp. 119–24, 237–43; id., *Collected Papers* i (1970), 374–5; Esgain, in O'Brien (ed.), *The New Nations in International Law and Diplomacy*, pp. 42–97; *British Digest* iib, Chap. 8; O'Connell i. 544–52; Reid, *International Servitudes in Law and Practice* (1932); id., 45 Hague *Recueil* (1933, III), 5–68; Váli, *Servitudes of International Law* (2nd ed., 1958); Hyde i. 510–15; Whiteman ii. 1173–1224; Rousseau iii. 43–6; *Répertoire suisse* ii. 1049–53.

[6] The subject has been regarded with great caution by tribunals, although they have not rejected the concept in principle: see the *North Atlantic Coast Fisheries* arbitration (1910), *R.I.A.A.* xi. 167; Briggs, p. 313; Hague Court Reports i. 141; Green, p. 301; *British Digest* iib, 585 (and see the comment at pp. 405–6); and the *Wimbledon* (1923), P.C.I.J., Ser. A, no. 1, p. 24; Green, p. 311 See also Judge Moreno Quintana, diss. op., *Right of Passage* case, I.C.J. Reports (1960), p. 90.

wireless stations, customs houses, or military bases, and so on. Again, the rights may take the form of an obligation on the neighbour to abstain from building in a given zone or from militarization of a defined area. The similarity to servitudes in municipal law and the influence of civil law doctrines on the writers have led to the advocacy of a concept of servitudes in international law, *jura in re aliena*, involving a relation of territory to territory, unaffected by change of sovereignty in either state, and terminable only by mutual consent, by renunciation on the part of the dominant state, or by consolidation of the territories concerned.[1] However, the majority of modern writers consider the category to be useless and, indeed, misleading.[2] It is certainly true that treaties, and local custom, may create obligations of a local character which survive a change in the sovereignty of one or both of the parties, but such instances are explicable without any reference to a concept of servitudes. Moreover, if the concept is adopted it is very difficult to explain why certain similar restrictions on territory are not transmissible, and further, why certain restrictions, clearly not like servitudes, are transmissible.

The concept is useless but the subject-matter to which it has been applied by various writers does have some real problems, and some brief account of these is necessary. At the outset two matters must be set apart. First, customary international law creates analogous accommodation rights in the case of the right of innocent passage through the territorial sea[3] and certain rights and duties of neighbourhood.[4] Secondly, in certain conditions, a multilateral treaty may create permanent local restrictions as part of an 'objective regime' in order to pursue an end of international public policy, as for example the neutralization of a sensitive area. The nature and basis of such 'objective regimes' varies, and the proper context of the problems is the law of treaties.[5] In general it is dangerous to argue that, if transmissibility arises from the principles of state succession[6] and, or, the law of treaties,[7]

[1] See Reid, op. cit., p. 25. Other advocates: Váli, op. cit.; Verzijl, *International Law in Historical Perspective* iii (1970), 413–28; O'Connell, op. cit.; Lauterpacht, op. cit.; and Oppenheim i. 535–43 (view of author and editor); Schücking, diss. judgment, the *Wimbledon*, *supra*, pp. 43 seq. Hall, *International Law* (8th ed.), pp. 203–5, bases servitudes on agreement. See also Parry, *British Digest* iib, 373–409.

[2] See McNair, op. cit.; id., *Law of Treaties* (1961), p. 656; Guggenheim i. 394–7; Schwarzenberger, op. cit.; Hyde i. 513; Briggs, p. 319; Brierly, pp. 190–4. See also the Commission of Jurists, Aaland Islands dispute, 1920, *British Digest* iib, 771.

[3] *Supra*, p. 203. [4] *Supra*, p. 285.

[5] See *infra*, pp. 619–22. On the status of mandates and trust territories see *supra*, pp. 181–2. Cf. McNair, *Law of Treaties* (1961), Chap. XXXIX [6] See Chapter XXVIII.

[7] On the effect of treaties on third states see *infra*, p. 619–22. See also the *Free Zones* case, Ser. A/B, no. 46, p. 145; and Armand-Ugon, diss. op., I.C.J. Reports (1960), p. 81.

then this proves the existence of a legal category 'servitude'.

Two situations may arise. The original parties to a treaty may stipulate for the granting of rights 'for ever' or use other words suggesting irrevocability. There is no question of transmissibility here,[1] and everything turns on the interpretation of the provisions. Thus, such language may be intended to exclude termination by the outbreak of war[2] or the operation of the *clausula rebus sic stantibus*.[3] More interesting are the cases in which local obligations affecting user of territory are considered to survive changes of sovereignty. Four possibilities exist.

(1) Rights of passage and the like may rest on a local custom acquiesced in by transferees of the territory.[4]

(2) If a successor in title participates in the enjoyment of rights which have their sources in a composite arrangement involving reciprocal benefits and duties, then, by the operation of estoppel, obligations of a territorial nature may devolve.[5] The estoppel could also be regarded as a consequence of various equitable principles, and especially the rule that one cannot both approbate and reprobate. Thus, if a frontier regime is established by agreement between A and B and part of the consideration for the agreement of B is the granting of grazing rights across the frontier in B's favour, then C, territorial successor to B, must accept or reject the arrangement as a whole: it cannot reject the frontier regime, but accept and enjoy the grazing rights.[6]

(3) Another application of principles of equity is involved in the principle that a state, by transferring territory to C, cannot derogate from a previous grant of territorial rights to B, such as a right of navigation: *nemo plus juris*

[1] See the *North Atlantic Coast Fisheries* arbitration, *supra*, in which by treaty Great Britain had granted a liberty of fishing 'forever' to inhabitants of the United States. The real issue was the extent to which a grantor can regulate the rights granted: see *infra*, p. 376. See also Schwarzenberger, op. cit., pp. 210–12.

[2] *Infra*, p. 614.

[3] *Infra*, pp. 616–18.

[4] *Right of Passage* case, I.C.J. Reports (1960), p. 6 at pp. 40, 43; Hall, p. 203.

[5] Cf. Judge Anzilotti, *Diversion of Water* case, P.C.I.J., Ser. A/B, no. 70 (1937), p. 50, on the principle *inadimplenti non est adimplendum* (a party which has failed to execute a treaty cannot rely on it). See also Váli, op. cit., p. 321.

[6] Cf. the Ethiopian–Somali dispute over grazing rights in the Haud: on which see Latham Brown, 5 *I.C.L.Q.* (1956), 245–64; 10 *I.C.L.Q.* (1961), 167–78. See also Fitzmaurice, *Yrbk., I.L.C.* (1960), ii. 99–100.

transferre quam ipse habet (no one can give a greater interest than he himself has).[1]

(4) The three principles already mentioned may be complemented by other applications of the principle that the grant of rights should be reasonably effective. For example, if state A, which is the riparian sovereign of a river giving access to the sea, is granted a right of navigation on the river, the waters of which are under the sovereignty of B, the grantor, then it is arguable that A may construct and use jetties which penetrate B's sovereignty in order to implement the right of navigation.[2]

Of these four principles, the third is perhaps the most controversial and difficult of application. If state A, on becoming independent, or receiving a parcel of territory from B, allows C to retain a military base on the territory concerned, the basis of the right is probably now the agreement or acquiescence of A. If B had not reserved such a right in its grant to A, then B will answer to C, but the right of C cannot be 'sanctioned' at the expense of A. Nor, in this case, can the difficulty be avoided by saying that the right involved is a 'local obligation' serving other territory held by C, and even if it were, to speak of a 'local obligation' may be to resurrect the concept of servitude.

2. *Other Restrictions on Territorial Supremacy*

Restrictions on the liberty of states to regulate the affairs of their territories as they wish are legion, stemming from treaty, local custom, estoppel, and the rules of customary law. Some of these restrictions have been classified in the two previous sections, but more comprehensive classification could be attempted.[3] However, to list such restrictions is simply to collect a great number of widely diverse topics ranging over much of international law. The nature of the restrictions vary, as is apparent if one compares the right of innocent passage through the territorial sea,[4] the obligation to avoid conditions on state territory causing harm to other states or their nationals,[5] the right of in-

[1] McNair, *Law of Treaties* (1961), pp. 656–9; O'Connell, 30 *Can. B.R.* (1952), 810–15; id., *Law of State Succession* (1st ed.), pp. 53–6. See also Fitzmaurice, loc. cit.

[2] On the position of the Shatt-al-Arab see Lauterpacht, 9 *I.C.L.Q.* (1960), p. 208 at pp. 226–32.

[3] Cf. Schwarzenberger, *International Law* i (3rd ed.), Part III; Fitzmaurice, 92 Hague *Recueil* (1957, II), 186–90; Sørensen, 101 Hague *Recueil* (1960, III), 182–98; Hyde i. 510–639.

[4] *Supra*, p. 203. [5] *Infra*, p. 439.

dividual or collective self-defence which permits the use of force against or within other states, and the great mass of treaty obligations relating to labour standards, international traffic, commerce, nationality, and many other fields. Important restrictions concern shared resources and amenities.[1]

3. *External Imposition of Governmental Functions without the Consent of the Sovereign*

Executive and administrative powers may be exercised by alien authorities under the rules of belligerent occupation[2] in time of war and by forces taking enforcement action under Chapter VII of the United Nations Charter.[3]

4. *The Regulation of Rights*

To observe that the definition of the precise content and modalities of rights is often a source of great difficulty is no doubt to state the obvious, but the problem may become acute in those cases in which a state or its nationals are accorded privileges of user in respect of the territory of another.[4] In the case of a right of innocent passage through the territorial sea, the coastal state has the right to make regulations in respect of the passage,[5] and it is clear that if a considerable degree of control were permitted the content of the right of passage would evaporate and the residue would amount to no more than a discretionary tolerance accompanied perhaps by certain immunities.

The problem is illustrated by three cases in international jurisprudence. In the *North Atlantic Coast Fisheries* arbitration[6] the United States claimed that Great Britain had no right to make regulations for a fishery in which American citizens had been granted a liberty by a Convention of 1818. The tribunal decided that regulations could be made if they were *bona fide* and not in violation of the treaty and also: '(1) appropriate or necessary for

[1] *Supra*, Chapter XII.

[2] The concept of belligerent occupation is not confined to enemy forces: *supra*, p. 371. See generally Greenspan, *The Modern Law of Land Warfare* (1959).

[3] On the relevance of consent to the presence of peace-keeping forces not acting under Chapter VII, see the controversial opinion of Bowett, *United Nations Forces*, pp. 231–2, 412–27.

[4] See McNair, *Law of Treaties* (1961), pp. 762–5. The content of legal privileges is a persistent problem in municipal law: cf. *Southam* v. *Smout* [1964] 1 Q.B. 308.

[5] See *supra*, pp. 203–7, on the passage of merchant ships and warships. On the position of warships using international straits see pp. 206–7, 282–3.

[6] Hague Court Reports 141; Briggs, p. 313; Green, p. 301; *British Digest* iib, 585.

the protection and preservation of such fisheries, or (2) desirable or necessary on grounds of public order or morals without unnecessarily interfering with the fishery itself; and in both cases equitable and fair as between local and American fishermen. . . .'

The *Asylum* case between Peru and Colombia arose in part from treaty provisions recognizing a right to give political asylum in embassies in 'urgent cases'. Colombia, the state which had granted asylum in its embassy in Peru to Haya de la Torre, a Peruvian politician, claimed the right to qualify the offence with which he was accused as 'political' and also to decide that an 'urgent case' had arisen. The further question was raised by Colombia in a claim that the territorial state was bound to give the guarantees necessary for the departure of the refugee from the country. In its first judgment[1] given on the case, the International Court of Justice decided that Colombia was not entitled to qualify the nature of the alleged offence, and that whilst the offence alleged was political, the present case was not an 'urgent case' within the meaning of the Havana Convention of 1928. The Court also held that Peru was not bound to allow the refugee to depart. The outcome was that Peru was not bound to allow departure and Colombia was not bound to hand over the political offender although asylum had been granted improperly. In a later judgment[2] the Court took the view that the terms of the Havana Convention simply failed to provide a solution to the problem, and it urged the parties to reach a friendly composition. In the *Right of Passage* case[3] Portugal argued that the right of passage from Daman to two enclaves inland was not a discretionary competence for India, although India, as the territorial sovereign of the intervening territory, had the right of regulation and control. The Court held[4] that it was within this right of regulation and control for India to refuse passage when there was tension in intervening Indian territory because of political events in the enclaves.

The subject is not susceptible to facile generalization, and each problem will have its form determined by the nature of the dispute, the facts, and the general context.[5] Where the nature of a

[1] I.C.J. Reports (1950), p. 266; Green, p. 362. See generally Lauterpacht, *The Development of International Law by the International Court*, pp. 142–8.

[2] I.C.J. Reports (1951), p. 71.

[3] I.C.J. Reports (1960), p. 6; Int. L.R. 31, p. 23. [4] pp. 44–5.

[5] See, for example, the issues on concurrence of jurisdiction in the case of ports and visiting forces: *supra*, pp. 316, 367. On the position of Berlin, access to the city, and residual occupation rights in West and East Germany see Quincy Wright, 55 *A.J.* (1961), 959–65; Bathurst, 38 *B.Y.* (1962), 255–306; Lauterpacht, 8 *I.C.L.Q.* (1959), 202–12. Further

right is not spelled out clearly in a treaty or local custom, numerous general principles may be brought to bear, including abuse of rights,[1] the principle of implied powers,[2] the presumption against derogation from a grant,[3] and the dependence of sovereignty over enclaves on the right alleged to exist.[4] Principles of effectiveness[5] and public policy may be relevant, for example the need for finality in territorial settlements,[6] equality of application of local law in respect of minority treaties,[7] and the special requirements of international fluvial law.[8] In the case of a right of passage the subject-matter may be significant and so the passage of armed forces may be *prima facie* generative of wide jurisdictional immunities.[9] Numerous other questions arise, each of which require treatment in depth, and it must suffice here to give them brief notice. To what extent is the given right susceptible to the effects of state succession[1] or war? Is the right subject to the *clausula rebus sic stantibus*[2] or its equivalent outside the law of treaties? What are the relations of the right to the principles of the *jus cogens*,[3] for example the right of self-defence and the principles of non-intervention and self-determination?[4] Is the right subject to the restrictions of the law of neutrality?[5]

Another source of problems arises when, in the case of exceptional rights over another's sovereignty or over a *res communis* (for example, jurisdiction in a contiguous zone of the high seas),[6] one considers the legality of forcible self-help. Who has to stand

examples: *British Digest* vi. 21, 29 seq.; *U.S. Nationals in Morocco*, I.C.J. Reports (1952), p. 176; *Saudi Arabia* v. *Arabian–American Oil Co.*, Int. L.R. 27, at pp. 214–17.

1 *Infra*, p. 443.

2 Cf. *supra*, p 60; *infra*, pp. 686–8.

3 Cf. Lauterpacht, 9 *I.C.L.Q.* (1960), p. 209 at pp. 226–32.

4 *Right of Passage* case, I.C.J. Reports (1960), pp. 66 (sep. op., Judge Wellington Koo), 84 (diss. op., Judge Armand-Ugon), 108–9 (diss. op., Judge Spender), 135, 137–8 (diss. op., Fernandes, Judge *ad hoc*).

5 I.C.J. Reports (1960), pp. 82–3 (diss. op., Judge Armand-Ugon).

6 See Lauterpacht, *The Development of International Law by the International Court*, pp. 233–4.

7 Ibid., pp. 257–62.

8 Ibid., pp. 234–5; Schwarzenberger, *International Law* i (3rd ed.), 218–23.

9 Cf. the *Right of Passage* case, *supra*, and especially the diss. op. of Judge Moreno Quintana, I.C.J. Reports (1960), p. 89. See also *supra*, pp. 368–71, on the position of visiting forces.

1 See Chapter XXVIII. This question has been primarily responsible for the persistence by some writers in the notion of state servitudes: *supra*, p. 372.

2 *Infra*, pp. 616–18. Cf. Schwarzenberger, op. cit., pp. 210–12.

3 *Infra*, pp. 512–15.

4 On self-determination generally see *infra*, pp. 593–6; cf. I.C.J. Reports (1960), p. 95 (diss. op., Judge Moreno Quintana).

5 This was the issue in the *Wimbledon* (1923), P.C.I.J., Ser. A, no. 1; Green, p. 311. See also I.C.J. Reports (1960), p. 25.

6 *Supra*, pp. 210–11.

down or be accused of unlawfully pre-empting a legal issue? In principle, the territorial *privilege*[1] is subject to curtailment in case of dispute: the claim to the privilege cannot be supported by self-help which would render the right, *ex post facto*, extraterritorial, and serious breaches of the peace are not a justifiable means of upholding exceptional rights. This type of problem is very well illustrated by the *Corfu Channel* case (Merits), which has been considered elsewhere.[2]

[1] The qualification as an 'exceptional right' or 'privilege', and the incidents attaching, will depend to some extent on general considerations as to whether there is a presumption in favour of the territorial sovereign (*supra*, pp. 288–9), and the relation of the subject-matter to domestic jurisdiction (*supra*, pp. 291–5).

[2] *Infra*, pp. 441–3.

PART VII

RULES OF ATTRIBUTION

(apart from Territorial Sovereignty and State Jurisdiction)

CHAPTER XVIII

THE RELATIONS OF NATIONALITY

1. *The Doctrine of the Freedom of States in Matters of Nationality*[1]

As special rapporteur of the International Law Commission,[2] Manley O. Hudson expressed the view: 'In principle, questions of nationality fall within the domestic jurisdiction of each state.' This proposition already had high authority behind it, and there is no doubt that it expresses the 'accepted view'. The impetus to a wide acceptance of the principle enunciated by Hudson was given by the dictum of the Permanent Court in the advisory opinion concerning the *Tunis and Morocco Nationality Decrees*:[3]

> The question whether a certain matter is or is not solely within the jurisdiction of a State is an essentially relative question; it depends upon the development of international relations. Thus, in the present state of international law, questions of nationality are, in the opinion of this Court, in principle within this reserved domain.

Whatever the intrinsic meaning and value of the statement of the Permanent Court *as such*,[4] its influence must be examined in terms of the construction placed upon it by others, to the effect that states are exclusively in control of nationality matters. Numerous textbooks and standard works have repeated the statement in the *Nationality Decrees* case, or have stated in their own words propositions obviously inspired by it.[5]

[1] Generally on nationality see Whiteman viii. 1–193; Weis, *Nationality and Statelessness in International Law* (1956); van Panhuys, *The Role of Nationality in International Law* (1959); de Castro, 102 Hague *Recueil* (1961, I), 521–634; Bar-Yaacov, *Dual Nationality* (1961). See also Brownlie, 39 *B.Y.* (1963), 284–364; and *British Digest* v.

[2] *Yrbk., I.L.C.* (1952), ii, p. 3 at p. 7. See also Hudson, *Cases* (2nd ed., 1936), p. 201; (3rd ed., 1951), p. 138.

[3] P.C.I.J., Ser. B, no. 4 (1923), p. 24; Whiteman viii. 37–42.

[4] See further Brownlie, 39 *B.Y.* (1963), 286–8.

[5] See, for example, Ralston, *The Law and Procedure of International Tribunals* (1926),

There are compelling objections of principle to the doctrine of the freedom of states in the present context. However, before these are considered it is necessary to recall the high significance which the concept of nationality has in the law. Thus a state, a national of which has suffered a wrong at the hands of another state, has the right to exercise diplomatic protection. This, the principle of nationality of claims, is all-important, in spite of certain qualifications to it recognized lately.[1] In former times, and, in the opinion of some jurists, even in the period of the United Nations Charter, the law recognized a right of forcible intervention to protect the lives and property of nationals.[2] Numerous duties of states in relation to war and neutrality, resting for the most part on the customary law, are framed in terms of the acts or omissions by nationals which states should prevent and, in some cases, punish. Aliens on the territory of a state produce a complex of legal relations consequent on their status of non-nationals. Acts of sovereignty may give rise to questions of international responsibility when they affect aliens or their property; witness the problems considered under the titles 'denial of justice', 'expropriation', and the like. Aliens may be expelled for sufficient cause and their home state is bound to receive them. Nationals will not, whilst aliens may, be extradited. Nationality provides a normal (but not exclusive) basis for the exercise of civil and criminal jurisdiction and this even in respect of acts committed abroad.

At the outset one might predicate a presumption of effectiveness and regularity which would abruptly resolve the apparent conflict between the reliance of so many institutions of the law on the concept of nationality, so far as application and enforcement are concerned, and the alleged freedom of states in the conferment of nationality. Nationality is a problem, in part of attribution, and regarded in this way resembles the law relating to territorial sovereignty.[3] National law prescribes the extent of the territory of a state, but this prescription does not preclude a

p. 160; ibid., Suppl., p. 76; Brierly, pp. 283, 357. See further Oppenheim i. 643. But see the first edition, i. 348–9, para. 293, where the original context reduces the significance of the statement.

[1] See *infra*, pp. 481, 662–3.

[2] Generally see Brownlie, *International Law and the Use of Force by States* (1963), pp. 289–301; Bowett, *Self-defence in International Law* (1958), pp. 87–105.

[3] Parry, *Nationality and Citizenship Laws of the Commonwealth and the Republic of Ireland* i. 17–19, regards the analogy of territory as 'very attractive', but he also remarks that it should not be pushed too far (see p. 21). However, for the purpose of comment on the possible *results* of a certain type of doctrine the analogy would seem to be perfectly valid.

forum which is applying international law from deciding questions of title in its own way, using criteria of international law. Sovereignty which is in principle unlimited, even by the existence of other states, is ridiculous, whether dominion is sought to be exercised over territory, sea, airspace, or populations. In a related matter, the delimitation of the territorial sea, the Court in the *Fisheries* case allowed that in regard to rugged coasts the coastal state would seem to be in the best position to appraise the local conditions dictating the selection of base lines, but the tenor of the judgment was not in support of legal autonomy, and the Court stated:[1]

> The delimitation of sea areas has always an international aspect; it cannot be dependent merely upon the will of the coastal State as expressed in its municipal law. Although it is true that the act of delimitation is necessarily a unilateral act, because only the coastal State is competent to undertake it, the delimitation with regard to other States depends upon international law.

This passage is of considerable importance, since the origins of nationality as a status are very similar to the process of delimitation here dealt with.

It is important to avoid reliance on general statements purporting to establish the boundaries of the reserved domain in abstract form.[2] Everything depends on the way in which a particular issue arises. Nationality is not capable of performing a role confined to the reserved domain or the realm of state relations: in principle it has two aspects, either of which may be dominant, depending on the facts and type of dispute. The approach of the International Court in the *Nottebohm* case[3] would seem to be perfectly logical in this respect. The Court said:[4]

> It is for Liechtenstein, as it is for every sovereign State, to settle by its own legislation the rules relating to the acquisition of its nationality, and to confer that nationality by naturalization granted by its own organs in accordance with that legislation.[5] It is not necessary to determine whether international law imposes any limitations on its freedom of decision in this domain[6]. . . . Nationality serves above all to determine that the person upon whom it is conferred enjoys the rights and is bound by the obligations which the law of the State in question grants to or imposes on its nationals.

[1] I.C.J. Reports (1951), p. 116 at p. 132. See also Judge McNair, pp. 160–1; and Judge Read, pp. 189–90; and further, Fitzmaurice, 30 *B.Y.* (1953), 11. Cf. the *Asylum* case, I.C.J. Reports (1950), p. 266 at pp. 273–5.

[2] See de Visscher, *Theory and Reality in Public International Law* (1957), pp. 222–3; and *supra*, p. 295.

[3] I.C.J. Reports (1955), p. 4.

[4] I.C.J. Reports (1955), pp. 20–1.

[5] Cf. *Yrbk., I.L.C.* (1954), ii. 164 (Belgian comment), 173 (United States comment).

[6] See *infra*, p. 383.

This is implied in the wider concept that nationality is within the domestic jurisdiction of the State.

But the issue which the Court must decide is not one which pertains to the legal system of Liechtenstein. It does not depend on the law or on the decision of Liechtenstein whether that State is entitled to exercise its protection . . . To exercise protection, to apply to the Court, is to place oneself on the plane of international law. It is international law which determines whether a State is entitled to exercise protection and to seise the Court.[1]

2. *Opinions of Governments on the Issue of Autonomy*

The significance of the views of governments, expressed in replies to questions of the Preparatory Committee for the Hague Codification Conference, does not need emphasis. Incidentally but usefully, these replies provide a commentary on the advisory opinion concerning the *Nationality Decrees in Tunis and Morocco*.[2] In its reply the German Government stated:[3]

The general principle that all questions relating to the acquisition or loss of a specific nationality shall be governed by the laws of the State whose nationality is claimed or contested should be admitted. The application of this principle, however, should not go beyond the limits at which the legislation of one State encroaches on the sovereignty of another. For example, a State has no power, by means of a law or administrative act, to confer its nationality on all the inhabitants of another State or on all foreigners entering its territory. Further, if the State confers its nationality on the subjects of other States without their request, when the persons concerned are not attached to it by any particular bond, as, for instance, origin, domicile or birth, the States concerned will not be bound to recognize such naturalization.

The British reply[4] states the principle of exclusive jurisdiction and continues:

The mere fact, however, that nationality falls in general within the domestic jurisdiction of a State does not exclude the possibility that the right of the State to use its discretion in legislating with regard to nationality may be restricted by duties which it owes to other States (see *Tunis and Morocco Case* . . .). Legislation which is inconsistent with such duties is not legislation which there is any obligation upon a State whose rights are ignored

[1] See also the *Fisheries* case, I.C.J. Reports (1951), p. 116, at p. 132, quoted *supra*, p. 382.

[2] *Supra*, p. 380.

[3] *League of Nations, Conference for the Codification of International Law, Bases of Discussion*, I, *Nationality* (1929), V. 1. 13.

[4] Ibid., pp. 17, 169. The replies of the Dominions and India are identical or substantially similar.

to recognize. It follows that the right of a State to legislate with regard to the acquisition and loss of its nationality and the duty of another State to recognize the effects of such legislation are not necessarily coincident.

Even if the discretion of the State in the former case may be unlimited, the duty of the State in the latter case is not unlimited. It may properly decline to recognize the effects of such legislation which is prejudicial to its own rights as a State.

It is only in exceptional cases that this divergence between the right of a State to legislate at its discretion with regard to the enjoyment or non-enjoyment of its nationality and the duty of other States to recognize such legislation would occur. The criterion is that the legislation must infringe the *rights* of the State as apart from its *interests*.

The last paragraph of this reply confines the area of divergence to 'exceptional cases'. However, if exceptional cases are admitted to exist the force of emphasis on discretion in legislation is much diminished. Obviously there are limits to the discretion, and these are not concealed by the device whereby the exercise of the discretion occurs but is not recognized by other states. In terms of international law this would then seem to be a discretion within the limits set by the divergence referred to in the British reply. In other words, the principle is admitted. Moreover, there is a general duty to bring national law into conformity with obligations under international law;[1] and in this connexion the opinion has been expressed[2] that where a state adopts legislation on its face contrary to its obligations the legislation may itself constitute the breach of an obligation. In such a case, however, potential plaintiff states must await the occurrence of actual damage before presenting a claim. The contradiction and misconception inherent in the theory of divergence are to be found in the replies of other governments. Thus the majority relate the duty to recognize foreign nationality legislation to fulfilment of international obligations, but do not always place this in direct relation to the right to determine nationality. In view of the element of contradiction and the rules noted above, the statements in the replies of governments to the effect that 'in principle' the question of nationality falls within the exclusive competence of states lose much of their effect.[3]

[1] *Supra*, p. 37.
[2] Fitzmaurice, 92 Hague *Recueil* (1957, II), 89.
[3] Or, more precisely perhaps, they lose the effect with which they have been invested by writers.

3. *The Convention Concerning Certain Questions Relating to the Conflict of Nationality Laws*[1]

At the Hague Codification Conference of 1930 the First Committee stated in its report[2] that although nationality 'is primarily a matter for the municipal law of each State, it is nevertheless governed to a large extent by principles of international law'. In spite of the fact that the committee could not agree on the principles to which they referred, the Conference did produce a Convention of some interest, though of limited importance. Article 1 thereof provides:[3] 'It is for each State to determine under its own law who are its nationals. This law shall be recognized by other States in so far as it is consistent with international conventions, international custom, and the principles of law generally recognized with regard to nationality.' It will be at once apparent that the antithesis between autonomy in legislation and the limited duty of recognition, which is evident in the replies of governments, recurs. The antithesis taken together with the independent force of the second part of the article, deprives the principle of autonomy of its integrity. However, the antithesis might perhaps equally be said to make the provision a legal curiosity, of little strength, and not giving respectability to any proposition. Article 18, paragraph 2, provides in part that the inclusion of the principles and rules stated in the Convention 'shall in no way be deemed to prejudice the question whether they do or do not already form part of international law'. In relation to Article 1 this takes one neither forwards nor backwards. But, with its limitations, Article 1 remains a useful authority for the view that international law sets limits to the power of a state to confer nationality.[4]

4. *Nationality Rules Commonly Adopted by States*

Certain principles concerning conferment of nationality are adopted in the legislation of states often enough to acquire the

[1] *League of Nations Treaty Series*, vol. 179, p. 89; *Laws Concerning Nationality*, U.N. Legislative Series, ST/LEG/SER.B/4, July 1954, p. 567. In force 1 July 1937. Twenty-seven states signed but did not ratify. Thirteen states have ratified or acceded to the Convention.

[2] *League of Nations, Conference for the Codification of International Law, Acts of the Conference*, II, *Report of the 1st Committee* (1930), V. 8. 2–3.

[3] This text was adopted by the First Committee by thirty-eight votes to two and by the Conference by forty votes to one: *Acts of the Conference*, II, *Minutes of the 1st Committee* (1930), V. 15. 19–36, 205–9; ibid. I, *Plenary Meetings* (1930), V. 14. 38–41. See also Sixth Session, Asian–African Legal Consultative Committee, 1964, Whiteman viii. 82.

[4] Thus Córdova, *Yrbk., I.L.C.* (1953), ii. 167, paras. 13–15.

status of 'general principles'. It is proposed to give a relatively short exposition[1] of these principles while postponing a general consideration of their precise legal status. Without prejudging too much the question of their legal status, account will be taken of the existence of a sufficiency of adherence to a principle to establish the principle as 'normal' though not necessarily adopted generally in the sense of either a simple or absolute majority.

The two main principles on which nationality is based are descent from a national (*jus sanguinis*) and the fact of birth within state territory (*jus soli*).

Jus sanguinis. Weis[2] remarks that *jus sanguinis* and *jus soli* are 'the predominant modes of acquisition of nationality'. In 1935 Sandifer[3] concluded that legislation in forty-eight states followed the *jus sanguinis* principally and referred to 'the widespread extent of the rule of *jus sanguinis*, and its paramount influence upon the law of nationality throughout the world'. There is no reason to think that this assessment is out of place today.[4] The Harvard Research survey polled seventeen states with law based solely on *jus sanguinis*; two equally on *jus sanguinis* and *jus soli*; and twenty-six principally on *jus soli* and partly on *jus sanguinis*. Experts[5] commonly regard the two principles as permissible criteria, but do not always indicate an opinion on their precise legal status. Van Panhuys[6] considers the two principles to be sanctioned by customary law.

In regard to the modalities of the *jus sanguinis*, Sandifer[7] calculated that forty-seven states had rules under which the status of the father governed (conditional in fourteen cases); thirty-five had rules under which the status of either parent or both governed (conditional in twenty-two cases); and twenty-nine, including the United States, had rules under which the status of the unmarried mother governed.

Jus soli. The role of *jus soli* will be evident from what has gone

[1] For extended surveys see Córdova, Special Rapporteur, *Yrbk., I.L.C.* (1953), ii. 167, 170 seq. (Part I); *Survey of the problem of multiple nationality prepared by the Secretariat*, A/CN.4/84, *Yrbk., I.L.C.* (1954), ii. 52, 63 seq. (Chap. I); Harv. Research, 23 *A.J.* (1929), Spec. Suppl., p. 24; Sandifer, 29 *A.J.* (1935), 248.

[2] Op. cit., p. 98. See also Hudson, *Yrbk., I.L.C.* (1952), ii, p. 3 at p. 7.

[3] 29 *A.J.* (1935), at pp. 256, 278.

[4] See new legislation in Parry, *Nationality and Citizenship Laws of the Commonwealth and Republic of Ireland*, 2 vols.; and U.N. Legislative Series, *Supplement to the Volume on the Laws concerning Nationality* 1954 (1959), ST/LEG/SER.B/9.

[5] Preparatory Committee of the Hague Codification Conference, *Bases of Discussion*, p. 20 (excised in the Committee on Nationality of the Conference by eighteen votes to seventeen); Mervyn Jones, *British Nationality Law and Practice*, pp. 10–11; Guggenheim i. 315–16; Makarov, 74 Hague *Recueil* (1949, I), pp. 364–5.

[6] Op. cit., pp. 160–1.

[7] Op. cit., pp. 254, 255, 258.

before. However, it may be remarked that, as a principle, it has a relative simplicity of outline, with fairly clear exceptions, when compared with *jus sanguinis*. Indeed, in terms of adherence to a particular system, with a minor degree of dilution, *jus soli* seems to have predominance in the world.[1] Except in so far as there may exist a presumption against statelessness, it is probably incorrect to regard the two most important principles as mutually exclusive: in varying degrees the law of a very large number of states rests on both, and recent legislation gives no sign of any change in the situation. However, the Harvard draft provided in Article 3 that states must choose between the two principles.[2]

Of particular interest are the special rules relating to the *jus soli*, appearing as exceptions to that principle, the effect of the exceptions being to remove the cases where its application is clearly unjustifiable. A rule which has very considerable authority stipulated that children born to persons having diplomatic immunity shall not be nationals by birth of the state to which the diplomatic agent concerned is accredited. Thirteen governments stated the exception in the preliminaries of the Hague Codification Conference. In a comment[3] on the relevant article of the Harvard draft on diplomatic privileges and immunities it is stated: 'This article is believed to be declaratory of an established rule of international law.' The rule receives ample support from the legislation of states[4] and expert opinion.[5] The Convention on Certain Questions relating to the Conflict of Nationality Laws of 1930 provides in Article 12: 'Rules of law which confer nationality by reason of birth on the territory of a State shall not apply automatically to children born to persons enjoying diplomatic immunities in the country where the birth occurs.'

In 1961 the United Nations Conference on Diplomatic Intercourse and Immunities adopted an Optional Protocol concerning Acquisition of Nationality,[6] which provided in Article II:

[1] According to Sandifer, p. 256, twenty-nine states followed *jus soli*; and the study by the International Union for Child Welfare (1950) concluded that, of forty-nine states, thirty-five relied principally on the *jus soli*. See also *Yrbk., I.L.C.* (1953), ii. 170–1; ibid., (1954), ii. 63 seq.

[2] Loc. cit., p. 27. See further Weis, op. cit., pp. 97–8, where he states: 'In the absence of historical examples it is a matter of conjecture whether a nationality law based equally on *jus soli* and *jus sanguinis* would be regarded as inconsistent with international law or the general principles of law.'

[3] 26 *A.J.* (1932), Suppl., p. 133. See also the Harvard draft on nationality, ibid. 23 (1929), Spec. Suppl., p. 13, Art. 5.

[4] See the U.N. Legislative Series, *Laws Concerning Nationality* (1954), Supplementary Volume, 1959.

[5] Córdova, *Yrbk., I.L.C.* (1953), ii. p. 166 at p. 176 (Art. III); Guggenheim i. 317.

[6] 18 April 1961; 500 U.N.T.S., 223. See Johnson, 10 *I.C.L.Q.* (1961), 597. The Proto-

'Members of the mission not being nationals of the receiving State, and members of their families forming part of their household, shall not, solely by the operation of the law of the receiving State, acquire the nationality of that State.' Some states extend the rule to the children of consuls,[1] and there is some support for this from expert opinion.[2] The United Nations Conference on Consular Relations adopted an Optional Protocol Concerning Acquisition of Nationality containing a provision similar to that concerning diplomats.[3] In a few instances legislation[4] and other prescriptions[5] exclude the *jus soli* in respect of the children of persons exercising official duties on behalf of a foreign government. Another exception quite commonly adopted concerns the children of enemy alien fathers born in territory under enemy occupation.

Extensions of the jus soli. The Harvard Research draft[6] refers to 'territory or a place assimilated thereto', and states have generally applied the principle of the *jus soli* to birth on ships and aircraft registered under the flag. Legislation formerly in force in Argentina[7] referred to birth in a 'legation or warship of the Republic', and the later legislation extends to birth 'in an international zone under the Argentine flag'.[8] Where apparent conflict may arise, as in the case of birth on a foreign ship in territorial waters, it is tolerably clear that the child does not in principle acquire *ipso facto* the nationality of the littoral state.[9] This is an obvious case where the matter is not one of exclusive jurisdiction. Moreover, the analogy is with the concept of aliens in transit, which appears in some laws, the presence being somewhat incidental and brief. However, some states, including the United States, Italy, and Japan, do at least claim the faculty of treating birth within their waters as productive of nationality.[1] Yet it

col, in Article II, reproduces the text of Article 35 of the draft articles of the I.L.C.: *Yrbk., I.L.C.* (1958), ii, p. 89 at p. 101.

[1] See *Laws Concerning Nationality* (1954), pp. 1, 152, 248, 459; *Supplement* (1959), p. 15.

[2] *Yrbk., I.L.C.* (1953), ii. 176–7.

[3] 24 April 1963; 596 U.N.T.S., 469. See also *Yrbk., I.L.C.* (1961), ii. 122, art. 52.

[4] For example, the Canadian Citizenship Act 1946, as amended, sect. 5 (2); Constitution of Bolivia, 23 November 1946, as amended; Constitution of Brazil, 18 September 1946.

[5] Article 2 of the draft convention prepared by the Committee of Experts of the League of Nations.

[6] *Ubi supra.* See generally Córdova, *Yrbk., I.L.C.* (1953), ii. 177–9.

[7] *Laws Concerning Nationality* (1954), p. 11; cf. p. 595.

[8] Ibid., p. 595. The countries taking this view include the U.K., Commonwealth states, Germany, Belgium, and Norway.

[9] See Parry, op. cit., pp. 151–3, 230, 412, 426, 537, 950, 960.

[1] See *Yrbk., I.L.C.* (1953), ii. 178; Hackworth iii. 10.

would be strange if birth on a ship exercising the right of innocent passage had this consequence. In an attempt to avoid statelessness, Córdova, as rapporteur of the International Law Commission, proposed an article which subjected those born on ships and aircraft to the law of the state in the territory (or waters) of which the ship or aircraft was situated at the time.[1]

Involuntary naturalization of individuals. As rapporteur for the International Law Commission, Hudson expressed the following opinion:[2]

> Under the law of some States nationality is conferred automatically by operation of law, as the effect of certain changes in civil status: adoption, legitimation, recognition by affiliation, marriage.
>
> Appointment as teacher at a university also involves conferment of nationality under some national laws.
>
> While these reasons for the conferment of nationality have been recognized by the consistent practice of States and may, therefore, be considered as consistent with international law, others have not been so recognized.

Some of these categories may be considered briefly.

Marriage. A survey carried out by the Secretary-General of the United Nations in 1953 showed that a wife automatically acquired the nationality of her husband in twenty-two states, that in forty-four states acquisition was conditional, and that in four states there was no effect. In some states the principle of family unity has prevailed, but the modern tendency is to favour sexual equality. The development of opinion has culminated in the Convention on the Nationality of Married Women opened for signature by the General Assembly of the United Nations on 29 January 1957.[3] The Hague Convention of 1930 merely provides that naturalization of the husband during marriage shall not involve a change in the nationality of the wife except with her consent. The Convention of 1957 favours the principle of the equality (and hence independence) of the wife, but compromises to some extent. Thus each contracting state agrees that neither the celebration nor the dissolution of marriage between one of its nationals and an alien, nor change of nationality by the husband during marriage, shall affect the wife's nationality automatically.

[1] *Yrbk., I.L.C.* (1953), ii. 177. See now the United Nations Convention on the Reduction of Statelessness, signed 30 August 1961, Art. 3 (test of flag or registration).

[2] *Yrbk., I.L.C.* (1952), ii. 8. The rubric employed is: 'Conferment of nationality by operation of law.'

[3] Resol. 1040 (XI). Text: *Laws Concerning Nationality*, Supplement (1959), p. 91. In force in 1958. See the British Nationality Act 1965, c. 34; and *Mejia* v. *Regierungsrat des Kantons Bern*, Int. L.R. 32, p. 192.

However, it is provided that the alien wife of a national of a contracting state may, at her request, acquire her husband's nationality by means of privileged naturalization procedures.

Legal recognition or legitimation. It is widely accepted in legislation that the child follows the father's nationality.[1]

Adoption. That the minor acquires the nationality of the adoptive parent is also generally recognized in legislation, but there are considerable variations from the norm.

Acquisition of domicile or analogous links. Hudson, rather curiously, refers[2] to appointment as a teacher at a university as a mode recognized by the law, but omits other important items to some extent, at least, *eiusdem generis*. Among the omissions are residence, domicile, and immigration *animo manendi*. Similarly, it is common to permit resumption of nationality, for example where a marriage which changed the nationality of the *de cujus* is now dissolved, by a renewal of domicile in the state concerned. Also akin to domicile is the conferment of nationality on members of particular ethnic or other defined groups belonging to the population of a state. In many states nationals of certain categories, such as naturalized citizens, citizens by registration (in Commonwealth countries), and analogous instances, may by acquisition of domicile abroad lose their nationality.[3]

In certain cases states have protested against legislation permitting involuntary naturalization of foreigners resident for a certain period on national territory or acquiring real estate in the territory.[4] However, it is important to determine the exact bases of such protests. Thus the United States was concerned to a great extent with the principle of voluntary expatriation. Other states, without being very articulate as to the reasons justifying their protests, were in substance reserving their rights and at the same time intimating that these matters were not within the discretion of the territorial sovereign.[5] The British view seems to have been that conferment of nationality on the basis of a number of years' residence, provided that due notice is given and a declaration of a contrary intention may be made, was lawful.[6] The available evidence does not indicate that states are hostile to

[1] Sandifer, 29 *A.J.* (1935), 259; *Yrbk., I.L.C.* (1953), ii. 180–1. See the British Nationality Act, 1948, s. 23 (1). But cf. Weis, op. cit., p. 114.

[2] Loc. cit. Cf. Austria, Citizenship Act 1949, Art. 2(4), 6.

[3] Cf. the United Nations Convention on the Reduction of Statelessness, Art. 7.

[4] Reliance is placed on the materials set out in Weis, pp. 105 seq.

[5] See the Law Officer's opinion quoted by Weis, p. 106.

[6] See Weis, p. 107 and *British Digest* v. 28, 250. However, the British view may well have been that in appropriate circumstances what occurred was a voluntary naturalization.

domicile as a basis for conferment of nationality (as opposed to a temporary residence without *animus manendi*).

'Voluntary' naturalization. The position is stated as follows by Weis:[1]

> Naturalization in the narrower sense may be defined as the grant of nationality to an alien by a formal act, on the application of the *de cujus*. It is generally recognized as a mode of acquiring nationality. The conditions to be complied with for the grant of naturalization vary from country to country, but residence for a certain period of time would seem to be a fairly universal requisite.

Hudson remarks:[2] 'Naturalization must be based on an explicit voluntary act of the individual or of a person acting on his behalf.' Some jurists have concluded that prolonged residence is a pre-condition for a naturalization which conforms with international law.[3] Such a conclusion is probably sound, but in regard to *voluntary*[4] naturalization two points must be borne in mind. First, the voluntary nature of the act supplements other social and residential links. Not only is the act voluntary but, in regard to obtaining nationality, it is specific: it has that very objective. The element of deliberate association of individual and state is surely important and should rank with birth and descent, not to mention marriage, legitimation, and adoption. Secondly, whilst it is true that a considerable number of states allow naturalization on easy terms, the form of the legislation quite often presents the relaxed conditions as available exceptionally.[5]

Nationality ex necessitate juris. The rubric is convenient, but not in all respects satisfactory, since acquisition by marriage, legitimation, and adoption might be so described. However, the cases to be mentioned are sufficiently clear to justify the somewhat question-begging heading. The first group of generally recognized rules consists in modalities of the *jus soli*. There is in the legislation of many countries a provision that a child of

[1] Op. cit., p. 101. See also *infra*, pp. 397–8.

[2] *Yrbk., I.L.C.* (1952), ii. 8. His rubric is: 'Naturalization in the narrower sense. Option.' In his terminology naturalization means every nationality acquired subsequent to birth.

[3] See *infra*, pp. 406 seq.

[4] Voluntary *sub modo*, since the individual does not have any control over the conditions under which naturalization may occur or under which it may be revoked. There is no right to naturalization unless this is conferred by treaty.

[5] See, for example, the Dominican Republic, Naturalization Act no. 1683 of 16 April 1948; *Laws Concerning Nationality* (1954), p. 126, Art. 18: 'The President of the Republic may, as a special privilege, grant Dominican nationality by decree to such aliens as he considers worthy of exemption from the usual Dominican naturalization formalities because of services rendered to the Republic.'

parents unknown is presumed to have the nationality of the state on the territory of which it is found until the contrary is proved. Also in a great many instances it is provided that the rule applies to children born of parents of unknown nationality or who are stateless. The principal rule as to foundlings appears in the Hague Convention on Certain Questions relating to the Conflict of Nationality Laws, which provides in Article 14: 'A foundling is, until the contrary is proved, presumed to have been born on the territory of the State in which it was found.'[1]

5. *Legal Status of the 'General Principles'*

A proportion, if not perhaps all, of the principles considered above are generally recognized principles as far as municipal law of the various states is concerned. Weis is very cautious in assessing such material in terms of state practice. He says:[2]

> Concordance of municipal law does not yet create customary international law; a universal consensus of opinion of States is equally necessary. It is erroneous to attempt to establish rules of international law by methods of comparative law, or even to declare that rules of municipal law of different States which show a certain degree of uniformity are rules of international law.

This statement of principle is unexceptionable in so far as the reversal of the statement would result in a proposition obviously much too dogmatic. However, in substance, Weis is thought to underestimate the significance of legislation as evidence of the opinion of states.[3] In the case of the territorial sea, the evidence of state practice available to the International Law Commission was chiefly in the form of legislation, and the comments of governments received by the Commission concentrated to some extent on the nature of their own legislation.

It may be said that, particularly in the field of nationality, the necessary *opinio juris et necessitatis* is lacking; but insistence on clear evidence of this may well produce capricious results. The fact is that municipal law overwhelmingly rests on significant links between the *de cujus* and the state. Such lack of uniformity as there is in nationality laws is explicable not in terms of a lack

[1] See also the United Nations Convention on the Reduction of Statelessness, 1961, Article 2.

[2] Op. cit., p. 98; see also p. 101. Similar views in Makarov, 74 Hague *Recueil* (1949, I), 304. Cf. Oppenheim i. 651 seq.

[3] Cf. the United Nations Legislative Series.

of *opinio juris*, but by reference to the fact that inevitably municipal law makes the attribution in the first place, and also to the occurrence of numerous permutations and hence possible points of conflict in legislation on a subject-matter so mobile and complex. There is no evidence that there is an absence of *opinio juris*, and, on the contrary, in spheres where conflict on the international plane is easily foreseeable, the rules are there to meet the case; witness the rules relating to children of diplomats and birth on ships and aircraft.

In view of considerations of this sort, the conclusions of the Court in the *Nottebohm* case are not particularly novel.[1] After considering the evidence[2] for the doctrine of the real or effective link favoured by the Court, the judgment proceeds:[3]

> The character thus recognized on the international level as pertaining to nationality is in no way inconsistent with the fact that international law leaves it to each State to lay down the rules governing the grant of its own nationality. The reason for this is that the diversity of demographic conditions has thus far made it impossible for any general agreement to be reached on the rules relating to nationality, although the latter by its very nature affects international relations. It has been considered that the best way of making such rules accord with the varying demographic conditions in different countries is to leave the fixing of such rules to the competence of each State. On the other hand, a State cannot claim that the rules it has thus laid down are entitled to recognition by another State unless it has acted in conformity with this general aim of making the legal bond of nationality accord with the individual's genuine connection with the State which assumes the defence of its citizens by means of protection as against other States.
>
> . . . According to the practice of States, to arbitral and judicial decisions and to the opinions of writers, nationality is a legal bond having as its basis a social fact of attachment, a genuine connection of existence, interests and sentiments, together with the existence of reciprocal rights and duties. It may be said to constitute the juridical expression of the fact that the individual upon whom it is conferred, either directly by the law or as the result of an act of the authorities, is in fact more closely connected with the population of the State conferring nationality than with that of any other State. Conferred by a State, it only entitles that State to exercise protection vis-à-vis another State, if it constitutes a translation into juridical terms of the individual's connection with the State which has made him its national.

[1] The more precise implications of the decision are examined *infra*, pp. 406–20.

[2] See *infra*, pp. 409–12. The Court says, I.C.J. Reports (1955), p. 22: 'National laws reflect this tendency when, *inter alia*, they make naturalization dependent on conditions indicating the existence of a link, which may vary in their purpose or in their nature but which are essentially concerned with this idea. The Liechtenstein Law of 4 January 1934 is a good example.' For the Liechtenstein Law see ibid., pp. 13–14.

[3] I.C.J. Reports (1955), p. 23.

This important statement of principle and policy was supported by eleven members of the Court, there being only three dissenting opinions.

6. *The Logical Application of Rules of International Law*

The manner in which rules of international law often make use of the terms 'national' or 'nationality' has been noticed previously.[1] If these rules are to work effectively, or at all, there must be important limitations on the powers of individual states in the matter of attribution of persons for purposes of international law. Some of these limitations must now be considered.

Mandated and Trust Territories.[2] In principle the status of the inhabitants of mandated and trust territories cannot be a domestic question. The mandatory does not have sovereignty over the territory,[3] nor does the administering authority over a trust territory.[4] It would seem that in principle the inhabitants cannot be nationals of the administering power, and thus, *in one sense*, they have no nationality. Weis observed:[5] 'The position of these persons is somewhat anomalous since they have, in consequence, no nationality in the sense of international law.' With respect this seems to be a *petitio principii*, since the absence of nationality *qua* internal law of the administering power, and the absence of nationality *eo nomine* conferred by some other source, does not render the inhabitants stateless. For various purposes of the law they are attributable to the territory itself. Judicial decisions, such as *R.* v. *Ketter*,[6] do not take the matter very far, since they merely establish that the *de cujus* is not a national of the administering power, without deciding what his status is otherwise. The decisions, and particularly those concerning South-West Africa,[7] often turn on questions of state succession. The existence of some system of attribution is recognized by the admission that the administering power may exercise the right of diplomatic protection in respect to the population of the territories.

[1] *Supra*, p. 381.

[2] See, in particular, Weis, op. cit., pp. 22–8; van Panhuys, op. cit., pp. 65–8. On Chapter XI of the United Nations Charter see *infra*, p. 567.

[3] Judge McNair, I.C.J. Reports (1950,) p. 128, at p. 150; Article 22 of the League Covenant.

[4] United Nations Charter, Chapter XII.

[5] Op. cit., p. 27.

[6] [1940] 1 K.B. 787; *Ann. Digest* 9 (1938–40), no. 21.

[7] *Rimpelt* v. *Clarkson*, *Ann. Digest* 14 (1947), no. 21; *Westphal et Uxor* v. *Conducting Officer of Southern Rhodesia* (1948), 2 S.A.L.R. 18; *Ann. Digest* 15 (1948), no. 54. See also, on the 'C' class mandates, *Wong Man On* v. *The Commonwealth and Others* (1952), 86 C.L.R. 125; Int. L.R. 19 (1952), no. 58, on which see O'Connell, 31 *B.Y.* (1954), 458.

States without nationality legislation. It may happen that a state has not adopted any nationality laws on the modern pattern. Such cases are increasingly rare, but the Yemen probably constitutes a recent example.[1] Historically, before the existence of general statutory definitions, nationality was related to domicile (to some extent it still is), and in fact the two concepts were not differentiated. Recurrent examples of the absence of nationality legislation arise from the creation of new states. Of necessity—if they are states—they must possess a population which is their own. In a decision on the status of former Palestine citizens[2] prior to the enactment of the Israeli Nationality Law of 1952, a judge of the District Court of Tel-Aviv observed:[3]

> So long as no law has been enacted providing otherwise, my view is that every individual who, on the date of the establishment of the State of Israel was resident in the territory which to-day constitutes the State of Israel, is also a national of Israel. Any other view must lead to the absurd result of a State without nationals—a phenomenon the existence of which has not yet been observed.

If a new state, relying on the absence of a municipal law, tried to deport a part of its permanent population, it would be acting in clear breach of its legal duties and might even involve its government in acts punishable as genocide.

Persons outside national legislation. The legislation of a number of states has categorized the population concerned into those who had a higher status, usually designated 'citizens', and others. Thus, in the case of the United Kingdom, the class of British protected persons is not regarded as consisting of 'British Subjects': but, with some significant exceptions,[4] such persons were and are considered to have the status of national for purposes of international law. In the past Italian law knew a distinction between citizens and colonial subjects, and in substance the latter were regarded as nationals in the international sphere. American law has the category '"non-citizen" nationals'. The

[1] Nepal adopted a Citizenship Act in 1952. Cf. Parry, *Nationality and Citizenship Laws of the Commonwealth*, pp. 355 seq.

[2] Palestine citizenship had ceased to exist: *Hussein* v. *Inspector of Prisons*, 6 November 1952; see Int. L.R. 17 (1950), 112.

[3] *A.B.* v. *M.B.*, Int. L.R. 17 (1950), 110. However, the same court in another case assumed the absence of nationality until the Nationality Law: *Oseri* v. *Oseri*, ibid., p. 111 (and cf. the *Shifris* case, ibid.). See also Rosenne, 81 *J.D.I.* (1954), p. 4, n. 3, and cf. p. 6. See further *Malapa* v. *Public Prosecutor*, Int. L.R. 28, p. 80.

[4] Where the protected state may be considered to have separate international personality and to have a nationality of its own; and when the individual derives the status from connexion with a British mandated or trust territory.

legal necessity for making attribution in the absence of any internal provisions governing the status of a group, and also in cases where a deliberate denial of citizenship occurs, is apparent from two international cases. In an arbitral award of 22 January 1926 the status of Cayuga Indians, who had migrated from the United States to Canada, was established on the basis of factual connexion. They were held to have become British nationals, and the assumption was that, for purposes of international law, they had previously been attached to the United States.[1] In *Kahane (Successor)* v. *Parisi and Austrian State*[2] the tribunal in substance regarded Rumanian Jews as Rumanian nationals, since Rumania, whilst withholding citizenship, did not consider them to be stateless. However, the main point of the decision was to establish the meaning of the term 'ressortissant' in the Treaty of St. Germain.[3]

Cases of state succession: see Chapter XXVIII, section 5 (a).

7. *State Responsibility and the Doctrine of the Genuine Link*

States cannot plead provisions of internal law in justification of international wrongs, and they are responsible for conditions on their territory which lead to the infliction of harm on other states. Delictual responsibility for damage arising from activities of persons on state territory will exist whether the delinquents are nationals or not.[4] However, many important duties of a specific nature are prescribed by reference to nationals of a state. Thus Oppenheim[5] states the existence of a duty to admit nationals expelled from other states and, the corollary, the duty not to expel nationals. Yet obviously *ad hoc* denationalization would provide a ready means of evading these duties. In appropriate circumstances responsibility would be created for the breach of duty if it were shown that the withdrawal of nationality was itself a part of the delictual conduct, facilitating the result.[6] Again, states could avoid rules governing the treatment of aliens if they could *at their discretion* impose nationality on aliens resident in or passing

[1] Award: 20 *A.J.* (1926), 574; *R.I.A.A.* vi. 173; Green, p. 64.

[2] *Ann. Digest* 5 (1929–30), no. 131.

[3] Arts. 249, 256.

[4] Cf. *Corfu Channel* case (Merits), I.C.J. Reports (1949), p. 4. As to activities outside state territory see McNair, *Opinions* ii. 288–9.

[5] i. 646, 695. See also Weis, op. cit., pp. 49–60 (very helpful); and *Co-operative Committee on Japanese Canadians* v. *A.-G. for Canada, Ann. Digest* 13 (1946), at p. 26.

[6] See Weis, pp. 58–9, 127; Fischer Williams, 8 *B.Y.* (1927), 55–60; Guggenheim i. 318; Jennings, 20 *B.Y.* (1939), p. 98 at pp. 112–13. Generally on denationalization see *infra*, pp. 404, 556.

through state territory, however brief the sojourn. Similar considerations apply to the law of belligerent occupation[1] and the law of neutrality.[2]

The principles needed to solve this type of problem are simple enough if, on the facts of the case, the manipulation of the law of nationality was part and parcel of the delictual conduct. However, it is possible to postulate a general principle of *genuine* link relating to the *causa* for conferment of nationality (and the converse for deprivation), a principle distinguishable from that of effective link. Significantly enough, authors,[3] with support from state practice and the jurisprudence of international tribunals,[4] have often stated the rule that a diplomatic claim cannot be validly presented if it is based on a nationality which has been fraudulently acquired. Admittedly the rule is often formulated with the acts of the *de cujus* in mind, but in principle it is applicable to fraud on the part of the administration of a state. In the *Nottebohm* case[5] Guatemala contended that Liechtenstein had acted fraudulently in granting nationality to Nottebohm, and, further, that Nottebohm himself had acted fraudulently in applying for and obtaining the certificate of naturalization. The Court did not concern itself with these arguments explicitly, but, in adverting to Nottebohm's motive of acquiring neutral status at the end of the judgment,[6] the Court accepted the substance of the argument: in this context the doctrine of genuine link, in the narrow sense, and the broad concept of effective link were brought into close relation.[7] In a dissenting opinion, Judge Klaestad considered that as regards fraud by Nottebohm the issue could not be decided apart from the merits.[8] Judge Read,

[1] Thus the German ordinance of 1942, which authorized the grant of nationality to certain classes of the population in territories not subject to German sovereignty but occupied by Germany, was not bound to be recognized by third states, as it was contrary to international law: see Guggenheim, I.C.J. Reports (1955), p. 54.

[2] In the *Nottebohm* case the Guatemalan argument, *per* Rolin, was that, because the motive of Nottebohm, a German national, was to acquire neutral status by his naturalization, there was no genuine link. This point was taken by the Court at the end of its judgment, I.C.J. Reports (1955), p. 26. See *infra*, p. 412, n. 5. The dissenting judges regarded the question as a part of the issues concerning abuse of rights and fraud: I.C.J.Reports (1955), pp. 32 (Klaestad), 48–9 (Read), 64–5 (Guggenheim). However, there was little or no evidence that Liechtenstein was attempting to avoid her neutral duties or that damage had been caused to Guatemala as a result of the naturalization. Nottebohm's motives could not easily be imputed to Liechtenstein.

[3] See, *inter alia*, Weis, op. cit., pp. 214–17, 219, 246; Makarov, 74 Hague *Recueil* (1949, I), 331–4.

[4] See, *inter alia* the *Salem* case, *Ann. Digest* 6 (1931–2), no. 98; *Flegenheimer* claim, Int. L.R. 25 (1958, I), p. 91 at pp. 98–101.

[5] I.C.J. Reports (1955), p. 4.

[6] p. 26; see *supra*, n. 2.

[7] See further *infra*, p. 418.

[8] I.C.J. Reports (1955), pp. 31–3.

also dissenting, considered that he could not, in dealing with a plea in bar, look at the evidence as to fraud, but he did not regard the motive of avoiding belligerent status (if this were the case) as amounting to fraud.[1] Guggenheim, Judge *ad hoc*, expresses views similar to those of Read.[2]

In applying the principle of genuine link, two considerations are relevant. In the first place, there is a presumption of the validity of an act of naturalization, since the acts of governments are presumed to be in good faith. Secondly, this is reinforced by the concept of nationality as a status, since an act of conferment being acted upon is not to be invalidated except in very clear cases.[3] However, it is not entirely clear that the rule as to inquiry into fraudulent naturalization can be used to support a general principle of genuine link. The Conciliation Commission in the *Flegenheimer* claim justified the rule in terms of procedure and judicial necessity.[4]

8. *Nationality of Claims*

When a government or court is concerned with the principle of diplomatic protection,[5] which rests primarily on the existence of the nationality of the claimant state attaching to the individual or corporation concerned both at the time of the alleged breach of duty[6] and at the time when the claim is presented, the issue is clearly placed on the international plane.[7] Situations will arise in which reference to the relevant national rules cannot give a solution.

In many cases the *de cujus* has nationality in both the claimant and defendant states. The discussions of this problem are generally presented by assigning the available evidence to two propositions, which are assumed to be incompatible. The first rule[8] is to be found in Article 4 of the Hague Convention of 1930: 'A State may not afford diplomatic protection to one of its

[1] Ibid., pp. 48–9. Read points out that at the time of the naturalization Guatemala was making every effort to maintain neutrality. At p. 26, the judgment of the Court refers to 'his status as a national of a belligerent State', and, earlier, at p. 25, states that, when he applied for naturalization, Nottebohm had been a German national from the time of his birth. It would seem that the Court indirectly admits the fact that Nottebohm felt bound by his German ties. Cf. Read at p. 47 (surely he is inconsistent: cf. his views at pp. 48–9); and Guggenheim, at pp. 64–5.

[2] Ibid., pp. 64–5. However, he regards the German nationality as the basis for 'belligerent status'. [3] See Jennings, 121 Hague *Recueil* (1967, II), 458–60.

[4] Int. L.R. 25 (1958, I), p. 91 at p. 98. [5] See further *infra*, pp. 480 seq.

[6] The right of protection may extend to instances in which harm is merely apprehended.

[7] *Nottebohm* case, I.C.J. Reports (1955), p. 4 at pp. 20–1.

[8] Proponents: van Panhuys, op. cit., pp. 73–81; Guggenheim i. 312; Kunz, 54 *A.J.* (1960), 558; Batiffol, *Droit international privé* (2nd ed.), p. 87.

nationals against a State whose nationality such person also possesses.' The other rule is that the effective nationality governs the question,[1] and was applied by the Permanent Court of Arbitration in the *Canevaro* case,[2] and the Italian-United States Conciliation Commission in the *Mergé* claim.[3] In the *Nottebohm* case the International Court stated,[4] with reference to 'the real and effective nationality': 'International arbitrators have decided in the same way numerous cases of dual nationality, where the question arose with regard to the exercise of protection.'

Two points may be made. First, the principle of effective link is not to be regarded as forcing a choice. If the facts are consistent with a substantial connexion with both states,[5] then the individual cannot expect international law to give him a privileged position as against other nationals of the two states—as would happen if he has a remedy in the international forum against his own government. Where, however, a choice can be made, then the principle of equality is not necessarily infringed, although it might be if tenuous links acknowledged by a municipal law were allowed to render the claim inadmissible. As a matter of principle the two rules usually cited in opposition are not incompatible.[6] The second point is that latitude may be allowed in this and other situations where the question is that of admissibility and the outcome does not directly affect the status of the individual.[7]

A different case of dual nationality is presented when one of two states of a dual national claims against a third state and the latter pleads that the other nationality of the *de cujus* is the effective or dominant nationality. A substantial jurisprudence supports the principle of the inopposability of the nationality of a third state in an international claim. In the *Salem* case[8] the tribunal found that Salem was a Persian national at the time of his Ameri-

[1] See Weis, pp. 191–2, for the continental literature.

[2] Hague Court Reports, p. 284; *R.I.A.A.* xi. 405.

[3] *R.I.A.A.* xiv, p. 236 at pp. 241–8; Int. L.R. 22 (1955), p. 443 at pp. 449–57 (the international jurisprudence is collected here); Green, p. 507. See also the cases set out in Int. L.R. 24 (1957), 452 seq.; *Flegenheimer* claim, ibid. 25 (1958, I), at pp. 147–50; *R.I.A.A.* xiv, p. 327 at pp. 374–8; *Turri* claim, Int. L.R. 30, p. 371; the *Mathison* case, *R.I.A.A.* ix. 485; the *Schmeichler-Pagh* case, 92 *J.D.I.* (1965), p. 689 (Danish Supr. Ct.); and *Shareholders of the Z.A.G.* v. *A. Bank*, Int. L.R. 45, 436 at p. 443 (Kammergericht, Berlin).

[4] I.C.J. Reports (1955), p. 22. Cf. the *Reparation case*, ibid. (1949), p. 186.

[5] See 39 *B.Y.* (1963), pp. 360–1.

[6] Cf. Hyde ii. 1131; Briggs, op. cit., p. 516; and Verzijl, in the *Georges Pinson* case, *Ann. Digest* 4 (1927–8), nos. 194, 195, quoted Int. L.R. 22 (1955), at p. 451. See also the *Spaulding* claim, *R.I.A.A.* xiv. 292; Int. L.R. 24 (1957), at pp. 454–5.

[7] See further *infra*, pp. 480 seq., and cf. the nature of the relation between diplomatic protection and nationality, pp. 401–2.

[8] *Ann. Digest* 6 (1931–2), no. 98; *R.I.A.A.* ii, p. 1161 at p. 1188.

can naturalization, and held that it was not open to Egypt to invoke the Persian nationality against the claimant state, the United States: 'the rule of International Law being that in a case of dual nationality a third Power is not entitled to contest the claim of one of the two Powers whose national is interested in the case by referring to the nationality of the other Power'. The tribunal referred to *Mackenzie* v. *Germany*,[1] but that case depended on a strict application of American law relating to expatriation and is not entirely in point. The same rule has been affirmed by the Italian-United States Conciliation Commission in its decision in the *Flegenheimer* claim.[2] However, in the *Mergé* claim the same Commission made it clear that for the Commission it was a question of treaty interpretation, and the working rule laid down was:[3] '(8) United States nationals who did not possess Italian nationality but the nationality of a third State can be considered "United States nationals" under the Treaty, even if their prevalent nationality was the nationality of the third State.'

The rule of inopposability invites some comment. In the *Salem* case the tribunal disapproved of the principle of effectiveness, whereas in the *Mergé* claim the Commission approved of the principle where the dual nationality was that of the two states in dispute. One may ask whether and on what basis the principle is to be confined to certain permutations only. The short answer probably is, as it was in *Nottebohm*, that the issue is that of opposability as between the two parties. However, in treating the issue thus it must surely be relevant, on some facts at least, to point to the dominant nationality of a third state.[4] This precise issue was not before the Court in *Nottebohm*, but the general principles propounded there extend logically to the present problem. The formulations of the Court refer in general terms to 'the courts of third States'.[5] However, it must be emphasized that the

[1] German-U.S. Mixed Claims Commission; *R.I.A.A.* vii. 288; 20 *A.J.* (1926), 595. See Schwarzenberger, *International Law* (3rd ed.), p. 366. The umpire declared that 'while the American Department of State *may in the exercise of its sound discretion* well decline to issue a passport to, or intervene on behalf of, or otherwise extend diplomatic protection to an American by birth of foreign parents so long as he resides in the country of the nationality of his parents, it is not believed that it has, by departmental rule or otherwise, asserted the power to strip of American citizenship one so born': *R.I.A.A.* vii, at p. 290. My italics.

[2] Int. L.R. 25 (1958, I), at pp. 149–50; *R.I.A.A.* xiv, at p. 377.

[3] Int. L.R. 22 (1955), at p. 456; *R.I.A.A.* xiv, at p. 247. See also the *Vereano* claim, Int. L.R. 24 (1957), 464; *R.I.A.A.* xiv. 321, and *Flegenheimer* claim, Int. L.R. 25 (1958, I), at p. 150; *R.I.A.A.* xiv, at p. 377.

[4] Cf. the problems of *jus tertii* in the law of conversion: see Atiyah, 18 *Mod.L.R.* (1955), 97.

[5] I.C.J. Reports (1955), p. 22. Cf. ibid., p. 21. However, on p. 22 there are two such

existence of a 'third nationality' will not be an automatic bar.

The last situation to consider is one in which *prima facie* the *de cujus* has one nationality or none. This was the problem in *Nottebohm*,[1] and the Court, by a large majority, stated and applied the principle of the real or effective link. In the *Flegenheimer* claim the Italian-United States Conciliation Commission distinguished *Nottebohm* on the ground that the case concerned opposability for the purposes of admitting the claim against Guatemala, but in substance the Commission disapproved of the principle of effective nationality as it was formulated by the Court in *Nottebohm*.[2] Any conclusion on the question obviously depends on the view held about the principle of effective nationality.[3]

9. *Diplomatic Protection*

It is trite learning that, with some exceptions,[4] states may only exercise diplomatic protection in respect of their nationals. The issue here is on the international plane and cannot be resolved by simple reference to the internal law of the states involved. A number of the problems have been discussed in terms of the question of the nationality of claims and, subsequently,[5] some comment will be made on the consequences of *Nottebohm* from the point of view of the effectiveness and availability of diplomatic protection. The assumption or, more correctly, the effect of the way in which the law is generally expressed is that diplomatic protection depends on nationality, but in reality the relation of the two is more complex. In the absence of formal evidence of ties with a particular state, the interest of a government in an individual, and especially the exercise or attempt to exercise protection in respect of that individual, may provide cogent evidence of nationality.[6] Moreover, if a right of protection arises by virtue of lawful administration of territory, then it would seem that nationality may be said to arise from the fact of the right of pro-

references and the latter reference is: 'the courts of third States, when they have before them an individual whom two other States hold to be their national, . . .'. But the passages on pp. 22 and 23, taken as a whole, are general in effect: see *infra*, pp. 414–15. See also the *Laurent* case, Anglo-American Claims Commission, 1853, Hornby's *Report*, p. 299, where Mexican domicile of British subjects was a bar to claims against the United States, a view repudiated by the Commission in 1871: see *British Digest* v. 315–22.

[1] Nottebohm had lost his German nationality as a consequence of the acquisition of Liechtenstein nationality in 1939. See Loewenfeld, 42 *Grot. Soc.* (1956), p. 13; Guggenheim, I.C.J. Reports (1955), p. 55.

[2] On the general significance of *Nottebohm* see *infra*, pp. 406 seq.

[3] See *infra*, p. 406.

[4] *Infra*, pp. 481, 684.

[5] *Infra*, p. 418.

[6] See also *infra*, p. 403, on the question of estoppel.

tection.[1] This is, in part at least, the justification for treating British protected persons and similar categories of persons[2] in other systems as nationals of the administering power on the international plane. Persons not enjoying the protection of the state of their nationality (by internal law) are known as '*de facto* stateless', and the International Law Commission has considered means of alleviating their position.[3] If the effective link test were applied, then it might be that a refusal to give diplomatic protection would be regarded *on the international plane* as a severing of the more important links with the given state.

Three further observations are called for. First, it is important to notice, though it may seem obvious, that there is an element of circularity in much that is said about this subject. In the absence of any internal law provisions[4] or evidence of facts giving nationality by birth and other titles under internal provisions, a state may still claim to protect its population by virtue of its international competence, its sovereignty, and its very statehood (these three quantities being identical for the present purpose).[5] If one accepts the existence of rules of attribution set by international law, then it is inelegant and illogical to say that diplomatic protection depends on 'nationality', especially when from the context the writer appears to refer to internal law. Secondly, what has been said is subject to the possible existence of the rule that neither state of a dual national may exercise diplomatic protection against the other.[6] Thirdly, diplomatic protection does not depend on nationality in either the internal or international sense in certain cases, because the right to protect may arise from a process of delegation by one sovereign to another or in other cases of representation in international relations.[7]

[1] In the *Cayuga Indians* case, the tribunal said, with reference to the Cayuga Indians in Canada: 'These Indians are British Nationals. They have been settled in Canada, under the protection of Great Britain and, subsequently, of the Dominion of Canada, since the end of the eighteenth or early years of the nineteenth century.' (*R.I.A.A.* vi, p. 175 at p. 177.) See also *Rothmann* v. *Austria and Hungary*, ibid., p. 253; *Margulies* v. *Austria and Hungary*, ibid., p. 279. Both these cases turn on the interpretation of an American statute, however. See further the *Mathison* case, ibid. ix, p. 485 at pp. 490, 491–2; *Valeriani* v. *Amuna Bekri Sichera*, *Ann. Digest* 8 (1935–7), no. 120; *Logan* v. *Styres et al.*, 20 D.L.R. (2d.) (1959), p. 416, Int. L.R. 27, p. 239 (as to the Six Nations Indians of Ontario); *British Digest* v. 388–91.

[2] See Parry, *Nationality and Citizenship Laws of the Commonwealth*, pp. 11–15.

[3] See, for example, *Yrbk., I.L.C.* (1954), i. 18 (246th Meeting); ibid. (1954), ii. 38 (draft article).

[4] See *supra*, p. 395.

[5] See the cases *supra*, n. 1, and note the significance of the phrase 'under the protection of the Crown', e.g. in *Logan* v. *Styres*.

[6] *Supra*, pp. 398–9.

[7] Poland conducted the external relations of Danzig by virtue of the treaty of 9 Novem-

10. *Nationality by Estoppel*

For the purpose of the discussion it is assumed, and the assumption is surely correct, that estoppel or *préclusion* is a principle of international law.[1] It seems that the principle can be applied to cases involving sovereignty over territory, and there is no reason why it should not be applied to the status of individuals. Indeed, in many cases where the basic facts concerning the individual are ambiguous,[2] the conduct of governments will provide the answer. Express declarations and admissions by diplomatic representatives may create an estoppel in the view of a court.[3] However, acts of administration of an incidental or routine nature, and in the absence of any dispute or apprehension thereof, may not have this effect. Thus in the *Nottebohm* case[4] Liechtenstein argued that Guatemala had recognized the naturalization in Liechtenstein on the basis of the entry of a visa in the Liechtenstein passport and official acts relating to the control of aliens. The Court observed:[5]

> All of these acts have reference to the control of aliens in Guatemala and not to the exercise of diplomatic protection. When Nottebohm thus presented himself before the Guatemalan authorities, the latter had before them a private individual: there did not thus come into being any relationship between governments. There was nothing in all this to show that Guatemala then recognized that the naturalization conferred upon Nottebohm gave Liechtenstein any title to the exercise of protection.

Admissions and absence of dispute by the parties in the face of a court will normally[6] be relied upon by a tribunal in matters of nationality.[7] In some cases the tribunal has been prepared to rely on the conduct of governments in the absence of any declaration

ber 1920. The whole question of protected states and criteria of statehood comes up. So also the diplomatic protection of the inhabitants of mandates arises from a concept akin to representation: cf. *Malapa* v. *Public Prosecutor*, Int. L.R. 28, p. 80. See further the *Pugh* claim, *Ann. Digest* 7 (1933–4), no. 97; Parry, *Nationality and Citizenship Laws of the Commonwealth*, pp. 122–3.

[1] See Bowett, 33 *B.Y.* (1957), 176–202; MacGibbon, 7 *I.C.L.Q.* (1958), 468; and *infra*, p. 637.

[2] Cf. in a different sphere the *Temple* case, I.C.J. Reports (1961), p. 17.

[3] *Société De Bienfaisance* v. *Siag*, *Ann. Digest* 6 (1931–2), no. 122; *Taamy* v. *Taamy*, ibid. 8 (1935–7), no. 128. Cf. the *Nottebohm* case, I.C.J. Reports (1955), p. 4 at pp. 17–20.

[4] I.C.J. Reports (1955), p. 4 at pp. 17–19. For a different conclusion see Judge Read's dissenting opinion at pp. 47–8, and cf. Guggenheim, Judge *ad hoc*, ibid., p. 53.

[5] At p. 18.

[6] But see 39 *B.Y.*, pp. 344–7, on nationality as a status. Presumably the doctrine of effective link would justify a court in refusing to rely on admissions (if it were free to do so under the terms of the *compromis*).

[7] *Expropriated Religious Properties* case, *R.I.A.A.* i, p. 7 at p. 46.

directly alluding to the issue. In the *Hendry* claim[1] the Mexican-United States General Claims Commission held that Mexico, the respondent state, was estopped from denying the American nationality of the deceased, Hendry, by reason of it having discharged him from employment because he was an American. However, in the *Flegenheimer* claim[2] the Italian-United States Conciliation Commission rejected an Italian argument that the the claim was inadmissible because at the date of the acts complained of Flegenheimer's apparent nationality (in their phrase) was German, because he had used a German passport in dealings with the Italian authorities. This argument failed on the facts, but the Commission noted 'that the doctrine of apparent nationality cannot be considered as accepted by the Law of Nations'.

11. *Compulsory Change of Nationality*

Existing practice and jurisprudence does not support a general rule that deprivation of nationality is illegal.[3] The analogue of deprivation of nationality is provided by the cases described as compulsory change of nationality and 'collective naturalization'. The whole pattern of rules and the practice of states is based on the assumption that in terms of administration states set the conditions under which nationality is acquired and lost. The law concerned may call for expressions of will on the part of individuals directly, or indirectly, by their establishing residence or service in the armed forces, but the conditions are set by the law.

[1] *R.I.A.A.* iv. 616. Cf. the *Kelley* claim, ibid., p. 608. See also *British Digest* v. 89, 369–70, 374, 379–80, 461.

[2] Int. L.R. 25 (1958, I), p. 91, at p. 151. The Commission went on: 'In international jurisprudence one finds decisions based on the "non concedit venire contra factum proprium" principle which . . . allows a Respondent State to object to the admissibility of a legal action directed against it by the national State of the allegedly injured party, when the latter has neglected to indicate his true nationality, or has concealed it, or has invoked another nationality at the time the fact giving rise to the dispute occurred, or when the national State has made erroneous communications to another State thus fixing the conduct to be followed by the latter.'

[3] See the conclusions of Hudson, *Yrbk., I.L.C.* (1952), ii. 10, and Weis, op. cit., pp. 126, 127, 242–3. Standard works on international law do not state such a rule, but this is in some cases a consequence of their general position on the freedom of states in matters of nationality. See Oppenheim i. 657–8, and Guggenheim i. 318. See also *Lempert* v. *Bonfol*, *Ann. Digest* 7 (1933–4), no. 115 at pp. 293–4; *U.S. ex rel. Steinvorth* v. *Watkins*, ibid. 14 (1947), no. 41. An important fact, generally ignored by writers on the subject, is that municipal laws providing for deprivation normally provide for this in cases where residence and acts of allegiance have occurred abroad. See also the United Nations Convention on the Reduction of Statelessness, 1961, Art. 8; Weis, op. cit., pp. 122–31; and the Universal Decl. of Human Rights, Art. 15, para. 2.

Nevertheless tribunals have occasionally stated in terms that international law does not permit compulsory change of nationality.[1] The United States, the United Kingdom, France, and other states have often protested against 'forced naturalization provisions', as they are sometimes called, in the laws of various Latin-American states.[2] This practice is bound up with the rule that international law does not permit states to impose their nationality on aliens resident abroad.[3] It is to be doubted whether this rule is correctly stated thus. The present writer would submit that the rule, and the practice referred to above, represents yet another aspect of the principle of effective link,[4] and is not to be stated unconditionally. The objective principle to emerge from the practice concerned is simply that nationality is not to be conferred on those already having a nationality unless the new nationality is based upon adequate links. Similarly, an illegal deprivation of nationality (for example on a racial basis) may become irreversible if the individual voluntarily establishes himself elsewhere at a stage when 'resumption' of the original citizenship would have been possible.[5]

12. *The Functional Approach to Nationality*

In spite of the reiteration from time to time of the principle that nationality depends on municipal law, it is common for legislation and judicial decisions to create functional nationality[6] whereby parts of national law are applied on the basis of allegiance, residence, and other connexions. There seems to be general acquiescence in this splitting up of the legal content of nationality for particular purposes. Thus legislation in many countries has defined the enemy alien in functional terms and without de-

[1] *In re Rau, Ann. Digest* 6 (1931–2), no. 124; decisions referred to ibid., p. 251 n. (*Occelli* and *Barcena*, decisions of the Italian-Mexican and Spanish-Mexican Claims Commissions); *Compulsory Acquisition of Nationality Case*, Int. L.R. 32, p. 166, referring to Article 1 of the Conv. on Conflict of Nationality Laws, 1930.

[2] e.g. laws referring to the purchase of land. For references: Briggs, pp. 461–2; and cf. Hudson, *Yrbk., I.L.C.* (1952), ii. 8.

[3] See Morgenstern, note in *Ann. Digest* 15 (1948), 211; and *In re Krüger*, Int. L.R. 18 (1951), no. 68 at p. 259 (referring to Universal Declaration of Human Rights, Art. 15, para. 2).

[4] Cf. Guggenheim i. 317; Makarov, 74 Hague *Recueil* (1949, I), 305.

[5] See *Oppenheimer* v. *Cattermole* [1973] Ch. 264; C.A.; [1975] 2 W.L.R. 347, H.L.; Mann, 89 *L.Q.R.* (1973), 194; id., 48 *B.Y.* (1976–7), 43–5, 50–1. Cf. *Loss of Nationality (Germany) Case*, Int. L.R., 45, 353.

[6] A different type of functionalism may occur when a forum is prepared to disregard dual nationality where policy demands a choice. Examples have already occurred earlier (see *supra*, pp. 398–9). Note also the provision in the staff regulations and rules of the United Nations which makes it mandatory for the Secretary-General to select a single nationality for the purpose of the staff rules: see *Julhiard* v. *Secretary-General of the United Nations*, Int. L.R. 22 (1955), 809.

pendence on the 'technical' nationality of the country in question. The control test has been widely applied to corporations[1] and goods in determining enemy character. Moreover, the use of factual tests occurs equally widely when the issue is one of the law of war and neutrality, for example taking under the law of prize.[2] However, France,[3] Germany, Italy, and Japan, among others refer to formal nationality of individuals and the flag of vessels. Moreover, in the context of treaties rules are often functional rather than declaratory as to general status. Thus in the *IMCO* case[4] the issue was the interpretation of the phrase 'the largest ship-owning nations' in Article 28 of the Convention for the Establishment of the Inter-Governmental Maritime Consultative Organization, and the advisory opinion delivered rested on an inquiry into the legislative history of the provision and usage in other maritime conventions. In construing the phrase 'nationals of the United Nations' in the peace treaties after the Second World War, a court is likely to adopt an approach which will give effect to the intentions of the parties.[5] In the Geneva Convention on the Status of Refugees of 1951, Article 16, paragraph 3, provides that a refugee must be treated, in states parties to the Convention in which he is not habitually resident, on the same footing as a national of the state in which he is resident for certain purposes including access to the courts.[6] The Vienna Convention on Diplomatic Relations[7] restricts the conferment of privileges and immunities in the case of members of the mission if they are nationals of the receiving state or 'permanently resident' therein.

13. *The Principle of Effective Link and the Judgment in the* Nottebohm *Case*

Prologue. The thesis of the present writer is that, seen in a proper perspective, the decision in the *Nottebohm* case is a natural

[1] *Daimler* v. *Continental Tyre Co.* [1916] 2 A.C. 307; *Contomichalos* v. *Drossos* (1937), *Gazette des Tribinaux Mixtes d'Egypte*, 28 (1937–8), 49. See further Watts, 33 *B.Y.* (1957), 78–83, and *infra*, pp. 421 seq.

[2] *The Arsia, Ann. Digest* 16 (1949), no. 206; *The Nyugat*, Int. L.R. 24 (1957), 916; *The S.S. Lea Lott*, ibid. 28. 652; *The Inginer N. Vlassopol*, ibid. 18 (1951), no. 223; *The Nordmeer, Ann. Digest* 13 (1946), no. 172; *The Athinai*, ibid. 12 (1943–5), no. 128. Cf. *The Unitas* [1950] A.C. 536 on the conclusiveness of a vessel's flag and limitations thereon.

[3] However, by legislation and administrative action France has modified her position and introduced residence as an additional test.

[4] *Constitution of the Maritime Safety Committee of the Inter-Governmental Maritime Consultative Organization*, I.C.J. Reports (1960), p. 23; and see Simmonds, 12 *I.C.L.Q.* (1963), 56.

[5] See the *Mergé* claim, Int. L.R. 22 (1955), 456.

[6] See *Grundel* v. *Bryner*, Int. L.R. 24 (1957), 483.

[7] See *supra*, p. 357.

reflection of a fundamental concept which has long been inherent in the materials concerning nationality on the international plane. The doctrine of the effective link has been recognized for some time in continental literature[1] and the decisions of some municipal courts.[2] The recognition is commonly in connexion with dual nationality, but the particular context of origin does not obscure its role as a general principle with a variety of possible applications. Several members of the International Law Commission were proponents of the principle (out of the context of dual nationality) during the fifth session.[3]

The reply of the German Government of 1929[4] to the Preparatory Committee of the Hague Codification Conference declared that 'a State has no power . . . to confer its nationality on all the inhabitants of another State or on all foreigners entering its territory . . . if the State confers its nationality on the subjects of other States without their request, when the persons concerned are not attached to it by any particular bond, as, for instance, origin, domicile or birth, the States concerned will not be bound to recognize such naturalization'. The internal legislation of states makes general use of residence, domicile, immigration *animo manendi* (with an intent to remain permanently), and membership of ethnic groups associated with the state territory, as connecting factors.[5] International law has rested on the same principles in dealing with the situations where a state has no nationality legislation and when certain parts of the population are outside nationality legislation. There is interesting evidence of reliance on settlement together with the existence of the political and diplomatic protection of a particular sovereign. The principle of effective link is considered to underlie much of the state practice on state succession and the continuity of states and to support the concept of *ressortissant* found frequently in treaties.[6]

[1] See Weis, pp. 191–2; Int. L.R. 22 (1955), 452–4. See also Lipstein [1977] *Camb. L.J.* 55–6, referring to Basdevant, 5 *Rev. de droit int. privé* (1909), 41, 60.

[2] *Magalhais* v. *Fernandes*, *Ann. Digest* 10 (1941–2), no. 83; *In re Heinz S*, ibid. 11 (1919–42), no. 98. See also the *Johann Christoph* (1854), 2 Sp. Ecc. and Ad. 2; and the German Federal Constitutional Court, Int. L.R. 19 (1952), no. 56, p. 320; and see *supra*, p. 399. For a pronouncement to the contrary see *The King* v. *Burgess, Ex parte Henry*, *Ann. Digest* 8 (1935–7), no. 19 at p. 67.

[3] *Yrbk., I.L.C.* (1953), i. 180, para. 24, p. 186, paras. 5, 7; p. 239, paras. 45, 46 (Yepes); p. 181, paras. 32, 33, p. 218, para. 63 (Žourek); p. 184, para. 57, p. 237, para. 24 (François); p. 239, para. 50 (Amado).

[4] *Supra*, p. 383.

[5] On the recognition of foreign divorce decrees by the English courts see *Indyka* v. *Indyka* [1969] 1 A.C. 33.

[6] See Weis, op. cit., pp. 8–10; and *Kahane* (*Successor*) v. *Parisi and Austrian State*, *supra*, p. 396.

The Issues in the Nottebohm *case (second phase).*[1] In this case Liechtenstein claimed damages in respect of the acts of the Government of Guatemala in arresting, detaining, expelling, and refusing to readmit Nottebohm and in seizing and retaining his property without compensation. In the counter-memorial Guatemala asked the Court to declare the claim of Liechtenstein inadmissible, in part 'because Liechtenstein had failed to prove that M. Nottebohm, for whose protection it was acting, properly acquired Liechtenstein nationality in accordance with the law of that Principality; because even if such proof were provided, the legal provisions which would have been applied cannot be regarded as in conformity with international law; and because M. Nottebohm appears in any event not to have lost, or not validly to have lost, his German nationality'. In the final submissions, the third point was developed and the inadmissibility was contended for 'on the ground that M. Nottebohm appears to have solicited Liechtenstein nationality fraudulently, that is to say, with the sole object of acquiring the status of a neutral national before returning to Guatemala, and without any genuine intention to establish a durable link, excluding German nationality, between the Principality and himself'.

In its judgment the court regarded the plea relating to Nottebohm's nationality as fundamental. The issue was one of admissibility, and the Court observed:[2]

> In order to decide upon the admissibility of the Application, the Court must ascertain whether the nationality conferred on Nottebohm by Liechtenstein by means of a naturalization which took place in the circumstances which have been described, can be validly invoked as against Guatemala, whether it bestows upon Liechtenstein a sufficient title to the exercise of protection in respect of Nottebohm as against Guatemala . . . what is involved is not recognition [of acquisition of Liechtenstein nationality][3] for all purposes but merely for the purposes of the admissibility of the Application, and, secondly, that what is involved is not recognition by all States but only by Guatemala.

[1] I.C.J. Reports (1955), p. 4; Green, p. 503; Bishop, p. 492. Literature: Kunz, 54 *A.J.* (1960), 536–71; Mervyn Jones, 5 *I.C.L.Q.* (1956), 230–44; Loewenfeld, 42 *Grot. Soc.* (1956), 5–22; de Visscher, 60 *R.G.D.I.P.* (1956), 238–66; Bastid, *Revue critique de droit international privé,* 45 (1956), 607–33; Maury, 23 *Zeit. für ausl. und. int. Privatrecht* (1958), 515–34; Perrin, *Recueil d'études en hommage à Paul Guggenheim* (1968), pp. 853–87; Grossen, *Festgabe Gutzwiller* (1959), pp. 489–502; Makarov, 16 *Z.a.ö. R.u.V.* (1955–6), 407–26; Lipstein and Loewenfeld, in *Gedächtnisschrift Ludwig Marxer,* (1963), pp. 275–325; Knapp, *Annuaire Suisse* (1960), 147–78; De Burlet, *Revue belge de d.i.*, 1976, pp. 75–89. The effect of the decision is under-estimated in O'Connell ii. 678–81, and the evidence for the effective link principle is not reported.

[2] I.C.J. Reports (1955), pp. 16–17. See also pp. 20, 21.

[3] The writer's parenthesis.

In the event, having applied the doctrine of the effective link to the facts, the Court held the claim to be inadmissible. Critics of the decision[1] and the dissenting judges[2] have pointed out that Guatemala had not argued the case on the basis that there was no effective link, and also that the precise *ratio* of the decision was the question of opposability as against Guatemala. The truth of this is obvious, but the effect of such formal arguments in limiting the significance of the judgment is negligible. The tendency to look for very precise grounds for decision is a common characteristic of judicial technique, and few jurists seriously believe that, apart from cases of treaty interpretation, the pronouncements of the Court can be placed in quarantine by formal devices.[3] Furthermore, the Court develops its views on the social bases of and legal policy concerning nationality in a manner which indicates the importance of the pronouncements on the genuine or effective link.[4] In any case, the fact that admissibility was involved was only a detour in the argument. As the Court said:[5] 'To exercise protection, to apply to the Court, is to place oneself on the plane of international law. It is international law which determines whether a State is entitled to exercise protection and to seise the Court.' The Court did not base its decision on estoppels as against Liechtenstein, but rested on the existence or not of a right of protection, an issue the outcome of which would logically affect states in general and not just the parties.[6] In view of all this it is not surprising to find authoritative acknowledgments of the general significance of the decision in the work of the International Law Commission[7] and other bodies.[8]

Evidence of the 'link' doctrine relied on by the Court. Commentators who are unsympathetic to the conclusions of the Court on questions of principle commonly emphasize the generality

[1] e.g. Mervyn Jones, op. cit., pp. 238–9; Kunz, op. cit., pp. 541, 552.

[2] See Judge Klaestad, I.C.J. Reports (1955), p. 30; Judge Read, ibid., pp. 35, 38, 39–40; Guggenheim, Judge *ad hoc*, p. 53 (cf. p. 62). See further the decision of the Italian–United States Conciliation Commission in the *Flegenheimer* claim, Int. L.R. 25 (1958, I), p. 91, at pp. 148–50.

[3] Cf. the effect of the *Fisheries* case, I.C.J. Reports (1951), p. 116.

[4] See *supra*, pp. 392–3.

[5] p. 20. [6] Cf. Guggenheim at pp. 60, 63, and Kunz, op. cit., p. 564.

[7] *Yrbk., I.L.C.* (1956), ii. 278–9 (draft article on nationality of ships and comment); ibid. (1956), i. 36, 66–7, 70–2 (p. 72, the genuine link test adopted by 9 votes to 3, with 3 abstentions). *Nottebohm* is not referred to expressly in these materials, but the terminology used, and the existence of a general problem beyond that of dual nationality, make the connexion clear. For the replies of governments on the nationality of ships, see *Yrbk., I.L.C.* (1956), ii. 14–16.

[8] See 51 *Annuaire de l'Inst.* (1965), ii. 269, Resolution II, art. 4; and *Foreign Relations Law of the U.S., Restatement, Second*; 1962; para. 26 (and see Briggs, 61 *A.J.* (1967), 214 for criticism).

of the passages dealing with the preceding practice on which the Court purported to rely.[1] The survey is, in the view of the present writer, unsatisfactory if it is regarded in isolation and weighed simply as a material assessment of practice and jurisprudence. Moreover, to those who regard the approach of the Court as a novelty,[2] the inadequacy of exposition in this connexion is a particular source of disquiet. Three points would seem to be worth consideration here. First, to those who felt that the 'link' theory was self-evident, and well supported in the legal materials, it would not be apparent that a very full *exposé* was necessary. Secondly, the somewhat varied collection of propositions and references to previous practice reads not as a survey but rather as an attempt at further and better particulars as to the logical necessity of the *general principle* for which the Court was contending. The relevant section of the judgment commences[3] well before the 'survey of materials', and the logical burden of the section as a whole is that, to settle issues on the plane of international law, principles have to be applied apart from the rules of national laws. The major point is made on the basis of a 'general principle of international law' and not on the basis of a rule which could be classified as a customary rule of the usual sort. Thirdly, the critics of the judgment are probably seeking materials which support the 'link' theory explicitly as a specific rule. Not all the materials support any rule in this way, but there is much material, surveyed earlier in this chapter, which supports the general principle. There was very little on the international plane which expressly *denied* the effective link doctrine, and the incidental rejection of it in the *Salem* case[4] was regarded by contemporaries as a novelty.[5]

At any rate, it is true that, taken individually, the pieces of evidence deployed by the Court are not completely cogent. Thus it is plausible for Judge Read[6] to say that the provision on dual nationality in the Statute of the Court[7] has nothing to do with

[1] pp. 21–3. However, the Court does not, as a general rule, seem ready to undertake an examination of the details of practice and jurisprudence in its judgments; see the *Fisheries* case. The judgments seem to present the conclusions on these matters, in summary form.

[2] See Mervyn Jones, op. cit., pp. 240–2; Kunz, op. cit., pp. 552, 555; Judge Read, I.C.J. Reports (1955), pp. 39–40; Perrin, op. cit., p. 874.

[3] At p. 20.

[4] *Supra*, pp. 399–400.

[5] See *Ann. Digest* 6 (1931–2), no. 98 at p. 192, note by Hersch Lauterpacht, and Mervyn Jones, op. cit., p. 242, n. 14.

[6] Diss. op., I.C.J. Reports (1955), p. 40.

[7] Article 3 provides: '1. The Court shall consist of fifteen members, no two of whom may be nationals of the same State. 2. A person who for the purposes of membership in the Court could be regarded as a national of more than one State shall be deemed to be a national of the one in which he ordinarily exercises civil and political rights.' See the judgment of the Court at p. 22.

diplomatic protection. The Court was obviously as aware of this as he was, but the majority judges were concerned with a general principle. Again, the references by the Court[1] to bilateral treaties concluded by the United States with other states since 1868, the so-called Bancroft Treaties, and to the Pan-American Convention of 13 August 1906, do not provide unequivocal evidence on the effective link as a part of general international law. As Judge Read points out,[2] the treaty restrictions on the power to protect naturalized persons who return to their country of origin may indicate a lack of reliance on a rule of positive law.

Judge Read[3] and others[4] have also contended that the Court[5] relied irrelevantly on the principles adopted by arbitral tribunals in dealing with cases of double nationality,[6] since in the *Nottebohm* case the facts did not present this problem. Nottebohm either had Liechtenstein nationality or none. However, in establishing logical positions it may be that the critics have the onus of proving why the doctrine of effectiveness only applies to certain permutations of fact. Commentators who regard the rejection of the doctrine of effective link in the *Salem* case as odd do not explain the oddity by saying that in that case Egypt was pleading the nationality of a third state.[7] The principle of effectiveness is thus not restricted to dual nationality of the two parties to the dispute. If the principle exists it applies to the *Nottebohm* permutation also.

Both the majority and the minority opinions on the Court almost completely neglect the state practice apart from conventions.[8] The judgment of the Court merely states:[9]

> The practice of certain States which refrain from exercising protection in favour of a naturalized person when the latter has in fact, by his prolonged absence, severed his links with what is no longer for him anything

[1] pp. 22–3.

[2] p. 41. He also says: 'even within that part of the Western hemisphere which is South of the 49th Parallel, the ratifications of the multilateral Convention were not sufficiently general to indicate consensus of the countries concerned'. See also Guggenheim, pp. 59–60; and Kunz, op. cit., p. 557.

[3] At pp. 41–2.

[4] See Kunz, op. cit., pp. 556–9; Guggenheim, I.C.J. Reports (1955), p. 59.

[5] p. 22.

[6] See *supra*, p. 385, and the *Mergé* claim, Int. L.R. 22 (1955), p. 443, at pp. 450–2; *R.I.A.A.* xiv, p. 236 at pp. 246–8.

[7] See Mervyn Jones, op. cit., p. 242, n. 14.

[8] There is a reference by the Court to national laws on naturalization: 'National laws reflect this tendency when, *inter alia*, they make naturalization dependent on conditions indicating the existence of a link. . . .' (p. 22). Kunz (p. 553) and Mervyn Jones (p. 236) are much too grudging in their assessment of national legislation; see *supra*, pp. 385 seq.

[9] p. 22.

but his nominal country, manifests the view of these States that, in order to be capable of being invoked against another State, nationality must correspond with the factual situation.

This consideration is far from conclusive.[1] Both sides seem to ignore the cumulative effect of the evidence set out earlier.[2] However, Guggenheim, judge *ad hoc*, reviews a number of issues, including the proposition that ownership of land is not by itself a sufficient legal title for the grant of nationality, and remarks[3] 'all these situations are, however, somewhat exceptional'. One may doubt if they are exceptional, but the point is that the *principle* of inopposability is accepted by him in this passage.

Judge Read completes his review of the evidence relied on by the majority with the statement:[4] 'It is noteworthy that, apart from the cases of double nationality, no instance has been cited to the Court in which a State has successfully refused to recognize that nationality, lawfully conferred and maintained, did not give rise to a right of diplomatic protection.' Here the phrase 'lawfully conferred' takes much force away from the proposition: no doubt Judge Read would agree that the imposition of nationality on aliens in transit through national territory is unlawful or, at least, inopposable. Thus, the question is begged. The non-opposability of nationality in internal law is obscured in the law of war and neutrality by the use of other or of supplementary connecting factors, but the effect is the same.[5] Enemy control may displace the 'nationality' of a person or goods or vessels for purposes of international law. Moreover, state practice has for long recognized the converse of Read's statement: absence of internal conferment does not lead to absence of a power of diplomatic protection.[6]

The principle applied to the facts. Nottebohm was German by birth and was still a German national when he applied for naturalization in Liechtenstein in October 1939. He had left Germany in 1905, but maintained business connexions with that country. As a consequence of naturalization in Liechtenstein he

[1] See *supra*, p. 402. [2] *Supra*, pp. 383 seq.

[3] p. 54. [4] p. 42.

[5] It is significant that the Court states at the end of the judgment (p. 26): 'Naturalization was asked for not so much for the purpose of obtaining a legal recognition of Nottebohm's membership in fact in the population of Liechtenstein, as it was to enable him to substitute for his status as a national of the belligerent State that of a national of a neutral State, with the sole aim of thus coming within the protection of Liechtenstein. . . . Guatemala is under no obligation to recognize a nationality granted in such circumstances. See also Hudson, 50 *A.J.* (1956), p. 1, at p. 5. For the seeker after the narrowest *ratio decidendi* this would seem to be the answer.

[6] *Supra*, pp. 395–6.

lost his German nationality.[1] The Court decided that the effective nationality was not that of Liechtenstein (but without characterizing the links with Guatemala in terms of effective nationality):[2]

> He had been settled in Guatemala for 34 years. He had carried on his activities there. It was the main seat of his interests. He returned there shortly after his naturalization, and it remained the centre of his interests and of his business activities. He stayed there until his removal as a result of war measures in 1943. He subsequently attempted to return there, and he now complains of Guatemala's refusal to admit him . . . In contrast, his actual connections with Liechtenstein were extremely tenuous . . . If Nottebohm went to Liechtenstein in 1946, this was because of the refusal of Guatemala to admit him . . . These facts clearly establish, on the one hand, the absence of any bond of attachment between Nottebohm and Liechtenstein and, on the other hand, the existence of a long-standing and close connection between him and Guatemala, a link which his naturalization in no way weakened.

The Court went on to consider the motive for and circumstances of the naturalization.[3]

The application of the principle of the link or *rattachement* to the facts of this case has been criticized from two points of view. The first approach deals with the alleged subjectivity of the test and is bound up with consideration of its attributes from the point of view of policy. The second approach is to say that *at the material time* the effective nationality was that of Liechtenstein. The question whether an absence of connexion when the nationality was originally acquired can be cured by later events[4] was not considered by the Court. As a question of principle it is surely consonant with the doctrine of effective link to permit curing by subsequent changes. In its judgment the Court approves the view 'that, in order to be capable of being invoked against another State, nationality must correspond with the factual situation'. The events which related to the merits of the dispute occurred between 1943 and 1951, and for nine years, between 1946 and the beginning of the case, Nottebohm had resided in Liechtenstein. His applications to return to Guatemala in 1946 could perhaps be explained by the necessity to protect his interests and property there.[5] However, while it might be argued that in 1955 his effective nationality was that of Liechtenstein, when the principal losses and acts complained of occurred it was not:[6] it is doubtful, to say the least, if after receiving a wrong a

[1] See Guggenheim, I.C.J. Reports (1955), p. 55. [2] pp. 25–6.

[3] *Supra*, p. 412, n. 5. [4] Mervyn Jones, op. cit., p. 241, n. 8, thinks not.

[5] See Judge Read, I.C.J. Reports (1955), p. 44.

[6] The latest decree relating to expropriation occurred in 1951. The application of the

national can then take on another nationality and, after a lapse of time, *retroactively* acquire a champion in the form of a 'foreign' state against the state of his former nationality.

The criteria of effectiveness. The principle of real and effective nationality applied by the Court is one of relatively close, factual connexion. The Court said:[1]

> International arbitrators have decided in the same way numerous cases of dual nationality . . . They have given their preference to the real and effective nationality,[2] that which accorded with the facts, that based on stronger factual ties between the person concerned and one of the States whose nationality is involved. Different factors are taken into consideration, and their importance will vary from one case to the next: the habitual residence of the individual concerned is an important factor,[3] but there are other factors such as the centre of his interests, his family ties, his participation in public life, attachment shown by him for a given country and inculcated in his children, etc.

Further on,[4] the Court refers to practice of certain states which 'manifests the view of these States that . . . nationality must correspond with the factual situation'. On the next page[5] of the judgment, in the same general context, there are references to the individual's 'genuine connection' and 'genuine connections' with the state, to nationality as based upon 'a social fact of attachment,[6] a genuine connection of existence, interests and sentiments, together with the existence of reciprocal rights and duties', and to nationality as 'the juridical expression of the fact that the individual . . . is in fact more closely connected[7] with the population of the State conferring nationality than with that of any other state'.

In discussion of the draft Conventions on the Elimination, and the Reduction, of Future Statelessness at its fifth session, the International Law Commission was concerned to discover the criteria which states would accept as creating a sufficient link between individual and state. Criticism, in relation to the reduction of future statelessness, was directed at a draft article

relevant decrees to Nottebohm's property occurred as early as 1944 at least. The series of decrees concerning the property of aliens started in 1941.

[1] I.C.J. Reports (1955), p. 22. See also Córdova, *Yrbk., I.L.C.* (1954), ii, p. 42, at p. 50; the Secretariat survey, ibid., p. 52, at p. 108, paras. 365–6.

[2] The phrase recurs later on the same page of the judgment and twice on p. 24.

[3] See Córdova, *ubi supra*, for the precedents.

[4] p. 22. [5] p. 23.

[6] Cf. p. 26, reference to 'bond of attachment'.

[7] See also, on p. 24 of the judgment, the references to 'factual connections between Nottebohm and Liechtenstein', and the 'social fact of a connection': pp. 22 seq. contain several other references to 'connection' and 'link'.

which in part provided that[1] 'if a person does not acquire any nationality at birth, either *jure soli* or *jure sanguinis*, he shall subsequently acquire the nationality of the State in whose territory he is born'. As a result of the criticism the final draft[2] contained the provision (in paragraph 2): 'The national law of the Party may make preservation of such nationality dependent on the person being normally resident in its territory until the age of eighteen, and provide that to retain nationality he must comply with such other conditions as are required from all persons born in the Party's territory.' Whilst the provision is rather tangential, it reflects the concern of the Commission to provide for the establishment of sufficiently close links. Yepes pointed out in discussion that *jus soli* countries made acquisition by birth conditional: the place of birth was a matter of chance, and nationality could not be left to chance.[3] In his phrase,[4] 'there must be a genuine relation between the individual and the nation', and he proposed habitual residence, the domicile of the parents, and option as links.[5] Žourek spoke of the need to prove the 'solidity' of the individual's link with the state, and suggested that this was not provided by 'a mere formality—the place of birth and the fact of residence'.[6] François stated[7] that the draft article[8] resting on an unconditional *jus soli* 'was contrary to a basic principle of law to which the Netherlands attached great importance, namely, that there should be a link between countries and the individuals to whom they granted their nationality'. In general the discussion showed the difficulty of codifying the factual criteria. Thus Córdova's draft on the reduction of future statelessness[9] set out the links sufficient to support nationality of the country of birth, viz., residence until military age, option for that nationality on reaching military age, and service in the armed forces of that state. These criteria received considerable criticism.[1]

The principle, as expounded by the Court in *Nottebohm*, rests on all relevant facts in the given case, although habitual residence is an important factor. Three questions as to its application re-

[1] See *Yrbk., I.L.C.* (1953), ii. 187. [2] Ibid., p. 228.

[3] Ibid. (1953), i. p. 180, para. 24. [4] Ibid., p. 186, para. 7 (and see para. 5).

[5] Ibid., p. 239, para. 45. See the draft proposals at pp. 215, 220.

[6] Ibid., p. 218, para. 63. Cf. ibid., p. 181, paras. 32, 33. Cf. Amado, p. 239, para. 50, where he speaks of 'a sufficient link'.

[7] Ibid., p. 184, para. 57.

[8] Ibid. (1953), ii. p. 170. See Córdova's justification for this form in the draft on elimination of future statelessness, ibid., pp. 174–5.

[9] Ibid., p. 187 (and see the comment by the Rapporteur at pp. 188–9).

[1] Ibid. (1953), i. 213 seq.

quire immediate notice. First, it is said by Judge Read[1] that the criteria on which it rests are vague and subjective, and he states: 'Nationality, and the relation between a citizen and the State to which he owes allegiance, are of such a character that they demand certainty.... There must be objective tests, readily established, for the existence and recognition of the status.' The form which such comment takes has certain flaws. The object of the test—to discover the effective nationality—is neither vague nor subjective. The 'tests' referred to are merely the relevant facts, which are 'objective'. It is true that there is the element of appreciation, of assessing facts, and this may lead to subjectivity. Yet if the difficulties of applying rules to facts were a bar to useful application of rules many significant outcrops of jurisprudence would stand as monuments to futility. Moreover, Judge Read himself applies the tests[2] and reaches a conclusion which he clearly regards as logical and definite.[3] Ignoring the fundamental incongruity of the principle of autonomy on the international plane, one may question the assumption that reference to national laws gives certain and objective criteria. In the *Nottebohm* situation this was hardly the case; even after investigation of the facts on the issue of admissibility by the Court, not all was clear: the obvious point surely is that in regard to cosmopolitans like Nottebohm no test is going to lead to nice results. A second question arising from the decision is whether an effective nationality can exist in the absence of a formal status in the internal law of the state concerned.[4] The statements of principle in the judgment and the finding[5] that Nottebohm's close connexion was with Guatemala lead to the conclusion that it can so exist. Of course, in many of the cases which lead to disputes, the facts on which internal law depends for its determination may not be established, or it may not be possible to establish the fact of the act of government creating the formal link. In many cases it will not be clear whether loss of nationality occurred *ipso facto* or only from the date of the issue of a certificate or other declaration of status by the state concerned.[6] Thirdly, it may be asked whether naturalization has certain special features

[1] I.C.J. Reports (1955), p. 46. See also Guggenheim, ibid., pp. 55–7.

[2] However, he uses his own terminology, referring to 'the establishment of legal relationships', and 'a series of legal relationships, rights and duties'.

[3] I.C.J. Reports (1955), pp. 46–8.

[4] Reuter, 103 Hague *Recueil* (1961, II), 612, thinks not.

[5] I.C.J. Reports (1955), p. 26.

[6] Cf. Guggenheim, I.C.J. Reports (1955), p. 55, on Nottebohm's loss of German nationality.

in the context of effective nationality: this leads on to the next rubric, and will be dealt with thereunder.

Effective links and the interests of governments. The judgment in *Nottebohm* presents the principle of effective nationality in terms of the links between the life of the person concerned and the population or community of a state and of a 'social fact of attachment'.[1] However, members of the International Law Commission who espoused the same principle (admittedly in a different context) during its fifth session were prone to stress the duality of relevant links, and to show concern for the loyalty of the individual toward the state, which on the international plane had the responsibility for protection of the individual. Thus Yepes[2] referred to 'a genuine relationship between the individual and the nation'. In his dissenting opinion Judge Read in effect provided his own interpretation of the principle of effective link, although he opposed the principle as such. In his words,[3] 'the State is a concept broad enough to include not merely the territory and its inhabitants but also those of its citizens who are resident abroad but linked to it by allegiance. . . . In the case of many countries such as China, France, the United Kingdom and the Netherlands, the non-resident citizens form an important part of the body politic, and are numbered in their hundreds of thousands or millions.' In his view Nottebohm by his own conduct and that of Liechtenstein became a member of that body politic, 'the country of his allegiance'. These considerations would seem to be perfectly valid, and the general formulations of the Court could accommodate the more 'political' factors.[4] Certainly the reference by the Court to interests and intentions of the individual could include questions of allegiance. In a case where a businessman has international connexions and social mobility, residence and interests may provide no choice and political ties may then take on particular significance.

In connexion with political ties it is perhaps justifiable to regard the voluntary creation of such ties between individual and state by naturalization as a link of special strength. This con-

[1] See especially p. 23; quoted *supra*, p. 414. But at p. 24 the Court uses the phrase 'bond of allegiance'.

[2] *Yrbk., I.L.C.* (1953), i. 186, para. 7. And see *supra*, p. 415.

[3] I.C.J. Reports (1955), pp. 44–5. Cf. p. 46 for a further reference to allegiance.

[4] The Court includes, in a list of relevant factors, 'attachment shown by him for a given country and inculcated in his children'; judgment, at p. 22. See also the *Canevaro* case, *R.I.A.A.* xi. 405, in which exercise of political rights and request to hold public office were important factors. Cf. the form of certain provisions in the United Nations Convention on Reduction of Statelessness, 1961, especially Art. 8.

sideration appears to have weighed with Judge Read,[1] and the judgment of the Court is not really inimical to such a view. On the facts *as the Court saw them* the naturalization was not a real attempt to join Liechtenstein as a community, and, by reason of the motive involved, 'it was lacking in the genuineness requisite to an act of such importance'.[2] The matter of political ties may also arise in a rather different light when acts of protection and 'holding out' as a national have occurred. Where the facts of the individual connexions are ambiguous the conduct of a government may provide a determinant.[3] Here, however, we approach the realm of estoppel, and, in principle, estoppel properly so-called could produce a result incompatible with the principle of effective link.

The relation of genuine and effective links. There is general agreement that naturalization on the basis of fraud or duress is voidable, and this rule relates to the question of genuine link in a narrow context.[4] In the *Nottebohm* judgment a broader doctrine of 'genuine connexion'[5] appears in intimate relation with the, more frequent, references to 'real and effective nationality' and the like. It is probably correct to treat the two elements as aspects of the same thing, the references to genuineness being intended to emphasize that the quality and significance of factual relations with a given country are to be taken into account. Where the individual has material and family connexions in several states, inquiry into motive and intention may become important. In the *Nottebohm* decision itself the Court gives some prominence at the end of its judgment to the purpose for which, in its view, Nottebohm sought naturalization in a neutral state.[6] As a general principle 'genuine connexion' is valuable, but in relation to special problems the principle may beg too many questions, presenting issues rather than providing solutions.[7] Genuineness is a very relative concept.

The effect of Nottebohm *on diplomatic protection.* Of the implications of the *Nottebohm* judgment in the realm of policy, critics have concentrated on what is, in their view, a very unfortunate

[1] I.C.J. Reports (1955), p. 44. See also *supra*, p. 391, and cf. Córdova, *Yrbk., I.L.C.* (1953), ii. 189, para. J.

[2] Ibid., p. 26.

[3] Cf. Judge Read, ibid., pp. 44–5, referring *inter alia* to Nottebohm obtaining the diplomatic protection of Liechtenstein in October 1943, and on commencement of the confiscation of his properties.

[4] *Supra*, p. 396.

[5] I.C.J. Reports (1955), p. 23 (phrase used twice).

[6] See *supra*, p. 412, n. 5.

[7] See the *I.M.C.O.* case, 1960: Pleadings, Oral Arguments and Documents, pp. 364–6 (Seyersted); 383 (Vallat). The whole question of registration of ships remains delicate, but see *infra*, p. 424, for the provision in Article 5 of the Convention on the High Seas.

severance of diplomatic protection and nationality.[1] The practical result of the decision is seen to be a narrowing of the ambit of diplomatic protection.[2] Paul de Visscher,[3] on the other hand, takes the view that the field of diplomatic protection seems to have been extended by the principle of effective nationality. Before commenting on these opinions it may be remarked that the consequences of an affirmation of the principle of effective nationality are unlikely to be radical, because in a vast number of cases the effective nationality matches the formal nationality. In difficult cases like that of *Nottebohm* it will be the case that the approach on the basis of national rules will produce results no more certain than the 'real link' method. In many of these cases the national law or laws do not stand in isolation, but are overlaid by many other equally relevant facts, presumptions, and evidence of official acts and declarations: in establishing a proper basis for protection the 'real link' method probably gives reasonably satisfactory answers. Furthermore, if the exercise of diplomatic protection ignores the requirement of genuine connexion, the state which it is sought to hold to account may refuse to recognize the right of protection. Long-resident refugees are an important source of problems, and it would seem likely that the link doctrine is potentially more helpful here than reference to national laws. The latter method leaves the refugee stateless or links him to a community which he has tried to quit permanently in many cases.

Fears that effective nationality produces a narrow regime will be the less justified if the doctrine is applied in a liberal way. There is probably nothing in *Nottebohm* or the other sources of principle to prevent an approach which is not too exacting in the matter of effectiveness. The application of the principle in *Nottebohm* appeared to be strict because of the factors involved: the individual concerned had a variety of links with two states, the issue was between the two best candidates, and on the Court's view of the facts the question of *genuine* attachment was prominent.[4] Professor Jennings[5] has remarked: 'If the law is to work in practice, . . . the presumption created by a juridical fact such as voluntary naturalization must be regarded by any tribunal as a very strong presumption, not easily rebutted.'

[1] See Judge Read, I.C.J. Reports (1955), p. 46.

[2] See Mervyn Jones, 5 *I.C.L.Q.* (1956), 244; Eagleton, 50 *A.J.* (1956), 919–20; *Annuaire de l'Institut* (1965), i. 75–80, 167–8; Knapp, *Annuaire suisse* (1960), 147–78.

[3] 60 *R.G.D.I.P.* (1956), 263–4.

[4] *Supra*, p. 412.

[5] 121 Hague *Recueil* (1967, II), 459.

On 30 August 1961 there was signed the United Nations Convention on the Reduction of Statelessness,[1] the detailed provisions of which rely on various criteria of factual connexion and evidence of allegiance. The United Nations Conference which gave rise to the Convention also adopted a resolution[2] recommending 'that persons who are stateless *de facto* should as far as possible be treated as stateless *de jure* to enable them to acquire an effective nationality'. Dr. Weis remarks[3] that the Convention and recommendation 'clearly reflect the importance which is attached to an increasing degree to effectiveness of nationality'.

[1] Text: 11 *I.C.L.Q.* (1962), 1090. In force 1975.

[2] Ibid., p. 1096.

[3] Ibid., p. 1087. He points out that delegates at the Conference tended to speak in terms of effective links: references, ibid., n. 38.

CHAPTER XIX

SOME RULES OF ATTRIBUTION: CORPORATIONS AND SPECIFIC ASSETS

1. *General Aspects*

THE assignment of persons and property to particular legal persons is normally approached through the concept of nationality and primarily the nationality of individuals and corporations for purposes of diplomatic protection. Yet it is clear that the problem of attribution must be solved in a variety of contexts including rules concerning jurisdiction and jurisdictional immunities. It has lately become apparent that the problems of jurisdiction can be solved on a satisfactory basis by the use of the principle of substantial connexion affirmed in the *Nottebohm* case.[1] Analogues of 'nationality for purposes of diplomatic protection' can be multiplied: in various contexts, 'substantial connexion' is employed as a substitute for the concept of nationality, or 'nationality', when used, is defined in terms of substantial connexion. The necessity for rules of attribution of a functional kind, not tied to an unworkable principle[2] of reference to municipal law and the autonomy of states in matters of 'nationality', is apparent when the issues of 'nationality' on the plane of international law are related to corporations, ships, aircraft, other national assets, and the assets of international organizations.

2. *Corporations*[3]

The attribution of legal persons (*personnes morales*) to a particular state for the purpose of applying a rule of domestic or

[1] *Supra*, p. 393. [2] *Supra*, pp. 380 seq.

[3] On the issues of diplomatic protection and admissibility of claims see the literature cited *infra*, p. 485. Otherwise see Ginther, 15 *Österreichische Zeit. für Öff. Recht* (1966), 27–59; Whiteman viii. 17–22; Schwarzenberger i. 388–412; Hackworth iii. 420–34; Walker, 50 *A.J.* (1956), 373–93; Vagts, 74 *Harv. L.R.* (1961), 1489–1551; Note, ibid., 1429–51; Kronstein, 52 *Col.L.R.* (1952), 983–1002; Radnay, 16 *Syracuse L.R.* (1965), 779–97; Steiner and Vagts, *Transnational Legal Problems* (1968), 56–87; Domke, 3 *I.L.Q.* (1950), 52–9; Rabel, *Conflict of Laws* (2nd ed., 1960), pp. 31–93; Batiffol, *Droit international privé* (5th ed., 1970), i. 233–62; Loussouarn and Bredin, *Droit du commerce international* (1969), pp. 251–309; Katz and Brewster, *The Law of International Transactions and Relations* (1960), pp. 171–202; Goldman, 90 *J.D.I.* (1963), 321–89; Caflisch, 24 *Ann. Suisse* (1967), 119–60; Mann, 88 *L.Q.R.* (1972), 57–82 (also in Mann, *Studies in International Law* (1973), pp. 524–52); Verzijl, *International Law in Historical Perspective* v. 111–44.

international law is commonly based upon the concept of nationality. The borrowing of a concept developed in relation to individuals is awkward in some respects but is now well established. A major point of distinction is the absence of legislative provisions in municipal law systems which create a national status for corporations: domestic nationality laws do not concern themselves with corporations. The consequences of this are twofold. First, the nationality must be derived either from the fact of incorporation, i.e. creation as a legal person, within the given system of domestic law, or from various links including the centre of administration (*siège social*), and the national basis of ownership and control. Secondly, the content of the nationality tends to depend on the context of the particular rule of law involved: nationality appears more as a functional attribution or tracing and less as a formal and general status of the kind relating to individuals.

A major issue concerning corporations is the right to exercise diplomatic protection in respect of the corporation and its shareholders. It is convenient to reserve this question for the discussion of admissibility of claims in Chapter XXI.

Rules of municipal law may make use of the concept of nationality of legal persons even in the absence of special legislation creating such a status as such. Important areas of domestic law referring to the nationality of corporations are constitutional law, private international law (conflict of laws), the law relating to trading with the enemy and taxation.

On the plane of international law and relations a great many treaty provisions define 'nationals' to include corporations (with functions of private law) for various purposes. Treaty provisions may or may not adopt the conflict of laws rule[1] that the law of the place of creation determines whether an association has legal personality. For the purposes of the particular treaty unincorporated associations, including partnerships, may be assimilated to corporations. Public corporations may also be included.[2]

Treaties of commerce create standards of treatment in relation to 'nationals' and, or, 'companies' of the contracting parties. The Treaty of Commerce, Establishment and Navigation of 1959 between the United Kingdom and Iran defines 'companies' thus:[3]

[1] Rabel, op. cit., pp. 69–72.

[2] See the cases of *German Interests in Polish Upper Silesia* (1926) and *Peter Pázmány University* (1933), *infra*, p. 423.

[3] Cmnd. 698, Article 2, para. 4. See also the Treaty of Friendship, Commerce and Navigation, U.S. and Italy, 1948, 79 U.N.T.S. 171, Article II. See further Feliciano, 118 Hague *Recueil* (1966, II), 262–83.

The term 'companies'—

(a) means all legal persons except physical persons;

(b) in relation to a High Contracting Party means all companies which derive their status as such from the law in force in any territory of that High Contracting Party to which the present Treaty applies;

(c) in relation to a country means all companies which derive their status as such from the law in force in that country.

The Treaty establishing the European Economic Community provides in Article 58 that corporations created under the law of a member state and having their 'siège statutaire', 'administration centrale', or 'principal établissement' within the Community are assimilated, for the purposes of the chapter on the right of establishment, to individuals who are 'ressortissant des États membres'.[1] For this purpose corporations include all legal persons whether of public or private law other than non-profit-making bodies.

Bilateral treaties concerned with double taxation contain rules of attribution which may invoke the concepts of nationality, residence, or fiscal domicile, whilst defining the crucial points of contact, which are commonly management and control.[2] Air transport agreements may require that airlines acquiring a foreign carrier permit satisfy a condition of substantial ownership and effective control by nationals of the other contracting party.[3] Important provisions ascribing a national character to corporations and other associations appear in peace treaties, agreements on reparation for war losses, treaties of cession, and agreements for compensation in case of nationalization and other events causing loss to foreign interests on state territory. In the *Peter Pázmány University*[4] case, the Permanent Court found that the University, as a legal person in Hungarian law, was a Hungarian national for the purpose of submitting a claim to restitution of property under Article 250 of the Treaty of Trianon, 1920. In general treaty provisions employ a variety of criteria including siège social,[5] the national source of actual control, ownership, and place of creation.

[1] See also Conv. Establishing the European Free Trade Association, 1959, Article 16, para. 6; European Conv. on Establishment of Companies, 1966, Article 1.

[2] Ginther, op. cit., pp. 40–6; and see *Compagnie Financière de Suez et l'Union Parisienne* v. *United States*, 492 F. 2nd 798 (U.S. Ct. of Claims, 20 February 1974); 68 *A.J.* (1974), 738; *Digest of U.S. Practice*, 1974, 532.

[3] See *Aerolineas Peruanas, S.A., Foreign Permit Case*, Int. L.R. 31, p. 416, U.S. Civil Aeronautics Board.

[4] P.C.I.J. Ser. A/B, no. 61 (1933), at pp. 228–32; Whiteman viii. 21. See also *German Interests in Polish Upper Silesia*, P.C.I.J. Ser. A, No. 7, pp. 73, 74–5 (1926).

[5] This concept of French law overlaps with residence and domicile. Normally the siège

3. *Ships*[1]

In the maintenance of a viable regime for common use of the high seas the law of the flag and the necessity for a ship to have a flag are paramount.[2] The opinion commonly expressed by jurists was strongly in favour of the unqualified freedom of each state to determine for itself the conditions under which national status could be conferred on vessels.[3] This view of state competence suffers from the organic faults considered in a wider setting in the previous chapter. The act of conferment of nationality (registration) is within the competence of states, but registration is in principle only evidence of nationality, and valid registration under the law of the flag state does not preclude issues of validity under international law. The *Nottebohm* principle applies equally here, and the Convention on the High Seas of 1958[4] provides in Article 5, paragraph 1:[5]

> Each State shall fix the conditions for the grant of its nationality to ships, for the registration of ships in its territory, and for the right to fly its flag. Ships have the nationality of the State whose flag they are entitled to fly. There must exist a genuine link between the State and the ship; in particular, the State must effectively exercise its jurisdiction and control in administrative, technical and social matters over ships flying its flag.

The International Law Commission[6] had preferred a reference to 'a genuine link' without any further specification. The Commission observed: 'While leaving States a wide latitude in this

social is the place where the administrative organs operate and where general meetings are held. However, tribunals may insist that the siège social should not be nominal and thus relate the test to that of effective control. See Schwarzenberger, op. cit., pp. 393–5; and *Bakalian and Hadjthomas* v. *Banque Ottomane*, 93 *J.D.I.* (1966), 117.

[1] See especially Whiteman ix. 1–51; Meyers, *The Nationality of Ships* (1967); Jennings, 121 Hague *Recueil* (1967, II), 460–5; Harolds, 28 *Fordham L.R.* (1959), 295–315; Singh, 107 Hague *Recueil* (1962, III), 38–64; Johnson, 8 *Indian Yrbk. of Int. Affairs* (1959), 3–15; Schwarzenberger, *International Law* i (3rd ed.), 412–18; Pinto, 87 *J.D.I.* (1960), 344–69; Watts, 33 *B.Y.* (1957), 52–84; Goldie, 39 *B.Y.* (1963), 220–83; de Visscher, *Les Effectivités du droit international public* (1967), pp. 139–44; Laun in *Gedächtnisschrift Ludwig Marxer* (1963), pp. 327–68; Fay, 77 *R.G.D.I.P.* (1973), 1000–80; Verzijl, *International Law in Historical Perspective* iv. 196–200; v. 144–50. See also U.N. Legis. Series, *Laws Concerning the Nationality of Ships* (1955); and references *infra*. On the status of those born on ships: *supra*, pp. 388–9.

[2] *Supra*, p. 242.

[3] See Gidel i. 80; Rienow, *The Test of the Nationality of a Merchant Vessel* (1937), pp. 218–19; Harv. Research, 29 *A.J.* (1935), Spec. Suppl. pp. 518–19. Cf. the *Muscat Dhows*, *R.I.A.A.* xi. 83, (1905).

[4] *Supra*, p. 237.

[5] See further Whiteman ix. 7–17; *Yrbk., I.L.C.* (1956), ii. 278–9; U.N. Conference on the Law of the Sea, Off. Recs. i. 78, 83, 85, 91, 108, 111, 112; iv. 61 seq.; the *I.M.C.O.* case, Pleadings (1960), pp. 357–8 (Riphagen), 364–8 (Seyersted), 383 (Vallat); Permanent Statute of the Free Territory of Trieste, Art. 33, 42 *A.J.* (1948), Suppl. p. 97; Jessup, 59 *Columbia L.R.* (1959), p. 234 at p. 256; id., sep. op., *Barcelona Traction* case (Second Phase), I.C.J. Reports (1970), at pp. 184, 186–9.

[6] *Yrbk., I.L.C.* (1956), ii. 278–9.

respect, the Commission wished to make it clear that the grant of its flag to a ship cannot be a mere administrative formality, with no accompanying guarantee that the ship possess a real link with its new State.' Professor Jennings[1] has remarked that 'the assumption that the "genuine link" formula, invented for dealing with people, is capable of immediate application to ships and aircraft, smacks of a disappointing naiveté' and, further, that 'a provision which might seem to encourage governments to make subjective decisions whether or not to recognize the nationality of this aircraft or that vessel is clearly open to abuse and for that reason to grave criticism.'

The provision above has met with criticism from partisans of the exclusive competence of states to ascribe national character to vessels.[2] The United States Department of State has adopted a position which involves interpreting the provision in such a way that the requirement of a genuine link is not a condition for recognition of the nationality of the ship but an independent obligation to exercise jurisdiction and control effectively.[3]

Treaties may contain specialized rules of attribution.[4] In the *I.M.C.O.* case[5] the International Court was asked to give an advisory opinion on the proper constitution of the Maritime Safety Committee of the Inter-Governmental Maritime Consultative Organization. The relevant convention provided, in Article 28(a), that 'The Maritime Safety Committee shall consist of fourteen Members elected by the Assembly from the Members, governments of those nations having an important interest in maritime safety, of which not less than eight shall be the largest ship-owning nations . . .' Panama and Liberia had not been elected and they and other states contended that the proper test was registered tonnage and not beneficial ownership by nationals. The Court found that the reference in the convention was solely to registered tonnage. This conclusion depended on the construction of the text and was assumed to be consistent with the general

[1] 121 Hague *Recueil*, (1967, II), 463.

[2] See McDougal, Burke and Vlasic, 54 *A.J.* (1960), 25–116; McDougal and Burke, *The Public Order of the Oceans*, pp. 1008–140; Boczek, *Flags of Convenience* (1962). The debate relates to the use of flags of convenience by American interests in competition with European shipping.

[3] Whiteman ix, p. 27, at p. 29. For the contrary view: Recommendation 108, General Conference of the I.L.O., 1958; Meyers, op. cit., p. 225 (144 votes to 0, 3 abstentions).

[4] See, for example, the Conv. on Fishing and Conservation of the Living Resources of the High Seas, 1958, art. 14; Peace Treaty with Italy, 42 *A.J.* (1948), Suppl.; p. 47, art. 78(9)(c); Annex VI, Art. 33.

[5] I.C.J. Reports (1960), p. 150; Int. L.R. 30, p. 426. See Simmonds, 12 *I.C.L.Q.* (1963), 56–87; Colliard, *Annuaire français* (1960), 338–61; Rosenne, 65 *R.G.D.I.P.* (1961), 507–17; de Visscher, *Les Effectivités*, p. 143.

purpose of the Convention. The Court thus found it unnecessary to examine the argument that registration was qualified by the requirement of a genuine link. With little or no justification the United States Department of State regards this as evidence in support of its position relating to Article 5 of the High Seas Convention.[1]

The courts of the United States have refused to apply local law to the internal management of vessels in American ports flying Honduran or Liberian flags which had close contacts with the United States.[2] This refusal to go behind the law of the flag and the fact of registration was based in part upon the construction of the relevant Treaty of Friendship, Commerce and Consular Rights and in part upon the general principle governing jurisdiction over ships in port.[3]

The Informal Composite Negotiating Text of 1977 (Third United Nations Conference on the Law of the Sea) contains draft provisions which retain the requirement of genuine link (Article 91). However, this draft article does not retain the association of 'genuine link' with the effective exercise of jurisdiction by the flag state: such duties are prescribed in a separate article (Article 94).

4. *Aircraft*[4]

The Convention for the Regulation of Aerial Navigation of 1919,[5] and later the Chicago Convention of 1944,[6] provided that the nationality of aircraft is governed by the state of registration. The former stipulated that registration could only take place in the state of which the owners were nationals, whilst the latter merely forbids dual registration. Neither Convention applied in time of war, and the latter Convention does not apply to state aircraft, i.e. 'aircraft used in military, customs and police services'. The Tokyo Convention on Offences Committed on Board Aircraft[7] provides that the state of registration has jurisdiction over offences and acts committed on board. The

[1] Whiteman ix, p. 27 at p. 29.

[2] *McCulloch* v. *Sociedad Nacional*; *McLeod* v. *Empresa Hondurena; National Maritime Union* v. *Empresa Hondurena*, 372 U.S. 10 (1963); Int. L.R. 34, p. 51; Whiteman ix. 30; *Incres* v. *International Maritime Workers Union*, 372 U.S. 24 (1963); Int. L.R. 34, p. 66.

[3] *Supra*, p. 316.

[4] See de Visscher, 48 Hague *Recueil* (1934, II), 294–301; id., *Les Effectivités*, pp. 144–6; Honig, *The Legal Status of Aircraft* (1956); Nys, *Rev. française de droit aérien* (1964), pp. 159–83; Mankiewicz, *Ann. français* (1952), p. 685 at pp. 686–90; Whiteman ix. 376–90, 429–41; Cooper, 17 *Journ. of Air Law and Com.* (1950), pp. 292–316.

[5] Articles 5–10. [6] Articles 17–21. [7] *Supra*, p. 319.

more recent provisions may be thought to support a doctrine of freedom in conferring national status by registration, in contrast to Article 5 of the Convention on the High Seas.[1] However, in the absence of flags of convenience in air traffic, it may be that the issue was left on one side by the authors, the assumption being that registration in practice depended on the existence of substantial connexions. In the absence of substantial connexions the state of registry will not be in a position to ensure that the aircraft is operated in accordance with the Chicago Convention. However, the application of a genuine link test is by no means straightforward and, as in the case of naturalization of individuals, registration is itself a presumptively valid and genuine connexion of some importance.[2] The problem is to isolate the role of registration: it may merely certify status under national law for the purpose of administering the particular convention.[3] Obviously the *Nottebohm* principle[4] ought to apply to aircraft as it does to ships. It must surely apply at the least to discover to which state non-civil aircraft belong, but it is probable that even where the Chicago Convention applies, issues of diplomatic protection are not precluded by registration. In bilateral treaties the United States has reserved the right to refuse a carrier permit to an airline designated by the other contracting party 'in the event substantial ownership and effective control of such airlines are not vested in nationals of the other contracting party'.[5]

In principle, aircraft of joint operating agencies, for example, Air Afrique, must be registered in one of the states involved. However, in 1967 the Council of the International Civil Aviation Organization adopted a resolution requiring the constitution of a joint register in such cases for the purposes of Article 77 of the Chicago Convention and the designation of a state as recipient of representations from third states.[6] The resolution applies both to joint operating agencies and intergovernmental agencies.

International agreement is called for on the legal status of dif-

[1] See Marakov, *Annuaire de l'Inst.* 48 (1959), i. 359 seq.; ibid., 49 (1961), ii. 328 seq. Cf. *Affaire F. OABV*, *Ann. français* (1958), 282.

[2] See Jennings, 121 Hague *Recueil*, pp. 460–6.

[3] But parties to the Chicago Convention may be precluded from contesting nationality based on registration: see Cheng, *The Law of International Air Transport* (1962), pp. 128–31.

[4] *Supra*, p. 393.

[5] See *Aerolineas Peruanas*, S.A., *Foreign Permit Case*, Int. L.R. 31, p. 416.

[6] See Whiteman ix. 383–90; Fitzgerald, 5 *Canad. Yrbk.* (1967), pp. 193–216; *Annuaire Français*, 1967, p. 528; I.L.A., *Report of the Fifty-Second Conference*, 1966, pp. 228–86; I.L.A., *Report of the Fifty-Third Conference*, 1968, pp. 147–56; Cheng, *Yrbk. of Air and Space Law*, 1966, 5–31; Venkatramiah, 11 *Indian Journ.* (1971), 435–58.

ferent types of air-cushion craft, including hovercraft and hydrofoils.

5. *Space Vehicles*[1]

The Space Treaty of 1967[2] does not employ the concept of nationality in relation to objects launched into outer space. Article VIII of the Treaty provides in part that the state of registration 'shall retain jurisdiction and control over such object, and over any personnel thereof, while in outer space or on a celestial body'. In the Convention on Registration of Objects Launched into Outer Space it is provided that the launching State shall maintain a register of space objects.[3] Each State of registry has a duty to furnish certain information to the Secretary-General of the United Nations.

6. *Property in General*

Ownership in international law is normally seen either in terms of private rights under national law, which may become the subject of diplomatic protection and state responsibility, or in terms of territorial sovereignty. However, rules of attribution exist which must create a counterpart of ownership on the international plane. This is the case for state ships, aircraft, space vehicles, and national treasures.[4] Many treaties confer 'property' or 'title' without referring this to the national law of the *situs* or to any other local law.[5] Transfers of materials may reserve 'title' to the transferor. Thus the United States agreed to lend a

[1] See McDougal, Lasswell and Vlasic, *Law and Public Order in Space* (1963), pp. 513–87; Goedhuis, 109 Hague *Recueil* (1963, II), pp. 301–8; Lachs, 113 Hague *Recueil* (1964, III), pp. 55–61; I.L.A., *Report of the Fifty-Second Conference*, 1966, p. 215; I.L.A., *Report of the Fifty-Third Conference*, 1968, pp. 170–85.

[2] *Supra*, p. 267.

[3] Adopted by the U.N. General Assembly on 12 November 1974; in force 15 September 1976; for the text: 14 I.L.M. (1975), 43; *Digest of U.S. Practice*, 1974, p. 401.

[4] See the Cambodian claim in the *Temple* case, I.C.J. Reports (1962), p. 6, for restitution of sculptures and other objects; and the Jordanian claim to the Temple Scroll, acquired by Israel, UNESCO, Executive Board meeting, October 1969. See further Williams, 15 *Canad. Yrbk.* (1977), 146–72; U.N. General Assembly Resolution on Restitution of Works of Art, 11 November 1977. Note also the case of a sunken Soviet submarine (see Rubin, 69 *A.J.* (1975), 855–8), and the Agreement between the U.K. and U.A.R. concerning the Tutankhamen Exhibition (*Treaty Series* No. 19 (1972), Cmnd. 4898), Art. 1(4).

[5] See the Soviet-Swedish Agreement on Construction of Embassy Buildings, 1958; 428 U.N.T.S., no. 6184; and various agreements on disposition of defence equipment, hydraulic works on frontier waters, and proprietary rights in river waters. See also the contract between the International Atomic Energy Agency, the Government of the United States, and the Government of Pakistan for the transfer of enriched uranium and plutonium for a reactor, 1962; 425 U.N.T.S., no. 6114.

vessel to the Philippines for five years, title to remain in the United States and the transferee having the right to place the vessel under its flag.[1] In the arbitration concerning *Monetary Gold* (1953)[2] Sauser-Hall, sole arbitrator, referred in his award to a concept of 'patrimoine nationale' which could extend to gold functioning as a monetary reserve, although the gold did not belong to the state concerned by its national law but to a private bank under foreign control. In general the notion of state immunity provides a paradigm of 'title' on the international plane.

The issue of title arises in more specialist contexts in which the concept of 'title' plays little or no active role, the outcome depending on the particular rules of law applicable. Problems of this kind concern the disposition of vessels taken in prize,[3] title to booty of war,[4] the taking of reparation in kind, the effect of territorial cession on public property in the territory concerned,[5] and claims by the victors of 1945 to German assets in neutral countries.[6]

7. *Assets of International Organizations*[7]

If one approaches the problem of attribution by reference to the rules concerning states, then negatives are prominent: organizations cannot have territorial sovereignty[8] and have no competence to confer nationality on persons or assets. Nevertheless the functional competence of organizations may include significant powers of jurisdiction and a regime of jurisdictional immunities, and both jurisdiction and the immunities of assets from national jurisdictions[9] are analogues of ownership. It is undoubtedly the case that the resources of the International

[1] Agreement of 1961; 433 U.N.T.S., no. 6232.

[2] Int. L.R. 20 (1953), p. 441 at pp. 469 seq.: *R.I.A.A.* xii, p. 13 at pp. 43 seq. See further 49 *A.J.* (1955), 403; Lalive, 58 *R.G.D.I.P.* (1954), 438; Fawcett, 123 Hague *Recueil* (1968, I), 248–51. Cf. *Monetary Gold Removed from Rome in 1943*, I.C.J. Reports (1954), p. 19. See also the *Standard Oil* case, *R.I.A.A.* ii, p. 777 at p. 795.

[3] Municipal legislation in some states confers nationality of the captor states on lawful prizes.

[4] Oppenheim ii. 401–2.

[5] See *German Interests in Polish Upper Silesia* (1926), P.C.I.J., Ser. A, no. 7, p. 41; *Peter Pázmány University* (1933), P.C.I.J., Ser. A/B, no. 61, p. 237; U.N.Trib. in Libya, *R.I.A.A.* xii. 363.

[6] See Mann, 24 *B.Y.* (1957), 239–57; Simpson, 34 *B.Y.* (1958), 374–84.

[7] See generally Chapter XXX.

[8] *Supra*, pp. 178–9.

[9] See the Convention on the Privileges and Immunities of the United Nations, 1946, sect. 3; and Jenks, *International Immunities*, pp. 52–3.

Monetary Fund and buffer stocks established under international commodity agreements are forms of property title to which is not derived from any system of municipal law.[1] In the case of ships used in furtherance of the purposes of an organization, there is obviously a case for allowing the organization to fly its own flag and exercise some protection over the vessel. The question of competence is still open, and there are some serious obstacles. The law of the flag is an instrument for ensuring compliance with various rules; but an organization will normally lack the means of exercising the appropriate jurisdiction and there will be no applicable law.[2] Aircraft operated by the United Nations or other intergovernmental organizations must, it seems, use a state registration, provided the relevant treaty provisions (in the Chicago Convention) allow this.[3] The problem of accession to the Convention on the Liability of Operators of Nuclear Ships by organizations has been considered by a Standing Committee of the Diplomatic Conference on Maritime Law, which failed to reach agreement.[4]

[1] See further Fawcett, 123 Hague *Recueil* (1968, I), 237–40; id., 44 *B.Y.* (1970), 173–4.

[2] The first Law of the Sea Conference could not agree on the subject. The Convention on the High Seas leaves the question open (Article 7). See François, *Yrbk., I.L.C.* (1956), ii. 102; ibid. (1963), ii. 178; Jennings, 121 Hague *Recueil* (1967, II), pp. 467–8; McDougal and Burke, *The Public Order of the Oceans*, pp. 773–7; Singh, 107 Hague *Recueil* (1962, III), 134–61; O'Connell, pp. 100, 608; Meyers, *Nationality of Ships* (1967), pp. 323–51. Fishing vessels of the United Nations Korean Reconstruction Agency and one of the vessels of the United Nations Emergency Force in Egypt carried a United Nations flag without having any state registration. On other occasions vessels with a national registration have flown a United Nations flag.

[3] See Mankiewicz, *Ann. français* (1962), 691–717; Cheng, op. cit., pp. 131–2; Whiteman ix. 383–90; FitzGerald, 5 *Canad. Yrbk.* (1967), 193–216.

[4] Sørensen, *Manual*, pp. 259–60.

PART VIII
THE LAW OF RESPONSIBILITY

CHAPTER XX
THE RESPONSIBILITY OF STATES

1. *The Relations of the Subject*

In international relations as in other social relations, the invasion of the legal interest of one subject of the law by another legal person creates responsibility[1] in various forms determined by the particular legal system. International responsibility is commonly considered in relation to states as the normal subjects of the law, but it is in essence a broader question inseparable from that of legal personality in all its forms. For the sake of convenience the question whether organizations and individuals have the capacity to make claims and to bear responsibility on the international plane has been treated separately.[2] However, whilst the treatment is conventional in singling out state responsibility, it is specialized in two respects. First, the question of the treatment of aliens and their property on state territory[3] is reserved for Chapter XXIII. This subject is an aspect of substantive law, and, logically, if it is to be included, then so also ought expositions of all the rights and duties of states. Nevertheless the treatment of aliens will be dealt with incidentally in connexion with the general problems of responsibility. Secondly, the question of exhaustion of local remedies so often dealt with under our general rubric is segregated as being a part of a separate issue, that of the admissibility of claims. Whilst certain aspects of admissibility require treatment in this chapter (section 14), the subject receives further consideration in Chapter XXI.

2. *The Basis and Nature of State Responsibility*[4]

Today one can regard responsibility as a general principle of international law, a concomitant of substantive rules and of the supposition that acts and omissions may be categorized as

[1] See *infra*, pp. 433–4. [2] *Infra*, pp. 577 seq., 684–6.

[3] Including the problems concerning the international minimum standard, denial of justice, and expropriation.

[4] See especially Jiménez de Aréchaga, in Sørensen (ed.), *Manual* (1968), pp. 533–72; Schwarzenberger, *International Law* (3rd ed.), i. 562–83; Sørensen, 101 Hague *Recueil*

illegal by reference to the rules establishing rights and duties. Shortly, the law of responsibility is concerned with the incidence and consequences of illegal acts, and particularly the payment of compensation for loss caused. However, this, and many other generalizations offered on the subject, must not be treated as dogma, or allowed to prejudice the discussion which follows. Thus the law may prescribe the payment of compensation for the consequences of legal or 'excusable' acts, and it is proper to consider this aspect in connexion with responsibility in general.[1] A scientific treatment of the subject is hindered by the relatively recent generalization of the notion of liability. In the Middle Ages treaties laid down particular duties and specified the liabilities and procedures to be followed in case of breach. In recent times the inconvenience of private reprisals,[2] the development of rules restricting forcible self-help, and the work of the International Court, have contributed towards a more normal conception of responsibility from the point of view of the rule of law. Of course the notions of reparation and restitution in the train of illegal acts had long been part of the available stock of legal concepts in Europe, and the classical writers, including Grotius, often referred to reparation and restitution in connexion with unjust war.[3]

(1960, III), 217–26; García Amador, 94 Hague *Recueil* (1958, II), 369–99, 462–7; Reports by García Amador, *Yrbk., I.L.C.* (1956), ii. 173, Chap. III; and ibid. (1957), ii. 105, Chap. I; ibid. (1960), ii. 57–66; Report of Sub-Committee, ibid. (1963), ii. 227–59; Secretariat papers, ibid. (1964), ii. 125–71; Note by Ago, ibid. (1967), ii. 325–7; Secretariat papers, ibid. (1969), ii. 101–24; Ago, First Report, ibid., 125–56; Second Report, *Yrbk., I.L.C.* (1970), ii. 177–97; Third Report, ibid. (1971), ii. (pt. 1), 199–274; Fourth Report, ibid. (1972), ii. 71–160; Fifth Report, ibid. (1976) ii (pt. 1), 3–54; Sixth Report, A/CN. 4/302, (1977); Seventh Report, A/CN. 4/307 (and add.) (1978); Eighth Report, A/CN. 4/318 (and add.) (1979); Reports of I.L.C. to U.N. General Assembly, *Yrbk., I.L.C.* (1973) ii. 165–98; ibid. (1974) ii (pt. 1), 269–90; ibid. (1975) ii. 51–106; ibid. (1976) ii. (pt. 2), 69–122; Münch, *Das Völkerrechtliche Delikt* (1963); Tunkin, *Theory of International Law* (1974), pp. 396–425; Reuter, 103 Hague *Recueil* (1961, II), 583–97; Accioly, 96 Hague *Recueil* (1959, I), 353–70; Rousseau, *Droit international public*, pp. 356–61; de Visscher, *Bibliotheca Visseriana* ii. (1924), 89–119; Strupp, *Das völkerrechtliche Delikt* (1920); Anzilotti, *Cours de droit international* i. (1929), 466 seq.; Cohn, 68 Hague *Recueil* (1929, II), 209–325; Ago, ibid., 419–554; Eagleton, *The Responsibility of States in International Law* (1928); Berlia, in *Études en l'honneur de G. Scelle* ii. 875–94; Basdevant, 58 Hague *Recueil* (1936, IV), 656–75; Kelsen, *Principles of International Law*, pp. 9–13, 19 seq. 114 seq.; Cheng, *General Principles of Law*, pp. 163–80; Carlebach, *La Problème de la faute et sa place dans la norme du droit international* (1962); Parry, 90 Hague *Recueil* (1956, II), 657–98; Quadri, 113 Hague *Recueil* (1964, III), 453–77; Queneudec, *La Responsabilité internationale de l'Etat pour les fautes personnelles de ses agents* (1966); Kouris, 72 *R.G.D.I.P.* (1968), 269–72; *Répertoire suisse de d.i.* iii. 1673–1796; Verzijl, *International Law in Historical Perspective* vi. 616–774.

[1] See *infra*, p. 443.

[2] Formerly sovereigns authorized private citizens to perform acts of reprisal (special reprisals) against the citizens of other states: Wheaton, *Elements* (1866), paras. 291, 292.

[3] See Gentili, *De Iure Belli Libri Tres*, Book, II, Ch. iii; Grotius, *De Iure Belli ac*

The nature of state responsibility[1] is not based upon delict in the municipal sense, and 'international responsibility' relates both to breaches of treaty and to other breaches of a legal duty. There is no harm in using the term 'international tort' to describe the breach of duty which results in loss to another state,[2] but the term 'tort' could mislead the common lawyer. The compendious term 'international responsibility' is used by tribunals and is least confusing. In any case, as McNair points out,[3] 'there is sometimes a tendency amongst lawyers to apply the normal rules of human responsibility, both contractual and delictual, to State responsibility too literally and too readily'.

The relevant judicial pronouncements are as follows. In a report on the *Spanish Zone of Morocco Claims*[4] Judge Huber said: 'Responsibility is the necessary corollary of a right. All rights of an international character involve international responsibility. If the obligation in question is not met, responsibility entails the duty to make reparation.' In its judgment in the *Chorzów Factory* (Jurisdiction)[5] proceedings, the Permanent Court stated that: 'It is a principle of international law that the breach of an engagement involves an obligation to make reparation in an adequate form. Reparation therefore is the indispensable complement of a failure to apply a convention and there is no necessity for this to be stated in the convention itself.'

In the judgment on the *Chorzów Factory* (Indemnity)[6] the Court said:

> . . . it is a principle of international law, and even a general conception of law, that any breach of an engagement involves an obligation to make reparation. In Judgment No. 8[7] . . . the Court has already said that repara-

Pacis, Book III, Ch. x, para. 4. Cf. the discussion of reparation in connexion with the armistice conditions and peace treaties, 1918–21: Brownlie, *International Law and the Use of Force by States*, pp. 135–9. See also the Statute of the International Court, Art. 36 (2), c, d.

[1] The question of criminal responsibility of states may arise: see Pella, 51 *R.G.D.I.P.* (1947), 1–27; Brownlie, op. cit., pp. 150–4; 44 *Annuaire de l'Inst.* (1952), i. 361–457; *Yrbk., I.L.C.* (1964), ii. 125–8.

[2] See Schwarzenberger, *International Law* i. 562, 563, 571, 581; the *Union Bridge Company* claim (1924), *R.I.A.A.* vi, p. 138 at p. 142; and Jenks, *The Prospects of International Adjudication*, pp. 514–33.

[3] *Opinions* ii. 198.

[4] Translation; French text, *R.I.A.A.* ii, p. 615 at p. 641. See also *Coenca Bros.* v. *Germany*, *Ann. Digest* 4 (1927–8), no. 389.

[5] (1927), P.C.I.J., Ser. A, no. 9, p. 21. This is quoted in part in the advisory opinion in the *Reparation* case, I.C.J. Reports (1949), p. 184; Green, p. 146.

[6] (1928), P.C.I.J., Ser. A, no. 17, p. 29; Green, p. 607. See also ibid., pp. 27, 47; the *Peace Treaties* case, I.C.J. Reports (1950), p. 228; and *Phosphates in Morocco* (Preliminary Objections) (1938), P.C.I.J., Ser. A/B, no. 74, p. 28.

[7] *Supra*, n. 5.

tion is the indispensable complement of a failure to apply a convention, and there is no necessity for this to be stated in the convention itself.

The *Corfu Channel* case involved a finding that Albania was liable for the consequences of a mine-laying in her territorial waters and the absence of a warning of the danger:[1] 'These grave omissions involve the international responsibility of Albania. The Court therefore reaches the conclusion that Albania is responsible under international law for the explosions which occurred . . . and for the damage and loss of human life which resulted from them, and that there is a duty upon Albania to pay compensation to the United Kingdom.'

These pronouncements show that there is no acceptance of a contract and delict (tort) dichotomy. However, the emphasis on the duty to make reparation does present a broad concept akin to civil wrongs in municipal systems. The law of claims is of course *in personam* in its operation, and parties may waive their claims. However, the idea of reparation does not always work well, and tends to give too restrictive a view of the legal interests protected and the *locus standi* of plaintiffs.[2] The duty to pay compensation is a normal consequence of responsibility, but is not coterminous with it.

In general, broad formulae on state responsibility are unhelpful and, when they suggest municipal analogies, a source of confusion. Thus it is often said that responsibility only arises when the act or omission complained of is *imputable* to a state.[3] Imputability would seem to be a superfluous notion, since the major issue in a given situation is whether there has been a breach of duty: the content of 'imputability' will vary according to the particular duty, the nature of the breach, and so on.[4] Imputability implies a fiction where there is none, and conjures up the idea of vicarious liability where it cannot apply. Unhappily Oppenheim[5] draws a distinction between original and vicarious state responsibility. Original responsibility flows from acts committed by, or with authorization of, the government of a state; vicarious responsibility flows from unauthorized acts of the agents of the state, or nationals, and of aliens living

[1] I.C.J. Reports (1949), p. 23. See *infra*, p. 441, on the main aspects of the case.

[2] See further *infra*, pp. 457, 466.

[3] See e.g. Sørensen, op. cit., p. 223. The writers use the term in several senses: cf. Kelsen, *Principles of International Law*, pp. 119–20 (2nd ed.), p. 199; Anzilotti, 13 *R.G.D.I.P.* (1906), 291; Accioly, op. cit., pp. 358–9. See also Reuter, op. cit., pp. 602–4.

[4] See *infra*, pp. 435 seq. See also Quadri, 113 Hague *Recueil*, pp. 457–9.

[5] i. 337–8, 341. See further Kelsen, op. cit. (2nd ed.), pp. 119–200.

within the territory of the state. It is to be admitted that the legal consequences of the two categories of acts may not be the same; but there is no fundamental difference between the two categories, and, in any case, the use of 'vicarious responsibility' here is surely erroneous.

3. *Boundaries of Responsibility*

In general.[1] It is intended to consider available defences subsequently,[2] although of course the use of the category 'defence' may be rather arbitrary, involving assumptions about the incidence of the burden of proof on particular issues. When the general problem is approached, the impression received is that those general principles which may be extracted are too general to be of practical value, a quality which belongs to general principles offered in books on the English law of tort and crime. Thus in principle an act or omission which produces a result which is on its face a breach of a legal obligation gives rise to responsibility in international law, whether the obligation rests on treaty, custom, or some other basis.[3] However, many rules prescribe the 'actus reus' without being very explicit about the 'mental state', or degree of advertence, required from the state organs involved. This is a common fault even in the case of the nominate torts of English law,[4] and many of our criminal statutes use question-begging terms like 'knowingly'.[5] Moreover, the issues in inter-state relations are often analogous to those arising from the activities of employees and enterprises in English law, where the legal person held liable is incapable of close control over its agents and rules employing metaphors based on the intention (*dolus*)[6] or negligence (*culpa*)[7] of natural persons tend to be unhelpful. In some cases it is *relationship* rather than fault in the ordinary sense which is held to justify liability. Thus in international law objective tests are usually employed to determine responsibility, although of course it can happen that governments, as groups of morally responsible *natural* persons, are capable of proven *dolus* or *culpa*. Moreover, in certain types of case, *dolus* and *culpa* have a special role to play.[8]

[1] See Judge Azevedo, I.C.J. Reports (1949), pp. 82 seq.; Schwarzenberger, op. cit., pp. 581–93. [2] *Infra*, pp. 464–6. [3] See *infra*, p. 634, on unilateral acts.

[4] The meaning of intention in the law of tort remains to some extent mysterious, and an observer using criminal law methods of analysis would find many questions unanswered in trespass and conversion.

[5] See Glanville Williams, *Criminal Law* (2nd ed.), pp. 140 seq.; Edwards, *Mens Rea in Statutory Offences*.

[6] See *infra*, p. 440. [7] See *infra*, p. 439. [8] See *infra*, p. 440.

4. *Objective Responsibility*

Technically, objective responsibility rests on the doctrine of the voluntary act: provided that agency and causal connexion are established, there is a breach of duty by result alone. Defences, such as act of third party, are available, but the defendant has to exculpate himself.[1] In the conditions of international life, which involve relations between highly complex communities, acting through a variety of institutions and agencies, the public law analogy of the *ultra vires* act is more realistic than a seeking for subjective *culpa* in specific natural persons who may, or may not, 'represent' the legal person (the state) in terms of wrongdoing.[2] Where, for example, an officer in charge of a cruiser on the high seas orders the boarding of a fishing vessel flying another flag, there being no legal justification for the operation, and the act being in excess of his authority, a tribunal will not regard pleas that the acts were done in good faith, or under a mistake of law, with any favour.[3] Moreover, in municipal systems of law, the precise mode of applying a *culpa* doctrine, especially in the matter of assigning the burden of proof, may result in a regime of objective responsibility.

It is believed that the practice of states and the jurisprudence of arbitral tribunals and the International Court have followed the theory of objective responsibility[4] as a general principle (which may be modified or excluded in certain cases). Objective tests of responsibility were employed by the General Claims Commission set up by a Convention between Mexico and the United States in 1923 in the well-known *Neer*[5] and *Roberts*[6] claims, and in the *Caire* claim,[7] Verzijl, President of the Franco-Mexican Claims Commission, applied

the doctrine of the objective responsibility of the State, that is to say, a

[1] See Judge Azevedo, I.C.J. Reports (1949), pp. 85–6.

[2] Attention may also be drawn to the vicarious liability (if it is correctly so-called) of the employer in English law for the acts of employees in many cases where the employer's liability can hardly rest on personal fault *a fortiori* if the employer is a corporation.

[3] See the *Jessie* (1921), *R.I.A.A.* vi. 57; the *Wanderer* (1921), ibid. 68; the *Kate* (1921), ibid. 77; the *Favourite* (1921), ibid. 82.

[4] See Borchard, 1 *Z.a.ö. R.u.V.* (1929), p. 223 at pp. 224–5; Schwarzenberger, *International Law* i. (3rd ed.), 632–41; Guggenheim ii. 52; Starke, 19 *B.Y.* (1938), 115; Basdevant, 58 Hague *Recueil* (1936, IV), 670–5; Cheng, *General Principles of Law*, pp. 218–32 (very helpful). See further Meron, 33 *B.Y.* (1957), p. 85, at pp. 93 seq.; and *infra*, p. 449.

[5] (1926), *R.I.A.A.* iv, p. 60 at pp. 61–2; Briggs, p. 613.

[6] (1926), *R.I.A.A.* iv, p. 77 at p. 80; Briggs, p. 549.

[7] (1929), *R.I.A.A.* v, p. 516 at pp. 529–31; Green, p. 650.

responsibility for those acts committed by its officials or its organs, and which they are bound to perform, despite the absence of *faute* on their part... The State also bears an international responsibility for all acts committed by its officials or its organs which are delictual according to international law, regardless of whether the official organ has acted within the limits of his competency or has exceeded those limits... However, in order to justify the admission of this objective responsibility of the State for acts committed by its officials or organs outside their competence, it is necessary that they should have acted, at least apparently, as authorised officials or organs, or that, in acting, they should have used powers or measures appropriate to their official character...

A considerable number of writers support this point of view, either explicitly,[1] or implicitly, by considering the questions of imputability, causation, and legal excuses without adverting to the question of *culpa* and *dolus*.[2] At the same time certain eminent opinions have supported the Grotian view that *culpa* or *dolus malus* provide the proper basis of state responsibility in all cases.[3] A small number of arbitral awards[4] give some support to the *culpa* doctrine: for example, in the *Home Missionary Society* case[5] the tribunal referred to a 'well-established principle of international law that no government can be held responsible for the act of rebellious bodies of men committed in violation of its authority, where it is itself guilty of no breach of good faith, or of no negligence in suppressing insurrection'. However, many of the awards cited in this connexion are concerned with the standard of conduct required by the law *in a particular context*, for example claims for losses caused by acts of rebellion,

[1] See *supra*, p. 436, n. 4. See also Anzilotti, 13 *R.G.D.I.P.* (1906), 14; *Opere* ii (i), 180 seq.

[2] See Sibert, *Traité* i. 309 seq.; and García Amador, Rapporteur, *Yrbk., I.L.C.* (1956), ii. 186; ibid. (1957), ii. 106.

[3] See Oppenheim i. 343 (also in 1st ed.); Lauterpacht, 62 Hague *Recueil* (1937, IV), 359–64; id., *Private Law Sources and Analogies*, pp. 134–43; Eagleton, *The Responsibility of States in International Law*, p. 209; Verdross, *Völkerrecht*, 5th ed., p. 377; Ago, 68 Hague *Recueil* (1939, II), 498. See also Accioly, op. cit., pp. 364–70, for an enumeration of the writers.

[4] Cases cited in this connexion are: the *Casablanca* case (1909), Hague Court Reports i. 110; *R.I.A.A.* xi. 119: *Cadenhead* (1914), 8 *A.J.* (1914), 663; *Iloilo* claims (1925), *R.I.A.A.* vi. 158, 160; *Pugh* claim (1933), *R.I.A.A.* iii. 1439; *Award on the Wal-Wal Incident* (1935), *R.I.A.A.* iii. 1657 (but see Schwarzenberger, op. cit., pp. 636–7). See also the *Davis* case (1903), *R.I.A.A.* ix. 460, 463; *Salas* case, ibid. x. 720.

[5] (1920), *R.I.A.A.* vi, p. 42 at p. 44. During a rebellion in the Protectorate of Sierra Leone the Home Missionary Society, an American religious body, suffered losses. The United States alleged that in the face of a crisis the British Government failed to take the proper steps for the maintenance of order and that the loss of life and damage was the result of this neglect and failure of duty. The claim was dismissed because (1) there was no failure of duty on the facts; (2) there had been an assumption of risk.

of private individuals, of the judiciary, and so on.[1] Thus in the *Chattin* claim[2] the General Claims Commission described the judicial proceedings in Mexico against Chattin as 'being highly insufficient' and referred, *inter alia*, to 'an unsufficiency of governmental action recognizable by every unbiased man'. Chattin had been convicted on a charge of embezzlement and sentenced by the Mexican court to two years' imprisonment. The Commission referred to various defects in the conduct of the trial and remarked that 'the whole of the proceedings discloses a most astonishing lack of seriousness on the part of the Court'. Furthermore, both writers[3] and tribunals[4] may use the words *faute* or fault to mean a breach of legal duty, an unlawful act. *Culpa*, in the sense of culpable negligence, will be relevant when its presence is demanded by a particular rule of law. Objective responsibility would seem to come nearer to being a *general* principle, and provides a better basis for maintaining good standards in international relations and for effectively upholding the principle of reparation.

The proposition that the type of advertence required varies with the legal context provides an introduction to the judgment of the International Court in the *Corfu Channel* case,[5] which is considered by Hersch Lauterpacht[6] to contain an affirmation of the *culpa* doctrine. In fact the Court was concerned with the particular question of *responsibility* for the creation of danger in the North Corfu Channel by the laying of mines, warning of which was not given. The basis of responsibility was Albania's knowledge of the laying of mines.[7] The Court considered 'whether it has been established by means of indirect evidence that Albania has knowledge of mine-laying in her territorial waters independently of any connivance on her part in this operation'. Later on it concluded that the laying of the minefield 'could not

[1] See *infra*, pp. 445 seq.

[2] (1927), *R.I.A.A.* iv. 282; Briggs, p. 666; Bishop, p. 753; Green, p. 645. See also Huber, Rapporteur, *Spanish Zone of Morocco* claims, *R.I.A.A.* ii. 644–6.

[3] See Accioly, op. cit., pp. 369–70.

[4] See the *Prats* case (1868), Moore, *Arbitrations* iii, p. 2886 at pp. 2894–5; *Russian Indemnity* case (1912), Hague Court Reports i, p. 532 at p. 543. See further Cheng, loc. cit.

[5] I.C.J. Reports (1949), p. 4. See further *infra*, p. 441.

[6] See Oppenheim i. 343, referring to I.C.J. Reports (1949), p. 18. And cf. Lauterpacht, *The Development of International Law by the International Court*, p. 88. See also *Répertoire suisse* iii. 1695.

[7] See García Amador, 94 Hague *Recueil* (1958, II), 387; id., *Yrbk., I.L.C.* (1960), ii. 62–3; Schwarzenberger, *International Law* (3rd ed.), i. 632–4; Cheng, *General Principles of Law*, pp. 231–2; Jiménez de Aréchaga, in Sørensen (ed.), *Manual*, p. 537; id., *Yrbk., I.L.C.* (1963), ii. 236. Judge Badawi, dissenting, supported a doctrine of fault which was in fact based on the notion of the unlawful, voluntary, act: I.C.J. Reports (1949), pp. 65–6.

have been accomplished without the knowledge of the Albanian Government' and referred to 'every State's obligation not to allow knowingly its territory to be used for acts contrary to the rights of other States'.[1] Liability thus rested upon violation of a particular legal duty. The use of circumstantial evidence to establish Albania's knowledge does not alter the fact that knowledge was a condition of responsibility. The Court was not concerned with *culpa* or *dolus* as such, and it fell to Judge Krylov[2] and Judge *ad hoc* Ečer[3] to affirm the doctrine of *culpa*.

5. *Culpa*

The term *culpa* is used to describe types of blameworthiness based upon reasonable foreseeability, or foresight without desire of consequences (recklessness, *culpa lata*). Although *culpa* is not a general condition of liability, it may play an important role in certain contexts. Thus where the loss complained of results from acts of individuals not employed by the state, or from activities of licensees or trespassers on the territory of the state, the responsibility of the state will depend on an unlawful omission. In this type of case questions of knowledge may be relevant in establishing the omission or, more properly, responsibility for failure to act. This type of relevance goes to the *actus reus*, as it were, and is not necessarily related to the *culpa* principle.[4] However, tribunals may set standards of 'due diligence' and the like, in respect of the activities, or failures to act, of particular organs of state.[5] Thus the 'subjective element' constitutes the type of duty, the actual object of imputation. In effect, since looking for specific evidence of a lack of proper care on the part of state organs is often a fruitless task, the issue becomes one of causation.[6] In the *Lighthouses* arbitration[7] between France and Greece one of the claims arose from the eviction of a French firm from their offices in Salonika and the subsequent loss of their stores in a fire which destroyed the temporary premises. The Permanent Court of Arbitration said:

> Even if one were inclined . . . to hold that Greece is in principle responsible for the consequences of that evacuation, one could not . . . admit a

[1] I.C.J. Reports (1949), pp. 18, 22.
[2] Ibid., pp. 71–2, quoting Oppenheim (7th ed.), i. 311.
[3] I.C.J. Reports (1949), pp. 127–8, also quoting Oppenheim.
[4] Cf. the *Corfu Channel* case, *supra*, p. 425. See also Lévy, 65 *R.G.D.I.P.* (1961), 744–64.
[5] See generally *infra*, pp. 445 *seq.*
[6] García Amador, *Yrbk., I.L.C.* (1960), ii. 63.
[7] *R.I.A.A.* xii. 217–18; Int. L.R. 23 (1956), 352–3.

causal relationship between the damage caused by the fire, on the one part, and that following on the evacuation, on the other, so as to justify holding Greece liable for the disastrous effects of the fire . . . The damage was neither a foreseeable nor a normal consequence of the evacuation, nor attributable to any want of care on the part of Greece. All causal connection is lacking, and in those circumstances Claim No. 19 must be rejected.

In any case, as Judge Azevedo pointed out in his dissenting opinion in the *Corfu Channel* case,[1] the relations of objective responsibility and the *culpa* principle are very close:[2] the effect, at least, of the judgment was to place Albania under a duty to take reasonable care to discover activities of trespassers.[3]

When a state engages in lawful activities, responsibility may be generated by *culpa* in the execution of the lawful measures.[4] The existence and extent of *culpa* may effect the measure of damages,[5] and, of course, due diligence, or liability for *faute* or *culpa*, may be stipulated for in treaty provisions.

6. *Intention and Motive*

The fact that an *ultra vires* act of an official is accompanied by malice on his part, i.e. an intention to cause harm, without regard to whether or not the law permits the act, does not affect the responsibility of his state.[6] Indeed, the principle of objective responsibility dictates the irrelevance of intention to harm, *dolus*, as a condition of liability: and yet general propositions of this sort should not lead to the conclusion that *dolus* cannot play a significant role in the law. Proof of *dolus* on the part of leading organs of the state will solve the problem of 'imputability' in the given case, and, in any case, the existence of a deliberate intent to injure may have an effect on remoteness of damage as well as helping to

[1] I.C.J Reports (1949), p. 85.

[2] See García Amador, *ubi supra*, p. 63.

[3] Cf. *Sedleigh-Denfield* v. *O'Callaghan* [1940] A.C. 880, a nuisance case in which it was emphasized by their Lordships that liability was not based on negligence.

[4] e.g. of sequestration of Italian property in Tunisia by the French Government after the defeat of Italy: *In re Rizzo*, Int. L.R. 22 (1955), p. 317 at p. 322. The Conciliation Commission said: 'the act contrary to international law is not the measure of sequestration, but an alleged lack of diligence on the part of the French State—or, more precisely, of him who was acting on its behalf—in the execution of the said measure . . .'. See also the *Ousset* claim, ibid., p. 312 at p. 314; the *Philadelphia-Girard National Bank* case (1929), *R.I.A.A.* viii. 67, 69; and *Yrbk., I.L.C.* (1969), ii. 103 (paras. 6–8).

[5] See the cases of *Janes* (1926), *R.I.A.A.* iv. 82; Briggs, p. 605; Bishop, p. 771; *Baldwin* (1842), Moore, *Arbitrations* iv. 3235; and *Rau* (1930), Whiteman, *Damages in International Law*, p. 26.

[6] e.g. *Baldwin* (1842), Moore, *Arbitrations* iv. 3235; Meron, 33 *B.Y.* (1957), 95–6.

establish the breach of duty.[1] Malice may justify the award of 'penal' damages.[2]

Motive and intention are frequently a specific element in the definition of permitted conduct. Thus the rule is stated that expropriation of foreign property is unlawful if the object is that of political reprisal or retaliation.[3] Again, action ostensibly in collective defence against an aggressor will cease to be lawful if the state concerned in the action is proved to be intent on using the operation for purposes of annexation.[4] Similarly, where conduct on its face unlawful is sought to be justified on the grounds of necessity or self-defence,[5] the intention of the actor is important, since it may remove all basis for the defences.[6] Difficulty may arise in many cases where states have legal powers not conditioned by the existence of particular motives for their exercise: if such powers are used in such a way as to cause damage to another state, or to disregard human rights, is the conduct involved rendered illegal? This raises the question of abuse of rights, which is pursued later.[7]

7. *The Individuality of Issues: the* Corfu Channel *Case*

At this stage it is perhaps necessary to stress that over-simplification of the problems, and too much reliance on general propositions about objective responsibility, *culpa*, and intention, can result in a lack of finesse in approaching particular issues. Legal issues, particularly in disputes between states, have an individuality which resists a facile application of general rules. Much depends on the assignment of the burden of proof, the operation of principles of the law of evidence, the existence of acquiescence and estoppels, the nature of the *compromis*, and the precise nature of the relevant substantive rules or treaty provisions. This note of caution can be justified by reference to the *Lotus*,[8] *Corfu Channel*,[9] and *Fisheries*[1] cases in the International Court.

The most interesting of these is perhaps the *Corfu Channel*

[1] *Dix* case, *R.I.A.A.* ix, p. 119, at p. 121; cf. *Monnot* vase, ibid., p. 232, at p. 233.

[2] See *infra*, pp. 459, 463. [3] See *infra*, pp. 538–9.

[4] See Brownlie, *International Law and the Use by Force by States*, pp. 408–9. See also *supra*, p. 203, on innocent passage through the territorial sea.

[5] See *infra*, p. 465.

[6] Of course, action in good faith is not necessarily justified by reason of the mistake as to necessity for action.

[7] pp. 443–5. [8] *Supra*, pp. 255, 301.

[9] I.C.J. Reports (1949), p. 4. [1] *Infra*, pp. 186 seq.

case.[1] The approach adopted by the majority of the Court fails to correspond neatly with either the *culpa* doctrine or the test of objective responsibility. 'Intention' is a question-begging category and appears in the case only in specialist roles. Thus, in the case of the British passage 'designed to affirm a right which had been unjustly denied' by Albania, much turned on the nature of the passage.[2] Taking all the circumstances into account, the Court held that the passage of two cruisers and two destroyers, through a part of the North Corfu Channel constituting Albanian territorial waters, was an innocent passage. As to the laying of the mines which damaged the destroyers *Saumarez* and *Volage*, the Court looked for evidence of knowledge of this on the part of Albania. The case also illustrates the interaction of the principles of proof and responsibility. The Court said:[3]

> ... it cannot be concluded from the mere fact of the control exercised by a State over its territory and waters that that State necessarily knew, or ought to have known, of any unlawful act perpetrated therein, nor yet that it necessarily knew, or should have known, the authors. This fact, by itself and apart from other circumstances, neither involves *prima facie* responsibility nor shifts the burden of proof.
>
> On the other hand, the fact of this exclusive territorial control exercised by a State within its frontiers has a bearing upon the methods of proof available to establish the knowledge of that State as to such events. By reason of this exclusive control, the other State, the victim of a breach of international law, is often unable to furnish direct proof of facts giving rise to responsibility. Such a State should be allowed a more liberal recourse to inferences of fact and circumstantial evidence ...
>
> The Court must examine therefore whether it has been established by means of indirect evidence that Albania has knowledge of mine-laying in her territorial waters independently of any connivance on her part in this operation. The proof may be drawn from inferences of fact, provided they leave *no room* for reasonable doubt. The elements of fact on which these inferences can be based may differ from those which are relevant to the question of connivance.

The decision raises another issue. At the time of the British mission 'designed to affirm a right', there had been no finding that the North Corfu Channel was an 'international strait',[4] and the question of passage for warships through the territorial

[1] See generally Brownlie, *International Law and the Use of Force by States*, pp. 283–9; Wilhelm, 15 *Annuaire suisse* (1958), 116–30.

[2] I.C.J Reports (1949), p. 30. The right was that of passage through an international strait: see ibid., pp. 28–30.

[3] p. 18. [4] See *supra*, p. 281.

sea, whether or not forming part of such a strait, was controversial. No attempt at peaceful settlement had been made, and the naval mission was an affirmation of what were, at the time, only *putative* rights.[1] Against this it could be said that Albania, by her policy of exclusion, supported on a previous occasion by fire from coastal batteries, had also adopted an *ex parte* view of her right to exclude warships. However, it is possible that in such a case there is a presumption in favour of the right of the coastal state; and, in any case, the British action on 22 October remained nonetheless a forcible affirmation of *putative* rights. The better course would have been to regard the naval mission as illegal,[2] and to consider whether the laying of mines without warning was a legal means of dealing with trespassers even for a small state with no navy of its own. It is probable that the nature of the *compromis* prevented such an approach, which would have avoided the necessity of holding that the naval mission was involved in an innocent passage as well as the Court's unhappy assimilation of putative rights and legal rights, in a dispute which in part concerned the law applicable.

8. *Liability for Lawful Acts. Abuse of Rights*

It may happen that a rule provides for compensation for the consequences of acts which are not unlawful in the sense of being prohibited.[3] Thus, in the Convention on the High Seas of 1958, Article 22 provides for the boarding of foreign merchant ships by warships where there is reasonable ground for suspecting piracy and certain other activities. Paragraph 3 then provides: 'If the suspicions prove to be unfounded, and provided that the ship boarded has not committed any act justifying them, it shall be compensated for any loss or damage that may have been sustained.' One is reminded here of the doctrine of incomplete privilege.[4]

Several systems of law know the doctrine of abuse of rights,[5]

[1] The status of the North Corfu Channel was very doubtful: see Brüel, *Festschrift für Rudolf Laun* (1953), p. 259 at pp. 273, 276.

[2] See the dissenting opinions of Judges Azevedo, I.C.J. Reports (1949), p. 109; and Krylov, ibid., p. 75. Self-help remains self-help whichever view of the law on the subject of the action is subsequently upheld.

[3] See Sørensen, 101 Hague *Recueil* (1960, III), 221–3; Quadri, 113 Hague *Recueil*, pp. 461–5.

[4] See *infra*, pp. 465–6.

[5] See Gutteridge, 5 *Camb. L.J.* (1933), 22–45; Lawson, *Negligence in the Civil Law*, pp. 15–20. See further the decision of the I.L.O. Admin. Trib. in *McIntire* v. *F.A.O.* (1954), Int. L.R. 21 (1954), 356.

exemplified by Article 1912 of the Mexican Civil Code:[1] 'When damage is caused to another by the exercise of a right, there is an obligation to make it good if it is proved that the right was exercised only in order to cause the damage, without any advantage to the person entitled to the right.' This doctrine[2] has had limited support from the dicta of international tribunals.[3] In the case concerning *Certain German Interests in Polish Upper Silesia*[4] it was held that, after the peace treaty came into force and until the transfer of sovereignty over Upper Silesia, the right to dispose of state property in the territory remained with Germany. Alienation would constitute a breach of her obligations if there was 'a misuse[5] of this right'. In the view of the Court German policy amounted to no more than the normal administration of public property. In the *Free Zones* case the Court held that French fiscal legislation applied in the free zones (which were in French territory), but that 'a reservation must be made as regards the case of abuse of a right, an abuse which, however, cannot be presumed by the Court'.[6] It is not unreasonable to regard the principle of abuse of rights as a general principle of law.[7] However, whilst it is easy to sympathize with exponents of the doctrine, the delimitation of its function is a matter of delicacy. After considering the work of the International Court, Lauterpacht observes:[8]

[1] Cf. Art. 226 of the German civil code.

[2] Generally, on abuse of rights in international law, see Oppenheim i. 345–7; Lauterpacht, *The Function of Law in the International Community*, pp. 286–306; id., *The Development of International Law by the International Court*, pp. 162–5; Schwarzenberger, *International Law and Order*, 84–109; also in 42 *Grot. Soc.* (1956), 147–79; Cheng, *General Principles of Law*, pp. 121–36; Politis, 6 Hague *Recueil* (1925, I), 1–109; García Amador, 94 Hague *Recueil* (1958, II), 377–82; id., *Yrbk., I.L.C.* (1960), ii. 58–60; Guggenheim, 74 Hague *Recueil* (1949, I), 249–54; Kiss, *L'Abus de droit en droit international* (1953); Fitzmaurice, 27 *B.Y.* (1950), 12–14; 30 *B.Y.* (1953), 53–4; 35 *B.Y.* (1959), 210–16; Whiteman v. 224–30; Ago, Second Report, U.N. Doc. A/CN.4/233, paras. 48, 49; Iluyomade, 16 *Harv. Int. L.J.* (1975), 47–92; Taylor, 46 *B.Y.* (1972–3), 323–52; Goodwin-Gill, 47 *B.Y.* (1974–5), 79–86, 154–5.

[3] Citations often involve *ex post facto* recruitment of arbitral awards, e.g. the *Portendick* claim (1843), Lapradelle and Politis i. 512, and the collection of references to the principle of good faith. See also *Yrbk., I.L.C.* (1953), ii. 219, para. 100.

[4] (1926), P.C.I.J., Ser. A, no. 7, p. 30; Green, p. 533.

[5] The Court said: 'Such misuse cannot be presumed, and it rests with the party who states that there has been such misuse to prove his statement.'

[6] (1930), P.C.I.J., Ser. A, no. 24, p. 12. See also *Free Zones* case (1932), P.C.I.J., Ser. A/B, no. 46, p. 167; Green, p. 741. References in separate and dissenting opinions are as follows: I.C.J. Reports (1948), pp. 79, 80; ibid. (1955), p. 120. Cf. Judge Anzilotti, *Electricity Company of Sofia* case (1939), P.C.I.J., Ser. A/B, no. 77, p. 98. A constant exponent of the doctrine was Judge Alvarez: I.C.J. Reports (1949), p. 47; ibid. (1950), p. 15; ibid. (1951), pp. 149 seq.; ibid. (1952), pp. 128–33.

[7] See Cheng and Lauterpacht, cited, note 2, *supra*. See also Kiss, op. cit., pp. 193–6 (a general principle of international law).

[8] *The Development of International Law by the International Court*, p. 164. See also

> These are but modest beginnings of a doctrine which is full of potentialities and which places a considerable power, not devoid of a legislative character, in the hands of a judicial tribunal. There is no legal right, however well established, which could not, in some circumstances, be refused recognition on the ground that it has been abused. The doctrine of abuse of rights is therefore an instrument which . . . must be wielded with studied restraint.

In some cases the doctrine explains the genesis of a rule of existing law, for example the principle that no state has a right to use or permit the use of its territory in such a manner as to cause injury by fumes to the territory of another.[1] Often it represents a plea for legislation or, which is nearly the same thing, the modification of rules to suit special circumstances. In general what is involved is the determination of the qualities of a particular category of permitted acts: is the power or privilege dependent on the presence of certain objectives? The presumption in the case of acts *prima facie* legal is that motive is irrelevant: but the law may provide otherwise. When the criteria of good faith, reasonableness, normal administration, and so on are provided by an existing legal rule, reference to 'abuse of rights' adds nothing. Similarly, in the case of international organizations, responsibility for excess of authority, *détournement de pouvoir*,[2] exists independently of any general principle of abuse of rights. In conclusion it may be said that the doctrine is a useful agent in the progressive development of the law, but that, as a general principle, it does not exist in positive law. Indeed it is doubtful if it could be safely recognized as an ambulatory doctrine, since it would encourage doctrines as to the relativity of rights[3] and result, outside the judicial forum, in instability.

9. *Responsibility for the Acts of State Organs, Officials, Revolutionaries, and Others*

(a) *General aspects*. The subject of state responsibility suffers from too much categorization. The question of liability of the legal person, the state, is overlaid by categories of imputability,[4]

Schwarzenberger, 42 *Grot. Soc.* (1956). 147–79; Verzijl, *International Law in Historical Perspective*, i. 316–20.

[1] See the *Trail Smelter* arbitration (1941), *Ann. Digest* (1938–40), no. 104; *R.I.A.A.* iii. 1905. See also the *Corfu Channel* case, *supra*, p. 441.

[2] See Fawcett, 33 *B.Y.* (1957), 311–16; Valentine, 35 *B.Y.* (1959), 174–222. On the logically distinct question of *ultra vires* acts by international organizations, *infra*, p. 698; and by state organs, *infra*, p. 449.

[3] Cf. Bowett's views discussed *supra*, p. 147, n. 6.

[4] See *supra*, p. 434.

direct and indirect responsibility, and of responsibility for acts of special groups, viz., state organs,[1] revolutionaries, and individuals. Strictly, every breach of duty on the part of states must arise by reason of the act or omission of one or more of the organs of state, and, since in many contexts the principle of objective responsibility applies, the emphasis is on causal connexion and the 'conduct appropriate' to the given situation. 'Liability for the acts of State organs, etc.' is coextensive with the whole range of legal duties, and yet the categories are commonly employed solely in connexion with special problems of the responsibility of states for harm to resident aliens.[2] The association of propositions with a particular area of delict is unfortunate, since the nature of the harm determines the extent of liability for the acts and omissions of organs and individuals. Standards of conduct may be relatively strict in the case of foreign diplomatic and consular agents[3] present on state territory or harms caused by armed forces[4] or explosives[5] within the territory to the interests of a foreign state, but less strict elsewhere. The presence of *dolus* may affect the nature of causation in a given case.[6] Particular rules and fact situations are more important than general propositions about responsibility for the acts of the judiciary or other categories of official: the categories provide only very general guidance.[7] Thus there may be responsibility for *ultra vires* acts of officials[8] and yet no responsibility for the acts of an official, acting with apparent authority, proved to have acted under the orders of a foreign power. Many cases provide nothing more than examples of the standard of conduct required. The status of the individual actor is only a factor in establishing 'imputability', or causal connexion between the corporate entity of the state and the harm done.

In some cases the categories of 'tortfeasor' provide no help at all. In the *Corfu Channel* case[9] Albania was held responsible for the consequences of mine-laying in her territorial waters by

[1] And further, special treatment of the legislative, executive, judiciary, military forces, officials generally, and *ultra vires* acts of officials.

[2] See further Chapter XXIII. This association in the literature of the subject is less justified today when other topics, for example the law concerning the use or threat of force, and the development of weapons, have at least an equal claim to special treatment.

[3] See the *Chapman* claim (1930), *R.I.A.A.* iv. 632; Briggs, p. 697; 8 *Canad. Yrbk.* (1970), 355–6; Cole, 41 *B.Y.* (1967), at pp. 390–2.

[4] But see *infra*, pp. 452, 465, on civil and international war.

[5] See the *Corfu Channel* case, *supra*, pp. 438, 441.

[6] *Supra*, p. 440.

[7] Cf. the treatment in McNair, *Opinions* ii. 207 seq., Oppenheim i. 357–69; and Schwarzenberger, *International Law* (3rd ed.), i. 613–31 (the most judicious treatment).

[8] *Infra*, p. 449.

[9] *Supra*, p. 441.

reason of the knowledge by the Albanian authorities of the presence of the mines. There was no finding as to the agency which did the mine-laying, and it was possible that a third state was involved. Similarly, a neutral state may be responsible for allowing armed expeditions to be fitted out within its jurisdiction which subsequently carry out belligerent operations against another state.[1] With these extensive reservations, attention may be directed to the problems associated with particular categories of organs and persons.

(b) *State organs*[2]

(i) *Executive and administration.*[3] In the *Massey Claim*[4] the United States recovered an award of 15,000 dollars by reason of the failure of the Mexican authorities to take adequate measures to punish the killer of Massey, a United States citizen working in Mexico. The opinion of Commissioner Nielsen stated:[5] 'I believe that it is undoubtedly a sound general principle that, whenever misconduct on the part of [persons in state service], whatever may be their particular status or rank under domestic law, results in the failure of a nation to perform its obligations under international law, the nation must bear the responsibility for the wrongful acts of its servants.' Unreasonable acts of violence by police officers and a failure to take the appropriate steps to punish the culprits will also give rise to responsibility.[6] Except for the operation of the local remedies rule,[7] the distinction between higher and lower officials has no significance for the placing of responsibility on the state.[8] In each case it will be for the relevant rule of law applied to the particular facts to establish whether responsibility flows from the act of the official as such or from the insufficiency of the measures taken by other organs to deal with the consequences of the act of the official.

[1] See the *Alabama* arbitration (1872), Moore, *Arbitrations* i. 653; Green, p. 27; Briggs, p. 1026.

[2] On the acts of heads of states, members of governments, and diplomatic envoys see Oppenheim i. 358–9.

[3] See García Amador, 94 Hague *Recueil* (1958, II), 403; id., *Yrbk., I.L.C.* (1956), ii. 187; ibid. (1957), ii. 107, 109; Accioly, 96 Hague *Recueil* (1959, I), 373, 392–4; McNair, *Opinions* ii. 207–19; Schwarzenberger, *International Law* (3rd ed.), i. 615–18; Whiteman vii. 807–19.

[4] (1927), *R.I.A.A.* iv. 155; Briggs, p. 680. The claim was brought on behalf of the widow individually and as guardian of two minor children of herself and Massey. See also the *Way* claim (1928), *R.I.A.A.* iv. 391.

[5] Ibid., at p. 159.

[6] *Roper* claim (1927), *R.I.A.A.* iv. 145; *Pugh* claim (1933), *R.I.A.A.* ii. 1439.

[7] On which see *infra*, p. 495.

[8] See the *Massey* claim and *Way* claim, *ubi supra*; Schwarzenberger, op. cit., pp. 617–618; Briggs, p. 697. For another opinion: Borchard, *Diplomatic Protection of Citizens Abroad*, pp. 185–90 (but see Briggs' comment).

(ii) *Armed forces*. The same principles apply to this category of officials, but it is probably the case that a higher standard of prudence in their discipline and control is required, for reasons which are sufficiently obvious.[1] Commissioner Nielsen, in his opinion on the *Kling Claim*,[2] said: 'In cases of this kind it is mistaken action, error in judgment, or reckless conduct of soldiers for which a government in a given case has been held responsible. The international precedents reveal the application of principles as to the very strict accountability for mistaken action.'

(iii) *Federal units, provinces, and other internal divisions*.[3] A state cannot plead the principles of municipal law, including its constitution, in answer to an international claim.[4] Arbitral jurisprudence contains examples of the responsibility of federal states for acts of authorities of units of the federations.[5]

(iv) *The legislature*.[6] This organ is in normal circumstances a vital part of state organization and gives expression to official policies by its enactments. The problem specific to this category is to determine when the breach of duty entails responsibility. Commonly, in the case of injury to aliens, a claimant must establish damage consequent on the implementation of legislation or the omission to legislate.[7] However, it may happen that, particularly in the case of treaty obligations,[8] the acts and omissions of the legislature are without more creative of responsibility. If a

[1] See Huber in the *Spanish Zone of Morocco* claims (1925), *R.I.A.A.* ii, p. 617 at p. 645; Freeman, 88 Hague *Recueil* (1955, II), 285. Cf. the *Caire* case (1929), *R.I.A.A.* v, p. 516 at pp. 528–9. See also the *Chevreau* case (1931), *R.I.A.A.* ii. 1115; the *Naulilaa* case (1928), ibid., p. 1013; *Eis Claim*, Int. L.R. 30, p. 116; *García and Garza* case, *R.I.A.A.* iv. 119; Bishop, p. 764; and the report of a League of Nations Commission of Inquiry, 1925, for which see Conwell-Evans, *The League Council in Action*, pp. 155–60; Garner, 20 *A.J.* (1926), 337. See also Whiteman viii. 825–30.

[2] (1930), *R.I.A.A.* iv., p. 575 at p. 579; Briggs, p. 686 at p. 689.

[3] See Accioly, 96 Hague *Recueil* (1959, I), 388–91; Schwarzenberger, *International Law* i. (3rd ed.), 625–7; McNair, *Opinions* i. 36–7.

[4] *Supra*, pp. 36–7.

[5] *Youmans* claim (1926), *R.I.A.A.* iv. 110; Briggs, p. 705; *Mallén* claim (1927), *R.I.A.A.* iv. 173; Briggs, p. 823; Bishop, p. 767; *Pellat* claim (1929), *R.I.A.A.* v. 534. See also Rousseau, p. 358.

[6] See Sibert, 48 *R.G.D.I.P.* (1941–5), 5–34; García Amador, 94 Hague *Recueil* (1958, II), 401–2; id., *Yrbk., I.L.C.* (1956), ii. 182, 186; ibid. (1957), ii. 107, 108; Accioly, 96 Hague *Recueil* (1959, I), 374–5; McNair, *Opinions* ii. 219–21; Schwarzenberger, *International Law* (3rd ed.), i. 614–15; Fitzmaurice, 92 Hague *Recueil* (1957, II), 89–90; Rousseau, pp. 370–3; Briggs, pp. 695–6; Guggenheim ii. 7–9; Jiménez de Aréchaga, in Sørensen (ed.), *Manual*, pp. 544–6.

[7] See the *Mariposa* claim (1933), *R.I.A.A.* vi, p. 338 at pp. 340–1.

[8] Where, on a reasonable construction of the treaty, a breach creates a claim without special damage. In any case, representations may be made and steps to obtain redress, *quia timet* may be taken. On the Panama Canal Tolls controversy between Great Britain and the United States, see McNair, *Law of Treaties* (1961), pp. 547–50; Hackworth vi. 59.

treaty creates an obligation to incorporate certain rules in domestic law, failure to do so entails responsibility for breach of the treaty. Professor Schwarzenberger[1] observes:

> It is a matter for argument whether the mere existence of such legislation or only action under it constitutes the breach of an international obligation. Sufficient relevant *dicta* of the World Court exist to permit the conclusion that the mere existence of such legislation may constitute a sufficiently proximate threat of illegality to establish a claimant's legal interest in proceedings for at least a declaratory judgment.[2]

(v) *The judicature.*[3] The activity of judicial organs relates substantially to the rubric 'Denial of justice', which will be considered subsequently in Chapter XXIII on the treatment of aliens. However, it is important to bear in mind, what is perhaps obvious, that the doings of courts may affect the responsibility of the state of the forum in other ways.[4] Thus in respect of the application of treaties McNair[5] states: '. . . a State has a right to delegate to its judicial department the application and interpretation of treaties. If, however, the courts commit errors in that task or decline to give effect to the treaty or are unable to do so because the necessary change in, or addition to, the national law has not been made, their judgments involve the State in a breach of treaty.'

(vi) Ultra vires *acts of organs and officials.*[6] It has long been apparent in the sphere of domestic law that acts of public authorities which are *ultra vires* should not by that token create immunity from legal consequences. In international law there are other reasons for disregarding a plea of illegality under domestic law. Moreover, the lack of express authority cannot be decisive as to the responsibility of the state. Arbitral jurisprudence and the majority of writers support the rule that states may be responsible for *ultra vires* acts of their officials committed within their apparent authority or general scope of authority.[7] An act

[1] Op. cit., p. 614. [2] See ibid., pp. 604–5 and see *infra*, p. 458.

[3] On the category 'judicial officer' see the *Way* claim (1928), *R.I.A.A.* iv, p. 391 at p. 400. Generally see Jiménez de Aréchaga, in Friedmann, Henkin and Lissitzyn (eds.), *Transnational Law in a Changing Society* (1972), pp. 171–87.

[4] In 1941 the Supreme Court of Eire assumed jurisdiction over certain Latvian and Estonian vessels over which the Soviet Government claimed ownership. The Soviet Government regarded the judgment as illegal and held the Irish Government responsible. See the *Ramava* [1942] Ir. R. 148, 171; *Ann. Digest* 10 (1941–3), no. 20; and 75 *Irish L.T.* (1941), 215.

[5] *Law of Treaties* (1961), p. 346.

[6] See Meron, 33 *B.Y.* (1957), 85–114; García Amador, *Yrbk., I.L.C.* (1957), ii. 107, 109–10; Accioly, 96 Hague *Recueil* (1959, I), 360–3; Briggs, pp. 616–17; Guggenheim ii. 5–7; Anzilotti, *Cours* i. 470–4; Freeman, 88 Hague *Recueil*, 290–2; Quadri, 113 Hague *Recueil* (1964, III), 465–8; *Yrbk., I.L.C.* (1975) ii. 61–70.

[7] Meron, loc. cit; Jiménez de Aréchaga, in Sørensen, *Manual*, p. 548. See also the *Bases*

of arrest by a police officer, in fact carrying out a private policy of revenge, but seeming to act in the role of police officer to the average observer, would be within the category. The rule accords generally with a regime of objective responsibility.

In the *Union Bridge Company* case[1] a British official of the Cape Government Railways appropriated neutral (American) property during the Second Boer War, mistakenly believing it was not neutral: the tribunal considered that liability was not affected by the official's mistake or the lack of intention on the part of the British authorities to appropriate the material, stating that the conduct was within the general scope of duty of the official. In the *Caire Claim*[2] a captain and a major in the Conventionist forces in control of Mexico had demanded money from M. Caire under threat of death, and had then ordered the shooting of their victim when the money was not forthcoming. In holding Mexico responsible for this act, Verzijl, President of the Commission, said:

> The State also bears an international responsibility for all acts committed by its officials or its organs which are delictual according to international law, regardless of whether the official or organ has acted within the limits of his competency or has exceeded those limits . . . However, in order to justify the admission of this objective responsibility[3] of the State for acts committed by its officials or organs outside their competence, it is necessary that they should have acted, at least apparently, as authorized officials or organs, or that, in acting, they should have used powers or measures appropriate to their official character . . .

In the *Youmans* case[4] the Commission stated: 'Soldiers inflicting personal injuries or committing wanton destruction or looting always act in disobedience of some rules laid down by superior authority. There could be no liability whatever for such misdeeds if the view were taken that any acts committed by soldiers

of Discussion of the Conference for the Codification of International Law, 1930, for the views of governments and the proposals of the Preparatory Committee (see Meron, pp. 101–2). Basis no. 13 was adopted by the Third Committee of the Conference as Article 8 (2): 'International responsibility is . . . incurred by a State if damage is sustained by a foreigner as a result of unauthorized acts of its officials performed under cover of their official character, if the acts contravene the international obligations of the State. International responsibility is, however, not incurred by a State if the official's lack of authority was so apparent that the foreigner should have been aware of it, and could, in consequence, have avoided the damage.'

[1] (1924), *R.I.A.A.* vi. 138; 19 *A.J.* (1925), 215.

[2] (1929), *R.I.A.A.* v. p. 516, at p. 530; *Ann. Digest* 5 (1929–30), no. 91; Green, p. 650. For other examples of mistaken action see *supra*, p. 436.

[3] See *supra*, pp. 436 seq.

[4] (1926), *R.I.A.A.* iv, p. 110 at p. 116; 21 *A.J.* (1927), p. 571 at p. 578; Briggs, p. 705 at p. 711; *Ann. Digest* 3 (1925–6), no. 162.

in contravention of instructions must always be considered as personal acts.' It is not always easy to distinguish personal acts and acts within the scope of (apparent) authority. In the case of higher organs and officials the presumption will be that there was an act within the scope of authority.[1] Where the standard of conduct required is very high, as in the case of military leaders and cabinet ministers in relation to control of armed forces, it may be quite inappropriate to use the dichotomy of official and personal acts: here, as elsewhere,[2] much depends on the type of activity and the related consequences *in the particular case*.[3]

Students of the English rules as to the liability of employers for the torts of employees may well suspect that the concepts of 'apparent authority' and 'general scope of authority' are means to an end and are not to be examined too closely. It is not difficult to find cases in which the acts of state agents were clearly *ultra vires* and yet responsibility has been affirmed. *Youmans*[4] was such a case, where troops sent to protect aliens besieged by rioters joined in the attack, in which the aliens were killed. In some cases the decisions for responsibility may be buttressed by circumstances indicating negligence by superior officers. So in the *Zafiro*[5] the United States was held responsible for looting by the civilian crew of a merchant vessel employed as a supply vessel by American naval forces, under the command of a merchant captain who in turn was under the orders of an American naval officer. The tribunal emphasized the failure to exercise proper control in the circumstances.[6] What really matters, however, is the amount of control *which ought to have been exercised* in the particular circumstances, not the amount of actual control.[7]

[1] But see the *Bensley* case, Moore, *Arbitrations* iii. 3018 (responsibility denied for the personal act of the governor of a Mexican state). [2] See *supra*, pp. 434, 441.

[3] Cf. the finding of the International Military Tribunal for the Far East on the operations by the Japanese Kwantung Army at Nomonhan in 1939: Judgment (Far Eastern Comm. text), pp. 331–3; Brownlie, *International Law amd the Use of Force by States*, pp. 210–11. [4] *Supra*, p. 450, n. 4.

[5] (1925), *R.I.A.A.* vi. 160; 20 *A.J.* (1926), 385; *Ann. Digest* 3 (1925–6), no. 161. See also the *Metzger* case (1903), *R.I.A.A.* x. 417; the *Roberts* case, ibid. ix. 204; the *Crossman* case, ibid., p. 356.

[6] Viz., the absence of civil or military government in Manila during the Spanish–American war. The tribunal might seem to overemphasize the need for failure to control, but the case is different from those in which unauthorized acts of armed forces occur within the area of established sovereignty of the state to which the armed forces belong: cf. the *Caire* case, *supra*.

[7] See *Case of Ireland against the United Kingdom*, Europ. Ct. of H.R., 18 January 1978, Judgment, paras. 158–9; the *Gordon* case (1930), *R.I.A.A.* iv. 586; 25 *A.J.* (1931), 380; *Ann. Digest* 5 (1929–30), no. 103 (army doctors at target practice with privately acquired pistol); and the *Morton* case, ibid., p. 428 (murder in a *cantina* by a drunken officer off

Meron[1] uses the concept of 'abuse of governmental means' to cover the cases involving acts committed outside the apparent scope of authority, but this does not provide a firm basis for the decisions, and those he mentions can be explained in other, less coherent, terms. In any case the decisions and diversity of fact situations are resistant to the categories of writers.[2]

(c) *Mob violence, insurrection, revolution, and civil war.*[3] The general principles considered below apply to a variety of situations involving acts of violence either by persons not acting as agents of the lawful government of a state, or by persons acting on behalf of a rival or candidate government set up by insurgents. The latter may be described as a '*de facto* government'. In the case of localized riots and mob violence, substantial neglect to take reasonable precautionary and preventive action and inattention amounting to official indifference or connivance will create responsibility for damage to foreign public and private property in the area.[4] The principles stated with reference to various types of situation are all derivatives of the standard of due diligence.

Lord McNair[5] extracts five principles from the reports of the legal advisers of the British Crown on the responsibility of lawful governments for the consequences of insurrection and rebellion. The first three principles are as follows:

(i) A State on whose territory an insurrection occurs is not responsible for loss or damage sustained by a foreigner unless it can be shown that the Government of that State was negligent in the use of, or in the

duty); and cf. the *Mallén* case (1927), ibid., p. 173; Bishop, p. 767; 21 *A.J.* (1927), 803; the *Henriquez* case, ibid. x. 727.

[1] 33 *B.Y.* (1957), p. 85 at pp. 105–13.

[2] Cf. Schwarzenberger, *International Law* (3rd ed.), i. 616. Oppenheim i. 362 refers to 'a wide and altogether unrestricted vicarious responsibility' for unauthorized acts.

[3] See García Amador, *Yrbk., I.L.C.* (1957), ii. 121–8; Accioly, 96 Hague *Recueil* (1959, I), 395–403; Schwarzenberger, *International Law* (3rd ed.), i. 627–30; Briggs, pp. 697–721; McNair, *Opinions* ii. 238–73, 277; *British Digest* vi. 175–99; Borchard, *The Diplomatic Protection of Citizens Abroad*, pp. 213–45; Harv. Research, 23 *A.J.* (1929), Spec. Suppl., pp. 188–96; Oppenheim i. 366–9; Silvanie, 33 *A.J.* (1939), 78–103; Hackworth v. 657–82; Rousseau, pp. 376–81; Eagleton, *Responsibility*, pp. 125–56; Whiteman viii. 819–24, 830–7; de Visscher, *Les Effectivités du droit international public* (1967), pp. 120–1; 8 *Canad. Yrbk.* (1970), 356–7; Jiménez de Aréchaga in Sørensen (ed.), *Manual* pp. 561–4; Akehurst, 43 *B.Y.* (1968–9), 49–70; *Répertoire suisse* iii. 1738–43; Verzijl, op. cit., vi. 694–705; *Yrbk., I.L.C.* (1964), ii. 152–4; ibid. (1969), ii. 106–7; ibid. (1975), ii. 70–83.

[4] *Ziat, Ben Kiran claim, R.I.A.A.* ii. 730; *Youmans* case, ibid. iv. 110; Whiteman viii. 831 (claim against Libya); U.K. and Indonesia, Exchange of Notes, 1 Dec. 1966, *Treaty Series* No. 34 (1967), Cmnd. 3277; Cole, 41 *B.Y.* (1965–6), 390–2; *Noyes* case (1933), *R.I.A.A.* vi. 308; *Pinson* case (1928), *R.I.A.A.* v. 327; *Sarropoulos* v. *Bulgaria* (1927), 7 Recueil des décisions des tribunaux arbitraux mixtes, p. 47 at p. 50; *Ann. Digest*, 4 (1927–8) no. 162; Hackworth v. 657–65.

[5] Op cit., p. 245.

failure to use, the forces at its disposal for the prevention or suppression of the insurrection;

(ii) this is a variable test, dependent on the circumstances of the insurrection;

(iii) such a State is not responsible for the damage resulting from military operations directed by its lawful government unless the damage was wanton or unnecessary, which appears to be substantially the same as the position of belligerent States in an international war.

These principles are substantially similar to those presented by writers of various nationalities. The general rule of non-responsibility[1] rests on the premises that, even in a regime of objective responsibility, there must exist a normal capacity to act, and a major internal upheaval is tantamount to *force majeure*. This is straightforward enough, but uncertainty arises when the qualifications put upon the general rule are examined. At the outset it will be noted that the general rule and the qualifications are stated in respect of damage to aliens on the territory of the state: this is unfortunate, since the nature of the qualifications (the conditions of responsibility) may vary according to the object of harm, so that, for example, if a diplomatic or consular agent is involved, a higher standard of conduct will be required.[2] There is general agreement among writers that the rule of non-responsibility cannot apply where the government concerned has failed to show due diligence. However, the decisions of tribunals and the other sources offer no definition of 'due diligence'. Obviously no very dogmatic definition would be appropriate, since what is involved is a standard which will vary according to the circumstances. And yet, if 'due diligence' be taken to denote a fairly high standard of conduct the exception would overwhelm the rule. In a comment on the Harvard Research draft[3] it is stated that: 'Inasmuch as negligence on the part of the government in suppressing an insurrection against itself is improbable, the claimant should be deemed to have the burden of showing

[1] See also Huber, *Spanish Zone of Morocco* claims (1924), *R.I.A.A.* ii, p. 615 at p. 642; and *R.I.A.A.* ii. 730. Cf. the *Home Missionary Society* case (1920), *R.I.A.A.* vi, p. 42 at p. 44; *Pinson* claim (1928), *R.I.A.A.* v. 327; Green, p. 722 (also for a discussion of the terms 'insurrection' and 'revolution'); *Sambiaggio* claim (1903), *R.I.A.A.* x. 500 (and see the index); Briggs, p. 715; *Volkmar* case (1903), *R.I.A.A.* ix. 317; *Santa Clara Estates Company* case (1903), ibid., p. 455; *Standard–Vacuum Oil Company Claim*, Int. L.R. 30, p. 168; *Socony Vacuum Oil Company Claim*, Int. L.R. 21 (1954), 55. Cf. also *Mossé* case, *R.I.A.A.* xiii. 486; *Treves* case, ibid., xiv. 262; *Levi* case, ibid., 272; *Fubini* case, ibid. 420. See also the *Gelbtrunk Claim*, ibid. xv. 463; Briggs, p. 713.

[2] Moreover, it is sometimes said that resident aliens have consented to certain types of risk.

[3] p. 194.

negligence; and claims commissions have so held....' The rapporteur for the International Law Commission on state responsibility, García Amador,[1] concludes that the basic principle is that there is a presumption against responsibility, and proposes the following provision:[2] 'The State is responsible for injuries caused to an alien in consequence of riots, civil strife or other internal disturbances if the constituted authority was manifestly negligent in taking the measures which, in such circumstances, are normally taken to prevent or punish the acts in question.' There is some authority for the view that the granting of an amnesty to rebels constitutes a failure of duty and an acceptance of responsibility for their acts on the basis of a form of estoppel: but in many cases this inference will be unjustified.[3]

The other two principles propounded by Lord McNair[4] are generally accepted:

(iv) such a State is not responsible for loss or damage caused by the insurgents to a foreigner after that foreigner's State has recognized the belligerency of the insurgents;

(v) such a State can usually defeat a claim in respect of loss or damage sustained by resident foreigners by showing that they have received the same treatment in the matter of protection or compensation, if any, as its own nationals (the plea of *diligentia quam in suis*).[5]

Victorious rebel movements are responsible for illegal acts or omissions by their forces occurring during the course of the conflict.[6] They also become responsible for the illegalities of the previous government.[7]

10. *Agency and Joint Tortfeasors*

The notion of agency may be applied to a number of legal relationships. Thus the concept extends or could extend to such diverse topics as diplomatic representation and other aspects of the law governing acts of personal agents of states and

[1] *Yrbk., I.L.C.* (1957), ii. 121–3.
[2] See also ibid., p. 121, Art. 12, para. 1.
[3] See Accioly, 96 Hague *Recueil* (1959, I), 402–3; Rousseau, pp. 379–80.
[4] *Ubi supra*, p. 452.
[5] See also García Amador, *Yrbk., I.L.C.* (1957), ii. 122, para. 8.
[6] Ibid., pp. 121 (Art. 12, para. 2), 128 (quoting *Bases of Discussion* of the Hague Codification Conference and the Harvard Research); Rousseau, p. 380; Schwarzenberger, *International Law* (3rd ed.), i. 627–9; Hackworth, v. 681 seq.; Borchard, op. cit., p. 241; *Pinson* claim (1928), *R.I.A.A.* v. 327; Green, p. 722; *Bolivar Railway Company* case (1903), *R.I.A.A.* ix. 445.
[7] *Supra*, p. 85 on continuity of governments.

organizations, the distinction between acts of officials for which a state is responsible and his 'personal' acts, the continuity of governments, including the responsibility of states for acts of previous revolutionary regimes, and the giving of diplomatic protection to non-nationals. A vital question, which has a close relation to the responsibility of states, is the extent to which a declaration of war by a state affects those states politically dependent upon it.[1] The protecting state may by virtue of the legal relations between it and the protected state *ipso facto* have control over the latter's foreign relations. In other cases a state *prima facie* independent may be sufficiently under the control of another for agency to be established.

Two issues more directly affecting state responsibility demand attention. The first concerns both the transferred servant and the case of an official acting in different capacities. The *Chevreau* case[2] illustrates the latter situation. In that case part of the French claim against the United Kingdom related to loss flowing from the negligence of the British consul in Persia, acting at the material time as agent for the French consul, and the tribunal rejected this part of the claim. Formal capacity may create an estoppel, or at least a presumption of fact, in such cases, but on particular facts a control test may be necessary to do justice. The second problem concerns the dependent state.[3] In the case where the putative dependent state cannot be regarded as having any degree of international personality[4] because of the extent of outside control, then the incidence of responsibility is no longer in question. In other cases a state may by treaty or otherwise assume international responsibility for another government.[5] In dealing with the *Spanish Zone of Morocco Claims*[6] Huber said

> . . . it would be extraordinary if, as a result of the establishment of the Protectorates, the responsibility incumbent upon Morocco in accordance

[1] See Oppenheim i. 191, 193, 196 (n. 1), 206–7 (notes); McNair, *Opinions* i. 39; *Katrantsios* v. *The Bulgarian State*, *Ann. Digest* 3 (1925–6), no. 27; *van Hoogstraten* v. *Low Lum Seng*, ibid. 9 (1938–40), no. 16.

[2] (1931), *R.I.A.A.* ii, p. 1115 at p. 1141. See also *Prince Sliman Bey* v. *Minister for Foreign Affairs*, Int. L.R. 28, p. 79.

[3] See Schwarzenberger, *International Law* (3rd ed.), i. 624–5.

[4] See *supra*, p. 74.

[5] The basis of responsibility may then rest either on the actual extinction of the personality of the protected state or on estoppel. Cf. *Studer* (*United States*) v. *Great Britain* (1925), *R.I.A.A.* vi. 149; *A.J.* (1925), 790. See also Guggenheim ii. 26–7. Cf. agreements for indemnification of the agent: *Zadeh* v. *United States*, Int. L.R. 22 (1955), 336; *Oakland Truck Sales Inc.* v. *United States*, ibid. 24 (1957), 952.

[6] (1925), *R.I.A.A.* ii, p. 615 at pp. 648–9. See also *Trochel* v. *State of Tunisia*, Int. L.R. 20 (1953), 47.

with international law were to be diminished. If the responsibility has not been assumed by the protecting Power, it remains the burden of the protected State; in any case, it cannot have disappeared. Since the protected State is unable to act without an intermediary on the international level, and since every measure by which a third State sought to obtain respect for its rights from the Cherif, would inevitably have an equal effect upon the interests of the protecting Power, it is the latter who must bear the responsibility of the protected State, at least by way of vicarious liability... the responsibility of the protecting State... is based on the fact that it is that State alone which represents the protected State in international affairs...

However, in cases where the dependent state retains sufficient legal powers to maintain a separate personality and the right to conduct its own foreign relations, the incidence of responsibility will depend on the circumstances: here, if the suzerain,[1] or state in an analogous position, is responsible on the facts, the responsibility will not be vicarious or derivative.[2]

The principles relating to joint responsibility of states are as yet indistinct, and municipal analogies are unhelpful. A rule of joint and several liability in delict is probably not justified in the conditions of state relations. Practice in the matter of reparation payments for illegal invasion and occupation rests on the assumption that Axis countries were liable on the basis of individual causal contribution to damage and loss, unaffected by the existence of co-belligerency.[3] However, if there is joint participation in specific actions, for example where state A supplies planes and other material to state B for unlawful dropping of guerrillas and state B operates the aircraft, what is to be the position? Must a plaintiff proceed by making a joint claim against both tortfeasors, or against the operator of the aircraft for all the damage, or may it go against states A and B separately for proportions of damages? In the *Corfu Channel* case the Court was untroubled by the possibility that another state had laid the mines in Albanian waters, and, as compensation is the principal object of international claims, it would seem that, if a confederate were later identified in such a case, the joint tortfeasor would be immune

[1] See *supra*, p. 119.

[2] See Schwarzenberger, loc. cit., and the *Brown* claim (1923), *R.I.A.A.* vi, p. 120 at pp. 130–1; Briggs, p. 215. Conceivably there could exist a joint liability.

[3] But cf. the *obiter dictum* of the U.S. Court of Claims in *Anglo-Chinese Shipping Co. Ltd.* v. *United States*, Int. L.R. 22 (1955), p. 982 at p. 986. See also claims by the United Arab Republic in respect of the Suez attack in 1956, and claims against individual states involved in the joint occupation of Germany and Austria.

from liability to pay compensation, though not perhaps from liability to measures of satisfaction.[1]

11. *The Types of* Damnum[2] *and the Forms and Function of Reparation*[3]

In general. These subjects must be treated with caution, since the problems involved lead back to substantial issues as to the nature of responsibility and are far from being a mere appendix to the law of state responsibility. Other aspects of the subject also justify circumspection. In the first place, whilst the science of responsibility in municipal law is helpful, in the sphere of international relations there are to be found important elements, including the rules as to satisfaction,[4] which would look strange in the law of tort and contract. Secondly, the terminology of the subject is in disorder, a fact which in part reflects differences of opinion on matters of substance. The usage adopted by the present writer is as follows. The term 'breach of duty' denotes an illegal act or omission, an 'injury' in the broad sense. 'Damage' denotes loss, *damnum*, whether this is a financial quantification of physical injury or damage, or of other consequences of a breach of duty. 'Reparation' will be used to refer to all measures which a plaintiff may expect to be taken by a defendant state: payment of compensation (or restitution), an apology, the punishment of the individuals responsible, the taking of steps to prevent a recurrence of the breach of duty, and any other forms of satisfaction. 'Compensation' will be used to describe reparation in the narrow sense of the payment of money as a 'valuation' of the wrong done. Confusion arises in the case where compensation is paid for a breach of duty which is actionable without proof

[1] In the case of several concurrent tortfeasors a tortfeasor sued separately will benefit from a reduction of damages: see the *Zafiro* (1925), *R.I.A.A.* vi. 160. See further Adam, *Les Organismes internationaux spécialisés* i. 119–23.

[2] i.e. injury or loss in the broad legal sense.

[3] See generally García Amador, *Yrbk., I.L.C.* (1956), ii. 209–14; ibid. (1958), ii. 67–70; ibid. (1961), ii. 2–45; and in 94 Hague *Recueil* (1958, II), 462–87; Schwarzenberger, *International Law* (3rd ed.), i. 653–81; Cheng, *General Principles of Law*, pp. 233–40; Briggs, pp. 742–7; Eagleton, 39 *Yale L.J.* (1929), 52–75; Kozhevnikov (ed.), *International Law*, pp. 130–3. See further Whiteman, *Damages in International Law*, 3 vols. (1937–43); Reitzer, *La Réparation comme conséquence de l'acte illicite en droit international* (1938); Personnaz, *La Réparation du préjudice en droit international public* (1938); Ralston, *The Law and Procedure of International Tribunals* (1926), pp. 241–69; id., Supplement (1936), pp. 115–34; Jiménez de Aréchaga, in Sørensen (ed.), *Manual*, pp. 564–72; Przetacznik, 78 *R.G.D.I.P.* (1974), 919–74; Verzijl, op. cit., vi. 742–71; Subilia, *L'Allocation d'intérêts dans la jurisprudence internationale* (1972); Bollecker-Stern, *Le Préjudice dans la théorie de la responsabilité internationale* (1973).

[4] See *infra*, p. 459.

of particular items of financial loss, for example the violation of diplomatic or consular immunities, trespass in the territorial sea or illegal arrest of a vessel on the high seas. The award of compensation for such illegal acts is sometimes described as 'moral' or 'political' reparation, terms connected with concepts of 'moral' and 'political' injury, and it is this terminology which creates confusion, since the 'injury' is a breach of *legal* duty in such cases and the only special feature is the absence of a neat method of quantifying loss, as there is, relatively speaking, in the case of claims relating to death, personal injuries, and damage to property.[1] It may happen that the particular rule of law makes loss to individuals or some other form of 'special damage' a condition of responsibility.

In the ordinary type of claim the object is similar to that of an action in the municipal sphere. In the *Chorzów Factory* (Indemnity) case[2] the Permanent Court declared that:

> The essential principle contained in the actual notion of an illegal act—a principle which seems to be established by international practice and in particular by the decisions of arbitral tribunals—is that reparation must, as far as possible, wipe out all the consequences of the illegal act and re-establish the situation which would, in all probability, have existed if that act had not been committed. Restitution in kind, or, if this is not possible, payment of a sum corresponding to the value which a restitution in kind would bear; the award, if need be, of damages for loss sustained which would not be covered by restitution in kind or payment in place of it—such are the principles which should serve to determine the amount of compensation due for an act contrary to international law.

The normal type of claim has these objectives and primarily aims at the protection of the interests of the claimant state: it is thus to be distinguished from the type of case in which the individual state is seeking to establish its *locus standi* in order to protect legal interests not identifiable with that state alone or with any existing state.[3] Before attention is turned to the principal topics of restitution and compensation, two other forms of remedy associated with the normal type of claim, but having features of their own, must be considered, viz., the declaratory judgment and satisfaction.

Declaratory judgments.[4] In some cases a declaration by a court

[1] Even then, the 'compensation' awarded for a broken limb is an exaction for the legal wrong involved, and not all aspects of the injury, e.g. pain and suffering, can be 'quantified' in simple terms of compensation and equivalence.

[2] (1928), P.C.I.J., Ser. A, no. 17, p. 47; Green, p. 607.

[3] See *infra*, pp. 466–73.

[4] See Lauterpacht, *The Development of International Law by the International Court*, pp. 205–6; 250–2; Rosenne, *The Law and Practice of the International Court*, pp. 125–6,

as to the illegality of the act of the defendant state constitutes a measure of satisfaction (or reparation in the broad sense).[1] However, international tribunals may be empowered or may assume the power to give a declaratory judgment in cases where this is, or is considered by the parties to be, the appropriate and constructive method of dealing with a dispute and the object is not primarily to give 'satisfaction' for a wrong received.[2] Whilst the International Court is unwilling to deal with hypothetical issues and questions formulated in the abstract, it has been willing to give declaratory judgments,[3] and in some cases, for example those concerning title to territory, it may in any case be appropriate to give a declaratory rather than an executory form to the judgment.[4] The applicant states in the *South West Africa* cases[5] were seeking a declaration that certain legislation affecting the territory was contrary to the obligations of South Africa under the Mandate. The propriety of giving a declaratory judgment raises very difficult issues as to *locus standi* and the nature of a legal interest which will be dealt with later on.[6]

Satisfaction.[7] Satisfaction may be defined as any measure which the author of a breach of duty is bound to take under customary law or under an agreement by the parties to a dispute, apart from restitution or compensation. Satisfaction is an aspect of reparation in the broad sense. However, it is not easy to distinguish between pecuniary satisfaction and compensation in the case of breaches of duty not resulting in death, personal injuries, or damage to or loss of property. Claims of this sort are commonly expressed as a claim for an 'indemnity'. If there is a distinction, it would seem to be in the intention behind the demand. If it is predominantly that of seeking a token of regret and acknowledgement of wrongdoing then it is a matter of satisfaction. The

619–21; García Amador, *Yrbk., I.L.C.* (1961), ii. 14–16; Gross, 58 *A.J.* (1964), 419–23; Shihata, *The Power of the International Court to Determine its own Jurisdiction*, pp. 216–19; Borchard, 29 *A.J.* (1935), 488–92; Ritter, *Ann. français*, 1975, 278–93.

[1] See *infra*.

[2] See *Arabian–American Oil Co.* v. *Saudi Arabia*, Int. L.R. 27, p. 117 at pp. 144–6.

[3] See *Certain German Interests in Polish Upper Silesia* (1926), P.C.I.J., Ser. A, no. 7, p. 18; and the *Interpretation of Judgments Nos. 7 and 8 (The Chorzów Factory)* (1927), ibid., no. 13, pp. 20, 21. And cf. the *Mavrommatis* case (1925), ibid., no. 5, p. 51, and see *infra*, p. 461, on the *Corfu Channel* case.

[4] See the *Eastern Greenland* case (1933), P.C.I.J., Ser. A/B, no. 53, pp. 23, 24, 75.

[5] I.C.J. Reports (1962), p. 319; ibid. (1966), p. 6; and see *infra*.

[6] *Infra*, pp. 466 seq.

[7] See García Amador, *Yrbk., I.L.C.* (1961), ii. 19–28; Schwarzenberger, *International Law* (3rd ed.), i. 658–9; Jiménez de Aréchaga, in Sørensen, *Manual*, p. 572; Whiteman viii. 1211–14. See further Bissonnette, *La Satisfaction comme mode de réparation en droit international* (1952).

objects of satisfaction are three, which are often cumulative: apologies or other acknowledgment of wrongdoing by means of a salute to the flag or payment of an indemnity; the punishment of the individuals concerned; and the taking of measures to prevent a recurrence of the harm. In the *I'm Alone*[1] case the Canadian Government complained of the sinking on the high seas of a liquor-smuggling vessel of Canadian registration by a United States coastguard vessel, as a climax to a hot pursuit which commenced outside United States territorial waters but within the inspection zone provided for in the 'Liquor Treaty' between Great Britain and the United States. The Canadian claim was referred to Commissioners appointed under the Convention concerned, and in their final report the following appears:

> We find as a fact that, from September, 1928, down to the date when she was sunk, the *I'm Alone*, although a British ship of Canadian registry, was *de facto* owned, controlled, and at the critical times, managed, and her movements directed and her cargo dealt with and disposed of, by a group of persons acting in concert who were entirely, or nearly so, citizens of the United States, and who employed her for the purposes mentioned[2]... The Commissioners consider that, in view of the facts, no compensation ought to be paid in respect of the loss of the ship or the cargo.
>
> The act of sinking the ship, however, by officers of the United States Coast Guard, was, as we have already indicated, an unlawful act; and the Commissioners consider that the United States ought formally to acknowledge its illegality, and to apologize to His Majesty's Canadian Government therefor; and, further, that as a material amend in respect of the wrong the United States should pay the sum of $25,000 to His Majesty's Canadian Government; and they recommend accordingly.

A number of ancillary questions remain. It is sometimes suggested that an affront to the honour of a state or intention to harm are preconditions for a demand for satisfaction, but this is very doubtful. Such elements may enter into the assessment of compensation,[3] as also may the failure to undertake measures to prevent a recurrence of the harm or to punish those responsible. Measures demanded by way of apology should today take forms which are not humiliating and excessive.[4]

[1] Whiteman, *Damages* i. 155–7; *R.I.A.A.* iii. 1609; Green, p. 472; Briggs, p. 385. See Hyde, 29 *A.J.* (1935), 296–301; Fitzmaurice, 17 *B.Y.* (1936), 82–111. See also the *Borchgrave* case (Preliminary Objections) (1937), P.C.I.J., Ser. A/B, no. 72, no. 73, p. 5; and the *Panay* incident, *Documents on International Affairs* (R.I.I.A., 1937), p. 757; Hackworth, v. 687–9.

[2] i.e., smuggling liquor.

[3] See *infra*, p. 463, on 'penal damages'.

[4] Cf. Stowell, *Intervention in International Law*, pp. 21–35, on measures of 'expiation' demanded in the past, and, on the *Tellini* incident, see Eagleton, 19 *A.J.* (1925), 304.

There is no evidence of a rule that satisfaction is alternative to and, on being given, exclusive of a right to compensation for the breach of duty.[1] In the *Corfu Channel* case[2] the Court declared that the mine-sweeping operation by the Royal Navy in Albania's territorial waters was a violation of her sovereignty, and then stated: 'This declaration is in accordance with the request made by Albania through her Counsel, and is in itself appropriate satisfaction.' In spite of the terminology, this is not an instance of satisfaction in the usual meaning of the word: the declaration is that of a court and not a party, and is *alternative* to compensation. No pecuniary compensation had been asked for by Albania and a declaration of this kind was therefore the only means of giving an effective decision on the matter.[3]

Restitution in kind and restitution in integrum.[4] To achieve the object of reparation tribunals may give 'legal restitution', in the form of a declaration that an offending treaty, or act of the executive, legislature, or judicature, is invalid.[5] Such action can be classified either as a genuine application of the principle of *restitutio in integrum* or as an aspect of satisfaction. Restitution in kind, specific restitution, is exceptional, and the vast majority of claims conventions and *compromis* (agreements to submit to arbitration) provide for the adjudication of pecuniary claims only.[6] Writers[7] and, from time to time, governments and tribunals[8] assert a right to specific restitution, but, whilst it is safe to

[1] No mandatory rule, that is: parties to a dispute may agree otherwise.

[2] I.C.J. Reports (1949), p. 4 at p. 35. See also the *Carthage* and the *Manouba* (1913), Hague Court Reports i, p. 329 at p. 335 and p. 341 at p. 349; *R.I.A.A.* xi. 457 at 460, and 471 at 476. And see Parry, 90 Hague *Recueil* (1956, II), 674–93.

[3] Cf. Judge Azevedo, dissenting, I.C.J. Reports (1949), pp. 113–14; *Aerial Incident* case (Prelim. Objections), I.C.J. Reports (1959), p. 127 at pp. 129–31; and see Sørensen, 101 Hague *Recueil* (1960, III), 230. And see further, on the powers of the European Court of Human Rights, Robertson, *Human Rights in Europe*, pp. 103–5.

[4] García Amador, *Yrbk., I.L.C.* (1961), ii. 17–18; Baade, 54 *A.J.* (1960), 814–30; Wortley, 55 *A.J.* (1961), 680–3; Schwarzenberger, *International Law* (3rd ed.), i. 656–7; Jiménez de Aréchaga in Sørensen (ed.), *Manual*, pp. 565–7.

[5] Such action is unusual, but see the *Martini* case (1930), *R.I.A.A.* ii, p. 975 at p. 1002. See also Robertson, *Human Rights in Europe*, p. 85; McNair, *Opinions* i. 78; and the *Barcelona Traction* case, I.C.J. Reports (1964), p. 6; (Second Phase), I.C.J. Reports (1970), p. 4; *South West Africa* cases (Second Phase), I.C.J. Reports (1966), p. 6 (with particular reference to the laws of *apartheid*).

[6] See also the General Act for the Pacific Settlement of International Disputes, 1928, Art. 32. A revised General Act came into force on 20 September 1950, 71 U.N.T.S., p. 101.

[7] See especially Mann, 48 *B.Y.* (1976–7), 1–65, at pp. 2–5; Verzijl, op. cit. vi. 742.

[8] See the *Walter Fletcher Smith* claim (1927), *R.I.A.A.* ii, p. 913 at p. 918; Whiteman, *Damages* ii. 1409; *Central Rhodope Forests* (1933), *R.I.A.A.* iii, p. 1405 at p. 1432; *Ann. Digest* 7 (1933–4), no. 39 at p. 99; Whiteman ii, p. 1460 at p. 1483. In the latter two awards restitution was not considered appropriate for practical reasons. See further Whiteman

assume that this form of redress has a place in the law, it is difficult to state the conditions of its application with any certainty. In the disputes arising out of the Mexican oil expropriations of 1938 and the Iranian measures in respect of the oil industry in 1951, some of the states the corporations of which were affected[1] demanded restitution, but eventually agreed to compensation. In many situations it is clear that a remedy which accommodates the internal competence of governments,[2] whilst giving redress to those adversely affected, is to be preferred: restitution is too inflexible. At the same time it will not do to encourage the purchase of impunity by the payment of damages. In exceptional cases customary law or treaty may create obligations to which is annexed a power to demand specific restitution. Thus in the *Chorzów Factory* case[3] the Permanent Court took the view that, the purpose of the Geneva Convention of 1922 being to maintain the economic *status quo* in Polish Upper Silesia, restitution was the 'natural redress' for violation of or failure to observe the treaty provisions. There is much that is uncertain, but it would seem that territorial disputes may be settled by specific restitution, although the declaratory form of judgments of the International Court masks the element of 'restitution'.[4] In imposing obligations on aggressor states to make reparation for the results of illegal occupation, the victims may be justified in requiring restitution of 'objects of artistic, historical or archaeological value belonging to the cultural heritage of the [retro]ceded territory'.[5]

Restitution has appeared in rather different contexts to those considered above. Peace treaties normally deal with the detailed

iii. 1581–2; and cf. the *Interhandel* case, I.C.J. Reports (1959), p. 6. See also *Texaco* v. *Libyan Government*, 17 *Int. Leg. Materials* (1978), 1; 104 *J.D.I.* (1977), 350; Award on Merits, paras. 92–112.

1 In the first case, the U.K. and the Netherlands; in the second the U.K.

2 See *supra*, pp. 109 seq., on sovereignty and jurisdiction; *infra*, pp. 533–4, 547, on acquired rights and concessions.

3 (1927), P.C.I.J., Ser. A, no. 9, p. 28. See also ibid., no. 17, p. 47; Green, p. 607; *Italian Rep*. v. *Fed. Rep. of Germany*, Int. L.R. 29, p. 442 at pp. 474–6. See further Baade, op. cit., pp. 822–7. It is normal to release vessels mistakenly captured in prize in neutral waters (see Whiteman, *Damages* ii. 1139), but there may be no obligation to replace foreign property requisitioned in wartime in kind (Hackworth vi. 649). But cf. on the obligations of unlawful belligerents, Art. 78 of the Italian Peace Treaty, and the *Duc de Guise* claim, Int. L.R. 18 (1951), 423.

4 See generally *supra*, p. 458, and in particular the *Eastern Greenland* case and the *Temple* case. In the latter the Court found, *inter alia*, that Thailand was obliged to restore to Cambodia any sculpture, stelae, fragments of monuments, and pottery which might have been removed by the Thai authorities.

5 See the Italian Peace Treaty, Arts. 12, 37, 78 and Annex XIV, para. 4, and cf. the *Franco-Ethiopian Railway Co.* claim (1956), Int. L.R. 24 (1957), 602. See further Part III of the Final Act of the Paris Conference on Reparations, para. A (text: Int. L.R. 20 (1953), 441).

problems arising from war measures of requisition, confiscation, and sequestration, and the solutions propounded may not depend in all cases on the illegality of the original seizure.[1] 'Restitution' was also used to describe the exercise of powers by the Allies to gather in monetary gold, looted by the Germans, to be used in satisfying reparation claims.[2] Finally, by virtue of their joint assumption of supreme power in Germany in 1945, the Allied powers enacted legislation concerning restitution and compensation by means of a civil remedy within German law, to victims of the National Socialist regime.[3]

12. *Compensation*, *Damages* (Dommages-Intérêts)

The general aspects of reparation and satisfaction have been considered already, and it remains to refer to certain problems concerning assessment of pecuniary compensation.[4] International tribunals face the same problems as other tribunals in dealing with indirect damages and deal with the issues in much the same way.[5] It is important to appreciate, even if the tribunals are often obscure in this respect, the intrinsic connexion between 'remoteness' and 'measure of damages', on the one hand, and, on the other, the rules of substance. The particular context of a breach of duty, i.e. the nature of the duty itself and the mode of breach, may determine the approach to the question of damages.[6] For the sake of argument, it may be that the rule of law is simply that if harm is caused by negligence in the course of some lawful activity then compensation is payable.[7] The scale of compensation will in such a case be less ambitious than that applicable to activity unlawful at birth, for example unprovoked attacks on the vessels of another state. There is some debate as to the possibility of penal damages in international law.[8] The problem concerns in part the

[1] See Fitzmaurice, 73 Hague *Recueil* (1948, II), 324 seq.; Whiteman viii. 1203–11. Cf. the Settlement Conv., 1952–4, on which see the *Apostolidis* case, Int. L.R. 34, p. 219.

[2] See Treaty Series no. 56 (1947), Cmd. 7173; and the arbitration on *Gold Looted by Germany from Rome in 1943*, *R.I.A.A.* xii. 13; Int. L.R. 20 (1953), 441; and the *Monetary Gold* case, I.C.J. Reports (1954), p. 19. See also, on the liquidation of assets in neutral countries, Simpson, 34 *B.Y.* (1958), 374–84.

[3] See Bentwich, 32 *B.Y.* (1955–6), 204–17.

[4] See the literature cited *supra*, p. 457; and further Salvioli, 28 Hague *Recueil* (1929, III), 235–86; Yntema, 24 *Columbia L.R.* (1924), 134–43; *Fisheries* case, Pleadings, I, p. 101.

[5] See Schwarzenberger i. 664–81; Cheng, *General Principles of Law*, pp. 233–40.

[6] Cf. Jennings, 37 *B.Y.* (1961), 156–82; Salvioli, op. cit., p. 268; and the *Dix* case, *R.I.A.A.* ix. 119, 121. On causation see also Cheng, op. cit., pp. 241–53.

[7] See *supra*, pp. 440, 443. Cf. the rule that expropriation of alien property is lawful if compensation is paid: *infra*, pp. 533 seq.

[8] See García Amador, *Yrbk., I.L.C.* (1956), ii. 211–12; Schwarzenberger i. 673–4.

granting of compensation for non-political loss, i.e. breach of legal duties as such, for example by unlawful intrusion into the territorial sea. Compensation in such cases is not correctly described as 'penal damages'.[1] However, it is true to say that tribunals are cautious in approaching cases of non-material loss,[2] and there is no simple solution to the problem of assessment. Thus in the *Janes* claim[3] the United States presented a claim based on a failure by Mexico to take adequate steps to apprehend the murderer of an American citizen. The award saw liability in terms of the damage caused to the individuals concerned rather than to the United States,[4] and gave compensation to the relatives of Janes for the 'indignity' caused by the non-punishment of the criminal. However, the United States was making no claim apart from that 'on behalf of' the dependants of Janes, and the Claims Commission was concerned to translate the Mexican breach of duty into damages. The problem was, as it were, one of quantification rather than ascription.

13. *Justifications*[5]

Classifications of 'defences' or 'justifications' are conventional and not very logical. Separate treatment of quantities as 'defences' should denote the existence of a legal burden of proof on the proponents of defences, but this is not always the case. Moreover, in international law the incidence of the burdens of proof is not dependent on a plaintiff-defendant relation as found in systems of municipal law.[6] Again, emphasis on objective responsibility and the specialized nature of many groups of rules narrows the scope of generally accepted defences. Extinctive prescription, and acquiescence and waiver, are usually considered as issues of admissibility of claims.[7]

[1] Cf. *supra*, on the *I'm Alone* and *Corfu Channel* cases. See the *Lusitania* claims (1923), 18 *A.J.* (1924), p. 361 at p. 368; and Cheng, op. cit., pp. 235–8.

[2] See Parry, 90 Hague *Recueil* (1956, II), 669 seq.

[3] (1925), *R.I.A.A.* iv. 82; Briggs, p. 605; Bishop, p. 771. See Brierly, 9 *B.Y.* (1928), 42–49; Jennings, 121 Hague *Recueil* (1967, II) 496. Another problem is the effect of waiver of a right to restitution on damages: see Salvioli, op. cit., p. 238; Jennings, 37 *B.Y.*, p. 172.

[4] See Article I of the General Claims Convention of 1923, set out in Briggs, p. 639.

[5] See Guggenheim ii. 57–63; Schwarzenberger i. 641–6; García Amador, *Yrbk., I.L.C.* (1956), ii. 208–9; McNair, *Opinions* ii. 221–37; Whiteman viii. 837–50; Ago, Eighth Report to I.L.C. (1979), A/CN. 4/318/Add. 1, 2, 3. On the invalidity and termination of treaties see *infra*, pp. 610 seq. On the relations to *jus cogens*, *infra*, pp. 512–15.

[6] See Lauterpacht, *The Development of International Law by the International Court*, pp. 363–7.

[7] See *infra*, pp. 505–6, Claimant's wrongdoing may be regarded also as a matter of admissibility: see *infra*, p. 507.

Tribunals accept defences of assumption of risk of the particular harm[1] and contributory negligence.[2] These defences have operated in practice in cases concerning harm to aliens, and the conduct of the individuals concerned has been treated as assumption of risk and so on. The defences also apply, of course, where conduct of organs of the claimant state amounts to assumption of risk or contributory negligence. *Force majeure*[3] will apply to acts of war[4] and under certain conditions to harm caused by insurrection and civil war.[5] However, necessity as an omnibus category probably does not exist, and its availability as a defence depends on specialized rules.[6] In particular contexts in the law of war, military necessity may be pleaded, and the right of angary allows requisition of ships belonging to aliens lying within the jurisdiction in time of war or other public danger.[7] The use of force in self-defence, collective self-defence, and defence of third states now involves a specific legal regime, though it related in the past to the ambulatory principle of self-preservation.[8] Armed reprisals are clearly excluded by the law of the United Nations Charter, but the propriety of economic reprisals and the plea of economic necessity is still a matter of controversy.[9] A useful principle is that of incomplete privilege according to which the defendant is privileged to commit what would otherwise be a trespass, but upon the terms that he shall compensate the plaintiff for any damage caused.[1] The right of

[1] *Home Missionary Society* case (1920), *R.I.A.A.* vi. 42. Cf. *Yukon Lumber* case (1913), *R.I.A.A.* vi, p. 17 at p. 20. See also Whiteman viii. 842–5; Brownlie, *Festschrift für F.A. Mann* (1977), pp. 309–19.

[2] *Davis* case (1903), *R.I.A.A.* ix. 460.

[3] See U.N. Secretariat Study, ST/LEG/13, 27 June 1977 (390 pp.).

[4] *American Electric and Manufacturing Co.* case, *R.I.A.A.* ix. 145; *Russian Indemnity* case (1912), *R.I.A.A.* xi., p. 421 at p. 443; and the *Lighthouses* arbitration (1956), Int. L.R. 23 (1956), 354; *R.I.A.A.* xii, p. 220, at p. 242. Cf. *Kelley* claim (1930), *R.I.A.A.* iv. 608; *Chevreau* case (1930), *R.I.A.A.* ii, p. 1113 at p. 1123. On special problems affecting contracts by state enterprises see Mann, 9 *I.C.L.Q.* (1960), 691–4; Domke, 53 *A.J.* (1959), pp. 788–806; and Riad, 108 Hague *Recueil* (1963, I), 646–52.

[5] *Spanish Zone of Morocco* claims (1924), *R.I.A.A.* ii, p. 615 at p. 642. See further *supra*, pp. 452–4.

[6] Jiménez de Aréchaga in Sørensen (ed.), *Manual*, pp. 542–4. But cf. Cheng, *General Principles of Law*, pp. 73–4, 223–31.

[7] McNair, *Opinions* iii. 398.

[8] See Brownlie, *International Law and the Use of Force by States* (1963); id., 37 *B.Y.* (1961), 183–268; Bowett, *Self-defence in International Law* (1958). On the use of force to enforce laws in a contiguous zone see *supra*, p. 215. On problems concerning threat of force cf. Glanville Williams, *Criminal Law Review* (1957), p. 219 at p. 221. Cf. Cheng, op. cit., pp. 69–102.

[9] On economic necessity see Ronning, *Law and Politics in Inter-American Diplomacy* (1963), pp. 55–6.

[1] Described as such in American doctrine on the law of tort: Harper and James, *The*

angary is conditioned in this way. However, attractive as such a doctrine might be in municipal law, in international relations it would encourage too many breaches of the peace if widely adopted.

14. *The Nature of a Legal Interest*: Locus Standi[1]

The types of international claim considered so far in this chapter involve direct harm to the legal rights of the plaintiff state in a context of delict, but it can happen that individual states may ground a claim either in a broad concept of legal interest or in special conditions which give the individual state *locus standi* in respect of legal interests of other entities. In the *South West Africa* cases[2] Ethiopia and Liberia made applications to the International Court in which the Court was asked to affirm the status of South-West Africa as a territory under mandate, and to declare that South Africa had violated various articles of the Mandate Agreement and Article 22 of the Covenant of the League of Nations in consequence of certain aspects of her administration of South-West Africa and, in particular, of the practice of *apartheid*. To found the jurisdiction of the Court the applications relied on Article 7 of the Mandate and Article 37[3] of the Statute of the Court, and the Union of South Africa, in its objections to the jurisdiction, submitted that Ethiopia and Liberia had no *locus standi* in the proceedings. Article 7 of the Mandate provides, in part:

> The Mandatory agrees that, if any dispute whatever should arise between the Mandatory and another Member of the League of Nations relating to the interpretation or the application of the provisions of the Mandate, such dispute, if it cannot be settled by negotiation, shall be submitted to the Permanent Court of International Justice . . .

Apart from the issue as to survival of jurisdiction of that Court by reason of Article 37 of the Statute of the present Court,

Law of Torts i. 60–4; *Vincent* v. *Lake Erie Transportation Company* (1910), 109 Minn. 456. Statements in Oppenheim i. 298, 343, n. 2, contain a similar doctrine. See also Ross, *A Textbook of International Law* (1947), p. 248.

[1] On the related question of third-party intervention before the International Court see Fitzmaurice, 34 *B.Y.* (1958), 124–9.

[2] *South West Africa* cases (Preliminay Objections), I.C.J. Reports (1962), p. 319; Int. L.R. 37, p. 3. See Verzijl, 11 *Neths. Int. L.R.* (1963), 1–25; and the literature cited *infra*.

[3] This part of the argument based on Art. 37 is not relevant to the subject at present under discussion. See *infra*, p. 720.

South Africa argued that neither Ethiopia nor Liberia was 'another Member of the League of Nations' as required for *locus standi* by Article 7 of the Mandate. The Court rejected this argument as contrary to the meaning of the article.[1] Another objection to the jurisdiction rested on the proposition that the dispute brought before the Court by the applicants was not a dispute as envisaged in Article 7, in particular because it did not affect any material interests of the applicant states or their nationals. As a matter of interpretation of Article 7 the Court rejected this argument also:[2]

> For the manifest scope and purport of the provisions of this Article indicate that the Members of the League were understood to have a legal right or interest in the observance by the Mandatory of its obligations both toward the inhabitants of the Mandated Territory,[3] and toward the League of Nations and its Members.

Having rejected these and other South African preliminary objections, the Court held that it had jurisdiction to decide the merits of the dispute.[4] In his separate opinion Judge Jessup[5] argued at length that 'international law has long recognized that States may have legal interests in matters which do not affect their financial, economic, or other "material", or, say, "physical" or tangible interests', and referred to provisions for settlement of disputes in minorities treaties, the Genocide Convention, and the Constitution of the International Labour Organization, cases in which all states had a legal interest in the protection of general interests of mankind.

This highly interesting decision, by a narrow majority, can of course be confined to the specific issue of the interpretation of Article 7 of the Mandate Agreement. It is significant that the dissenting judges were much more cautious on the nature of a legal interest. Thus President Winiarski expressed himself as follows:[6]

> The relevant words of Article 7 cannot be interpreted in such a way as to conflict with the general rule of procedure according to which the Applicant State must have the capacity to institute the proceedings, that is to

[1] I.C.J. Reports (1962), pp. 335–42. Emphasis was placed on the importance of effective judicial protection of the 'sacred trust of civilization'.

[2] Ibid., p. 343.

[3] See further Judge Bustamante, separate opinion, ibid., pp. 355–6, 374, 378, 380; and Verzijl, op. cit., at p. 25.

[4] By eight votes to seven.

[5] I.C.J. Reports (1962), pp. 424–33.

[6] Ibid., pp. 455–7. See also the joint dissenting opinion of Spender and Fitzmaurice, pp. 547–9; and the dissenting opinion of Morelli, pp. 569–71.

say, a subjective right, a real and existing individual interest which is legally protected. 'No interest, no action': this old tag expresses in a simplified, but, on the whole, correct form the rule . . . of international law. We have seen it in the *Mavrommatis* case.[1] In the *Wimbledon* case[2] the Permanent Court of International Justice met the objection raised by Germany by saying . . . that 'each of the four Applicant Powers has a clear interest in the execution of the provisions relating to the Kiel Canal, since they all possess fleets and merchant vessels flying their respective flags' . . . [the Applicants] assert that they have a sufficient legal interest . . .: 'a legal interest in seeing to it through judicial process that the sacred trust of civilization created by the Mandate is not violated'. But such a legally protected interest has not been conferred on them by any international instrument. . . .

Subsequently the view of the dissenting judges was to prevail. In the *South West Africa* cases (Second Phase),[3] contrary to the expectations of those appearing before the Court, the merits were not dealt with. There had been certain changes in the membership of the Court, and the minority of 1962 now appeared as a majority.[4] The view of the majority in 1966 was that the question of the legal interest of the applicants had not been finally settled in the first phase of the proceedings. A fine distinction was drawn between the right to invoke a jurisdictional clause and the question of legal interest, the latter being an issue of merits.[5] The Court disagreed with the view that the issue of legal interest was a question of admissibility disposed of in 1962. Even if the issue were treated as one of admissibility it would fall to be dealt with at the second phase.[6] In the event the Court treated the issue of legal interest as one of merits. In the view of the 'minority' of seven judges the consequence was to violate the principle of *res judicata* by reopening a question settled at the first phase.

[1] (1925), P.C.I.J., Ser. no. 5.

[2] (1923), P.C.I.J., Ser. A, no. 1, p. 20; Green, p. 311.

[3] I.C.J. Reports (1966), p. 6; Int. L.R. 37, p. 243. For comment see Cheng, *Curr. Leg. Problems* (1967), 181–212; Katz, *The Relevance of International Adjudication* (1968), chap. 4; Higgins, 42 *Int. Affairs* (1966), 573–99; Falk, 21 *Int. Organization* (1967), 1–24; Jennings, 121 Hague *Recueil* (1967, II), 507–11; Nisot, 3 *Revue belge* (1967), 24–36; de Visscher, *Aspects récents du droit procédural de la Cour Internationale de Justice*, pp. 17–28; Gross, 120 Hague *Recueil* (1967, I), 375–84; Dugard, 83 *S.A.L.J.* (1966), 429–60; Fleming, 5 *Canad. Yrbk.* (1967), 241–52. See also on the concept of *actio popularis*, Seidl-Hohenveldern, *Comunicazioni e Studi*, XIV (1975), 803–13; Schwelb, 2 *Israel Yrbk. of Human Rights* (1972), 46–56.

[4] The decision was by seven votes, together with the casting vote of the President (Spender, Fitzmaurice, Winiarski, Spiropoulos, Morelli, Gros, and Van Wyk, the *ad hoc* Judge for South Africa). The 'minority' of seven Judges consisted of Wellington Koo, Koretsky, Tanaka, Jessup, Padilla Nervo, Forster, and Mbanefo, the *ad hoc* Judge for Ethiopia and Liberia.

[5] I.C.J. Reports (1966), pp. 36–8.

[6] pp. 42–3.

On the matter of the legal interest of the applicants the Court took up the general position of the minority on the Court in 1962. It is important to record precisely what the Court in 1966 said on the issue of legal interest. The Court was concerned with the interpretation of a particular instrument, the Mandate for South West Africa, and refused to apply the teleological principle of interpretation of treaties.[1] As a matter of interpretation, individual states only had a legal interest in respect of certain provisions of the Mandate characterized by the Court as the 'special interests' provisions, for example those concerning freedom for missionaries who were nationals of members of the League of Nations to enter and reside in the territory for the purpose of prosecuting their calling.[2] The applicants were not invoking interests protected by such provisions but referred to various provisions classified by the Court as 'conduct' provisions in respect of which the only supervision provided for was through the political organs of the League of Nations.[3]

Aside from the issue of interpretation of the relevant instrument, the Court made certain statements of general application. In considering the argument that interpretation of the Mandate should proceed in the light of the necessity for effectiveness in the system of supervision, the Court said:[4]

> Looked at in another way moreover, the argument amounts to a plea that the Court should allow the equivalent of an '*actio popularis*', or right resident in any member of a community to take legal action in vindication of a public interest. But, although a right of this kind may be known to certain municipal systems of law, it is not known to international law as it stands at present . . .

It is important to notice that the dissenting judges (the 1962 majority view) did not assert the existence of such a general principle. The difference of view consisted of two principal elements: (a) the minority of 1966 did not regard judicial supervision, as opposed to supervision by political organs, as very exceptional, and consequently were more prone to interpret the relevant provisions to the effect that individual states had an interest in observance of the instrument concerned; (b) the minority of 1966 were prepared to regard the common interest of the contracting parties in enforcement of a certain type of multilateral treaty as a normal feature of international law and relations

[1] pp. 35, 47–8. On this principle see *infra*, p. 629.
[2] pp. 19–23, 31–2, 43–4.
[3] On the issue of supervision see *infra*, p. 645.
[4] p. 47.

and, in the process of interpretation, not to be ruled out as an eccentric possibility.[1]

The difference between the two sides of the Court is virtually one of presumption and style of interpretation in approaching the economic and social aspects of international relations. The Court in 1966 took an empirical view of legal interest as a general issue and refused to restrict the concept, as a matter of general principle, to provisions relating to a material or tangible object:[2]

Next, it may be said that a legal right or interest need not necessarily relate to anything material or 'tangible', and can be infringed even though no prejudice of a material kind has been suffered. In this connection, the provisions of certain treaties and other international instruments of a humanitarian character, and the terms of various arbitral and judicial decisions, are cited as indicating that, for instance, States may be entitled to uphold some general principle even though the particular contravention of it alleged has not affected their own material interests;—that again, States may have a legal interest in vindicating a principle of international law, even though they have, in the given case, suffered no material prejudice, or ask only for token damages. Without attempting to discuss how far, and in what particular circumstances, these things might be true, it suffices to point out that, in holding that the Applicants in the present case could only have had a legal right or interest in the 'special interests' provisions of the Mandate, the Court does not in any way do so merely because these relate to a material or tangible object. Nor, in holding that no legal right or interest exists for the Applicants, individually as States, in respect of the 'conduct' provisions, does the Court do so because any such right or interest would not have a material or tangible object. The Court simply holds that such rights or interests, in order to exist, must be clearly vested in those who claim them, by some text or instrument, or rule of law;—and that in the present case, none were ever vested in individual members of the League under any of the relevant instruments, or as a constituent part of the mandates system as a whole, or otherwise.

Very similar issues were raised by the *Northern Cameroons* case (Preliminary Objections),[3] arising from an application by the Cameroons of 30 May 1961 which requested the Court to declare that the United Kingdom, as administering authority for the Cameroons, failed to fulfil its obligations under the Trusteeship Agreement relating to that territory. On 21 April 1961 the

[1] See Wellington Koo, I.C.J. Reports (1966), pp. 225–9; Koretsky, pp. 242–8; Tanaka, pp. 251–4; Jessup, pp. 352–88; Padilla Nervo, pp. 461–4; Forster, pp. 478–82; Mbanefo, pp. 501–5.

[2] pp. 32–3. Cp. Winiarski, quoted *supra*.

[3] I.C.J. Reports (1963), p. 15; 58 *A.J.*, p. 488; Int. L.R. 35, p. 353; and see Gross, 58 *A.J.* (1964), 415–31; Johnson, 13 *I.C.L.Q.* (1964), 1143–92; Verzijl, 11 *Neths. Int. L.R.* (1964), 25–33.

General Assembly of the United Nations approved the results of a plebiscite in the Northern Cameroons and declared that British administration should terminate on 1 June 1961, when it would become a province of the Federation of Nigeria. The background of the application was the dissatisfaction on the part of the Cameroons Government with the manner in which preparations for the plebiscite were made and a belief that maladministration had resulted in a plebiscite which favoured union with Nigeria and not the Cameroons. The application was based on Article 19 of the Trusteeship Agreement (which was still in force when the application was made), a provision similar to Article 7 of the Mandate Agreement for South-West Africa.[1] The Court held that there was a dispute in existence, thus disposing of the preliminary objections of the United Kingdom.[2] However, having established the *right* to exercise jurisdiction, the Court went on to decide against the *propriety* of exercising jurisdiction in this case. Since the Cameroons was not seeking reparation or a finding which would invalidate the union with Nigeria, the issue was 'remote from reality' in the Court's view. The Court said:[3]

> The function of the Court is to state the law, but it may pronounce judgment only in connection with concrete cases where there exists at the time of the adjudication an actual controversy involving a conflict of legal interests between the parties. The Court's judgment must have some practical consequence in the sense that it can affect existing legal rights or obligations of the parties, thus removing uncertainty from their legal relations. No judgment on the merits in this case could satisfy these essentials of the judicial function.

A part of the judgment in the *Cameroons* case was devoted to the question whether in the case it would be proper to give a declaratory judgment. The Court thought not, since the treaty in question—the Trusteeship Agreement—was no longer in force and there was no opportunity for a future act of interpretation or application in accordance with the judgment.[4] It is not easy to justify this refusal in the light of the declaration in the *Corfu Channel* case[5] on the illegality of Operation Retail (in regard to which Albania did not ask for any reparation), and several dissenting judges thought that the *Corfu Channel* case

[1] *Supra*, p. 466.

[2] I.C.J. Reports (1963), p. 27. On the definition of a 'dispute' see *infra* on admissibility.

[3] Ibid., pp. 33–4. See also the separate opinion of Fitzmaurice, pp. 97–100.

[4] Ibid., p. 37. See also Wellington Koo, sep. op., p. 41; Fitzmaurice, sep. op., p. 97.

[5] I.C.J. Reports (1949), p. 4 at p. 36. See further *supra*, p. 461. See also the *Right of Passage* case: I.C.J. Reports (1960), p. 6 and Gross, op. cit., pp. 427–8.

should have been followed.[1] More difficult is the determination of the difference between the *Cameroons* and *South West Africa* cases in regard to the nature of a legal interest. In this respect the two adjudication clauses involved were identical, though, as adjudication clauses in different contexts, they might call for different interpretations.[2] In his dissenting opinion in the *South West Africa* cases (Second Phase)[3] Judge Jessup stated that, since the Applicants were in effect asking for a declaratory judgment and not an award of damages for their individual benefit, after the decision in 1962 they were entitled to a declaratory judgment without any further showing of interest.[4] On this view the only distinction between the two cases is that the legal and political situation in the *Cameroons* case had precluded any pertinent pronouncement by the court. In the *Nuclear Tests Case* (Australia v. France)[5] four Judges were of the opinion that the purpose of the claim was to obtain a declaratory judgment. The majority of the Judges thought otherwise and, in the light of a French undertaking not to continue tests, held that the dispute had disappeared.

In these cases much turns on the interpretations of the relevant adjudication clause, the definition of a dispute, and notions of judicial propriety. However, assuming that the hurdles of jurisdiction, admissibility,[6] and propriety are surmounted, there is no inherent limitation of the concept of legal interest to 'material' interests. In this respect generalization is to be avoided, and the law is still developing. Thus states acting in collective self-defence, or a war of sanction against an aggressor, would seem to have a claim for costs and losses, although the evidence is not as yet very abundant.[7] 'Protective' claims in

[1] See I.C.J. Reports (1963), pp. 150–1 (Badawi), pp. 170, 180 (Bustamante), and p. 196 (Beb a Don). The suggested method of distinguishing the *Corfu Channel* case in the separate opinion of Fitzmaurice, ibid., p. 98, n. 2, is attractive but not conclusive. See also the separate opinion of Morelli, pp. 140–1.

[2] The majority judgment (see p. 35) in substance ignored this aspect of things. See, however, the separate opinion of Spender, ibid., pp. 65–73, and the dissenting opinion of Bustamante, pp. 156 seq.

[3] I.C.J. Reports, 1966, p. 328.

[4] He quotes from the separate opinion of Fitzmaurice in the *Cameroons* case, pp. 99, 100.

[5] I.C.J. Reports, 1974, p. 253; Joint Diss. Op. at pp. 312–21; and see Ritter, *Ann. français*, 1975, 278–93.

[6] See *infra*, Chapter XXI.

[7] See Brownlie, *International Law and the Use of Force by States*, p. 148. Cf. McNair, 17 *B.Y.* (1936), p. 150 at p. 157, where he says of the General Treaty for the Renunciation of War (Kellogg-Briand Pact): 'it is a reasonable view, though I cannot assert it be an established opinion, that a breach of the pact is a legal wrong not merely against the victim of the resort to armed force but also against the other signatories of the Pact'.

respect of 'dependent' peoples may have special features; for example, a tribunal should be reluctant to reject a claim on account of prescription or laches of the protecting sovereign.[1] Such claims, and the type of legal interest which they represent, may be founded on the principle of self-determination[2] as a part of *jus cogens*[3] and on the General Assembly Declaration on the Granting of Independence to Colonial Countries and Peoples.[4]

15. *Causes of Action*

As a practical matter it is important to establish the precise subject of the particular legal dispute. In diplomatic correspondence it is helpful if the complainant state indicates with reasonable clarity what it is complaining about, and in particular, whether a legal demand is being advanced as opposed to a mere remonstrance or request for reparation or political action irrespective of the legal issues (as may happen). As a question of instituting proceedings before an international tribunal, the relevant special agreement or application employed to start proceedings must indicate the subject of the dispute and the parties.[5] In the case of proceedings by application the precise issue will be isolated by the tribunal in the light of the pleadings in general and the final submissions in particular.[6] There are no rigid forms of action in international law but the definition of the cause of action may have significance beyond the exercise, just noticed, by which a tribunal decides what it has to decide on the merits.

(a) Objections to jurisdiction *ratione temporis* or based upon the reserved domain of domestic jurisdiction require consideration of what is the subject of the dispute.[7]

(b) A tribunal may have to apply the principle of *res judicata* and thus decide whether in previous proceedings a particular issue was disposed of finally and without possibility of revision in proceedings affecting the same general subject-matter.[8]

[1] See the *Cayuga Indians* case (1926), *R.I.A.A.*, vi, p. 173 at p. 189. See *supra*, p. 62 and *infra*, p. 506; on the European Convention of Human Rights and the European Court of Human Rights, *infra*, pp. 574–5, 584 seq. On the question of 'common interest' see Art. 25 of the Statute of the European Court: Robertson, *Human Rights in Europe*, p. 231.

[2] *Infra*, p. 593–6. [3] *Infra*, pp. 512–15. [4] *Infra*, p. 594.

[5] See Article 40 of the Statute of the International Court. See the comment by Mann, 46 *B.Y.* (1972–3), pp. 504–5, referring to the *Norwegian Loans* case, I.C.J. Reports, 1957, p. 9.

[6] Cf. *Fisheries* case, I.C.J Reports (1951), p. 126; *Interhandel* case, ibid. (1959), p. 19.

[7] *Right of Passage* case (Merits), I.C.J. Reports (1960), pp. 32–6.

[8] See Rosenne, *The Law and Practice of the International Court* ii. 623–30.

(c) The operation of the rule of admissibility of claims requiring prior exhaustion of local remedies in certain cases may call for careful examination of the nature of the dispute as presented to the relevant municipal court and the dispute as presented on the international plane. It must be decided whether local remedies were available in respect of the particular harms complained of.[1] In the same connection a tribunal must consider whether the issue is exclusively one of national law.[2]

(d) In presenting the merits of a claim there may be some advantage in relating the evidence to more than one category of unlawful activity. Thus in the *Barcelona Traction* case[3] Belgium presented the general pattern of action by the Spanish courts and administrative authorities as amounting to a despoliation of the property of the Barcelona Traction Company. There was no expropriation or direct forced transfer as such, but the effect of wrongfully entertaining and enforcing bankruptcy proceedings, as alleged, and enabling a private Spanish group to purchase the assets of the Barcelona Traction group at a ridiculously low price, as alleged, was to bring about a despoliation, an unlawful deprivation of property. The facts relied upon were presented in terms of four legal categories: abuse of rights; usurpation of jurisdiction; denial of justice *lato sensu*; denial of justice *stricto sensu*. The claims for damage and reparation were not apportioned in relation to these heads separately but to each and all of them. In the *Nuclear Tests Cases*[4] the Applicant States had some difficulty in relating the deposit of radioactive fall-out to existing legal categories.[5]

The concept of causes of action also concerns two other issues. First, the requirement that the applicant state establish a legal interest may be described in terms of a need to show a cause of action.[6] This is simply a question of the use of words. Secondly, there is a relatively unexplored territory reminiscent of the problems in the Common Law of relating the form of action to the

[1] See Read, diss. op., *Norwegian Loans* case, I.C.J. Reports (1957), pp. 98–100; Lauterpacht, sep. op., ibid., p. 39.

[2] See Lauterpacht, sep. op., ibid., pp. 36–8.

[3] I.C.J. Reports (1970), p. 4 at pp. 15–25, Final Submissions, preamble, and sections I–V. See also Tanaka, sep. op., pp. 146, 153. There may also be certain hazards in this type of presentation since the abuse of rights content in the *Barcelona* case seemed to contradict certain other positions.

[4] Australia v. France, I.C.J. Reports, 1974, p. 253; New Zealand v. France, ibid., p. 457.

[5] See, in particular the *Pleadings, Nuclear Tests Cases*, 2 vols. (Australia v. France), Vol. I, p. 14; Handl, 69 *A.J.* (1975), 50–76.

[6] See Jennings, 121 Hague *Recueil* (1967, II), 507–11.

heads of damage. For example, in the English Law of torts it is easier to obtain recovery for financial loss if this can be presented as a head of 'damage' related to a recognized head of 'liability', such as nuisance, or presented as the damages flowing from an acceptable type of loss, such as negligence causing physical harm. In international claims comparable issues have arisen. Thus, there is an interaction between the availability of local remedies and the type of harm which can be the subject of an international claim. Thus it may happen that a contract (governed by a system of private law) is broken by a diplomatic agent or government agency for which immunity from the local jurisdiction is claimed and in respect of which no remedy may exist in the national law of the state of origin. In such a case the state of the nationality of the other party to the contract will have a claim, arising from the breach of contract, on the international plane. Such transposed causes of action are difficult to characterize.[1] A similar problem arises in denial of justice cases where the 'cause of action' is the fact that local law or local executive intervention excludes recourse to the local courts by the alien seeking a remedy. In this case the international wrong is the exclusion from the local courts, but the heads of damage will reflect the private law issues for which a local remedy was sought.

16. *Control of Discretionary Powers*[2]

Many rules of general international law and treaty provisions are concerned to confer or describe spheres of state competence and employ concepts such as territorial sovereignty, sovereign rights, jurisdiction, contiguous zone (see Chapter XIB), and power of administration. In these instances activities by a state exercising such a competence which cause harm to other states may raise issues comparable to the control of discretionary powers of ministers and public bodies in municipal law. International tribunals may from time to time insist that a competence be exercised 'reasonably' or 'in good faith'.[3] In the *South West Africa* cases (Second Phase) (1966),[4] South Africa as Mandatory

[1] See Jessup, sep. op., *Barcelona Traction* case (Second Phase), I.C.J. Reports (1970), p. 168. Compare the items of loss in the *Janes* case, *supra*, p. 464; the *General Electric Company Claim*, Int. L.R. 30, p. 140 at pp. 142–3; and the *Singer Claim*, ibid., p. 187 at p. 197.

[2] See also Chapter XVII, section 4, on the regulation of rights.

[3] See *supra*, pp. 443–5, on abuse of rights. Cf. *First Admissions* case, I.C.J. Reports (1948), at pp. 91–2 (Joint dissent). See also *Rutili* v. *Minister of the Interior* [1976] 1 C.M.L.R. 140, Europ. Ct. of Justice.

[4] I.C.J. Reports (1966), p. 4. See further *infra*, p. 596.

was given 'full power of administration and legislation over the territory' by the Mandate. This power was expressed to be 'subject to the Mandate'. One judge[1] argued that this involved an extensive grant of discretionary power. Other members[2] of the International Court took the view that the discretionary power of the Mandatory was limited by a legal principle or standard of equality or non-discrimination in racial matters.[3]

In truth no power is in the ultimate sense 'discretionary', since the notion of power involves an idea of design, of a *defined* objective, purpose or competence. The use of the term 'discretionary power' relates normally to one of three conceptions:

(a) a presumption in favour of the holder of the power or powers, which is a factor in assessing responsibility or interpreting the limits set by treaty provisions;
(b) an area of functions in principle free of restraint subject only to certain special norms, rules or standards, for example, a standard of equality or non-discrimination relating to (all or one of) race, citizenship, sex, or religion;
(c) the existence of a margin of appreciation in the exercise of a legal power or the application of a legal category to particular circumstances. An example is the establishment of straight base-lines for a territorial sea which 'must not depart to any appreciable extent from the general direction of the coast'.[4]

17. *Ultra-hazardous Activities*

Many systems of municipal law contain rules creating 'absolute' or relatively strict liability for failure to control operations which create a serious or unusual risk of harm to others. Such rules are based, in part at least, upon principles of loss distribution and liability imposed upon the effective (insured) defendant. It is the general opinion that international law at present lacks such a principle,[5] although Dr. Jenks[6] has proposed that the law

[1] Van Wyk (*Ad Hoc* Judge, for South Africa), at pp. 150–2.

[2] See, in particular, Tanaka at pp. 283–5, 301–2; Jessup at pp. 433–8; Padilla Nervo at pp. 466–9; Forster at pp. 480–1.

[3] *Infra*, p. 596.

[4] See the *Fisheries* case, I.C.J. Reports (1951), at pp. 133, 141–2; and the Convention on the Territorial Sea, Art. 4, *supra*, p. 190.

[5] Sørensen, p. 539.

[6] 117 Hague *Recueil* (1966, I), p. 105 at pp. 176–96. See also Goldie, 14 *I.C.L.Q.* (1965), 1189–1264; Quadri, 113 Hague *Recueil* (1964, III), 468–71; Whiteman viii. 763–9. Dupuy, *La Responsabilité Internationale des États pour les Dommages d'Origine technologique et industrielle* (1976).

be developed on the basis of a Declaration of Legal Principles Governing Ultra-Hazardous Activities Generally which would be adopted by the United Nations General Assembly. Caution is required in accepting the statement that the existing law lacks such a principle. Confusion arises because the operation of the normal principles of state responsibility may create liability for a great variety of dangerous activities on state territory or emanating from it. In truth the division between fault liability and strict liability is not as sharp as it is said to be in the textbooks of municipal law.[1] It follows that the regime of objective responsibility in international law provides some measure of protection in respect of dangerous activities.

Particular problems have been dealt with in multilateral conventions. Thus, absolute liability has been recognized in respect of nuclear installations[2] and the operation of nuclear ships.[3] This liability exists as a civil liability under the applicable system of municipal law. The precise rules governing harm caused by objects launched into space have been agreed in the form of the Convention on International Liability for Damage Caused by Space Objects of 1972.[4]

[1] See Lawson, *Negligence in the Civil Law*, p. 43.

[2] Paris Conv. on Third Party Liability in the Field of Nuclear Energy, 1960; 55 *A.J.* (1961), 1082; Brussels Conv. Suppl. to the Paris Conv.; 2 *Int. Leg. Materials* (1963), 685; Vienna Conv. on Civil Liability for Nuclear Damage; ibid., 727. See further Hardy, 36 *B.Y.* (1960), 223–49; id., 10 *I.C.L.Q.* (1961), 739–59; Arangio-Ruiz, 107 Hague *Recueil* (1962, III), p. 503 at pp. 575–630; and Cigoj, 14 *I.C.L.Q.* (1965), 809–44.

[3] Brussels Conv. on Liability of Operators of Nuclear Ships, 1962; 57 *A.J.* (1963), 268.

[4] See U.N. Gen. Ass. resol. 2777 (XXVI) of 29 November 1971; and 10 *Int. Leg. Materials* (1971), 965.

CHAPTER XXI

THE ADMISSIBILITY OF STATE CLAIMS

1. *Introductory*

A STATE presenting an international claim to another state, either in diplomatic exchanges or before an international tribunal, has to establish its qualifications for making the claim, and the continuing viability of the claim itself, before the merits of the claim come into question.[1] In the case where the claim is presented before a tribunal the preliminary objections may be classified as follows.[2] Objections to the jurisdiction, if successful, stop all proceedings in the case, since they strike at the competence of the tribunal to give rulings as to the merits or admissibility of the claim. An objection to the substantive admissibility of a claim invites the tribunal to reject the claim on a ground distinct from the merits—for example, undue delay in presenting the claim. In normal cases the question of admissibility can only be approached when jurisdiction has been assumed, and issues as to admissibility, especially those concerning the nationality of the claimant and the exhaustion of local remedies, may be closely connected with the merits of the case. Even if a claim is not rejected on grounds of lack of jurisdiction or inadmissibility, a tribunal may decline to exercise its jurisdiction on grounds of judicial propriety:[3] this was the outcome of the *Cameroons* case.[4]

[1] Generally see Witenberg, 41 Hague *Recueil* (1932, III), 5–132.

[2] See Fitzmaurice, 34 *B.Y.* (1958), 12–14; id., separate opinion in the *Cameroons* case, I.C.J. Reports (1963), pp. 100 seq.; Rosenne, *The Law and Practice International Court*, pp. 296–313; Winiarski, dissenting opinion in the *South West Africa* cases, I.C.J. Reports (1962), p. 449; Morelli, dissenting opinion, ibid., pp. 573–4; Bustamante, dissenting opinion in the *Cameroons* case, I.C.J. Reports (1963), pp. 180–1; and Shihata, *The Power of the International Court to Determine its Own Jurisdiction*, pp. 107–12.

[3] See Fitzmaurice, 34 *B.Y.* (1958), 21–2, 36–9; separate opinion in the *Cameroons* case, I.C.J. Reports (1963), 100–8; Rosenne, op. cit., pp. 256–7. Fitzmaurice, I.C.J. Reports (1963), p. 103, describes questions of propriety as 'of a wholly antecedent or, as it were, "pre-preliminary" character'. See also Bustamante, ibid., pp. 181–3; Beb a Don, pp. 189 seq.

[4] *Supra*, p. 470. See also Gross, 58 *A.J.* (1964), p. 415 at pp. 423–9. The Court, I.C.J. Reports (1963), p. 28, did not find it necessary to deal with the issue of admissibility.

2. *Diplomatic Negotiations*[1]

In the *Right of Passage* case (Preliminary Objections)[2] India made a preliminary objection as follows: 'Portugal, before filing her Application in the present case, did not comply with the rule of customary international law requiring her to undertake diplomatic negotiations and continue them to the point where it was no longer profitable to pursue them. . . .' The Court said that, assuming the contention had substance, the condition related in the objection had been complied with 'to the extent permitted by the circumstances of the case'.[3] It is very doubtful if the customary law recognizes such a condition,[4] and the flexible and empirical nature of diplomatic negotiations render inappropriate a comparison with the local remedies rule.[5] However, prior recourse to diplomatic negotiations may provide material evidence of the existence of a legal dispute, and an adjudication clause in a treaty may contain the condition.[6]

3. *Legal Disputes*

In the *South West Africa* cases (Preliminary Objections)[7] the third preliminary objection advanced by the Republic of South Africa ran as follows:[8] 'the conflict or disagreement alleged by [the Applicants] to exist between them and the Government of the Republic of South Africa, is . . . not a "dispute" as envisaged in Article 7 of the Mandate for South West Africa, more particularly in that no material interests of the Governments of Ethiopia and/or Liberia or of their nationals are involved therein or affected thereby'. The Court held that there was a dispute within the meaning of Article 7 of the Mandate.[9] Yet irrespective of the existence of a dispute within the meaning of the adjudication clause relevant to the proceedings, there was a prior question

[1] See Bourquin, in *Hommage d'une génération de juristes au Président Basdevant* (1960), pp. 43–55; Witenberg, op. cit., pp. 22–6; Soubeyrol, 68 *R.G.D.I.P.* (1964), 319–49; Reuter, *Comunicazioni e Studi*, XIV (1975), 711–33.

[2] I.C.J. Reports (1957), p. 125 at p. 130. Cf. ibid., pp. 132–3.

[3] Ibid., pp. 148–9.

[4] See Hudson, *The Permanent Court of International Justice 1920–42*, pp. 413–16; Waldock, 32 *B.Y.* (1955–6), 266, n. 1; Bourquin, op. cit., pp. 48–50; and Case no. 1, Arbitration Tribunal for the Agreement on German External Debts, 34 *B.Y.* (1958), p. 363 at p. 366. But see Witenberg, loc. cit.

[5] See *infra*, p. 495.

[6] See the *Mavrommatis* case, P.C.I.J., Ser. A, no. 2, p. 13; the *South West Africa* cases, I.C.J. Reports (1962), p. 319, and the *Cameroons* case, ibid. (1963), p. 15.

[7] I.C.J. Reports (1962), p. 319; see *supra*, pp. 466–8.

[8] I.C.J. Reports (1962), p. 327.

[9] Ibid., pp. 342–4. See also Judge Bustamante, sep. op., pp. 379–84; Judge Jessup, sep. op., pp. 422–33; Judge van Wyk, diss. op., pp. 658–62.

of admissibility—was there a legal dispute in existence in any case? Early in the judgment[1] the Court dealt with this point, holding that there was a dispute in this sense and quoting the definition of a dispute in the *Mavrommatis* case[2] as 'a disagreement on a point of law or fact, a conflict of legal views or of interests between two persons'. In the *Nuclear Tests Case* (Australia v. France)[3] the application of the concept of a 'legal dispute' involved considerable differences of opinion within the International Court.

4. *Absence of a Legal Interest of the Plaintiff*

The existence of a legal interest[4] on the part of a plaintiff is a question distinct from the existence of a *dispute* relating to a legal interest alleged to exist by the plaintiff state. At the same time the nature of the claim and the existence of a dispute are closely connected questions.[5] In the *Cameroons* case[6] the Court treated the issue as to the existence of a legal interest on the part of the applicants as a matter of judicial propriety.[7] Nevertheless, some members of the Court treated it as an issue of admissibility,[8] and Judge Wellington Koo[9] refers to the existence of a legal interest as 'the indispensable basis of a justiciable dispute'.

5. *Diplomatic Protection: the Nationality of Claims*

The problem of attribution of individuals to particular states and the relations of diplomatic protection and nationality have been explored previously.[1] A normal and important function of nationality is to establish the legal interest of a state when nationals, and legal persons with a sufficient connexion with the

[1] Ibid., p. 328.

[2] P.C.I.J., Ser. A, no. 2, p. 11. See further Judge Morelli, diss. op., I.C.J. Reports (1962), pp. 564–71. The same issue arose in the *Cameroons* case, I.C.J. Reports (1963), p. 15 at pp. 20 (U.K. preliminary objections), 27. See also Judge Wellington Koo, sep. op., ibid., pp. 43–4; Judge Fitzmaurice, sep. op., pp. 105, 108–11; Judge Morelli, sep. op., pp. 131–41; Judge Bustamante, diss. op., pp. 164–7. See also the *Peace Treaties* case, I.C.J. Reports (1950), p. 74, and Cassese, *Comunicazioni e Studi*, XIV (1975), 173–200.

[3] I.C.J. Reports, 1974, p. 253.

[4] See generally *supra*, pp. 466–73. On the admissibility of claims for cumulative harm arising in part before statehood of the applicant, see Judge Fitzmaurice, I.C.J. Reports (1963), p. 129; White, *Camb. L.J.* (1965), p. 9 at p. 11; and Lauterpacht, *Recognition*, p. 60, n.1.

[5] Judge Morelli, sep. op., I.C.J. Reports (1963), p. 132.

[6] *Supra*, p. 470.

[7] See *supra*, p. 478.

[8] Judge Fitzmaurice, sep. op., I.C.J. Reports (1963), pp. 101, 105; Judge Badawi, diss. op., pp. 150–3; Judge Bustamante, pp. 170–2, 181. Cf. Judge Morelli, sep. op., p. 132. Cf. the *South West Africa* cases, *supra*, pp. 466–70, and see President Winiarski, I.C.J. Reports (1962), pp. 449–57.

[9] I.C.J. Reports (1963), pp. 44–6 (sep. op.).

[1] *Supra*, Chapter XVIII.

state,[1] receive injury or loss at the hands of another state. The subject-matter of the claim is the individual and his property: the claim is that of the state.[2] Thus if the plaintiff state cannot establish the nationality of the claim, the claim is inadmissible because of the absence of any legal interest of the claimant.[3] However, the variety of problems involved necessitates separate and somewhat extended treatment of the principle of nationality of claims. At the outset certain important exceptions to the principle must be noticed.[4] A right to protection of non-nationals[5] may arise from treaty or an *ad hoc* arrangement establishing an agency. The other generally accepted exceptions are alien seamen on ships flying the flag of the protecting state[6] and members of the armed forces of a state. If the injured party was in the service of the claimant state the latter may be said to have suffered harm to a legal interest although the victim was an alien.[7]

The operation of the nationality rule.[8] The rule is generally stated as follows:[9] 'from the time of the occurrence of the injury until the making of the award the claim must continuously and without interruption have belonged to a person or to a series of

[1] See *infra*, pp. 485–90.

[2] See *infra*, Chapter XXIV, on the position of the individual in international law and the question of human rights.

[3] *Panevezys-Saldutiskis Railway* (1939), P.C.I.J., Ser. A/B, no. 76; Briggs, p. 725. But legal interest may exist on some other basis: Fitzmaurice, 27 *B.Y.* (1950), 24–5.

[4] See Schwarzenberger, *International Law* (3rd ed.), i. 592–6; Parry, 30 *B.Y.* (1953), 257; id., *Nationality and Citizenship Laws of the Commonwealth* i. 12; Oppenheim i. 347. On the *Reparation* case, see *infra*, p. 684. On the relevance of a common national status in the Commonwealth: Parry, *Nationality and Citizenship Laws*, pp. 114–23; Fawcett, *The British Commonwealth in International Law*, p. 185. On the position of aliens employed in diplomatic and consular services: Fitzmaurice, 27 *B.Y.* (1950), 25, n.1.

[5] That is, apart from the question of persons internationally attributable to a state, but outside internal nationality legislation: see *supra*, pp. 395–6.

[6] See Watts, 7 *I.C.L.Q.* (1958), 691–712. But see Schwarzenberger, op. cit., pp. 593–4.

[7] Fitzmaurice, op. cit., p. 25. Cf. the *Reparation* case, *infra*, p. 684.

[8] Questions of nationality, including multiple and effective nationality, are discussed *supra*, Chapter XVIII. On diplomatic protection and the operation of the nationality rule see generally Hurst, 7 *B.Y.* (1926), 163–82; Sinclair, 27 *B.Y.* (1950), 125–44; Blaser, *La Nationalité et la protection juridique internationale de l'individu* (1962); Borchard, 43 *Yale L.J.* (1934), 359–92; id., *Bibliotheca Visseriana* (1923), iii. 1–53; id., *Annuaire de l'Inst.* 36 (1931), i. 256 seq.; ibid., 36 (1931), ii. 201 seq.; ibid., 37 (1932), 235 seq., 479 seq.; ibid., 51 (1965), i. 5–225; ibid., ii. 157–253, 260–2; Parry, 90 Hague *Recueil* (1956, II), 699–712; García Amador, 94 Hague *Recueil* (1958, II), 426–39; id., *Yrbk., I.L.C.* (1956), ii. 199–203; id., *Yrbk., I.L.C.* (1958), ii. 61–7; Witenberg, 41 Hague *Recueil* (1932, III), 44–50; Lillich, 13 *I.C.L.Q.* (1964), 899–924. See further: Lillich, *International Claims, Their Adjudication by National Commissions* (1962); id., *International Claims, Their Preparation and Presentation* (1962); id., 17 *Curr. Leg. Problems* (1964), 157–83; id., *International Claims: Postwar British Practice* (1967); Martin, 44 *Grot. Soc.* (1958–9), 243–63; Drucker, 49 *A.J.* (1955), 477–86; O'Connell ii. 1032–52; Weston, *International Claims: Postwar French Practice* (1971); Whiteman viii. 1216–91; *Répertoire suisse* ii. 607–55; Feller, *The Mexican Claims Commissions 1923–1934* (1935); Lillich and Weston, *International Claims: Their Settlement by Lump Sum Agreements*, 2 vols. (1975).

[9] Oppenheim i. 347–8; Briggs, pp. 733–4.

persons (a) having the nationality of the State by whom it is put forward, and (b) not having the nationality of the State against whom it is put forward'. International agreements, and internal legislation putting these into effect, may avoid the principle or vary and refine the conditions of continuity.[1] The principle of continuity has been criticized because it permits incidental matters, e.g. change of nationality by operation of law including cession of territory, to affect reasonable claims, and also because, if the legal wrong is to the state of origin, then the wrong has matured at the time of injury and is unaffected by subsequent changes in the status of the individual. The essence of the rule is probably a desire to prevent the individual choosing a powerful protecting state by a shift of nationality.[2] This view does not support the application of the principle in cases of involuntary changes brought about by death or state succession[3] and there is a respectable body of opinion which would reject the principle altogether.[4] The principle appears to be well-entrenched in the practice of states, but it may be modified in cases of state succession.[5]

The first part of the rule of continuity does not give rise to too much difficulty: the relevant nationality must exist at the time of injury.[6] The second part of the rule is variously stated in terms of nationality continuing until the 'presentation of the award', or the filing of a claim before a tribunal, or the formal presentation of a diplomatic claim in the absence of submission to a tribunal. However, the majority of governments[7] and of writers[8] take the date of the award or judgment as the critical date. In any case

[1] See Lillich, 13 *I.C.L.Q.* (1964), 900–4; Sinclair, op. cit., p. 142. A common critical date is that of the coming into force of the treaty governing the settlement of claims. See also the *Orinoco Steamship Co.* case, *R.I.A.A.* ix. 180; and *Padavano* claim, Int. L.R. 26 (1958, II), 336.

[2] See Borchard, 43 *Yale L.J.* (1934), 359–92 especially at pp. 377–80; and Briggs, pp. 733–5.

[3] See Borchard, op. cit., pp. 388–9. The awkward results of the rule appear in the following cases of state succession. Tanganyika became independent in 1961 and Zanzibar in 1963. In 1964 the two states formed a union. Thus the populations concerned were the subjects of two changes of nationality.

[4] *Annuaire de l'Inst.* (1931), ii. 201–12; ibid. (1932), 479–529; Jennings, 121 Hague *Recueil*, pp. 474–7; O'Connell ii. 1033–9; Fitzmaurice, sep. op., *Barcelona Traction* case (Second Phase), I.C.J. Reports (1970), pp. 99–103.

[5] See the resol. of the Institute of Int. Law, *Annuaire*, 51 (1965), p. 260. See also Jessup, sep. op., *Barcelona Traction* case (Second Phase), I.C.J. Reports (1970), p. 202; and Chapter XXVIII, section 5.

[6] Most writers state the rule in this way. But cf. Rousseau, pp. 362–3.

[7] *Bases of Discussion*, Hague Codification Conference, 1930, iii. 140–5.

[8] e.g. Hurst, 7 *B.Y.* (1926), 180; Oppenheim, loc. cit.; Sørensen, pp. 576–7. See also Huber, *Spanish Zone of Morocco* claims, *R.I.A.A.* ii, p. 615 at p. 706; *Ann. Digest* 2 (1923–4), 189; *Eschauzier* claim (1931), *R.I.A.A.* v, p. 207 at p. 209; *Kren* claim, Int. L.R. 20 (1953), 233; and Schwarzenberger, *International Law* (3rd ed.), i. 597–8.

much depends on the terms of the agreement creating the machinery for the settlement of claims.

Succession on death.[1] The nationality of an heir must be that of the state of which the decedent on whose behalf the claim would have been made was a national: in other words the principle of continuous nationality is applied to the beneficial interest in the property.[2] Since the beneficial interest is crucial a claim will be denied if the residuary legatee does not have the requisite nationality although the executrix has.[3] It may happen that a claims commission will presume continuity of nationality in the heirs of the deceased creditor.[4]

Assignment of claims.[5] If during the critical period a claim is assigned to or by a non-national of the claimant state, the claim must be denied. However, assignment does not affect the claim if the principle of continuity is observed.

Agents and procurators.[6] International jurisprudence would presumably adopt the principle of procuration or agency, but here, as elsewhere, it is the nationality of the real or beneficial owner which matters. If a person with a power of attorney successfully presents a claim to a domestic tribunal of the defendant state the claimant is bound by the acts of the attorney and is barred from presenting the claim to another tribunal.[7]

Beneficial owners.[8] The principle to be followed is set forth in the decision of the United States Foreign Claims Settlement Commission in the *American Security and Trust Company* claim:[9] 'It is clear that the national character of a claim must be tested by

[1] See Diena, 15 *R.D.I.L.C.* (1934), 173–93; Blaser, op. cit., pp. 39–44; Schwarzenberger, op. cit., p. 599; Briggs, p. 735; Hurst, 7 *B.Y.* (1926), 166–74; Hackworth v. 788–94, 805, 849–51.

[2] See the *Stevenson* claim (1903), *R.I.A.A.* ix. 385; *Flack* claim (1929), *R.I.A.A.* v. 61; *Eschauzier* claim (1931), ibid., p. 207; *Gleadell* (1929), ibid., p. 44; *Ann. Digest* 5 (1929–30), no. 17; *Kren* claim, Int. L.R. 20 (1953), 233; *Bogovic* claim, ibid., 21 (1954), 156. Cf. *Hanover Bank* claim, ibid., 26 (1958, II), 334.

[3] See *Gleadell, supra.* But see Diena, op. cit., p. 186.

[4] *Straub* claim, Int. L.R. 20 (1953), 228.

[5] Witenberg, op. cit., pp. 71–2; Hyde ii. 899–900; Hackworth v. 846–8; *Perle* claim, Int. L.R. 21 (1954), 161; *First National City Bank of New York* claim, ibid., 26 (1958, II), 323; *Dubozy* claim, ibid., p. 345. See also *Batavian National Bank* claim, ibid., p. 346 (on assignment after filing of claim).

[6] See Moore, *Arbitrations*, pp. 4681, 4683; Blaser, op. cit., pp. 45–6. Cf. I.C.J. Reports (1970), pp. 93–9, 135–6, 211–19, 352–3.

[7] *Nartnick* claim, Int. L.R. 21 (1954), 149.

[8] See Lillich, 13 *I.C.L.Q.* (1964), 922–3; Drucker, 36 *Grot. Soc.* (1950), 112–13.

[9] (1957), Int. L.R. 26 (1958, II), 322. See also *Binder-Haas* claim, Int. L.R. 20 (1953), 236; *Knesevich* claim, Int. L.R. 21 (1954), 154; *First National City Bank of New York* claim, Int. L.R. 26 (1958, II), 323; *Methodist Church* claim, ibid., p. 279; *Hanover Bank* claim, ibid., p. 334; *Chase National Bank* claim, ibid., p. 483; Jessup, sep. op., *Barcelona Traction* case (Second Phase), I.C.J. Reports (1970), pp. 218–19.

the nationality of the individual holding a beneficial interest therein rather than by the nationality of the nominal or record holder of the claim. Precedents for the foregoing well-settled proposition are so numerous that it is not deemed necessary to document it with a long list of authorities. . . .'

Thus in that case the claim was denied, as the beneficiaries were not nationals of the United States although the trustee presenting the claim was. Treaties, and internal legislation regulating the consequences of international settlements for lump sums, may allow trustees to claim irrespective of the nationality of the beneficiaries.[1]

Insurers.[2] Insurers may claim on the basis of subrogation provided the principle of continuity of nationality is satisfied. Subrogation may be regarded as a form of assignment or a form of representation: in any case it could be supported as a general principle of law.[3] This at least represents the practice of the United States Foreign Claims Settlement Commission in the recent past. There are cogent arguments against allowing the nationality of the insurer to affect the nationality of the claim. In particular, because of the practice of reinsurance, the ultimate bearer of loss is not readily ascertainable.[4] However, if the insurer's interest is established and the principle of continuity is satisfied there would seem to be no very good reason for denial of a claim, although there is authority for the view that the insurer should bear the risks in the contemplation of the policy and should not qualify for protection.[5]

Partnership claims.[6] In principle, as a firm is not a legal person in English law, partners who are British nationals would receive protection as individuals to the extent of their interest in the

[1] See U.K. Orders in Council relating to settlements with Yugoslavia and Czechoslovakia: [1952] 1 S.I. 1096–7 (no. 1414); [1952] 1 S.I. 1092–3 (no. 1413).

[2] See Ritter, 65 *R.G.D.I.P.* (1961), 765–802; Blaser, *La Nationalité et la protection juridique internationale de l'individu*, pp. 47–50; McNair, *Opinions* ii. 290–2; Hackworth v. 809–12; O'Connell ii. 1050–2; Meron, 68 *A.J.* (1974), 628–47.

[3] See the *Federal Insurance Company* claim, Int. L.R. 26 (1958, II), 316, in which the U.S. Foreign Claims Settlement Commission said: 'By virtue of [a] . . . principle, recognized and applied alike by courts of law and equity . . . an insurer who indemnifies the person who has suffered loss through another's wrongdoing, thereby acquires, to the extent of such indemnification, the assured's rights against the wrong-doer . . .' See also the *Continental Insurance Company* claim, ibid., p. 318.

Cf. the third preliminary objection of Bulgaria in the *Aerial Incident* case (Preliminary Objections), I.C.J. Reports (1959), p. 127 at p. 133. The Court did not find it necessary to deal with this objection.

[4] Schwarzenberger, *International Law* (3rd ed.), i. 599–600.

[5] Guggenheim i. 311, n.2. This was the position taken by the British Government in 1929.

[6] Lillich, 13 *I.C.L.Q.* (1964), 907–8; *British Digest* v. 481–502.

partnership. However, post-war British claims practice, reflected in settlement agreements and Orders in Council, has in general permitted claims by firms constituted under English law, as such, irrespective of the nationality of the partners.

Corporations.[1] The 'nationality' of a corporation for purposes of public international law, and more especially with regard to exercise of diplomatic protection, is a quality not easily distinguished in the available sources from questions of municipal law and functional rules for the determination of 'enemy character' in connexion with trading with the enemy, prize law, and so on.[2] Since a corporation is a legal person and rules as to diplomatic protection distinguish corporate and other entities, a preliminary question should arise as to which system of law is to be used to classify the entity as corporate or not, or, more precisely, whether the firm or association concerned has legal personality distinct from that of its members as individuals.[3] Reference to the country under whose law the entity was constituted is, on the plane of international law, neither a necessary nor a sufficient test and, in any case, internal law frequently does not provide rules as to the 'nationality' of associations whether with or without legal personality. In fact reference to 'nationality' of 'corporations' as a means of ascertaining the admissibility of international claims is clumsy. It is significant that agreements on settlement of claims frequently contain *ad hoc* definitions of nationality which deal, in part, with corporations.[4]

The evidence of state practice and jurisprudence is very

[1] See generally Schwarzenberger, *International Law* (3rd ed.), i. 387–412; Beckett, 17 *Grot. Soc.* (1931), 175–94; McNair, *Opinions* ii. 32–9; P. de Visscher, 102 Hague *Recueil* (1961, I), 427–62; Kronstein, 52 *Columbia L.R.* (1952), 983–1002; Williams and Chrussachi, 49 *L.Q.R.* (1933), 334–49; Hackworth iii. 420, v. 840; Watts, 33 *B.Y.* (1957), 79–83; Jones, 26 *B.Y.* (1949), 226–32; Parry, *Nationality and Citizenship Laws of the Commonwealth* i. 133–42; Rundstein, Guerrero, and Schücking, 22 *A.J.* (1928), Spec. Suppl., pp. 157–214; Nial, 101 Hague *Recueil* (1960, III), 314–22; Bindschedler, 90 Hague *Recueil* (1956, II), 231–42; O'Connell ii. 1039–43, 1047–8; *British Digest* v. 503–35; de Hochepied, *La Protection diplomatique des Societés et des actionnaires* (1965); Petrén, 109 Hague *Recueil* (1963, II), 503 seq.; Ginther, 16 *Öst. Zeit. für Öff. Recht* (1966), 27–83; Khalid Al-Shawi, *The Role of the Corporate Entity in International Law* (1957); Harris, 18 *I.C.L.Q.* (1969), 275–317; Goldman, 90 *J.D.I.* (1963), 321–89; Feliciano, 118 Hague *Recueil* (1966, II), 284–95; Caflisch, *La Protection des sociétés commerciales et des intérêts indirects en droit international public* (1969; *Répertoire suisse* ii. 635–51; Diez de Velasco, 141 Hague *Recueil* (1974, I), 93–185. On the nationality and diplomatic protection of the Suez Canal Company see P. de Visscher, 62 *R.G.D.I.P.* (1958), 425–9; Scelle, *Annuaire français* (1956), pp. 12–13; Huang, 51 *A.J.* (1957), 278–89; White, *Nationalisation of Foreign Property*, pp. 76–81; and see further Chapter XIX, section 2.

[2] *Supra*, pp. 405–6.

[3] In some systems associations other than corporations in the English style receive legal personality, and the recent tendency in English law is to give procedural capacity to unincorporated bodies.

[4] See Lillich, 13 *I.C.L.Q.* (1964), 908–11.

difficult to evaluate: the right of protection is discretionary, and many treaties and judicial decisions are concerned with very narrow questions and do not provide a suitable basis for generalization. However, certain somewhat provisional conclusions may be offered. In the first place there is very little evidence in support of the view that a state may present a claim on behalf of a corporation on the sole basis of its incorporation under its law.[1] In general the evidence supports a doctrine that some substantial and effective connexion between the legal entity and the claimant state is required,[2] but there is no certainty as to the criteria for determining such connexion. Of course, there is probably no point in seeking rigid principles.

British and American practice requires the existence of a substantial beneficial interest owned by nationals in the corporation,[3] and Italy and Switzerland have relied on this criterion in making agreements, though not exclusively. In many instances the beneficial interest exists in connexion with a corporation incorporated under the law of the claimant state, but the crucial question is whether, on the basis of the beneficial interest, protection may be exercised in respect of a corporation incorporated in another state, and even in the defendant state. The present writer would give an affirmative answer to this as an issue of principle, but the sources give no unequivocal answer.[4]

The other principles supported by a modicum of practice and jurisprudence must be considered. It will be seen that they are

[1] Parry, op. cit., p. 139. For a different view: Beckett, op. cit., p. 185; Moore, *Digest* vi. 641–2; Vallat, *International Law and the Practitioner*, p. 25. (Parry remarks that the proposition is 'unsupported by any convincing precedent'.) See, however, the cases discussed by Schwarzenberger, *International Law* (3rd ed.), i. 397–402, and especially the *Standard Oil Company* case (1926), *R.I.A.A.* ii. 779; 8 *B.Y.* (1927), 156; 22 *A.J.* (1928), 404. On the *Agency of Canadian Car and Foundry Company* case (1939) see Bishop, p. 825; Parry, op. cit., pp. 139–40; Watts, 33 *B.Y.* (1957), 80–1.

[2] See Schwarzenberger, op. cit., pp. 389–90, 411–12; White, *Nationalisation of Foreign Property*, p. 67; de Visscher, 102 Hague *Recueil* (1961, I), 446–62; C. de Visscher, *Théories et réalités* (4th ed.), pp. 303–4; id., *Les effectivités du droit international*, pp. 131–4; Caflisch, op. cit. For the contrary view: Harris, op. cit., who favours a modification of the 'established rule'. See also *supra* in regard to individuals, and *U.K. Contemp. Practice* (1962), ii. 194.

[3] See Lillich, loc. cit.; White, *Nationalisation of Foreign Property*, pp. 62–5; Watts, 33 *B.Y.* (1957), 80–3. See also the *Westhold Corporation* claim, Int. L.R. 20 (1953), 266; *Cisatlantic* claim, ibid. 21 (1954), 293. On the whole, the jurisprudence of arbitral tribunals is inconclusive: Schwarzenberger, op. cit., pp. 406–10. See further the *I'm Alone* (1933–5), *R.I.A.A.* iii. 1609; Briggs, p. 385; Green, p. 472. *Contra: Interoceanic Railway of Mexico* claim (1931), *R.I.A.A.* v. p. 178 at p. 184.

[4] See Parry, op. cit., p. 140; Jones, 26 *B.Y.* (1949), 227–31; and Watts, op. cit., pp. 81–2. In particular see the *Delagoa Bay Railway* claim, Moore, *Arbitrations*, p. 1865; *British Digest* v. 559; and the *Standard Oil Company* case (1926), *R.I.A.A.* ii. 779; 8 *B.Y.* (1927), 156.

difficult to distinguish and are cognates of the concept of substantial connexion. One of these principles depends on the *siège social* of the corporation, which seems to mean the place where its administrative organs function, the centre of control.[1] Tribunals have also relied on the 'domicile' of a corporation, defining it in terms similar to the usual explanation of *siège social*.[2] The control test, resting on the seat of economic control and influence, has appeared in a number of treaties.[3] In a number of cases tribunals have applied two or more of the available criteria in conjunction. Thus in the *Flack* claim[4] the nationality of the company was held to depend on incorporation, domicile, and *siège social*, in each case in London.

As a whole the legal experience suggests that a doctrine of real or genuine link has been adopted, and, as a matter of principle, the considerations advanced in connexion with the *Nottebohm* case apply to corporations.[5] However, a caution is needed against easy acceptance of any general proposition as a definitive summary of the law. Much depends on the terms of the relevant agreements. Dr. Parry[6] ends his discussion thus:

> The conclusion to be drawn might thus appear to be that in the sphere of the right of protection the test of nationality of corporations is control. Or, if it be not control, it is substantial interest. But since it is possible that the shareholding interest of the nationals of two or more States might be equal and equally substantial, it is more than arguable that the apparent cases of protection of corporations are really cases of protection of individual shareholders and provide no evidence whatsoever as to what principle governs the nationality of corporations.

It may be pointed out that, if a doctrine of substantial connexion is employed, some but not all of the difficulties of classi-

[1] See de Visscher, 102 Hague *Recueil* (1961, I), 437–9; Schwarzenberger, op. cit., pp. 393–5; Judge Jessup, sep. op., *Barcelona Traction* case (Second Phase), I.C.J. Reports (1970), p. 183. Cf. the *Canevaro* case (1912), Hague Court Reports i, p. 284 at p. 287; and the *Wimbledon*, P.C.I.J., Ser. A, no. 1, p. 182 and C3, Suppl., p. 3.

[2] Schwarzenberger, op. cit., pp. 395–7. See the *Madera Company* claim (1931), *R.I.A.A.* v. 156; 28 *A.J.* (1934), 590.

[3] de Visscher, op. cit., pp. 439–45 (criterion criticized); Schwarzenberger, op. cit., pp. 402–6. See also Judge Jessup, *ubi supra*.

[4] (1929), *R.I.A.A.* v. 61.

[5] See *supra*, pp. 393, 406 seq., and de Visscher, 102 Hague *Recueil* (1961, I), 450–7. de Visscher points out that the notion of 'nationality' is superfluous here. See further the *Canevaro* case, *supra*, p. 399 and the *I'm Alone*, *supra*, p. 460. In the case of the Suez Canal Company writers (*supra*, p. 485, n. 1) have applied a control test. However, commercial control may not be the only criterion in the case of an organization with an important *public* function on the territory of a particular state and there may be some analogy with the ties of allegiance of individuals. Function matters as well as ownership and control: cf. *infra*, p. 495, on state interests in corporations. See also Judge Gros, sep. op., *Barcelona Traction* Case (Second Phase), I.C.J. Reports, 1970, pp. 278–81.

[6] Op. cit., p. 141.

fication of an entity as a legal person are avoided. If the place of incorporation is not a sufficient criterion, one still has to choose a system which decides whether separate legal personality exists or not, for example in the case of a partnership. Tribunals seem to rely on municipal law in this respect, but in fact, by demanding the existence of *siège social*, control, domicile, and so on, they would seem to require a guarantee that the grant of personality is reasonable and not a device for limiting the proper sphere of protection of other governments.[1]

The Barcelona Traction *case and the protection of corporations.* The decision in the *Barcelona Traction* case (Second Phase) is considered fully below. For the present the case must be considered in relation to the diplomatic protection of corporations. The Barcelona Traction Company was incorporated under Canadian law and had its registered office in Canada. The International Court, in reaching the conclusion that Belgium had no capacity to espouse the claims of the, as alleged, Belgian shareholders in the Company, considered the argument that such a claim was the only possibility of redress for the loss suffered since the company's national state lacked capacity to act on its behalf. This argument raised the question whether Canada was the national state of Barcelona Traction. The Court explained its view that Canada was the national state in these terms:[2]

> In allocating corporate entities to States for purposes of diplomatic protection, international law is based, but only to a limited extent, on an analogy with the rules governing the nationality of individuals. The traditional rule attributes the right of diplomatic protection of a corporate entity to the State under the laws of which it is incorporated and in whose territory it has its registered office. These two criteria have been confirmed by long practice and by numerous international instruments. This notwithstanding, further or different links are at times said to be required in order that a right of diplomatic protection should exist. Indeed, it has been the practice of some States to give a company incorporated under their law diplomatic protection solely when it has its seat (*siège social*) or management or centre of control in their territory, or when a majority or a substantial proportion of the shares has been owned by nationals of the State concerned. Only then, it has been held, does there exist between the corporation and the State in question a genuine connection of the kind familiar from other branches of international law. However, in the particular field of the diplomatic protection of corporate entities, no absolute test of the 'genuine connection' has found general acceptance. Such tests as have been applied are of a relative nature,

[1] Cf. the *Canevaro* case, *ubi supra*; and *Ruden & Co.* (1870), Lapradelle and Politis ii. 588.

[2] I.C.J. Reports (1970), p. 42. See also Judge Ammoun, sep. op., pp. 295–6, 300; and the very qualified expressions of Judge Fitzmaurice, p. 83.

and sometimes links with one State have had to be weighed against those with another. In this connection reference has been made to the *Nottebohm* case. In fact the Parties made frequent reference to it in the course of the proceedings. However, given both the legal and factual aspects of protection in the present case the Court is of the opinion that there can be no analogy with the issues raised or the decision given in that case.

In the present case, it is not disputed that the company was incorporated in Canada and has its registered office in that country. The incorporation of the company under the law of Canada was an act of free choice. Not only did the founders of the company seek its incorporation under Canadian law but it has remained under that law for a period of over 50 years. It has maintained in Canada its registered office, its accounts and its share registers. Board meetings were held there for many years; it has been listed in the records of the Canadian tax authorities. Thus a close and permanent connection has been established, fortified by the passage of over half a century. This connection is in no way weakened by the fact that the company engaged from the very outset in commercial activities outside Canada, for that was its declared object. Barcelona Traction's links with Canada are thus manifold.

This passage is of considerable importance. The Court rejects the analogy of the *Nottebohm* case[1] and the 'genuine connection' principle applied in that case in the context of the naturalization of individuals. Nevertheless, the authority of this expression of opinion is reduced by three circumstances. First, since neither Belgium nor Spain contested the Canadian character of the Barcelona Traction Company the reference to the issue of 'genuine connection' was quite without point.[2] Secondly, the Court in fact takes the trouble to set out the 'manifold' links of the company with Canada. Thirdly, there is a considerable body of opinion both on the Court[3] and elsewhere[4] in favour of the application of the *Nottebohm* principle to the diplomatic protection of limited companies. It would seem that the process whereby an individual embarks on a voluntary naturalization and the incorporation of a company in the country of choice are significantly similar. Fears that the 'genuine' or 'effective' link principle will lead to instability and absence of diplomatic protection are by no means groundless. However, the *Nottebohm* principle is essentially the assertion that in referring to institutions of municipal law,

[1] *Supra*, p. 406.

[2] See the judgment at pp. 42–3, and the Joint Declaration of Judges Petrén and Onyeama, I.C.J. Reports (1970), p. 52.

[3] See the Joint Declaration of Judges Petrén and Onyeama (previous note); and the separate opinions of Judges Fitzmaurice, ibid., pp. 79–83; Tanaka, p. 129 (but cf. pp. 140–141); Jessup, pp. 182–91, 195, 204–7; Padilla Nervo, p. 254; Gros, pp. 279–83. See also the diss. op. of Riphagen, Judge *ad hoc*, pp. 346–8, 351–2.

[4] See the material considered *supra*, pp. 485–7.

international law has a reserve power to guard against giving effect to ephemeral, abusive, and simulated creations. Moreover, there is probably a presumption of validity in favour of the nationality created by incorporation and, in the case of multinational corporate bodies, no very exacting test of substantial connexion should be applied.

Shareholders.[1] There is considerable authority for the view that shareholders must rely upon the diplomatic protection available in favour of the corporation in which they have invested. The shareholders may receive diplomatic protection from the state of their nationality in certain situations namely, when the act of the respondent state affects the shareholder's legal rights (for example, the right to receive dividends) as such, and also when the company has ceased to exist in law in the place of incorporation. Other exceptions may exist but they are controversial. The admissibility of claims on behalf of shareholders was at issue in the *Barcelona Traction* case (Second Phase.)[2] An account of the law must focus on this decision, resting as it did upon a majority judgment the reasoning of which was supported by twelve judges.

The Barcelona Traction Company was incorporated in Canada in 1911 and had its head office in Toronto. The company was a holding company and formed a number of subsidiary companies for the purpose of developing the production and distribution of electric power in the Spanish province of Catalonia. Some of the subsidiaries were incorporated under Canadian law and had registered offices in Canada; the others were incorporated under Spanish law and had registered offices in Spain. The Belgian contention was that by the outbreak of the Second World War

[1] Whiteman viii. 1269–91; Hyde ii. 904–8; Hackworth v. 827–45; *British Digest* v. 535–71; C. de Visscher, 15 *R.D.I.L.C.* (1934), 624–51; Beckett, 17 *Grot. Soc.* (1931), 188–94; Jones, 26 *B.Y.* (1949), 225–58; Bagge, 34 *B.Y.* (1958), 169–75; P. de Visscher, 102 Hague *Recueil* (1961, I), 463–79; Feliciano, 118 Hague *Recueil* (1966, II), 295–310; Lillich, 13 *I.C.L.Q.* (1964), 911–21; id., *International Claims: Postwar British Practice*, pp. 40–52; Weston, *International Claims: Postwar French Practice*, pp. 167–71; Nial, 101 Hague *Recueil* (1960, III), 311–22; Kiss, in Université de Paris, Institut de droit comparé, *La personnalité morale et ses limites* (1960), pp. 179–210; Caflisch, *La Protection des Sociétés Commerciales et des Intérêts Indirects en Droit International Public* (1969); de Hochepied, *La Protection diplomatique des Sociétés et des actionnaires* (1965); Sørensen, pp. 579–81; O'Connell ii. 1043–9; Jiménez de Aréchaga, 4 *Phil. Int. L.J.* (1965), 71–98; Clay, 45 *Georgetown L.J.* (1956), 1–19; Diez de Velasco, 141 Hague *Recueil* (1974, I), 93–185.

[2] I.C.J. Reports (1970), p. 3; 9 *Int. Leg. Materials* (1970), 227; Bishop, p. 837; for comment see Briggs, 65 *A.J.* (1971), 327–45; Lillich, ibid., 522–32; Metzger, ibid., 532–41; Caflisch, 31 *Z.a.ö. R.u.V.* (1971), 162–96; C. de Visscher, 6 *Revue belge* (1970), i–iv; id., 7 *Revue belge* (1971), 1–6; id., *Théories et réalités* (4th ed.), pp. 303–5; Higgins, 11 *Virginia Journ. of Int. Law* (1971), 327–43; various items, 23 *Revista española* (1971), nos. 2–3; Seidl-Hohenveldern, 22 *Öst. Z. für öff. R.* (1971–2), 255–309; Grisel, 17 *Ann. Suisse* (1971), 31–48; Mann, 67 *A.J.* (1973), 259–74.

the share capital of Barcelona Traction was in large part held by Belgian nationals, the principal shareholder being a Belgian company called Sidro.[1] During the Second World War large blocks of shares were transferred to American nominees and, for a time, were vested in a trustee. In the Belgian view the ownership of these remained Belgian. In the immediate postwar period the Spanish authorities refused to authorize foreign currency transfers to service sterling bonds issued by Barcelona Traction. As a consequence in 1948 three Spanish holders of recently acquired bonds brought bankruptcy proceedings against Barcelona Traction. Eventually Barcelona Traction and the subsidiary companies were declared bankrupt in Spain, and by 1952 the assets in Spain and the management of the subsidiaries had passed to Spanish interests as a result of a complicated series of proceedings in the Spanish courts.

As a result of the bankruptcy proceedings, Spain received diplomatic representations from several governments and from Canada in particular. Canada took little or no further action after 1952 and, after a failure to negotiate a settlement, Belgium submitted the dispute to the International Court of Justice,[2] claiming reparation for losses[3] caused to Belgian shareholders in Barcelona Traction as a consequence of various unlawful acts[4] by the Spanish courts and administrative authorities. In the Belgian view the bankruptcy proceedings were contrived with the object of transferring the control of the group of companies to Spanish interests and leading to the 'total despoliation' of the group.

The Court held that Belgium lacked a legal interest in the subject matter of the claim and hence did not proceed to the merits. Judge Jessup held that the Belgian ownership of the shares had not been established. Judge Gros held that the company lacked a genuine connection with the Belgian economy. Judge Tanaka decided in favour of Belgium on the issue of admissibility

[1] The principal shareholder in Sidro was another company, Sofina, in which, it was alleged, Belgian interests were preponderant.

[2] An earlier Application in 1958 was discontinued, a step which Spain as Respondent did not oppose. In 1964 the Court, on a new Application of 1962, rejected two Spanish preliminary objections relating to jurisdiction and joined the other preliminary objections (relating to non-exhaustion of local remedies and lack of *jus standi* in respect of the shareholders) to the merits. The Spanish objection on the basis of lack of *jus standi* had two branches (a) absence of Belgian ownership of the shares in question; (b) the absence of a right of diplomatic protection in respect of shareholders by a state other than the national state of the company.

[3] A sum equivalent to 88 per cent of the net value of the business at the time of the bankruptcy declaration in 1948, plus incidental damage and certain expenses. Apart from the interest element the total claimed was some 84 million dollars.

[4] On the issues of state responsibility raised by Belgium see *supra*, p. 474.

but held in favour of Spain on the merits. The other twelve Judges of the Court[1] participated in the reasoning of the majority judgment, though Judge Fitzmaurice[2] had serious misgivings concerning 'an unsatisfactory state of the law that obliges the Court to refrain from pronouncing on the substantive merits of the Belgian claim, on the basis of what is really—at least in the actual circumstances of this case—somewhat of a technicality'.

The Court[3] accepted the mechanism of the limited liability company (*société anonyme*) as a general feature of national legal systems which had become a fact of international economic life. The shareholder takes advantage, as he is entitled to do, of the device of incorporation. If the company is harmed, this indirectly causes prejudice to the shareholders; but in such a case what is affected is a simple interest and not the *rights* of the shareholders. The shareholders must look to the company and thence to the national state of the company for action. The Court was unimpressed by the argument that, in the absence of protection by Canada (which had ceased substantial diplomatic activity in 1952), the shareholders should have alternative protection. The Court simply pointed out that Canada had the power to exercise protection but such power was discretionary—it was a right, not an obligation.[4] Various issues as to the policy of the law are explored in the judgment and, among the considerations which found favour with the Court was the following:[5]

> The Court considers that the adoption of the theory of the diplomatic protection of shareholders as such, by opening the door to competing diplomatic claims, could create an atmosphere of confusion and insecurity in international economic relations. The danger would be all the greater inasmuch as the shares of companies whose activity is international, are widely scattered and frequently change hands.

The Court recognized that the shareholder has an independent basis for protection if the act complained of is aimed at the direct rights of the shareholder as such, for example, the right to any dividend.[6] Apart from that case, the question remained whether there were special circumstances in which the corporate veil could be lifted in the interest of the shareholders. Treaties and decisions concerned with the treatment of enemy and allied property in the two world wars and the treatment of foreign

[1] Riphagen, *ad hoc* Judge for Belgium, dissented.

[2] I.C.J. Reports (1970), p. 64.

[3] See especially pp. 34–8. See also the separate opinions of Judges Morelli, pp. 231–42; Padilla Nervo, pp. 244–64; and Ammoun, pp. 296–333.

[4] pp. 41–5. See also at p. 37. [5] pp. 48–50 at p. 49.

[6] p. 36.

property in cases of nationalization were forms of *lex specialis* and were not of general application. In the view of the Court[1] the only special circumstance was the case of the company having ceased to exist as a corporate entity capable in law of defending its rights in the relevant municipal courts.

The carefully argued separate opinions of Judges Tanaka,[2] Jessup,[3] and Gros[4] supported the diplomatic protection of shareholders as a principle.[5]

The Court rejected two propositions for which there had been some support in the sources of the law, and which thus deserve some consideration.

(i) Protection for shareholders may be justified when the corporation is 'completely paralysed' or 'practically defunct'.

The Court held that shareholders could only receive protection as such when the corporation had ceased to exist in law. This was not true of Barcelona Traction since, in spite of its economic paralysis in Spain and state of receivership in Canada, the Company still existed and was capable of legal action. The Court remarked that the description 'practically defunct' 'lacks all legal precision'.[6] On the other hand Judges Fitzmaurice,[7] Tanaka,[8] and Gros,[9] with the support of a fair amount of other opinion,[1] would assimilate the absence of effective personality with formal termination of corporate existence, on the basis that in the context of diplomatic protection the internal law criteria are to be applied with moderation.

(ii) Protection may be exercised where the corporation has the nationality of the very state responsible for the acts complained of.

The Court remarked that 'whatever the validity of this theory

[1] pp. 40–1. [2] pp. 121 seq., especially pp. 130–5. [3] pp. 168–201.

[4] pp. 268–79, on condition that the investments in question are 'connected with the national economy' of the protecting state.

[5] Also in support of the principle: Nial, op. cit., pp. 320–2; Lillich, op. cit.; Wortley, *Expropriation*, pp. 11–12, 144; Judge Wellington Koo, *Barcelona Traction* case (Preliminary Objections), I.C.J. Reports (1964), pp. 53–64; Verzijl, 12 *Neths. Int. L.R.* (1965), 34–40; Feliciano, op. cit.; C. de Visscher, *Les effectivités du droit international public*, pp. 134–8; de Hochepied, op. cit., Jones, op. cit. (with some caution); *Proceedings, A.S.I.L.* (1969), 30–53. See further the *Ziat Ben Kiran* claim, *R.I.A.A.* ii. 729; *Ann. Digest* 2 (1923–4), no. 102. Against the principle: Jiménez de Aréchaga, op. cit.; id., in Sørensen, pp. 579–81; Bagge, op. cit., p. 171. See also *Arbitration between the United States and the Reparation Commission* (1926), *R.I.A.A.* ii. 779; 8 *B.Y.* (1927), 156.

[6] p. 41. See also Judges Jessup, pp. 193–4; Padilla Nervo, pp. 256–7; Ammoun, pp. 318–20; and Beckett, op. cit., pp. 190–1.

[7] pp. 72–5. [8] p. 134.

[9] p. 276. See also Riphagen, Judge *ad hoc*, pp. 344–5.

[1] P. de Visscher, op. cit., p. 477; Bindschedler, 90 Hague *Recueil* (1956, II), 237–8. British practice is in accord: *British Digest* v. 564; Hackworth v. 840–3. See also Feliciano, op. cit., p. 304.

may be, it is certainly not applicable to the present case, since Spain is not the national State of Barcelona Traction'.[1] However, Judges Fitzmaurice,[2] Tanaka,[3] and Jessup[4] supported this form of protection, primarily on the basis that in such a case no claim on behalf of the company would be possible on the international plane since the company has local nationality. The separate opinions of Judges Morelli,[5] Padilla Nervo,[6] and Ammoun[7] rejected this form of protection and the authorities are much divided on the issue.[8] In truth the exception, if it exists, is anomalous 'since it ignores the traditional rule that a State is not guilty of a breach of international law for injuring one of its own nationals'.[9] It is arbitrary to allow the shareholders to emerge from the carapace of the corporation in this situation but not in others. If one accepts the general considerations of policy advanced by the Court then this alleged exception to the rule is disqualified.

Interests in ships and aircraft.[1] The question of the nationality of ships and aircraft arises in a variety of contexts,[2] and many of the rules are of a functional kind.[3] In fact much that is written on the subject is not concerned with the problems of diplomatic protection, and it is not appropriate to fasten on general propositions about the nationality of ships, primarily relating to jurisdiction, as relevant to the issue of the admissibility of claims. In general the principle of real or genuine link[4] supported in the *Nottebohm* case[5] ought to apply here, and there is evidence for the view that *bona fide* national ownership, rather than registration or authority to fly the flag, provides the appropriate basis for protection of ships.[6] The determination of national ownership leads into the issues concerning beneficial interest, corporations,

[1] p. 48 and see, however, Judge Padilla Nervo, sep. op., I.C.J. Reports (1970), p. 257.
[2] pp. 72–4. [3] p. 134. [4] pp. 191–3.
[5] p. 240. [6] pp. 257–9. [7] p. 318.
[8] In favour of protection: Beckett, 17 *Grot. Soc.* (1932), 189–93; C. de Visscher, 61 *R.D.I.L.C.* (1934), 624, 651; P. de Visscher, 102 Hague *Recueil* (1961, I), 478–9; Petrén, 109 Hague *Recueil* (1963, II), 506, 510; Judge Wellington Koo, sep. op., *Barcelona Traction* case (Preliminary Objections), I.C.J. Reports (1964), p. 58; Jones, op.cit., p. 257; Caflisch, op. cit., pp. 153 seq.; Kiss, op. cit. See also Vallat, *International Law and the Practitioner*, p. 28; Whiteman viii. 1272–4. Opposing protection: Jiménez de Aréchaga, 4 *Phil. Int. L.J.* (1965), 93–4; id., in Sørensen, p. 580; Diez de Velasco, 141 Hague *Recueil* (1974, I), 163–6. See also O'Connell ii. 1043; *Kunhardt Case* (1903), *R.I.A.A.* ix. 171; *Baasch and Römer Case* (1903), *R.I.A.A.* x. 723; *Brewer, Moller and Company Case*, *R.I.A.A.* x. 433; *El Triunfo Case*, *R.I.A.A.* xv. 467. [9] Judge Jessup, sep. op., p. 192.
[1] See especially Watts, 33 *B.Y.* (1957), 52–84; and also Schwarzenberger, *International Law* (3rd ed.), i. 412–18; Briggs, pp. 330–3; Rienow, *The Test of the Nationality of a Merchant Vessel* (1937); Rousseau, pp. 416–18.
[2] *Supra*, pp. 203, 242–3, 316–19, 424–6. [3] See *supra*, pp. 405–6.
[4] See generally, *supra*, pp. 392 seq. [5] I.C.J. Reports (1955), p. 4.
[6] Watts, op. cit., pp. 73–83.

and shareholders considered previously. It would seem that the position is the same in the case of aircraft.

State interests in corporations.[1] Governments may themselves hold shares in corporations, and some novel issues may arise, for example concerning the need to exhaust local remedies,[2] when the corporation makes a claim which is adopted by the government under the law of which the corporation is constituted. In the *Anglo-Iranian Oil Company* case[3] the United Kingdom supported a claim in which it had a direct interest. A question arises as to the eligibility of corporations in which governments have interests to claim sovereign immunity.[4]

Subrogation. The term subrogation may describe the transfer of liabilities as a consequence of the principle of state succession (assuming that the principle could operate in this way).[5] The term more correctly describes the process of 'transfer' on the basis of agreement between the successor state and the claimant, or estoppel, in which case issues as to the existence and meaning of the agreement or estoppel concern the admissibility of the claim.[6]

6. *Exhaustion of Local Remedies*[7]

An important rule of admissibility applies to cases of diplomatic protection as opposed to instances of direct injury to the state. A claim will not be admissible on the international plane

[1] See Johnson, 4 *I.L.Q.* (1951), 159–77; McNair, *Opinions* ii. 39.

[2] See *infra*, section 6. [3] I.C.J. Reports (1951), p. 89.

[4] McNair, loc. cit., referring to a case in which the U.S. District Court for the District of Columbia granted immunity to the Anglo-Iranian Oil Company Ltd., basing its decision on the 'public purpose' of the Company: 47 *A.J.* (1953), 502.

[5] Cf. Schwarzenberger, *International Law* (3rd ed.), i. 175–9; and the *Lighthouses* arbitration (1956), P.C.A., *R.I.A.A.* xii. 188–9; Int. L.R. 23 (1956), p. 659 at p. 668. On state succession see Chapter XXVIII.

[6] See the *Mavrommatis* case (1924), P.C.I.J., Ser. A, no. 2, at p. 28; and *Blabon et al.* v. *United States*, Int. L.R. 28, p. 195.

[7] Or, 'épuisement des recours locaux', 'épuisement préalable des recours internes'. See generally, Fawcett, 31 *B.Y.* (1954), 452–8; Bagge, 34 *B.Y.* (1958), 165–9; Amerasinghe, *State Responsibility for Injuries to Aliens*, pp. 169–269; id., 12 *I.C.L.Q.* (1963), 1285–1325; id., 25 *Z.a.ö.R.u.V.* (1965), 445–77; id., 36 *Z.a.ö.R.u.V.* (1976), 727–59; Schwarzenberger, *International Law* (3rd ed.), i. 602–12; Garcia Amador, *Yrbk., I.L.C.* (1958), ii. 55–61; Verzijl, *Annuaire de l'Inst.* 45 (1954), i. 5 seq.; ibid. 46 (1956), 1 seq.; Reuter, 103 Hague *Recueil* (1961, II), 613–19; Briggs, pp. 632–7; id., 50 *A.J.* (1956), 921–7; Fitzmaurice, 37 *B.Y.* (1961), 53–64; Law, *The Local Remedies Rule in International Law* (1961); Jenks, *The Prospects of International Adjudication*, pp. 527–37; Whiteman viii. 769–807; de Visscher, 52 Hague *Recueil* (1935, II), 421–32; Sørensen, pp. 582–90; Mummery, 58 *A.J.* (1964), 389–414; Schwebel and Wetter, 60 *A.J.* (1966), 484–501; Head, 5 *Canad. Yrbk.* (1967), 142–58; Jennings, 121 Hague *Recueil* (1967, II), 480–6; Przetacznik, 21 *Öst. Zeit. für öff. R.* (1971), 103–12; P. de Visscher, 136 Hague *Recueil* (1972, II), 167–76; Chappez, *La Règle de l'épuisement des voies de recours internes* (1972); Cançado Trindade,

unless the individual alien or corporation concerned has exhausted the legal remedies available to him in the state which is alleged to be the author of injury.[1] This is a rule which is justified by practical and political considerations and not by any logical necessity deriving from international law as a whole. The more persuasive practical considerations advanced are the greater suitability and convenience of national courts as forums for the claims of individuals and corporations, the need to avoid the multiplication of small claims on the level of diplomatic protection, the manner in which aliens by residence and business activity have associated themselves with the local jurisdiction,[2] and the utility of a procedure which may lead to classification of the facts and liquidation of the damages.[3] The role of the local remedies rule is seen more readily if three situations are distinguished.[4]

(1) When the act complained of is a breach of an international agreement or customary law, and is not a breach of local law, then the rule is inapplicable.

(2) When the act complained of is a breach of local law only, then it is only the subsequent conduct of the state of the forum which can create responsibility. If the authorities there interfere with the course of justice or certain standards are not observed, then a denial of justice has occurred and responsibility results from it.

(3) When the act complained of is a breach both of the local law and of an international agreement or customary law, the rule of the exhaustion of local remedies applies. In this type of case the function of the rule is procedural: it is a question of admissibility and not of substance.[5]

However, the distinction between the first and third situations does not depend entirely on the question whether there has been a breach of the local law. The incidence of the procedural rule is a difficult problem,[6] and probably any answer will be incomplete if the empirical nature of the rule and its dependence on criteria

16 *Indian Journ.* (1976), 187–218; id., 12 *Revue belge* (1976), 499–527. See also Ago, Sixth Report on State Responsibility, I.L.C. Doc., A/CN.4/302, Add. 2 and Add. 3, 5 and 14 July 1977.

[1] The application of the rule may be avoided by agreement.

[2] Cf. the problems of the real or genuine link in the context of nationality, *supra*, pp. 392 seq.

[3] See McNair, *Opinions* ii. 197–8, 312. See also Borchard, *Diplomatic Protection of Citizens Abroad*, p. 817.

[4] See Fawcett, op. cit.

[5] Fawcett, op. cit.; Judge Lauterpacht, sep. op., *Norwegian Loans* case, I.C.J. Reports (1957), p. 9 at pp. 39–41. Fawcett is of opinion that the objection would not be admitted if the claim were not for judgment and damages but for a declaration only; on this point see also Simmonds, 10 *I.C.L.Q.* (1961), 537, 545; Amerasinghe, *State Responsibility*, p. 204. For a contrary view: Sørensen, p. 582. See also *Case of Ireland against the United Kingdom*, Europ. Ct. of Human Rights, Judgment, 18 January 1978, para. 159; ibid., Judge Fitzmaurice, sep. op., paras. 8–11.

[6] On which see Meron, 35 *B.Y.* (1959), 83–101.

of reasonableness are ignored. The distinction which is commonly drawn is between cases of direct injury to a state, for example by inflicting damage on its warships[1] or the commission of acts directed against its ambassador, and cases of diplomatic protection, in which the interest of an individual (or other legal entity of private law) is affected and the legal interest of the state depends on the nationality of the individual concerned. It is only in the latter case that the exhaustion of local remedies is a condition of admissibility on the international plane. However, in drawing the distinction one is perhaps only stating the problem rather than providing the basis for a solution. Reliance on the existence or not of a breach of local law is not entirely satisfactory, since, in some cases normally regarded as examples of direct injury to a state, it is not clear that there is no breach of the local law of the defendant state. Meron[2] argues that the rule cannot apply in cases of direct injury by reason of the maxim *par in parem, non habet jurisdictionem*, but it could be said that the maxim loses much of its force if it rests on the difference between direct and indirect injury (in the persons of nationals) to states. In the latter case states in the first instance leave the determination of issues to the internal law after all.

Conditions of application of the local remedies rule. The existence of the rule is undoubted and its application in practice is very common. Nevertheless, not a little confusion and complexity are presented by the conditions in which the rule is applied.

(a) *What is the precise function of proceedings in the local courts?* The rule is often described rather loosely in terms of the possibility of 'obtaining redress' in the local courts. As an issue of admissibility the local proceedings are regarded retrospectively, but when proceedings are begun in the local courts various issues of law and fact may be at large. It will not always be clear whether there is a breach of international law, or local law, or of either. The alien claimant in the local courts may be able to seek a remedy for a breach of international law *as such*, or may employ a remedy of local law which involves no reference to matters of international law but gives substantial reparation for the harm complained of. Even in the case of direct injury to the interests of a foreign state, for example, damage to warships caused by agents of the state in which remedies are sought, it is not possible to *assume* that no remedy exists in municipal law.[3] The local proceedings may actually establish that an instance of state responsi-

[1] Cf. the *Corfu Channel* case (Merits), I.C.J. Reports (1949), p. 4.

[2] Op. cit., pp. 84–5.

[3] Cf. Jennings, 121 Hague *Recueil* (1967, II), 482.

bility has occurred but it is surely incorrect to state[1] that resort to local remedies is 'required . . . in order to determine . . . whether or not [such] an act or omission is incompatible with international law'. The local proceedings may simply establish that a particular rule of local law stands in the way of redress and leave aside both the issue of compatibility of that rule with international law, and the whole question of whether the dispute has an international character.[2] Thus in general the exhaustion of local remedies will involve using such local procedures as are available to protect interests which correspond *as closely as may be and in practical terms* with the interests involved in a subsequent international claim.[3]

(b) *The local remedies rule only applies when effective remedies are available in the national system.* In certain circumstances recourse to local remedies is excused. The remedies to be exhausted comprise all forms of recourse as of right, including administrative remedies of a legal nature 'but not extra-legal remedies or remedies as of grace'.[4] The best test appears to be that an effective remedy must be available 'as a matter of reasonable possibility'.[5] No effective remedy is available if a point of law which could have been taken on appeal has previously been decided by the highest court,[6] or if the only issue on appeal would be one of fact and the higher courts lack the power to review findings of fact.[7] However, the local law may be uncertain on such issues as the principles of sovereign immunity, the Act of State doctrine, or the interpretation of gold clauses, and the consequence is that an international tribunal should show caution in drawing conclusions on the availability of a local remedy.[8] It must be noted, however, that a fair number of writers[9] and arbitral awards[1] have been willing to presume ineffectiveness of

[1] See Briggs, 50 *A.J.* (1956), at pp. 925–6; also in Whiteman viii. 786–7.

[2] See Lauterpacht, sep. op., I.C.J. Reports (1957), p. 38.

[3] See the *Finnish Ships Arbitration* (*infra*) and the *Interhandel* case (*infra*). Cf. Amerasinghe, pp. 196–7. See further Bustamante y Rivero, I.C.J. Reports (1970), pp. 57–63; Tanaka, ibid., pp. 147–8.

[4] Brierly, p. 281, citing the *Finnish Ships Arbitration* (1934), *R.I.A.A.* iii. 1479.

[5] See Lauterpacht, sep. op., *Norwegian Loans* case, I.C.J. Reports (1957), p. 39; Fitzmaurice, 37 *B.Y.* (1961), 59–64; Tanaka, sep. op., *Barcelona Traction* case (Second Phase), I.C.J. Reports (1970), pp. 144–5; Gros, sep. op., ibid., p. 284.

[6] *Panevezys* v. *Saldutiskis Railway* case, P.C.I.J., Series A/B, no. 76; *X* v. *Austria*, Int. L.R. 30, p. 268.

[7] *Finnish Ships Arbitration* (1934), *R.I.A.A.* iii. 1484 at p. 1535.

[8] Lauterpacht, sep. op., I.C.J. Reports (1957), pp. 39–40.

[9] Sørensen, pp. 589–90; Oppenheim i. 361–2; Amerasinghe, *State Responsibility*, pp. 196–7, 242–4.

[1] e.g. *Forests in Central Rhodopia* (Merits), *Ann. Digest* (1933–4), no. 39; *R.I.A.A.* iii. 1405, 1420; 28 *A.J.* (1934), 773, 789.

remedies from the circumstances, for example on the basis of evidence that the courts were subservient to the executive.[1] A final and major point remains. A remedy is effective if it does justice to the claim in the local courts: 'a remedy cannot be *ineffective* merely because, if, the claimant is in the wrong, it will not be *obtainable*'.[2]

(c) *Should the local courts have jurisdiction in accordance with international law?* It may be that no effective remedy is available if the local courts do not have jurisdiction in relation to the matter in issue *in terms of local law*[3] (see (b) above). A different issue is whether the local remedies rule can apply when, according to international law, the local courts could not have jurisdiction over the matter in issue. Judge Fitzmaurice[4] has expressed the opinion that it could not, since no question of local remedies could arise in respect of proceedings which were a nullity in terms of international law, either as a consequence of excess of jurisdiction or on some other ground, such as lack of notification of proceedings.

(d) *Issues arising from executive action.* It is sometimes said to be the law that the rule does not apply when the issue arises from measures taken by 'the constitutional or legislative power or the highest executive organs'.[5] This view is too dogmatic since remedies may be available whatever the constitutional status of the agency taking the measure concerned. The test remains that of the reasonable possibility of an effective remedy.[6]

(e) *In cases of diplomatic protection does the rule apply only if a sufficient link existed between the alien and the respondent state?* Some authorities hold the opinion that local remedies need not be exhausted unless, at the time of the original harm alleged, the alien has established some voluntary connexion with the territory or jurisdiction of the respondent state.[7] This view receives no

[1] See the *Brown* claim (1923), *R.I.A.A.* vi. 120; Briggs, p. 215. See also Whiteman, p. 784; Tanaka, sep. op., *Barcelona Traction* case (Second Phase), I.C.J. Reports (1970), pp. 145–7.

[2] Fitzmaurice, 37 *B.Y.* (1961), 60.

[3] See the Estonian argument and the Court's acceptance of the principle in the *Panevezys–Saldutiskis Railway* case, P.C.I.J., Ser. A/B, no. 76, p. 18; Whiteman viii. 773.

[4] sep. op., *Barcelona Traction* case (Second Phase), I.C.J. Reports (1970), pp. 103–10. See also Riphagen, Judge *ad hoc*, ibid., pp. 355–6; Amerasinghe, *State Responsibility*, pp. 185–187; Jennings, 121 Hague *Recueil* (1967, II), 485–6.

[5] See Verzijl, *Annuaire de l'Inst.*, 45 (1954), i. 112; Whiteman viii. 785; *Annuaire de l'Inst.*, 46 (1956), 266. See also the *U.S.* v. *Bulgaria*, I.C.J. Pleadings, quoted in Whiteman viii. 783–4; and Lauterpacht, *Collected Papers* i. 397–8.

[6] See the judgment in the *Interhandel* case, I.C.J. Reports (1959), p. 27. See also Sørensen, p. 587.

[7] See Sørensen, p. 583; Meron, 35 *B.Y.* (1959), 94–100; Amerasinghe, *State Responsibility*, pp. 182–7; O'Connell ii. 950–2; *Aerial Incident* case (*Israel* v. *Bulgaria*), I.C.J. Pleadings (1959), pp. 531–2; Whiteman viii. 793. See also Reuter, 103 Hague *Recueil*, p. 615; *British Digest* vi. 253; Jennings, 121 Hague *Recueil* (1967, II), 485–6.

explicit support from the decided cases though it can be reconciled with the *Finnish Ships* and *Ambatielos* cases (see below) by recourse to a broad definition of the link required and retrospective rationalization.[1] As a matter of principle the outcome depends upon one's view of the major basis in policy of the local remedies rule. If the major objective is to provide an alternative, relatively more convenient, recourse to that of proceeding on the international plane then no condition as to a link will apply. If the rule is related to assumption of risk by the alien and the existence of a proper basis for exercise of national jurisdiction, then the requirement of a voluntary link, such as residence, is good sense.

(f) *The rule applies only in connexion with state responsibility for an unlawful act.* This is the assumption in the literature and jurisprudence of the subject and the Arbitral Tribunal for the Agreement on German External Debts has decided[2] that the rule, as a consequence, cannot apply where the applicant state makes no claim for damages but merely requests a decision on the interpretation and application of a treaty.

The operation of the local remedies rule will now be examined in the light of the leading cases.

Finnish Ships *arbitration*.[3] During the First World War, at a time when Finland was a part of Russia, the Russian Government requisitioned certain ships belonging to Finnish shipowners which were transferred to the British Government. The vessels were used in the service of the Allies, and at the end of the war the Finnish Government made claims against the British Government for compensation, on behalf of the owners, for the hire of some ships used, and the loss of others, in the Allied service. The claims were unfruitful, and, under the Indemnity Act, 1920, the owners submitted the claims to the Admiralty Transport Arbitration Board. In 1926 the Board dismissed the claims on the ground that the requisition complained of was by and on behalf of the Russian Government. There was no appeal from this finding of fact. Appeal was possible on points of law to the Court of Appeal and the House of Lords, but the owners did not appeal. Eventually the two governments agreed to submit to Bagge, the sole arbitrator, the question: 'Have the Finnish

[1] Against the link requirement: Harvard Draft, 1961; 55 *A.J.* (1961), p. 577, art. 19 (and see Whiteman viii. 793–4); Am. Law Institute, Restatement, Second, *Foreign Relations Law*, paras. 206–10.

[2] *Swiss Confederation* v. *German Federal Republic (No. 1)* (1958), Int. L.R. 25 (1958, I), p. 33 at pp. 42–50; and see Johnson, 34 *B.Y.* (1958), 363–8.

[3] (1934), *R.I.A.A.* iii. 1479; *Ann. Digest* 7 (1933–4), no. 91; Briggs, p. 620. See also Fachiri, 17 *B.Y.* (1936), 19–36; Borchard, 28 *A.J.* (1934), 729–33; Hostie, 43 *R.G.D.I.P.* (1936), 327–57.

shipowners or have they not exhausted the means of recourse placed at their disposal by British law?' By reason of the failure to appeal the British Government argued that the remedies had not been exhausted. The Finnish Government contended that, in view of the finding of fact, the right of appeal was illusory and ineffective since an appeal was bound to fail. The arbitrator pointed out[1] that he was not concerned with the merits of the claim before the Board. The test of effectiveness was applied on the assumption that all allegations of fact in the claim were true. On this basis, he found that the appealable points of law in the judgment of the Board 'obviously would have been insufficient to reverse the decision of the Arbitration Board as to there not being a British requisition, and that, in consequence, there was no effective remedy against this decision'.[2] His answer to the question submitted to him was therefore that the local remedies had been exhausted.

Ambatielos *arbitration*.[3] In 1919 Mr. Ambatielos, a Greek national, concluded a contract for the purchase of nine steamships, then under construction, with the United Kingdom Government. In due course Ambatielos sought remedies for loss resulting from late delivery of some of the vessels and cancellation of the contract of purchase in respect of two others. However, as the Board of Trade had instituted proceedings in the Court of Admiralty on mortgage deeds executed on some of the ships in 1920, the claim of Ambatielos was, by agreement between the parties, put forward as a defence to the proceedings. Mr. Justice Hill gave judgment (January 1923) for the United Kingdom Government for possession and sale of certain vessels which had been delivered and for principal and interest due under the mortgage deeds. On appeal to the Court of Appeal Ambatielos asked for leave to call as a witness Major Laing, the British civil servant who had negotiated the contract for purchase of the ships. Leave was refused, and after judgment Ambatielos did not appeal to the House of Lords. In 1953 the International Court of Justice held[4] that the United Kingdom was bound to submit to arbitration the dispute as to the validity of the claim of Ambatielos under the Anglo-Greek Treaty of Commerce and Navigation of 1886. Under an agreement concluded in 1955 the claim was

[1] *R.I.A.A.* iii. 1499, 1503–4. [2] Ibid., pp. 1535 seq.

[3] (1956), Award, H.M.S.O., 1956; *R.I.A.A.* xii. 83; Int. L.R. 23 (1956), 306; ibid. 24 (1957), 291; Green, p. 657. See also Pinto, 84 *J.D.I.* (1957), 540–615; Amerasinghe, op. cit., pp. 1296 seq. (dealing, *inter alia*, with the opinions of Alfaro and Spiropoulos).

[4] I.C.J. Reports (1953), p. 10; Int. L.R. 20 (1953), 547. See also the *Ambatielos* case (Preliminary Objection), I.C.J. Reports (1952), p. 28; Int. L.R. 19 (1952), no. 96.

thus submitted to a Commission of Arbitration. The Greek claim consisted of the main claim A, for compensation for breach of the contract of sale, an alternative claim B based on unjust enrichment for return of a part payment of the price, and another alternative claim C in connexion with the cancellation of the purchase of two of the vessels as from the date of judgment instead of the date on which the mortgage deeds were signed. The United Kingdom submitted, *inter alia*, that the procedural remedies in the English courts had not been exhausted.

One of the principal Greek arguments was that the rule was not applicable because the remedies open to Ambatielos were ineffective. The Commission applied the test propounded in the *Finnish Ships* arbitration, viz., that the truth of the facts on which the claimant bases the claim must be assumed in determining the applicability of the rule. On the application of the rule the Commission observed:

> . . . 'local remedies' include not only reference to the courts and tribunals, but also the use of the procedural facilities which municipal law makes available to litigants before such courts and tribunals. It is the whole system of legal protection, as provided by municipal law, which must have been put to the test . . .

It is clear, however, that it cannot be strained too far:

> In the view of the Commission the non-utilisation of certain means of procedure can be accepted as constituting a gap in the exhaustion of local remedies only if the use of these means of procedure were essential to establish the claimant's case before the municipal courts.

The Commission found that the local remedies had not been exhausted. As regards claim A, Ambatielos had failed to exhaust local remedies by not calling Major Laing as witness in the High Court[1] and by not exhausting his rights of appeal. In the case of claim B, such remedies as were available for unjust enrichment in English law had not been tried. Nor had any claim of the kind presented in claim C been put forward in the English court: the claim before Mr. Justice Hill had been for non-delivery and was the converse of the claim for non-cancellation of the purchase of two vessels on the date of the mortgage deeds.

The Interhandel *case*.[2] In 1942 the United States Government vested most of the shares of the General Aniline and Film Com-

[1] The Commission made the assumption that the testimony would have had the effect of establishing the claim.

[2] I.C.J. Reports (1959), p. 6; Bishop, p. 808. See also Meron, 35 *B.Y.* (1959), 89–92; Simmonds, 10 *I.C.L.Q.* (1961), 495–547; Briggs, 53 *A.J.* (1959), 547–63; C. de Visscher, 63 *R.G.D.I.P.* (1959), 413–33.

pany (G.A.F.) as enemy property under the provisions of the Trading with the Enemy Act, 1917. The majority of G.A.F. shares were owned by Interhandel, a Swiss firm, which, in the opinion of the United States Government, was under the control of I.G. Farben. The view of the Swiss Government was that, after remodelling in 1940, Interhandel had completely severed its ties with I.G. Farben, although in 1945 the Swiss Government had ordered a provisional blocking of Interhandel's assets. In 1946 the Washington Accord was signed between France, the United Kingdom, and the United States and, on the other side, Switzerland. This agreement provided, *inter alia*, for the liquidation of property in Switzerland owned or controlled by Germans in Germany, the unblocking of Swiss assets in the United States, and the submission of disputes as to the application of the Accord to arbitration. The dispute remained unsettled, and in 1948, on an appeal by Interhandel under the Accord procedure, the Swiss Authority of Review annulled the provisional blocking of assets. The Swiss Government claimed that the Allied powers were bound by this decision and claimed that the vested property should be restored or that there should be resort to the arbitration procedure provided for in the Accord. The United States Government contended that the Washington Accord and the ruling of the Swiss Authority of Review did not apply to property vested in the United States.

In 1958 proceedings on the preliminary objections of the United States began in the International Court as a consequence of a Swiss application which invoked the optional clause of the statute. The Swiss application was made only after litigation by the corporation in the United States' courts between 1948 and 1957. The third preliminary objection of the United States, though framed as an objection to jurisdiction, was in effect directed against the admissibility of the application by reason of the non-exhaustion of local remedies. On the position in the United States courts the International Court observed:[1]

The Court has indicated in what conditions the Swiss Government, basing itself on the idea that Interhandel's suit had been finally rejected in the United States courts, considered itself entitled to institute proceedings by its Application of October 2nd, 1957. However, the decision given by the Supreme Court of the United States on October 14th, 1957 . . . granted a writ of *certiorari* and readmitted Interhandel into the suit. The judgment of that Court on June 16th, 1958, reversed the judgment of the Court of Appeals dismissing Interhandel's suit and remanded the case to the District Court. It was thenceforth open to Interhandel to avail itself again

[1] I.C.J. Reports (1959), pp. 26–7.

of the remedies available to it under the Trading with the Enemy Act, and to seek the restitution of its shares by proceedings in the United States courts. Its suit is still pending in the United States courts. The Court must have regard to the situation thus created.

Switzerland had argued that the local remedies rule did not apply, since the failure of the United States to comply with the decision of the Swiss Authority of Review, based on the Washington Accord, constituted a direct breach of international law, causing immediate injury to the rights of the applicant state. The Court rejected the argument:[1] '. . . the Court would confine itself to observing that such arguments do not deprive the dispute which has been referred to it of the character of a dispute in which the Swiss Government appears as having adopted the cause of its national, Interhandel,[2] for the purpose of securing the restitution to that company of assets vested by the Government of the United States'. The objection based on the local remedies rule was therefore upheld[3] in regard to the principal submission of the applicant. In its alternative claim, the applicant asked the Court to declare its competence to decide whether the United States was under an obligation to submit the dispute to arbitration or conciliation. The Court[4] agreed with the United States contention that this claim involved the same interest as the principal claim and stated that 'the grounds on which the rule of the exhaustion of local remedies is based are the same, whether in the case of an international court, arbitral tribunal, or conciliation commission'. Thus the objection applied to the alternative claim also.

Dogmatic criticism of the decision in the *Interhandel* case is inappropriate, since much depended on matters of appreciation. Nevertheless two criticisms might be thought to have cogency. In the first place, particularly in respect of the alternative claim, it is very doubtful if the facts disclosed that the only interest of Switzerland was that of Interhandel and that no direct injury to the applicant was involved.[5] There was no remedy available to the latter in the United States courts for breach of treaty rights. Secondly, litigation lasting ten years and on which no term had been placed might not be regarded as 'adequate' or 'effective'.[6]

[1] Ibid., p. 28. See also p. 27.

[2] No preliminary objection similar to that in the *Nottebohm* case, *supra*, pp. 406 seq., was advanced, although the facts seem to have warranted such an objection.

[3] By nine votes to six. [4] p. 29.

[5] See the dissenting opinions of Judge *ad hoc* Carry, p. 32, and of Judges Winiarski, pp. 83–4, Armand-Ugon, pp. 87–9, and Lauterpacht, p. 120. See also Simmonds, op. cit., pp. 540–5.

[6] Judge Armand-Ugon, at p. 87, referring to the *Finnish Ships* arbitration.

Other applications of the rule. The rule as to exhaustion of local remedies has prominence in the practice of the European Commission of Human Rights and the European Court of Human Rights,[1] and this new affirmation of the rule is a strong indication that it still accords with the attitude of governments to international petitions and claims. However, some jurists[2] claim to find evidence that tribunals are tending to restrict the ambit of the rule. Instances to support this view certainly exist,[3] but as a general perspective it is difficult to maintain, witness the *Interhandel* decision. A further possible application of the rule is in the case of claims by international organizations in respect of injuries to their agents. In principle the rule would seem to apply here, but the law may develop on other lines.[4]

7. *Extinctive Prescription*[5]

The lapse of time in presentation may bar an international claim in spite of the fact that no rule of international law lays down a time limit. Special agreements may exclude categories of claim on a temporal basis, but otherwise the question is one for the discretion of the tribunal. The rule is widely accepted by writers and in arbitral jurisprudence.[6] In the *Gentini*[7] case Ralston, Umpire, observed: 'The principle of prescription finds its foundation in the highest equity—the avoidance of possible injustice to the defendant. . . .' Commonly a state claim will be

[1] See *infra*, pp. 584–8. See also the International Covenant on Civil and Political Rights, art. 41 (1) (c); Brownlie, *Documents*, p. 162.

[2] See e.g. Reuter, 103 Hague *Recueil* (1961, II), 615–16.

[3] See the decision of the Court of Justice of the European Communities, Case 6/60, *Humblet* v. *État Belge*, *Recueil de la jurisprudence de la Cour* (1960), p. 1125; and cf. Case no. 1, Arbitration Tribunal for the Agreement on German External Debts, 34 *B.Y.* (1958), 363.

[4] See Eagleton, 76 Hague *Recueil* (1950, I), 351–2; Hardy, 37 *B.Y.* (1961), 525–6. See generally, *infra*, p. 684, on the competence of organizations in bringing international claims. Of course, the United Nations cannot provide local remedies for claims against itself, but perhaps a claims tribunal could be created for this purpose.

[5] Or, 'préscription libératoire'. See generally King, 15 *B.Y.* (1934), 82–97; Politis and C. de Visscher, *Annuaire de l'Inst.* 32 (1925), 1–24; García Amador, *Yrbk., I.L.C.* (1958), ii. 61 (Article 23), 67; *Ambatielos* case, I.C.J. Pleadings (1953), index; Ralston, *Law and Procedure of International Tribunals*, pp. 375–83, Suppl., pp. 185–7; Oppenheim i. 349–50; Schwarzenberger, *International Law* (3rd ed.), i. 565–70; C. de Visscher, in *Hommage d'une génération de juristes au Président Basdevant* (1960), pp. 525–33; Pinto, 87 Hague *Recueil* (1955, I), 438–48; Cheng, *General Principles of Law*, pp. 373–86; Hackworth v. 713–18.

[6] See King, op. cit., and also the *Ambatielos* claim (1956), *R.I.A.A.* xii. 103; Int. L.R. 23 (1956), 306; and the *Lighthouses* arbitration (1956), *R.I.A.A.* xii. 186; Int. L.R. 23 (1956), 659.

[7] (1903), *R.I.A.A.* x. 552–5. See also the *Spader* claim (1903), *R.I.A.A.* ix. 223.

denied because of the difficulty the defendant has in establishing the facts, but where there is no clear disadvantage to the defendant tribunals will be reluctant to allow lapse of time *simpliciter* to bar claims in the conditions in which state relations are conducted. Broad considerations of justice predominate. Thus in the *Cayuga Indians Claim*[1] a protected minority were not held to be prejudiced by delay on the part of the territorial sovereign.

On some sets of facts prescription will be associated with questions of acquiescence and estoppel,[2] and a number of cases which are regarded as instances of prescription are in fact based on lapse of time as evidence of acquiescence or waiver.[3] The distinction between prescription and acquiescence is important: in the latter case lapse of time and considerations of equity are less germane than precise evidence of acts of the parties. In cases of state succession and subrogation it would be necessary to establish acquiescence binding on particular legal persons, whereas prescription is a 'universal' basis of inadmissibility.

8. *Waiver of Claims*[4]

Abandonment of claims may occur by unilateral acts of waiver, acquiescence implied from conduct, and by agreement. As in cases of diplomatic protection the state is asserting its own competence, it follows that the state may compromise or release the claim, leaving the individual or corporation concerned without any remedy.[5] Conversely the waiver of a claim by the national in his private capacity does not bind his government.[6]

9. *Other Grounds of Inadmissibility*

Other grounds exist which deserve brief notice. An objection *ratione temporis* will raise a question of admissibility when it

[1] (1926), *R.I.A.A.* vi. 173; 20 *A.J.* (1926), 574; *Ann. Digest* 3 (1925–6), no. 181; Bishop, p. 51. See also Oppenheim i. 350, n. 2.

[2] See generally *infra*, pp. 634, 637.

[3] See *Sarropoulos* v. *Bulgarian State* (1927), *Recueil des décisions des tribunaux arbitraux mixtes* vii. 47; *Ann. Digest* 4 (1927–8), no. 173. Cf. Schwarzenberger, op. cit.

[4] See Witenberg, op. cit., pp. 31–33; García Amador, *Yrbk., I.L.C.* (1958), ii. 57–8; Suy, *Les Actes juridiques unilatéraux en droit international public*, pp. 154–7; *Haas* v. *Humphrey* (1957), Int. L.R. 24 (1957), 316; *Wollemborg* claim (1956), ibid., p. 654; *R.I.A.A.* xiv. 283. On the Calvo Clause see *infra*, pp. 546–7.

[5] See Briggs, pp. 722–3. Cf. *Public Trustee* v. *Chartered Bank of India, Australia and China*, Int. L.R. 23 (1956), p. 687 at pp. 698–9; *Austrian Citizen's Compensation Case*, Int. L.R. 32, p. 153; *Inao Horimoto* v. *The State*, ibid., p. 161; *Togen Akiyama* v. *The State*, ibid., p. 233; *Jews Departed from Hungary Case*, ibid. 44, p. 301.

[6] The decision in the *Tattler* claim (1920), *R.I.A.A.* vi. 48; Briggs, p. 723; Bishop, p. 821; is in error. Cf. *First National City Bank of New York* claim (1957), Int. L.R. 26 (1958, II), p. 323 at p. 325.

involves the submission that at the relevant time the applicant state, or claimant in other circumstances, had no *locus standi*, for example because there was a lack of legal personality.[1] It is obvious that failure to comply with the rules of court of the tribunal in making an application may provide a ground for an objection as to admissibility, although tribunals may be reluctant to give too much significance to matters of form.[2] Analogously to the local remedies rule, it may happen that a respondent can establish that adequate remedies have been or ought to be obtained in another tribunal, whether national or international.[3] Moreover, there will be a residue of instances in which questions of inadmissibility and 'substantive' issues are difficult to distinguish. This is the case with the doctrine of 'clean hands', according to which a claimant's involvement in activity illegal under either municipal or international law may bar the claim.[4]

10. *Counter-Claims*[5]

Much that has been said above will apply, *mutatis mutandis*, to counter-claims. However, the overriding requirement, apart from questions of jurisdiction, is that the counter-claim should have a sufficient connexion with the claim itself.[6]

11. *Foreign Acts of State in Municipal Courts*

One form of the Act of State doctrine is the rule that municipal courts will not pass on the validity of the acts of foreign governments performed in their capacities as sovereigns within their

[1] See the *Cameroons* case, I.C.J. Reports (1963), pp. 46–7 (Judge Wellington Koo, sep. op.), 127–30 (Judge Fitzmaurice, sep. op.), 169 (Judge Bustamante, diss. op.). Both sides in the case treated the objection as a jurisdictional one.

[2] See Witenberg, op. cit., pp. 90–4; the *Cameroons* case, I.C.J. Reports (1963), pp. 27–8, 42–3 (Judge Wellington Koo), 173–4 (Judge Bustamante). See also, on procedural inadmissibility, the latter at pp. 172–3.

[3] See the *Ottoz* claim, Int. L.R. 18 (1951), no. 136; the *Nartnick* and *Mayer* claims, Int. L.R. 21 (1954), pp. 149, 150 respectively; and see the defendant's arguments in *Luther* v. *Sagor* [1921] 1 K.B. 456; [1921] 3 K.B. 532. On litispendence as an analogue of the local remedies rule see Jenks, *Prospects of International Adjudication*, p. 527.

[4] See Witenberg, op. cit., pp. 63–70; Hackworth v. 709–18; Rousseau, p. 367; Salmon, *Ann. français* (1964), 225–66; Miaja de la Muela, *Mélanges offerts à Juraj Andrassy*, pp. 189–213. Cf. the defence of public policy in the common law of tort. Cf. García Amador, *Yrbk., I.L.C.* (1958), ii. 53–4; ibid. (1961), ii. 53, art. 19.

[5] See Rosenne, *The Law and Practice of the International Court* i. 434–6.

[6] See the *Asylum* case, I.C.J. Reports (1950), p. 266 at pp. 280–1, 288; and the *Orinoco Steamship Co.* case, *R.I.A.A.* ix, p. 180 at p. 201.

own territories. In this form the rule has been applied to foreign expropriation measures by courts in various states[1] and by the United States Supreme Court in the *Sabbatino* case.[2] The rule has obvious significance in the field of jurisdiction, and a variety of considerations of policy are thought to support it, including the need to leave the executive unencumbered in its conduct of international relations. There is, however, an aspect of the rule which justifies its mention in a chapter on the admissibility of state claims. The issue of admissibility is considered in the context of international tribunals, but, as is clear from study of the local remedies rule, admissibility is bound up with the maintenance of a sensible relationship between national and international courts. The Act of State doctrine, from this point of view, is a congener of the local remedies rule: certain issues are better left to procedures on the international plane.[3] But it is not a converse of that rule, as the incidents of its operation are very different.

What is called the *Sabbatino* principle, involving judicial self-limitation *vis-à-vis* the executive, has received criticism. However, the principle has been reaffirmed by the Supreme Court in *First National City Bank* v. *Banco Nacional de Cuba*.[4] The more recent developments indicate the difficulty in finding a satisfactory alternative.[5] In *Alfred Dunhill* v. *Republic of Cuba*[6] the Supreme Court employed the 'restrictive theory' of sovereign immunity as the basis for refusal to recognize repudiation of commercial obligations of a state instrumentality as an act of state.

[1] On these decisions see Münch, 98 Hague *Recueil* (1959, III), 442–6 and *infra*, p. 539, n. 8. See also Note, 62 *Columbia L.R.* (1962), 1278–1312; and the *Indonesian Corporation* case, 13 *Neths. Int. L.R.* (1966), 58.

[2] *Banco Nacional de Cuba* v. *Sabbatino*, 376 U.S. 398 (1964); see Henkin, 64 *Columbia L.R.* (1964), 805–32; and Simmonds, 14 *I.C.L.Q.* (1965), 452–92. An attempt to limit the effect of the decision took the form of the Foreign Assistance Act of 1965, the so-called Second Hickenlooper Amendment. For comment: Note, 4 *N.Y.U. Journ. of I.L.* (1971), 260–74.

[3] Cf. the doctrine of sovereign immunity, *supra*, Chapter XV, and cf. also *Bulgarian State* v. *Takvorian*, Int. L.R. 21 (1954), 265.

[4] 406 U.S. 759 (1972); 11 *I.L.M.* 811.

[5] See Lowenfeld, 66 *A.J.* (1972), 795–814.

[6] 96 Sup. Ct. 1854 (1976); 15 *I.L.M.* 735.

CHAPTER XXII

SOME INCIDENTS OF ILLEGALITY AND THE CONCEPT OF *JUS COGENS*[1]

1. *The Varying Content of Illegality*

THE law of responsibility has a precarious existence in a decentralized system of international relations, lacking compulsory jurisdiction and automatically applicable enforcement procedures. Much of the law consists of rules of competence and functional co-operation,[2] and the normal instance is not a tribunal but diplomatic exchange and negotiated settlement. Thus acceptance of the delictual character of breaches of treaty and other rules and the appearance of sophisticated, municipal, principles of responsibility, linked to damages rather than the political 'indemnity' or 'satisfaction', are relatively recent. Rules develop in the customary law as liberties and prohibitions with no very precise definition of the content of illegality involved.

Beyond the incidence of responsibility for causing material harm, there exists a variety of situations in which the illegality is conditioned in special terms. Even in the normal sphere of international responsibility, acts of trespass, for example an intrusion into the territorial sea of another state not causing 'material harm', are regarded by some as an exceptional form of delict.[3] Some jurists are of opinion that states may bear a criminal responsibility for certain categories of wrongdoing, including the launching of aggressive war;[4] and, irrespective of the criminality of the act *qua* act of state, criminal responsibility of individuals participating may exist under international law.[5] In several instances the illegality is relative or conditional. Illegality may result only if no compensation is paid,[6] and may be excluded as a

[1] See generally, Guggenheim, 74 Hague *Recueil* (1949, I), 195–268; Fitzmaurice, 92 Hague *Recueil* (1957, II), 117–28; Jennings, *Cambridge Essays in International Law* (1965), pp. 64–87; Baade, 39 *Indiana L.J.* (1964), 497–559; Cahier, 76 *R.G.D.I.P.* (1972), 645–97; Mann, 48 *B.Y.* (1976–7), 1–65; Verzijl, *International Law in Historical Perspective* vi (1973), 50–104; P. de Visscher, 136 Hague *Recueil* (1972, II), 90–94.

[2] There is a strong analogy with principles of constitutional and administrative law.

[3] *Supra*, pp. 457, 463. See especially Parry, 90 Hague *Recueil* (1956, II), 674 seq. Cf. the status of *ultra vires* jurisdictional acts unaccompanied by any immediate enforcement or material harm, for example unlawful extension of nationality law.

[4] *Supra*, p. 433, n. 1 for references to the literature. [5] *Infra*, pp. 561–4.

[6] Cf. the law of expropriation, *infra*, pp. 531 seq.; and see *supra*, pp. 465–6, on incomplete privilege.

consequence of bilateral relations determined by estoppel or acquiescence.[1] The legality of reprisal is conditioned in part by a prior commission of a delict by the state against which the reprisal is directed.[2]

2. *Objective Consequences of Illegal Events*

Illegal conduct may produce a legal regime contingent on the existence of the conduct rather than its illegality. Thus an 'armed conflict' or 'war', the inception of which may have been the result of a breach of the United Nations Charter, will nevertheless draw in its train most[3] of, if not all, the rules governing the conduct of war. Similarly, states have in some instances at least operated a principle of effectiveness.[4] Thus, where control of territory results from illegal annexation, it may be good policy to recognize grants of nationality by the wrongdoer, since nationality may be regarded as a status and nullification of grants may have harmful consequences.[5] In the law relating to acquisition of territorial sovereignty, including the delimitation of a territorial sea, and to rights of passage and other privileges, illegal activity may produce valid results by the operation of prescription, acquiescence, and estoppel.[6] Here the illegal conduct is merely a *causa sine qua non* and does not of itself produce legal consequences.

3. *General Wrongs: Abuse of State Competence*

The notion of *delicta juris gentium*, as opposed to torts as reparation obligations between tortfeasor and claimant, takes four forms: (1) that of high illegality or breach of *jus cogens*, as in the case of genocide (see section 5, *infra*); (2) reference to cases where international law recognizes a general competence to exercise jurisdiction to apprehend, and perhaps to punish, irrespective of the nationality of the wrongdoer, as in the case of

[1] *Infra*, pp. 634 seq. For examples of relativity in the law of belligerent occupation see Baxter, 27 *B.Y.* (1950), 235 seq. Cf. *Dralle* v. *Republic of Czechoslovakia*, Int. L.R. 17 (1950), no. 41 at p. 165. See also *Arbitral Award Case*, I.C.J. Reports (1960), p. 192; ibid., pp. 221–3, diss. op., Judge Urrutia Holguín.

[2] See Fitzmaurice, op. cit., p. 119.

[3] For a possible qualification, see *infra*, pp. 514, n. 5, 536, n. 2.

[4] See generally Touscoz, *Le Principe d'effectivité dans l'ordre international* (1964); Lauterpacht, *The Development of International Law by the International Court*, pp. 227 seq.

[5] See Brownlie, 39 *B.Y.* (1963), 326–7, 344–5.

[6] *Supra*, pp. 163–4.

piracy;[1] (3) acts which harm all states indiscriminately and which are difficult to trace to particular tortfeasors, as in the case of successive nuclear tests in the atmosphere;[2] (4) acts infringing principles of law creating rights the beneficiaries of which do not have legal personality or, more correctly, do not have presently effective means of protecting their rights, as, for example, non-self-governing peoples and the populations of mandate or trust territories.[3] These categories are, of course, related in their application to particular subject-matter: thus the principle of self-determination involves (1) and (4).

The abusive exercise of a state competence without material harm to some other state raises issues similar to those apparent in the *South West Africa* cases,[4] where the mandatory's abuse of competence was in issue and the question was whether states not harmed in their material interests were allowed to raise the issues. Thus a state may extend its nationality to part of the population of another state, deprive a part of its permanent population of nationality, legislate for a criminal jurisdiction of aliens well beyond the limits set by international law, refuse to accept responsibility for its territorial sea, or fail to exercise criminal jurisdiction when it alone has competence.[5] In these cases no justiciable issue arises until acts of administration and enforcement infringe the legal interest of another state.

In principle proceedings in municipal courts involving excess of jurisdiction are 'null and void *ab initio*, and without effect on the international plane'.[6]

4. Ex injuria non oritur jus

The principle that no benefit can be received from an illegal act has been stated by jurists in the context of international law[7]

[1] Cf. the treaties concerning repression of slavery and prostitution: Oppenheim i. 733–4; and Schwelb, 9 *I.C.L.Q.* (1960), 668. The approach here is in terms of a duty to apprehend and punish and it is not clear that the wrongdoing is to be classified as an 'international crime'.

[2] See *supra*, p. 285–6.

[3] See *infra*, pp. 566–7; on the problems of *locus standi* before tribunals, *supra*, pp. 466–73. On the principles of self-determination, *infra*, pp. 593–6.

[4] *Supra*, pp. 466–70.

[5] Cf. the position of contributing states in relation to United Nations forces in the Congo.

[6] Judge Fitzmaurice, sep. op., *Barcelona Traction Case*, I.C.J. Reports, 1970, pp. 103–6 at p. 106 (para. 72).

[7] See Verzijl, 15 *R.D.I.* (La Pradelle) (1935), 284–339; Lauterpacht, 62 Hague *Recueil* (1937, IV), 287–96; Guggenheim, op. cit. See also Lauterpacht, *Recognition*, pp. 409 seq., 421 seq.

and applied by tribunals. In the *Eastern Greenland*[1] case the Permanent Court took the view that Norway could not rely on her decree of 1931 affecting the disputed area, as Denmark had a prior title.[2] Municipal courts have often refused to give extra-territorial recognition to acts regarded as illegal under international law.[3] The principle itself leads to the wide field of problems as to the nullity of *ultra vires* acts, problems which cannot be properly approached by way of abstract generalizations.[4] Reference to the principle *ex injuria non oritur jus* does not provide a safe guide to the solution of specific problems. For example, acquiescence of a State may confirm the validity of an award of an arbitrator which was *in limine* open to challenge on the ground of excess of jurisdiction.[5]

5. Jus Cogen [6]

Jurists have from time to time attempted to classify rules, or rights and duties, on the international plane by use of terms like 'fundamental' or, in respect to rights, 'inalienable' or 'inherent'. Such classifications have not had much success, but have inter-

[1] *Supra*, pp. 133, 146. Other judicial applications of the principle are listed in Oppenheim i. 142, n. 1.

[2] Cf. Judge Anzilotti, diss., P.C.I.J., Ser. A/B, no. 53 at pp. 94–5. See also *supra*, p. 126, on title.

[3] See *In re Krüger*, Int. L.R. 18 (1951), no. 68; *Singapore Oil Stocks* case, Int. L.R. 23 (1956), 810; Green, p. 698; *Civil Air Transport Inc.* v. *Central Air Transport Corp.*, Int. L.R. 19 (1952), no. 20 at p. 97.

[4] See Jennings and Baade, *supra*, p. 509, n. 1. On the *ultra vires* acts of organizations see *infra*, pp. 698 seq. See also Chapter IV, section 7.

[5] See *Arbitral Award made by the King of Spain on 23 December 1906*, I.C.J. Reports, 1960, p. 192.

[6] See generally Schwelb, 61 *A.J.* (1967), 946–75; Verdross, 60 *A.J.* (1966), 55–63; Scheuner, 27 *Z.a.ö. R.u.V.* (1967), 520–32; Barberis, ibid., 30 (1970), 19–45; Schwarzenberger, 43 *Texas L.R.* (1965), 455–78; and, less fully, in *Curr. Leg. Problems* (1965), 191–214; C. de Visscher, 75 *R.G.D.I.P.* (1971), 5–11; *Concept of Jus Cogens in International Law*, Conf. on Int. Law, Langonissi (Greece), 1966 (1967); Mosler, 25 *Ann. suisse* (1968), 9–40, Paul, 21 *Ost. Zeit. für öff. R.* (1971), 19–49; Ago, *Yrbk., I.L.C.* (1970), ii. 177, 184 (para. 23); ibid. (1971), ii (pt. 1), 199, 210 (para. 41); ibid. (1976), ii (pt. 1), 3, 31–2 (paras. 98–9); Marek, in *Recueil d'études en hommage à Paul Guggenheim*, pp. 426–59; Riesenfeld, 60 *A.J.* (1966), 511–15; Virally, *Annuaire français* (1966), 5–29; Nisot, *Revue Belge* (1968), 1–8; Monaco, 125 Hague *Recueil* (1968, III), 202–12; Guggenheim, *Traité* (2nd ed.), i. 128–9; Morelli, 51 *Rivista di d.i.* (1968), 108–17; Schweitzer, 15 *Archiv des V.* (1971), 197–223; P. de Visscher, 136 Hague *Recueil* (1972, II), 102–11; Sztucki, *Jus Cogens and the Vienna Convention on the Law of Treaties* (1974); Mann, *Festschrift für Ulrich Scheuner* (1973), pp. 399–418; Wolfke, 6 *Polish Yrbk.* (1974), 145–62; Rozakis, *The Concept of Jus Cogens in the Law of Treaties* (1976); Crawford, 48 *B.Y.* (1976–7), 146–8; Nageswar Rao, 14 *Indian Journ.* (1974), 362–85; Sinclair, *The Vienna Convention on the Law of Treaties* (1973), pp. 110–31.

mittently affected the interpretation of treaties by tribunals.[1] In the recent past some eminent opinions have supported the view that certain overriding principles of international law exist, forming a body of *jus cogens*.[2]

The major distinguishing feature of such rules is their relative indelibility. They are rules of customary law which cannot be set aside by treaty or acquiescence but only by the formation of a subsequent customary rule of contrary effect. The least controversial examples of the class are the prohibition of aggressive war,[3] the law of genocide, the principle of racial non-discrimination,[4] crimes against humanity, and the rules prohibiting trade in slaves and piracy. In the *Barcelona Traction* case (Second Phase),[5] the majority judgment of the International Court, supported by twelve Judges, drew a distinction between obligations of a state arising *vis-à-vis* another state and obligations 'towards the international community as a whole'. The Court said:

> Such obligations derive, for example, in contemporary international law, from the outlawing of acts of aggression, and of genocide, as also from the principles and rules concerning the basic rights of the human person, including protection from slavery and racial discrimination.

Other rules which may[6] have this special status include the principle of permanent sovereignty over natural resources[7] and the principle of self-determination.[8]

The concept of *jus cogens* was accepted by the International

[1] On sovereignty and the restrictive interpretation of treaties see Lauterpacht, op. cit., pp. 300–6, and *supra*, p. 288.

[2] See Lauterpacht, 27 *B.Y.* (1950), 397–8; id., *Yrbk., I.L.C.* (1953), ii. 154–5, esp. para. 4; Fitzmaurice, 30 *B.Y.* (1953), 30; id., 92 Hague *Recueil* (1957, II), 120, 122, 125. See also *In re Flesche, Ann. Digest* 16 (1949), no. 87 at p. 269. For an early source: Anzilotti, *Opere* i. 289 (3rd Ital. ed., 1927; also in *Cours de droit international* (1929), i. 340). See further *North Sea Continental Shelf Cases*, I.C.J. Reports, 1969, pp. 97–8 (Padilla Nervo, sep. op.), 182 (Tanaka, diss. op.), 248 (Sørensen, diss. op.).

[3] McNair, *Law of Treaties* (1961), pp. 214–15.

[4] See the 1966 edn. of this book, p. 417; Judge Tanaka, diss. op., *South West Africa* cases (Second Phase), I.C.J. Reports (1966), p. 298; Judge Ammoun, sep. op., *Barcelona Traction* case (Second Phase), I.C.J. Reports (1970), p. 304; Judge Ammoun, sep. op., *Namibia* opinion, ibid. (1971), pp. 78–81. See further *infra*, p. 596. The principle of religious non-discrimination must have the same status as also the rather neglected principle of non-discrimination as to sex.

[5] I.C.J. Reports (1970), p. 3 at p. 32. See also *In re Koch*, Int. L.R. 30, p. 496 at p. 503; *Assessment of Aliens Case*, Int. L.R. 43, p. 3 at p. 8; *Tokyo Suikosha Case*, 13 *Japanese Ann. of I.L.* (1969), p. 113 at p. 115.

[6] The writer is referring to candidate rules and uses tentative language, a fact not observed by all of those referring to the text of the 1966 edn.

[7] See the relevant U.N. Declaration *infra*, p. 540.

[8] Judge Ammoun, sep. op., *Barcelona Traction* case (Second Phase), I.C.J. Reports (1970), p. 304.

Law Commission[1] and incorporated in the final draft on the law of treaties in 1966, Article 50[2] of which provided that: 'a treaty is void if it conflicts with a peremptory norm of general international law from which no derogation is permitted and which can be modified only by a subsequent norm of general international law having the same character.' The Commission's commentary makes it clear that by 'derogation' is meant the use of agreement (and presumably acquiescence as a form of agreement) to contract out of rules of general international law. Thus an agreement by a state to allow another state to stop and search its ships on the high seas is valid, but an agreement with a neighbouring state to carry out a joint operation against a racial group straddling the frontier which would constitute genocide, if carried out, is void since the prohibition with which the treaty conflicts is a rule of *jus cogens*. After some controversy, the Vienna Conference on the Law of Treaties reached agreement on a provision (Article 53)[3] similar to the draft article except that, for the purposes of the Vienna Convention on the Law of Treaties, a peremptory norm of general international law is defined as 'a norm accepted and recognized by the international community of States as a whole as a norm from which no derogation is permitted and which can be modified only by a subsequent norm of general international law having the same character'. Charles de Visscher[4] has pointed out that the proponent of a rule of *jus cogens* in relation to this article will have a considerable burden of proof.

Apart from the law of treaties the specific content of norms of this kind involves the irrelevance of protest, recognition, and acquiescence: prescription cannot purge this type of illegality. Moreover, it is arguable that *jus cogens* curtails various privileges, so that, for example, an aggressor would not benefit from the rule that belligerents are not responsible for damage caused to subjects of neutral states by military operations.[5] Many problems

[1] See *Yrbk., I.L.C.* (1963), ii, p. 187 at pp. 198 (art. 37), 211 (art. 45), 216 (art. 53). See also McNair, op. cit., pp. 213–18; Lauterpacht, *Yrbk., I.L.C.* (1953), ii. 154–5; and Fitzmaurice, ibid. (1958), ii. 27 (art. 17), 40.

[2] See *Yrbk., I.L.C.* (1966), ii. 247–9. See also pp. 261 (art. 61), 266 (art. 67).

[3] See also Articles 64 and 71.

[4] *Théories et réalités en droit international* (4th ed.), pp. 295–6. See also id., 75 *R.G.D.I.P.* (1971), 5–11.

[5] See McNair, *Opinions* ii. 277; and Schwarzenberger (3rd ed.), i. 646. Authority also exists for the view that an aggressor does not acquire title to property acquired even if the confiscation and requisition were within the Hague Regulations: references, Brownlie, *International Law and the Use of Force by States*, p. 406, n. 3. Scope for reliance on doctrines of reprisal and necessity will be reduced. Can the principle of universal jurisdiction

remain: more authority exists for the category of *jus cogens* than exists for its particular content,[1] and rules do not develop in customary law which readily correspond to the new categories. However, certain portions of *jus cogens* are the subject of general agreement, including the rules relating to the use of force by states, self-determination, and genocide. Yet even here many problems of application remain, particularly in regard to the effect of self-determination on the transfer of territory. If a state uses force to implement the principle of self-determination, is it possible to assume that one aspect of *jus cogens* is more significant than another?[2]

6. *The Obligation of Putting an End to an Illegal Situation*

When competent organs of the United Nations make a binding determination that a situation is illegal, the states which are addressees of the resolution or resolutions concerned are under an obligation to bring that situation to an end.[3] Much depends on the precise manner in which such resolutions spell out the consequences. However, in the ordinary course the consequence of the illegality will involve a 'duty of non-recognition'. This duty may be observed irrespective of or in the absence of any directives from the United Nations if in the careful judgment of the individual state a situation has arisen the illegality of which is opposable to states in general.

In 1970 the Security Council adopted Resolution 276 in which that organ recognized the decision of the General Assembly to terminate the mandate of South West Africa and to assume direct responsibility for the territory until its independence. The same decision of the General Assembly declared that the presence of South African authority in South West Africa (otherwise Namibia) as well as all acts by that Government concerning Namibia were illegal and invalid. In Resolution 283 the

develop in relation to *jus cogens*? Cf. the *Eichmann* case, *supra*, p. 305. Should the principle of self-determination, as an aspect of *jus cogens*, be used to widen concepts of legal interest and *locus standi*? Cf. the *South West Africa* cases (Second Phase), I.C.J. Reports (1966), p. 6, on which see *supra*, p. 468.

[1] See the trenchant comment by Schwarzenberger, who regards the principle as a source of instability in treaty relations: op. cit.; also in *International Law* (3rd ed.), i. 425–7; and *The Inductive Approach to International Law*, pp. 85–107. See further a reply by Verdross, 60 *A.J.* (1966), 55–63. It is useful to note that the Declaration on Principles of International Law Concerning Friendly Relations and Co-operation Among States, adopted by the U.N. General Assembly on 24 October 1970 (see 65 *A.J.* (1971), 243), makes no reference to peremptory norms.

[2] See further *supra*, Chapter VII, section 24.

[3] See the *Namibia* opinion, I.C.J. Reports (1971), p. 54.

Security Council called upon all states to take specific steps consequential upon the illegality of the South African presence, including the termination of diplomatic and consular representation as far as such relations extend to Namibia, the ending of dealings relating to the territory by state enterprises and the withdrawal of financial support from nationals and private corporations that would be used to facilitate trade or commerce with Namibia.

In Resolution 284 (1970) the Security Council asked the International Court for an Advisory Opinion in response to the question: 'What are the legal consequences for States of the continued presence of South Africa in Namibia, notwithstanding Security Council resolution 276 (1970)?' In its Opinion [1] the Court considered a variety of issues including the legal status of the General Assembly resolution by which the Mandate was terminated.[2] The Court held [3] that as a consequence of Security Council resolution 276 (1970), which was mandatory within the terms of the United Nations Charter, member states were under an obligation to recognize the illegality and invalidity of South Africa's continued presence in Namibia. In the Opinion it was recognized that the precise determination of appropriate measures was a matter for the political organs. Thus the Court would 'confine itself to giving advice on those dealings with the Government of South Africa which, under the Charter of the United Nations and general international law, should be considered as inconsistent with the declaration of illegality and invalidity made in paragraph 2 of resolution 276 (1970), because they may imply a recognition that South Africa's presence in Namibia is legal'. Matters touched upon in this connexion included treaty relations in cases in which South Africa purported to act on behalf of or concerning Namibia, diplomatic relations, and economic dealings. The Opinion excepted acts such as registration of births, deaths, and marriages from the taint of invalidity. Finally, the Court expressed the view that the illegality of the situation was opposable to all states and not merely to members of the United Nations.

[1] I.C.J. Reports (1971), p. 16. [2] *Supra*, p. 178.

[3] pp. 54–6 of the Opinion; supported by 11 votes to 4 (see p. 58). By 13 votes to 2 it was held that, the continued presence of South Africa in Namibia being illegal, South Africa was under an obligation to withdraw its administration immediately. Judges Fitzmaurice and Gros, dissenting, considered that the Mandate had not been validly terminated. Passages in separate and dissenting opinions dealing with the legal consequences of the presence of South Africa in Namibia are as follows: pp. 89–100 (Ammoun); 119–20 (Padilla Nervo); 133–7 (Petrén); 147–9 (Onyeama); 165–7 (Dillard); 217–19 (de Castro); 295–8 (Fitzmaurice). See Dugard, 88 *S. African L.J.* (1971), 460–77.

In legal terms the consequences of illegality, or 'the duty of non-recognition', are distinct from the application of economic and military sanctions, voluntary or mandatory, as a consequence of United Nations resolutions as, for example, in relation to Rhodesia consequent upon the unilateral declaration of independence by the Smith regime.[1] Politically speaking, the practical consequences of non-recognition are similar to non-military sanctions.[2] It may be true, as Judge Petrén suggests in his Separate Opinion, that the resolutions relating to Namibia impose certain duties which go beyond the effects of mere non-recognition in general international law.[3]

[1] See resols. of 1965 and 1966: 60 *A.J.* (1966), 921–6; 61 *A.J.* (1967), 652–5; resols. of 1968: 7 *Int. Leg. Materials* (1968), 897, 1402. See also 9 *Int. Leg. Materials* (1970), 636.

[2] See Judge Petrén, sep. op., I.C.J. Reports (1971), pp. 127, 134–7.

[3] Ibid., pp. 134–7. See also Judges Onyeama, sep. op., p. 148; Dillard, sep. op., p. 165; Fitzmaurice, diss. op., p. 297.

PART IX

THE PROTECTION OF INDIVIDUALS AND GROUPS

CHAPTER XXIII

INJURY TO THE PERSONS AND PROPERTY OF ALIENS ON STATE TERRITORY

1. *State and Individual*

THE legal consequences of belonging to a political community with a territorial base have not changed a great deal since the feudal era, in spite of changes in the theory used to describe or explain the relation.[1] Ties of allegiance, citizenship, and nationality have provided the basis for the legal community of the state, whether the state was regarded primarily as an organic unity expressed in terms of 'personal' sovereignty or as a territorial domain. Modern practice tends toward the latter view, but has not wholly abandoned the doctrine of Vattel. Vattel, in a much quoted passage,[2] stated that an injury to a citizen is an injury to the state. His principle is often described as a fiction, but it is surely inadequate so to characterize the legal relation between a 'corporate' legal person and its membership. In any case Vattel was not contending that any harm to an alien was an injury to his state: the relation simply provides a necessary basis for principles of responsibility and protection.[3] On the one hand, the state has a certain responsibility for the acts of its citizens or other persons under its control of which its agents know or ought to know and which cause harm to the legal interest of another state. On the other hand, the state has a legal interest represented by its citizens, and those harming its citizens may have to account to the state protecting the latter. This accountability may take the form of subjection to the extra-territorial application of the national criminal law to acts harming citizens.[4] More important

[1] On the position of the individual in international law see Chapter XXIV.

[2] *Le Droit des gens*, Bk. 11, Chap. vi, para. 71.

[3] But see Ammoun, sep. op., *Barcelona Traction* case (Second Phase), I.C.J. Reports (1970), pp. 290–4 (and cf. the same opinion at p. 300, para. 10).

[4] Generally on jurisdiction: *supra*, Chapter XIV.

than this, however, is the diplomatic protection exercised by a state, in respect of its nationals.[1] If nationals are subjected to injury or loss by an agency for which another state is responsible in law, then, whether the harm occurs in the territory of a state, or *res communis*, i.e. the high seas or outer space, or in *terra nullius*, the state of the persons harmed may present a claim on the international plane.

The last proposition begs many questions involving the conditions under which responsibility arises, and the principal object of the present chapter is to examine these conditions. The general principles of 'imputability', including responsibility for the unauthorized acts of officials, have been considered in Chapter XX.

2. *Admission, Expulsion, and Liabilities of Aliens*

The problems of responsibility naturally arise most frequently when aliens and their assets are stationed on state territory, and, by way of preliminary, something must be said of the incidence of aliens within the state. In principle this is a matter of domestic jurisdiction: a state may choose not to admit aliens or may impose conditions on their admission.[2] Internal economic policies and aspects of foreign policy may result in restrictions on the economic activity of aliens.[3] National policy may require prohibition or regulation of the purchase of immovables, ships, aircraft, and the like, and the practice of certain professions by aliens. Provisions for the admission of aliens in treaties of friendship, commerce, and navigation are qualified by references to 'public order, morals, health or safety'.[4]

As might be expected, expulsion is also within the discretion of the state,[5] but tribunals and writers have at times asserted the

[1] The concept of nationality is examined in Chapter XVIII. The means of establishing the existence of the legal interest based on nationality, and other issues of admissibility, are considered *supra*, pp. 480 seq. Exceptionally, a state may have a legal interest in an individual on some basis other than nationality, e.g. if the individual enters the state service: *supra*, p. 481. On the right of protection of the United Nations in respect of persons in its service see *infra*, p. 684.

[2] This is the view of modern authorities, e.g. Oppenheim i. 675. For British practice see McNair, *Opinions* ii. 105–8; and *Musgrove* v. *Chun Teeong Toy* [1891] A.C. 272. See generally on admission and exclusion of aliens: Goodwin-Gill, *International Law and the Movement of Persons between States* (1978); *Répertoire suisse* ii. 698–973. *British Digest* vi. 9–77; Verdross, 37 Hague *Recueil* (1931, III), 338–47; Hackworth iii. 549–52, 690–705, 717 seq.; Puente, 36 *A.J.* (1942), 252–70. On the effect of the European Conv. on Human Rights on admission and expulsion see 23 Int. L.R. (1956), 393; 33 *B.Y.* (1957), 317; and Int. L.R. 28, pp. 208, 246. On the law of the E.E.C. see the *Movement of Workers* case, Int. L.R. 40, p. 289. See also the European Conv. on Establishment, *Europ. Treaty Series* No. 19.

[3] See further *supra*, p. 262.

[4] e.g., treaty between the United States and Italy, 1948; Briggs, p. 530.

[5] See *British Digest* vi. 83–241; Hackworth iii. 690–705; McNair, *Opinions* ii. 109–12;

existence of limitations on this discretion.[1] In particular, the power of expulsion must be exercised in good faith and not for an ulterior motive. Whilst the expelling state has a margin of appreciation in applying the concept of 'ordre public', this concept is to be measured against human rights standards. The latter are applicable also to the manner of expulsion.[2] In certain conditions expulsion may constitute genocide or may infringe the principle of non-discrimination (racial or religious) which is part of customary international law. Expulsion which causes specific loss to the national state receiving groups without adequate notice would ground a claim for indemnity as for incomplete privilege.[3] Finally, and most important of all, the expulsion of persons who by long residence have acquired *prima facie* the effective nationality[4] of the host state is not a matter of discretion, since the issue of nationality places the right to expel in question.

The liabilities of alien visitors under their own and under the local law lead to overlapping and conflicting claims of the state of origin and the host state in various areas of jurisdiction, including anti-trust regulation, legislation governing labour and welfare standards, monetary regulations, and taxation.[5] The principles on which conflicts of jurisdiction may be approached have been considered in Chapter XIV, and it is at present the intention to examine the limits of the competence of the host state in placing liabilities on aliens of a special kind, viz., duties to serve in the armed forces, militia, or police and to submit to requisitions in time of emergency.[6] The legal position is not in all respects clear. Thus there is authority and principle to support the rule that an alien cannot be required to serve in the regular armed forces or

de Boeck, 18 Hague *Recueil* (1927, III), 443–650; *British Practice* (1964), 209–11; ibid. (1966), 111–15; ibid. (1967), 112–14; Whiteman viii. 850–63. On asylum and extradition see *supra*, pp. 314–15; *infra*, pp. 558–9.

[1] See generally Goodwin-Gill, op. cit., pp. 201–310; and in 47 *B.Y.* (1974–5), 55–156; and also Oppenheim i. 692–3; Hackworth iii. 690; *British Digest* vi. 112 seq.; Wooldridge and Sharma, 23 *I.C.L.Q.* (1974), 397–425.

[2] The view is sometimes expressed that the expelling state must have complied with its own law: *British Digest* vi. 151–2; Goodwin-Gill, op. cit., pp. 263–81; and 47 *B.Y.* (1974–5), pp. 122–35.

[3] Cf. *supra*, pp. 465–6.

[4] *Supra*, pp. 393, 406 seq.

[5] For a very useful survey of such claims see Katz and Brewster, *The Law of International Transactions and Relations, Cases and Materials* (1962), pp. 550–778.

[6] For British practice see *British Digest* vi. 359–422; McNair, *Opinions* ii. 113–37. See also Parry, 31 *B.Y.* (1954), 437–52; id., *Nationality and Citizenship Laws of the Commonwealth* i. 120–1.

the host state.[1] However, American and recent Australian practice supports the view that the alien admitted with a view to permanent residence has an obligation to serve in local militia and police forces and also in forces to be used in external defence.[2] Where the alien has participated in the local political franchise the obligation may also arise.[3] The basis for obligations of this kind is the reciprocity between residence and local protection, on the one hand, and the responsibilities of a 'functional' citizenship. In some cases the long residence and local connexions may create a new, effective, nationality opposable to the state of origin.[4]

3. *General Principles*

The exercise of diplomatic protection in respect to nationals visiting or resident in foreign countries has subsisted, with some changes of terminology and concept, since the late Middle Ages. Practice with modern features appears in the late eighteenth century, when the grant of special reprisals, an indiscriminate right of private war, to citizens harmed by aliens disappeared. It is the nineteenth century which produced political and economic conditions in which the status of aliens abroad became a problem of wide dimensions. The history has been primarily but not entirely concerned with the conflict of interest between investor states and the economically exploited hosts to foreign capital. In the century after 1840 some sixty mixed claims commissions were set up to deal with disputes arising from injury to the interests of aliens.[5] Literature on protection of aliens from the point of view of investor states grew particularly after about 1890, and influential contributions were made by the Italian Anzilotti and the American jurists Moore, Borchard, and Eagleton.[6]

[1] Sørensen, pp. 489–90; Verdross, op. cit., p. 379; Oppenheim i. 681; Kozhevnikov (ed.), *International Law*, pp. 161, 164; Guggenheim i. 348; *Polites* v. *Commonwealth of Australia*, 70 C.L.R. 60, 70, per Latham, C.J. The law of war and neutrality may reinforce the position when the host state is involved in civil or foreign war.

[2] See Greig, *Austral. Yrbk.* (1967), 249–56; *British Practice* (1966), p. 107; Whiteman viii. 540–73.

[3] The analogue is the principle of allegiance or effective connexion as a basis for criminal jurisdiction over aliens: *supra*, pp. 306, 309.

[4] *Supra*, pp. 393, 406 seq.

[5] Claims settlement conventions included conventions between Mexico and the United States of 1839, 1848, 1868, and 1923; the Venezuelan arbitrations of 1903 involving claims of ten states against Venezuela; and conventions between Great Britain and the United States of 1853, 1871, and 1908.

[6] See Anzilotti, 13 *R.G.D.I.P.* (1906), 5–29, 285–309, also in *Opere* ii. (1) (1956), 151–207; Moore, *Digest* vi, Chap. XXI; Borchard, *The Diplomatic Protection of Citizens Abroad*

The area of law under discussion has always been one of acute controversy, and, in the period since 1945, concepts of economic independence and political and economic principles favouring nationalization and the public sector in national economies have made considerable headway. The legal reasoning offered on precise issues stems from a small number of general principles and the nature of the relation between them. It is always admitted that presumptively the ordering of persons and assets is an aspect of the domestic jurisdiction of a state and an incident of its sovereign equality and independence in the territorial sphere. Customary law contains long established exceptions to the territorial competence of states, the chief of which is the immunity from local jurisdiction of the premises and personnel of diplomatic missions.[1] Exceptions may of course be created by treaty, and in the past immunity for aliens has been coupled with the privilege of the sending state in maintaining a special system of courts for nationals on the territory of the receiving state. This arrangement, known as a regime of capitulations, applied in countries such as China, Iran, Turkey, and Egypt in the past.[2] Apart from special cases supported by custom or treaty, the territorial competence of the state subsists, and the alien is admitted, in the discretion of the sovereign, as a visitor who as such has a duty to submit to the local law and jurisdiction. If the alien acquires domicile or permanent residence he is even more obviously obliged to accept local duties, including perhaps the duty to serve in the armed forces. However, residence abroad does not of itself deprive an individual of the protection of his own government. In the past writers have rested the right of protection on the right of self-preservation or a 'right of intercourse': the correct way of justifying diplomatic protection and the nationality of claims would seem to be the very existence of the relation of nationality and the general absence of an alternative and better means of grounding protection in existing law.[3] Where the state authorities cause injury to the alien visitor, for example in the form of brutality by police officials, then the legal position is clear. The host state is responsible, but, as a condition for the presentation of the claim by the state of the alien,

(1915); and Eagleton, *The Responsibility of States in International Law* (1928). See further Dunn, *The Protection of Nationals* (1932), and Freeman, *The International Responsibility of States for Denial of Justice* (1938). The treatise by Borchard had particular influence.

[1] See *supra*, Chapter XVI.

[2] Oppenheim i. 682–6.

[3] Cf. Cavaré, *Makarov Festgabe*, pp. 54–80.

the latter is required to exhaust the remedies available (where this is so) in the local courts.[1] The reasons for this particular condition of admissibility are practical: small claims by individuals are handled better in municipal courts, governments dislike the multiplication of claims for diplomatic intervention, and it is reasonable, for the resident alien especially, to submit to the local system of justice.

Much more difficult are the cases where the alien is harmed by acts or omissions which are on their face merely a normal exercise of the competence of organs of administration and government of the host state. These situations include the malfunction of judicial organs dealing with acts which are breaches of the local law affecting the interests of the alien, so-called 'denial of justice',[2] and also general legislative measures, not directed at aliens as such, affecting the ownership or enjoyment of foreign-owned assets. There has always been a current of opinion to the effect that the alien, having submitted to the local law, can only expect treatment on a basis of equality with nationals of the host state. This view is pressed particularly in relation to the lack in most cases of any *major* interest of the state of the alien in respect to injuries to nationals. It is also said that the status of the alien is not the subject of a privilege as 'alien', but is simply that of an 'individual' within the territorial sovereignty and jurisdiction of the host state.[3] The issues raised by such arguments must now be considered.

4. *The Standard of National Treatment*[4]

There has always been considerable support for the view that the alien can only expect equality of treatment under the local law because he submits to local conditions with benefits and burdens and because to give the alien a special status would be contrary to the principles of territorial jurisdiction and equality.

[1] *Supra*, p. 495. Cf. *British Digest* vi. 253, 345, 347.

[2] *Infra*, pp. 529–31.

[3] See the opinions of Guha Roy, 55 *A.J.* (1961), 863–91. See also Anand, 56 *A.J.* (1962), p. 383 at pp. 400–3; Sinha, 14 *I.C.L.Q.* (1965), p. 121 at pp. 127–8; Castañeda, 15 *Int. Organisation* (1961), 38–48; and the debate in the International Law Commission, *Yrbk., I.L.C.* (1957), i. 154 seq.

[4] See the works cited *supra*, p. 521, n. 6, and, further: Strisower, *Annuaire de l'Inst.* (1927), i. 455–98; Verdross, 37 Hague *Recueil* (1931, III), 327–406; Harv. Research, 23 *A.J.* (1929), Spec. Suppl., pp. 131–399; Jessup, 46 *Columbia L.R.* (1946), pp. 903–28; and in *A Modern Law of Nations*, pp. 94–122; Roth, *The Minimum Standard of International Law Applied to Aliens* (1949); Sohn and Baxter, 55 *A.J.* (1961), 545–84; García Amador, *Yrbk., I.L.C.* (1956), ii. 201–3; *British Digest* vi. 247–440, *passim*, e.g. p. 343 but cf. pp. 291, 292); Whiteman viii. 704–6; García Amador, Sohn and Baxter, *Recent Codifications of the Law of State Responsibility for Injuries to Aliens* (1974).

Before examining the validity of the principle of national treatment, it must be observed that it is agreed on all hands that certain sources of inequality are admissible. Thus it is not contended that the alien should have political rights in the host state as of right. Moreover, the alien must take the local law as he finds it in regard to regulation of the economy and restriction on employment of aliens in particular types of employment. Access to the courts may be maintained, but with modified rules in ancillary matters: thus an alien may not have access to legal aid and may have to give security for costs.[1] More general variations may of course be created by treaty. The various standards of treatment commonly employed in treaties are as follows: those of reciprocity, the open door, good neighbourliness, and of identical, national, most-favoured-nation, equitable, and preferential treatment.

The principle of national treatment had support from many jurists both in Europe and Latin America prior to 1940,[2] from a small number of arbitral awards,[3] and from seventeen of the states at the Hague Codification Conference in 1930.[4] At the latter twenty-one states opposed the principle, although some opponents had on occasion supported it in presenting claims to international tribunals.[5]

5. *The International Minimum Standard*

Since the beginning of the present century legal doctrine has opposed an 'international minimum standard', 'a moral standard for civilized states', to the principle of national treatment.[6] A

[1] The *cautio judicatum solvi* of civil law systems.

[2] Including Strupp, De Louter, Sibert, Nys, Alvarez, and Yepes. See also the citations by Herz, 35 *A.J.* (1941), p. 243 at p. 259, n. 66. The equality principle was advocated as early as 1868 by the Argentinian jurist Calvo.

[3] See the *Canevaro* case (1912), P.C.A., Hague Court Reports i. 285; 6 *A.J.* (1912), 746; *R.I.A.A.* xi. 397; *Cadenhead* case (1914), 8 *A.J.* (1914), 663; and the *Standard Oil* case (1926), 8 *B.Y.* (1927), 156; 22 *A.J.* (1928), 404; *R.I.A.A.* ii, p. 781 at p. 794.

[4] See Roth, op. cit., pp. 72–4. See also the report of Guerrero of 1916, 20 *A.J.* (1926), Spec. Suppl., pp. 176 seq.

[5] e.g. the United States in the *Norwegian Ships* arbitration (1922), *R.I.A.A.* i. 307; Green, p. 3. See also the Havana Convention of 1928, Art. 5, 23 *A.J.* (1929), Spec. Suppl., p. 234; draft Conv. proposed by the Paris Conference on the Treatment of Aliens, 1929, Art. 17, Roth, p. 71; and the Montevideo Convention of 1933, Art. 9, 28 *A.J.* (1934), Suppl., p. 75.

[6] Leading proponents include Anzilotti, Verdross, Borchard, Oppenheim, Guggenheim, de Visscher, Scelle, and Jessup. See the citations by Roth, op. cit., p. 88; and Herz, 35 *A.J.* (1941), 260; and materials cited *supra*, notes 2–5. See also American Law Institute, Restatement, Second, *For. Relations Law*, pp. 501–7; and Whiteman viii. 697–704.

majority of the states represented at the Hague Codification Conference supported the international standard, and this standard is probably affirmed in the Declaration of the United Nations General Assembly adopted in 1962 on Permanent Sovereignty over Natural Resources.[1] The standard has also enjoyed the support of many tribunals and claims commissions. Thus in the *Neer Claim*[2] the General Claims Commission set up by the United States and Mexico expressed the law as follows:

> . . . the propriety of governmental acts should be put to the test of international standards . . . the treatment of an alien, in order to constitute an international delinquency should amount to an outrage, to bad faith, to wilful neglect of duty, or to an insufficiency of governmental action so far short of international standards that every reasonable and impartial man would readily recognize its insufficiency.

6. *The Two Standards in Perspective*

The controversy concerning the national and international standards has not remained within the bounds of logic, and this is not surprising, as the two viewpoints reflect conflicting economic and political interests. Thus those supporting the national treatment principle are not necessarily committed, as is sometimes suggested, to the view that municipal law has supremacy over international law: it is quite possible to contend that, as a matter of international law, the standard of treatment is to be defined in terms of equality under the local law. Protagonists of national treatment point to the role the law associated with the international standard has played in maintaining a privileged status for aliens, supporting alien control of large areas of the national economy, and providing a pretext for foreign armed intervention. The experience of the Latin-American states and others dictates extreme caution in handling the international standard, but it is necessary to distinguish between, on the one hand, the question as to the content of the standard and the mode of application and, on the other hand, the core principle, which is simply that the territorial sovereign cannot in all circumstances avoid responsibility by pleading that aliens and nationals had received equal treatment. Thus if a national law provides that all persons of a

[1] Examined *infra*, pp. 540–3.

[2] (1926), *R.I.A.A.* iv. 60; Briggs, p. 613. See also the *Roberts* claim (1926), *R.I.A.A.* iv. 41; Briggs, p. 549; the *Hopkins* claim (1926) *R.I.A.A.* iv. 411; Briggs, p. 204; and *British Claims in the Spanish Zone of Morocco* (1925), *R.I.A.A.* ii, p. 617 at p. 644. See also the cases on expropriation cited *infra*, pp. 534 seq.

particular race resident within the state shall be sterilized[1] it will not satisfy the state of an alien within the category to point to the equal application of the law. Conversely, the rules of international law authorize at least a measure of discrimination, for example in matters of taxation and exchange control. In any case the host state owes a special duty to aliens acting as diplomatic or consular agents or in some other official capacity.[2]

A source of difficulty has been the tendency of writers and tribunals to give the international standard a too ambitious content, ignoring the odd standards observed in many areas under the administration of governments with a 'Western' pattern of civilization within the last century or so. Another cause of difficulty, connected with the first, has been the extension of delictual responsibility to the malfunction of administrative and judicial organs, as in the field of denial of justice. This aspect involves the imposition of the law of delict where the true analogy is the use of administrative law remedies to enforce a proper use of legal powers.[3] It will be suggested later that in regard to non-exercise or malfunction of legal powers the standard of national treatment rule has some significance, at least as creating a presumption of absence of *dolus* (intention).

The basic point would seem to be that there is no single standard. Circumstances, for example the outbreak of war,[4] may create exceptions to the international treatment rule, even where this applies in principle. Where a reasonable care or due diligence standard is applicable, then *diligentia quam in suis*[5] might be employed, and would represent a more sophisticated version of the national treatment principle. *Diligentia quam in suis* would allow for the variations in wealth and educational standards between the various states of the world and yet would not be a mechanical national standard, tied to equality. Though the two are sometimes confused, it is not identical with national treatment. There is support for the view that *diligentia quam in suis* has long been accepted as the standard in relation to harm re-

1 A form of genocide, on which see *infra*, p. 562.

2 See Chapters XV and XVI.

3 See further *infra*, pp. 529–31, on denial of justice. See also *supra*, p. 523.

4 See H.M.S.O., *Manual of Military Law* iii, Chap. III (1958); and Seeger, *Le Statut personnel des étrangers ennemis et la Convention de Genève du 12 août 1949 relative à la protection des civils* (1958).

5 I.e. national treatment but on the basis of the standard *ordinarily* observed by the particular state in its own affairs. References to such a standard: Judge Huber, *British Claims in Spanish Morocco* (1924), *R.I.A.A.* ii, p. 617 at p. 644; McNair, *Opinions* ii. 198, 245, 247, 250, 254, 258–66.

sulting from insurrection and civil war.[1] Finally, there are certain overriding rules of law including the proscription of genocide which are clearly international standards.[2]

A recent development has been the appearance of attempts to synthesize the concept of human rights and the principles governing the treatment of aliens. Thus García Amador, rapporteur of the International Law Commission on the subject of state responsibility, presented in his second report a draft chapter with the rubric 'violation of fundamental human rights'.[3] The first article provided:

1. The State is under a duty to ensure to aliens the enjoyment of the same civil rights, and to make available to them the same individual guarantees as are enjoyed by its own nationals. These rights and guarantees shall not, however, in any case be less than the 'fundamental human rights' recognized and defined in contemporary international instruments.
2. In consequence, in case of violation of civil rights, or disregard of individual guarantees, with respect to aliens, international responsibility will be involved only if internationally recognized 'fundamental human rights' are affected.

In the article which follows, the expression 'fundamental human rights' is expanded by an enumeration, which is stated not to be exhaustive, of rights, e.g. inviolability of privacy, home, and correspondence, and respect for honour and reputation.

This particular synthesis of human rights and the standard of treatment for aliens involves codifying the 'international minimum standard', raising that standard, extending it to new subject matter, and relating internal affairs and local law to international responsibility to a degree which the majority of states would find intolerable. Moreover, the standard is unconscionably vague, and the draft provides that the rights and freedoms enumerated 'may be subjected to such limitations or restrictions as the law expressly prescribes for reasons of internal security, the economic well-being of the nation, public order, health and morality or to secure respect for the rights and freedoms of others'.[4] Moreover,

[1] *Supra*, pp. 452–4, and McNair, loc. cit.

[2] See *Barcelona Traction* case (Second Phase), I.C.J. Reports (1970), p. 4 at p. 32; and see *infra*, Chapter XXIV.

[3] *Yrbk., I.L.C.* (1957), ii. 112. Generally on the individual in international law and human rights see *supra*, Chapter XXIV. See also Jessup, *A Modern Law of Nations*, pp. 94–122 and in 46 *Columbia L.R.* (1946), 903–28; Parry, 90 Hague *Recueil* (1956, II), 653–725; Cavaré, in *Makarov Festgabe* (1958), pp. 54–80; Blaser, *La Nationalité et la protection juridique internationale de l'individu* (1962).

[4] For criticisms of the draft see the discussion in *Yrbk., I.L.C.* (1957), i. 154 seq., and for the rapporteur's answer, ibid., ii. 49.

as the Indian member of the Commission pointed out,[1] the draft of rights and freedoms involved the application to economic relations between states of the standard of right which the non-Communist European states had hitherto prescribed for themselves in their domestic affairs: a standard of a particular economic and social system was held out as the universally just standard. The present writer considers that it is not possible to postulate an international minimum standard which in effect supports a particular philosophy of economic life at the expense of the host state.[2] It is certainly the case that since 1945 developments concerning human rights have come to provide a new content for the international standard based upon those human rights principles which have become a part of customary international law. These principles include the principle of non-discrimination on grounds of race,[3] the prohibition of genocide,[4] and the prohibition of torture and of inhuman or degrading treatment or punishment. A careful synthesis of human rights standards and the modern 'treatment of aliens' standards is called for.[5] The concept of discrimination calls for more sophisticated treatment in order to identify unreasonable (or material) discrimination as distinct from the different treatment of non-comparable situations.[6]

7. *Relevant Forms of Delictual Responsibility*

The general principles of state responsibility were examined in the previous chapter, and they are applicable to cases where aliens are injured, whether this occurs within or without the territory of the defendant state. Thus one might expect to rely upon a rule that a state is liable for failure to show due diligence in matters of administration, for example by failing to take steps to apprehend the murderer of an alien. However, the position is far more complex. In the first place, as we have seen, there is no single standard but different standards relating to different situations.[7] Furthermore, reference to a particular standard presumes that the activity

[1] *Yrbk., I.L.C.* (1957), i. 158 (Pal).

[2] See Fischer Williams, 9 *B.Y.* (1928), p. 1 at pp. 20, 25.

[3] *Infra*, pp. 596–8.

[4] *Infra*, pp. 562–3.

[5] This was pointed out in the first edition of this work of 1966, alongside criticism of García Amador's formulation. See McDougal, Lasswell and Chen, 70 *A.J.* (1976), 432–69, for a full discussion.

[6] See McDougal, Lasswell and Chen, op. cit., pp. 450–1; Wex, 15 *Canad. Yrbk.* (1977), 198 at pp. 222–6.

[7] *Supra*, pp. 445 seq.

concerned is outside the reserved domain of domestic jurisdiction and is the subject of international duties. But in the cases of nationalization (or general expropriation), and termination by governments of concession agreements, this is the major issue. International law is not a system replete with nominate torts or delicts, but the rules are specialized in certain respects. Thus reference may be made to the source of harm, such as unauthorized acts of officials, insurrection, and so on,[1] or to the object and form of harm, as, for example, territorial sovereignty, diplomats and other official agents, or injury to nationals. The category of injury to nationals involves the problems considered in the preceding sections and also certain special topics, the principal of which are denial of justice and expropriation. These will now be considered, together with other related subjects.

8. *Denial of Justice*[2]

The term 'denial of justice' has been employed by claims tribunals so as to be coextensive with the general notion of state responsibility for harm to aliens,[3] but it is widely regarded as a particular category of deficiencies on the part of the organs of the host state, principally concerning the administration of justice. It has been pointed out that the term has been given such a variety of definitions that it has little value and the problems could be discussed quite adequately without it.[4] However, if the phrase has a presumptive meaning, the best guide to this is probably the Harvard Research draft,[5] which provides as follows:

Article 9. A State is responsible if an injury to an alien results from a denial of justice. Denial of justice exists when there is a denial, unwarranted delay or obstruction of access to courts, gross deficiency in the administration

[1] Cf. *supra*, pp. 449 seq.

[2] See Freeman, *The International Responsibility of States for Denial of Justice* (1938); Eagleton, 22 *A.J.* (1928), 538–59; Lissitzyn, 30 *A.J.* (1936), 632–46; Spiegel, 32 *A.J.* (1938), 63–81; McNair, *Opinions* ii. 295–322; Harvard draft, 23 *A.J.* (1929), Spec. Suppl., pp. 173–87; Fitzmaurice, 13 *B.Y.* (1932), 93–114; Puente, 43 *Michigan L.R.* (1944), 383–406; de Visscher, 52 Hague *Recueil* (1935, II), 369–440; Sørensen, pp. 550–7; Whiteman viii. 706–20, 726–35, 863–85; García Amador, *Yrbk., I.L.C.* (1957), ii. 110–12; Adede, 14 *Canad. Yrbk.* (1976), 73–95. See also *supra*, pp. 519–23.

[3] See the tribunal in the *Robert E. Brown* claim (1923), Briggs, p. 215, *R.I.A.A.* vi. 120.

[4] See Lissitzyn, op. cit., pp. 645, 646; Jessup, 46 *Columbia L.R.* (1946), 913; Briggs, pp. 679–80.

[5] *Ubi supra*, p. 173. Similar definitions and approval of this definition in Fitzmaurice, op. cit., p. 108; Dunn, op. cit., p. 148; Freeman, op. cit., p. 97; McNair, op. cit., p. 295; Briggs, p. 679. See also Restatement, Second, *For. Relations Law*, pp. 502–3, 534–48; Tanaka, sep. op., *Barcelona Traction* case (Second Phase), I.C.J. Reports (1970), at pp. 144, 156; Padilla Nervo, sep. op., ibid., pp. 252, 265.

of judicial or remedial process, failure to provide those guarantees which are generally considered indispensable to the proper administration of justice, or a manifestly unjust judgment. An error of a national court which does not produce manifest injustice is not a denial of justice.

A somewhat more restricted definition received some support at the Hague Codification Conference in 1930:[1]

Article 8, paragraph 2. A State is responsible as a result of the fact that, in a manner incompatible with the international obligations of the State, the foreigner has been hindered by the judicial authorities in the exercise of his right to appear in Court, or has encountered in his proceedings unjustifiable obstacles or delays implying a refusal to do justice.

The rubric 'Denial of Justice' concerns the application to certain aspects of state administration of the international standard. Latin-American opinion would limit the concept to a duty to allow foreigners easy access to the courts which would duly exercise jurisdiction, without any inquiry into the quality of the justice given.[2]

The most controverted issue is the extent to which erroneous decisions may constitute denial of justice. There is authority for the view that an error of law accompanied by a discriminatory intention is a breach of the international standard.[3]

In the present context the international standard has been applied ambitiously by tribunals and writers and difficulties have arisen. First, the application of the standard may involve decisions upon very fine points of national law and the quality of national remedial machinery.[4] Thus, in regard to the work of the courts, a distinction is sought to be made between error and 'manifest injustice'.[5] Secondly, the application of the standard in this field seems to contradict the principle that the alien, within some limits at least, accepts the local law and jurisdiction. Thirdly, the concept of denial of justice embraces many instances where the harm to the alien is a breach of local law only and the 'denial' is a failure

[1] *Acts*, p. 158, quoted by Jiménez de Aréchaga, in Sørensen, pp. 556–7. The relevant Committee did not complete its work, however; see Freeman, op. cit., pp. 634–713

[2] See the report of Guerrero quoted in Briggs, p. 678. See also Whiteman viii. 727 (Inter-Am. Juridical C'ee Report, 1961).

[3] See Jiménez de Aréchaga, in Friedmann, Henkin and Lissitzyn, *Essays in Honor of Philip C. Jessup* (1972), pp. 171–87, at pp. 179–85, referring to the submissions of both Parties in the *Barcelona Traction Case*, I.C.J. Reports, 1970, p. 3; Whiteman viii. 727–31; and see Adede, op. cit., p. 91. See further O'Connell ii. 948.

[4] Cp. the discussion in the article by Mann, 42 *B.Y.* (1967), 26–9.

[5] See McNair, op. cit., p. 305; and *British Digest* vi. 287–95.

to reach a non-local standard of competence in dealing with the wrong in the territorial jurisdiction. Thus the concept of the foreign state wronged in the person of its nationals is extended to cases where the primary wrong is a breach of municipal law alone. We are concerned with what may be in part an eccentric application of the principles of responsibility in this context,[1] and it would be better if such claims were regarded as resting on an equitable basis only. The existence of the rule of admissibility that the alien should first exhaust local remedies is a partial reflection of the special character of claims on behalf of aliens against the host state.[2]

Distinct from these problems is the situation where a foreign court acts outside the area of state competence permitted by international law in punishing aliens for breaches of national law: the *ultra vires* act creates responsibility just as much as the illegal acts of other parts of the machinery of state.[3]

9. *Expropriation of Foreign Property* [4]

A state may place conditions on the entry of an alien on its territory and may restrict acquisition of certain kinds of property

[1] Cf. Parry, 90 Hague *Recueil* (1956, II), 695–6; and the *Janes* case, discussed *supra*, p. 464. The application of principles of responsibility is eccentric in the context of international relations: of course there is no objection of legal principle to extension of responsibility to cases of maladministration.

[2] *Supra*, p. 495. Cp. Guha Roy, 55 *A.J.* (1961), p. 863 at p. 877. See further Ténékidès, 14 *R.D.I.L.C.* (1933), 514–35; de Visscher, 52 Hague *Recueil* (1935, II), 421–32.

[3] See McNair, *Opinions* ii. 311, and *supra*, p. 449.

[4] See Fachiri, 6 *B.Y.* (1925), 159–71; id., 10 *B.Y.* (1929), 32–55; Fischer Williams, 9 *B.Y.* (1928), 1–30; Herz, 35 *A.J.* (1941), 243–63; Friedman, *Expropriation in International Law* (1953); Bindschedler, 90 Hague *Recueil* (1956, II), 179–306; Foighel, *Nationalization and Compensation* (1964); Wortley, *Expropriation in Public International Law* (1959); Gillian White, *Nationalisation of Foreign Property* (1961); Domke, 55 *A.J.* (1961), 585–616; McNair, 6 *Neths. Int. L.R.* (1959), 218–56; Rolin, ibid., pp. 260–75; Verdross, ibid., pp. 278–87; Fouilloux, *La Nationalisation et le droit international public* (1962); Petrén, 109 Hague *Recueil* (1963, II), 492–575; García Amador, *Yrbk., I.L.C.* (1959), ii. 2–24; Int. Law Assoc., Report of the Forty-Eighth Conference, 1958, pp. 130–239; *Annuaire de l'Inst.* 43, i. 42–132; 44, ii. 251–323; 52, i. 402–527, 656–732; 52, ii. 400–63, 523–6, 560, 565; American Law Institute, Restatement, Second, *Foreign Relations Law of the United States* (1965), pp. 553–75; Whiteman viii. 1020–1185; Delson, 57 *Columbia L.R.* (1957), 755–86; Ronning, *Law and Politics in Inter-American Diplomacy*, pp. 33–62; Bishop, *Cases*, (3rd ed.), pp. 863–7; id., 115 Hague *Recueil* (1965, II), 403–14; Sohn and Baxter, 55 *A.J.* (1961), 545–84; Steiner and Vagts, *Transnational Legal Problems*, pp. 314–70; Miller and Stanger (eds.), *Essays on Expropriations* (1967); Amerasinghe, *State Responsibility for Injuries to Aliens*, pp. 121–68; Lillich (ed.), *The Valuation of Nationalized Property in International Law*, 3 vols. (1972–5); *Répertoire suisse* ii. 661–98; Orrego Vicuña, 67 *A.J.* (1973), 711–27; Francioni, 24 *I.C.L.Q.* (1975), 255–83.

by aliens. Apart from such restrictions, an alien individual, or a corporation controlled by aliens, may acquire title to property within a state under the local law. The subject-matter may be shares in enterprises, single items such as estates or factories, or, on a monopoly basis, major areas of activities such as railways and mining. In a number of countries foreign ownership has extended to proportions of between fifty and one hundred per cent of all major industries, resources, and services such as insurance and banking. Even in *laisser-faire* economies, the taking of private property for certain public purposes and the establishment of state monopolies have long been familiar. Since the Soviet revolution and the extension of the public sector in many economies, both socialist and non-socialist, the conflict of interest between foreign investors and their governments and the hosts to foreign capital, seeking to obtain control over their own economies, has become more acute. The terminology of the subject is by no means settled, and in any case form should not take precedence over substance. The essence of the matter is the deprivation by state organs of a right of property either as such, or by permanent transfer of the power of management and control.[1] The deprivation may be followed by transfer to the territorial state or to third parties, as in systems of land distribution as a means of agrarian reform. The process is commonly described as expropriation. If compensation is not provided, or the taking is regarded as unlawful, then the taking is sometimes described as confiscation. Expropriation of one or more major national resources as part of a general programme of social and economic reform is now generally referred to as nationalization or socialization.

State measures, *prima facie* a lawful exercise of powers of government, may affect foreign interests considerably without amounting to expropriation. Thus foreign assets and their use may be subjected to taxation, trade restrictions involving licences and quotas,[2] or measures of devaluation.[3] Whilst special facts

[1] On the various procedures of taking see Sohn and Baxter, 55 *A.J.* (1961), 553, 559; Domke, ibid., pp. 588–90; Christie, 38 *B.Y.* (1962), 307–38; Whiteman viii. 1006–20; Weston, 16 *Virginia Journ. of I.L.* (1975–6), 103–75. On concession agreements see *infra*, pp. 547–51.

[2] Treaties may make such restrictions unlawful: e.g. under the GATT (*supra*, p. 262), the EFTA Treaty, 1960, and bilateral commercial treaties.

[3] Currency depreciation is lawful unless it is discriminatory: *Tabar claim*, Int. L.R., 20 (1953), p. 211; *Zuk claim*, ibid., 26 (1958, II), p. 284; *Furst claim*, ibid., 42, p. 153; *British Digest* vi. 350; Wortley, op. cit., pp. 107–9; 5 *Canad. Yrbk.* (1967), 268; Whiteman viii. 982–8. Treaty obligations exist, *inter alia*, under I.M.F. agreements: Mann, 26 *B.Y.* (1949), pp. 263–70. See also *Re Keim*, Int. L.R. 44, p. 102.

may alter cases, in principle such measures are not unlawful and do not constitute expropriation. If the state gives a public enterprise special advantages, for example by direction that it charge nominal rates of freight, the resulting *de facto* or quasi-monopoly is not an expropriation of the competitors driven out of business:[1] it might be otherwise if this were the primary or sole object of a monopoly regime. Taxation which has the precise object and effect of confiscation is probably unlawful.[2]

10. *The Compensation Rule*

The rule supported by all leading 'Western' governments and a majority of jurists in Europe and North America is as follows: the expropriation of alien property is lawful if adequate, effective, and prompt compensation[3] is provided for. In principle, therefore, expropriation, as an exercise of territorial competence, is lawful, but the compensation rule makes the legality conditional. The justifications for the rule are based on the assumptions prevalent in a liberal regime of private property and in the principle that foreign owners are to be given the protection accorded to private rights of nationals, provided that this protection involves the provision of compensation for any taking. These assumptions are used to support the compensation principle as yet another aspect of the international minimum standard governing the treatment of aliens.[4] The emphasis is on respect for property rights as 'acquired rights'[5] and as an aspect of

[1] See the *Oscar Chinn* case (1934), P.C.I.J., Ser. A/B, no. 63; World Court Reports iii. 416. See further Christie, op. cit., pp. 322, 334–6. This decision is also authority for the view that goodwill is not an item of property separate from an enterprise.

[2] See *British Practice* (1964), 202–6; Whiteman viii. 980, 1016, 1044; *Tax on Mortgagors' Gains Case*, Int. L.R. 44, p. 149 at pp. 153–4.

[3] The formula appears in a Note from the U.S. Secretary of State, Cordell Hull, to the Mexican Government dated 21 July 1938: Briggs, p. 556; Bishop, p. 851; Hackworth iii. 655. The formula also appears in various modern commercial treaties: e.g. the Anglo-Japanese Commercial Treaty of 1963, art. 14; see Almond, 13 *I.C.L.Q.* (1964), 925 at p. 949. See also Whiteman viii. 1085–9. It is also commonly stipulated that the taking should be 'in the public interest', but see *infra*, p. 545. On the criteria of adequacy, effectiveness, and promptness, see García Amador, *Yrbk., I.L.C.* (1959), ii. 16–24; White, pp. 235–43; Domke, 55 *A.J.* (1961), 603–10; Sohn and Baxter, ibid., pp. 553 (Art. 10/4), 559–60; I.C.J. Pleadings, *Anglo-Iranian Oil Co.* case (United Kingdom v. Iran), pp. 100 seq.; Jiménez de Aréchaga, *Yrbk., I.L.C.* (1963), ii. 237–44; Cole, 41 *B.Y.* (1965–6), 374–9; Whiteman, viii. 1143–85; Metzger, 50 *Virginia L.R.* (1964), 603–7.

[4] On which, *supra*, p. 524.

[5] The statements of the Permanent Court on the principle of respect for vested or acquired rights occur in the context of state succession; see *infra*, p. 535, n. 4. See generally García Amador, *Yrbk., I.L.C.* (1959), ii. 3–10; Foighel, op. cit., pp. 124–8. See also the *Lighthouses* arbitration (1956), P.C.A., *R.I.A.A.* xii. 155, 236.

human rights.[1] Reference is also made to general principles of law, including those of unjust enrichment and abuse of rights. The principle of acquired rights is thought by many to be unfortunately vague, and the difficulty is to relate this principle to other principles of law: in short this and other general principles beg too many questions. Constitutional provisions,[2] legislation providing for compensation,[3] and municipal court decisions[4] provide a general guide but no more than that, since local versions of public policy are not necessarily significant for international law.

Whatever the nature of the justifications offered for the compensation rule, it has received considerable support from state practice and the jurisprudence of international tribunals. The United Kingdom, the United States, and France have supported the rule in relation to Mexican agrarian reform, post-war nationalization in Eastern Europe, the Iranian law of 1951 nationalizing the oil industry, the nationalization of the Suez Canal by Egypt, and so on.[5] Agreements involving provision for

[1] Cf. the Additional Protocol to the European Convention on Human Rights, Art. 1: Robertson, *Human Rights in Europe* (1963), p. 196. See also *Gudmundsson* v. *Iceland*, *Yrbk. of the European Conv.* iii. 394, 424; Int. L.R. 30, p. 253 at pp. 265 seq. See generally Chapter XXIV.

[2] See Shawcross, 102 Hague *Recueil* (1961, I), p. 339 at p. 347.

[3] See White, op. cit., pp. 184–93.

[4] Many of these depend on the public policy of the forum and conflict of laws rules. However, see the *S.S. Elise*, *Ann. Digest* 15 (1948), no. 50 at p. 200; *Anglo-Iranian Oil Co.* v. *Idemitsu Kosan Kabushiki Kaisha*, Int. L.R. 20 (1953), 305; the *Rose Mary* [1953] 1 W.L.R. 246; Int. L.R. 20 (1953), 316; *In re Rhein-Main-Donau A.G.*, Int. L.R. 21 (1954), 212. See further Gihl, *Liber Amicorum Algot Bagge*, pp. 56–66; and cf. *Czechoslovak Agrarian Reform* case, *Ann. Digest* 4 (1927–8), no. 94.

[5] The pre-1914 practice involved the following cases: the Sicilian sulphur monopoly granted to a French company, thus harming British subjects (1836), 28 *B.F.S.P.*, 1163–242; 29 id., 175–204, 1225; 30 id., 111–20; the *Charlton* case (1841), 31 *B.F.S.P.*, 1025–32; the *Finlay* case (1846), 39 *B.F.S.P.*, 410; *British Digest* vi. 341; the *King* case (1853), Moore, *Digest* vi. 262; Whiteman, *Damages* ii. 1387; the *Savage* case (1852), Moore, *Arbitrations* ii. 1855; the *Delagoa Bay Railway* case (1900), Martens, *N.R.G.* (2nd Ser.), Vol. 30, 329; *British Digest*, v. 535; Whiteman, *Damages* iii. 1694; La Fontaine, *Pasicrisie*, p. 398 (Portugal conceded the principle of compensation); *Portuguese Religious Properties* case (1920), *R.I.A.A.* i. 7; Hague Court Reports ii. 1; the proposal for an insurance monopoly in Uruguay (1911), Hackworth v. 588; the Italian life insurance monopoly (1912), ibid. On the work of the Brussels Conference, 1921, see McNair, *Opinions* i. 9, and Wortley, op. cit., p. 61. On the Cannes Conference of 1922 see H. of C., Sess. Papers XXIII, 1922 (but see Friedman, pp. 19, 101–3). More modern practice includes the following: U.S. Notes to Mexico in 1938 and 1940, Hackworth iii. 655, 658, 662; Briggs, pp. 556, 559; Bishop (3rd ed.), pp. 851, 860; 33 *A.J.* (1939), Suppl., pp. 181–207; U.K. Note to Mexico, 1938, Cmd. 5758; U.K. minute to Poland, Treaty Series no. 23 (1948), Cmd. 7403 (cf. Fawcett, 27 *B.Y.* (1950), 372–3); U.K. Memorial, *Anglo-Iranian Oil Co.* case, I.C.J. Pleadings (1951), pp. 100–9; U.S. Note to Guatemala, 28 August 1953, 29 *Dept. of St. Bull.* (1953), 357, 359; protests of France, U.K., and U.S. on Suez Canal Company nationalization, 1956; U.S. views on Cuban and Ceylonese nationalizations, 56 *A.J.* (1962), 166; 58 *A.J.* (1964), 168; U.K. reaction to Indonesian measures, *British Practice*

some sort of compensation in the form of the 'lump sum settlement' are numerous, but jurists are in disagreement as to their evidential value: many agreements rest on a bargain and special circumstances, and it is difficult to see whether the compensation principle is assumed as the general norm or has been eroded by the frequency of compromise.[1] Although some awards were in substance diplomatic compromises,[2] a good number of international tribunals have supported the compensation rule and the principle of acquired rights.[3] *Dicta* in a number of decisions of the Permanent Court,[4] involving treaty interpretation and the effects of state succession on various categories of property, may be regarded as supporting the compensation principle, which is supported also by a majority of jurists in Western countries.[5]

(1964), 194–200; to Tanzanian nationalization of banks, ibid., 1967, 118–20. In 1958 it was stated (by Brandon, Int. Law Assoc., Forty-Eighth Conference) that 54 U.N. members were on record as supporting the compensation principle. However, it is doubtful if all states in this tally accept the 'adequate, effective, and prompt' formula. Cp. also the Netherlands Note to Indonesia, 18 December 1959, 54 *A.J.* (1960), 484; Kiss, *Répertoire* iv, paras. 655–66.

[1] See White, op. cit., pp. 193–243; Friedman, pp. 86–101; Fawcett, 27 *B.Y.* (1950), 372–3; Drucker, 10 *I.C.L.Q.* (1961), 238–54; Shawcross, op. cit., pp. 348–50; Lillich, 16 *Syracuse L.R.* (1964–5), 735–6; id., *The Protection of Foreign Investment* (1965), pp. 167–88; Lillich and Weston, *International Claims: Their Settlement by Lump Sum Agreements*, 2 vols. (1975); Whiteman viii. 1107–29.

[2] See the *Delagoa Bay Railway* and *Expropriated Religious Properties* cases, *supra*, p. 534, n. 5.

[3] *Norwegian Ships* arbitration (1921), P.C.A., *R.I.A.A.* i. 307, 338; Green, p. 3; Hague Court Reports ii. 40; *French Claims against Peru* (1921), P.C.A., *R.I.A.A.* i. 215; Hague Court Reports ii. 31; 16 *A.J.* (1922), 480; *Landreau* claim (1921), *R.I.A.A.* i. 347, 365; *Spanish Zone of Morocco* claims (1925), *R.I.A.A.* ii. 615, 647; *Ann. Digest* 2 (1923–4), no. 85; *Hopkins* claim (1927), *R.I.A.A.* iv. 41; 21 *A.J.* (1927), 160; *Ann. Digest* 3 (1925–6), no. 167; Briggs, p. 204; *Goldenberg* claim (1928), *R.I.A.A.* ii. 901, 909; 3 *R.D.I.* (1929), 559; *Hungarian Optants* case (1927), *Rec. T.A.M.* vii. 138; arbitral award between Portugal and Germany (1930), *R.I.A.A.* ii. 1035, 1039; *Ann. Digest* 5 (1929–30), 150, 151; *Shufeldt* claim (1930), *R.I.A.A.* ii. 1079, 1095; 24 *A.J.* (1930), 799; *Mariposa* claim (1933), *R.I.A.A.* vi. 338; *de Sabla* claim (1933), *R.I.A.A.* vi. 358, 366; *Ann. Digest* 7 (1933–4), no. 92 at p. 243; *Arabian-American Oil Co.* v. *Saudi Arabia* (1958), Int. L.R. 27, p. 117 at pp. 144, 168, 205.

See also the *El Triunfo* case (1901), *R.I.A.A.* xv. 467; Bishop, p. 788; *Upton* (1903), *R.I.A.A.* ix. 234; and *Selwyn* (1903), ibid., p. 380.

[4] See *German Interests in Polish Upper Silesia* (1926), P.C.I.J., Ser. A, no. 7, pp. 21, 22, 33, 42; World Court Reports i. 510, 523–4; Green, p. 533; *Chorzów Factory* case (Jurisdiction) (1927), Ser. A, no. 9, pp. 27, 31; and no. 13, p. 19; World Court Reports i. 646, 677; *Chorzów Factory* case (Indemnity) (1928), Ser. A, no. 17, pp. 46, 47; Green, p. 607 (cf. Fischer Williams, 9 *B.Y.*, 8–10); *German Settlers in Poland* (1923), Ser. B, no. 6, pp. 23, 24, 38; Green, p. 174; *Peter Pázmány University* (1933), Ser. A/B, no. 61, p. 243.

[5] See McNair, Rolin, Verdross, Wortley, White, and Petrén, cited *supra*, p. 531, n. 4. See also García Amador's report, *Yrbk., I.L.C.* (1959), ii. 2–24; Sørensen, 101 Hague *Recueil* (1960, III), 176 seq.; Fitzmaurice, 92 Hague *Recueil* (1957, II), 128; Guggenheim

Jurists supporting the compensation rule recognize the existence of exceptions, the most widely accepted of which are as follows:[1] under treaty provisions; as a legitimate exercise of police power, including measures of defence against external threats; confiscation as a penalty for crimes; seizure by way of taxation or other fiscal measures; loss caused indirectly by health and planning legislation and the concomitant restrictions on the use of property; the destruction of property of neutrals as a consequence of military operations, and the taking of enemy property as part payment of reparation for the consequences of an illegal war.[2]

11. *The Principle of National Treatment*[3]

A number of jurists[4] and a few tribunals[5] have subscribed to the view that an alien cannot complain provided he receives the same treatment as nationals: if nationals of the expropriating state receive no compensation the alien can expect none. Sir John Fischer Williams has pointed out that a general dogma as to the inviolability of private property can no more be erected into an international duty than other political and economic doctrines. Thus the exceptions to the compensation rule noticed above indicate the relativity of acquired rights even in states founded on private enterprise principles. For reasons offered earlier, it is not thought that the national treatment principle provides a reliable general formula. In relation to expropriation, as

i. 333–4; Briggs, p. 569; Shawcross, 102 Hague *Recueil* (1961, I), 339, 369; O'Connell, pp. 776–85.

[1] See Friedman, op. cit., pp. 1–3; Wortley, pp. 40–57; Guggenheim i. 333; Herz, 35 *A.J.* (1941), 251–2; *Yrbk., I.L.C.* (1959), ii. 11–12, paras. 43, 44; Sohn and Baxter, 55 *A.J.* (1961), 553, 561–2, Art. 10 (5); Fischer Williams, 9 *B.Y.* (1928), 22–8; Petrén, op. cit., pp. 525–36.

[2] See the *AKU* case, Int. L.R. 23 (1956), 21; *Prince Salm-Salm* case, ibid. 24 (1957), 893. This view is controversial, however. See further *Assets of Hungarian Company in Germany* case, Int. L.R. 32, p. 565; *Re Dohnert, Muller, Schmidt & Co.*, ibid., p. 570.

[3] See further *supra*, p. 523.

[4] See Dunn, 28 *Col. L.R.* (1928), 166–80; Cavaglieri, 38 *R.G.D.I.P.* (1931), 257–96; Brierly, *Law of Nations* (6th ed.), p. 284; Fischer Williams, 9 *B.Y.* (1928), 28–9. See further Herz, 35 *A.J.* (1941), 259, n. 66.

[5] See the *Canevaro* case, P.C.A. (1912), Hague Court Reports i. 285; 6 *A.J.* (1912), 746; *R.I.A.A.* xi. 397; *Standard Oil Co. Tankers* (1926), *R.I.A.A.* ii. 781, 794; 8 *B.Y.* (1927), 156; 22 *A.J.* (1928), 404.

elsewhere, it plays a subsidiary role in the context of the positive legal principles.[1]

12. *Control of Major National Resources*

The classical model for expropriation has long been the taking of a single item of property, and the analogy has been the wrongful taking of property in private law. Cases in which expropriation is allowed to be lawful in the absence of compensation are within the narrow concept of public utility prevalent in *laisser-faire* economic systems, i.e. exercise of police power, health measures, and the like. The fact is that a large proportion of the members of the community of states now regard the existence of a public sector as an important aspect of national independence and economic development. Many of the poorer states have accepted foreign investment at the expense of economic, and therefore political, independence. It is all very well to say that nationalization is possible—providing prompt and adequate compensation is paid. In reality this renders any major economic or social programme impossible, since few states can produce the capital value of a large proportion of their economies promptly. It is common for the poorer economies to be subjected to foreign ownership to a great extent,[2] and the analogy of private law ownership clashes sharply with the desire of states to govern their own economies. This impasse has led some eminent jurists to distinguish between general expropriation (nationalization, or socialization), on the one hand, and, on the other, small-scale expropriation. In the case of nationalization of a major industry or natural resource compensation would be on a basis of payments phased out over a period and calculated with reference to the general economic position in the state concerned. In other words, compensation of private interests is accommodated to the competence to nationalize.[3] Jurists from socialist countries have

[1] See further *supra*, pp. 523, 526, *infra*, p. 544, and cf. Fischer Williams 9 *B.Y.* (1928), 28–9; Friedman, pp. 133, 210.

[2] See the percentages for the Polish economy in 1946, quoted in Friedman, p. 32.

[3] See the opinions of Lauterpacht, 62 Hague *Recueil* (1937, IV), 346; id., *International Law: Collected Papers* i (1970), 387–90; Sørensen, pp. 485–9; Bishop, 115 Hague *Recueil* (1965, II), 409–10; Amerasinghe, *State Responsibility for Injuries to Aliens*, pp. 121–68; Oppenheim i. 352; La Pradelle, *Annuaire de l'Inst.* 43 (1950, I), 60–6; de Visscher, *Theory and Reality in Public International Law*, pp. 193–5; Henri Rolin, *Annuaire de l'Inst.*, 43 (1950, I), 97; id., 6 *Neths. Int. L.R.* (1959), 272; Friedman, op. cit., pp. 206–11; Guggenheim i. 334–5. See also Baade, 54 *A.J.* (1960), 804, notes 22, 23. Cf. the Mexican Note to the U.S. of 3 August 1938, Briggs, p. 558; Hackworth iii. 657. For Asian and Latin-American opinions see *Yrbk., I.L.C.* (1957), i. 154 seq. See further Petrén, op. cit., pp. 545 seq.; Sohn and Baxter, 55 *A.J.* (1961), 553 (art. 10, para. 4), 559–60.

placed emphasis on the need to relate the assessment of compensation to the profits obtained and the indirect harm caused to the economy by speculative development.[1] The principle of nationalization unsubordinated to a full compensation rule may be supported by reference to principles of self-determination, independence, sovereignty, and equality.[2] Equitably based, the lump sum settlement (*indemnité globale forfaitaire*) short of the prompt, adequate, and effective standard has become common, and some authors regard the practice as evidence of an *opinio juris*.[3]

13. *Expropriation Unlawful* per se

The position achieved by the preceding discussion is as follows:

(1) Expropriation for certain public purposes, e.g. exercise of police power and defence measures in wartime, is lawful even if no compensation is payable.

(2) Expropriation of particular items of property is unlawful unless there is provision for the payment of prompt, adequate, and effective compensation.

(3) Nationalization, i.e. expropriation of a major industry or resource, is unlawful only if there is no provision for compensation payable on a basis compatible with the economic objectives of the nationalization, and the viability of the economy as a whole.

Thus expropriation under (2) and (3) is unlawful, if at all, only *sub modo*, i.e. if appropriate compensation is not provided for. The controversial differences between (2) and (3) are the basis on which compensation is assessed and the absence of prompt payment in (3). However, whatever may be the relation of these two categories, there is evidence of a category of types of expropriation which are illegal apart from a failure to provide for compensation, in which cases lack of compensation is an additional element in, and not a condition of, the illegality. It has

[1] See Katzarov, 84 *J.D.I.* (1957), 6–51. Cf. the U.S. Court of Appeals in *Banco Nacional de Cuba* v. *Sabbatino* (1962), 56 *A.J.* (1962), p. 1085 at pp. 1098–101; and in the Supreme Court, 376 U.S. 398 (1964); Bishop, p. 877; 58 *A.J.* (1964), 779; *Anglo-Iranian Oil Co. Ltd.* v. *S.U.P.O.R.*, Int. L.R. 22 (1955), 23.

[2] See the resolutions of the U.N. General Assembly considered below.

[3] See Rolin, *ut supra*; id., 6 *Neths. Int. L.R.* (1959), 273. For doubts as to the *opinio juris*, see Sørensen, 101 Hague *Recueil* (1960, III), 180 and Bindschedler, 90 Hague *Recueil* (1956, II), 297. See further Fawcett, 27 *B.Y.* (1950), 372–5; García Amador, *Yrbk., I.L.C.* (1959), ii. 20–4. At the very least, the requirement of 'promptness' has been overshadowed by post-war practice: see on this the *Anglo-Iranian* case, I.C.J. Pleadings (1951), p. 106.

been suggested that this category includes interference with the assets of international organizations[1] and taking contrary to promises amounting to estoppels.[2] Certainly it includes seizures which are a part of crimes against humanity or genocide, involve breaches of international agreements,[3] are measures of unlawful retaliation or reprisal against another state,[4] are discriminatory, being aimed at persons of particular racial groups or nationals of particular states,[5] or concern property owned by a foreign state and dedicated to official state purposes.[6]

The practical distinctions between expropriation unlawful *sub modo*, i.e. only if no provision is made for compensation, and expropriation unlawful *per se* would seem to be these: the former involves a duty to pay compensation only for direct losses, i.e. the value of the property, the latter involves liability for consequential loss (*lucrum cessans*);[7] the former confers a title which is recognized in foreign courts (and international tribunals), the latter produces no valid title.[8]

[1] See Delson, 57 *Columbia L.R.* (1957), 771.

[2] Friedmann, 50 *A.J.* (1956), 505. On estoppel see *infra*, p. 637.

[3] Cf. *German Interests in Polish Upper Silesia* (Merits) (1926), P.C.I.J., Ser. A, no. 7; Green, p. 533; *Chorzów Factory* case (Indemnity) (1928), Ser. A, no. 17, pp. 46–7; Green, p. 607.

[4] Netherlands Note to Indonesia, 18 December 1959, 54 *A.J.* (1960), 484; U.S. Notes to Libya, 8 July 1973, *Digest of U.S. Practice*, 1973, 334–5; 20 June 1974, ibid., 1975, 490–1; U.S. Court of Appeals, *Banco Nacional de Cuba* v. *Sabbatino* (1962), 56 *A.J.*, p. 1085 at pp. 1101–4; *Banco Nacional de Cuba* v. *First National City Bank*, 270 F. Supp. 1004 (1967); Int. L.R. 42, p. 45; Seidl-Hohenveldern, in *Essays Presented to Kollewijn and Offerhaus* (1962), pp. 470–9; Rolin, 6 *Neths. Int. L.R.* (1959), 274. An obvious difficulty is to determine when a reprisal is lawful: in principle it should be a reaction to a prior breach of legal duty and be proportionate.

[5] There is much authority for this: see White, op. cit., pp. 119–44; McNair, 6 *Neths. Int. L.R.* (1959), 247–9; Rolin, ibid., pp. 269–70; Herz, 35 *A.J.* (1941), 243, 249, 259; Sørensen, 101 Hague *Recueil* (1960, III), 178; U.S. Court of Appeals, *Banco Nacional de Cuba* v. *Sabbatino* (1962), 56 *A.J.* (1962), 1104–5; *In re Helbert Wagg & Co. Ltd.* [1956] 1 Ch. 323; Int. L.R. 22 (1955), 480; *Bank Indonesia* v. *Senembah Maatschappij*, Int. L.R. 30, p. 28. And see *infra*, pp. 596–8.

The test of discrimination is the intention of the government: the fact that only aliens are affected may be incidental, and, if the taking is based on economic and social policies, it is not directed against particular groups simply because they own the property involved. See I.C.J. Pleadings, *Anglo-Iranian Oil Co.* case (1951), p. 97; *Anglo-Iranian Oil Co. Ltd.* v. *S.U.P.O.R.*, Int. L.R. 22 (1955), p. 23 at p. 39; Whiteman viii. 1041–57.

[6] White, op. cit., pp. 151–3.

[7] See Sørensen, 101 Hague *Recueil* (1960, III), 178–9; Fatouros, *Government Guarantees to Foreign Investors* (1962), pp. 307–9. Some writers require specific restitution in the latter case; see Baade, 54 *A.J.* (1960), 807–30; 56 *A.J.* (1962), 504–5; Wortley, 55 *A.J.* (1961), 680–3. See also Sohn and Baxter, ibid., p. 556; Jennings, 37 *B.Y.* (1961), 171–3.

[8] See Domke, 54 *A.J.* (1960), 305–23; id., ibid. 55 (1961), 610–16; Baade, 54 *A.J.* (1960), 801–35; id., ibid. 56 (1962), 504–7; Seidl-Hohenveldern, ibid., pp. 507–10; id., 49 *Michigan L.R.* (1951), 851–68. The writers are not agreed on these questions, and municipal courts often recognize measures lawful under the *lex situs*: *Luther* v. *Sagor* [1921] 3 K.B. 532; *In re Helbert Wagg & Co. Ltd.* [1956] 1 Ch. 323; Int. L.R. 22 (1955), 480; *Dutch Tobacco Firms in Indonesia*, Int. L.R. 28, p. 16. The issues before municipal courts

14. *The General Assembly Resolution of 1962 on Permanent Sovereignty over Natural Resources*

The materials on which an assessment of the rules governing expropriation must be based include important projects canvassed within the United Nations. In 1955 the Third Committee of the General Assembly adopted a draft article, as a part of the Human Rights Covenants, on the right of self-determination, the second paragraph of which stated: 'The peoples may, for their own ends, freely dispose of their natural wealth and resources without prejudice to any obligations arising out of international economic co-operation, based upon the principle of mutual benefit, and international law. In no case may a people be deprived of its own means of subsistence.' The concept of economic self-determination stemmed from a General Assembly resolution of 21 December 1952.[1] Much later, work in the U.N. Commission on Permanent Sovereignty over Natural Resources and the Economic and Social Council culminated in the adoption of Resolution 1803 (XVII) by the General Assembly on 14 December 1962.[2] The resolution was in the form of a Declaration on Permanent Sovereignty over Natural Resources. The *consideranda* to the resolution refer, *inter alia*, to 'the inalienable right of all States freely to dispose of their natural wealth and resources in accordance with their national interests', and to 'respect for the economic independence of States', and stipulate that the resolution has no bearing on the subject of succession of states and governments.

The substance of the Declaration is as follows:

1. The right of peoples and nations to permanent sovereignty over their natural wealth and resources must be exercised in the interest of their national development and of the well-being of the people of the State concerned;

2. The exploration, development and disposition of such resources, as

are influenced by the operation of rules of conflict of laws (see Verzijl, in *Makarov Festgabe*, p. 531) and the act of state doctrine (see *supra*, p. 507). See further Münch, 98 Hague *Recueil* (1959, III), 411–503.

[1] Resol. 626 (VII). See also Resols. 1314 (XIII), 12 December 1958, and 1515 (XV), 15 December 1960. See generally Hyde, 50 *A.J.* (1956), 854–67; and U.N. Secretariat study, *The Status of Permanent Sovereignty over Natural Wealth and Resources* (1962). Resol. 626 (VII) was cited in *Anglo-Iranian Oil Co. Ltd.* v. *S.U.P.O.R.*, Int. L.R. 22 (1955), p. 23 at p. 40; and *Anglo-Iranian Oil Co.* v. *Idemitsu Kosan Kabushiki Kaisha*, ibid. 20 (1953), p. 305 at p. 313.

[2] Adopted by 87 votes to 2, 12 abstentions. See Gess, 13 *I.C.L.Q.* (1964), 398–449 (text of resol., p. 400) and Fischer, *Ann. français* (1962), pp. 516–28; *Texaco* v. *Libyan Government*, 17 *Int. Leg. Materials* (1978), 1; 104 *J.D.I.* (1977), 350, Award on Merits, paras. 68, 80–1, 83–4, 87–8. See further Resol. 2158 (XXI) adopted on 25 November 1966 by 104 votes to 0, 6 abstentions; 6 *Int. Leg. Materials* (1967), 147; *British Practice* (1966), p. 205.

well as the import of the foreign capital required for these purposes, should be in conformity with the rules and conditions which the peoples and nations freely consider to be necessary or desirable with regard to the authorization, restriction or prohibition of such activities;

3. In cases where authorization is granted, the capital imported and the earnings on that capital shall be governed by the terms thereof, by the national legislation in force, and by international law. The profits derived must be shared in the proportions freely agreed upon, in each case, between the investors and the recipient State, due care being taken to ensure that there is no impairment, for any reason, of that State's sovereignty over its natural wealth and resources;

4. Nationalization, expropriation or requisitioning shall be based on grounds or reasons of public utility, security or the national interest which are recognized as overriding purely individual or private interests, both domestic and foreign. In such cases the owner shall be paid appropriate compensation, in accordance with the rules in force in the State taking such measures in the exercise of its sovereignty and in accordance with international law. In any case where the question of compensation gives rise to a controversy, the national jurisdiction of the State taking such measures shall be exhausted. However, upon agreement by sovereign States and other parties concerned, settlement of the dispute should be made through arbitration or international adjudication;

5. The free and beneficial exercise of the sovereignty of peoples and nations over their natural resources must be furthered by the mutual respect of States based on their sovereign equality;

6. International co-operation for the economic development of developing countries, whether in the form of public or private capital investments, exchange of goods and services, technical assistance, or exchange of scientific information, shall be such as to further their independent national development and shall be based upon respect for their sovereignty over their natural wealth and resources;

7. Violation of the rights of peoples and nations to sovereignty over their natural wealth and resources is contrary to the spirit and principles of the Charter of the United Nations and hinders the development of international co-operation and the maintenance of peace;

8. Foreign investment agreements freely entered into by, or between, sovereign States shall be observed in good faith; States and international organizations shall strictly and conscientiously respect the sovereignty of peoples and nations over their natural wealth and resources in accordance with the Charter and the principles set forth in the present resolution.

15. *The Charter of Economic Rights and Duties of States*

Since 1972 the less developed states have pressed for the establishment of a 'new deal' in their relations with the industrialized nations. This pressure was reflected, in particular, in the United Nations General Assembly Resolution 3201(S-VI) of 1 May 1974[1] containing a Declaration on the Establishment of a New International Economic Order. On 12 December 1974 the General Assembly adopted the Charter of Economic Rights and Duties of States (120 votes in favour; 6 against; 10 abstentions).[2] The states voting against the resolution were: Belgium, Denmark, German Federal Republic, Luxembourg, the United Kingdom and the United States.

For present purposes the leading principles of the Charter are to be found in Article 2, as follows:

1. Every State has and shall freely exercise full permanent sovereignty including possession, use and disposal, over all its wealth, natural resources and economic activities.'

2. Each State has the right:

. . . (c) to nationalize, expropriate or transfer ownership of private property, in which case appropriate compensation should be paid by the State adopting such measures, taking into account its relevant laws and regulations and all circumstances that the State considers pertinent. In any case where the question of compensation gives rise to a controversy, it shall be settled under the domestic law of the nationalizing State and by its tribunals, unless it is freely and mutually agreed by all States concerned that other peaceful means be sought on the basis of the sovereign equality of States and in accordance with the principle of free choice of means.

What effect, if any, do these formulations have on customary international law? Such resolutions are vehicles for the evolution of state practice and each must be weighed in evidential terms according to its merits. The Charter has a strong political and programmatic flavour and does not purport to be a declaration of pre-existing principles. The opinion has been expressed that Article 2 of the Charter is merely a *de lege ferenda* formulation.[3] This view is contradicted by evidence that Article 2 (2) (c) is regarded by many states as an emergent principle, applicable *ex nunc*. In the first place, the language harks back to paragraph 4 of the 1962 Resolution (above). Secondly, the attitude of states

[1] 13 *Int. Leg. Materials* (1974), 715; 68 *A.J.* (1974), 798. See also Resolution 3202 (S-VI), ibid., 720.

[2] Resolution 3281 (XXIX), 14 *Int. Leg. Materials* (1975), 251; 69 *A.J.* (1975), 484. For comment see Lillich, 69 *A.J.* (1975), 359–65; Castañeda, *Ann. français*, 1974, 31–56; Virally, ibid., 57–77; Brower and Tepe, 9 *Int. Lawyer* (1975), 295–318; Haight, ibid., 591–604; Feuer, 79 *R.G.D.I.P.* (1975), 273–320; White, 24 *I.C.L.Q.* (1975), 542–52; id., 16 *Virginia J.I.L.* (1975–6), 323–45; Mahiou, 12 *Revue belge* (1976), 421–50; Salem, 102 *J.D.I.* (1975), 753–800; Rao, 16 *Indian Journ.* (1976), 351–70; Jiménez de Aréchaga, Hague *Recueil* (1978, I), 297–310. See also the Declaration of Lima, 26 March 1975, Second General Conference of UNIDO; 14 *Int. Leg. Materials* (1975), 826.

[3] *Texaco* v. *Libyan Government*, *supra*, Award on Merits, paras. 88–9. However, this approach is modified in paras. 90–1.

opposed to Article 2 indicates all too clearly that governments are aware of the need to 'contract out' of such formulations by reservations of position either by explanations of negative votes and abstention or by the making of specific reservations after adoption of a resolution by consensus (without formal vote).[1]

Assuming that the provisions of Article 2 are to be reckoned with, as evidence of new customary law, what are the consequences? The concept of permanent sovereignty over natural resources reinforces the existing principle that taking for public purposes is lawful. The compensation principle is not, as such, denied. Recent comment has neglected to notice that, if the term 'compensation' has an objective content, then failure by the local courts to provide 'compensation' would be contrary to the principles of Article 2. It is also clear that liability for denial of justice may arise if certain standards are not observed.[2] Moreover, expropriation contrary to treaty, or in breach of an independent principle of customary law, for example, the principle of non-discrimination on grounds of race or religion, will continue to be unlawful. It has been stated[3] that the reference to the domestic law of the nationalizing state is intended to give general recognition to the Calvo doctrine,[4] but in fact the reference to domestic law is exclusively in relation to 'compensation' and, as it has been suggested above, this is by no means a reference to domestic law willy-nilly.

In conclusion it is to be emphasized that, assuming that Article 2 of the Charter does bring about a change in the customary law, whatever this might be, the United States and its associates will not be bound since they have adopted the role of persistent objectors.[5]

16. *Conclusions on Expropriation*

The Declaration of 1962 set out above, which constitutes evidence of the existing law,[6] places emphasis on the rights of the state host to or receiving foreign assets and aid and in a general

[1] See 13 *Int. Leg. Materials* (1975), 715 at pp. 744, 749, 753, 759, 762.

[2] Cf. Castañeda, *Ann. français*, 1974, at pp. 51, 54; *Texaco* v. *Libyan Government*, *supra*, Award on Merits, paras. 90–1.

[3] Lillich, 69 *A.J.* (1975), 359 at p. 361.

[4] On which see *infra*, pp. 546–7.

[5] On the persistent objector: *supra*, pp. 10–11. In the Second Committee of the General Assembly Article 2 (2) (c) of the Charter attracted negative votes or abstention from 22 delegations.

[6] See U.K. note to the Government of Iraq, 4 September 1967; *British Practice* (1967), p. 121.

way contradicts the simple thesis of acquired rights. However, its actual formulations tend to cover up the real differences of opinion on the law by reference to international law and the payment of 'appropriate compensation'. Question-begging though the provisions may be, it is significant that the right to compensation, on whatever basis, is recognized in principle. In view of the real differences of opinion, any statement of conclusions can only be provisional. Indeed, some authorities regard the law relating to compensation for expropriated alien property to be substantially uncertain.[1] The present position, including the elements of confusion, can be expressed in a number of independent propositions.

(1) A considerable number of states insist that expropriation can only take place on payment of adequate, effective compensation. However, in practice deferred payments are regarded as sufficient provided effective compensation takes place.[2] The requirement of promptness has become subordinated to the other conditions and also to economic realities relating to payment of large sums.
(2) Neither the principle of acquired rights nor that of national treatment provide reliable guidance.
(3) The majority of states accept the principle of compensation, but not on the basis of the 'adequate, effective, and prompt' formula.[3]
(4) Where major natural resources are concerned, cogent considerations of principle reinforced by the declaration of 1962, militate against the 'adequate, effective, and prompt' formula.[4]
(5) The view that only local legislation need be complied with[5] is not reflected in state practice generally or the declaration of 1962.
(6) Certain categories of expropriation are illegal *per se* and not merely in the absence of appropriate compensation.[6]
(7) Reference to reprisal action, as a type of expropriation

[1] See Bishop, 115 Hague *Recueil* (1965, II), 405–11.
[2] See Foighel, op. cit., pp. 255–7; I.C.J. Pleadings, *Anglo-Iranian Oil Co.* case, pp. 100 seq.
[3] See the references in the article by Gess, *ut supra*, pp. 427–9, to the General Assembly debate on the Declaration of 1962, which provides for 'appropriate compensation'. See further Jiménez de Aréchaga, Hague *Recueil* (1978, I), 21, 297–310.
[4] See Lauterpacht, 62 Hague *Recueil* (1937, IV), 346; and Sohn and Baxter, 55 *A.J.* (1961), 553 (Art. 10 (4)), 559–60.
[5] See Vilkov, *Soviet Year Book of I.L.* (1960), 76.
[6] *Supra*, pp. 538–9.

illegal *per se*, only leads to secondary questions as to the legality of the reprisal.

(8) Reference to general principles that expropriation must be for purposes of public utility, or that it must not be 'arbitrary', only causes confusion.[1] The determination of public utility is primarily a matter for individual states, and categories of illegality (see proposition (6)) can only depend on particular rules of international law.

(9) The 'orthodox' compensation rule is stated to have exceptions, principally on the basis of police power.[2] Here the concept of public utility in certain societies is employed to explain cases where no compensation is payable. The exceptions are an embarrassment since, as a matter of principle, this position is not very different from the view taken by some states with a different view of public utility, viz., that the compensation rule does not apply, at least in the 'adequate, effective, and prompt' form.

17. *Legal Devices Adopted by Investors and Hosts to Foreign Capital*

There is a large literature on the means of protecting foreign investment, and suggestions are made for the creation of multilateral investment codes.[3] In practice legal protection (apart from general international law) is based upon bilateral investment and aid agreements, guarantees to investors by the governments of capital-exporting states, and agreements between the investor and the recipient state. Investor states attempt to keep issues out of the national courts of the latter by appropriate clauses on jurisdiction in case of dispute and on choice of applicable law.[4] On the proposal of the World Bank an International

[1] See Gillian White, op. cit., pp. 149–50, who states that the rule against non-discrimination suffices. But absence of discrimination is not by itself a sufficient guide to legality. For references to public utility see Herz, 35 *A.J.* (1941), 252–3; *Yrbk., I.L.C.* (1959), ii. 15–16; Sohn and Baxter, p. 553 (Art. 10); McNair, 6 *Neths. Int. L.R.* (1959), p. 218 at pp. 243–7; and the Declaration of the U.N. General Assembly of 1962, *supra*, p. 525.

[2] *Supra*, p. 536.

[3] See 12 *Stanford L.R.* (1960), 606–37; Domke, 105 *U. Pa. L. Rev.* (1957), 1033–43; Fatouros, *Government Guarantees to Foreign Investors* (1962); id., in Friedmann and Pugh (eds.), *Legal Aspects of Foreign Investment* (1959), pp. 699–733; 66 *Harv. L.R.* (1953), 514–24; Snyder, 10 *I.C.L.Q.* (1961), 469–94; Gros, *Mélanges Rolin* (1964), pp. 125–33; I.L.A., *Report of the Fifty-Second Conference* (1966), pp. 819–60; *Report of the Fifty-Third Conference* (1968), pp. 667–707; Schwarzenberger, *Foreign Investments and International Law* (1969); 71 *Harv. L.R.* (1958), 1102–22; Lillich, *The Protection of Foreign Investment* (1965); Rubin, *Foreign Development Lending: Legal Aspects* (1971).

[4] See Sereni, 96 Hague *Recueil* (1959, I), 133–232; Spofford, 113 Hague *Recueil* (1964, III), 121–234; Metzger, 50 *Virginia L.R.* (1964), 594–627.

Centre for the Settlement of Investment Disputes has been set up.[1] The Centre has jurisdiction over 'any legal dispute arising directly out of an investment, between a Contracting State (or any constituent subdivision or agency of a State designated to the Centre by that State) and a national of another Contracting State, which the parties to the dispute consent to in writing to submit to the Centre'. Investor governments, however, are not committed to the view that concession agreements involving recipient states and foreign corporations are 'international agreements' and not contracts of private law.[2]

States receiving foreign investment have long sought means of assimilating the foreign investor and their own nationals, and in treaties they seek to establish a standard of equal treatment or reciprocity. In making concession contracts with aliens, it has been the practice of Latin-American governments to insert a 'Calvo clause', under which the alien agrees not to seek the diplomatic protection of his own state and submits matters arising from the contract to the local jurisdiction.[3] The majority of jurists and governments have hitherto denied the validity of such clauses, but international tribunals have since 1926 given them a degree of acceptance.[4] In principle, a clause in a contract of private law cannot deprive a state of the right of diplomatic protection or an international tribunal of jurisdiction. However, a tribunal may interpret the agreement which confers jurisdiction in such a way as to incorporate the clause, particularly where the alien contractor is seeking to use diplomatic protection as a means of avoiding his obligations. In any case the operation of the local remedies rule often makes the clause superfluous,[5]

[1] Conv. on the Settlement of Investment Disputes between States and Nationals of Other States; opened for signature 18 March 1965; in force 14 October 1966; 575 U.N.T.S. 159; 4 *Int. Leg. Materials* (1965), p. 532. See Moore, 18 *Stanford L.R.* (1966), 1359–80; Schwarzenberger, op. cit., pp. 135–52; and literature cited *infra*, p.

[2] See *infra*, pp. 547–51.

[3] See Lipstein, 22 *B.Y.* (1945), 130–45; Shea, *The Calvo Clause* (1955); Briggs, pp. 648–50; García Amador, *Yrbk., I.L.C.* (1958), ii. 58–9; O'Connell ii. 1059–66; Sørensen, pp. 590–3; Whiteman viii. 916–33; Freeman, 40 *A.J.* (1946), 121–47; Summers, 19 *Virginia L.R.* (1932–3), 459–84; Feller, *The Mexican Claims Commissions 1922–1934* (1935), pp. 185–200; Graham, 6 *Texas Int. Law Forum* (1970–1), 289–308; *Rogers*, 72 *A.J.* (1978), 1–16. The 'clause' (there is no single type) is named after the Argentinian jurist responsible for the device. See further Agreement of Cartagena, Decision of Commission, No. 24, December 1970, Common Regime on Foreign Investments, 11 *Virginia Journ. of I.L.* (1971), 264.

[4] See the *North American Dredging Co.* claim (1926), *R.I.A.A.* iv. 26; Briggs, p. 640; Green, p. 639; Bishop, p. 811 (American-Mexican Claims Commission); and comment in Sørensen, p. 592.

[5] The Calvo clause would not be superfluous in a case like the *North American Dredging Co.* claim (last note) since the Convention by which the adjudicating Commission was constituted contained a specific waiver of the local remedies rule.

since, subject to what is said below, breach of a private law contract is not an international wrong and the right of diplomatic protection will arise only if there is a denial of justice in the course of exhausting remedies in the local courts.[1] The clause is not superfluous if the agreement conferring jurisdiction upon an international tribunal excludes the operation of the local remedies rule but incorporates by reference the effect of the Calvo clause (or is so interpreted). The practical effect of the clause in arbitrations has been to prevent contractual disputes being the object of diplomatic protection or inter-state proceedings in the absence of a denial of justice.

18. *Breaches and Annulment of State Contracts*

Governments make contracts of various kinds with aliens or legal persons of foreign nationality: loan agreements (including the issue of state bonds), contracts for supplies and services, contracts of employment, agreements for operation of industrial and other patent rights under licence, agreements for the construction and operation of transport or telephone systems, and agreements conferring the sole right, or some defined right, to exploit natural resources on payment of royalties. The last two categories can be described as 'concession agreements', but there is no firm reason for regarding 'concession agreements' as a term of art or, assuming they can form a defined category, as being significantly different from other state contracts.[2] The contracting government may act in breach of contract, legislate in such a way as to make the contract worthless (for example, by export or currency restrictions), use its powers under domestic law to annul the contract, or repudiate the contract by means illegal in terms of the domestic law. What, then, is the position in terms of international law?

In principle, the position is regulated by the general principles governing the treatment of aliens. Thus, the act of the contracting government will entail state responsibility if by itself or in combination with other circumstances, it constitutes a denial of justice (in the strict sense) or an expropriation contrary to international law. The general view[3] is that a breach of contract (as

[1] On which, *supra*, p. 529.

[2] Some authorities insist on treating concessions as a special category, e.g. O'Connell ii. 976–97. For another view: Sohn and Baxter, 55 *A.J.* (1961), 566–7. On the position of bonds see Hyde ii. 1005. See also Mann, 54 *A.J.* (1960), at pp. 589–90.

[3] Mann, 54 *A.J.* (1960), 572–91 (also, *Studies in International Law* (1973), pp. 302–26); Jessup, *A Modern Law of Nations* (1948), p. 104; id., 46 *Columbia L.R.* (1946), p. 913; Dunn, *The Protection of Nationals* (1932), pp. 165–7, 171; Amerasinghe, 58 *A.J.* (1964), 881–913; id., *State Responsibility for Injuries to Aliens* (1967), pp. 66–120; Bishop, pp.

opposed to its confiscatory annulment) does not create state responsibility on the international plane. On this view the situation in which the state exercises its executive or legislative authority to destroy the contractual rights as an asset comes within the ambit of expropriation.[1] It follows that such action will lead to state responsibility in the same conditions as expropriation. Thus, it is often stated that the annulment is illegal if it is arbitrary and, or, discriminatory.[2] These terms cover two situations. First, action directed against persons of a particular nationality[3] or race is discriminatory. Secondly, action which lacks a normal public purpose is 'arbitrary'. A government acting in good faith may enact exchange control legislation or impose trade restrictions which incidentally (and without discrimination) lead to the annulment or non-enforceability of contractual rights. It is difficult to treat such action as illegal on the international plane.[4]

There is a school of thought which supports the view that the breach of a state contract by the contracting government of itself creates international responsibility.[5] Jennings[6] has argued persuasively (though with some deliberate caution) that there are no basic objections to the existence of an international law of contract. He points out that in the field of nationality,[7] for example, rights

792–4; id., 115 Hague *Recueil*, 399–400; Hyde, *International Law* (2nd ed., 1947), ii. 988–90; Fitzmaurice, 37 *B.Y.* (1961), 64–5, Borchard, *Diplomatic Protection*, ch. 7; Briggs, pp. 664–5; Eagleton, *Responsibility* (1928), pp. 157–68; Metzger, 50 *Virginia L.R.* (1964), 607–8; Lipstein, 22 *B.Y.* (1945), 134–5; Feller, *The Mexican Claims Commissions 1923–1934* (1935), p. 174; Foighel, *Nationalization and Compensation* (1964), pp. 178–93; Petrén, 109 Hague *Recueil*, 523–4; Wengler, 76 *R.G.D.I.P.* (1972), 313–45; Rigaux, 67 *Revue critique de d. i. privé* (1978), 435–59.

The position of O'Connell ii. 976–1010, is broadly the same but concession contracts and bond obligations are treated as legally distinct categories. See further Fatouros, *Government Guarantees to Foreign Investors* (1962), pp. 232–301.

[1] See the *Shufeldt Claim* (1930), *R.I.A.A.* ii. 1083; Wortley, *Expropriation*, pp. 55–7; Gillian White, *Nationalisation*, pp. 162–79. Cf. *Feierabend Claim*, Int. L.R. 42, p. 157; *Hexner Claim*, ibid., 169. See also *Valentine Petroleum Arbitration* (1967), Int. L.R. 44, p. 79 at pp. 85–91; *Texaco* v. *Libyan Government*, 17 *Int. Leg. Materials* (1978), 1; 104 *J.D.I.* (1977), 350.

[2] See, for example, Mann, op. cit., pp. 574–5; Sohn and Baxter, op. cit., pp. 566–70; Whiteman viii. 933, 942.

[3] On this issue see *supra*, p. 539.

[4] Some authorities would regard this on the same basis as expropriation lawful *sub modo*; see Gillian White, *Nationalisation*, pp. 162–3, 178. Cf. also O'Connell ii. 986–9; García Amador, *Yrbk., I.L.C.* (1959), ii. 14–15, 24–36; Hyde, 105 Hague *Recueil* (1962, I), 322–3.

[5] See Oppenheim i. 344; Schwebel, 53 *Proc. A.S.I.L.* (1959), 266–73; Harv. Research, 1929, art. 8, 23 *A.J.* (1929), Spec. Suppl., pp. 167–8 (but the comment considerably modifies the text); Carlston, 52 *A.J.* (1958), 760–79; I.L.A., *Report of the Forty-Eighth Conference* (1958), p. 161. See also Am. Law Inst., Restatement, Second, *Foreign Relations Law*, paras. 193–5. O'Connell ii. 993–4, comes close to this position in respect of concession contracts. See further *Annuaire de l'Inst.* (1952), ii. 318.

[6] 37 *B.Y.* (1961), 156–82.

[7] See Chapter XVIII.

created in municipal law may be evaluated according to international law standards. Again, the cases of contractual situations giving rise to denial of justice to be found in arbitral jurisprudence are treated as cases of contract when the issues of remedy and reparation are dealt with. Jennings also refers to the Calvo clause,[1] which, in so far as it has validity on the international plane, is not a mere question of domestic jurisdiction. Exponents of the international law character of state contracts also use arguments based upon the doctrine of acquired rights[2] and the principle of *pacta sunt servanda*, and refer to certain decisions of international tribunals.[3]

Apart from the merits of these arguments, it has to be recognized that there is little solid evidence that the position they tend to support corresponds to the existing law. The practice of the leading capital-exporting states, the United States[4] and the United Kingdom[5] clearly requires some element, beyond the mere breach of contract, which would constitute a confiscatory taking or denial of justice *stricto sensu*. On analysis most of the arbitral decisions cited in support of the view that breach of contract by the contracting state is an international wrong are found not to be in point, either because the tribunal was not applying international law or because the decision rested on some element apart from the breach of contract.[6] There is no evidence that the principles of acquired rights and *pacta sunt servanda* have

[1] *Supra*.

[2] See Jennings, op. cit., pp. 173–5, 177; O'Connell ii. 984–5; Hyde, 105 Hague *Recueil* (1962, I), 315–18. The award in *Saudi Arabia* v. *Arabian-American Oil Co.* (*supra*, p. 535) referred to acquired rights as a 'fundamental principle'. See also McNair, 33 *B.Y.* (1957), p. 1 at pp. 16–18.

[3] For example, the *Delagoa Bay Railway* case (*supra*, p. 534, n. 5); *El Triunfo* claim (*supra*, p. 535, n. 3); *Landreau* claim (ibid.); *Shufeldt* claim (ibid.); *Rudloff case*, *R.I.A.A.* ix. 244; and *Saudi Arabia* v. *Arabian-American Oil Co.* (*supra*, p. 535, n. 3). See also the *Sapphire-N.I.O.C.* arbitration, Int. L.R. 35, p. 136; see Lalive, 13 *I.C.L.Q.* (1964), 987–1021; and *Texaco* v. *Libyan Government*, 17 *Int. Leg. Materials* (1978), 1; 104 *J.D.I.* (1977), 350; see Lalive, ibid., pp. 319–49; Rigaux (op. cit. *supra*, p. 547, n. 3).

[4] Moore, *Digest*, vi. 705; Hackworth v. 611; Whiteman viii. 906–7. For a different view of the U.S. position see Wetter, 29 *Univ. of Chicago L.R.* (1962), p. 275 at pp. 305–22; Sohn and Baxter, 55 *A.J.* (1961), p. 573.

[5] Pre-1900 items; McNair, *Opinions* ii. 201–4; *British Digest* vi. 358. See further *Anglo-Iranian Oil Co. Case, Pleadings*, U.K. Memorial, pp. 83–6, 96–8; *Ambatielos Case, Pleadings*, pp. 389, 475; *British Practice* (1966), 108–11. The position of France, the U.K., and U.S. on the nationalization of the Suez Canal Company by Egypt in 1956 rested on the special character of the Company as an 'international agency' and on the allegation of breaches of the Convention of Constantinople: see 6 *I.C.L.Q.* (1957), 314; Whiteman iii. 1084–1130. However, compensation was paid to stockholders for the nationalization: E. Lauterpacht (ed.), *The Suez Canal Settlement* (1960).

[6] See Mann, op. cit., pp. 575–80; Amerasinghe, *State Responsibility*, pp. 77–84. The award in *Saudi Arabia* v. *Arabian-American Oil Co.* (*ut supra*, pp. 144–6) had a declaratory character as the principle of acquired rights had been recognized by both parties.

the particular consequences contended for. Exponents of acquired rights doctrine commonly give it a modified form which leaves room for exercise of local legislative competence. Moreover, if one is to apply general principles of municipal law then it becomes apparent that government contracts have a special status and in some systems lack enforceability.[1] It is a striking fact that in English law[2] when the executive receives money paid over by a foreign government in settlement of contract claims (on an *ex gratia* or some other basis), the executive is under no legal duty to pay over the sums received to the private claimants. The arguments based upon acquired rights could be applied to a number of reliance situations created by the host state by the grant of public rights such as citizenship or permission to reside or to work. The distinction drawn by partisans of responsibility in contract situations between loan agreements, concessions, and other contracts is unsatisfactory. Why do they prefer their reasoning only in certain contract or reliance situations?

There is a further issue which requires consideration. In the proceedings arising from the Iranian cancellation of the 1933 Concession Agreement between the Iranian Government and the Anglo-Iranian Oil Company, the United Kingdom contended that violation of an explicit undertaking in a concession by the government party not to annul was illegal quite apart from the law relating to expropriation on payment of adequate compensation.[3] This view almost certainly does not represent the positive law but it is not without merit.[4] An undertaking not to annul by legislative action is a voluntary acceptance of risk comparable to the undertaking given by an alien in the form of a Calvo clause.

The rules of public international law accept the normal operation of rules of private international law and when a claim for breach of a contract between an alien and a government arises, the issue will be decided in accordance with the applicable system of municipal law designated by the rules of private international law. Further questions are raised if the parties to a state contract expressly choose an applicable law other than a particular system of local law, either 'general principles of law' or public

[1] Note also that decisions of English courts have upheld legislative abrogation of gold clauses: *R.* v. *International Trustee* [1937] A.C. 500. See also *Kahler* v. *Midland Bank* [1950] A.C. 24 and Mann, *The Legal Aspect of Money* (3rd ed.), pp. 126 seq., 146 seq.

[2] And this is typical: *infra*, pp. 590–1.

[3] U.K. Memorial, *Anglo-Iranian Oil Co. Case, Pleadings*, pp. 86–93. See comment by Mann, 54 *A.J.* (1960), 587; and cf. *Digest of U.S. Practice*, 1975, pp. 489–90.

[4] A few writers give it support: White, op. cit., pp. 163, 175–9; O'Connell ii. 993–4. See also *Radio Corporation of America* case, *R.I.A.A.* iii. 1621.

international law.[1] A choice by the parties of public international law is assumed by some writers to place the contract on the international plane but this cannot be correct since a state contract is not a treaty and cannot involve state responsibility as an international obligation.[2]

19. *Foreign Investment Agreements*

The United Nations General Assembly Declaration on Permanent Sovereignty over Natural Resources[3] provides in paragraph 8 that 'foreign investment agreements freely entered into *by or between*[4] sovereign states shall be observed in good faith'. This provision may be subject to the principles concerning justifiable expropriation set out in paragraph 4 of the Declaration. If this is not the case, then the resolution is strong evidence for the view that 'foreign investment agreements' have a status in international law superior to that of other state contracts.[5]

[1] See McNair, 33 *B.Y.* (1957), 1–19; Sereni, 96 Hague *Recueil* (1959, I), 133–232; Mann, 35 *B.Y.* (1959), 34–7; id., 42 *B.Y.* (1967), 1–37; O'Connell, ii. 977–84, 990–1; Weil, 128 Hague *Recueil* (1969, III), 120–88; *Annuaire de l'Inst.*, 57, I, 192–265; Mann *et al.*, *Revue belge*, 1975, 562–94; the *Abu Dhabi* arbitration, 1 *I.C.L.Q.* (1952), 247; Int. L.R., 18 (1951), no. 37; and *Texaco* v. *Libyan Government*, 17 *Int. Leg. Materials* (1978), 1; 104 *J.D.I.* (1977), 350.

[2] *Annuaire de l'Inst.*, 57, I, 246–7 (Report of van Hecke). For a different view: *Texaco Award* (previous note), paras. 26, 46–8, 71, *per* Dupuy, Sole Arbitrator.

[3] Resolution 1803 (XVII); *supra*.

[4] My italics.

[5] See *British Practice* (1967), p. 121; Gess, 13 *I.C.L.Q.* (1964), at pp. 439–42; and see the *Texaco Award* (note 1 above), para. 68.

CHAPTER XXIV

THE PROTECTION OF INDIVIDUALS AND GROUPS: HUMAN RIGHTS AND SELF-DETERMINATION

1. *Sovereignty and Domestic Jurisdiction*

An attempt to assess modern developments concerning the protection of the individual, more especially against his own government, must take into account the matrices of customary or general international law. To impose responsibility on a state on the international plane, it is necessary for the complainant to establish that the matter is subject to international law or, more precisely, is not a matter purely within the area of discretion which international law designates as sovereignty. The modern rule is stated in terms of the reserved domain of domestic jurisdiction and bears very closely on the question of human rights.[1]

While there is some difference of opinion, Article 2, paragraph 7, of the United Nations Charter is probably in substance a restatement of the classical rule.[2] Three points arise immediately. First, this provision is concerned with the special question of 'constitutional' competence of the organs of the United Nations, and it may be that its precise content is not therefore identical with the rule of general international law apart from the Charter. However, even if the rules are not identical, since the principles of the Charter are so prominent in the practice of states, interpretation of the provision in Article 2, paragraph 7, by organs of the United Nations will no doubt influence the general law. The second point is that the reservation is inoperative when a treaty obligation is concerned.[3] And, thirdly, the domestic jurisdiction

[1] Generally on sovereignty and domestic jurisdiction, *supra*, Chapter XIII. On the individual in international law generally Jessup, *A Modern Law of Nations* (1948), pp. 68–93; Lauterpacht, *International Law and Human Rights* (1950); Nørgaard, *The Position of the Individual in International Law* (1962); Spiropoulos, *L'individu en droit international* (1928); Ténékidès, *L'individu dans l'ordre juridique international* (1933); Hill, 28 *Am. Pol. Sci. Rev.* (1934), 276; Korowicz, 50 A.J. (1956), 533–62; Lauterpacht, 63 *L.Q.R.* (1947), 438, 64 *L.Q.R.* (1948), 97 (also in Lauterpacht, *International Law: Coll. Papers*, ii. 487–533); Sperduti, 90 Hague *Recueil* (1956, II), 733–838; Ezejiofor, *Protection of Human Rights under the Law* (1964); Rousseau ii. 695–774.

[2] Quoted *supra*, p. 293.

[3] See *Peace Treaties* case, I.C.J. Reports (1950), pp. 65, 70–1; *Nationality Decrees in Tunis and Morocco*, P.C.I.J., Ser. B, no. 4, at p. 24 (1923).

reservation does not apply if the United Nations agency is of the opinion that a breach of a specific legal obligation relating to human rights in the Charter itself has occurred. In practice, organs of the United Nations have further reduced the effect of the reservation, by construing certain provisions relating to human rights, which might seem only hortatory, as presenting definite and active legal obligations. This development has related primarily to questions of human rights and self-determination arising under Chapters IX and XI of the Charter.

It has been easy for the political organs to find justification in the wide-ranging Charter provisions for discussion as 'of international concern' of a great number of issues arising from methods of government in many areas of the world. Moreover, the liberal practice under Articles 55 and 56[1] of the Charter could drastically change the concept of domestic jurisdiction. The extent to which 'defendant' states can now rely on some type of formal interpretation of Article 2, paragraph 7, is in doubt. If care is not taken, too much can be proved, and the substance of Article 2, paragraph 7, will disappear. One commentator has suggested that the meaning it bears is that, even where international obligations of a state are involved, the United Nations is precluded from penetrating, without the state's consent, behind its authority over its own territory, nationals, ships, and aircraft, except in cases of enforcement action for the maintenance or restoration of peace.[2] This means that for the most part the United Nations must confine itself to discussion and recommendations 'without teeth', but in fact considerable political pressure results from such proceedings, especially in the General Assembly.

2. *Rights Conferred by Treaty*

In examining the relations of individuals in terms of the ordinary canons of international law, it is obvious that states can agree to confer special rights on individuals, and such agreements existed before the appearance of the Charter with its general provisions on the subject. In the *Danzig Railway Officials* case,[3] the Permanent Court of International Justice said: 'It cannot be disputed that the very object of an international agreement, according to the intention of the contracting Parties, may be the adoption by the Parties of some definite rules creating individual

[1] Quoted *infra*, pp. 569–70. [2] Waldock, 106 Hague *Recueil* (1962, II), 188–91.
[3] P.C.I.J., Ser. B, no. 15 (1928).

rights and obligations and enforceable by the national courts.'[1] In general, treaties do not create direct rights and obligations for private individuals, but, if it was the intention of the parties to do this, effect can be given to the intention. Thus, in accordance with the agreement between Danzig and Poland regulating conditions of employment of officials taken into the Polish railway service, the Danzig railway officials had a right of action against the Polish railway administration for recovery of claims based on the agreement.

3. *The Individual and the State*

Effective nationality. The intimate relation between individual and state, recognized by international law, is apparent from the rules on diplomatic protection, but authoritative exposition of the nature of nationality on the international plane has lately elaborated that relation. The need for certain links between an individual and a state as a basis for conferring nationality was emphasized by various members of the International Law Commission in the debates on elimination and reduction of statelessness.[2] Habitual residence and the question of allegiance recur in these discussions. The final development of this work was the adoption by a United Nations Conference in 1961 of a Convention on Reduction of Statelessness,[3] which rests conferment, renunciation, and deprivation of nationality on various social links between individual and state.

In its judgment in the *Nottebohm* case[4] the International Court of Justice expounded the principle that, for nationality to be opposable to other states on the international plane, there must be a real and effective link, a genuine connexion, between the state and the individual concerned. Some jurists have expressed the fear that diplomatic protection will be less effective as a result of the decision, and it has been said that a person held to have no effective nationality will not have the protection of international conventions relating to stateless persons.[5] The latter

[1] Id. at 17–18; see Lauterpacht, *The Development of International Law by the International Court* (1958), pp. 173–6; Verzijl, *Jurisprudence of the World Court* i. 136–140. See also the European Convention for the Protection of Human Rights and Fundamental Freedoms, 4 Nov. 1950, Cmd. no. 8969 (Treaty Series no. 71 of 1953), on which see *infra*, pp. 574–5.

[2] See *Yrbk., I.L.C.* (1953), i. 180–1, 184, 186, 218, 237, 239.

[3] For text, see 11 *I.C.L.Q.* (1962), 1090.

[4] I.C.J. Reports (1955), p. 4 at pp. 22–3. Generally on effective nationality and the *Nottebohm* case see Chapter XVIII.

[5] Courts are reluctant to hold that statelessness exists: see *Ministry of Home Affairs* v.

point is a criticism perhaps of the content of such conventions. It should be noted that the principle of effective nationality would restrict the ambit of protection only if a considerable quantum of links were required; it does not follow from *Nottebohm* that the principle will apply restrictively.

Other aspects of the relation. The reference to nationality does not exhaust the legal aspects of the individual in relation to the state. Thus the state may be responsible for activity on its territory which injures other states or their nationals even if performed by aliens.[1] The exercise of criminal jurisdiction may extend to non-nationals on state territory under certain conditions, even with respect to treason. Aliens may expect to be prosecuted in states where they indulge in such activity, and they cannot seek shelter behind the personality of their own state (unless they are beyond the area of effective jurisdiction of the prosecuting state).

Mobility of population, economic stress, and inequalities and political divisions which cut across international boundaries have, since the nineteenth century, created a series of instances in which the individual ceases to follow the classical legal model. Thus numerous incongruities between national laws have produced statelessness and multiple nationality. Similarly, political strife may produce acts of deprivation of nationality by some states as a measure of security; and in other instances large numbers of refugees may retain a *de jure* nationality for which they have no use and so are referred to as '*de facto* stateless'.

Multiple nationality is inconvenient in its consequences, but particular sources of friction, e.g. conscription, have often been dealt with by treaty. Moreover, states frequently tolerate dual nationality, and there may be a trend towards increased acceptance of it.[2] In any event statelessness in its various forms is the real problem. Certain forms of statelessness arising from gaps in national law, as was the case of the Rumanian Jews,[3] or from an

Kemali, Int. L.R. 40, p. 191 at p. 195; Ct. of Cassation, Italy, referring to the Univ. Decl. of Human Rights, art. 15 (see *infra*, p. 556).

[1] See *Corfu Channel* case (Merits), I.C.J. Reports (1949), p. 4 at pp. 18–23; Brownlie, 7 *I.C.L.Q.* (1958), 712–35.

[2] See *Nottebohm* case, I.C.J. Reports (1955), p. 4 at pp. 42–3 (dissenting opinion). Nevertheless, the International Law Commission has considered means of reducing its causes. See *Yrbk., I.L.C.* (1952), ii, at pp. 11–12. See also the treaty practice of Communist states since 1956, referred to in Bar-Yaacov, *Dual Nationality* (1961), pp. 83–4; and the Conv. on Reduction of Cases of Multiple Nationality and Military Obligations in Cases of Multiple Nationality, European Treaty Series no. 43, signed 6 May 1963; 58 *A.J.* (1964), 573.

[3] Cf. *Valeriani* v. *Amuna Bekri Sichera*, *Ann. Digest* 8 (1935–7), no. 120; *Kahane (Successor)* v. *Parisi and the Austrian State*, *Ann. Digest* 5 (1929–30), no. 131.

absence of nationality law when a new state comes into being, may be remedied by reference to habitual residence (or domicile) in conjunction with other principles of law concerning state responsibility and the nature of statehood and territorial sovereignty.

Since 1920 statelessness has been an increasing problem,[1] and after work by the International Law Commission, a United Nations Convention on Reduction of Statelessness was adopted at a conference in 1961 and came into force in 1975.[2] The Convention creates obligations for the granting of nationality on the basis of residence conditions (five to ten years), with qualifications (offences against national security, and sentence, on any criminal charge, to imprisonment for five years or more, disqualify). Article 1 relates to persons born in state territory who would otherwise be stateless. In addition, other provisions control deprivation of nationality,[3] and thus Article 9 prohibits deprivation on racial, ethnic, religious, or political grounds. The conference at which the Convention was drawn up also adopted a resolution recommending that persons who are stateless *de facto* should as far as possible be treated as stateless *de jure* to enable them to acquire an effective nationality. In 1960 the Convention relating to the Status of Stateless Persons came into force.[4]

Another family of problems concerns the extent to which the individual can contract out of or sever his connexion with his state. In the first place, is there a right of expatriation? The Universal Declaration of Human Rights prescribes, in Article 15, paragraph 2, that 'No one shall be arbitrarily deprived of his nationality nor denied the right to change his nationality'. In the light of existing practice, however, the individual does not have this right,[5] although the provision in the Universal Declaration may influence the interpretation of internal laws and treaty rules. In some cases, if the individual does succeed in establishing a new and effective nationality, this may be opposable to other

[1] See U.N. Department of Social Affairs, *A Study of Statelessness*, U.N. Doc. no. E/1112, and add. 1, Sales no. 1949, XIV, at 2 (1949). The extent of the problem is clearly recognized in *Re Immigration Act and Hanna*, Int. L.R. 24 (1957), 465. See also Mutharika, *The Regulation of Statelessness under International and National Law* (1977).

[2] See Weis, 11 *I.C.L.Q.* (1962), 1073. For text of the Convention, see id. at p. 1090; Brownlie, *Human Rights*, p. 170.

[3] United Nations Convention on the Reduction of Statelessness, Arts. 8, 9.

[4] 360 U.N.T.S., 117; Brownlie, *Human Rights*, p. 153.

[5] Oppenheim i. 648–9. A resolution of the United States Congress in 1868 acknowledged the right of expatriation as 'a natural and inherent right of all people', 66 Stat. 267 (1868). See also *Yrbk., I.L.C.* (1954), ii at p. 61, paras. 37–8; Maury, *Hommage d'une génération de juristes au Président Basdevant*, pp. 378–82; Fischer Williams, 8 *B.Y.* (1927), p. 45 at pp. 52–3; *Digest of U.S. Practice*, 1974, pp. 73–5.

states including the 'losing' state. Recent instruments have contained the principle of freedom to leave any country, including one's own.[1]

When a state succession occurs, the affected population normally will automatically acquire the nationality of the successor state.[2] However, liberal sentiment and the influence of the principle of self-determination have led some writers to assert a right of option.[3] It is certainly true that many treaties of cession provide rights of option, but their existence may militate against the view that general international law recognizes such a right. At least in cases of universal succession, non-resident citizens of the state extinguished may, by the better view, escape acquisition of the nationality of the successor state by remaining abroad. In addition, there is an American practice disapproving compulsory acquisition of nationality but this relates primarily to cases in which alien residents in Brazil and elsewhere could become naturalized on what were, in the view of the United States, slender grounds.[4]

Machinery has long been sought to provide refugees with a certain status regardless of the fact that they were often stateless *de jure* or *de facto*. The problem is particularly difficult because governments are not always willing to distinguish between those who are victims of political upheaval and those who, while on foreign soil, are active partisans against their own governments. Even 'passive' refugees may be used as a political bargaining factor, and the host state may delay a process of assimilation which would terminate the pressure refugees *en masse* may exert, politically, on the state of origin.

A detailed account of developments calculated to alleviate the condition of refugees is not possible here,[5] but the following may be noted. By a Convention Relating to the International Status of Refugees of 28 October 1933[6] the contracting parties assumed obligations toward Russian and Armenian refugees. In 1946 the United Nations General Assembly adopted the Constitution of the International Refugee Organization, which functioned until

[1] Int. Covenant on Civil and Political Rights, 1966, art. 12; Europ. Conv. on Human Rights, Fourth Protocol, 1963, art. 2 (in force, 1968). In both cases broadly defined restrictions are permitted.

[2] *Infra*, pp. 658–63.

[3] See Fauchille, *Droit international public* i, Pt. 1, p. 857; Kaufmann, 54 Hague *Recueil* (1935, IV), 373.

[4] See Briggs, pp. 460–2.

[5] See e.g., Weis, 48 *A.J.* (1954), 193–221; Grahl-Madsen, *The Status of Refugees in International Law*, 2 vols. (1966); Aga Khan, 149 Hague *Recueil* (1976, I), 287–352.

[6] Cmd. no. 5347 (Treaty Series no. 4 of 1937).

1952, when its main functions were taken over by the office of the United Nations High Commissioner for Refugees. In 1951 at Geneva a United Nations conference adopted a Convention on the Status of Refugees[1] which by 1971 was in force between some fifty-six states. This provides national treatment with regard to some rights such as freedom of religion, 'most-favoured-nation treatment' with regard to wage-earning employment and the right of association, and stipulates that, in other contexts, including education other than elementary education, refugees are to receive treatment as favourable as possible and not less favourable than that accorded to aliens as a class.[2] In 1954 another United Nations conference adopted a Convention Relating to the Status of Stateless Persons[3] which applies to 'a person who is not considered as a national by any State under the operation of its law'. In general this provides a status equal to that of refugees, but with respect to certain rights, including wage-earning employment, the standard of treatment is lower, the criterion being treatment not less favourable than that accorded to aliens as a class.

The interests of the individual appear in another complex relation with his own and other states in the law concerning extradition and political asylum. In the normal case the process of extradition accords with good policy. The values of justice are preserved and the interest of the requesting state in exercising jurisdiction is recognized. Moreover, the individual is not allowed to escape responsibility for the common types of crimes (*mala in se*).

There is no duty to extradite,[4] however, and even where a treaty exists, exception is made for persons accused of political offences. Since the late nineteenth century liberal tendencies have favoured the practice of granting asylum to political offenders. Efforts, so far only in the realm of *lex ferenda*, have been made to create a right of asylum for the individual, in place of the discretion which states at present have. The Universal Declaration of Human Rights prescribes a right 'to seek

[1] United Nations Conference of Plenipotentiaries on the Status of Refugees and Stateless Persons, Geneva, 1951, Final Act and Convention Relating to the Status of Refugees, U.N. Doc. no. A/CONF.2/108; Brownlie, *Human Rights*, p. 135 (with changes of Protocol). See further the Protocol of 1966, on which see Weis, 42 *B.Y.* (1967), p. 39. Text: ibid., p. 67; 606 U.N.T.S., p. 267; in force, 1967.

[2] See *U.K. Contemp. Practice* (1962), i, at 71–2; Schwelb, 9 *I.C.L.Q.* (1960), p. 654 at p. 660.

[3] United Nations Conference on the Status of Stateless Persons, New York, 1964, Final Act and Convention Relating to the Status of Stateless Persons, U.N. Doc. No. E/CONF. 17/5/Rev. 1; Brownlie, *Human Rights*, p. 153.

[4] Except perhaps in the case of war criminals.

and to enjoy in other countries asylum from persecution', which is not to be invoked in the case of prosecutions 'arising from non-political crimes or from acts contrary to the purposes and principles of the United Nations'.[1] In 1962, during discussion in the Third Committee of the General Assembly of the Draft Covenant on Civil and Political Rights, some states supported the inclusion of a new article on the right of asylum.[2] At the moment two sources of difficulty exist: the uncertainty of the concept of political offences and the tendency, within military and political alliances, to refuse asylum to persons considered by allies to be politically dangerous. The United Nations Declaration on Territorial Asylum of 1967 contains certain principles which states should observe in granting asylum on their territory:[3] work is proceeding on a draft convention.[4]

4. *Nationality and the Concept of Territory*

In the previous section the individual was seen in relation to the state, and it is now proposed to look at another type of relation which has influenced the legal regime. As illustrated above, the doctrine of effective nationality emphasizes the social bases of the individual's legal relations. This doctrine reflects the reliance of some important treaties,[5] as well as municipal laws,[6] on habitual residence or domicile. The basic ideas would seem to be that belonging to a community is important and that a stable community is normally related to a particular territorial zone. In the normal case, territory, both socially and legally, connotes population, and to regard a population, in the normal case, as related to particular areas of territory is to recognize a political reality which underlies modern territorial settlements. Similarly, one may refer also to the ideas inherent in the concepts of mandated and trust territories and the principles of Chapter XI of the United Nations Charter relating to non-self-governing territories.[7]

[1] Universal Declaration of Human Rights, 6 Dec. 1948, U.N. Doc. no. A/811, Art. 14.

[2] See *U.K. Contemp. Practice* (1962), i, at pp. 221–2.

[3] U.N. Gen. Ass. resol. 2312 (XXII) of 14 Dec. 1967; 62 *A.J.* (1968), 822. For text and comment see Weis, 7 *Canad. Yrbk.* (1969), 92–149.

[4] See *Digest of U.S. Practice*, 1975, 156–8.

[5] See, e.g., U.N. Legis. Series, *Laws Concerning Nationality* (1954), pp. 586–93. The Treaties of St. Germain refer to persons born of parents 'habitually resident or possessing rights of citizenship [*pertinenza-heimatrecht*] as the case may be there ...'; *Laws Concerning Nationality*, p. 590. See also the Italian Peace Treaty, 10 Feb. 1947, Art. 19; *Laws Concerning Nationality*, p. 589.

[6] See, e.g., *Laws Concerning Nationality*, at pp. 136–7, 268, 293.

[7] See *South West Africa* cases, I.C.J. Reports (1962), pp. 319, 354–7, 374, 378, 380,

This concept of territory is perhaps inherent in the rule that state succession results in automatic change of nationality.[1] The population has a 'territorial' or local status, and sovereignty here involves clear responsibilities toward the people concerned. Thus, the United Nations Convention on Reduction of Statelessness provides in Article 10:

1. Every treaty between Contracting States providing for the transfer of territory shall include provisions designed to secure that no person shall become stateless as a result of the transfer . . .
2. In the absence of such provisions a Contracting State to which territory is transferred or which otherwise acquires territory shall confer its nationality on such persons as would otherwise become stateless as a result of the transfer or acquisition.

A problem which is not yet solved concerns the conditions under which transfer or exchange of population may occur. Examples of population exchange to remove minority problems are to be found in treaties between the states directly concerned.[2] The movement of ethnic Germans sanctioned by the Potsdam Agreement may be justified as a part of the sanctions and measures of security imposed by the principal members of a coalition which had fought a lawful war of collective defence against Nazi Germany.[3] However, it will not be easy in every case to decide whether the principle of local status has the effect of qualifying the application of other rules.

5. *The Individual as Representative and Agent*

It is worth recording the role which individuals play in discharging responsibilities on the international plane. The time has long since passed when representatives were regarded rather literally as fragments of the sovereign dignity of personal rulers who personified the state. Embassies, diplomatic missions, and consular officials today have a variety of functions and are an important form of liaison in a decentralized system. The legal status of diplomatic missions and consuls has lately been the subject of general conventions adopted by United Nations con-

429–32, 479–82; *International Status of South West Africa*, I.C.J. Reports (1950), pp. 128, 133; *Namibia* Opinion, I.C.J. Reports, 1971, p. 16; Int. L.R., 49, 2.

[1] See *Yrbk., I.L.C.* (1954), ii. 61, para. 39; Briggs, p. 503; Oppenheim i. 551, 571, 656–7; Rousseau iii. 343. But see O'Connell, *The Law of State Succession*, p. 249; Weis, *Nationality and Statelessness in International Law*, pp. 149, 153–4.

[2] *Accord Greco-Turc du 1er Décembre 1926*, P.C.I.J., Ser. C, no. 15–1, at p. 83 (1926). Generally: Balladore Pallieri, *Annuaire de l'Inst.* 44 (1952), i. 138–50.

[3] See Brownlie, *International Law and the Use of Force by States*, pp. 408–9.

ferences in 1961 and 1963 respectively.[1] Duly authorized representatives may create obligations for their states as a result of personal acts, or may bring into existence informal agreements relating to important matters.[2] Moreover, votes and declarations at international conferences and in organs of the United Nations can have an indirect but significant law-making function, providing cogent evidence of the practice of states on such legal questions as interpretation of particular treaties, and, of course, the United Nations Charter itself.

6. *The Individual and International Criminal Responsibility*

Since the latter half of the nineteenth century it has been generally recognized that there are acts or omissions for which international law imposes criminal responsibility on individuals and for which punishment may be imposed, either by properly empowered international tribunals or by national courts and military tribunals. These tribunals exercise an international jurisdiction by reason of the law applied and the constitution of the tribunal, or, in the case of national courts, by reason of the law applied and the nature of jurisdiction (the exercise of which is justified by international law). In the Charter of the International Military Tribunal annexed to the Agreement for the Prosecution and Punishment of the Major War Criminals of the European Axis, signed on 8 August 1945, Article 6 provides in part as follows:

> The following acts, or any of them, are crimes coming within the jurisdiction of the Tribunal for which there shall be individual responsibility:
>
> (a) Crimes against peace. Namely, planning, preparation, initiation or waging of a war of aggression or a war in violation of international treaties, agreements, or assurances, or participation in a common plan or conspiracy for any of the foregoing.
>
> (b) War crimes. Namely, violations of the laws or customs of war...
>
> (c) Crimes against humanity. Namely, murder, extermination, enslavement, deportation, and other inhumane acts committed against any civilian population before or during the war or persecutions on political, racial, or religious grounds in execution of or in connection with any crime within the jurisdiction of the Tribunal, whether or not in violation of the domestic law of the country where perpetrated.[3]

[1] See further Chapter XVI. [2] See further *infra*, pp. 633 seq.

[3] Text in 39 *A.J.* (1945), Suppl., pp. 258, 259–60. See generally Woetzel, *The Nuremberg Trials in International Law* (2nd impression rev. 1962). On the Tokyo Tribunal,

On the question of individual responsibility the tribunal stated in the judgment:

> It was submitted that international law is concerned with the actions of sovereign States, and provides no punishment for individuals; and further, that where the act in question is an act of State, those who carry it out are not personally responsible but are protected by the doctrine of the sovereignty of the State. In the opinion of the Tribunal, both these submissions must be rejected. That international law imposes duties and liabilities upon individuals as upon States has long been recognized . . . the very essence of the Charter is that individuals have international duties which transcend the national obligations of obedience imposed by the individual State. He who violates the laws of war cannot obtain immunity while acting in pursuance of the authority of the State, if the State in authorising action moves outside its competence under international law.

The category of war crimes was certainly orthodox law in 1945, and crimes against humanity were to a great extent war crimes writ large. While the tribunal refused to regard acts committed before 1939 as within its jurisdiction, the latter category extended to the murder of German Jews and Jews and others from co-belligerents of Germany. Furthermore, crimes against peace were defined authoritatively and prosecuted for the first time at Nuremberg. But whatever the state of the law in 1945, Article 6 of the Nuremberg Charter has since come to represent general international law. The Agreement to which the Charter was annexed was signed by the United States, United Kingdom, France, and U.S.S.R., and nineteen other states subsequently adhered to it. In a resolution adopted unanimously on 11 December 1946, the General Assembly affirmed 'the principles of international law recognized by the Charter of the Nuremberg Tribunal and the judgment of the Tribunal'.

The concept of crimes against humanity led to the adoption by the General Assembly of the Convention on the Prevention and Punishment of the Crime of Genocide.[1] In Article I of the Convention the contracting parties 'confirm' (the phrasing is perhaps significant) that genocide (defined in Article II) 'is a

see Sohn, *Cases on United Nations Law* (1956), p. 904; Horwitz, 'The Tokyo Trial', *Int. Conciliation* (1950), p. 475. See also the *Eichmann* case, Int. L.R. 36, p. 5, on which see works cited *supra*, p. 305; and *In re Koch*, Int. L.R. 30, p. 496.

[1] U.N. Gen. Ass., Off. Rec., 3rd Sess., Resolution 174 (A/180) (1948); text in 45 *A.J.* (1951), Suppl., p. 7; Brownlie, *Human Rights*, p. 116. In force between at least 73 states, including the United Kingdom. The United States has not ratified the Convention. See generally Drost, *The Crime of State* (1959), ii; Lemkin, *Axis Rule in Occupied Europe* (1944); Robinson, *The Genocide Convention* (1960); Kunz, 43 *A.J.* (1949), 738–46; Whiteman xi. 848–74; 58 *Yale L.J.* (1949), 1142; Goldenberg, 10 *Western Ontario L.R.* (1971), 1–55. See also *Reservations to Genocide Convention*, I.C.J. Reports (1951), p. 23.

crime under international law which they undertake to prevent and to punish'. It is apparent from the enforcement provisions of the Convention and the present reliance on national tribunals to repress international crime that many problems of international criminal jurisdiction remain to be solved.

Article VI provides:

> Persons charged with genocide or any of the other acts enumerated in Article III shall be tried by a competent tribunal of the State in the territory of which the act was committed, or by such international penal tribunal as may have jurisdiction with respect to those Contracting Parties which shall have accepted its jurisdiction.

In all these cases the individual bears responsibility under international law which is determined in jurisdictions the competence of which is based upon international law.[1] In substance the Geneva Conventions of 1949[2] provide for individual responsibility for serious breaches of obligations which are laid down therein (although many of the obligations and the correlative responsibilities existed already in general international law). Parties to the Conventions are under a duty to search for persons, regardless of their nationality, alleged to have committed or to have ordered to be committed a grave breach of a Convention and to prosecute them before their own courts. The Conventions avoid the term 'war crimes' in relation to 'grave breaches', but there can be no doubt that the latter constitute war crimes and are concerned with individual responsibility for breaches of the laws of war. The ambiguity is to be explained by a desire to emphasize the obligations of the contracting states to suppress and punish the acts prohibited.[3] The language employed in the British *Manual of Military Law* (Part III: *The Law of War on Land*) leaves no doubt that the individual is regarded as being bound directly by the laws of war.[4]

Although this chapter is devoted to describing existing practice, it is relevant to note that, in spite of extensive consideration of the problem in committees of the General Assembly,

See further the Convention on the Suppression and Punishment of the Crime of *Apartheid*, adopted by the U.N.G.A., 30 November 1973; 13 *Int. Leg. Materials* (1974), 50; *Digest of U.S. Practice*, 1973, 128–32.

[1] On the relation between responsibility under international law and universality of jurisdiction see *supra*, p. 305.

[2] Misc. no. 4 (1950), Cmd. 8033; 75 U.N.T.S. Generally, Draper, *The Red Cross Conventions* (1958).

[3] See Oppenheim ii. 394–5; Baxter, 28 *B.Y.* (1951), 382–93; Roling, 12 *Revue belge* (1976), 8–26.

[4] H.M.S.O. (1958), para. 1. The revision of this part of the *Manual* was carried out by Sir Hersch Lauterpacht.

the likelihood of setting up an international criminal court is very remote.[1]

7. *International Protection of Human Rights*[2]

Events of the Second World War and concern to prevent a recurrence of catastrophes associated with Fascist internal policies led to increased concern for the legal and social protection of human rights and fundamental freedoms. A notable pioneer in the field was Hersch Lauterpacht, who stressed the need for an International Bill of the Rights of Man.[3] The provisions of the United Nations Charter also provided a dynamic basis for development of the law. The more important results of the drive to protect human rights will be recorded in due course, but at the outset some comment may be made on the forms assumed by the campaign. Inevitably it has carried to the international forum the ideologies and concepts of freedom of the various leading states, and ideological differences between socialism and capitalism have influenced the debates. The political aspects to the campaign could hardly have been avoided, and its diversity has probably been rewarding to some extent.[4]

Early Developments. In the nineteenth century a number of

[1] Materials in Sohn, *Cases on United Nations Law* (1956), pp. 1003–19. See further Mueller and Wise (eds.), *International Criminal Law* (1965), pp, 513–627; Bridge, 13 *I.C.L.Q.* (1964), 1255–81.

[2] On techniques of supervision and protection see also *infra*, Chapter XXVII.

[3] See Lauterpacht, *International Law and Human Rights* (1950); Lauterpacht, *An International Bill of the Rights of Man* (1945). See further Robertson, *Human Rights in the World* (1972); Brownlie, *Basic Documents on Human Rights* (1971); Eide and Schou (eds.), *International Protection of Human Rights* (1968); *René Cassin: Amicorum Discipulorumque Liber* I (1969), II (1970), III (1971); Khol, *Zwischen Staat und Weltstaat* (1969); Carey, *U.N. Protection of Civil and Political Rights* (1970); Waldock, in *The European Convention on Human Rights, I.C.L.Q.*, Suppl. Public. no. 11 (1965), pp. 1–23; Ganji, *International Protection of Human Rights* (1962); Mirkine-Guetzévich, 83 Hague *Recueil* (1953, II), 261–371; Moskowitz, *Human Rights and World Order* (1958); Ezejiofor, *Protection of Human Rights under the Law* (1964); Robinson, *The Universal Declaration of Human Rights* (1958); McDougal and Bebr, 58 *A.J.* (1964), 603–41; Schwelb, *Human Rights and the International Community* (1964); 11 *Howard L.J.* (Spring 1965); McDougal, Lasswell, and Chen, 63 *A.J.* (1969), 237–69; Robertson (ed.), *Human Rights in National and International Law* (1968); Weston *et al.*, 53 *Iowa L.R.* (1967), 268–365; Gotlieb (ed.), *Human Rights, Federalism, and Minorities* (1970); Sohn and Buergenthal, *International Protection of Human Rights* (1973); and *Basic Documents on the International Protection of Human Rights* (1973); Higgins, 48 *B.Y.* (1976–7), 281–320; I.L.A., *Report of the Fifty-Fifth Conference*, 1972, pp. 539–624; *Report of the Fifty-Sixth Conference*, 1974, pp. 203–22; *Report of the Fifty-Seventh Conference*, 1976, pp. 475–540; Humphrey, in Bos (ed.), *The Present State of International Law* (1973), pp. 75–105; Schachter, 24 *New York Law School L.R.* (1978), 63–87. See also works cited *supra*, p. 552, *infra*, p. 574; and in Chapter XXVII.

[4] Thus the International Commission of Jurists, in the Declaration of Delhi, modified its programme to allow for the importance given to social and economic rights by people from 'underdeveloped countries'. See 2 *Journ. of the Int. Comm. of Jurists* (1959), 7–54.

rather elastic legal doctrines permitted forcible intervention on the territory of states, and one strand of the contemporary doctrine concerned humanitarian intervention.[1] The doctrine was vague, and the principle was employed when the facts revealed a desire to advance the interests of the intervening state. A possible case of genuine humanitarian action is provided by the French occupation of parts of Syria and the policing of the coast by warships from August 1860 to June 1861 to prevent the recurrence of massacres of Maronite Christians. However, the institution belonged to an era of unequal relations, and few jurists think that it has a place in modern law in its classical form.

Within the regime of the United Nations Charter, intervention may occur in pursuance of a decision under Chapter VII of the Charter or, otherwise, within the general competence of the General Assembly to take 'measures' under Articles 11 and 14.[2] In the Congo crisis such measures were initiated with the consent of the state concerned and, on one view of the facts, were a form of humanitarian intervention.

In the broader sphere of diplomatic protection of nationals abroad, controversy centres on the existence and meaning of the 'international standard' of treatment, and the question of individual protection merges with the less altruistic and conflicting positions of investor-creditor states and 'underdeveloped states'. At the same time the practice relating to denial of justice concerns certain basic and uncontroversial human rights.[3]

Treaty protection of national minorities. Although there were no clauses on protection of minorities in the Covenant of the League of Nations, the opportunity was taken to associate the general peace settlement and the machinery of the League with obligations in regard to treatment of minorities.[4] The resulting network of obligations constituted the first full-blooded effort on the political and legal level to provide for the protection of minorities. The treaties were in three groups. The first were minorities treaties between the principal Allied and associated powers, on the one hand, and Poland, Czechoslovakia, Greece, and

[1] See Brownlie, *International Law and the Use of Force by States*, pp. 338–42. On intervention to protect nationals, see ibid., pp. 289–301. See further Franck and Rodley, 67 *A.J.* (1973), 275–305; Lillich (ed.), *Humanitarian Intervention and the United Nations* (1973).

[2] See *Certain Expenses of the United Nations*, I.C.J. Reports (1962), p. 151.

[3] See *supra*, pp. 529–31.

[4] See generally Nørgaard, *The Position of the Individual in International Law*, pp. 109–21; Rousseau ii. 739–65; Humphrey, in Bos (ed.), *The Present State of International Law* (1973), pp. 80–1. For a bibliography, see Oppenheim, i. 711.

others, on the other hand. The second group took the form of special chapters in the peace treaties with Bulgaria, Austria, Hungary, and Turkey. Thirdly, special conventions relating to the Memel Territory and Upper Silesia had minority clauses. The treaties provided as follows: protection of life and liberty and the free exercise of religion without discrimination on grounds of language, race, or religion; for nationals of the treaty parties there was to be equality before the law and with respect to civil and political rights; further, there was to be freedom of organization for religious and educational purposes and provision by the state for the elementary instruction of children in their own language in districts where a minority formed a considerable proportion of the population.

The machinery of protection was, it seems, to some extent effective in providing supervision, and much useful work was done, although it would have been possible, had political conditions permitted it, to have exercised more effective control. The clauses were placed under the guarantee of the League and could not be modified without the consent of the Council. Any Council member had the right to bring to its attention any infraction or danger of infraction, and the Council could then 'take such action and give such directions as it may seem proper in the circumstances'. Apart from the arrangement for Upper Silesia there was no right of individual petition, but large numbers of petitions were dealt with by the Council and they provided a very necessary source of information. Disputes between states went to the Council and then to the Permanent Court. In cases involving minorities clauses, the Court applied a principle of effective interpretation and insisted that equality of treatment must exist in fact as well as in law.[1] Human rights provisions figured in the peace treaties with Hungary, Rumania, and Bulgaria in 1947, but the machinery of protection did not survive political division between the wartime Allies.[2] Finland and Italy, and Austria (in the State Treaty of 1955), assumed similar obligations. The United Nations has not shown much practical interest in the protection of minorities as a general issue.[3]

The mandates system and trust territories. The arrangements for

[1] *Minority Schools in Albania*, P.C.I.J., Ser. A/B, no. 64, at p. 18 (1935); *Polish Nationals in Danzig*, P.C.I.J., Ser. A/B, no. 44, at p. 28 (1932). See generally Lauterpacht, *The Development of International Law by the International Court*, pp. 257–62; Ezejiofor, op. cit., pp. 38–51.

[2] See *Interpretation of Peace Treaties*, I.C.J. Reports (1950), p. 221.

[3] On the background see Humphrey, 62 *A.J.* (1968), 869–88. But see the U.N. Commission on Human Rights, 30th. sess., 1977, Resolutions 5 (XXX) and 6 (XXX) and the Report of Capotorti, E/CN. 4/Sub. 2/304 and Add. 1–7.

giving a special status to the inhabitants of certain territories under the system of mandates of the League of Nations and the concept of trusteeship in the United Nations Charter are substantially the same. About the mandate, the International Court has said:[1] 'The Mandate was created, in the interests of the inhabitants of the territory, and of humanity in general, as an international institution with an international object—a sacred trust of civilization.' The importance of the international status of such a territory led the Court to avoid the technical problems —not always an easy task—and hold that South Africa is bound by her obligations as mandatory in respect of South West Africa prior to the termination of the Mandate in 1966. The Union having refused to enter into a trusteeship agreement within the scheme of the United Nations Charter, the machinery of enforcement provided by the Charter had to be attached to the surviving mandate.[2] The Court has been determined to promote the exercise of effective supervision over South West Africa.[3]

The trusteeship system, presented in Chapter XII of the Charter, is comprehensive, and Article 76 emphasizes the duties of the administering authority to promote self-government or independence and to encourage respect for human rights and fundamental freedoms. Control is entrusted to the Trusteeship Council (Chapter XIII of the Charter) under the authority of the General Assembly, except in the case of strategic areas, which are supervised by the Security Council (Article 83). The Mandates Commission and now the Trusteeship Council were given the power to receive and consider petitions from the inhabitants of the territories.[4] Moreover, the Trusteeship Council has power to send periodic visiting missions to trust territories, and its general powers and willingness to go against the wishes of the administering authority have given its work an aspect very different from that of the old Mandates Commission.

Non-self-governing territories. Chapter XI of the United Nations Charter is entitled 'Declaration regarding non-self-governing territories', and under Article 73 thereof members 'recognize the principle that the interests of the inhabitants of these territories are paramount, and accept as a sacred trust of civilization

[1] See I.C.J. Reports (1950), p. 128 at p. 132.

[2] See *International Status of South West Africa*, I.C.J. Reports (1950), p. 128; *South West Africa* cases, ibid. (1962), p. 319. See further *South West Africa* cases (Second Phase), ibid. (1966), p. 6; and the *Namibia* Opinion, ibid. (1971), p. 16; Int. L.R., 49, 2.

[3] On the issues of legal interest and the nature of a dispute see *supra*, pp. 466–73.

[4] See Nørgaard, op. cit., pp. 121–38. At present the Trusteeship Council is responsible for the Trust Territory of the Pacific Islands.

the obligation[1] to promote to the utmost . . . the well-being of the inhabitants of these territories, and, to this end . . . to develop self-government . . .'.

Unlike the trusteeship provisions this chapter makes little or no express provision for effective supervision by United Nations organs. However, in practice the General Assembly has adopted a vigorous policy of implementation of the ill-defined obligation in Article 73. The Assembly established a committee, as a subsidiary organ, with powers of supervision, and assumed a power to designate specific territories as 'non-self-governing' for the purposes of Chapter XI.[2] Since 1963 the scene has been dominated by the Declaration on the Granting of Independence to Colonial Countries and Peoples of 1960[3] and the special committee of seventeen, later twenty-four, set up to implement the Declaration. The key to these developments is the principle of self-determination and the increase of Afro-Asian membership in the General Assembly. The persistence of the committee and disputes over its competence in relation to certain matters culminated in the withdrawal from membership of the United Kingdom, the United States (in 1971), Italy (1970), and Australia (1969).

The International Labour Organization. Although its work may appear specialized, the International Labour Organization (I.L.O.) has in fact for two generations done an immense quantity of work towards giving practical expression to a number of very important human rights and towards establishing standards of treatment. Its agenda has included forced labour, freedom of association, discrimination in employment, equal pay, social security, and the right to work.[4] The I.L.O.'s Constitution has a tripartite character, and there is separate representation of employers and workers, as well as governments, in the Governing Body and in the General Conference. In addition, there are provisions for union and employer organizations to make repre-

[1] Cf. *International Status of South West Africa*, I.C.J. Reports (1950), at pp. 132–3; and the *South West Africa* cases, ibid. (1962), pp. 329 seq.

[2] See Waldock, 106 Hague *Recueil* (1962, II), 27–31; Higgins, *The Development of International Law through the Political Organs of the United Nations*, pp. 110 seq. On domestic jurisdiction, *supra*, p. 293.

[3] See *infra*, p. 594.

[4] See Jenks, *The International Protection of Trade Union Freedom* (1957), id., *Human Rights and International Labour Standards* (1960); id., *Social Justice in the Law of Nations* (1970); *The I.L.O. and Human Rights* (Report of the Director-General (Part I) to the International Labour Conference, Fifty-Second Session, 1968); Brownlie, *Human Rights*, pp. 257–326; McNair, *The Expansion of International Law*, pp. 29–52; International Labour Office, *The Impact of International Labour Conventions and Recommendations* (1976).

sentations and complaints. This constitutional procedure was augmented in 1949 when the I.L.O. Governing Body established a fact-finding and conciliation commission on freedom of association.[1]

The procedure for enforcement of I.L.O. conventions is important. The Constitution requires member states to make separate annual reports upon the measures taken by them to give effect to conventions adopted by it, and these reports are examined closely by a committee of experts, which may raise questions with the governments concerned. A member state may file a complaint with the International Labour Office if it is dissatisfied with another member's observance of a convention by which it is bound. The complaint may be referred to a commission of inquiry, and any government concerned in the complaint may refer the findings of the commission to the International Court of Justice. In February 1962 the first commission of inquiry reported, having been appointed upon a complaint by Ghana against Portugal alleging the existence of forced labour in Portuguese African territories contrary to the Convention Concerning the Abolition of Forced Labour of 1957.[2] It is clear that such inquiries have a judicial aspect, and the composition of the commission just referred to reinforces this view.[3] Moreover, the breadth of subject-matter open to inquiry in this manner indicates a considerable erosion of domestic jurisdiction.

Human rights and the Charter of the United Nations. The clauses concerning human rights in the Charter provide a foundation for, and an impetus to further improvement in, the protection of human rights. In the preamble the members 'reaffirm faith in fundamental human rights, in the equal rights of men and women . . .'. Article 1 defines the purposes of the United Nations to include co-operation 'in promoting and encouraging respect for human rights and for fundamental freedoms for all without distinction as to race, sex, language, or religion'. Of key importance is Article 55, which states that 'the United Nations shall promote: (a) higher standards of living, full employment, and conditions of economic and social progress and development. . . . (c) universal respect for, and observance of, human rights and

[1] See Nørgaard, op. cit., at pp. 139–58.

[2] 45 I.L.O. Official Bull., no. 2, Supp. no. II (1962); Int. L.R. 35, p. 285. Both governments accepted the findings. For a further inquiry into a Portuguese complaint against Liberia: 46 I.L.O. Official Bull., no. 2, Suppl. no. II (1963); Int. L.R. 36, p. 351. See also Vignes, *Annuaire français* (1963), pp. 438–59; Osieke, 47 *B.Y.* (1974–5), 315–40.

[3] See *South West Africa* cases, I.C.J. Reports (1962), pp. 427–8 (sep. op. of Judge Jessup).

fundamental freedoms for all . . .'. Article 56 provides: 'All Members pledge themselves to take joint and separate action in co-operation with the Organization for the achievement of the purposes set forth in Article 55.'[1]

As treaty provisions applicable to the Organization and its members these prescriptions are of paramount importance. Article 55 is perhaps oblique—the United Nations 'shall promote'. However, Article 56 is stronger and involves the members; and the political and judicial organs of the United Nations have interpreted the provisions as a whole to constitute legal obligations.[2] Two possible sources of weakness require notice. First, the legal obligation is general in provenance, and work has gone forward to supplement the Charter by the adoption of covenants giving more specific content to rights protected and providing more sophisticated enforcement procedures. Thus, while it may be doubtful whether states can be called to account for every alleged infringement of the rather general Charter provisions, there can be little doubt that responsibility exists under the Charter for any substantial infringement of the provisions, especially when a class of persons, or a pattern of activity, are involved.

The second source of weakness is the absence of precise definition. If the intention of the draftsmen is respected, it will be clear that the concept of human rights has a core of reasonable certainty. Moreover, in 1948 the General Assembly adopted a Universal Declaration of Human Rights[3] which is comprehensive and has to some extent affected the content of national law, occasionally being expressly invoked by tribunals.[4] The De-

[1] Other references to human rights exist in Articles 62, 68, and 76. Article 76 refers to the encouragement of respect for human rights in stating the basic objectives of the trusteeship system. Where attempts were made by private individuals in the United States to invoke the provisions of Articles 55 and 56, relief was denied on the basis that the Charter, while binding on the United States as a treaty, was not self-executing. See *Rice* v. *Sioux City Memorial Park Cemetery, Inc.*, 245 Iowa 147, 60 N.W. 2d 110 (1953), Int. L.R. 20 (1953), 244; *Fujii* v. *State of California*, 28 Cal. 2d 718, 242 P. 2d 617 (1952), Int. L.R. 19 (1952), 312; *Comacho* v. *Rogers*, 199 F. Supp. 155 (1961); Int. L.R. 32, p. 368. See further *Re Drummond Wren* (1945), 3 D.L.R. 674, *Ann. Digest* 12 (1943–5), no. 50; *Re Noble and Wolfe* (1948), 4 D.L.R. 123; (1949), 4 D.L.R. 475; (1951), 1 D.L.R. 321; *Ann. Digest* 16 (1949), No. 100; *Oyama* v. *State of California* (1948), 332 U.S. 633; *Ann. Digest* 16 (1949), no. 79.

[2] See the Adv. Op. on Namibia: I.C.J. Reports (1971), at pp. 56–7. See further Schwelb, 66 *A.J.* (1972), 337-51.

[3] Whiteman v. 237; Brownlie, *Basic Documents*, p. 132; id., *Human Rights*, p. 106. See Oppenheim i. 744–6; Waldock, 106 Hague *Recueil* (1962, II), 198–9.

[4] e.g. *In re Flesche*, *Ann. Digest* (1949), at p. 269; *The State* (*Duggan*) v. *Tapley*, Int. L.R. 18 (1951), at p. 342; *Robinson* v. *Sec.-Gen. of the U.N.*, Int. L.R. 19 (1952), at p. 496; *Extradition of Greek Nationals* case, Int. L.R. 22 (1955), at p. 524; *Beth-El Mission* v.

claration is not a legal instrument, and some of its provisions, for example the reference to a right of asylum, could hardly be said to represent legal rules. On the other hand, some of its provisions either constitute general principles of law or represent elementary considerations of humanity.[1] Perhaps its greatest significance is that it provides an authoritative guide, produced by the General Assembly, to the interpretation of the provisions in the Charter.[2] No doubt there is a great area of ambiguity, but the indirect legal effect of the Declaration is not to be underestimated, and it is frequently regarded as a part of the 'law of the United Nations'.[3]

The political organs of the United Nations have been prepared to exercise a general power of investigation and supervision in this field,[4] but there is a lack of specific machinery for dealing with complaints. The existing agencies have difficulty in dealing with particular cases; discussion normally centres on political implications rather than settlement of actual cases. Nevertheless publicity, fact-finding machinery, and other 'measures' under Article 14 of the Charter can achieve useful objectives.

The Commission on Human Rights. The nearest approach to permanent machinery for supervision of the problem of protection is the Commission on Human Rights set up by the Economic and Social Council in 1946. The Commission, however, with the approval of the Economic and Social Council, early on decided that it had no power to take any action in regard to any complaints concerning human rights. The Commission receives thousands of private communications, which are in substance complaints, and the governments concerned are invited to reply, after being given an indication of the nature of the complaint.[5] In the recent past the Commission has had a more active role in investigating alleged violations of human rights.[6] The principal functions of the Commission have been to prepare the texts of the Universal Declaration, the Convention on the Political Rights of

Minister of Social Welfare, Int. L.R. 47, 205. See further Skubiszewski, 2 *Polish Yrbk.*, pp. 99–105 and cf. *De Meyer* v. *État belge*, Int. L.R. 47, 196.

[1] Cf. *Corfu Channel* case (Merits), I.C.J. Reports (1949), p. 4 at p. 22.

[2] See Waldock, op. cit., p. 199. But see Oppenheim i. 745.

[3] See Schwelb, op. cit., at pp. 673–5; and Waldock, *I.C.L.Q.*, Suppl. Public. no. 11 (1965), p. 1 at p. 14. See also Security Council Resolution 310 (1972); comment by Schwelb, 22 *I.C.L.Q.* (1973), 161–3.

[4] In practice, Article 2, paragraph 7 has not been very restrictive. See *supra*, p. 293.

[5] The complainant's identity is not divulged. See generally Nørgaard, op. cit., pp. 104–7. See also Art. 64 of the Charter for the power of the Economic and Social Council to obtain reports from members on progress in the field of human rights.

[6] See Chapter XXVII, section 4.

Women, and draft covenants supplementing the Universal Declaration. In addition studies are undertaken and a useful *Yearbook on Human Rights* is published.[1]

The International Covenants, 1966. The adoption of the Universal Declaration of Human Rights was widely regarded as a first step toward the preparation of a Covenant, which would be in the form of a treaty. The Declaration, of course, was contained in a resolution of the General Assembly and was not intended to be binding. After extensive work in the Commission on Human Rights and the Third Committee of the General Assembly, the latter in 1966 adopted two Covenants and a Protocol: the International Covenant on Economic, Social, and Cultural Rights; the International Covenant on Civil and Political Rights; and an Optional Protocol to the latter.[2]

The Covenants, which came into force in 1976, have legal force as treaties for the parties to them and constitute a detailed codification of human rights. The Covenant on Economic, Social, and Cultural Rights contains various articles in which the parties 'recognize' such rights as the right to work, the right of everyone to social security and to an adequate standard of living for himself and his family. The type of obligation is programmatic and promotional, except in the case of the provisions relating to trade unions (Article 8). Each party 'undertakes to take steps . . . to the maximum of its available resources, with a view to achieving progressively the full realization of the rights recognized in the present Covenant by all appropriate means, including particularly the adoption of legislative measures'. The rights recognized are to be exercised under a guarantee of non-discrimination but there is a qualification in the case of the economic rights 'recognized' in that 'developing countries . . . may determine to what extent they would guarantee' such rights to non-nationals. The machinery for supervision consists of an obligation to submit reports on measures adopted, for transmission to the Economic and Social Council of the United Nations.

[1] See further, Humphrey, *René Cassin: Amicorum Discipulorumque Liber I*, p. 108; id., 62 *A.J.* (1968), 869–88; I.L.A., *Report of the Fifty-Fifth Conference*, 1972, pp. 571–8; Marie, *La Commission des Droits de l'Homme de l'O.N.U.* (1975).

[2] For the texts see Brownlie, *Basic Documents* (2nd ed.), pp. 151, 162, 181; id., *Human Rights*, pp. 199, 211, 232; 30 *Z.a.ö. R.u.V.* (1970), 349, 365, 394. For comment: Schwelb, 62 *A.J.* (1968), 827–68; id., in Eide and Schou (eds.), *International Protection of Human Rights* (1967), pp. 103–29; Capotorti, ibid., pp. 131–48; Schwelb, in *René Cassin: Amicorum Discipulorumque Liber I* (1969), pp. 301–24; Newman, *Public Law* (1967), 274–313; Robertson, 43 *B.Y.* (1968–9), 21–48. On the problem of co-ordination between the Covenants and the European Conv. on Human Rights see Chapter XXVII, section 11.

The International Covenant on Civil and Political Rights is more specific in delineation of rights, stronger in statement of the obligation to respect the rights specified, and better provided with means of review and supervision. The provisions clearly owe much to the European Convention on Human Rights and the experience based upon it. Article 2, paragraph 1, contains a firm general stipulation: 'Each State Party to the present Covenant undertakes to respect and to ensure to all individuals within its territory and subject to its jurisdiction the rights recognized in the present Covenant, without distinction of any kind, such as race, colour, sex, language, religion, political or other opinion, national or social origin, property, birth, or other status'.[1] The rights are defined with as much precision as can reasonably be expected and relate to the classical issues of liberty and security of the person, equality before the law, fair trial, and the like. There is an obligation to submit reports on measures adopted to give effect to the rights recognized by the Covenant to a Human Rights Committee. There is also a complaints procedure under which parties may complain of non-compliance, subject to a bilateral attempt at adjustment and prior exhaustion of domestic remedies, provided that such complaints are only admissible if both the states concerned have recognized the competence of the Committee to receive complaints (the procedure under Article 41). The Committee may make use of *ad hoc* Conciliation Commissions in resolving issues raised in this manner. In addition the Optional Protocol[2] to this Covenant provides for applications to the Human Rights Committee created by the Covenant from individuals subject to its jurisdiction who claim to be victims of violations of the provisions of the Covenant, and who have exhausted all available domestic remedies. The state charged with a violation is under an obligation to submit to the Committee 'written explanations or statements clarifying the matter and the remedy, if any, that may have been taken by that state'. Subsequently, the Committee 'shall forward its views to the State Party concerned and to the individual'. Thus no public determination of the issue on a judicial or quasi-judicial basis results, in contrast to the possibilities provided in the European Convention to be considered later.

[1] However, the firmness of the stipulation is placed in question by paragraph 2, which makes it apparent that states may become parties on the basis of a *promise* to bring their legislation into line with the obligations of the Covenant: see Robertson, 43 *B.Y* (1968–9), at p. 25.

[2] The Protocol enters into force three months after deposit of the tenth instrument of ratification or of accession.

General conventions on human rights. The work of the I.L.O. has already been mentioned, but, to make the record more complete, it is necessary to draw attention to the vast amount of ground covered by multilateral conventions covering particular areas such as racial discrimination, freedom of information, the political rights of women, slavery, and forced labour.[1] In addition, conventions now exist relating to major issues like genocide and the problem of refugees and stateless persons.

Regional machinery for protection. Machinery for the protection of human rights may be created on a regional basis. The European Convention for the Protection of Human Rights and Fundamental Freedoms,[2] together with its Protocols, is a comprehensive bill of rights on the Western liberal model, born of the Council of Europe. The contracting parties undertake to secure to 'everyone within their jurisdiction' the rights and freedoms defined in section I of the Convention. The precise definition there has enabled some of the parties to incorporate the rights in their national law as self-executing provisions. In order to make the draft acceptable to governments certain qualifications on its field of application had to be incorporated. Article 17 provides: 'Nothing in this Convention may be interpreted as implying for any State, group or person any right to engage in any activity or perform any act aimed at the destruction of any of the rights and freedoms set forth herein. . . .' Article 15 permits measures derogating from the obligations under the Convention 'in time of war or other public emergency threatening the life of the

[1] For examples, see Schwelb, 9 *I.C.L.Q.* (1960), 654; Brownlie, *Human Rights*, Parts II–V.

[2] Signed on 4 November 1950; entered into force on 3 September 1953. Text of Conv. and five Protocols: Brownlie, *Basic Documents*, pp. 206 seq.; id., *Human Rights*, pp. 339 seq.; 45 *A.J.* (1951), Suppl., p. 24; 58 *A.J.* (1964), 331. See further the European Social Charter, signed on 18 October 1961, entered into force on 26 February 1965. Text: Brownlie, *Human Rights*, p. 366, *Treaty Series*, No. 38 (1965), Cmnd. 2643. See generally Fawcett, *The Application of the European Convention on Human Rights* (1969); Monconduit, *Commission européenne des Droits de l'Homme* (1965); *Mélanges offerts à Polys Modinos* (1968); Guradze, *Die Europäische Menschenrechts Konvention* (1968); Beddard, 16 *I.C.L.Q.* (1967), 206–17; Robertson, *Human Rights in Europe* (1963); id., 27 *B.Y.* (1950), 145–63, 28 *B.Y.* (1951), 359–65, 28 *B.Y.* (1952), 452–4; Modinos, 11 *I.C.L.Q.* (1962), 1097–108; Waldock, 34 *B.Y.* (1958), 356–63; Waldock *et al.*, *I.C.L.Q.*, Suppl. Public. no. 11 (1965); Vasak, *La Convention européenne des Droits de l'Homme* (1964); Weil, *The European Convention on Human Rights* (1963); id., 57 *A.J.* (1963), 804–27; *Yearbook of the European Convention on Human Rights* (1958–); Eissen, *Annuaire français* (1959), pp. 618–58; Greenberg and Shalit, 63 *Columbia L.R.* (1963), 1384–412; Castberg, *The European Convention on Human Rights* (1974); Jacobs, *The European Convention on Human Rights* (1975); Higgins, 48 *B.Y.* (1976–7), 281–320. All members of the Council of Europe are parties except Spain and Liechtenstein (which have signed the Conv.), 19 states in all. The Convention may apply to overseas territories: Art. 63.

nation'. However, no derogation shall be made under this provision from Articles 2 (right to life) (except in respect of deaths resulting from lawful acts of war), 3 (torture and inhuman punishment), 4 (1) (slavery or servitude), and 7 (no retrospective punishment).

The principal organ (for practical purposes) is the Commission of Human Rights, to which every complaint goes. Any party may refer an alleged breach of the Convention by another party to the Commission. In addition, parties may by declaration recognize the competence of the Commission to receive petitions from any person, non-governmental organization, or group of persons claiming to be victims of violation of the Convention. The machinery of protection is considered in greater detail subsequently.[1]

The work of the Commission and the Court has provided valuable material on the elaboration of the provisions on civil liberties and the concept of exhaustion of local remedies.[2] However, the procedure used is far from expeditious, and the amount of direct protection conferred is somewhat limited. At the same time the working of the machinery has exposed anomalies in national systems of law, and the Convention has influenced decisions of national courts[3] and the policy of the national legislatures involved.[4] It is possible that the European experiment may influence the creation of similar regional treaties. Developments have taken place in Latin America. In 1960 an Inter-American Commission on Human Rights was set up as an appendage of the Organization of American States.[5] The Ameri-

[1] *Infra*, pp. 584–8.

[2] See the International Law Reports (1957 seq.), Part VI, A, I; Fawcett, *Curr. Leg. Problems* (1971), 246–56. See the reports on the European Convention, compiled each year by the Council of Europe; the latest being Doc. H(79)1.

[3] See Golsong, 33 *B.Y.* (1957), 317–21; id., 38 *B.Y.* (1962), 445–56; Buergenthal, *I.C.L.Q.*, Suppl. Public. no. 11 (1965), pp. 79–106; Petzold, 46 *B.Y.* (1972–3), 401–4; 47 *B.Y.* (1974–5), 356–61; Khol, 18 *Am. Journ. Comp. Law* (1970), 237; *s.* v. *Free State of Bavaria*, Int. L.R. 45, 316; *Association Protestante* v. *Radiodiffusion-Télévision Belge*, Int. L.R. 47, 198.

[4] The *De Becker* case (see Robertson, *Human Rights in Europe*, p. 63) resulted in a change in Belgian legislation. The work of the Commission has, for example, focused on the West German and Austrian practice of permitting long terms of detention pending trial. See Scheuner, in Eide and Schou (eds.), *International Protection of Human Rights*, pp. 193–215.

[5] See Schreiber, *The Inter-American Commission on Human Rights* (1970); Cabranes, 65 *Michigan L.R.* (1967), 1147, 1164–73; Vasak, *La Commission interaméricaine des Droits de l'Homme* (1968); Tardu, 70 *A.J.* (1976), 778–800; Gros Espiell, 145 Hague *Recueil* (1975, II), 1–55.

can Convention on Human Rights,[1] signed in 1969, provides for a Commission and a Court.

8. *Recent Developments*

There can be little doubt that the main issue is the implementation of the existing stock of standards and, in that connection, the reduction of the gap between international commitments and the domestic performance of governments. At the same time the problems relating to human rights in some fields are of genuine complexity and difficulties are not to be ascribed exclusively to the delinquencies and inadequacies of governments.

Two developments stand out. The first is the adoption of the Final Act of the Conference on Security and Co-operation in Europe in Helsinki on 1 August 1975. This contains a declaration of principles under the heading 'Questions Relating to Security in Europe'.[2] The Final Act was signed by representatives of 35 states, including the United States and the U.S.S.R. It constitutes an important statement of intent but is not legally binding.[3] The declaration of principles includes a section entitled 'Respect for human rights and fundamental freedoms, including the freedom of thought, conscience, religion or belief'. The text contains a commitment to act in conformity with existing obligations in the field of human rights. This hardly breaks new ground but at least the instrument involves the United States, which has stayed outside most of the multilateral treaties on human rights.

In 1975 the United Nations General Assembly, by consensus, adopted a Declaration[4] on the Protection of All Persons from being subjected to Torture and Other Cruel, Inhuman or Degrading Treatment or Punishment. The prohibited conduct is 'condemned as a denial of the purposes of the Charter of the United Nations and as a violation of human rights and fundamental freedoms proclaimed in the Universal Declaration of Human Rights'.

[1] Text: Brownlie, *Human Rights*, p. 399; 65 *A.J.* (1971), 679; 9 *Int. Leg. Materials* (1970), 101.

[2] Text: 14 *Int. Leg. Materials* (1975), 1292; *Digest of U.S. Practice*, 1975, 8; 70 *A.J.* (1976), 417. For comment: Russell, 70 *A.J.* (1976), 242–72.

[3] See the final clauses and Schachter, 71 *A.J.* (1977), 296–304.

[4] Resolution 3452 (XXX), 9 December 1975; *Digest of U.S. Practice*, 1975, 217. See further U.N.G.A. Resolutions 3448 (XXX), 9 December 1975; 31/124, 16 December 1976; 32/118, 16 December 1977, concerning the protection of human rights in Chile; and *Case of Ireland against the United Kingdom*, Europ. Ct. of Human Rights, Judgment of 18 January 1978; 17 *Int. Leg. Materials* (1978), 680.

9. *The Individual before Tribunals Exercising International Jurisdiction*[1]

Any tribunal which has cognizance of legal questions not determinable by any national jurisdiction will be regarded as constituting an international tribunal.[2] This definition will include tribunals set up by treaty as well as tribunals functioning within the context of the governing instrument of an international organization, such as the administrative tribunals of the United Nations. Moreover, it is thought justifiable to have regard to the nature of the jurisdiction as well as that of the court. Thus any national tribunal which is given jurisdiction by municipal law over questions of international law, for example responsibility for war crimes, or genocide, and which exercises that jurisdiction in accordance with international law, may also be considered to be exercising an 'international jurisdiction'.

As a further preliminary to the inquiry some remarks may be made about its general object and relevance. It is common for writers to pursue problems relating to the status of the individual in international law in terms of the large theoretical question as to whether the individual is a 'subject' of international law. The present inquiry is obviously relevant to this question, but for two reasons it is proposed to conduct it outside the context of doctrinal and terminological disputes on the subject. First, whilst the writer shares the views of writers on the subject on the need to reinforce the protection of human rights, he considers that the promotion of such objects is best served by an examination of the practical problems involved in giving individuals access to international courts and in imposing responsibility for breaches of international law on individuals. Secondly, to say the individual is, or is not, a 'subject' of international law is, in either case, to say too much and to beg a great many questions. The individual does not bear normal responsibility for breaches of obligations imposed by the customary law of nations

[1] See von der Heydte, 107 Hague *Recueil* (1962, III), 297–357; Rousseau ii. 731–8; Korowicz, *Introduction to International Law*, pp. 343–89; Sperduti, 90 Hague *Recueil* (1956, II), 788–824; Gormley, *The Procedural Status of the Individual before International and Supranational Tribunals* (1966). See further *supra*, p. 561.

[2] See Redslob, *Traité*, pp. 71, 72; and Anzilotti, *Cours de droit international* (1929), p. 136. *Contra*, Korowicz, *Introduction to International Law*, pp. 349–50, and Lauterpacht, *International Law and Human Rights*, p. 50. It is not intended to discuss the right of individuals or groups to present petitions to political bodies such as the Trusteeship Council or committees of the General Assembly. This subject, though of great interest, would seem to fall outside the category of international jurisdictions concerned with legal disputes. See Nørgaard, op. cit., pp. 99 seq., and *infra*, Chapter XXVII.

because most of these obligations can only rest on states and governments, and, further, he cannot bring international claims. Yet there is no rule that the individual cannot have some degree of legal personality, and he has such personality for certain purposes.[1] Thus the individual as such is responsible for crimes against peace and humanity and for war crimes. Treaties may confer procedural capacity on individuals before international tribunals. It is not helpful therefore to pose the question as one of legal personality in all respects or not at all. The problem, it is suggested, responds to an empirical approach. Although there is no rule that individuals cannot have procedural capacity before international jurisdictions, the assumption of the classical law that only states have procedural capacity is still dominant and affects the content of most treaties providing for the settlement of disputes which raise questions of state responsibility,[2] in spite of the fact that frequently the claims presented are in respect of losses suffered by individuals and private corporations.

The Statute of the International Court of Justice. Article 34, paragraph 1, of the Statute of the Court provides simply: 'Only States may be parties in cases before the Court.' The problem of conferring upon individuals a capacity to appear before the Court was discussed in 1920 by the committee of jurists appointed to draft a statute, but only two out of its ten members were favourable towards admitting individuals as parties before the Court. The practice of the Court does not envisage the legal representatives of individuals appearing at the bar of the Court, holding a watching brief, receiving copies of the pleadings, or being allowed in any way, for example, as *amicus curiae*, to state their views.[3]

Although both in law and practice the rules governing access are relaxed in some respects in the exercise of the Court's advisory competence, nothing in the Statute permits individuals to take part in advisory proceedings. The possibility that injustice might result caused the Council of the League of Nations to propose a special pre-trial procedure and to forgo some of its own procedural rights before the Court when, on 14 December 1939,

[1] Cf. Sørensen, 101 Hague *Recueil* (1960, III), 141–4; Oppenheim i. 638. A large number of writers regard the individual as a subject of international law. See works cited *supra*, p. 552.

[2] See Hudson, *International Tribunals* (1944), pp. 67–8; Simpson and Fox, *International Arbitration* (1959), pp. 34–41, 94–111. Also: Drucker, 10 *I.C.L.Q.* (1961), 238–54.

[3] See Rosenne, *The Law and Practice of the International Court* (1965), pp. 736–9; Korowicz, op. cit., pp. 343–4; Hudson, *The Permanent Court of International Justice 1920–1942* (1943), p. 396; Briggs, pp. 94–5.

it decided to request an advisory opinion in the matter of the *Former Officials of the Governing Commission of the Saar Territory*. The resolution allowed the complainants to lodge a memorandum, addressed to the League, with the Secretariat, and within a time limit thereafter the Secretary-General was to furnish the complainants with a 'statement of the point of view of the League' regarding the memorandum. A further round of written statements was envisaged, at the option of the complainants, and all these documents were subsequently to be transmitted to the Court together with the request for the advisory opinion. Finally, the League renounced the exercise of the right to present written and oral statements to the Court under Article 66 of the Statute 'if the same possibility cannot be given to the petitioners, since it does not wish to have greater opportunities of furnishing information to the Court than the petitioners themselves'.[1] In the *United Nations Administrative Tribunal* case[2] a different procedure was adopted by the General Assembly of the United Nations. The advisory opinion arose here from Resolution 785A (VIII) of 9 December 1953, and had its source in the discussion of the supplementary estimates. The issue raised was the finality of awards of the U.N. Administrative Tribunal, and this obviously affected the legal position of individuals who were judgment creditors against the Organization under the awards. In the course of the proceedings the Federation of International Civil Servants' Associations approached the Registrar and inquired whether the Statute of the Court, or whether the Court at its discretion, would allow the Federation to place its views before the Court. In his reply the Registrar stated that the Court is not authorized to receive written or oral statements 'from a body such as your Federation'. Subsequently, a firm of New York lawyers, who had appeared before the Administrative Tribunal on behalf of the staff members involved, requested an opportunity to submit a written memorandum and to participate in oral argument, as its clients were 'directly affected by the judgments of the Tribunal which assess their conduct and award them compensation for breach of contract. It is the finality of these judgments which is the subject of the proceeding before the Court.' In the communication to the Court it was admitted that neither the Charter, nor the Statute, nor the Rules of Court, make provision for the appearance of private individuals. However, it was pointed out

[1] See Rosenne, op. cit., p. 737; and Gross 52 *A.J.* (1958), 16–40.

[2] I.C.J. Reports (1954), p. 47. The account which follows is based on Rosenne, pp. 737–9.

that the rules in advisory proceedings are more flexible than those applying to contentious cases, and the practice adopted with regard to the International League for the Rights of Man in the *South West Africa* case[1] was referred to. Further, it was stated that the proceeding before the Court was the result of proceedings instituted by the staff members and carried to the point of final judgment by the Administrative Tribunal. Throughout the proceedings before the Administrative Tribunal the views of the Secretary-General were presented by the Legal Department of the United Nations, and the views of the staff members by the undersigned counsel: and 'it would be unreasonable to change this procedure in the midst of the litigated controversy'.[2] On the instructions of the President of the Court, the Registrar replied that the Court 'would be bound by the limitations set forth' in Article 66, paragraph 2, of the Statute and 'would therefore not be authorized to request or receive written or oral statements either from your clients or on their behalf from the Counsel who represented them before the Administrative Tribunal'.[3] Further reference to the operation of the administrative tribunals of the U.N.O. and its specialized agencies will be made below.

Criminal responsibility of individuals. Having stated the basic position assumed by the classical law and by general international law at the present time, the exceptions to the general rule may be considered. The exceptions existing in customary or general international law consist in acts or omissions for which international law imposes criminal responsibility on individuals, and for which responsibility may be established and punishment imposed, either by properly empowered international tribunals or by national courts.[4]

Claims against states: treaties conferring procedural capacity. Apart from the sphere of international crimes, which in any case involves 'procedural capacity' of a special and restricted type, it is in the context of particular treaty provisions that the individual has received procedural capacity of the more normal kind, viz., the capacity to bring claims against states. Several important multilateral treaties have contained such provisions. Hague Convention XII of 1907[5] provided for the establishment of an International Prize Court, and Articles 4 and 5 permitted neutral

[1] I.C.J. Reports (1950), p. 128, at p. 130. The International League was given the right to submit a written statement on legal issues.

[2] *U.N. Administrative Tribunal* case, I.C.J. Pleadings, p. 394.

[3] Ibid., p. 397.

[4] See further *supra*, pp. 561–4.

[5] Scott, *The Hague Conventions* (1915), pp. 189–90.

individuals to claim rights against a foreign state before the Court. The individual could be forbidden by his own state to institute a proceeding, as the state might institute proceedings in his stead. The Convention was not ratified, and Hudson's opinion was that the opening of the proposed court to individuals had little influence on later developments.[1]

The Central American Court of Justice which functioned from 1908 to 1918 could be seised of questions which private individuals of one of the five Central American republics

> may raise against any of the other contracting Governments, because of the violation of treaties or conventions, and other cases of an international character; no matter whether their own Government supports said claim or not; and provided that the remedies which the laws of the respective country provide against such violation shall have been exhausted or that denial of justice shall have been shown.

The Court dealt only with five cases brought by individuals, and held four of them to be inadmissible on the ground that internal remedies had not been exhausted. The other case was decided against the claim of the individual.[2]

Of greater practical importance were the mixed arbitral tribunals set up in accordance with Articles 296, 297, 304, and 305 of the Treaty of Versailles and the corresponding articles of the other peace treaties after the First World War. Before these tribunals individual citizens of the victor states could bring claims against nationals and governments of the defeated states. The tribunals dealt with a large number of claims and functioned for about ten years.[3] Their significance is, however, limited by a number of factors. They were part and parcel of dictated peace treaties, and their decisions turned to a large extent on points of private law and the interpretation of the peace treaties. They included enforcement provisions of unusual strength as a result of their origin, and in some of the more important cases governments intervened in support of their nationals.[4]

[1] *The Permanent Court of International Justice 1920–1942* (1943), p. 75.

[2] The relevant Convention was signed on 20 December 1907. Literature: Hudson, 26 *A.J.* (1932), 759–86; id., *The Permanent Court of International Justice 1920–1942* (1943), pp. 42–70. The ten cases with which the Court dealt did not provide any significant experience.

[3] See *Recueil des décisions des Tribunaux Arbitraux Mixtes institués par les Traités de Paix* (1922–30); Guggenheim i. 285–6; Lauterpacht, *International Law and Human Rights*, p. 50; Simpson and Fox, op. cit., pp. 16–17.

[4] When claimants did not avail themselves of the assistance of agents appointed by their governments and pursued their claims unaided, this apparently had an adverse effect on the efficient working of the tribunals.

Particular interest attaches to the Arbitral Tribunal of Upper Silesia set up by the German-Polish Convention of 15 May 1922.[1] Before this tribunal individuals had the capacity to make direct claims to vested rights against their own and foreign governments. The rules of procedure of the tribunal (Articles 16 to 24 of the Convention) made no distinction between the representatives of the governments and private individuals as parties in disputes. The individual was thus given full procedural capacity for the purposes of this important Convention.

Other bilateral treaties of varying importance have allowed the presentation of claims directly by individuals.[2] By an Agreement of 10 August 1922, between the United States and Germany, a Mixed Claims Commission was set up to hear claims by American citizens against Germany for damage to property, rights, and interests in Germany, other claims for injury to persons or property as a consequence of war, and debts due to American citizens by the German Government or German nationals.[3] Many agreements of this type, and the awards made by the tribunals or commissioners appointed under them, refer to nationals of the parties as 'claimants', and the measure of damages is normally applied in terms of personal loss without any heads relating to losses by the state, e.g. loss of industrial production or potential, or damages for infringements of sovereignty. However, they do not give claimants procedural capacity, but commonly provide that the governments concerned 'may designate agents and counsel who may present oral or written arguments to the Commissioner under such conditions as he may prescribe'.[4]

Practice after the Second World War has varied considerably in the matter of the settlement of claims by nationals. The peace treaties of 1947 did not revive the system established by the Treaty of Versailles and treated the settlement of claims as a matter between states. However, the Convention on the Settlement of Matters arising out of the War and the Occupation

[1] See Kaeckenbeeck, *The International Experiment of Upper Silesia* (1942); Korowicz, op. cit., pp. 353–7; and *Steiner and Gross* v. *Polish State*, *Ann. Digest*, 4 (1927–8), no. 188. See *supra*, p. 565 on the system of protection of minorities.

[2] See Rousseau ii. 732–6; Guggenheim i. 285, n. 2; and the *Aboilard* case, *R.I.A.A.* xi. 71.

[3] *R.I.A.A.* vii. 13.

[4] *R.I.A.A.*, *passim*. See also Lauterpacht, op. cit., p. 49; García Amador, 94 Hague *Recueil* (1958, II), 474–87 (on the question of damages). Cf. *Lighthouses* arbitration (France/Greece), P.C.A., 24 July 1956, Int. L.R. 23 (1956), p. 659 at pp. 669–71. On measure of damages generally: the *Lusitania* cases (1923), *R.I.A.A.* vii. 32; *Chorzów Factory* case (Indemnity) (1928), P.C.I.J. Ser. A, no. 17; *Corfu Channel* case (Assessment of Compensation), I.C.J. Reports (1949), p. 244; and *supra*, pp. 463–4.

signed on 26 May 1952 [1] with the German Federal Republic makes interesting arrangements in this respect. The Charter annexed to the Convention sets up an Arbitral Commission to which there is a direct access by nationals or residents of the states or territorial entities referred to in the Charter and by corporate bodies constituted under the laws of those states and entities.

In general, claims settlements have followed the traditional pattern in recent years, but a number of international organizations have now come into being in the context of which tribunals exist with specialist functions, the performance of which involves conferment of procedural capacity, or lesser rights of access, on legal persons other than governments and states. The most interesting of these developments depend upon treaties which are part of the general movement towards integration of political and economic life in Western Europe. It will be convenient to treat of the European economic institutions first.

The Court of Justice of the European Communities. The European Coal and Steel Community has a Court of Justice which was established in December 1952.[2] The function of the Court is to ensure the rule of law in the interpretation and application of the treaty constituting the Community and of its implementing regulations. Article 33 of the treaty provides in part:

> The Court shall have jurisdiction in actions brought by a Member State or by the Council to have decisions or recommendations of the High Authority declared void on grounds of lack of competence, infringement of an essential procedural requirement, infringement of this Treaty or of any rule of law relating to its application, or misuse of powers. . . .
>
> Undertakings or the associations referred to in Article 48 may, under the same conditions, institute proceedings against decisions or recommendations concerning them which are individual in character or against general decisions or recommendations which they consider to involve a misuse of powers affecting them.

Persons who may appeal directly to the Court are: (1) individuals who have acquired or regrouped rights or assets; (2)

[1] 49 *A.J.* (1955), Suppl., p. 116; Germany no. 1 (1955), Cmd. 9368, p. 88; Simpson and Fox, op. cit., pp. 37–9. Note also the Conciliation Commission provided for in Article 83 of the Italian Peace Treaty: rules of procedure in 45 *A.J.* (1951), Suppl., p. 84 (see Articles 4 and 7); and see Seidl-Hohenveldern, *The Austrian–German Arbitral Tribunal* (1972); id., *Ann. français*, 1969, 266–75.

[2] Treaty constituting the Community, signed 18 April 1951; in force 25 July 1952; *Treaty Series* No. 2 (1973), Cmnd. 5189. See, on the Court of Justice: Valentine, *The Court of Justice of the European Communities*, 2 vols. (1965); id., 36 *B.Y.* (1960), 147–222; Lever, 41 *Grot. Soc.* (1958–9), 205; Donner, in *Legal Problems of the European Economic Community and the European Free Trade Association, I.C.L.Q.*, Suppl., no. 1 (1961), p. 66; Wall, *The Court of Justice of the European Communities* (1966); Brinkhorst and Schermers, *Judicial Remedies in the European Communities: A Casebook* (1969).

buyers whose interests are impaired; (3) persons who are directly interested in the result of action taken by the High Authority; and (4) persons fined by the High Authority of the Community for a breach of the treaty's obligations. The first two cases before the Court were brought by private corporations.

In 1958 a Court of Justice of the European Communities was set up which supersedes the Court referred to above and is common to the European Economic Community, the Coal and Steel Community, the Euratom. The Rome Treaty provides that the Court of the European Economic Community may review the legality of the acts of the Council and of the Commission. Individuals and private corporations may appeal to the Court, the Council, and the Commission. Under certain conditions there is a right of reference to the Court from decisions of national tribunals. Under Article 173 of the Rome Treaty and Article 146 of the Euratom Treaty individuals have a right to demand annulment of decisions, regulations, and other acts affecting them.[1]

In several cases the Court of Justice has referred to the relevance of obligations of Member States under human rights treaties.[2]

The European Convention for the Protection of Human Rights and Fundamental Freedoms. Undoubtedly the most significant developments have been on the basis of the European Convention for the Protection of Human Rights and Fundamental Freedoms signed on 4 November 1950.[3] The human rights protected by the treaty are to be enforced by three organs, the European Commission of Human Rights, the European Court of Human Rights, and the Committee of Ministers of the Council of Europe.

The Commission, manifestly, has not got the powers of a court, but in its handling of petitions it may be said to be acting judicially, and the procedure for hearing petitions is of interest. Any high contracting party may refer to the Commission any alleged breach of the Convention (Article 24).[4] However, in

[1] Treaty establishing the European Economic Community, 25 March 1957, in 4 *European Year Book* (1958), 413. Conv. relating to certain Institutions common to the European Communities, of the same date, 5 *European Year Book* (1959), 587; *Treaty Series* No. 1 (1973), Cmnd. 5179-II. See generally Robertson, *European Institutions*, 2nd ed. (1966); *Cour de Justice des Communautés européennes, Recueil de la jurisprudence de la Cour*; Bebr, *Judicial Control of the European Communities* (1962); Toth, 24 *I.C.L.Q.* (1975), 659–706. On Euratom, *supra*, p. 261.

[2] See *Nold* v. *Commission* [1974] 2 C.M.L.R. 338, 354; *Rutili* v. *Minister of the Interior* [1976] 1 C.M.L.R. 140, 155.

[3] See *supra*, p. 574.

[4] Thus a state may support the rights of nationals of other states: see, for example, *Denmark, Norway, Sweden and Netherlands* v. *Greece* (1967); *Ireland* v. *United Kingdom* (1971).

addition, individual complainants are given *locus standi* before the Commission. This right of individual petition (Article 25) was described by the Legal Committee of the Consultative Assembly of the Council of Europe as 'a right of individuals to seek a remedy directly', but in the treaty it has been made a 'right' only at the option of governments. The government concerned must have recognized the competence of the Commission to receive petitions from individuals by express declaration.[1] With this limitation, the Commission may receive petitions addressed to the Secretary-General of the Council of Europe from any person, non-governmental organization, or group of individuals claiming to be the victim of a violation by one of the parties of the rights protected by the Convention. The Commission shall accept petitions after all domestic remedies have been exhausted 'according to the generally recognized rules of international law' (Article 26). These words were added in order to refer to the jurisprudence according to which improper delay by national tribunals is deemed to be an exhaustion of local remedies. A considerable proportion of applications are rejected as 'manifestly ill-founded' (Article 27 (2)). The main duty of the Commission is to investigate alleged breaches of the Convention, for which purpose the states concerned are to provide the necessary facilities, and to secure, if possible, an amicable settlement (Article 28). If negotiation has failed, the Commission is to report to the Committee of Ministers of the Council of Europe, making such proposals as it thinks fit (Articles 31 and 32). The decision of the latter is transmitted to the governments concerned. The Committee of Ministers is competent (1) when a matter cannot be referred to the Court because the states concerned have not recognized its competence; (2) when a matter, which has not been resolved by a friendly settlement, is not referred to the Court although the states concerned have recognized its competence.

However, the individual applicant is allowed to be represented by lawyers before the Commission. In front of the Court the Commission appears by Delegates whose duty is to assist the Court. Such assistance may include the reporting of the views of the applicant. The Delegates may be 'assisted' by lawyers of the

[1] Fourteen of the members have recognized the competence of the Commission to receive individual petitions, viz., Austria, Belgium, Denmark, Federal Republic of Germany, Iceland, Ireland, Italy, Luxembourg, Netherlands, Norway, Portugal, Sweden, Switzerland, and the United Kingdom. On the function of the Commission see Monconduit, *Commission européenne des Droits de l'Homme* (1965).

applicant.[1] Reference of a case to the Court can only be by a Government or by the Commission.

Proceedings in the Lawless *case*. The European Court of Human Rights was ultimately set up at Strasbourg on 21 January 1959. Only states parties to the Convention, and the Commission of Human Rights can bring cases before the Court (Articles 46–8) and its jurisdiction is compulsory only for those states making express declarations of acceptance (Article 46).[2] The Committee of Ministers is an alternative instance in the scheme. The individual does not have access to the Court, yet he is, in substance, an interested party, a complainant, and obviously his case must be presented to the Court as well as that of the government against which he has brought his petition. The problem as to how this should be done was raised in the course of hearing preliminary objections in the first case brought before the Court, that of the petition of Lawless, an Irish citizen, against his government.[3] This raised an important question as to the interpretation of Article 15 of the Convention, which gives states the right of derogating from their obligations under the Convention 'in time of war or other public emergency threatening the life of the nation'. In determining the questions of interpretation the Commission was divided and decided to refer the case to the Court for an authoritative decision in addition to transmitting its report to the Committee of Ministers. The Court had now to decide what was the role of the Commission in these circumstances. *Inter alia*, was the Commission to appear as a party to the proceedings? Was the Commission to act as the advocate of the individual applicant? And if it was not to act as his advocate, by what means, if at all, was the point of view of the applicant to be put to the Court?[4]

In accordance with the rules of court and the Commission's rules of procedure the Commission appointed delegates to take

[1] See the *Sunday Times* case (1978); and Europ. Ct. press release B(77)65.

[2] The compulsory jurisdiction of the Court has been recognized by fifteen states: Austria, Belgium, Denmark, Federal Republic of Germany, France, Iceland, Ireland, Italy, Luxembourg, the Netherlands, Norway, Portugal, Sweden, Switzerland, and the United Kingdom (the latter in 1966, initially for three years). For comment on the Court's role see Rolin, 11 *Howard L.J.* (1965), pp. 442–51; Sørensen, in *René Cassin: Amicorum Discipulorumque Liber I*, p. 333. The Second Protocol to the Conv. empowers the Court to give advisory opinions at the request of the Committee of Ministers on certain legal questions concerning the interpretation of the Conv. and the Protocols.

[3] See Int. L.R. 31, p. 276; Robertson, 36 *B.Y.* (1960), 343–54; *Yearbook of the European Convention* (1960), pp. 474, 492; O'Higgins, *Camb. L.J.* (1962), pp. 234–51; Pelloux, *Annuaire français* (1961), pp. 251–66.

[4] See Robertson, op. cit., p. 348.

part in the consideration of the case before the Court. The principal delegate of the Commission, in his opening address to the Court in the *Lawless* proceedings, stated that it was impossible for the Commission to depart from its objectivity and impartiality or to identify itself either with the government or the individual. On 30 March 1960 the Commission had adopted a new Rule 76 of its rules of procedure. Under this rule, when a case brought under Article 25 is subsequently referred to the Court, the Secretary of the Commission shall immediately notify the applicant, and, unless the Commission shall otherwise decide, the Secretary shall also in due course communicate to him the Commission's report, informing him that he may, within a time limit, submit to the Commission his written observations on the said report. The Commission will then decide what action to take in respect of the observations. In the *Lawless* proceedings the Commission communicated its report to the applicant and invited his observations thereon, with a view to transmitting them, if this was considered appropriate, to the Court as one of the Commission's documents in the case. In its memorial the Commission asked the Court to give leave for this to be done and also to give directions as to the right of the Commission to communicate to the Court the comments of the applicant in regard to matters arising in the proceedings.[1] The Irish Government strongly objected to the procedure proposed and stated that the Commission 'attempts by a subterfuge to bestow on the individual the quality of a party before the Court'. The Court gave judgment on a variety of preliminary objections and questions of procedure on 14 November 1960. It accepted, implicitly at least, the validity of Article 76 of the Commission's rules of procedure. On the request of the Commission for leave to communicate to the Court the applicant's observations on its own report and on other points arising in the proceedings, the Court reserved the right to make a decision on these questions at a later date, as it had not at that time been able to examine the merits of the case. It did, however, remark that 'it is in the interests of the proper administration of justice that the Court should have knowledge of and, if need be, take into consideration, the applicant's point of view'.[2]

[1] During the oral hearings the President of the Commission cited the opinion of the I.C.J. in the *Administrative Tribunal of the I.L.O.* case, I.C.J. Reports (1956), p. 77 at p. 86. On which see *infra*, p. 588.

[2] *Yearbook* (1960), p. 516.

Judgment on the merits was delivered on 1 July 1961.[1] On the questions of procedure raised in a submission by the principal delegate of the Commission the Court gave judgment on 7 April 1961. *Inter alia*, the Court stated:[2]

> *Whereas* in its judgment of 14th November 1960 the Court declared that there was no reason at this stage to authorize the Commission to transmit to it the written observations of the Applicant on the Commission's Report:
>
> *Whereas* in the said Judgment . . . the Court has recognized the Commission's right to take into account [*de faire état*] the Applicant's views on its own authority, as a proper way of enlightening the Court;
>
> *Whereas* this latitude enjoyed by the Commission extends to any other views the Commission may have obtained from the Applicant in the course of the proceedings before the Court;
>
> *Whereas*, on the other hand, the Commission is entirely free to decide by what means it wishes to establish contact with the Applicant and give him an opportunity to make known his views to the Commission;
>
> *Whereas* in particular it is free to ask the Applicant to nominate a person to be available to the Commission's delegates;
>
> *Whereas* it does not follow that the person in question has any *locus standi in judicio*.
>
> For these reasons,
>
> Decides unanimously:
>
> . . . that at the present stage the written observations of the Applicant . . . are not to be considered as part of the proceedings in the case;
>
> . . . that the Commission has all latitude, in the course of debates and in so far as it believes they may be useful to enlighten the Court, to take into account the views of the Applicant concerning either the Report or any other specific point which may have arisen since the lodging of the Report;
>
> . . . that it was for the Commission, when it considered it desirable to do so, to invite the Applicant to place some person at its disposal (in order to make known to the Court the Applicant's point of view on any specific points arising in the course of the debates), subject to the reservations indicated above.

Advisory Opinion of the International Court of Justice on Judgments of the Administrative Tribunal of the International Labour Organization. Lastly, brief attention may be directed to administrative tribunals of international organizations.[3] The Statute of the Administrative Tribunal of the United Nations was adopted

[1] Text: 4 *Yearbook of the European Convention* (1961), 438; Int. L.R. 31, p. 290.

[2] At pp. 442–4.

[3] See Korowicz, op. cit., pp. 367–78; Nørgaard, op. cit., pp. 289–303; Bastid, 92 Hague *Recueil* (1957, II), 343–517. The Administrative Tribunals of the League of Nations existed from 1928 to 1946.

by the General Assembly on 24 November 1949. The tribunal is competent to hear applications alleging non-observance of contracts of employment and terms of employment of staff members of the U.N. Secretariat. Applications may be made by staff members, their legal successors in case of their death, and any other person who can show that he or she is entitled to rights under any contract or terms of employment. Article 11, paragraph 1, of the Statute provides:

If a Member State, the Secretary-General or the person in respect of whom the judgment has been rendered by the Tribunal (including anyone who succeeded to that person's rights on his death) objects to the judgment on the ground that the Tribunal has exceeded its jurisdiction or competence or that the Tribunal has failed to exercise jurisdiction vested in it, or has erred on a question of law relating to the provisions of the Charter of the United Nations, or has committed a fundamental error in procedure which has occasioned a failure of justice, such Member State, the Secretary-General or the person concerned may . . . make written application to the Committee established by paragraph 4 of this Article asking the Committee to request an advisory opinion of the International Court of Justice on the matter.

As a United Nations official, the individual thus has procedural capacity before the tribunal equal to that of the organs of the U.N. However, when an advisory opinion is sought problems analogous to those of the *Lawless* case will arise: in particular, how is the International Court to have access to the views of the officials concerned? The question has arisen in practice in the case of judgments of the Administrative Tribunal of the I.L.O. in respect of which advisory opinions may be requested by international organizations under certain conditions. In 1955 an advisory opinion was requested by the Executive Board of the U.N.E.S.C.O., which referred to the Court the question of the validity of certain decisions of the I.L.O. tribunal.[1] The Court considered that it ought to comply with the request for an opinion, and, in coming to this decision, made some comments on the procedural aspect of the question of equality between U.N.E.S.C.O. and the officials concerned before the Court. The Court stated:[2]

Here the absence of equality flows . . . from the provisions of the Statute

[1] Advisory opinion, *Judgments of the Administrative Tribunal of the I.L.O.*, I.C.J. Reports (1956), p. 77. The request was made under Article XII of the Statute of the Tribunal of the I.L.O. See also Rosenne, *The Law and Practice of the International Court*, pp. 686–90; Gross, 52 *A.J.* (1958), 16–40. Several organizations use the I.L.O. Tribunal: I.C.J. Reports, (1956), p. 79.

[2] I.C.J. Reports (1956), p. 86.

of the Court. In the form of advisory proceedings, the Court has before it a challenge the result of which will affect the right of the officials to the benefit of the Judgments of the Tribunal and the obligation of U.N.E.S.C.O. to comply with them. The judicial character of the Court requires that both sides directly affected by these proceedings should be in a position to submit their views and their arguments to the Court.

In the case of U.N.E.S.C.O., the Statute and the Rules of Court constitute no obstacle in this respect . . . In the case of the officials, the position is different.

It was with that difficulty that the Court was confronted. The difficulty was met, on the one hand, by the procedure under which the observations of the officials were made available to the Court through the intermediary of U.N.E.S.C.O. and, on the other hand, by dispensing with oral proceedings. The Court is not bound for the future by any consent which it gave or decisions which it made with regard to the procedure thus adopted. In the present case, the procedure which has been adopted has not given rise to any objection on the part of those concerned. It has been consented to by counsel for the officials in whose favour the Judgments were given. The principle of equality of the parties follows from the requirements of good administration of justice. These requirements have not been impaired in the present case by the circumstance that the written statement on behalf of the officials was submitted through U.N.E.S.C.O. Finally, although no oral proceedings were held, the Court is satisfied that adequate information has been made available to it.

Conclusion: state control of private claims. Customary international law still maintains the rule that it is the state which has the capacity to present international claims, even though in many cases the claim is substantially that of a private person.[1] In its judgment in the *Mavrommatis Palestine Concessions* case[2] the Permanent Court observed: 'By taking up the case of one of its subjects and by resorting to diplomatic action or international "judicial" proceedings on his behalf, a State is in reality asserting its own rights—its rights to ensure, in the person of its subjects, respect for the rules of international law.'[3] This statement was repeated in the *Nottebohm* case (Second Phase).[4]

As international society is ordered at present, the law operates

[1] For examples, see e.g. *Nottebohm* case, I.C.J. Reports (1955), p. 4; *Ambatielos* case, ibid. (1953), p. 10; *Anglo-Iranian Oil Co.* case, ibid. (1952), p. 93; *Haya de la Torre* case, ibid. (1951), p. 71; *Asylum* case, ibid., p. 266. But see García Amador, 94 Hague *Recueil* (1958, II), 414–22. See also *Shimoda* v. *The State*, Int. L.R., 32, p. 626 at pp. 635–42.

[2] P.C.I.J., Ser. A, no. 2 (1924).

[3] Ibid., at p. 12. See also *Panevezys-Saldutiskis Railway*, P.C.I.J., Ser. A/B, no. 76, at p. 16 (1939); *Serbian Loans*, P.C.I.J., Ser. A, no. 20, at p. 17 (1929); League of Nations Conference for the Codification of International Law, *Bases of Discussion*, p. 13; *Kgdm. of Greece* v. *Fed. Rep. of Germany*, Int. L.R. 34, p. 219 at pp. 227–31.

[4] I.C.J. Reports (1955), p. 4 at p. 24.

primarily through the states, and the individual sees international law in many respects as an order concerned with the delegation or delimitation of competences. With certain exceptions the state has a competence to protect its nationals by diplomatic action. But the state has no obligation to aid an individual in presenting a claim.[1] Moreover, even when a claim is presented and compensation is paid over, the state is not a trustee or agent for the nationals with respect to whom the claim was made. This is the view of the English courts[2] and the United States Court of Claims.[3]

Although in recent times individuals have been given procedural capacity in special contexts for presentation of claims,[4] these variations have not affected the general rule. Nor is the rule weakened by the appearance of cases in which claims do not depend on the existence of the link of nationality. The most important of these, the presentation of claims by the United Nations in respect of injury to persons in its service[5] and the protection of alien seamen on ships flying the flag,[6] rest on practical considerations. The essence of the matter is the assumption, at least in the field of admissibility, that the state is wronged in the person of its national;[7] thus the claimant state must establish that the individual concerned was a national when the delict occurred as well as at the time of presentation of the claim. However, the factors commonly considered by tribunals to be relevant in calculating damages in cases where there has been denial of justice are complex and reflect in great part the reality that, for example, the relatives of the deceased are the real claimants.[8]

Broadly speaking, the procedural position of the individual has not changed very much since 1920. At the same time certain changes have occurred which are of considerable interest and significance in spite of the fact that their effects are quantitatively small. They result partly from a movement to improve pro-

[1] See *Digest of U.S. Practice*, 1973, 332–4; P. de Visscher, 136 Hague *Recueil* (1972, II), 158; *Barcelona Traction Case*, I.C.J. Reports, 1970, p. 4 at p. 44.

[2] See *Civilian War Claimants' Association Ltd.* v. *The King* [1932] A.C. 14. For the position in Norway: Seyersted, 12 *Scand. Studies in Law* (1968), 121–49; and in Switzerland: Drucker, 15 *I.C.L.Q.* (1967), 1157–60.

[3] Cf. *Blabon* v. *United States*, 173 F. Supp. 799 (Ct. Cl. 1959); Int. L.R. 28, 195; and see *Aris Gloves* v. *United States*, 420 F. 2d. 1386 (Ct. Cl. 1970); 64 *A.J.* (1970), 948.

[4] See *supra*, pp. 580–3.

[5] See *Reparation* case (1949), I.C.J. Reports, p. 174.

[6] See *supra*, p. 481.

[7] Thus, a state may waive a claim based on a wrong to its national. See *Public Trustee* v. *Chartered Bank of India, Australia and China*, Int. L.R. 23 (1956), p. 687 at pp. 698–9; *Austrian State Treaty Case*, ibid., 40, p. 184.

[8] See *Janes* (United States *v.* Mexico) (1926), *R.I.A.A.* iv. 82, 90–8; Brierly, 9 *B.Y.* (1928), p. 42 at pp. 46–8. Cf. *supra*, pp. 546–7, on the Calvo clause.

tection of human rights and partly from purely practical considerations. The latter are prominent in the proceedings relating to *Judgments of the Administrative Tribunal of the I.L.O.* Even if the individual is not to be given procedural capacity, a tribunal interested in doing justice effectively must have proper access to the views of individuals whose interests are directly affected, whether or not they are parties as a matter of procedure.

It would perhaps be a more helpful approach if writers on the subject were to advert to the precise difficulties involved in giving procedural capacity to individuals before international tribunals. It is obvious that the major inhibiting factor is political. A significant number of governments are reluctant to assent to any arrangement which might seem to confer international personality on individuals, even if the capacity involved is very restricted and specialized. Until 1965 the United Kingdom did not accept the jurisdiction of the European Court of Human Rights on this ground.[1] Moreover, the European Convention itself has considerable qualifications to its provisions on the basis of political requirements. A right of derogation exists 'in time of war or other public emergency threatening the life of the nation' (Article 15). The Commission has applied Article 17[2] in such a way as to exclude the German Communist Party from the protection of the Convention.[3]

More interesting than the political factors, however, and more within the competence of the jurist, are the practical questions involved in giving procedural capacity to individuals. There is considerable difference between giving the individual full procedural capacity and, or, the right to initiate proceedings, on the one hand, and arranging for a state, or international organization, or a part thereof acting as *amicus curiae* (cf. the European Commission of Human Rights) to 'represent' the individual in an indirect way, supplying the tribunal with the views of the individual whose rights and interests are directly affected by the proceedings. In the former case especially questions of legal

[1] Foreign Secretary, House of Commons Debates, vol. 574, col. 867, 29 July 1957; 7 *I.C.L.Q.* (1958), 92. See also Hudson, *International Tribunals*, pp. 166–72, 201–2; Korowicz, *Introduction to International Law*, pp. 382–5.

[2] Text: 'Nothing in this Convention may be interpreted as implying for any State, group or person any right to engage in any activity or perform any act aimed at the destruction of any of the rights and freedoms set forth herein or at their limitation to a greater extent than is provided for in the Convention.'

[3] Appeal by German C.P. against decision of the Federal Constitutional Court of 17 August 1956 declaring it to be illegal and dissolving it. Several member states of the Council of Europe have large Communist Parties.

costs loom large, and arrangements for legal aid would be very necessary.[1]

10. *The Principle of Self-Determination*[2]

It is not necessarily the case that there is a divorce between the legal and human rights of groups, on the one hand, and individuals, on the other. Guarantees and standards governing treatment of individuals tend, by their emphasis on equality, to protect groups as well: this is obviously so in regard to racial discrimination. Many instruments of the type recorded earlier stipulate for rights 'without distinction as to race, sex, language, or religion'.[3] However, in certain contexts, such as trusteeship in the United Nations Charter, the rights of a certain population as such are protected.

The rights of important groups as such become particularly prominent in connexion with the principle, or right, of self-determination,[4] viz., the right of cohesive national groups ('peoples') to choose for themselves a form of political organization and their relation to other groups. The choice may be independence as a state, association with other groups in a federal state, or autonomy or assimilation in a unitary state. Until recently the majority of Western jurists assumed or asserted that the principle had no legal content, being an ill-defined concept of policy and morality.[5] Since 1945 developments in the

[1] In proceedings under the European Convention, the Council of Europe provides free legal aid.

[2] See Mirkine-Guetzévitch, 83 Hague *Recueil* (1953, II), 326–51; Rousseau ii. 17–35; Nawaz, *Duke L.J.* (1965), pp. 82–101; Scelle, *Spiropoulos Festschrift* (1957), pp. 385–91; Wengler, 10 *Rev. Hell. de d.i.* (1958), 26–39; Levin, *Soviet Year-Book of I.L.* (1962), pp. 45–8 (Eng. summary); Tunkin, *Theory of International Law* (1974), pp. 60–9; Lachs, 1 *Indian Journ.* (1960–1), 429–42; Whiteman v. 38–87; id., xiii. 701–68; Emerson, 65 *A.J.* (1971), 459–75; Sørensen, pp. 509–10; Bastid, in *Mélanges offerts à Juraj Andrassy*, pp. 13–30; Verzijl, *International Law in Historical Perspective* i. 321–36; Kaur, 10 *Indian Journ.* (1970), 479–502; Fawcett, 132 Hague *Recueil* (1971, I), pp. 387–91; Rigo Sureda, *The Evolution of the Right of Self-Determination: A Study of United Nations Practice* (1973); Calogeropoulos-Stratis, *Le Droit des peuples à disposer d'eux-mêmes* (1973); Crawford, 48 *B.Y.* (1976–7), 149–73; Brossard, 15 *Canad. Yrbk.* (1977), 84–145; Sinha, 14 *Indian Journ.* (1974), 332–61; Jiménez de Aréchaga, Hague *Recueil* (1978, I), 99–111.

[3] Cf. U.N. Charter, Art. 1 (3); European Conv. for the Protection of Human Rights, Art. 14. Many applications to the European Commission of Human Rights from Belgian sources have concerned the rights of communities in relation to the language question in Belgium.

[4] French equivalents are: droit des peuples à disposer d'eux-mêmes, droit ou principe de libre disposition, d'auto-disposition, de libre détermination.

[5] Prior to 1945 references in the legal sources are rare. See, however, the report of the Committee of Jurists on the Aaland Islands question in 1920: see Padelford and Andersson,

United Nations, and the influence of Afro-Asian and Communist opinion, have changed the position, and some Western jurists now admit that self-determination is a legal principle.[1] The generality and political aspect of the principle do not deprive it of legal content: in the *South West Africa* cases (Preliminary Objections)[2] the International Court regarded the terms of Article 2 of the Mandate Agreement concerned as disclosing a legal obligation, in spite of the political nature of the duty 'to promote to the utmost the material and moral well-being and the social progress of the inhabitants of the territory'.

Although reference is often made to the declarations in the Atlantic Charter of 14 August 1941,[3] the key development was the appearance of references to 'the principle of equal rights and self-determination of peoples' in Article 1, paragraph 2, and Article 55 of the United Nations Charter.[4] Many jurists and governments were prepared to interpret these references as merely of hortatory effect, but the practice of United Nations organs has established the principle as a part of the law of the United Nations. In Resolution 637 A (VII) of 16 December 1952[5] the General Assembly recommended, *inter alia*, that 'the States Members of the United Nations shall uphold the principle of self-determination of all peoples and nations'. Most important is the Declaration on the Granting of Independence to Colonial Countries and Peoples adopted by the General Assembly in 1960[6] and referred to in a series of resolutions concerning specific territories since then.[7] The Declaration regards the

33 *A.J.* (1939), p. 465 at p. 474. Cf. Briggs, p. 65; Hyde i. 363, 389; Hackworth i. 422. The principle is referred to in Soviet treaties concluded in the period 1920–2.

[1] See Scelle, op. cit.; Starke, *An Introduction to International Law* (7th ed.), p. 57; Quincy Wright, 98 Hague *Recueil* (1959, III), 193; Wengler, op. cit.

[2] I.C.J. Reports (1962), p. 319. Cf. the division of opinion in the *South West Africa* cases (Second Phase), ibid. (1966). p. 6.

[3] Text: 35 *A.J.* (1941), Suppl., p. 191. Adherence by the U.S.S.R. and other states in a Declaration of 1 January 1942: 36 *A.J.* (1942), Suppl., p. 191.

[4] See also Chapters XI (Declaration Regarding Non-Self-Governing Territories) and XII (international trusteeship system), and *supra*, pp. 566–8.

[5] See Sohn, *Cases and Materials on United Nations Law*, p. 805. The Commission on Human Rights and the Third Committee have been concerned with the subject, and it appears in the Covenants on Civil and Political Rights and Economic, Social, and Cultural Rights, *supra*, p. 572. The principle was invoked during discussion by the General Assembly, *inter alia*, of the Algerian, Tunisian, and Cyprus cases: Sohn, pp. 420 seq., 812 seq.; and Rosalyn Higgins, *The Development of International Law through the Political Organs of the United Nations*, pp. 90–106.

[6] Resol. 1514 (XV); Whiteman, xiii. 701–68. Se also Resol. 1314 (XIII).

[7] The G.A. established a Special Committee to implement the Declaration. See the resols. on implementation of the Decl. in *U.K. Contemp. Practice* (1962, II), 280–2, 287; ibid. (1963, II), 216–20; *British Practice*, 1964, 173, 237; *U.N. Monthly Chronicle* (June 1965), pp. 55 seq. (July 1965), p. 47. See also Resol. 2145 (XXI), set out *supra*, p. 176.

principle of self-determination as a part of the obligations stemming from the Charter, and is not a 'recommendation', but is in the form of an authoritative interpretation of the Charter.[1] The principle has been incorporated in a number of international instruments.[2] However, a number of governments continue to deny that it exists as a legal principle.[3] The United States[4] and many other governments support the principle, which appears in the Declaration of Principles of International Law concerning Friendly Relations adopted without vote by the United Nations General Assembly in 1970.[5] The Advisory Opinion of the International Court relating to the *Western Sahara*[6] confirms 'the validity of the principle of self-determination' in the context of international law.

The present position is that self-determination is a legal principle, and that United Nations organs do not permit Article 2, paragraph 7, to impede discussion and decision when the principle is in issue.[7] Its precise ramifications in other contexts are not yet worked out, and it is difficult to do justice to the problems in a small compass. The subject has three aspects. First, the principle informs and complements other general principles of international law,[8] viz., of state sovereignty, the equality of states, and the equality of peoples within a state. Thus self-determination is employed in conjunction with the principle of non-intervention in relation to the use of force and otherwise.[9] Secondly, the concept of self-determination has been applied in the different context of economic self-determination.[1] Lastly,

[1] See Waldock, 106 Hague *Recueil* (1962, II), 33; Annual Report of the Secretary-General (1961), p. 2. Cf. Judge Moreno Quintana, I.C.J. Reports (1960), pp. 95–6.

[2] The Pacific Charter, 8 September 1954, *Dept. of St. Bull.* 31 (1954), 393; Communiqué of the Bandung Conference, 24 April 1955, *Annuaire français* (1955), p. 723; Decl. of the Belgrade Conference of Non-Aligned Countries, 6 September 1961 (25 states); Decl. of the Cairo Conference of Non-Aligned Countries, October 1964 (47 states), 4 *Indian Journ.* (1964), 599. See also U.N. General Assembly Resol. 1815 (XVII): *U.K. Contemp. Practice* (1962, II), 290; and Resol. 1966 (XVIII), ibid. (1963, II), 225.

[3] For statements of the British view: *U.K. Contemp. Practice* (1963, II), 83; ibid. (1964, I), 11. Reference to Japanese opinion: Gess, 13 *I.C.L.Q.* (1964), 414.

[4] See 61 *A.J.* (1967), 595; statement in U.N. Gen. Ass., 12 October 1966.

[5] Resol. 2625 (XXV), Annex. Text: 65 *A.J.* (1971), 243; Brownlie, *Basic Documents*, p. 32.

[6] I.C.J. Reports, 1975, p. 12 at pp. 31–3. See also the *Namibia Opinion*, ibid., 1971, p. 16 at p. 31.

[7] On domestic jurisdiction: *supra*, pp. 291 seq. On the practice of U.N. organs in the present connexion see Higgins, loc. cit.

[8] On these general principles *supra*, p. 19. On the relation of self-determination to *jus cogens* see *supra*, p. 512.

[9] Cp. the Punta del Este Declaration, 56 *A.J.* (1962), 601, 607; and the U.N. General Assembly resols. on the Hungarian situation in 1956 (see Higgins, op. cit., pp. 184–5, 211).

[1] See the Declaration on Permanent Sovereignty over Natural Resources, *supra*, p. 540,

the principle appears to have corollaries which may include the following: (1) if force be used to seize territory and the object is the implementation of the principle, then title may accrue by general acquiescence and recognition more readily than in other cases of unlawful seizure of territory;[1] (2) the principle may compensate for a partial lack of certain *desiderata* in the fields of statehood and recognition;[2] (3) intervention against a liberation movement may be unlawful and assistance to the movement may be lawful; (4) territory inhabited by peoples not organized as a state cannot be regarded as *terra nullius* susceptible to appropriation by individual states in case of abandonment by the existing sovereign.

11. *The Standard of Non-discrimination*

The Charter of the United Nations, which entered into force in 1945, contains a significant number of references to 'human rights and fundamental freedoms for all without distinction as to race, sex, language or religion'.[3] These somewhat general and to some extent promotional provisions have provided the background to the appearance of a substantial body of multilateral conventions and practice by the organs of the United Nations. By 1965, at the latest, it was possible to conclude that the principle of respect for and protection for human rights had become recognized as a legal standard.[4] In 1970 the majority of the International Court, consisting of twelve judges, delivering judgment in the *Barcelona Traction* case (Second Phase)[5] referred to obligations *erga omnes*[6] in contemporary international law which included 'the principles and rules concerning the basic rights of the human person, including protection from slavery and racial discrimination'.

There is indeed a considerable support for the view that there is in international law today a legal principle of non-discrimination which at the least applies in matters of race.[7] This principle is based, in part, upon the United Nations Charter, especially Articles 55 and 56, the practice of organs of the United Nations,

and Article 1 common to the Covenants produced by the Third Committee of the General Assembly, *supra*, p. 555.

[1] See further *supra*, p. 163.

[2] See *supra*, Chapters IV and V and, on *locus standi*, pp. 466–73.

[3] See Articles 1 (3), 13 (1), 55, 56, 62 (2), and 76.

[4] Judge Tanaka, diss. op., *South West Africa* cases (Second Phase), I.C.J. Reports (1966), at p. 300; *Namibia Opinion*, ibid. (1971), p. 57, para. 131.

[5] I.C.J. Reports (1970), p. 3 at p. 32.

[6] i.e. binding on all states and also having the status of peremptory norms (*jus cogens*), on which see *supra*, pp. 512–15.

[7] See the diss. ops. of Judge Tanaka, I.C.J. Reports (1966), at pp. 286–301; and Padilla Nervo, ibid., pp. 455–6, 464, 467–9. Cf. the sep. op. of Judge Van Wyk, ibid., pp. 154–5,

in particular resolutions of the General Assembly condemning *apartheid*, the Universal Declaration of Human Rights, the International Covenants on Human Rights and the European Convention on Human Rights.[1] An alternative view is that there is no legal principle of racial non-discrimination as such but the international practice supports instead such a standard or criterion as an aid to interpretation of treaties, including the Mandate agreement in issue in the *South West Africa* cases.[2]

There is a growing body of legal materials on the criteria by which illegal discrimination may be distinguished from reasonable measures of differentiation, i.e. legal discrimination.[3] The principle of equality before the law allows for factual differences such as sex or age and is not based on a mechanical conception of equality. The distinction must have an objective justification;[4] the means employed to establish a different treatment must be proportionate to the justification for differentiation;[5] and there is a burden of proof on the party seeking to set up an exception to the equality principle.[6] The provisions of Article 1 of the International Convention on the Elimination of All Forms of Racial Discrimination, 1966,[7] are of particular interest:

1. In this Convention, the term 'racial discrimination' shall mean any distinction, exclusion, restriction or preference based on race, colour, descent, or national or ethnic origin which has the purpose or effect of nullifying or

158–72. See further Whiteman v. 244–6; and viii. 376–83; Huston, 53 *Iowa L.R.* (1967), 272–90. On the issue of sexual equality see Daw, 12 *Malaya L.R.* (1970), 308–36; Brownlie, *Human Rights*, p. 183; McDougal, Lasswell and Chen, 69 *A.J.* (1975), 497–533.

[1] See Art. 14, on which see Fawcett, note 3, *infra*; Eissen, *Mélanges offerts à Polys Modinos* (1968), pp. 122–45; Guggenheim, *René Cassin: Amicorum Discipulorumque Liber* I (1969), p. 95.

[2] See the diss. op. of Judge Jessup, I.C.J. Reports (1966), pp. 432–3, 441.

[3] See Fawcett, *The Application of the European Convention on Human Rights*, pp. 232–44; McKean, 44 *B.Y.* (1970), 177; Vierdag, *The Concept of Discrimination in International Law with Special Reference to Human Rights* (1973); *Minority Schools in Albania* (1935), P.C.I.J., Ser. A/B, no. 64. *Association Protestante* v. *Radiodiffusion-Télévision Belge*, Int. L.R. 47, 198; *Beth-El Mission* v. *Minister of Social Welfare*, Int. L.R. 47, 205. On discrimination on grounds of sex see: *Chollet (née Bauduin)* v. *Commission*, Court of Justice of Europ. Comm., *Recueil*, 18 (1972), 363; *Zanoni* v. *E.S.R.O.*, Int. L.R. 51, 430; *Artzet* v. *Secretary-General*, ibid., 438; *Leguin* v. *Secretary-General*, ibid., 451.

[4] See Judge Tanaka, I.C.J. Reports (1966), at pp. 302–16; *Belgian Linguistics* case (Merits), Europ. Ct. of Human Rights Judgment of 23 July 1968, Int. L.R. 45, 136, pp. 163–6, 173–4, 180–1, 186, 199–201, 216–17; *National Union of Belgian Police* case, Europ. Ct. of H.R., Ser. A, Vol. 19, pp. 19–22; *Swedish Engine Drivers' Union* case, ibid., Vol. 20, pp. 16–17; *Schmidt and Dahlström* case, ibid., Vol. 21, pp. 16–18; *Case of Engel and Others*, ibid., Vol. 22, pp. 29–31.

[5] *Belgian Linguistics* case, last note; *Societé X, W et Z* v. *République Fédérale d'Allemagne*, Europ. Comm. of H.R., Collection of Decisions, Vol. 35, p. 1.

[6] Judge Tanaka, diss. op., I.C.J. Reports (1966), at p. 309.

[7] Brownlie, *Basic Documents in International Law*, p. 190.

impairing the recognition, enjoyment or exercise, on an equal footing, of human rights and fundamental freedoms in the political, economic, social, cultural or any other field of public life.

2. This Convention shall not apply to distinctions, exclusions, restrictions or preferences made by a State Party to this Convention between citizens and non-citizens.

3. Nothing in this Convention may be interpreted as affecting in any way the legal provisions of States Parties concerning nationality, citizenship or naturalization, provided that such provisions do not discriminate against any particular nationality.

4. Special measures taken for the sole purpose of securing adequate advancement of certain racial or ethnic groups or individuals requiring such protection as may be necessary in order to ensure such groups or individuals equal enjoyment or exercise of human rights and fundamental freedoms shall not be deemed racial discrimination, provided, however, that such measures do not, as a consequence, lead to the maintenance of separate rights for different racial groups and that they shall not be continued after the objectives for which they were taken have been achieved.[1]

The issue of non-discrimination in relation to treatment of aliens has been considered elsewhere. It is noteworthy that there is more or less authority for propositions which employ non-discrimination (on the basis of nationality) as a principle limiting the normal liberties of States in particular contexts, including expropriation,[2] currency devaluation,[3] taxation,[4] and the export trade.[5] It would be reasonable to suppose that arbitrary discrimination in the exercise of the power to expel aliens would be unlawful. There are two issues in such cases. First, whether the particular liberty is subject to limitation of this type: if the particular standard of non-discrimination is *jus cogens* (as in racial discrimination), the answer will be affirmative. Secondly, whether standards have developed for determining the distinction between lawful differentiation and unlawful, arbitrary, discrimination.

11. *Evaluation and Synthesis*

The foregoing discussion reveals the diversity of the relations the individual has in international legal experience. It is clear that legal developments have done much that is constructive, but it is

[1] Cp. Judge Tanaka, diss. op., I.C.J. Reports (1966), at pp. 306–10, in which he takes the view that any distinction on a racial basis is contrary to the principle of non-discrimination.

[2] *Supra*, p. 539. [3] *Supra*, p. 532. [4] *Supra*, p. 533.

[5] See Fawcett, 123 Hague *Recueil* (1968, I), 267–74, with particular reference to GATT.

equally clear that political conditions determine the extent and permanence of the progress made in terms of legal obligations and institutions. In closing, three points may be made to place the problem of the individual in international relations in perspective. Theoretical controversy as to whether the individual is a subject of the law is not always very fruitful in practical terms, and the issue is always viewed with the idea of proving that he is a subject *vel non*. He probably is *in particular contexts*, although some would say that this is true only when he has true procedural capacity. The second point is that the individual must be seen in the context of the organized community in which he lives, and, therefore, his individual condition will depend on general social and economic advancement in that community. Some very difficult issues at once arise which are not solved by general formulas of the conventional kind about human rights. A government may desire to control the economy of the state and to create a public sector which, in its view, is necessary to proper economic growth. If full compensation must be paid (and it is often said that the 'human rights' of the investors and corporations concerned are to be protected in this way), nationalization on any scale is impossible, at least on 'prompt and adequate' terms.[1] There is then a collision of interest which may be resolved at the expense of the human rights of the national community as a whole. Finally, many states in the General Assembly of the United Nations see human rights issues as bound up with community rights to self-determination: the Charter is concerned with the equality of states and peoples. Self-determination and racial equality are prominent issues in the world forum, as evidenced by the attitude of the majority of member states toward Rhodesia and South Africa.

For the future, work on individual human rights may tend towards a synthesis of the 'civil liberties' model and programmes of social and economic advancement for communities devastated by poverty. The economic gap between the industrial nations and Latin American and the Afro-Asian world is widening, and legal development should reflect the most urgent needs of the world today.

[1] See *supra*, pp. 533 seq.

PART X

INTERNATIONAL TRANSACTIONS

CHAPTER XXV

THE LAW OF TREATIES

1. *Introductory*[1]

A GREAT many international disputes are concerned with the validity and interpretation of international agreements, and the practical content of state relations is embodied in agreements. The great international organizations, including the United Nations, have their legal basis in multilateral agreements. Since it began its work the International Law Commission[2] has concerned itself with the law of treaties, and in 1966 it adopted a set of seventy-five draft articles.[3]

These draft articles formed the basis for the Vienna Conference which in two sessions (1968 and 1969) completed work on the Vienna Convention on the Law of Treaties, consisting of eighty-five articles and an Annex. The Convention[4] is not yet in force and requires thirty-five ratifications as a condition of entering into

[1] The principal items are: the Vienna Convention on the Law of Treaties (see note 4); the commentary of the International Law Commission on the Final Draft Articles, *Yrbk., I.L.C.* (1966), ii, p. 172 at pp. 187–274; Whiteman xiv. 1–510; Rousseau, *Droit international public*, i (1970), 61–305; Guggenheim, *Traité* (2nd ed.), i. 113–273; McNair, *Law of Treaties* (1961); Harvard Research, 29 *A.J.* (1935), Suppl.; O'Connell i. 195–280; Sørensen, pp. 175–246; Jennings, 121 Hague *Recueil* (1967, II), 527–81; Am. Law Institute, Restatement, Second, *Foreign Relations Law* (1965), 359–496; Fawcett, 30 *B.Y.* (1953), 381–400; *Répertoire suisse* i. 5–209. See further: Rousseau, *Principes généraux du droit international public*, i (1944); Basdevant, 15 Hague *Recueil* (1926, V), 539–642; Detter, *Essays on the Law of Treaties* (1967); Holloway, *Modern Trends in Treaty Law* (1967); Gotlieb, *Canadian Treaty-Making* (1968); *British Practice* (1964), pp. 78–85; 1966, 154–9; various authors, 27 *Z.a.ö. R.u.V.* (1967), 408–561; ibid., 29 (1969), 1–70, 536–42, 654–710; Verzijl, *International Law in Historical Perspective* vi (1973), 112–612.

[2] On which *supra*, p. 31.

[3] The principal items are as follows: International Law Commission, Reports by Brierly, *Yrbk.* (1950), ii; (1951), ii; (1952), ii; Reports by Lauterpacht, *Yrbk.* (1953), ii; (1954), ii; Reports by Fitzmaurice, *Yrbk.* (1956), ii; (1957), ii; (1958), ii; (1959), ii; (1960), ii; Reports by Waldock, *Yrbk.* (1962), ii; (1963), ii; (1964), ii; (1965), ii; (1966), ii; Draft articles adopted by the Commission, I, Conclusion, Entry into Force and Registration of Treaties, *Yrbk.* (1962), ii. 159; 57 *A.J.* (1963), 190; *Yrbk.* (1965), ii. 159; 60 *A.J.* (1966), 164; Draft Articles, II, Invalidity and Termination of Treaties, *Yrbk.* (1963), ii. 189; 58 *A.J.* (1964), 241; Draft Articles, III, Application, Effects, Modification and Interpretation of Treaties, *Yrbk.* (1964), ii; 59 *A.J.* (1965), 203, 434; Final Report and Draft, *Yrbk.* (1966), ii. 172; 61 *A.J.* (1967), 263.

[4] Text: 63 *A.J.* (1969), 875; 8 *Int. Leg. Materials* (1969), 679; 29 *Z.a.ö. R.u.V.* (1969), 711; Brownlie, *Documents*, p. 233. For the preparatory materials see: items in note 3; *United Nations Conference on the Law of Treaties, First Session, Official Records*, A/CONF.

force.[1] The Convention is not as a whole declaratory of general international law: it does not express itself so to be (see the preamble). Various provisions clearly involve progressive development of the law; and the preamble affirms that questions not regulated by its provisions will continue to be governed by the rules of customary international law. Nonetheless, a good number of articles are essentially declaratory of existing law and certainly those provisions which are not constitute presumptive evidence of emergent rules of general international law.[2] The provisions of the Convention are regarded as a primary source already: as, for example, in the oral proceedings before the International Court in the *Namibia* case. In its Advisory Opinion in that case the Court observed:[3] 'The rules laid down by the Vienna Convention . . . concerning termination of a treaty relationship on account of breach (adopted without a dissenting vote) may in many respects be considered as a codification of existing customary law on the subject.'

The Convention was adopted by a very substantial majority at the Conference[4] and constitutes a comprehensive code of the main areas of the law of treaties. However, it does not deal with (a) treaties between states and organizations, or between two or more organizations;[5] (b) questions of state succession;[6] (c) the effect of war on treaties.[7] The Convention is not retroactive in effect.

A provisional draft of the International Law Commission[8] defined a 'treaty' as

> any international agreement in written form, whether embodied in a single instrument or in two or more related instruments and whatever its particular designation (treaty, convention, protocol, covenant, charter, statute, act, declaration, concordat, exchange of notes, agreed minute, memorandum of agreement, *modus vivendi* or any other appellation), concluded between two or more States or other subjects of international law and governed by international law.

39/11; *Second Session*, A/CONF. 39/11, Add. 1; Rosenne, *The Law of Treaties* (1970). For comment see Reuter, *La Convention de Vienne sur le droit des traités* (1970); Elias, *The Modern Law of Treaties* (1974); Sinclair, 19 *I.C.L.Q.* (1970), 47–69; id., *The Vienna Convention on the Law of Treaties* (1973); Kearney and Dalton, 64 *A.J.* (1970), 495–561; Jennings, 121 Hague *Recueil* (1967, II), 527–81; Deleau, *Ann. français* (1969), 7–23; Nahlik, ibid., 24–53; Frankowska, 3 *Polish Yrbk.* (1970), 227–55.

[1] Article 84. [2] Cf. *North Sea Continental Shelf Cases*, *supra*, p. 13.

[3] I.C.J. Reports (1971), p. 16 at p. 47. See also *Appeal relating to Jurisdiction of ICAO Council*, I.C.J. Reports, 1972, p. 46 at p. 67; *Fisheries Jurisdiction Case*, I.C.J. Reports, 1973, p. 3 at p. 18; and Briggs, 68 *A.J.* (1974), 51–68.

[4] 79 votes in favour; 1 against; 19 abstentions.

[5] *Infra*, p. 681. [6] *Infra*, p. 665. [7] See *infra*, p. 614.

[8] *Yrbk., I.L.C.*, 1962, ii. 161.

The reference to 'other subjects' of the law was designed to provide for treaties concluded by international organizations, the Holy See, and other international entities such as insurgents.[1]

In the Vienna Convention, as in the Final draft of the Commission, the provisions are confined to treaties between states (Article 1). Article 3 provides that the fact that the Convention is thus limited shall not affect the legal force of agreements between states and other subjects of international law or between such other subjects. Article 2 (1) (a) defines a treaty as 'an international agreement concluded between States in written form and governed by international law, whether embodied in a single instrument or in two or more related instruments[2] and whatever its particular designation'. These provisions leave open the issue concerning the status of agreements between states and private individuals or corporations and which are governed by national law. In the *Anglo-Iranian Oil Co.* case[3] the International Court rejected the contention that a concessionary contract was a treaty or convention within the meaning of the Iranian Declaration accepting the compulsory jurisdiction of the Court under its Statute, Article 36.[4] Article 2 stipulates that the agreements to which the Convention extends be 'governed by international law' and thus excludes the various commercial arrangements, such as purchase and lease, made between governments and operating only under one or more national laws.[5] The capacity of particular international organizations to make treaties depends on the constitution of the organization concerned.[6] The International Law Commission is reviewing the subject of agreements concluded by international organizations.

2. *Conclusion of Treaties*[7]

(a) *Form.*[8] The manner in which treaties are negotiated and brought into force is governed by the intention and consent of

[1] See Chapter III on legal personality.

[2] The conclusion of treaties in simplified form is increasingly common. Many treaties are made by an exchange of notes, the adoption of an agreed minute and so on. See: *Yrbk., I.L.C.* (1966), ii. 188 (Commentary); Hamzeh, 43 *B.Y.* (1968–9), 179–89; Smets, *La Conclusion des accords en forme simplifiée* (1969); Gotlieb, *Canadian Treaty-Making* (1968).

[3] I.C.J. Reports (1952), pp. 111–12. [4] *Infra*, p. 723.

[5] See Mann, 33 *B.Y.* (1957), 20–51; id., 35 *B.Y.* (1959), 34–57; and cf. the *Diverted Cargoes* case, *R.I.A.A.* xii, p. 53, at p. 70. See also *British Practice* (1967), p. 147.

[6] On the capacity of members of federal states: *supra*, pp. 62–3, 79.

[7] The effect on the validity of treaties of non-compliance with internal law is considered in section 5. On participation in multilateral treaties, see *infra*, p. 631.

[8] On 'gentleman's agreements' see E. Lauterpacht, *Festschrift für F. A. Mann* (1977), 381–98. See also *Digest of U.S. Practice*, 1974, 195–9.

the parties. There are no substantive requirements of form, and thus, for example, an agreement may be recorded in the minutes of a conference. In practice form is governed partly by usage, and thus form will vary according as the agreement is expressed to be between states, heads of states, governments (increasingly used), or particular ministers or departments. The Vienna Convention applies only to agreements 'in written form' but Article 3 stipulates that this limitation is without prejudice to the legal force of agreements 'not in written form'. Obviously substantial parts of the Convention are not relevant to oral agreements: the fact remains that important parts of the law, for example, relating to invalidity and termination, will apply to oral agreements.[1]

(b) *Full Powers and signature.*[2] The era of absolute monarchs and slow communications produced a practice in which a sovereign's agent would be given a Full Power to negotiate and to bind his principal. In modern practice, subject to a different intention of the parties, a Full Power involves an authority to negotiate and to sign and seal a treaty. In the case of agreements between governments Full Powers, in the sense of the formal documents evidencing these and their reciprocal examination by the negotiators, are often dispensed with.[3]

The successful outcome of negotiation is the adoption and authentication of the agreed text. Signature has, as one of its functions, that of authentication, but a text may be authenticated in other ways, for example by incorporating the text in the final act of a conference or by initialling. Apart from authentication, the legal effects of signature are as follows. Where the signature is subject to ratification, acceptance, or approval (see below), signature does not establish consent to be bound. However, signature qualifies the signatory state to proceed to ratification, acceptance, or approval and creates an obligation of good faith to refrain from acts calculated to frustrate the objects of the treaty.[4] Where the treaty is not subject to ratification, acceptance, or approval, signature creates the same obligation of good faith and establishes consent to be bound. Signature does not create an

[1] See Whiteman xiv. 29–31; *Yrbk., I.L.C.* (1966) ii. 190, Art. 3, Commentary, para. 3.

[2] See Mervyn Jones, *Full Powers and Ratification* (1946); I.L.C. draft, Articles 1 (i) (d) (e), 4–7, 10–11; *Yrbk., I.L.C.* (1962), ii. 164 seq.; Waldock, ibid., pp. 38 seq.; *Yrbk., I.L.C.* (1966), ii. 189, 193–7; Whiteman, xiv. 35–45; Vienna Conv., Arts. 7–11.

[3] Other exceptions exist in modern practice. Thus Heads of State, Heads of Government, and Foreign Ministers are not required to furnish evidence of their authority.

[4] See Vienna Conv., Article 18; *Upper Silesia* case, P.C.I.J., Ser. A, no. 7, p. 30; McNair, op. cit., pp. 199–205; Fauchille, *Traité* i, Pt. iii, p. 320.

obligation to ratify.[1] In recent times signature has not featured in the adoption of all important multilateral treaties: thus the text may be adopted or approved by the General Assembly of the United Nations by a resolution and submitted to member states for accession.[2]

(c) *Ratification.*[3] Ratification involves two distinct procedural acts: the first is the act of the appropriate organ of the state, which is the Crown in the United Kingdom, and may be called ratification in the constitutional sense; the second is the international procedure which brings a treaty into force by a formal exchange or deposit of the instruments of ratification. Ratification in the latter sense is an important act involving consent to be bound. However, everything depends on the intention of the parties, where this is ascertainable, and modern practice contains many examples of less formal agreements not requiring ratification and intended to be binding by signature. A problem which has provoked controversy concerns the small number of treaties which contain no express provision on the subject of ratification. The International Law Commission[4] at first considered that treaties in principle require ratification[5] and specified exceptional cases where the presumption was otherwise, for example if the treaty provides that it shall come into force upon signature. However, the Commission changed its view, partly by reason of the difficulty of applying the presumption to treaties in simplified form. Article 14 of the Vienna Convention regulates the matter by reference to the intention of the parties.

(d) *Accession, acceptance, and approval.*[6] 'Accession', 'adherence', or 'adhesion' occurs when a state which did not sign a treaty, already signed by other states, formally accepts its provisions. Accession may occur before or after the treaty has

[1] *Yrbk., I.L.C.* (1962), ii. 171. But see Lauterpacht, ibid. (1953), ii. 108–12; and Fitzmaurice, ibid. (1956), ii. 112–13, 121–2.

[2] See the Convention on the Privileges and Immunities of the United Nations, *infra*, pp. 682–3.

[3] See Whiteman xiv. 45–92; Mervyn Jones, op. cit.; Dehousse, *La Ratification des traités* (1935); Camara, *The Ratification of International Treaties* (1949); Fitzmaurice, 15 *B.Y.* (1934), 113–37; id., 33 *B.Y.* (1957), 255–69; Blix, 30 *B.Y.* (1953), 352–80; Frankowska, 73 *R.G.D.I.P.* (1969), 62–88.

[4] I.L.C. draft, Arts. 1 (1) (d), 12; *Yrbk., I.L.C.* (1962), ii. 171; Waldock, ibid., pp. 48–53. See the Final Draft, Arts. 2 (1) (b), 10, 11 and 13; *Yrbk., I.L.C.* (1966), ii. 197–8; and the Vienna Conv., Arts. 2 (1) (b), 11, 14, 16.

[5] See McNair, p. 133; Detter, *Essays*, 15–17. Some members of the Commission were of opinion that no specific rule on the question existed. See also *British Practice* (1964), i. 81–82. See also the *Ambatielos* case, I.C.J. Reports (1952), p. 43.

[6] I.L.C. draft, Arts. 1 (1) (d), 13–16. See the Final Draft, Arts. 2 (1) (b), 11, 12 and 13; *Yrbk., I.L.C.* (1966), ii. 197–201; Vienna Conv., Arts. 2 (1) (b), 11, 14–16.

entered into force. The conditions under which accession may occur and the procedure involved depend on the provisions of the treaty. Accession may appear in a primary role as the only means of becoming a party to an instrument, as in the case of a convention approved by the General Assembly of the United Nations and proposed for accession by member states.[1] Recent practice has introduced the terms 'acceptance' and 'approval' to describe the substance of accession. Terminology is not fixed, however, and where a treaty is expressed to be open to signature 'subject to acceptance', this is equivalent to 'subject to ratification'.

(e) *Expression of consent to be bound.* Signature, ratification, accession, acceptance, and approval are not the only means by which consent to be bound may be expressed. Any other means may be used if so agreed, for example an exchange of instruments constituting a treaty.[2]

3. *Reservations*[3]

In the Vienna Convention, a reservation is defined as 'a unilateral statement, however phrased or named, made by a State, when signing, ratifying, accepting, approving or acceding to a treaty, whereby it purports to exclude or to modify the legal effect of certain provisions of the treaty in their application to that State'. This definition begs the question of validity, which is determined on a contractual and not a unilateral basis. The formerly accepted rule for all kinds of treaty was that reservations were valid only if the treaty concerned permitted reservations and if all other parties accepted the reservation. On this basis a reservation constituted a counter-offer which required a new acceptance, failing which the state making the counter-offer would not become a party to the treaty. This view rests on a

[1] As in the case of the Convention on the Privileges and Immunities of the United Nations. See McNair, pp. 153–5.

[2] Vienna Conv., Arts. 11 and 13.

[3] I.L.C. draft, Arts. 1 (1) (f), 18–22; *Yrbk., I.L.C.* (1962), ii. 175–82; Waldock, ibid., pp. 60–8; Final Draft, Arts. 2 (1) (d), 16–20; *Yrbk., I.L.C.* (1966), ii. 189–90, 202–9; Vienna Conv., Arts. 19–23; Lauterpacht *Yrbk, I.L.C.* (1953), ii. 123–36; Fitzmaurice, 2 *I.C.L.Q.* (1953), 1–27; id., 33 *B.Y.* (1957), 272–93; Holloway, *Les Réserves dans les traités internationaux* (1958); id., *Recent Trends*, pp. 473–542; McNair, Chapter IX; Bishop, 103 Hague *Recueil* (1961), ii. 249–341; Anderson, 13 *I.C.L.Q.* (1964), 450–81; Whiteman xiv. 137–93; Detter, *Essays*, 47–70; Jennings, 121 Hague *Recueil* (1967, II), 534–41; Cassese, *Recueil d'études en hommage à Guggenheim*, pp. 266–304; Tomuschat, 27 *Z.a.ö. R.u.V.* (1967), 463–82; Kappeler, *Les Réserves dans les traités internationaux* (1958); Mendelson, 45 *B.Y.* (1971), 137–71; Ruda, 146 Hague *Recueil* (1975, III), 95–218; Bowett, 48 *B.Y.* (1976–7), 67–92; Imbert, *Les Réserves aux traités multilatéraux* (1979).

contractual conception of the absolute integrity of the treaty as adopted.[1]

In the period of the League of Nations (1920–46) the practice in regard to multilateral conventions showed a lack of consistency. The League Secretariat, and later the Secretary-General of the United Nations, in his capacity as depositary of conventions concluded under the auspices of the League, followed the principle of absolute integrity. In contrast the members of the Pan-American Union, later the Organization of American States, adopted a flexible system which permitted a reserving state to become a party *vis-à-vis* non-objecting states. This system, dating from 1932, promotes universality at the expense of depth of obligation. Thus a state making sweeping reservations could become a party though bound only in regard to two or three non-objecting states and, even then, with large reservations.

Following the adoption of the Convention on the Prevention and Punishment of the Crime of Genocide by the General Assembly of the United Nations in 1948, a divergence of opinion arose on the admissibility of reservations to the Convention, which contained no provision on the subject. The International Court was requested for an advisory opinion, and in giving its opinion[2] stressed the divergence of practice and the special characteristics of the Convention, including the intention of the parties and the General Assembly that it should be universal in scope. The principal finding of the Court was that 'a State which has made . . . a reservation which has been objected to by one or more of the parties to the Convention but not by others, can be regarded as being a party to the Convention if the reservation is compatible with the object and purpose of the Convention. . . .' In 1951 the International Law Commission rejected the 'compatibility' criterion as too subjective and preferred a rule of unanimous consent. However, in 1952 the General Assembly requested the Secretary-General of the United Nations to conform his practice to the opinion of the Court in respect of the Genocide Convention; and, in respect of *future*[3] conventions concluded under the auspices of the United Nations of which he was depositary, to act as depositary without passing upon the legal effect of documents containing reservations and leaving it to each state to draw legal consequences when reservations were communicated to them. In its practice the Secretariat adopted the

[1] See *Reservations to Genocide Convention*, I.C.J. Reports (1951), p. 15 at pp. 21, 24.

[2] Last note.

[3] Concluded after 12 January 1952, when the resolution was adopted.

'flexible' system for future conventions, and in 1959 the General Assembly reaffirmed its previous directive and extended it to cover *all* conventions concluded under the auspices of the United Nations, unless they contain contrary provisions. In 1962 the International Law Commission decided in favour of the 'compatibility' doctrine.[1] The Commission pointed out that the increase in the number of potential participants in multilateral treaties made the unanimity principle less practicable.

The Final Draft of the Commission was followed in most respects by the Vienna Convention. Article 19 of the Convention indicates the general liberty to formulate a reservation when signing, ratifying, accepting, approving or acceding to a treaty and then states three exceptions. The first two exceptions are reservations expressly prohibited and reservations not falling within provisions in a treaty permitting specified reservations and no others. The third class of impermissible reservations are cases falling outside the first mentioned classes in which the reservation is 'incompatible with the object and purpose of the treaty'.

Article 20 provides as follows for acceptance of and objection to reservations other than those expressly authorized by a treaty:

> 2. When it appears from the limited number of the negotiating States and the object and purpose of a treaty that the application of the treaty in its entirety between all the parties is an essential condition of the consent of each one to be bound by the treaty, a reservation requires acceptance by all the parties.
>
> 3. When a treaty is a constituent instrument of an international organization and unless it otherwise provides, a reservation requires the acceptance of the competent organ of that organization.
>
> 4. In cases not falling under the preceding paragraphs and unless the treaty otherwise provides:
>
> (a) acceptance by another contracting State of a reservation constitutes the reserving State a party to the treaty in relation to that other State if or when the treaty is in force for those States;
>
> (b) an objection by another contracting State to a reservation does not preclude the entry into force of the treaty as between the objecting and reserving States unless a contrary intention is definitely expressed by the objecting State;
>
> (c) an act expressing a State's consent to be bound by the treaty and containing a reservation is effective as soon as at least one other contracting State has accepted the reservation.

[1] Draft Articles 18 (1) (d) and 20 (2). The Commission rejected a 'collegiate' system which would require acceptance of the reservation by a given proportion of the other parties for the reserving state to become a party: cf. Anderson, op. cit. See also *British Practice* (1964), i. 83–4.

5. For the purposes of paragraphs 2 and 4 and unless the treaty otherwise provides, a reservation is considered to have been accepted by a State if it shall have raised no objection to the reservation by the end of a period of twelve months after it was notified of the reservation or by the date on which it expressed its consent to be bound by the treaty, whichever is later.

The 'compatibility' test is the least objectionable solution but is by no means an ideal regime,[1] and many problems remain. The application of the criterion of compatibility with object and purpose is a matter of appreciation, but this is left to individual states. How is the test to apply to provisions for dispute settlement, or to specific issues in the Territorial Sea Convention of 1958,[2] such as the right of innocent passage? In practical terms the 'compatibility' test approximates to the Latin-American system and thus may not sufficiently maintain the balance between the integrity and the effectiveness of multilateral conventions in terms of a firm level of obligation.

The reason for the approximation to the Latin-American system[3] is that each state decides for itself whether reservations are incompatible and some states might adopt a liberal policy of accepting far-reaching reservations. In practice, for extraneous reasons, the flexible system is working fairly well. Firstly, the process by which the texts of multilateral treaties are prepared is very thorough and involves careful working toward genuine consensus: at the end of the procedures there should not be too much cause for reservations. Secondly, the more important treaties tend to make express provision for the subject of reservations. Such special regulations may provide for decision on incompatibility by a majority rule (e.g. if at least two-thirds of the parties object) and prohibit reservations to the more fundamental provisions.

4. *Entry into Force, Deposit, and Registration*[4]

The provisions of the treaty determine the manner in which

[1] See Waldock, *Yrbk., I.L.C.* (1962), ii. 65–6; I.L.C., 1966 Report, ibid. (1966), ii. 205–6; Sinclair, 19 *I.C.L.Q.* (1970), 53–60.

[2] *Supra*, pp. 183 seq.

[3] For the Standards on Reservations adopted in 1973 by the Org. of Am. States see *Digest of U.S. Practice*, 1973, 179–81. For the history: Ruda, op. cit., pp. 115–33.

[4] I.L.C. drafts, Arts. 23–5; *Yrbk., I.L.C.* (1962), ii. 182–3; Waldock, ibid., pp. 68–73; Final Draft, Arts. 21, 22, and 75; *Yrbk., I.L.C.* (1966), ii. 209–10, 273–4; Vienna Conv., Arts. 24, 25, 80. On registration see Whiteman xiv. 113–26; McNair, Chap. X; Brandon, 29 *B.Y.* (1952), 186–204; id., 47 *A.J.* (1953), 49–69; Boudet, 64 *R.G.D.I.P.* (1960), 596–604; Broches and Boskey, 4 *Neths. Int. L.R.* (1957), 189–92, 277–300; Higgins, *The Development of International Law by the Political Organs of the United Nations*, pp. 328–36; Detter, *Essays*, pp. 28–46.

and the date on which the treaty enters force. Where the treaty does not specify a date, there is a presumption that the treaty is intended to come into force as soon as all the negotiating states have consented to be bound by the treaty.[1]

After a treaty is concluded, the written instruments, which provide formal evidence of consent to be bound by ratification, accession, and so on, and also reservations and other declarations, are placed in the custody of a depositary, who may be one or more states, or an international organization. The depositary has functions of considerable importance relating to matters of form, including provision of information as to the time at which the treaty enters into force.[2] The United Nations Secretariat plays a significant role as depositary of multilateral treaties.

Article 102 of the Charter of the United Nations[3] provides as follows:

> 1. Every treaty and every international engagement entered into by any Member of the United Nations after the present Charter comes into force shall as soon as possible be registered with the Secretariat and published by it.
> 2. No party to any such treaty or international engagement which has not been registered in accordance with the provisions of paragraph 1 of this Article may invoke that treaty or engagement before any organ of the United Nations.

This provision is intended to discourage secret diplomacy and to promote the availability of texts of agreements. The *United Nations Treaty Series* includes agreements by non-members which are 'filed and recorded' with the Secretariat as well as those 'registered' by members. The Secretariat accepts agreements for registration without conferring any status on them, or the parties thereto, which they would not have otherwise. However, this is not the case where the regulations governing the article provide for *ex officio* registration. This involves initiatives by the Secretariat and extends to agreements to which the United Nations is a party, trusteeship agreements, and multilateral agreements of which the United Nations is a depositary. It is not yet clear in every respect how wide the phrase 'every international engagement' is, but it seems to have a very wide scope. Technical intergovernmental agreements, declarations

[1] Vienna Conv., Art. 24 (2).

[2] Vienna Conv., Arts. 76, 77; Rosenne, 61 *A.J.* (1967), 923–45; ibid., 64 (1970), 838–52; Whiteman xiv. 68–92.

[3] A similar but not identical provision appeared in Article 18 of the Covenant of the League of Nations: McNair, pp. 180–5.

accepting the optional clause in the Statute of the International Court, agreements between organizations and states, agreements between organizations, and unilateral engagements of an international character[1] are included.[2] Paragraph 2 is a sanction for the obligation in paragraph 1, and registration is not a condition precedent for the validity of instruments to which the article applies, although these may not be relied upon in proceedings before United Nations organs.[3] In relation to the similar provision in the Covenant of the League the view has been expressed that an agreement may be invoked, though not registered, if other appropriate means of publicity have been employed.[4]

5. *Invalidity of Treaties*[5]

(a) *Provisions of internal law.*[6] The extent to which constitutional limitations on the treaty-making power can be invoked on the international plane is a matter of controversy, and no single view can claim to be definitive. Three main views have received support from writers. According to the first, constitutional limitations determine validity on the international plane.[7] Criticism of this view emphasizes the insecurity in treaty-making that it would entail. The second view varies from the first in that only 'notorious' constitutional limitations are effective on the international plane. The third view is that a state is bound irrespective of internal limitations by consent given by an agent properly authorized according to international law. Some advocates of this view qualify the rule in cases where the other state

[1] McNair, p. 186, and see *infra*, p. 634.

[2] If an agreement is between international legal persons it is registrable even if it be governed by a particular municipal law; but cf. Higgins, op. cit., p. 329. It is not clear whether special agreements (*compromis*) referring disputes to the International Court are required to be registered.

[3] If the instrument is a part of the *jus cogens* (*supra*, p. 512), should non-registration have this effect?

[4] *South West Africa* cases (Preliminary Objections), I.C.J. Reports (1962), p. 319 at pp. 359–60 (sep. op. of Judge Bustamante) and 420–2 (sep. op. of Judge Jessup). But cf. joint diss. op. of Judges Spender and Fitzmaurice, ibid., p. 503.

[5] See also *infra*, p. 622, on conflict with prior treaties. As to capacity of parties, *supra*, p. 601. See generally: Elias, 134 Hague *Recueil* (1971, III), 335–416.

[6] See *Yrbk., I.L.C.* (1963), ii. 190–3; Waldock, ibid., pp. 41–6; I.L.C., Final Report, *Yrbk., I.L.C.* (1966), ii. 240–2; McNair, Chap. III; Blix, *Treaty-making Power*; Lauterpacht, *Yrbk., I.L.C.* (1953), ii. 141–6; P. de Visscher, *De la conclusion des traités internationaux* (1943), pp. 219–87; id., 136 Hague *Recueil* (1972, II), 94–8; Geck, 27 *Z.a.ö. R.u.V.* (1967), 429–50; *Digest of U.S. Practice*, 1974, 195–8.

[7] This was the position of the International Law Commission in 1951; *Yrbk.* (1951), ii. 73.

is aware of the failure to comply with internal law or where the irregularity is manifest. This position, which involves a presumption of competence and excepts manifest irregularity, was approved by the International Law Commission, in its draft Article 43, in 1966. The Commission stated that 'the decisions of international tribunals and State practice, if they are not conclusive, appear to support' this type of solution.[1]

At the Vienna Conference the draft provision was strengthened and the result appears in the Convention, Article 46:

1. A State may not invoke the fact that its consent to be bound by a treaty has been expressed in violation of a provision of its internal law regarding competence to conclude treaties as invalidating its consent unless that violation was manifest and concerned a rule of its internal law of fundamental importance.

2. A violation is manifest if it would be objectively evident to any State conducting itself in the matter in accordance with normal practice and in good faith.

(b) *Representative's lack of authority.*[2] The Vienna Convention provides that if the authority of a representative to express the consent of his state to be bound by a particular treaty has been made subject to a specific restriction, his omission to observe the restriction may not be invoked as a ground of invalidity unless the restriction was previously notified to the other negotiating states.

(c) *Corruption of a state representative.* The International Law Commission decided that corruption of representatives was not adequately dealt with as a case of fraud[3] and an appropriate provision appears in the Vienna Convention, Article 50.

(d) *Error.*[4] The Vienna Convention, Article 48,[5] contains two principal provisions which probably reproduce the existing law and are as follows:

1. A State may invoke an error in a treaty as invalidating its consent to be bound by the treaty if the error relates to a fact or situation assumed by that State to exist at the time when the treaty was concluded and formed an essential basis of its consent to be bound by the treaty.
2. Paragraph 1 shall not apply if the State in question contributed by its

[1] *Yrbk., I.L.C.* (1966), ii. 240–2.

[2] I.L.C. draft, Art. 32; *Yrbk., I.L.C.* (1963), ii. 193; Waldock, ibid., pp. 46–7; Final Draft, Art. 44; *Yrbk., I.L.C.* (1966), ii. 242; Vienna Conv., Art. 47.

[3] *Yrbk., I.L.C.* (1966), ii. 245.

[4] See Lauterpacht, op. cit., p. 153; Fitzmaurice, op. cit., pp. 25, 35–7; Waldock, op. cit., pp. 48–50; Oraison, *L'Erreur dans les traités* (1972).

[5] See also *Yrbk., I.L.C.* (1966), ii. 243–4.

own conduct to the error or if the circumstances were such as to put that State on notice of a possible error.[1]

(e) *Fraud.*[2] There are few helpful precedents on the effect of fraud. The Vienna Convention provides[3] that a state which has been induced to enter into a treaty by the fraud of another negotiating state, may invoke the fraud as invalidating its consent to be bound by the treaty. Fraudulent misrepresentation of a material fact inducing an essential error is dealt with by the provision relating to error.

(f) *Coercion of state representatives.*[4] The Vienna Convention, Article 51, provides that 'the expression of a State's consent to be bound by a treaty which has been procured by the coercion of its representative through acts or threats directed against him shall be without legal effect'. The concept of coercion extends to blackmailing threats and threats against the representative's family.

(g) *Coercion of a state.*[5] The International Law Commission in its draft of 1963 considered that Article 2, paragraph 4, of the Charter of the United Nations, together with other developments, justified the conclusion that a treaty procured by the threat or use of force in violation of the Charter of the United Nations shall be void. Article 52 of the Vienna Convention so provides.[6] An amendment with the object of defining force to include any 'economic or political pressure' was withdrawn. A Declaration condemning such pressure appears in the Final Act of the Conference.

(h) *Conflict with a peremptory norm of general international law* (jus cogens). See Chapter XXII, section 5.

(i) *Unequal treaties.* The doctrine of international law in Communist states, invoked by their representatives in organs of

[1] See the *Temple* case, I.C.J. Reports (1962), p. 26. See also the sep. op. of Judge Fitzmaurice, ibid., p. 57.

[2] See Lauterpacht, ibid. (1953), ii. 152; Fitzmaurice, ibid. (1958), ii. 25, 37; Waldock, ibid. (1963), ii. 47–8; Oraison, 75 *R.G.D.I.P.* (1971), 617–73.

[3] Article 49. See also the Final Draft, *Yrbk., I.L.C.* (1966), ii. 244–5.

[4] Fitzmaurice, op. cit., pp. 26, 38; Waldock, op. cit., p. 50; Final Draft, Art. 48; *Yrbk., I.L.C.* (1966), ii. 245–6.

[5] I.L.C. draft, Art. 36; *Yrbk., I.L.C.* (1963), ii. 197; Waldock, ibid., pp. 51–2; Lauterpacht, op. cit., pp. 147–52; McNair, pp. 206–11; Brownlie, *International Law and the Use of Force by States*, pp. 404–6; Fitzmaurice, *Yrbk., I.L.C.* (1957), ii. 32, 56–7; ibid. (1958), ii. 26, 38–9; Bothe, 27 *Z.a.ö. R.u.V.* (1967), 507–19; Jennings, 121 Hague *Recueil*, pp. 561–3; Ténékidès, *Annuaire français*, 1974, 79–102; *Fisheries Jurisdiction Case* (United Kingdom v. Iceland), I.C.J. Reports, 1973, p. 3 at p. 14; Briggs, 68 *A.J.* (1974), 51 at pp. 62–3.

[6] See also the Final Draft, Art. 49; *Yrbk., I.L.C.* (1966), ii. 246–7; Whiteman xiv. 268–70; Kearney and Dalton, 64 *A.J.* (1970), 532–5.

the United Nations, holds treaties not concluded on the basis of the sovereign equality of the parties to be invalid.[1] An example of such a treaty is an arrangement between a powerful state and a state still virtually under its protectorate, whereby the latter grants extensive economic privileges and, or, military facilities. Whilst 'Western' jurists oppose the doctrine on the ground that it is too vague, the principle is regarded as entirely just by newly independent states, and it is no longer confined to the thinking of jurists from Communist states.[2] Apart from the presence or absence of general agreement on the content of the principle, a proportion of its dominion may be exercised through the rules concerning capacity of parties, duress (*supra*), fundamental change of circumstances (*infra*, section 6 (h)), and the effect of peremptory norms of general international law, including the principle of self-determination (*supra*, pp. 593–6 and *infra*, section 6 (i)).

6. *Termination and Suspension of Treaties*[3]

(a) *Pacta sunt servanda*. The Vienna Convention prescribes a certain presumption as to the validity and continuance in force of a treaty,[4] and such a presumption may be based upon ***pacta sunt servanda*** as a general principle of international law: a treaty in force is binding upon the parties and must be performed by them in good faith.[5]

(b) *State succession*.[6] Treaties may be affected when one state succeeds wholly or in part to the legal personality and territory of another. The conditions under which the treaties of the latter survive depend on many factors, including the precise form and origin of the 'succession' and the type of treaty concerned.

[1] See Kozhevnikov (ed.), *International Law*, pp. 248, 280–1; Lester, 11 *I.C.L.Q.* (1962), 847–55; Detter, 15 *I.C.L.Q.* (1966), 1069–89. The principle has been advanced both as affecting essential validity and as a ground for termination.

[2] See Sinha, 14 *I.C.L.Q.* (1965), p. 121 at pp. 123–4.

[3] See generally *Annuaire de l'Institut*, 49, i (1961); 52, i, ii (1967); Fitzmaurice, *Yrbk., I.L.C.* (1957), ii. 16–70; McNair, Chaps. XXX–XXXV; Tobin, *Termination of Multipartite Treaties*; Detter, *Essays*, pp. 83–99; Whiteman xiv. 410–510; Capotorti, 134 Hague *Recueil* (1971, III), 419–587; Haraszti, *Some Fundamental Problems of the Law of Treaties* (1973), pp. 229–425.

[4] Article 42. See also I.L.C. draft, Art. 30; *Yrbk., I.L.C.* (1963), ii. 189; Final Draft, Art. 39; ibid. (1966), ii. 236–7.

[5] See the Vienna Conv., Art. 26; the I.L.C. Final Draft, Art. 23; *Yrbk., I.L.C.* (1966), ii. 210–11; and McNair, Chap. XXX.

[6] See Chapter XXVIII, pp. 665–9. In its work on the law of treaties the International Law Commission put this question aside: Final Draft, Art. 69; *Yrbk.* (1966), ii. 267; and see the Vienna Conv., Art. 73.

Changes of this kind may of course terminate treaties apart from categories of state succession (section (h), *infra*).

(c) *War and armed conflict.*[1] Hostile relations do not automatically terminate treaties between the parties to a conflict. Many treaties, including the Charter of the United Nations, are intended to be no less binding in case of war, and agreements such as the Geneva Conventions of 1949 are intended to regulate the conduct of war. However, in state practice many types of treaty are regarded as at least suspended in time of war, and war conditions may lead to termination of treaties on grounds of impossibility or fundamental change of circumstances. In many respects the law on the subject is uncertain. Thus, it is not yet clear to what extent the illegality of the use or threat of force has had effects on the right (where it may be said to exist) to regard a treaty as suspended or terminated.[2]

(d) *Operation of the provisions of a treaty.* A treaty may of course specify the conditions of its termination, and a bilateral treaty may provide for denunciation by the parties.[3] Where a treaty contains no provisions regarding its termination the existence of a right of denunciation depends on the intention of the parties, which can be inferred from the terms of the treaty and its subject-matter, but, according to the Vienna Convention, the presumption is that the treaty is not subject to denunciation or withdrawal.[4] Some important law-making treaties, including the Conventions on the Law of the Sea of 1958, contain no denunciation clause. Treaties of peace are presumably not open to unilateral denunciation.

(e) *Termination by agreement.* Termination or withdrawal may take place by consent of all the parties.[5] Such consent may be implied. In particular, a treaty may be considered as terminated if all the parties conclude a later treaty which is intended to supplant the earlier treaty or if the later treaty is incompatible with its provisions.[6] The topic of 'desuetude', which is probably

[1] See McNair, Chap. XLIII; Briggs, pp. 934–46; Scelle, 77 *J.D.I.* (1950), 26–84; La Pradelle, 2 *I.L.Q.* (1948–9), 555–76; Edwards, 44 *Grot. Soc.* (1958), 91–105; Whiteman xiv. 490–510. The question was put aside by the International Law Commission: Final Draft, Art. 69; *Yrbk.* (1966), ii. 267; and see the Vienna Conv., Art. 73.

[2] I.L.C. draft, Part II, commentary; *Yrbk., I.L.C.* (1963), ii. 189, para. 14.

[3] Vienna Conv., Art. 54; I.L.C. Final Draft, Art. 51; *Yrbk., I.L.C.* (1966), ii. 249.

[4] Vienna Conv., Art. 56; I.L.C. draft, Art. 39; *Yrbk., I.L.C.* (1963), ii. 200–1; Waldock, ibid., pp. 64–70; Fitzmaurice, ibid. (1957), ii. 22; McNair, pp. 502–5, 511–13; I.L.C., Final Draft, Art. 53; *Yrbk.* (1966), ii. 250–1.

[5] Vienna Conv., Art. 54; I.L.C. Draft, Art. 40, *Yrbk.* (1963), ii. 203–3; I.L.C. Final Draft, Art. 54, *Yrbk.* (1966), ii. 251–2.

[6] Vienna Conv., Art. 59; I.L.C. Draft, Art. 41, *Yrbk.* (1963), ii. 203–4; I.L.C. Final

not a term of art, is essentially concerned with discontinuance of use of a treaty and its implied termination by consent.[1] However, it could extend to the distinct situation of a unilateral renunciation of rights under a treaty. Moreover, irrespective of the agreement of the parties, an ancient treaty may become meaningless and incapable of practical application.[2]

(f) *Material breach.*[3] It is widely recognized that material breach by one party entitles the other party or parties to a treaty to invoke the breach as a ground of termination or suspension. This option by the wronged party is accepted as a sanction for securing the observance of treaties. However, considerable uncertainty has surrounded the precise circumstances in which such right of unilateral abrogation may be exercised, particularly in respect of multilateral treaties. Article 60 of the Vienna Convention[4] deals with the matter with as much precision as can be reasonably expected:

1. A material breach of a bilateral treaty by one of the parties entitles the other to invoke the breach as a ground for terminating the treaty or suspending its operation in whole or in part.

2. A material breach of a multilateral treaty by one of the parties entitles:

(a) the other parties by unanimous agreement to suspend the operation of the treaty in whole or in part or to terminate it either:

(i) in the relations between themselves and the defaulting State, or

(ii) as between all the parties.

(b) a party specially affected by the breach to invoke it as a ground for suspending the operation of the treaty in whole or in part in the relations between itself and the defaulting State;

(c) any party other than the defaulting State to invoke the breach as a ground for suspending the operation of the treaty in whole or in part with respect to itself if the treaty is of such a character that a material breach of its provisions by one party radically changes the position of every party with respect to the further performance of its obligations under the treaty.

Draft, Art. 56; *Yrbk.* (1966), ii. 252–3. See also the sep. op. of Judge Anzilotti, *Electricity Company of Sofia* case, P.C.I.J., Ser. A/B, no. 77, p. 92. See also *infra*, p. 622.

[1] See I.L.C. Final Draft, Art. 39, Commentary, para. 5; *Yrbk.* (1966), ii. 237; Fitzmaurice, *Yrbk., I.L.C.* (1957), ii. 28, 47–8, 52; McNair, pp. 516–18; *Yuille, Shortridge Arbitration*, Lapradelle and Politis, ii. 105; *Nuclear Tests Case* (Australia v. France), I.C.J. Reports, 1974, p. 253 at pp. 337–8 (Joint Diss. Op.), 381 (De Castro, diss.).

[2] See Parry, in Sørensen, p. 235.

[3] McNair, pp. 553–71; Sinha, *Unilateral Denunciation of Treaty Because of Prior Violations of Obligations by Other Party* (1966); Detter, *Essays*, pp. 89–93; Fitzmaurice, *Yrbk., I.L.C.* (1957), ii. 31, 54–5; *Tacna-Arica Arbitration*, *R.I.A.A.* ii. 929, 943–4; *Ann. Digest* (1925–6), no. 269; Whiteman xiv. 468–78; Briggs, 68 *A.J.* (1974), 51–68.

[4] See also I.L.C. Draft, Art. 42, *Yrbk., I.L.C.* (1963), ii. 204; Waldock, ibid., pp. 72–7; Final Draft, Art. 57; ibid. (1966), ii. 253–5.

3. A material breach of a treaty, for the purposes of this article, consists in:[1]

(a) a repudiation of the treaty not sanctioned by the present Convention; or

(b) the violation of a provision essential to the accomplishment of the object or purpose of the treaty.

4. The foregoing paragraphs are without prejudice to any provision in the treaty applicable in the event of a breach.

5. Paragraphs 1 to 3 do not apply to provisions relating to the protection of the human person contained in treaties of a humanitarian character, in particular to provisions prohibiting any form of reprisals against persons protected by such treaties.

(g) *Supervening impossibility of performance.*[2] The Vienna Convention provides[3] that a party 'may invoke the impossibility of performing a treaty as a ground for terminating it if the impossibility results from the permanent disappearance or destruction of an object indispensable for the execution of the treaty'. Situations envisaged include the submergence of an island, the drying up of a river, or destruction of a railway, by an earthquake or other disaster. The effect of impossibility is not automatic, and a party must invoke the ground for termination.

(h) *Fundamental change of circumstances.*[4] The principles have been expressed in Article 62 of the Vienna Convention as follows:

1. A fundamental change of circumstances which has occurred with regard to those existing at the time of the conclusion of a treaty, and which was not foreseen by the parties, may not be invoked as a ground for terminating or withdrawing from the treaty unless:

[1] This definition was applied by the International Court in the *Namibia Opinion*, I.C.J. Reports (1971), pp. 46–7, in respect of South African violations of the Mandate for South West Africa (Namibia) and the consequent termination of the Mandate by the United Nations General Assembly.

[2] See generally McNair, pp. 685–8; Fitzmaurice, *Yrbk., I.L.C.* (1957), ii. 50–1.

[3] Art. 61 (1); I.L.C. draft, Art. 43, *Yrbk., I.L.C.* (1963), ii. 206; Waldock, ibid., pp. 77–9; Final Draft, Art. 58, ibid. (1966), ii. 255–6. Another example of impossibility arises from the total extinction of one of the parties to a bilateral treaty, apart from any rules of state succession which might allow devolution: see Waldock, loc. cit. and ibid., commentary at pp. 206–7.

[4] I.L.C. draft, Art. 44, *Yrbk., I.L.C.* (1963), ii. 207; Waldock, ibid., pp. 79–85; Final Draft, Art. 59, ibid. (1966), ii. 256–60; Fitzmaurice, ibid. (1957), ii. 56–65; McNair, pp. 681–91; Rousseau, *Principes généraux du droit international public* i. 580–615; Chesney Hill, *The Doctrine of 'Rebus sic Stantibus'* (1934); Harvard Research, *ut supra*, pp. 1096–126; van Bogaert, 70 *R.G.D.I.P.* (1966), pp. 49–74; Whiteman xiv. 478–90; Detter, *Essays*, pp. 95–9; Lissitzyn, 61 *A.J.* (1967), 895–922; Poch de Caviedes, 118 Hague *Recueil* (1966), ii. 109–204; Schwelb, 29 *Z.a.ö. R.u.V.* (1969), 39–70; Note, 76 *Yale L.J.* (1967), 1669–87; Pastor Ridruejo, 25 *Ann. suisse* (1968), 81–98; Verzijl, *Festschrift für Walter Schätzel* (1960), pp. 515–29; Haraszti, *Some Fundamental Problems of the Law of Treaties* (1973), pp. 327–420; id., 146 Hague *Recueil* (1975, III), 1–94; Jasudowicz, 8 *Polish Yrbk.* (1976), 155–81; *Répertoire suisse* i. 178–86.

(a) the existence of those circumstances constituted an essential basis of the consent of the parties to be bound by the treaty; and

(b) the effect of the change is radically to transform the extent of obligations still to be performed under the treaty.

2. A fundamental change of circumstances may not be invoked as a ground for terminating or withdrawing from a treaty:

(a) if the treaty establishes a boundary; or

(b) if the fundamental change is the result of a breach by the party invoking it either of an obligation under the treaty or of any other international obligation owed to any other party to the treaty.

3. If, under the foregoing paragraphs, a party may invoke a fundamental change of circumstances as a ground for terminating or withdrawing from a treaty it may also invoke the change as a ground for suspending the operation of the treaty.

An example of a fundamental change would be the case where a party to a military and political alliance, involving exchange of military and intelligence information, has a change of government incompatible with the basis of alliance. The majority of modern writers[1] accept the doctrine of *rebus sic stantibus* which is reflected in this provision. The doctrine involves the implication of a term that the obligations of an agreement would end if there has been a change of circumstances. As in municipal systems, so in international law it is recognized that changes frustrating the object of an agreement and apart from actual impossibility may justify its termination. Some jurists dislike the doctrine, regarding it as a primary source of insecurity of obligations, more especially in the absence of a system of compulsory jurisdiction. The Permanent Court in the *Free Zones* case[2] assumed that the principle existed while reserving its position on its extent and the precise mode of its application. State practice and decisions of municipal courts[3] support the principle, for which three juridical bases have been proposed. According to one theory the principle rests on a supposed implied term of the treaty, a basis which involves a fiction and, where it does not, leaves the matter as one of interpretation. A second view is to import a 'clausula' *rebus sic stantibus* into a treaty by operation of law, the clause operating automatically. The third view, which represents the modern law, is that the

1 British writers have always been reluctant to accept the principle: cf. Brierly, pp. 335–9.

2 (1932), P.C.I.J., Ser. A/B, no. 46, pp. 156–8; *Ann. Digest* (1931–2), p. 362 at p. 364; Bishop, p. 144; Green, p. 741. The Court observed that the facts did not justify the application of the doctrine, which had been invoked by France.

3 e.g. *Bremen* v. *Prussia, Ann. Digest* 3 (1925–6), no. 266; *In re Lepeschkin*, ibid., 2 (1923–4), no. 189; *Sransky* v. *Zivnostenska Bank*, Int. L.R. 22 (1955), 424–7.

principle is an objective rule of law, applying when certain events exist, yet not terminating the treaty automatically, since one of the parties must invoke it. The International Law Commission and the Convention exclude treaties fixing boundaries from the operation of the principle in order to avoid an obvious source of threats to the peace.

In the *Fisheries Jurisdiction Case* (United Kingdom v. Iceland)[1] the International Court accepted Article 62 of the Vienna Convention as a statement of the customary law but decided that the dangers to Icelandic interests resulting from new fishing techniques 'cannot constitute a fundamental change with respect to the lapse or subsistence' of the jurisdictional clause in a bilateral agreement.

(i) *New peremptory norm.* A treaty becomes void if it conflicts with a peremptory norm of general international law (*jus cogens*) established after the treaty comes into force.[2] This does not have retroactive effects on the validity of a treaty.

7. *Invalidity, Termination, and Suspension: General Rules*[3]

The application of the regime of the Vienna Convention concerning the invalidity, termination, and suspension of the operation of treaties is governed by certain general provisions. The validity and continuance in force of a treaty and of consent to be bound is presumed (Article 42).[4] Certain grounds of invalidity must be invoked by a party[5] and so the treaties concerned are not void but *voidable*. These grounds are: incompetence under internal law, restrictions on authority of representative, error, fraud, and corruption of a representative. The same is true of certain grounds of termination namely, material breach, impossibility, and fundamental change of circumstances. On the other hand a treaty is *void* in case of coercion of a state (invalidity), and conflict with an existing or emergent peremptory norm (*jus cogens*) (invalidity or termination). Consent to be bound by a

[1] I.C.J. Reports, 1973, p. 3 at pp. 20–1. See also ibid., p. 49 (Fed. Rep. of Germany v. Iceland); and Briggs, 68 *A.J.* (1974), 51–68.

[2] Vienna Conv., Art. 64; I.L.C. draft, Art. 45; *Yrbk., I.L.C.* (1963), ii. 211; Waldock, ibid., pp. 77, 79 (para. 8); Final Draft, Art. 61; ibid. (1966), ii. 261; Fitzmaurice, ibid. (1957), ii. 29–30, 51. See also *supra*, p. 612. Generally on *jus cogens* see Chapter XXII, section 5.

[3] See further the Vienna Conv., Arts. 69–72 and 75; and Cahier, 76 *R.G.D.I.P.* (1972), 672–89.

[4] See also Article 26 and *supra*.

[5] On the procedure see Articles 65–8. See further Briggs, 61 *A.J.* (1967), 976–89.

treaty procured by coercion of the representative of a state 'shall be without any legal effect' (Article 51, invalidity). The rules governing separability of treaty provisions (Article 44), that is, the severance of particular clauses affected by grounds for invalidating or terminating a treaty, do not apply to the cases of coercion of a representative, coercion of a state or conflict with an *existing* peremptory norm (*jus cogens*). Provisions in conflict with a *new* peremptory norm may be severable, however.[1]

8. *Application and Effects of Treaties*[2]

(a) *Justification for non-performance or suspension of performance.* The grounds for termination have been considered in section 6, and the requirements of essential validity in section 5. However, the content of those categories does not exhaust the matters relevant to justification for non-performance of obligations, an issue which can arise irrespective of validity or termination of the *source* of obligation, the treaty itself. The topic of justification belongs to the rubric of state responsibility (Chapter XX, section 13). Clearly a state may plead necessity, or *force majeure*, for example, the effects of natural catastrophe or foreign invasion.[3] In the same connexion legitimate military self-defence in case of armed conflict and civil strife provides a more particular justification.[4] Non-performance by way of legitimate reprisals raises highly controversial issues of the scope of reprisals in the modern law.[5] The Vienna Convention does not prejudge any question of state responsibility (Article 73).

(b) *Obligations and rights for third states.*[6] The maxim *pacta tertiis nec nocent nec prosunt* expresses the fundamental principle that a treaty applies only between the parties to it. The final draft

[1] See *Yrbk., I.L.C.* (1966), ii. 238–9, 261. For comment on this distinction see Sinclair, 19 *I.C.L.Q.* (1970), 67–8.

[2] Vienna Conv., Arts. 28–30, 34–8; I.L.C. draft, Arts. 55–64; 59 *A.J.* (1965), 210 seq.; Final Draft, Arts. 24–6, 30–4.

[3] See U.N. Secretariat Study, ST/LEG/13, 27 June 1977.

[4] See Fitzmaurice, *Yrbk., I.L.C.* (1959), ii. 44–5, 64–6.

[5] Fitzmaurice, ibid., pp. 45–6, 66–70; McNair, p. 573; Schwarzenberger i. 537. Cf. Article 2 (3) of the United Nations Charter.

[6] Vienna Conv., Arts. 34–8; I.L.C. draft, Arts. 58–62; 59 *A.J.* (1965), 217–27; Final Draft, Arts. 30–4; *Yrbk., I.L.C.* (1966), ii. 226–31; Fitzmaurice, *Yrbk., I.L.C.* (1960), ii. 69–107; Rousseau, *Principes généraux* i. 452–84; Jiménez de Aréchaga, 50 *A.J.* (1956), 338–57; McNair, pp. 309–21; Lauterpacht, *The Development of International Law by the International Court*, pp. 306–13; Guggenheim (2nd ed.), i. 197–204; Lachs, 92 Hague *Recueil* (1957, II), pp. 313–19; Detter, *Essays*, 100–18; Whiteman xiv. 331–53; Jennings, 20 *I.C.L.Q.* (1971), 433–50; Cahier, 143 Hague *Recueil* (1974, III), 589–736; Rozakis, 35 *Z.a.ö. R.u.V.* (1975), 1–40; *Répertoire suisse* i. 139–48.

of the International Law Commission and the Vienna Convention refer to this as the 'general rule', and it is a corollary of the principle of consent and of the sovereignty and independence of states. Article 34 of the Convention provides that 'a treaty does not create either obligations or rights for a third State without its consent'.

The existence and extent of exceptions to the general rule have been matters of acute controversy. The Commission was unanimous in the view that a treaty cannot by its own force create obligations for non-parties. The Commission did not accept the view that treaties creating 'objective regimes', as, for example, the demilitarization of a territory by treaty or a legal regime for a major waterway, had a specific place in the existing law.[1] Article 35 of the Vienna Convention provides that 'an obligation arises for a third State from a provision of a treaty if the parties to the treaty intend the provision to be the means of establishing the obligation and the third State expressly accepts that obligation in writing'.

However, two apparent exceptions to the principle in respect of obligations exist. Thus a rule in a treaty may become binding on non-parties if it becomes a part of international custom.[2] The Hague Conventions concerning rules of land warfare and, perhaps, certain treaties governing international waterways fall within this category. Further, a treaty may provide for lawful sanctions for violations of the law which are to be imposed on an aggressor state.[3] The Vienna Convention contains a reservation in regard to any obligation in relation to a treaty which arises for an aggressor state 'in consequence of measures taken in conformity with the Charter of the United Nations with reference to the aggression' (Article 75). The precise status of Article 2, paragraph 6, of the United Nations Charter is a matter of some interest. Kelsen,[4] among others, holds the view that the provision creates duties, and liabilities to sanctions under the enforcement provisions of the Charter, for non-members. Assuming that this was the intention of the draftsmen, the provision can only be reconciled with general principles by reference to the status of the principles in Article 2 as general or customary international law.

More controversial is the conferment of rights on third parties,

[1] See McNair, p. 310, and see further *supra*, pp. 279, 373.

[2] Vienna Conv., Art. 38; I.L.C. Final Draft, Art. 34; *Yrbk., I.L.C.* (1966), ii. 230.

[3] *Yrbk., I.L.C.* (1966), ii. 227, Art. 31, Commentary, para. 3; ibid., Art. 70, p. 268.

[4] *The Law of the United Nations*, pp. 106–10. *Contra*, Bindschedler, 108 Hague *Recueil* (1963, I), 403–7. Cf. McNair, pp. 216–18.

the *stipulation pour autrui*. Not infrequently treaties make provisions in favour of specified third states or for other states generally, as in the case, it would seem, of treaties concerning certain of the major international waterways, including, on one view, the Panama Canal.[1] The problem is to discover when, if at all, the right conferred becomes perfect and enforceable by the third state. The rule is that the third state only benefits in this sense if it expressly or implicitly assents to the creation of the right, a proposition accepted by the leading authorities.[2] Another view, supported by some members of the International Law Commission, was that the right which it was intended to create in favour of the third state was not conditional upon any specific act of acceptance by the latter.[3] Some authority for this view exists in the judgment in the *Free Zones* case.[4] In that case the rights contended for by Switzerland, viz., the benefit of a free customs zone in French territory under multipartite treaties to which France was a party, but Switzerland was not, rested in fact on agreements of 1815 and 1816 to which Switzerland was a party.[5] However, the statement by the Court appears to accept[6] the principle that the creation of rights for third states is a matter only of the intention of the grantor states.

In its Final Report the Commission took the view that the two opposing views, referred to above, did not differ substantially in their practical effects. Article 36 of the Vienna Convention creates a presumption as to the existence of the assent of the third state:

1. A right arises for a third State from a provision of a treaty if the parties to the treaty intend the provision to accord that right either to the third State, or to a group of States to which it belongs, or to all States, and the third State assents thereto. Its assent shall be presumed so long as the contrary is not indicated, unless the treaty otherwise provides.

2. A State exercising a right in accordance with paragraph 1 shall comply with the conditions for its exercise provided for in the treaty or established in conformity with the treaty.

The third state may, of course, disclaim any already inhering

[1] *Supra*, pp. 275–9.

[2] Rousseau and McNair *ut supra*. See the Final Draft, 1966, Art. 32.

[3] See Lauterpacht, Fitzmaurice, Jiménez de Aréchaga, *ut supra*.

[4] (1932), P.C.I.J., Ser. A/B, no. 46, pp. 147–8. See also the Committee of Jurists on the Aaland Islands question; 29 *A.J.* (1935), Suppl., Pt. III, pp. 927–8; and *Jews Deported from Hungary Case*, Int. L.R. 44, p. 301 at pp. 314–15.

[5] See McNair, pp. 311–12.

[6] See the comment by Cahier, op. cit., pp. 629–30, who refers to the ambiguity in the reference by the Court to acceptance of the right 'as such' by the third state.

right expressly or tacitly through failure to exercise the right. The right of a third state may not be revoked or modified by the parties if it is established that it was intended that this could only occur with the consent of the third state: Article 37 (2).

(c) *Treaties having incompatible provisions.*[1] The relation of treaties between the same parties and with overlapping provisions is primarily a matter of interpretation, aided by presumptions. Thus it is to be presumed that a later treaty prevails over an earlier treaty concerning the same subject-matter. A treaty may provide expressly that it is to prevail over subsequent incompatible treaties, as in the case of Article 103 of the Charter of the United Nations. Further, it is clear that a particular treaty may override others if it represents a norm of *jus cogens.*[2]

9. *Amendment and Modification of Treaties*[3]

The amendment[4] of treaties depends on the consent of the parties, and the issue is primarily one of politics. However, the lawyer may concern himself with procedures for amendment, as a facet of the large problem of peaceful change in international relations. Many treaties, including the Charter of the United Nations (Articles 108 and 109), provide for the procedure of amendment. In their rules and constituent instruments, international organizations create amendment procedures which in some cases show considerable sophistication. In the League Covenant (Article 19) and, less explicitly, in the Charter of the United Nations (Article 14) provision for peaceful change was made as a part of a scheme to avoid threats to the peace.

Apart from amendment, a treaty may undergo 'modification' when some of the parties conclude an '*inter se* agreement' altering the application of the treaty between themselves alone.[5]

[1] Vienna Conv., Arts. 30, 59; I.L.C. draft, Art. 63; 59 *A.J.* (1965), 227–40; Final Draft, Arts. 26, 56; *Yrbk., I.L.C.* (1966), ii. 214–17, 252–3; Lauterpacht, ibid. (1953), ii. 156; ibid. (1954), ii. 133; Fitzmaurice, ibid. (1958), ii. 27, 41–5; Waldock, ibid. (1963), ii. 53–61; McNair, pp. 215–24; Rousseau, *Principes généraux* i. 765–814; Jenks, 30 *B.Y.* (1953), 401–53; Cahier, 76 *R.G.D.I.P.* (1972), 670–2.

[2] *Supra*, p. 512.

[3] Vienna Conv., Arts. 39–41; I.L.C. draft, Arts. 65–8; 59 *A.J.* (1965), 434–45; Final Draft, Arts. 35–8; *Yrbk., I.L.C.* (1966), ii. 231–6; *Annuaire de l'Inst.* 49 (1961), i. 229–91; 52 (1967), i. 5–401; Handbook of Final Clauses, ST/LEG/6, pp. 130–52; Hoyt, *The Unanimity Rule in the Revision of Treaties* (1959); Blix, 5 *I.C.L.Q.* (1956), 447–65, 581–96; Whiteman xiv. 436–42; Detter, *Essays*, pp. 71–82.

[4] There is no distinction of quality between 'amendment' of particular provisions and 'revision' of the treaty as a whole.

[5] Vienna Conv., Art. 41.

Modification may also result from the conclusion of a subsequent treaty[1] or the emergence of a new peremptory norm of general international law.[2] The Final Draft of the International Law Commission[3] provided that 'a treaty may be modified by subsequent practice in the application of the treaty establishing the agreement of the parties to modify its provisions'. This article was rejected at the Vienna Conference on the ground that such a rule would create instability.[4] This result is unsatisfactory. In the first place Article 39 of the Convention provides that a treaty may be amended by agreement without requiring any formality for the expression of agreement. Secondly, a consistent practice may provide cogent evidence of *common* consent to a change. Thirdly, modification of this type occurs in practice: witness the inclusion in practice of fishing zones as a form of contiguous zone for the purposes of the Territorial Sea Convention.[5] The process of interpretation through subsequent practice (section 10 (f)) is legally distinct from modification, although the distinction is often rather fine.

10. *Interpretation of Treaties*[6]

(a) *Competence to interpret.* Obviously the parties have competence to interpret a treaty, but this is subject to the operation of other rules of the law. The treaty itself may confer competence on an *ad hoc* tribunal or the International Court. The Charter of

[1] See *supra*, p. 603.

[2] See pp. 512–15.

[3] Art. 38, *Yrbk., I.L.C.* (1966), ii. 236.

[4] *Official Records, First Session*, pp. 207–15. See also Kearney and Dalton, 64 *A.J.* (1970), 525.

[5] *Supra*, p. 215. See also U.S. and France, *Air Transport Services Agreement Arbitration*, 1963, Int. L.R. 38, p. 182; *R.I.A.A.* xvi. 5; Award, Part IV, sect. 5.

[6] Rousseau, *Principes généraux*, pp. 631–764; id., *Droit international public* i (1970); Guggenheim, *Traité* (2nd ed.), i. 245–68; Whiteman xiv. 353–410; McDougal, Lasswell, and Miller, *The Interpretation of Agreements and World Public Order* (1967); McNair, Chaps. XX–XXVIII; Fitzmaurice, 28 *B.Y.* (1951), 1–28; id., 33 *B.Y.* (1957), 203–38; Lauterpacht, *The Development of International Law by the International Court*, esp. pp. 116–41; id., 26 *B.Y.* (1949), 48–85; *Annuaire de l'Inst.* 43 (1950), i. 366–460; 44 (1952), ii. 359–401; 46 (1956), 317–49; de Visscher, *Problèmes d'interprétation judiciare en droit international public* (1963); Sinclair, 12 *I.C.L.Q.* (1963), 508–51; Degan, *L'Interprétation des accords en droit international* (1963); Stone, *Sydney L.R.* (1953–4), 344–68; Hogg, 43 *Minnesota L.R.* (1958–9), 369–441, ibid., 44 (1959–60), 5–73; Berlia, 114 Hague *Recueil* (1965, I), 287–332; Jennings, 121 Hague *Recueil* (1967, II), 544–52; Bernhardt, *Die Auslegung völkerrechtlicher Verträge* (1963); Sinclair, 19 *I.C.L.Q.* (1970), 60–6; Jacobs, 18 *I.C.L.Q.* (1969), 318–46; Schwarzenberger, *International Law and Order*, pp. 110–28; Gross, *A.S.I.L. Proceedings* (1969), pp. 108–22; Rosenne, 5 *Columbia Journ. of Transnational Law* (1966), 205–30; Yasseen, 151 Hague *Recueil* (1976, III), 1–114; Haraszti, *Some Fundamental Problems of the Law of Treaties* (1973), pp. 13–228.

the United Nations is interpreted by its organs, which may seek advisory opinions from the Court of the Organization.[1]

(b) *The status of 'rules of interpretation'*. Jurists are in general cautious about formulating a code of 'rules of interpretation', since the 'rules' may become unwieldy instruments instead of the flexible aids which are required.[2] Many of the 'rules' and 'principles' offered are general, question-begging, and contradictory. As with statutory interpretation, a choice of a 'rule', for example of 'effectiveness' or 'restrictive interpretation', may in a given case involve a preliminary choice of meaning rather than a guide to interpretation. The International Law Commission in its work confined itself to isolating 'the comparatively few general principles which appear to constitute general rules for the interpretation of treaties'.

(c) *The text and the intentions of the parties*. The Commission and the Institute of International Law[3] have taken the view that what matters is the intention of the parties *as expressed in the text*, which is the best guide to the more recent common intention of the parties. The alternative approach regards the intentions of the parties as an independent basis of interpretation. The jurisprudence of the International Court supports the textual approach,[4] and it is adopted in substance in the relevant provisions of the Vienna Convention:[5]

ARTICLE 31

General rule of interpretation

1. A treaty shall be interpreted in good faith in accordance with the ordinary meaning to be given to the terms of the treaty in their context and in the light of its object and purpose.

2. The context for the purpose of the interpretation of a treaty shall comprise, in addition to the text, including its preamble and annexes:

(a) any agreement relating to the treaty which was made between all the parties in connection with the conclusion of the treaty;

(b) any instrument which was made by one or more parties in connection with the conclusion of the treaty and accepted by the other parties as an instrument related to the treaty.

[1] See further, *infra*, p. 701.

[2] For the case in favour of having rules: Beckett, *Annuaire de l'Inst.* 43 (1950), i. 435–40.

[3] *Ut supra*, p. 502. The first rapporteur of the Institute, Lauterpacht, preferred more direct investigation of intention.

[4] See Fitzmaurice, *ut supra*.

[5] On interpretation of treaties authenticated in two or more languages see Art. 33; and Hardy, 37 *B.Y.* (1961), 72–155.

3. There shall be taken into account, together with the context:

(a) any subsequent agreement between the parties regarding the interpretation of the treaty or the application of its provisions;

(b) any subsequent practice in the application of the treaty which establishes the agreement of the parties regarding its interpretation;

(c) any relevant rules of international law applicable in the relations between the parties.

4. A special meaning shall be given to a term if it is established that the parties so intended.

ARTICLE 32

Supplementary means of interpretation

Recourse may be had to supplementary means of interpretation, including the preparatory work of the treaty and the circumstances of its conclusion, in order to confirm the meaning resulting from the application of article 31, or to determine the meaning when the interpretation according to article 31:

(a) leaves the meaning ambiguous or obscure; or

(b) leads to a result which is manifestly absurd or unreasonable.

This economical code of principles follows exactly the Final Draft of the International Law Commission.[1] At the Vienna Conference the United States proposed an amendment with the object of removing the apparent hierarchy of sources by combining the two Articles, and thus giving more scope to preparatory work and the circumstances in which the treaty was concluded. This proposal received little support. In its Commentary[2] the Commission emphasized that the application of the means of interpretation in the first article would be a single combined operation: hence the heading 'General rule' in the singular. The various elements present in any given case would interact. The Commission pointed out that the two articles should operate in conjunction, and would not have the effect of drawing a rigid line between 'supplementary' and other means of interpretation. At the same time the distinction itself was justified since the elements of interpretation in the first article all relate to the agreement between the parties 'at the time when or after it received authentic expression in the text'. Preparatory work did not have the same authentic character 'however valuable it may sometimes be in throwing light on the expression of agreement in the text'.

(d) *Textual approach: natural and ordinary meaning.*[3] The first

[1] Arts. 27, 28. [2] *Yrbk., I.L.C.* (1966), ii. 219–20.

[3] There seems to be no real difference between the principle of actuality (or textuality) and the principle of natural and ordinary meaning in the scheme of Fitzmaurice.

principle stated in Article 31 of the Vienna Convention is that 'a treaty shall be interpreted in good faith in accordance with the ordinary meaning to be given to the terms of the treaty . . .'.[1] In the advisory opinion on the *Polish Postal Service in Danzig*[2] the Permanent Court observed that the postal service which Poland was entitled to establish in Danzig under treaty was not confined to operation inside the postal building, as 'postal service' must be interpreted 'in its ordinary sense so as to include the normal functions of a postal service'. A corollary of the principle of ordinary meaning is the principle of integration: the meaning must emerge in the context of the treaty as a whole[3] and in the light of its objects and purposes.[4] Another corollary is the principle of contemporaneity: the language of the treaty must be interpreted in the light of the rules of general international law in force at the time of its conclusion,[5] and also in the light of the contemporaneous meaning of terms.[6] The doctrine of ordinary meaning involves only a presumption: a meaning other than the ordinary meaning may be established, but the proponent of the special meaning has a burden of proof.[7] Other logical presumptions exist. Thus general words following or perhaps preceding special words are limited to the genus indicated by the special words (the *ejusdem generis* doctrine); and express mention excludes other items (*expressio unius est exclusio alterius*).

(e) *Context to be used*. The context of a treaty for purposes of interpretation comprises, in addition to the treaty, including its preamble[8] and annexes, any agreement or instrument related to the treaty and drawn up in connexion with its conclusion.[9]

(f) *Subsequent practice*. The parties may make an agreement regarding interpretation of the treaty. It follows also that reference may be made to 'subsequent practice in the application of

[1] See the *Admissions* case, I.C.J. Reports (1950), p. 8.

[2] (1925), P.C.I.J., Ser. B, no. 11 at p. 37. See also the *Eastern Greenland* case (1933), P.C.I.J., Ser. A/B, no. 53 at p. 49; U.S.–Italy Arbitration, *Interpretation of Air Transport Services Agreement*, *R.I.A.A.* xvi. 75 at p. 91.

[3] See the Vienna Conv., Art. 31 (1); *Competence of the I.L.O. to Regulate Agricultural Labour* (1922), P.C.I.J., Ser. B, nos. 2 and 3, p. 23; *Free Zones* case (1932), Ser. A/B, no. 46, p. 140.

[4] See the Vienna Conv., Art. 31 (1); *U.S. Nationals in Morocco*, I.C.J. Reports (1952), pp. 183–4, 197–8.

[5] See the *Grisbadarna* case, *R.I.A.A.* xi. 159–60. Generally on inter-temporal law *supra*, p. 131.

[6] *U.S. Nationals in Morocco*, *supra*, p. 132. See also Fitzmaurice, 33 *B.Y.* 225–7.

[7] For critical comment on the concept of natural or plain meaning see Lauterpacht, *The Development of International Law by the International Court*, pp. 52–60.

[8] See Fitzmaurice, 33 *B.Y.* 227–8.

[9] See the Vienna Conv., Art. 31 (2).

the treaty which clearly establishes the understanding of all the parties regarding its interpretation'.[1] Subsequent practice by individual parties also has some probative value.

(g) *Practice of organizations.*[2] In a series of important advisory opinions the International Court has made considerable use of the subsequent practice of organizations in deciding highly controversial issues of interpretation.[3] Two points arise. The first is that constitutionally members who were outvoted in the organs concerned may not be bound by the practice.[4] Secondly, the practice of political organs involves elements of politics and opportunism, and what should be referred to, subject to the constitutional issue, is the reasoning *behind* the practice, which can reveal its legal relevance, if any.[5]

(h) *Preparatory work.* When the textual approach, on the principles referred to already, either leaves the meaning ambiguous or obscure, or leads to a manifestly absurd or unreasonable result, recourse may be had to further means of interpretation, including the preparatory work of the treaty and the circumstances of its conclusion.[6] Moreover, such recourse may be had to verify or confirm a meaning that emerges as a result of the textual approach.[7] In general the International Court, and the Permanent Court before it, have refused to resort to preparatory work if the text is sufficiently clear in itself.[8] On a number of occasions the Court has used preparatory work to confirm a conclusion reached by other means.[9] Preparatory work is an aid to be employed with

[1] See the Vienna Conv., Art. 31 (3) (b); *Yrbk., I.L.C.* (1966), ii. 221, para. 15; *Air Transport Services Agreement Arbitration* (1963), Int. L.R. 38, p. 182 at pp. 245–8, 256–8; *Air Transport Services Agreement Arbitration* (1965), *R.I.A.A.* xvi, p. 75 at pp. 99–101. See also Fitzmaurice, 28 *B.Y.* 20–1; 33 *B.Y.* 223–5, where subsequent practice is commended for its 'superior *reliability*' as an indication of meaning. For the jurisprudence see also Rousseau, pp. 704–7, and McNair, pp. 424–9. See further Cot, 70 *R.G.D.I.P.* (1966), 632–66.

[2] See Engel, 16 *I.C.L.Q.* (1967), 865–910; Judge Spender, *Expenses* case, I.C.J. Reports (1962), pp. 187 seq.; Judge Fitzmaurice, ibid., pp. 201–3.

[3] *Competence of the General Assembly*, I.C.J. Reports (1950), p. 9; *I.M.C.O.* case, ibid. (1960), pp. 167 seq.; and the *Expenses* case, ibid. (1962), pp. 157 seq.

[4] See further *infra*, pp. 696 seq.

[5] See the sep. op. of Judge Spender in the *Expenses* case, pp. 187 seq. The I.L.C. did not deal with the problem in the present draft: 59 *A.J.* (1965), 456 (para. 14).

[6] See the Vienna Conv., Art. 32, *supra*; *Yrbk., I.L.C.* (1966), ii. 222–3, paras. 18–20; Jennings, 121 Hague *Recueil*, pp. 550–2.

[7] See further Lauterpacht, *The Development of International Law by the International Court*, pp. 116–41; 48 *Harv. L.R.* (1935), 549–91; McNair, Chap. XXIII.

[8] *Admissions* case, I.C.J. Reports (1948), p. 63; *Competence of the General Assembly*, ibid. (1950), p. 8. See Fitzmaurice, 28 *B.Y.* 10–13; 33 *B.Y.*, 215–20; Hambro, *Case Law of the International Court*, various vols., Pt. I, Chap. II (e).

[9] For example, *Convention of 1919 concerning the Work of Women at Night* (1932), P.C.I.J., Ser. A/B, no. 50, p. 380; Bishop, p. 166.

discretion, since its use may detract from the textual approach, and, particularly in the case of multilateral agreements, the records of conference proceedings, treaty drafts, and so on may be confused or inconclusive. The International Law Commission has taken the view that states acceding to a treaty and not taking part in its drafting cannot claim for themselves the inadmissibility of the preparatory work, which could have been examined before accession.[1]

(i) *Restrictive interpretation.*[2] In a number of cases the Permanent Court committed itself to the principle that provisions implying a limitation of state sovereignty should receive restrictive interpretation.[3] As a general principle of interpretation this is question-begging and should not be allowed to overshadow the textual approach: in recent years tribunals have given less scope to the principle.[4] However, in cases which give rise to issues concerning regulation of rights and territorial privileges the principle may operate:[5] in these instances it is not an 'aid to interpretation' but an independent principle. The principle did not find a place in the provisions of the Vienna Convention.

(j) *Effective interpretation.*[6] The principle of effective interpretation is often invoked, and suffers from the same organic defects as the principle of restrictive interpretation. The International Law Commission did not give a separate formulation of the principle, considering that, as a matter of the existing law, it was reflected sufficiently in the doctrines of interpretation in good faith in accordance with the ordinary meaning of the text (paragraph (d) above).[7] The International Court has generally subordinated the principle to the textual approach.[8] In the *Peace Treaties* case[9] the Court made this clear and avoided revision of the treaties by refusing to remedy a fault in the machinery for settlement of disputes not curable by reference to the texts themselves.

[1] Differing thus from the *River Oder Commission* case (1929), P.C.I.J., Ser. A, no. 23. See further Sinclair, 12 *I.C.L.Q.* (1963), at pp. 512–17; *Arbitral Comm. on Property, etc., in Germany*, Int. L.R. 29, p. 442 at pp. 460–8.

[2] See Lauterpacht, 26 *B.Y.* (1949), 48–85; id., *The Development of International Law by the International Court*, pp. 300–6; McNair, pp. 765–6.

[3] e.g. *River Oder Commission* case, *ut supra*, p. 26.

[4] See, however, *De Pascale Case, R.I.A.A.* xvi. 227; *De Leon Case*, ibid., 239. Cf. *Droutzkoy Case*, ibid., p. 273, at p. 292.

[5] *Supra*, pp. 364 seq.

[6] See n. 3, p. 627, *supra*; *Annuaire de l'Inst.* 43 (1950), i. 402–23; McNair, Chap. XXI.

[7] *Yrbk., I.L.C.* (1966), ii. 219, para. 6.

[8] Fitzmaurice, 28 *B.Y.* 19–20; 33 *B.Y.*, 211, 220–3.

[9] I.C.J. Reports (1950), p. 229. See also the *South West Africa* cases (Preliminary Objections), ibid. (1962), pp. 511–13 (diss. op. of Judges Spender and Fitzmaurice); *South West Africa* cases (Second Phase), ibid. (1966), pp. 36, 47–8.

(k) *The teleological approach.*[1] The International Law Commission and the Vienna Convention gave a cautious qualification to the textual approach by permitting recourse to further means of interpretation when the latter 'leads to a result which is manifestly absurd or unreasonable in the light of the objects and purposes of the treaty'.[2] Somewhat distinct from this procedure is the more radical teleological approach according to which a court determines what the objects and purposes are and then resolves any ambiguity of meaning by importing the substance 'necessary' to give effect to the purposes of the treaty. This may involve a judicial implementation of purposes in a fashion not contemplated in fact by the parties. At the same time the textual approach in practice often leaves the decision maker with a choice of possible meanings and in exercising that choice it is impossible to keep considerations of policy out of account. Many issues of interpretation are by no means narrow technical enquiries.

In advisory opinions concerning powers of organs of the United Nations, the International Court has adopted a principle of institutional effectiveness and has freely implied the existence of powers which in its view were consistent with the purposes of the Charter.[3] This tendency reached its apogee in the opinion given in the *Expenses* case, and the problems raised by this decision are considered elsewhere.[4]

The teleological approach has many pitfalls. However, in a small specialized organization, with supranational elements and efficient procedures for amendment of constituent treaties and rules and regulations, the teleological approach, with its aspect of judicial legislation, may be thought to have a constructive role to play. Yet the practice of the Court of the European Communities has not shown any special attraction to this approach,[5] and it would seem that the delicate treaty structure with its supranational element dictates a generally textual and relatively conservative approach to texts. In any case the Court has a special

[1] See Fitzmaurice, 28 *B.Y.*, 7–8, 13–14; 33 *B.Y.*, 207–9.

[2] I.L.C., Final Draft, Art. 28; Vienna Conv., Art. 32.

[3] The cases are cited *infra*, pp. 686–8. See further the *International Status of South West Africa*, I.C.J. Reports (1950), p. 128, the *South West Africa* cases, ibid. (1962), p. 319, and the *Namibia Opinion*, ibid. (1971), p. 16 at pp. 47–50. See also the opinions of Fitzmaurice, in the *Expenses* case, I.C.J. Reports (1962), pp. 198 seq. See further Gordon, 59 *A.J.* (1965), 794–833. Cf., however, the Joint Dissent of Fitzmaurice and Spender in the *South West Africa* cases, I.C.J. Reports (1962), at pp. 511–22; and the view of the Court in the *South West Africa* cases (Second Phase), I.C.J. Reports (1966), pp. 36, 47–8.

[4] *Infra*, pp. 698 seq.

[5] On the practice: Sinclair, op. cit., pp. 517–24; McMahon, 37 *B.Y.* (1961), 320–50. Generally on the European Court see *supra*, pp. 583–4.

character as a 'community' rather than an 'international' court, and in terms of functions it approximates to an administrative tribunal employing principles which reflect administrative law concepts of legal systems within the Community.

11. *Classification of Treaties*

A number of distinguished writers have developed or supported classifications of treaties. Lord McNair long ago pointed to the variety of functions which the treaty performs and the need to free ourselves from the traditional notion that the treaty is governed by a single undifferentiated set of rules.[1] As he suggests, some treaties, dispositive of territory and rights in relation to territory, are like conveyances in private law. Treaties involving bargains between a few states are like contracts; whereas the multilateral treaty creating either a set of rules, such as the Hague Conventions on the Law of War, or an institution, such as the Copyright Union, is 'law-making'. Moreover, the treaty constituting an institution is akin to a charter of incorporation. It is certainly fruitful to contemplate the unique features of parts of the large terrain to which the law of treaties applies and to expect the development of specialized rules. Thus it is the case that the effect of war between parties varies according to the type of treaty involved. However, Lord McNair and others have tended to support the position that the genus of treaty (the contents of the genus may themselves be a matter of dispute) produces fairly *general* effects on the applicable rules. Thus the law-making character of a treaty is said (1) to rule out recourse to preparatory work as an aid to interpretation; (2) to avoid recognition by one party of other parties as states or governments; and (3) to render the doctrine of *rebus sic stantibus* inapplicable.[2] More especially, Lord McNair,[3] Sir Gerald Fitzmaurice,[4] and Sir Humphrey Waldock,[5] among others, have regarded certain treaties as creating an 'objective regime' creating rights and duties for third states. Examples given include the treaty regimes for international waterways,[6] regimes for demilitarization,[7] and

[1] 11 *B.Y.* (1930), 100–18; also in *The Law of Treaties* (1961), pp. 739–54. See also Rousseau, *Principes généraux* i. 132–41, 677, 728–64; Vitta, *Ann. français* (1960), pp. 225–38. On the special role of multilateral treaties see Lachs, 92 Hague *Recueil* (1957, II), pp. 233–341.

[2] See McNair, *ut supra*.

[3] *Law of Treaties* (1961), Chap. XIV.

[4] *Yrbk., I.L.C.* (1960), ii. 96 seq. (with considerable caution).

[5] 106 Hague *Recueil* (1962, II), 78–81 (with some caution).

[6] *Supra*, pp. 270–9.

[7] See the Committee of Jurists on the Aaland Islands question, 29 *A.J.* (1935), Suppl., Pt. III, pp. 927–8.

treaties creating organizations.[1] Significantly the International Law Commission deliberately avoided any classification of treaties along broad lines and rejected the concept of the 'objective regime' in relation to the effects of treaties on non-parties.[2] The Commission has accepted specialized rules in a few instances,[3] but has been, correctly it would seem, empirical in its approach. In formulating the general rules of interpretation the Commission did not consider it necessary to make a distinction between 'law-making' and other treaties.[4] The drafts of the Commission and the Vienna Convention treat the law of treaties as essentially a unity.[5] The evidence is that jurists are today less willing to accept the more doctrinal versions of the distinction between treaty-contract (*vertrag*) and treaty-law (*vereinbarung*),[6] the latter category representing multilateral treaties making rules for future conduct and framing a generally agreed legislative policy. The contrast intended is thus between the bilateral political bargain and the 'legislative act' produced by a broad international conference. But in fact the distinction is less clear: for example, it is known that political issues and cautious bargaining lie behind law-making efforts like the Geneva Conventions on the Law of the Sea. Further, the distinction obscures the real differences between treaty-making and legislation in a municipal system.[7]

12. *Participation in General Multilateral Treaties*

In an early draft (Article 1 (1) (c)) the International Law Commission defines a 'general multilateral treaty' as 'a multilateral treaty which concerns general norms of international law and deals with matters of general interest to States as a whole'. Such a treaty has been described as 'the nearest thing we yet have to a general statute in international law'.[8] United Nations practice in convening a conference to draw up a treaty is to leave the question of composition to a political organ, the General Assem-

[1] Cf. the *Reparation* case, *infra*, p. 678.

[2] *Supra*, section 8 (b); *infra*, section 12. See also, in the context of aids to interpretation, 59 *A.J.* (1965), 449–50 (commentary on the draft).

[3] See the Vienna Conv., Art. 62 (2), *supra*, p. 616. Cf. the provisions on reservations, *supra*, pp. 607–8.

[4] *Yrbk., I.L.C.* (1966), ii. 219, para. 6. But note the view of Berlia, 114 Hague *Recueil*, 287 at p. 331.

[5] See Dehaussy, *Recueil d'études en hommage à Guggenheim*, pp. 305–26.

[6] For the history see Lauterpacht, *Private Law Sources*, para. 70.

[7] Waldock, op. cit., pp. 74–6.

[8] Ibid., p. 81. See also Lachs, *ut supra*.

bly, and a number of Communist states[1] have been excluded as a result. In the Commission it was proposed that states should have a right to become parties to this type of treaty. This solution was adopted in a provisional draft in the insubstantial form that the right existed except where the treaty or the rules of an international organization provide otherwise.[2] The Final Draft of the Commission contained no provision on the subject and amendments intended to give 'all States a right to participate in multilateral treaties' were defeated at the Vienna Conference.[3]

[1] For a long time Mongolia; also China, East Germany, North Vietnam, and North Korea. These states were not represented at the Law of the Sea Conference in 1958.

[2] I.L.C. draft, Art. 8; *Yrbk., I.L.C.* (1962), ii. 167–9; Waldock, ibid., pp. 53–8.

[3] *Yrbk., I.L.C.* (1966), ii. 200; U.N. Secretariat Working Paper, A/CN.4/245, 23 April 1971, pp. 131–4. See also Lukashuk, 135 Hague *Recueil* (1972, I), 231–328.

CHAPTER XXVI

OTHER TRANSACTIONS; AGENCY AND REPRESENTATION

1. *Informal Agreements*

THE law of treaties does not contain mandatory requirements of form, and the rapporteurs on the subject of the International Law Commission have admitted the validity of unwritten agreements.[1] In the *Panevezys-Saldutiskis Railway* case[2] the Permanent Court accepted the view that participation by two states, parties to a dispute, in the adoption of a resolution by the Council of the League of Nations constituted a binding 'engagement'. Again, in the *Eastern Greenland* case[3] the Court placed reliance in part on an oral statement by the Norwegian Minister of Foreign Affairs, Mr. Ihlen, to the Danish Minister accredited to Norway, relating to Norwegian acceptance of the Danish claim to the whole of Greenland. Though apparently unilateral, the Court regarded this statement, and a Danish disclaimer of interests in Spitzbergen, as interdependent.

2. *Quasi-Legislative Acts*

The nature of a mandate agreement[4] was in issue in the *South West Africa* cases (Preliminary Objections).[5] The applicant states founded jurisdiction on its nature as 'a treaty or convention in force' providing for reference of disputes to the Permanent Court and kept alive in this respect by Article 37 of the Statute of the present Court.[6] In its preliminary objections South Africa, the mandatory state, contended, *inter alia*, that the Mandate was not *ab initio* a 'treaty or convention', since its original authority was a resolution of the Council of the League of Nations. The Court held that the Mandate was an agreement in spite of the

[1] See the sep. op. of Judge Jessup, *South West Africa* cases (Preliminary Objections), I.C.J. Reports (1962), pp. 402–5.

[2] (1931), P.C.I.J., Ser. A/B, no. 42, pp. 115, 116. See also McNair, *Law of Treaties* (1961), p. 14.

[3] (1933), P.C.I.J., Ser. A/B, no. 53 at pp. 71–3. See also McNair, op. cit., pp. 9–10; and Hambro, *Festschrift für Jean Spiropoulos*, pp. 227–36.

[4] See *supra*, p. 566.

[5] I.C.J. Reports (1962), p. 319. Cf. *South West Africa* cases (Second Phase), I.C.J. Reports (1966), p. 6; *Namibia* Opinion, ibid. (1971), p. 16.

[6] See *infra*, p. 720.

confirmation by the Council of the League.[1] However, in a joint dissenting opinion, Judges Spender and Fitzmaurice took a different view, concluding that the Mandate was 'a quasi-legislative act of the League Council'.[2] As the Court itself pointed out, the Mandate Agreement had special features. These may be described as 'quasi-legislative': but it does not follow that it is not a 'treaty or convention', for certain purposes at least. Similar problems arise in the case of trusteeship agreements under Chapter XII of the United Nations Charter.[3] The Permanent Court assimilated mandates to treaties for purposes of interpretation.[4] However, in the context of interpretation such quasi-legislative acts cannot be approached in quite the same way as bilateral treaties.[5]

3. *Unilateral Acts*

(a) *In general.* Acts and conduct of governments may not be directed towards the formation of agreements and yet are capable of creating legal effects in a great many ways. The formation of customary rules and the law of recognition are two of the more prominent categories concerned with the 'unilateral' acts of states. Some authors have been prepared to bring unilateral acts, including protest, promise, renunciation, and recognition, within a general concept of 'legal acts', either contractual or unilateral, based upon the manifestation of will by a legal person.[6] The writer is of opinion that this approach may provide a useful framework for discussion of problems and yet may obscure the variety of legal relations involved. Moreover, analysis in terms of categories of 'promise', 'protest', and the like is superficial, and tends to confuse conditioning facts and legal consequences. In terms of result, a great deal will depend on the context in which a 'protest' occurs, including the surrounding circumstances and especially the effect of relevant rules of law.[7]

[1] At pp. 330–1 of the judgment.

[2] Ibid., pp. 482–90. See also the diss. op. of Judge Basdevant, p. 461. Cf. sep. op. of Judge Morelli, *Northern Cameroons* case, I.C.J. Reports (1963), p. 142; and *Namibia* Opinion, ibid. (1971), pp. 266–8, Judge Fitzmaurice, diss. op.; pp. 338–9, Judge Gros, diss. op.

[3] See Detter, *Law Making by International Organizations*, pp. 187–201.

[4] *Mavrommatis Palestine Concessions* case, P.C.I.J., Ser. A, No. 2.

[5] See Hardy, 37 *B.Y.* (1961), 76–8.

[6] See especially Suy, *Les Actes juridiques unilatéraux en droit international public* (1962), at p. 22. See further Dehaussy, 92 *J.D.I.* (1965), 41–66; Kiss, 65 *R.G.D.I.P.* (1961), 317–31; Rousseau i. (1970), 416–32; Jacqué, *Elements pour une théorie de l'acte juridique en droit international publique* (1972); Verzijl, *International Law in Historical Perspective* vi (1973), 105–11.

[7] See the treatment by Venturini, 112 Hague *Recueil* (1964, II), 367–467. See also Reuter, 103 Hague *Recueil* (1961, II), 547–82.

(b) *Unilateral declarations.* A state may evidence a clear intention to accept obligations *vis-à-vis* certain other states by a public declaration which is not an offer or otherwise dependent on reciprocal undertakings from the states concerned.[1] Apparently the terms of such a declaration will determine the conditions under which it can be revoked.[2] In 1957 the Egyptian Government made a Declaration on the Suez Canal and the Arrangements for its Operation[3] in which certain obligations were accepted. The Declaration was communicated to the Secretary-General of the United Nations together with a letter which explained that the Declaration was to be considered as an 'international instrument' and registered as such by the Secretariat. Such a declaration may implicitly or otherwise require acceptance by other states as a condition of validity.[4]

In the *Nuclear Tests Case* (Australia v. France)[5] the International Court held that France was legally bound by publicly given undertakings, made on behalf of the French Government, to cease the conduct of atmospheric nuclear tests. The criteria of obligation were: the intention of the State making the declaration that it should be bound according to its terms; and that the undertaking be given publicly. There was no requirement of a *quid pro quo* or of any subsequent acceptance or response. With one exception[6] the Judges expressing views in separate or dissenting opinions made no reference to this matter. As a result of the French undertaking, so interpreted, the dispute, it was held, had disappeared and 'the claim advanced by Australia no longer has any object'. Whilst the principle applied by the Court—that a unilateral declaration may have certain legal effects—is not new, when the declaration is not directed to a specific State or States but is expressed *erga omnes*, as here, the detection of an intention to be legally bound, and of the structure of such intention, involves very careful appreciation of the facts. In the

[1] See McNair, op. cit., p. 11; Brierly, *Yrbk., I.L.C.* (1950), ii. 227; Lauterpacht, ibid. (1953), ii. 101 seq.; Judge Jessup, sep op., *South West Africa* cases (Preliminary Objections), I.C.J. Reports (1962), pp. 402–4, 417–18; Fitzmaurice, 33 *B.Y.* (1957), pp. 229–30; *Répertoire suisse* i. 213 (and see iii. 1326).

[2] Cf. Fitzmaurice, *Yrbk., I.L.C.* (1960), ii. 79 (Art. 12), 81 (Art. 22), 91, 105.

[3] *Supra*, p. 276.

[4] Cf. the Austrian Declaration of 1955, contained in a Statute on Austria's permanent neutrality; on which see Kunz, 50 *A.J.* (1956), 418–25.

[5] I.C.J. Reports, 1974, p. 253 at pp. 267–71. See also *Nuclear Tests Case* (New Zealand v. France), ibid., p. 457 at pp. 472–5. For comment see: Carbone, 1 *Ital. Yrbk.* (1975), 166–72; Rubin, 71 *A.J.* (1977), 1–30

[6] Judge de Castro, diss. op., I.C.J. Reports, 1974, p. 372 at pp. 373–4, accepting the principle, but deciding on the facts that the French statements lay within 'the political domain'.

North Sea Continental Shelf Cases[1] the International Court stated that unilateral assumption of the obligations of a convention by conduct was 'not lightly to be presumed', and that 'a very consistent course of conduct' was required in such a situation.

(c) *Reliance on voidable transactions.* A specific instance of waiver, reinforced by estoppel (see *infra*), is provided for in Article 45 of the Vienna Convention on the Law of Treaties:[2]

> A State may no longer invoke a ground for invalidating, terminating, withdrawing from or suspending the operation of a treaty under articles 46 to 50[3] or articles 60 and 62,[4] if, after becoming aware of the facts:
>
> (a) it shall have expressly agreed that the treaty is valid or remains in force or continues in operation, as the case may be; or
>
> (b) it must by reason of its conduct be considered as having acquiesced in the validity of the treaty or in its maintenance in force or in operation, as the case may be.

(d) *Evidence of inconsistent rights.* Unilateral declarations involve, in principle at least, concessions which are intentional, public, coherent, and conclusive of the issues. However, acts of acquiescence and official statements may have probative value as admissions of rights inconsistent with the claims of the declarant in a situation of competing interests, such acts individually not being conclusive of the issues. Thus in the *Eastern Greenland* case[5] the Court attached significance to the fact that Norway had become a party to several treaties which referred to Danish sovereignty over Greenland as a whole, Norway having contended that Danish sovereignty had not been extended over the whole of Greenland. The legal significance of this type of admission depends on the aspect of inconsistency between the admission and the position later taken on the disposition of legal rights in a sphere in which the claims are in conflict.

(e) *Estoppel and status.* On the basis of stability in matters of status, rather than principles of good faith and consistency, nationality[6] and diplomatic protection[7] may rest on estoppel. Official conferment of status may be upheld although in the first instance acquisition of the status rested on error of fact or law.

[1] I.C.J. Reports, 1969, p. 4 at p. 25 (paras. 27–8).

[2] See the Final Draft, 1966, Art. 42; *Yrbk., I.L.C.* (1966), ii. 239, Commentary.

[3] *Supra*, pp. 610–12. [4] *Supra*, pp. 615–17.

[5] (1933), P.C.I.J., Ser. A/B, No. 53, pp. 70–1. See also the *Minquiers* case, I.C.J. Reports, 1953, p. 47 at pp. 66–7, 71–2, and see further *supra*, pp. 163–5.

[6] *Supra*, pp. 403–4.

[7] On the relation of this and nationality, *supra*, pp. 401–2. See further *British Digest* v. 89, 369–70, 374, 379–80, 461, 467–73.

This form of estoppel does not depend on reliance having been placed upon the representation by another state.[1]

(f) *Opposable situations.* Acceptance of the existence of rights inconsistent with those contended for provides evidence for the competitor when the dispute is resolved subsequently (para. (d), *supra*). This acceptance may be circumstantial and indirect. However, when the competitor's claim or encroachment is palpable, and a dispute is already known to exist, the other side may damage its case seriously by its recognition or acquiescence. The counterpart to the latter is the protest of a state disputing the claim or, at the least, reserving its rights. Acquiescence,[2] recognition, or implied consent may have the result of conceding lawfully held rights to a usurper, subject to the operation of rules of *jus cogens* preventing this.[3] A similar yet somewhat distinct role appears when a state is claiming rights on a basis which is plausible to some extent, and yet rests either on an ambiguous state of fact, or on a contention that the law has changed or provides an exception in its favour. Here acquiescence by the 'loser' involves an acceptance of the legal basis of the opponent's claim, and perhaps such acquiescence can be more readily proved than in the case of the state faced by an undoubted usurper.[4]

(g) *Law-creating conduct.* Depending on the nature of a claim, recognition or protest in reaction to it may provide evidence of the development of customary rules.[5] If the claim or conduct is presented as resting on law, or, though novel, does not inevitably collide with existing rules, then recognition or protest are evidence for and against the creation of rules unless they are intended otherwise, as where they represent purely political attitudes or are part of a bilateral arrangement.

4. *Estoppel* (Préclusion)

There is a tendency among writers to refer to any representation or conduct having legal significance as creating an estoppel,

[1] Cf. the definition of Bowett, *infra*, p. 638.

[2] On acquiescence and protest generally see MacGibbon, 30 *B.Y.* (1953), 293–319; 31 *B.Y.* (1954), 143–86. On prescription and acquiescence in regard to acquisition of territory *supra*, pp. 156 seq. See also Bowett, 33 *B.Y.* (1957), 197–201; Cahier, in *Recueil d'études en hommage à Paul Guggenheim*, pp. 237–65; Barale, *Ann. français* (1965), 389–427; Bentz, 67 *R.G.D.I.P.* (1963), 44–91.

[3] On *jus cogens, supra*, pp. 512–15.

[4] See the *Fisheries* case, I.C.J. Reports (1951), at pp. 138–9, and *supra*, pp. 186 seq., in relation to the Norwegian system of straight baselines for delimiting the territorial sea.

[5] See generally Chapter I, and MacGibbon, 33 *B.Y.* (1957), 115–45.

precluding the author from denying the 'truth' of the representation, express or implied. By analogy with principles of municipal law, and by reference to decisions of international tribunals, Dr. Bowett[1] has stated the essentials of estoppel to be: (1) a statement of fact which is clear and unambiguous; (2) this statement must be voluntary, unconditional, and authorized; and (3) there must be reliance in good faith upon the statement either to the detriment of the party so relying on the statement or to the advantage of the party making the statement. A considerable weight of authority[2] supports the view that estoppel is a general principle of international law, resting on principles of good faith and consistency, and shorn of the technical features to be found in municipal law. Without dissenting from this as a general and preliminary proposition, it is necessary to point out that estoppel in municipal law is regarded with great caution, and that the 'principle' has no particular coherence in international law, its incidence and effects not being uniform.[3] Thus before a tribunal the principle may operate to resolve ambiguities and as a principle of equity and justice:[4] here it becomes a part of the evidence and judicial reasoning. Elsewhere, its content is taken up by the principles noted in the last section, which are inter-related and yet are specialized to some degree.[5]

Recent examples of judicial application of the principle are the *Arbitral Award by the King of Spain*[6] and the *Temple* case.[7] In the

[1] 33 *B.Y.* (1957), p. 176 at p. 202. This author takes some pains to isolate estoppel from other things. See further Dominicé, in *Recueil d'études en hommage à Paul Guggenheim*, pp. 327–65, at pp. 364–5.

[2] See Judges Alfaro and Fitzmaurice in the *Temple* case, I.C.J. Reports (1962), pp. 39–51, 61–5; Bowett, loc. cit.; MacGibbon, 7 *I.C.L.Q.* (1958), 468–513; Lauterpacht, *The Development of International Law by the International Court*, pp. 168–72; Report of the International Law Commission on the Law of Treaties, *Yrbk., I.L.C.* (1963), ii. 212–13; Waldock, ibid., pp. 39–40; Report of I.L.C., *Yrbk., I.L.C.* (1966), ii. 239. For more cautious statements see Rousseau, *Principes généraux*, p. 912 n.; Rousseau, *Droit international public* i. (1970), 387–9; and McNair, *Law of Treaties*, Chap. XXIX; Suy, op. cit., p. 64, n. 3. See also sep. op., Judge Mbanefo, *South West Africa* cases, I.C.J. Reports (1962), p. 440.

[3] See the diss. op. of Judge Spender, *Temple* case, I.C.J. Reports (1962), p. 143.

[4] Cf. Cheng, *General Principles of Law*, pp. 141–58; Schwarzenberger, 87 Hague *Recueil* (1955, I), 312 seq.; Lauterpacht, *ut supra*; Bowett, op. cit., p. 195.

[5] See the comments of Venturini, op. cit., pp. 370–4. Bowett uses the principle of reliance to isolate 'simple' or 'true' estoppel from the other principles. However, in some contexts, such as renunciation, reliance is not active in determining legal consequences. Nor does his distinction as to statements of fact have much viability. See further Vallée, 77 *R.G.D.I.P.* (1973), 949–99.

[6] I.C.J. Reports (1960), p. 192 at p. 213. See Johnson, 10 *I.C.L.Q.* (1961), 328–37.

[7] I.C.J. Reports (1962), p. 6 at p. 32. See Johnson, 11 *I.C.L.Q.* (1962), 1183–204; and, on the relation of estoppel and acquisition of territory, *supra*, p. 164. See further the *Argentine–Chile Frontier* case, Award of 1966, Int. L.R. 38, p. 10 at pp. 76–9.

former case Nicaragua challenged the validity of the award on several grounds: the Court held the award valid and stated that it was no longer open to Nicaragua, who, by express declaration and by conduct, had recognized the award as valid, to challenge its validity. In the *Temple* case Thailand sought to avoid a frontier agreement on the ground of error. In this case also the Court held that Thailand was precluded by her conduct from asserting that she did not accept the treaty. These cases support a particular type of estoppel (see section 3, para. (c), *supra*), but the rule concerned could operate independently of any general doctrine of estoppel.

5. *Agency and Representation*

(a) *States and organizations as agents.* States and organizations of states act as agents for various purposes, including the making of treaties.[1]

(b) *State organs.* The state organs include the head of state, head of government, heads of executive departments, and diplomatic representatives.[2] However, the legal boundaries of the state are not to be defined in simple terms, a view supported by the experience of municipal law. Specific authority may be given to individuals constituting delegations to conferences or special missions to foreign governments.[3] The existence of authority in a particular instance may be a matter regulated in part by international law. Thus, in treaty-making and in the making of unilateral declarations a Foreign Minister is presumed to have authority to bind the state he represents.[4] Moreover, the quality of 'the state' varies on a functional basis: thus 'sovereign immunity' from other state jurisdictions extends to the agents of the state, including its armed forces and warships, and state property in general.[5]

(c) *Analogues of agency.* The notion of agency lacks precision beyond its more obvious 'contractual' applications. Rules tend to be functional and specialized. Thus the law of state responsibility employs the concept of agency and yet imposes liability

[1] See Chapter XXIX, section 2.

[2] See *British Digest* vii; Sørensen, 101 Hague *Recueil* (1960, III). 58–68; *Yrbk., I.L.C.* (1962), ii. 164–6.

[3] On *ad hoc* diplomacy see Chapter XVI.

[4] Cf. *Eastern Greenland* case (1933), P.C.I.J., Ser. A/B, no. 53, p. 71; McNair, *Law of Treaties*, pp. 73–5; and Vienna Conv. on the Law of Treaties, 1969, Art. 7 (2) (a).

[5] Or, at least, property used for public purposes. On sovereign immunity see Chapter XV. On the immunity of armed forces see Chapter XVII, sect. 1 (e).

for unauthorized acts of officials.[1] In the law concerning the jurisdictional immunity of states, immunity may depend on a notion of state *function* rather than control in a simple sense.[2] Elements or analogues of agency appear in the law of state succession,[3] where subrogation may occur as a result of a change of sovereignty; in the law of nationality and diplomatic protection;[4] in the concept of ownership by states;[5] in the law governing the extent of state jurisdiction,[6] particularly where extra-territorial jurisdiction is claimed over state organs as such;[7] and in the rules governing representation on the international plane of peoples with a protected status under the law, including the populations of trust territories.[8]

[1] *Supra*, p. 449. On the *ultra vires* acts of organizations, see *infra*, pp. 698 seq.
[2] *Supra*, p. 342, n. 1. See also Riad, 108 Hague *Recueil* (1963, I), 565–660.
[3] *Infra*, Chapter XXVIII. [4] *Supra*, Chapter XVIII. [5] *Supra*, p. 428.
[6] *Supra*, Chapter XIV. Cf. also the concept of a command structure in the law of war: see Draper, 12 *I.C.L.Q.* (1963), 387–413; Bowett, *United Nations Forces*, Chap. 15.
[7] Cf. Seyersted, 14 *I.C.L.Q.* (1965), 31–82, 493–527.
[8] *Supra*, pp. 62, 466–73, 566–8.

CHAPTER XXVII

TECHNIQUES OF SUPERVISION AND PROTECTION

1. *Introductory*

In the discussion of the subject of human rights (Chapter XXIV) various institutions and procedures concerned with enforcement and protection were noticed. However, there is a more general significance of such institutions and procedures, since they may apply to a variety of subject matters apart from human rights. It is therefore useful to present a summary view of the techniques of supervision and protection developed in the practice of international affairs.[1] Naturally, the techniques of implementation of treaties, and the regimes and standard setting contained within them, overlap with two other major topics namely, the peaceful settlement of disputes and enforcement action by the Security Council or regional agencies. It should also be stressed that the normal and primary means of implementation is the express or implied obligation placed upon states parties to the particular treaty to take appropriate legislative and administrative steps.

2. *Reporting Procedures*

Multilateral conventions commonly require parties to report periodically on the implementation of the obligations of the particular convention. Among such conventions are the Slavery Convention of 1926 (as amended by the Protocol of 1953), the Convention on the Elimination of All Forms of Racial Discrimination of 1966 and the International Covenants on Human

[1] The more useful surveys are: Khol, *Zwischen Staat und Weltstaat* (1969); Van Asbeck, *Liber Amicorum J.P.A. François* (1959), pp. 27–41. Capotorti, in Eide and Schou (eds.), *International Protection of Human Rights* (1968), pp. 131–48; Carey, 53 *Iowa L.R.* (1967), 291–324; id., *U.N. Protection of Civil and Political Rights* (1970); Schwelb, 62 *A.J.* (1968), 827–68; Studies Prepared by the Sec.-Gen., U.N. Documents E/CN.4/AC.21/L.1, 30 December 1966; A/CONF.32/6, 20 June 1967; Sohn, 62 *A.J.* (1968), 909–12; Golsong, 110 Hague *Recueil* (1963, III), 7–150; Korey, *Int. Conciliation*, No. 570 (Nov. 1968); Berthoud, *Le contrôle international de l'exécution des conventions collectives* (1946); Landy, *The Effectiveness of International Supervision* (1966); Valticos, *Mélanges Modinos* (1968), 331–56; id., 123 Hague *Recueil* (1968, I), 315–407; Schwebel (ed.), *The Effectiveness of International Decisions* (1971); International Labour Office, *The Impact of International Labour Conventions and Recommendations* (1976); Fischer and Vignes (eds.), *L'Inspection International* (1976); Schreiber, 145 Hague *Recueil* (1975, II), 297–398.

Rights, also of 1966.[1] The I.L.O. Constitution requires each member to make annual reports concerning measures taken to give effect to all Conventions binding the member. An *Ad Hoc* Committee on Periodic Reports of the U.N. Commission on Human Rights considers reports submitted by member states and members of specialized agencies.

3. *Fact-finding Bodies*[2]

Governments are normally sensitive to the results of investigations which have an authoritative character, this depending on the composition of the body concerned and its adherence to certain standard principles of fair and competent enquiry. Fact-finding may occur as a part of a general procedure, or as a preliminary to negotiation and conciliation. Thus an important part of the work of the European Commission of Human Rights is the eliciting of facts and the compilation of a report.[3] Fact-finding bodies have been created by United Nations organs from time to time. The U.N. Human Rights Commission established in 1967 an *Ad Hoc* Working Group of Experts to investigate various aspects of human rights in southern Africa, including the situation of prisoners and detainees in South Africa, and in 1969 a similar group was established to investigate allegations concerning violations by Israel of the Geneva Convention Relative to the Protection of Civilian Persons in Time of War.

4. *Political Supervision*

The Mandate agreements and Minorities Treaties of 1919–20 provided for supervision of the arrangements contained therein by the Council of the League of Nations.[4] The United Nations General Assembly has on a significant number of occasions taken a position concerning situations involving breaches of human rights provisions in treaties including the United Nations Charter. Examples of such action relate to the application of the Peace Treaties with Bulgaria, Hungary, and Rumania and numerous resolutions on racial discrimination in general and *apartheid* in particular. Political pressure by the General Assembly may involve a continuing element of inquiry and reporting by a

[1] See especially Capotorti, op. cit., pp. 134–8.

[2] See Ermacora, 1 *Revue des Droits de l'Homme* (1968), 180–218.

[3] See Article 31 of the European Convention and *supra*, p. 584. On the I.L.O. Commissions of Enquiry see *supra*, p. 569.

[4] See further *supra*, 565–6.

subsidiary body.[1] The Commission on Human Rights of the Economic and Social Council has in recent years adopted a more prominent role as a part of the system of political protection.[2] In 1967 the Economic and Social Council authorized the Commission to 'make a thorough study of situations which reveal a consistent pattern of violations of human rights . . . and report, with recommendations thereon, to the Economic and Social Council'. Since 1947 the Commission has had no power to take action on complaints by individuals. Now, however, all communications received by the Secretary-General in this connection, together with the replies of governments thereon, may be considered if they 'appear to reveal a consistent pattern of gross and reliably attested violations' of human rights.[3] The work is carried out by the Sub-Commission on the Prevention of Discrimination, and ultimately—the procedure is slow—the Commission reports to the Economic and Social Council. It is a condition of admissibility of a communication that domestic remedies shall have been exhausted 'unless it appears that such remedies would be ineffective or unreasonably prolonged'.

Those cases not settled by the European Commission of Human Rights and consequently the subject of a Report to the Committee of Ministers, may be resolved by the latter body, which is a political instance, unless the case is referred to the European Court of Human Rights under Article 48 of the Convention.[4]

5. *Complaints Procedures Apart from Adjudication*

(a) *Complaints as evidence.* Complaints from individuals, non-governmental organizations and governments may provide evidence on which an organ may take appropriate action even

[1] Cf. the Special Committees on the Situation with Respect to the Implementation of the Declaration on the Granting of Independence to Colonial Countries and Peoples (1961); on Apartheid (1962); and to Investigate Israeli Practices Affecting the Human Rights of the Population of the Occupied Territories (1968). See Khol, 3 *Revue des Droits de l'Homme* (1970), 21–50.

[2] See Humphrey, 62 *A.J.* (1968), 869–88; Van Boven, 15 *Neths. Int. L.R.* (1968), 374–93; Schreiber, 145 Hague *Recueil* (1975, II), 351–9; I.L.A., *Report of the Fifty-Fifth Conference*, 1972, 539–624 (note reports by Humphrey and Schwelb); I.L.A., *Report of the Fifty-Sixth Conference*, 1974, 209–13; I.L.A., *Report of the Fifty-Seventh Conference*, 1976, 511–14; *Review of the Int. Comm. of Jurists*, 1977–8 (commentaries).

[3] Economic and Social Council, Resolution 1503 (XLVIII) of 27 May 1970; 64 *A.J.* (1970), 1023. See further Carey, 66 *A.J.* (1972), 107–9; and ibid., p. 240 (resol. of Sub-commission, 14 Aug. 1971). See also the *Ad Hoc* Working Groups of Experts created in 1967: *supra*. The Commission appointed a Special Rapporteur on Apartheid in 1967.

[4] *Supra*, pp. 584–6.

when, taken individually, the complaints have no status which would justify or require consideration or action.[1]

(b) *Individual Petitions.*[2] We are concerned here with situations in which individuals and non-governmental organizations have a right under treaty to present petitions which will be considered and acted upon, as individual complaints, by an organ under a prescribed procedure. It is not easy to characterize such instances: they are in a general way analogous to public inquiries and administrative bodies with quasi-judicial functions. Petitions from the people of a mandated territory[3] were partly a matter of information for the Permanent Mandates Commission but rejections were accompanied by reasons. Within the Trusteeship system of the United Nations,[4] petitioners are more nearly parties to the procedure, which is quasi-judicial. The outcome of the procedure is that the Trusteeship Council may make a recommendation to the administering authority concerned. Petitions from associations of employers or workers are accepted and acted upon within the I.L.O. system.[5] The International Convention on the Elimination of All Forms of Racial Discrimination establishes a procedure for individual petitioning.[6] The Optional Protocol to the International Covenant on Civil and Political Rights[7] and the American Convention on Human Rights[8] also provide optional procedures for individual petitions. It is common for such recourse to be conditioned by a prior exhaustion of all available domestic remedies.

(c) *Complaints by States.*[9] The Human Rights Committee established by the International Covenant on Civil and Political Rights has a competence (which must be recognized by parties to the Covenant) 'to receive and consider communications to the effect that a State Party claims that another State Party is not fulfilling its obligations under the present Covenant'.[1] Similar provisions exist in other conventions, including that on the Elimination of All Forms of Racial Discrimination,[2] the Constitu-

[1] See the powers of the U.N. Commission on Human Rights described in Section 4. Cp. also the practice of the General Assembly's Special Committees on Colonialism and *Apartheid.*

[2] See Nørgaard, *The Position of the Individual in International Law* (1962), pp. 99–172; Parson, 13 *Wayne L.R.* (1967), 678–705.

[3] *Supra*, pp. 566–7. [4] See the U.N. Charter, Article 87.

[5] I.L.O. Constitution, Articles 24 and 25.

[6] Article 14. The competent body is the Committee on the Elimination of Racial Discrimination (Article 8): see I.L.A., *Report of the Fifty-Fifth Conference*, 1972, pp. 585–608 (Schwelb). [7] Brownlie, *Basic Documents on Human Rights*, p. 232.

[8] Ibid., p. 399, Articles 44–51.

[9] On the position under the European Convention on Human Rights see p. 584.

[1] Article 41. [2] Article 11.

tion of the I.L.O.,[1] and the Protocol to the U.N.E.S.C.O. Convention Against Discrimination in Education.[2]

6. *Judicial Supervision*

Since 1919 the political supervision of guarantees in treaties has been reinforced by a system of judicial supervision based upon the Permanent Court of International Justice or its successor. The Polish Minority Treaty of 1919 provided (Article 12, paragraph 3) as follows:

> Poland further agrees that any difference of opinion as to questions of law or fact arising out of these Articles between the Polish Government and any one of the Principal Allied and Associated Powers or any other Power, a member of the Council of the League of Nations, shall be held to be a dispute of an international character under Article 14 of the Covenant of the League of Nations. The Polish Government hereby consents that any such dispute shall, if the other party thereto demands, be referred to the Permanent Court of International Justice. The decision of the Permanent Court shall be final and shall have the same force and effect as an award under Article 13 of the Covenant.

It is to be noted that recourse to this type of procedure has been minimal in practice. Nevertheless, the conception of supervision by a reasonably neutral judicial organ on the basis of an *actio popularis*, in which the Applicant State need allege no injury to legal rights representing its individual interest, is of great value.[3] Similar adjudication clauses appeared in the Mandate agreements and the application of these has been a matter of considerable difficulty.[4] In the *South West Africa* cases[5] the International Court in the First Phase of the cases in 1962 upheld the effectiveness of judicial supervision in recognizing the right of the Applicant States to invoke the jurisdictional clause in the Mandate Agreement.[6] The Separate Opinions of Judges McNair and Read in the proceedings on a request for an Advisory Opinion in 1950 emphasized the nature of judicial supervision based upon the principle that *any* Member of the League of Nations had a legal interest in the implementation of the provisions of the

[1] Article 26; see further *supra*, p. 568.

[2] *U.K. Treaty Series*, no. 23 (1969), Cmnd. 3894.

[3] See the *Interpretation of the Statute of the Memel Territory*, P.C.I.J., Series A/B, No. 47, p. 243.

[4] See the *Mavrommatis Palestine Concessions* (Jurisdiction) Case, 1924, P.C.I.J., Series A, No. 2. Judges de Bustamante and Oda dissented.

[5] See generally *supra*, p. 466.

[6] I.C.J. Reports (1962), p. 319, at pp. 342–4. See also the diss. ops. at the Second Phase: I.C.J. Reports (1966), pp. 244–8 (Koretsky), 255–7 (Tanaka), 356–79 (Jessup).

Mandate.[1] On the other hand a substantial minority of judges in the First Phase[2] and a formal[3] majority of seven judges in the Second Phase[4] of the *South West Africa* cases, whilst not denying the principle of judicial supervision, adopted the view that the principle, based on a broad notion of legal interest in the observance of the treaty provisions apart from harm to a 'material interest', was exceptional, and on a number of grounds gave a narrow interpretation to the jurisdictional clause in the Mandate for South West Africa.

Adjudication clauses substantially similar to the provision in issue in the *South West Africa* cases exist in a number of multilateral conventions including the Genocide Convention, the International Convention on the Elimination of All Forms of Racial Discrimination, the Convention on the Political Rights of Women, and the International Convention for the Prevention of the Pollution of the Sea by Oil. Whether the particular clause supports an *actio popularis* will be partly a question of interpretation and partly dependent upon the development of rules of *jus cogens*.[5]

7. *Quasi-judicial Bodies*

The complaints procedures considered in Section 5 above might be described as 'quasi-judicial' since the term is rather general and could apply to any complaints procedure. However, certain procedures may result in findings which are quasi-judicial decisions in that (a) they apply rules of law to facts established by due process; (b) the finding is binding and not simply the basis for a mere recommendation to the state concerned. The findings of the European Commission of Human Rights are essentially judicial on these criteria and they provide the basis upon which the Committee of Ministers, in the absence of a reference to the European Court, may decide whether there has been a violation of the Convention (Article 32).[6] The Commissions of Inquiry within the I.L.O. system could perhaps be regarded as somewhat comparable.

[1] Ibid. (1950), pp. 158, 164–5, respectively.

[2] I.C.J. Reports (1962), pp. 449–55 (Winiarski), 463–4 (Basdevant), 466–7, 479–81, 484, 520–1, 547–60 (Joint diss. op. of Spender and Fitzmaurice), 598–600, 660–2 (Van Wyk). Judge Morelli dissented on the ground that there was no 'dispute' within the meaning of the jurisdictional clause.

[3] By the casting vote of the President.

[4] I.C.J. Reports (1966), p. 6 at pp. 38–41, 43–7.

[5] *Supra*, p. 512.

[6] See McNair, *The Expansion of International Law* (1962), pp. 13–16.

8. *Negotiation and Conciliation*

A high proportion of procedures for investigation and complaint are linked with provisions for negotiation, good offices, and conciliation to achieve a friendly settlement. Provisions of this type appear in the European Convention on Human Rights,[1] the International Covenant on Civil and Political Rights,[2] the International Convention on the Elimination of All Forms of Racial Discrimination,[3] the American Convention on Human Rights,[4] and the Protocol to the U.N.E.S.C.O. Convention Against Discrimination in Education.[5] In 1967 the Economic and Social Council transmitted a draft proposal for the establishment of a United Nations High Commissioner's Office for Human Rights to the General Assembly for consideration.[6] The roles to be foreseen for such an office include negotiation and informal intercession. The proposal has not been fruitful hitherto.

9. *Other Control Procedures*

Bodies may be given powers to investigate and if necessary call upon governments to take remedial measures, independently of any complaints procedure and irrespective of the existence of a 'dispute' between any of the parties to the particular convention. Under the Single Convention on Narcotic Drugs, 1961,[7] the International Narcotics Control Board has such powers.

10. *The Types of Rules*

The obligations contained in treaties are infinitely various and their content is a matter of interpretation in the particular case. However, certain provisions are only directory or programmatic. Thus the International Covenant on Economic, Social, and Cultural Rights[8] contains a number of provisions exemplified

[1] *Supra*, p. 574. [2] Articles 41, 42. See Schwelb, 62 *A.J.* (1968), 827–68.
[3] Articles 11–14. [4] Articles 48–51.
[5] Adopted in 1962; *U.K. Treaty Series* No. 23 (1969), Cmnd. 3894.
[6] For a Secretariat Study see U.N. Document E/CN.4/AC.21/L.1. See also Macdonald, 5 *Canad. Yrbk., I.L.* (1967), 84–117; Clark, *A United Nations High Commissioner for Human Rights* (1972); Humphrey in I.L.A., *Report of the Fifty-Sixth Conference*, 1974, pp. 210–11.
[7] 520 U.N.T.S., 151; *Treaty Series* No. 34 (1965), Cmnd. 2631; Article 14. See also the powers of the Council under the International Sugar Agreement, 1968, *Treaty Series* No. 93 (1969), Cmnd. 4210, Article 58; the Council under the International Coffee Agreement, *Treaty Series* No. 103 (1969), Cmnd. 4211, Article 48; the Council under the Wheat Trade Convention, *Treaty Series* No. 1 (1969), Cmnd. 3840, Articles 19, 20; and the role of the EFTA Council, on which see Szokoloczy-Syllaba, 20 *I.C.L.Q.* (1971), 519–34. And see the more recent agreements for coffee, etc.
[8] Brownlie, *Basic Documents*, p. 139.

by the recognition of the right to work in Article 6.[1] There the States Parties agree to 'take appropriate steps to safeguard the right' and 'the steps to be taken . . . to achieve the full realization' of the right to work include 'technical and vocational guidance and training programmes, policies and techniques' with appropriate objectives. Most treaty provisions set precise standards and have a more defined content although even direct prescriptions may refer to 'reasonable measures', or prohibit 'unjustifiable interference',[2] thus allowing a certain discretion.[3]

It is justifiable to argue that the method of interpretation to be adopted should be appropriate to the type of provision involved. Thus in certain matters affecting humanitarian interests or the functioning of the United Nations, the International Court has on some occasions at least favoured the principle of effectiveness.[4] The Advisory Opinion on the *International Status of South West Africa* of 1950 rests to a considerable extent on the principle or assumption of the effectiveness of international supervision.[5] Thus it was held that South Africa was obliged to accept the supervision of the General Assembly of the United Nations in respect of the Mandate in spite of the demise of the League of Nations, the original foundation of the Mandates system, and the disappearance of the League Council, the original source of political supervision. In contrast, the judgment in the contentious proceedings in 1966 involved a rejection of the argument from necessity.[6]

11. *Problems of Co-ordination: Regional Bodies*

The view has been expressed that violations of human rights can best be dealt with on a regional basis and the Commission on Human Rights of the Economic and Social Council has established an *ad hoc* Study Group on Regional Commissions.[7] Of course, regional institutions concerned with the protection of

[1] See Schwelb, in Eide and Schou (eds.), *International Protection of Human Rights*, pp. 103–29. Note especially Article 2 (3). Cf. Schwelb, in *René Cassin: Amicorum Discipulorumque Liber I*, pp. 301–32; Whiteman v. 244–6; Judge Fitzmaurice, sep. op., *Expenses* case, I.C.J. Reports (1962), at pp. 213–15.

[2] See the provisions of the Continental Shelf Convention, for example.

[3] *Supra*, p. 475. [4] *Supra*, p. 628.

[5] I.C.J. Reports (1950), p. 128 at pp. 133–4, 136–7. Cp. Lauterpacht, *The Development of International Law by the International Court*, pp. 277–81.

[6] I.C.J. Reports (1966), p. 6 at pp. 34–6, 44–8. Note also the Judgment, p. 19, which seems to assume that the finding of 1950 was not to be taken for granted. See further Cheng, 20 *Curr. Legal Problems* (1967), p. 181 at pp. 184–93.

[7] See the Report, U.N. Document E/CN.4/966; and E/CN.4/972, p. 80.

human rights already exist in Europe and Latin America. No doubt a proliferation of institutions is inevitable, though not perhaps desirable, and issues of co-ordination necessarily arise.[1] The Human Rights Commission or the proposed U.N. Commissioner for Human Rights could be given the responsibility for measures of co-ordination.

Problems arise from the relation of the European Convention on Human Rights and the International Covenant on Civil and Political Rights.[2] Thus there is an overlap between the optional procedure for inter-state complaints provided for in Article 41 of the Covenant and that provided for in Article 24 of the European Convention.[3] The Covenant does not prohibit recourse to other methods of settlement (Article 44) but under Article 62 of the European Convention the Contracting Parties agree that they will not, except by special agreement, submit a dispute to a means of settlement other than those provided for in the Convention.

12. *Certain Other Issues: Inspection Procedures*

The material set forth in this chapter by no means exhausts the experience available. In certain contexts other than protection of human rights reporting and inspection procedures have been developed or considered extensively.[4] The concept of inspection by an impartial agency is to be found in the Statute of the International Atomic Energy Agency and the Treaty establishing Euratom. Adversary inspection, or the reciprocal right to inspect the other party to investigate suspected violations, appears in the

[1] See Vasak, 1 *Revue des Droits de l'Homme* (1968), 164–79; Werners, 15 *Neths. Int. L.R.* (1968), 394–413.

[2] Modinos, 1 *Revue des Droits de l'Homme* (1968), 41–69; Robertson, 43 *B.Y.* (1968–9), 21–48; Eissen, 30 *Z.a.ö.R.u.V.* (1970), 237–62, 646–9. On the relation to the Inter-American system: Tardu, 70 *A.J.* (1976), 778–800.

[3] See Resol. (70) 17 of the Committee of Ministers of the Council of Europe, adopted by the Ministers' Deputies on 15 May 1970, in which the Committee 'declares that, as long as the problem of interpretation of Article 62 of the European Convention is not resolved, States Parties to the Convention which ratify or accede to the U.N. Covenant on Civil and Political Rights and make a declaration under Article 41 of the Covenant should normally utilize only the procedure established by the European Convention in respect of complaints against another Contracting Party to the European Convention relating to an alleged violation of a right which in substance is covered both by the European Convention (or its protocols) and by the U.N. Covenant on Civil and Political Rights, it being understood that the U.N. procedure may be invoked in relation to rights not guaranteed in the European Convention (or its protocols) or in relation to States which are not Parties to the European Convention.'

[4] See Gotlieb, *Disarmament and International Law* (1965), pp. 130–68; Johnston, *The International Law of Fisheries* (1965), pp. 253 seq.; Whiteman iv. 977 seq.; Simsarian, 60 *A.J.* (1966), 502–10.

Antarctica Treaty,[1] various conventions concerning high seas fisheries,[2] and bilateral agreements for co-operation in the peaceful uses of atomic energy.[3] The Antarctica Treaty also provides an example of regulation which is intended to be effective as against third parties: the issues involved are noticed elsewhere.[4]

[1] *Supra*, p. 265.

[2] Example: Int. Conv. for the High Seas Fisheries of the North Pacific Ocean, 1953, 205 U.N.T.S., p. 65; 48 *A.J.* (1954), Supp., p. 71. See further Carroz and Roche, 6 *Canad. Yrbk.* (1968), 61–90.

[3] e.g. U.S.-U.S.S.R., Treaty on Underground Nuclear Explosions for Peaceful Purposes, 1976; 15 *Int. Leg. Materials* (1976), 891.

[4] *Supra*, p. 619. See further Jennings, 20 *I.C.L.Q.* (1971), 433–52.

PART XI

TRANSMISSION OF RIGHTS AND DUTIES

CHAPTER XXVIII

STATE SUCCESSION[1]

1. *State Succession as a Category*

STATE succession arises when there is a definitive replacement of one state by another in respect of sovereignty over a given territory in conformity with international law. The political events concerned include total dismemberment of an existing state, secession, decolonization of a part of a state, merger of existing states and partial cession or annexation of state territory. In the case of the replacement of a mandate or trusteeship by a sovereign state, the definition needs an amendment since in those cases it is not sovereignty but a special type of legal competence which is replaced. In general the process involved is that of a permanent displacement of sovereign power and thus temporary changes resulting from belligerent occupation or grants of exclusive possession of territory by treaty are excluded. Distinct also is the case where one state acts as the delegate or agent of another for legal purposes.

When the sovereignty of one state replaces that of another state then a number of legal problems arise. Is the successor state bound by all or any of the treaties of the predecessor? Do the inhabitants of the territory concerned automatically become nationals of the successor? Is the successor state affected by inter-

[1] The principal items of literature are as follows: O'Connell, *State Succession in Municipal Law and International Law*, 2 vols. (1967); id., 130 Hague *Recueil* (1970, II), 95–206; Zemanek, 116 Hague *Recueil* (1965, III), 187–300; Castrén, 78 Hague *Recueil* (1951, I), 379–506; Whiteman ii, Chap. IV; Schwarzenberger, *International Law* (3rd ed.); 164–79; Jennings, 121 Hague *Recueil* 1967, II), 437–51; *Yrbk., I.L.C.* (1962), ii. 101, 131; (1963), ii. 95, 260; (1968), ii. 1, 87, 94, 213; (1969), ii. 23, 45, 69; (1970), ii. 25, 61, 102, 136, 170; (1971), ii (pt. 1), 143, 157; (1971), ii (pt. 2), 111; (1972), ii. 1, 60, 61, 223; (1973), ii. 3, 198; (1974), ii (pt. 1), 1, 89, 91, 162; (1975), ii. 106; (1976), ii (pt. 1), 55; (1976), ii (pt. 2), 122; Rousseau iii (1977), 329–511; Verzijl, *International Law in Historical Perspective* vii (1974); Bardonnet, *La Succession d'États à Madagascar* (1970); *Répertoire suisse* iii. 1297–1403; Bedjaoui, 130 Hague *Recueil* (1970, II), 455–586. See also U.N. Legislative Series, ST/LEG/SER.B/14 (1967); ST/LEG/SER.B/17 (1978).

national claims involving the predecessor, by the predecessor's national debt and its other obligations under the system of municipal law now supplanted? It is of great importance to note that the phrase 'state succession' is employed to *describe* an area, or a source of problems: the term does not connote any principle or presumption that a transmission or succession of legal rights and duties occurs. The phrase 'state succession' is well established in spite of its misleading suggestion of the municipal law analogy of continuity of legal personality in a man's general property, passing as an inheritance, this involving a complete or 'universal succession'.

The subject of state succession is at present under examination by the International Law Commission, which acknowledges that the work involves in part the progressive development of the law. Part of the work has culminated in the Vienna Convention on Succession of States in Respect of Treaties.[1] State succession is an area of great uncertainty and controversy. This is due partly to the fact that much of the state practice is equivocal and could be explained on the basis of special agreement and various rules distinct from the category of state succession. Indeed, it is perfectly possible to take the view that not many settled legal rules have emerged as yet.[2] The account which follows is necessarily provisional to a degree but may help somewhat by indicating ways in which existing principles of international law bear on the problems.

2. *The Pre-emption of Problems by Treaty, Acquiescence, and Estoppel*

A number of major issues have been dealt with in the past by multilateral peace treaties which actually constituted new states and regulated succession problems as a part of the territorial rearrangement. Thus the Treaty of St. Germain of 1919 provided for the responsibility of the successor states of the Austro-Hungarian Monarchy for the public debts of the predecessor.[3] Provisions of the Italian Peace Treaty of 1947, and the United Nations resolution on 'Economic and Financial Provisions Relating to Libya' determined various questions concerning the

[1] Opened for signature on 23 August 1978.

[2] Cf. *Yangtze (London) Ltd.* v. *Barlas Bros. (Karachi) Ltd.*, Int. L.R. 34, p. 27 at pp. 32–3, S.C. of Pakistan; *Pales Ltd.* v. *Ministry of Transport*, Int. L.R. 22 (1955), p. 113 at p. 122, S.C. of Israel (as Ct. of Civil Appeals); Guggenheim, *Traité*, i. 461.

[3] Art. 203 of the Treaty. See also Tripartite Claims Comm., Admin. Decision No. 1, *R.I.A.A.* vi. 203; and the *Ottoman Debt Arbitration* (1925), *R.I.A.A.* i. 529.

relations of Italy and its former colony of Libya.[1] On other occasions the conduct of states may produce informal novation by means of unilateral declarations and forms of acquiescence or estoppel. In 1958 when the United Arab Republic was created by the Union of Egypt with Syria, the Minister of Foreign Affairs of the Union made a statement, as follows, in a Note to the Secretary-General of the United Nations: '. . . all international treaties and agreements concluded by Egypt or Syria with other countries will remain valid within the regional limits prescribed on their conclusion and in accordance with the principles of international law'. Such a declaration of itself could not bind third states parties to treaties with the former states of Egypt and Syria. However, third states appear to have acquiesced in the position adopted by the United Arab Republic and the United States expressly took cognizance of the assurance given.[2]

On a considerable number of occasions the inheritance or devolution of treaty rights and obligations has been the subject of agreements between the predecessor and successor states.[3] The United Kingdom has made such agreements with Burma, Ceylon, the Federation of Malaya, Ghana, Cyprus, the Federation of Nigeria, Sierra Leone, Jamaica, Trinidad and Tobago, The Gambia, and Malta. Such agreements promote certainty and stability of relations. They also create certain problems. First, the agreement may appear to be a part of the bargain exacted by the outgoing colonial power at independence and the new state may seek legal means of disputing its validity and application.[4] Secondly, third states cannot be legally bound by inheritance agreements unless by express declaration or conduct they agree to be bound.[5]

3. *Territorial Sovereignty and Domestic Jurisdiction*

After a change of sovereignty various issues may be raised in the context of municipal law, viz., the destiny of the property of

[1] U.N. Tribunal in Libya, decisions of 18 February 1952 and 31 January 1953, *R.I.A.A.* xii. 356; Int. L.R. 24 (1957), 103 and (1958, I), 2.

[2] Whiteman ii. 959–62, 1014. See also Waldock, *Yrbk., I.L.C.* (1971) ii (pt. 1), 145–53; *Yrbk., I.L.C.* (1972), ii. 272–7; ibid. (1974) ii (pt. 1), 236–41.

[3] See generally E. Lauterpacht, 7 *I.C.L.Q.* (1958), 524–30; O'Connell, op. cit., ii. 352–73.

[4] See on unequal treaties', *supra*, p. 612; and *infra*, p. 670, on issues concerning *jus cogens*.

[5] See the U.K.–Venezuela Agreement, 1966, Art. VIII, *British Practice* (1966), p. 72; Waldock, Second Report, *Yrbk., I.L.C.* (1969), ii. 54–62; *Yrbk., I.L.C.* (1972), ii. 236–41; ibid. (1974) ii (pt. 1), 183–7.

the ceding or former state, the continuity of the legal system, the status of private property rights, including rights deriving from contracts and concessions concluded under the former law, and nationality problems. Hyde [1] and other writers have maintained that the municipal law of the predecessor remains in force until the new sovereign takes steps to change it. O'Connell [2] and other modern authorities [3] support a principle of vested or acquired rights. This principle is to the effect that a change of sovereignty has no effect on the acquired rights of foreign nationals. The principle has received support from tribunals [4] but it is a source of confusion since it is question-begging and is used as the basis for a variety of propositions. For some, it means simply that private rights are not affected by the change of sovereignty as such. For others it appears to mean that the successor state faces restrictions on its powers in relation to private rights of aliens additional to the ordinary rules of international law governing treatment of aliens apart from a case of succession. Moreover, writers often fail to relate the concept of acquired rights to the other principles affecting a change of sovereignty. The new sovereign receives the same sort of sovereignty as the transferor has had, and this involves normal powers of legislation and jurisdiction deriving from sovereign equality and the reserved domain of domestic jurisdiction. Survival of the old law depends on the consent of the new sovereign.[5] Indeed some proponents of acquired rights formulate the principle in a qualified form. Thus O'Connell [6] states that 'the principle of respect for acquired rights in international

[1] Hyde i. 397 seq. See also Briggs, p. 237.

[2] *International Law* i. 377–81, 388–9; *State Succession* (2nd ed.), Chaps. 6 and 10; 130 Hague *Recueil* (1970, II), 134–46.

[3] Oppenheim i. 160, n. 3. See also Waldock, *Yrbk., I.L.C.* (1969), i. 74–5; Tsuruoka, ibid., 87–8. Zemanek, op. cit., p. 279, points out that only when one assumes that the chain of continuity is broken does it become necessary to have recourse to a special rule on vested rights.

[4] *Lighthouses* case, *R.I.A.A.* xii, p. 155 at p. 236; *Forests of Central Rhodopia* case, *R.I.A.A.* ii, p. 1389 at pp. 1431–6. See also *infra*, p. 656.

[5] Briggs, p. 237; Guggenheim, p. 136; Kaeckenbeeck, 17 *B.Y.* (1936), p. 1 at pp. 13 seq.; Rosenne, 27 *B.Y.* (1950), p. 267 esp. at pp. 273, 281–2; Zemanek, op. cit., p. 281; Bedjaoui, *Yrbk., I.L.C.* (1968), ii. 115; and ibid. (1969), ii. 69. See the debate: *Yrbk., I.L.C.* (1969), i. 53 seq., and Bedjaoui, 130 Hague *Recueil* (1970, II), 531–61. Various writers have pointed out that the often-quoted passage in the case of *German Settlers in Poland* (1923), (P.C.I.J. Series B, No. 6, p. 36; Briggs, p. 222; Green, p. 174) that, in the instance of German territory transferred to Poland after the First World War, German law had continued to operate in the territory in question, is a factual statement that German law was continued in force after the cession. See further *L. and JJ.* v. *Polish State Railways*, Int. L.R. 24 (1957), 77, Polish Supreme Court.

[6] *State Succession* at p. 266. O'Connell (at p. 107) points out that the principle of continuity of law is only a presumption. See also 130 Hague *Recueil* (1970, II), 141.

law is no more than a principle that change of sovereignty should not touch the interests of individuals more than is necessary,' and goes on to say that the successor state which alters or cancels acquired rights must comply with the minimum standards of international law. In the case of decolonization, the continuation of the pre-independence economic structure, which commonly involves extensive foreign ownership of major resources, would produce a situation in which political independence and formal sovereignty were not matched by a normal competence to regulate the national economy. The declaration of the United Nations General Assembly on 'Permanent Sovereignty over Natural Resources'[1] contains a proviso thus:

> Considering that nothing in paragraph 4 below in any way prejudices the position of any Member State on any aspect of the question of the rights and obligations of successor States and Governments in respect of property acquired before the accession to complete sovereignty of countries formerly under colonial rule.

(a) *State Property.*[2] It is generally conceded that succession to the public property of the annexed or ceding state is a principle of customary international law and the jurisprudence of the Permanent Court of International Justice supports this position.[3] Another approach would be to say that the 'principle' is really a presumption that acquisition of state property is inherent in the grant of territorial sovereignty and is a normal consequence of the acquisition of sovereignty in situations apart from a grant or cession.

(b) *Public Law Claims and Public Debts.*[4] It follows from what has already been said that the successor state has a right to take up fiscal claims belonging to the former state, including the right to collect taxes due.

Much more a matter of controversy is the fate of the public debts of the replaced state. It may be that there is no rule of

[1] *Supra*, p. 540.

[2] See *Yrbk., I.L.C.* (1970), ii. 131; ibid. (1971) ii (pt. 1), 157; ibid. (1973), ii. 3; ibid. (1974), ii (pt. 1), 91; ibid. (1975), ii. 110; ibid. (1976), ii (pt. 1), 55; ibid. (1976), ii (pt. 2), 122; 16 *Int. Leg. Materials* (1977), 1249, 1255.

[3] *Peter Pazmany University* case (1933), P.C.I.J., Series A/B, No. 61 at p. 237. See also *Haile Selassie* v. *Cable and Wireless, Ltd.* (No. 2), [1939] Ch. 182, 195; Briggs, p. 213. On the definition of state property see Schwarzenberger, *International Law* i. (3rd ed.), i. 167–9; U.N. Tribunal for Libya, *supra*; and Guggenheim i. (1953), 468–9. See also Bedjaoui, *Yrbk., I.L.C.* (1968), ii. 106–8, and ibid. (1970), ii. 131, 144–51.

[4] In addition to the literature referred to *supra*, p. 651, see Int. Law Assoc., Report of the Fifty-Third Conference, 1968, 598 at pp. 598, 603; Lauterpacht, *International Law: Collected Papers* iii. 121–37; Bedjaoui, *Yrbk., I.L.C.* (1971) ii (pt. 1), 185; 16 *Int. Leg. Materials* (1977), 1249, 1255 (Part II of draft).

succession established,[1] but some writers[2] have concluded that in cases of annexation or dismemberment, as opposed to cession, where the ceding state remains in existence, the successor is obliged to assume the public debts of the extinct state. Zemanek[3] confines succession to the situation where before independence an autonomous political dependency has through the agency of the metropolitan power contracted a 'localized debt' which is automatically attributed to the new state after separation. In practice municipal courts will enforce obligations of the predecessor state against the successor only when the latter has recognized them.[4] In principle public debts are subject to the same regime as state contracts and concessions (see below).[5]

(c) *State Contracts and Concessions.* As in the case of all rights acquired under the municipal law of the predecessor state, rights deriving from state contracts and concessions are susceptible to change by the new sovereign. Limitations on such interference derive only from any relevant international standards concerning aliens or human rights in general.[6] However, a number of writers[7] state the principle that the acquired rights of a concessionaire must be respected by a successor state.[8] There is a certain anomaly in the selection of concessions as beneficiaries of the principle, which could be related to other matters, including

[1] See the *Ottoman Debt Arbitration* (1925) *R.I.A.A.* i, p. 531 at p. 573; Brierly, p. 159; Rousseau iii. 426–70; Hackworth i. 539; Castrén, 68 Hague *Recueil* (1951, I), 458–84 at p. 465; Guggenheim i. (1953), 469; *Franco-Ethiopian Railway Company Claim*, Int. L.R. 24 (1957), p. 602 at p. 629.

[2] Feilchenfeld, *Public Debts and State Succession* (1931); Sack, 80 *Univ. of Penn. L.R.* (1931), 608; Briggs, p. 234; Oppenheim i. 166–7; Sørensen (ed.), *Manual*, p. 293. See further O'Connell, *State Succession* i. 369 seq.; and the *Lighthouses Arbitration*, Int. L.R. 23 (1956), at p. 659.

[3] Op. cit., pp. 255–70. See also Guggenheim i. (1953), 472; Bedjaoui, *Yrbk., I.L.C.* (1968), ii. 109–10; and *Pittacos* v. *État Belge*, Int. L.R. 45, 24 at pp. 31–2.

[4] See, for example, *West Rand Central Gold Mining Company* v. *The King* [1905] 2 K.B. 391; *Shimshon Palestine Portland Cement Company Ltd.* v. *A.-G.*, Int. L.R. 17 (1950), 72, Israel S.C. (sitting as Ct. of Civil Appeals); *Dalmia Dadri Cement Company Ltd.* v. *Commissioner of Income Tax*, Int. L.R. 26 (1958, II), 79, India, S.C. Many of the municipal decisions rest on special doctrines and Act of State in particular.

[5] Cf. Brierly, pp. 157–9. On the concept of odious debts see Int. Law Assoc., Fifty-Fourth Conference, Report of the Committee on Succession of States.

[6] See Chapters XXIII and XXIV; Castrén, *Yrbk., I.L.C.* (1969), i. 63, para. 45; Ruda, ibid., 82, para. 39; Ago, ibid., 88, para. 22; Guggenheim i. (1953), 474; Schwarzenberger, op. cit., p. 173, commenting on the case of *Certain German Interests in Polish Upper Silesia* (1926), P.C.I.J. Series A, No. 7, pp. 21, 22; I.L.A., *Report of the Fifty-Fifth Conference*, 1972, p. 654 at p. 660.

[7] For example: Rousseau iii. 393–425; O'Connell, *State Succession* i. 304 seq. esp. at p. 345 (but see also p. 266 and *supra*, p. 654); Guggenheim i. (1953), 476–7. Oppenheim i. 162, is cautious on this issue.

[8] See *supra*, pp. 653–4, on the principle. See also Bedjaoui, *Yrbk., I.L.C.* (1968), ii. 115–17; *Répertoire suisse* iii. 1394–1403.

contracts of employment and pension rights. It will be appreciated that judicial pronouncements to the effect that the mere change of sovereignty does not cancel concession rights[1] do not give support to the acquired rights doctrine in the form that *after* the change of sovereignty the new sovereign must maintain the property rights of aliens acquired before the change of sovereignty.

In the *Lighthouses Arbitration*[2] between France and Greece before the Permanent Court of Arbitration certain claims were concerned with an alleged Greek responsibility for breaches of concessions occurring prior to extension of Greek sovereignty over the autonomous state of Crete. These claims raise issues of succession in the context of state responsibility which are examined below. However, the Tribunal also approached the matter on the basis of recognition and adoption by Greece of the violation of the concession contract occurring before and even after the change of sovereignty over the island in question. The Tribunal said:[3]

> '. . . the Tribunal can only come to the conclusion that Greece, having adopted the illegal conduct of Crete in its recent past as autonomous State, is bound, as successor State, to take upon its charge the financial consequences of the breach of the concession contract. Otherwise, the avowed violation of a contract committed by one of the two States . . . with the assent of the other, would, in the event of their merger, have the thoroughly unjust consequence of cancelling a definite financial responsibility and of sacrificing the undoubted rights of a private firm holding a concession to a so-called principle of non-transmission of debts in cases of territorial succession, which in reality does not exist as a general and absolute principle. In this case the Greek Government with good reason commenced by recognising its own responsibility.

The short point remains that territorial change *of itself* neither cancels nor confers a special status on private rights. Where the private rights involve a substantial foreign control of the economy, then some modern exponents of the principle of vested or acquired rights are moved to formulate certain large qualifications concerning 'odious concessions' or 'concessions contrary to the public policy of the successor state',[4] for example, a major

[1] *Sopron-Köszeg Railway Case* (1929), *R.I.A.A.* ii. 961, 967.

[2] Int. L.R. 23 (1956), 79; *R.I.A.A.* xii. 155; Green, p. 182. Of some interest, though depending on treaty provisions, is the *Mavrommatis Jerusalem Concessions Case* (1925), P.C.I.J., Series A, No. 5, pp. 21, 27.

[3] Int. L.R. 23 (1956), at p. 92; *R.I.A.A.* xii, at p. 198; Green at p. 191.

[4] Zemanek, 116 Hague *Recueil* (1965, III), at pp. 282–9 (and note p. 288). See also Sørensen (ed.), *Manual*, p. 292; and 44 *Annuaire de l'Inst.* (1952), ii. 472.

concession granted on the eve of independence and involving vital resources. Qualified to this degree, the principle would seem to lose its viability.

4. *The Interaction of Rules of Law*

A common fault of writers is to classify issues primarily as 'succession' and consequently to consider particular issues in isolation from the matrix of rules governing the subject-matter, which might involve, for example, the law of treaties or nationality. It has been pointed out earlier in this chapter that principles of acquiescence and estoppel are often dominant, and in the previous section the issues of succession to state property and private law rights were related to general principles of international law governing transfers of sovereignty. The need to consider problems precipitated by a change of sovereignty in relation to the particular body of legal principles is illustrated very well by the law relating to nationality and the law of treaties.

5. *Particular Legal Issues*

(a) *Nationality.*[1] The problem involved is that of the nationality of inhabitants of territory which is the subject of a change of sovereignty.[2] If assumptions as to matters of principle may be made at the outset, the writer's opinion is that no help is to be derived from the categories of the law of state succession.[3]

In the submission of the present writer, the evidence is overwhelmingly in support of the view that the population follows the change of sovereignty in matters of nationality. At the end of the First World War the Versailles and associated treaties contained a number of provisions, more or less uniform in content, relating to changes of sovereignty which exhibited all the variations of

[1] On the position of corporations after a change of sovereignty see *Caisse Centrale* v. *Société Générale*, Int. L.R. 41, 369; Mann, 88 *L.Q.R.* (1972), 57–82; also in Mann, *Studies* (1973), pp. 524–52.

[2] See the rubrics employed by Weis, *Nationality and Statelessness in International Law*, p. 139, and Hudson, *Yrbk., I.L.C.* (1952), ii. 8.

[3] Cf. Weis, pp. 140, 150. At p. 150 he observes: 'Most of the principles referred to in connection with universal succession apply, *mutatis mutandis*, to the effects of partial succession on nationality. This is, however, subject to two qualifications: (a) questions of nationality will, in cases of partial succession, more frequently be regulated by treaty; and (b) since the predecessor State continues to exist, two nationalities, the nationality of the predecessor and that of the successor State, are involved. There thus arises not only the question of acquisition of the new nationality, but also that of the loss of the old nationality.' These qualifications hardly raise serious issues of principle.

state succession.[1] Thus the Minorities Treaty signed at Versailles provided as follows:

Article 4 (cp. Art. 3). Poland admits and declares to be Polish nationals *ipso facto* and without the requirements of any formality persons of German, Austrian, Hungarian or Russian nationality who were born in the said territory of parents habitually resident there, even if at the date of the coming into force of the present Treaty they are not themselves habitually resident there.

Nevertheless, within two years after coming into force of the present Treaty, these persons may make a declaration before the competent Polish authorities in the country in which they are resident stating that they abandon Polish nationality, and they will then cease to be considered as Polish nationals. In this connexion a declaration by a husband will cover his wife and a declaration by parents will cover their children under 18 years of age.

Article 6. All persons born in Polish territory who are not born nationals of another State shall *ipso facto* become Polish nationals.

The Treaties of St. Germain, Trianon, and Paris[2] have similar provisions, except that the Treaties of St. Germain and Trianon refer to persons born of parents 'habitually resident or possessing rights of citizenship [pertinenza—heimatrecht] as the case may be there'. It is thought that the precedent value of such provisions is considerable in view of their uniformity and the international character of the deliberations preceding the signature of these treaties. The objection that they give a right of option does not go very far, since the option is a later and additional procedure. Only if and when the option is made does the nationality of the successor state terminate: there is no statelessness before then. The treaty of peace with Italy of 1947 provided in Article 19 that Italian citizens domiciled, in the sense of habitual residence, in territory transferred shall become citizens of the transferee; and a right of option is given.

State practice evidenced by the provisions of internal law is to the same effect. The law of the United Kingdom has been expressed as follows by Lord McNair:[3]

The normal effect of the annexation of territory by the British Crown, whatever may be the source or cause of the annexation, for instance, a

[1] See *Laws Concerning Nationality* (1954), pp. 586 seq. See also the Treaty of Neuilly-sur-Seine, Arts. 51 and 52, ibid., p. 587; and the Treaty of Lausanne, Arts. 30–6, ibid.

[2] Art. 4. The Treaty of Paris concerned Rumania. See also *Markt* v. *Prefect of Trent*, *Ann. Digest* 10 (1941–2), no. 76. See also Caggiano, 2 *Ital. Yrbk.* (1976), 248 at pp. 264–71.

[3] *Opinions* ii. 24.

treaty of cession, or subjugation by war, is that the nationals of the State whose territory is annexed, if resident thereon, become British subjects; in practice, however, it is becoming increasingly common to give such nationals an option, either by the treaty of cession or by an Act of Parliament, to leave the territory and retain their nationality.

The present law is represented by section 11 of the British Nationality Act, 1948, which provides as follows:

If any territory becomes a part of the United Kingdom and colonies, His Majesty may by Order in Council specify the persons who shall be citizens of the United Kingdom and Colonies by reason of their connection with that territory; and those persons shall be citizens of the United Kingdom and Colonies as from a date to be specified in the Order.

There is no reason to believe that this provision has altered the principle as it was assumed to be before 1948.[1] The change is really one of procedure: there is now a prescribed mode for settlement of the precise categories of person who were to acquire British citizenship. The practice of the United States is to confer nationality on nationals of the predecessor state resident in the territory,[2] although on occasion persons who were 'citizens' of the territory annexed acquired citizenship.[3] In view of the state practice it is hardly surprising to find works of authority stating that persons attached to territory change their nationality when sovereignty changes hands.[4] Somewhat surprising is the caution of Dr. Weis in his conclusion on these issues. In his view:[5]

[1] Parry, *Nationality and Citizenship Laws of the Commonwealth*, pp. 274–5. The Act, he says, 'merely enacts the principle explained, that the matter is one for regulation in its discretion by the Crown'. Before 1949 there was no statutory provision expressly regulating annexation as a mode of acquiring the status of British subject: in other words, section 11 is concerned with a matter of internal competence.

[2] Moore, *Digest* iii. 311 seq.; Hackworth iii. 116 seq.

[3] Annexations of Hawaii and Texas: see Hackworth iii. 119; and Moore iii. 314. Soviet practice: *Laws Concerning Nationality* (1954), pp. 463, 464 (decrees relating to Lithuania, Estonia, Latvia, Bessarabia, and Northern Bukovina). See also the French law of 1945, ibid., p. 152.

[4] See Oppenheim i. 551, 571, 656–7; Rousseau iii. 343; Hyde ii. 1090; Briggs, p. 503. See further the opinion of the U.S. Attorney-General quoted by Briggs, p. 503, and the Harvard draft, Art. 18, 23 *A.J.* (1929), Spec. Suppl., p. 61.

[5] p. 149. Under the rubric 'Partial succession' he concludes (pp. 153–4) '. . . one may speak of a positive rule of international law on nationality to the effect that, under international law and provided the territorial transfer is based on a valid title, the predecessor State is under an obligation *vis-à-vis* the successor State to withdraw its nationality from the inhabitants of the transferred territory if they acquire the nationality of the successor State. In the absence of explicit provisions of municipal law there exists a presumption of international law that the municipal law of the predecessor State has this effect.' A formula involving a presumption as to the effect of municipal law is infelicitous. Other authors are

To sum up, it may be said that there is no rule of international law under which the nationals of the predecessor State acquire the nationality of the successor State. International law cannot have such a direct effect, and the practice of States does not bear out the contention that this is inevitably the result of the change of sovereignty. As a rule, however, States have conferred their nationality on the former nationals of the predecessor State, and in this regard one may say that there is, in the absence of statutory provisions of municipal law, a *presumption* of international law that municipal law has this effect.

Variations of practice, and areas of doubt, certainly exist, but by their nature they are hardly inimical to the general rule. Some difficulties merely concern modalities of the general rule itself.[1] Thus the position of nationals of the predecessor state who at the time of the transfer are resident outside the territory the sovereignty of which changes is unsettled. The rule probably is that, unless they have or acquire a domicile in the transferred territory, they do not acquire the nationality of the successor state.[2] This, it seems, is the British doctrine.[3]

The general principle is that of a substantial connexion with the territory concerned by citizenship or residence or family relation to a qualified person. This principle is perhaps merely a special aspect of the general principle of the effective link.[4] However, it could be argued that for the individuals concerned, at the moment of transfer, the connexion with the successor state is fortuitous. Whatever the merits of this, the link, in cases of territorial transfer, has special characteristics. Territory, both

of similarly cautious opinions: see Graupner, 32 *Grot. Soc.* (1946), p. 87 at p. 92; Mervyn Jones, *British Nationality Law* (1956), pp. 20–6; Parry, 28 *B.Y.* (1951), 426–7. See also Whiteman viii. 104–12.

[1] By analogy, the validity of the baseline principle in the law of the territorial sea was not thought to be affected by the absence (at least before 1958) of clear evidence as to its application to all permutations arising in coastal formations and relations.

[2] See Oppenheim i. 572; Weiss, pp. 145–8, 155–8; 159; O'Connell, *The Law of State Succession*, p. 253; Mervyn Jones, pp. 23–4; *Slouzak Minority in Teschen* (*Nationality*) case, *Ann. Digest* 11 (1919–41), no. 93; *Ministry of Home Affairs* v. *Kemali*, Int. L.R., 40, 191; *North Transsylvania Nationality* case, ibid., 43, 191. Cf. *In re Andries*, Int. L.R. 17 (1950), no. 26 (dual nationality arising).

[3] McNair, *Opinions* ii. 21–6; Weis, p. 145. Parry, op. cit., pp. 163–4, 275, is of the opinion that the rule was uncertain. See also *Murray* v. *Parkes* [1942] 2 K.B. 123.

[4] *Supra*, pp. 393 seq. See also the Secretariat survey of 14 May 1954, *Yrbk., I.L.C.* (1954), ii. 61, para. 39: 'The opinion is widely held that, in case of change of sovereignty over a territory by annexation, or its voluntary cession by one State to another, the annexing State is obliged to grant its nationality to the inhabitants of the territory concerned who were citizens of the ceding State, at least if they have, at the time of annexation, their permanent residence in the ceded territory. In most instances these questions are settled by treaty. . . .' And cf. the United Nations Convention on the Reduction of Statelessness, 1961, Art. 10.

socially and legally, is not to be regarded as an empty plot: territory (with obvious geographical exceptions) connotes population, ethnic groupings, loyalty patterns, national aspirations, a part of humanity, or, if one is tolerant of the metaphor, an organism.[1] To regard a population, in the normal case, as related to particular areas of territory, is not to revert to forms of feudalism but to recognize a human and political reality, which underlies modern territorial settlements. Modern thinking on human rights and the principle of self-determination has the same basis, and the latter has tended to create demands for changes in territorial sovereignty. If these assumptions are justifiable, it may be worthwhile to draw on the ideas inherent in the concepts of mandated and trust territories, and the principles of Chapter XI of the United Nations Charter.[2] Sovereignty denotes responsibility, and a change of sovereignty does not give the new sovereign the right to dispose of the population concerned at the discretion of the government. The population goes with the territory: on the one hand, it would be illegal, and a derogation from the grant, for the transferor to try to retain the population as its own nationals, and, on the other hand, it would be illegal for the successor to take any steps which involved attempts to avoid responsibility for conditions on the territory, for example by treating the population as *de facto* stateless or by failing to maintain order in the area. The position is that the population has a 'territorial' or local status, and this is unaffected whether there is a universal or partial successor and whether there is a cession, i.e. a 'transfer' of sovereignty, or a relinquishment by one state followed by a disposition by international authority.[3] In certain cases other considerations arise. Where there is a question of the continuity of states difficulties will arise which do not depend on nationality law, and in principle the result will be as in other cases of state succession.[4] When a new status is created by international quasi-legislative acts, as in case of the

[1] See the treatment in Vattel, *Le Droit des gens* i. Chap. XIX.

[2] See further the *South West Africa* cases, I.C.J. Reports (1962), p. 319 at pp. 354–7; 374, 378, 380 (Judge Bustamante, sep. op.), 422, 429–32 (Judge Jessup, ind. op.), 479–82, 541 seq. (Judges Spender and Fitzmaurice, joint diss. op.).

[3] It may happen that title is renounced without the territory becoming a *res nullius*. Relinquishment is thus distinct from abandonment, and is usually accompanied by recognition of title in another state, or recognition of a power of disposition to be exercised by another state or group of states. See, for example, the Treaty of St. Germain, 10 September 1919, Arts. 36, 43, 46, 47, 53, 54, 59, 89–91.

[4] See *Costa* v. *Military Service Commission of Genoa*, *Ann. Digest* 9 (1938–40), no. 13, *United States, ex rel. Reichel* v. *Carusi*, ibid. 13 (1946), no. 49; *Re Tancredi*, Int. L.R. 17 (1950), no. 50; Austrian Supreme Court, Int. L.R. 26 (1958, II), p. 40 at p. 42; German

creation of a mandate regime or trust territory, there may be no automatic change.[1] Lastly, though it cannot be dealt with here, the question of the legality of population transfer (apart from voluntary exercise of rights of option) arises.

(b) *Diplomatic claims and the principle of continuous nationality.* The operation of the nationality rule has been examined in Chapter XXI. In principle the requirement of continuity of nationality between the time of injury and the presentation of the claim (or, in cases of resort to judicial settlement, the making of the award) is not satisfied if the individual concerned suffers a change of nationality as a result of a change of territorial sovereignty. At least one of the arguments used to support the continuity principle, namely that it prevents the injured citizen choosing his own protector by a shift of nationality, has no application to a change of nationality in the present connexion. The rule of continuous nationality would adversely affect the whole citizen population of Tanzania after the voluntary union of Tanganyika and Zanzibar. In some cases of transfer the predecessor and successor states may act jointly in espousing claims on behalf of persons of their nationality successively, but this solution is inapplicable in case of mergers and dismemberment of states. It is surely the case that the correct solution in principle is a rule of substitution or subrogation, putting the successor in charge of claims belonging to the predecessor. This would be consonant with the conception of an effective change of sovereignty.

In the *Panevezys–Saldutiskis Railway* case[2] the Permanent Court was concerned with an Estonian claim and a Lithuanian

Federal Republic, Supreme Administrative Court, ibid. 21 (1954), 175; Federal Constitutional Court, ibid. 22 (1955), 430 (cf. Weis, op. cit., pp. 156–8); Federal Supreme Court, in *In re Feiner*, ibid. 23 (1956), 367, and in the *Austro-German Extradition* case, ibid., p. 364. In the last two cases the Court observed: 'Nor are there any binding rules of international law governing the question of acquisition and loss of nationality in the event of State succession.' However, decisions permitting Germans nationality arising from the Anschluss to subsist after the re-establishment of Austria in 1945 seem to rest on the rule that extraterritorial residence avoids the result of the change of sovereignty. Cf. *Austrian Nationality* case, Int. L.R. 20 (1953), 250; *Loss of Nationality (Germany) Case*, Int. L.R. 45, 353. On 17 May 1956 the German Federal Republic enacted a law under which those who were German nationals by virtue of the Anschluss ceased to be such on 26 April 1945. However, such persons were entitled to regain German nationality by declaration, with retroactive effect, to the date of loss, that they had had 'permanent residence' since 26 April 1945 'within the territory of the German Reich as constituted on 31 December 1937 (Germany)': *Laws Concerning Nationality*, Supplement (1959), p. 122.

[1] See *Westphal et Uxor* v. *Conducting Officer of Southern Rhodesia*, *Ann. Digest* 15 (1948), no. 54; Parry, *Nationality and Citizenship Laws of the Commonwealth*, p. 668.

[2] (1939), P.C.I.J., Series A/B, No. 76; World Court Reports, iv. 341; Briggs, p. 725.

counter-claim relating to the property of a company established under the law of the Russian Empire and operating in the territory which in 1918 constituted the new states of Estonia and Lithuania. In 1923 the company became an Estonian company with registered offices in Estonia. Estonia subsequently claimed compensation for the assets of the company remaining in Lithuania of which Lithuania had taken possession in 1919 and the Court upheld the Lithuanian preliminary objection based upon non-exhaustion of local remedies. The only judgment[1] delivered which concerned the principle of continuity of nationality expressly in the context of state succession was the dissenting opinion of Jonkheer van Eysinga.[2] He referred to the 'inequitable results' of a rule requiring continuity and concluded that it had not been established that the rule could not resist the normal operation of the law of state succession.

(c) *Transmissibility of State Responsibility*. The preponderance of authority is in favour of a general rule that liability for an international delict is extinguished when the wrongdoing state ceases to exist either by annexation or voluntary cession.[3] It seems that such liability is 'personal' and there is no good reason for succession to responsibility. This reasoning clearly cannot have general application and is less cogent in relation to voluntary merger or voluntary dissolution.[4] Nor does it apply when a successor state accepts the existence of succession, thus creating an estoppel in various particular respects.[5] In the *Lighthouses Arbitration*[6] it was held in connexion with one claim that Greece had by her conduct adopted an illegal act by the predecessor state and recognized her responsibility. Recently certain writers[7] have chal-

[1] But one may argue that the majority judgment (p. 16) deals with the point when it holds that the principle of continuity applied. However, the issue was whether there was proof of the Estonian nationality of the company concerned *at the time of injury* in 1919, i.e., when state succession had already occurred: see the sep. op. of de Visscher and Rostworowski, at pp. 27–8.

[2] At pp. 32–5. See also O'Connell, *State Succession* i. 537–41, Jennings, 121 Hague *Recueil* (1967, II), 476; and Monnier, *Ann. français* (1962), 68–72.

[3] Oppenheim, i. 162; Hurst, 5 *B.Y.* (1924), 163; Guggenheim i. (1953), 474; Rousseau, iii. 505–11; Briggs, p. 233; *Brown Claim* (1923), *R.I.A.A.* vi. 120; Briggs, 215; *Hawaiian Claims* (1925), *RI.A.A.* vi. 157; Monnier, *Ann. français* (1962), 65–90.

[4] Cf. the *Lighthouses Arbitration*, above; and Brierly, pp. 160–1. However, the decision rests on the element of adoption of the wrongful act by Greece and thus is not in principle inconsistent with the other authorities. The P.C.A. nevertheless is sceptical as to the existence of any general rule and refers to 'the vagaries of international practice and the chaotic state of authoritative writings': Int. L.R. 23 (1956), at pp. 91–2; *R.I.A.A.* xii, at p. 198. See further Verzijl, *International Law in Historical Perspective* vii. 219–28.

[5] *Infra*. p. 672. [6] *Supra*, p. 657.

[7] See, in particular, O'Connell, *State Succession* i. 482–6; and Jennings, 121 Hague *Recueil* (1967, II), 449–50.

lenged the application of a rule of non-transmission of responsibility to claims in respect of wrongful deprivation of private property: apparently this position is a logical extension of the view that rights under concessions survive changes of sovereignty.

The substantial problem would appear to be the doubtful status of the local remedies rule when, for example, a taking of property has occurred under the law of the previous sovereign. If the new state refuses to accept continuity of the municipal law, then a possible but not a necessary consequence is that no 'local remedies' are available and in any case international responsibility does not pass to the successor. If continuity of the legal system is accepted, does it follow that the successor by providing 'local remedies' is estopped from contesting succession to responsibility after such remedies have been exhausted?

(d) *Claims to Territory and the Benefit of Local Customs.*[1] In both the *Right of Passage* case (Merits)[2] and the *Temple* case (Merits)[3] the successor states in relation to local customs and boundary treaties, respectively, relied on the materiality of evidence of the position before transfer of sovereignty by the United Kingdom and France, respectively. The basis for this in both cases was recognition. In the *Island of Palmas*[4] and *Clipperton Island*[5] cases the United States and Mexico, respectively, were claiming as successors to Spain.

(e) *The Law of Treaties: In General.*[6] It seems to be generally accepted that in cases of 'partial succession', i.e. annexation or cession, where the 'losing' state is not extinguished, no succession to treaties can occur. Of course, existing treaties of the acquiring state will apply *prima facie* to the territories concerned. The rest of the area of problems is approached on the basis, first, that the law of treaties is the prime reference and thus the fact of succession must be fitted into that context, and, secondly, that the case where a continuing identity of legal personality is established is reserved for separate treatment.[7]

When a new state emerges it is not bound by the treaties of the

[1] See Bedjaoui, *Yrbk., I.L.C.*, 1968, II, 112–14. On boundary treaties see *infra*, p. 667.

[2] I.C.J. Reports (1960), p. 6; on which see *supra*, pp. 10, 377.

[3] Ibid. (1962), p. 6. [4] *Supra*, p. 144. [5] *Supra*, p. 145.

[6] In addition to the literature referred to *supra*, p. 651. see *Yrbk., I.L.C.* (1950), ii. 206–18; the Int. Law Assoc., Report of the Fifty-Third Conference, 1968, p. 596; and Report of the Fifty-Fourth Conference, 1970; Int. Law Assoc., *The Effect of Independence on Treaties* (1965); Mochi Onory, *La Succession d'états aux traités* (1968); Udokang, *Succession of New States to International Treaties* (1972); Goerdeler, *Die Staatensukzession in Multilateralen Verträgen* (1970); O'Connell, in: I.L.A., *The Present State of International Law* (1973), pp. 331–8.

[7] *Infra*, p. 671.

predecessor sovereign by virtue of a principle of state succession. In many instances the termination of a treaty affecting a state involved in territorial changes will be achieved by the normal operation of provisions for denunciation or the doctrine of fundamental change of circumstances.[1] However, as a matter of general principle a new state, *ex hypothesi* a non-party, cannot be bound by a treaty, and in addition other parties to a treaty are not bound to accept a new party, as it were, by operation of law.[2]

The rule of non-transmissibility applies both to secession of 'newly independent states' (that is, to cases of decolonization) and to other appearances of new states by the union or dissolution of states. The distinctions drawn by the International Law Commission in this respect in its drafts are not reflected by the practice of states.[3] This is not to deny that considerations of principle and policy may call for a different outcome in the case of a union of states. However, the distinction between a secession and the dissolution of federations and unions is unacceptable, both as a proposition of law and as a matter of principle.

To the general rule of non-transmissibility (the 'clean state' doctrine) certain important exceptions are often stated to exist. These may now be considered.

(i) *Treaties evidencing rules of general international law.* Certain multilateral conventions contain rules which are generally accepted as declaratory of general international law, as, for example, the Convention on the High Seas and parts of the Convention on the Continental Shelf.[4] A successor state is bound by such rules in the same way as other states.

(ii) '*Objective regimes*' *and localized treaties in general.* A number of writers, including O'Connell[5] and McNair,[6] have taken the view that there is a category of dispositive or localized

[1] *Supra*, p. 616.

[2] Oppenheim, i. 158–9; McNair, *Law of Treaties* (1961), pp. 592, 600–1, 629, 655; Brierly, p. 153; Sørensen (ed.), *Manual*, pp. 294–5, 298–9; Jennings, 121 Hague *Recueil* (1967, II), 442–6; Guggenheim i. 463; *Yrbk., I.L.C.* (1970), ii. 31–7; ibid. (1972), ii. 227, 250–4; ibid. (1974), ii (pt. 1), 7–9, 168–9, 211–14. See further Report of the Fifty-Third Conference, I.L.A., 1968, pp. xiii, 589 seq.; *Yrbk., I.L.C.* (1950), ii. 214–18 (the Israeli practice), in particular para. 23; 69 *A.J.* (1975), 863–4 (U.S. practice).

[3] Reports to U.N. Gen. Ass.; *Yrbk., I.L.C.* (1972), ii. 250, 286; ibid. (1974), ii (pt. 1), 211, 252. The evidence set forth in the Reports does not satisfy the criteria of a rule of customary law. See further the Vienna Conv. on Succession of States in Respect of Treaties, 1978, Art. 1, and Parts III and IV.

[4] See Chapters X and XI.

[5] *State Succession* ii. 12–23, 231 seq.

[6] *Law of Treaties*, pp. 655–64. See also Zemanek, op. cit., pp. 239–44; Rousseau iii. 491–4; Oppenheim i. 159; Sørensen (ed.), *Manual*, pp. 297–8; Guggenheim i. (1953), 465. See further: *Répertoire suisse* iii. 1333–4, 1339–40, 1358–92.

treaties concerning the incidents of enjoyment of a particular piece of territory in the matter of demilitarized zones, rights of transit, navigation, port facilities, and fishing rights. This category of treaties in their view is transmissible. The subject-matter overlaps considerably with the topic of international servitudes considered elsewhere.[1] The present writer, in company with others,[2] considers that there is insufficient evidence in either principle or practice for the existence of this exception to the general rule. First, much of the practice is equivocal and may rest on acquiescence. Secondly, the category is very difficult to define[3] and it is not clear why the treaties apparently included should be treated in a special way. Supporters of the alleged exception lean on materials which are commonly cited as evidence of an independent concept of state servitudes.[4] However, the Vienna Convention on Succession of States in Respect of Treaties of 1978 provides that a succession of states shall not affect obligations, or rights, 'relating to the use of territory', and 'established by a treaty for the benefit of any territory of a foreign state and considered as attaching to the territories in question' (Article 12).

(iii) *Boundary treaties*. Many jurists, who are unable to accept the existence of the category of localized treaties as an exception to the 'clean slate' rule, nevertheless regard boundary treaties as a special case depending on clear considerations of stability in territorial matters. It would seem that the question depends on normal principles governing territorial transfers: certainly the change of sovereignty does not as such affect boundaries.[5]

(iv) *Certain other categories*. The majority of writers are of the view that no other exceptions exist. However, a number of authorities consider that in the case of general multilateral or 'law-making' treaties there is a transmission. The view of O'Connell[6] is that in such cases the successor state is obliged by operation of law. However, the actual practice does not support this

[1] *Supra*, p. 372.

[2] See, for example, Castrén, 78 Hague *Recueil* (1951, I), 448–9. Sceptical are Brierly, p. 154; and Jennings, 121 Hague *Recueil* (1967, II), 442.

[3] See the miscellany in McNair.

[4] See *Free Zones* Case (1932), P.C.I.J., Series A/B, No. 46; World Court Reports, ii. 448; Green, p. 741; and *The Wimbledon* (1923), P.C.I.J., Series A, No. 1; World Court Reports, i. 163; Green, p. 311. On state servitudes see *supra*, pp. 372–5.

[5] On the principle of *uti possidetis* see *supra*, p. 137. See also O'Connell, *State Succession* ii. 273; Waldock, *Yrbk., I.L.C.* (1968), ii. 92–3; Bedjaoui, ibid., 112–14; Waldock, *Yrbk, I.L.C.* (1972), ii. 44–59; ibid., 298–308; ibid. (1974), ii (pt. 1), 196–208.

[6] Op. cit., i. 212–29. See also Jenks, 31 *B.Y.* (1952), 105, whose conclusions are essentially *de lege ferenda*.

thesis but rather indicates that the successor has an *option* to participate in such a treaty in its own right irrespective of the provisions of the final clauses of the treaty on conditions of participation.[1] It is probable that the regular acquiescence of states parties to such conventions and of depositaries in such informal participation indicates an *opinio juris*. However, there is some difficulty in producing a neat definition of general multilateral treaties for this purpose. The type includes the Conventions on the Privileges and Immunities of the United Nations, White Slave Traffic, Narcotic Drugs, Obscene Publications, Slavery, the Law of the Sea, Customs Facilities for Touring, various Customs conventions, Refugees, I.L.O. Conventions, the Geneva Conventions of 1949 on the conduct of war, and the Warsaw Convention for the Unification of Certain Rules relating to International Carriage by Air.[2] Common characteristics are the generality of participation allowed for in the conventions themselves, and the primary object of providing a comprehensive code of rules or standards for the particular subject-matter.[3] The constitutions of international organizations are not in the class.[4]

In practice problems of succession are dealt with by devolution agreements,[5] by original accession to conventions by new States and by unilateral declarations. In 1961 the Government of Tanganyika made a declaration to the Acting Secretary-General of the United Nations in the following terms:[6]

> As regards bilateral treaties validly concluded by the United Kingdom on behalf of the territory of Tanganyika, or validly applied or extended by the former to the territory of the latter, the Government of Tanganyika is willing to continue to apply within its territory on a basis of reciprocity, the terms of all such treaties for a period of two years from the date of independence . . . unless abrogated or modified earlier by mutual consent. At the expiry of that period, the Government of Tanganyika will regard such of these treaties which could not by the application of rules of customary international law be regarded as otherwise surviving, as having terminated.

[1] See Waldock, *Yrbk., I.L.C.* (1968), i. 130–1, paras. 47–8, and pp. 145–6, paras. 14–16; Castañeda, ibid., p. 137, paras. 37–41; Waldock, *Yrbk., I.L.C.* (1970), ii. 37–60; *Yrbk., I.L.C.* (1972), ii. 254–72; ibid. (1974), ii (pt. 1), 214–36; and Indonesian Note in U.N. Legis. Series ST/LEG/SER B/14, *Materials on Succession of States* (1967), p. 37. See further the Secretariat studies in *Yrbk., I.L.C.* (1968), ii. 1; (1969), ii. 23; (1970), ii. 61.

[2] U.N. Secretariat Memo. A/CN4/150, *Yrbk., I.L.C.* (1962), ii. 106, Chap. II.

[3] See Jennings, 121 Hague *Recueil* (1967, II), 444.

[4] See *infra*, p. 670. [5] *Supra*, p. 653.

[6] *Materials on Succession of States*, p. 177. See also Seaton and Maliti, *Tanzania Treaty Practice* (1973); Waldock, *Yrbk., I.L.C.* (1969), ii. 62–8; *Yrbk., I.L.C.* (1972) ii. 241–6; ibid. (1974), ii (pt. 1), 187–93.

... The Government of Tanganyika is conscious that the above declaration applicable to bilateral treaties cannot with equal facility be applied to multilateral treaties. As regards these, therefore, the Government of Tanganyika proposes to review each of them individually and to indicate to the depositary in each case what steps it wishes to take in relation to each such instrument—whether by way of confirmation of termination, confirmation of succession or accession. During such an interim period of review, any party to a multilateral treaty which has prior to independence been applied or extended to Tanganyika may, on the basis of reciprocity, rely against Tanganyika on the terms of such treaty.

This approach has been adopted, though with variations, by a considerable number of states in a similar situation.[1] In a general way such declarations combine a vague or general recognition[2] that certain unspecified treaties do survive as a result of the application of rules of customary law with an offer of a grace period in which treaties remain in force on an interim basis without prejudice to the declarant's legal position and with a requirement of reciprocity.[3] These arrangements are consistent with the existence of an option to participate in multilateral treaties but are not positive evidence in support of such an option. The practice based on such declarations supports the view that what eventually occurs is either termination or novation as the case may be in respect of the particular treaty.

The actual practice concerning the optional continuance of treaties in force is, it will be appreciated, not confined to multilateral conventions.[4] The question arises whether the practice in relation to general multilateral conventions is to be interpreted on the basis that the new state has the option to participate as of right. The answer is, probably, yes, but this can only be a tentative view and the practice in the case of continuance (apart from a new accession) of treaties of all types may be explicable simply as a novation of the original treaty by the new state and the other pre-existing, contracting party or parties.[5]

[1] Including Uganda, Kenya, Barbados, Guyana, Swaziland, Nauru, Mauritius, Botswana, Lesotho, Zambia, Burundi, Rwanda and Malawi. See also U.N. Legislative Series, *Materials on Succession of States*, p. 233 (Malagasy Note); and Waldock, Second Report, *Yrbk., I.L.C.* (1969), ii. 62–8.

[2] See the Zambian declaration.

[3] But see *Molefi* v. *Principal Legal Adviser*, Int. L.R. 39, p. 415, Lesotho High Ct., 1969; [1971] A.C. 182, P.C., in which the Privy Council treated a declaration of this type as an accession to the 1951 Convention Relating to the Status of Refugees.

[4] See the unilateral declarations noted above; Zemanek, op. cit., p. 243; I.L.A., *The Effect of Independence on Treaties* (1965), pp. 99–100, 109, 144 seq.; *Materials on Succession of States*, pp. 37, 42, 218.

[5] See the U.K. view on a bilateral treaty with France as affecting Laos: *Materials on Succession of States*, pp. 188–9; *Yrbk., I.L.C.* (1969), ii. 60.

(f) *Constitutions of International Organizations.*[1] The prevailing doctrine is to the effect that in so far as new states may succeed to treaty obligations of their predecessors under principles of general international law, such principles have no application to membership in international organizations. The position is determined by the provisions of the constitution of the particular organization. In the case of the United Nations all newly independent states are required to apply for membership in the United Nations. However, the member states by general tacit agreement or acquiescence may treat particular cases in a special way. When an original Member of the United Nations, India, was partitioned in 1947 the General Assembly treated the surviving India as the successor to pre-1947 India and admitted Pakistan as a new member of the United Nations. The union of Egypt and Syria in 1958 as the United Arab Republic and the dissolution of the union in 1961 resulted in informal consequential changes in membership of the Organization rather than formal admission, in the first instance of the United Republic, and in the second instance of the restored Egypt (still the United Arab Republic) and Syria.

(g) *The Law of Treaties: Succession to signature, ratification and reservations.* Within the existing possibilities of inheritance of treaties, there is considerable practice to the effect that a new state can inherit the legal consequences of a ratification by a predecessor of a treaty which is not yet in force, but it is doubtful if a new state can inherit the consequences of signature of a treaty which is subject to ratification.[2] A further issue, as yet unsettled, is whether a state 'inheriting' or continuing the treaties of a predecessor inherits the latter's reservations or is entitled to make reservations and objections of its own.[3]

(h) *Jus Cogens: Succession in relation to the principle of self-determination.* Several members of the International Law Commission have pointed out[4] that rules concerning succession must conform with any existing principles of *jus cogens*.[5] Points about *jus cogens* are made with particular reference to the principle of

[1] O'Connell, *State Succession* ii. 183–211; Zemanek, op. cit., pp. 245–54; Schachter, 25 *B.Y.* (1948), 101–9; Whiteman ii. 1016–27; U.N. Doc. A/CN4/149 and Add. 1, *Yrbk., I.L.C.* (1962), ii. 101; ibid., p. 106 at paras. 144–9; *Yrbk., I.L.C.* (1968), ii. 1; (1969), ii. 23; Green, in Schwarzenberger (ed.), *Law, Justice and Equity* (1967), pp. 152–67.

[2] See *Yrbk., I.L.C.* (1962), ii. 124, paras. 143, 151.

[3] See Gaja, i. *Italian Yrbk.* (1975), 52–68; Waldock, *Yrbk., I.L.C.* (1970), ii. 46–52. See also the Vienna Conv. on Succession of States in Respect of Treaties, 1978, Arts. 18, 19, 20, 32, 33, 36, 37.

[4] *Yrbk., I.L.C.* (1968), i. 102, para. 35 (Bedjaoui); p. 125, paras. 22, 23 (Ustor); p. 125, paras. 26–8 (Castañeda); p. 132, para. 69 (Tabibi); p. 138, para. 57 (Bartoš); p. 144, para. 63 (El-Erian).

[5] *Supra*, p. 512.

self-determination[1] and the possible continuance of political and economic domination after formal independence has been attained. The legal status of devolution treaties and economic concessions standing over from the pre-independence regime may be challenged on this basis in particular circumstances.[2]

6. *Relevance of the Political Form of Territorial Change*

There is clearly some relation between the nature of the territorial change and the transmissibility of rights and duties. Thus it is generally agreed that a cession of a part of territory will not affect the treaties of the parties to the transfer. Similarly, there are reasons of principle for approaching the issue of state responsibility differently in the cases of merger or voluntary dissolution of states. However, apart from the results of empirical enquiry in the context of such legal categories as treaties or state responsibility, there seems to be little or no value in establishing, as major *legal* categories, concepts of cession, dismemberment, merger, decolonization, and the like.[3] It may be that decolonization attracts special principles but there is no *general* significance in the distinction between decolonization, dismemberment, secession, and annexation. Too ready a reliance on such distinctions produces harmful results. In the first place, particular factual situations are presented as though they are legal categories. Secondly, distinctions are made in the legal rules adduced which may seem anomalous or invidious. Thus O'Connell[4] employs the category of 'annexation' and accepts the view that annexation terminates 'personal' treaties. He adopts a different approach to survival of treaties in the case of 'grants of independence' without explaining adequately why there should be such a different outcome.

This much having been said, the factual and political events producing a change of sovereignty may nevertheless have legal relevance in particular circumstances. Thus if the successor either

[1] *Supra*, p. 593.

[2] See Bedjaoui, *Yrbk., I.L.C.* (1968), ii. 115–17; and (1969), i. 53–6; Bartoš, ibid., 56–7.

[3] But see Bedjaoui, *Yrbk., I.L.C.* (1968), ii. 100–1. Other members of the Int. Law Comm. adopted a similar point of view: *Yrbk., I.L.C.* (1969), i. 53 seq.

[4] *State Succession* ii, Chaps. 2 and 8. O'Connell and Jennings (121 Hague *Recueil* at pp. 447–8) regard 'evolution towards independence' within the British Commonwealth as creating a continuity in personality with the pre-independence colonial government. This view is not reflected in the relevant legal position except in the rather different case where a protectorate is held to have had international personality before the subordinate status was removed: see Zemanek, 116 Hague *Recueil* (1965, III), 195–202; U.N. Legis. Series, *Materials on Succession of States* (1967), p. 184. Cf. also Rosenne, 27 *B.Y.* (1950), 267.

repudiates or acknowledges political continuity with the predecessor then this may produce some effects of preclusion or estoppel in respect of legal matters. Thus Poland refused to accept that there was continuity after she regained her independence in 1918.[1] There will be a presumption against continuity in cases where the political and legal machinery of change has involved relinquishment of sovereignty followed by reallocation in the form of a multilateral territorial settlement, as in the case of the peace treaties in Europe in 1919–20.[2] Similarly, there will be a presumption against continuity in the case of a forcible secession or its equivalent, as in the case of the appearance of Israel.[3] In those instances in which there is no 'transfer' of sovereignty then it is inappropriate to argue from the principle of a *grant* of sovereignty. Of course, the reference to either acknowledged or repudiated political (and thus legal) continuity with a predecessor state raises problems for third states which are not bound to accept the political determination of the putative successor.[4] The recognition of continuity by third states must be an important element since assessment of political continuity is very much a matter of choice and appreciation.[5] This is also the case where complicated political change produces a double succession within a short space of time as in the case of India and Pakistan, and Senegal and Mali. Normally, of course, these matters will be regulated by treaty: thus, for example, Turkey as a new political entity was held to be identical with the Ottoman Empire in provisions of the Treaty of Lausanne.[6]

7. *Doctrine of Reversion*[7]

It is possible that a continuity by virtue of general recognition by third states (see the last section) arises in the form of a reversion. Thus the successor state may be regarded as recovering a political and legal identity displaced by an intervening period of dismemberment or colonization.[8] Such cases will be rare and the logical consequences of a doctrine of reversion may create a threat to the security of legal relations: thus it would follow that the

[1] *Yrbk., I.L.C.* (1963), ii. 129, paras. 305 seq.; p. 131, paras. 326 seq.

[2] *Supra*, p. 139 and cf. *R.I.A.A.* i, p. 429 at pp. 441–4. Special provision was made in the treaties for the maintenance of public debts.

[3] U.N. Legis. Series, *Materials on Succession of States* (1967), p. 38; *Shimshon Palestine Portland Cement Factory Ltd.* v. *A.-G.*, Int. L.R. 17 (1950), 72.

[4] Whiteman ii. 758–9; *Répertoire suisse* iii. 1337–57.

[5] *Supra*, p. 85.

[6] See also the *Ottoman Debt Arbitration, R.I.A.A.* i, p. 529 at pp. 571–4, 590–4, 599.

[7] See Alexandrowicz, 45 *International Affairs*, (1969), 465–80; Jain, 9 *Indian Journ. of I.L.* (1969), 525–7.

[8] Cf. the history of Poland and India.

successor would not be bound by territorial grants or recognition of territorial changes by the previous holder. The suggestion has been made that, quite apart from recognition by third states, in a case of post-colonial reversion, the principle of self-determination may create a presumption in favour of the successor state.[1] This raises large issues of the relation between principles of *jus cogens*, of which self-determination [2] is an example in the view of some authorities, and the law relating to state succession.[3]

[1] See the dissenting opinion of Judge Moreno Quintana in the *Right of Passage* case, I.C.J. Reports, (1960), p. 6 at pp. 93–6, especially at p. 95. Cf. Bedjaoui, *Yrbk., I.L.C.* (1968), i. 128, para. 10.

[2] *Supra*, p. 593. [3] See *supra*, section 5 (h).

CHAPTER XXIX

OTHER CASES OF TRANSMISSION OF RIGHTS AND DUTIES

1. *Succession between International Organizations*[1]

It happens from time to time that an international organization is dissolved and its functions are in substance assumed by a new organization with similar objects and composition. When the League of Nations was dissolved in 1946, practical arrangements had been made for the transfer of its property and certain of its functions to the United Nations. There was no automatic transfer and the element of continuity depended on the consent of the United Nations.[2] In the case of functions under treaties, transfer of functions to the United Nations required the consent of the parties to the treaties. Instruments containing acceptances of the jurisdiction of the Permanent Court of International Justice (which was dissolved in 1946) were deemed to be acceptances of the jurisdiction of the new Court by specific provisions in the new Statute.[3]

There is no rule of automatic succession between organizations. In the Advisory Opinion on the *International Status of South West Africa*[4] the International Court was concerned to discover the legal consequences of the dissolution of the League of Nations, the organs of which had supervised the execution of the Mandate[5] for South West Africa and South Africa's refusal to conclude a Trusteeship Agreement. On a number of grounds not relating to any principle of succession between organizations, the Court found that the Mandate continued to exist. It also found that the appropriate organs of the United Nations were to exercise the supervisory functions of the League of Nations in spite of the fact that such functions 'were neither expressly transferred to the United Nations nor expressly assumed by that organization'.[6]

[1] Fitzmaurice, 29 *B.Y.* (1952), 8–10; Chiu, 14 *I.C.L.Q.* (1965), 83–120; Hahn, *Duke L.J.* (1962), 379–422, 522–57; also in 13 *Öst. z. für off. R.* (1963–4), 167–239; Bowett, *International Institutions* (3rd ed.), pp. 336–41; O'Connell i. 396–9; Judge Fitzmaurice, diss. op., *Namibia Opinion*, I.C.J. Reports (1971), pp. 227–63; Schwarzenberger, *International Constitutional Law* (1976), pp. 99–114; Schermers, *International Institutional Law* ii. 645–69.

[2] See Whiteman xiii. 263–300.

[3] See *infra*, p. 720.

[4] I.C.J. Reports (1950), p. 128. See also *South West Africa* cases (Preliminary Objections); ibid. (1962), p. 319; and the *Namibia Opinion*, ibid. (1971), p. 16. See generally Cheng, 20 *Curr. Leg. Problems* (1967), 181–212.

[5] On which see *supra*, p. 181.

[6] Ibid., p. 136.

The reasoning of the Court is not easy to characterize. The principal basis of this finding was 'the necessity for supervision' which continued to exist despite the disappearance of the supervisory organ under the Mandates system—the Council of the League of Nations. Judge Fitzmaurice, as he now is, has expressed the view that the Advisory Opinion is authority for the proposition that an 'automatic devolution' of functions from one organization to another *may* occur and that in certain conditions there is a presumption that such a devolution occurs.[1] If the Court was purporting to construe the provisions of the United Nations Charter and relying upon a teleological or purposive approach to interpretation, then Judge Fitzmaurice was in error.[2] However, the principle of necessity may seem to go beyond mere treaty interpretation and, if that be so, then *in effect* the Court was discovering a case of 'automatic' succession.[3]

Judge Fitzmaurice has his own view of the matter.[4] He considers that 'there are only three ways in which the United Nations could, upon the dissolution of the League, have become invested with the latter's powers in respect of mandates as such: namely, (a) if specific arrangement to that effect had been made, —(b) if such a succession must be implied in some way,—or (c) if the mandatory concerned—in this case South Africa—could be shown to have consented to what would in effect have been a *novation* of the reporting obligation, in the sense of agreeing to accept the supervision of, and to be accountable to, a new and different entity, the United Nations, or some particular organ of it.' With respect, this formulation must be correct. The essential difference between Judge Fitzmaurice and the Court as a whole probably consists in the manner of application of these principles to the evidence of what actually happened upon the dissolution of the League.

2. *Cases of Agency*

States may act on behalf of other states for various purposes, provided that authority to do so exists and is not exceeded. States

[1] 29 *B.Y.* (1952), 8. See also Oppenheim i. 168–9; Lauterpacht, *The Development of International Law by the International Court*, pp. 277–81.

[2] See Schwarzenberger i. 178; Bowett, op. cit., p. 340; Chiu, op. cit., pp. 105–6. See also Cheng, op. cit., pp. 187–91.

[3] The formulations of the Court in the *Namibia Opinion*, I.C.J. Reports (1971), at pp. 28–45, do not take the matter any further.

[4] I.C.J. Reports (1971), p. 227. See also the Joint Dissent of Judges Spender and Fitzmaurice, *South West Africa* cases, I.C.J. Reports (1962), at pp. 516 seq.

may appoint other states as agents for various purposes, including the making of treaties. This agency may arise from the existence of a relation of federation or dependence or protection[1] or otherwise.[2] By agreement an organization may become an agent for member states, and others, in regard to matters outside its normal competence and a state may act as agent for an organization.[3]

3. *Assignment*

In considering the effects of a devolution agreement[4] the International Law Commission has pointed out that it was 'extremely doubtful' whether such a purported assignment by itself could change the position of any of the interested states. The Vienna Convention on the Law of Treaties contains no provisions regarding assignment of rights or obligations. As the Commission has pointed out: 'The reason is that the institution of "assignment" found in some national systems of law by which under certain conditions contract rights may be transferred without the consent of the other party to the contract does not appear to be an institution recognized in international law.'[5]

[1] Cf. *supra*, pp. 76–9.

[2] See the I.L.C. Report on the Law of Treaties, 59 *A.J.* (1965), 203 at p. 209, referring to the Belgo-Luxembourg Economic Union, under which treaties may be concluded by one state on behalf of the Union. See also the Utilities Claims Settlement Agreement between the Government of the United States as Unified Command, on its own behalf and on behalf of Certain Other Governments, and the Government of the Republic of Korea, 1958, *Treaty Series* No. 57 (1959), Cmnd. 796.

[3] *Infra*, p. 690.

[4] On which see *supra*, p. 653.

[5] *Yrbk., I.L.C.* (1969), ii. 56, para. 10. For a different view: Mann, 30 *B.Y.* (1953), 475–8 (also in Mann, *Studies* (1973), pp. 360–5); and see also Starke, 13 *Indian Journ.* (1973), 519–29.

PART XII

INTERNATIONAL ORGANIZATIONS AND TRIBUNALS

CHAPTER XXX

INTERNATIONAL ORGANIZATIONS

1. *Introductory*

In the nineteenth century states advanced from the bilateral treaty and reliance on diplomatic contact to other forms of co-operation. The Congress of Vienna heralded an era of international conferences and multilateral treaties, and later there appeared administrative unions such as the European Danube Commission, and the International Telegraph Union. After 1920 the League of Nations and the United Nations provided the more developed notion of universal peace-keeping institutions, and there appeared an ever-increasing number of specialized institutions concerned with technical, economic, and social co-operation. Permanent organizations with executive and administrative organs paralleled but did not completely replace the system of *ad hoc* diplomacy involving, *inter alia*, conferences.[1] The general study of international organization and the multiplicity of institutions and agencies is a department of the political and social sciences, and in the present chapter the object is to indicate only the legal problems arising from the function of organizations of states.[2]

2. *Legal Personality*[3]

The international community has no legal and administrative process comparable to that of incorporation in municipal law,

[1] Cf. the United Nations Conferences on the Law of the Sea and other subjects. On *ad hoc* diplomacy: Chapter XVI, section 11.

[2] See especially Bowett, *The Law of International Institutions* (3rd ed., 1975); Reuter, *International Institutions* (1958; 5th French ed., 1967); Chaumont, *Les Organizations internationales* (1961); Colliard, *Institutions internationales* (4th ed., 1967); Morgenstern, 48 *B.Y.* (1976–7), 241–57; Rousseau ii. (1974), 449–691; Schwarzenberger, *International Constitutional Law* (1976); Schermers, *International Institutional Law* (1972), 2 vols.; Kirgis, *International Organizations in Their Legal Setting* (1977).

[3] Generally see *supra*, Chapter III.

but it is significant that the latter may recognize unincorporated associations as legal persons.[1] Where there is no constitutional system for, as it were, recognizing and registering associations as legal persons, the primary test is functional. Indeed, it would be fatuous to work from an abstract model in face of the existence of some 170 organizations of states. In the *Reparation* case[2] the International Court was asked for an advisory opinion on the capacity of the United Nations, as an organization, to bring an international claim in respect of injury to its personnel, on the lines of diplomatic protection, and in respect of injury to the United Nations caused by the injury to its agents. The Charter did not contain any explicit provision on the legal personality of the Organization,[3] but the Court drew on the implications of the Charter as a whole:[4]

> The subjects of law in any legal system are not necessarily identical in their nature or in the extent of their rights, and their nature depends upon the needs of the community. Throughout its history, the development of international law has been influenced by the requirements of international life, and the progressive increase in the collective activities of States has already given rise to instances of action upon the international plane by certain entities which are not States. This development culminated in the establishment in June 1945 of an international organization whose purposes and principles are specified in the Charter of the United Nations. But to achieve these ends the attribution of international personality is indispensable.
>
> The Charter has not been content to make the Organization created by it merely a centre 'for harmonizing the actions of nations in the attainment of these common ends' (Article I, para. 4). It has equipped that centre with organs, and has given it special tasks. It has defined the position of the Members in relation to the Organization by requiring them to give it every assistance in any action undertaken by it (Article 2, para. 5), and to accept and carry out the decisions of the Security Council; by authorizing the General Assembly to make recommendations to the Members; by giving the Organization legal capacity and privileges and immunities in the territory of each of its Members; and by providing for the conclusion of agreements between the Organization and its Members. Practice—in particular the conclusion of conventions to which the Organization is a party—has confirmed this character of the Organization, which occupies a position in certain respects in detachment from its Members, and which is under a duty to remind them, if need be, of certain obligations. It must be added that the Organization is a political body, charged with political tasks

[1] Cf. *Knight and Searle* v. *Dove* [1964] 2 Q.B. 631; and see Wedderburn, 28 *Mod. L.R.* (1965), 62–71.

[2] I.C.J. Reports (1949), p. 174; Briggs, p. 85; Green, p. 146; Bishop, p. 233.

[3] Article 104 relates solely to legal capacity of the Organization in the municipal law of Member States, on which see Bridge, 18 *I.C.L.Q.* (1969), 689.

[4] I.C.J. Reports (1949), pp. 178–9.

of an important character, and covering a wide field namely, the maintenance of international peace and security, the development of friendly relations among nations, and the achievement of international co-operation in the solution of problems of an economic, social, cultural or humanitarian character (Article I); and in dealing with its Members it employs political means. The 'Convention on the Privileges and Immunities of the United Nations' of 1946 creates rights and duties between each of the signatories and the Organization (see, in particular, Section 35). It is difficult to see how such a convention could operate except upon the international plane and as between parties possessing international personality.

In the opinion of the Court, the Organization was intended to exercise and enjoy, and is in fact exercising and enjoying, functions and rights which can only be explained on the basis of the possession of a large measure of international personality and the capacity to operate upon an international plane. It is at present the supreme type of international organization, and it could not carry out the intentions of its founders if it was devoid of international personality. It must be acknowledged that its Members, by entrusting certain functions to it, with the attendant duties and responsibilities, have clothed it with the competence required to enable those functions to be effectively discharged.

Accordingly, the Court has come to the conclusion that the Organization is an international person. That is not the same thing as saying that it is a State, which it certainly is not, or that its legal personality and rights and duties are the same as those of a State. Still less is it the same thing as saying that it is 'a super-State', whatever that expression may mean. It does not even imply that all its rights and duties must be upon the international plane, any more than all the rights and duties of a State must be upon that plane. What it does mean is that it is a subject of international law and capable of possessing international rights and duties, and that it has capacity to maintain its rights by bringing international claims.

The criteria of legal personality in organizations may be summarized as follows:

(1) a permanent association of states, with lawful objects, equipped with organs;
(2) a distinction, in terms of legal powers and purposes, between the organization and its member states;
(3) the existence of legal powers exercisable on the international plane and not solely within the national systems of one or more states.[1]

[1] See further Jenks, 22 *B.Y.* (1945), 267–75; Ginther, *Die völkerrechtliche Verantwortlichkeit internationaler Organisationen gegenüber Drittstaaten* (1969); Skubiszewski, 12 *Annuaire français* (1966), p. 544 at pp. 556–60; Quadri, 113 Hague *Recueil* (1964, III), 423–33; Seyersted, 34 *Acta Scandinavica* (1964), 46–61; id., 4 *Indian Journ.* (1964), 1–74, 233–68; Pescatore, 103 Hague *Recueil* (1961, II), 27–52, 67–74; Dupuy, 100 Hague *Recueil* (1960, II), 467–88, 529–61; Fawcett, 34 *B.Y.* (1957), 313–14; Broches, 98 Hague *Recueil* (1959, III), 323–9; Weissberg, *The International Status of the United Nations* (1961); Carroz and Probst, *Personalité juridique internationale et capacité de conclure des traités de*

These criteria relate to delicate issues of law and fact and are not always easy to apply. However, many important institutions undoubtedly have legal personality, including the specialized agencies of the United Nations (such as the International Labour Organization), the European Communities (European Economic Community, the Coal and Steel Community, and Euratom), and the Council of Mutual Economic Assistance (COMECON); and, as will appear subsequently, the really difficult questions concern the particular capacities of the organization as a legal person and its relations to members, third states, and other organizations. Before these questions are considered it may give more point to the criteria summarized above if certain distinctions are drawn. Thus an organization may exist but lack the organs and objects necessary for legal personality: the British Commonwealth is an association of this kind. Similarly, a multilateral convention may be institutionalized to some extent, making provision for regular conferences, and yet not involve any separate personality.[1] Joint agencies of states,[2] for example an arbitral tribunal or river commission, may have restricted capacities and limited independence, but the difference between a limited functional independence, with executive and jurisdictional powers, and legal personality is only a matter of degree. This is also the case with the agencies and subsidiary organs of organizations, such as the High Commissioner for Refugees and the Technical Assistance Board in relation to the United Nations.[3] If an organization has considerable independence and power to intervene in the affairs of member states, the latter may come to have a status akin to that of membership in a federal union. It may be noted also that, whilst an organization with legal personality is normally established by treaty, this is by no means necessary and the source could equally be the resolution of a conference of states or a uniform practice.[4] The constitutional basis of the United Nations Conference on Trade and Development (UNCTAD) and of the United Nations Industrial

l'O.N.U. et des institutions spécialisées (1953); Bishop, 115 Hague *Recueil* (1965, II), 261–8; Tunkin, 119 Hague *Recueil* (1966, III), 7–66; Morozov, in Tunkin (ed.), *Contemporary International Law* (1970), 118–40; Osakwe, 65 *A.J.* (1971), 502–21.

[1] Cf. conflicting decisions of Italian courts on the status of the North Atlantic Treaty Organization: *Branno* v. *Ministry of War*, Int. L.R. 22 (1955), 756; *Mazzanti* v. *H.A.F.S.E.*, ibid., p. 758.

[2] See further *supra*, p. 65. Cf. the Commonwealth Secretariat Act, 1966.

[3] See *supra*, p. 65; Reuter, *Hommage à Président Basdevant*, pp. 415–40; and Dale, 23 *I.C.L.Q.* (1974), 576–609.

[4] On the formation of the World Tourism Organization see Gilmour, 18 *Neths. Int. L.R.* (1971), 275–98. Cf. *Zoernsch* v. *Waldock* [1964] 1 W.L.R. 675, Green, p. 153, on the constitution of an organ of an organization.

Development Organization (UNIDO) must be found in resolutions of the General Assembly.[1]

Finally, some other relations of the subject-matter may be mentioned. An institution may lack the features of an 'organization' and yet have legal personality on the international plane. Thus the 'Contracting Parties' of the General Agreement on Trade and Tariffs have some legal personality, partly by reason of the exercise by them of a quasi-judicial function in the complaint procedures between contracting parties. Moreover, a formal presentation may concentrate too much on 'international legal personality', ignoring the powers of organizations, and institutions like the GATT, to make local law contracts such as leases of buildings. In practice the latter competence may flow from the international legal personality.

3. *Performance of Acts in the Law*

The analogue for the successful exercise of legal functions in international relations is the state, in spite of the obvious dangers of assuming automatic and extensive parallels. The most viable type of organization will have a number of legal powers similar to those normally associated with statehood. The enumeration of acts in the law which organizations may perform will establish the dynamics of the subject and provide a necessary background to the subjects of implied powers and interpretation of basic instruments developed later. At the same time the individuality of each organization must be emphasized: in the first instance the evidence of legal capacity is to be found in the constituent treaty of the particular organization.

(a) *The treaty-making power.*[2] The existence of legal personality does not of itself support a power to make treaties, and everything depends on the terms of the constituent instrument of the

[1] See Gutteridge, *The United Nations in a Changing World*, pp. 75–85.

[2] See Parry, 26 *B.Y.* (1949), 108–49; Schneider, *Treaty-Making Power of International Organizations* (1959); Seyersted, 37 *B.Y.* (1961), 449–51; Kasme, *La Capacité des Nations Unies de conclure des traités* (1960); Broches, op. cit., pp. 329 seq.; Pescatore, op. cit., pp. 55–67; Dupuy, op. cit., pp. 489 seq.; Detter, 38 *B.Y.* (1962), 421–44; Karunatilleke, 75 *R.G.D.I.P.* (1971), 12–91; Hungdah Chiu, *The Capacity of International Organizations to Conclude Treaties, and the Special Legal Aspects of the Treaties So Concluded* (1966); Whiteman xiii. 28–31; Zemanek (ed.), *Agreements of International Organizations and the Vienna Convention on the Law of Treaties* (1971); *Yrbk., I.L.C.* (1974), ii (pt. 2), 3 (biblio.). The specific provisions of drafts of the International Law Commission on the law of treaties applied to the treaties of states only, but the Commission has recognized that in principle it considers the international agreements to which organizations are parties to fall within the scope of the law of treaties: *Yrbk., I.L.C.* (1963), ii. 177–8 (paras. 113–5). See I.L.C., Final Draft on the Law of Treaties, 1966, Art. 3; *Yrbk., I.L.C.* (1966), ii. 190; and the Vienna Conv. on the Law of Treaties, 1969, Art. 3. See also Report of the I.L.C., 1977; Provisional Draft Articles on treaties concluded between states and International Organizations or between International Organizations; 16 *Int. Leg. Materials* (1977), 1260 (on

organization. The constituent instrument does not normally confer a general treaty-making power, but this may be established by interpretation of the instrument as a whole and resort to the doctrine of implied powers (*infra*). The United Nations Charter contains provisions expressly authorizing certain agreements, such as the trusteeship agreements (Chapter XII) and relationship agreements with the specialized agencies (Articles 57 and 63). However, the United Nations, together with other organizations, has concluded headquarters agreements with states and agreements on co-operation with other organizations, although the constituent instrument contains no express authority for these types of agreement. In practice organizations readily assume a treaty-making power.

(b) *Privileges and immunities*.[1] In order to function effectively, international organizations require a certain minimum of freedom and legal security for their assets, headquarters, and other establishments and for their personnel and representatives of member states accredited to the organizations. By analogy with the privileges and immunities accorded to diplomats, the requisite privileges and immunities in respect of the territorial jurisdiction of host states are provided for but in this context on the basis of treaty and not customary law. There is as yet no customary rule supporting international immunities,[2] but it could happen that the fulfilment of obligations of membership involving activity on state territory by the organization demanded a certain amount of immunity without special agreement.[3] In any case the international immunities are highly specialized and inevitably vary a great deal. In contrast to diplomatic privileges and immunities the functional basis is much more dominant, and, as experience with United Nations peace-keeping forces shows, the relationship with the host state will depend a great deal on the specific function involved and all the circumstances.[4] Naturally the immunity given to judges of the International Court and other holders of judicial offices is of special importance and

the basis of the work of Reuter as Rapporteur); and *Annuaire de l'Inst.* (1973), 55, 214–415.

[1] Bowett, *The Law of International Institutions* (3rd ed.), pp. 308–23; Jenks, *International Immunities* (1961); Kunz, 41 *A.J.* (1947), 828–62; Perrin, 60 *R.G.D.I.P.* (1956), 193–237; Lalive, 84 Hague *Recueil* (1953, III), 291–385; Weissberg, op. cit., pp. 141–69; Brandon, 28 *B.Y.* (1951), 90–113; Schröer, 75 *R.G.D.I.P.* (1971), 712–41; Whiteman xiii. 32–188; Secretariat Study, *Yrbk., I.L.C.* (1967), ii. 154–324; El-Erian, ibid., 133–53; ibid. (1968), ii. 119–62; ibid. (1969), ii. 1–21; ibid. (1970), ii. 1–24; ibid. (1971), II (pt. 1), 1–142; Michaels, *International Privileges and Immunities* (1971).

[2] This is the general opinion. For other views: Lalive, op. cit., p. 304; Weissberg, op. cit., p. 144.

[3] Bowett, op. cit., p. 310.

[4] See especially Bowett, *United Nations Forces*, pp. 428–67.

is equated to diplomatic privileges.[1] As in the case of diplomatic immunities, international immunities are subject to waiver.

Article 105 of the United Nations Charter provides that 'the Organization shall enjoy in the territory of each of its members such privileges and immunities as are necessary for the fulfilment of its purposes', and, further, that 'representatives of the Members of the United Nations and officials of the Organization shall similarly enjoy such privileges and immunities as are necessary for the independent exercise of their functions in connection with the Organization'. If the constituent treaty contains only general stipulations, then further arrangements are necessary. In the case of the United Nations the principal instrument involved is the General Convention on the Privileges and Immunities of the United Nations.[2] The United Nations and the United States concluded a Headquarters Agreement in 1947.[3] For constitutional and other reasons states implement treaty obligations of this kind by municipal legislation, and in the United Kingdom the applicable legislation is the International Organizations Act, 1968.[4]

The question of privileges and immunities is governed by the Vienna Convention on the Representation of States in their Relations with International Organizations of a Universal Character,[5] adopted in 1975. It is to apply to permanent missions constituting representation of the sending State to the organization concerned, and also delegations sent to an organ or a conference convened by the organization. The provisions have been criticized by a number of governments on the basis that the interest of the host State receives insufficient protection. The privileges and immunities are modelled on the provisions of the Vienna Convention on Diplomatic Relations.[6] The United States, for example, does not accept that the provisions of the present

[1] See Article 19 of the Statute of the International Court; and 93 *J.D.I.* (1966), p. 176.

[2] Approved by the General Assembly on 13 February 1946. Text: 1 U.N.T.S., 15. See *M.* v. *Organisation des Nations Unies et Etat Belge*, Int. L.R. 45, 446. There is a separate Convention on the Privileges and Immunities of the Specialized Agencies, approved on 21 November 1947. Text: 33 U.N.T.S., 261.

[3] 11 U.N.T.S. 18. See *U.S.* v. *Melekh*, 190 F. Supp. 67; 193 F. Supp. 586; Int. L.R. 32, p. 308; *U.S. ex rel. Casanova* v. *Fitzpatrick*, 214 F. Supp. 425; Int. L.R. 34, p. 154; *People* v. *Coumatos*, 224 N.Y.S. 2d 507; Int. L.R. 35, p. 222.

[4] See also the Diplomatic and Other Privileges Act, 1971. See further *Zoernsch* v. *Waldock* [1964] 1 W.L.R. 675; Green, p. 153.

[5] Text: 69 *A.J.* (1975), 730; *Digest of U.S. Practice*, 1975, p. 40. The Conv. requires 35 ratifications or accessions before it comes into force. For comment: Fennessy, 70 *A.J.* (1976), 62. For the Report of the International Law Commission, see *Yrbk., I.L.C.* (1971), ii (pt. 1), 278.

[6] See Chapter XVI.

Convention represent the existing international law on the subject.[1]

(c) *Capacity to espouse international claims.* In the advisory opinion in the *Reparation* case, quoted in part earlier, the International Court held unanimously that the United Nations was a legal person with capacity to bring claims against both member and non-member[2] states for direct injuries to the Organization. The power to espouse claims for direct injuries was regarded, it seems, as a concomitant of legal personality, since the Court leaned on the general ambience of purposes and functions as it did when examining the preliminary issue of personality. However, the Court[3] expressed its conclusion in terms of implied powers and effectiveness, of which more later. A similar reasoning may apply to other organizations.[4] The capacity to espouse claims thus depends (1) on the existence of legal personality and (2) on the interpretation of the constituent instrument in the light of the purposes and functions of the particular organization.[5] In contrast, the existence of immunities is not conditioned by separate legal personality on the part of the agency concerned.

(d) *Functional protection of agents and persons entitled through them.*[6] The Court in the *Reparation* case used similar reasoning[7] to justify its opinion that the United Nations could espouse claims for injury to its agents on the basis of a functional protection. This view provoked several dissenting opinions,[8] and certainly this capacity cannot readily be invoked for other organizations, especially when their functions do not include peace-keeping.[9] A problem which remains to be solved is the determination of priorities between the state's right of diplomatic protection and the organization's right of functional protection.[1]

[1] See *Digest of U.S. Practice*, 1973, pp. 25–9, referring to Article 36 of the I.L.C. draft articles (n. 5, *supra*).

[2] I.C.J. Reports (1949), pp, 184–5, 187. [3] At p. 180.

[4] For extension of the principle to the European Communities: Pescatore, op. cit., pp. 218–19. See also Broches, op. cit., pp. 323–9 (on the International Bank).

[5] Sørensen, 101 Hague *Recueil* (1960, III), 139, relates the capacity directly to legal personality.

[6] See El-Erian, *Yrbk., I.L.C.* (1963), ii. 159 at pp. 181–3; Eagleton, 76 Hague *Recueil* (1950, I), 369–72; Hardy, 37 *B.Y.* (1961), 516–26; *Yrbk., I.L.C.* (1967), ii. 218–19.

[7] I.C.J. Reports (1949), pp. 181–4. Cf. *Jurado* v. *I.L.O.* (*No. 1*), Int. L.R. 40, p. 296.

[8] See Hackworth, p. 196, Badawi, p. 205, and Krylov, p. 217. Winiarski, p. 189, in general shared the views of Hackworth.

[9] Pescatore, pp. 219–21, denies the capacity for the European Communities. Cp. Bowett, *The Law of International Institutions* (3rd ed.), p. 303–4.

[1] I.C.J. Reports (1949), pp. 185–6; Bowett, *United Nations Forces*, pp. 151, 242–8, 448.

(e) Locus standi *before international tribunals.* When an organization has legal personality it ought in principle to have *locus standi* before international jurisdictions. Everything depends on the statute governing the tribunal or the *compromis* concerned. Whilst certain organizations have access to the International Court through its advisory jurisdiction, the Statute still confines *locus standi* to states (Article 34).[1]

(f) *Responsibility.*[2] Organizations may have extensive functions involving the conclusion of treaties, the administration of territory, the use of armed forces, and the provision of technical assistance. If an organization has a legal personality distinct from that of the member states, and functions which in the hands of states may create responsibility, then it is in principle reasonable to impute responsibility to the organization. In a very general way this follows from the reasoning of the Court in the *Reparation* case. However, regard must be had to each set of circumstances. In relation to the use of forces under the authority of the United Nations in peace-keeping operations, the general principle is that the issue of financial responsibility is determined by the relevant agreements between governments contributing forces and the United Nations,[3] and between the latter and the host state. There is no evidence of a presumption in law that the United Nations bears either an exclusive or a primary responsibility for the tortious acts of such forces, and the law remains undeveloped. In practice the United Nations has accepted responsibility for the acts of its agents.[4] However, in the case of more specialized organizations with a small number of members, it may be necessary to fall back on the collective responsibility of the member states.[5] There is a strong presumption against a delegation of responsibility by a state to an organization arising

[1] *Infra*, p. 716. See, on the whole question, Jenks, *The Prospects of International Adjudication*, pp. 185–224 (also in 32 *Grot. Soc.* (1946), 1–41).

[2] Eagleton, op. cit., pp. 385–404; Bowett, *United Nations Forces*, pp. 57, 149–50, 242–8; García Amador, *Yrbk., I.L.C.* (1956), ii, p. 173 at pp. 189–90; Seyersted, 37 *B.Y.* (1961), 420–3, 431, 473–5; FitzGerald, 3 *Canad. Yrbk. of I.L.* (1965), 265–80; Ginther, *Die Völkerrechtliche Verantwortlichkeit internationaler Organisationen gegenüber Drittstaaten* (1969); *Yrbk., I.L.C.* (1967), ii. 219–20. See also the Western European Union Conv. of 1958; 7 *I.C.L.Q.* (1958), 568; Cmnd. 389; the U.N. General Assembly Decl. on Outer Space, fifth principle, *supra*, p. 267; and Art. 6 of the Outer Space Treaty, *supra*, p. 270.

[3] See *Nissan* v. *A.-G.* [1970] A.C. 179; Int. L.R. 44, p. 359; for comment see 43 *B.Y.* (1968–9), 217–26.

[4] See *Yrbk. of the United Nations*, 1965, p. 138; Whiteman xiii. 28; *M.* v. *Organisation des Nations Unies et État Belge*, Int. L.R. 45, 446.

[5] On the position of the European Communities: Pescatore, op. cit., pp. 211–26. See further Seyersted, 34 *Acta Scandinavica* (1964), 62–75.

simply from membership therein. Evidence must be sought of the intention of the states establishing the particular organization. In certain cases the organization may be conceived of as incurring liabilities in the course of its activities and as a vehicle for the distribution of costs and risks.[1]

(g) *Administration of territory*. See Chapter VIII, section 2.

(h) *Right of mission*.[2] The constituent instrument of an organization may expressly or by implication permit the sending of official representatives to states and other organizations. Though there is a similarity to the sending of diplomatic missions in state relations the analogy cannot be pressed very far.

(i) *Recognition of states*. See *supra*, Chapter V, section 9.

4. *Interpretation of the Constituent Instrument: Inherent and Implied Powers*[3]

The constitutional structure of an international organization involves a nice distribution of powers between the organization and the reserved domain of domestic jurisdiction of member states, and also between the various organs of the organization itself. Considerable problems of interpretation may arise in two contexts. First, the issue may be faced before any action is taken. If a competent organ holds that action contemplated would be *ultra vires*, then procedures for amendment may be followed: in Article 235 of the European Economic Community Treaty the Council of the Community is given power to make appropriate provision. Secondly, the challenge to constitutionality may occur during the process of decision-making, or even after action has been taken, as was the case in the disputes within the United Nations over expenditure on the peace-keeping force placed in Egypt in 1956 and the United Nations operation in the Congo. Basically the problems are those of treaty interpretation, complicated by the fact that political organs may determine the conditions in which an issue is adjudicated upon and the consequences of any judicial opinion on interpretation.

The International Court has applied the doctrine of implied

[1] See Ginther, op. cit. For example: the European Launcher Development Organization; European Space Research Organization. See further the Conv. on Liability for Damage Caused by Space Objects, 1972, Art. XXII.

[2] See further Pescatore, op. cit., pp. 187–97; Seyersted, op. cit., pp. 21–4.

[3] See Bindschedler, 108 Hague *Recueil* (1963, I), 312–418; Vallat, 97 Hague *Recueil* (1959, II), 203–91; McMahon, 37 *B.Y.* (1961), 320–50; Hexner, 53 *A.J.* (1959), 341–70; Lauterpacht, *The Development of International Law by the International Court*, pp. 267–81; Rosenne, *Comunicazioni e Studi*, XII (1966), 21–89.

powers in interpreting the United Nations Charter. In the *Reparation* case the Court observed in its advisory opinion[1] that 'the rights and duties of an entity such as the Organization must depend upon its purposes and functions as specified or implied in its constituent documents and developed in practice'. In practice the reference to implied powers may be linked to a principle of institutional effectiveness. Thus in the same opinion[2] the Court stated: 'Under international law, the Organization must be deemed to have those powers which, though not expressly provided in the Charter, are conferred upon it by necessary implication as being essential to the performance of its duties.' The Court has also held that a capacity to establish a tribunal to do justice between the Organization and staff members 'arises by necessary intendment out of the Charter', there being no express provision in this regard.[3] Judicial interpretation may lead to expansion of the competence of an organization if resort be had to the teleological principle according to which action in accordance with the stated purposes of an organization is *intra vires* or at least is presumed to be.[4] The view has also been expressed that, when the issue of interpretation relates to the constitution of an organization, a flexible and effective approach is justifiable.[5] Obviously the judicial power of appreciation is wide, and the principles enunciated in this fashion may be used as a cloak for extensive legislation. The process of interpretation cannot be subordinated to arbitrary devices. Thus in his dissenting opinion in the *Reparation* case[6] Judge Hackworth observed: 'Powers not expressed cannot freely be implied. Implied powers flow from a

[1] I.C.J. Reports (1949), p. 174 at p. 180.

[2] At p. 182. See also the *International Status of South West Africa* case, I.C.J. Reports (1950), p. 128 at pp. 136–8; the *Voting Procedure* case, ibid. (1955), p. 67; the *Petitioners* case, ibid. (1956), p. 23; and *South West Africa* cases (Preliminary Objections), ibid. (1962), p. 319 at pp. 328–9, 331 seq. On the *Namibia* Opinion of 1971 see *supra*, p. 515.

[3] *Effects of Awards of Compensation made by the U.N. Administrative Tribunal*, I.C.J. Reports (1954), p. 47 at pp. 56–7.

[4] See the *Expenses* case, I.C.J. Reports (1962), p. 151 at pp. 167–8; Green, p. 768; Bishop, p. 262; and *infra*, pp. 701 seq. See also the separate opinion of Judge Fitzmaurice, I.C.J. Reports (1962), pp. 204–5; id., 28 *B.Y.* (1951), 7–8, 13–14; id., 33 *B.Y.* (1957), 207–9. See further, the *Namibia Opinion*, I.C.J. Reports (1971), p. 16 at pp. 47–9, and especially p. 52. See also ibid., p. 132 (Judge Petrén, sep. op.); pp. 150, 163–4, (Judge Dillard, sep. op.); pp. 184–9 (Judge de Castro, sep. op.); pp. 223–4, 279–95 (Judge Fitzmaurice, diss. op.); pp. 338–41 (Judge Gros, diss. op.).

[5] Vallat, 97 Hague *Recueil* (1959, II), 249–50.

[6] I.C.J. Reports (1949), at p. 198. See also the dissenting opinions of Judges Winiarski and Moreno Quintana in the *Expenses* case, I.C.J. Reports (1962), at pp. 230, 245, respectively; the joint dissenting opinion of Judges Spender and Fitzmaurice in the *South West Africa* cases (Preliminary Objections), ibid., pp. 511 seq.; and Judge Fitzmaurice, diss. op., *Namibia* case, I.C.J. Reports (1971), pp. 281–2.

grant of expressed powers, and are limited to those that are 'necessary' to the exercise of powers expressly granted.' Moreover, where a particular issue calls for a measure of appreciation, a great deal must depend on the context and the interplay of various relevant principles. In the context of the United Nations Charter, the principles of implied powers and effectiveness may beg the very question at issue, and, in any case, such principles must be related to Article 2 (1) of the Charter, which states that 'the Organization is based on the principle of the sovereign equality of all its Members', and also to Article 2 (7), which refers to the domestic jurisdiction of states. Particular care should be taken to avoid an automatic implication, from the very fact of legal personality,[1] of particular powers, such as the power to make treaties with third states[2] or the power to delegate powers.[3]

5. *Relations with Member States*

(a) *Decision-making*. Decisions by international conferences and organizations can in principle only bind those states accepting them. Indeed, in the League of Nations decisions could only be taken on a basis of unanimity. Today the principle of majority decision is commonly adopted, and voting rules may vary considerably between various organizations and organs of the same organization.[4] In some bodies, such as the International Monetary Fund, weighted voting has been introduced, and in the United Nations Security Council the five permanent members have a voting privilege known as the 'veto'. The trend away from the principle of unanimity and other aspects of the existing voting systems create considerable problems of controlling the powers of organizations. The constitutional issues arising from disputes over interpretation of the basic instrument and decisions alleged to be *ultra vires* will be noticed later on.[5]

[1] See Seyersted, *Acta Scandinavica*, 34 (1964), 28 seq.; and 37 *B.Y.* (1961), 453–8, for this type of approach.

[2] See Pescatore, op. cit., p. 62; but see *Commission* v. *Council* [1971] C.M.L.R. 335; and see Akehurst, 46 *B.Y.* (1972–3), 439 at p. 440.

[3] See Reuter, *Hommage à Président Basdevant*, p. 415 at pp. 426, 431–7; and *Meroni & Cie et al.* v. *The High Authority*, Int. L.R. 25 (1958, I), 369; Valentine, *The Court of Justice of the European Communities* ii. 590. See further Giardina, 1 *Ital. Yrbk.* (1975), 99–111.

[4] See Jenks, 22 *B.Y.* (1945), p. 11 at pp. 33–42; Bowett, op. cit. (3rd ed.), pp. 357–62; Skubiszewski, 18 *Int. Organization* (1964), 700–805; Jenks, *Cambridge Essays*, pp. 48–63.

[5] *Infra*, pp. 698 seq. These problems recur in relation to amendment of constitutional texts and apportionment of expenses of organizations. On the latter see Bowett, op. cit., pp. 363–6 and *infra*, pp. 678, 680. On procedures for revision of constitutional texts see especially Detter, op. cit., pp. 34–41.

(b) *Domestic jurisdiction.*[1] The type of international co-operation undertaken through an organization and its constituent treaty will normally leave the reserved domain of domestic jurisdiction untouched. Action in pursuit of particular objects rests on the basis of agreement in the constituent instrument, and any administrative or executive measures or recommendations by organs of the organization relate to governments and, whilst perhaps creating obligations to take certain steps within the national jurisdiction, do not of themselves affect state organs within that sphere. Since the constitution of an organization usually defines its objects and powers with some care, an express reservation of domestic jurisdiction will not always be necessary.[2] When the powers of the organization are extensive, as in the case of the United Nations, an express reservation occurs (Article 2 (7) of the Charter). However, the Charter does not allow the reservation to affect the application of enforcement measures against states under Chapter VII.[3] Encroachment on domestic jurisdiction is most striking when government functions are delegated to an institution for particular purposes. Thus in the European Economic Community agreements concluded by the Community are binding on member states.[4] Moreover, the same Community has quasi-legislative powers over matters normally within the sphere of a national legislature, for example in regard to customs tariffs.[5] The Court of Justice of the European Communities and the High Authority of the European Coal and Steel Community have direct jurisdiction over the industries concerned within member states.[6] These extensive powers are delegated by treaty, of course, but the effect on domestic matters is significant and has caused the evocative but not very exact term 'supranational' to be applied to the Communities.[7] However, the law of the European Economic Community does not confer on institutions of the Community the right to annul the legislative or administrative acts of a member state. Such annulment must occur through the organs of the state.[8]

[1] See generally *supra*, pp. 291–7; see also *infra*, on the relation of organizations to municipal law.

[2] On practice within the European Communities: Hahn, 108 Hague *Recueil* (1963, I), 201–2, 207–9.

[3] On the relation of Article 2 (7) to action taken outside Chapter VII, see Bowett, *United Nations Forces*, pp. 196–200, 282–3.

[4] Similarly in the case of agreements concluded by the Commission of Euratom.

[5] E.E.C. Treaty, Articles 189–92. See also Article 14 of the European Coal and Steel Community Treaty. See further Erades, 15 *I.C.L.Q.* (1966), pp. 117–32.

[6] Note also the system of the European Convention of Human Rights, *supra*, p. 574.

[7] See Hahn, op. cit., pp. 211–91; Verzijl, *International Law in Historical Perspective* i. 283–92; *Internationale Handelsgesellschaft Case* [1972] C.M.L.R. 255.

[8] *Humblet* v. *Belgium* (1960), Int. L.R. 29, p. 56 at pp. 59–61.

(c) *Agency*. By agreement between the states and the organization concerned, the latter may become an agent for member states, and others, in regard to matters outside its ordinary competence.[1] Conversely, a state may become an agent of an organization for a particular purpose, for example, as an administering authority of a trust territory under Article 81 of the United Nations Charter.

(d) *The law applicable*.[2] An organization obviously enters into a variety of legal relations both on the international plane and with persons of private law within particular systems of municipal law. In principle the relations of the organization with other persons of international law will be governed by international law, including general principles of law, with the norms of the constituent treaty predominating when relations with member states of the organizations are concerned. When an issue arises from relations with persons of private law, the question may be regulated by a choice of law provision in a treaty which refers to a system of municipal law or to 'general principles of law'. Otherwise, everything will depend on the forum before which the issue is brought and the rules of conflict of laws applicable. An organization of the type of the European Economic Community involves complex relations, which cannot be referred wholly to a single legal system: indeed, the treaties governing the European Communities do not specify the sources of law to be used by the Court of Justice of the Communities. In practice the Court uses a variety of sources, viz., the basic treaties, the regulations, decisions, and directives of the leading organs, and the jurisprudence of the member states, these being welded into a workable Community law in the practice of the Court.[3]

6. *The Functional Concept of Membership*[4]

Whilst organizations are normally composed of states, a number of organizations have operated in effect a functional

[1] Examples of subrogation by agreement in Pescatore, op. cit., pp. 112–14.

[2] On the related questions of the control of acts of organizations and the power of interpretation of constituent instruments see *infra*, pp. 698 seq. On choice of law see Bowett, *The Law of International Institutions* (3rd ed.), pp. 326–30; Fawcett, 36 *B.Y.* (1960), p. 321 at pp. 336–40; Jenks, *The Proper Law of International Organizations* (1962); Seyersted, 122 Hague *Recueil* (1967, III), 434–624; Valticos, *Annuaire de l'Inst.*, 1977, i. 1–191.

[3] See Bebr, *Judicial Control of the European Communities* (1962), pp. 26–9; McMahon, 37 *B.Y.* (1961), 320–50; Brinkhorst and Schermers, *Judicial Remedies in the European Communities* (1969). See also *International Fruit Co. N.V.* v. *Produktschap voor Groenten en Fruit*, [1975] 2 C.M.L.R. 1, on the relevance of public international law.

[4] See Fawcett, 36 *B.Y.* (1960), p. 321 at pp. 340–1; id., *The British Commonwealth in International Law*, pp. 229–31.

concept of membership compatible with their special purposes. Thus the Universal Postal Union is a union of postal administrations, the International Monetary Fund a union of currency areas, and the World Meteorological Organization a union of states and territories having their own meteorological service. In this type of membership regime dependent territories have a functional equality with sovereign states. However, in some organizations[1] dependent territories are given 'associate' membership although in practice they may have an equality with other members.

7. *Relations with States not Members*

The general rule is that only states parties to a treaty are bound by the obligations contained in it, and this rule applies in principle to the constituent instruments of organizations of states. An exception to the rule appears in the Charter of the United Nations, Article 2 (6) of which provides: 'The Organization shall ensure that States which are not Members of the United Nations act in accordance with the Principles so far as may be necessary for the maintenance of international peace and security.'

The exception[2] rests on the special character of the United Nations as an organization concerned primarily with the maintenance of peace and security in the world and including in its membership the great powers as well as the vast majority of states. Whilst third states are not in principle bound by the basic treaty of an international organization, the possession of legal personality by an organization may give rise to certain obligations on the part of non-member states under general international law. Thus an organization may possess a capacity to bring international claims against both members and non-members.[3]

In the *Reparation for Injuries*[4] case the International Court, with little elaboration, regarded a power to bring claims against non-members of the United Nations as a sort of corollary of the

[1] The I.T.U., W.H.O., I.M.C.O., U.N.E.S.C.O., and F.A.O.

[2] For the view that the provision does not bind non-members: Bindschedler, 108 Hague *Recueil* (1963, I), 404–6. For the more usual view, accepted in the text: Kelsen, *The Law of the United Nations*, pp. 85–6, 106–10. The view, surely incorrect, is sometimes expressed that regional organizations can take enforcement action against non-members without the authorization of the Security Council (Article 53 (1)). On the selective blockade of Cuba in 1962, *inter alia* directed against the U.S.S.R., an extra-regional power, see Campbell, 16 *Stanford L.R.* (1963–4), 160–76; Wright, 57 *A.J.* (1963), 546–65; Giraud, 67 *R.G.D.I.P.* (1963), 501–44; Nizard, 66 *R.G.D.I.P.* (1962), 486–545. See also Akehurst, 42 *B.Y.* (1967), 175–227.

[3] *Supra*, p. 684.

[4] I.C.J. Reports (1949), p. 174 at pp. 184–5. See also the *Namibia Opinion*, ibid. (1971), p. 16 at p. 56.

power to do so in respect of member states. The Court produced a statement which represents an assertion of political and constitutional fact rather than a reasoned conclusion:

> On this point, the Court's opinion[1] is that fifty States, representing the vast majority of the members of the international community, had the power, in conformity with international law, to bring into being an entity possessing objective international personality, and not merely personality recognized by them alone, together with capacity to bring international claims.

It is sometimes appropriate and necessary for courts, both national and international, to state propositions of this type. The difficulty which remains arises from the fact that the statement, being related to the setting up of the United Nations, a special case, provides no useful guide for other cases.

It has been suggested that a rule is forming according to which an organization as a legal person can expect the same immunities and privileges as a state,[2] but the general equation of the legal personality of organizations with that of states would be incautious.[3] Certainly, third states may and do enter into agreements with organizations which are valid on the international plane.[4] It is also probable that a principle operates to the effect that constitutional limitations within the structure of the organization cannot be pleaded by the organization, or third states, as a justification for avoiding their mutual obligations.[5] Non-member states may also enter into relations with an organization by means of special missions and vice versa. However, the existence of a legal personality in an organization does not connote a whole range of legal capacities, and the constituent instrument remains the prime determinant of specific powers in the matter of relations with third states. This is particularly obvious when it is necessary to inquire to what extent, if at all, the agreements concluded by an organization bind the members of the organization also.

8. *Relations Between Organizations*[6]

To appreciate the importance of relations between organi-

[1] The only opposing view was that of Judge Krylov, at pp. 218–19.

[2] Sørensen, 101 Hague *Recueil* (1960, III), 139.

[3] However, see Seyersted, 34 *Acta Scandinavica* (1964), 3–112.

[4] On the agreements between the International Bank and Switzerland, a non-member, see Broches, 98 Hague *Recueil* (1959, III), 374–84. See further Pescatore, op. cit., pp. 55–6, 59–60, 95 seq.

[5] See the *Expenses* case, I.C.J. Reports (1962), p. 151 at p. 168; the separate opinion of Judge Fitzmaurice, ibid., pp. 199–200; and Seyersted, op. cit., pp. 32–40.

[6] See Jenks, 28 *B.Y.* (1951), 29–89; id., 77 Hague *Recueil* (1950, II), 157–301; Dupuy, 100 Hague *Recueil* (1960, II), 461–587; Pescatore, op. cit., pp. 198–204.

zations of states it is necessary to recall the variety and number of organizations. The United Nations has a special relation with the 'specialized agencies', viz., the International Labour Organization, the Universal Postal Union, the International Telecommunications Union, the Food and Agricultural Organization, the World Health Organization, the United Nations Educational, Scientific and Cultural Organization, the International Civil Aviation Organization, the International Maritime Consultative Organization, the World Meteorological Organization, the International Monetary Fund, the International Bank for Reconstruction and Development, and the International Finance Corporation. A great many regional institutions now exist, including the Council of Europe, the Organization of African Unity, the Arab League, and the Organization of American States. Moreover, specialized institutions may appear within a region, as, for example, the European Economic Community, and the Council for Mutual Economic Assistance (COMECON). Political conditions, functional requirements, and historical development have created a decentralized system, and the United Nations itself acts through its various organs, like the Economic and Social Council, which maintains functional and regional commissions.

As persons in international law, organizations may enter into legal relations with one another[1] and conclude agreements with each other valid on the international plane. Thus the United Nations has a series of relationship agreements with the specialized agencies.[2] Moreover, there is no reason why one organization should not become a member of another.[3] Clearly in all this the problem of co-ordination looms large. The United Nations Charter (Articles 56 et seq.) and many other constituent instruments contain provisions concerned with co-ordination. Co-ordination depends in practice on agreements and administrative practice, but some machinery for co-ordination has been created by the Economic and Social Council through the Administrative Committee on Co-ordination and the Committee for Programme and Co-ordination. There is also the Enlarged Committee, which reports to the General Assembly. The co-operative, advisory, and specialized nature of much activity by organizations makes jurisdictional conflict of the type occurring

[1] The issues of competence on the internal constitutional plane and its relation to external acts in the law are in principle the same as in the case of agreements with third states: *supra*, p. 692.

[2] And also with the International Atomic Energy Agency.

[3] This seems not to have occurred in practice as yet. See Pescatore, op. cit., p. 203.

between states unlikely. However, when regional organizations claim extensive powers for the maintenance of regional peace and security, important issues of competence arise in relation to the United Nations Charter, which places regional organizations [1] in the position of subordinates or delegates in the matter of 'enforcement action' directed against threats to peace, breaches of the peace, and acts of aggression.[2]

9. *Relation to Municipal Law*[3]

An organization will necessarily enter into relations within particular systems of municipal law, both in the state in which the headquarters is sited and in the course of its activities there and elsewhere. The extent to which the particular system recognizes its legal personality will depend on the local law as modified by the obligations of any relevant agreement. Thus the Treaty of Rome provides (Article 211) that the European Economic Community shall be accorded legal capacity in each member state to the greatest extent accorded to corporate entities ('les personnes morales'). The effect of such provisions is of course dependent on the constitutional doctrine of each state on the incorporation of the agreements into internal law.[4] In the case of the International Civil Aviation Organization the Constitution makes no provision as to the precise content of its legal personality, and as a consequence the status of the organization varies according to the unco-ordinated municipal laws of the member states. To refuse all legal protection on state territory to personnel and assets of an organization may entail international responsibility quite apart from treaty obligations. Private law disputes relating to property or operations of the organization will be settled according to the principles of conflict of laws, apart from the effect of the jurisdictional immunity of the organization

[1] The issue exists apart from the possession of legal personality by the body concerned. The Charter, in Chapter VIII, refers to 'regional arrangements or agencies'. It is an open question whether the North Atlantic Treaty Organization, and the Warsaw Pact association have legal personality. Probably they have, whether or not they are regional arrangements.

[2] See Chapters VII and VIII of the Charter. On this aspect of the events in Guatemala in 1953 and Cuba in 1962, see Fawcett, 103 Hague *Recueil* (1961, II), 372–83; Jiménez de Aréchaga, 111 Hague *Recueil* (1964, I), 423–526 and items cited *supra*, p. 691, n. 2. Conflicts could also occur between regional security organs with overlapping spheres of action.

[3] See O'Connell, 67 *R.G.D.I.P.* (1963), 26–9, 34; Skubiszewski, 2 *Polish Yrbk.*, 80–108; Schreuer, 27 *I.C.L.Q.* (1978), 1–17. On the effect on validity of treaties of constitutional limitations within the legal systems of the parties, see *supra*, p. 610 and Broches, 98 Hague *Recueil* (1959, III), 387–408.

[4] *Supra*, pp. 49, 52–3.

as defined by the relevant agreement, or, perhaps, arising from general international law.

There are many other aspects of the relation to municipal law. Thus the organization may impinge on matters of domestic jurisdiction in the course of its activities, and, as has been pointed out already, close links between the municipal and international planes exist in the machinery of the European Communities.[1] When issues are adjudicated on the international plane, reference to principles of municipal systems as a source of law may occur, as, for example, by the Court of Justice of the European Communities in connexion with *détournement de pouvoir*. Moreover, where legal relations within an organization are concerned, as in the case of staff contracts, municipal law or general principles derived from several municipal systems may be applied by adoption.[2]

10. *Law-making by Organizations*[3]

The varied roles played by organizations may be distinguished as follows:

(a) *Sponsorship of treaty-making*. The United Nations has convoked diplomatic conferences for the purposes of drafting and opening for signature important multilateral treaties, as for example the four Conventions on the Law of the Sea of 1958. The constituent instrument of an organization may contain provisions giving the organization an initiating power, and streamlining the procedure, in respect of amendments to the instrument.

(b) *Forums for state practice*. Statements on legal questions by governments through their representatives in organs and committees of organs provide evidence of customary law. So it is also with the voting on resolutions concerned with legal matters, for

[1] The Netherlands Constitution of 1953 provides for incorporation into internal law of decisions of international organizations. See also Merle, *Annuaire français* (1958), pp. 341–60; Bebr, *Judicial Control of the European Communities*, pp. 178–236; Erades, *ubi supra*, p. 689. [2] See Jenks, *The Proper Law of International Organizations*, pp. 25 seq.

[3] Skubiszewski, 18 *Int. Organization* (1964), 790–805; id., 41 *B.Y.* (1965–6), 198–274; id., *Recueil d'études en hommage à Guggenheim*, 508–20; Merle, *Annuaire français* (1958), pp. 341–60; Tammes, 94 Hague *Recueil* (1958, II), 265–364; Waldock, 106 Hague *Recueil* (1962, II), 26–35, 96–193; Hahn, 108 Hague *Recueil* (1963, I), 226–34; Virally, *Annuaire français* (1956), pp. 66–96; Johnson, 32 *B.Y.* (1955–6), 97–122; Sørensen, 101 Hague *Recueil* (1960, III), 91–108; Sloan, 25 *B.Y.* (1948), 1–33; Lachs, *Mélanges Rolin*, pp. 157–70; Detter, *Law Making by International Organizations* (1965); Gross, 19 *Int. Organization* (1965), 537–61; Saba, 111 Hague *Recueil* (1964, I), 607–90; McMahon, 41 *B.Y.* (1965–66), 1–102; Yemin, *Legislative Powers in the United Nations and Specialized Agencies* (1969); Sandorski; *Polish Yrbk.* (1966–7), 208–21; Buergenthal, *Law-making in the International Civil Aviation Organization* (1969); Cheng, 5 *Indian Journ.* (1965), 23–48.

example the resolution of the General Assembly affirming the principles of the Nuremberg Charter.[1]

(c) *Prescriptive resolutions.* A resolution not in itself binding[2] may prescribe principles of international law and be, or purport to be, merely declaratory. However, the mere formulation of principles may elucidate and develop the customary law.[3] When a resolution of the General Assembly touches on subjects dealt with in the United Nations Charter, it may be regarded as an authoritative interpretation of the Charter: obvious examples are the Universal Declaration of Human Rights[4] and the Declaration on the Granting of Independence to Colonial Countries and Peoples[5] contained in resolutions of the General Assembly. Resolutions on new legal problems provide a means of corralling and defining the quickly growing practice of states, whilst remaining hortatory in form.[6]

(d) *Channels for expert opinion.* Organizations often establish bodies of legal experts in connexion with projects for the codification or progressive development of the law, the most important being the International Law Commission of the United Nations General Assembly,[7] and, like governments, organizations have a staff of legal advisers from whom proceed expert and highly influential opinions.[8]

(e) *Decisions of organs with judicial functions.* Clearly decisions of judicial organs, such as the Court of Justice of the European Communities, may contribute to the development of the law of treaties, principles of interpretation, and general international law.[9] The specialized function of such bodies may of course limit their contribution to the latter.

(f) *The practice of political organs.* Political organs, and particularly the General Assembly and Security Council of the United Nations, make numerous recommendations and decisions relating to specific issues, which involve the application of general international law, or, where there is no identity of the two, the provisions of the Charter or some other constituent instrument.

[1] See further *supra*, p. 562.

[2] Thus resolutions of the United Nations General Assembly are recommendations creating *prima facie* no legal obligation. See, however, Judge Lauterpacht, separate opinion, *South West Africa* (Voting Procedure), I.C.J. Reports (1955), p. 67 at pp. 118–19, 122; Skubiszewski, *A.S.I.L. Proc.* (1964), pp. 153–62; and *Digest of U.S. Practice*, 1975, p. 85.

[3] See *supra*, p. 14. [4] *Supra*, p. 570. [5] *Supra*, p. 594.

[6] See the declaration of principles governing activities in outer space: *supra*, p. 267.

[7] On which see *supra*, p. 31.

[8] On the legal opinions of the U.N. Secretariat: Schachter, 25 *B.Y.* (1948), 91–125.

[9] See McMahon, 37 *B.Y.* (1961), 320–50.

Such practice provides evidence of the state of the law and also of the meaning of texts, and has considerable legal significance.[1] However, as with the practice of states, the nature of the particular decision and the extent to which legal matters were considered must be examined before much legal weight is given to the decision. Furthermore, to give legal significance to an omission of an organ to condemn[2] is hazardous in the extreme, since this omission turns often on the political attitude of the majority in the organ concerned. Moreover, many jurists regard the decisions of political organs in terms of the arithmetic of voting, the decisions being taken to represent the views of *n* states in the majority and their legal cogency being roughly on a scale *n* majority divided by *n* minority states. Obviously states cannot by their control of numbers of international organizations raise in some sense the value of their state practice by reference to the 'practice of organizations'.[3]

In certain instances a consistent and uniform interpretation by members of an organ placed upon a persistent practice, for example, in matters of voting, adopted *by that organ* will be opposable to *all* Members provided that there is substantial evidence of general acceptance by Members of the organization. On this basis in its Advisory Opinion in the *Namibia* case[4] the International Court rejected the South African argument that the key Security Council resolution was invalid since two permanent members had abstained. The consistent practice of the members of the Security Council had been to interpret such abstention as not constituting a bar to the adoption of resolutions in spite of the provisions of Article 27, paragraph 3, of the Charter which refer to the 'concurring votes' of the permanent members.

(g) *Powers of legislation delegated to organizations.* In certain instances states have delegated important law-making powers to organizations. Thus the High Authority of the European Coal and Steel Community may make decisions and regulations which are legally effective within the legal systems of member states.

[1] See Higgins, *The Development of International Law Through the Political Organs of the United Nations* (1963); id., 64 *A.J.* (1970), 1–18; id., *Proc. A.S.I.L.* (1970), 37–48; and Schachter, 58 *A.J.* (1964), 960–5. On the interpretation of the United Nations Charter by the organs see further *infra*, pp. 699–704.

[2] See the statements by Higgins in 37 *B.Y.* (1961), p. 269 at p. 319. Cf. Schachter, 59 *A.J.* (1965), 168.

[3] Cf. Sørensen, op. cit., pp. 100–1, 105–6. For views on the reliability of subsequent practice of organs in interpretation of the Charter see the separate opinions of Judges Spender and Fitzmaurice in the *Expenses* case, I.C.J. Reports (1962), at pp. 187 seq., 210 seq., respectively, and Gross, 17 *Int. Organization* (1963), p. 1 at pp. 14 seq.

[4] I.C.J. Reports (1971), p. 16 at p. 22.

Other forms of delegation exist involving various procedures for acceptance of the regulations by members. Some organs, for example the World Health Assembly of W.H.O. or the Council of I.C.A.O., may make regulations by majority decision, leaving states to contract out by express rejection or by entering reservations.

(h) *External practice of organizations.* Organizations may make agreements with member and non-member states and with other organizations, and may present international claims and make official pronouncements on issues affecting them. Subject to what has been said above about the need for care in evaluating acts of political organs, the practice of organizations provides evidence of the law.

(i) *Internal law-making.* Organizations have considerable autonomy in making rules on internal matters such as procedure and the relations of the organization and its staff. Resolutions of organs of the United Nations on questions of procedure create internal law for members. However, questions of internal powers, for example concerning budgetary control, have a delicate relation to issues as to external *ultra vires*, if budgetary approval were given to sums allocated for operations under resolutions alleged to be *ultra vires* the Charter as a whole.[1] The United Nations has developed a code of staff regulations and rules governing the conditions of service of its officials, and the General Assembly has established a United Nations Administrative Tribunal to adjudicate upon applications alleging non-observance of employment contracts of staff members of the Secretariat.[2]

11. *Control of Acts of Organizations*

(a) *Responsibility under general international law.* As we shall gather later, there is no compulsory system for review of the acts of organizations by bodies external to them. In this situation the 'normal' controls, such as they are, are provided by general international law. The correlative of legal personality and a capacity to present international claims is responsibility.[3] Moreover, when creating institutions states cannot always hide behind the organization when its activities cause damage to the interests

[1] See the *Expenses* case, *infra*, pp. 699, 702–3.

[2] See Sohn, *Basic Documents of the United Nations*, pp. 242–68; Jenks, *The Proper Law of International Organizations*, pp. 25 seq.; *Effect of Awards of Compensation made by the U.N. Administrative Tribunal*, I.C.J. Reports (1954), p. 47. [3] *Supra*, p. 685.

of states or other organizations. General international law provides criteria according to which an organization may be held to be unlawful in conception and objects, and, apart from this, particular acts in the law may be void if they are contrary to a principle of the *jus cogens*.[1]

(b) *Internal political control.* The question of control in practice turns on the powers of the executive and deliberative organs and the constitutional limitations under which these political organs are placed.[2] The division of competence between organs and the limits to the powers of the organization as a whole may be carefully drawn, and, as in the Charter of the United Nations, the obligations set out in the relevant instrument may be expressed to apply to the organization itself, and the organs.[3] Interpretation of the constituent treaty by organs is the general rule. In the United Nations Charter, reference to the International Court depends on the readiness of political organs to request an advisory opinion, and any opinion given is not necessarily acted upon subsequently. Similarly, with bodies like the International Monetary Fund, which is concerned with politically sensitive issues, judicial powers are conferred on the executive board or other executive organ and there is no provision for direct judicial control by a separate judicial organ.[4] In the *Namibia* Opinion[5] the International Court remarked that 'undoubtedly, the Court does not possess powers of judicial review or appeal in respect of the decisions taken by the United Nations organs concerned'. However, in the same Advisory Opinion the Court did consider the validity of acts of organs 'in the exercise of its judicial function and since objections have been advanced . . .'

Organs may produce an impressive and consistent case law on points of interpretation. However, political organs may support constitutional developments which are distinctly controversial and regarded as *ultra vires* the organs by a minority of member states. The most obvious examples are the machinery created by the Uniting for Peace Resolution of the General Assembly of the United Nations in 1950 and the use of that machinery for the creation of a United Nations Emergency Force in 1956 to serve

[1] On this see *supra*, pp. 512–15.

[2] See generally Bindschedler, 108 Hague *Recueil* (1963, I), 312–418; and Hahn, ibid., pp. 195–297.

[3] See the Charter, Articles 2, 24 (2), and 55.

[4] On the I.M.F. see Fawcett, 36 *B.Y.* (1960), 321–42. On the European Free Trade Association see Darwin, ibid., pp. 354–9. On the International Bank, see Broches, op. cit., pp. 312–13. On the I.L.O., see Osieke, 48 *B.Y.* (1976–7), 259–80. See also Hexner, 53 *A.J.* (1959), 341–70.

[5] I.C.J. Reports (1971), p. 16 at p. 45. See further *supra*, p. 515.

in Egypt. A minority of states contended that only the Security Council had the power to take enforcement action, and on this basis they refused to contribute to the expenses incurred in carrying out the operation in Egypt. A similar situation arose when the Security Council gave a mandate to the Secretary-General to organize forces for operations in the Congo (ONUC). There is no automatic recourse which can settle disputes on points of interpretation by members; individual states have no right to request opinions, and minority opinion can be overridden. States in a minority may withdraw from the organization, acquiesce in what they regard as illegal operations, resist military forces acting under putative authority of the organization, or withhold financial contribution. The latter course was adopted in the cases of UNEF and ONUC, and eventually the General Assembly requested an advisory opinion from the Court.[1] Even at this juncture political control was prominent. The request was formulated in a manner calculated to narrow the issue somewhat artificially to the interpretation of 'expenses of the Organization within the meaning of Article 17, paragraph 2, of the Charter of the United Nations'. Moreover, the Court's opinion was sought retrospectively, long after the actions were authorized and enormous expenditure incurred.[2]

(c) *External political control.* Organizations usually lack external restraints, but exceptionally one organization may be made subordinate to another in one or more respects. Thus 'regional arrangements and agencies' are regulated in a general way by Chapter VIII of the United Nations Charter, and more particularly by Article 53 (1), which provides that no enforcement action shall be taken by such arrangements or agencies 'without the authorization of the Security Council'.[3]

(d) *Direct judicial control.*[4] Organizations are commonly given immunity on a functional basis from municipal law,[5] but policy

[1] On the *Expenses* case see further *infra*, p. 702. See also Fitzmaurice, sep. op., I.C.J. Reports (1962), pp. 203–4; Winiarski, diss. op., at p. 232; and Bustamante, diss. op., at pp. 304–5. Similar issues arose when the General Assembly terminated the Mandate for South West Africa: see the *Namibia* Opinion, I.C.J. Reports (1971), p. 16. See also Waldock, 106 Hague *Recueil* (1962, II), 35–6; and cf. Fawcett, 33 *B.Y.* (1957), 311–16. Generally on the legal effect of illegal acts of organizations see E. Lauterpacht, in *Cambridge Essays*, pp. 88–121; Cahier, 76 *R.G.D.I.P.* (1972), 645, 659; Osieke, 48 *B.Y.* (1976–7), 259–80.

[2] See Judge Basdevant, I.C.J. Reports (1962), p. 237.

[3] Cf. *supra*, pp. 691, 694.

[4] See generally on judicial control the proceedings of the Institute of International Law: *Annuaire de l'Inst.* (1952), 44, i. 224 seq.; (1954), 45, i. 265 seq.; (1957), 47, i. 5 seq.; (1957), 47, ii. 274 seq. Text of resolutions: ibid., pp. 476, 488, 52 *A.J.* (1958), 105.

[5] *Supra*, p. 682.

may favour a different regime. Thus the International Bank is subject to suit in a member state by private legal persons but not by member states.[1] Direct judicial control of the acts of organizations by a specially created organ is rare, but it appears in a developed form in the European Communities, which share a Court of Justice.[2] This Court has considerable powers of review in respect of acts of organs of the Communities on grounds of incompetence, violation of the relevant treaty or rules for its application, procedural irregularity, and *détournement de pouvoir*.[3] The European Economic Community Treaty provides for a reference to a judicial organ of the question of compatibility with the basic treaty of an agreement at the stage of negotiation.[4]

(e) *External rights of appeal.* Some organizations, such as the Food and Agricultural Organization, rely on their own organs to decide disputes, but provide a right of appeal to an appropriate international court or arbitral tribunal.[5] Certain constituent treaties provide for recourse to arbitration.[6]

(f) *Interpretation by advisory opinions* (and see para. (b) above). The General Assembly and Security Council of the United Nations, and the specialized agencies, have the power to request the International Court for advisory opinions.[7] This procedure has been described as involving 'indirect' judicial control of organizations, but this is misleading. The opinions are only 'advisory' it is true, but they are influential and may relate to matters of high controversy. Moreover, the opinions come from a body less closely integrated with the institution controlled than the judicial organ of the European Communities, and thus the control is more 'external' in some measure.[8] The 'direct' control of the Court of the European Communities exists in a highly specialized political and legal context.

The supranational European institutions are not subject to 'external' judicial interpretation whilst the Charter of the United Nations is. Moreover, the International Court has been unwilling to refuse to give opinions on the ground that the issue was

[1] See Broches, op. cit., p. 309.

[2] See Valentine, 36 *B.Y.* (1960), 174–222; id., *The Court of Justice of the European Communities* i; Bebr, *Judicial Control of the European Communities* (1962); McMahon, 37 *B.Y.* (1961), 320–50.

[3] See Fawcett, 33 *B.Y.* (1957), 311–16. Very simply, the term means the arbitrary exercise of a discretionary power. [4] Article 228 of the E.E.C. Treaty.

[5] See the F.A.O. Constitution, Article 17.

[6] See the I.T.U. Constitution, Article 28 (2); U.P.U. Constitution, 1964, Article 32; U.P.U. General Regulations, Article 126. [7] *Infra*, p. 728.

[8] It is noteworthy that the specialized agencies have not shown readiness to request advisory opinions: cf. Fawcett, 36 *B.Y.* (1960), p. 321 at p. 327.

political.[1] In the *Expenses* case[2] the Court faced an issue on which members of the United Nations were completely divided, the constitutional basis for the use of armed forces in UNEF and ONUC.[3] The issue took the form of a request for an interpretation of Article 17 (2) of the Charter, but in substance the obligations of members were in issue and not merely the budgetary competence of the General Assembly in making resolutions authorizing expenditures for the operations concerned. The Court pursued a policy of 'institutional effectiveness' and stated that 'when the Organization takes action which warrants the assertion that it was appropriate for the fulfilment of one of the stated purposes of the United Nations, the presumption is that such action is not *ultra vires* the Organization'.[4] The majority opinion held that the operations were in pursuance of the stated purposes and that member states were bound by the resolutions of the General Assembly authorizing the expenditures involved, which were 'expenses of the Organization' under Article 17 (2). The reasoning of the Court has been subjected to cogent criticism by Gross.[5] The main points of criticism are as follows. The General Assembly can only make recommendations, yet the Court's view permits non-obligatory recommendations to result in binding financial obligations. This gives the General Assembly a supranational budgetary power denied to more closely integrated communities. Moreover, the presumption against *ultra vires* runs contrary to the principle of the sovereign equality of members and points to creation of 'a super state'.[6] As a matter of treaty interpretation, the Court's approach to Article 17 (2) was open to grave doubt. Further, reference by the Court to the subsequent practice of organs as an aid to interpretation involved the use of evidence which did not unequivocally bear on the issues before the Court.[7] Many lawyers may warm to any decision which gives more power to the Organization, but the Organi-

[1] *Infra*, p. 730.

[2] I.C.J. Reports (1962), p. 151; Green, p. 768; Bishop, p. 262; Int. L.R. 34, p. 281. For comment see Gross, 16 *Int. Organization* (1963), 1–35; Jennings, 11 *I.C.L.Q.* (1962), 1169–83; Simmonds, 13 *I.C.L.Q.* (1964), 854–98; Verzijl, 10 *Neths. Int. L.R.* (1963), 1–32; Bindschedler, 108 Hague *Recueil* (1963, I), 353–64; E. Lauterpacht, *Cambridge Essays*, pp. 106 seq.

[3] See generally Bowett, *United Nations Forces* (1964).

[4] I.C.J. Reports (1962), p. 168. See also Judge Fitzmaurice, at pp. 204, 208; Morelli, at p. 223; Bustamante, diss. op., at p. 298. Another opinion concerning the issue of *ultra vires* is the *IMCO* case, I.C.J. Reports (1960), p. 150; Green, p. 778.

[5] Op. cit.

[6] Cf. I.C.J. Reports (1949), p. 179. See also I.C.J. Pleadings (*Expenses* case), pp. 134, 403, 425; Winiarski, diss. op., I.C.J. Reports (1962), at pp. 230, 232; Moreno Quintana, diss. op., at p. 248; Bustamante, diss. op., at pp. 302, 304–5.

[7] See Judge Spender, I.C.J. Reports (1962), pp. 187 seq.; Judge Fitzmaurice, pp. 210 seq.; Winiarski, diss. op., at pp. 230–2.

zation is not an abstraction, and political alliances, however transient, may give direction to decisions of political organs. To speak of 'institutional effectiveness' or 'implied powers' is to beg a great many questions.[1] The issue in the case was both legal and political, and the choice before the Court involved large assumptions about the structure of the Charter. This type of judicial control does not settle the problem of reconciling major divisions between member states: indeed, the present opinion may have exacerbated a crisis which might have had a disastrous outcome but was settled by negotiation.[2]

The general issues presented by the *Expenses* case also attended the termination of the Mandate for South West Africa by a General Assembly resolution, consequential action by the Security Council, and a request by the latter to the Court for an Advisory Opinion on the legal consequences for states of the presence of South Africa in South West Africa (Namibia) in defiance of the resolutions.[3] The view of the South African and French Governments presented to the Court was that the relevant resolutions of the General Assembly and Security Council were *ultra vires*. On this question the Court observed:[4]

> Undoubtedly, the Court does not possess powers of judicial review or appeal in respect of the decisions taken by the United Nations organs concerned. The question of the validity or conformity with the Charter of General Assembly resolution 2145 (XXI) or of related Security Council resolutions does not form the subject of the request for advisory opinion. However, in the exercise of its judicial function and since objections have been advanced the Court, in the course of its reasoning, will consider these objections before determining any legal consequences arising from those resolutions.

Nevertheless a significant minority[5] of Judges preferred the principle that any relevant issue of law was a matter for the Court

[1] See Moreno Quintana, diss. op., at p. 245; 'Each organ has its due function. The implied powers which may derive from the Charter so that the Organization may achieve all its purposes are not to be invoked when explicit powers provide expressly for the eventualities under consideration.' See also Koretsky, diss. op., at pp. 272–4; and the views of Judges Hackworth, Spender, and Fitzmaurice cited *supra*, p. 687, n. 6.

[2] The United States invoked Article 19 of the Charter in consequence of the opinion and for a whole session no voting took place in the General Assembly. See 4 *Int. Leg. Materials* (1965), 1000.

[3] I.C.J. Reports (1971), p. 16. See further *supra*, p. 515.

[4] At p. 45 of the Opinion. See also pp. 71 (Judge Ammoun, sep. op.); 105 (Padilla Nervo); 180–2 (de Castro).

[5] See pp. 130–1 (Judge Petrén, sep. op.); 141–5 (Judge Onyeama, sep. op.); 151–2 (Judge Dillard, sep. op.); 301–4 (Judge Fitzmaurice, diss. op.); 331–2 (Judge Gros, diss. op.).

and accepted the corollary that the legal qualities of the basic resolutions could be relevant to the legal consequences of South African rejection of the resolutions. In short, if a political organ refers a matter to the principal judicial organ of the United Nations, the latter is entitled and, indeed, bound to act as such.[1]

(g) *Administrative tribunals*. A number of organizations possess their own administrative tribunals to hear disputes concerning staff contracts.[2]

[1] See also the Advisory Opinion in the *Expenses* case, I.C.J. Reports (1962), p. 151 at p. 157. The issue was not raised in such a sharp form in the *Expenses* case in which the terms of the request for an Opinion directly raised the issue whether expenditures had been validly authorized: see the *Namibia* case, p. 181 (Judge de Castro, sep. op.).

[2] The U.N. Administrative Tribunal and the I.L.O. Tribunal serve a number of other organizations. See further Bowett, op. cit., pp. 283–94; Bastid, 92 Hague *Recueil* (1957, II), 347–517; Akehurst, *The Law Governing Employment in International Organizations* (1967) and items cited *supra*, pp. 578–80. On the machinery for review of decisions of the U.N. Administrative Tribunal see Advisory Opinion on *Application for Review of Judgement No. 158*, I.C.J. Reports, 1973, p. 166.

CHAPTER XXXI

THE JUDICIAL SETTLEMENT OF INTERNATIONAL DISPUTES

1. *Peaceful Settlement in General*

THE settlement of disputes between states by judicial action is only one facet of the enormous problem of the maintenance of international peace and security. In the period of the United Nations Charter the use of force by individual states as a means of settling disputes is impermissible. Peaceful settlement is the only available means.[1] However, there is no obligation in general international law *to settle* disputes, and procedures for settlement by formal and legal procedures rest on the consent of the parties. The context of judicial settlement in international relations is thus very different to that of the function of municipal courts, and this type of settlement is relatively exceptional in state relations. The object of this chapter is to consider the technical problems involved in legal process between states. The large field of settlement by political means, including action by organs of international organizations, must be left on one side.[2] Yet it must not be thought that there is a complete divorce between the two approaches to settlement. Political organs, like the General Assembly and Security Council of the United Nations, may and often do concern themselves with evidence and legal argument, although the basis for action remains primarily political.[3] The General Assembly, in particular, has provided a useful forum for settling disputes although its work in this respect tends to be forgotten. So also governments conducting negotiations with a view of settling disputes commonly take legal advice, and confidential legal advice from specialist advisers to the executive may be weighty and reasonably

[1] On the legal regulation of the use of force by states see Whiteman xii. 1–495; Brownlie, *International Law and the Use of Force by States* (1963); Bowett, *Self-Defence in International Law* (1958).

[2] See Chapters VI and VII of the U.N. Charter; Stone, *Legal Controls of International Conflict*, pp. 67 seq.; Goodrich, Hambro and Simons, *Charter of the United Nations* (3rd ed., 1969); Kelsen, *The Law of the United Nations* (1951); Sohn, *Cases on United Nations Law*, 2nd ed. (1967); *Repertory of Practice of U.N. Organs*; Vallat, *Cambridge Essays*, pp. 155–77. Generally on international organizations see Chapter XXX.

[3] See Higgins, *The Development of International Law through the Political Organs of the United Nations* (1963); id., 64 *A.J.* (1970), 1–18; Schachter, 58 *A.J.* (1964), 960–5.

objective.[1] Conversely, primarily judicial machinery may be given powers to act in a legislative (and thus political) capacity, witness the power of the International Court of Justice to decide *ex aequo et bono* if the parties agree thereto.[2]

2. *Arbitration*[3]

In both national and international legal history, the mature judicial process develops out of relatively informal administrative and political procedures. International practice has long included negotiation, good offices, and mediation as informal methods of settling disputes.[4] Treaties establishing machinery for peaceful settlement frequently provide for these methods and also for conciliation. Conciliation is distinct from mediation and grew out of the commissions of inquiry provided for in the Hague Conventions for the Pacific Settlement of International Disputes of 1899 and 1907 and the commissions which figured in the series of arbitration treaties concluded by the United States in 1913 and 1914 (the Bryan treaties). Conciliation has a semi-judicial aspect, since the commission of persons empowered has to elucidate the facts, may hear the parties, and must make proposals for a settlement which, normally, do not bind the parties.

Before conciliation appeared as an established technique, the process of arbitration had long been a part of the scene, having the same political provenance. However, the practice of arbitration evolved as a sophisticated procedure similar to judicial settlement. Modern arbitration begins with the Jay Treaty of 1794 between the United States and Great Britain, which provided for adjudication of various legal issues by mixed commissions. The popularity of arbitration increased considerably

[1] See McNair, *International Law Opinions* i, preface, p. xix. Cf. *A British Digest of International Law compiled principally from the archives of the Foreign Office* (1965–).

[2] See *infra*, p. 727.

[3] See generally Simpson and Fox, *International Arbitration* (1959); Hudson, *International Tribunals, Past and Future* (1944); Carlston, *The Process of International Arbitration* (1946); Sohn, 108 Hague *Recueil* (1963, I), 9–113; Ralston, *The Law and Procedure of International Tribunals* (1926); Suppl. (1936); Stuyt, *Survey of International Arbitrations, 1794–1970* (1972); Witenberg, *L'Organisation judiciaire, la procédure et la sentence internationales* (1937); I.L.A., *Report of the Fifty-Second Conference* (1966), pp. 287–356; Whiteman xii. 1020–1152; Mosler and Bernhardt (eds.), *Judicial Settlement of International Disputes* (1974), pp. 417–552; Verzijl, *International Law in Historical Perspective* viii (1976), 161–323; Sohn, 150 Hague *Recueil* (1976, II), 195–294.

[4] On these, and on conciliation, see Oppenheim ii. 6–20; Hackworth vi. 1–57. On conciliation see further *Annuaire de l'Inst.* (1959), i. 5–130; Cot, *La Conciliation internationale* (1968); Bar-Yaacov, *The Handling of International Disputes by Means of Inquiry* (1974); David Davies Memorial Institute, *International Disputes: The Legal Aspects* (1972).

after the successful *Alabama Claims* arbitration of 1872 between the United States and Great Britain.[1] In this early stage of experience arbitral tribunals were often invited by the parties to resort to 'principles of justice and equity' and to propose extra-legal compromises. However, by the end of the century, arbitration was primarily if not exclusively associated with a process of decision according to law and supported by appropriate procedural standards. In recent times the distinction between arbitration and judicial settlement has become formal. The contrasts are principally these: the agreement for submission to arbitration (*compromis*) would be more likely to allow settlement on extra-legal principles (but this power may be conferred on a court); the agency of decision in arbitration would be designated 'arbitral tribunal', 'umpire';[2] the tribunal consists of an odd number, usually with national representatives (but this element may be present in standing courts); the arbitral tribunal is usually created to deal with a particular dispute or class of disputes; and there is more flexibility than there is in a system of compulsory jurisdiction with a standing court.[3] More significant than the differences between judicial settlement and arbitration as large categories are the variations of arbitral procedures, some of which are akin to a compulsory jurisdiction, and the differences between legal and political disputes.[4]

3. *Permanent Court of Arbitration*

Between 1900 and 1920 the Permanent Court of Arbitration was the major organization for arbitration. It was set up under the Hague Convention for the Pacific Settlement of International Disputes of 1899[5] and consists not of a court but of machinery for the calling into being of tribunals. There is the Permanent Administrative Council and the International Bureau, which

[1] Award: Moore, *Arbitrations* i. 653. Great Britain was required to pay 15,500,000 dollars.

[2] There is no fixed terminology, and judicial functions are carried out by agencies labelled 'mixed claims commission', or even 'conciliation commission' (as in the case of the Conciliation Commissions set up to hear claims arising under Article 83 of the peace treaty with Italy, 1947).

[3] See the circular of the Secretary-General of the P.C.A. of 3 March 1960, 54 *A.J.* (1960), 933.

[4] Cf. Sohn, op. cit.

[5] Most states supporting the 'Court' became parties to the Convention of 1899. The Convention of 1907, which received few ratifications, was not radically different. 71 states participate in the Court. See generally Hudson, *Permanent Court of International Justice 1920–1942* (1943), pp. 6–36; Guyomar, *Annuaire français* (1962), pp. 377–90; François, 87 Hague *Recueil* (1955, I), 461–551; id., 9 *Neths. Int. L.R.* (1962), 264–72.

acts as a secretariat or registry for the tribunals set up. The basis of the 'Court' is a panel of arbitrators to which parties may nominate a maximum of four persons. When parties to the Convention agree to submit a dispute to the Permanent Court of Arbitration, each appoints two arbitrators from the panel, and the four arbitrators select an umpire. Thus a tribunal is constituted only to hear a particular case. The Permanent Court of Arbitration has had a useful but hardly spectacular existence. Between 1900 and 1932 twenty cases were heard, but since then only three cases have been dealt with.[1]

4. *Codes of Arbitral Procedure*

Apart from provisions relating to the Permanent Court of Arbitration, the Hague Conventions of 1899 and 1907 contain a code of arbitral procedure which applies to tribunals created under the Permanent Court machinery or by other means unless the parties have agreed on special rules of procedure. In 1953 the International Law Commission adopted a draft Convention on Arbitral Procedure,[2] which did not find favour with governments and was reformulated as a set of Model Rules on Arbitral Procedure.[3] The object of the draft Convention was to provide for cases where the validity of awards is challenged on various grounds,[4] and also to safeguard the effectiveness of the obligation to arbitrate arising from agreement. A key issue in any agreement to arbitrate is the appointment of the arbitrators,[5] and especially the neutral member of a tribunal or commission. Treaties normally contain carefully drawn provisions on the appointment of the neutral member, but the relevant provisions in the peace treaties with Bulgaria, Hungary, and Rumania of 1947 failed because failure by one side to appoint its own member of the tribunal rendered them inoperative.[6] This

[1] In recent years attempts have been made to revive interest in the P.C.A.

[2] See *Yrbk.*, *I.L.C.* (1953), ii. 201, 208; and A/CN.4/92, *Commentary on the Draft Convention on Arbitral Procedure* (1955).

[3] *Yrbk.*, *I.L.C.* (1958), ii. 81. The Model Rules were adopted by the U.N. Gen. Ass. in Resol. 1262 (XIII), 14 Nov. 1958. They are optional.

[4] e.g. that the tribunal exceeded the powers conferred in the agreement to arbitrate. Cf. *Case Concerning the Arbitral Award by the King of Spain*, I.C.J. Reports (1960), p. 192.

[5] See Sohn, op. cit., pp. 60–81; Johnson, 30 *B.Y.* (1953), 152–77.

[6] In a request for an advisory opinion the General Assembly submitted the following question to the Court: 'If one party fails to appoint a representative to a Treaty Commission under the Treaties of Peace . . . where that party is obligated to appoint a representative to the Treaty Commission, is the Secretary-General of the United Nations authorized to appoint the third member of the Commission upon the request of the other

problem was considered by the International Law Commission at its fourth, fifth, and tenth sessions, and the material part of the provision finally adopted is as follows:[1]

2. If the tribunal is not constituted within three months from the date of the request made for the submission of the dispute to arbitration, or from the date of the decision on arbitrability, the President of the International Court of Justice shall, at the request of either party, appoint the arbitrators not yet designated. If the President is prevented from acting or is a national of one of the parties, the appointments shall be made by the Vice-President. If the Vice-President is prevented from acting or is a national of one of the parties, the appointments shall be made by the oldest member of the Court who is not a national of either party.

Critics of this provision regard it as in conflict with the principle of the autonomy of the parties in international arbitration and as creating a procedure halfway between arbitration and normal legal procedure.

5. *Judicial Settlement*

It is not intended to draw a sharp line between arbitration and judicial settlement: the latter category can properly be applied to the work of any international tribunal settling disputes between states in accordance with rules of international law. Moreover, the more institutionalized types of jurisdiction developed historically from arbitral experience. Apart from the International Court of Justice, judicial settlement includes the activity of many *ad hoc* arbitral tribunals[2] and mixed commissions, and of specialized tribunals of a semi-permanent character,[3] including the United Nations Tribunal in Libya,[4] the United Nations Tribunal in Eritrea, the Supreme Restitution Court of the

party to a dispute according to the provisions of the respective Treaties?' The Court replied in the negative: *Interpretation of Peace Treaties* (Second Phase), I.C.J. Reports (1950), p. 221. The Court remarked (p. 229); 'It is the duty of the Court to interpret the Treaties, not to revise them.'

[1] *Yrbk., I.L.C.* (1958), ii. 83; Article 3. See also the European Conv. for the Peaceful Settlement of Disputes, 1957, 320 U.N.T.S., 243, Art. 21.

[2] See, in particular, the *Rann of Kutch Arbitration* (1968), Int. L.R. 50, 2; *Beagle Channel Arbitration* (1977), 17 *Int. Leg. Materials* (1978), 632; *Delimitation of the Continental Shelf* (U.K. and France), Decisions of 30 June 1977 and 14 March 1978.

[3] See generally *Annuaire français*, 'Chroniques'; and International Law Reports (ed. Lauterpacht); Mosler and Bernhardt (eds.), *Judicial Settlement of International Disputes* (1974), pp. 83–190, 285–416; Jessup, *The Price of International Justice* (1971).

[4] See *Italy* v. *Libya*, Int. L.R. 22 (1955), 103.

German Federal Republic,[1] the Arbitral Commission on Property, Rights, and Interests in Germany,[2] the Arbitral Tribunal and Mixed Commission for the Agreement on German External Debts,[3] the Property Commissions set up as a consequence of Article 15 (a) of the Peace Treaty with Japan,[4] and the International Centre for Settlement of Investment Disputes between states and nationals of other states.[5] Two circumstances are paramount: (1) the existence of a dispute; and (2) decision by a tribunal which, in virtue of its source of authority, composition, immunity from local jurisdiction, and powers of jurisdiction, is international rather than national.[6] The definition of a 'dispute' and the nature of a legal interest have been considered elsewhere.[7] The international character of the tribunal is a question of both its organization and its jurisdiction. A municipal tribunal may apply international law and when it does so is no longer *merely* an organ of the national system of law:[8] but it is not acting independently of the national system, it is not settling issues between legal persons on the international plane, and its jurisdiction does not rest on agreement on the international plane.[9] *For the present purpose*, therefore, the municipal tribunal would not be an international tribunal. Whilst the advisory jurisdiction of the International Court will be considered, what

[1] Conv. on the Settlement of Matters Arising out of the War and the Occupation of 1952, amended by the Paris Protocol, 1954, 49 *A.J.* (1955), Suppl., pp. 69, 83. Cf. *Casman* v. *Herter*, 117 F. Supp. 285; Int. L.R. 28. 592; Application no. 235/56, *Yearbook of the European Conv. on Human Rights* (1958–9), p. 256 at p. 288.

[2] Conv. on the Settlement of Matters Arising out of the War and the Occupation, 49 *A.J.* (1955), Suppl., pp. 69, 113.

[3] Agreement on German External Debts, 27 February 1953, 333 U.N.T.S., 3; Cmd. 8781.

[4] Agreement of 1952; 138 U.N.T.S., 183. See Int. L.R. 29 and 30; and Summers and Fraleigh, 56 *A.J.* (1962), 407–32.

[5] Text of Convention establishing the centre: 60 *A.J.* (1966), 892; U.K. Arbitration (International Investment Disputes) Act, 1966, Sched. See Lauterpacht, *Recueil d'études en hommage à Paul Guggenheim*, pp. 642–64; Delaume, 93 *J.D.I.* (1966), 26–49; Broches, *Liber Amicorum for Martin Domke*, pp. 12–22; id., 136 Hague *Recueil* (1972, II), 331–410; Roulet, 22 *Annuaire Suisse* (1965), 121–54.

[6] On the concept of international jurisdiction: Cavaré, *Annuaire français* (1956), pp. 496–509; Nørgaard, *The Position of the Individual in International Law*, pp. 179–96, 216 seq.; Korowicz, *Introduction to International Law*, pp. 349–50.

[7] *Supra*, pp. 466–73, 479–80.

[8] See further *supra*, pp. 577–8.

[9] Cf. the Foreign Claims Settlement Commission in the United States and the Foreign Compensation Commission in the United Kingdom. See Lillich, *International Claims: Their Adjudication by National Commissions* (1962); id., 13 *I.C.L.Q.* (1964), 899–924; id., *International Claims: Post-war British Practice* (1967); the *Flegenheimer* claim, Int. L.R. 30, p. 532; Freidberg, 10 *Virginia J. of Int. Law* (1970), 282–99; Weston, ibid., 223–81; Weston, *International Claims: Postwar French Practice* (1971). A municipal court, e.g. the Swiss Federal Tribunal, may be appointed by agreement to arbitrate in an international dispute.

follows is concerned primarily with the problems of contentious jurisdiction in ordinary international claims. It is, of course, the case that the judicial function is employed in other contexts by states and organizations.[1] Thus the Court of Justice of the European Communities[2] has a competence in relation to appeals against decisions of organs of the Communities for annulment (*recours en annulation*),[3] suits for damages against Community organs, and appeals against decisions imposing penalties.[4] Again, commissions of inquiry set up by the International Labour Organization to investigate breaches of I.L.O. conventions,[5] and decisions to permit waiver in the GATT system, have a judicial aspect.[6] These bodies, together with the Committee of Ministers, the Commission, and Court, acting within the European Convention on Human Rights,[7] perform a variety of judicial functions as administrative and review tribunals. Provision for settlement of disputes by arbitration appears in the constituent instruments of international organizations, such as the Universal Postal Union,[8] in commodity agreements, such as the International Coffee Agreement of 1968,[9] and in bilateral air transport agreements.[1]

[1] Recent institutions are the Court of Arbitration of the French Community created in 1959; Whiteman i. 564; and the Commission of Mediation, Conciliation and Arbitration of the Org. of African Unity; 3 Int. Leg. Materials, 1116.

[2] See *supra*, p. 583.

[3] See Valentine, 36 *B.Y.* (1960), 174–222; Bebr, *Judicial Control of the European Communities* (1962), pp. 37–112; and Brinkhorst and Schermers, *Judicial Remedies in the European Communities, A Case Book* (1969).

[4] For comment on the work of the Court in general see *Annuaire français* (1958 seq.), 'Chroniques'; Riesenfeld, 56 *A.J.* (1962), 724–8; 59 *A.J.* (1965), 325–35; Reuter, *Recueil d'études en hommage à Paul Guggenheim*, pp. 665–86. On the Court of Justice of the European Communities and other courts with an administrative function: Nørgaard, *The Position of the Individual in International Law*, pp. 263 seq. See further Wengler, *Annuaire de l'Inst*, 44 (1952), i. 224–91; ibid., 45 (1954), i. 265 seq.; ibid., 47 (1957), i. 5 seq.; ibid., ii. 274 seq.

[5] *Supra*, pp. 568–9.

[6] General Agreement on Tariffs and Trade, Cmd. 8048, Art. 23. See 40 *B.Y.*, p. 53. On settlement of disputes in economic organizations see Detter, *Annuaire français* (1960), pp. 796–7; Darwin, 36 *B.Y.* (1960), 354–9. For developments in U.N.E.S.C.O. see Saba, 111 Hague *Recueil* (1964, I), 653–6. On the functions of the I.C.A.O. Council see Buergenthal, *Law-Making in the International Civil Aviation Organization*, pp. 123–97. On the powers of the International Frequency Registration Board, see Evensen, 115 Hague *Recueil* (1965, II), 534–40; International Telecommunications Conv., 1965, art. 13.

[7] *Supra*, pp. 574, 584–8.

[8] Constitution, 1964, art. 126. See also the Int. Telecommunications Conv., 1965, art. 28 (2), Annex 3.

[9] Art. 44; and see the arbitration reported in 8 *Int. Leg. Materials* (1969), 564. The latest instrument is the Agreement of 1976.

[1] Recent cases: Award, 1963, U.S.–France; *R.I.A.A.* xvi. 5; 3 *Int. Leg. Materials* (1964), 668; Adv. op., 1965, U.S.–Italy; *R.I.A.A.* xvi. 75; 4 *Int. Leg. Materials* (1965), 974. See Larsen, 61 *A.J.* (1967), 496–520.

6. *The Permanent Court of International Justice and the International Court of Justice*[1]

The 'World Court' is the label commonly applied to the Permanent Court of International Justice and the International Court of Justice, the latter appearing as a new creation in 1945 but being substantially a continuation of the earlier body. The Permanent Court began to function in 1922, but as a new standing tribunal it grew out of previous experience. Arbitral practice contributed to the development in two ways. Its positive influence shows in the similarity in certain respects between the Court and arbitral practice, viz., the institution of national judges,[2] the power to decide *ex aequo et bono*,[3] the use of special agreements to establish jurisdiction, and the application of some basic principles, for example, that in the absence of agreement to the contrary, an international tribunal has the right to decide questions of its own jurisdiction.[4] The negative influence was the more decisive, since criticism of the Permanent Court of Arbitration, to the effect that it was not a standing court and could not develop a jurisprudence, led to proposals for and a good measure of agreement on a draft Convention Relative to the Creation of a Permanent Court of Arbitral Justice at the Second Hague Peace Conference in 1907. The Convention failed of adoption because of disagreement on the number of judges on the Court, some representatives requiring as many judges as there were states members of the Court.[5]

[1] Generally see Rosenne, *The Law and Practice of the International Court*, (1965); id., *The World Court: What It is and How It Works* (1973); id., *Documents on the International Court of Justice* (1974); Guyomar, *Commentaire du Règlement de la Cour internationale de Justice* (1973); various writers, *Comunicazioni e Studi*, XIV (1975); Fitzmaurice, 29 *B.Y.* (1952), 40–62; 34 *B.Y.* (1958), 8–161; Hudson, *The Permanent Court of International Justice, 1920–1942* (1943); Anand, *Compulsory Jurisdiction of the International Court of Justice* (1961); id., *Studies in International Adjudication* (1969); de Visscher, *Aspects récents du droit procédural de la Cour Internationale de Justice* (1966); Gross, 65 *A.J.* (1971), 253–326; Foster, 7 *Canad. Yrbk.* (1969), 150–91; Dubisson, *La Cour internationale de justice* (1964); *Yearbook of the International Court of Justice*. See also McNair, *The Development of International Justice* (1954); Whiteman xii. 1153–1471.

[2] See *infra*, p. 716. [3] See *infra*, p. 727.

[4] *Nottebohm* case (Preliminary Objection), I.C.J. Reports (1953), p. 111 at p. 119. See further *supra*, p. 20, for references to arbitral decisions in the practice of the Court.

[5] As 46 states were invited to the conference, there would be a tribunal of 46 judges, in three groups sitting at various periods: see Scott, 2 *A.J.* (1908), 772–810; Hudson, op. cit., 80–4. For the proposal for an International Prize Court in 1907 see Hudson, op. cit., pp. 71–9. On the not very successful Central American Court of Justice, which functioned from 1908 to 1918, see Hudson, op. cit., pp. 42–70; id., 26 *A.J.* (1932), 759–86; Mosler and Bernhardt (eds.), *Judicial Settlement of International Disputes* (1974), pp. 315–22.

In 1920 the Council of the League of Nations appointed an advisory committee of jurists to prepare a draft Statute for a Permanent Court of International Justice.[1] The draft Statute sprang from three sources: the draft Convention of 1907, a proposal of neutral states for compulsory jurisdiction, and the Root-Phillimore plan for the election of judges, of which more subsequently. The draft Statute provided for compulsory jurisdiction, but in the Council and the Assembly of the League the great powers and their supporters were able to prevail in their opposition to this. In the Assembly, however, a weak compromise was agreed on in the form of the 'optional clause'.[2] As amended, the Statute came into force in 1921. A defect in the Statute was that it contained no provision for its own amendment and all changes required unanimous approval from the parties, a slow procedure. After the Second World War the Permanent Court could have been revived, but the committee seised of the problem at the San Francisco conference decided to create a new court, two important considerations being the dislike of bodies related to the League of Nations felt by the United States and Soviet Union, and the problem of amending the Statute if the old Court were to be related to the United Nations Organization.[3]

The new court has a much closer relation with the United Nations than the old had with the League. The Charter provides (Article 92) that the International Court of Justice is 'the principal judicial organ of the United Nations', and all members of the latter are *ipso facto* parties to the Statute of the Court (Article 93).[4] In substance if not in form, the new Court is a continuation of the old: the Statute is virtually the same; jurisdiction under instruments referring to the old Court has been transferred to the new;[5] and there is continuity in the jurisprudence of the Court. The new Statute contains provisions on its amendment (Articles 69 and 70).

7. *Organization of the Court*[6]

The problem which merits particular notice is the appoint-

[1] See Art. 14 of the League Covenant.

[2] *Infra*, p. 723. [3] See Hudson, 51 *A.J.* (1957), 569–73.

[4] On the relation to the United Nations see further *infra*, pp. 714–15, 719.

[5] See *infra*, p. 720.

[6] In the remainder of the chapter, references to 'the Court' denote the functioning of the two Courts except where the context determines otherwise.

ment of judges,[1] the key point in the creation of a standing international tribunal in which states may have confidence. The Statute of the Court goes far towards maintaining the independence of judges once appointed. No member of the Court may exercise any political or administrative function, or engage in any other occupation of a professional nature (Article 16, para. 1), or act as agent or counsel in any case, or participate in the decision of a case with which he has previously been connected in some other capacity (Article 17). Dismissal can only occur on the basis of the unanimous opinion of the other members of the Court (Article 18, para. 1). Members engaged on business of the Court have diplomatic privileges and immunities (Article 19).[2] Salaries are fixed by the General Assembly and may not be decreased during the term of office and are free of all taxation (Article 32).

However, the conditions governing the appointment of judges and the machinery of nomination and election are political in character. The membership of the Court cannot be equal to that of the United Nations, since it must have viability as a tribunal,[3] and yet its composition must be broad enough to give states sufficient confidence to resort to the Court. Before 1929 there was a Court of eleven. The present Court has fifteen judges with partial or 'regular' elections of five judges every three years.[4] Article 2 of the Statute provides that 'the Court shall be composed of a body of independent judges, elected regardless of their nationality from among persons of high moral character, who possess the qualifications required in their respective countries for appointment to the highest judicial offices, or are jurisconsults of recognized competence in international law'. This formula takes in professors, professional lawyers, and civil service appointees: in practice many judges of the Court have been former advisers to national Foreign Offices.[5] In other provisions of the Statute the question of nationality acquires significance.

[1] See generally, Lauterpacht, *The Function of Law in the International Community*, pp. 156–7, 202–41; Rosenne, *Law and Practice*, pp. 165–210; Guerrero, *Annuaire de l'Inst*, 44 (1952), ii. 439–52; Huber *et al.*, ibid., 45 (1954), i. 407–554, and ii. 60–106; Hambro, *Festgabe für Makarov* (1958), p. 141; Gross (ed.), *The Future of the International Court of Justice* (1976), in particular, pp. 377–441 (Rosenne).

[2] See *Armand Ugon* v. *Banco Italiano del Uruguay*, 93 *J.D.I.* (1966), p. 176.

[3] It has been suggested that the maximum allowing for viability and successful collective functioning is seventeen. Proposals to increase the number of judges were made in the United Nations in 1956–7: Schwelb, 64 *A.J.* (1970), p. 880 at p. 882.

[4] Members may be re-elected. In the general election in 1946 the allocation of three, six, and nine year terms was settled by lot. The quorum is nine.

[5] See the *I.C.J. Yearbook* for biographical notes on the judges.

It is provided that no two members may be nationals of the same state (Article 3, para. 1), and Article 9 requires electors to bear in mind 'that in the body as a whole the representation of the main forms of civilization and of the principal legal systems of the world should be assured'. The principle stated is unimpeachable, but it is difficult to translate into practice, and in any case the system of election ensures that the composition of the Court reflects voting strength and political alliances in the Security Council and General Assembly. The permanent members of the Security Council normally have judges on the Court.[1] Until recently Latin America was over-represented, having four judges. Asian and African representation has increased somewhat lately.[2]

Nomination of candidates for election to the Court (Statute, Articles 4–7) is by the national groups of the Permanent Court of Arbitration:[3] members of the United Nations not so represented may create national groups for the purpose. Groups may and often do nominate persons of other nationalities.[4] The system of nomination is a (probably unsuccessful) attempt to have independent persons nominated. However, the national groups are themselves nominated by governments, and nominations are sent through Foreign Offices. In spite of criticism the system of indirect nomination, as opposed to direct nomination by governments, was maintained in the new Statute of 1945.

The system of election is based on the Root-Phillimore plan of 1920 and involves independent, simultaneous, voting by the Security Council and the General Assembly. States which are parties to the Statute of the Court but not members of the United

[1] Since 1960 there has been no Chinese judge.

[2] The election of October 1963 produced the following composition: 6 Europeans, 2 Latin Americans, 2 Africans, 3 Asians, 1 Australian, 1 North American. However, analysis of the composition may proceed on quite other criteria. Politically, the Latin-American and Asian states represented on the Court were associates of the West. The African states were Egypt, which obviously has Arab ties, and Senegal, which is a political associate of France. There were two judges from European Communist states. As from 5 February 1970 the Court had the following composition: 6 Europeans, 2 Latin Americans, 3 Africans (Sub-Saharan), 2 Asians, 1 Lebanese, 1 North American. The Europeans include judges from Poland and the U.S.S.R. The other judges are from states associated politically with the West, some very closely. Non-aligned States are unrepresented unless Nigeria and Lebanon are so classified. In 1977 the composition was similar, with the substitution for the Lebanese national of a Syrian judge. This type of analysis should not be allowed to obscure the actual legal status of the judges as individuals, who are not representatives of states.

[3] Cf. *supra*, p. 707.

[4] Article 6 provides: 'Before making these nominations, each national group is recommended to consult its highest court of justice, its legal faculties and schools of law, and its national academies and national sections of international academies devoted to the study of law.' See Baxter, 55 *A.J.* (1961), 445.

Nations are permitted[1] to take part in the procedures of nomination and election: for elections the General Assembly is thus specially augmented. Candidates must obtain an absolute majority in both organs to be elected (Article 10 of the Statute). In practice the Security Council and General Assembly do not vote independently, and more or less discreet consultation occurs.[2] In post-war elections political calculations have been prominent, and the attitude of judges in particular cases has on occasion affected the voting when candidates have been presented for re-election.[3] The political basis for elections has been the object of adverse comment, particularly with regard to the post-1945 system of partial elections every three years, but it is difficult to see a way out: the political basis for elections would seem to be a condition of the Court's existence.[4]

A further concession to the political conditions of the Court's existence is to be found in Article 31 of the Statute. This provides that a party to a case before the Court has a right, in effect, to representation on the Court by a national judge, and, if there is no judge of its nationality, a judge *ad hoc* may be appointed (who may be of some other nationality). The judge *ad hoc* is appointed by the party concerned and commonly supports its view of the case when on the bench.[5] The institution is reminiscent of the national commissioners in *ad hoc* arbitral bodies and is justified if at all by expediency alone.

8. *Jurisdiction of the Court in Contentious Cases*[6]

The Court has jurisdiction in contentious cases between

[1] General Assembly Resol. 264 (III), 8 October, 1948.

[2] For procedures to deal with deadlock, see Articles 11 and 12 of the Statute. Informal consultation is used to obviate resort to a joint conference. See further Sørensen, pp. 700–1.

[3] For comment on particular elections: Rosenne, pp. 924–31; Hudson, 46 *A.J.* (1952), 38–9; Simpson, 37 *B.Y.* (1961), 527–35; Hogan, 59 *A.J.* (1965), 908–12.

[4] On the appointment of judges to the Court of the European Communities see Valentine, *The Court of Justice of the European Communities* (1965), 8, 17–30; and, for the European Commission and Court of Human Rights, Robertson, *Human Rights in Europe*, pp. 43 seq., 92 seq.; and Golsong, in *I.C.L.Q.*, Suppl. Public. no. 11 (1965), pp. 38 seq.

[5] On voting in the Court: Rosenne, pp. 939–48; Suh, 63 *A.J.* (1969), 224–36. Generally on individual and dissenting opinions: Anand, 14 *I.C.L.Q.* (1965), 788–808.

[6] See especially Shihata, *The Power of the International Court to Determine its Own Jurisdiction* (1965); Fitzmaurice, 34 *B.Y.* (1958), 8–138; Rosenne, pp. 267–506; Hambro, 25 *B.Y.* (1948), 133–57; id., 76 Hague *Recueil* (1950, I), 125–215; Hudson, *The Permanent Court of International Justice 1920–1942*, pp. 405–82; Abi-Saab, *Les exceptions préliminaires dans la procédure de la Cour internationale* (1967); Grisel, *Les exceptions d'incompétence et d'irrecevabilité dans la procédure de la cour internationale de justice* (1968); Starace, *La Competenza della corte internazionale di giustizia in materia contenziosa* (1970).

states,[1] on the basis of the consent of the parties. The Court has often referred to the fact that the jurisdiction of the Court to hear and decide a case on the merits depends on the will of the parties.[2] This principle, reflected in Article 36 of the Statute, rests on international practice in the settlement of disputes and is a corollary of the sovereign equality of states.[3] As it has been pointed out elsewhere,[4] the competence of a tribunal to deal with the merits of a claim may be challenged on a number of grounds. Objections to the jurisdiction strike at the competence of the tribunal to give rulings as to the merits or admissibility of the claim. An objection to the admissibility of a claim, for example on the ground that local remedies have not been exhausted, involves a challenge to the validity of a claim distinct from issues as to jurisdiction or merits. Normally the question of admissibility can only be approached when jurisdiction has been assumed, and issues of admissibility, especially those concerning the nationality of the claimant and the exhaustion of local remedies, may be closely connected with the merits of the case. It is possible for cases to go through three phases, involving distinct proceedings concerned successively with preliminary objections to jurisdiction, preliminary objections to admissibility, and the ultimate merits of the case. In practice, the Court may join certain types of preliminary objection to the merits. For example, objections to jurisdiction by reference to the concept of domestic jurisdiction, or the existence of a dispute before the date of acceptance of jurisdiction in an instrument excluding past disputes, involve issues which could not be pronounced upon without prejudging the merits.[5] Finally, the Court may decline to exercise a juris-

On the use of the terms 'competence' and 'jurisdiction': Fitzmaurice, 29 *B.Y.* (1952), 40–2; 34 *B.Y.* (1958), 8–9.

[1] Article 34, para. 1, of the Statute provides: 'Only states may be parties in cases before the Court.' See further *supra*, p. 578.

[2] See, for example, the *Anglo-Iranian Oil Co.* case, I.C.J. Reports (1952), at pp. 102–3; and the *Monetary Gold* case, ibid. (1954), at p. 32. See further Fitzmaurice, 34 *B.Y.* (1958), 66–97.

[3] *Supra*, pp. 287 seq. In their joint dissenting opinion in the *South West Africa* cases (Preliminary Objections), I.C.J. Reports (1962), p. 319 at pp. 473–4, Judges Spender and Fitzmaurice stated that the Court has a duty to be satisfied beyond a reasonable doubt that jurisdiction does exist.

[4] *Supra*, Chapter XXI.

[5] *Right of Passage* case (Preliminary Objections), I.C.J. Reports (1957), p. 125 at pp. 149–52. See also Rosenne, pp. 464–6; Fitzmaurice, 34 *B.Y.* (1958), 23–5; Lauterpacht, *The Development of International Law by the International Court*, pp. 113–15; Shihata, pp. 113–16; the *Barcelona Traction* case (Preliminary Objections), I.C.J. Reports (1964), p. 6 at pp. 41–7; Morelli, diss. op., ibid., pp. 97–115; ibid. (Second Phase), I.C.J. Reports (1970), p. 51; Bustamante y Rivero, sep. op., p. 57; Fitzmaurice, sep. op., pp. 110–13; Tanaka, sep. op., p. 115; Gros, sep. op., p. 268 n., Ammoun, sep. op., pp. 286–7; Rip-

diction which it has, or which may be found to exist in the given case, on grounds of judicial propriety.[1]

As a further preliminary, consideration must be given to the effects of becoming a party to the Statute of the Court.[2] States do not submit to the jurisdiction of the Court as a result of signing the Statute, and some further expression of consent is required. On the other hand, states not parties to the Statute are not unconditionally barred from the Court.[3] Signature of the Statute, though it may not ground jurisdiction in the ordinary way, does have some important consequences. In the first place, without more, parties to the Statute are bound to accept the jurisdiction of the Court to determine its own competence (the *compétence de la compétence*): Article 36 (6) of the Statute provides that 'In the event of a dispute as to whether the Court has jurisdiction, the matter shall be settled by the decision of the Court'.[4] Secondly, the Statute in Article 41 supports a jurisdiction to indicate 'interim measures of protection' (or, 'provisional measures') to preserve the respective rights of the parties. Unless there are circumstances which make it apparent that there is no consent to the jurisdiction, the Court will assume the power to indicate such measures, without prejudice to the question of the jurisdiction

hagen, diss. op., pp. 356–7. In the *Interhandel* case (Preliminary Objections), I.C.J. Reports (1959), at pp. 27–9, the Court refused to join an objection of non-exhaustion of local remedies to the merits: for comment see Jenks, pp. 532–4; Shihata, pp. 279–82. See further on the relation of issues of admissibility and merits and also on the status of decisions on preliminary objections, the *South West Africa* cases (Second Phase), I.C.J. Reports (1966), p. 6 (see Cheng, 20 *Curr. Leg. Problems* (1967), p. 181, at pp. 199–205); and the *Nuclear Tests Case* (Australia v. France), I.C.J. Reports, 1974, p. 253.

[1] See the *Cameroons* case, I.C.J. Reports (1963), p. 15; *supra*, p. 470.

[2] Article 93 (1) of the United Nations Charter provides that all members of the Organization are *ipso facto* parties to the Statute of the Court, and Art. 35 (1) of the Statute states that the Court shall be open to parties to it. Article 93 (2) of the Charter provides that a state which is not a member of the United Nations may become a party to the Statute of the Court 'on conditions to be determined in each case by the General Assembly upon the recommendation of the Security Council'. Switzerland, Liechtenstein, and San Marino have become parties under this provision.

[3] Article 35 (2) of the Statute stipulates as follows: 'The conditions under which the Court shall be open to other states shall, subject to the special provisions contained in treaties in force, be laid down by the Security Council, but in no case shall such conditions place the parties in a position of inequality before the Court.' In the *Corfu Channel* case (Preliminary Objections), I.C.J. Reports (1947–8), p. 53, Art. 35 (2) was not regarded as exclusive in effect: see Rosenne, pp. 278–84.

[4] See the *Nottebohm* case (Preliminary Objection), I.C.J. Reports (1953), pp. 119–20, where the Court regarded this power as grounded in international law apart from any explicit provision in the Statute. See further Shihata, op. cit.; Fitzmaurice, 34 *B.Y.* (1958), 25–31; Berlia, 88 Hague *Recueil* (1955, II), 109–54. On the power of the Court to determine the jurisdiction of another international tribunal see the *Ambatielos* case (Merits: Obligation to Arbitrate), I.C.J. Reports (1953), p. 10, and Fitzmaurice, op. cit., pp. 31–66.

of the Court to deal with the merits of the case.[1] Lastly, under Article 62 of its Statute the Court has power to permit third-party intervention in cases in which a state has an interest of a legal nature which may be affected by the decision in the case.[2]

9. *Heads of Jurisdiction*

(a) *Matters specially provided for in the Charter of the United Nations.* Article 36 (1) of the Statute includes within the jurisdiction 'all matters specially provided for in the Charter of the United Nations'. These words were inserted during the drafting of the present Statute in the expectation that the Charter would contain some provision for compulsory jurisdiction. Apart from a controversial construction of Article 36 (3) of the Charter, no such provision was made. In the *Corfu Channel* case (Preliminary Objections)[3] the United Kingdom argued that Article 36 (1) of the Statute could be referred to Article 36 (1) and (3) of the Charter, which provide for reference of legal disputes to the Court on the recommendation of the Security Council; and, further, that a recommendation involved a decision which was binding in accordance with Article 25 of the Charter. The Court did not find it necessary to deal with the point, but in a joint separate opinion seven judges rejected the argument, *inter alia* on the ground that in its normal meaning the term 'recommendation' was non-compulsory.[4]

(b) *Consent* ad hoc: *jurisdiction by special agreement and unilateral application.* The consent of the parties may be given *ad hoc* to the exercise of jurisdiction over a dispute which already exists. Normally, as in the *Minquiers and Ecrehos*[5] case between France and the United Kingdom, the consent will take the form of a special agreement (*compromis*). However, the special agreement is

[1] *Anglo-Iranian Oil* case, I.C.J. Reports (1951), p. 89 at pp. 92–3. See further Shihata, pp. 179–80; Fitzmaurice, op. cit., pp. 107–19; Lauterpacht, *The Development of International Law by the International Court*, pp. 110–13; the joint dissent of Winiarski and Badawi, I.C.J. Reports (1951), pp. 96–8; and the separate opinion of Lauterpacht, *Interhandel* case, I.C.J. Reports (1951), p. 117. A further issue concerns the binding nature of orders indicating interim measures: see Lauterpacht, op. cit., pp. 252–4; Fitzmaurice, op. cit., pp. 122–4.

[2] On intervention under Articles 62 and 63 of the Statute in general: Rosenne, pp. 430–4; Fitzmaurice, op. cit., pp. 124–9.

[3] I.C.J. Reports (1947–8), p. 15.

[4] Ibid., pp. 31–2. Jurists generally agree with the joint separate opinion: see Fitzmaurice, 29 *B.Y.* (1952), 31–2, 44; Oppenheim ii. 115. For a different approach: Rosenne, pp. 342–4; Gross, 120 Hague *Recueil* (1967, I), 351–5.

[5] I.C.J. Reports (1953), p. 47. In this case a special agreement was employed, although the parties had both accepted jurisdiction under the optional clause (Statute, Article 36 (2)).

not an essential requirement of form, and the Court has taken the view that consent *ad hoc* may arise where the plaintiff state has accepted the jurisdiction by a unilateral application followed by a separate act of consent by the other party, either by a communication to the Court or by taking part in the initiation of proceedings.[1] In other words, the voluntary jurisdiction is not to be restricted by requirements of form, and Article 36 (1) of the Statute states simply that 'the jurisdiction of the Court comprises all cases which the parties refer to it'.

(c) *Consent* ante hoc: *treaties and conventions.*[2] Article 36 (1) of the Statute refers also to 'all matters specially provided for . . . in treaties and conventions in force'.[3] A great many multilateral and bilateral treaties contain clauses granting jurisdiction in advance over classes of disputes arising from their subject-matter.[4] Although the jurisdiction is by the consent of the parties, like all types of jurisdiction in the present context, it can be described as 'compulsory' in the sense that agreement, in binding form, is given in advance of the appearance of particular disputes. However, the label 'compulsory jurisdiction' is often used to describe simply jurisdiction arising under Article 36 (2) of the Statute.[5]

(d) *Transferred jurisdiction: Articles 36 (5) and 37 of the Statute.*[6] The Statute of the Permanent Court provided for jurisdiction on the basis of compromissory clauses in treaties or conventions, and when the Statute was redrafted in 1945 it was desired to save such clauses. Article 37 of the new Statute thus provides:

> Whenever a treaty or convention in force provides for reference of a matter to a tribunal to have been instituted by the League of Nations, or to the Permanent Court of International Justice, the matter shall, as between the parties to the present Statute, be referred to the International Court of Justice.

[1] *Corfu Channel* case (Preliminary Objections), I.C.J. Reports (1948), pp. 27–8. See further Hudson, pp. 435–8; Fitzmaurice, 29 *B.Y.* (1952), 43–4; id., 34 *B.Y.* (1958), 79–80; Rosenne, pp. 319–22 (and see Rosenne's earlier work (1957), pp. 265–6); Jenks, *The Prospects of International Adjudication*, pp. 24 seq.; and *infra*, section (f).

[2] See Lawson, 46 *A.J.* (1952), p. 219 at pp. 223–9; Fitzmaurice, 34 *B.Y.* (1958), 73–4; Rosenne, pp. 332–5; *Ambatielos* case (Preliminary Objections), I.C.J. Reports (1952), p. 28 at p. 39; Briggs, in *Recueil d'études en hommage à Guggenheim*, pp. 628–41.

[3] i.e., in force on the date of the institution of proceedings. Nor can a unilateral suspension of a treaty *per se* render jurisdictional clauses inoperative: *Appeal relating to the Jurisdiction of the ICAO Council*, I.C.J. Reports (1972), p. 46 at pp. 53–4.

[4] See *I.C.J. Yearbook* (1976–7), p. 80. On the drafting of compromissory clauses: Guggenheim, *Annuaire de l'Inst.* (1954), 45, i. 310–43; ibid. (1956), 46, 178–264.

[5] See the *Ambatielos* case, I.C.J. Reports (1952), at p. 39.

[6] See Rosenne, pp. 335–42, 376–9; Fitzmaurice, 34 *B.Y.* (1958), 137–8.

Two limitations are prominent here: the treaty or convention must be 'in force' between the litigating states, and all the parties to the dispute must be parties to the new Statute. Article 37 has operated to support jurisdiction in the *Ambatielos* case (Preliminary Objection),[1] the *South West Africa* cases (Preliminary Objections),[2] and the *Barcelona Traction* case (Preliminary Objections).[3] The application of Article 37 to particular situations leads to a variety of difficult questions which are, however, incidental to the operation of Article 37 itself. An issue bearing directly on the effect of the article was highlighted by the *Aerial Incident* case (Preliminary Objections).[4] There the issue was the survival of a Bulgarian declaration of acceptance of jurisdiction under the optional clause (Statute, Article 36 (2)), made in 1921. Article 36 (5) of the Statute of the present Court, drafted in 1945, provides:

> Declarations made under Article 36 of the Statute of the Permanent Court of International Justice and which are still in force shall be deemed, as between the parties to the present Statute, to be acceptances of the compulsory jurisdiction of the International Court of Justice for the period which they still have to run and in accordance with their terms.

The Government of Israel, as plaintiff, argued that the effect of the declaration of 1921 was revived when Bulgaria again became a party to the Statute on joining the United Nations in 1955, as a consequence of Article 36 (5). The majority of the Court interpreted the latter to apply only to states which were signatories of the 1945 Statute, prior to the dissolution of the Permanent Court, and not to a state in the position of Bulgaria, not a signatory, and becoming a party to the Statute many years later as an automatic consequence of admission to the United Nations.[5] The Court emphasized that a different construction would run counter to the principle that the jurisdiction of the Court is founded on the consent of states.[6] In a carefully reasoned

[1] I.C.J. Reports (1952), p. 28.

[2] Ibid. (1962), p. 319 at pp. 334–5. Cf. the joint dissenting opinion of Spender and Fitzmaurice, ibid., at pp. 469, 494–503, 505–6, 512–13; the separate opinion of Bustamante, pp. 367, 376–7; separate opinion of Jessup, pp. 415–16; the separate opinion of Mbanefo, pp. 437–8; the dissenting opinion of Van Wyk, pp. 613–15. See also the *Status of South West Africa* case, I.C.J. Reports (1950), p. 128 at p. 138.

[3] I.C.J. Reports (1964), p. 6.

[4] Ibid. (1959), p. 127. See Gross, 57 *A.J.* (1963), 753–66.

[5] See also the separate opinion of Badawi, p. 148. In the separate opinion of Armand-Ugon, p. 152, the view is taken that Article 36 (5) only applies to declarations of acceptance for a fixed term and not to declarations, such as that of Bulgaria in 1921, without a time limit.

[6] At p. 142 of the judgment.

joint dissenting opinion,[1] Judges Lauterpacht, Wellington Koo, and Spender interpreted Article 36 (5) in a different way, taking the view that declarations, in regard to that provision, and treaties and conventions, in regard to Article 37, did not lose validity on the dissolution of the Permanent Court on 18 April 1946.[2] As a consequence of a formalistic approach to points of interpretation, the joint dissent reduces the consensual basis of the Court's jurisdiction in this context to a shadow. The problem left over was this: if the view in the joint dissent, that Articles 36 (5) and 37 were to be treated alike, was correct, then the majority interpretation of 36 (5) could be used to reduce the effect of Article 37. In the *South West Africa* cases (Preliminary Objections) the issue was not faced: the Court was influenced by the need to exercise effective supervision over a territory with a special status, and, in any case, the parties were all signatories of the Statute at San Francisco. But in the *Barcelona Traction* case the principal second preliminary objection of Spain raised the issue: Spain was not a party to the Statute before the dissolution of the Permanent Court in 1946. The Court held that Article 37 could not be approached in this way and that the date on which the respondent became a party to the Statute was irrelevant.[3] The decision in the *Aerial Incident* case[4] was distinguished on the following grounds: (1) a different category of instrument was involved in Article 37; (2) the phrase 'in force' in Article 37 bore on the instrument containing the jurisdictional clause and not the clause; (3) the *Aerial Incident* case was *sui generis* and could have gone in favour of Bulgaria on other grounds. As a further reason for not following the *Aerial Incident* decision, the Court pointed out that a decision concerning Article 37 must affect a considerable number of treaties and general multilateral conventions.[5] On the plane of formal logic the distinctions offered are not in all respects impressive, and the Court would seem to have tempered consistency with expediency.[6]

[1] p. 156.

[2] pp. 163, 166, 171, 180–2. See also Jessup, I.C.J. Reports (1962), p. 415.

[3] I.C.J. Reports (1964), pp. 26–39. See also the *Nuclear Tests Case* (Australia v. France), ibid. (1974), pp. 332–3 (Joint Diss. Op.), 375–80 (De Castro, diss.).

[4] I.C.J. Reports (1959), p. 127. See also the *Temple* case (Preliminary Objections), I.C.J. Reports (1961), p. 17, distinguished in the present decision at p. 30.

[5] I.C.J. Reports (1964), pp. 29–30. Article 36 (5) has now ceased to be of importance, as no optional clause declarations exist which need to be saved.

[6] Spender and Wellington Koo did not discern any decisive distinction (pp. 47, 51–3). Spiropoulos considered that the *Aerial Incident* judgment was decisive in the present case (p. 48). In his separate opinion Tanaka concluded that the present decision 'substantially over-ruled' the *Aerial Incident* decision (pp. 65–77): only by expressly over-

(e) *Consent* ante hoc: *declarations under the optional clause.*[1] Article 36 (2) of the Statute, commonly referred to as the optional clause, provides as follows:

> The state parties to the present Statute may at any time declare that they recognize as compulsory *ipso facto* and without special agreement, in relation to any other state accepting the same obligation, the jurisdiction of the Court in all legal disputes concerning:
>
> (a) the interpretation of a treaty;
> (b) any question of international law;
> (c) the existence of any fact which, if established, would constitute a breach of an international obligation;
> (d) the nature or extent of the reparation to be made for the breach of an international obligation.

Acceptance of jurisdiction is by means of unilateral declarations deposited with the Secretary-General of the United Nations, the declarant state being bound to accept jurisdiction *vis-à-vis* any other declarant so far as the acceptances coincide. On the principle of reciprocity, the lowest common factor in the two declarations is the basis for jurisdiction, and thus a respondent state can take advantage of a reservation or condition in the declaration of the applicant state.[2] The independent declarations are binding in the senses that they can only be withdrawn in accordance with the law of treaties and operate contractually with a suspensive condition, viz., the filing of an application by a state with a coincident declaration.[3] This type of jurisdiction involves acceptance of jurisdiction in advance for categories of disputes which are contingencies.[4] The commitment *ante hoc*, in relation to any other state fulfilling the conditions of the Statute,

ruling the previous decision could the Court have reconciled considerations of consistency with those of policy. In dissenting opinions Morelli and Armand-Ugon (Judge *ad hoc*) held that Article 37 ceased to operate after the dissolution of the Permanent Court (pp. 86–97, 134–59, respectively).

1 See Waldock, 32 *B.Y.* (1955–6), 244–87; Briggs, 93 Hague *Recueil* (1958, I), 229–363; Rosenne, pp. 364–421; Fischer Williams, 11 *B.Y.* (1930), 63–84; Fitzmaurice, 34 *B.Y.* (1958), 74–9; Vulcan, 18 *Acta Scandinavica* (1947–8), 30–55.

2 See the *Electricity Company of Sofia and Bulgaria* case (1939), Ser. A/B, no. 77, pp. 80–2; *Anglo-Iranian Oil Company* case, I.C.J. Reports (1952), p. 93, at p. 103; *Case of Certain Norwegian Loans*, ibid. (1957), p. 9 at pp. 23–4.

3 The declarations are valid without ratification, but may be made subject to ratification. They are registered as 'international agreements' under Art. 102 of the Charter. On their interpretation: I.C.J. Reports (1952), p. 103. On the question whether two optional clause declarations are a form of treaty *inter se*: *Nuclear Tests Case* (Australia v. France, I.C.J. Reports (1974), pp. 352–6 (Joint Diss. Op.).

4 In practice acceptances under Article 36 (2) can be made in such a way as to apply to particular disputes.

is usually described as a compulsory jurisdiction, although, as in the case of jurisdiction by treaty or convention, the basis is ultimately consensual. The basis of the optional clause lay in a compromise, first achieved in 1920, and maintained in the new Statute in 1945, between a system of true compulsory jurisdiction based on unilateral applications by plaintiffs, and jurisdiction based on treaties concluded independently. The expectation was that a general system of compulsory jurisdiction would be generated as declarations multiplied. The conception was sound enough, but the conditions in which the system has functioned have reduced its effectiveness. In 1934 there were forty-two declarations in force, the number reducing to thirty-two by 1955 but increasing since then.[1] The point is of course that since 1955 the figures represent a low proportion of the total of independent states (some 147 are parties to the Statute of the Court). The negative factors are principally the lack of confidence in international adjudication on the part of governments, the practice, accepted by the Court, of making declarations subject to various reservations and conditions, frequently arbitrary in extent and ambiguous in form, and the tactical advantages of staying out of the system.

Before the nature of certain of the conditions and reservations is examined, some general points must be made about the drafting of Article 36 (2). In the first place, the paragraph refers to 'all legal disputes', whereas paragraph (1) refers to 'all cases' and 'all matters', an indication that the latter is not restricted to 'disputes'. However, both paragraphs involve the distinction between legal and political issues, and the distinction is less easy to maintain if no 'dispute' exists.[2] In spite of the reference to legal disputes in Article 36 (2), some declarations state the limitation as a reservation. More important in practice is the condition of reciprocity in Article 36 (2), expressed in the words 'in relation to any other state accepting the same obligation'.[3] This condition is a part of the Statute itself and applies to declarations expressed to be made 'unconditionally'. It follows that reservations as to reciprocity in acceptances are superfluous.

[1] The *I.C.J. Yearbook* (1976–7), p. 49, lists 45 acceptances. For the text of the U.K. decl. of 1969 see Misc. No. 4 (1969), Cmnd. 3872; 18 *I.C.L.Q.* (1969), p. 769. On the new Canadian decl. of 1970 see Macdonald, 8 *Canad. Yrbk.* (1970), 3–38.

[2] On the definition of a dispute: *supra*, pp. 479–80. On the important question of justiciability and the distinction between legal and political disputes see Lauterpacht, *The Function of Law in the International Community* (1933); Sohn, 108 Hague *Recueil* (1963, I), 41 seq.; 76–81; Brownlie, 42 *B.Y.* (1967), 123–43.

[3] This does not mean, as it could be taken to mean, that the declarations must be identical. Generally, on reciprocity, see Briggs, op. cit., pp. 237–68.

Article 36 (3), rather confusingly, refers to a condition of reciprocity which is optional and not a part of the Statute: declarations may contain a suspensive condition referring to acceptance of compulsory jurisdiction by other states. An important point is that reciprocity applies when a case is submitted to the Court and not before: thus in the *Right of Passage* case (Preliminary Objections)[1] India was unsuccessful in her contention that reciprocity applied so as to allow the respondent to take advantage of a reservation in the declaration of the applicant, Portugal, of a right to exclude any given category or categories of disputes, on notification to the Secretary-General. Portugal had filed her application only three days after depositing her declaration.

Particular conditions and reservations met with require brief examination.[2]

(i) *Matters of domestic jurisdiction*. A plea that the issue concerned is a matter of domestic jurisdiction may appear as a preliminary objection or as a plea on the merits: strictly speaking the plea is available, apart from any reservation on the subject, in accordance with the general principles of international law.[3] One form of this reservation has created controversy. In 1946 the United States deposited a declaration with a reservation of 'disputes with regard to matters which are essentially within the domestic jurisdiction of the United States of America as determined by the United States of America', and seven other states have used this 'automatic' or 'peremptory' reservation.[4] In principle this form of reservation is incompatible with the Statute of the Court, since it contradicts the power of the Court to determine its own jurisdiction and is not a genuine acceptance of jurisdiction *ante hoc*.[5]

[1] I.C.J. Reports (1957), p. 125, at pp. 143–4, 147–8.

[2] For other reservations see Briggs, op. cit., pp. 296–308. Reservations as to reciprocity and legal disputes have been noted already.

[3] On the general question of domestic jurisdiction before international tribunals: *supra*, pp. 295–7. Many declarations, including the current U.K. declaration, contain no reservation concerning domestic jurisdiction.

[4] See generally Briggs, op. cit., pp. 328–63; Shihata, pp. 271–97; Gross, 56 *A.J.* (1962), 357–82; Henkin, 65 *A.J.* (1971), 374–7. The other declarations with this reservation were those of France (1947), Mexico (1947), Liberia (1952), South Africa (1955), India (1956), Pakistan (1957), the Sudan (1958), Malawi (1966), Philippines (1972). The French, Indian, and Pakistani declarations have been replaced by declarations with a non-automatic reservation. The South African declaration has been terminated. A British version was withdrawn in 1959 for events occurring after 26 November 1958 (see 52 *A.J.* (1958), 13; 8 *I.C.L.Q.* (1959), 198), and withdrawn wholly in 1963. See the *Yearbook* of the Court for declarations currently in force.

[5] The Court has avoided the issue when it has been raised, as in the *Case of Certain Norwegian Loans*, I.C.J. Reports (1957), p. 9; and the *Interhandel* case, ibid. (1959), p. 6. However, a number of judges have held the reservation to be illegal: see I.C.J. Reports

(ii) *Time-limits and reservations* ratione temporis.[1] Declarations may be expressed to be for a term of years, but some are expressed to be terminable after, say, six months' notice and some immediately on notice to the Secretary-General. Whilst a power of termination immediately on notice weakens the system of compulsory jurisdiction, it would seem to be compatible with the Statute of the Court.[2] Once the Court is seized of a case on the basis of declarations in force at the date of an application, the subsequent expiry of a declaration of one of the parties does not affect the Court's jurisdiction in that case.[3]

(iii) *Reservation of past disputes.* Reservation of past disputes as a type of reservation *ratione temporis* is common, and the reservation may be taken further, as in the 'Belgian formula', which refers to all disputes arising after a certain date 'with regard to situations or facts subsequent to the said date'. Disputes often have a long history, and this formula is ambitious. In its jurisprudence the Court has taken the view that the limitation takes in only situations or facts which are the source, the real cause, of the dispute.[4]

(f) *Consent* post hoc: forum prorogatum.[5] Lauterpacht writes[6] that 'exercise of jurisdiction by virtue of the principle of *forum prorogatum* takes place whenever, after the initiation of proceedings by joint or unilateral application, jurisdiction is exer-

(1957), pp. 42 seq. (Lauterpacht), pp. 68–70 (Guerrero); ibid. (1959), pp. 55–9 (Spender), 76–8 (Klaestad), 92–4 (Armand-Ugon), 97 seq. (Lauterpacht). See also *Annuaire de l'Inst.* (1959), ii. 359 (resol. 2); Guerrero, *Festschrift für Jean Spiropoulos* (1957), pp. 207–12; Jennings, 7 *I.C.L.Q.* (1958), 355–63; Goldie, 9 *U.C.L.A. Law Rev.* (1961–2), 277–359; and Simmonds, 10 *I.C.L.Q.* (1961), 522–32. Juristic opinion is against the validity of the reservation: Oppenheim ii. 62–3; Hudson, 41 *A.J.* (1947), 9–14; Waldock, 31 *B.Y.* (1954), 131–7; Briggs, op. cit., p. 363; id., 53 *A.J.* (1959), 301–18; Jennings, loc. cit. Note the cautious comment of Rosenne, pp. 395–9.

[1] Generally on competence *ratione temporis*: Briggs, op. cit., pp. 269–95; Rosenne, pp. 329–31; id., *The Time Factor in the Jurisdiction of the International Court of Justice* (1960); Debbasch, 64 *R.G.D.I.P.* (1960), 230–59; Soubeyrol, *Annuaire français* (1959), pp. 232–57.

[2] See the view of the Court on an analogous reservation in the *Right of Passage* case (Preliminary Objections), I.C.J. Reports (1957), p. 125 at pp. 143–4. See further Briggs, op. cit., pp. 273–7.

[3] *Nottebohm* case (Preliminary Objection), I.C.J. Reports (1953), p. 111 at pp. 122–3. See also Fitzmaurice, 34 *B.Y.* (1958), 14–19.

[4] See the *Phosphates in Morocco* case, P.C.I.J., Ser. A/B, no. 74, pp. 23–4; *Electricity Company of Sofia and Bulgaria* case, ibid., no. 77, p. 82; *Right of Passage* case (Merits), I.C.J. Reports (1960), p. 6 at pp. 33–6. See further Briggs, op. cit., pp. 279–95.

[5] See Rosenne, pp. 283–4, 322, 344–63; Shihata, pp. 128–35; Waldock, 2 *I.L.Q.* (1948), 377–91; Lauterpacht, *The Development of International Law by the International Court*, pp. 103–7; Fitzmaurice, 34 *B.Y.* (1958), 80–6; Stillmunkes, 68 *R.G.D.I.P.* (1964), 665–86; Winiarski, *Festschrift für Jean Spiropoulos* (1957), pp. 445–52.

[6] Op. cit., p. 103.

cised with regard either to the entire dispute or to some aspects of it as the result of an agreement, express or implied . . .'. The principle operates because the Statute and rules of court as interpreted contain no mandatory rules as to specification of the formal basis on which the applicant founds jurisdiction, nor as to the form in which consent is to be expressed. Consent may take the form of an agreement on the basis of successive acts of the parties, and the institution of proceedings by unilateral application is not confined to cases of compulsory jurisdiction. Thus, in the *Corfu Channel* case (Preliminary Objection),[1] after the United Kingdom had made a unilateral application, Albania accepted the jurisdiction in an official communication to the Court. Informal agreement, agreement inferred from conduct, or a formal agreement, in each case *after* the initiation of proceedings, may result in prorogated jurisdiction. However, the Court will not accept jurisdiction unless there is a real, and not merely apparent, consent.[2] Resort to technical constructions in order to promote jurisdiction in particular cases may in the long run discourage appearances before the Court, and the judicial practice has not developed *forum prorogatum* as a true principle of estoppel. 'Automatic and compulsory' jurisdiction, in so far as it occurs at all, is confined to (1) instances in the practice of the Court where preliminary objections in fact independent of the merits are joined to the merits without the consent of both parties;[3] (2) the operation of Articles 36 (5) and 37 prior to the dissolution of the Permanent Court and, on one view, subsequently;[4] (3) the competence to decide on matters of jurisdiction and similar powers based on the Statute.[5]

(g) *Jurisdiction to decide* ex aequo et bono.[6] Article 38 (2) of the Statute gives the Court power to decide a case *ex aequo et bono* if the parties agree to this. This provision qualifies Article 38 (1), which refers to the function of the Court as being to decide 'in

[1] I.C.J. Reports (1947–8), at p. 27. But the institution of proceedings was based on a special agreement.

[2] See the *Ambatielos* case, I.C.J. Reports (1952), p. 28 at p. 39; and the *Anglo-Iranian Oil Company* case, ibid., p. 93 at p. 114.

[3] See the dissenting opinion of Armand-Ugon in the *Barcelona Traction* case (Preliminary Objections), I.C.J. Reports (1964), p. 6 at p. 164. See also the dissenting opinion of Morelli, ibid., pp. 97 seq., on the entertainment of 'preliminary objections' inadmissible as such. On the effect of the *non ultra petita* rule on jurisdiction see Rosenne, pp. 326–7; and Fitzmaurice, 34 *B.Y.* (1958), 98–107.

[4] *Supra*, p. 720.

[5] *Supra*, p. 718. On incidental jurisdiction: Rosenne, pp. 422–36; Briggs, 66 *R.G.D.I.P.* (1960), 217–29.

[6] See Lauterpacht, op. cit., pp. 213–23; Fitzmaurice, op. cit., pp. 132–7; Rosenne, pp. 323–6.

accordance with international law' such disputes as are submitted to it.[1] The exercise of this power, which has not yet occurred, may not be easy to reconcile with the judicial character of the tribunal.

10. *The Advisory Jurisdiction of the Court*[2]

Article 65 (1) of the Statute provides as follows: 'The Court may give an advisory opinion on any legal question at the request of whatever body may be authorized by or in accordance with the Charter of the United Nations to make such a request.' The Charter in Article 96 empowers the General Assembly and Security Council so to request, and provides that on the authorization of the General Assembly a similar power may be given to other organs and to specialized agencies.[3] The uses of the advisory jurisdiction are to assist the political organs in settling disputes and to provide authoritative guidance on points of law arising from the function of organs and specialized agencies. Thus some requests for opinions relate to specific disputes or situations, like those emanating from the League Council under the old Statute,[4] and the various opinions relating to South West Africa (Namibia);[5] and such requests involve use of political organs as an indirect means of seizing the Court of precise disputes. Other requests, as in the cases concerning the *Competence*

[1] It seems also to qualify Article 36 (2), which refers to 'all legal disputes'. But under Article 36 (2) (and possibly 36 (1)) the existence of a 'legal dispute' is a precondition for jurisdiction, on whatever basis the dispute is decided.

[2] Hudson, *The Permanent Court of International Justice, 1920–1942*, pp. 483–524; id., 42 *A.J.* (1948), 15–19, 630–2; id., 37 *Harv. L.R.* (1923–4), 970–1001; Rosenne, pp. 651–757; id., 39 *B.Y.* (1963), 1–53; Lauterpacht, op. cit., pp. 107–10, 248–50, 352–8; Fitzmaurice, 29 *B.Y.* (1952), 45–55; id., 34 *B.Y.* (1958), 138–49; Sloan, 38 *Calif. L.R.* (1950), 830–59; Greig, 15 *I.C.L.Q.* (1966), pp. 325–68; Gross, 120 Hague *Recueil* (1967, I), pp. 319–440; Keith, *The Extent of the Advisory Jurisdiction of the International Court of Justice* (1971); Pratap, *The Advisory Jurisdiction of the International Court* (1972); Pomerance, *The Advisory Function of the International Court in the League and U.N. Eras* (1973); Waldock, *Aspects of the Advisory Jurisdiction of the International Court of Justice* (1976); Reisman, 68 *A.J.* (1974), 648–71.

[3] Authorizations have been given to the Economic and Social Council, the Trusteeship Council, the Interim Committee of the General Assembly, the Committee on Applications for Review of the Judgments of the United Nations Administrative Tribunal, the various specialized agencies (with the exception of the Universal Postal Union), and the International Atomic Energy Agency. Agreements to which the United Nations or a specialized agency is a party may contain obligations to request and to accept advisory opinions: see Rosenne, pp. 682–6.

[4] For example, the case of *Nationality Decrees in Tunis and Morocco*, P.C.I.J., Ser. B, no. 4 (1923). The disputants here had not been able to agree on arbitration.

[5] Arising out of South Africa's refusal to recognize the international status of South West Africa as a territory under mandate.

of the Assembly[1] and *Reservations to the Genocide Convention*,[2] have involved fairly general and abstract questions. The origin of many requests in actual disputes, and the very nature of the judicial function, have given a contentious aspect to advisory proceedings. Thus Article 68 of the Statute provides that the Court shall be guided by the provisions applicable in contentious cases 'to the extent to which it recognizes them to be applicable'.[3] In the *Eastern Carelia* case[4] the Council of the League of Nations asked for an opinion on a dispute between Finland and the Soviet Union, the latter objecting to the exercise of jurisdiction, and the Court refused jurisdiction on the ground that the requesting organ was not competent to request an opinion in the circumstances: no state can be compelled to submit disputes to a tribunal without its consent, and the Soviet Union was not bound by the League Covenant. In the *Namibia*[5] and *Western Sahara*[6] cases the *Eastern Carelia* case was distinguished on the basis that the situations involved did not constitute a dispute: and in each case the political organ making the request for an opinion was concerned in the exercise of *its own* functions under the Charter of the United Nations, and not the settlement of a particular dispute.[7]

Whilst there is no separate proceeding to deal with preliminary objections, as there is in contentious proceedings, and perhaps should be in advisory procedure, objections to the jurisdiction arise frequently and relate both to jurisdiction as such and to propriety. Objections to jurisdiction might involve the incapacity of the requesting body either *in limine*[8] or in relation to the subject-matter of the request, as where a plea of domestic jurisdiction is made.[9]

1 I.C.J. Reports (1950), p. 4. The issue was whether under Article 4 of the Charter the General Assembly had a power to admit to membership unilaterally.

2 I.C.J. Reports (1951), p. 15. Here the issue was the conditions under which reservations to multilateral conventions could be made.

3 Article 83 of the Rules of Court provides for appointment of judges *ad hoc* if the request concerns 'a legal question actually pending between two or more States'.

4 P.C.I.J., Ser. B, no. 5 (1923). The rule still holds, although in the *Peace Treaties* case, I.C.J. Reports (1950), p. 65, the Court distinguished the *Eastern Carelia* case, *inter alia* by emphasizing its duty to comply with the request of another organ of the United Nations. See Lauterpacht, op. cit., pp. 352–8; Shihata, pp. 121–3. See further Gross, 120 Hague *Recueil* (1967, I), 359–70.

5 I.C.J. Reports (1971), p. 16 at pp. 23–4.

6 I.C.J. Reports (1975), p. 12 at pp. 24–6.

7 See further Waldock, *Aspects of the Advisory Jurisdiction of the International Court of Justice* (1976), pp. 3–10.

8 As in *Eastern Carelia* case (*supra*) and the *Peace Treaties* case, I.C.J. Reports (1950), p. 65.

9 See the *Peace Treaties* case, ibid., p. 70.

In practice objections have often challenged the power of the Court to deal with political questions. Article 65 of the Statute refers to 'any legal question', and the Court has taken the view that, however controversial and far reaching in their implications, issues of treaty interpretation, arising in the context of the United Nations Charter, are legal questions.[1] As the Court is unwilling to decline jurisdiction by adverting to the political implications of opinions, the issue then becomes one of propriety.[2] In the *Admissions*[3] and the *Expenses*[4] cases the Court concerned itself with issues of interpretation which had considerable political ramifications, and, significantly, the organs concerned were unable to act on these two opinions. In refusing to decline requests by virtue of its discretion in the matter of advisory jurisdiction, the Court has reiterated the view that as it is an organ of the United Nations a request for an advisory opinion should not, in principle, be refused.[5] Furthermore, the principle of the *Eastern Carelia* case, that the matter concerned a dispute between two states and jurisdiction could not be exercised without their consent, can be advanced as an issue both of jurisdiction and of propriety.[6]

11. *An Evaluation of the Court*[7]

In the period 1922–46 the Permanent Court dealt with thirty-three contentious cases and twenty-eight requests for

[1] See the *Admissions* case, I.C.J. Reports (1948), p. 61; *Competence of the General Assembly*, ibid. (1950), pp. 6–7; the *Expenses* case, ibid. (1962), p. 155. At the San Francisco conference it was decided not to grant a power to settle disputes on interpretation of the Charter: 13 UNCIO 668–9, 709–10. See also *Genocide* case, I.C.J. Reports (1951), p. 20.

[2] Objections to the advisory jurisdiction do not always stress the distinction between propriety and jurisdiction. See further on the distinction between legal and political questions, I.C.J. Reports (1948), pp. 69 seq. (ind. op. of Judge Alvarez), 75 seq. (ind. op. of Judge Azevedo), 94–5 (Judge Zoričić, diss. op.), 107–9 (Judge Krylov, diss. op.); I.C.J. Reports (1962), pp. 249–52 (Moreno Quintana); pp. 253–4 (Koretsky). A connected question raised in the *Expenses* case concerned the extent to which the requesting organ could limit the issues to be examined.

[3] *Conditions of Admission to Membership of the United Nations*, I.C.J. Reports (1947–8), p. 57. See also *Competence of the General Assembly*, ibid. (1950), p. 4; and Rosenne, 39 *B.Y.* (1963), 39–42.

[4] I.C.J. Reports (1962), p. 151.

[5] See the *Peace Treaties* case (First Phase), I.C.J. Reports (1950), pp. 71–2; *Reservations* case, ibid. (1951), p. 19; *Administrative Tribunal of the I.L.O.*, ibid. (1956), p. 86; the *Expenses* case, ibid. (1962), p. 155. Cf. Fitzmaurice, 29 *B.Y.* (1952), 53.

[6] See the *Peace Treaties* case, I.C.J. Reports (1950), pp. 70–1. See further Gross, 121 Hague *Recueil* (1967, II), 355–70.

[7] See generally Jenks, *The Prospects of International Adjudication* (1964); de Visscher, 50 *A.J.* (1956), 467–74; Stone, 'The International Court and the World Crisis', *Int. Conciliation* no. 536 (1962); Rosenne, 39 *B.Y.* (1963), 1–53; Gross, 56 *A.J.* (1962), 33–62;

advisory opinions; whilst from 1946 to 1978 the new Court has dealt with thirty-nine contentious cases[1] and sixteen requests for advisory opinions. The tempo of resort to the Court has if anything decreased since 1945, particularly in the matter of advisory opinions, and acceptance of compulsory jurisdiction under the optional clause has, in relation to the increase in the number of independent states, dwindled. The following factors explain the reluctance of states to resort to the Court: the political fact that hauling another state before the Court is often regarded as an unfriendly act; the greater suitability of other tribunals and other methods of review for both regional and technical matters; the general conditions of international relations; preference for the flexibility of arbitration in comparison with a compulsory jurisdiction; the lack of representation of Afro-Asia on the Court;[2] and distrust of the Court on the part of Communist and other states. Given the conditions of its existence, the Court has made a reasonable contribution to the maintenance of civilized methods of settling disputes, but it has not been at all prominent in the business of keeping the peace: indeed, the provisions of the United Nations Charter do not place emphasis on the role of the Court. In certain respects, however, the Court has been influential, viz., in the development of international law as a whole as a result of its jurisprudence[3] and in the giving of advisory opinions on the interpretation of the United Nations Charter[4] and other aspects of the law of international organizations.[5] Assessment of its jurisprudence ought not to be based on facile generalizations, and

id., 9 *Malaya L.R.* (1967), 10–19; id., 63 *A.J.* (1967), 74–85; id., 65 *A.J.* (1971), 253–326; id., 121 Hague *Recueil* (1967, II), 319–440; Sohn, *Proc. A.S.I.L.* (1964), pp. 131 seq.; Simpson, 81 *L.Q.R.* (1965), 308–11; Eek, in *Liber Amicorum in Honour of Alf Ross* (1969), p. 79 at pp. 89–93; Cheng, 20 *Yrbk. of World Affairs* (1966), 241–56; Dalfen, 6 *Canad. Yrbk.* (1968), 212–25; I.L.A., *Report of the Fifty-First Conference* (1964), pp. 23–117; Mosler and Bernhardt (eds.), *Judicial Settlement of Disputes* (1974); Gross (ed.), *The Future of the International Court of Justice* (1976), 2 vols.; Dugard, 16 *Virginia Journ. of I.L.* (1976), 463–504; P. de Visscher, 136 Hague *Recueil* (1972, II), 178–202. See also *Annuaire de l'Inst.* (1959), ii. 55–177, 358–66.

[1] This figure does not include eight unilateral applications in which the applicant did not allege that the Court had jurisdiction but requested the Court to communicate the application to the other party: e.g. *Case Concerning the Aerial Incident of September 4th, 1954*, I.C.J. Reports (1958), p. 158.

[2] See Shihata, 19 *Int. Organization* (1964–5), 203–22.

[3] See generally Lauterpacht, *The Development of International Law by the International Court* (1958); Fitzmaurice, vols. 27–9, 31–5 *B.Y.*; Hambro, *The Case Law of the International Court.*

[4] *Reparation for Injuries* case, I.C.J. Reports (1949), p. 174; *Admissions* case, ibid. (1947–8), p. 57; *Competence of the General Assembly*, ibid. (1950), p. 4; *Voting Procedure* (South West Africa), ibid. (1955), p. 67; the *Expenses* case, ibid. (1962), p. 151; *Namibia Opinion*, ibid. (1971), p. 16.

[5] *Supra*, Chapter XXX.

characterization of a particular decision as conservative or radical must depend on the view taken of the relevant pieces of law. British writers have been critical of decisions like those in the *Fisheries*,[1] *Reservations*,[2] and *Nottebohm*[3] cases as being too radical, and, whether this be so or not, it is certain that the Court has developed the law as often as it has applied it. When, in its advisory opinions[4] the Court has pronounced on the interpretation of the United Nations Charter, it has trenched boldly on political issues (which did not cease to be such because they were also legal issues) of the first magnitude. Whatever the prospect before the International Court, the usefulness of the judicial process in international relations continues to receive wide recognition, although the forms preferred are those of technical or specialized tribunals like the Court of the European Communities, regional tribunals, and *ad hoc* arbitrations.[5] The exclusion of organizations from the contentious jurisdiction of the International Court (Article 34 of the Statute) results in reference to arbitration in the provisions of agreements between organizations and states.[6]

In recent years a number of governments have taken an interest in modest steps to increase resort to the Court. Thus in 1970 the United States and eleven other Member States proposed an agenda item in the General Assembly entitled 'Review of the Role of the International Court of Justice'.[7] The outcome was a General Assembly resolution in 1974[8] which was essentially an advertisement, in very mild terms, of the availability of the Court. At the same session a more general resolution was adopted which called upon Member States to make full use of the methods of peaceful settlement of disputes provided for in the Charter of the United Nations, including judicial settlement.[9]

The Senate of the United States passed five resolutions in 1974 intended to bring about an increase in the work of the Court.[1] The International Court has produced amendments to the Rules of Court intended to provide greater flexibility in procedure and to avoid delays.[2] Further modifications were made in 1978.

[1] *Supra*, pp. 186 seq. [2] *Supra*, p. 606. [3] *Supra*, pp. 392, 406 seq.

[4] *Supra*, p. 731, n. 4. [5] See Simpson, op. cit. and *supra*, pp. 709–11.

[6] For example, in Headquarters Agreements, and loan and guarantee agreements with the International Bank. See also *supra*, p. 699. [7] See Gross, 66 *A.J.* (1972), 479–90.

[8] Resol. 3232 (XXIX), 12 Nov. 1974; adopted by consensus.

[9] Resol. 3283 (XXIX), 12 Dec. 1974; *Digest of U.S. Practice*, 1974, p. 649.

[1] See Sohn, 69 *A.J.* (1975), 92–96; and see the study resulting from one of the resolutions, produced by the Dept. of State in 1976: *Digest of U.S. Practice*, 1976, p. 650; 16 *Int. Leg. Materials* (1977), 187.

[2] Adopted on 10 May 1972; see Jiménez de Aréchaga, 67 *A.J.* (1973), 1–22.

INDEX